The wedge driven by Martin Kahler between the historical Jesus and the kerygmatic Christ was, according to Kermit Zarley, mishit. Instead, the wedge of misinterpretation needs to be driven between the New Testament's depiction of God's Son and the ecclesiastical Christ, the portrait of Jesus as redrawn by Christians under the influence of Platonic and Neo-Platonic philosophical categories. Readers of the New Testament and historians of Jesus should recognize this important thesis. In addition, Zarley combines a high view of Scripture with a thoroughly human Jesus and lands with a square stance on a unique tee box—an unusual form of unitarian theology. No one can read this book without being challenged.
Dr. Scot McKnight, Professor of New Testament,
Northern Seminary near Chicago

I am much impressed. It runs 600 pages, is thoroughly researched and documented, and fully in touch with the massive amount of scholarly discussion currently available on the Christology of the New Testament. . . . he has surely done his homework. . . . This work by our modern Servetus is a mortal wound to the doctrine of the Trinity. . . . it is a towering work that will stand for a long time to come.
Dr. James Tabor, Chair of Religious Studies,
Univ. of North Carolina at Charlotte

Kermit Zarley has provided another powerful witness against the complex, Greek philosophical definition of God and Jesus which have prevailed since the great Church councils. . . . Zarley's work needs to be read by every pastor in the land. He calls the church to a complete reappraisal of one of its core doctrines. He shows that God is a single Person, the Father . . . The implications of this invitation to reexamination of theology and Christology are huge. . . . a *tour de force* . . . extensive documentation.
Sir Anthony Buzzard, Professor emeritus of New Testament,
Atlanta Bible College

Probably the best book on the Trinity by a non-Trinitarian that I have ever read. The approach is thorough and systematic, but the style is very readable. . . . I bought a copy of Kermit's book in preparation for my debate with Rob Bowman in 2010. I recommend it highly; it's the best Unitarian apologetic on the market.
David Burke, Pastor-Teacher of the Christadelphian Church, Australia

I was a trinitarian for over 30 years when I began questioning what I had been taught and was teaching regarding the Person and identity of Jesus. . . . your explanation of Rev. 1:1 helped me see another text that shows that Jesus is not omniscient, and therefore not God, in His post-resurrectional state. You have many such moments of brilliance throughout your book, making it a truly revolutionary work. . . . The concept of Agent Christology is very powerful! Also God-in-Christ Christology. . . . this book is outstanding in establishing Jesus in His position as the exalted Messiah, while God the Father alone is God. . . . a well documented and thorough treatise.
Samuel Brown, Pastor and Former Missionary, Melbourne, Australia

Kermit Zarley has provided an unequalled analysis and comprehensive resource on a study of the nature of Jesus Christ. His book is over 580 pages long and has a bibliography of over 400 authors. Virtually every verse in the Bible (Old and New Testaments) that has ever been used in an attempt to demonstrate that Jesus is God is examined in depth. . . . The clear and simple truth regarding Jesus

Christ that he was and is a man, the Son of God, the Messiah of Israel—not a divine being or God—is amply demonstrated (e.g., John 17:3; 1 Cor. 8:4, 6; Eph.4:4-6). It may surprise some that Jesus never actually directly claimed to be God.

All Bible students including Christadelphians like me will appreciate the thoroughness of Zarley's expositions and his extensive references to recognised experts in language and history. As a resource for difficult passages of Scripture, 'Restitution' is probably unequalled. His longest chapter is on John's gospel—118 pages. Well-known . . . verses such as John 1:1, 1:18, and 20:28 are dealt with in detail.

Since mainstream Christianity holds the doctrine of the trinity as essential to salvation, Zarley's book, *The Restitution*, is controversial; but if correct, it exposes the world-wide and almost universal fundamental error held by most Christians. His examination of the history of Christology (99 pages) amply demonstrates how this disastrous change occurred. Zarley has therefore done us a great service in dispelling the mystery (and the mist!) surrounding the Bible's teaching on the nature of Jesus Christ.

Stephen Hill, Christadelphian Church minister, South Australia

I initially didn't think much of this fellow and just thought he was some bored guy with nothing to do and just craved for attention [due to my contest to guess who I was]. But then, I purchased his book, "The Restitution," and with no exaggeration my jaw dropped in surprise after seeing the absolutely outstanding scholarship displayed in this book. . . . This was a book that I have been craving for so long and kept telling myself that needed to be written. . . . [it] surveys the best scholarship has to offer on the topic of Christology . . . is the biggest and best contribution to Biblical Unitarian apologetics that I have seen so far and stands brilliantly side-by-side with the works of Anthony Buzzard against those (who unfortunately are in the majority) who believe that the Bible propagates the notion of the Trinity. My personal favorite is his detailed 30-page discussion on the Thomas calling Jesus "My Lord and My God" argument. In short, buy this book immediately. The small amount of money you will be putting for the amount of knowledge you would be receiving in return is indeed a great bargain!

Bassam Zawadi, Muslim apologist, Saudi Arabia

Anyone who thinks the Bible says God is a Trinity, or Jesus Christ is God, should read Kermit Zarley's *The Restitution*. It is a comprehensive study of biblical Christology. For some 1700 years, Christian churches have claimed the Bible says Jesus is God, or a God-Man. Zarley, a former Trinitarian for 22 years, challenges this assertion. He says the biblical view is not "God **is** Christ," but "God **in** Christ." That is, the One God of the Bible, Yahweh, worked in and through His human Messiah to reveal Himself to mankind (John 1:18; Heb 1:1) and to reconcile the world to Himself (2 Cor 5:19).

On the one hand, the book is a scholarly work that is well-documented with hundreds of mostly reference footnotes. On the other hand, it is very readable and accessible to the lay reader. It may be a bit of a daunting read from cover to cover (546 pages not including bibliography), but I found the reading only tedious in a couple places. The book will serve well as a reference for future study. Even if readers don't agree with Zarley's claims, Bible college and seminary students, teachers, pastors, and lay persons should read this book so they can better understand what they do believe.

Bill Schlegel, former Associate Professor of Bible, The Master's University, Israel Bible Extension. Host: *One God Report* Podcast

The
Restitution
Biblical Proof Jesus Is NOT God

Kermit Zarley

THE RESTITUTION: BIBLICAL PROOF JESUS IS NOT GOD

Copyright © 2008 by Kermit Zarley. All rights reserved. Except for brief quotations, no portion of this publication may be reproduced, stored in a retrieval system, or transmitted in any form or by any means—electronic, mechanical, photocopy, recording—without written permission of the author. Contact him at kermitzarley.com.

Unless otherwise noted, Scripture quotations are taken from the NEW AMERICAN STANDARD BIBLE®, Copyright© 1960, 1962, 1963, 1968, 1971, 1972, 1973, 1975, 1977, 1995 by The Lockman Foundation. Used by permission. www.Lockman.org.

Library of Congress Cataloging-in-Publication Data

Zarley, Kermit, 1941-
    The Restitution: Biblical Proof Jesus Is Not God
    Includes bibliographical references.
    1. Jesus Christ—Person and offices. 2. Jesus Christ—History of doctrines—Early church to the present. 3. Bible. N.T. Gospels—Criticism, interpretation, etc. I. Title.

Hardcover: ISBN 978-1-7352591-4-7
Softcover: ISBN 978-1-7352591-6-1
E-Book: ISBN 978-1-7352591-5-4

In 2023, this book's title was changed from The Restitution of Jesus Christ to the title The Restitution: Biblical Proof Jesus Is Not God. And the pseudonym is abandoned.

Cover design by Christy Eller

Contents

Preface xi
Abbreviations..xxi
Chapter One: Introduction..1

Part One: History of Church Christology

Chapter Two: Church Christology in the First Millennium............ 26
Chapter Three: Church Christology in the Second Millennium 71

Part Two: Messianism in the Old Testament

Chapter Four: Messianism in the Old Testament 121
    A. Introduction: Yahweh, Messiah, Son of God, and Monotheism
    B. "The Angel of the LORD"
    C. Daniel's "Son of Man"
    D. Problem Passages
        1. Is the Trinity in the book of Genesis?
        2. Is Messiah called "Mighty God" in Isaiah 9.6?
        3. What about *alma* and *Immanuel* in Isaiah 7.14?
        4. Is the Davidic Messiah called "Yahweh" in Jeremiah 23.6?

Part Three: Christology in the New Testament

Chapter Five: Christology of the Synoptists................................ 203
    A. Introduction
    B. Christology of Matthew
    C. Christology of Mark
    D. Christology of Luke
    E. The Limited Knowledge of Jesus
    F. The Trial of Jesus
    G. Problem Passages
        1. Does calling Jesus "Immanuel" in Matthew 1.23 mean He is God?
        2. Is the doctrine of the Trinity in Matthew 28.19?
        3. Does Jesus' authority to forgive sins in Mark 2.5 indicate He was God?
        4. Did Jesus identify Himself as God to the rich young man in Mark 10.18?
Chapter Six: Christology of John..277
    A. Introduction
    B. Problem Passages
        1. Is the Logos identified as God in John 1.1c?
        2. Did Jesus preexist in heaven?

3. Is Jesus called "the only begotten God" in John 1.18?
4. Who said in John 5.18 that Jesus was "making Himself equal with God"?
5. Did Jesus claim implicitly, in John 8.24, 28, 58, "I am Yahweh"?
6. What did Jesus mean in John 10.30, "I and the Father are one"?
7. Did Thomas call Jesus "my God" in John 20.28?
8. Is denial that Jesus is the Christ a denial of incarnation in 1 Jn 2.22?
9. Is "the Trinity" in 1 John 5.7?
10. Who is "the true God" in 1 John 5.20?

Chapter Seven: Christology of Paul 391
  A. Introduction
  B. Problem Passages
    1. Does "the church of God" in Ac 20.28 indicate that Jesus is God?
    2. Does Paul call Jesus Christ "God" in Romans 9.5?
    3. Does 2 Corinthians 8.9 indicate that Jesus preexisted?
    4. Does Galatians 2.20 say "the Son of God" or "(the) God and Christ"?
    5. What about "the Kingdom of Christ and God" in Ephesians 5.5?
    6. Does Philippians 2.6 say Jesus preexisted with "equality with God"?
    7. Does Jesus' "fulness (of Deity)" in Col 1.19 and 2.9 mean He is God?
    8. Is Christ Jesus "the God-man" in 1 Timothy 2.5?
    9. Is Christ Jesus "God manifest in the flesh" in 1 Timothy 3.16?
    10. Is Jesus Christ "our God" in 2 Thessalonians 1.12?
    11. Is Christ Jesus "our great God and Savior" in Titus 2.13?

Chapter Eight: Christology of the Author of Hebrews 458
  A. Introduction
  B. Problem Passages
    1. What does it mean in Hebrews 1.6 to worship Jesus?
    2. Is "the Son" called "God" in Hebrews 1.8?

Chapter Nine: Christology of Peter... 470
  A. Introduction
  B. Problem Passage
    1. Is Jesus called "our God and Savior" in 2 Peter 1.1?

Chapter Ten: Christology of The Apocalypse 477
  A. Introduction
  B. Problem Passages
    1. Is Christ identified as "the Lord God ... the Almighty" in Revelation 1.8?
    2. Does Revelation 13.8 say the Lamb was slain from the world's foundation?
    3. Does the worship of Jesus in heaven indicate that He is God?

Appendices..490
  A: The Doctrine of the Trinity
  B: The Nature of the Holy Spirit
  C: Modern Christologies

Glossary 516
Selected Bibliography..521
General Bibliography.. 523
  Primary Works Cited
  Secondary Works Cited

Complete Contents

Preface xi
Abbreviations.. xxi
Chapter One: Introduction... 1
The Fame of Jesus • Who Is Jesus? • What Is Christology? • The Significance of the Bible • Traditional Christology • The Quest for the Historical Jesus • How Jesus Identified Himself • How Others Identified Jesus • What Jesus Said About God • What Others Did Not Say About Jesus • The Resurrected Jesus • The Holy Spirit and Fulfilled Prophecy • The Jesus Movement • The Three Foremost Irrefutable Texts • The Scarcity of Biblical Texts • The Major Debated *Theos* Texts • The Debated Non-*Theos* Texts • Principles of Hermeneutics • More Important Considerations • Early Evangelistic Messages • Epilogue

Part One: History of Church Christology

Chapter Two: Church Christology in the First Millennium............ 26
Introduction • Greek Philosophy and Christian Theology • The Didache and 1 Clement • Pliny the Younger • Early Jewish Christianity • Ignatius • 2 Clement • Justin Martyr • Iranaeus • Sabellianism and Paul of Samosata • Tertullian • Origen • Summary of Ante-Nicene Christology • Two Church Centers • The Arian Controversy • The Council of Nicaea • The Nicene Creed • Arius Exonerated • Athanasius • Eusebius of Caesarea • Appolinaris • The Council of Constantinople • New Testament Credal Fragments • The Apostles' Creed • The Council of Ephesus • The Second Council of Ephesus • The Council of Chalcedon • The Second Council of Constantinople • Conclusions about Ecumenical Councils • Obliterating the Distinction between God and Son • The Athanasian Creed • Critical Thinking • Social Implications of Critical Thinking

Chapter Three: Church Christology in the Second Millennium 71
The Medieval Period • The Catholic Inquisition • The Protestant Reformation • Servetus • The Execution of Servetus • Reaction to the Execution of Servetus • The Socinians • Continental European Unitarianism • British Unitarianism • John Locke • Deism • British Arianism • Sir Isaac Newton: A Secret Arian? • Samuel Clarke: A Moderate Arian • William Whiston: A Zealous Arian • American Unitarianism • The Anabaptists • The Affects of Religious Intolerance • Credal Faith • Friedrich Schleiermacher • American Anti-Trinitarian Churches • Biblical Criticism • The Tubingen School • The History of Religions School • Liberal Theology • The Quest for the Historical Jesus • Death of the Quest • The New Quest • The Third Quest • Kenotic Christology • Other Modern Developments • The World Council of Churches • Christianity and Islam • Modern World Evangelism • British Scholars • The New Dutch Christology • Roman Catholic Scholars • Bible et christologie • Call for a Revised Christology • Conclusion

Part Two: Messianism in the Old Testament

Chapter Four: Messianism in the Old Testament 121
A. Introduction: Yahweh, Messiah, Son of God, and Monotheism
The Parting of Judaism and Christianity • Yahweh • The Messiah • Yahweh and Messiah Distinguished • Messiah as Yahweh's Agent • Yahweh as Messiah's God • The Son of God • The Shema and Jewish Monotheism • Trinitarian Monotheism? • The New History of Religions School

B. "The Angel of the LORD"
Introduction • The Meaning of *malak* • Adam and Eve • Hagar • Abraham • Isaac and Jacob • Manoah and his Wife • Moses • Moses and the Guardian Angel of Israel • The Transcendence of God • Joshua • Other Instances of the Angel of the LORD • The Angels Gabriel and Michael • Michael as the Guardian Angel of Israel • Michael Servetus and Michael the Archangel

   C. Daniel's "Son of Man"
Introduction • Daniel 7 • The Two Powers Heresy • The Jewish Saints Interpretation • Dating Daniel • The Worldwide People of God • Heaven's Royal Court • The Son of Man as King • The Worldwide Kingdom • The Son of Man as Suffering Servant • The Son of Man as "the Highest One" • The Son of Man as a Warrior-King • The Son of Man as a Divine Being? • Conclusion

   D. Problem Passages
      1. Is the Trinity in the book of Genesis?
Introduction • Switching from Plural to Singular • Four Primary Interpretations • The Form of God and Angels • Man in the Image of God • Elohim • Cherubim • Seraphim • Angels Called "gods" of "the Most High" • The Council of the Holy Ones • The Seven Spirits of God • Conclusion
      2. Is Messiah called "Mighty God" in Isaiah 9.6?
Introduction • English Versions • The Hebrew and Greek Texts • The Context • Commentators • Messianic Agency • Conclusion
      3. What about *alma* and *Immanuel* in Isaiah 7.14?
      4. Is the Davidic Messiah called "Yahweh" in Jeremiah 23.6?

Part Three: Christology in the New Testament

Chapter Five: Christology of the Synoptists 203
   A. Introduction
The Synoptic Gospels and their Authors • The Authenticity of the Sayings of Jesus • Priority and Dates of Authorship • Oral Tradition • The Christ, the Son of God • Only the Father is God • The Baptism of Jesus • The Voice Out of the Heavens • The Holy Spirit in the Life of Jesus • Acts of the Holy Spirit in the Life of Jesus • The Temptations of Jesus • The Humanity of Jesus • Angels Ministering to Jesus • The Miracles of Jesus • The Resurrection of Jesus • Summary

   B. Christology of Matthew
The Author and his Readers • Form, Structure, and Style • The Christ, the Son of God • The Virgin Birth • Worshipping Jesus • Jesus' Authority to Perform Miracles • The God of Jesus Christ • Summary

   C. Christology of Mark
The Author and his Readers • Structure and Style • The Author's Purpose • The Messianic Secret • Summary

   D. Christology of Luke
The Author and his Readers • Structure and Style • "Christ, the Son of God" • "the Most High (God)" • Jesus' Physical and Moral Development • Jesus' Dependence upon the Holy Spirit • Jesus as Prophet • Glorifying and Praising God • Jesus in Prayer • Preaching Jesus as "the Christ" • Preaching "the word" • Jesus' Resurrection, Ascension, Exaltation • Summary

   E. The Limited Knowledge of Jesus
Introduction • Textual Variance • History of Interpretation • Jesus' Ignorance of Other Future Matters • Jesus' Ignorance of Mundane Matters • Jesus' Supernatural Knowledge • Did Jesus "know all things"? • Conclusion

   F. The Trial of Jesus
Introduction • The Sanhedrin's Examination of Jesus • The Charge of Blasphemy • No Charge of Jesus Claiming to Be God • The Trial before Pilate • The Crucified Jesus • Conclusion

   G. Problem Passages
      1. Does calling Jesus "Immanuel" in Matthew 1.23 indicate that He is God?
      2. Is the doctrine of the Trinity in Matthew 28.19?
      3. Does Jesus' authority to forgive sins in Mark 2.5 indicate that He was God?
      4. Did Jesus identify Himself as God to the rich young man in Mark 10.18?

Chapter Six: Christology of John 277
   A. Introduction
The Author and his Readers • "The Jews" • The Traditional Interpretation of John • Comparing John with the Synoptics • Alleged Disparity & Consequent Dismissal • Reinterpreting John • Christocentric or Theocentric? • The Prologue • The Word • Wisdom Christology • The Humanity of Jesus • The Incarnation • Agent Christology • The Meaning of *theos* in John • The Invisibility of God • Distinguishing God and Christ • The Subordination of the Son • The Dependence of the Son • Truth and Life in the Son • The Resurrection of the Son • The Holy Spirit • The Superiority of God the Father • Only the Father Is God • The Son of God • The Revealer of God • The Purpose of the Fourth Gospel • Summary

   B. Problem Passages
      1. Is the Logos identified as God in John 1.1c?
Introduction • The Mini-Prologue • English Versions and the Greek Text • Dissecting the Three Clauses • Grammatical Problems • "the Word was divine" • "the Word was a god" • The Jehovah's Witnesses • "the Word was God" • The Anarthrous *theos* in John 1.1c • The Colwell Rule? • Harner vs. Colwell • "what God was, the Word was" •

"the Word had the same nature as God" • Linkage • Comparing John and the Author of Hebrews • Summary
2. Did Jesus preexist in heaven?
Introduction • The Spiritual Gospel • "He Existed before Me" in John 1.15, 30 • Angels Ascending and Descending in John 1.51 • Jesus Ascending and Descending in John 3.13 • "He Who Comes from Heaven" in John 3.31 • The Bread from Heaven in John 6.25-65 • Wisdom Christology • "I Am from Above" in John 8.23 • "The Glory...I had... Before" in John 17.5
3. Is Jesus called "the only begotten God" in John 1.18?
Introduction • The Greek NT and English Versions • The Meaning of *Monogenes* • Reasons for *Monogenes Theos* • Reasons against *Monogenes Theos* • Reasons for *Ho Monogenes Huios* • Reasons against *Ho Monogenes Huios* • Survey of Scholars • Conclusion
4. Who said in John 5.18 that Jesus was "making Himself equal with God"?
Introduction • Healing on the Sabbath • Keeping the Sabbath Holy • Equality with God? • Jesus' Disclaimer of Deity • Summary
5. Did Jesus claim implicitly, in John 8.24, 28, 58, "I am Yahweh"?
Introduction • The "I am" Sayings in Exodus 3.14 and Deutero-Isaiah • The Messianic Interpretation of John 8.24 • Jesus as "the Light of the World" • The Context of Jesus' "I am" Saying in John 8.24 • Jesus' Message from the Beginning • Jesus' "I am" Sayings with a Predicate • The "Son of Man" Interpretation of John 8.28 • Preexistence of Jesus in John 5.58? • A Different "I am" Saying • Jesus' "I am" Saying in John 18.5 • Summary
6. What did Jesus mean in John 10.30, "I and the Father are one"?
Introduction • Verse-by-verse Exposition • Summary
7. Did Thomas call Jesus "my God" in John 20.28?
Introduction • The Thomas Incident • Authenticity of Thomas' Confession • History of Interpretation of Thomas' Confession • An Address to Jesus • Nominatives as Vocatives? • Ascribing Divinity to Jesus • "The Lord" • "My God and Your God" • "The Only True God" • Jesus as the Father's Agent • *Seeing* the Father in Jesus • The "God in Christ" Interpretation • Source of Enlightenment and Glorification • Jesus' Response • More History of Interpretation • The Purpose of John's Gospel • Conclusion
8. Is denial that Jesus is the Christ, in John 2.22, a denial of incarnation?
9. Is "the Trinity" in 1 John 5.7?
Introduction • Erasmus and Textus Receptus • Evidence Against the Authenticity of 1 John 5.7 • Conclusion
10. Who is "the true God" in 1 John 5.20?
Introduction • English Versions • *Houtos* Refers to Jesus Christ • *Houtos* Refers to God the Father • Commentators • Conclusion

Chapter Seven: Christology of Paul 391
A. Introduction
Saul the Pharisee • Paul the Monotheistic Theologian • Paul the Evangelist • Paul's Gospel • Keeping the Gospel Pure • Only the Father is God • The God and Father of Jesus Christ • Distinguishing God and Christ • Distinguishing God and His Son • Christ: the Perfect Image of God • Adam Christology • God-in-Christ Christology • Lordship Christology • Yahweh Texts Applied to Jesus • Subordination Christology • The Invisibility and Immortality of God • "Maranatha" • The Spirit and Kingdom of God and Christ • The Preexistence of Jesus? • The Cosmic Christ • Summary
B. Problem Passages
1. Does "the church of God" in Acts 20.28 indicate that Jesus is God?
Introduction • The Greek Text and Versions • Two *Theou* Translations • Conclusions of Commentators
2. Does Paul call Jesus Christ "God" in Romans 9.5?
Introduction • Modern Greek New Testaments • Versions that Call Christ "God" • Versions that Do Not Call Christ "God" • Reasons for the One Person View • Reasons for the Two Person View • Survey of Commentators • Conclusion
3. Does Paul indicate in 2 Corinthians 8.9 that Jesus preexisted?
4. Does Galatians 2.20 say "the Son of God" or "(the) God and Christ"?
5. What about "the Kingdom of Christ and God" in Ephesians 5.5?
6. Does Paul say in Philippians 2.6 that Jesus had an "equality with God"?
Introduction • Two Interpretations • "The Form of God" • "Equality With God" • "Emptied Himself" • "God Highly Exalted Him" • "Every Knee Bow/Tongue Confess" • "Jesus Christ is Lord" • "The Name ... Above Every Name" • Conclusion
7. Does "fulness" in Colossians 1.19 and 2.9 mean Jesus is God?
8. Is Jesus Christ "our God" in 2 Thessalonians 1.12?
English Versions • Reasons for the Two Persons View • Reasons for the One Person View
9. Is Christ Jesus "the God-man" in 1 Timothy 2.5?
Introduction • God is "One" • The God-man? • Christ as Mediator • Conclusion
10. Is Christ Jesus "God manifest in the flesh" in 1 Timothy 3.16?

11. Is Christ Jesus "our great God and Savior" in Titus 2.13?
    Introduction • The Greek Text and English Versions • One Person View • Two Persons View • Survey of Scholars

Chapter Eight: Christology of the Author of Hebrews 458
A. Introduction
   The Author and his Style • Structure and Purpose • The Prologue • The Superiority of Jesus • The Sinless Humanity of Jesus • The Preexistence of Jesus? • Distinguishing God and Christ • The Subordination of the Son • Jesus' Prayers and Exaltation
B. Problem Passages
   1. What does it mean in Hebrews 1.6 to worship Jesus?
   2. Is "the Son" called "God" in Hebrews 1.8?
      Introduction • English Versions of Psalm 45.6-7 • Grammar of Psalm 45.6-7 • Setting of Psalm 45 • Jewish Monotheism • English Versions of Hebrews 1.8-9 • Grammar of Hebrews 1.8-9 • Context of Hebrews 1.8-9 • Literary Reasons • Scholastic Uncertainty • Summary

Chapter Nine: Christology of Peter 470
A. Introduction
   Peter: The Leader of the Apostles • Servant Christology • God Empowered Jesus to Do Miracles • Distinguishing God and Christ • Jesus Is the Christ • The Holy One of God Belongs to God • The God of Jesus Christ • Summary
B. Problem Passage
   1. Is Jesus called "our God and Savior" in 2 Peter 1.1?
      The Greek Text and English Versions • Reasons for the One Person View • Reasons for the Two Persons View • Commentators

Chapter Ten: Christology of The Apocalypse 477
A. Introduction
   The Author • Structure and Style • Jesus' Limited Knowledge • God and Christ Distinguished • The God of Jesus Christ • "The Lamb" and "the Word" • The Throne of God • Why No Holy Spirit? • "The Throne of David" • The Meaning of "Hallelujah" • Agent Christology
B. Problem Passages
   1. Is Christ identified as "the Lord God ... the Almighty" in Revelation 1.8?
   2. Does Revelation 13.8 say the Lamb was slain at the time of creation?
   3. Does the worship of Jesus in Heaven indicate that He is God?

Appendices 490
   A: The Church Doctrine of the Trinity
      Introduction • Historical Development • No Biblical Basis for the Word "Trinity" • Contradictory, Confusing,, Incomprehensible • Restitution of True Doctrine of God & Christ
   B: The Nature of the Holy Spirit
      The Church Doctrine of the Holy Spirit • The Spirit of God and the Spirit of Man • The Holy Spirit in the Old Testament • The Holy Spirit in the New Testament • Capitalizing Holy Spirit • Applying Personal Pronouns to the Holy Spirit • Personifying the Holy Spirit • Ascribing Impersonal Functions to the Holy Spirit • The Holy Spirit as the Spirit of the Father • Does Scripture Identify the Holy Spirit as God?
   C: Modern Christologies
      High and Low Christologies • A Hellenized Christology • A Late, Liturgical Christology • Development vs. Evolutionary Christology • Judaical and Anthropological Christologies • Functional vs. Ontological Christology • Process Christology

Glossary 516
Selected Bibliography 521
General Bibliography 523
   A. Primary Works Cited
   B. Secondary Works Cited

Preface

This book is about Christology. Christology is generally defined as the study of Christ. This book examines a particular aspect of Christology: whether Jesus is God. Nothing has occupied the center stage of Christian doctrine more than this question.

The traditional view that Jesus is God was developed during the early centuries of Christianity. The institutional Catholic Church decided officially at its First Ecumenical Council—the Council of Nicaea, held in CE 325—that Jesus was "very God of very God." This language meant that Jesus was fully God in every sense. In the next century, the Church wrestled with a related question: How can Jesus be both man and God? The Church officially answered this question at its Fifth Ecumenical Council—the Council of Chalcedon, held in CE 451—by establishing an elaborate christological dogma that has held its course as both Catholic and Protestant orthodoxy to the present. It was that Jesus is both man and God by possessing two natures: a human nature and a divine nature. *This belief—that Jesus is fully man and fully God—remains the heart of Christian theology.*[1]

This teaching—that Jesus is God—became so well established in the institutional Church that, in the intervening centuries until modern times, distinguished scholars wrote very little on this subject except in systematic theology books. They treated it as having been so thoroughly discussed and settled in the 4th and 5th centuries that it was no longer worthy of further investigation and debate.[2] To this day, none of the mainline church denominations have officially disavowed their doctrine that Jesus was and is fully God, nor have they revised any of their creeds containing this dogma. Yet there have been few books written recently for the public solely on defending the assertion that Jesus is God.[3]

This situation, however, began to change on the academic level during the 17th century with the emergence of Enlightenment in Europe. Out of it arose literary and historical criticism, and these were applied to the Bible as well as all church teachings. The historical origins of religions were examined too, especially that of Christianity, and so was the impact that these religions had on each other. The result was that during the 19th century, Nicene-Chalcedonian Christology was

---

[1] Martin Hengel, *Studies in Early Christology* (Edinburgh: T&T Clark, 1995), viii.
[2] Albert Schweitzer (*The Quest of the Historical Jesus: First Complete Edition* [orig. 1906], tr. and ed. from 2nd Ger. ed. by John Bowden [Minneapolis: Fortress, 2001], 5) alleges concerning Jesus, "the investigation of his life and historical personality were done away with."
[3] Larry W. Hurtado writes books that do so from the perspective of worship, and Richard Bauckham does likewise by placing Jesus and God in the same unique category; yet these authors avoid saying straighout that "Jesus is God" even though that is what they mean. For a new and biblically comprehensive book that says "Jesus is God," see Robert M. Bowman Jr. and J. Ed Komoszewski, *Putting Jesus in His Place: The Case for the Deity of Christ* (Grand Rapids: Kregel, 2007). See below for mention of M. Harris' book.

seriously challenged for the first time in church history, especially its doctrine of two-natures of Christ. It happened because there was a growing scholastic awareness of a disparity between this church *kerygma* (Gr. for "proclamation"), which came to be called "the Christ of faith," and "the Jesus of history" gleaned mostly from the first three gospels of the New Testament (NT). This awareness in disparity resulted in an ambitious academic pursuit, later called "the quest for the historical Jesus." It began quite unnoticeably in Germany in the late 18th century and thrust through vividly in the latter half of the 19th century. But this "Quest" allegedly died in the first half of the 20th century because radical historical critics deemed it impossible to recover the historical Jesus. Some of them even assessed Jesus as irrelevant to Christian faith. But the Quest revived during the mid-20th century and flourishes today, mostly because people could not stop believing that Jesus was the founder of Christianity.

Church history shows that the easiest way to identify Jesus is with titles. Thus, "title Christology" emerged during the 1950s and 1960s with the publication of several important books on this genre. Surprisingly, these authorities of title Christology often ignored whether the Greek NT applies the word *theos*, which means "God," to Jesus.[4] In fact, Oscar Cullmann in his benchmark book on title Christology—*The Christology of the New Testament* (1963)—even repudiates the importance of deciding whether the NT ever calls Jesus "God," though he believed that it does. He allots priority to several titles applied to Jesus and then treats the major, disputed NT *theos* texts on this subject in a scanty chapter with the following introduction:[5] "We shall therefore examine the texts relevant to this question with the explicit presupposition that Jesus' 'deity' by no means stands or falls with them."[6] This assertion suggests that Cullmann recognized that the view which he adopted—that the NT calls Jesus "God"—was somewhat weak.

On the other hand, contemporary NT scholar Murray Harris has written a very scholarly and technical book that focuses solely on examining these disputed *theos* texts in the NT that have been thought to identify Jesus as "God." In his *Jesus as God: The New Testament Use of Theos in Reference to Jesus* (1992), Harris stresses "the relative neglect of the study of *theos* as a christological title."[7] He observes that prior to his work, "there has never been a full-scale study of the NT use of *theos* as a christological term."[8] Harris contends that the NT unequivocally calls Jesus "God." His book is cited often herein.

In recent times, most NT scholars have regarded non-titular biblical texts about Jesus' identity as important as titular ones. Raymond Brown asserts that they are "more important."[9] He states, "If Jesus presented himself as one in whose life God was active, he did so not primarily by the use of titles ... the material that would have to be treated in discussing the divinity of Jesus in the New Testament is very broad in range."[10]

---

[4] E.g., Vincent Taylor, *The Names of Jesus* (London: MacMillan, 1954); R.H. Fuller, *The Foundations of New Testament Christology* (New York: Scribner, 1965); F. Hahn, *The Titles of Jesus in Christology: Their History in Early Christianity* (London: Lutterworth, 1969).
[5] *Theos* is the Greek word for "God." Originally, the NT documents were written in Greek.
[6] Oscar Cullmann, *The Christology of the New Testament*, rev. ed., tr. Shirley C. Guthrie and Charles A.M. Hall (Philadelphia: Westminster, 1963), 307.
[7] Murray J. Harris, *Jesus as God: The New Testament Use of Theos in Reference to Jesus* (Grand Rapids: Baker, 1992), 11.
[8] M. Harris, *Jesus as God*, 10.
[9] Raymond E. Brown, *Jesus God and Man: Modern Biblical Reflections* (New York: MacMillan, 1967), 2.
[10] R.E. Brown, *Jesus God and Man*, 2.

The Restitution: Biblical Proof Jesus Is Not God encompasses the whole range of biblical material that reputedly addresses the subject of whether Jesus is God. In doing so, it proposes an alternative, a revised Christology called "exclusive God-in-Christ Christology,"[11] which does not identify Jesus as God. This God-in-Christ Christology is strictly a "functional" or "spirit" Christology as opposed to the traditional Christology. The latter—that Jesus is God—is called "incarnational" Christology or "ontological" or "essence" Christology.

God-in-Christ Christology encapsulates the most concise explication of the great mystery of Jesus' identity as it is represented in the Bible. It appears most succinctly in St. Paul's brief christological statement, "God was in Christ" (2 Cor 5.19). This book contends that many biblical texts that have been interpreted to mean that Jesus was God really mean no more than that *God was in Jesus*. So, *this book's thesis is that God fully indwelt Jesus, yet Jesus was no more than a man*.

Although this book affirms Jesus' virgin birth, it insists that this doctrine does not necessitate that He is more than a man. Rather, the virgin birth merely likens Jesus to Adam before the fall, when he was without sin and capable of being an ideal, archetypal man as Jesus became. Thus, *Jesus was more of a man than sinful humans are* because He was as God intended man to be. John A.T. Robinson well states that Jesus "was totally and utterly a man—and had never been anything other than a man or more than a man."[12]

While this book diverges from Christian orthodoxy on the critical issue about whether or not Jesus is God, *this book affirms all other major doctrines of Christian orthodoxy about Jesus*. So, it adheres solidly to belief in Jesus as the virgin-born, sinless, miracle-working, resurrected, exalted Lord, Messiah of Israel, Son of Man, and Savior who accomplished salvation, made available for all humankind, through His sin-bearing, atoning death on the cross.

Examining carefully all of the scriptural data that addresses the subject of whether Jesus is God is a somewhat academic and tedious process. In order for any explanation of these biblical passages to be credible, it must interact with other major interpretations, especially those advocated by traditionalists. In doing so, I have attempted to avoid being overly-technical, as well as overly-simplistic, in order to target a wide readership that includes both Bible students as well as general readers who are unskilled in either biblical languages or theology. This format makes this book reader-friendly as well as the most comprehensive in scope and particular persuasion known to this author.[13]

In considering these relevant biblical passages, one's view of the inspiration of Scripture is critical. In modern times, those who have embraced alternative christologies, often being historical-critical scholars, have usually adopted views of the inspiration of Scripture that diverge markedly from conservative views, e.g., those held by church fathers.[14] So, most modern, alternative christologies *have not* been based on the historical integrity of the NT gospels. In contrast, *this book proposes an alternative Christology that is based on a conservative*

---

[11] I have chosen to label it a "God-in-Christ Christology" rather than a "Oneness Christology" because the latter can be construed to mean Sabellianism, which identifies Jesus and the Father as one being.
[12] John A.T. Robinson, *The Human Face of God* (Philadelphia: Westminster, 1973), 179. Robinson was the most distinguished biblical scholar with whom this book completely agrees regarding the identity of Jesus.
[13] See Mark H. Graeser, John A. Lynn, and John W. Schoenheit, *One God & One Lord: Reconsidering the Cornerstone of the Christian Faith*, 3rd ed. (Indianapolis: Christian Educational Services, 2003). Their book and mine share many arguments, but I've used none of them since I learned of it as mine went to press.
[14] Klaas Runia, *The Present-Day Christological Debate* (Downers Grove, IL: Inter-Varsity, 1984), 109.

view of the Bible. For instance, I treat all of Jesus' sayings in the NT gospels as historically authentic or reasonably representative of His "voice."

Some reviewers may allege that a conservative view of the inspiration of the Bible is incompatible with *the thesis of this book—that Jesus is the Son of God, not God*. On the contrary, it is just that these two concepts have seldom been joined together throughout church history since the dissolution of early Jewish Christianity, which this book follows.

Herein, I do not interact with historical-critical scholars as to why they dismiss certain Scriptures as historically inauthentic. To respond to this technical discipline would make this book too complicated for most readers and expand it unnecessarily.

Organizing the vast amount of biblical material relevant to this subject proved difficult. At first, I organized it according to subject matter, a method that is easier and is used in systematic theology. But I later changed course, conforming to the modern trend in biblical studies, and rearranged the material according to the beliefs of the principal NT authors and characters. The advantage of books written with this format is that they have far fewer presuppositions and thus tend to get at the truth more readily. Yet R.E. Brown well notes, "Books following this approach are often not easily readable."[15] Indeed, most of them are repetitive, technical, and written for scholars and advanced students. I have tried to overcome these obstacles with a writing style that targets novices, thus presuming nothing of my readers, and minimizing repetition (no mean task). Rather than attempting to arrange NT christologies according to their chronological development (surely an impossible task),[16] I have arranged them according to their location in the Bible.

Also in this book, each NT author is recognized as a theologian who wrote from his own distinctive theological and thematical perspectives and with his specific readers in mind. Therefore, the NT presents a diversity of christologies about Jesus.[17] Although some of them were no doubt developed earlier in the 1st century than others, making them more primitive, none of these NT christologies are regarded herein as either superior or in opposition to others. Rather, biblical christologies which may have developed later are viewed as complementing and/or supplementing prior ones, not contradicting them.

I believe it is incumbent upon those who do Christology, i.e., when it is possible to do so objectively and therefore reasonably, to integrate these diversities into a unified Christology that represents the totality of Scripture.[18] Indeed, O. Cullmann, in contrast to most of his historical-critical colleagues, recognized the validity of the concept which he called "the Christology of the New Testament."[19] The reason is that a conservative view of the Bible recognizes it as the mind of God. In contrast, some scholars cited in this book view diversities in Scripture as irreconcilable; e.g., they think that the

---

[15] Raymond E. Brown, *An Introduction to New Testament Christology* (New York: Paulist, 1994), 106n163.

[16] Cf. G.B. Caird, *New Testament Theology*, ed. L.D. Hurst (Oxford: Clarendon, 1994), 9-10.

[17] E.g., *Bible et christologie*, in Joseph A. Fitzmyer, *Scripture and Christology: A Statement of the Biblical Commission with a Commentary* (New York: Paulist, 1986), 2.2.2.2 (b) states: "Hence one may speak of the Christology of the Apostle Paul."

[18] *Bible et christologie*, 1.2.3.2; 2.2.2.2 (c).

[19] O. Cullmann, *Christology*, 6, 236, 315. See also Leander E. Keck, "Christology of the New Testament: What, Then, Is New Testament Christology," in *Who Do You Say that I Am?: Essays in Christology*, eds. Mark Allan Powell and David R. Bauer (Louisville, KT: Westminster John Knox, 1999), 185-200.

synoptists and the Apostle Paul did not believe Jesus was God, but the author of the Gospel of John did.

In this book, each NT author's Christology begins with an introduction. Assuming that each NT book and letter (whether multi-authored or not) is a literary unit, the general purpose of these introductions is to attempt to construct the Christology of each supposed author and thereby show that he *could not* have believed that Jesus was God. Following these introductions, these chapters examine closely those biblical texts that traditionalists have offered in support of their thesis that Jesus is God. I have labeled these Scriptures as "Problem Passages," and *the exegesis of these texts is the primary focus of this book.*

Bible quotations are from the *New American Standard Bible* (NASB) unless otherwise specified. I have chosen it rather than that preferred by most scholars—the RSV or NRSV—for three reasons. First, the NASB supports the traditional view that Jesus is God more than any other English version. I have capitalized pronouns that refer to God and Jesus merely to conform to the NASB and to facilitate that pronoun's reference.[20] Thus, capitalizing personal pronouns for Jesus is not intended to indicate He is God. Second, the NASB is the most word-for-word translation of the Greek and Hebrew texts of any modern English versions. Third, for the past few decades the NASB and the NIV have been the most popular Bible versions in American Evangelicalism—my church community.

Some readers will assess the tone of this book as both negative and reductionist. I concur. Due to the entrenched errors of classical (traditional) Christology, it is necessary to first focus on *who Jesus is not*. It is a fact of education that sometimes unlearning must precede learning. Don Cupitt well explains, "no one is going to be much interested in the construction of an alternative account of the meaning of Jesus unless he is first persuaded that the old account is indefensible."[21] The charge that God-in-Christ Christology alone is reductionist is correct when compared to the traditional approach. But being reductionist proves nothing. For instance, Catholics deem the Protestant view of Mary as reductionist.

This book alleges that the institutional church's classical doctrine of incarnation, which traditionalists often call a "high Christology," is *expansionist* and thus represents an unwarranted addition to the biblical portrait of Jesus. God-in-Christ Christology can be conceived as a *higher* Christology than incarnational Christology. For, Jesus was *more* "highly exalted" in heaven (Phil 2.9) if He was no more than a man, did not preexist, and did not regain a position previously held, all of which traditional Christology asserts. And traditionalists often fail to recognize that their Christology is *theo-logically reductionist*. Don Cupitt explains by alleging of their christocentrism, "It tended to create a cult of the divine Christ which let Deity [God the Father] itself fade into the background."[22] So, their supposedly "high Christology" results in a "low theology" that fails to recognize God's supremacy over all, including Christ, and thereby diminishes the honor due the Almighty.

What is the benefit of believing that Jesus was no more than a man, thus not God? Foremost, everyone ought to seek to know the truth purely for truth's sake.

---

[20] Suggested by Bob Hudson and Shelley Townsend, *A Christian Writer's Manual of Style* (Grand Rapids: Zondervan, 1998), 50.

[21] Don Cupitt, *Jesus and the Gospel of God* (London: Lutterworth, 1979), 11. See also A. Schweitzer, *The Quest of the Historical Jesus: First Complete Edition*, 3-5. I sometimes quote D. Cupitt approvingly. However, he has since become an apostate by undergoing a shocking theological change toward atheism.

[22] Don Cupitt, "The Christ of Christendom," in *The Myth of God Incarnate*, ed. J. Hick, 145.

This point can hardly be overemphasized, and I am surprised to find it so little appreciated by so many Christians. To believe in a Jesus who is not the actual, real Jesus of history is to believe in a fictional caricature of Jesus. To do so detracts to some degree from the truth of the Christian message about Jesus. Beyond this, the benefits to be gained from an exclusively God-in-Christ Christology, as opposed to traditional Christology, are both intellectual and devotional.

Intellectually, with an exclusively God-in-Christ Christology, God is viewed much more simply and clearly as a single, personal being rather than the abstract, complex, tri-personal "Godhead" of Trinitarianism. Biblically astute Trinitarians know quite well about the difficulty in understanding and explaining their doctrine. Moreover, every time they read the word "God" in the Bible they must scrutinize its context in order to determine whether it refers to the triune Godhead or to one of its three members. Similarly, when they read in the NT what Jesus did or said, there is always the question of whether He acted or spoke from the source of His human nature or His divine nature.

Devotionally, the strong tendency of traditional Christology toward Docetism, a fact well recognized by scholars, has led countless Christian believers to reason that it seems *easy* for Jesus Christ, being the God-man, to have resisted temptation, endured suffering and shame, and thus to have lived a sinless life. After all, God is perfect, cannot be tempted, and therefore cannot sin (cf. Mt 5.48; Jam 1.13). Some Christians find it difficult to relate to such a Jesus. In responding to the challenge to follow Him, they say, "How can you follow God because He is perfect?" On the other hand, if Jesus was not God, but more like us than previously thought—so that He had to struggle and persevere with the utmost determination of His will, simultaneously drawing mystically upon God's strength through the power of the Holy Spirit in order to resist temptation, eschew evil, and accomplish His mission of providing for us so great salvation—this realization can awaken a renewed and lasting appreciation for Jesus as Lord and Savior. Who cannot relate more easily to a Christ like this? *In viewing Jesus Christ as no more than a man, He becomes for us an even greater role model. Thus, His story is enhanced rather than diminished by an exclusively God-in-Christ Christology as compared to the traditional Christ-is-God Christology.* Finally, for those who object to the traditional incarnational Christology, this God-in-Christ Christology is certainly a more believable story.

Some readers will no doubt criticize this book for not identifying Jesus more precisely. For example, I have refrained from speculating on the relationship between God and the Johannine Logos, this Logos and Jesus, and how the Logos impacted Jesus' life. But this speculative mode of thinking is what led church fathers into their christological morass. They sought detailed answers to theological questions about the nature of the Logos and its relation to Jesus, Jesus' supposed preexistence and its time of origin, and thus the exact and full extent of Jesus' uniqueness. And how did the Holy Spirit figure in all of this? I believe Scripture is silent on such questions, so that these church fathers, in pursuing such things, exceeded scriptural bounds (cf. Deut 29.29; Ps 131.1).[23] Maurice Wiles observes that in the early centuries of Christianity, church fathers defined their doctrines of God and Christ with "an increasing degree of precision,"[24] to which John Macquarrie adds, "without having adequate grounds"

---

[23] D. Cupitt (*Jesus and the Gospel of God*, 13) rightly claims that the NT documents "leave the question of Jesus' metaphysical status quite open.... All that matters is that Jesus is pre-eminently the one through whom God gives eternal salvation."

[24] Maurice F. Wiles, *Explorations in Theology 4* (London: SCM, 1979), 47.

from Scripture.²⁵ A.E. Harvey likewise notes, "The gospel narratives in no way anticipate the later patristic interest in Jesus' precise relationship with God."²⁶

Church fathers amplified these mistakes by stating their dogmatic speculations sometimes in non-scriptural, metaphysical language and categories borrowed from Greek religio-philosophy. Since error tends to compound itself in time, in succeeding centuries the church fell into a labyrinth of heinous blunders of doctrinal complexity exacerbated by its ecumenical councils and creeds. Due to scriptural silence on these christological matters, these church fathers should have been more flexible by permitting some degree of intellectual freedom on these issues. *Until glory comes, the precise extent of Jesus' uniqueness must remain for us a mystery to contemplate rather than a problem to solve.*²⁷

Many scholars describe Jesus' uniqueness as "divine." I think the terms "divine," "divinity," "divine being," and "divine Sonship" do not adequately identify Jesus as God. I therefore refrain from using them. Scholars who do so rarely define them, and with good reason. For example, the English word "divine" has a very broad range of meaning, and so does *theios*, which is its Greek counterpart. Moreover, *theios* was available to the NT authors; yet they never applied it to Jesus in their canonical writings. Traditionalist I. Howard Marshall surmises that "to have asked an early Christian, 'Do you believe that Jesus is divine?' would have been a category that was not part of his thinking."²⁸ Even today, identifying Jesus as "divine" often results in confusion. A.E. Harvey observes that Christianity first spread into a Hellenistic culture that liberally applied the word *theios* to rulers and philosophers; yet he explains that "it did not imply that divine honours should be paid to [them]."²⁹ He cites both Philo and Josephus as examples of ancient writers who described OT heroes as "divine" without intending to designate them as "gods."³⁰ Frances Young explains concerning 1ˢᵗ century Christians living in Hellenistic lands, "That *theios* was a very general adjective with no incarnational overtones is clear from the fact that in a later period Christian saints and fathers could be so described.... men and things could have degrees of divinity."³¹ Indeed, some scholars opt for a "degree Christology," which means that Jesus is more than a man but less than fully God. Also, traditionalist Richard Bauckham questions the widespread practice of calling Jesus "divine." He says that for modern scholars the word "'divine'—is rarely faced with clarity.... it is also unclear what the attribution of divinity to Jesus in early Christology would really imply."³²

Similarly, I usually refrain from using the expressions "high Christology" and "low Christology" that are so common among scholars. The former suggests

---

²⁵ John Macquarrie, *Jesus Christ in Modern Thought* (London/Philadelphia: SCM/Trinity, 1990), 13.
²⁶ Anthony E. Harvey, *Jesus and the Constraints of History* (London: Duckworth, 1982), 167n75. Albert Schweitzer (*The Quest of the Historical Jesus: First Complete Edition*, 400) concludes concerning the earthly Jesus, "His life as a whole,... remained a mystery ever for the disciples."
²⁷ Cf. Adolf von Harnack, *What Is Christianity?* 2nd ed., rev., tr. Thomas Bailey Saunders (New York: Putnam's Sons, 1902), 135.
²⁸ I. Howard Marshall, *The Origins of New Testament Christology* (Leicester, England: Inter-Varsity, 1977), 104.
²⁹ A.E. Harvey, *Jesus and the Constraints of History*, 156.
³⁰ Ibid., 157.
³¹ Francis Young, "Two Roots of a Tangled Mass?" in *The Myth of God Incarnate*, ed. J. Hick, 100.
³² Richard Bauckham, *God Crucified: Monotheism and Christology in the New Testament* (Grand Rapids: Eerdmans, 1998), 5. Bauckham also cites Charles A. Gieschen (*Angelmorphic Christology: Antecedents and Early Evidence* [Leiden: Brill, 1998], 32-33), who lists a "criteria of divinity."

a lofty, more developed truth whereas the latter appears elementary and more incomplete.

Such questions about nuances of words may cause some novice readers to think, "What's all the fuss about?" and dismiss this book as a useless exercise in mundane linguistics. On the contrary, it is very important because throughout church history its leaders have made the supposed deity/divinity of Jesus Christ the supreme litmus test for deciding whether a person is a genuine Christian. Peter had written, "the prophets who prophesied of the grace that would come ... made careful search and inquiry, seeking to know what person or time the Spirit of Christ within them was indicating as He predicted the sufferings of Christ and the glories to follow" (1 Pt 1.10-11). Shouldn't we likewise search the Scriptures to understand if Christ was God or only that God was in Christ?

In 1961, distinguished form critic Vincent Taylor published a brief article entitled, "Does the New Testament Call Jesus God?" In it he insists, "The question may be asked, What is the value of the inquiry we are making?... I have no doubt that [its] importance is very great indeed. First, the habit of calling Jesus God tends to restrict unduly our understanding of the riches of the Divine Being."[33] Taylor further relates that, since the mid-20th century, traditional Christology "caused embarrassment" for Christian scholars. He explains, "honest historical criticism becomes very difficult" because "the Gospels clearly show that the knowledge of Jesus was limited,"[34] suggesting that He was not God.

Most churchgoers know little about the important advances achieved by biblical scholarship the past two centuries. It is sad that many could care less. One sensible reason is that most publications about theological progress are technical, contain foreign language material, and thus are incomprehensible to laypeople. One of the purposes of this book is to help bridge this gulf. In fact, Christianity now suffers a schism between academy and pew that is growing into a deepening crisis. Christian scholars often dismiss the laity as anti-intellectual, so that they speak and write mostly to themselves. And the laity generally rejects Bible scholars as lacking faith.[35] James D.G. Dunn acknowledges this problem and states, "suspicion and fear of scholarship is even more widespread in church circles in America than in Britain." But he exhorts, "Christians have nothing to fear from scholarship and little to fear from particular scholars. On the contrary, they should welcome the critically inquiring and investigative skills of scholars. For since Christians are also concerned with the truth, they should also want to be made aware of and delivered from untruth, in all its forms."[36]

Another reason people don't know about theological advance is that books about it can be rather large, from which they shy away. I recommend that such readers treat this book as a reference source, yet attempt to read at least the following portions: the first three chapters, all of the introductions in subsequent chapters, "The Trial of Jesus" in Chapter Five, and especially the commentary in Chapter Six on Jn 1.1c and Jn 20.28. I regard my commentary on Jn 20.28

---

[33] Vincent Taylor, "Does the New Testament Call Jesus God?" *ExpT* 73 (1961-62): 118. This article seems to have caused R.E. Brown to publish an article with the same title four years later, resulting in a book.
[34] V. Taylor, "Does the New Testament Call Jesus God?" 118.
[35] See Alister E. McGrath, "The Two Nations: Disillusionment with Academic Theology," in *The Future of Christianity* (Oxford: Blackwell, 2002), 120-55.
[36] James D.G. Dunn, *The Evidence for Jesus* (Philadelphia: Westminster, 1985), xiv, 103.

as the highlight of my research and the most critical portion of this book. Such readers may later desire to investigate various problem passages as they become aware of them.

The title of this book echoes the title of the last book by the Spaniard Michael Servetus, entitled *The Restitution of Christianity* (1553), which got him executed. The word "restitution" means "restoration." So, my objective in this book is to contribute to ongoing Jesus Research that hopefully will help lead to a reconstruction of traditional Christology that will reflect a restoration of the pristine faith of Jesus and His disciples. It was that Jesus was a perfectly righteous man who gained victory over sin and provided salvation for us by His atoning death on the cross, but not that He was God.

This book is a reprint, beginning in 2023, of *The Restitution of Jesus Christ* which was published in 2008. This former title is changed to *The Restitution: Biblical Proof Jesus Is Not God*. Also, the book's previous pseudonym, Servetus the Evangelical, is herein deleted. Neither of these changes requires this book to be a second edition since its content is not changed other than to correct typos and change this paragraph. I still identify with Michael Servetus in his courageous effort to identify God the Father as the only true God, the Almightly, and Jesus as Lord and Savior.

In attempting to recover the pristine faith of the first Christians about the identity of Jesus, I claim my right as a freeman in Christ as did the renowned poet John Milton when he defended his right to critique the church doctrine of the Trinity as follows:

> I only entreat that my readers will ponder and examine my statements in a spirit which desires to discover nothing but the truth, and with a mind free from prejudice. For without intending to oppose the authority of Scripture, which I consider inviolably sacred, I only take upon myself to refute human interpretations as often as the occasion requires, conformably to my right, or rather to my duty as a man.... But inasmuch as they [opposers] can lay claim to nothing more than human powers, assisted by that spiritual illumination which is common to all, it is not unreasonable that they should on their part allow the privileges of diligent research and free discussion to another inquirer, who is seeking truth through the same means and in the same way as themselves, and whose desire of benefiting mankind is equal to their own.[37]

Even some conservative scholars in mainline churches concur. Consider Aloys Grillmeier, a Roman Catholic scholar and foremost authority on patristic theology, who has been calling for a reconstruction of traditional Christology since 1965.[38]

My primary purpose in writing this book has *not* been to convince readers of my christological convictions. That is secondary. Rather, my primary purpose is to persuade readers that the Bible does not require that people believe in the traditional doctrine of the Trinity, the incarnation, and thus the deity of Christ, in order to become a true believer in Jesus. So, I insist that these teachings should not be included as elements in evangelistic messages or as faith-requirements for formal church membership. Assessing people as "non-Christian" solely on the basis of being non-Trinitarian ought to forever cease. I am of the opinion (I hope not too idealistic) that by God's love professing Christians can learn to extend liberty to each other regarding such issues and love one another. Granted, it

---

[37] John Milton, "The Christian Doctrine" [n.d.], in John Milton, *Complete Poems and Major Prose*, Book I, Ch. 5, ed. Merrit Y. Hughes (repr. New York: Odyssey, 1957), 932.

[38] Aloys Grillmeier, *Christ in Christian Tradition* [1965], tr. Alois Grillmeier (Philadelphia: Westminster, 1975), 495.

didn't happen much in the past; but those times of extreme religious intolerance have passed away. Such coerced, corporeal agreement on unessential doctrinal matters does not "preserve the unity of the Spirit in the bond of peace," but love does (Eph 4.3).

Indeed, we have inherited a tradition of anathemas pronounced by church officials upon dissident, non-traditionalist, yet professing Christians since the Council of Nicaea. Such adversity still continues unabated in many church communities today, bolstered by some traditionalist scholars. For example, I would hope that Murray Harris, upon further reflection, would withdraw his assertion that "any modern form of Christianity that has surrendered a wholehearted belief in Jesus' deity has drifted from its moorings and is at sea in a vessel that has forfeited its rating as 'Christian.'"[39] Similarly, in 1999 a doctrinal declaration was issued and signed by over a hundred evangelical Christian leaders, mostly Americans, which includes the following article: "We deny that any view of Jesus Christ which reduces or rejects his full deity is Gospel faith or will avail to salvation."[40] I could react as contrarily by charging that anyone who believes in the doctrine of the Trinity worships three gods and thereby violates the First Commandment, as Sir Isaac Newton alleged and the Koran states (*Quran* 5:72-73), and thus cannot be a true Christian. But I reject such allegations.

In conclusion, I contend that the NT verifies that anyone who (1) truly believes Jesus is the Christ, the sinless Son of God, who died for their sins and arose bodily from the dead, and (2) confesses Him as Lord, manifesting evidence in their life to that effect, is indeed a genuine Christian believer and should be accepted as such.[41]

---

[39] Murray J. Harris, *3 Crucial Questions About Jesus* (Grand Rapids: Baker, 1994), 103. Similarly, M. Hengel, *Studies in Early Christology*, viii-ix. Harris (*Jesus as God*, 12) uses the terms "deity," "God," and "Godhead" synonymously.

[40] Quoted from "The Gospel of Jesus Christ: An Evangelical Celebration," in *This We Believe: The Good News of Jesus Christ for the World*, gen. eds. John N. Akers, John H. Armstrong, and John D. Woodbridge (Grand Rapids: Zondervan, 2000), 245.

[41] D. Cupitt (*Jesus and the Gospel of God*, 19) rightly observes, "in the New Testament generally the mark of a Christian is not that he believes that Jesus is God but that he believes Jesus is Lord, Messiah and Son of God." William Barclay espoused a seemingly less-conditional evangel when he told an acquaintance of mine, "Young man, we are not saved by our theology but by our relationship with Jesus."

Abbreviations

General

Aram.	Aramaic	Lat.	Latin
b.	born	loc. cit.	*loco citato*, in the place cited
BCE	before the Common Era (BC)	mg	marginal reading
c.	*circa*, about (with regard to dates)	MT	Masoretic Text
CE	Common Era (AD)	n	note
cf.	*confer*, compare	n.d.	no date
ch(s).	chapter(s)	n.p.	no publisher
d.	died	NT	New Testament
ed.	editor, edition, edited by	OT	Old Testament
eds.	editors	op. cit.	*opere citato*, in the work cited
e.g.	*exempli gratia*, for example	orig.	original
Eng.	English	p., pp.	page, pages
ET	English Translation	par.	and parallel(s) in other gospel(s)
esp.	especially	R.	Rabbi
et al.	*et alii*, and others	repr.	reprint, reprinted
etc.	*et cetera*, and so forth	rev.	revised
Ger.	German	LXX	Septuagint, The
Gr.	Greek	Tg.	Targum
Heb.	Hebrew	tr.	translated by, translator(s)
ibid.	*ibidem*, in the same place	v., vv.	verse, verses
idem	the same	viz.	*videlicet*, namely
i.e.	*id est*, that is	vol(s).	volume(s)
		x	number of times (e.g., 2x=two times)

Books of the Bible

Old Testament

Gen	Genesis	Ps	Psalm		
Exo	Exodus	Prov	Proverbs		
Lev	Leviticus	Eccl	Ecclesiastes		
Num	Numbers	Isa	Isaiah		
Deut	Deuteronomy	Jer	Jeremiah		
Josh	Joshua	Eze	Ezekiel		
Jud	Judges	Dan	Daniel		
1 Sam	1 Samuel	Hos	Hosea		
2 Sam	2 Samuel	Oba	Obadiah		
1 Kgs	1 Kings	Mic	Micah		
2 Kgs	2 Kings	Hab	Habakkuk		
1 Chr	1 Chronicles	Zeph	Zephaniah		
2 Chr	2 Chronicles	Hag	Haggai		
Neh	Nehemiah	Zech	Zechariah		
Est	Esther	Mal	Malachi		

New Testament

Mt	Matthew	1 Tim	1 Timothy
Mk	Mark	2 Tim	2 Timothy
Lk	Luke	Tit	Titus
Jn	John	Heb	Hebrews
Ac	Acts	Jam	James
Rom	Romans	1 Pt	1 Peter
1 Cor	1 Corinthians	2 Pt	2 Peter
2 Cor	2 Corinthians	1 Jn	1 John
Gal	Galatians	2 Jn	2 John
Eph	Ephesians	3 Jn	3 John
Phil	Philippians	Rev	Revelation
Col	Colosians		
1 Th	1Thessalonians		
2 Th	2 Thessalonians		

Bible Versions, Commentaries, Journals, Dictionaries, Other

AB	Anchor Bible
AJT	*Asia Journal of Theology*
ANF	*Ante-Nicene Fathers*. Edited by Alexander Roberts, James Donaldson, et al. 1985-1987. 10 vols. Repr., Peabody, Mass., 1994
ASV	American Standard Version (1901)
AV, KJV	Authorized Version (=King James Version, 1611)
BAGD	Bauer, W., W.F. Arndt, F.W. Gingrich, and F.W. Danker. *Greek-English Lexicon of the New Testament and Other Early Christian Literature*. 2nd ed. Chicago, 1979
BC	Broadman Commentary
B-D-B	Brown, F., S.R. Driver, and C.A. Briggs. *The New Brown-Driver-Briggs-Gesenius Hebrew and English Lexicon: With an Appendix Containing the Biblical Aramaic*. [Orig. Oxford, 1907.] Edited by J.P. Green, Sr. Peabody, Mass., 1979
Berkeley	Holy Bible, The: The Berkeley Version in Modern English (1945, 1959). Gerrit Verkuyl.
Bib	*Biblica*
BJRL	*Bulletin of the John Rylands University Library of Manchester*
BSac	*Bibliotheca Sacra*
BT	*Bible Translator, The*
Cassirer	God's New Covenant: A New Testament Translation (1989). Edited by Heinz W. Cassirer
CBCNEB	Cambridge Bible Commentary: New English Bible
CBQ	*Catholic Biblical Quarterly*
CBSC	Cambridge Bible for Schools and Colleges
DDD	*Dictionary of Deities and Demons in the Bible*. Edited by K. van der Toorn, B. Becking, and P.W. van der Horst. Leiden, 1995
DHT	*Dictionary of Historical Theology, The*. Edited by Trevor A. Hart. Grand Rapids, 2000
DJG	*Dictionary of Jesus and the Gospels*. Edited by J.B. Green, S. Mc Knight. Downers Grove, 1992
DSS	Dead Sea Scrolls
EA	*Encyclopedia Americana* 27 (1956)
EB	*Encyclopaedia Britannica*. 11th ed.
EBC	Expositor's Bible Commentary, The, with the NIV
ESV	The Holy Bible, English Standard Version (2001)
ET	English Translation
ExpT	*Expository Times*
GNB	Good News Bible (1976; includes TEV)
Goodspeed	Complete Bible, The: An American Translation (1923, 1927; rev. ed. 1935). E.J. Goodspeed
HBD	*Harper's Bible Dictionary*. Edited by Paul T. Achtemeier et al. New York, 1985
Hermeneia	Hermeneia: A Critical and Historical Commentary on the Bible
HNTC	Harper's New Testament Commentaries
HTR	*Harvard Theological Review*
IB	Interpreter's Bible. Edited by G.A. Buttrick et al. 12 vols. New York, 1951-1957
ICC	International Critical Commentary
JB	Jerusalem Bible (1966)
JBL	*Journal of Biblical Literature*
JETS	*Journal (Bulletin) of the Evangelical Theological Society*
JPSTC	JPS Torah Commentary: The Traditional Hebrew Text with the new JPS Translation. Philadelphia, Jewish Publication Society.
JSNT	*Journal for the Study of the New Testament*
JTS	*Journal of Theological Studies*
K&D	Keil, C.F., and F. Delitzsch. *Commentary on the Old Testament*. Translated by J. Martin et al. 25 vols. Edinburgh, 1857-1878. 10 vols. Repr., Peabody, Mass., 1996

KJV/AV	King James Version (1611=Authorized Version)
LXX	Septuagint (Gr. OT)
MCNT	Meyer's Commentary on the New Testament. Edited by H.A.W. Meyer. 1st Eng. ed. 1883. Repr. Peabody, MA: Hendrickson, 1983.
M-H-T	Moulton-Howard-Turner. *A Grammar of New Testament Greek*
MNTC	Moffatt New Testament Commentary. Edited by James Moffatt
Moffatt	New Translation of the Bible, A (1913, 1925; rev. 1935). James Moffatt
MS, MSS	manuscript, manuscripts
MT	Masoretic Text (Heb. OT)
NA^{27}	*Novum Testamentum Graece*. 27th edition. Edited by Kurt Aland et al.
NAB	New American Bible (1970)
NASB	New American Standard Bible (1963, 1971)
NBC	The New Bible Commentary. 3rd edition
NBD	*New Bible Dictionary, The*. Edited by J.D. Douglas. Grand Rapids, 1962
NCBC	New Century Bible Commentary
NCE	*New Catholic Encyclopedia*. Edited by W.J. McDonald et al. 15 vols. New York, 1967
NEB	New English Bible (1961, 1970)
NIB	New Interpreter's Bible, The
NICNT	New International Commentary on the New Testament
NIDNTT	*New International Dictionary of New Testament Theology, The*. Edited by C. Brown. 4 vols. Grand Rapids, 1975-1985
NIGTC	New International Greek Testament Commentary
NIV	The Holy Bible, New International Version (1973, 1978)
NJPS	New JPS Translation, The. 2nd ed. (1999). (JPS=Jewish Publication Society)
NKJV	New King James Version (1982)
NJB	New Jerusalem Bible (1985)
NovT	*Novum Testamentum*
NPNF^1	*Nicene and Post-Nicene Fathers*: Series 1
NPNF^2	*Nicene and Post-Nicene Fathers*: Series 2
NRSV	The New Revised Standard Version Bible (1989)
NT	New Testament
NTC	New Testament Commentary
NTCERK	*New 20th Century Encyclopedia of Religious Knowledge*. 2nd ed. Edited by J.D. Douglas. Grand Rapids, 1991
NTS	*New Testament Studies*
NWT	New World Translation of the Christian Greek Scriptures. 1950. Rev. ed. Brooklyn, NY, 1951.
OLD	*Oxford Latin Dictionary*. Edited by P.G.W. Glare. Oxford: Clarendon, 1982.
OTP	*Old Testament Pseudepigrapha*. Edited by J.H. Charlesworth. 2 vols. New York, 1983
OT	Old Testament
PCB	Peake's Commentary on the Bible
Q	Quell ("sayings" source for synoptic gospels)
RB	*Revue Biblique*
REB	Revised English Bible (1989)
RSV	The Revised Standard Version Bible (1946, 1952, 2nd ed. 1971)
RV	Revised Version (1881, 1885)
SJT	*Scottish Journal of Theology*
SBLSP	*Society of Biblical Literature Seminar Papers*
Schurer	Schurer, Emil. *History of the Jewish People in the Age of Jesus Christ, The* (175 BC—AD 135)
SPS	Sacra Pagina Series
Str-B	Strack, H.L., and P. Billerbeck. *Kommentar zum Neuen Testament aus Talmud und Midrasch*. 6 vols. Munich, 1922-1961

T	Theology
TCNT	Twentieth Century New Testament (1904)
TDNT	Theological Dictionary of the New Testament. Edited by G. Kittel and G. Friedrich. Translated by G.W. Bromiley. 10 vols. Grand Rapids, 1964-1976.
TEV	New Testament in Today's English Version, The (1966)
Th To	Theology Today
TNTC	Tyndale New Testament Commentaries
TOTC	Tyndale Old Testament Commentaries
TR	Textus Receptus (Received Text)
TWOT	Theological Wordbook of the Old Testament. Edited by R.L. Harris, G.L. Archer, Jr., and Bruce K. Waltke. 2 vols. Chicago, 1980
UBS⁴	Greek New Testament, The. 4th edition. United Bible Societies.
WBC	Word Biblical Commentary
WC	Westminster Commentaries
WDCT	Westminster Dictionary of Christian Theology, The. Edited by Alan Richardson and John Bowden. Philadelphia, 1983.
ZNW	Zeitschrift für die neutestamentliche Wissenschaft und die Kunde der alteren Kirche
>	Indicates this book has a major comment on the scripture reference preceding this mark.

Pseudepigrapha, Apocrypha, Mishnah, Talmud, Targums, Other

Ascen. Isa.	Ascension of Isaiah	Pesiq. Rab.	Pesiqta Rabbati
Apoc. Abr.	Apocalypse of Abraham	Pss. Sol.	Psalms of Solomon
2-4 Bar.	2-4 Baruch	Sanh.	Sanhedrin
Ber.	Berakhot	Sir	Sirach/Ecclesiasticus
1-3 En.	1-3 Enoch	Sib Or	Sibylline Oracles
Gen. Rab.	Genesis Rabah	Ta'an.	Ta'anit
Jub	Jubilees	Tg. Ps.-J.	Targum Pseudo-Jonathan
1-2 Macc	1-2 Maccabees	Test. Abr.	Testament of Abraham
Ned.	Nedarim	Test. Levi	Testament of Levi
Pesah.	Pesahim	Wis	Wisdom

Apostolic Church Fathers

Barn.	Barnabas
1-2 Clem.	1-2 Clement

Chapter One
Introduction to Christology

The Fame of Jesus	The Resurrected Jesus
Who Is Jesus?	The Holy Spirit and Fulfilled Prophecy
What Is Christology?	The Jesus Movement
The Significance of the Bible	The Three Foremost Irrefutable Texts
Traditional Christology	The Scarcity of Biblical Texts
The Quest for the Historical Jesus	The Major Debated *Theos* Texts
How Jesus Identified Himself	The Debated Non-*Theos* Texts
How Others Identified Jesus	Principles of Hermeneutics
What Jesus Said About God	More Important Considerations
What Others Did Not Say About Jesus	Epilogue
Early Evangelistic Messages	

The Fame of Jesus

Jesus of Nazareth is the most famous man who ever lived. No one has ever had as profound an impact on human beings, especially in Western civilization, as has Jesus of Nazareth. He is the central figure of human history. The western calendar attests to this. And although He lived two thousand years ago, His tremendous influence on the world has not abated one bit. Christianity continues to have the largest number of adherents of any religion in the world. About two billion people, one third of the world's population, profess to be Christian. Thus, Jesus is just as relevant today as He ever has been, if not more so. In fact, far more books have been written about Jesus, from every conceivable angle, especially from a historical perspective lately, than any other human being. But how did he do it? How did this Jesus become the most famous man who has ever lived?

Very little is known about Jesus for the first thirty years of His life (cf. Lk 3.23). We learn from the four gospels of the New Testament (NT) that He was the first-born in a large Jewish family of peasant stock. We also are informed that He grew up as a rather precocious youth in Nazareth (Lk 2.40, 49-50). It was a small, obscure village located sixty-five miles north of Jerusalem in the Galilee of northern Israel. (Nazareth still exists today, having a population of about 60,000.) Here, Jesus assisted His (step) father Joseph as the town carpenter, which probably meant a woodcrafter (Mt 13.55; Mk 6.3).

But from the time that Jesus was about thirty years old until His death (Lk 3.23), we know a lot about Him.[1] We know that He was a deeply religious man

---

[1] E.P. Sanders, *The Historical Figure of Jesus* (New York: Penguin, 1993), xiii, 5, 54, 56; N.T. Wright, *Jesus and the Victory of God* (Minneapolis: Fortress, 1996), 123.

who gathered disciples and taught them about the God of Israel. We also know that He excelled at public speaking and delivering Jewish midrash, which is commentary on the Jewish Bible (Lk 4.16-30; Jn 10.30-38). This was especially true when He was engaged in controversy with His Jewish antagonists. Some of them postured themselves as experts on the Torah, which is the Law of Moses and a part of their Scriptures. Jesus was a Torah teacher, too.

Jesus often taught in parables. They are brief, fictitious, wisdom stories about real life situations that usually convey an ethical point. Jesus frequently told parables about the kingdom of God—what it is like and how to enter it. He compared the kingdom of God to a farmer sowing seed, a woman finding a lost coin, or a man discovering buried treasure in a field. Most people who heard Jesus tell about these vivid snapshots of life were enthralled with the simple, yet profound, lessons that He drew from them. Such stories were easy to remember, and so were His brief ethical and moral conclusions. Jesus therefore was a creative genius who did not teach as most teachers do—in abstract concepts that can be difficult to grasp and even harder to remember.

Some of the greatest Bible scholars and most intelligent and educated people in the world have spent their lives studying Jesus' teaching methods. Yet He apparently never had any formal education. He did not have advanced theological training by attending either of the two prominent schools of His time in Jerusalem—the school of Shammai and the school of Hillel. We read that one time when Jesus was teaching in the temple at Jerusalem, "The Jews therefore were marveling, saying, 'How has this man become learned, having never been educated'" (Jn 7.15; cf. Mk 6.2 par.).

One of the curious things about Jesus is that He didn't do the things that usually make people famous. For instance, He never wrote a book, never held a public office, and never marshaled an army. And even though He was an itinerant preacher, Jesus rarely traveled outside His tiny homeland. Whenever He did, He apparently didn't go more than fifty miles from home (cf. Mt 10.5-6; 15.24).[2] Most people who become famous spend their whole lives working hard to achieve such notoriety. In contrast, Jesus conducted His public ministry in such a short period of time,[3] perhaps only two or three years, and in such a small part of the world. Moreover, He never held an official religious position in Judaism and even refused to join any of its sects (Jn 2.24-25). So, Jesus didn't seem to have much going for Him in order to become the most famous person who has ever lived.

Not only that, until Jesus reached nearly mid-life He must not have been very well known outside of His hometown of Nazareth and its environs. Until He decided to join His cousin John the Baptist in becoming a public religious figure, Jesus had been no more than a common laborer. C.L. Blomberg says of Jesus, "even as the founder of a religious movement, he had little impact during his lifetime."[4] And distinguished Jesus researcher E.P. Sanders claims that for many years following Jesus' death, His fame was largely unknown beyond the confines of His own little country.[5]

---

[2] The NT gospels provide no evidence that Jesus ever traveled outside of Galilee, Judea, and Perea except (1) when His parents took Him as a child to Egypt to escape Herod's onslaught (Mt 2.13-21), (2) whenever He went through Samaria, and (3) a brief visit to Tyre and Sidon (Mt 15.21/Mk 7.24).
[3] Marcus J. Borg, *Jesus: A New Vision: Spirit, Culture, and the Life of Discipleship* (San Francisco: HarperSanFrancisco, 1987), 39. E.g., a large majority of 20th century scholars alleged that Josephus' mention of Jesus in his *Antiquities of the Jews*, 18.3.3, is either Christian interpolation or redaction.
[4] C.L. Blomberg, "Gospels (Historical Reliability)," in *DJG* 292.
[5] E.P. Sanders, *The Historical Figure of Jesus*, 49-51.

Yet the amazing history of the growth of Christianity—in which it started small, grew gradually, and later became a mammoth entity—coincides perfectly with something Jesus taught. He predicted that the kingdom of God which He preached would start very small—like a mustard seed, the tiniest seed in the garden—but grow to be the largest of all the plants in the garden (Mt 13.31-32/ Mk 4.31-32). Christianity did grow to become the largest plant in the world's garden of religions, and it still is to this day.

Who Is Jesus?

So, who was this man Jesus of Nazareth? This is perhaps the paramount question of all time; it is also the subject of this book.

Surely, Jesus was the most gifted of men. Regarding His words, He was a teaching rabbi, an itinerant preacher, a wisdom sage, and a seer-prophet. Regarding His deeds, Jesus was a charismatic healer, a miracle-worker, an exorcist, and a religious reformer. Through only word-of-mouth, large multitudes gathered excitedly to see Jesus perform His mighty works of wonder and hear His many pearls of extraordinary wisdom.

The common people received Jesus gladly. They "marveled" at seeing His many healings (Mt 8.27). And they "enjoyed listening to Him" (Mk 12.37). Oftentimes, the multitude "was astonished at His teaching" (Mk 11.18), so that "all the people were hanging on His words" Lk 19.48), pondering their profound meaning. They wondered how Jesus could do and say such amazing things and therefore who He really was.[6]

Now, the Jews had a very rich religious heritage. It was based mostly on the Law of Moses and secondarily on Israel's many prophets, among whom Moses was foremost. The God of these Hebrew people had promised through their prophets that someday He would send them a Messiah-King who would inaugurate a great kingdom in their midst and that it would spread all over the world. All of this was recorded in their Scriptures. This Messiah was expected to come from the tribe of Judah and the royal lineage of King David. The genealogies of Matthew and Luke do indeed include Jesus among David's descendants (Mt 1.1, 6; Lk 3.31). Jews believed from their Scriptures that this Messiah would be a military conqueror like David who would deliver them from their enemies. That, and Davidic lineage, is why they designated the Messiah as "the son of David."

Consequently, multitudes that saw and heard Jesus wondered if He could be this promised Messiah (Christ).[7] Some questioned if He was that great prophet about whom Moses had predicted that God would raise up like himself (Deut 18.15-19; Jn 6.14; 7.40).

Sometimes, the Jewish crowds became sharply divided in their speculation about Jesus' identity (Jn 7.43). Once, they tried to take Him by force and make Him a king; but He withdrew to a mountain to be alone and probably to pray (Jn 6.15).

So, Jesus often did the opposite of trying to become famous and powerful in this world. Sometimes, when He performed a miracle He would forbid the witnesses to tell others about it.[8] And He would give commands not to tell people that He was the Christ.[9]

---

[6] E.g., Mt 12.23; Mt 13.27/Mk 4.41/Lk 8.25; Jn 3.2; 7.40, 43; 8.53; 12.34.
[7] E.g., Jn 4.29; 7.26-27, 31, 41-42; 10.24-25; Mt 26.63/Mk 14.61; Lk 22.67, 70.
[8] E.g., Mt 8.4/Mk 1.44/Lk 5.14; Mk 5.43/Lk 8.56; Mk 7.36; cf. Mt 17.9/Mk 9.9; Mk 9.30.
[9] E.g., Mt 16.20/Mk 8.30/Lk 9.21; cf. Mk 1.24-25/Lk 4.34-35; Mk 1.34/Lk 4.41; Mt 12.16/Mk 3.11-12.

In contrast, Jewish religious officials were envious of Jesus and jealous of His popularity (Mt 27.18/Mk 15.10). When He taught the need for a personal and a national spiritual transformation, He sometimes singled them out by accusing them of impiety or hypocrisy. Rather than heed His call to repentance, they felt upstaged, their official status threatened, and they were appalled (e.g., Jn 11.47). Once they said among themselves about Jesus, "this man is performing many signs. If we let Him go on like this, all men will believe in Him and the Romans will come and take away our place and our nation" (Jn 11.47-48). Days later they said, "look, the world has gone after Him" (Jn 12.19).

These Jewish religious authorities earnestly desired to silence Jesus, to get rid of Him once and for all. To do so, they often engaged Him in debate, trying to trap Him in His words (Mt 22.15/Mk 12.13/Lk 20.20). They wanted to find Him guilty of teaching against the Torah (Jn 8.6). If successful, they could seriously discredit Him publicly and perhaps even charge Him with blasphemy. (According to the Torah, blasphemy incurred the death penalty; but the Jews' subjugation to the Romans prevented them from carrying it out.) During such disputes, Jesus often overpowered His adversaries with extraordinary spiritual acumen expressed in words of wisdom. And by frequently quoting Scripture, He demonstrated much skill at midrash (e.g., Mt 22.46), especially with the Torah.

Thus, a sharp contrast arose between the multitudes and Israel's religious rulers about their respective attitudes toward Jesus. The author of the NT Gospel of Luke highlights this difference. At the close of one of his narratives, Luke writes concerning Jesus, "And as He said this, all His opponents were being humiliated; and the entire multitude was rejoicing over all the glorious things being done by Him" (Lk 13.17).

Occasionally, the religious leaders themselves questioned Jesus specifically about His identity. Once they queried Him, apparently in a sarcastic tone, "Who are You?" (Jn 8.25). The next time they got into an argument with Jesus they challenged Him, "How long will You keep us in suspense? If You are the Christ, tell us plainly" (Jn 10.24).

Even Jesus' twelve apostles were sometimes mystified about His identity, despite the fact that they constantly accompanied Him during His public ministry. One time they were sailing together in a boat on Lake Galilee when a storm blew over which threatened to swamp the vessel. The disciples trembled and feared for their lives. Yet Jesus was fast asleep in the boat's stern. When they quickly awoke Him, "He arose, and rebuked the winds and the sea; and it became perfectly calm. And the men marveled, saying, 'What kind of man is this, that even the winds and the sea obey Him?'" (Mt 8.26-27).

Jesus regarded it supremely important for people to consider who He was and to come to a decision about it.[10] Once, during a rather sublime moment, Jesus asked His apostles privately and directly, "Who do people say that I am?" (Mk 8.27). After they offered various answers He inquired further, "'But who do you say that I am?' Peter answered and said to Him, 'You are the Messiah'" (Mk 8.29 NRSV).

What Is Christology?

The study of Jesus' identity and His significance is called Christology. Christian theologians regard Christology as preeminent among all theological studies. Biblical exegetes and theologians define Christology in three different

---

[10] Contra Albert Schweitzer (*Out of My Life and Thought: An Autobiography*, tr. C.T. Campion, Postcript by Everett Skillings [ET 1933, repr. New York: Henry Holt, 1949], 56), who alleged that Jesus "does not require of men today that they should be able to grasp either in speech or in thought who he is."

ways: (1) *narrowly*, the study of Jesus as the promised Messiah (Christ) of Israel; (2) *commonly*, the study of Jesus' entire identity (His Person); (3) *widely*, the study of Jesus' entire identity as well as His significance in a soteriological role (His work or function) in the purposes of God, hence everything about Him. In this book, the word "Christology" will be used as defined in #2, i.e., Jesus' entire identity, called "identity Christology,"[11] but with emphasis on whether He is God because this is what the institutional church has proclaimed with such vigor. It ought to be understood, however, that a thoroughgoing examination of Jesus' identity is inadequate if it ignores His significance for us as Lord and Savior.

Why study Christology? Some personal engagement with Christology is vital for every believer in Jesus. Widely esteemed Roman Catholic NT scholar R.E. Brown well explains, "Christian believers whose spiritual lives should be shaped by the Master, if they have not wrestled in some mature way with the identity of Jesus, are in danger of constructing a fictional Jesus ... most people answer the question of the identity of Jesus without any real struggle to gain precision about what the NT says.... Christology is so important an issue for religious adherence that one should not express judgments without seriously looking at the evidence."[12]

In studying identity Christology, it is imperative to first consider the meaning of the word God and how it should be used. The NT literature was written during the 1st century CE, and all of it has come down to us in the Greek language. The word for God in the Greek NT is *theos*. In 1st century Hellenism, *theos* was used very differently than it was used in the NT. Greek-speaking people applied *theos* to many supposed divine beings. But they also applied *theos* to humans and even to inanimate objects as well as to abstract concepts.[13] And in the Latin west, where the church prevailed in later centuries, the same was true of its Latin word for God—*deus*. In contrast, *theos* in the NT is used almost exclusively for the one and only God, the God of Israel, the God of the OT.

Therefore, in attempting to answer the question of whether Jesus is God, the word God must be understood in the context of Jesus' religious culture and that of the earliest Christians. This culture had its roots in the history recorded in the OT, which reached back to the patriarchs. If the 1st century Christians ever proclaimed Jesus as *theos* (Aram. *elah*), they would have meant that He was the God of Israel, the God of the OT, the one and only God. This is a far different use from how *theos* was used in Hellenism.

The Significance of the Bible

How does one study Christology in attempting to determine who Jesus was? Some explore the subject mostly from a philosophical or a mystical perspective, without much recourse to the Bible. But Maurice Wiles rightly comments, "Jesus of Nazareth was a historical figure and is known to us primarily through the records of the New Testament."[14] Therefore, the main focus for determining the identity of Jesus ought to be on what the four NT gospels say and don't say about Him.[15] Most Christians regard these gospels, actually the whole Bible, as

---

[11] Not many scholars use this well-suited terminology. Richard Bauckham frequently does in his book, *God Crucified: Monotheism and Christology in the New Testament* (Grand Rapids: Eerdmans, 1998).
[12] Raymond E. Brown, *An Introduction to New Testament Christology* (New York: Paulist, 1994), vi, 10-11.
[13] Pieter W. van der Horst, "God (II)," in *DDD*, 365-67.
[14] M. Wiles, *Explorations in Theology 4*, 22. Similarly, E.P. Sanders, *The Historical Figure of Jesus*, 3.
[15] The 1945 discovery of the Nag Hammadi library in Upper Egypt contained the first-known complete MS of the Gospel of Thomas. Some scholars, e.g., many Jesus Seminar Fellows, regard it as quite historically authentic, independent of the NT gospels, and the earliest record of (114) sayings of Jesus.

the criterion for a litmus test in examining one's Christology. Consequently, *this book will focus on the exegesis of the Bible, especially the four* NT *gospels, in order to determine what it proclaims about Jesus' identity.*

In the early centuries of church history, Christians became embroiled in many controversies about Jesus' identity. Each time it happened, they fervently searched the Scriptures to defend their positions.[16] These debates were often between two or three groups of professing Christians that were in opposition to each other. In fact, the major christological controversies of the early centuries of church history were of this latter type, in which all disputants appealed mostly to the NT, as well as patristic interpretations of it, in order to support their respective theses. Most of their arguments centered on the proper interpretation of the four gospels, especially the sayings of Jesus. An examination of these early, protracted, christological controversies confirms that *the gospels of the* NT *require substantial analysis in order to determine how these documents identify Jesus.*

How have Christians generally viewed these four NT gospels? Church fathers believed that the gospel writers (Evangelists) recorded historically authentic accounts of the works and words of Jesus. And they believed that subsequent scribal transmissions (hand copies) of those original documents were generally reliable. However, patristic textual critics who were familiar with the manuscript (MS) evidence, e.g., Jerome, the translator of the (Latin) Vulgate in the 5th century, did complain occasionally about MS variants. Nevertheless, church fathers believed that the original autographs of these four gospels were historically reliable and their transmissions trustworthy. And they viewed them on the same level as the Jewish Bible, which they received as divinely inspired, too. Most Christians throughout church history have embraced this conservative view of the inspiration of the Bible. (And it is the viewpoint adopted by this author as well.)

So, the primary question that Bible-believing Christians have asked down through the centuries is this: "What do these four NT gospels say about the identity of Jesus?"

Traditional Christology

Since the 2nd century, nearly all professing Christians have claimed that Jesus was and is both man and God. *The institutional church proclaimed in its first ecumenical council—the Nicene Council of 325* CE*—that Jesus is "very God of very God." These church fathers further declared that Jesus as God was the most distinctive feature of the Christian faith and absolutely essential to it. They therefore contended that a person must believe that Jesus is God in order to be a genuine Christian. Anyone who denied that Jesus is God was regarded as a non-Christian and therefore outside of the kingdom of God and without hope.* The teaching that Jesus is God is called "the deity of Christ."

Little has changed since. Catholics, Protestants, and Evangelicals alike still adhere to this traditional Christology—that it is absolutely necessary for people to believe that Jesus is God in order for them to be saved and therefore inherit eternal life.

Many Christians are even more stringent about it. They say that *if you don't believe that Jesus is God, you don't really believe in Jesus at all.* "It doesn't matter what else you believe about Jesus," they say. You can even believe that Jesus is the Christ, the Son of God, confess Him as Savior and Lord, believe that He lived a sinless and perfectly righteous life, performed many miracles, died on the

---

[16] Regarding early controversies, I presume the inclusion of the Christian "Scriptures" even though the Church did not officially sanction the NT until the late 4th century.

cross for your sins, arose alive from the dead, and ascended into heaven where He now sits exalted at the right hand of God, awaiting His second coming to the earth to consummate the worldwide kingdom of God on earth; but "if you don't believe in the deity of Christ, which means that Jesus Christ is God," so says most of the contemporary institutional church, "you are *not* a genuine Christian." For instance, popular American Presbyterian Reformed theologian R.C. Sproul states categorically, "A denial of Christ's deity is the essence of unbelief."[17]

In fact, most church officials still follow the patristic practice of not accepting people as candidates for formal church membership if it becomes apparent that they do not believe that Jesus Christ is God. In doing so, these ecclesiastical authorities clearly make belief in the supposed deity of Christ an essential element of Christian faith.

Scholars refer to Christians who believe that Jesus is God as "traditionalists." Such Christians insist that the deity of Christ is the very core of Christian doctrine. That is why they are so defensive about it. Many of them cling tenaciously to the conclusion that if Jesus was not God, and if the early Christians had not believed that He was God, there never would have been any Christianity. Norman Pittenger, an eminent process theologian and a contemporary traditionalist, puts it in no uncertain terms in asserting that without the deity of Christ, "Christianity is certainly destroyed."[18] Are these people right?

Jesus Research: The Quest for the Historical Jesus

In the past two centuries, there has arisen a growing movement among scholars to reexamine the subject of the identity of Jesus. In fact, as we embark upon the 21st century this scholarly pursuit, called Jesus Research, remains in the forefront of all theological and biblical studies. N.T. Wright, likely the United Kingdom's foremost Jesus researcher, points out that one of the most frequently asked questions today is this: "Is Jesus God?"[19]

This scholarly, ongoing, detailed investigation of the identity of Jesus is also called "the Quest for the Historical Jesus." We will learn more about it in Chapter Three. Suffice it to say for now that, by the use of historical-critical methods of investigation, this academic pursuit represents an attempt to go back in time, back beyond dogmatic church proclamations made especially in the 4th and 5th centuries, to the early church's primitive belief about Jesus during the 1st century. The purpose of this research in the minds of most of these notable scholars, called "questers," has been to *try to ensure that the contemporary church is centered on the real Jesus of history and not some caricature.*

This quest for the historical Jesus therefore rests upon the presupposition that there is a significant disparity between the belief of the 1st century Christians about Jesus' identity and that of the institutional church dogma that became established centuries later. In fact, some traditionalist scholars now acknowledge that recent critical scholarship has shown that some aspects of traditional Christology do not rest on a solid foundation.[20]

---

[17] R.C. Sproul, *Getting the Gospel Right: The Tie that Binds Evangelicals Together* (Grand Rapids: Baker, 1999), 135.
[18] W. Norman Pittenger, *The Word Incarnate: A Study of the Doctrine and Person of Christ* (San Francisco: Harper, 1959), 85.
[19] Tom Wright, *The Original Jesus: The Life and Vision of a Revolutionary* (Grand Rapids: Eerdmans, 1991), 78.
[20] Christian scholars often admit that it can take decades for some scholastic determination, of which there is a consensus, to pass down to the laity, especially when it clashes with traditional church dogma.

Some contemporary scholars spearheading this quest for the historical Jesus have attempted to go back beyond the beliefs of the early Christians to the self-awareness of Jesus. While it is difficult, if not impossible, to psychoanalyze Jesus solely from the NT gospels,[21] the starting point for discovering the identity of Jesus is surely Jesus Himself and thus, to some degree, His self-consciousness as revealed in these writings.[22]

The importance of the self-consciousness of Jesus for Christology cannot be overemphasized. If a person accepts the premise that both the pre- and post-Easter Jesus of the NT became the source and center of early Christianity, as this author does, *Jesus' self-consciousness is the preeminent issue to investigate in an attempt to determine His identity.* The institutional church and radical critics have surprisingly undervalued this aspect. In fact, they have opposed it, albeit for opposite reasons. *Any fundamental belief in Jesus' identity that cannot be connected to Jesus' self-consciousness, as gleaned from the NT gospels, is seriously flawed and represents a discontinuity in one's Christology.*

How Jesus Identified Himself

So, let us examine the NT gospels to see how Jesus identified Himself. In doing so, we first learn that He was most fond of applying to Himself the enigmatic title, "the Son of Man." Until modern times, Christian scholars have not regarded Jesus' adoption of this appellation as particularly significant. Church fathers thought it pertained only to Jesus' humanity and not to His supposed deity. Many scholars today think just the opposite.

Interestingly, except for Jesus' use of this "Son of Man" language, He seldom divulged His identity with the use of titles.[23] On rare occasions, Jesus did verbally indicate that He was the Messiah and/or the Son of God. One time, He privately and indirectly admitted to a Samaritan woman that He was "the Messiah" (Jn 4.25-26). Another time, Jesus asked His disciples who they thought He was. The Apostle Peter answered that He was "the Christ, the Son of the living God." This account by Matthew makes it evident that Jesus accepted Peter's reply (Mt 16.16-17). And once during the Feast of Dedication at Jerusalem, the Johannine Jesus admitted to His interlocutors, "I said, 'I am the Son of God'" (Jn 10.36). But Jesus finally owned both of these titles—the Messiah/Christ and the Son of God—at His examination before the Sanhedrin (Mt 26.63-64 par.). Later, we will investigate these and other titles as well as this examination.

But did Jesus ever claim to be God, as the institutional church asserts? Ask most Christians, "Where does the Bible say Jesus claimed to be God?" If they know their Bible well, they likely will answer, "He said, 'I and the Father are one'" (Jn 10.30>). But surely this brief statement does not represent an unequivocal declaration that He is God. One is struck with the thought, "Is this the best scriptural evidence traditionalists have to support their strong belief that Jesus thought He was God and said He was God?"

Indeed it is! Consequently, *in light of the traditional Christian view that Jesus is God, it is rather shocking to learn that the NT gospels do not contain a single saying of Jesus in which He unambiguously claimed to be God.* Thus, the gospels do not relate that Jesus ever said, "I am God" or the like, which is *ego eimi ho theos*

---

[21] Joseph A. Fitzmyer, *A Christological Catechism: New Testament Answers*, rev. ed. (New York: Paulist, 1991), 15.

[22] The terms "self-awareness" and "self-consciousness," as applied to Jesus, are used synonymously herein.

[23] R.E. Brown (*Jesus God and Man*, 23) acknowledges a "shortage of recorded self-identifying statements by Jesus."

in Greek and *anahelah* in Aramaic, the native language Jesus and all Jews spoke in Israel in those days. Some of the most distinguished New Testament scholars concur with A.E. Harvey in saying of Jesus, "there is no evidence whatsoever that he spoke or acted as if he believed himself to be 'a god,' or divine.'"[24] Michael Goulder asserts, "Being a monotheist, Jesus cannot have thought of himself sanely as being Yahweh,"[25] (Heb. YHWH), the OT name for God. And strong Trinitarian Brian Hebblethwaite concedes, "it is no longer possible to defend the divinity of Jesus by reference to the claims of Jesus" in the NT gospels.[26]

Take the Synoptic Gospels; scholars concur that they do not contribute hardly anything to indicate that Jesus is identified as God. Yes, the synoptists report that He healed many people, performed other miracles, and rose from the dead. And they reveal that Jesus exercised functions which many Jews, and subsequent traditionalist Christians, have thought were the sole prerogatives of God, such as claiming authority to forgive sins. And the synoptists, as well as other NT authors, relate that Jesus and some of His disciples applied OT texts to Jesus which, in their OT contexts, pertain strictly to Yahweh. But we will learn later that none of these things indicate that Jesus was God.

Therefore, we cannot overemphasize the question, Did Jesus *claim* to be God? Perhaps a more important question is, "Did Jesus *believe* He was God?" Of course, it is conceivable, but highly unlikely, that Jesus believed He was God without proclaiming it.

How Others Identified Jesus

If Jesus never identified Himself as God, how did His contemporaries identify Him? Over forty times in the NT gospels, God, men, women, angels, and even demons proclaim that Jesus is "the Christ" or "the Son of God." Except for calling Jesus "Lord," these are the two most prominent titles the NT Evangelists and their characters apply to Jesus. Here is a sampling of the testimony of the latter:

- Gabriel - "He will be great, and will be called the Son of the Most High" (Lk 1.32).
- Gabriel - "the holy offspring shall be called the Son of God" (Lk 1.35).
- God - "This is My beloved Son, in whom I am well-pleased" (Mt 3.17 par.).
- John the Baptist - "I have seen and I testify that this is the Son of God" (Jn 1.34 NIV).
- Nathaniel - "You are the Son of God; You are the King of Israel" (Jn 1.49).
- The Devil "If You are the Son of God" (Mt 4.3, 6 par.).
- Demon - "I know who You are—the Holy One of God" (Mk 1.24/Lk 4.34).
- Demons - "You are the Son of God" (Lk 4.41, and "they knew Him to be the Christ").
- Unclean spirits - "You are the Son of God" (Mk 3.11).
- Demoniac - "You, Jesus, Son of the Most High God" (Mk 5.7/Lk 8.28).
- Disciples in the boat - "You are certainly God's Son" (Mt 14.33).
- Peter - "Thou art the Christ, the Son of the living God" (Mt 16.16 par.).
- Peter - "You are the Holy One of God" (Jn 6.69).
- Martha - "I have believed that You are the Christ, the Son of God" (Jn 11.27).
- Centurion guard - "Truly this was the Son of God" (Mt 27.54).

---

[24] A.E. Harvey, *Jesus and the Constraints of History* (Philadelphia: Westminster, 1982), 168.
[25] Michael Goulder, "Incarnation or Eschatology?" in Michael Goulder, ed., *The Debate Continued: Incarnation and Myth* (London: SCM, 1979), 143.
[26] Brian Hebblethwaite, *The Incarnation: Collected Essays in Christology* (Cambridge: University, 1987), 74.

Except for the first two affirmations above, all of them were spoken to Jesus. The fact that He never disapproved of the application of such titles to Himself implies His tacit acceptance of them. The most important thing to glean from these appellations is that *the central theme of the four NT gospels is that Jesus is the Christ, the Son of God.*

But did Jesus' apostles, or the Evangelists, or any other characters mentioned in the NT gospels ever identify Him as God? Many Christians will answer that He was God because the NT repeatedly declares Him to be the Son of God. But that is a deduction, which will be addressed throughout this book, and not an express declaration. Some Christians who know their Bible will cite the Apostle Thomas' confession, in Jn 20.28>, in which He said to Jesus, "My Lord and my God." We will examine this utterance in a later chapter. Except for it, most NT scholars answer this question in the negative. A.E. Harvey explains, "the immediate followers of Jesus were strictly bound by the constraint of monotheism which, as Jews, they instinctively professed and in their attempts to declare who Jesus was they stopped well short of describing him as 'divine.'"[27]

What Jesus Said About God

Whether Jesus or others identified Him as God, the NT reveals that He did talk incessantly *about* God, calling Him "Father." What did Jesus say about God as Father?

Jesus was a Jew who spoke like a Jew. Jews usually distinguished themselves from Gentiles by their belief in one God. In contrast, most Gentiles believed in many gods. Being a Jew commonly meant believing in one God. Consequently, *Jesus affirmed that there is only one true God.* An example was when a Pharisee, a Torah-expert, asked Him what was the greatest commandment (Mt 22.34-36/Mk 12.28-34). Jesus answered by quoting the Shema. It includes the words: "THE LORD OUR GOD IS ONE LORD" (Mk 12.29). The man replied, "Right, Teacher. You have truly stated that HE IS ONE AND THERE IS NO ONE ELSE BESIDES HIM" (v. 32). This Pharisee surely meant that God is a single being, or personality, so that there are no other beings who are God.[28] Accordingly, Jesus could not be God, and this is surely how He understood the man's response. Mark informs that, rather than reprimand the fellow, "when Jesus saw that he had answered intelligently, He said to him, 'You are not far from the kingdom of God'" (Mk 12.34).

Thus, in accordance with the OT as well as Judaism, Jesus always thought and spoke of the one God, the God of Israel, as Someone other than Himself. As a Jew living in a strictly monotheistic religious culture, Jesus could not possibly have thought in any other way about it. If He had, we would surely know of it in the NT. One of the clearest gospel examples is when a man identified Jesus as "good Teacher." Jesus objected by replying, "Why do you call Me good? No one is good except God alone" (Mk 10.18>).

Nevertheless, the Johannine Jesus clearly preached that people must come to Him in order to get to God. He said, "I am the way,... to the Father" (Jn 14.6). The Johannine Jesus saw Himself as the only path for sinners to take in order to be reconciled with God.

The Johannine Jesus even declared that He had come to show people God (Jn 14.6-10). In fact, *Jesus' foremost claim about Himself was that God was uniquely present in Him. So, according to Jesus, He was not God but the Revealer*

---

[27] A.E. Harvey, *Jesus and the Constraints of History*, 167.
[28] See Isa 43.10-11; 44.6, 8; 45.5-6, 18, 21-22; 47.8, 10.

of the God who indwelt Him. This is the fundamental difference between traditional Christ-is-God Christology and that which is set forth in this book, called strictly a "God-in-Christ Christology." Many Christians unknowingly are confused about this important distinction. They do not understand that *God being in Christ is not the same as Christ being God.*

The main thing Jesus said about God was that He was always calling God "My Father." The OT only acknowledges God as the "father" of Israel nationally, not individually (Isa 63.16; 64.8; cf. Jer 3.4, 19). This corporate concept was based on God calling the nation of Israel "My son" (Ex 4.22-23; Hos 11.1). Jesus' opponents were offended at His somewhat unique and very personal style of calling God "My Father" and occasionally referring to Himself as "the Son (of God)." It certainly suggested that He claimed to have an extraordinarily intimate relationship with God (Jn 5.17-18).

Jesus thus spoke of "God" and "the/My Father" interchangeably.[29] His disciples soon adopted this usage, which is reflected virtually everywhere in the NT. Traditionalist theologian Karl Rahner explains, "*ho theos* [God] in the language of the New Testament signifies the Father,... All that is meant is that when the New Testament thinks of God, it is the concrete, individual, uninterchangeable Person who comes into mind, who is in fact the Father and is called *ho theos*."[30] Indeed, this practice traces back to Jesus.

Jesus sometimes called the Father "My God" (Mt 27.46; Mk 15.34; Jn 20.17). How could He do that if He Himself was God? Assuming that Jesus and the Father are separate beings, which they are, doesn't calling Jesus "God" suggest two Gods?

What Others Did Not Say About Jesus

It is also significant what Jesus' disciples *did not say* about Him. While arguments based on silence are usually weak, this NT silence is particularly striking. Setting aside Jn 20.28> for later examination, *the four NT gospels and the book of Acts do not contain any discussion or even a single statement in which Jesus' disciples identify Him as "God."*

The same is true of the gospel Evangelists. They never declare in their own words that Jesus is "God." Moreover, none of them provide any sort of treatise about such a notion. A.E. Harvey attributes this silence to the constraint of Jewish monotheism. He explains that "the New Testament writers appear to have submitted to this constraint, and to have avoided using the word 'god' or 'divine' of Jesus."[31]

Jesus and His apostles were Jews who knew their religion of Judaism well. Its main feature has always been monotheism—the belief in one God. Jews understood their God to be a single being or person. Jewish contemporary scholar Jacob Neusner states categorically, "Israel knows God as a person and ... a fully embodied personality."[32]

If the NT authors had believed that Jesus was God, why didn't they say so in their NT writings in the form of clear, didactic, propositional statements? G.H. Boobyer puts the question this way, "If the New Testament

---

[29] E.g., Jn 4.34-35; 6.27, 46; 8.41-42; 11.40-41; 14.1-2; 17.1-3; 20.17. Most notable are those instances in which two or all three synoptists record the same quotation of Jesus yet interchange "God" and "Father," e.g., Mt 12.50 and Mk 3.35;
[30] Karl Rahner, *Theological Investigations*, tr. Cornelius Ernst, 20 vols. (Baltimore: Helicon, 1961), 1:146.
[31] A.E. Harvey, *Jesus and the Constraints of History*, 157.
[32] Jacob Neusner and Bruce Chilton, *Jewish-Christian Debates: God, Kingdom, Messiah* (Minneapolis: Fortress, 1998), 218.

writers believed it vital that the faithful should confess Jesus as 'God,' is the almost complete absence of just this form of confession in the New Testament explicable?"[33]

Early Evangelistic Messages

How did the early Christians identify Jesus in their evangelistic messages recorded in the NT? Scholars call these messages the *kerygma*, a Greek word meaning "proclamation." The book of Acts is the main place to look for this kerygma. This book is unique in that it records the missionary, evangelistic activity of the early Christians.

Regarding titles, the book of Acts verifies that Jesus' first disciples preached mostly that He was the Messiah (Christ), the Son of God, Savior, and Lord.[34] *Yet there is no evidence in the book of Acts that the early Christians proclaimed Jesus as "God" in their evangelistic messages.*[35]

An example is the scared Philippian jailer. He exclaimed to the imprisoned Paul and his associates, "'what must I do to be saved? And they said, 'Believe in the Lord Jesus, and you shall be saved'" (Ac 16.30-31). Thus, they told him to believe in Jesus as Lord, not God. Catholic traditionalist R.E. Brown acknowledges, "The sermons which Acts attributes to the beginning of the Christian mission do not speak of Jesus as God."[36]

The book of Acts also relates instances in which the Jewish religious authorities arrested Jesus' disciples and interrogated them.[37] As the Sanhedrin had done in its interrogation of Jesus, it never accused these disciples of proclaiming Jesus as "God." This omission, too, strongly suggests that these disciples did not believe such a thing.

If the early Jewish Christians had believed that Jesus was God, why didn't they proclaim it in their evangelistic messages? Surely they would have deemed it more important to preach that Jesus is God than that He is the Christ, the Son of God.[38] The obvious reason that they didn't is that Jesus never identified Himself as God.

If it had been known especially in Judea that either Jesus or His disciples had proclaimed publicly that Jesus was God, it would have been impossible for such an assertion to have gone unchallenged by the religious establishment. And the volatile arguments that it would have aroused likely would not have escaped the book of Acts.[39]

While the kerygma in Acts reveals that the apostles and other early disciples *did not* believe Jesus was God, it shows that they esteemed Him very highly. For instance, they considered Him sinless, acknowledged that He did miracles, and eventually believed His every word. They praised Him as "Rabbi," "Master," and "Lord." They believed that He was the promised Messiah-King of Israel and that in the future He would usher in the glorious kingdom of God. Having forsaken all to follow Jesus, their hopes for the future were so bound up in Him. They believed that they would occupy prominent positions

---

[33] G.H. Boobyer, "Jesus As '*Theos*' in the New Testament," *BJRL* 50 (1967-68): 253.
[34] E.g., Ac 2.36; 3.6, 18, 20; 4.10; 5.31, 42; 9.20, 22; 10.36; 11.17; 13.23; 16.31.
[35] For these messages in the book of Acts, see Ac 2.14-40; 3.12-26; 4.8-12; 5.42; 9.20, 22; 10.34-43; 13.16-41; 16.30-31; 17.3, 18, 22-31; 18.5, 28; 20.21; 22.1-21; 26.2-29; 28.23, 31.
[36] R.E. Brown, *Jesus God and Man*, 30; cf. p. 33; idem, *An Introduction to New Testament Christology*, 190. See Appendix C: Modern Christologies/A Late, Liturgical Christology and Chapter Six/Jn 20.28>.
[37] E.g., Ac 4.3-22; 5.17-40; 6.8—7.60; 8.3; 21.30—26.32.
[38] We will see later that subsequent Christians made a mistake in equating "the Son of God" with "God."
[39] The accusation that Jesus claimed to be God will be considered later, in Jn 5.18> ; 10.33>.

of authority in that future kingdom because Jesus promised it to them (Mt 19.28; Lk 22.30).

But seeming tragedy struck. Jesus was arrested by a Roman cohort, taken to the Jewish religious authorities, interrogated by them, and accused of blasphemy. He was then tried, condemned, and crucified by Roman Governor Pilate. And His dead body was entombed. Jesus' disciples must have been so overwhelmed with grief and despair. They had not believed Him when He had foretold on various occasions that He would suffer and die at Jerusalem and rise from the dead on the third day.[40]

The Resurrected Jesus

On the morning of the third day following Jesus' crucifixion, the sealed stone was found rolled away and His tomb empty. The NT repeatedly explains that God (the Father) raised Jesus from the dead.[41] Jesus proved this to His disciples by appearing before many of them on various occasions, always conversing with them and at least once eating with them.[42] According to Paul, the risen Jesus appeared to over 500 believing brethren at one time (1 Cor 15.6). Then, forty days after Jesus' resurrection the disciples were standing with their Master on the Mount of Olives when they witnessed His departure from this world. Jesus ascended up into the sky before their very eyes, "and a cloud received Him out of their sight" (Ac 1.9). According to further NT tradition, Jesus then entered heaven where God invited Him to sit down with Him at His right hand on His throne.[43]

Christianity stands or falls on the resurrection of Jesus; without it, Christianity is inexplicable. For, it needs to be explained how Jesus could have publicly ministered for only two or three years and then died, and how His followers afterwards would have been so disillusioned and discouraged; yet only days later they were instantly and dramatically renewed with hope and vigor, launching a worldwide campaign to become fishers of men and thereby fulfill the mission for which Jesus had chosen and called them. They went about boldly proclaiming the good news of their resurrected, glorified, and exalted Lord.

So, these early Jewish Christians had such a strong conviction that Jesus had risen from the dead. They based this conviction on what they clearly had regarded as specific historical events. Like Judaism, Christianity was to become a very historical religion. In the years that followed, Jesus' apostles traveled far and wide throughout the known world, preaching about historical events in the life of Jesus as well as His remembered sayings. But these men *especially* proclaimed His bodily resurrection from the dead. They understood this supreme act as God's vindication of Jesus and confirmation that He was indeed the promised Messiah of Israel, the Son of God, of whom many prophecies in their Scriptures had foretold. Oftentimes, these disciples risked their lives for preaching about Jesus' resurrection.[44] Tradition says most of Jesus' apostles died martyr's deaths for publicly proclaiming such things. This unflinching, shining testimony of Jesus' followers is evidence that they believed so strongly that he had risen from the dead.

---

[40] Jn 2.18-22 cf. with Mk 14.58; 15.29; Mt 12.40; Mt 16.21-22/Mk 8.31-32/Lk 9.22; Mt 17.22-23/Mk 9.30-32/Lk 9.43-45; Mt 20.17-19/Mk 10.32-34/Lk 18.31-34; Mt 27.63; Lk 24.6-8; cf. Mt 16.4; Lk 11.29.
[41] E.g., Ac 2.24, 32; 3.15, 26; 4.10; 5.30; 10.40; 13.30, 34, 37; 17.31; Rom 10.9; 1 Cor 6.14; 15.15; Gal 1.1; Eph 1.20; Col 2.12; 1 Thes 1.10; 1 Pt 1.21.
[42] Mt 28; Mk 16; Lk 24; Jn 20; Ac 1.3; 17.31.
[43] E.g., Mk 16.19; Lk 22.69; Ac 7.55-56; Rom 8.34; Eph 1.20; Col 3.1; Heb 10.12; 12.2; 1 Pt 3.22.
[44] E.g., Ac 3.26—4.4; 4.18, 33; 6.8—7.60; 23.6-7; 17.18, 32; 24.21; 26.23-24.

Now, at the beginning of this chapter the question was posed, How did Jesus become the most famous person the world has ever known? We considered His amazing gifts as an answer. But the foremost answer of all is His resurrection from the dead. The resurrection of Jesus testifies most supremely to the uniqueness of Jesus and Christianity.

In light of such facts, the existence of Christianity therefore seems impossible if Jesus had not literally risen from the dead. The Apostle Paul insisted that the resurrection of Jesus is absolutely fundamental to faith in Him. Paul wrote to the Corinthian believers, saying, "if Christ has not been raised, your faith is worthless" (1 Cor 15.17). Without a doubt, the Christian "faith has its origin and progressive growth in Jesus' resurrection."[45] No other great religion can claim *that* for its founder, and none has ever tried.

The Holy Spirit and Fulfilled Prophecy

So, the foundation of Christianity has always been the proclamation that Jesus was the Christ, the Son of God, Lord, Savior, and that He arose from the dead. There are two other matters that need to be added to this list in what constitutes the seven pillars of the foundation of early Christianity: the coming of the Holy Spirit upon Jesus' disciples on that first day of Pentecost of the Christian era and Jesus' fulfillment of OT prophecies.

The OT affirms that the Holy Spirit had always been active in the world and often experienced by Israel. But such spiritual phenomena usually pertained to a select few, mostly Israel's prophets and kings. In contrast, something new and most world-changing happened only fifty days after Jesus' resurrection: the Holy Spirit came and filled all of Jesus' disciples with joy and produced outward supernatural manifestations in them. It was the beginning of a life-long affirmation to them of the truth about Jesus, in which they experienced God's power so strongly and vividly in their lives and ministries.

Also, in the early years following the Christ event, Jesus' disciples searched the OT to discover that He had fulfilled some of its prophecies. Like the power of the Holy Spirit in their lives, this realization of the fulfillment of OT prophecies in Jesus' life, death, and resurrection was so crucial in strengthening the disciples' faith. And citing these fulfillments of prophecy became very important elements in their evangelistic preaching, especially when their audience consisted mostly of their Jewish brethren.

The Jesus Movement

This early Christian movement therefore began as a sect of Judaism composed only of Jews. Scholars now call it "the Jesus Movement." At first, most of these followers of Jesus apparently continued to live in the Galilee, where Jesus had lived. And they did not forsake their custom of attending synagogues in their respective localities. Also, male heads of families, with family members often accompanying them, would make an occasional pilgrim trek to Jerusalem to gather at the temple with their Jewish brethren and worship God during annual festivals, especially Passover.[46] Despite their

---

[45] *Bible et christologie*, 1.2.3.1.
[46] Modern scholars have tended to identify the early Jewish Christians of Galilee and Judea as "Palestinian Christians" and their land as "Palestine," terms that conflict with modern usage. And they have used these terms anachronistically, since biblical lands were called "Judea," "Samaria," and "Galilee" in Jesus' time and afterwards. The Romans did not rename them "Palaestina" until the final Diaspora began, in 135 CE.

belief in Jesus as Messiah, these early disciples did not cut themselves off from Judaism.

Nevertheless, the early Jewish Christians pondered the meaning and implications of Jesus' life, death, resurrection, ascension, and heavenly exaltation. The result of these deliberations was that *the disciples integrated their veneration for Jesus with their former monotheistic faith, and they obviously felt that it did not infringe on their reverence for, and worship of, the one true God.* In other words, they devoted themselves to Jesus as Lord of their lives without feeling they had compromised their faith in Yahweh their God.

These early disciples could not contain their joy and excitement about what they had seen and heard, especially after they experienced the Holy Spirit coming upon them with such power at Pentecost. They immediately began to spread the gospel, the good news about their resurrected Lord Jesus. For a while they enjoyed favor with the people, having a positive reception to their message, and thus had peace (Ac 2.41, 47; 4.4; 9.31). But eventually the large majority of their countrymen began to reject their message and persecute them. Such opponents argued that Jesus could not possibly have been the Messiah because He died, and that by crucifixion, which they regarded as scandalous. They contended that there was nothing in their Scriptures about the Messiah dying; rather, He would deliver the nation from its enemies and reign forever as its king. The disciples conceded that Jesus had not fulfilled all of the messianic prophecies but that in the future He would return in glory and then do so. So, a very important element in their message was what later came to be called "the Second Coming of Christ." In fact, that is what the two angels at Jesus' ascension had foretold would happen someday (Ac 1.11).

Members of this Jesus Movement developed an oral tradition about Jesus in their cultic communities that was based on witnesses who saw and heard Jesus. This tradition no doubt was recited often at their gatherings. Eventually, these believers wrote down their oral traditions. These documents, and copies of them, were circulated among the believing communities. And these documents, along with letters written by respected individuals such as the Apostle Paul, were collected and read aloud during congregational church meetings (Col 4.16; 1 Th 5.27; 1 Tim 4.13). It is believed that out of this rich oral and literary tradition the NT gospels were compiled (Lk 1.1-3). In time, the Catholic Church recognized most of these collected gospels, books, and letters as the NT.

These NT documents reveal that these early Jewish Christians ascribed various lofty titles, attributes, and functions to the resurrected and heavenly-exalted Jesus. These believers probably thought previously that some of these descriptions should be reserved exclusively for God. But they would have changed their minds after the Christ event. One piece of evidence is that they submitted their prayerful petitions to God in the name of Jesus. And they composed hymns and songs of praise for both God and Jesus. They sang them with enthusiastic joy, uttering heartfelt thanks in the same breath to both.

Such devotion to Jesus Christ raises serious and thought-provoking questions. Precisely what sort of status did these early Jewish Christians ascribe to Jesus, especially regarding His relation to God the Father? In proclaiming Jesus' uniqueness, did they think that He, too, was God? Or did they ascribe a divinity to Him, but to a lesser extent? And what of their former monotheism? Did they continue to conform to it, in accordance with the faith of their forefathers, especially the Hebrew patriarchs? Or did they make a compromise by altering it? Put bluntly, was this Jesus Movement a heretical sect that had abandoned its monotheistic roots in Judaism? A.E. Harvey answers astutely:

> the earliest Christians could hardly have occupied themselves with the question posed by later theologians: whether, and in what sense, Jesus was "god." The Jewish people were severely and passionately monotheist. That God is one, and that only he is God, was the foundation of their religion and their whole way of life, and was explicitly endorsed by Jesus himself. Therefore, among those Jews who were first converted to Christ, the idea could not have been entertained for one moment that Jesus was *another* god.[47]

What eventually brought about the final schism between this new, budding flower that came to be called "Christianity" and its indestructible stem—Judaism? It was not so much that the Christians identified Jesus as Israel's promised Messiah, though they did and that was a prominent source of contention between Christianity and Judaism. Rather, Jewish scholar Jacob Neusner informs, "A review of the medieval disputations will turn up ample evidence that the Judaic party regarded the claim of incarnation as decisive proof of Christianity's implausibility—indeed, incomprehensibility. So it must follow that the parties parted company at incarnation,... [that] Jesus is God incarnate."[48]

This reason for the final schism between these two religions raises an important point. The NT reveals that the apostolic Christians preached that Jesus was the Messiah, not God; but the post-apostolic Christians preached that Jesus was the Messiah *and* God. Thus, *preaching that Jesus is God was a departure from biblical, apostolic Christianity.*

The Three Foremost Irrefutable Texts

Now let us return to the extant documents penned by the early believers in Jesus that have survived in the NT corpus, and let us see whether they say that Jesus is God.

Two major points will emerge repeatedly in this book to show that Jesus cannot be God and that the NT provides a massive amount of evidence affirming this. These two points are that (1) only the Father is God, and (2) Jesus Christ is distinguished from God. Three irrefutable texts that declare both of these points are as follows, with the first one being in Jesus' high-priestly prayer and the other two occurring in Paul's writings:

- "And this is eternal life, that they may know you, the only true God, and Jesus Christ, whom you have sent" (Jn 17.3 NRSV).
- "There is no God but one.... yet for us there is but one God, the Father, from whom are all things, and we exist for Him; and one Lord, Jesus Christ, by whom are all things, and we exist through Him" (1 Cor 8.4, 6).
- "There is one body and one Spirit, just as also you were called in one hope of your calling; one Lord, one faith, one baptism, one God and Father of all who is over all and through all and in all" (Eph 4.4-6).

These three texts establish without any doubt whatsoever that Jesus is not God. If there are other biblical texts which proclaim that Jesus *is* God, they conflict with these verses.

---

[47] A.E. Harvey, ed., *God Incarnate: Story and Belief* (London: SPCK, 1981), 52. Emphasis not mine.
[48] Jacob Neusner and Bruce Chilton, *Jewish-Christian Debates: God, Kingdom, Messiah* (Minneapolis: Fortress, 1998), 217. Cf. Allan F. Segal, *Two Powers in Heaven: Early Rabbinic Reports about Christianity and Gnosticism* (Leiden: Brill, 1977), 262.

The Scarcity of Biblical Texts

So, what about those biblical texts which traditionalists claim identify Jesus as God? Indeed, some traditionalist expositors cite not a few of them. Scholarly authorities on this subject usually classify these passages by separating them into two categories: (1) those believed to call Jesus "God" *explicitly*, having *theos* in the Greek text, and (2) those believed to do so *implicitly*, not having *theos* in the Greek text.

Regarding the first category, the Greek NT contains twenty-two instances that contain the word *theos* which various traditionalist expositors throughout church history have thought identify Jesus as "God."[49] However, the majority of recent traditionalist authorities—those who have written rather extensively on the subject of whether Jesus is God[50]—concede that most of these twenty-two biblical texts *do not* identify Jesus as "God" (Gr. *theos*). Murray Harris claims "only seven certain, very probable, or probable instances out of a total of 1,315 uses of *theos*" in the NT are applied to Jesus.[51] Harris provides a survey of twenty-seven of the most notable NT scholars who have written on this subject over the past century, and he observes, "the majority of [these] scholars hold that *theos* is applied to Jesus no fewer than five times and no more than nine times in the NT."[52] Indeed, Oscar Cullman proposes at least nine;[53] R.N. Longenecker thinks there are "only eight or nine;"[54] A.W. Wainwright identifies seven;[55] Karl Rahner reckons for only six;[56] R.E. Brown decides that three are certain and five are probable.[57]

Historical critics are inclined to decide that there are even fewer *theos* texts applied to Jesus in the NT. For example, Rudolf Bultmann decides on only one for certain, it being Jn 20.28, and perhaps two or three others having some degree of divinity applied to Jesus. He concludes, "Neither in the synoptic gospels nor in the Pauline epistles is Jesus called God; nor do we find him so called in the Acts of the Apostles or in the Apocalypse."[58] Vincent Taylor subscribes to Bultmann's conclusion by saying, "The one clear ascription of Deity to Christ" in the NT is Jn 20.28.[59]

Some traditionalist authorities therefore admit that their position is not firmly rooted in Scripture. Wainwright explains, "Indeed it might have been expected that the predicate *theos* would have been used of Jesus far more often in the pages of the New Testament."[60] And John Macquarrie remarks in his typically candid style, "it may strike us as rather odd that such an apparently central Christian affirmation as 'Jesus Christ is God' is so minimally attested

---

[49] Murray J. Harris, *3 Crucial Questions about Jesus* (Grand Rapids: Baker, 1994), 119n16.
[50] The foremost include (in alphabetical order) W. Barclay, G.H. Boobyer, R.E. Brown, O. Cullmann, M. Harris, B.A. Mastin, K. Rahner, E. Stauffer, and A.W. Wainwright. See "Selected Bibliography."
[51] M. Harris, *Jesus as God*, 274. See also p. 268.
[52] M. Harris, *Jesus as God*, 274.
[53] O. Cullman, *The Christology of the New Testament*, 308-14.
[54] R.N. Longenecker, *The Christology of Early Jewish Christianity*, 139.
[55] A.W. Wainwright, "The Confession 'Jesus is God' in the New Testament," 294.
[56] Karl Rahner, "Theos in the New Testament," in Rahner's *Theological Investigations* 1:136.
[57] R.E. Brown, *Jesus God and Man*, 23, 28-29.
[58] Rudolf Karl Bultmann, *Essays, Philosophical and Theological*, tr. J.C.G. Greig (New York: Macmillan, 1955), 275.
[59] V. Taylor, "Does the New Testament Call Jesus God? 118.
[60] A.W. Wainwright, *The Trinity in the New Testament* (London: SPCK, 1962), 66. Likewise, R.N. Longenecker, *The Christology of Early Jewish Christianity*, 141.

in the Scriptures that we have to hunt around for instances, and when we have found them, argue about what they really mean."[61]

Indeed. It is also surprising that, with the possible exception of Jn 1.1c, none of these NT *theos* texts are found in any treatise, however brief, which identifies Jesus. Traditionalist R.E. Brown readily admits concerning these *theos* texts, "none of the instances attempt to define Jesus essentially."[62] And he adds, "even in the New Testament works that speak of Jesus as God, there are also passages that seem to militate against such a usage."[63]

Some contemporary traditionalists have sought to defend their position by offering an explanation for this scarcity of biblical support. Their most common explanation has been that calling Jesus "God" was a late NT development, so that those passages that are presumed to call Jesus "God" were authored at a late date.[64] (See Appendix C: Modern Christologies.) R.E. Brown is representative of this position. He asserts, "The New Testament does call Jesus 'God,' but this is a development of the later New Testament books. In the Gospels, Jesus never uses the title 'God' of Himself."[65]

A few traditionalist scholars, e.g., M. Harris, reason that if the early Christians had called Jesus *theos* as regularly as they did the Father, Jews and pagan Gentiles alike would have tended to regard Christianity as ditheistic.[66] Harris therefore implies what R.N. Longenecker states outright,[67] that the early Christians largely avoided such an identification due to the likelihood of this misunderstanding. On the contrary, since when do we think that the first Spirit-filled, emboldened Christians formulated their theology in reaction to others, especially to non-believers? And why should we think that people in the 1st century would so react any more than people in any other century?

The Major, Debated *Theos* Texts

Scholars refer to these few texts, which arguably call Jesus "God," as "the major, debated *theos* texts." They are called "major" because they are considered of utmost importance compared to other *theos* texts that allegedly identify Jesus as "God." They are called "debated" because, except for Jn 20.28>, there exists considerable disagreement among modern scholars as to whether these passages call Jesus "God."

Indeed, upon examining these major, debated *theos* texts in various English translations of the Bible, it is surprising to learn that half or more of them are translated quite differently.[68] Some English versions translate these verses so that they read that Jesus is "God;" yet other reliable English versions do not

---

[61] J. Macquarrie, *Jesus Christ in Modern Thought*, 295.
[62] Raymond E. Brown, "Does the New Testament Call Jesus God?" *JTS* 26 (1965): 572.
[63] R.E. Brown, *Jesus God and Man*, 33.
[64] E.g., R.E. Brown, R.T. France, A.W. Wainwright, J.L. D'Aragon, and tentatively R.N. Longenecker.
[65] R.E. Brown, *Jesus God and Man*, 86.
[66] Murray J. Harris, "Titus 2:13 and the Deity of Christ," in *Pauline Studies: Essays Presented to Professor F.F. Bruce on His 70th*, eds. Donald A. Hagner and Murray J. Harris (Grand Rapids: Eerdmans, 1980), 265-66.
[67] R.N. Longenecker, *The Christology of Early Jewish Christianity*, 140-41.
[68] Of the eight major, disputed *theos* texts (so not including Jn 20.28 and 1 Jn 5.20), the following versions translate half as identifying Jesus as "God" and the other half as not: AV, RV, RSV, NEB. The NRSV even has five of the eight calling Jesus "God." So much for Christian Fundamentalists alleging the AV adheres to the true doctrine about Jesus more than modern versions do, especially the one preferred by (liberal) scholars!

translate them as calling Jesus "God," but that the word "God" (*theos*) in such cases refers to the Father.[69]

(Throughout this book, these two variations in either interpretation or translation of a passage that mentions both God and Jesus will be referred to as follows: (1) "the one Person view" identifies Jesus as "God," and (2) "the two Person view" mentions both God and Jesus as two separate Persons and therefore does not identify Jesus as "God.")

In addition, some modern Bible versions translate these major, contested *theos* texts a certain way while including an alternate translation as a footnote, or a "marginal reading" ("mg"), which states otherwise. Accordingly, some particular text of a modern English version of the Bible might have a reading that identifies Jesus as "God" while the alternate reading does not identify Jesus as God.

William Barclay well summarizes this rather confusing situation. He explains, "It is when we begin to examine the evidence that we run into very real difficulties. The evidence is not extensive. But we shall find that on almost every occasion in the New Testament in which Jesus seems to be called God there is a problem either of textual criticism or of translation. In almost every case we have to discuss which of two readings is to be accepted or which of two possible translations is to be accepted."[70] Barclay concludes, "One of the most vexed questions in Christian thought and language is whether or not we can directly and simply call Jesus "God.""[71]

Perhaps the most disturbing problem that Barclay hints at regards variants in the MS evidence.[72] Traditionalist D.A. Fennema observes, "Most of the passages which may call Jesus 'God' are plagued by textual variants or syntactical obscurity, either of which permits an entirely different interpretation of the passage."[73] Oscar Cullmann similarly states, "Passages which apply the designation 'God' to Jesus are not numerous, and some of them are uncertain from the standpoint of textual criticism. Even in ancient times some people apparently attributed undue importance to the question whether or not Jesus was to be called 'God' ... This explains the many textual variants precisely in the passages."[74] What Cullmann infers is the dreaded problem that textual critics sometimes encounter in the ancient Greek MSS of the NT or portions of it: scribal interpolations. These are unwarranted, purposeful, even fraudulent, insertions or alterations by copyists.

---

[69] See the chart published by Graeser-Lynn-Schoenheit (*One God & One Lord*, 618), which shows how the major English versions translate the major, disputed *theos* texts. This chart is reproduced from Victor Perry's journal article, "Problem Passages of the New Testament in Modern Translations: Does the New Testament Call Jesus God?" *ExpT* 87 (1975-76): 214-15. Incidentally, this chart shows that the NASB translates more of these texts as calling Jesus "God" than any other English Bible version. However, it wrongly cites the NEB as identifying Jesus as "God" in Jn 1.1c, surely a misunderstanding of that rendering.

[70] William Barclay, *Jesus As They Saw Him: New Testament Interpretations of Jesus* (London: SCM, 1962), 20-21.

[71] W. Barclay, *Jesus As They Saw Him*, 20.

[72] Textual criticism is indispensable to the Bible. See, e.g., Bruce M. Metzger, *The Text of the New Testament: Its Transmission, Corruption and Restoration*, 2nd ed. (New York: Oxford University, 1968); Kurt Aland and Barbara Aland, *The Text of the New Testament: An Introduction to the Critical Editions and to the Theory and Practice of Modern Textual Criticism* [1981], tr. Erroll F. Rhodes (Grand Rapids: Leiden, 1987).

[73] D.A. Fennema, "John 1.18: 'God the Only Son,'" *NTS* 31 (1985): 125.

[74] O. Cullmann, *Christology*, 307-08.

Many of these debated christological *theos* texts only contain grammatical problems that arise due to the unpunctuated Greek NT. That is, during the 1st century, when the documents that eventually comprised the NT were originally written in the Greek language, they had no punctuation, all letters were in upper case (uncials), and there were no spaces between words, as with the Hebrew Bible. Often, it is uncertain how the grammar of these critical verses in the Greek NT should be treated. Usually, the disputed text only concerns a brief phrase or a single word. The question may be whether to place a comma or a period in a certain place, or how to treat an indefinite (anarthrous) noun. These grammatical issues can be complex, if not incomprehensible, for most Bible readers because they do not know *koine* ("common") Greek.

This grammatical uncertainty becomes even more evident when perusing these verses in the better NT commentaries. M. Harris explains, "it is a curious fact that each of the [disputed *theos*] texts ... contains an interpretative problem of some description; actually, most contain two or three."[75] And A.E. Harvey alleges, "The New Testament writers ... show no tendency to describe Jesus in terms of divinity; the few apparent exceptions are either grammatically and textually uncertain or have an explanation which,... brings them within the constraint of Jewish monotheism."[76]

It is surprising to discover that, with the exception of perhaps only two of these NT *theos* passages, contemporary traditionalist authorities are about evenly divided as to whether these major *theos* passages call Jesus "God." For instance, R.T. France adduces, "in many cases the apparent direct attribution of divinity to Jesus melts away in the light of uncertainty about either the text, or the punctuation, or the syntax, leaving us with no undisputed (or almost undisputed!), direct attribution of divinity to Jesus outside the opening and closing declarations of the Gospel of John (Jn. 1:1; 1:18, 20:28)."[77]

Indeed, the two *theos* passages in the NT that traditionalist authorities have regarded as providing incontrovertible evidence that Jesus Christ is "God" are Jn 1.1c> ("the Word was God") and Jn 20.28> ("Thomas ... said to Him, 'My Lord and my God.'"). And this has held true among not only traditionalists but most historical critics. O. Cullmann calls these two texts "indisputable" evidence that Jesus is God;[78] M. Harris renders them "incontestable."[79] These two texts will be examined in detail in Chapter Six, and we will see that a few of these authorities only regard Jn 20.28 as indisputable.

The following table shows all nine major, debated christological texts (arranged in their NT order) which contain the word *theos* and their type(s) of problem(s) and genre. (A difficulty with syntax is herein regarded as a grammatical problem.)

---

[75] M. Harris, *Jesus as God*, 11.

[76] A.E. Harvey, *Jesus and the Constraint of History*, 157. Similarly, idem, "Christology and the Evidence of the New Testament," in *God Incarnate: Story and Belief*, ed. A.E. Harvey (London: SPCK, 1981), 52.

[77] R.T. France, "The Worship of Jesus: A Neglected Factor in Christological Debate?" in *Christ the Lord: Studies in Christology presented to Donald Guthrie*, ed. H.H. Rowdon, 23.

[78] O. Cullmann, *Christology*, 308.

[79] M. Harris, *Jesus as God*, 284.

Table 1: Jesus as *Theos* in the New Testament

Text	Problem(s)	Genre	Translation (NASB)
Jn 1.1c	punctuation grammatical	hymn (?)	In the beginning was the Word, and the Word was with God, and the Word was God.
Jn 1.18	textual grammatical	hymn (?)	No man has seen God at any time; the only begotten God, who is in the bosom of the Father, He has explained Him.
Jn 20.28	grammatical	confession	Thomas answered and said to Him, "My Lord and my God!"
Rom 9.5	punctuation grammatical	doxology	whose are the fathers, and from whom is the Christ according to the flesh, who is over all, God blessed forever. Amen.
2 Th 1.12	grammatical	doctrine	according to the grace of our God and the Lord Jesus Christ.
Tit 2.13	grammatical	prophecy	looking for the blessed hope and the appearing of the glory of our great God and Savior, Christ Jesus
Heb 1.8-9	textual grammatical contextual	Old Testament citation	But of the Son He says, THY THRONE, O GOD, IS FOREVER AND EVER,... THEREFORE GOD, THY GOD, HATH ANOINTED THEE
2 Pt 1.1	textual grammatical	salutation	by the righteousness of our God and Savior, Jesus Christ
1 Jn 5.20	grammatical	summary	we are in Him who is true, in His Son Jesus Christ. This is the true God and eternal life.

The genre of these *theos* texts is significant. The first four listed above, in Table 1, appear in a liturgical context. Only one out of the nine—1 Jn 5.20—can legitimately be classified as didactical. Due to this evidence, some scholars concede that in such instances these authors were not primarily concerned with the doctrinal precision of most of these texts. Some of these scholars thus recommend caution in appealing to liturgical or otherwise non-didactical NT material when seeking to determine the identity of Jesus. Wilhelm Bousset especially cautions about NT hymns, "Singing is something different from the hard, fixed formula of doctrine and even from prayer."[80] (See Appendix C: Modern Christologies.) Accordingly, Christology would have proceeded from exposition to hymnology rather than the reverse.[81]

---

[80] Wilhelm Bousset, *Kyrios Christos: A History of the Belief in Christ from the Beginnings of the Christianity to Iranaeus* [1913], tr. John Steely. ET of 5th ed. (Nashville, TN: Abingdon, 1970), 304-05. Christian hymns should reflect sound doctrine, which we can expect of those (and fragments) in the NT.
[81] Contra, e.g., L.W. Hurtado, *One God, One Lord: Early Christian Devotion and Ancient Jewish Monotheism* (London: SCM, 1988), 100-04; idem, *At the Origins of Christian Worship: The Context and Character of Earliest Christian Devotion* (Grand Rapids: Eerdmans, 1999), 72, 86-92; M. Hengel, *Studies in Early Christology*, 246-47.

Likewise, the categories in which these *theos* texts do not appear is significant as well. They are not in any of the following NT material: (1) the gospel sayings of Jesus, (2) the evangelistic speeches recorded in the book of Acts, (3) descriptive information about what the apostles preached, (4) definitions of the gospel, or (5) an author's didactic expositions in which he seeks to establish Jesus' identity. Obviously, these five categories are critical for determining what the NT teaches about the identity of Jesus.

In sum, this avalanche of evidence strongly suggests that grammatical problems in these few disputed *theos* texts should be resolved so that they do not call Jesus "God."

The Debated, Non-*Theos* Texts

Most traditionalists further contend that the following major, non-*theos* NT texts *implicitly* identify Jesus as God: Jn 5.18; 8.24, 28, 58; 10.30-33; Phil 2.5-11; Col 1.19; 2.9; 1 Tim 2.5; 3.16. (Note that the last three appear in what are regarded as hymns or hymnal fragments.) Some traditionalists cite the following minor, non-*theos* texts as also implicitly identifying Jesus as God: Mt 1.23; 28.19; Mk 2.5-12; 10.17-18 par.; Jn 3.13; Ac 20.28; Gal 2.20; Eph 5.5; 1 Jn 5.7; Rev 1.8.

As for the OT, many traditionalist scholars regard the following as major, implicit texts that substantiate that Jesus is God: Gen 1.26; 3.22; 11.7; Isa 7.14; 9.6. And many traditionalists cite OT quotations or allusions to OT texts which appear in the NT and are applied to Jesus as further evidence that He is God.

These debated *theos* and non-*theos* texts will be examined extensively throughout this book in their respective christologies, with most attention devoted to the major texts.

Principles of Hermeneutics

It is always wise to exercise caution when searching the Bible for isolated proof texts as evidence to support one's theology. Thus, it is quite dubious to decide whether the NT calls Jesus "God" primarily on the basis of the exegesis of these few, chief texts listed above. One reason, mentioned above, is that most of these contested passages have grammatical problems mostly because the Greek language lacked punctuation and precise grammatical rules in comparison with modern standards. For this and other reasons it should be recognized—even by those who advocate, as I do, a conservative view of the inspiration of the Bible—that *biblical writers, although inspired by the Holy Spirit, occasionally would have written words, phrases, or perhaps even a sentence which can justifiably be regarded as ambiguous to one degree or another*. Another reason is that the church's later theological considerations were unknown to these biblical authors. Thus, interpreters ought to exercise caution by avoiding anachronistic exegesis.

So, the question of whether the Bible identifies Jesus as God centers mostly on the proper translation or interpretation of these disputed passages listed above. Like any literature, *the Bible generally should be interpreted according to prudent principles of hermeneutics (interpretation)*. One hermeneutical principle that is well recognized by scholars is that the more complicated and ambiguous passages of a document should be interpreted in light of other relevant passages in that document (or other material written by the same author) which are deemed clear and simple. That is, *obscure texts should be interpreted according to clear ones*. Better stated, *clear texts take priority over obscure texts*. Church fathers generally recognized this principle and tried to implement it.

Church fathers also recognized the principle of quantity. They often argued that however reasonable an alleged heretic's interpretation of some Scripture might appear, it should be rejected when there is a far greater quantity of biblical testimony which they reckoned as supporting their own orthodox position. Tertullian explained this principle quite simply concerning Scripture, "the only proper course is to understand the few statements in the light of the many."[82] *If this hermeneutical principle of majority rule is applied to identity Christology, the biblical evidence overwhelmingly favors that Jesus is not God.* For example, the NT calls the Father "God" about 500 times whereas less than ten NT texts arguably call Jesus "God." And most of the latter concern only a word or a brief phrase rather than a full explanation.

More Important Considerations

It is vitally important to examine these major, disputed NT texts very carefully in formulating one's Christology. But the following considerations, some of which have already been mentioned above, are of even *more* paramount importance in determining whether the NT identifies Jesus as God:

- There is *no* NT evidence that Jesus ever claimed to be God.
- There *is* NT evidence that Jesus denied that He ever claimed to be God.
- At Jesus' hearing before the Sanhedrin, He was *not* accused of claiming to be God.
- The NT *constantly* distinguishes God and Jesus Christ as two separate individuals.
- The NT *repeatedly* identifies God exclusively as "the Father."
- The NT contains no unambiguous statement such as "Jesus (Christ) is God."

These major points will emerge repeatedly as we progress in this study.

Epilogue

The Bible warns against altering Scripture. When Moses gave the Israelites the Law, he said, "You shall not add to the word which I am commanding you, nor take away from it" (Deut 4.2). A biblical proverb reads, "Every word of God is tested;... Do not add to His words lest He reprove you, and you be proved a liar" (Prov 30.5-6).[83]

What about the Christian gospel? Did later church fathers unjustifiably *add* to the gospel of Jesus Christ when they made His supposed deity, and its corollary, the doctrine of the Trinity, essential matters of Christian belief? Or do these propositions represent accurate clarifications and elaborations of what was seminally concealed in the original gospel, so that God *enlightened* post-apostolic church fathers about these matters and *authorized* them to make these adjustments? Put plainly, do these doctrines—the deity of Christ and the Trinity—affirm or distort the "good news" that Jesus and His apostles gave to succeeding generations of Christians?[84] Bible scholar and Anglican churchman Brian Hebblethwaite asserts the common notion, "I cannot

---

[82] Tertullian, *Against Praxeas*, 20. Also, Athanasius (e.g., *Orations Against the Arians*, III, 29) often argued that his doctrine, esp. that pertaining to the Arian Controversy, mirrored the overall "scope of Scripture."

[83] Though a sobering thought, some Christians misapply the injunction in Rev 22.18-19 to the entire Bible.

[84] For the two classic, contrasting answers to this question, see Adolf von Harnack (ET *What is Christianity?* 1900], who answers negatively, and Alfred Loisy (*The Gospel and the Church* [1903], tr. Christopher Home [repr. Philadelphia: Fortress, 1976]), 177-78], who answers positively.

suppose the church's creedal faith to have been mistaken over so central a matter as the divinity of Christ."[85]

On the contrary, those whom the Catholic Church calls "the holy fathers" were human beings not unlike our fallible selves. It is therefore incumbent upon those who sincerely desire to know the truth to have a sober look at the history of the development of church Christology, especially the history of what the Catholic Church deems "the great and holy ecumenical councils." This we will do in the next chapter. In this process we will discover what a difference there is between the simple, yet profound, teachings of Jesus and the complicated, abstract arguments of church fathers in their councils and creeds. And we will learn that their Christology involves many irresolvable problems that further signal the need for this investigation. These difficulties regarding the pre-Easter Jesus will be considered in this book, and they can be set forth as follows:

- How could Jesus have been God since God is invisible to mortal humans?
- How could Jesus really have been tempted and be God, since "God cannot be tempted."
- How could Jesus have been God since He died but God cannot die?
- How could the pre-Easter Jesus have been God since only the Father possessed immortality?
- If Jesus was God, who is self-sufficient, then Jesus did not need the power of the Holy Spirit.
- If Jesus performed miracles with a divine nature, then He did not need the Holy Spirit's power.
- If Jesus performed miracles with a divine nature, then the Father did not do the works of Jesus.
- If Jesus did not know the time of His return, then He could not have been God, who knew.
- If Jesus had two natures, then He logically must have had two wills, which is non-human.
- God transcends His creation, so that being God is incompatible with being human.
- Jesus could not have been God because being human is incompatible with being God.
- If Jesus was a God-man, then He could not have been either fully God or fully man.
- If Jesus was co-equal with the Father, then the Father could not be "greater," as Jesus said.

---

[85] Brian Hebblethwaite, "*The Myth* and Christian Faith," in *Incarnation and Myth: The Debate Continued*, ed. Michael D. Goulder (Grand Rapids: Eerdmans, 1979), 16.

Part One
History of Church Christology

Chapter Two
Church Christology in the First Millennium

Introduction	Arius Exonerated
Greek Philosophy/Christian Theology	Athanasius
The Didache and 1 Clement	Eusebius of Caesarea
Pliny the Younger	Appolinaris
Early Jewish Christianity	The Council of Constantinople
Ignatius	New Testament Credal Fragments
2 Clement	The Apostles' Creed
Justin Martyr	The Council of Ephesus
Iranaeus	The Second Council of Ephesus
Sabellianism and Paul of Samosata	The Council of Chalcedon
Tertullian	The Second Council of Constantinople
Origen	Conclusions about Ecumenical Councils
Summary of Ante-Nicene Christology	Obliterating Distinction of God & Son
Two Church Centers	The Athanasian Creed
The Arian Controversy	The Trinity
The Council of Nicaea	Critical Thinking
The Nicene Creed	Social Implications of Critical Thinking

Introduction

Christians are supposed to believe in Jesus. But what does that mean? Christians are so named because they believe that Jesus is "the Christ," the Messiah God promised to Israel. Indeed, this is what the NT says; but Christians believe that the NT tells us a lot more about who Jesus is. Ernst Kasemann explains that according to the NT, and thus the early Christians, "[Christian] Faith means one thing only; to know who Jesus is."[1]

Most churchgoers simply believe whatever their church teaches them about who Jesus is, which is usually traditional Christology. But how did this traditional Christology develop, and is it a valid assessment of who the NT says that Jesus is? Because of modern scholarship, we possess a far greater knowledge of the historical development of traditional church Christology than previous generations did.[2]

---

[1] Ernest Kasemann, *The Testament of Jesus: A Study of the Gospel of John in the Light of Chapter 17* [1966], tr. Gerhard Krodel (Philadelphia: Fortress, 1968), 25.
[2] Maurice F. Wiles, "Christianity without Incarnation? in *The Myth of God Incarnate*, ed. J. Hick, 3.

Knowing the historical development of traditional beliefs about Jesus, supporting Scriptures of these beliefs, and interpretations of these Scriptures, plus the reputation of leading proponents of these beliefs, can significantly affect what we believe about Jesus; and it should. True faith is open, honest, rational, and reasonably self-critical. Christians therefore should be open to critical examination of their traditions. D.F. Strauss made the following classic statement on this subject: "The true criticism of dogma is its history."[3]

The historical development of traditional church Christology can be summarized as follows: (1) in the 2nd and 3rd centuries the church set forth as the "orthodox" Christian Faith that Jesus was "God," yet with certain qualifications; (2) but in the 4th century the institutional Church proclaimed Jesus as God absolutely, i.e., with *no* qualifications whatsoever; (3) in the 5th century the Church struggled to balance two concepts: (a) how to affirm the unity of God, while also maintaining the distinction between the Father and the Son as two separate Persons, and (b) how Jesus could be both God and man. Martin Hengel calls this development "the riddle of Christology."[4]

We now turn to this most fervent, protracted, complex struggle in church history.

Greek Philosophy and Christian Theology

After Jesus ascended into heaven, according to the NT many of the Jewish people, especially the religious authorities, persecuted His disciples, who also were Jews (Ac 8.1; 11.19). This persecution first centered in Jerusalem and its environs—in Judea. Some of these Jewish believers in Jesus sought to escape this persecution by dispersing into nearby Gentile lands. This resulted in a sort of "Jewish Christian Diaspora." Into the Gentile world these Jews went, spiritually armed with their life-changing message of the "good news" about their resurrected, heavenly-exalted Lord and Savior—Jesus Christ.

Throughout that first century, against many odds this initially Jewish movement sustained marked growth amidst some persecution in their Gentile homelands. The center of this Jesus Movement soon shifted from Jerusalem to Antioch, Syria. That is where Jesus' disciples were first called "Christians" (Ac 11.26). Due to this Diaspora, it didn't take long for the ethnic mix of the entire movement to change to consist of more Gentiles than Jews. Most scholars deem this transition as the beginning of "Christianity."

The eastern Roman world in which this infant church was first nurtured was permeated with a Greco-Roman culture of religio-philosophy known as "Hellenism." Hellenistic people believed in many ancient Greco-Roman philosophies and myths. They worshipped a multitude of gods and lords in beautifully adorned temples filled with idols of their gods. They regarded their gods as mystically connected to the Roman state. Honoring their gods was considered a patriotic, civic duty. Ironically, these pagans accused the Christians of being "atheists" because the Christians (1) did not believe in the Roman gods, (2) refused to sacrifice before their idols in the Roman temples, and (3) would not publicly confess allegiance to these idol-gods when called upon publicly to do so. Consequently, many Christians were hauled off to Roman tribunals where they were falsely accused of various things, such as anti-intellectualism, immoralities, and atheism.

---

[3] D.F. Strauss, *The Life of Jesus Critically Examined* [1835], tr. George Eliot (repr. London: SCM, 1973), 45.
[4] M. Hengel, *Studies in Early Christology*, xvii.

Faced with such charges, these Christians were forced to defend their religious convictions, both intellectually and morally. So, in the 2nd and early 3rd centuries there arose a host of learned, Gentile, Christian theologians in the Roman world, called "apologists," who did just that. They often made a public "apology" (defense) of their faith, i.e., a logical, rational explanation for Christian belief and righteous living.

Another formidable foe of traditional Christian belief in the 1st century was incipient Gnosticism. Its name derives from the Greek word *gnosis*, which means "knowledge." Gnosticism referred to a supposed esoteric knowledge that was dualistic, in which matter is regarded as evil and spirit as pure and therefore good. Later, so-called "Christian Gnostics" embraced the notion of two gods: (1) the evil god, called the Demiurge, who created the universe and was generally regarded as the god of the Jews and therefore the god of the OT, and (2) the good and loving god of the NT.

Some of the apologists, prior to their conversion to Christ, had been educated in Greek philosophy. In addition, the Jewish philosopher and theologian, Philo (c. 20 BCE—50 CE), a contemporary of Jesus, had a most profound and lasting influence on the religious and intellectual world of that time. He was a resident of the intellectual center of the Hellenistic world, Alexandria, Egypt, and he was an astute student of both Greek philosophy and the OT. Even though the apologists vigorously defended their faith against polytheistic paganism and Gnosticism, they were significantly influenced by Philo and thus much Greek philosophical thinking about God, called "classical theism."

For example, these apologists of the 2nd century followed Philo in asserting that *ho theos* (Gr. for "the god/God") identified solely the one true God, i.e., the God of the Jews and their Scriptures, whereas *theos* without the article could refer exclusively to the *logos* (Gr. for "Word," "Mind," or "Reason").[5] Both Jews and Greeks embraced the concept of the Logos and held various theories about it. These Logos theories represented attempts to explain the supposed paradox between God's transcendence and His relation to His creation. The Logos was thought to be the necessary, and therefore vital, link between God and His creation. Philo wrote, "the Logos is the God of us imperfect men."[6] He even called the Logos "the second deity/god" (Gr. *deuteros theos*). Yet Philo still distinguished the Logos from the one and only, true and living God.[7] Rabbinic Judaism therefore never regarded Philo as compromising strict monotheism.

Most notably, since the Christian gospel flourished early in lands permeated with polytheistic religions, some critical scholars have concluded that it must have become increasingly easier for Gentile converts to Christianity to think of God as a plurality of Persons.[8] Accordingly, Rudolf Bultmann makes a startling, but quite accurate, assessment of the early development of traditional Christology. He alleges that, following the writing of the NT, "it is only with the Apostolic Fathers that free unambiguous reference to Jesus Christ as 'our God' begins."[9] It thus behooves us to examine briefly some of this patristic (and other) literature of the post-apostolic age to which Bultmann refers, which we

---

[5] Philo, *On Dreams, That They Are God-Sent*, I, 229-30.
[6] Philo, *Allegorical Interpretation*, 3.207.
[7] Philo, *Questions and Solutions*, 2.62; idem, *On Dreams*, 1.229.
[8] E.g., Friedrich Schleiermacher, *The Christian Faith* [1830], tr. H.R. Mackintosh and J.S. Steward, 2nd ed. (Philadelphia: Fortress, 1928), 747.
[9] R. Bultmann, *Essays*, 276. The term "apostolic Fathers" designates church leaders during the period about 95-165 CE; the "apostolic age" designates the period about 30/33-95 CE.

will do chronologically. This examination will lead us to the infamous "Arian Controversy" and the "Ecumenical Councils" of the Catholic Church.

The Didache and 1 Clement

Only a few scholars cite The Didache as evidence that the early Christians called Jesus "God." The Greek word *Didache* means "Teaching." The Didache is a church manual written in about 95 CE. It is known as "The Teaching of the Twelve Apostles" even though they did not write it. Didache 10.6 addresses Jesus, "Hossana to the God of David." But this likely is corrupt, the original being, "Hosanna to the house of David."[10]

The lengthy First Epistle of Clement to the Corinthians, also known as 1 Clement, was written anonymously toward the close of the 1st century CE. Many church fathers believed that its author was the Apostle Paul's associate mentioned in Phil 4.3. Some early churches so revered this letter that they subjoined their copy of it to their collection of sacred documents, some of which were later included in the NT.

This letter of 1 Clement does not have any evidence that its author believed that Jesus Christ was God. On the contrary, it (1) mentions "God" and "Christ" together, thus clearly distinguishing them as separate Persons, (2) affirms the Father as "the true and only God," and (3) even poses the question: "Have we not one God and one Christ?"[11]

Pliny the Younger

When it comes to Christology, it seems that just about every traditionalist scholar worth his or her salt quotes "Pliny the Younger" in an attempt to confirm that Christians of the early 2nd century CE worshipped and believed in Jesus Christ as "God." The parade of scholars who so represent Pliny is pervasive; but a large majority of them misrepresent Pliny in translating his critical words by capitalizing the word "God."[12] In so doing, they exercise

---

[10] R.E. Brown (*An Introduction to New Testament Christology*, 191), who for support cites authority Jean Paul Audet (*Didache: Instructions des apotres* [Paris: J. Gabalda, 1958], 62-67).

[11] 1 Clement 43.9 and 46.5 in *ANF* 1:17.

[12] E.g., P. Schaff, *History of the Christian Church*, 2:546; E. Stauffer, "*theos*," in *TDNT* 3:106; R.E. Brown, *John i-xii*, 20, 24; idem, *Jesus God and Man*, 27; idem, *An Introduction to New Testament Christology*, 188; A.W. Wainwright, *The Trinity in the New Testament*, 66; idem, "The Confession 'Jesus is God' in the New Testament," 294; R.T. France, "The Worship of Jesus: A Neglected Factor in the Christological Debate," in *Christ the Lord: Studies in Christology Presented to Donald Guthrie*, ed. Harold H. Rowdon (London: Inter-Varsity, 1982), 30; Ralph P. Martin, "Some Reflections on New Testament Hymns," 49; Martin Hengel, "Christological Titles in Early Christianity," in *The Messiah: Developments in Earliest Judaism and Christianity*, ed. James Charlesworth (Minneapolis: Fortress, 1992), 425; idem, *Studies in Early Christology*, 263-64, 359-60, 364-65; Margaret Barker, *The Great Angel: A Study of Israel's Second God* (London: SPCK, 1992), 216; Gerald O'Collins, *Christology: A Biblical, Historical, and Systematic Study of Jesus* (Oxford: University, 1995), 136; Larry W. Hurtado, "The Binitarian Shape of Early Christian Worship," in *The Jewish Roots of Christological Monotheism: Papers from the St. Andrews Conference on the Historical Origins of the Worship of Jesus*, eds. Carey C. Newman et al. (Leiden: Brill, 1999), 205; idem, *At the Origins of Christian Worship: The Context and Character of Earliest Christian Devotion* (Grand Rapids: Eerdmans, 1999), 88. (At least Stauffer, Wainwright, Hengel, and Hurtado provide the exact Latin quotation along with their English translation.) Tertullian (*Apology*, 2.6) reports this Pliny-Trajan epistolary exchange; but there are two MS variants of his account regarding the last two words of the critical phrase, and neither of these variants correspond to Pliny's letter. These variants are: (1) "singing hymns to Christ and God," and (2) "singing hymns to Christ as God." Eusebius (*Ecclesiastical History*, 3.33) also relates this Pliny-Trajan exchange and reveals that he derived his information from Tertullian's *Apology*. But he quotes Tertullian with these words, "sang to Christ as to a god," which may indicate a third variant here in Tertullian's *Apology*.

isegesis, not exegesis, by inserting their own meaning into Pliny's phrase. A few scholars get it right, using "god," and those who do are usually quite distinguished.[13] The main reason is that during this time Latin was still written only in all capitals. Lower case (miniscule) was not introduced into the Latin script until about the 9th century CE.

Pliny's real name was Plinius Caecillius Secundus. As governor of Bithynia, Asia Minor (present Turkey), he carried on an extensive correspondence with Roman Emperor Trajan. In 112 CE, Pliny wrote one of several letters to the emperor, asking for his advice on how to properly judge people whom private prosecutors were hauling before Roman tribunals, mostly in Pontus in Asia Minor (cf. 1 Pt 1.1), for the crime of professing to be a "Christian."[14] Pliny explains that in his jurisdiction the Christians regularly "met on a stated day before it was light, and addressed a form of prayer to Christ, as to a god."[15]

Writing in Latin, Pliny's pertinent phrase is "*CARMENQUE CHRISTO QUASI DEO.*" The word *quasi* means "seeming," and our word "as" is a possible translation of it. Consequently, the last three words of this phrase can be translated as follows: "to Christ as (a) god" or "to Christ as if (a) god" but not "to Christ as God." As for the verb, *carmenque*, it means "a solemn or ritual utterance, usually sung or chanted." A prime example is "a religious hymn."[16] Most scholars translate *carmenque* as "sang a hymn" rather than "addressed a form of prayer." It is uncertain if the singing was antiphonal.

The NT verifies that the early Christians demonstrated their devotion to Jesus Christ by singing hymns about Him and to Him.[17] But there is no clear literary evidence, either in the NT or otherwise,[18] that the early Christians up to this time had ever intended to glorify Jesus Christ *as God* in their hymns.[19] Indeed, *all* NT hymns merely verify that the early Christians perceived Jesus as the supreme agent of God, not God Himself.[20]

---

[13] The following modern scholars translate Pliny's phrase with "a god" while Vermes has only "god:" Vincent Taylor, *The Person of Christ in New Testament Teaching* (London: Mac Millan, 1958), 202; C.H. Dodd, *The Founder of Christianity* (New York: Macmillan, 1970), 4; Jaroslav Pelikan, *The Christian Tradition: A History of the Development of Doctrine: The Emergence of the Catholic Tradition* (Chicago: University, 1971), 173; Martin Hengel, *Crucifixion in the Ancient World and the Folly of the Message of the Cross* (Philadelphia: Fortress, 1977), 2; G.W.H. Lampe, *God as Spirit: The Bampton Lectures, 1976* (Oxford: Clarendon, 1977), 163; Hans Kung, *Christianity: Essence, History, and Future* [1994], tr. John Bowden (New York: Continuum, 1995), 19, 132; Geza Vermes, *The Changing Faces of Jesus* (London: Penguin, 2000), 53; N.T. Wright, *The New Testament and the People of God* (Minneapolis: Fortress, 1992), 349; Larry W. Hurtado, *How on Earth Did Jesus Become a God? Historical Questions about Earliest Devotion to Jesus* (Grand Rapids: Eerdmans, 2005), 13.

[14] See A.N. Sherwin-White, *The Letters of Pliny: A Historical and Social Commentary* (Oxford: Clarendon, 1966), 694.

[15] *Letters of Gaius Plinius Caecilius Secundus*, in *The Harvard Classics*, tr. William Melmoth, rev. F.C.T. Bosanquet, 51 vols. (New York: P.F. Collier and Son, 1909), 10.96.

[16] *OLD*, 278.

[17] E.g., Eph 5.19; Phil 2.5-11; 1 Tim 3.16; cf. Rev 5.8-10, 13-14; 7.9-12.

[18] M. Hengel (*Studies in Early Christology*, 231, 247, emphasis not mine) observes that outside of the NT, "no *collection* of Christian psalms (or of prayers) originating in the first or second century *has been preserved*," but only as early as the 4th and 5th centuries.

[19] See commentary herein on Jn 1.1c>, Phil 2.6-7>, and 1 Tim 3.16>, which passages are generally believed to be in hymnal settings.

[20] Contra esp. Larry W. Hurtado (e.g., *One God, One Lord: Early Christian Devotion and Ancient Jewish Monotheism* [London: SCM, 1988], 104), who has written several books the past twenty years in which he asserts that the devotional life of the early church, e.g., NT hymns, reveals a belief that Jesus was God.

Also, Pliny's religious culture actually prohibited him from determining that the Christians sang to Jesus Christ as "God," as if Pliny himself believed that there exists only a single deity. N.T. Wright's word of caution applies here, in which he states, "I have frequently used 'god' instead of 'God'.... The modern usage, without the article and with a capital, seems to me actually dangerous. This usage,... implies that all users of the word are monotheists."[21] No Roman official at that time could have been a monotheist.

Typical of the Mediterranean world in antiquity, Roman citizens regarded it as their patriotic duty to worship their Graeco-Roman deities, of which there were several. Indeed, people of antiquity were very polytheistic, believing that their gods controlled human life, either for blessing or cursing. Thus, in certain vicinities of the Roman Empire and at certain times during the first three centuries of Christianity, Christians stood trial accused by the Roman state of being atheists because they refused to (1) renounce their faith in the one God and His Christ and (2) pay tribute to these pagan gods by either public confession or public prayer or make sacrificial offerings to their idols or both.

Moreover, the two letters by Pliny and Trajan which address this subject clearly confirm that this was such a time. For, Pliny informed the emperor that whenever his judicial courts sent him people condemned for the crime of professing to be "a Christian," he demanded that "they had repeated after me a formula of invocation to the gods and had made offerings of wine and incense to your statue (which I had ordered to be brought into court for this purpose along with the images of the gods), and furthermore had reviled the name of Christ: none of which things, I understand, any genuine Christian can be induced to do."[22] If these Christians refused Pliny's demands, he discloses that he had them executed. Emperor Trajan, in his letter of reply to Pliny, responded approvingly of the governor's handling of such situations. He only added, "anyone who denies that he is a Christian, and makes it clear that he is not by offering prayers to our gods, he is to be pardoned as a result of his repentance."[23] Notice that Emperor Trajan writes, "our gods."

This Pliny-Trajan correspondence clearly reveals that Governor Pliny *did not* believe that there was one God, or even that the one God of the Jews and Christians was the chief god. Rather, Pliny indicates that he believed in the many Roman gods, or at least postured himself as such. Consequently, he could not have believed that the Christians sang to, prayed to, or worshipped Jesus Christ as "God," as if he believed there was only one god. To do so would have made it evident that he did not believe in the Roman gods. And that would have placed him in the precarious position of being liable for execution himself, as were the Christians! Philosopher-theologian Don Cupitt is right in concluding, "Pliny ... *thought* that the believers sang hymns to Christ as if he were a god."[24] M. Harris concurs by explaining, "*Christo quasi deo*. Whatever this phrase meant to the Christians who reported the matter to Pliny, Pliny himself would doubtless have understood the phrase in the sense, 'to Christ as if to a god.'"[25] L. Hurtado surely

---

[21] N.T. Wright, *The New Testament and the People of God*, xiv.
[22] *Pliny Letters and Panegyricus in Two Volumes*, tr. Betty Radice, in *The Loeb Classical Library*, ed. E.H. Warmington (Cambridge, MA: Harvard, 1969), 289.
[23] *Pliny Letters and Panegyricus*, 291, 293.
[24] Don Cupitt, "Jesus and the Meaning of God," in *Incarnation and Myth: The Debate Continued*, ed. M.D. Goulder, 36. Emphasis mine. Cf. C.L. Blomberg, "Gospels (Historical Reliability)," 292.
[25] Murray Harris, "References to Jesus in Early Classical Authors," in *The Jesus Tradition Outside the Gospels*, ed. David Wenham (Sheffield, England: JSOT, 1985), 346.

errs by concluding that this phrase signifies that those Christians believed that "Jesus is somehow divine."[26]

Early Jewish Christianity

After 70 CE, early Jewish Christianity existed mostly in the Transjordan as a separate entity from mainstream Gentile Christianity.[27] Sometimes, it served as an intermediary between the predominantly Gentile church and Judaism. It seems most of its practitioners were called "Ebionites," meaning "the poor."[28] Little is known of these Jewish Christians except what can be gleaned from patristic writings about them and their literature.[29]

There seems to have been two kinds of Ebionites—Judaistic and Gnostic. Both types observed the Sabbath and adhered strongly to the Mosaic Law while exalting Jesus as a great prophet and Israel's promised Messiah. Most Ebionites seem to have denied Jesus' virgin birth yet affirmed His resurrection and heavenly ascension. Many of them observed the Eucharist and celebrated Sunday in commemoration of Jesus' resurrection. And most Ebionites had a profound eschatological expectation of Jesus' return.

But Ebionites were known mostly for insisting that Jesus was no more than a man, though a very virtuous one, and therefore not God. Many of them espoused Adoptionist Christology, in which they believed that the Logos-Christ descended upon Jesus at His baptism and departed from Him just prior to His crucifixion. This was due to their strong Gnostic presupposition that the Logos-Christ could not have suffered and died. Yet by the late 4th century, Ebionites apparently believed that Jesus was a preexistent, divine being.[30]

Ebionites also robustly repudiated the Apostle Paul. They denigrated him for not being an eyewitness of Jesus and accused him of being an apostate from the Mosaic Law.

These Ebionites began to decline in number in the 4th century, and they were not heard of anymore after the 5th century. Their strict observance of the Law

---

[26] L.W. Hurtado, *How on Earth Did Jesus Become a God?* 14.

[27] For modern treatments of early Jewish Christianity, see Georg Strecker, "Appendix 1: On the Problem of Jewish Christianity," in *Orthodoxy and Heresy in Earliest Christianity* [1934], Walter Bauer, tr. John E Steely et al, ed. Robert Kraft and Gerhard Krodel, 2nd ed. (Philadelphia: Fortress, 1971), 241-85; Ray A. Pritz, *Nazarene Jewish Christianity: From the End of the New Testament Period until Its Disappearance in the Fourth Century* (Leiden: Brill, 1988); A.F.J. Kiljn, *The Jewish Christian Gospel Tradition* (Leiden: Brill, 1992); Matt Jackson-McCabe, ed., *Jewish Christianity Reconsidered: Rethinking Ancient Groups and Texts* (Minneapolis: Fortress, 2007; Oskar Skarsaune and Reidar Hvalvik, eds, *Jewish Believers in Jesus: The Early Centuries* (Peabody, MA: Hendrickson, 2007). For a fairly recent and brief discussion, see H. Kung, *Christianity: Essence, History, And Future*, 98-108.

[28] Their name derives from the Greek word *ebion*, which translates the Hebrew *ha ebyonim*, meaning "the poor." Opponents of Ebionism charged that their name indicated a "poor opinion." However, both the Ebionites and the Qumran sectarians adopted this title because they likened poverty to genuine piety (Lk 1.53; 4.18 [Isa 61.1]; 6.20). In fact, the Ebionites dwelt mostly in the Transjordan, near the Qumran sect.

[29] The primary, non-extant works of Jewish Christianity are *The Gospel of the Hebrews*, *The Gospel of the Nazarenes*, and *The Gospel of the Ebionites*. The latter may have been a mutilated revision of the canonical Gospel of Matthew. See, e.g., Eusebius, *Ecclesiastical History*, 3.27; Georg Stecker, "Appendix 1: On the Problem of Jewish Christianity;" Jakob Jocz, *The Jewish People and Jesus Christ: The Relationship Between Church and Synagogue*, 3rd ed. (Grand Rapids: Baker, 1979), 191-200; Petri Luomanen, "Ebionites and Nazarenes," in *Jewish Christianity Reconsidered*, 81-118.

[30] Petri Luomanen ("Ebionites and Nazarenes," 99-100) relates that church father Epiphanius (*Panarion* 30.16.3) so describes them.

of Moses and opposition to Pauline teaching may have proved prime factors in their demise. Perhaps it had to do with Jesus' teaching about putting new wine into old wineskins, which doesn't work (Mk 2.22 par.). While Christianity had its roots in Judaism, it would not be bound by the Law of Moses but flourish in the freedom of the grace of Jesus Christ (cf. Jn 1.17).

A smaller Jewish Christian group, called "Nazarenes,"[31] held Jesus in even higher esteem. They believed that He was born of a virgin. And they did not chastise other Christians for refusing Mosaic observances. Neither did they denounce the Apostle Paul or his writings. Yet, like the Ebionites, they, too, asserted that Jesus was no more than a man. These Nazarenes seem to have best represented the earliest Jewish Christianity.[32]

Since church fathers were Gentiles impacted by Hellenism, they often suppressed, destroyed, and misrepresented the writings of these Jewish Christians. Hans Kung relates,

> Jewish Christianity always insisted on the historical fact that the Messiah and Lord Jesus of Nazareth was not a divine being, a second God, but a human being from among human beings.... Christian patristics for a long time understood Jewish Christianity uncritically (following the heresiological remarks of the church fathers) as a single heretical entity.... many scholars are devoting themselves to the exciting task of finding early **traces** of the many branches of Jewish Christianity.... present-day scholars see more the **continuity** of Jewish Christianity with the beginnings of early Christianity and less its heretical distortion. For them Jewish Christians are the **legitimate heirs of early Christianity**.[33]

There is a growing scholastic interest in early Jewish Christianity. This endeavor may prove significant for Christian origins. There is a current scholastic consensus that church fathers misrepresented these early Jewish Christians as Gnostics. Instead, Gnostic Ebionites were one of two branches of Ebionites and a distinct minority among them.

The early Jewish Christian belief in Jesus as a great prophet and the Messiah of Israel, yet no more than a man,[34] would later be revived in Islam, Enlightenment, Deism, Liberal Christian Theology, and among many researchers involved in the present-day Quest for the Historical Jesus. These movements will be examined in the next chapter.

Ignatius

In stark contrast to the Ebionites and Nazarenes, it seems that no one in the 2nd century declared more resolutely that Jesus was "God" than did Ignatius (c. 40-110/117 CE). This supposed Bishop of Antioch so glorified Christian martyrdom that he used it to bring about his own death. Sometime between 110 and 117 CE (the date is uncertain), while being transported by guards to Rome for his execution, Ignatius wrote seven letters to individual churches which many church officials later preserved and dearly treasured.[35] The subsequent influence

---

[31] Church fathers labeled them "Nazoraeans," as do many modern scholars. But they should not to be confused with a pre-Christian Jewish group of a similar name. All early Jewish Christians were at first called "Nazarenes" (Ac 24.5: Gr. *Nazoraion*; cf. Mt 2.23). Non Christian Jews also called them *nosrim*.
[32] Ray A. Pritz (*Nazarene Jewish Christianity*) claims Nazarenes originated from apostolic Christianity.
[33] H. Kung, *Christianity: Essence, History, and Future*, 97, 99, 103. Emphasis his.
[34] Affirmed by Justin Martyr, *Dialogue with Trypho*, 48.8.
[35] The fifteen letters ascribed to Ignatius are problematic. All modern scholars dismiss the first eight as spurious, and most of them accept only the shorter version of the remaining seven as authentic.

of these letters on the institutional church can hardly be overemphasized. Yet much of their content is arguably unflattering to their author.

Of first importance in these letters is that Ignatius repeatedly emphasizes the need for church unity by insisting on an unswerving loyalty to church bishops. Consequently, Bishop Ignatius is recognized as the fountain of the RCC's doctrine called "apostolic succession." (This doctrine still undergirds the RCC's hierarchical system of authority.) For, Ignatius incessantly urges his readers to revere and obey their bishop "as Jesus Christ" and do nothing without the direction of their bishop.[36] One reason for his rigid demand for uncritical loyalty to church leaders was his fear of doctrinal heresy infiltrating the church coupled with a perceived, heightened risk of church schism.[37] Thus, Ignatius was so intolerant of dissent that he could write dogmatically, "If any man follows him that makes a schism in the Church, he shall not inherit the kingdom of God" (Phil. 3).

Secondly, Ignatius so incredulously exhorted his readers to employ the art of silence that,[38] later, his writings became the catalyst for an unbridled excess of this practice among some Catholic monastics.

Thirdly, Ignatius so craved martyrdom that he inspired an ensuing morbid trend of an inordinate fanaticism for martyrdom, which the RCC later condemned. Indeed, even Jesus shrunk from the prospect of His necessary and imminent death (Mt 26.38-44 par.).

Due to these grievous errors that infiltrated the institutional Church primarily through Ignatius' letters, they should be read with caution. Church historian A. Cleveland Coxe observes that "the epistles ascribed to Ignatius have given rise to more controversy than any other documents connected with the primitive Church."[39]

Ignatius zealously desired "to attain unto God," as he put it. He meant becoming "a complete disciple" by following Jesus in martyrdom. To accomplish this, Ignatius voluntarily appeared before a Roman tribunal in his hometown of Antioch. He probably prodded officials to condemn him to death as a Christian. Regardless, it was his wish, and he got it. Whether he was tried and condemned at Antioch or Rome is uncertain. Roman soldiers transported him bound in chains to Rome for a final interrogation. There, he no doubt would have been given one last opportunity to recant his testimony. Finally, he was thrown into Rome's Flavian public amphitheatre and eaten alive by wild beasts.

---

[36] A compelling argument is that the NT does not sanction the office of bishop and its correlating three-tier system of authority. (See Phil 1.1; Ac 20.17, 28; 1 Tim 3.1-13; Tit 1.5-9.) For example, Luke and Paul use two Greek words, *presbuteros* ("elders") and *episkopos* ("overseer" or "bishop") interchangeably, which indicates their endorsement of a minimal two-tier system with a multiplicity of elders and deacons in each local, sizeable church congregation. Although the NT commands subjection to church leaders (Heb 13.17; 1 Pt 5.5), it does not authorize an indiscriminant submission to them (Ac 4.19; 5.29; 3 Jn 9), as in Ignatius' letters. While Paul exhorts the Corinthians, "Be imitators of me," he adds, "as I also am of Christ" (1 Cor 11.1). Also, the NT forbids church leaders from "lording it" over congregants (1 Pt 5.3; cf. Mt 20.25-26; 23.7-12; cf. 3 Jn 9-10). Interestingly, the church at Rome in its early history was governed only by a plurality ("college") of elders in mutual submission to one another. Cf. 1 Tim 3; Tit 1.

[37] The foremost authority of Ignatius has been J.B. Lightfoot. He (*The Apostolic Fathers Clement, Ignatius, and Polycarp: Revised Texts with Introduction, Notes, Dissertations, and Translations* [1889-90], 5 vols. [repr. Grand Rapids: Baker, 1981], Part Two, 1:39) observes, "The ecclesiastical order was enforced by him almost solely as a security for the doctrinal purity."

[38] E.g., Ignatius, *Trallians* 9.1.

[39] *ANF*, 1:46.

Six of Ignatius' seven letters were addressed to the Christian community in various cities in Asia Minor (present central Turkey). In reading these letters, one is impressed with Ignatius' courage and devotion to God and Christ. The following is one of Ignatius' celebrated, poetic, and passionate excerpts that reveal his martyr complex:

> I write to all churches, and I bid all men know, that of my own free will I die for God, unless ye should hinder me.... Let me be given to the wild beasts, for through them I can attain unto God. I am God's wheat, and I am ground by the teeth of wild beasts that I may be found pure bread. Rather entice the wild beasts, that they may become my sepulchre, and may leave no part of my body behind, so that I may not, when I am fallen asleep, be burdensome to anyone. Then shall I be truly a disciple of Jesus Christ,... Come fire and cross and grapplings with wild beasts, wrenching of bones, hacking of limbs, crushings of my whole body, come cruel tortures of the devil to assail me. Only be it mine to attain unto Jesus Christ.[40]

Many scholars allege that the letters of Ignatius belie a false humility (cf. Mt 6.1-18). For instance, church historian and traditionalist Philip Schaff asserts concerning Ignatius' letters, "There mingles also in all his extravagant professions of humility and entire unworthiness a refined spiritual pride and self-commendation."[41] One example is when he wrote, "I could unfold all the mysteries of the celestial hierarchy" (*Trall.* 5.3).

On the positive side, Ignatius' letters are replete with doctrinal statements that oppose incipient Docetism (Gr. *dokein*="to seem" or "to appear"). Docetism later became a branch of Gnosticism, and it flourished especially in Asia Minor. It was the belief that Jesus of Nazareth was completely God but not really a man. That is, Jesus only appeared to have a human body, but He was really a phantom. Docetism appealed to the doctrine of impassibility of classical theism—that Jesus' sufferings were only apparent and therefore not real. Ignatius is therefore to be commended in his letters for repeatedly opposing this early form of Docetism by affirming that Jesus was "really" a man who "actually" had a physical body.

But in refuting proto-Docetism, Ignatius seems to have uncritically accepted its primary tenant, that Jesus is God. For, *Ignatius emerges as the first patristic writer to unequivocally call Jesus Christ "God,"* which the following passages in his letters attest:
- "our God Jesus Christ" (*Eph.* 18.2; *Rom.* 3.3; *Pol.* 8.3).
- "Jesus Christ our God" (*Eph.* inscr.; twice in *Rom.* inscr.).
- "Jesus Christ ...our God" (*Eph.* 15.3).
- "Jesus Christ the God" (*Smyrn.* 1.1).
- "Jesus Christ ... my God" (*Rom.*6.3).[42]

These occurrences in Ignatius' letters led Rudolf Bultmann to make this judicious comparison: the NT reveals a distinct reticence in calling Christ "God," but "Ignatius on the contrary speaks of Christ as God as if it were a thing to be taken quite for granted."[43]

Thus, Ignatius made two bold but unwarranted and foolish leaps. One was from the pages of holy writ to such untenable ascriptions as "Jesus Christ our

---

[40] Ignatius, *Romans* 4.1; 5.9.
[41] P. Schaff, *History of the Christian Church*, 2:658-59. In contrast, J.B. Lightfoot (*Apostolic Fathers, Part Two*, 1:38) defends Ignatius by asserting, "No humility could be more real than his."
[42] It has been alleged that Ignatius also called Christ "God" in the following passages, with the last two disputed as interpolations: "blood of God" (*Eph.* 1.1; [cf. Ac 20.28]; "God of man" (*Eph.* 7.2); "God appeared in the likeness of man" (*Eph.* 19.3); "the passion of my God" (*Rom.* 6.3); "our God Jesus Christ" (*Trall.* 7.1); "Christ our God" (*Smyr.* 10.1).
[43] R. Bultmann, *Theology of the New Testament*, 1:129.

God;" the other was from the comfortable fellowship of the church at Antioch into the salivating mouths of starving lions at Rome's Coliseum!

Yet, in partial defense of Ignatius, whenever he called Christ "God" in his letters, he usually attached the pronoun "our," "my," etc. Such qualifiers seem to suggest that he embraced a persistent Hellenistic viewpoint, promulgated especially by Philo, that the Logos can properly be called "god/God" but not "the God." J.B. Lightfoot, preeminent authority on the epistles of Ignatius, adamantly espouses this assessment. He contends that "Ignatius does not appear ever to call Jesus Christ God absolutely.... Though Ignatius frequently speaks of Jesus Christ as God, it may be questioned whether he ever so styles Him without some explanatory or qualifying phrase."[44] A.C. McGiffert also insists that such evidence "does not mean that Ignatius identified Christ with the supreme God."[45]

Indeed! For the next two centuries church fathers seem to have uniformly called Jesus Christ "God," but not absolutely, i.e., without qualifying words.

2 Clement

For example, some scholars cite *2 Clement*, written about 165 CE, as extra-biblical evidence that identifies Jesus Christ as "God."[46] The opening words of this epistle are generally translated, "Brethren, we must think of Jesus Christ as of God." The author likely does not mean that "Jesus Christ" and "God" are equivalents but that Christians ought to think of Jesus as they do of God, that Jesus Christ is *like* God. For, the closing paragraph in this letter suggests that the author believes that only the Father is God absolutely. He writes, "To the only God, invisible, Father of truth, who sent forth to us the Savior." Moreover, the opening words, above, should be understood from what follows. The entire sentence reads, "Brethren, we must think of Jesus Christ as of God, as the judge of the living and the dead." Indeed, Christ will judge both the living and the dead on judgment day because God granted Him this authority, so that He will do so on behalf of God (e.g., Jn 5.22, 27; 2 Cor 5.10; cf. Rom 14.10).

Justin Martyr

Justin Martyr (c. 114-165 CE) was the most influential apologist of the 2nd century. He was a former philosopher who was converted to Jesus Christ. He afterwards recognized partial agreement between Greek philosophy and Christianity.[47] He became a theology instructor at Rome and a prolific writer. He supposedly represented what most Christians believed. His second name was appended after his death as a Christian martyr.

Ironically, Justin's influence was felt more in Egypt because he accepted much of the classical theism touted at Alexandria. He emphasized that God is transcendent and otherworldly. He also accepted Greek classical theism, that God is incomprehensible, ineffable, unapproachable, and that there exists a great gulf between God and the created world. So far, Justin's only difference with Greek religio-philosophy was that he believed that only the Logos, rather than additional intermediary aeons, was necessary to bridge the sin-chasm between God and man.

---

[44] J.B. Lightfoot, *The Apostolic Fathers, Part Two*, 1:289, 169, 26.

[45] A.C. McGiffert, *A History of Christian Thought* (New York: Scribner's Sons, 1954), 38.

[46] E.g., R. Bultmann, *Essays*, 276; R.E. Brown, *Jesus God and Man*, 32; idem, *An Introduction to New Testament Christology*, 191.

[47] Robert M. Grant, *Greek Apologists of the Second Century* (Philadelphia: Westminster, 1988), 50.

Justin's Christology was therefore centered strongly on a Logos concept, now called "Logos Christology." Justin equated the concepts of Logos and Son. He therefore embraced the partially Gnostic belief that the Logos-Son only preexisted as a power or an attribute of God but that it later emanated from God to become the Son of God through whom God created the universe. Justin believed that the Logos-Son did not eternally exist but that it had an origin. Justin explained the generation of the Logos-Son by employing the analogy of removing a burning brand from a fire, which results in two fires. Belief in this two-stage theory of the Logos-Son became quite prevalent among subsequent Christian apologists. In contrast, later traditionalists alleged that this theory made God's essence divisible, which they argued was impossible or else God could not be God.

Concerning the man, Jesus Christ, Justin Martyr wrote repeatedly that He was "God"[48] and that He had preexisted as the Logos-Son. In Justin's book, *Dialogue with Trypho*, he concludes, "Now I have proved at length that Christ is called God."[49]

While Justin could often call Jesus Christ "God" without attaching any qualifiers, he nevertheless did not intend to do so absolutely. Three times within a few paragraphs in *Dialogue with Trypho* he unabashedly calls Jesus Christ "another God" (Gr. *heteros theos*).[50] Justin likewise clings solidly to an essential subordinationism in his *Apology* by explaining concerning Jesus Christ that Christians are "holding Him in second place," after "the true God Himself ... we give to a crucified man a place second to the unchangeable and eternal God."[51] Justin further explains of Christ, "the first power after God the Father and Lord of all is the Word, who is also the Son."[52]

Irenaeus

Irenaeus (120-202 CE) was bishop of Lyons in Gaul (present France) for twenty-five years until his death. His monumental book, *Against Heresies*, "is one of the most precious remains of early Christian antiquity."[53] His writings had considerable influence on the western church.

Unlike Justin Martyr, Irenaeus disliked philosophy. He centered his Christology on the incarnation of the Son as the God-man. And he frequently supported his views with Scripture rather than philosophical arguments.

Irenaeus was very soteriological in his approach to Christology. He emphasized Jesus' mediatorship as the Revealer of God and Redeemer of man. Like the Apostle Paul in 1 Cor 15.22 and v. 45, Irenaeus adopted an incarnational, Adam Christology in which the Logos-Son became the archetypal man, Jesus, in order to restore what had been lost through Adam's fall.[54]

So, Irenaeus accepted the pre-incarnational Logos-Son Christology. But he departed from most of the other apologists by rejecting the two-stage hypothesis of it. Instead, he argued that the Logos-Son was eternal without affirming His preexistent, personal subsistence. Irenaeus wisely insisted that questions about both the generation and nature of the Logos were unanswerable due to a paucity

---

[48] E.g., Justin calls Christ "God" at least fifteen times in *Dialogue with Trypho* in the following places: 34.6; 36.2; 48.1; 55-57; 59.1; 61.3; 63.9; 113.7; 126-28. Also *1 Apology* 63.10.
[49] Justin Martyr, *Dialogue with Trypho*, 124.11.
[50] Justin Martyr, *Dialogue with Trypho*, 55-56; also 50.2.
[51] Justin Martyr, *Apology*, 1.13.2-3.
[52] Justin Martyr, *Apology*, 1.32.13.
[53] A. Cleveland Coxe in *ANF*, 1:311.
[54] E.g., Irenaeus, *Against Heresies*, 5.21.1.

of biblical revelation. To do so was mere speculation. He polemically alleged that those who do "cannot be in their right minds,... we should leave such knowledge in the hands of God."[55]

Irenaeus called Christ "God" perhaps more resolutely than his predecessors did. He asserted what later became the classical definition of the incarnation, that God actually became a man. For example, he wrote that "the Father is God and the Son is God; for that which is begotten of God is God."[56] Yet Irenaeus did not mean that the Son was God in an absolute sense, i.e., without qualification. For he could also state, "the Father Himself is alone called God."[57] Echoing 1 Cor 8.6, Irenaeus likewise affirmed "faith in one God, the Father Almighty, and in one Lord Jesus Christ, the Son of God."[58]

Finally, Irenaeus deemed the Father superior to the Son in both knowledge and dignity, and he often quoted Mt 24.36/Mk 13.32 and Jn 14.28 for support.[59] He concluded regarding the Father, "God holds the supremacy over all things," and thus over Christ.[60]

Sabellius and Paul of Samosata

So, as the 3rd century began to take shape, the large majority of professing Christians still believed in the one and only true God as a single Person, whom Jesus had called "the/My Father."[61] But they also believed that Jesus Christ was "God," only to a lesser extent. However, there was a growing fear among church leaders of a possible admixture of heathen beliefs with this established, supposedly pure, doctrine. Some Christians were concerned that their religion could become polytheistic because of their identification of both the Father and Jesus as "God," thus suggesting two Gods.

Consequently, "modalistic monarchianism" arose during the early 3rd century. It was an attempt to preserve the unity of God in the form of a strict monotheistic belief. Its chief spokesman was Sabellius, who was from Alexandria, Egypt. Little is known of him. He affirmed some important features of orthodoxy, viz., the virgin birth, the complete humanity of Jesus, and His being God. However, Sabellius reckoned God as a monad (unipersonal monarch) who manifests Himself in varying modes (hence modalistic). Sabellius identified three modes, naming them "Father," "Logos-Son," and "Spirit." He deemed these modes merely as attributes or powers that resided in the one God. Thus, while modalistic monarchians like Sabellius solidly affirmed Jesus' humanity, they either obscured the personal distinction between the Father and the Son or denied it altogether. Therefore, they came to be known mostly for identifying Jesus Christ as the Father.[62]

In approximately 260 CE, the Catholic Church officially condemned modalistic monarchianism, which had become known more popularly as "Sabellianism." Ever since, both Catholic and Protestant orthodoxy have regarded Sabellianism

---

[55] Irenaeus, *Against Heresies*, 2.28.6-7.
[56] Irenaeus, *Demonstratio*, 45; similarly *Against Heresies*, 1.8.5.
[57] Irenaeus, *Against Heresies*, 2.28.4.
[58] Irenaeus, *Against Heresies*, 1.3.6.
[59] E.g., Irenaeus, *Against Heresies*, 2.28.6, 8.
[60] Irenaeus, *Against Heresies*, 2.28.7.
[61] *EB*, 11th ed., 23:963. Cited by Anthony F. Buzzard and Charles F. Hunting, *The Doctrine of the Trinity: Christianity's Self-Inflicted Wound* (Morrow, GA: Atlanta Bible College/Restoration Fellowship, 1994), 4.
[62] Kenneth Scott Latourette, *A History of Christianity: Volume I: Beginnings to AD 1500*, rev. ed. (New York: Harper & Row, 1975), 144.

as one of the worst heresies in church history. This teaching has resurfaced periodically, most significantly in modern times among Pentecostal Christians, as we shall see in the next chapter.

Soon afterwards, another form of monarchianism emerged called "dynamistic monarchianism." Its adherents also sought to preserve the unity of God. But they insisted that only an impersonal power of God resided in Jesus Christ. Thus, dynamistic (Gr. *dynamis*="power") monarchians denied any personal presence of God in Jesus Christ. Most of them assented that God's power had always indwelt Jesus since His conception. Others insisted that it came upon Him either at His baptism or His resurrection. These last two viewpoints were labeled "adoptionism," and they are now referred to as "Adoption Christology." Some church historians have labeled monarchians as "unitarians."[63]

The foremost proponent of dynamistic monarchianism was Paul of Samosata. He was a civil official who became bishop of Antioch in 260 CE. He taught that the Logos (or Wisdom of God) and the Spirit of God were not separate and distinct *hypostases* (beings or subsistences) from God but the power of God, similar to mind and reason in humans. He also perceived Jesus as sinless but progressing toward divinity due to His increasing intimacy with God. In 269 CE, church bishops held a synod at Antioch deposing Paul of Samosata of his see, condemning his Christology, and excommunicating him.

Tertullian

Tertullian (c. 155-222 CE) was a former lawyer who converted to Christ in midlife and soon became a theologian. More than any other ante-Nicene church father, Tertullian is credited with developing the doctrine of the Trinity, especially its peculiar language. Much of it consists of legal terms. For example, Tertullian is recognized as the first Latin church father to use the word *trinitas* (trinity) to explain that God is one *substantia* (substance) manifested by three separate and distinct *personae* (persons), viz., the Father, the Son, and the Holy Spirit.[64] Tertullian was rhetorical and sarcastic, and he is known for this mostly in his opposition to the modalistic monarchian Praxeas. Tertullian alleges concerning Praxeas, "He says that the Father Himself came down into the Virgin, was Himself born of her, Himself suffered, indeed was Himself Jesus Christ."[65] Tertullian also says of Praxeas, "he put to flight the Paraclete, and he crucified the Father."[66] And he adds concerning Praxeas and other such monarchians, "they accuse us of preaching two and three gods while they claim that they are worshippers of one God."[67]

Tertullian, however, opposed later orthodoxy by teaching that prior to creation God was alone, but not without His impersonal Reason indwelling Him. Tertullian believed that the Logos was the later expression of Reason, which was God's own thought. He concluded that God only *became* the Father just prior to creation, when the Logos proceeded forth by generation to become God's

---

[63] E.g., P. Schaff, *History of the Christian Church*, 2:572-81.
[64] Tertullian, *Against Praxeas*, 3, 11-12. Actually, Theophilus, bishop of Antioch (ca. 115-181 or 188 CE; *Epistle to Autolycus II, xv*), in 180 CE became the first patristic writer to apply the Greek word *trias* (=L. *trinitas*=Eng. trinity) to God. But his concept of "God, and His Word, and His Wisdom," which latter he used interchangeably with the Holy Spirit, did not coincide with the later, final Trinitarian formula. Thus, Trinitarians usually do not credit him but Tertullian as the originator of their namesake term.
[65] Tertullian, *Against Praxeas*, 1.
[66] Tertullian, *Against Praxeas*, 1.
[67] Tertullian, *Against Praxeas*, 3.

deputy agent in creation as well as His Son. Tertullian therefore asserted that God "could not have been a Father before the Son ... [and] there was a time when there was no Son."[68] So, Tertullian did not subscribe to what later orthodoxy would designate as "the eternality" of the Son.

Later in his career, Tertullian discredited himself with Catholicism by joining the Montanists. It was a charismatic Christian sect whose members spoke in tongues and prophesied, and many of them advocated moral separatism and universal celibacy.

Origen

Origen (185-254 CE) is recognized as the first Christian systematic theologian. He first taught at the catechetical school at Alexandria, Egypt. Following his ouster there, on account of his doctrine, he founded a school at Caesarea, Palestine. Origen was probably the most influential post-apostolic theologian until Augustine. His appeal was most evident in the ensuing christological disputes of the next two centuries, when all parties in conflict tended to cite his writings for support. An interesting sidebar about Origen is that, right or wrong, at the tender age of nineteen he demonstrated his intense devotion to Christ by castrating himself in accordance with his understanding of Jesus' teaching on eunuchs in Mt 19.12.

As might be expected, Origen was a controversial fellow. He was sort of an original thinker who embraced some Greek philosophy by emphasizing the Logos or Wisdom in a Platonist, cosmological scheme. He thus viewed the Logos and all other beings (souls) as having eternally preexisted as "divine" and that God created the world through the Logos for the purpose of rehabilitating all of these fallen souls through punishment in order to restore them to their pre-fallen state of divinity. He also believed in the future immortality of all souls. Origen therefore clearly was a universalist. The Church later repudiated this particular Platonic teaching and sanctioned Origen for it.

In one place in Origen's writings he echoes Philo,[69] calling the Logos "the second god" (Gr. *ho deuteros theos*).[70] But he differs from Philo, as well as Tertullian and the other apologists, by insisting that the Logos always existed as a distinct, personal being separate from God.

Origen's most significant contribution to orthodox Christology was his doctrine of "eternal generation," which is an oxymoron. It means that God eternally generated (continually generates) the Logos. During the next century, this doctrine became the primary basis of the Arian controversy. T.E. Pollard acknowledges, "Perhaps Origen's greatest contribution to Trinitarian theology is his doctrine of eternal generation, yet its primary source for him is [not the Bible but] his Middle-Platonist cosmology" concerning the preexistence of souls.[71] As R.E. Brown correctly observes, "No NT passage states precisely that the Son coexisted from all eternity with the Father."[72]

While Origen conceived of the Logos-Son being co-eternal with the Father, he nevertheless did not believe they were co-equal. Rather, he repeatedly affirmed the essential subordination, and therefore inferiority, of the Son to the Father. To support this position, Origen frequently cited two of his favorite

---

[68] Tertullian, *Against Hermogenes*, 3.
[69] Philo, *Questions and Answers on Genesis*, 2.62; cf. *On Dreams*, 1.229. But note that Philo (*On Dreams*, 1.229; *Questions and Answers on Genesis*, 2.798) wrote more than once, "there is only one true God."
[70] Origen, *Fragment on Hebrews contra Celsum*, V, 39.
[71] T.E. Pollard, *Johannine Christology and the Early Church* (Cambridge: University, 1970), 95.
[72] R.E. Brown, *An Introduction to New Testament Christology*, 143.

sayings of Jesus: "The Father is greater than I," and the Father is "the only true God" (Jn 14.28; 17.3).

Summary of Ante-Nicene Christology

So, the sum of ante-Nicene, patristic Christology is that while leading church fathers such as Justin Martyr, Irenaeus, Tertullian, and Origen, did not hesitate to call Jesus Christ "God," they did not mean that He was equal in essence, and therefore shared the same nature, with God the Father. Rather, they only declared that Jesus Christ was "God" with qualification, thus not distancing themselves from strict monotheism as their successors did. So, they were neither Trinitarian nor Binitarian in the strict sense of those terms. Instead, they all viewed the Father, the Son, and the Holy Spirit in descending order regarding both dignity and essence, so that the Son was essentially subordinate to the Father and likewise the Spirit to the Son.[73] Irenaeus and Tertullian came the closest to what the Church later decided as orthodoxy concerning Jesus' identity.

These ante-Nicene fathers of the 2nd and 3rd centuries agreed on many cardinal elements of the Christian faith as passed down by the apostles and other early disciples of Jesus. *Yet, among these church fathers there existed a fluidity of opinion on speculative, christological matters.* Adolf von Harnack concludes concerning at least the first two centuries of Christianity that there were "very diverse conceptions of the Person, that is, of the nature of Jesus."[74] However, this situation was about to change dramatically.

Two Church Centers

It helps to have a mental picture of the background of the upcoming christological struggle. We have seen that the early Jesus Movement began with its center at Jerusalem but that it shifted on account of the early Jewish followers of Jesus being persecuted in their motherland by their own brethren in the flesh. The result was that two primary centers of Christianity developed elsewhere in the world. One was located at Antioch, Syria, and the other at Alexandria, Egypt. We have already seen that Antioch became the headquarters of the church soon after its persecution began at Jerusalem (Ac 11.19-30). Antioch was the third largest city in the Roman Empire at that time. Alexandria was the second largest city in the Roman Empire and the premier intellectual center of the world.

Presuppositionally, these two theological centers differed markedly. Christians at Antioch focused on the importance of Scripture and its proper interpretation. The result was they pioneered biblical exegesis. For this reason, and the threat of proto-Gnosticism, they first emphasized, and later sought to protect, the integrity of Jesus' humanity as presented in the NT gospels. They also regarded Jesus' Sonship as beginning only with His incarnation. On the other hand, Christian theologians at Alexandria were heavily influenced by Greek philosophy, with its metaphysics. They focused on the abstract, ontological significance of the Logos and its relation to both God and Jesus. They also viewed the Logos and the Son as having preexisted before Jesus' incarnation. Alexandria was to become the center of traditional (orthodox) Christology.[75]

---

[73] P. Schaff, *The History of the Christian Church*, 2:561-64. Some didn't attribute *hypostasis* to Holy Spirit.

[74] A. von Harnack, *History of Dogma*, 1:190.

[75] E.g., Arthur Darby Nock, *Essays on Religion and the Ancient World*, ed. Zeph Stewart, 2 vols. (Oxford: University, 1972), 2:574.

This christological difference resulted in these two centers of Christianity often opposing each other.

The Arian Controversy

In 318 CE, a christological controversy erupted at Alexandria, Egypt. It would have monumental importance for church Christology. Known as the Arian Controversy, it centered on the teaching of a church priest (presbyter) named Arius.[76]

Arius (c. 250-336 CE) was tall, slender, an eloquent speaker, and nearly seventy years old when this dispute broke out. He pastored a church in the Baucalis district of Alexandria, near the Great Harbor. He endeared himself to his many parishioners and other locals, most notably with his theological poetry put to music. Sometimes, Arius walked the city streets like a Pied Piper, chanting or singing his tunes with a joyous crowd scampering after him. He wrote a book, entitled *Thalia*, which contained his theology in both rhyme and prose. But, as with the fate of many books that the Church deemed heretical, *Thalia* was banned and therefore never survived posterity.

Arius was somewhat Antiochian in Christology. Briefly stated, he advocated an abstract monotheism by emphasizing the transcendence of God the Father while also affirming Jesus' humanity. Like the orthodox party that opposed him, Arius insisted that Jesus preexisted as a complete Person as both the Logos and Son of God (though Arius distinguished the two) and thus as a separate subsistence (Gr. *hypostasis*) from God the Father. Arius further acknowledged that Jesus was "God." But, unlike the orthodox party, he taught that Jesus was not God absolutely, so that only the Father is "the one, true God." The orthodox party accused Arius of not believing that Jesus was (fully) God. Yet Arius believed no differently on these matters than had his predecessors, the apologists.

The principal teaching of Arius that sparked such fierce contention was that he asserted that, sometime prior to the creation of the world, God created His Son as "the first born of all creation" (Col 1.15; cf. Rev 3.14). Arius therefore depicted the Son as a God-made creature, though uniquely distinct from all other creatures. Arius sometimes cited Tertullian by repeatedly stating concerning the Logos-Son, "There was when he was not." He meant that before creation and time, the Logos-Son did not exist.[77] As stated earlier, this idea requires that, prior to the Son's supposed creation, God was not Father.

Arius further asserted that the Son was created "out of nothing," thus not of God's essence. Accordingly, Jesus had a divine nature that was "like" that of the Father but not the same. And Arius asserted that Jesus' nature was alterable, since He possessed free will, yet He chose righteousness to become unalterable (cf. "wisdom" in Prov 8.22). Arius also claimed Jesus did not possess omniscience as an attribute of His divine nature. Citing Mt 24.36/Mk 13.32, Arius concluded that Jesus did not fully know the Father.

This Arian Controversy broke out when Arius wrote an explanatory letter to the bishop at Alexandria. In it, he defends his theology and that of his associates. It begins, "We acknowledge one God, alone unbegotten, alone everlasting, alone

---

[76] The so-called "orthodox party" (some historians prefer "the Athanasian party") unfairly labeled those who adopted the views of Arius as "Arians." And they also inappropriately labeled this dispute "the Arian Controversy." Arius was never much of a central figure in this quarrel, which lasted over fifty years.

[77] We must rely on the church fathers' transmission of Arius' teaching, with supposedly key quotations of certain phrases, since Arius' books were collected and destroyed by the authority of the Emperor's edict.

unbegun, alone true, alone having immortality, alone wise, alone sovereign." Arius also distinguishes this God in absolute terms, e.g., "the only true God" and "eternal One." And occasionally he applies the Greek philosophical term "Unoriginate" to this God, who later became Father. Arius styles the Son as "God Originate," therefore essentially subordinate to the Father.

Bishop Alexander objected vehemently. He was one of the most powerful bishops in the Roman Empire, with his jurisdiction encompassing much of North Africa. Bishop Alexander denounced Arius' teaching as heretical. He alleged that it rendered Christ as less than fully God and thus not God at all. He explained that God the Father generated the Logos-Son as a distinct personality but that, in order for Him to be fully God, there could never have been a time when the Logos-Son did not exist. The bishop opposed the apologists' teaching on this and affirmed Origen's contradictory doctrine of eternal generation. The bishop asserts, "God is always, the Son is always," and the Son is "the unbegotten begotten." Yet Bishop Alxander denies Origen's essential subordinationism and affirms the teaching of Dionysius (Origen's successor as head of the Alexandrian school), that there never was a time when God was not the Father.

This theological dispute intensified between Bishop Alexander, Arius, and their respective constituents. The battle grew so intense that the local populace took it violently into the streets. Consequently, in 318 CE Bishop Alexander summoned a synod of over a hundred bishops at Alexandria. The majority of them deposed Arius, condemned him and his supporting bishops, denounced them as "atheists," and banished them from the city.

But Arius could not be silenced. He traveled north, visiting many friends and spreading his views in the northeastern realm of the empire. In about 319 to 322 CE, two of Arius' influential bishop friends—Eusebius of Nicomedia and Eusebius of Caesarea—retorted on his behalf by convening synods of their own in their districts. These synods exonerated Arius and demanded his reinstatement at Alexandria.

This Arian Controversy escalated until it threatened the peace of the eastern branch of the Catholic Church. The question posed by the disputing parties went like this: Was the Son (1) created, and thus essentially subordinate to the Father, or (2) eternally generated, so as to be co-eternal and co-equal with the Father? The answers given by Arius and Bishop Alexander to this question laid the battle lines for what was to become, and remains to this day, *the greatest theological controversy in the history of the church.*

The Council of Nicaea (325 CE)

General Constantine (272-337 CE) became emperor of the Roman Empire in 312 CE. In that year, he was propelled toward that office when he achieved an inter-Roman military victory which caused him to embrace Christianity. As he and his troops marched toward Rome, they professedly saw ahead of them in the sky a flaming cross which was inscribed with the Greek words, E*n touto nika*, meaning, "By this, conquer." Constantine also claimed that that night he had a dream in which Jesus Christ appeared to him, showing him a cross, and commanding him to inscribe the sign of the cross on all of his soldiers' standards. The next day Constantine replaced his army's old standards, which had pagan symbols, with new standards having a symbol of a cross. Then they marched forth courageously and won the battle against the army of General Maxentius. In contrast, Maxentius had previously consulted an oracle for guidance in the battle.

Up to that time, the Roman world had never experienced freedom of religion. For any group of Roman citizens to legally practice a religion, Rome's administrative authorities had to approve it. Christianity had thus far never been approved. But in 313 CE, Constantine issued an edict acknowledging Christianity as a legitimate religion.

So, Constantine became the first professing Christian emperor. He sought to unify both his empire and the Church by intervening to settle the Arian Controversy. To do so, he sent a letter to the two original disputants. In it, he said he had made "careful inquiry into the origin and foundation of these differences" and that he had judged their "cause to be of a truly insignificant character and quite unworthy of such fierce contention." He concluded that such discussions should be "intended merely as an intellectual exercise."[78]

Traditionalists ever since have generally faulted this assessment by the emperor. They have deemed him a theological novice who failed to grasp the gravity of the issues being disputed. While their criticism has some merit, the emperor's assessment of this dispute does too. Constantine's advisor on church affairs was his friend and spiritual mentor, seventy year-old Hosius (Ossius), Bishop of Cordova, Spain. He seems to have had an impeccable reputation. (Athanasius so respected Hosius that he often called him "the Great."[79]) Hosius aided in drafting the emperor's letter and personally delivered it to the two disputants. Church historian K.S. Latourette surmises, "Constantine's words probably reflected the attitude of the average Christian layman" at that time.[80]

In early 325 CE, under the emperor's direction a regional synod of bishops met at Antioch to solve this matter. But they issued a polemical, anti-Arian, credal statement that only worsened the conflict. So, it seemed that stronger measures had to be taken.

So, that summer of 325 CE, Emperor Constantine convened and presided over what came to be called the Nicene Council. It was so-named due to its location in the city of Nicaea in Bithynia, Asia Minor (present Iznik, Turkey), forty-five miles southeast of Constantinople (present Istanbul, Turkey). Bishops were summoned from throughout the empire, and 318 reportedly attended. R.P.C. Hanson says this figure was exaggerated and that it "probably fell between 250 and 300."[81] But each bishop was accompanied by two presbyters and three servants, so that perhaps 2,000 men attended. All were guests of the emperor at his expense, and the affair lasted just over two months during mid-year.

The Council of Nicaea remains to this day the most important event in the history of post-apostolic Christianity.[82] The Catholic Church has always described it as "the first ecumenical council" and "the great and holy council" because it was to become the first and most illustrious of all subsequent ecumenical church councils. Yet, it was not really ecumenical because almost all of the attending bishops were from the eastern realm of the empire. This circumstance reflected

---

[78] Quoted by K.S. Latourette, *A History of Christianity: Volume I*, 153-54.

[79] P. Schaff, *History of the Christian Church*, 3:627n1.

[80] K.S. Latourette, *A History of Christianity: Volume I*, 154. Latourette adds, "We read that one of these who had suffered for his faith in the persecutions ... bluntly told the debaters that Christ did not 'teach us dialectics, art, or vain subtleties, but simple-mindedness, which is preserved by faith and good works.'"

[81] R.P.C. Hanson, *The Search for the Christian Doctrine of God*, 156.

[82] *The Almanac of the Christian World*, ed. Edythe Draper, 1991-92 ed. (Wheaton, IL: Tyndale, 1990), 303.

the decline of the West by this time, the reemergence of the East, the West's disregard for a controversy that would not be conducted in its native tongue of Latin and that it would be a semantical argument in Greek.

The atmosphere of this Nicene gathering was euphoric. Christianity had suffered persecution by the Roman state throughout much of its history of three centuries. Now, the emperor was a professing brother in Christ who was honoring his fellow Christians. Several of the attendees bore physical scars as wounds incurred from prior judicial torture for their refusal to recant their Christian testimony, especially in "the Great Persecution" of Christians in 303 to 311 CE.

No minutes of council meetings were ever recorded, which appears to have been purposeful. Although Arius attended these meetings, he was not allowed to speak because he was not a bishop. So, his bishop friends presented arguments on his behalf. Despite legend to the contrary, Athanasius could not have spoken since he was only a deacon.

One interesting story that happened during the Nicene council meetings deflates a most cherished childhood fantasy of the Western World: *Santa Claus slapped Arius in the face!* That's right. Richard Rubenstein reports that "a young Gallic bishop by the name of Nicholas, who afterwards became the legendary saint of Christmas celebrations, became so incensed by Arius' heretical declarations that he slapped the old man's face!"[83] He is the St. Nicholas who became renowned for giving gifts to needy children.

(St. Nicholas was bishop of what is now Demre, a coastal Turkish city. In 2002, the Turkey-based Santa Claus Foundation demanded of Italy that St. Nicholas' bones, which it alleges were stolen by pirates in the 11th century, be returned to Turkey.)

Despite such skirmishes, Emperor Constantine gladly assembled the council with pomp, majesty, and eloquence. The large meetings were held in one of his magnificent and sumptuous palaces, called the Judgment Hall. Since the emperor had just returned victorious in war, he stated in his opening address to the council, "Discord in the church I consider more fearful and painful than any war.... Delay not therefore my friends,... put away all causes of strife." Note the subtle nudge of political pressure!

Like many politicians, Emperor Constantine had a hidden agenda. He was determined to form a Christian theocracy with an enforceable religious doctrine under the slogan: "one God, one emperor, one kingdom, one church, one faith." But it never quite happened. Initial unity proved illusory and soon eluded the emperor; but dogma did not.

The Nicene Creed

The Nicene Council drafted a dogmatic statement about one page in length called the Nicene Creed. A creed is a statement of belief that often serves as a test of orthodoxy, meaning "right opinion." The Nicene Creed declared that the Son of God was "begotten not made." This language was intended as an ontological statement affirming eternal generation. But this creed's most important christological proposition was that it declared that Jesus Christ was "very God of very God," meaning "fully God of fully God" or "truly God of truly God." This language was inserted to oppose the Arian teaching of the inferiority of the Son,

---

[83] Richard E. Rubenstein, *When Jesus Became God: The Epic Fight over Christ's Divinity in the Last Days of Rome* (New York: Harcourt Brace, 1999), 77.

which Arians supported mostly by citing Jn 14.28. R.P.C. Hanson informs that the Nicene Creed "was constructed as a deliberately anti-Arian document."[84]

Such language seems strange to us moderns. But for those ancients, the words "very God" (Gr. *alethinon theon*) referred to a popular Hellenistic concept which had predated Christianity. Centuries earlier, Greeks employed *alethinon theon* to distinguish a primary god from lesser gods. Origen had even employed this word in his commentary on the Gospel of John to explain that the Father is exclusively "Very God" in distinction from Christ, whom we have already seen he regarded as essentially a lesser God/god.[85] Thus, the Nicene fathers departed from Origen's teaching, as well as that of their apologist predecessors, in styling Christ as "very God."

This Nicene debate therefore was largely a semantical disagreement. The creed's framers originally had intended to be guided by a principle followed previously in the Apostles' Creed. It was that *any binding credal formula must not include unscriptural language*. The reason given was that unscriptural words suggest that they are based upon unscriptural concepts. But traditionalist and patristic authority J.N.D. Kelly observes concerning this principle, that it "was only abandoned when it was seen that every conceivable text or biblical turn of phrase could be ingeniously distorted by the Arians to look like evidence in support of their speculations."[86]

Debate ensued primarily because the word *homoousios* was introduced into the creed.[87] By applying it to Jesus, it rendered Him as being of the "same substance" (Gr. *homo*=same; *ousia*=substance) with the Father. But at that time, *ousia* was capable of a variety of meanings, e.g., "being," "essence," or "reality," which were discussed.[88] What the creed's framers meant by *homoousios* was "consubstantiality," i.e., that Jesus and the Father are united in a common substance or nature. R.P.C. Hanson alleges,

> considerable confusion existed about the use of the terms *hypostasis* and *ousia* at the period when the Arian Controversy broke out.... The search for the Christian doctrine of God in the fourth century was in fact complicated and exasperated by semantic confusion, so that people holding different views were using the same words as those who opposed them, but unawares, giving them different meanings from those applied to them by those opponents.... the word *hypostasis* and the word *ousia* had pretty well the same meaning. They did not mean, and should not be translated, 'person' and 'substance,' as they were used when at last the confusion was cleared up and these two distinct meanings were permanently attached to these words in theology which dealt with the doctrine of God.[89]

Nowadays, the doctrine of the Trinity is generally defined succinctly in English as three Persons in one essence or substance. Hanson says this does not reflect the Nicene Creed's wording even though it is so claimed. He informs concerning the Greek word for person, "The word *prosopon* does not figure prominently in the Arian Controversy.... To denote that which God is as Three in distinction to what he is as One, the word might have been helpful

---

[84] R.P.C. Hanson, *The Search for the Christian Doctrine of God: The Arian Controversy, 318-381* [1988] (rep. Grand Rapids: Baker, 2005), 164.
[85] Origen, *Commentary on John*, 2.2.
[86] J.N.D. Kelly, *Early Christain Creeds*, 3rd ed. (Essex, England: Longman, 1972), 253.
[87] In 269 CE, the Synod of Antioch rejected *homoousios*, deeming that it supported Paul of Samosata's Christology. Eusebius feared it suggested that the essence of the Father was divisible. The western church used the word *consubstantial*, the Latin equivalent of the Greek word *homoousios*.
[88] J.N.D. Kelly, *Early Christian Creeds*, 243-49, 253.
[89] R.P.C. Hanson, *The Search for the Christian Doctrine of God*, 181.

in avoiding misunderstandings."[90] But he explains it was also used to mean "appearance," which could suggest Sabellianism, so it had to be avoided. And he claims that in the West, the Latin word for person, *persona*, was similarly inadequate.[91]

A middle party also formed that was led by Eusebius, the famed church historian and Bishop of Caesarea in Palestine. This group of bishops was unjustly labeled the "semi-Arian" party when, in fact, its intended purpose was to serve as a mediating influence in the controversy.[92] These bishops did, however, side with the Arians in objecting to unscriptural language in the creed. Both this middle party and the Arians assented to designating Jesus as *homoiousios*, meaning "similar" or "like substance" with the Father.

Thus, this disagreement at Nicaea centered mostly on the words *homoousios* and *homoiousios*, a difference of only the letter "i." Modern historian Edward Gibbon, in his highly-acclaimed seven-volume history of the Roman Empire, ridiculed this greatest of church controversies for hinging on only one letter in the Greek alphabet. He famously alleged, "the profane of every age have derided the furious contests which the difference of a single diphthong excited between the Homoousians and the Homoiousians."[93]

The problematic word *ousia* was also included in the Nicene Creed and applied to Jesus. But afterwards, the conflicting parties generally, but not officially, replaced it with the more precise word *hypostasis*, which means "subsistence," i.e., that which underlies an object or person. For example, while the Arians rejected *homoousios*, arguing that it suggested Sabellianism, they approved of *hypostasis* as referring to two different modes of subsistence of the one indivisible whole, i.e., the two separate Persons, viz., God the Father and Jesus Christ, being the one indivisible Godhead.

The majority of the bishops at Nicea did not at first readily acquiesce to this strange terminology. Many worried about such Pauline, pastoral admonitions as to be "nourished on the words of the faith" and "retain the standard of sound words" (1 Tim 4.6; 2 Tim 1.13; cf. 2 Pt 2.3). They felt further discomfort by Paul's warnings "not to wrangle about words, which is useless," and anyone who "does not agree with sound words, those of our Lord Jesus Christ,... is conceited and understands nothing; but he has a morbid interest in controversial questions and disputes about words, out of which arise envy, strife" (2 Tim 2.14; 1 Tim 6.3-4). J.N.D. Kelly relates, "Only a comparatively small group,... welcomed the language of the creed.... [the majority] had no desire to be saddled with an un-Scriptural term."[94]

At first, Emperor Constantine remained neutral in this dispute, often associating with the middle party. But seeing the obstinacy of the anti-Arian party to yield any ground whatsoever, and for the sake of ecclesiastical well-being and political expediency, he shifted his allegiance to them. The emperor then sought to assuage the fears of the dissenting bishops by redefining and minimizing the importance of *homoousios* and pressuring them to sign the creed.[95] Actually,

---

[90] R.P.C. Hanson, *The Search for the Christian Doctrine of God*, 206.

[91] R.P.C. Hanson, *The Search for the Christian Doctrine of God*, 206-07.

[92] The orthodox party unjustly applied this label to Eusebius and his associates, as if they were theologically more Arian than orthodox. It is more reasonable to call them "the middle party."

[93] Edward Gibbon, *The History of the Decline and Fall of the Roman Empire*, 7 vols. (London: Methuen, 1909), 2:373.

[94] J.N.D. Kelly, *Early Christian Creeds*, 254.

[95] J.N.D. Kelly, *Early Christian Creeds*, 254.

the crafty emperor approved of *homoousios* because its ambiguity enabled the creed's wider endorsement.[96] So much for politics!

Traditionalists have widely ignored Emperor Constantine's political coercion at the Nicene Council. Instead, they have touted the Council's unanimity, citing that all of its bishops, except Arius and his two bishop friends from Libya, signed the creed. Indeed they did, but under threat of imperial banishment! The emperor promptly expelled Arius and his two friends from the empire for refusing to sign the creed.[97] Then he made it a capital crime, punishable by death, to possess any of Arius' books. Officials afterwards collected all they could and burned them. Francis Young thus cautions, "The course of doctrinal development should never be studied in isolation from the historical context of the debates."[98] Indeed, that is the main reason for this lengthy chapter in this book.

To make matters worse, after dismissing the council the emperor sent a succession of edicts through his empire which served as imperial decrees establishing the validity of the Nicene Creed. In these edicts, the emperor states that the Nicene Creed is

> a signal benefit from the divine providence, in that, being freed from all error, we acknowledge one and the same faith. Henceforth it will not be in the power of the devil to do any thing against us; for all his insidious machinations are utterly removed....
> ....Arius alone, who first sowed this evil among you,... was found to be overcome by diabolical art and influence. Let us receive, therefore, that doctrine [the creed] which was delivered by the Almighty. Let us return to our beloved brethren, from whom this shameless minister of satan has separated us.... this man, who is evidently an enemy of the truth,... For what was approved by three hundred bishops can only be considered as the pleasure of God.... For whatever is transacted in the holy councils of the bishops, is to be referred to the divine will.... [and] the cruelty of the devil is taken away by divine power through my instrumentality.

Many church congregations still regularly recite the Nicene Creed, but in an abbreviated form. The latter third of it—which heaps anathemas (a list of condemnations) on Arius and his followers as having no part in the Catholic (Universal) Church and thus deemed estranged from God and His salvation and condemned to hell—is *not* recited and thus remains unknown to most such church folk.

Interestingly, the Nicene Creed portrays only a Binitarian faith.[99] The subject of the Holy Spirit was not even discussed by the Council. Throughout the 2nd and 3rd centuries, there existed no consensus of opinion among church fathers on the nature of the Holy Spirit. Some thought the Holy Spirit (Spirit of God) was merely an impersonal power or attribute of God. Others ascribed personality to the Holy Spirit. A few refused to speculate about the matter, refusing to go beyond the express declarations of Scripture. P. Schaff explains, "the doctrine of the Holy Spirit was far less developed, and until the middle of the fourth century was never a subject of special controversy."[100] At the time of the Nicene Council, the Church clearly had not developed what later became the doctrine of the Trinity. (See Appendix B: The Nature of the Holy Spirit.)

---

[96] J.N.D. Kelly, *Early Christain Creeds*, 250. R. Bultmann (*Essays*, 273) alleges that most confessional formulas are intentionally drafted ambiguously in order to enlist the largest possible endorsement.
[97] Eusebius of Caesarea procrastinated but signed the next day.
[98] Frances Young, "A Cloud of Witnesses," in *The Myth of God Incarnate*, ed. J. Hick, 28.
[99] Maurice F. Wiles ("Origins of the Doctrine of the Trinity," *JTS* 8 [1957]: 99) claims that the entire Ante-Nicene period was "as much binitarian as trinitarian."
[100] P. Schaff, *History of the Christian Church*, 2:560.

Arius Exonerated

The anti-Arians (Orthodox) deemed Arius worse than an infidel. They reasoned that it would be better to deny Christ openly than to profess faith in Him while deceiving people into believing that He was some sort of demigod, as they alleged that Arius did. The progenitor of this raging rhetoric was the youthful, articulate Athanasius (c. 297-373 CE). He had been Bishop Alexander's protégé and assistant during the Nicene Council.

Arius and the Arians, despite their offenses, have been seriously misrepresented in church history. This is due mostly to the fact that posterity never had access to Arius' writings. As is often the case with alleged heretics, their writings were destroyed by imperial decree. Also, the anti-Arians in their own writings sometimes distorted Arian theology. Patristic authority Maurice Wiles explains, "Athanasius is not only responsible for creating the concept of Arianism; he is also responsible for determining how the concept has been understood in the subsequent history of the church. That understanding has been affected far more by the polemical account given by Athanasius than by the precise teaching either of Arius himself or of the so-called Arians."[101] Francis Young adds, "It is unjust to Arius to describe his doctrine as utterly unbiblical."[102] Indeed, he and the Arians sought to support their doctrines from Scripture just as much as the anti-Arians did. Fortunately, there recently has been an ongoing revision of the history of this conflict as well as Arian theology.[103]

Arius soon lost patience with the whole ordeal. In a letter to the emperor, he threatened to start another church if he was not immediately reinstalled. That really riled the emperor. He immediately dispatched a hostile letter, declaring Arius a non-Christian and threatening to make life very difficult for both him and his associates if they did not succumb to the emperor's imperial authority. This literary exchange prompted one more meeting between Arius and the emperor, wherein Arius apologized for his letter. The emperor then reciprocated by forgiving Arius and promising to reinstall him.

On the surface, Emperor Constantine appears to have been fickle. But Richard Rubenstein probably captures the true sentiment of the situation:

> To watch Constantine alternate between approval of the two enemies, Arius and Athanasius, gives one the impression of an unstable, vacillating man. The impression is not entirely accurate. True, the emperor was easily moved to anger or affection.... But the matter goes beyond this. The dispute itself also caused shifts of opinion, because each side seemed to have seized on an indispensable portion of the truth. Many people less volatile than Constantine found themselves drawn first to one side, then the other.[104]

Rubenstein also sums up quite well the effect of the Nicene Creed on strict monotheistic belief. He remarks, "Doctrinally, this is the point at which Christianity breaks decisively with its parent faith and with other forms of monotheism ... For Nicene Christians, incorporating Jesus into the Godhead was the way to preserve and extend the worship of Christ without sacrificing

---

[101] Maurice F. Wiles, *Archetypal Heresy: Arianism Through the Centuries* (Oxford: Clarendon, 1996), 6.
[102] F. Young, "A Cloud of Witnesses," 26.
[103] E.g., see Robert C. Gregg and Dennis E. Groh, *Early Arianism: A View of Salvation* (Philadelphia: Fortress, 1981); Rowan Williams, *Arius: Heresy and Tradition* (London: Darton, Longman and Todd, 1987); M. Wiles, *Archetypal Heresy*; R.P.C. Hanson, *The Search for the Christian Doctrine of God: The Arian Controversy, 318-381* (Edinburgh: T.&T. Clarke, 1988).
[104] R. Rubenstein, *When Jesus Became God*, 115.

monotheism. For others, defining Jesus as God incarnate sacrificed monotheism by definition."[105]

Less than three years later the emperor completely changed his mind! Emperors are allowed to do that, you know, especially vacillating ones! Emperor Constantine was persuaded toward Arianism by Bishop Eusebius of Caesarea and the emperor's sister, who had become an Arian. Constantine thus recalled the exiled Arius for an interview and required him to simultaneously submit a more conciliatory credal statement of his own. When Arius obliged, the emperor summoned a council of bishops to Nicomedia to study Arius' creed. In early 328 CE, the emperor and the Council of Nicomedia somewhat overturned the Nicene Creed by approving of Arius' creed, which did not have the word *homoousios*. This was quite a change in the emperor's disposition, which traditionalists rarely mention. The emperor then exonerated Arius and wrote to Bishop Alexander, directing him to reinstate Arius to the city of Alexandria and his church.

But the insolent bishop refused. Instead, he wrote the emperor, declaring that there was no place in the Catholic Church for unrepentant heretics the likes of Arius. The emperor quickly dispatched another letter to the insubordinate bishop, demanding his submission. So, Bishop Alexander sent Athanasius as his agent to convince the emperor. While Athanasius was en route, Bishop Alexander died unexpectedly. Athanasius then rushed back to Alexandria to become installed as successor to the deceased bishop.

New Bishop Athanasius also refused to reinstate Arius. So the emperor wrote a threatening letter to him, demanding that he accept Arius and his supporters as fellow Christians or else the emperor would send officials to forcibly expel the defiant bishop from his cherished position. Athanasius shot back in a letter, saying that he would not obey the emperor because Arius and his crowd were "enemies of Jesus Christ." Not so says historian E. Gibbon; citing sources, he claims Arius' "most implacable adversaries have acknowledged the learning and blameless life of that eminent presbyter."[106]

In 335 CE, a council of over a hundred bishops met at Tyre, Lebanon, to hear charges of terrorism, torture, and even a murder lodged against Athanasius and his associates. It even sent a team of investigators to Alexandria. After the council received that report, it condemned Athanasius and advised the emperor to depose him of his see and expel the bishop from Alexandria. Bishop Athanasius then hurried to the capital at Constantinople to personally plead his case before the emperor. Constantine summoned representative bishops of the Council of Tyre and heard both their arguments and those of Athanasius. During one heated exchange, the insolent bishop lost his cool and reportedly shouted at the emperor, "Be warned. God will judge between you and me."[107]

That did it! Constantine immediately condemned Athanasius and deported him far from Egypt, to the frontier of Gaul. There he remained until the emperor died two years later. It was Roman custom to return all forced exiles upon the death of the emperor.

But just before Emperor Constantine died, in 336 CE he summoned the eastern bishops to consider Arius' doctrine one more time. They examined the creed that Arius recently had submitted. This time, the emperor personally entered into interrogations of Arius. The result was that Arius was acquitted of

---

[105] R. Rubenstein, *When Jesus Became God*, 210.

[106] E. Gibbon, *The History ... of the Roman Empire*, 2:364.

[107] R. Rubenstein (*When Jesus Became God*, 130) cites Timothy D. Barnes (*Constantine and Eusebius* [Cambridge, MA: Harvard, 1981], 240).

heresy and his revised teaching was approved as orthodox. The emperor then declared that Arius would be readmitted to the fellowship of the Catholic Church at Constantinople on a set day as a jubilant celebration in recognition of the end of the Arian Controversy.

But in a twist of seeming fate, the night before the planned ceremony the aged Arius was suddenly stricken with abdominal cramps and died instantly. Athanasius and some of his supporters alleged that Arius' unexpected death was no mere coincidence but (you guessed it) the judgment of God! (Oh, yeh! What of Bishop Alexander's unexpected death in light of his insubordination to the emperor?) But some of the Arians would not be outdone by such a pernicious attack on their beloved patriarch; they countered with the protest that Athanasius had sent agents who poisoned Arius.

The fact that Arius had eventually compromised his position slightly, just for the sake of the peace of the Church, is to his credit. Plus, his literary works were burned, so his theology cannot be accurately assessed by posterity. Besides, at the time of the Nicene Council, Arius was an elderly man of perhaps sixty-five years of age, whereas Athanasius was full of youthful exuberance, being only twenty-seven years of age. R. Rubenstein concludes concerning Arius, "his devotion to Christ and the Church was genuine, as was his desire to live at peace with other Christians, even if he and they differed in matters of doctrine."[108] Wisdom teaches that living by the Golden Rule sometimes require a diet of theological tolerance and perhaps swallowing some pride by eating a slice of humble pie.

Despite Arius' exoneration, both his and Athanasius' episodes of forced exile could not be erased from church history. This precedent bode ill for the future of the church. P. Schaff observes, "This is the first example of the civil punishment of heresy; and it is the beginning of a long succession of civil persecutions for all departures from the Catholic faith. Before the union of church and state, ecclesiastical excommunication was the extreme penalty. Now banishment and afterwards even death were added."[109]

Athanasius

As for Athanasius, many Christians have thought that, humanly speaking, he saved Christianity from extinction. It's because, for the next fifty years, Athanasius—who was very small in physical stature but very large in indomitable spirit—became the preeminent, staunch defender of the Nicene Creed.

At first, Athanasius defended the Nicene Creed's unscriptural language. He argued, "If the expressions are not in so many words in the Scriptures, yet they contain the sense of the Scriptures."[110] Later, he avoided semantical arguments by not using *homoousios* and other controversial, unscriptural language. In fairness to Athanasius, he noted correctly that the Arians' favorite descriptive words for Jesus and the Father, which were "Originate" and "Unoriginate," respectively, were not found in Scripture either.

Athanasius' Christology was based squarely on soteriology. Church historian and traditionalist P. Schaff remarks, "It was the passion and the life-work of Athanasius to vindicate the deity of Christ, which he rightly regarded as the corner-stone of the edifice of the Christian faith, and without which he could conceive no redemption."[111] Indeed, Athanasius argued that Jesus Christ had to

---

[108] R. Rubenstein, *When Jesus Became God*, 102.
[109] P. Schaff, *History of the Christian Church*, 3:360.
[110] Athanasius, "Letters Concerning the Decrees of the Council of Nicaea," 5.21.
[111] P. Schaff, *History of the Christian Church*, 3:890.

be God in order for His sacrificial, atoning death to be completely efficacious, i.e., to satisfy the just demands of a holy God as an effective payment for our sins. Earlier, Irenaeus had insisted the same, that if Christ was not God then there is no salvation.[112]

Traditionalists have propounded this argument ever since, and many of them have attributed much significance to it.[113] Most recently, leading conservative Evangelical theologian Alister McGrath asserts, "Unless Jesus is God, it is impossible for Jesus to save us."[114] Even moderately traditionalist John Macquarrie questions that if Christians were to abolish the doctrines of the incarnation and the Trinity, "What kind of doctrine of atonement remains possible?"[115]

But traditionalists who make this argument usually do so arbitrarily. That is, they provide neither rationale nor scriptural support for their position.[116] Some think Anselm of Canterbury (1033-1117) made the definitive statement on this issue in his famous *Cur Deus Homo*. Yet even he offers very little rationale in it for his position. He merely reasons, "if any other being [than God] should rescue man from eternal death, man would rightly be adjudged as the servant of that being ... For he,... would now be the servant of a being who was not God."[117] So what! Whoever serves Jesus Christ also serves God the Father (cf. Jn 5.23; 12.44; 13.20; Phil 2.9-11).

Actually, God is the One who ultimately saves,[118] but He does it through Jesus Christ. Jesus saves all right (1 Tim 1.15; Heb 7.25), only in the sense that He provided salvation by offering Himself as the sin sacrifice. Yet "there is only one Lawgiver and Judge, the One who is able to save and to destroy" (Jam 4.12), and that is God. God is the one who saves, ultimately, because only He forgives and justifies those who believe. Don Cupitt rightly concludes that, although God saves through Jesus, "it does not follow that the one through whom salvation is given must be himself co-equal with God."[119]

Moreover, this soteriological argument does not correspond to God's covenantal requirements for Israel regarding the Levitical animal sacrifices, which anticipated Jesus' death as the archetypal sacrifice. That is, God required Israel to offer animal sacrifices being without spot and blemish and therefore having no defect. Jesus fulfilled this symbolic requirement for an expiatory sacrifice, not by being God but by being without sin as our Passover, viz., the Lamb of God. Moreover, the author of Hebrews clearly distinguishes God and Christ concerning this transaction by relating that Jesus "offered Himself without blemish to God" (Heb 9.14).

---

[112] Irenaeus, *Against Heresies*, 3.18.7.

[113] E.g., Charles Hodge, *Systematic Theology*, 3 vols. (orig. 1871-73; repr. Grand Rapids: Eerdmans, 1986), 1:485; F.P. Cotterell, "The Christology of Islam," in *Christ the Lord*, ed. H.H. Rowdon, 291-296; Klaas Runia, "Continental Christologies," in *Crisis in Christology: Essays in Quest of Resolution*, ed William R. Farmer (Livonia, MI: Truth, 1995), 21; *This We Believe: The Good News of Jesus Christ for the World*, gen. eds. John N. Akers, John H. Armstrong, and John D. Woodbridge (Grand Rapids: Zondervan, 2000), 73.

[114] E.g., Alister McGrath, *"I Believe:" Exploring the Apostles' Creed* (Downers Grove, IL: InterVarsity, 1991), 41.

[115] John Macquarrie, "Christianity without Incarnation? Some Critical Comments," in *The Truth of God Incarnate*, ed. Michael Green (Grand Rapids: Eerdmans, 1977), 144.

[116] E.g., Karl Barth, *Church Dogmatics*, ed. G.W. Bromiley and T.F. Torrance, tr. G.W. Bromiley, 14 vols. (Edinburgh: T. & T. Clark, 1975), 2:403, 405.

[117] Anselm, *Cur Deus Homo*, 1:5; cf. 2:6. His catechetical presentation is self-serving if not self-conceited.

[118] E.g., Jn 1.13; 1 Cor 1.21; 2 Tim 1.8-9; Tit 3.4-5.

[119] D. Cupitt, *Jesus and the Gospel of God*, 17.

An underlying reason for Athanasius' soteriological scheme—in which God Himself is the sin sacrifice—is the perceived divine goal of the deification of man.[120] For, Athanasius wrote concerning the Logos-Son, "He was made man that we might be made God."[121] In fact, Athanasius repeatedly calls Christians *theoi*,[122] usually translated "gods" or "deified." But we should not be so shocked at Athanasius sounding like a modern-day Mormon! Irenaeus had written earlier, "We have not been made gods in the beginning, but at the first men, then at length gods."[123] Traditionalists don't tell you these tidbits.

Most Christians have rightly objected to this patristic notion of the deification of man. For example, Stephen Smalley remarks, "The NT never admits the possibility of human beings becoming 'deified' even in reference to 'participating in the divine nature' at 2 Pet 1:4."[124] Indeed, the NT only claims that believers in Jesus are made "sons/children (of God)" by adoption.[125] Yet the chief idea of the Eastern Orthodox Church in medieval times was the deification of man through faith in Jesus Christ.[126]

Closely related to this soteriological argument was the creaturely argument. Athanasius and other church fathers asserted that Jesus had to be God in order to save humankind. Athanasius argued that if God created the preexistent Jesus, as Arius had insisted of the Logos, Jesus could not save anyone since a creature cannot save another creature. Traditionalists have offered this argument ever since. But it is quite arbitrary, irrelevant, unsupported by Scripture, and apparently borrowed from Greek philosophy.

Consider this startling inference: if the anti-Arian party headed by Athanasius was correct—that a person *must* believe that Jesus is fully, and therefore eternally, God in order to be saved—then all preceding apologists and other Christians were not saved either, which is preposterous! Recall that the apologists taught that Jesus was God, but, as Arius later did, they insisted that He was not God absolutely. They did not postulate that Jesus, as the preexistent Logos, was eternally generated. In fact, Irenaeus, who came closest to later orthodoxy, had chided those who delved into the matter of the generation of the Logos, insisting that God had not provided any revelation on it in holy writ.

Exegetically, Athanasius led the orthodox party in constantly refuting Arian objections by interpreting the christological portions of the NT with a theological grid that Maurice Wiles calls the "two-nature exegesis."[127] This grid presupposes that every time Jesus spoke or acted, He did so from the sole source of one of His two natures—either His human nature or His divine nature. Wiles concludes,

---

[120] See the seminal book on this subject by Jules Gross, published recently in English, *The Divinization of the Christian According to the Greek Fathers* [1938], tr. Paul A. Onica (Anaheim, CA: A&C, 2002).
[121] Athanasius, *On the Incarnation*, 54. The word Athanasius used herein is *theopoiethomen*, which is best rendered "God" according to Archibald Robertson (*NPNF*², 4:65n5) and signifies deification.
[122] E.g., Athanasius, *Orations Against the Arians*, 2.70; 3.19-20, 23, 25, 33, 39.
[123] Irenaeus, *Against Heresies*, 4.38.4. Irenaeus (*Against Heresies*, 4, preface) also wrote, "We have shown that no one else is called God by the Scriptures except the Father of all, and the Son, and those who possess the adoption," i.e., Christians.
[124] Stephen Smalley, *1, 2, 3 John*, in WBC 51, 142.
[125] Mt 5.9, 45; Lk 6.35; 20.36; Rom 8.14, 19, 23; 9.26 (Hos 1.10); Gal 3.26; 4.5-6. However, see Ps 58.1; 82.6; Jn 10.34>.
[126] Jaroslav Pelikan, *The Christian Tradition: A History of the Development of Doctrine: The Spirit of Eastern Christendom (600-1700)* (Chicago: University, 1974), 10.
[127] Maurice F. Wiles, *The Spiritual Gospel: The Interpretation of the Fourth Gospel* (Cambridge: University, 1960), ch. 8.

"The two-nature exegesis was thus an essential feature in the whole case of Athanasius against the Arians."[128]

This hermeneutical method apparently originated among some Christian expositors in reaction to Gnosticism as early as the 3rd century. For, the Valentinian Gnostics had supported their dualism (soul is pure and eternal but flesh is evil) by asserting that Jesus possessed only a divine nature and therefore neither a real human nature nor a physical body. Origen is the first church father known to oppose this heresy with the proposal that the earthly Jesus always spoke or acted at any given moment either from the source of His human nature or His divine nature, but never both simultaneously. Here is another example of how orthodox Christology developed in reaction to its opposition. Indeed, orthodoxy often developed by means of antithesis.[129]

Origen's two-nature exegetical method was adopted by other prominent church fathers, especially Tertullian. Later, the Church officially sanctioned this hermeneutical method and applied it as a theological grid for interpreting all of Jesus' words and works recorded in the NT. John Hick raises serious questions about this method. He inquires, "if Jesus had two consciousnesses, did these alternate, so that sometimes those around him were conversing with a human being and sometimes with God?"[130] Also, when some such person speaks or acts from the source of his or her divine nature, can that person at that moment be regarded as truly, and thus fully, human?

Athanasius often argued against the Arians' concept of the Logos by insisting, "God is not a man."[131] But couldn't this retort be used against Athanasius, the Arians, and all others who shared the viewpoint that the Father generated the Logos-Son before the creation of the world, regardless of the question of the eternality of the Logos? That is, how do we know for sure that Jesus preexisted as the Son of God? We will see that this dogma was questioned many centuries later, in which it was alleged that the Bible supports the concept of Jesus preexisting His incarnation as the Logos, but not as the Son. (And this is what Tertullian meant when he asserted that God was not always the Father.) Indeed, the angel Gabriel announced to the Virgin Mary that her "holy offspring shall be called the Son of God" (Lk 1.35), as if this title refers solely to Jesus as a human being. In contrast, Athanasius and all these churchmen understood "the Son of God" title for Jesus as referring primarily to a pre-incarnational generation of the Logos-Son. So, *post-apostolic church fathers erred by thinking that God has generative powers comparable to that of man, though not fleshly.* They didn't get this idea from Jews or their Scriptures, but from Greek metaphysical, theistic philosophy.

Athanasius was a polemicist extraordinaire who was fond of name-calling. He labeled the Arians as "Ario-maniacs." He uses this term liberally in his book, *Orations Against the Arians*. Therein, he alleges that Arians are like their "father the devil" and that Arianism is a "harbinger of Antichrist."[132] He often calls Arians "Christ's enemies" and even "atheists."[133] Yet we have seen that Arians believed the same as Athanasius did concerning many fundamental Christian

---

[128] M. Wiles, *The Spiritual Gospel*, 116.

[129] Ernst Kasemann (*Essays on New Testament Themes* [London: SCM, 1964], 16) states, "Knowledge proceeds by antithesis."

[130] John Hick, "Critique by John Hick," in *Encountering Jesus: A Debate on Christology*, Stephen T. Davis, ed. et al. (Atlanta: John Knox, 1988), 69.

[131] Athanasius, *Orations Against the Arians*, 1.28; 2.34.

[132] Athanasius, *Orations Against the Arians*, 1.1.

[133] E.g, Athanasius, *Orations Against the Arians*, 3.37, 47, 50, 55, 57-58, 64, 67.

teachings about Jesus. Their conflict regarded only the question of the eternal generation of the Logos-Son.

Trinitarian R.P.C. Hanson has authored the standard resource on the development of church Christology during the Arian Controversy, a rubric he says is a misnomer.[134] He claims that (1) Hilary, Bishop of Potiers, started the idealization of Athanasius even though he never met him; (2) "The historians of the nineteenth century were even more laudatory" of him; (3) "The twentieth century, however, has in many instances altered the favourable verdict."[135] Hanson reveals that Athanasius' theological opponents accused him of committing undeserved beatings, woundings, imprisonments, and even murders, so that all Eastern bishops, who were mostly Arian, refused to communicate with him for at least twenty years.[136] The Council of Tyre, consisting of 85 bishops, met to examine a long list of charges about Athanasius' behavior and affirmed that they were true. Hanson concurs and concludes, "we find Athanasius behaving like an employer of thugs hired to intimidate his enemies ... Athanasius in following this policy set an evil example to his successors of the use of force and intrigue."[137] Hanson admits that Athanasius' opponents could have been guilty of some exaggeration or propaganda; but he cites the discovery in modern times of papyrus evidence which clearly proves such transgressions.[138]

Athanasius' retort to these allegations is typical of cultists. He disassociates life and theology, as if they are unrelated. Jesus indicated otherwise when he prayed, "I praise You, Father, Lord of heaven and earth, that You have hidden these things from the wise and intelligent and have revealed them to infants" (Mt 11.25/Lk 10.21). And He taught in His Sermon on the Mount, "Not everyone who says to Me, 'Lord, Lord,' will enter the kingdom of heaven; but he who does the will of My Father who is in heaven" (Mt 7.21). Hanson relates, "No one ever seriously accused Athanasius of heresy, but his writings suggest time and time again that accusations of misconduct as a bishop should be ignored in order to concentrate upon the doctrinal issues."[139] In contrast, Jesus taught that true knowledge of God and His Son can only be obtained through humility and obeying God.

Athanasius had a checkered career. Arian emperors banished him from the Roman Empire five times, forcing him to suffer exile for twenty years. But each time an emperor who embraced Nicene orthodoxy ascended to the throne, he quickly recalled Athanasius from exile and reinstated him to his see. Consequently, the orthodox party eventually honored their valiant hero with the title "Athanasius the Great," and some subsequent church fathers labeled him "the father of orthodoxy."[140]

In the decades that followed the Nicene Council, its creed failed to accomplish the aspirations of Emperor Constantine, Athanasius, or his orthodox party. In fact, for many years the Nicene Creed was not well received among most

---

[134] R.P.C. Hanson, *The Search for the Christian Doctrine of God*, xvii. He says, "'the Arian Controversy' is a serious misnomer.... He was the spark that started the explosion, but ... he was of no great significance."
[135] R.P.C. Hanson, *The Search for the Christian Doctrine of God*, 239-40.
[136] R.P.C. Hanson, *The Search for the Christian Doctrine of God*, 249-54.
[137] R.P.C. Hanson, *The Search for the Christian Doctrine of God*, 254-55.
[138] R.P.C. Hanson, *The Search for the Christian Doctrine of God*, 251-54. The papyrus was published in 1924 by H.I. Bell in his book, *Jews and Christians in Egypt*. Hanson (p. xx) says, "though this was published nearly sixty years ago the significance of it has not yet sunk in everywhere."
[139] R.P.C. Hanson, *The Search for the Christian Doctrine of God*, 244.
[140] P. Schaff, *History of the Christian Church*, 3:885-86.

Christians mostly due to its unscriptural language. Each succeeding emperor adopted either an Arian or a Nicene Christology, and they usually enforced it upon the whole church by exiling dissidents. Paradoxically, for the next fifty years after the Nicene Council, which was held in the East, the West adhered to the Nicene Creed whereas Arianism prevailed in the East.

Eusebius of Caesarea

Eusebius (c. 263-c. 340 CE), bishop of Caesarea in Palestine, was the foremost church historian of the early centuries of Christianity and the most learned of all the bishops during his time. We have seen that he played a significant role as a moderating voice at the Nicene Council. In fact, the Nicene Creed was drafted partly in response to a creed submitted earlier by Eusebius, which was called "the Creed of Caesarea."

The Christology of Bishop Eusebius was quite Philonic, apologist, and Origenist. As Arius, he emphasized the Father's transcendence as Almighty God. Unlike Arius, he identified Jesus, as Origen did, as "a second God."[141] Eusebius supported his Christology mostly by citing Jn 17.3, in which Jesus called the Father "the only true God."

Eusebius differed with Arius by asserting that the Father generated the Logos-Son from His own essence "before all ages." Eusebius agreed with Arius by insisting that the Logos-Son only possessed eternity in a derivative sense. So, Eusebius differed sharply with the orthodox party, and agreed with the Arians, in denying that the Son is co-equal and co-eternal with the Father, thus affirming He is inferior and posterior to the Father.

Apollinaris

Apollinaris (c. 310-c. 390 CE) was bishop of Laodicea, Syria, and a friend of Athanasius. He first rose to fame by publicly refuting the cynical philosopher Porphery as well as the apostate Emperor Julian. Apollinaris is most known for being the first church father to raise acutely the negative implications of the doctrine of the two full natures in Christ. He alleged that it suggested two personalities. To avoid this error, Apollinaris defended the unity of Christ's Person by insisting that Jn 1.14 means that the Logos only assumed a human body and not a human will or a human spirit. Thus, he asserted that Jesus had one indivisible nature by affirming His supposed deity yet denying His full humanity. Apollinaris compared his doctrine to mixing water with wine.

Apollinaris' opponents argued against him soteriologically. They insisted that if Christ did not possess a full human nature then, psychologically, He would have been an incomplete human being. Accordingly, Jesus could not have served as our example, and He could not have qualified as the full Redeemer of our body, mind, spirit, and will.

In 375 CE, Apollinaris seceded from the Catholic Church to form his own sect. His followers became known as "Apollinarians." Two succeeding synods, as well as the next ecumenical council, condemned Apollinarianism for being contradictory.

The Council of Constantinople (381 CE)

Following the Nicene Council, the fires of this credal quarrel burned brightly for over fifty years. From 351 to 360 alone, Emperor Constantius convened and personally presided over no less than nine councils of bishops for the sole

---

[141] Eusebius, *Demonstratio Evangelica*, 1.5, 10.

purpose of trying to settle the Arian Controversy. Each of these nine councils drafted a more minimalist creed compared to the Nicene Creed. Usually, these creeds omitted *homoousios*, and sometimes they altered the phrase "very God of very God." Yet the controversy only intensified.

This ongoing credal controversy became a pitiful spectacle as an advertisement of Christianity to the pagan Roman world. Sometimes, it resulted in public riots, bloodshed, and an occasional death in the major metropolises. One contemporary historian of that time, a non-Christian named Ammianus, concluded, "no wild beasts are such enemies of mankind as are most Christians in their deadly hatred of one another."[142]

This credal controversy led to a brief overturn of Christianity as a legitimate state religion and the resuming of the persecution of Christians. It happened when Emperor Constantius died, in 360, and his talented and educated nephew, Julian, succeeded him to the throne. Ever since, Christians have called this emperor "Julian the Apostate." It is because he had been a professing Christian and then turned back to paganism, doing everything in his imperial power to restore it. But after only two years in office, this gallant emperor expired in a fierce military battle.

Later, Christian novice Emperor Theodosius emerged to stomp out the smoldering embers of the Arian Controversy and halt its shifting of imperial allegiances. In 380, he declared Christianity the sole, official religion of the Roman Empire. He issued an edict requiring that all Roman citizens confess the Nicene Creed or suffer imperial punishment. The next year he sanctioned this edict as law by summoning bishops to Constantinople in what the Catholic Church later deemed "the Second Ecumenical Church Council."

As at Nicaea, this council was called "the Council of Constantinople" due to its location, and it drafted "the Creed of Constantinople." This creed represents a modified Nicene Creed, reiterating its main principles. Its main contribution to creeds is that it adds a statement which affirms both the personality and full deity of the Holy Spirit. And since the anathemas of the Nicene Creed were no longer relevant, they were not included.

Three theologians had a major influence in drafting the Creed of Constantinople and thereby settling the Arian Controversy. Called "the three Cappadocians," they were Basil the Great of Caesarea in Cappadocia (330-379 CE), Gregory of Nazianzen (c. 330-390 CE), and Basil's younger brother, Gregory of Nyssa (331/340-c. 395 CE). Before this, the Church usually employed interchangeably the words *ousia* and *hypostasis*, meaning subsistence, just as Greek speakers usually used them.[143] The three Cappadocians changed this by redefining them as religious terms.[144] They insisted God is one *ousia*, meaning substance, in three *hypostases*, meaning subsistences—the Father, the Son, and the Holy Spirit—and these three are co-equal and co-eternal. But these three *hypostases*, called "the Trinity," did not escape the charge of tritheism. Thus, Basil published a book entitled *Against Those Who falsely Accuse Us of Saying That There Are Three Gods*.

The Council of Constantinople therefore represents the Catholic Church's official formulation of the full doctrine of the Trinity as well as the final victory for the orthodox party. Since that time, the Christology

---

[142] R. Rubenstein (*When Jesus Became God*, 194) cites W.H.C. Frend (*The Rise of Christianity* [Philadelphia: Fortress, 1984], 601).
[143] J.N.D. Kelly, *Early Christian Creeds*, 244.
[144] J. Pelikan, *The Emergence of the Catholic Tradition*, 219-220.

promulgated in the creeds of especially Nicaea and Constantinople has not been challenged seriously within mainline Christian churches to the present time except some scholars within Germany's Lutheran Church have refuted it.

So, Emperor Theodosius was most responsible for the formation of the Council of Constantinople as well as its creed. But his reputation is very disconcerting, which should be cause for alarm. After the council, he issued another edict requiring the allegiance of all Roman citizens to its creed, in which he declared that any dissidents were "madmen" and "heretics." Later, in 394 CE, Theodosius began punishing pagans for their refusal to adopt Catholic Christianity. And he later proved himself a madman in his reaction to a city riot in Thessalonica that caused the death of one of his officials. The emperor then invited the entire unsuspecting Thessalonian population to be entertained in the city-arena. About 7,000 attended, and he had them all massacred as punishment for the riot.[145]

Gregory of Nazianzen was very widely esteemed by the Catholic Church.[146] He presided over the Council of Constantinople for awhile (but resigned) because he was the Bishop of Constantinople, a position he had accepted reluctantly after being pressured by his father, a bishop himself. Apparently, the process of becoming a bishop, as well as the selection of bishops to attend church councils and synods, could sometimes be ethically questionable. Gregory provides an insider critique of this process. He alleges that "the highest clerical places are gained not so much by virtue, as by iniquity; no longer the most worthy, but the most powerful, take the episcopal chair."[147] Sometime after this council, Gregory was summoned to a synod; but he declined in a letter by explaining, "to tell the truth, I am inclined to shun every collection of bishops, because I have never yet seen that a synod came to a good end, or abated evils instead of increasing them. For in those assemblies (and I do not think I express myself too strongly here) indescribable contentiousness and ambition prevail.... Therefore I have withdrawn myself."[148]

New Testament Credal Fragments

Church councils drafting creeds arouses the question of whether the NT provides any credal statements as a sure foundation and, if so, whether their doctrinal content validates these subsequent church creeds. A perusal of the NT shows that it *does not* provide any elaborate credal statements that establish a definitive identity of Jesus, much less of the Holy Spirit. However, the NT *does* have some very brief, primitive credal fragments. The foremost are as follows, with the first one being a formula that the early Christians sometimes uttered when they baptized new converts:

- Jesus is "Lord" (1 Cor 12.3; e.g., Rom 10.9; Phil 2.11; cf. Ac 8.16; 19.5; 1 Cor 6.11).
- Jesus is "the Christ" (Ac 9.22; 1 Jn 2.22; cf. Ac 2.36; 16.31; 17.3; 18.5, 28; 20.21).
- Jesus is "the Son of God" (1 Jn 4.15; 5.5; cf. Mt 16.16 par.; Ac 9.20; Rom 1.3-4)

---

[145] R. Rubenstein, *When Jesus Became God*, 224.
[146] P. Schaff (*History of the Christian Church*, 3:347) relates that a church historian named Socrates praised Gregory of Nazianzen as the most spiritually devout and eloquent man of his age.
[147] Quoted by P. Schaff, *History of the Christian Church*, 3:252.
[148] Quoted by P. Schaff, *History of the Christian Church*, 3:347.

More thoroughgoing confessional statements are found in Rom 1.3-4; 8.34; 1 Cor 8.6; 15.3-7; Phil 2.6-11; 1 Tim 2.5; 3.16; 6.13-16; 2 Tim 2.4. Credal authority J.N.D. Kelly surmises concerning these and other such NT evidence:

> It is clear that "God, Who has raised the Lord Jesus from the dead," had become a stereotyped tag or cliche before the third generation of the first century.... Explicit Trinitarian confessions are few and far between; where they do occur, little can be built upon them.... It cannot be too often repeated that, in the proper sense of the terms, no creed, confession or formula of faith can be discovered in the New Testament, with the possible exception of such curt slogans as *Kurios Iesous* [Lord Jesus].[149]

It will be observed that none of these NT confessional fragments or brief statements identifies either Jesus or the Holy Spirit as "God."

The Apostles' Creed

The question of whether the church should have elaborate creeds that exceed this brief but simple confessional, christological data in the NT has often been fiercely debated throughout church history. This extended dispute takes us back to the most popular creed in the history of Christianity—the Apostles' Creed.

Jesus' apostles did not write the Apostles' Creed.[150] Its date of origin no doubt preceded that of the Nicene Creed. The Apostles' Creed has been thought to contain the essential elements of the Christian faith, so that there was no further need for any more creeds. The Apostles' Creed declares "God" as "the Father Almighty." It describes Jesus as God's "only begotten Son, our Lord." And it affirms Jesus' virgin birth by means of the Holy Spirit. So, it calls God "the Father," but it does not identify Jesus as God.

Both the Nicene and Constantinople creeds, on the other hand, extend far beyond the Apostles' Creed by asserting that Jesus is fully God. Don Cupitt correctly concludes that "the true New Testament teaching is preserved in the Apostles' creed, and the Nicene creed goes a crucial step beyond anything that the New Testament says."[151] In sum, *neither the NT nor the Apostles' Creed declares that Jesus Christ is God.*

Eusebius had submitted his own creed at the Nicene Council. It incorporated the structure of the Apostles' Creed, with some phrases being copied verbatim. The framers of the Nicene Creed used Eusebius' draft as a basis and thereby indirectly patterned the Nicene Creed after the Apostles' Creed. But they added that Jesus is "God from God."

The Council of Ephesus (431 CE)

Despite the settling of the Arian Controversy, these first two ecumenical councils and their creeds only seemed to stoke more fires of controversy. Deciding that Jesus was eternally, fully God led to the inevitable question: How can Jesus be both God and man? The institutional church now began to argue this question most vociferously.

Church fathers had ill-framed this question due to their incorrect presupposition that Jesus is God. They should have asked something like this: "How did Jesus relate to God and reveal Him to humankind, and what does this say about Jesus' identity?"

---

[149] J.N.D. Kelly, *Early Christian Creeds*, 21-23.

[150] Studies in the late 19th century show that the common view during the Middle Ages, that Jesus' chosen apostles formulated the Apostles' Creed, is a myth. See J.N.D. Kelly, *Early Christian Creeds*, 3.

[151] D. Cupitt, *Jesus and the Gospel of God*, 19.

Instead, this prolonged christological debate often centered on Jesus' birth and the supposed generation of the pre-existent Logos-Son. Regarding the former, the majority of Christians passionately professed Mary—the mother of Jesus—as *Theotokos* (Gr. "God-bearing"), meaning "mother of God." By this time, many Christian theologians reasoned that if Jesus was God, Mary, His mother, must be "the mother of God."

Nestorius (c. 386-451 CE), Bishop of Constantinople, consented to Jesus Christ having two natures. Yet he, too, objected to calling Mary *Theotokos* by insisting that God could not be born. So, like his deceased teacher—Theodore of Mopsuestia—Nestorius substituted the Greek word *Christotokos* ("Christ-bearing"), meaning "mother of Christ."

Emperor Theodosius II summoned a church council at Ephesus, in Asia Minor (present Turkey), to resolve these issues. The majority of those who attended condemned Nestorius most vehemently for rejecting the application of *Theotokos* to Mary. They also wrongly charged him with denying any union between the two natures. However, some followers of Nestorius, called "Nestorians,"[152] did later propose that because Jesus Christ had two natures He also must have had two personalities.

Due to Nestorius' christological views, he suffered persecution the remainder of his life in an obscure, forced exile. Yet Nestorian Christianity later flourished mostly in Persia (and spread throughout the Near East), where it enjoyed a good reputation. In fact, faithful remnants of the Nestorian Church still exist in Iran to this day.

Church historians regard this Third Ecumenical Council as a sham.[153] It consisted of a series of mutual incriminations and anathemas, with the two opposing parties not even meeting. P. Schaff relates, "Now followed a succession of mutual criminations, invectives, arts of church diplomacy and politics, intrigues, and violence, which gives the saddest picture of the uncharitable and unspiritual Christianity of that time."[154]

Even though this Council of Ephesus was later denounced by its successor, the word *Theotokos* afterwards became the supreme test of orthodox Christology.[155] In fact, rejecting the view that Mary was *Theotokos* was regarded as a denial of Christ's deity. This *Theotokos* doctrine prepared the way for the subsequent Catholic development of an unrestrained mariolotry. Ephesus had long been the home of the popular pagan cult of Diana. By now, the Ephesian Christians were known for attempting to replace it with the worship of the Virgin Mary.

The Second Council of Ephesus (449 CE)

In opposition to Nestorianism, Monophysitism arose next. The etymology of the word Monophysite is that *mono* means "one" or "single," and *physis* means "nature." Therefore, Monophysites urged the unity of Christ's person by means of the Logos subsuming human nature at the incarnation. Monophysites thus

---

[152] P. Schaff (*History of the Christian Church*, 3:730-31) informs that these followers of Nestorius—who rejected Catholic mariolatry, the use of images, and the doctrine of purgatory—merely called themselves "Chaldean Christians" or "Assyrian Christians" due to their liturgical language, whereas their opponents called them "Nestorians." Indeed, throughout church history the orthodox church has typically identified its opponents in this manner, e.g., "Arians," "Socinians," and "Unitarians," and thereby denied their own label of identification, not accepting them as such, which in most cases was "Christian" or "brethren."

[153] E.g., P. Schaff, *History of the Christian Church*, 3:347-48.

[154] P. Schaff, *History of the Christian Church*, 3:725.

[155] P. Schaff, *History of the Christian Church*, 3:421.

denied two separate natures in Jesus and insisted on a single, deified human nature.[156] Opponents alleged that Monophysitism blurred or mixed the two natures and thus failed to adequately distinguish them. Monophysites countered that two natures logically required two Persons.

At first, Cyril, and then Eutyches, led these Monophysites. Both men insisted that God, as Christ, was born, suffered, and died. These precepts contradicted several features of classical theism that had been adopted by post-apostolic Christianity from Hellenism, e.g., that God is eternal, immutable, impassible, and immortal. While these Monophysites were ideologically divided, their united rallying cry was that Jesus was "God crucified."

Consequently, another council was convened at Ephesus. This Fourth Ecumenical Council consisted of 135 bishops who surprisingly exonerated Eutyches and the other Monophysites. Since this council's decisions represented a departure from the precepts set forth by its predecessors, it came to be known as "the Council of Robbers."

The Council of Chalcedon (451 CE)

This Monophysite doctrine of the blending of two natures in Christ, making them indistinguishable, could not go unchallenged. Pope Leo "the Great" convinced the new emperor, Marcian, of the necessity of another church council. Then he wrote a long letter, heralded as the *Tome*, to the emperor which outlined the points in dispute and delineated his view that Jesus possessed both a human nature and a divine nature. We have seen that this two-nature concept had originated earlier, during the 3rd century.

So, the Fifth Ecumenical Council was called to resolve this complex dispute about the supposed humanity and divinity of Jesus. Called "the Council of Chalcedon," since it was held in Chalcedon, near Constantinople (in present Turkey), it exceeded all previous councils in attendance, having nearly 600 bishops. This council (1) annulled the previous declarations of the "Robber's Council," (2) affirmed Mary as *Theotokos*, and (3) adopted Leo's christological declarations in his *Tome* almost verbatim.

With regard to the identity of Jesus, this Council of Chalcedon set forth the following affirmations in its confessional statement, called "The Definition of Faith:"

> Following, then, the holy Fathers, we all with one voice teach that it should be confessed that our Lord Jesus Christ is one and the same Son, the Same perfect in godhead, the Same perfect in manhood, truly God and truly man,...
> ... of the Virgin Mary, the mother of God; one and the same Christ, Son, Lord, Only-begotten, known in two natures, [which exist] without confusion, without change, without division, without separation;... not parted or divided into two persons.

So, the Council of Chalcedon declares that Jesus had two natures, a divine nature and a human nature, and that they are distinct while united in one Person. It also declares that "even the prophets ... and our Lord Jesus Christ himself taught us" these things.

The most important christological language of this confession is that which distinguishes the purported two natures. In fact, this brief explanation of the two natures, coupled with the Nicene Creed's description of Jesus as "very God

---

[156] The native Coptic Church of both Egypt and Ethiopia still flourishes today in their homelands, and this church has always been Monophysitic. It traces its origin back to the Ethiopian eunuch official mentioned in Ac 8.26-39 and is therefore one of the oldest churches surviving in the world today.

of very God," was to become the institutional church's preeminent explanation of Jesus' uniqueness.

The emperor adjourned the Council with a prayer, thanking Christ for restoring peace to the church. Then he warned that anyone teaching contrary to the Council's christological declarations would suffer the dire consequences of imperial punishment. Like his predecessor, Emperor Constantine, Emperor Marcian had laid down the precondition that the Council resolve this christological dispute that was threatening chaos in his empire. He later issued edicts banning all Monophysites from the empire and had their writings burned, just as Constantine had done with Arius and his writings.

Throughout church history, "Chalcedon," as that council came to be called, has been regarded as second in christological importance to the Council of Nicea. It is amazing that later non-Catholics, e.g., Protestants, accepted uncritically Chalcedonian Christology—that Jesus Christ is both man and God by possessing two natures—yet they rigorously opposed the Chalcedonian affirmation that Mary is *Theotokos*.

Chalcedon's confessional statement resolved little. Instead, its assertions soon raised important questions never addressed before. For instance, if Jesus had two distinct and separate natures, yet He was not two persons, mustn't He also have had two wills—a divine will and a human will? And what about two consciousnesses and two souls? The upshot of the Council of Chalcedon was that it aroused more theological questions than it resolved, as had previous councils. John Hick explains, "The result is that we inherit the original Chalcedonian formula but with no clearly spelled out meaning attached to it."[157]

Traditionalist and church historian P. Schaff informs that these new and inflamed controversies, which began at Chalcedon and continued for more than a hundred years,

> brought theology little appreciable gain, and piety much harm; and they present a gloomy picture of the corruption of the church.... theological speculation sank towards barren metaphysical refinements; and party watchwords and empty formulas were valued more than real truth....
> The external history of the controversy is a history of outrages and intrigues, depositions and banishments, commotions, divisions, and attempted reunions. Immediately after the council of Chalcedon bloody fights of the monks and the rabble broke out.[158]

Roman Catholic scholar Aloys Grillmeier has been the foremost authority on the history of patristic theology and the ecumenical church councils. He concurs with Schaff by alleging, "Chalcedon became a stumblingblock, the starting-point of a schism which from then on was to split the imperial Church, and ... would continue to afflict the Church—right up to the present."[159]

The Second Council of Constantinople (680 CE)

Many years later a sixth ecumenical council was held, again at Constantinople. Due to the conclusions determined at Chalcedon,[160] it should come as no surprise that this second Council of Constantinople asserted

---

[157] John Hick, *The Metaphor of God Incarnate: Christology in a Pluralistic Age*, 2nd ed. (Louisville: WJK, 2005), 48.
[158] P. Schaff, *History of the Christian Church*, 3:764.
[159] Aloys Grillmeier, *Christ in Christian Tradition: Volume Two, From the Council of Chalcedon (451) to Gregory the Great (590-604)* [1986], tr. Pauline Allen and John Cawte (Atlanta: Knox, 1987), 3-4.
[160] E.g., William Temple, *Christus Veritas: An Essay* (London: MacMillan, 1924), 135; V. Taylor, *The Person of Christ*, 295.

that Jesus Christ had two wills and two consciousnesses—one human and one divine, respectively. (Recall that Apollinaris had formed his one-nature Christology out of fear that the orthodox, two-nature Christology suggested two personalities.) This opinion, called "Dyotheletism," came close to the Nestorian two Persons view. This council therefore condemned the opposing view, in which Christ had one will, called "Monotheletism," as heretical and anathematized those adherents. Yet subsequent Christendom never accepted the conclusions of this second Council of Constantinople—that Jesus had two wills and two centers of consciousness.

Conclusions about the Ecumenical Church Councils

So, over a period of about 355 years Roman emperors and Catholic Church officials convened six ecumenical church councils in the eastern realm of the empire, all in present-day Turkey. These councils were convened primarily to resolve christological disputes concerning the identity of Jesus. The christological resolutions of these six councils can be summed up as follows: during Jesus' incarnation He was both fully God and fully man by possessing both a complete, divine nature, it being equal in all respects to those of God the Father and the Holy Spirit, as well as a thoroughly human nature, which results in His having two wills and two consciousnesses, respectively. However, this doctrine of double wills and consciousnesses was soon abandoned. Church fathers developed this classical Christology by employing the following methodologies:

- They departed from the time-honored principle of defining the Christian faith only by the use of words of an auxiliary language that clearly translate scriptural words. Instead, they sought to encapsulate what they perceived as the true teaching of the Bible with the use of non-biblical, philosophical words and categories borrowed from Hellenism that were not commensurate with the words of the Bible.[161]
- They often formed their Christology in reaction to alleged heresy rather than basing it solely on the exegesis of Scripture.
- They delved into "the secret things" which belong only to the LORD (Deut 29.29; cf. Ps 131.1), things that God has not revealed to us and concerning which Scripture is silent. These church fathers thus purported to know that which could not be known. And they sought to impose their speculative, theological determinations on all professing Christians, oftentimes making such doctrines essential to Christian faith.
- They succumbed to imperial involvement in church affairs and thereby made the church unnecessarily vulnerable to political pressure.[162] This situation resulted in the political union of church and state and thus a different kind of religious persecution.

The influence of "heresy" on the development of church doctrine can hardly be over-exaggerated. Maurice Wiles offers two reasons why: (1) theology that develops in opposition to disputants invariably tends to be overstated,[163] and (2) "it was often the heretic who determined the general lines along which doctrine should develop."[164]

---

[161] Contra C.F.D. Moule (*The Holy Spirit* [1978] [repr. Grand Rapids: Eerdmans, 1979], 57), who insists upon the "continued value and indispensability" of such controversial language.
[162] Many scholars and church historians so attest. N.T. Wright (*Jesus and the Victory of God*, 541) insists that you cannot "separate theology from politics."
[163] M. Wiles, *Explorations in Theology 4*, 45-46.
[164] Maurice Wiles, *The Making of Christian Doctrine* (Cambridge: University, 1967), 33.

Many scholars have recognized this departure of the institutional church from the primitive Christian message—that Jesus is the Christ, the Son of God. *The New Catholic Encyclopedia* states concerning the final formulation of the doctrine of the Trinity, that "among the Apostolic Fathers, there had been nothing even remotely approaching such a mentality or perspective."[165] And Jewish scholar Joseph Klausner well observes of the patristic era, "The Messiahship of Jesus became secondary to his deity."[166]

Nevertheless, traditionalists have defended this development by insisting that later church fathers needed time to reflect upon the meaning of the Christ-event and that their explanations (some would call them "additions") of the gospel were biblically accurate. Some traditionalists have contended that the theological positions that emerged victorious from controversy did so as evidence of their veracity as well as God's sovereignty.

On the contrary, F. Young gets it right by alleging, "There are strong reasons then for seeing the patristic development and interpretation of incarnational belief, not as a gradual dawning of the truth inspired by the Holy Spirit, but as a historically determined development which led to the blind alleys of paradox, illogicality and docetism."[167]

Obliterating the Distinction between God and His Son

Another very significant error that church fathers committed as they developed their Christology was that they *obliterated* the biblical distinction between the terms "God" and "(the) Son (of God)," the latter as applied to Jesus.[168] It happened because they ignored the Jews' use of the expression, "son of God," which Jews applied mostly to the king of Israel, and its use in their Scriptures (e.g., 2 Sam 7.14; Ps 2.7). Instead, church fathers substituted the Greek, metaphysical, religio-philosophical understanding of "son of God." Jewish Christian authority Geza Vermes explains, "to a Jew,... son of God could refer, in an ascending order, to any of the children of Israel; or to a good Jew; or to a charismatic holy Jew; or to the king of Israel; or in particular to the royal Messiah; and finally, in a different sense, to an angelic or heavenly being. In other words, 'son of God' was always understood metaphorically in Jewish circles. In Jewish sources, its use never implies participation by the person so-named in the divine nature."[169]

In contrast, Athanasius often interchanged the terms "God" and "Son (of God)." He argued, in opposition to the Arians, that the orthodox doctrine "proclaims our Lord Jesus Christ as God and Son of the Father" and "that he was ever God and is the Son."[170] So, Athanasius and all other post-apostolic church fathers arbitrarily abandoned the Jews' strictly functional meaning for the term "son (of God)," verified in their Scriptures, and defined its application to Jesus as indicating the generation of the pre-incarnational Logos-Son from the Father's substance (essence).[171] Their reasoning went like this: (1) the Father is God; (2) the NT expression, "the Son of God," refers to God generating ("begetting")

---

[165] NCE 14:299.
[166] Joseph Klausner, *The Messianic Idea in Israel: From Its Beginning to the Completion of the Mishnah*, tr. W.F. Stinespring (New York: MacMillan, 1955), 528.
[167] F. Young, "A Cloud of Witnesses," 29.
[168] Geza Vermes, *Jesus the Jew: A Historian's Reading of the Gospels* (Philadelphia: Fortress, 1973), 212-13; idem, *The Changing Faces of Jesus*, 32.
[169] Geze Vermes, *Jesus in His Jewish Context* (Minneapolis: Fortress, 2003), 66.
[170] Athansius, *Orations Against the Arians*, 2.10; 3.29.
[171] So says D. Cupitt (*Jesus and the Gospel of God*, 13).

His Son with respect to the Son's divine nature prior to His incarnation; (3) in the human realm a physical man generates a physical son, who is born in the likeness of his physical father to become a man like his father; (4) likewise, God the Father generated the Son in His own likeness, thus to become God.

This patristic reasoning continued to prevail, but its influence has sharply waned in the theological academy in the past two centuries, so that few distinguished critical scholars have embraced it.[172] Yet James D.G. Dunn, in his critique of this reasoning, well observes of Christianity-at-large, "it is generally taken for granted, axiomatic, part of the basic definition of what Christianity is, that to confess Jesus as 'the Son of God' is to confess his deity, and very easily assumed that to say 'Jesus is the Son of God' means and always has meant that Jesus is the pre-existent, second person of the Trinity."[173]

Church fathers therefore erred by interpreting the expression, "(the) Son of God," *metaphysically* as it is applied to Jesus. That is, they accepted Greek religio-philosophical teaching that gods metaphysically generate sons just as men physically procreate sons. These church fathers thereby concluded that God metaphysically generated a Son.

The NT expression, "the Son of God," as applied to Jesus should be understood *metaphorically* and thus relationally, in which the genitive "of" distinguishes Son from God. That is why Nels Ferre rightly contends, "Jesus is not God but the Son of God."[174]

Neither does this traditionalist interpretation of "the Son of God" coincide with the NT. For it never equates Jesus' identity as the Son of God with the supposed notion of His being God. And the traditionalists' comparison of eternal generation with physical generation collapses because a human father chronologically precedes his son whereas eternal generation teaches that the Father and the Son are the same age—eternal.

Moreover, many church fathers and their successors even obliterated the common understanding of the word "God." By attempting to clarify their doctrine of God, they often substituted the non-biblical expression "the godhead/Godhead." This term denotes an abstract, multi-personality that is difficult for us moderns to relate to because there is nothing like it in the human realm. This is not the case with the English word "God," which is commonly understood to signify a single personality. Therefore, whether traditionalists are aware of it or not, they are constantly compelled to distinguish each biblical instance of the word "God" as to whether it refers to the triune "Godhead" or "the Father." When it is the latter, some avoid interchanging "God" and "the Father," opting only for the qualifying expression "God the Father." So, using the term "Godhead" can result in expunging the word "God" from our minds and thus from our devotional life.

This raises the question: What is the effect on Christian piety of this obliteration of distinction in terms? Many Christians trained in orthodoxy, though perhaps unaware, hold confusing images of God and His Son. Such confusion can inhibit believers in the knowledge of their faith because (1) conceiving of a personal relationship with the supposed Godhead is an abstract concept, and (2) conceiving of Christ as God makes believers less likely to relate to Him in their trials and temptations. Oscar Cullmann recognized the latter problem

---

[172] One is O. Cullmann (*Christology*, 305), who asserts, "'Son of God,' then, means complete participation in the Father's deity."

[173] J.G.D. Dunn, *Christology in the Making*, 12-13. Some traditionalists have erroneously interpreted 1 Jn 2.23 ("Whoever denies the Son does not have the Father") to mean denying that the Son is God.

[174] N.F.S. Ferre, "Is the Basis of the World Council Heretical?" *ExpT* 74 (1962-63): 67.

and therefore alleged, "Despite its official condemnation, Monophysitism still dominates the religious thinking of the average Catholic. Jesus and God are often no longer distinguished even by terminology. The question has rightly been raised whether the need for veneration of Mary has not perhaps developed so strongly among the Catholic people just because this confusion has made Jesus himself remote from the believer."[175] Indeed, many Roman Catholics identify more readily with Mary than with Jesus because they reckon Jesus as God and thus deem Him less approachable.

The Athanasian Creed

So, a distinctly Trinitarian view of God emerges in the combined dogma of the first six ecumenical church councils. Yet this historical development lacked clarity in understanding the Trinity. Amazingly, none of these creeds or statements of the church councils mention the word "trinity" even though patristic use of it had preceded them all.

Consequently, the Athanasian Creed was drafted to resolve this problem. It was created in the 5th century, or later, by unknown authors in Gaul (present France; exact date unknown). This Athanasian Creed thereafter became the institutional church's primary resource for defining the doctrine of the Trinity.[176] It declares "the catholic faith" as "one God in Trinity, and Trinity in Unity; neither confounding the persons, nor dividing the substance." It has often been alleged that in several places this document suffers from doublespeak. For instance, it explains that all three members of the Trinity are "uncreate," "incomprehensible," "almighty," and "coeternal." Then it adds that "there are not three incomprehensibles, nor three uncreated, but one uncreated and one incomprehensible." And it says the same regarding the words "eternal" and "almighty."

The Athanasian Creed rightly affirms that "there are not three Gods, but one God." It explicitly denies the essential subordination of the Son by asserting, "in this Trinity none is afore or after the other; none is greater or less than another. But the whole three persons are coeternal together, and coequal…. He therefore that will be saved must thus think of the Trinity." Thus, the Athanasian Creed requires that an individual believe in the final formulation of the doctrine of the Trinity in order to receive eternal salvation.

Throughout subsequent church history, both Catholic and mainline Protestant denominations endorsed the Athanasian Creed as well as its declared exclusivity for salvation. And the three preeminent, post-apostolic teachers of the church— Augustine, Thomas Aquinas, and John Calvin—endorsed the entire contents of this creed.

Critical Thinking

So, during the early centuries of Christianity, traditional church Christology was hammered out mostly by speculative theologians influenced by Greek metaphysics. No doubt most people of the pew were intellectually incapable of grasping these subtle theological nuances with which these theologians had deeply engaged themselves. Most Christians regarded this set of orthodox dogmas as mysteries to accept by faith primarily because they recognized

---

[175] O. Cullmann, *Christology*, 306-07n1. Likewise, James D.G. Dunn, *A New Perspective on Jesus: What the Quest for the Historical Jesus Missed* (Grand Rapids: Baker, 2005), 16.

[176] The RCC accepts the Athanasian Creed, but rightly acknowledges that Athanasius did not produce it.

Catholic Church authority. Besides, this traditional Christology attributed the highest possible status to Jesus, which seemed to them to best honor Him.

Ever since, many devout Christians have believed that the ecumenical church councils could not have been wrong on such a fundamental issue as the deity of Christ. Some even think, like Emperor Constantine did briefly concerning the Nicene Creed, that God would have prevented "the holy fathers" from succumbing to error in drafting the creeds just as God preserved the writers of Scripture from error in holy writ. Maurice Wiles asserts, "Some people have looked to the formal utterances of those councils as the proper starting point [for Christology], the authoritative basis for our affirmations about the person of Christ. But it would be an odd procedure to adopt. They were dependent on the same sources of Scripture and the subsequent experience of the church that are open to us."[177] Indeed, blind trust in church authorities is naïve to say the least.

Sometimes, church history has not been written by honest truth seekers but by vain victors of disputes. Don Cupitt assesses, "What we have been taught to call 'orthodoxy' was in fact merely the form of Christianity which happened to triumph over the others."[178] And Hans Kung likewise concludes, "today we know that the history of theology and the church, too, was predominantly written by the victors at the expense of the losers—along dogmatic or church-political lines."[179] Indeed, oftentimes these winners of theological debate afterwards persuaded political authorities to collect and burn all of their opponents' writings while their own remained preserved for posterity. Much of what we know about their opponents' teaching has proceeded from these victors, who often misrepresented their enemies. It is worth repeating—that is why critical investigation of the historical development of dogma is so essential to discovering the truth.

In addition, Christians have tended to defend uncritically their belief in the deity of Christ because the chief skeptics of Christianity have usually denied the supernatural. Consequently, in defending their belief that Jesus exercised supernatural powers and arose from the dead, many Christians have overreacted to such opposition by ascribing *too much* to Jesus. And they have often done so while engaged in conflict with those who were not skeptics, but professing Christians like themselves.

The result has been that traditionalist Christians have alleged that any Christology that departs from that which was officially established by the Nicene and Chalcedonian Church councils of the 4th and 5th centuries is "reductionist" and thus should be rejected as heretical and non-Christian. On the contrary, *the Nicene-Chalcedonian Christology of the institutional Catholic Church represents a departure from the true gospel handed down by the apostles of Jesus Christ, and this departure was "expansionist." We can err by ascribing too much to Jesus Christ just as we can err by ascribing too little to Him. When Christians ascribe too much to Jesus, they inevitably ascribe too little to God the Father. Therefore, when traditionalists have been expansionist in their Christology, it automatically made them reductionist in their theology proper.*

The antidote against such error is to think critically of everything people do, including ourselves. Many of the world's worst crimes have been committed in the name of "God" and/or religion. None are more renowned than the crucifixion of Jesus. Christians should strive to be "noble-minded" like the Bereans; for,

---

[177] Maurice F. Wiles, "Can We Still Do Christology?" in *The Future of Christology: Essays in Honor of Leander E. Keck*, eds. Abraham J. Malherbe and Wayne A. Meeks (Minneapolis, MN: Fortress, 1993), 235.
[178] Don Cupitt, "The Christ of Christendom," 145.
[179] H. Kung, *Christianity: Essence, History and Future*, 153.

after Paul preached to them, they "examined the Scriptures daily, to see whether these things were so" (Ac 17.10-11).

God calls people to healthy introspection, self-criticism, and repentance—change of mind. Individual believers and the corporate church should strive to develop a spirit of critical analysis, even inquiring into their own theological convictions. Ultimately, being able to think critically about theology derives from a healthy self-criticism like that of King David (Ps 139.23-24; cf. 51.17). Without such honesty and openness, we cannot spiritually hear a word from God. Don Cupitt warns, "Religion without self-criticism easily becomes rigid, superstitious and unspiritual."[180] America's beloved novelist Mark Twain may have been right when he said, "Education consists mostly of unlearning."

Since Vatican II, many Bible scholars in the RCC have been thinking critically. For instance, in 1983 the Pontifical Biblical Commission produced a superb summary of Christology that serves as a model of critical analysis. Entitled *Bible et christologie*, it surprisingly is a little critical of its own traditional Christology. In fact, its definition of the core of the Christian faith does not include the deity of Christ, as the following attests:

> "*True faith* is faith in Jesus Christ, the Son of God, who has come 'in the flesh,' who has revealed to human beings the name of the Father, who 'has given himself as a ransom for all,' who rose on the third day, who has been taken up into glory, who sits at God's right hand, and whose glorious coming is awaited at the end of time. A Christology that would not profess all these things would be departing from the testimony of apostolic tradition."[181]

Yet, currently in the Western World there exists a generation gap about critical thinking. The secular university cultivates an objective spirit of inquiry that results in critical investigation. Consequently, the educated younger generation is quite familiar with the critical thinking process and puts it to use.[182] In contrast, the older generation's response to critical inquiry is often one of resistance and then a hardened defensiveness. Such opposition to the normal process of truth-seeking perplexes the younger generation.

Maybe something Jesus taught applies to this predicament. He once said, "No one sews a patch of unshrunk cloth on an old garment; otherwise the patch pulls away from it, the new from the old, and a worse tear results. And no one puts new wine into old wineskins; otherwise the wine will burst the skins,... but one puts new wine into fresh wineskins" (Mk 2.21-22). The older generation as a whole may be too much like the old garment and the old wineskins and therefore incapable of thinking critically about Jesus' identity. Perhaps it is only the younger generation(s) of critical thinkers that can be like the fresh wine by not being so indoctrinated with traditional identity Christology and therefore capable of seeing and believing the true identity of the real, historical Jesus.

Social Implications of Critical Thinking

For those not accustomed to objectivity, critical thinking can make them feel *very* uncomfortable. For us Christians, it can be disconcerting to anticipate the reaction of our Christian friends if they learn that we have changed to believe in some non-traditional, unpopular theology. How will we be treated? We cringe at the possibility of rejection by church and friends. It can affect us emotionally, socially, occupationally, and financially.

---

[180] Don Cupitt, "Religion and Critical Thinking," *Theology* 86 (1983): 246.
[181] *Bible et christologie*, 2.2.3.1. Emphasis not mine.
[182] So says M. Wiles, *Explorations in Theology* 4, 4.

But where is our loyalty? We must ask ourselves, "Am I loyal to what my church says, to what church fathers and their ecumenical councils determined, or to God and His Christ as I understand them through the Holy Scriptures?" There *can* be a difference. The institutional church *can* be wrong, and a study of church history sadly reveals this many times. Former Roman Catholic priest Michael Norwood still professes to be a Christian yet denies that Jesus is God. He cautions, "institutional resistance to such discussion is likely to be very strong. Any conclusions that might weaken the case for Jesus being 'true God' would confront the official church with a major challenge to its authority."[183]

Consider how often Jesus challenged religious authorities by confronting them about their theological errors and hypocritical practices. His critique forced Him to move from His hometown (Mt 4.13). It even cost Him His life, though in God's providence. While few Christians are called to suffer martyrdom, we need to seriously ask ourselves, "Am I committed to seeking the truth about God and His Christ no matter what the cost?"

Through the centuries, a large majority of professing Christians believed in the doctrine of the Trinity, so that Jesus Christ is God. Yet majority opinion does not make it true. D.A. Carson, referring to another subject, states a true principle that can be applied to Christology by saying, "Since when has majority opinion defined what is true, even majority evangelical opinion? Logically speaking, a proposition is either true (that is, it accords with reality and is held to be true by omniscience), or it is not, even if not one person believes it. Of course one should be very careful and humble before disagreeing dogmatically with what the majority of believers (whoever they are) have held to be true; but the fact that they believe it does not make it true."[184] James D.G. Dunn writes similarly, "we must attempt the exceedingly difficult task of shutting out the voices of early fathers, Councils and dogmaticians down the centuries, in case they drown the earlier voices, in case the earlier voices were saying something different, in case they intended their words to speak with different force to their hearer."[185] Eminent evangelical leader and scholar John Stott states, "The hallmark of authentic Evangelicalism is not the uncritical repetition of old traditions but the willingness to submit every tradition, however ancient, to fresh biblical scrutiny and, if necessary, reform."[186]

Two colossal barriers to critical thinking are bias and party spirit. Our belief system can become so ingrained in our thinking that it can be difficult to objectively analyze what we believe. It thus becomes almost impossible for a person thoroughly indoctrinated in some ideology to momentarily *detach* themselves from the grip of their ideological grid and genuinely consider, *with openness*, the validity or non-validity of other ways of thinking. When so confronted, such people almost always resort to a totally defensive mentality. As Don Cupitt puts it, "To this day most people retain a deeply engrained habit of reading Christendom's dogmas into the New Testament, and many theologians still struggle to reconcile the New Testament with developed Christianity."[187]

Evangelicals now constitute the largest and most active religious group in North America. Despite its phenomenal growth, Evangelicalism has undergone considerable intellectual decline. Evangelical Mark Noll, an authority on

---

[183] Michael Norwood, *Is Jesus God? Finding Our Faith* (New York: Crossroad, 2001), 104.
[184] D.A. Carson, *The King James Version Debate: A Plea for Realism* (Grand Rapids: Baker, 1979), 55.
[185] J.G.D. Dunn, *Christology in the Making*, 13-14.
[186] John Stott in an interview in Roy Mc Cloughry, "Basic Stott: Candid Comments on Justice, Gender, and Judgment," *Christianity Today*, January 8, 1996, p. 28.
[187] D. Cupitt, *Jesus and the Gospel of God*, 8-9.

Evangelical Theology, documents its precipitous fall in his provocative yet widely acclaimed book, *The Scandal of the Evangelical Mind* (1994). It begins with this startling but humorous sentence, "The scandal of the evangelical mind is that there is not much of an evangelical mind."[188] Evangelicals spiritually hinder themselves if they continue to ignore, or refuse to engage, the leading theological thinkers of their time.

Party spirit leads to party rivalry. It causes people to keep their ideology in a lock box. By refusing to interact with opposing views, people become blind to the pervasive, negative impact of party loyalty. Wise King Solomon wrote, "I have seen that every labor and every skill which is done is the result of rivalry between a man and his neighbor. This too is vanity and striving after wind" (Eccl 4.4). Robert Hall puts it this way:

> "Whatever holds back a spirit of inquiry is favourable to error, whatever promotes it, to truth. But nothing, it will be acknowledged, has a greater tendency to obstruct the spirit of inquiry, than the spirit and feeling of party. Let a doctrine, however erroneous, become a party distinction, and it is at once entrenched in interests and attachments which make it extremely difficult for the most powerful artillery of reason to dislodge it."[189]

For a lesson in bias and party spirit, read some of the patristic writings. A classic example is Athanasius in his very polemical *Orations Against the Arians*. The ancients had schools that trained students in such vitriolic rhetoric. Athanasius was a master of it. M. Wiles concludes concerning such vicious, verbal attacks, "Abuse of one's opponents is frequently a sign of the weakness of the case that one is making out against them."

Now that we have examined briefly the first millennium of the history of church Christology, we turn to look at its second millennium. That is when Enlightenment took root across Europe, causing many Europeans to think critically about Catholic dogma. The result was that they protested vehemently against some of it, to which we now turn.

---

[188] Mark A. Noll, *The Scandal of the Evangelical Mind* (Grand Rapids: Eerdmans, 1994), 3.
[189] Robert Hall, *Works*, 1:352. Cited by A. Buzzard and C. Hunting, *The Doctrine of the Trinity*, 3.

Chapter Three
Church Christology in the Second Millennium

The Medieval Period	Some Anti-Trinitarian Churches
The Catholic Inquisition	Biblical Criticism
The Protestant Reformation	The Tubingen School
Michael Servetus	The History of Religions School
Arrest, Trial & Execution of Servetus	Liberal Theology
Reaction to the Execution of Servetus	The Quest for the Historical Jesus
The Socinians	Death of the Quest
Continental European Unitarianism	The New Quest
British Unitarianism	The Third Quest
John Locke	Kenotic Christology
Deism	Other Modern Developments
British Arianism	The World Council of Churches
Sir Isaac Newton: A Secret Arian?	Christianity and Islam
Samuel Clarke: A Moderate Arian	Modern World Evangelism
William Whiston: A Zealous Arian	British Scholars
American Unitarianism	The New Dutch Christology
The Anabaptists	Roman Catholic Scholars
The Affects of Religious Intolerance	Bible et christologie
Credal Faith	Call for a Revised Christology
Friedrich Schleiermacher	Conclusion

The Medieval Period

As we move forward in our investigation of the history of church Christology beyond the six ecumenical church councils, in 325 to 680, we find that hardly anything was added to it during most of the medieval period (c. 590-1294). While the eastern and western branches of the Catholic Church officially divided in 1054, called "the Great Schism," they have remained in complete agreement christologically to this day. Both the Eastern Orthodox Church and the Roman Catholic Church have officially retained all of the Nicene-Chalcedonian Christology. And both denominations have claimed to be fully Trinitarian by endorsing the Athanasian Creed, which designates all three Persons of the Trinity as co-equal and co-eternal.

However, the foremost theological disagreement between these two monolithic churches, which persists to this day, regards the procession of the Holy Spirit. This dispute pertains to the doctrine of the Trinity, not Christology.

It goes back to the Council of Constantinople (381 CE), which consisted of Greek-speaking bishops of the eastern branch of the Church. In their Constantinopolitan Creed, due to Jn 15.26 they augmented the Nicene Creed to include the idea that "the Holy Spirit ... proceeds from the Father."

In the West, King Reccared of Spain called a church council at Toledo in 589. He read a Latin exposition declaring that the Holy Spirit "proceeds from the Father and the Son," i.e., equally. The added words, "and the Son" (L. *filioque*), were called the Filioque Clause. This double procession was not revolutionary, but echoed common opinion in the West. The king's exposition included the anathema, "Whoever does not believe in the Holy Spirit, or does not believe that He proceeds from the Father and the Son, and denies that He is coeternal and coequal with the Father and the biblical Son, let him be anathema."

Greek-speaking bishops of the East objected to this Filoque Clause. They either held steadfast to the shorter phrase, "from the Father," in the Constantinopolitan Creed, or they augmented the addition by rendering it, "from the Father and through the Son."

Latin-speaking bishops of the western branch of the Church objected to this word "through" and others. They alleged that the eastern bishops made the Son and the Spirit essentially subordinate to the Father and thereby impugned the doctrine of the Trinity. The eastern bishops denied this, though they continued to assert that the Father is both the "Source" and "Cause" of the existence of the other two members of the Trinity.

After that, the most notable addition to traditional Christology was spearheaded by Thomas Aquinas (1225-1274), the most celebrated theologian of medieval times. Though not an original thinker, he taught that Jesus possessed "the beatific vision."[1] Aquinas meant that since Jesus was God He necessarily lived by sight and thus not by faith, having a full, complete vision of God. Accordingly, Jesus was not omniscient but acquired complete knowledge experientially on all topics, called "infused knowledge." In other words, Jesus' knowledge superseded that of all generations, both past and future.

The Scholastics adopted the beatific vision, so that it was widely held in the latter period of the Middle Ages.[2] In doing so, they lost sight of their scriptural moorings by wandering into the dense fog of Trinitarian speculation. They sank into a morass of irrationality that ended in tritheism—belief in three gods—to which Trinitarianism leads.

Aquinas' doctrine of the beatific vision unveils one of the absurdities to which traditional, identity Christology can lead. Aquinas states, "When the divine reality is not hidden from sight, there is no point in faith. From the first moment of his conception Christ had the full vision of God in his essence ... Therefore he could not have had faith."[3] In accordance with traditional Christology, this reasoning is quite logical. But it is wrong because it is based on a wrong premise—that Jesus Christ is God. Instead, the NT gospels make it quite obvious that Jesus was a man of faith, i.e., faith in God His Father.

The RCC honors St. Augustine and St. Aquinus as the two greatest theologians in Catholic Church history following the apostolic era, with Thomas Aquinas receiving top honors. Yet both men sorely lacked biblical language skills. Unfortunately, they had a major impact on the Church's developing

---

[1] Thomas Aquinas, *Summa Theologica*, III, g.11-12.
[2] Gerald O'Collins, *Christology: A Biblical, Historical, and Systematic Study of Jesus* (Oxford: University, 1995), 255n16.
[3] T. Aquinas, *Summa Theologica*, 3.7.3.

policy regarding forced confessions as well as conversions, especially as it pertained to those whom the Church deemed as heretics.

Augustine (354-430) had advocated forcing non-Christians to confess Catholic faith. For his sole scriptural support he cited Jesus' parable in Lk 14.15-24. It is about a man who prepared a big dinner, sent out invitations, and then told his servants, "Go out into the highways and along the hedges, and compel them to come in, that my house may be filled" (v. 23). Augustine allegorically interpreted the man as Christ, the house as the Catholic Church, and the servants as Christian evangelists. He explains,

> "Whom thou shalt find wait not till they choose to come, compel them to come in.... let the heretics come from the hedges, here they shall find peace. For those who make hedges, their object is to make divisions. Let them be drawn away from the hedges, let them be plucked up from among the thorns. They have stuck fast in the hedges, they are unwilling to be compelled. 'Let us come in,' they say, 'of our own good will.' This is not the Lord's order, 'Compel them,' saith he, 'to come in.' Let compulsion be found outside, the will will arise within."[4]

Augustine adopted this notion of forced confessions due to his extreme view on the sovereignty of God as well as his own conversion experience. Thus, he writes concerning Christian conversion, "we have been ... not only led, but even forced" by God.[5]

Thomas Aquinas went one step further. While ironically proclaiming love as the greatest of all human virtues, the "Angelic doctor," as he was called, asserted the right of the church-state to punish heretics with death.[6] He says in his famous *Summa Theologica*, "much more reason is there for heretics, as soon as they are convicted of heresy, to be not only excommunicated but even put to death."[7] He further explains that for the Church to safeguard itself from a heretic, "it delivers him to the secular tribunal to be exterminated thereby from the world by death."[8] Thomas Aquinas' influence paved the way for the despicable treatment lying just ahead for dissenters of Roman Catholic dogma.

The Catholic Inquisition

During the 12th century, there had been isolated incidents in Catholic Europe of the execution of religious heretics. But this situation worsened dramatically in the early 13th century with the creation of the infamous "Catholic Inquisition."

"Gospel" means "good news." What we are about to embark upon is not good news. Ironically, the RCC thought it was safeguarding the good news by instituting its Inquisition. On the contrary, in this process of self-protection the Church turned out to be *fighting against* the good news, so that the Catholic Inquisition became *very bad news*.

People usually don't want to hear bad news when it's about them or the group to which they belong. The natural inclination is to cover it up. But this impulse, to either conceal or ignore the truth, does not originate from the wisdom of God. Wise King Solomon explained that "in much wisdom there is much grief, and increasing knowledge results in increasing pain" (Eccl 1.18). Nevertheless,

---

[4] Augustine, *Homilies on the Gospels*: Sermon 42, 8 in *NPNF¹*, 6:449.
[5] Augustine, *Homilies on the Gospels*: Sermon 42, 1 in *NPNF¹*, 6:447.
[6] P. Schaff, *History of the Christian Church*, 5:673, 675.
[7] T. Aquinas, *Summa Theologica*, P(26)-Q(11)-A(3).
[8] T. Aquinas, *Summa Theologica*, vol. 3, The Second Part of The Second Part (Part I) or p. 150.

knowledge of history *can* help succeeding generations to avoid repeating past atrocities, not that it necessarily will.

The most abominable atrocities ever committed in the name of Christianity are the innumerable episodes of persecution, arrest, interrogation, torture, exile, and execution of presumed heretics that the Roman Catholic Church carried out throughout Europe for several centuries by means of its Inquisition. This Catholic Inquisition was an outgrowth of another abominable atrocity—the "Holy Crusades."

The trans-national, so-called "Holy Crusades" were anything but holy. They were a series of seven armed pilgrimages by European nations, all united under the banner of the Christian symbol of the cross. Their aim was to conquer the Holy Land and reclaim its spiritual citadel, Jerusalem, and on the way there to defeat Islam militarily. These Crusades began in France in 1095 and ended there in 1270. But it was a local crusade in southern France that initially prompted the formation of the Catholic Inquisition.

The Albigensian Crusade was "a holy war" declared by Pope Innocent III in 1209. (It was much like some Islamic clerics recently have done by declaring *jihad* against the West.) It was directed primarily against a large, widespread but divided heretical cult called "The Cathari." It was a strange sect which advocated a syncretistic belief system that included religious toleration. But the European church-states viewed it as rebellious. According to church historian P. Schaff, The Cathari disagreed among themselves about Gnostic dualism but agreed in denouncing the following gamut: the RCC, but especially its hierarchy, sex in marriage, the rite of water baptism, belief in the resurrection of the dead, the OT, and even John the Baptist.[9] Surprisingly, Schaff concludes that this sect emphasized piety and that its "doctrine seems to have highly exalted Christ."[10]

This Church war against The Cathari lasted twenty years. In its first year, Catholic France reportedly put 20,000 Cathari folks to death in one town alone. But such brutality didn't work; instead, it strengthened the resolve of leaders of such movements.

So, Pope Gregory IX decided on a different strategy. He instituted the Papal Inquisition in 1227/31. He chose the Dominic Order of preaching monks, who were well trained in Roman Catholic theology, and sent them to visit suspected regions for the purpose of rooting out heretics. The Franciscans soon joined them in this effort. These monks were called "the Inquisitors" because they would "inquire" of the townspeople of anyone suspected of either heresy or non-Christian practices and arrest them. At first they tried to persuade them to confess the alleged misdeeds. Inquisition policy was that the accused were always presumed guilty until proven innocent. Also, the identity of the accusers was always withheld publicly. Torture was used often and profusely in order to obtain forced confessions. The two most gruesome torture devices used were "the iron maiden" and "the rack." If victims still refused to confess, the RCC confiscated their property and turned the accused over to the state for automatic expulsion or execution.

Eventually, this dreaded Inquisition spread from France into Germany and then Italy. Prior to the Reformation, the evangelical Waldensians suffered the most at the hands of these heresy hunters. The Catholic Inquisition fearfully gripped most of Europe for 250 years before arriving full-blown in Spain.

---

[9] P. Schaff, *History of the Christian Church*, 5:474-76.
[10] P. Schaff, *History of the Christian Church*, 5:476.

The Spanish Inquisition was the worst of all regional Catholic Inquisitions. It began in 1478 against Spain's Moors (African Muslims) and Jews. These two peoples were usually given the choice of forced Catholic conversion or banishment from the state. But, as in the rest of Europe earlier, sometimes they were executed. In 1492 alone, Spain's King Ferdinand and Queen Isabella sent Christopher Columbus sailing the ocean blue to discover the New World and convert its natives to Catholic Christianity; and that same year these co-monarchs sent the Catholic Inquisitors throughout Spain to capture, arrest, and expel 800,000 Jews and Muslims for refusing to profess Catholic Christianity. Within less than a generation, the Spanish Inquisition executed about 20,000 Jews. This scourge lasted 350 years before it was abolished in 1834 as the last Catholic Inquisition stronghold in Europe. The Catholic Inquisition therefore lasted 600 years.

Even to this day, nothing impedes Christian evangelism in Europe more than the memory of the heinous history of the Crusades and the Inquisition. This history teaches us that using force to accomplish religious conversion usually has the opposite effect.

The Protestant Reformation

Take the Protestant Reformation. It began in Germany in 1517 at a time when most European countries exercised the union of church and state, the church being solely the RCC. These Catholic European states usually had laws against "blasphemy" and "heresy," with RCC dogma as the standard rule. In the early stages of the Protestant Reformation, sometimes the Protestants were brought to trial for allegedly breaking these laws, and sometimes they were not. So, there was no consistency.

Such laxity in enforcement of religious laws against heresy caused the RCC to strengthen its Inquisition in order to better identify and arrest alleged heretics. In the centuries that followed, several tens of thousands of Protestants were put to death by Catholic governments in what came to be called "the Counter Reformation."

As for the theological development within the Protestant Reformation, in its early years its leaders were mostly occupied with the accuracy of certain soteriological Catholic doctrines, e.g., justification and absolution (with its monetary indulgences), which had developed during medieval times. The slogan of the Protestant Reformation was *sola scriptura* (L. "only Scripture"). Ironically, the movement failed to scrutinize the Catholic doctrine of the Trinity and therefore its corollary, the deity of Christ, in light of Scripture. Also ironically, Martin Luther (1483-1546), the founder of the Protestant Reformation, objected to the word "trinity" as being non-biblical; yet he fully-embraced the traditional doctrine of the Trinity, with its two-nature Christology. In fact, Luther once wrote unabashedly, "I know of no other God except the one called Jesus Christ."[11]

Years later, this lack of doctrinal scrutiny resulted in a most contemptible blight against the career of John Calvin (1509-1564). He was the preeminent Bible teacher of the Protestant Reformation. In 1553, Calvin hailed officials of the Catholic Inquisition to arrest a Spanish medical doctor for his anti-Trinitarian views. Then Calvin orchestrated a citywide trial that resulted in putting this man to death in a gruesome, public execution.

---

[11] Quoted in Paul Althaus, *The Theology of Martin Luther*, tr. Robert C. Schultz (Philadelphia: Fortress, 1966), 191.

Michael Servetus

That man was Michael Servetus (Sp. Miguel Serveto Conesa, 1511-1553).[12] Born in Villeneu(f)ve, Spain, to a devoted Catholic family of nobility, his father was a notary and his mother was a Jew. A child prodigy, he grew up in the early stages of the Spanish Inquisition, when the government forced adherence to Catholic Christianity and thus its doctrine of the Trinity. This religious persecution by the RCC aroused serious questions in Servetus' youthful mind. While studying law at the French University of Toulouse at the age of seventeen, he became shocked at his first reading of the Bible, which he did in its original languages. He concluded that the Bible did not support the doctrine of the Trinity. He also asserted that Christians should not demand adherence to doctrines that are unessential to their faith, as was this doctrine, especially if unsupported by the Bible.

Consequently, at the youthful age of twenty, Servetus naively set himself to the daunting task of correcting this supposed theological error. As an assistant to Quintana, confessor of Emperor Charles V, Servetus became familiar with some of the inner workings of the RCC, and he was dismayed by it. Spurned of a requested hearing with his church and then denied interviews with Protestant leaders (except Oecolampadius), especially in France and Switzerland, he quickly wrote and published his first theological book. Entitled *On the Errors of the Trinity* (1531), it consisted of only 119 pages.[13] Early Protestant leader Wolfgang Capito wrote that "the book became remarkably popular."[14] Even at that early age, Servetus was fluent in Spanish, Latin, Hebrew, and Greek, the last two being the original languages of the Bible. Servetus' father apparently had trained him in these languages during his youth, and he later learned Arabic as well.

In his book, Servetus affirms the sole authority of the Bible in doctrinal matters and denies that it contains either the doctrine of the Trinity or its terminology. He lodges a scathing rebuke against the Church, asserting that its inclusion of the doctrine of the Trinity in Church creeds reveals that they are mere inventions of men. He contends that the Bible designates the Holy Spirit only as God's "activity," i.e., the power of God, and thus not a person. He alleges that the Trinity doctrine, as proclaimed in the Athanasian Creed, is an insuperable and unnecessary obstacle in the conversion of Jews and Muslims to Christianity. And he rightly insists that he believes in the Trinity as generally taught by the apologists. Finally, Servetus contends that the Protestant Reformation had not gone far enough and that he is attempting to reestablish pre-Nicene, biblical Christianity.

As for Servetus' Christology, he denies the eternal generation of the Son. This free-thinking Spaniard affirms the virgin birth and claims that Jesus' Sonship began at His incarnation, in accordance with Lk 1.32-35. So, Servetus denies that Jesus preexisted. He argues that Scripture only verifies that the Logos preexisted as a manifestation of God the Father, not as a separate Person from Him, and it united with Jesus at His conception. Servetus even admits that Jesus

---

[12] I have allotted an inordinate amount of space to Servetus, not only because I have drawn my pseudonym from him. He knew six languages and practiced six intellectual professions. P. Schaff (*History of the Christian Church*, 8:786) says Servetus "was one of the most remarkable men in the history of heresy."

[13] The full title (but in Latin) is *On the Errors of the Trinity. In seven books, by Michael Servetus, Spaniard from Aragonia, also known as Reves*.

[14] Indebted to Marian Hillar with Claire S. Allen, *Michael Servetus: Intellectual Giant, Humanist, and Martyr* (Lanham, MD: University Press of America, 2002), 26.

is God by agreeing with the apologists in explaining that His divinity is derived solely from the Father. Yet Servetus affirms the following major elements of Church orthodoxy: Jesus was the Christ who performed miracles, died for our sins, arose alive from the tomb, appeared to His disciples, and ascended into heaven where He was exalted by sitting at God's right hand, and now awaits His second coming.

As with the writings of the ante-Nicene fathers, whom Servetus cites liberally for support, *On the Errors of the Trinity* suffers from much Logos speculation and not a little incongruity. But it reveals that Servetus had a considerable knowledge of the Bible as well as patristic and Scholastic literature. Andrew M.T. Dibb gives an unbiased critique of Servetus' book, saying, "The Trinitatus is not an easy book to master. Although liberally annotated with Biblical and Patristic references, Servetus makes it difficult for a reader to follow his argument. It seems to have little cohesion and the outline of his argument is difficult to follow. However, although it is often obscure, there is a progression of ideas in the Trinitatus that can be roughly illustrated under the paradigm that Christ is a man, Christ is the Son of God, Christ is God,"[15] but not fully God as determined at Nicaea.

One year after Servetus published this first of his theological works, he published a booklet entitled *Dialogues on the Trinity* to further clarify his previous views. In it, he even describes his previous book as a "barbarous, confused and incorrect book" that is "incomplete and written as though by a child for children."[16] That same year Servetus published another book entitled *On the Justice of Christ's Reign*.

The danger of being anti-Trinitarian in the early Protestant Reformation cannot be over-exaggerated. Both the Roman and Protestant churches agreed on the doctrine of the Trinity, treating it as foundational to Christianity. As Servetus' book about the Trinity circulated in Europe, governmental authorities usually banned it and confiscated copies to burn them. Servetus, fearing for his safety, abandoned his passion for theology, returned to France, and disguised his identity, changing his name to Michel de Villeneuve. In this the doctor provided a clue to his identity, since his birthplace was Villaneuva de Sijena.

While in France, this brilliant and multi-talented Spaniard attained several notable achievements as a consummate multi-professional. He became an editor and a translator of classics, temporarily a university mathematics professor, then an inventor, and briefly a pioneer in geography. But most of all, Servetus attended medical school in Paris and became a distinguished physician. His twelve-year medical practice in Vienna included his being the personal physician for the archbishop. His keen intellect was manifested when he discovered and wrote about the pulmonary circulation of the blood more than a century before the medical community discovered it. Servetus also translated and edited the famous Santes Pagnini Bible. He added a preface to it, in which he recommends the study of the history of the Hebrew people in order to achieve a better understanding of the Bible. Servetus was an indefatigable researcher. He read much Judaica, the writings of Greek philosophers, and church fathers. Because of his many skills and a critical mind, modern scholars recognize Michael Servetus as a forerunner of biblical criticism. Some historians even regard him as "the father of the freedom of conscience."

---

[15] Andrew M.T. Dibbs, *Servetus, Swendenborg and the Nature of God* (Lanham, MD: University Press of America, 2005), 67.
[16] *Dialogues on the Trinity*, Greeting.

Because of Servetus' knowledge of Hebrew, he correctly argued that the common Hebrew word for "God," the plural *elohim*, does not provide for a trinity of Persons in a supposed Godhead. For this and other reasons, Jewish scholar Louis Israel Newman concludes, "it is apparent that Servetus was equipped for Biblical exegesis far better than his contemporaries."[17] Indeed, in many ways Servetus was a man ahead of his time.

But this alias Dr. Michel de Villeneuve could no longer restrain his penchant for expounding with the pen God's truth, as he perceived it. After twenty years of public silence on theology, and despite a successful medical practice and peaceful life at Vienna, he was discontented. So he resumed his theological career by writing and publishing another provocative book, in 1552, this one under his real name. It was his magnum opus, being 734 pages in length, and it contained his treatise on the circulation of the blood. Entitled *Christianismi restitutio* (ET *The Restitution of Christianity*), he meant its restoration. Catholics and Protestants alike detested it just as vehemently as they did his first book. To make matters much worse, back in 1546 Servetus had started a lengthy correspondence with the astute John Calvin that lasted for over a year, with Servetus writing thirty letters to Calvin. (The two simultaneously had been students in Paris.) The tenor of these letters soon deteriorated dramatically, with Servetus hurling a cascade of invectives at Calvin. Indeed, the excitable Spaniard could be very obstinate and caustic in controversy. But then, Calvin was a well-known master of rhetoric himself.

John Calvin had been made master of Geneva, Switzerland. The city offered him the post, and his friend, Guillaume Farel, a fanatical Reformer, had threatened Calvin with God's judgment if he refused to accept it. Geneva afterwards became the capital of the Reformed churches and a sort of model theocracy. Calvin instituted much restrictive legislation there. Citizens were reprimanded and even punished for not greeting him with the title "Master." Many of them declared him a tyrant. Although John Calvin was small in stature, even frail and often rather sickly, he admitted to having a violent temper and absolutely no tolerance whatsoever for criticism of himself.

Marian Hillar is a contemporary authority on Servetus as well as Calvin's role in the execution of Servetus. Hillar alleges:

> "Calvin in fact established a dictatorship, becoming a civil and religious dictator. Geneva was nicknamed Protestant Rome and Calvin himself—the Pope of the Reformation.... Calvin introduced an absolute control of the private life of every citizen. In his doctrine every man was a wretched being not worthy of existence, a sinner and evil doer, 'trash' (*une ordure*). He instituted a 'spiritual police' to supervise constantly all Genevese and they were subjected to periodical inspections in their households by the '*police des moeurs*.' Anything that smacked of pleasure—music, song, laughter, theater, amusement, dancing, playing cards, even skating— was declared '*paillardise*' and severely punished. Calvin managed to destroy the normal bonds between people and simple decency inducing them to spy upon each other. His method of intimidation and terror was so refined that it involved control of every petty activity."[18]

The Arrest, Trial, and Execution of Servetus

Because of Servetus' last book, Calvin summoned the Catholic Inquisitors to arrest him in Vienne, France. They promptly did so on April 4, 1553. But the doctor outwitted his captors and escaped. Later, he headed for northern Italy

---

[17] Louis Israel Newman, *Jewish Influences on Christian Reform Movements* (New York: Columbia University, 1925), 534.
[18] M. Hillar, *Michael Servetus*, 153-54.

where he planned to practice medicine among new groups of anti-Trinitarians, many of them Anabaptists.

Unfortunately for Servetus, it seems that he could not avoid traveling through Geneva. And mostly on account of Master Jean Calvin, Geneva had strict Sabbatical laws. One of them was the mandatory requirement of church attendance on Sunday.

Servetus apparently feared arrest if discovered breaking the "Christian Sabbath." So he took a calculated, but foolish, risk. On August 13th, 1553, he attended the large church where Calvin pastored and preached every Sunday. A parishioner uncannily recognized the doctor and quickly informed the Master. Calvin hailed the heresy-hunting Inquisitors to arrest Servetus again, this time charging him as an escaped prisoner.

During the next seventy-five days, Calvin led Geneva's other thirteen Protestant pastors—called "the Venerable Company of Pastors" and members of the Little Council of Geneva—in an intense doctrinal interrogation of Servetus and his two main books. Due to Calvin's frail health and civil governing duties, it was orchestrated by him but conducted by his student secretary living at Calvin's home—Nicholas de la Fontaine. These judges were incensed at Servetus' denial of the doctrine of the Trinity and thus Jesus' eternal-divine Sonship. Servetus had asserted in his first book that the post-Nicene Trinity was "a Cerberus" (a pagan, three-headed, monster god.) But these pastors were further repulsed at Servetus' denial of infant baptism and the immortality of the soul. Calvin was especially irritated with Servetus labeling his opponents as "Trinitarians."

The civil court directed Calvin to write a draft of the interrogation, with Servetus' annotations appended. It consisted of thirty-eight extracts from Servetus' two books. Calvin pronounced these extracts "partly impious blasphemies, partly profane and insane errors, and all wholly foreign to the Word of God and the orthodox faith." This document was submitted to four major cities in Switzerland for the judgment of their city councils and church pastors. They ruled Servetus guilty and seemed to approve of his execution.

Switzerland was like most European states in that it was a church-state. Geneva's court condemned Servetus in accordance with the Codex of Justinian. Established by the Roman Empire during the 6th century, it prescribed the death penalty for those denying the church doctrine of the Trinity or infant baptism, thus advocating rebaptism as adults. Servetus had committed both infractions. These were the only two legal charges brought against him. The Geneva Reformers, however, had earlier abolished all (Catholic) canon laws, so that this was not the legal basis for their condemnation of Servetus.

Purposeful judicial irregularities were made in the trial of Michael Servetus.[19] Although he was entitled by law to counsel, which he requested, it was refused on the illegitimate grounds that he was intelligent enough to defend himself. When Calvin and the others completed their lengthy interrogation of Servetus, they pronounced him guilty of grave heresy and blasphemy against "the Lord God Jehovah" for publishing his two main books and that such infractions were deserving of death. The court had authority to try defendants accused of crimes committed within Geneva's jurisdiction, yet this was never mentioned in the

---

[19] M. Hillar (*Michael Servetus*, 187-88) lists the following legal irregularities: (1) Servetus was refused counsel without reason, despite requesting it twice and being guaranteed such by law; (2) he was tried for his book on the Trinity despite it being published twenty-three years prior and in another state; (3) he never published or dogmatized in Geneva; (4) the accusation that *The Restitution of Christianity* corrupted Christians was baseless since it had just been published and not one copy had been sold.

trial. Nor was an attempt made to prove that Servetus committed such crimes in Geneva or that any of his books had ever been sold there, much less been there. And the court never stated the legal basis for its condemnation of Servetus. It only was inferred in its judgment that the accused was guilty of breaking the Mosaic law of blasphemy as stated in Lev 24.16 and perhaps Deut 13.

Ironically, seven years earlier Calvin had vowed in a letter to his friend Farel about Servetus, that "if he come here [to Geneva] ... I will never permit him to depart alive." Calvin only stated his opposition to burning Servetus at the stake; but the other pastors surprisingly overruled him. As a consolation, they offered Servetus hanging rather than tortuous burning on the condition that he confess to them the words, "Jesus Christ, the eternal Son of God." The accused remained steadfast in his convictions and refused.

Servetus was presented with his condemnation and death sentence only a few hours before his execution. He apparently did not expect it, since he was shocked when so informed. He quickly requested a meeting with Calvin, pleading for his forgiveness. But the Reformer stayed true to his convictions as well, refusing to grant a pardon.

Servetus was executed on the Plateau of Champel just outside Geneva during midday on October 27, 1553. M. Hillar relates the scene as follows: "No cruelty was spared on Servetus as his stake was made of bundles of the fresh wood of live oak still green, mixed with the branches still bearing leaves. On his head a straw crown was placed sprayed with sulfur. He was seated on a log, with his body chained to a post with an iron chain, his neck was bound with four or five turns of a thick rope. This way Servetus was being fried at a slow fire for about a half hour before he died. To his side were attached copies of his [last] book" by a chain.[20] With a large crowd witnessing the proceeding, and in a moment of hushed solemnity, the executioner reached forth with his fiery torch and ignited the mass of kindling surrounding its victim. Flames quickly arose and engulfed his emaciated body. For a while, the accused heretic uttered painful shrieks and groans. Just before he expired, and recalling the consolation that had been offered to him only hours prior, he cried out with a loud, penetrating voice, "Oh Jesus Christ, Son of the eternal God, have mercy upon me." Even in his last dying breath, Michael Servetus passionately held to his convictions, proclaiming what he had perceived to be original, biblical Christology. Church historian and strong Trinitarian P. Schaff admits concerning Servetus, "it is evident that he worshipped Jesus Christ as his Lord and Savior."[21]

So, Protestant leaders afflicted Michael Servetus with martyrdom in his forty-second year. Yet this alias Dr. Michel de Villeneuve—physician, physiologist, humanist, and scholar—was a devout follower of Jesus Christ. Throughout that final day of his life, Servetus portrayed a most exemplary spirit. This proud and illustrious Spaniard refrained from his usual vitriolic attacks on his accusers. Instead, chained to the stake, he humbly and graciously prayed out loud, asking God to pardon all his accusers, even John Calvin.

What a contrast was the indomitable Jean Calvin, Master of Geneva! The famous Reformer afterwards never recanted of his participation in this dastardly deed. Despite an angry uproar against Servetus' execution, which news spread like wildfire in much of Europe, the arguably dictatorial Calvin remained stubbornly impenitent the rest of his life about this Servetus affair. The next year he published a book defending his action, saying, "Whoever shall maintain that

---

[20] M. Hillar, *Michael Servetus*, 185. Historians are divided on which book it was and if one or two.
[21] P. Schaff, *History of the Christian Church*, 8:789,

wrong is done to heretics and blasphemers in punishing them makes himself an accomplice in their crime and guilty as they are. There is no question here of man's authority; it is God who speaks,... Wherefore does he demand of us ... to combat for His glory."[22] Calvin implores the two Mosaic laws against blasphemy even though they apply to those guilty of idolatry or blasphemy against Yahweh.[23]

On the contrary, Servetus was a devout worshipper of Yahweh as the one and only true God. And he exalted Jesus as the Christ, God's special Son, and the only Savior from sin for all humankind. Thus, this application of the two Mosaic laws of blasphemy against Servetus is absolutely baseless. Actually, Servetus' faith corresponded much more closely to the Jewish concept of Yahweh as the one God than did the traditional, Trinitarian view of God held by Calvin and all other leading Reformers and Catholics.

Reaction to the Execution of Servetus

Granted, religious intolerance was the spirit of the age. Countless religious people were then executed as heretics. Prior to Servetus, in 1415, Roman Catholic leaders tried and burned Englishman John Hus at the stake for alleged heresy. P. Schaff reports that in the Catholic Netherlands, in 1567-1573, as many as 100,000 professing Christians were put to death and 30,000 in 1546 in Holland and Friesland, all "for the offences of reading the Scriptures, of looking askance at a graven image, or of ridiculing the actual presence of the body and blood of Christ in a wafer."[24] Most leading Reformers at one time or another sought refuge from the long arms of the law of Catholic Inquisitors. Yet all leading Reformers approved of the execution of Servetus. Mild-mannered Melanchthon even deemed it "a pious example which deserved to be remembered to all posterity."

Later historians unanimously disagreed. Historian Edward Gibbon, author of the critically-acclaimed *The History of the Decline and Fall of the Roman Empire* (1776), wrote that he personally felt "more scandalized at the single execution of Servetus" than certain murderous atrocities that had occurred in both Spain and Portugal in his lifetime, which even involved the death of large multitudes.[25] P. Schaff, similarly, calls the demise of Servetus "the most thrilling tragedy in the history of the Reformation."[26] M. Hillar concludes, "To evaluate his [Servetus'] significance and recognize his role one has to look at the issue from a neutral perspective in an intellectual environment free from religious domination. Such an intellectual position was not possible for historical reasons until the nineteenth century."[27]

In 1903, on the 350th anniversary of Servetus' death, a group of John Calvin's distant relatives and Geneva Calvinists assembled at the site of Servetus' execution to ceremoniously denounce their forebear's role in the Spanish martyr's death. And, to Calvin's further disgrace, they erected a monument of block granite, measuring three meters in size, which still stands there today. On one side it reads, "On the 27 of October, 1553, died at the stake in Champel, Michael Servetus of Villeneuve of Aragon, born on the 29 of September, 1511." On the

---

[22] John Marshall, *John Locke, Toleration and Early Enlightenment Culture* (Cambridge: University, 2006), 325.
[23] Calvin also argued against interpreting Jesus' parable of the wheat and the tares as implying religious toleration of heretics (Mt 13.29 par.), and he did the same concerning Gamaliel's wise counsel (Ac 5.34).
[24] P. Schaff, *History of the Christian Church*, 8:813-14.
[25] Quoted in P. Schaff, *History of the Christian Church*, 8:689.
[26] P. Schaff, *History of the Christian Church*, 7:66.
[27] M. Hillar, *Michael Servetus*, 240.

other side it reads, "As reverent and grateful sons of Calvin, our great Reformer, repudiating his mistake, which was the mistake of his age, and according to the true principles of the Reformation and Gospel, holding fast to the freedom of conscience, we erect this monument of reconciliation on 28 October, 1903."

A theology that would cause the leading biblical exegete of the great Protestant Reformation to condemn and execute a man for the charge of blasphemy—even though he passionately believed in Jesus as his Lord and Savior, affirmed His resurrection, and even declared Him as God, though essentially subordinate to the Father—suggests that *John Calvin's theology should be held suspect just as much as that of Michael Servetus*! To accept the common presumption about Calvin's theology, as so many have done, or to separate Calvin's life from his theology, is to perpetuate his hideous transgression.[28]

No one should think that this Servetus affair represents a single blip on the radar screen of John Calvin's life. Earlier, in 1547, native Genevan Jacques Gruet sided with old Genevan families that resented the tyrannical power exercised by Calvin and the other pastors of the Consistory. Calvin was implicated in an incident in which someone placed a placard in one of the city's churches that read, "When too much has been endured revenge is taken." For this altercation and the charge of being involved in a French plot to invade Geneva, at the behest of Calvin and the other pastors Gruet was arrested, tried, condemned, and beheaded. In another incident, Jerome Bolsec, a former Roman Catholic monk, temporarily switched affiliation to the Reformed side and immigrated to Geneva. In 1551, he spoke out against Calvin's doctrine of unconditional predestination. For this infraction he was arrested, imprisoned, and tried by the Geneva Council. Calvin tried to get him condemned to death, but he failed only because other Swiss churches objected.

The memory of Servetus has not been lost. In the 20th century, several monuments and statues were erected in remembrance of him, especially in Spain. Spanish streets, schools, and hospitals were named after him. And there is a growing movement dedicated to the memory of Servetus and affirmation of the principles for which he died.[29]

Historian and Unitarian, Earl Morse Wilbur, has been recognized as the foremost authority on Servetus. He concludes that Michael Servetus unwittingly influenced the direction the Protestant movement took regarding Trinitarianism. Wilbur relates that until Servetus' first publication, "it had not been quite clear what attitude the newly reformed part of Christendom would finally take toward the traditional trinitarian dogma." Wilbur provides the following examples to show that "the leaders of Protestant thought were plainly wavering about it, in view of its lack of clear scriptural support."[30]

- Calvin disapproved of the Athanasian Creed and even slighted the Nicene Creed.
- Zwingli and others were quite unsound in their exposition of the Trinity.
- Melanchthon earlier ignored Trinitarianism, deeming it unessential to salvation.[31]

---

[28] Consider Servetus' affirmation of Jesus as the Christ and Son of God with the treatment he received by these pastoral Reformers in light of Jn 20.30-31; 1 Jn 4.7-8, 11, 15, 20-21; 5.1, 5; cf. Mt 7.20-21.
[29] E.g., Servetus International Society, Michael Servetus Institute, Unitarian Universalists.
[30] *The Two Treatises of Servetus on the Trinity* in *The Harvard Theological Studies*, tr. Earl Morse Wilbur (1932; repr. New York: Kraus, 1969), xvi-xvii. See also Earl Morse Wilbur, *Our Unitarian Heritage: An Introduction to the History of the Unitarian Movement* (Boston: Beacon, 1925), 40-42.
[31] *The Two Treatises of Servetus on the Trinity*, xvii.

Melanchthon is a prime example of how the early Reformers changed. He wrote a friend about the Reformers' subsequent carte blanche acceptance of Trinitarianism and divulged, "I have always feared that serious difficulties would one day arise."[32]

Wilbur therefore suggests that, given time, the Reformers might have critically examined the Trinitarian teaching and dismissed it as biblically unsound. He continues, "The outbreak of Servetus interfered with all of this; and in the face of the Catholic criticism which the Reformers still feared might have such serious results for their movement, they made haste to assert their orthodoxy on this point."[33]

So, in the name of Jesus Christ these pastors of the Reformation executed Michael Servetus. Fearing a backlash, they hastily sealed records of their interrogations. These remained hidden from the public for nearly two centuries. Sin always tries to cover-up.

Throughout Europe, neither church nor state objected to Servetus' execution. In fact, many other church states, even Protestant ones, had their own executions of heretics. For instance, two years prior, in 1551, the Archbishop of Canterbury Thomas Cranmer led Church of England officials in arresting surgeon George van Parris. He was tried, found guilty of heresy, and burned to death at the stake for refusing to recant of his testimony, "that God the Father is only God and that Christ is not very God."[34]

Nevertheless, news of Servetus' martyrdom spread quickly across Europe, and much of the populace became outraged about it. A foment of anti-Trinitarianism arose, mostly in eastern and central Europe, but especially in the land where Servetus was headed on his way to his untimely death—the home of the Vatican.

The Socinians

In Italy, a lawyer named Laelius Socinus (Ital. *Lelio Sozzini*; 1525-1562) soon had a major, though indirect, impact on the spread of anti-Trinitarianism. He was both a student of classics and a moral humanist who had doubts about Roman Catholicism, particularly its doctrine of the Trinity. He later witnessed the public trial of Servetus, in which the accused was allowed to debate his views with those of his judges. Laelius Socinus took notes of the proceeding and bequeathed them, along with the rest of his property, to a teenage nephew showing intellectual promise.

That was Faustus Socinus (Ital. *Fausto Sozzini*; 1539-1604). Like his uncle Laelius, Faustus became a lawyer. Years later, he was stirred by reading his uncle's account of Servetus' trial. It caused him to abandon his law practice in Italy and migrate to Switzerland and then Poland. There, where others of like faith had preceded him, in 1579 Faustus Socinus began organizing anti-Trinitarians into a movement that included many Italian immigrants. And he was not impeded politically in his efforts. By that time, intellectual freedom prevailed in Poland, mainly due to a lack of central government.

---

[32] Cited from P. Schaff, *History of the Christian Church*, 8:719.
[33] *The Two Treatises of Servetus on the Trinity*, xvii. Wilbur relates that Calvin endorsed it in a full treatment in his *Institutes of the Christian Religion*; Melanchthon, later in his *Loci*, made it absolutely essential for salvation; and all subsequent Protestant confessions unequivocally included it.
[34] Cited by Buzzard and Hunting (*The Doctrine of the Trinity*, 142) from G.H. Williams, *The Radical Reformation* (Philadelphia: Westminster, 1962), 779-80.

Before Socinus arrived in Poland, the Polish Brethren had not wanted to separate from mainstream Christianity and form their own sect. But they felt forced into it when the orthodox Reformed churches of Poland disassociated from them. Therefore, in order to perpetuate their movement, in 1565 these brethren formed the "Minor Reformed Church of Poland." When Socinus arrived years later, he quickly became its foremost leader and eventually the most important figure in the history of Unitarianism.

Like Servetus, Faustus Socinus purposed to restore primitive Christianity as he understood it. He proved an able leader, spokesman, and debater for this non-Trinitarian movement. Socinus systematized the movement's beliefs and wrote voluminously on theology. He appealed to both the authority of the NT as well as human reasoning.

Early adherents of this non-Trinitarian movement referred to themselves simply as "Christian" or "brethren." But outsiders labeled them "Socinians," which eventually stuck. These Socinians possessed a strong sense of individuality. They also tended to be highly educated, intellectual, and cultured. They believed passionately in the principles of freedom of conscience, reason, and religious toleration even more than they did in their own peculiar theological convictions. Consequently, Socinians made a major contribution to the development of the humanist movement and the Age of Rationalism.

Catholics and orthodox Protestants supported their doctrinal positions by claiming the authority of both the Bible and the ecumenical church creeds. In contrast, Socinians were vehemently anti-credal. The closest Socinus ever came to drafting a creed was when his associates asked him to revise their foremost catechism shortly before his death. He obliged and it was published the next year, in 1605.[35] It was called "the Racovian Catechism" (L. *Racovia*) because it was published at Rakow, Poland, the movement's headquarters. As a catechism, it proclaimed the supposed fundamentals of the Christian faith in question-and-answer format. Widely circulated throughout Europe, it was never intended to be doctrinally binding on Socinians; and it never was. The primary precepts of the Racovian Catechism can be condensed as follows:

1. Man is mortal in both soul and body.
2. Eternal life comes only through the correct knowledge of God and Jesus Christ.
3. The one, true God is a single person: the Father.
4. Jesus was born miraculously of a virgin and therefore was a true man. He lived a sinless life, wrought miracles, died, and arose alive from the dead. The resurrected Jesus ascended into heaven, where He now resides exalted at God's right hand, awaiting his return to earth to judge the living and the dead.
5. Jesus' resurrection is more important than his death. The (only) significance of his death is that he showed us the way to return to God and be reconciled to him.
6. We must acknowledge Jesus Christ, who has divine power over us, as also being God, but only by office, not nature. And whosoever does not adore Christ for his sublime majesty, and seek his aid through prayer, is not a Christian.
7. The Holy Spirit is not a person, but the power of God bestowed upon men.
8. There is no original sin or predestination.

---

[35] Socinus died before completing his revision, which was finished by two other Socinian scholars.

9. There is only one sacrament: the Lord's Supper.
10. Water baptism merely symbolizes inward faith, so that infant baptism is unscriptural.

The principal theological doctrine that defined Socinians was, like that of the earlier Arians, their assertion that only the Father is the one true God. Their key biblical text for this proposition was Jn 17.3. Positively, this doctrine of the unity of God gave them an affinity with Jews and Muslims. Negatively, Socinians became known for their anti-Trinitarian views. Also like the Arians, Socinians regarded Jesus as God, but only in a derivative sense. Therefore, Socinians held a fairly high view of Jesus. Socinus himself regarded anyone who did not "worship" Jesus Christ as no better off than an atheist.

Continental European Unitarianism

Adherents of these Socinian beliefs enjoyed religious freedom in only two countries: Poland and Transylvania (present western Hungary). They were first called "Unitarians" in Transylvania in the year 1600, mostly due to their emphasis on the unity of God. Many Reformed churches in this region gradually changed to become Unitarian. By the end of the 16th century, about 500 Unitarian churches existed in Transylvania and parts of Hungary, even more than in the larger region of Poland.[36] In contrast to the Socinians of Poland, most of these Unitarians in Transylvania and Hungary eventually repudiated praying to, and worshipping, Jesus Christ.

Socinians and Unitarians were often mistaken as Arian in Christology. The two primary doctrinal differences between Socinians and Arians concerned preexistence and atonement. Arians acknowledged the personal preexistence of Jesus as the Logos whereas Socinians left this matter undecided, while generally denying it. Also, Arians affirmed orthodoxy by attributing a vicarious atoning significance to Jesus' death while Socinians only regarded it as an example of humiliation and submission to God.

Socinians and Unitarians alike propagated these views in their homelands mostly through public debates held with consenting, orthodox, Protestant theologians. These elaborate events were often advertised, well attended, and lasted for several days.

Due to religious intolerance in other European countries, Socinians and Unitarians could only spread their views abroad through their avalanche of publications.[37] These writings sometimes caused later orthodox Protestant churches to change theologically on their own to become Unitarian.

In 1660, the Polish Socinians met an ignoble fate. The State of Poland cooperated with both Catholics and Protestants by passing a law that forced all Socinians into exile. Some of them suffered martyrdom because of it. Thus began the long, pitiful history of the persecution of Socinians and Unitarians. Poland subsequently put many of them to death as condemned heretics. The institutional church and state often worked unitedly to accomplish this tragedy. Nevertheless, Socinian and Unitarian teachings did not cease but spread into Western Europe, first taking root in Holland and then England.

---

[36] E.M. Wilbur, *Our Unitarian Heritage*, 230-31.
[37] E.M. Wilbur (*Our Unitarian Heritage*, 157n1) recounts that, until their expulsion from Poland, the Socinians published "some 500 separate works or editions."

British Unitarianism

Unitarianism was not really imported to England. It formed mostly on its own among some dissenting Presbyterian (Puritan) churches. It began through the influence of that venerable educator, John Biddle (1615-1662). He is often called "the father of English Unitarianism." Biddle was so biblically oriented that it was often said that he memorized the entire NT, except for the book of Revelation, in both English and Greek.

Biddle, soon after becoming a Unitarian, wrote and published a book in 1647 which espoused views similar to those of Servetus.[38] In it, Biddle asserts that the Holy Spirit is an impersonal emanation from God. And he also translated into English, and published, the Racovian Catechism and other Unitarian writings. He publicly debated his Unitarian beliefs with Bishop Ussher, renowned for his biblical chronology. After that, and solely in reaction to Biddle, England passed a heresy law. It was called, of all things, "the Draconian Ordinance." ("Dracon" derives from the Greek word *drakon*, meaning "dragon.") For all this, Biddle was incarcerated for nearly half his life and died in prison.

In 1689, England reversed itself by passing "The Toleration Act." This legislation precipitated the so-called "Trinitarian Controversy" throughout England, which lasted for the next sixty years, until 1750. During this period, many public debates were held with regard to Trinitarianism, and both sides published a plethora of books and tracts on this subject. And the Unitarian Church of England became established in the late 18th century.

Back in the 1530s, England had created its own state church, called "the Anglican Church." In 1571, England's parliament passed an act requiring their religious ministers to subscribe to the Anglican Church's "Thirty-Nine Articles of Religion," a process called "subscription." "The Articles," as they came to be known, included the doctrine of the Trinity and an endorsement of the Athanasian Creed. A protest movement arose against this subscription, and its constituents were called "the Dissenters." They consisted mostly of Presbyterians, General Baptists, and Independents. Three hundred years later, in 1871, England finally relented and abolished its subscription, but not The Articles.

John Locke

A book that caused no little controversy in England during this period was John Locke's *The Reasonableness of Christianity* (1695).[39] Locke was a philosopher as well as an education and political theorist who wrote important books on all of these subjects. The highlight of the U.S. Declaration of Independence—"we hold these truths to be self-evident, that all men are endowed by their creator with certain inalienable rights, and among these are life, liberty and the pursuit of happiness"—is traced back to Locke's book entitled *Second Treatise on Civil Government* (1690). In fact, renewed interest in John Locke's writings has surged from the late 20th century to the present.

As a Christian layman, John Locke refuted what he called "systems of divinity." He opposed systematic theology and attempted to rely solely on the Bible. In his famous book, *The Reasonableness of Christianity*, he argues that the Bible teaches that to become a genuine Christian, and therefore be "saved," regardless of any other theological beliefs a person may hold, it is only necessary to believe the following: (1) the one God exists, (2) God sent Jesus, (3) Jesus is the

---

[38] John Biddle, *Twelve Questions or Arguments drawn out of Scripture, wherein the commonly received Opinion touching the Deity of the Holy Spirit is clearly and fully refuted* (1647).
[39] Another important book was by Oxford educator Dr. Arthur Bury entitled *The Naked Truth* (1690).

Messiah, and (4) Jesus died and was resurrected. Concerning Jesus being "the Son of God," Locke preempted biblical criticism on this one by citing the Jews' practice of interchanging their terms "Messiah" and "the Son of God," so that these should be understood synonymously as applied to Jesus. Locke rejected identifying Jesus by employing Greek metaphysics and thus the two-nature Christology of Chalcedon. For this reason, he was often accused incorrectly of being a Unitarian. Like Unitarians, however, Locke omitted any atonement concept as essential to saving faith.

The hallmark of John Locke's theology is his refreshing simplicity of the gospel. First, he cites Jesus quoting Isa 61.1, that the "POOR HAVE THE GOSPEL PREACHED TO THEM" (Mt 11.5/Lk 7.22; cf. Lk 4.18). Then this brilliant philosopher-theologian, who minces no words, ends his book by contending on behalf of intellectually common folk,

> 'Tis well if Men of that rank (to say nothing of the other Sex) can comprehend plain propositions, and a short reasoning about things familiar to their Minds, and nearly allied to their daily experience.... Had God intended that none but the Learned Scribe, the disputer or wise of this World, should be Christians, or be Saved, thus Religion should have been prepared for them; filled with speculations and niceties, obscure terms, and abstract notions.... And if the poor had the Gospel Preached to them, it was, without doubt, such a Gospel, as the poor could understand, plain and intelligible: And so it was, as we have seen, in the preaching of Christ and his Apostles.[40]

This is what John Locke meant by the *reasonableness* of Christianity,[41] that its saving message precluded such complexities as Trinitarianism, eternal generation, and the like.

Deism

Deism began in England in the mid-17th century. It spread throughout Europe and North America, flourishing there for about a century. Deism grew out of Enlightenment, partly in reaction to the religious intolerance of the Reformation. Deism consisted of an intellectual rationalism that was based solely on reason and natural law. Thus, Deism was anti-supernaturalistic, generally skeptical of divine revelation and therefore the Bible, and generally opposed to orthodox Christianity.

Pure Deists believed in a personal, transcendent Supreme Being who created a "clockwork universe," meaning that He did not afterwards intervene in human affairs. Moderate Deists, however, postulated that God was immanent in the individual human conscience, if not active in human affairs. Regarding theological dogma, all Deists were known most for rejecting the Christian doctrines of the incarnation and the Trinity. Some of them were a bit hazy on whether the one God was a personal being. They frequently employed the words "Providence," "God of Nature," or "the Deity" rather than "God."

Deism remained an ideological movement that never formed into a particular school of thought or cultus. Actually, classical Deists were opposed to organized, institutional religion. Yet many of those who declared themselves as Deists were not without influence in society. Several founding forefathers of the USA were Deists. Thomas Jefferson (1743-1826), the author of the U.S.

---

[40] J. Locke, *The Reasonableness of Christianity, As Delivered in the Scriptures* (London: 1695), 303-04.
[41] John C. Higgins-Biddle, ed., John Locke's *The Reasonableness of Christianity, As Delivered in the Scriptures: Edited with an Introduction and Notes* (Oxford: Clarendon, 1999), xxi.

Declaration of Independence and the third U.S. president, was a thorough-going Deist. (Some authorities, however, claim that it is more accurate to classify him as "a Freethinker.") Moderate Deists included George Washington (1732-1799), the first U.S. president, and Benjamin Franklin (1706-1790), the great inventor, publisher, politician, and Renaissance man.

Thomas Jefferson opposed much of organized Christian religion when he helped get "the establishment clause" into the First Amendment to the U.S. Constitution. It reads, "Congress shall make no law respecting an establishment of religion." Jefferson was most opposed to Presbyterianism. In his writings, he frequently denounces John Calvin, calling him an "Atheist." Jefferson later wrote the following harshly rhetorical attack on Presbyterianism, citing the Servetus episode:

> The Presbyterian clergy are the loudest, the most intolerant of all sects; the most tyrannical and ambitious, ready at the word of the law-giver, if such a word could now be obtained, to put their torch to the pile, and to rekindle in this virgin hemisphere the flame in which their oracle, Calvin, consumed the poor Servetus, because he could not subscribe to the proposition of Calvin, that magistrates have a right to exterminate all heretics to the Calvinistic creed! They pant to re-establish by law that holy inquisition which they can now only infuse into public opinion.[42]

Later, in Germany, Deism helped stir the emergence of both biblical criticism and the History of Religions School. In the U.S., Thomas Jefferson became one of the first biblical critics among American Deists when, in the winter of 1819-1820, he produced a composite harmony of the four NT gospels. Entitled *The Life and Morals of Jesus of Nazareth*, it was published posthumously, in 1904. It emphasizes the ethical teachings of Jesus. But as a purely rationalistic work, it excludes all gospel narrative that depicts Jesus as a healer and miracle-worker, and it excises his resurrection and post-resurrection appearances as well.

British Arianism

Along with the appearance of Unitarianism in England, there arose a profound reemergence of the old Arianism. The theologies of these two groups were similar, and for this reason many people confused the two groups and thus their respective theologies. Anyone identified as an anti-Trinitarian, or even just a heretic, was often labeled "Arian." The primary theological difference between Unitarians and these new Arians was that Unitarians generally *did not* believe in the personal preexistence of Jesus, though they formed no such dogma, and Arians *did* believe in it, though not in eternal preexistence.

During the 18th century, many noble English folk and clergymen changed their theology to become non-Trinitarian or anti-Trinitarian. They usually became Unitarian, Arian, or something in between. Many were labeled "Arian" because they adhered to some form of personal preexistence of Jesus. But they distinguished themselves from the old Arians by minimizing its theological importance mostly due to the lack of scriptural data, especially explanatory material, on this subject. Some of them went public with their heterodoxical theology; others, to protect their careers and social life, did not.

John Milton (1608-1674) was a prime example of the latter. This famous English poet was the foremost, thoroughgoing Arian and anti-Trinitarian of the 17th century. Apparently to avoid public rejection and sustain his literary career, he remained a secret proponent of Arianism all of his life. (The Toleration Act

---

[42] Paul Leicester Ford, ed., *The Works of Thomas Jefferson*, 14 vols. (1904-05), 4:322.

was not passed until after his lifetime.) Milton's extensive christological book, *The Christian Doctrine*, was published posthumously according to his will, but not until 150 years after his death.[43] In it, like Servetus, he alleges that the Protestant Reformation's retrieval of true Christianity from the corruptions of Catholicism was incomplete, especially regarding Trinitarianism.[44]

Sir Isaac Newton: A Secret Arian?[45]

The most renowned English anti-Trinitarian of the 17th and 18th centuries was the brilliant Sir Isaac Newton (1642-1727). One of history's greatest mathematicians and scientists, Newton is most famous for discovering the law of gravity. Like Milton, he was a devout Christian and a theological writer. Only in recent years has it become known that Newton wrote more on theology and alchemy than on mathematics and science combined. He especially studied biblical prophecies and often testified that the fulfillment of them strengthened his faith immeasurably in the existence and providence of God.

Many conflicting opinions have been written about Sir Isaac Newton's theological proclivities. This is partly due to his obsession to remain publicly silent about his anti-Trinitarian views in order to avoid being drawn into controversy. Newton, however, was quite conversant about his unorthodox theology with his closest friends, especially those included in what became known as "the inner circle of Sir Isaac Newton." John Locke was the first person Newton talked to about his anti-Trinitarian views. Locke, with whom Newton carried on an extensive literary correspondence, once wrote of Isaac Newton's "great knowledge in the Scriptures, wherein I know few his equals."[46]

In order for Sir Isaac Newton to continue his illustrious career at Cambridge, it became necessary that he meet the requirements of ordination to keep his fellowship. But the thought of becoming an ordained minister in the Church of England caused him much consternation. Why? Subscription! He believed there were serious discrepancies between the Church of England's Thirty-Nine Articles and the NT as well as between the Articles themselves. In all good conscience, Newton wasn't sure he could subscribe to all of the Articles. For instance, Article One is about the Trinity and Article Two affirms classical incarnation, eternal generation, and two-nature Christology. Yet Article Six reads: "Holy Scripture containeth all things necessary to salvation; so that whatsoever is not read therein, nor may be proved thereby, is not to be required of any man, that it should be believed as an article of the Faith, or be thought requisite or necessary to salvation." This matter about the Trinity disturbed Newton immensely. So, in 1672, Sir Isaac, who was a voracious reader, laid aside his other work and plunged into a deep study of the NT and patristic writings of the 2nd through the 4th centuries. This ordeal lasted over three years. In the meantime, Cambridge officials wouldn't wait on his decision; they resolved their dilemma by invoking a special dispensation in order to establish a new chair for Newton.

Much has come to light in the late 20th century regarding the secret theological beliefs of Sir Isaac Newton. What was his theology? He regarded the Bible as divine revelation and thus the sole source for determining answers to questions about God that go beyond natural revelation. The primary precept of

---

[43] See John Milton, "The Christian Doctrine," in Book I, Ch. 5 in *Complete Poems and Major Prose*, ed. Merritt Y. Hughes (repr. New York: Odyssey, 1957), 932-64.
[44] Ibid., 1,7,10, 17.
[45] Much of what follows about Isaac Newton is gleaned from M. Wiles, *Archetypal Heresy*, 77-93.
[46] E.S. De Beer, ed, *The Correspondence of John Locke*, 8 vols. (Oxford: Clarendon, 1979), 7:772-74 (=no. 3275 of April 30, 1703). Indebted to M. Wiles, *Archetypal Heresy*, 78-79.

his faith was that "whenever it is said in the Scriptures that there is one God, it means the Father."[47] Newton's foremost christological text that he used to support this maxim was 1 Cor 8.6. Thus he writes, "We are forbidden to worship two Gods, but we are not forbidden to worship one God and one Lord."[48] Newton also distinguished degrees of worship; he assigned *ultimate* worship to God as Creator and a *lesser* worship to Jesus Christ as God's agent in both creation and redemption. He argued that worshipping two or more beings *equally*, as in the doctrine of the Trinity, is an infraction against the First of the Ten Commandments and is therefore *idolatry*. (Interestingly, and just the opposite, during the Arian Controversy of the 4th century the orthodox party accused the Arians of idolatry for believing in, and therefore worshipping, the Father as God but Jesus Christ as "a demi-god.")

Like the Arians and apologists before them, Newton cited Jn 1.1c in contending that both the Father and the Logos are god, but the Logos only in a secondary, derivative sense. Newton thus subscribed to the personal preexistence of Jesus as the Logos; but he insisted that this precept is unessential to saving faith. He rightly claimed that in at least the 2nd century CE, Christians who believed in the personal preexistence of Jesus *did not* regard those professing Christians who believed otherwise as heretics devoid of salvation. Consequently, this preexistence issue, which Newton knew quite well was the decisive factor distinguishing Unitarians and Arians, he deemed insignificant.

Therefore, it generally has been thought that Isaac Newton was Arian in theology; but this is really incorrect, and he detested the Arian label. Newtonian scholar Stephen D. Snobelen concludes, "Attempts to align Newton with any single theological tradition will end in failure. Newton was an eclectic theologian."[49]

Isaac Newton has also been falsely accused of being a Deist by denying divine immanence. Not true! He taught the very intriguing concept that God does not directly accomplish any activity that He can delegate to others. Newton articulates this principle most succinctly by saying, "God does nothing by himself which he can do by another."[50]

Newton faults the Arians, Athanasius, and most ante-Nicene and Nicene church fathers for allowing Greek and Gnostic teachings, as well as unscriptural language, to infiltrate the Church. He contends that the primary way to understand God is as the moral and good Sovereign of the universe. Newton thus dismisses metaphysical concepts—described by using such words as "substance," "essence," "eternal generation," and "consubstantiality"—as being beyond both the realm of scientific observation and, more importantly, the revelation of Scripture.

Isaac Newton was much more anti-Athanasius than pro-Arian, and he could not withhold proclaiming it. Though abhorring disputes, he risked controversy by publishing a book most critical of Athanasius.[51] In it, he repeatedly indicts Athanasius for "forgery" in falsely representing patristic writings and lying about historical events to strengthen his theological position. Newton heaps

---

[47] Yahuda MS 14, p. 25. Indebted to M. Wiles, *Archetypal Heresy*, 79n80. All subsequent citations of Isaac Newton's writings herein are taken from this book by Wiles.
[48] Yahuda MS 15, p. 46.
[49] Stephen Snobelen, "Isaac Newton, heretic: the strategies of a Nicodemite," www.isaac-newton.org, 416.
[50] Martin Bodmer MS 9 (CH 18.88), p. 1. Indebted to M. Wiles, *Archetypal Heresy*, 83n99.
[51] Isaac Newton, *Paradoxical Questions concerning the morals of Athanasius and his followers* (c. early 1690s; Keyes MS 10). See also R.P.C. Hanson, "The Behaviour of Athanasius," in Hanson's *The Search for the Christian Doctrine of God: The Arian Controversy*, 239-73.

mountains of scorn on Athanasius for the doctrinal corruption the Church suffered on account of the Arian Controversy. He admits that his severe judgment of Athanasius is due to his feeling personally embarrassed at Athanasius having frustrated the purposes of God and causing Newton the personal aggravation of having to keep much of his own theological beliefs private. *AMEN, brother*!

One of Sir Isaac Newton's friends, Hopton Haynes, claimed that Newton once told him, "the time will come when the doctrine of the incarnation shall be exploded as an absurdity equal to transubstantiation."[52]

Samuel Clarke: A Moderate Arian[53]

Highly respected Samuel Clarke (1675-1729) was Newton's closest friend the last two decades of Newton's life. Clarke had a profound influence on England's Trinitarian Controversy. As a theologian, philosopher, and an author of many classics, his accolades include having been a member of the Newtonian inner circle, Chaplain to Queen Anne, and being "regarded as the greatest English theologian of his time."[54] Clarke, too, studied the ante-Nicene and Nicene fathers and consequently changed theologically to become a moderate Arian. For most Christian folk then familiar with the term "Arian," besides indicating heresy it connoted ignorance and folly. When Clarke went public with his brand of Arianism, for a while this erudite scholar was an enigma to most English folk.

In 1712, Samuel Clarke published his magisterial and non-polemical book, *The Scripture-Doctrine of the Trinity*. He was to become most known for it. For decades, it remained the benchmark refutation of the doctrine of the Trinity. In this book, Clarke advocates a sort of semi-Arian, subordinationist Christology in which Jesus Christ is God but essentially inferior to the Father and thus deserving of a lesser worship. Nevertheless, Clarke argues that his presentation of the Trinity coincides with the Anglican Church's Articles. Largely due to this book, Clarke was forced to acquiesce to political pressure from England's Upper House of Convocation by promising never to preach or teach his heterodox views again. He honorably kept this promise the rest of his life.

Clarke's theology can be summarized as follows: (1) like Newton, whenever the Scriptures mention the "one God," it always refers to "the Father;" (2) the Father alone is self-existent whereas the Son and the Holy Spirit are not; (3) the Son preexisted, but the Scriptures do not reveal how the Son metaphysically derives from the Father, and speculation on this matter should be avoided; (4) the Scriptures sometimes designate the Son as "God," but only regarding His relative attributes and dominion over us; (5) the exalted Son possesses all divine powers, yet He remains essentially subordinate to the Father; and (6) both prayer and worship directed to the Son ultimately glorify the Father.

William Whiston: A Zealous Arian

William Whiston (1667-1752) was a scientist, a theologian, and a translator of classics. He is most known for his translation of the complete works of Flavius Josephus, the renowned Jewish historian of the late 1st century who wrote the most complete history of the Jewish people. But Whiston was primarily a historian who excelled at knowledge of patristic writings. It happened because

---

[52] S. Snobelen, "Isaac Newton, heretic," 389. Taken from Richard Baron, *Cordial For Low Spirits*, 3 vols. (London, 1763), 1:i, xviii-xix.
[53] For a recent and excellent overview of the theologies of Samuel Clark and William Whiston, see M. Wiles, *Archetypal Heresy*, 93-134.
[54] Earle Morse Wilbur, *A History of Unitarianism*, 2 vols. (Cambridge, MA: Harvard, 1952), 1:239.

his friend Samuel Clarke persuaded Whiston toward Arianism and, in the process, challenged him to study the church fathers.

Whiston thereafter dedicated the remainder of his life to an impassioned project to convert England's church leaders to an even more thoroughgoing Arianism than that of Clarke. And he capped his literary career by writing a five-volume Christology entitled *Primitive Christianity Revived* (1711-12). The brilliant but eccentric William Whiston, however, did not convince hardly a soul about Arianism, and his fearless public-stand cost him dearly. For example, due to the recommendation of his friend Sir Isaac Newton, Whiston succeeded Newton to his chair at Cambridge upon Newton's retirement in 1703; but in 1710, Whiston was expelled from this position for his Arian views. Sadly, Whiston was denied gainful employment the remaining forty-two years of his life.

Newton had warned Whiston not to go public with his anti-Trinitarianism. When Whiston did so, in 1711, he suffered public accusations of heresy. Then he implicated Newton, deeming him morally weak in staying silent. Sir Isaac ended their relationship.

Unlike Newton, Whiston never complained of being labeled an Arian even though he didn't like Arius. In fact, Whiston aligned himself theologically more with Eusebius and his middle party in the Arian-Nicene conflict. Like Newton, Whiston also wrote and published against Athanasius.[55] He accused Athanasius of being "a notorious forger and liar."[56] Actually, Whiston was more incensed with what he conceived as an anti-Christian character of Athanasius than he was with his doctrinal matters. And Whiston constantly accuses Athanasius of misrepresenting his opponents, most of whom were Arians.

In sum, Newton, Clarke, and Whiston believed that Arianism generally reflected primitive Christianity. And these three men rejected "orthodoxy"—a label they refused, substituting for it "Athanasianism"—deeming it the archetypal heresy.[57] However, their British Arianism did not survive much beyond the 18th century mostly because it assigned varying degrees of divinity between Jesus and God.

American Unitarianism

Now let us return to Unitarianism. For those churchgoers who really know the old church hymns and still love to sing them in church, here is a shocker: the beloved hymn writer, Isaac Watts (1674-1748), became a Unitarian late in life after professedly studying the doctrine of the Trinity, and therefore the deity of Christ, for twenty years.

We might expect that Unitarianism would sail across the Atlantic. Indeed it did, with much vigor. If you are an American, and you don't know about the significant role that Unitarianism played in early American history, then you don't know early American history very well! Get this: five U.S. presidents were professedly Unitarian. The two most prominent were John Adams (1735-1826), leader of the Continental Congress, and Thomas Jefferson.[58] Jefferson

---

[55] William Whiston, "Suspicions Concerning Athanasius," in *An Historical Preface to Primitive Christianity Revived* (London, 1711).
[56] William Whiston, *Historical Memoirs of the Life and Writings of Dr. Samuel Clarke* (London, 1730), 178, 601.
[57] M. Wiles, *Archetypal Heresy*, 5.
[58] Other famous, early American Unitarians were Samuel Morse, inventor of the Morse Code and the telegraph, Alexander Graham Bell, inventor of the telephone, and poets Charles Dickens, Robert Burns, and Henry Wadsworth Longfellow.

once wrote, "there is not a young man now living in the U.S. who will not be a Unitarian." Like Jefferson, many Unitarians professed Deism.

Unitarianism came to "the New World" soon after the Puritans landed there. They established "Congregational" churches in Massachusetts that were Calvinistic in doctrine yet more democratic in polity. In 1663, Puritans founded Harvard College mostly to educate their young ministers. By 1805, it was liberal and anti-Trinitarian, favoring Unitarianism. The Congregationalist churches began splitting over Harvard's theological change. As in England, a theological war erupted throughout Massachusetts regarding Trinitarianism, and this debate lasted for the next thirty years. By 1840, one wing of these churches, consisting of 125 of them located mostly in the Boston area, had changed theologically to become Unitarian. The other wing, consisting of 400 churches located mostly in the rest of Massachusetts, remained Trinitarian and thus orthodox.[59]

Today, American Unitarianism is much more liberal than the original Socinianism of Poland, the old Unitarianism of Continental Europe and England, or its American forebears. In 1961, American Unitarians merged with the Universalists to form the Unitarian Universalist Association. Most of its members describe themselves as religious "humanists;" some are avowed agnostics or atheists; a bare few claim to be "Christian." Some pundits account for this liberalizing trend on the basis of the Unitarian legacy of freedom of conscience, local church autonomy, and anti-credalism. Indeed, Unitarians were always ecclesiastically free to individually choose their own theology.

Most American Unitarian Universalists nowadays believe that Jesus' significance does not extend beyond His being a great religious figure, perhaps the greatest in history, and therefore a model for living. These modern Unitarians also deny the existence of hell and eternal punishment, and most of them advocate universalism. Apparently due to this liberal change in Unitarianism, it seems to have had no noticeable impact on either 20th century Jesus Research or the lingering anti-Trinitarian movement.[60] Yet, ironically, traditionalist J.C. O'Neill observes the impact of biblical criticism on the NT and concludes, "today the Socinian reading of the historical evidence is widely accepted by many New Testament scholars, at least for the earlier strata of the New Testament."[61]

The Anabaptists

The more radical and mystical Anabaptist (re-baptized) movement arose in Europe during the early period of the Reformation as well. It was a loose, rather unorganized, but widespread lay movement of mostly common folk who merely called themselves "Christian" or "brothers and sisters." Like Unitarians, Anabaptists denied infant baptism, for which they acquired their name. It was applied to them by those Reformers who opposed them. Anabaptists rejected this label for a while, arguing that "believers' baptism," as they called it, was not rebaptism.

Anabaptists were the forerunners of today's Baptists. They held a wide variety of beliefs. Most were moralists and pacifists who emphasized freedom of conscience and separation of church and state. Because Anabaptists spurned public office, they did not avail themselves of much civil protection. Also, like Unitarians, Anabaptists subscribed wholeheartedly to the Apostles' Creed

---

[59] E.M. Wilbur, *Our Unitarian Heritage*, 427.
[60] *WDCT* 591.
[61] J.C. O'Neill, *Who Did Jesus Think He Was?* (Leiden: Brill, 1995), 1.

and generally rejected the later ecumenical creeds. Some Anabaptists were anti-Trinitarian. Anabaptists were also non-clerical, faulted the Reformers for refusing the authority of Scripture regarding ethics and ecclesiology, and championed a further restoration of NT Christianity. Consequently, both Catholics and Protestants often viewed Anabaptists and Unitarians alike.

During the 16th century and thereafter, countless Anabaptists and Unitarians were persecuted and/or exiled for their faith by Catholic and Protestant ecclesiastical leaders and political officials. Many of them suffered martyrdom. In contrast, whenever anti-Trinitarians enjoyed the state's favor, which was seldom (Unitarians of Transylvania), they *never* persecuted their religious opponents.[62] In contrast, by the mid-16th century 30,000 European Anabaptists had been put to death, mostly in Holland.[63] Religious heresy continued to be prosecuted as a capital crime in England until 1612, in Geneva until 1687, in Scotland until 1697, and in Poland until 1776, except for a brief respite in 1552-1560. Until then, only Anabaptists and Unitarians defended religious toleration.[64]

The Effects of Religious Intolerance

One of the effects of centuries of all of this theological intolerance of European Catholics and Protestants toward dissenters was that religion declined substantially there during the 20th century. Those institutional churches had made themselves so odious to much of un-churched Europe, especially educated people. Even today, historians often cite Europe's legacy of the Crusades and the Inquisition as practically insurmountable intellectual barriers for many Europeans, who remain intransigent to the gospel of Jesus Christ. Thus, a widespread religious cynicism continues to pervade Europe to this day.

In 1902, authority Adolf von Harnack observed this church history of religious intolerance by describing the question of Jesus' identity as

> one which lands us in the great sphere of controverted questions which cover the history of the Church from the first century up to our own time. In the course of this controversy men put an end to brotherly fellowship for the sake of a *nuance*; and thousands were cast out, condemned, loaded with chains and done to death. It is a gruesome story. On the question of 'Christology' men beat their religious doctrines into terrible weapons, and spread fear and intimidation everywhere.[65]

In contrast, the United States became a blessed refuge for religious dissent. In fact, the U.S. became the world's beacon of religious freedom and toleration. Perhaps that is one reason this "one nation under God" (added to "The Pledge of Allegiance" in 1954) became the source of much Christian evangelization of the world during the 20th century. Today, according to pollsters the U.S. far exceeds Europe—its motherland—in church attendance per capita of population.

Credal Faith

Returning to the subject of credal faith, whereas Unitarians and Anabaptists rejected the Athanasian Creed, the leading European Protestant denominations received it with surprising respect, as witnessed in their confessional

---

[62] E.M. Wilbur, *Our Unitarian Heritage*, 231.
[63] E.M. Wilbur, *Our Unitarian Heritage*, 231.
[64] M. Hillar, *Michael Servetus*, 232.
[65] A. von Harnack, *What Is Christianity?*, 134.

statements.⁶⁶ Both the Belgic Confession (1566) and the Synod of Dort (1619) specifically endorsed it as authoritative. And one of the Anglican Church's Articles declares that the Athanasian Creed "ought thoroughly to be received and believed." Also, its Book of Common Prayer ordered that this creed be recited by church members in place of the Apostles' Creed on no less than thirteen specified holy days throughout the year.

In the U.S., it has not been any different. The constitution of the Lutheran Church in America declares the Athanasian Creed as one of the "true declarations of the faith of the Church." The Protestant Episcopal Church of America does likewise by professedly adhering to The Thirty-Nine Articles of the Church of England. So it is with the United Methodist Church, which is based on John Wesley's refined condensation of The Thirty-Nine Articles. As for Presbyterian denominations, most endorse the Westminster Confession (1642), which adopts the same Trinitarianism as that of the Athanasian Creed.

Regarding church scholars, Protestants have always been freer to question their theological traditions than have their Catholic counterparts. For example, Arminian Dutch theologians were the first Protestants to question eternal generation. They inquired how anyone can be generated by, or proceed from, God and also be equally God. So they adopted a subordinationist Trinitarianism, in which Jesus was regarded as essentially inferior to the Father, similar to the Christology of the apologists. The result was that these Arminian scholars accepted the Nicene Creed but interpreted it as subordinationist, and they rejected the Athanasian Creed.⁶⁷ A century later in America, Nathaneal Emmons (1745-1840), Congregationalist Moses Stuart (1780-1852), and Methodist Adam Clark (1762-1832) did likewise. Stuart and Clark went a step further by rejecting both eternal generation and eternal (divine) Sonship. They therefore agreed with their predecessor, Michael Servetus, that Jesus being "the Son of God" refers only to His filial relationship with God the Father and thus His incarnation, as in Lk 1.35, not preexistence.

Friedrich Schleiermacher

Friedrich Schleiermacher (1768-1834) was a brilliant and socially-inclined German scholar who is generally acknowledged as the most influential Protestant theologian ever. Called "the father of Liberal Theology" (some would insist "Modern Theology"), Schleiermacher debated whether or not the Christian faith is a supernatural religion. He believed Jesus literally rose from the dead and that He and the apostles did some miracles,⁶⁸ but these propositions were not an important focus for Schleiermacher.

Schleiermacher was a pietist who emphasized self-consciousness, actually a God-consciousness, with the feeling of total dependence upon God. Thus, he attributed Jesus' uniqueness to His "absolutely powerful God-consciousness," assigning an unprecedented "existence of God in Him."⁶⁹ Schleiermacher therefore was a strong proponent of a solely God-in-Christ Christology, opposing traditional Christology by denying Jesus was God.

---

⁶⁶ J.N.D. Kelly, *The Athanasian Creed: The Paddock Lectures for 1962-1963* (London: Adam & Charles Black, 1964), 48.
⁶⁷ E.g., Curcellaeus (1586-1659), Limborch (1633-1712), Le Clerc (1657-1736), Coleridge (1772-1834).
⁶⁸ Friedrich Schleiermacher, *The Christian Faith* [1821], 2nd ed. 1830, tr. H.R. Mackintosh and J.S. Steward (Philadelphia: Fortress, 1928), 448-50; idem, *The Life of Jesus*, 431-81.
⁶⁹ F. Schleiermacher, *The Christian Faith*, 387. On pp. 400-24, Schleiermacher uses the expression "the being of God in Christ/Him" no less than fourteen times. And he uses other similar expressions therein, too.

Schleiermacher made a penetrating, critical analysis of Chalcedonian, two-nature Christology. He concluded that it is both confusing and futile. He further argued that it is impossible to objectify God as consisting of various characteristics comprising a nature. And he contended that it is impossible for two such entirely diverse "natures"—a human nature and a divine nature—to subsist together in one individual. He cited the historical difficulty, indeed impossibility, of finding a balance between joining the supposed two natures together in one person without mixing them to form a third nature and keeping the two natures separate in order to affirm, and thus not deny, the unity of the person.[70]

Schleiermacher was also a severe critic of Trinitarianism. He observed that it was formulated during the height of controversy. He alleged that it is incoherent, speculative, and clearly unsupported in the Gospel of John. In fact, this gospel played a profound role in the development of Schleiermacher's theology. He also contended that Trinitarianism betrays a very subtle, essential subordinationism, in which Trinitarians presume divine attributes ascribed to the Father, yet they are constantly compelled to prove the same for both Jesus Christ and the Holy Spirit. Schleiermacher exposed the Reformers' failure to scrutinize the Catholic doctrine of the Trinity in this oft-quoted summary: "We have the less reason to regard this doctrine as finally settled since it did not receive any fresh treatment when the Evangelical (Protestant) Church was set up; and so there must still be in store for it a transformation which will go back to its very beginning.... we should strive to secure freedom for a thoroughgoing criticism of the doctrine in its older form, so as to prepare the way for, and introduce, a reconstruction of it."[71]

Thus, Schleiermacher was one of the first Protestant pioneers to begin blazing a trail through the thick, entangled overgrowth of patristic orthodoxy that had blurred the NT picture of the historical Jesus and thus had been overlooked by the early Reformers.

Some Anti-Trinitarian Churches

The Groningen School arose within the Reformed Church of Holland during the second quarter of the 19th century. Known for its Christology, it asserted that Christ was not God but that God was in Christ, thus denying the orthodox doctrine of the Trinity. It emphasized education, foreign missions, personal piety, and thus ethics. It affirmed Jesus' miracles and resurrection, but viewed His death only as an example of suffering, thus not as an atonement for sin. The famous artist, Vincent van Gogh, was influenced by this sect because his father was a pastor in it and his uncle a famous theologian in it.

The first anti-Trinitarian American to assert that only the Father is God and Jesus is "divine," and to extend these doctrines denominationally, was Alexander Campbell (1788-1866). He was a Kentucky preacher who emigrated from Ireland. Campbell's "Christian Restorationist Movement" resulted in the union of various Methodist, Baptist, and Presbyterian churches to form a new denomination called the "Christian Church." It was non-credal and congregational in polity. In the early 20th century, a schism broke out within this church denomination that resulted in the formation of two others named "the Disciples of Christ" and "the

---

[70] F. Schleiermacher, *The Christian Faith*, 391-96.

[71] F. Schleiermacher, *The Christian Faith*, 747, 749, cf. 396. Similarly, D. Cupitt, *Jesus and the Gospel of God*, 73-74.

Churches of Christ." All three of these denominations soon severed their anti-Trinitarian roots to avoid being marginalized by the church-at-large.

Presently, the two largest anti-Trinitarian groups in the U.S. are a portion of the Pentecostal movement and the Jehovah's Witnesses. Both originated in the U.S. during the early 20th century. A split occurred among Pentecostals during WWI over the doctrine of the Trinity. It resulted in the creation of the United Pentecostal Church, known mostly for being anti-Trinitarian and baptizing in "Jesus' Name only" (cf. Ac 2.38; 8.16; 10.48; 19.5). This church exemplifies a return to Sabellianism with its "Oneness" doctrine, i.e., God the Father is one Person who became the man Jesus. In contrast, The Assemblies of God, the largest Pentecostal church in the world, has embraced Trinitarianism. Like mainline Protestant denominations, it employs the Matthean Trinitarian baptismal formula (Mt 28.19>). (As for the Jehovah's Witnesses, who are Arian in Christology, see Chapter Seven/Jn 1.1c>.)

Biblical Criticism

The Renaissance and Enlightenment periods emerged in the 16th through the 18th centuries. These movements gave birth to an amplified literary criticism. This method of analysis was applied to many intellectual disciplines, especially literary classics, but also historical and religious documents.

The Bible was not exempt; literary criticism was applied to it as well. Called "biblical criticism," it was the utilization of what came to be called "the historical-critical method" of analyzing Scripture. These terms were not originally intended to connote a negative, cynical view of the Bible, as one might expect; rather, they were intended to indicate an objective and thus unprejudiced, careful appraisal of it. However, much of this critical scholarship of the Bible became quite skeptical of both divine revelation and supernaturalism. Conservatives labeled it, pejoratively, "higher criticism."

Nevertheless, biblical criticism flourishes today in all sectors of Christian academia. Categories that have emerged within biblical criticism are "source criticism," "form criticism," and "redaction criticism." These disciplines have considerably affected how scholars do Christology. Even conservative biblical scholars now recognize the benefits of a judicious, non-radical use of these modern tools of scholarship.

Biblical criticism began in Germany. From the time that German monk Martin Luther lit the fires of the Protestant Reformation, Germany remained the world's center for biblical studies. In the centuries that followed, until the last few decades, the rest of the world merely responded to innovative theological ideas coming out of Germany.

This fact probably seems strange to most readers because of what happened in the mid-20th century: the rise of German Nazism, Germany's role in WWII, and the resulting Holocaust. During the decades following this triad of foreboding evils, a long dark shadow was cast over the national German Lutheran Church because of its complacency, if not complicity, in these most somber events from which it is still recovering.

The Tubingen School

The historical-critical method of interpreting the NT came into existence during the mid-19th century in Tubingen, Germany. It first happened among a nucleus of eight professors who banded together in an ad hoc group called "the Tubingen School." Most of them taught theology or philosophy during the daytime at the University of Tubingen. This group held together in two ways: (1) meeting in the evenings, usually daily, at the same inn to discuss mostly theological subjects and (2) publishing a quarterly journal entitled *Theologische Jahrbucher*.

This Tubingen School was founded and headed by Ferdinand Christian Baur (1792-1860). His father, a Lutheran pastor, trained young Ferdinand in orthodox theology and sent him to be educated at the Lutheran seminary at the University of Tubingen. Later called "the Old Tubingen School," it was founded by the famous NT scholar John Albert Bengel. This school became known for its orthodoxy, especially its adherence to supernaturalism and the divine inspiration of the Bible. But Bengel's grandson, E.G. Bengel, was not orthodox in theology, and he became Baur's most influential professor there. E.G. Bengel caused the school to abandon Chalcedonian Christology and ascribe a very limited divinity to Jesus, i.e., in the sense that Jesus only taught divine truths.

F.C. Baur later founded his even more liberal school in Tubingen in opposition to the historically more conservative Old Tubingen School. The emergence of this new quasi-school was instigated with the publication of a very erudite and influential book authored by Baur's close friend and pupil, D.F. Strauss (1808-1874). Entitled *Life of Jesus* (1835), its viewpoint was anti-supernatural, making the book very controversial. Ironically, Strauss was never recognized as either a scholar or a member of Baur's new Tubingen School since he was not a resident of Tubingen. D.F. Strauss was an avowed pantheist (some would say atheist) and a marvelous lecturer. Toward the end of his rather miserable life, Strauss publicly denied being a Christian and demanded a secular funeral.

Strauss coined two lasting expressions that he set in discontinuity with each other. "The Christ of faith" referred to the church's dogmatic proclamations of a Jesus who was historically inauthentic, but "the Jesus of history" referred to the actual, historical Jesus.

Not surprisingly, this new Tubingen School was generally regarded throughout Germany as the bastion of unbelief and therefore a center of apostasy. Its members were constantly engaged in controversy with other scholars. Nevertheless, because of this school's continuing and profound influence to this day, historian Horton Harris wrote in 1975 concerning this Tubingen School, "It was *the most important theological event in the whole history of theology from the Reformation to the present day.*"[72]

How so? Baur was most responsible for establishing the historical-critical method of the interpretation of the Bible.[73] He based this method on the presupposition of non-supernaturalism if not anti-supernaturalism. He also coined the expressions "Christology from below" and "Christology from above," which scholars still use. Both refer to the starting point of doing Christology: (1) "from below" starts with Jesus being a man, as Bauer asserted of the Synoptic Gospels, and (2) "from above" starts with Jesus being an ontological, preexistent Person, if not God, as Baur insisted the Gospel of John affirms.

About the only thing orthodox about this new Tubingen School was, as Scott J. Hafemann says, that its "critical investigation of the Bible established itself as orthodoxy within the world of scholarship."[74] On account of this Tubingen School's remarkable and lasting influence, which continues to the present time,

---

[72] Horton Harris, *The Tubingen School: A Historical and Theological Investigation of the School of F.C. Baur* [1975] (repr. Grand Rapids: Baker, 1990), xvii. Emphasis not mine.

[73] H. Harris, *The Tubingen School*, 53.

[74] Scott J. Hafemann, "F.C. Bauer," in *Historical Handbook of Major Biblical Interpreters*, ed. D.K. McKim, 289.

it is surprising that this very small quasi-school only existed for twenty-five years, from 1835 to Baur's death in 1860.

The History of Religions School

Like everything else, religions do not operate in a vacuum. Most religious people are influenced by other cultures, worldviews, and contemporary religions they encounter. This process is called "historical conditioning." The history of the Hebrew people in their ancestral land is a prime example, though an important purpose of the giving of the Torah was to negate such. But the subsequent reality was that the Hebrew/Jewish religion was very much influenced from the outside, and so was its later cousin—Christianity.

And so, from about 1880 to 1920, German historical-critical scholars developed an academic movement called the "History of Religions School" (Ger. *Religionsges-chichtliche Schule*). Eventually centered in Gottingen, Germany, it was a comparative study of religions that employed historical-critical and supposedly scientific methods. It focused mostly on feverishly critiquing the impact of religions on each other, most particularly the influence of other religions on Christianity, in order to further discover their origins. By exposing the influence of Greek religio-philosophy on various aspects of classical Christian theology, these historians sought to overthrow the traditional, Chalcedonian, ontological Christology and supplant it with a very "functional Christology" that was concerned almost exclusively with the acts of Jesus and His relationship to God as His loving, heavenly Father. Prominent names in this movement were Otto Pfleiderer (1839-1908), William Wrede (1859-1906), Johannes Weiss (1863-1914), Hermann Gunkel (1862-1932), Ernst Troeltsch (1865-1923), and especially Wilhelm Bousset (1865-1920).

The results of this historical investigation were rather negative. Early Christianity was regarded as a thoroughly hellenized religion. W. Bousset, and later, R. Bultmann, alleged that the incarnation dogma was borrowed from the Gnostic Redeemer Myth. So, Jesus was viewed as no more than a great prophet who performed no supernatural acts, but mostly preached the imminent end of the world (which did not occur). Jesus therefore was deemed to be of moral but no theological relevance for modern folk.

This History of Religions School did not last long because some of its conclusions eventually proved false. For example, it was discovered that the Gnostic Redeemer Myth did not exist prior to the 2nd century CE, so that it could not have been the source of the church doctrine of the incarnation.[75] On the positive side, however, this historical discipline established by the History of Religions School did stimulate further research.

In another related development, in the latter half of the 19th century conservative scholars in Germany, and then England, reacted to the debate between "higher criticism" (radical criticism) of the History of Religions School and classical, dogmatic, church theology by developing an intermediate position called "biblical theology." Its advocates adopted fewer presuppositions than in classical theology. They usually coordinated them into a systematic theology and tried to restore a more Jewish understanding of Jesus.

---

[75] E.g., Martin Hengel, *The Son of God: The Origin of Christology and the History of Jewish-Hellenistic Religion* [1975], tr. John Bowden (Philadelphia: Fortress, 1976), 33-34.

Liberal Theology

Liberal Theology came to the fore in mainstream Protestantism during the latter 19th century and extended well into the first half of the 20th century. Called "liberalism" and, later, "modernism" by its many foes, it represented a further development of English Deism of the 17th century and especially German rationalism of the 18th century, which was spearheaded by H.S. Reimarus (1694-1768). Liberal theologians characterized Jesus as no more than a moral-reforming prophet and sage. They thus denied that He performed miracles or arose from the dead, and they attributed no atoning significance to His death, only rendering it as a model of suffering. These Liberals therefore (1) centered upon Jesus' moral teaching and its personal application to discipleship, (2) advocated social improvement, and (3) expounded an anthropocentric theology and optimistic humanism. But the latter largely led to the demise of Liberal Theology following the two world wars.

German historical-critical scholar Adolf von Harnack (1851-1930) was also the son of a conservative theology professor and emerged as the leader of Liberal Theology. In his massive and monumental seven-volume *History of Dogma*,[76] Harnack attacks the method of the development of church dogma in general and thereby demolishes, at least in the eyes of much German academia, Nicene-Chalcedonian Christology in particular. For example, Harnack and others[77] followed Schleiermacher by showing convincingly that the NT does not ascribe to Jesus a metaphysical nature and thus not two natures.

Also in this period, liberal Protestant scholars produced a slew of publications called "Life of Jesus" books. Harnack did too, and his popular volume was entitled in English, *What is Christianity?*[78] In it, Harnack alleges that the church dogma that Jesus is God is "a perversion" of the Bible. He asserts, "There can be no sense of development with respect to the gospel; it has not developed but was fully given in Jesus Christ."[79]

Three years later, Roman Catholic scholar Alfred Loisy published *The Gospel and the Church* as a rebuttal to Harnack's book.[80] It became the foremost basis of the RCC's defense of its development of Christology in the 2nd through the 5th centuries CE. But in comparing these two books, it was Harnack's critique of classical Christology that proved most compelling, at least from a scriptural standpoint. Consider the NT epistle of Jude, in which the author writes "about our common salvation" and exhorts readers to "contend earnestly for the faith which was once for all delivered to the saints" (Jude 3).

In *What is Christianity?*, Harnack typifies other liberal Protestant authors who portray Jesus as no more than a prophet. Yet they tout the historical-critical-grammatical method of biblical interpretation as "scientific" and thus foolproof. And they claim that this literary method had overcome the failure of church fathers to be objective.

But Harnack discredited himself severely by his unwavering and patriotic support of Germany's involvement in WWI and his advisory role to Kaiser

---

[76] Adolf von Harnack, *History of Dogma* [1886-89], 7 vols., tr. Neil Buchanan et al. (London: Williams and Norgate, 1896-99).

[77] E.g., Rudolf Karl Bultmann, *Jesus and the Word* [1926] (New York: Scribner's Sons, 1934), 215-16.

[78] Adolf von Harnack, *What Is Christianity?* [1900], tr. Thomas B. Saunders (NY: Harper, 1957). This title does not reflect its original, *Das Wesen des Christentums* (1900), meaning "The Essence of Christianity."

[79] A. Harnack, *What is Christianity?*, 262, 218.

[80] Alfred Loisy, *The Gospel and the Church* [1903], tr. Christopher Home (repr. Philadelphia: Fortress, 1976).

Wilhelm, which were regarded as a serious detachment from Christian ethics. Harnack appeared hypocritical, which disillusioned many of his admirers. But the demise of Liberal Theology occurred later, mostly because the two world wars extinguished its fiery flame of human optimism.

The Quest for the Historical Jesus

Albert Schweitzer (1875-1965) was a famous German historical-critical scholar of the NT who devoted most of his life to being a medical missionary in Africa. But before he did, in 1906 he published a book entitled *The Quest of the Historical Jesus* (1906; ET 1910). This tome had such an enormous impact on the academic, Christian community that it recently has been acclaimed "the greatest twentieth-century book on Jesus."[81] It is a documentation of previous critical investigation of the life of Jesus by German scholars, from 1778 to 1906. Schweitzer, a self-professed Unitarian, alleged that these historical-critical scholars had soundly refuted Chalcedonian, two-nature Christology as being "a deception" that had "prevented the leading spirits of the Reformation from grasping the idea of a return to the historical Jesus. This dogma had first to be shattered before people could once more go out in quest of the historical Jesus."[82] Schweitzer further elucidated metaphorically of Jesus, that these scholars had "loosed the bands by which He had been riveted for centuries to the stony rocks of ecclesiastical doctrine."[83] On the academic level, Schweitzer's assault on Calcedonian Christology was damaging and proved lasting.

To make a comparison, Liberal Theology had generally rejected the idea that Jesus preached an eschatological kingdom, whereas Schweitzer insisted that Jesus was a fanatical figure who preached the imminent end of the world and the simultaneous manifestation of the eschatological kingdom, but that subsequent history proved Him wrong. Also opposite of Liberal Theology, Schweitzer concluded that the endeavor to further pursue a quest for the historical Jesus was misguided and futile.

Death of The Quest

A reaction thus arose to this quest for the historical Jesus and the Life of Jesus books that it spawned. These liberal portraits of Jesus came to be perceived as merely characterizations of contemporary culture if not the liberal authors themselves. George Tyrrell (1861-1909) made the following clever and famous statement about it: "the Christ that Harnack sees, looking back through nineteen centuries of Catholic darkness, is only the reflection of a Liberal Protestant face, seen at the bottom of a deep well."[84] Scholars dubbed this investigation analyzed by Schweitzer as the "Old Quest" because it proved "unscientific" and allegedly died. Ironically, these Old Questers were not as unbiased as they had professed to be; they, too, treated the biblical material very presuppositionally.

Although it took a while for people to learn about it, no one sounded the death knell of the Old Quest more than did German dogmatic theologian Martin

---

[81] This acclamation is by preeminent translation authority, John Bowden, in Albert Schweitzer, *The Quest of the Historical Jesus: First Complete Edition*, ed. John Bowden (Minneapolis: Fortress, 2001), xi.
[82] A. Schweitzer, *The Quest of the Historical Jesus: First Complete Edition*, 5.
[83] A. Schweitzer, *The Quest of the Historical Jesus: First Complete Edition*, 478.
[84] George Tyrrell, *Christianity at the Cross-Roads* (London: Longmans, 1909), 44. See also A. Schweitzer, *The Quest of the Historical Jesus: First Complete Edition*, 6.

Kahler (1835-1912). He wrote an essay, first published in German in 1892,[85] in which he took up the subject of the quest for the historical Jesus, framing it with Strauss' two expressions—"the Jesus of history" and "the Christ of faith."[86] Recall that the former referred to the historically-authentic, pre-Easter Jesus, the latter to the faith proclaimed by the church. This Christ of faith, also called "proclamation" (Gr. *kerygma*), centered on identifying the post-Easter Jesus as "God" and emphasizing soteriology.[87] Kahler contended, as Strauss had, that these two concepts are in complete discontinuity and that a choice must be made between them. Opposite of Strauss, Kahler's choice was, "The real Jesus is the preached Christ."[88] But Kahler injected a red herring by alleging that the quest cannot produce a biography of Jesus that meets modern standards. With this argument he overthrew "the Jesus of history," alleging that it is impossible to ascertain Jesus from the gospel records. Kahler's position would eventually prove tenuous because it completely disconnected the Christian faith from the One whom most Christians regarded as its Founder, and it raised doubts about the significance of the real Jesus. Yet Kahler's views were to have a very profound impact on the most academically-accomplished NT scholar of the 20th century.

That was Rudolf Bultmann (1884-1976). He arose to spur the demise of critical investigation of the life of Jesus. A period thus ensued, called "The No Quest," that lasted until the mid-20th century.[89] Bultmann championed a radical, form-critical analysis of the Bible and an existentialist hermeneutic. His skeptical, anti-supernaturalistic conclusion was that the NT contains myths, e.g., Jesus' miracles and bodily resurrection. He regarded these as layers of husks that needed to be removed in order to get to the kernel. Bultmann therefore insisted that the NT gospels be "demythologized," resulting in disassociating the Jesus of history from the kerygmatic, post-Easter Christ of faith. He emphasized the latter and went so far as to allege that the NT gospels provide no reliable history of Jesus, so that the historical Jesus cannot be either the founder of Christianity or the origin of church Christology. He only insisted that Christianity adhere to belief that the man, Jesus of Nazareth, did indeed exist. So, Bultmann dismissed the quest for the historical Jesus as being irrelevant and futile in this renowned statement, "We can, strictly speaking, know almost nothing about the life and personality of Jesus since the early Christian sources [the NT gospels] show no interest in either."[90] On the positive side, Bultmann must be credited for emphasizing (1) the need for divine forgiveness, bestowed on the basis of

---

[85] Martin Kahler, *The So-called Historical Jesus and the Historic, Biblical Christ* [1892], tr. Carl E. Braaten (Philadelphia: Fortress, 1964).

[86] D.F. Strauss, *The Christ of Faith and the Jesus of History* [1865], tr. and ed. L.E. Keck (Philadelphia: Fortress, 1977).

[87] However, the expression "Christ of faith" seems inadequate. It suggests no more than belief that Jesus is the Christ whereas it is intended to refer to "the proclaimed, post-Easter Christ," who was declared as God.

[88] M. Kahler, *The So-Called Historical Jesus and the Historic, Biblical Christ*, 66.

[89] However, Dale C. Allison (*Resurrecting Jesus: The Earliest Christian Tradition and Its Interpreters* [New York: T. & T. Clark, 2005], 1-18, 23-26) provides a compelling assessment that an ongoing and therefore uninterrupted quest had continued throughout the 20th century.

[90] Rudolf Karl Bultmann, *Jesus and the Word* [1926], tr. Louise Pettibone Smith and Erminie Huntress Lantero (New York: Scribner's Sons, 1934), 9. This viewpoint has since been abandoned by contemporary scholars. E.g., N.T. Wright ("A Biblical Portrait of God," *The Changing Face of God: Lincoln Lectures in Theology 1996* [n.p.: Lincoln Cathedral Publications, 1996], 26) asserts, "If we do not know much of anything about Jesus, early Christianity remains inexplicable."

personal decision regarding the cross of Christ, and (2) pursuit of the virtue of self-denial.

The New Quest

In contrast, in 1953 one of Bultmann's former students, Ernst Kasemann (1906-1998), revived the quest for the historical Jesus. Now called "the New Quest," it began rather ironically with a lecture he delivered to the annual gathering of Bultmann and his former graduate students from the University of Marburg.[91] In this speech, Kasemann agrees with his teacher, as well as neo-orthodox theologian Karl Barth (1886-1968), that the NT gospels cannot be trusted in their entirety in presenting a historically-authentic life of Jesus. Yet Kasemann asserts that there must necessarily be a joining together of the Christ of faith with the Jesus of history by means of diligent, historical research. And he points out that some scholars had already begun to do so convincingly. Kasemann's primary reason is that no matter how much redaction material overlays the gospel records as we have them, it is quite obvious that the Evangelists understood their accounts to be solidly grounded in the historical facts of Jesus' life, death, and resurrection.

Thus began the post-Bultmanian era. Although Kasemann agreed with Bultmann, that a reconstruction of the historical Jesus was not possible, he nevertheless thereafter attempted to identify the supposedly authentic, primitive, "bare bones" christological texts in the NT. He did so largely by employing the same principles used in textual criticism for establishing a criterion of authenticity. One of those principles is "double dissimilarity," referred to as a "minimalist view" of the gospels. Kasemann's famous lecture resulted in several Bultmanian scholars also attempting to connect the Christ of faith with a reconstruction of the Jesus of history. Like Kasemann, some of them also returned to the traditional belief in the literal, bodily resurrection of Jesus.[92]

An interesting sidebar is that years earlier, in 1937, the German Gestapo arrested and imprisoned Kasemann for preaching against Nazi nationalism from Isa 27.13. And during this imprisonment he wrote the first draft of a book sympathetic to Jews, entitled *The Wandering People of God*. Kasemann thus not only revived The Quest; his positive approach to Jewish people helped set the stage for the development of its next level.

Another positive result from this critical analysis of Jesus was that some scholars determined that the NT contained many different christologies. (See Appendix C: Modern Christologies.) These christologies came to be classified as "from below" (functional Christology) or "from above" (ontological or essence Christology). Functional Christology focused on biblical texts, primarily those contained in the Synoptics, that portray God as acting through the man Jesus. Ontological, traditional Christology was generally perceived to be found only in the Johannine writings and perhaps some Pauline texts and the book of Hebrews because these supposedly depict the incarnation, i.e., the preexistent Jesus as literally coming down from heaven to become a man. These critics usually deemed a functional Christology as an authentic representation of the pristine faith of the early Christians; and they alleged that ontological Christology was strictly a later, fictional development.

---

[91] It was a paper, entitled "The Problem of the Historical Jesus," that was later translated and published in English in Kasemann's *Essays on New Testament Themes*, 15-47.
[92] J.D.G. Dunn (*Christology in the Making*, 3n16) provides a list of no less than sixty scholars whose books on the resurrection of Jesus were published during the 1950s and 1960s.

The Third Quest

In the last quarter of the 20th century, the so-called "Third Quest" for the historical Jesus arose with a clamor and continues to this day. It represents a broader investigation into the question, "Who was Jesus of Nazareth?" Its emphasis has been on understanding Jesus as a Jewish religious figure within the religious, social, and political milieu of 1st century Palestine. Distinguished contemporary Jesus researcher E.P. Sanders regards the NT gospels as fairly reliable for discovering the Jewishness of the historical Jesus. In contrast to Bultmann's assertion—that we know next to nothing about Jesus—Sanders insists, "We know a lot about Jesus."[93] The consensus of Third Quest scholars has been that Jesus was a Jewish prophet who preached the present and eschatological kingdom. An increasing number of Jewish scholars contributed to this Quest by reclaiming Jesus as a Jew, but only historically and thus without encountering Jesus spiritually.[94]

During more than the past century several liberal Jewish scholars contributed to the theme of the Jewishness of Jesus, though they did not represent any sort of official position of Judaism. They especially aided historical Jesus research, and thereby the investigation of Christian origins, in its pursuit of the study of ancient Jewish literature.

During the 1990s "The Jesus Seminar," which epitomizes the liberal wing of the Third Quest, gained considerable attention. Founded by Robert Funk in 1985, it now consists of about two hundred scholars.[95] The Seminar's main purpose has been to evaluate the authenticity of each purported saying of Jesus in the four NT gospels as well as the non-canonical Gospel of Thomas. Its findings were published in 1993 in a book entitled *The Five Gospels: The Search for the Authentic Words of Jesus*.[96] In this book, the Seminar allots no historical veracity whatsoever to any of the Johannine sayings of Jesus except one, in Jn 4.44. The Seminar assesses varying degrees of authenticity to what appears to be a slight majority of the synoptic sayings of Jesus.

The combined three stages of the quest for the historical Jesus are now referred to as "Life of Jesus Research" or simply "Jesus Research." This critical investigation of the life of Jesus continues unabated today, spreading most significantly in recent decades beyond seminary walls into the halls and classrooms of secular university campuses.[97] In fact, as we embark upon the 21st century, the Third Quest for the historical Jesus remains steadfastly in the forefront of all theological and biblical studies in the Western World.

---

[93] E.P. Sanders, *The Historical Figure of Jesus* (New York: Penguin, 1993), ix.
[94] Jakob Jocz, *The Jewish People and Jesus Christ: A Study in the Relationship Between the Jewish People and Jesus Christ* (London: SPCK, 1949), 7.
[95] Robert W. Funk, *Honest to Jesus: Jesus for a New Millennium* (New York: HarperSanFrancisco, 1996), 7. R. Funk's (p. 305) radical imbalance emerges when he states unabashedly, "Jesus himself should not be, must not be, the object of faith. That would be to repeat the idolatry of the first believers."
[96] Robert W. Funk and Roy W. Hoover, *The Five Gospels: The Search for the Authentic Words of Jesus* (New York: Polebridge Press, 1993). This book furnishes a list of seventy-four scholars who were "Fellows of the Jesus Seminar" at the time of its publication.
[97] M. Wiles (*Explorations in Theology 4*, ix) wrote in 1979, "Most theologians writing in England at the present time have an official position in the university rather than in the church. Though often ordained ministers of a church, it is the university which pays them and which provides the primary setting for their work."

Kenotic Christology

Recall that Chalcedonian Christology asserts that Jesus possessed both a human nature and a divine nature and that the latter consisted of all of the attributes of deity.

However, the NT gospels provide no substantial evidence that Jesus possessed, let alone exercised, the divine attributes of omnipotence, omnipresence, and omniscience. (Theologians designate these as God's "relative," "metaphysical" or "incommunicable" attributes in distinction from His "moral," "essential," "immanent" or "communicable" attributes of love, justice, truth, righteousness, holiness, etc.) Indeed, the NT begins with the synoptic portrait of a very human Jesus, and it cannot be harmonized easily with the ontological, classical Christology that became fully established at Chalcedon.

Consequently, during the early 17th century a debate arose among Lutheran theologians at the two most prominent universities in Germany, at Tubingen and Giessen, over how to resolve this perplexing problem. These professors endeavored to preserve their belief in the two natures of Jesus—that He was both fully man and fully God—and thereby affirm Nicene-Chalcedonian Christology.[98] Both schools thus taught that Jesus possessed all of the attributes of deity during His incarnation. The Tubingen school, however, proposed that Jesus *concealed* His relative attributes, so that He did not reveal them externally, but used them secretly. On the other hand, the Giessen school insisted that Jesus did not conceal His relative attributes but merely *chose not to exercise* them.[99]

Both of these proposals presented serious difficulties. For one thing, how could Jesus be God, and therefore possess omniscience, when He divulged that He did not know the time of His second coming (Mt 24.36/Mk13.32>)? These German Lutheran theologians answered that Jesus really *did know* in His divine nature, but in His human nature He either *knew only secretly* or *chose not to know*. So, according to Mt 24.36 and Mk 13.32 Jesus was expressing Himself solely from the source of His human nature. But this explanation did not escape the charge of duplicity, which impugns the moral integrity of Jesus. That is, how could Jesus be deemed an honest man if He said He did not know something when in fact He did? Also, both of these proposals arouse suspicion that Jesus was psychologically imbalanced and perhaps even the victim of a multi-personality disorder. Later, J.A.T. Robinson alleged that a God-man suggests an image of a hybrid.[100]

Interest thus waned in this dispute until the mid-19th century. Then German scholar Gottfried Thomasius (1802-1873), followed later by English scholars W.F. Gess (1819-1891) and Charles Gore (1853-1932), revived interest in this dispute by seeking to overcome these difficulties with a slightly different nuance. Thomasius proposed in his book *Christi Person und Werke* (1853) that at the incarnation the Logos *laid aside* His relative divine attributes of omniscience, omnipotence, and omnipresence out of necessity in becoming a man. So, Thomasius conceded that these divine attributes are incompatible with being fully human. For example, how can a human being be omnipresent?

Thomasius based his proposal on Phil 2.6-7>. He interpreted the phrases "form of God" and "equality with God" therein as referring to Christ's

---

[98] Colin Brown, "*kenos*," in *NIDNTT* 1:548.
[99] Some later scholars, e.g., V. Taylor (*The Person of Christ*, 293), contended that Jesus possessed these latent, relative attributes but that we cannot be sure if He realized it and that He had choice not to use them.
[100] John A.T. Robinson, "Need Jesus Have Been Perfect?" in *Christ Faith and History: Cambridge Studies in Christology*, eds. S.W. Sykes and J.P. Clayton (Cambridge: University, 1972), 39.

preincarnate state, i.e., His personal preexistence as the Logos when He was equal to God in essence, sharing all of His divine attributes. Thomasius insisted that at the incarnation the Logos "emptied" (Gr. *kenos*=empty; *kenoo*=to empty) Himself of all of His relative attributes. Thomasius' dependence on the word "emptied," in v. 7, gave rise to the label "kenosis theories" or "Kenotic Christology." By the end of the century, Kenotic Christology was declining in Germany whereas most British and American scholars were adopting some form of it.[101] Gore taught similarly in his books *Lux Mundi* (1889) and *Dissertations* (1895). Kenotic Christology was a middle ground between hardline traditionalists and historical critics.

However, scholars eventually realized that Thomasius' approach also encountered more problems than it resolved. While it safeguarded the humanity of Jesus, I.A. Dorner (1809-1884) alleged that a change in deity contradicts immutability (deity can't change), which is another divine attribute posited by classical theism. And such a divesting of *any* divine attributes would seem to represent a *reduction* in deity. That opposed what Paul had taught, that "all the fulness of Deity" existed in the earthly Jesus (Col 2.9; cf. 1.19).

More recently, an increasing number of traditionalist scholars have insisted that the only thing the Logos emptied Himself of at the incarnation was His majestic glory. Indeed, in Jesus' High Priestly prayer He seems to have asked the Father to restore to Him His pre-creation glory (Jn 17.5). However, Phil 2.7 provides no hint of an emptying of glory or of any particular divine attribute. Besides, this interpretation of a self-emptying of glory does not really resolve the two-nature dilemma.

Two-nature Christology came under further scrutiny in the 20th century with the rise of the discipline of psychology. Carl Jung alleged that the notion of Jesus having two natures was incompatible with the NT gospel portrait of Jesus as one who exemplifies what Jung termed "individuation," meaning psychological "undividedness." Jung thus claimed that two-nature Christology weakens the Christ-image as the archetypal self.[102]

Due to such insuperable difficulties in applying kenosis theories to the Jesus of the NT gospels, and especially to Phil 2.6-7, by the early second half of the 20th century Kenotic Christology had fallen out of favor with the majority of distinguished scholars.[103] Not only did they insist that the NT does not support it, they deemed it anthropologically and psychologically unsound as well as a diminishing of deity. Horace Bushnell, who adopted mostly a God-in-Christ Christology, well said of Jesus, "I shall not decompose him and label off his doings, one to the credit of his divinity, and another to the credit of his humanity. I shall receive him in simplicity of faith, as my one Lord and Savior."[104]

Nevertheless, this traditional two-nature exegesis of Scripture is still advocated by many Bible expositors today, especially those in the growing Evangelical movement.

---

[101] John Stewart Lawton, *Conflict in Christology* (New York: Macmillan, 1947), 164.

[102] Carl G. Jung, *Aion* in *The Collected Works of C.G. Jung* (New York: Routledge, 1959), 41-42.

[103] So says V. Taylor (*The Person of Christ*, 78), though he continued to embrace it. See also John Knox, *The Humanity and Divinity of Christ: A Study of Pattern in Christology* (Cambridge: University, 1967), 100-03; Donald M. Baillie, *God Was in Christ* (New York: Scribner's Sons, 1948), 94-98.

[104] Horace Bushnell, *God in Christ* (Hartford: Brown and Parsons, 1849), 164.

Other Modern Developments

In the late 19th and early 20th centuries, James Denney (1856-1917) was one of the most distinguished theologians of his generation. He carried on an extensive and lengthy correspondence with Sir W. Robertson Nicoll that included the subject of Jesus' identity. Denney had written a widely acclaimed book entitled *Jesus and the Gospel*. Nicoll wrote to Denney about it, alleging that he had failed to unequivocally affirm that Jesus is God. Denney wrote back, "If a man does not worship Christ, I do not care what he thinks,... [but] a form of proposition which in our idiom suggests inevitably the precise equivalence of Jesus and God does some kind of injustice to the truth."[105]

During the second quarter of the 20th century, the prolific Swiss theologian Karl Barth (1886-1968) arose to prominence. He reacted to his education in Liberal Theology by returning to Protestant orthodoxy to establish "neo-orthodoxy." Although Barth was difficult to comprehend, much of the Protestant Church adopted his neo-orthodoxy in its struggle against Liberal Theology. Barth affirmed the Trinity most vigorously in his monumental *Church Dogmatics* (13 vols., 1936-1977), yet he tried to redefine it. He was very christocentric in his theology, with his point of departure being the preexistence of Jesus. One of Barth's key points was his very arbitrary proposition that God has revealed Himself in Jesus Christ so that Christ reveals God, and whoever reveals God must be God as well. Thus, similar to Athanasius' argument that only God can save humans, Barth asserted that only God can reveal God. In a 1946 popular lecture series on the Apostles' Creed, Barth treaded conspicuously close to Docetism. Like his spiritual forebear, Martin Luther, Barth proclaimed, "This Jesus of Nazareth,... this man is the Jehovah of the Old Testament, is the Creator, is God himself."[106] Bultmann and Barth therefore eventually distanced themselves until they represented opposite ends of the christological spectrum.

The venerable C.S. Lewis (1898-1963) was an authority on English literature. Converted from atheism to Christianity, he became widely acclaimed as a fiction author. In 1943, he published his classic on Christian apologetics entitled *Mere Christianity*. It is one of the most famous books ever written that purports to define the Christian religion. In it, Lewis proclaims that the very essence of Christianity is that Jesus Christ is God and that He claimed to be God.[107] But Lewis does not support this latter assertion scripturally. Yet he describes Jesus as "a man who goes about talking as if He was God."[108] Then Lewis pens the following popular piece that some scholars call "the *trilemma* argument:"

> I am trying to prevent anyone saying the really foolish thing that people often say about Him: "I'm ready to accept Jesus as a great moral teacher, but I don't accept His claim to be God." That is the one thing we must not say. A man who was merely a man and said the sort of things Jesus said would not be a great moral teacher. He would either be a lunatic--on the level with the

---

[105] James Denney, *Letters of Principal James Denney to W. Robertson Nicoll (1883-1917)* (London: Hodder and Stoughton, 1920), 57. Quoted in *The Methodist Recorder* (1939); V. Taylor, "Does the New Testament Call Jesus God?" 116.

[106] Karl Barth, *Dogmatics in Outline* (London: SCM, 1949), 84.

[107] C.S. Lewis, *Mere Christianity* (New York: MacMillan, 1943). Lewis only offers implicit scriptural support by asserting that Jesus' claim to forgive sins (Mk 2.5>) "makes sense only if He really was ... God" (p. 55). He also insists that God became man (pp. 39, 91, 140), Jesus Christ is God (pp. 7-8, 55, 56, 60, 61, 63, 162), and Jesus claimed to be God (pp. 56, 63, 143, cf. 54). And Lewis has a large section on the doctrine of the Trinity, which doctrine he asserts "matters more than anything else in the world" (p. 153).

[108] C.S. Lewis, *Mere Christianity*, 54; idem, *The Case for Christianity* (New York: MacMillan, 1943), 44.

man who says he is a poached egg--or else he would be the Devil of Hell. You must make your choice. Either this man was, and is, the Son of God: or else a madman or something worse. You can shut him up for a fool, you can spit at him and kill him as a demon; or you can fall at his feet and call him Lord and God. But let us not come with any patronising nonsense about his being a great human teacher. He has not left that open to us. He did not intend to.

We are faced, then, with a frightening alternative. This man we are talking about either was (and is) just what He said or else a lunatic, or something worse.... I have to accept the view that He was and is God.[109]

To his credit, Lewis was opposing the liberal teaching of a moralistic Jesus whose life and death had no more significance than as a worthy moral example for us to follow. Yet, in this paragraph Lewis illogically leads us to choose between only three options regarding Jesus' identity: either He is (1) a lunatic, (2) the devil, or (3) God. Notice that Lewis herein follows the patristic practice of incorrectly equating the terms "God" and "the Son of God," the latter as applied to Jesus.[110] Lewis adds, "I have explained why I have to believe that Jesus was (and is) God.... I believe it on His authority."[111] Again, he provides no scriptural support and thus no statement by Jesus to affirm this assertion.

C.S. Lewis always disavowed being a theologian. He said modestly, "I am a very ordinary layman of the Church of England."[112] Indeed, his brilliant intellect, combined with such an unassuming nature, was the secret to so much admiration for C.S. Lewis.

J.A.T. Robinson surely had Lewis' trilemma argument in mind when he protested:

We are often asked to accept Christ as divine because he claimed to be so--and the familiar argument is pressed: 'A man who goes around claiming to be God must either be God--or else he is a madman or a charlatan' ... And, of course, it is not easy to read the Gospel story and to dismiss Jesus as either mad or bad. Therefore, the conclusion runs, he must be God.

I am not happy about this argument. None of the disciples in the Gospels acknowledged Jesus because he claimed to be God, and the Apostles never went out saying, "This man claimed to be God, therefore you must believe in him."[113]

No one has worked Lewis' trilemma argument more than American Evangelical Josh McDowell.[114] This popular, public speaker and evangelist is one of the world's leading voices declaring that Jesus is God. He has authored over 100 books, with over 42 million copies in print. But his lengthy, apologetic works consist mostly of quotations rather than structured arguments. He doesn't interact with leading Jesus researchers.[115] Without discussion, McDowell presupposes that the NT identification of Jesus as the Son of God means that He

---

[109] C.S. Lewis, *Mere Christianity*, 55-56; also almost verbatim in *The Case for Christianity*, 45.
[110] C.S. Lewis was usually a very logical thinker and a cogent author. However, in his best-selling book, *The Screwtape Letters*, on pp. 116-120 he implicitly defends traditional Christology against the biblical criticism of his time by illogically arguing that any quest for the historical Jesus is the work of the devil and that Christians therefore should ignore such an endeavor.
[111] C.S. Lewis, *Mere Christianity*, 63.
[112] E.g., C.S. Lewis, *Mere Christianity*, 6, cf. 39. Lewis is answering the question about "what Christians believe" (p. 43), i.e., "the belief that has been common to nearly all Christians at all times" (p. 6).
[113] John A.T. Robinson, *Honest to God* (Philadelphia: Westminster, 1963), 71-72. See also D. Cupitt, *Jesus and the Gospel of God*, 15.
[114] E.g., Josh McDowell, *The New Evidence that Demands a Verdict* (Nashville: Thomas Nelson, 1999), 157; idem, *Evidence for Christianity* (Nashville: Thomas Nelson, 2006), 378.
[115] E.g., British scholars Geza Vermes, N.T. Wright, and James D.G. Dunn and American scholars E.P. Sanders, Marcus J. Borg, and John Domminic Crossan, all of them prolific writers.

is God.[116] And in identifying Jesus as God, he rarely cites modern writers with opposing views and treats the critical, biblical texts very sparingly.[117]

Likewise, some traditionalist expositors fail to distinguish between the concepts of God *being in* Christ and Christ *being* God. British expositor John R.W. Stott seems to make this error. He is an esteemed worldwide church leader, pastor, educator, and author in the burgeoning evangelical community. Following C.S. Lewis, John Stott authored the highly-acclaimed *Basic Christianity* (1958). In it, he asserts rather startlingly, "If Jesus was not God in human flesh, Christianity is exploded."[118] Then he expounds almost in the same breath, "The Christian claim is that we can find God in Jesus Christ."[119] Indeed we can, but God *in* Christ is not the same as Christ *being* God, as Stott seems to imply.

Nels Ferre, on the other hand, recognizes this important distinction in concepts. He explains, "There is a decisive difference between the affirmation that Jesus Christ is God and Saviour and that God was in Christ reconciling the world to Himself."[120]

The World Council of Churches

Talk about declaring unequivocally that Jesus Christ is "God and Saviour," that is exactly what the World Council of Churches (WCC) did when it was first formed in 1948 at Amsterdam. It drafted a brief, one sentence, confessional statement as the basis for its existence. Called the "basis statement," it declares, "The World Council of Churches is composed of Churches which acknowledge Jesus Christ as God and Saviour."

When the WCC was created, the liberal and modernist vs. fundamentalist and conservative debate among Christian churches was in full swing on both sides of the Atlantic. The conservative Eastern Orthodox and Roman Catholic Churches feared the liberalism that was permeating some quarters of Protestantism. Consequently, this assertion by the WCC—that Jesus Christ is God—was inserted into its basis statement to appease these Catholics and thereby secure the largest possible membership.[121]

"God and Saviour" in this basis statement apparently was drawn from Tit 2.13> as rendered in some versions. Catholic R.E. Brown thought so, and he deemed this an "unfortunate" development by claiming that this translation of Tit 2.13 is "uncertain."[122]

No one objected more strenuously to this WCC basis statement than did Rudolf Bultmann. And he is generally recognized as the most brilliant NT scholar of the 20th century. In 1951, Bultmann delivered a famed lecture in which he alleged, "The formula 'Christ is God' is false in every sense in which God is understood as an entity which can be objectified, whether it is understood in an Arian or Nicene, an Orthodox or a Liberal sense. It is correct, if 'God' is understood here as the event of God's acting. But my question is, ought one not rather to avoid such formulae on account of misunderstanding and cheerfully

---

[116] E.g., J. McDowell, *Evidence for Christianity*, 352-56, 366-67, 374.
[117] E.g., J. McDowell, *The New Evidence that Demands a Verdict*, 141-48; idem, *Evidence for Christianity*, 369-74.
[118] John R.W. Stott, *Basic Christianity*, 2nd ed. (Downers Grove, IL: Inter-Varsity, 1971), 8.
[119] J.R.W. Stott, *Basic Christianity*, 9.
[120] Nels F.S. Ferre, "Is the Basis of the World Council Heretical?" *ExpT* 74 (1962-63): 67.
[121] N.F.S. Ferre, "Is the Basis of the World Council Heretical?" 66-67.
[122] R.E. Brown, *Jesus God and Man*, 18.

content oneself with saying that he is the Word of God?"[123] Bultmann later wrote, "in describing Christ as 'God' the New Testament still exercises great restraint."[124] Vincent Taylor declared this remark "an understatement."[125]

But Bultmann's controversial objection fell on deaf ears within the WCC. Instead, WCC authorities later *augmented* this basis statement by inserting the phrase, "according to the scriptures." And they later *expanded* it to include the full Trinitarian formula as follows: "the one God, Father, Son and Holy Spirit."

Nels Ferre was a charter member of the WCC's Faith and Order Commission. Its purpose was to examine christological issues. Ferre, too, objected to this basis statement, even at the time of its formulation. But he discloses that his objection was not addressed. Ferre provides the following reasons why he charged the basis statement with error:

1. "[It] is severely heretical from the point of view of the Christian faith;... It is true neither to the full, central New Testament picture of Christ nor to its historical development by the fathers of the Church.... The statement of the World Council, 'Jesus is God,' is sheer Docetism. It makes no mention of Jesus' humanity. Jesus is not God but the Son of God." (Ferre rightly distinguishes a significant difference between the terms "God" and "the Son of God," the latter as it pertains to Jesus.)
2. "It stands in the way of effective relations to other religions and to the world in general. If the basis were both Christian and true, then I should not mind either its offensiveness or its poverty as a means of communicating and relating the faith.... the basis constitutes a false obstacle to communication with the other religions of the world.... Is it not unfortunate to have to carry on such conversation from an untenable and divisive basis?"[126]

What about inter-dialogue among Christian denominations? Catholic scholar R.E. Brown points out that "in Protestant-Catholic dialogue a preference on the part of some Protestants for avoiding the phraseology 'Jesus is God' is quite prevalent."[127] In 1979, D. Cupitt claimed, "few theologians would accept that formula without qualification."[128]

Christianity and Islam

Judaism, Christianity, and Islam are the three great monotheistic religions of the world. It would be remiss in this book not to at least consider briefly the theology of Islam, since this religion rivals Christianity as the second largest religion in the world.

The teachings of Islam are not as far removed from biblical Christianity as is commonly thought in the West.[129] Many Christian scholars and historians acknowledge, now, that Islam was founded under the influence of remnants of Jewish Christianity.[130]

---

[123] R. Bultmann, *Essays*, 287.
[124] Rudolf Karl Bultmann, *Theology of the New Testament*, 2 vols. (London: SCM, 1952-55), 1:129.
[125] V. Taylor, "Does the New Testament Call Jesus God?" 118.
[126] N.F.S. Ferre, "Is the Basis of the World Council Heretical?" 67-68.
[127] R.E. Brown, *Jesus God and Man*, 3.
[128] Don Cupitt, "Jesus and the Meaning of God," in *Incarnation and Myth: The Debate Continued*, ed. M.D. Goulder, 31.
[129] For a recent, brief, and unusually favorable assessment of Islam by a world-class Roman Catholic scholar spearheading dialogue with it, see H. Kung, *Christianity: Essence, History, and Future*, 105-10.
[130] E.g., O. Cullmann, *Christology*, 50.

Many untutored Christians have thought that because Muslims call their God "Allah," they must worship another god than that of the Judeo-Christian faith. On the contrary, *allah* is merely the Arabic word for "god." Plus, Islam recognizes Allah as the God of the original Bible. (Muslims allege, as does the Koran, that the Bible was not transmitted properly through the ages and is therefore corrupted.) Whether Islam's Allah and the Judeo-Christian God are characterized the same or differently is another matter.

The creed of Islam is called "the Shahada." This Arabic word means "to testify" or "to bear witness." The Shahada is a brief formula: "There is no God but Allah, and Mohammed is his prophet." The first half of Shahada is very similar to the beginning of the Jews' Shema: "YHWH is our God; YHWH is one." According to Islam, merely reciting the Shahada is what makes a person a Muslim. Muslims are required to recite the Shahada regularly every day, just as Jews are required to recite the Shema twice a day.

Many Jews and Muslims believe they are truly monotheistic and that Christians are not monotheistic but tritheistic, i.e., worshipping three gods. Of course, Trinitarians strongly object to this portrayal. We have seen that many anti-Trinitarians who also claim to be Christian agree with this assessment and allege that Trinitarianism is the greatest theological obstacle to inter-religious dialogue for Christians with Jews and Muslims.

While Muslims reject the deity of Christ, they esteem Jesus highly. They regard Him and Mohammed as two of the four greatest prophets of Allah, Mohammed being the last and greatest. Muslims also ascribe to Jesus a most virtuous life, although they do not acknowledge that He was sinless. They also affirm that Jesus did miracles (Qur'an 5:110) and that He was Israel's Messiah. Muslims even believe that Jesus ascended into heaven and that He will literally return to earth in glory. Muslims strongly affirm the resurrection and judgment day, two most prominent themes in the Koran, and that Jesus will have an important role in administering them. So, the Koran calls Jesus, "Illustrious in this world and the next" (Qur'an 3.45). Yet Muslims insist that Jesus was no more than a man.

Few Christians know that Muslims believe strongly in the virgin birth of Jesus. It is clearly stated in their Koran (Qur'an 19.16-22; 21.91; 66.12). Yet they do not attribute a virgin birth to Mohammed, which seems to make Jesus greater in dignity. And Muslims affirm an Adam Christology, in which Adam and Jesus entered the world supernaturally. In contrast, many professing Christian scholars of the 20th century rejected the concept of the virgin birth and thus treated the two NT infancy narratives about Jesus as fiction. And not a few of these scholars denied that Jesus did miracles or arose from the dead.

Mohammed was a caravan trader prior to his religious conversion at age forty. During his many treks from Mecca to Damascus and other cities, he apparently had much contact with Jewish Christians. (Also, Mohammed's hometown of Medina, formerly Yathrib, was founded by Jews.) They must have been remnants of the Nazarenes because Mohammed seems to have adopted from them his belief in Jesus' virgin birth and strong resistance to trinitarianism. Historian Joan Taylor says concerning the word *Nazoraeans*, "the Aramic-derived word and its cognates (as opposed to the Greek-derived term 'Christians') became the normative reference to believers in Christ in Persia, Arabia, Armenia, Syria, and Palestine."[131]

---

[131] Joan E. Taylor, *Christians and Holy Places: The Myth of Jewish Christian Holy Origins* (Oxford: University, 1993), 24n17. Quoted by Wolfram Kinzig, "The Nazoraeans," in *Jewish Believers in Jesus*, O. Skarsaune and R. Hvalvik, eds. 470.

The only major christological differences between Islam and biblical Christianity regard (1) the supremacy of Jesus, (2) how He died, and (3) His death's soteriological significance. Muslims are not in agreement about the historical circumstances of Jesus' death, and thus His resurrection, because the Koran is unclear about it (Qur'an 4:157-58). Some Muslims believe Jesus died on the cross; others think He was crucified but didn't die; most believe He was never crucified but that someone else, who resembled Him, was crucified. Muslims allege that even if Jesus died on a cross, He could not have atoned for sins. Like Jews, Muslims deplore Jesus' cross as a scandal, linking it with the Crusades.

Muslims deny that Jesus was the Son of God. They argue that monotheism does not logically allow for God to have an actual son. But this denial must be understood in accordance with traditional Christology as well as the common Muslim misunderstanding of it. Muslims reject the church dogma that Jesus is the ontological Son who is essentially equal to God. The Koran states, "Allah is one, the Eternal God,... none is equal to him" (Qur'an 112.3). In fact, the Koran condemns any person to hell who equates a human being with Allah (e.g., Qur'an 4.48). But most Muslims wrongly think that Christians teach that Jesus is the Son of God by literal procreation, in which God engaged in sexual relations with Mary, resulting in the Child Jesus being conceived in Mary's womb. There has been considerable ignorance on the part of both Christians and Muslims about each other's faith. Consequently, inter-religious dialogue between them should be encouraged.

The Islamic Empire, called "the Caliphate," extended from Spain to the Indus River in the 9th-11th centuries. Certain esteemed Muslim scholars of the early 9th century wrote lucidly against the incarnation, appealing almost entirely to the NT. They argued that Christianity departed from its original traditions, citing comparisons between the NT and patristic writings. One of these scholars, Ali al-Tabari, was a Christian missionary who converted to Islam at age seventy. He alleged that the four gospels and Paul's letters contain about 20,000 verses that characterize Jesus as human; yet Christians, especially the Nicean church fathers, interpreted them in light of a mere ten "unclear statements" in the NT. (He refers mostly to the major *theos* texts listed in Chapter One.) Historian David Thomas explains that "for him Christian doctrines about Christ have nothing to do with the origins of Christianity itself."[132] Indeed, these Muslim theologians argued as follows: (1) there is no explanation in the Bible of how God became a man, (2) it is unreasonable to assert that Jesus is God if He died, and (3) the church's two-nature doctrine of Christ is most illogical. Thus, these Muslim scholars argued as did Jewish Christians before them.

Modern World Evangelism

What about Christian evangelists and missionaries around the world in recent times? Do they believe that the deity of Christ is essential to their message of salvation?

In 1974, 2,700 evangelists from 150 nations gathered in Lausanne, Switzerland, for the first "International Congress on World Evangelism."[133] It was convened by the Billy Graham Evangelistic Association and attended by

---

[132] David Thomas, ed. and tr., *Early Muslim Polemic against Christianity: Abu Isa al-Warraq's "Against the Incarnation"* (Cambridge: University, 2002), 41.
[133] The next time the Congress was held, in 1989, 6,000 evangelists attended.

the world-renowned evangelist himself. This Congress formed the "Lausanne Committee for World Evangelization," which is still the largest evangelical organization in the world that promotes Christian evangelism. The Congress also drafted a statement of faith, called "the Lausanne Covenant." Its first article begins, "We affirm our belief in the one-eternal God, Creator and Lord of the world, Father, Son and Holy Spirit." This statement is more likely to be understood as modalistic monarchianism than as trinitrarianism, as it is intended.

In 1983, 3,800 evangelists from 132 nations met in Amsterdam to attend the "First International Conference for Itinerant Evangelists."[134] This Conference drafted a set of articles that defined their noble mission of world evangelization. Called "The Amsterdam Affirmations," they begin, "We confess Jesus Christ as God, our Lord and Savior, who is revealed in the Bible." This statement implies that the salvation message preached by the attending evangelists includes the proposition that Jesus is God and that this axiom is supported in the Bible. Yet we saw clearly in Chapter One that none of the evangelistic messages recorded in the NT declare that Jesus Christ is God.

In 1999, a group of fifteen Evangelical leaders drafted an extensive doctrinal statement of approximately ten pages in length that purportedly defines the NT gospel. It is entitled, "The Gospel of Jesus Christ: An Evangelical Celebration." This drafting committee included leading Evangelical scholars J.I. Packer, D.A. Carson, R.C. Sproul, and John Woodbridge. Over 200 Evangelical leaders and scholars signed this declaration. The list of signatories includes such illustrious men of God as Billy Graham, Bill Bright, Jerry Falwell, Pat Robertson, Charles Colson, John Stott, Charles Swindoll, John Walvoord, and many other well-known names.[135] Their statement describes Jesus Christ as "God the Son, the second Person of the Holy Trinity." It continues, "We affirm that faith in Jesus Christ as the divine Word (or Logos, John 1:1), the second Person of the Trinity, co-eternal and co-essential with the Father and the Holy Spirit (Heb. 1:3), is foundational to faith in the Gospel. We deny that any view of Jesus Christ which reduces or rejects his full deity is Gospel faith or will avail to salvation. We affirm that Jesus Christ is God incarnate (John 1:14)."[136] The drafters claim that their statement reflects the major creeds of Christianity. Indeed. But do these excerpts from it reflect the Bible?

British Scholars

In contrast, during the 1960s an increasing number of distinguished British scholars began questioning whether the NT identifies Jesus as God. William Barclay wrote in 1962, "One of the most vexed questions in Christian thought and language is whether or not we can directly and simply call Jesus God."[137] That same year Vincent Taylor wrote about identifying Jesus as "God," saying, "Some scholars do speak of Him in this way, while others who hold the highest estimate of His Person hesitate to use this name and feel a sense of uneasiness when they hear it applied to Him."[138] The following year John A.T. Robinson

---

[134] The next time the Conference was held, in 1986, 8,000 evangelists attended.
[135] *This We Believe: The Good News of Jesus Christ for the World*, eds. John N. Akers, John H. Armstrong, and John D. Woodbridge (Grand Rapids: Zondervan, 2000), 18, 249-52.
[136] Quoted from *This We Believe*, 239, 245. Also see it in *Christianity Today*, June 1999.
[137] W. Barclay, *Jesus As They Saw Him*, 20.
[138] V. Taylor, "Does the New Testament Call Jesus God?" 116. Raymond E. Brown (*The Epistles of John* in AB, 626) later stated the same thing, that "there is an uneasiness (sometimes unexpressed) among scholars about NT texts that call Jesus 'God.'"

penned this statement, "The New Testament says that Jesus was the Word of God, it says that God was in Christ, it says that Jesus is the Son of God; but it does not say that Jesus was God, simply like that."[139] Robinson wrote briefly on the church doctrine of the Trinity, in which he reveals that he "attempted to contribute to the reconstruction that lies ahead,"[140] echoing Schleiermacher's quote above. Then Robinson summarizes the claims of Jesus with this classic statement, *"Jesus never claims to be God, personally; yet he always claims to bring God, completely."*[141]

In 1968, American G.H. Boobyer reported, "the last thirty or forty years has been leading an increasing number of reputable New Testament scholars to the conclusion that Jesus ... certainly never believed himself to be God." Boobyer added, "critical study of the Gospels discloses a Jesus with no consciousness of being God and making no claim to be God."[142] *A complete discontinuity between Jesus' claims about Himself and assertions about Him by church fathers would prove to be a fatal flaw in traditional Christology.* As Boobyer indicates, this is the conclusion to which critical study leads.

The most significant Christological development in Britain during the last quarter of the 20th century was the book, *The Myth of God Incarnate* (1977).[143] In this series of essays, seven contributing British scholars, all of them members of the Church of England in good standing, oppose the classical understanding of incarnation—that God literally became a man. They allege that the doctrine of incarnation (1) was a later development not supported in the earliest NT texts, (2) its hypostatic union of two natures in Jesus is incoherent, and (3) it is unessential to Christian faith. This book stirred a maelstrom throughout the United Kingdom, arousing a scholarly debate that resulted in the publication of other books on the incarnation, some favorable and others not.[144]

One of the contributing authors to *The Myth of God Incarnate* was Don Cupitt. He asserts therein, "The New Testament does not teach the later standard doctrine that Jesus is a distinct, divine person co-equal, co-essential and co-eternal with God the Father. It exalts Jesus as high as is possible without compromising monotheism."[145]

A.E. Harvey, later chaplain of Westminster Abbey, agreed with these authors. He alleged that in the NT there is no "direct evidence that Jesus was divine." He concluded, "the doctrine of the divinity of Christ, the whole enterprise must be abandoned."[146]

Traditionalist Klaas Runia has summarized this academic situation as a "new mood in European theology, which became manifest at the end of the sixties and

---

[139] J.A.T. Robinson, *Honest to God*, 70.
[140] John A.T. Robinson, *The Priority of John* [1985], Amer. ed., ed. J.F. Coakley (Oak Park, IL: Meyer-Stone, 1987), 397. He did so esp. in "The Fourth Gospel and the Church's Doctrine of the Trinity," in *Twelve More New Testament Studies*, 171-80.
[141] J.A.T. Robinson, *Honest to God*, 73. Emphasis mine. This statement by Robinson probably best sums up the thesis of this (my) book.
[142] G.H. Boobyer, "Jesus As 'Theos' in the New Testament," 251-52.
[143] John Hick, ed., *The Myth of God Incarnate* (London: SCM, 1977). See the enthusiastic Arab-Muslim response to it in the book by Abdus-Samad Sharafuddin entitled *About "The Myth of God Incarnate:" An Impartial Survey of its Main Topics* (Jeddah, Saudi Arabia, 1978).
[144] The following scholars opposed it: Don Cupitt, *The Debate About Christ* (1979); Michael Goulder, ed., *Incarnation and Myth: The Debate Continued* (1979).
[145] D. Cupitt, *Jesus and the Gospel of God*, 18.
[146] A.E. Harvey, "Christology and the Evidence of the New Testament," in *God Incarnate: Story and Belief*, A.E. Harvey, ed. (London: SPCK, 1981), 52.

throughout the seventies, and was evidenced by a clear and consistent rejection of Chalcedon and its doctrine of the two natures of Christ united in the person of the Son, that is, the second Person of the Trinity. The starting point of the new Christologies is that Jesus is man, and no more than man."[147]

The New Dutch Christology

Nowhere has this alternative Christology movement been more prominent than in Holland. It has not been a revival of Liberal Theology—which was antisupernatural and reckoned no saving significance to Jesus' death—but has been more conservative. Called "the New Dutch Christology," it started in 1966. The RCC's Piet Schoonenberg was its pioneer with his book, *The Christ* (1969).[148] In it, he asserts that we should not think of Jesus as a God-man but as God-in-man, which is God-in-Christ Christology. But in an apparent attempt to remain Roman Catholic, Schoonenberg attempted to reinterpret the ecumenical creeds and the doctrine of the Trinity. Theologian Ellen Flesseman-van Leer agreed with Schoonenberg's reconstructed Christology, except she denied the virgin birth. She went a step further by affirming Jesus' mission as Savior, Redeemer, and Reconciler. She also assented to Jesus' literal resurrection from the dead. Then she adds,

> I cannot believe in a trinitarian God ... The Son Jesus Christ is not God, but a man who is so fully one with God that I encounter God in him; and the Spirit is not an entity alongside God the Father, but is God himself who shares himself with me, the power of his presence,.... The doctrine of the trinity is not explicitly formulated by any ecclesiastical council.... It is generally recognized in our time that the trinitarian formula is incomprehensible for people today.... I regard it as nothing lost if we drop this doctrine,... [and] the traditional doctrine of the incarnation.[149]

Perhaps the most important proponent of the New Dutch Christology has been theologian Hendrikus Berkhof. In his book, *Christian Faith* (1979), he clearly affirms the cardinal Christian doctrines regarding Jesus, except for the virgin birth, and says of Him,

> In the New Testament, nothing is proclaimed about him which would be nonhuman or extra-human.... Jesus is man, the perfected covenant man, *the* new man, the eschatological man.... Are there two subjects in him? No, he is not a dual being.
>
> ....
>
> Can we then, however, still speak of God's becoming man? That, however, is an expression which is not derived from the NT.... there are a few times, on account of the intimate union of God and man in him, Jesus is called "God" (in any case in John 20:28; Tit. 2:13, and 1 John 5:20),... What we have here is a covenantal functionality which only in this way agrees with the numerous statements in which Jesus distinguishes himself from God, or is distinguished from God by the writers.[150]

While these theologians should not be ignored, they often ignore critical NT texts altogether, or their exegetical treatment of them generally leaves something to be desired.

---

[147] Klass Runia, "Continental Christologies," in *Crisis in Christology*, ed. W.R. Farmer, 15.
[148] Piet Schoonenberg, *The Christ: A Study of the God-man Relationship in the Whole of Creation and in Jesus Christ* [1969], tr. Della Couling (New York: Herder and Herder, 1971).
[149] Ellen Flesseman-van Leer, *A Faith for Today* [1972], tr. John E. Steely (Macon, GA: Association of Baptist Professors of Religion, 1980), 88-89.
[150] Hendrikus Berkhof, *Christian Faith: An Introduction to the Study of Faith* [1979], tr. Sierd Woudstra, rev. ed. (Grand Rapids: Eerdmans, 1986), 291, 294). Emphasis not mine.

Roman Catholic Scholars

Recall that Roman Catholic scholars have not enjoyed the freedom to question their theological traditions, and therefore freely explore theological studies, as their Protestant counterparts have been.[151] For instance, during the first half of the 20th century the RCC thoroughly expunged from its ranks what it perceived as "Modernism" in order to preserve the christological determinations of its ancient ecumenical councils.[152] Roman Catholic scholar Joseph A. Fitzmyer wrote in 1986 that this Church reaction "cast a dark cloud of fear over Catholic biblical studies in the first part of this [20th] century and induced a mentality of suspicion about any kind of critical or historical study of the Gospels and the NT—a mentality that still persists among many pastors, teachers, and faithful in the Church today."[153]

But the scholastic climate within Roman Catholicism changed dramatically in the second half of the 20th century. It began rather unnoticeably in the 1940s under Pope Pius XII.[154] But the date most cited is 1964, when Vatican II opened a window of fresh air in the RCC that has been inhaled theologically ever since.

However, substantial change in monolithic organizations often takes time. Take, for instance, two of the most distinguished RCC theologians in the latter half of the 20th century: Dutchman Edward Schillebeeckx and Swiss Hans Kung.[155] Church officials attempted to silence them somewhat because they did not admit in their writings that Jesus Christ is God, though they did affirm that God was in Christ. Kung even outright denies classical incarnation. Consequently, the RCC forever banned him from teaching Roman Catholics. Kung's Christology can be summed up as follows: Jesus is God's agent *par excellence*, who reveals the one true God. Joseph A. Fitzmyer, however, points out that throughout Kung's several publications he fails to discuss the two most important biblical texts that traditionalists contend affirm Christ's deity: Jn 1.1c> and 20.28>.[156]

In 1980, the esteemed RCC's Pontifical Biblical Institute's commission, which consisted of twenty elite scholars worldwide, issued a cautious statement approving form-criticism as applied to the Bible. This statement supported a previous one it had made, in 1964.[157] Due to such changes, Protestant theologian John Macquarrie wrote in 1990, "the leadership in theology today belongs to Roman Catholic writers."[158]

There is often a considerable lag time for theological developments to pass from the academic level down to church laity. One reason, mentioned earlier by Catholic R.E. Brown, is that there was a problem with Church authorities "instructing Catholic biblical scholars not to discuss delicate subjects on a popular level.... We simply have to face the fact that the discussion of delicate subjects cannot be kept from the public."[159]

---

[151] R.E. Brown, *Jesus God and Man*, 39-45; idem, *An Introduction to New Testament Christology*, 7-8.
[152] The RCC began this purging by excommunicating theologian Alfred Loisy in 1908. For an account of it, see Bernard B. Scott, "Introduction," in A. Loisy's *The Gospel and the Church*, xi-xiii.
[153] J.A. Fitzmyer, *Scripture & Christology*, 64-65.
[154] R.E. Brown, *An Introduction to New Testament Christology*, 9.
[155] See esp. Edward Schillebeeckx, *Jesus: An Experiment in Christology* [1974], tr. Hubert Hoskins (New York: Seabury, 1979); Hans Kung, *On Being a Christian* [1974], tr. Edward Quinn (Garden City: Doubleday, 1976); idem, *Does God Exist?: An Answer for Today*, tr. Edward Quinn (Garden City, NY: Doubleday, 1980).
[156] J.A. Fitzmyer, *Scripture & Christology*, 80.
[157] Pontifical Biblical Commission, *On the Historical Truth of the Gospels* (1964).
[158] J. Macquarrie, *Jesus Christ in Modern Thought*, 304.
[159] R.E. Brown, *Jesus God and Man*, 42n7.

Bible et christologie

In 1983, the Pontifical Biblical Commission issued its benchmark document on Christology entitled *Bible et christologie* (The Bible and Christology). It analyzes various modern christological approaches and well summarizes what the Bible affirms about Christology. This document advocates an integrated, unified Christology resulting from a consideration of all the relevant biblical data, and it rejects the tendency of historical-critical scholars to focus only on what they presume to be older NT writings, as if only these reflect the pristine Christian faith. The following excerpt is a surprising self-critique of the RCC's unscriptural terminology contained in its Nicene and Chalcedonian creeds.

> 1.2.1. *The approach of Classical Theology* encounters two hazards:
> 1.2.1.1. The formulation of doctrine about Christ *depends* more on *the language of theologians of the patristic period and the Middle Ages* than on the language of the New Testament itself, as if this ultimate source of the revelation (about him) were less accurate and less suited to setting forth a doctrine in well-defined terms.
> 1.2.1.2. Recourse to the New Testament, if it is had with the sole concern of defending or establishing the so-called "traditional" doctrine in its "classical" formulation, runs the risk of *not being open*, as it ought to be, to *certain critical questions* that cannot be avoided in the exegetical area.... So it can happen that doctrinal propositions are made to rest on critical conclusions that are too "conservative," when in reality they are controversial [emphasis not added].
> ....
> 1.2.2.1. The "auxiliary" languages employed in the Church in the course of centuries do not enjoy the same authority, as far as faith is concerned, as the "referential language" of the inspired [NT] authors,... distinctions and analyses necessary for research cannot be made if the express affirmations of Scripture are done away with.

The Commission chose American NT scholar Joseph A. Fitzmyer to write a commentary on this document. Published in 1986, Fitzmyer explains that what the commission meant by the above words was that "the NT data about Christ had been reconceptualized or reformulated" by the ecumenical church councils, even risking denial of scriptural teaching itself.[160] In 1991, Fitzmyer further wrote about Chalcedon's presupposition that Jesus possessed two natures and thus two intellects. He alleges, "the New Testament gives no inkling of the teaching of Chalcedon. That council not only reformulated in other language the New Testament data about Jesus' constitution, but also reconceptualized it in the light of the current Greek philosophical thinking. And that reconceptualization and reformulation go well beyond the New Testament data."[161]

Call for a Revised Christology

So, it is no longer only non-Catholic, liberal, or critical scholars the likes of Schleiermacher, Harnack, and Bultmann who have called for a reconstruction of church Christology. As Jesus studies mount, Richard France observes that many contemporary NT scholars of various church backgrounds and theological persuasions admit to a "widespread dissatisfaction with the classical statement of the Council of Chalcedon," thus recognizing the need for a reconstructed Christology.[162] Traditionalist Klaas Runia admits that, since the early 1980s, the Third Quest for the historical Jesus has launched "a thoroughgoing reconsideration and reconstruction of the traditional Christology."[163]

---

[160] J.A. Fitzmyer, *Scripture & Christology*, 57.
[161] J.A. Fitzmyer, *A Christological Catechism*, 102.
[162] Richard T. France, "Christology," in NT*CERK*, 182.
[163] K. Runia, *The Present-Day Christological Debate*, 66.

Besides dissenting Catholics Schillebeeckx and Kung, even some distinguished, conservative Catholic scholars have been calling for a revision of traditional Christology. Consider Aloys Grillmeier, the world's foremost authority on patristic theology. Over thirty-five years ago he began insisting, "the demand for a complete reappraisal of the Church's belief in Christ right up to the present day is an urgent one."[164]

Finally, we have seen that the last two centuries have produced the disciplines of biblical criticism, the History of Religions School, and three stages of Jesus Research, all of which have resulted in thrusting NT scholarship to a higher level. G.H. Boobyer therefore queries, "In the light of the knowledge now at the disposal of New Testament scholarship—knowledge so much greater than that possessed by the Fathers—does not this christological problem call for a fresh and far more thoroughgoing elucidation?"[165]

Don Cupitt has well summarized the development of Christology to the present:

> Classical Christianity had assumed the unity of scripture and tradition, and while that was assumed it was impossible to question the process of development. People then did not have our sort of historical consciousness. They took it absolutely for granted that Jesus, Paul, and the contemporary church were all unanimous. But once a real historical development of doctrine was admitted things could never be the same again. The Protestants might like to pretend that the New Testament taught a single faith, and that the New Testament faith was identical with the faith they themselves professed. But in the end they could not help recognizing doctrinal differences ... between the New Testament and their own doctrines. Today we have to admit that the age of religious innocence is over. Once we understand biblical criticism and the human, historically conditioned character of religious ideas, our viewpoint must change....
>
> To see this is to realize that the age of dogmatic Christianity is ending and that we are moving into a new era. The change of outlook that is called for is very considerable. It is not a shift from conservative definiteness to liberal woolliness, but a shift from dogmatic to critical faith.[166]

Consequently, some people are now calling for a thoroughgoing reformation, just as the Anabaptists, Socinians, and Unitarians did during the early Protestant Reformation. A few of these folks are calling themselves "New Reformation Christians." Don Cupitt concludes, "So today a reformation more thorough than Luther's is called for: there is no other way of restoring the real Jesus to his proper centrality in Christian faith."

Summary

The following is a summary of the major reasons showing an urgent need for a reexamination of the identity of Jesus leading to a revised church Christology:
- The patristic church was heavily influenced by Hellenistic ideas about God that could not be adequately substantiated from Scripture. Furthermore, in modern times reputable scholars from both inside and outside the church have increasingly challenged many prominent features of classical theism upon which traditional Christology was founded.
- The terms, and therefore categories, employed in the development of traditional Christology were borrowed from metaphysical ideas of Greek religio-philosophy. This terminology was not intelligible for succeeding

---

[164] Aloys Grillmeier, *Christ in Christian Tradition* [1965], tr. Alois Grillmeier (Philadelphia: Westminster, 1975), 495.
[165] G.H. Boobyer, "Jesus As 'Theos' in the New Testament," 251.
[166] D. Cupitt, *Jesus and the Gospel of God*, 22-23.

generations or very useful in biblical exegesis. Instead, the identity of Jesus needs to be described in contemporary language that is both understandable to moderns as well as biblically harmonious. The result will inevitably be a more functional, and less ontological, Christology.

- The disparity between the various stages of christological belief that developed during the first four centuries of Christianity—that of the apostles (1st century CE), apologists (2nd-3rd centuries), and orthodox (4th-5th centuries)—gives the appearance that church Christology departed from its moorings and has remained in this condition ever since.
- The church doctrine of the Trinity is contradictory and nonsensical, lacks biblical support, and has no parallel in human existence, i.e., it contrasts with uni-personal man bearing the image of God (which we will see in the next chapter).
- Traditional two-nature Christology is incompatible with the modern disciplines of anthropology and psychology and is employed as a forced grid in NT gospel exegesis.
- Traditional Christology has always tended toward Docetism, and recent Jesus Research increasingly resists this tendency and insists on a more human Jesus.

With this historical sketch of two millennia of church Christology now complete, we turn around to look farther back in time, prior to church history and the Christ event, to examine the roots of church Christology.

Part Two
Messianism in the Old Testament

Chapter Four
Messianism in the Old Testament

A. Introduction: Yahweh, Messiah, Son of God, Monotheism

The Parting of Judaism and Christianity	Yahweh as Messiah's God
Yahweh	The Son of God
The Messiah	The Shema and Jewish Monotheism
Yahweh and Messiah Distinguished	Trinitarian Monotheism?
Messiah as Yahweh's Agent	The New History of Religions School

The Parting of Judaism and Christianity
The most unusual and profound phenomena in the history of religion are probably the emergence of Christianity from Judaism and the subsequent strained relationship between these two great monotheistic religions. While the schism that later took place between them was no doubt inevitable, both of them have suffered much from it. This is especially true regarding their perception of the same God they both profess to worship.

We have seen that the early Jesus Movement consisted entirely of Jews and that it originally existed in Galilee and Judea as a rather loose and unofficial sect of Judaism. But this situation was short-lived. This Jesus Movement soon spread beyond the confines of its birthplace into Gentile lands. When the majority of its adherents were no longer Jews, but Gentiles, scholars now recognize this development as "(Gentile) Christianity." Since Jesus originally had gathered disciples around Him, and they afterwards established this movement, Jesus became indirectly linked to it as the founder of Christianity.[1]

Jesus, however, always remained connected to His own people, the Jews, if not to their religion of Judaism. He traveled and ministered mostly in His home region of Galilee. There, He preached and taught Jews about the kingdom God promised long ago to Israel in its Holy Scriptures. After choosing His apostles, "These twelve Jesus sent out after instructing them, saying, 'Do not go in the way of the Gentiles, and do not enter any city of the Samaritans; but rather go to the lost sheep of the house of Israel'" (Mt 10.5-6).

This development is remarkable because Galilee contained many Gentile citizens. It even had totally Gentile cities. Galilee also was nearly surrounded by

---
[1] See C.H. Dodd, *The Founder of Christianity* (New York: MacMillan, 1970). Jesus' founding of Christianity should be distinguished from His approval of its later development.

Gentiles. In fact, centuries earlier the prophet Isaiah called this land, "Galilee of the Gentiles" (Isa 9.1). One time, Jesus and His apostles departed westward from Galilee to enter briefly into the Syrophoenician (Gentile) territory of Tyre and Sidon. Jesus apparently did not intend to minister there to Gentiles because He encountered a Gentile woman who begged Him to cast a demon out of her little daughter and He first replied to her, "I was sent only to the lost sheep of the house of Israel" (Mt 15.24).

Jesus also regularly attended the annual festivals at Jerusalem and taught at the temple there. In delivering His kingdom messages, He often stressed the urgency of repentance and the necessity of receiving God's salvation by faith for both the individual and the nation. He once said, "Salvation is from the Jews" (Jn 4.22). Even though Jesus became the founder of what was to become the largest religion in the world, consisting almost entirely of Gentiles worldwide, He never severed Himself from His Jewish roots.

According to the NT, even though the Jewish religious leaders at Jerusalem were the most culpable for the condemnation and execution of Jesus, the subsequent Jesus Movement did not begrudge Judaism enough to soon separate from it. Jesus' original disciples and their Jewish converts remained connected to their mother religion by continuing to attend synagogues on the Sabbath and make annual pilgrim treks to Jerusalem to attend its festivals, primarily Passover, but also Pentecost and Tabernacles.

These believers did, however, hold additional meetings of their own in their homes. The format of these gatherings was apparently much like those of the synagogue. But they were further predicated on the model Jesus had established with His apostles during the Last Supper, when they had gathered together to eat what may have been the Passover meal and Jesus instituted the Eucharist (Mk 14.22-25 par.). They held it in "a large upper room" (Mk 14.15 par.). Two of Jesus' post-resurrection appearances probably occurred there (Jn 20.19, 26). After that, when He ascended from Mount Olivet to heaven in the presence of His disciples, Luke relates, "they returned to Jerusalem with great joy, and were continually in the temple, praising God" (Lk 24.52-53). Luke adds, "And day by day continuing with one mind in the temple, and breaking bread from house to house, they were taking their meals together with gladness and sincerity of heart, praising God, and having favor with all the people" (Ac 2.46).

At first, Jews of the homeland responded warmly to Jesus' disciples and their evangelistic message. Thousands were converted at single gatherings (Ac 2.37-41; 4.4). But it was not so with the religious leaders at Jerusalem. They persecuted these disciples just as they had done to Jesus (Ac 4-5; cf. Mt 13.9-11 par.; Jn 16.2). And they eventually influenced not only their countrymen to do likewise but Diaspora Jews as well (Ac 6-7).

One of those Diaspora Jews was Saul, a Pharisee from Tarsus (Ac 8—9.2; present Turkey). He was going around getting Christians thrown in jail and heartily contributing to getting some of them martyred. When he dramatically converted to faith in Jesus, and fervently began preaching everywhere about his new Lord (Ac 9.3—31), this Saul, also named "Paul," encountered much stiff opposition from his Jewish brethren.

Nevertheless, Paul's heart always yearned for the salvation of his people (Rom 9.1-3). None of the early Christians had nearly the impact in ministering to the church or evangelizing the world that Paul had. For a time, he preached "to the Jew first, and also to the Greek" (Rom 1.16; 2.9-10). Later, Paul and Barnabas, his early missionary associate, made an important shift in their evangelistic outreach. Due to intense opposition from Jews they changed their focus from evangelizing Diaspora Jews to bringing the gospel to the more receptive Gentiles (Ac 13.46). This change in ministry outreach contributed immensely to transforming the Jesus Movement into Gentile Christianity.

The persecution of the Jewish Christians, especially those living in Jerusalem and surrounding Judea, was severe and long lasting. They not only suffered religiously but socially and financially. For many years during Paul's missionary journeys, he collected financial contributions from Gentile church communities to which he ministered. Then he delivered these monies to persecuted Jewish Christians living in Jerusalem and Judea.[2]

This intensifying persecution of the early Jewish Christians caused some of them to emigrate and settle in Gentile lands. This resulted in more spreading of the Christian message. In the final years leading up to the fall of Jerusalem, in 70 CE, the remaining Jewish Christians living there and its environs fled eastward, beyond the Jordan River, some going to Pella. This entire exodus is called "the Jewish Christian Diaspora," and it is a significant aspect of the rupture between early Jewish Christianity and Judaism.

Scholars call the split between Judaism and Christianity "the Parting of the Ways." An important turning point was the banning of Jewish Christians from the synagogues. Perhaps it was originally elicited by the Council of Jamnia in the 80s and 90s, though the date is uncertain. The Talmud is full of rules demanding complete separation from "heretics" (Heb. *minim*; plural *min*). In the Talmud, *minim* refers sometimes to a Gnostic, but often to a Jewish Christian. The latter were treated as traitors and regarded as worse than heathen. Jews also point to a Jewish text signaling the final parting, called "the Eighteen Benedictions," meaning "blessings." In medieval times, the eminent sage Maimonides (1135-1204) gave final form to these declarations. Yet Jews claim that the origin of these Benedictions reaches back to Rabbi Gamaliel II at the end of the 1st century CE (*b. Ber.* 28b). Actually, the Twelfth Benediction, called in Hebrew the *Birkat ha-Minim*, is not a blessing but a curse. Added later, in the early 2nd century CE, it condemns all *min* and demands that their names be erased from the Book of Life believed to be kept in heaven (e.g., Ex 32.33; Ps 69.28). Thus, Judaism's traditional assessment of Jesus has always been the following: "He practiced sorcery and enticed Israel to apostasy."[3]

The early Jewish Christians responded to the opposition of their Jewish brethren by strongly affirming the veracity of their Lord Jesus Christ and delivering a scathing indictment against Judaism. They first claimed that (1) Jesus' resurrection signified God's vindication of Him and verification of His messiahship, (2) Jesus' empty tomb and the failure of authorities to recover His body was solid evidence for His resurrection, (3) Jesus' atoning death rendered the temple sacrifices no longer expiatory and therefore somewhat irrelevant, and (4) part of the Mosaic Law was no longer obligatory. After the destruction of the temple, in 70 CE, Jewish Christians further claimed that that event (1) confirmed the above propositions, (2) fulfilled Jesus' prophecy about that destruction (Mt 23.36-39—24.2 par.; Lk 21.20-24), and (3) served as God's judgment for Israel's sins, especially its rejection of Jesus as Israel's Messiah. Some of these arguments proved compelling to many Jews. Scholars now believe that, soon following the destruction of the temple, there was a marked influx in Jewish Christianity. Nevertheless, most Jews bristled at these assertions, which, of course, resulted in a further parting of the ways.

---

[2] E.g., Ac 11.29-30; 24.17; Rom 15.25-27; 1 Cor 16.1-3.
[3] *Sanh.* 43a; cf. Mt 12.24/Mk 3.22.

Contemporary Jewish writer David Klinghoffer explains that during the early centuries of the Common Era, and more so in medieval times, rabbis opposed Christianity for especially four reasons. He observes, in their order of importance, "The top four are the seeming reversion from monotheism to the worship of multiple deities [Father, Son, Holy Spirit]; the problem of Christianity's abrogation of the law of the Torah; the true Messiah; and the person of Jesus himself." Klinghoffer says of the first reason, "In Talmudic and other early rabbinic literature, the most often heard polemical theme directed against Christians has to do with the charge that the latter worshipped two gods. Not three, as in later Christian formulations—the Father, Son, and Holy Spirit—but two. In the first centuries of our [common] era, not all Christians had yet become formal Trinitarians, for the Holy Spirit had not yet joined the pantheon."[4]

So, for the first three centuries following the Christ event, Judaism was bitterly opposed to Jewish Christianity. Yet Judaism remained quite unconcerned of its Gentile counterpart. But with the subsequent dissolution of Jewish Christianity, beginning in the 4th century CE, the chief opponent of Judaism now became Gentile Christianity. It had expanded, united with the Roman state, and thereafter frequently persecuted the Jews. Christian Jewish scholar Jakob Jocz provides the following sad, but balanced, summary of the extraordinary and lasting separation between Judaism and Gentile Christianity:

> Generations of Jews have lived and passed into oblivion, and though surrounded by Christianity on every side, have never actually faced the truth about Jesus. Equally little have they known about Christianity itself. To the son of Israel, his Christian neighbour remained a Gentile who believed in three gods, worshipped the Cross and hated the Jews. A large measure of the guilt for this state of affairs falls upon the Church itself; an equally large measure falls upon the spiritual leaders of Judaism.... It is no exaggeration to say that the empirical Church, i.e., the Church of history, has shown herself the greatest enemy of the Jewish people. The Church has, therefore, been the first and foremost stumbling-block in the Jewish appreciation of Jesus.[5]

From the 1st century CE through the Middle Ages, Judaism sought to erase Jesus of Nazareth from its consciousness. Catholic anti-Semites characterized Jews as "Christ killers" if not "God-killers," which further exacerbated the bitter division between Judaism and Christianity. The medieval unification of church and state resulted in Jews being confined to ghettos, especially in Catholic Europe and Russia.

By the 18th century, however, Enlightenment had brought about the emancipation of Jews in western culture. But it resulted in much apostasy from Judaism and an internal division between its orthodoxy and liberalism. The latter eventually formed two branches mostly in the U.S.: Conservative Judaism and Reform Judaism.

Toward the end of the 19th century, leaders of the more liberal Reform Judaism felt that, intellectually, they could no longer ignore Jesus of Nazareth or, morally, follow their ancestors in condemning Him as an apostate. As was happening in the liberal wing of Christianity, especially in Germany, they began to reconstruct the historical Jesus. This literary activity caused many Jews to

---

[4] David Klinghoffer, *Why the Jews Rejected Jesus: The Turning Point in Western History* (New York: Doubleday, 2005), 132.

[5] Jakob Jocz, *The Jewish People and Jesus Christ: A Study in the Relationship Between the Jewish People and Jesus Christ* (London: SPCK, 1949), 64, 92.

reexamine their attitude toward this alleged sorcerer and messianic pretender without it conjuring up any religious or spiritual implications.

Thus, during the 20th century liberal Jewish scholars contributed significantly to the rediscovery of the Jewishness of Jesus. They refuted much unflattering Jewish legend about Him.[6] The result has been that liberal Jewish scholarship has (1) reclaimed Jesus as a Jew and even learned to appreciate Him as an ethical teacher and a moral reformer, (2) connected Him to the Torah, the Prophets, and even Judaism, while also minimizing originality in His teaching,[7] (3) denied that He founded Christianity, alleging that Paul did that, and (4) some of these Jewish scholars have even faulted those Jewish religious leaders for their part in the condemnation and execution of Jesus.[8] Nonetheless, these liberal Jewish scholars generally have continued to reject Jesus as Israel's Messiah. And, in marked opposition to Orthodox Judaism, sometimes they have negated the very idea of a Jewish Messiah while still subscribing to the idea of a future messianic age.

Since Christianity originated from Judaism, and both of these religions treat the OT as Scripture, knowing the OT and the nature of both pre-Christian and 1st century CE Judaism is essential to discovering Christian origins and thus the real Jesus. Specifically, to understand what the early Christians (and ultimately Jesus) meant by their belief in "God" and their identification of Jesus as "Lord," "Messiah/Christ," and "the Son of God," we need to seek to understand what these words mean in the OT and how Judaism understood them, especially in Jesus' time. To avoid such an investigation, as the post-apostolic church largely did, is to reconstruct a Gentile Jesus that is somewhat contrary to the Jesus of the NT. The same is true of the prominent OT figure, "the angel of the LORD," as well as Jesus' favorite expression of self-designation, "the Son of Man." Not to be forgotten is the divisive issue of Trinitarianism. So, in this chapter we will explore these and similar subjects in the OT as they relate to the question of whether Jesus is God. In Chapter Five we will begin examining the application of such OT titles to Jesus in the NT.

Yahweh

The Hebrews had a proper name for their God. Transliterated into English, it is *yhwh*, which scholars usually capitalize as YHWH. (Ancient Hebrew script consisted only of consonants; it had no vowel points until they were introduced in the 6th through the 8th centuries CE.) This name for Israel's God occurs 6,823 times in the MT. English Bibles usually translate it "the Lord," but place "Lord" in small capitals as LORD or LORD to distinguish it from the same translation for the Hebrew word *Adonay*, which also means "Lord."

Jews also refer to God's name as *Hashem*, translated "the Name." The Hebrew word *shem*, meaning "name," occurs often in the MT. Sometimes it refers to a human being; but usually it refers to God. *Hashem* often appears in the MT alongside YHWH; together, they are translated in English versions, "the name of the LORD."

---

[6] Some distinguished, non-Christian Jewish scholars, with their relevant works appended, who have characterized Jesus quite favorably include the following: C.G. Montefiore, *The Synoptic Gospels*, 2 vols. (London, 1909); idem, *Some Elements of the Religious Teaching of Jesus* (London, 1910); H.G. Enelow, *A Jewish View of Jesus* (New York, 1920); Joseph Klausner, *Jesus of Nazareth, His Life, Times and Teaching* (ET 1925); idem, *The Messianic Idea in Israel* (1955); Martin Buber, *Two Types of Faith* (1951).
[7] A few eminent Christian scholars have agreed with Jewish scholars that Jesus was not original in His teaching. E.g., A. Harnack (*History of Dogma*, 1:41) asserted, "Jesus Christ brought no new doctrine."
[8] All of these seven points are gleaned from J. Jocz, *The Jewish People and Jesus Christ*, 144-45.

The meaning of God's name—YHWH—remains somewhat uncertain. The only information about it in the Bible is in Ex 3. Therein, "the angel of the LORD appeared" to Moses from within a miraculously-burning bush that was not consumed by the fire (Ex 3.2). God, apparently being represented by an angel, engaged Moses in conversation. God told Moses that He would lead the Hebrew people out of bondage in Egypt and give them a land, the land of Canaan, which came to be known much later as "the promised land." When Moses asked God "what" (Heb. *mah*) His name was (v. 13), Moses apparently was inquiring about the meaning of God's name, since this name was already known.[9] That is why God first replied, "'I AM WHO I AM;' and He said, 'Thus you shall say to the sons of Israel, "I AM has sent me to you"'" (v. 14). In the next sentence, God mentions His name when He commands Moses to "say to the sons of Israel, 'The LORD [YHWH] ... has sent me to you'" (v. 15). Thus, when God said to Moses, "I AM," He clearly meant, "I am YHWH." In fact, this is exactly how the Decalogue (Ten Commandments) begins, "I am the LORD [YHWH] your God" (Ex 20.2; Deut 5.6).[10] More particularly, the words in v. 14, "I AM WHO I AM,"[11] translate the Hebrew words *'ehyeh 'aser 'ehyeh*, so that "I AM" translates *'ehyeh*. This word derives from the Hebrew verb *hayah* (or *hawah*), which is usually translated "(be)came," "become," or preferably "(to) be." Herein, it means "the Self-Existent One," "the Self-Subsistent One," or the like. But a few scholars think *hayah* means, "causes to be," a rendering that corresponds with Martin Buber's contention that the LXX translation of *'ehyeh*, here, which is *ego eimi* ("I am"), is Hellenistic, incorrect, and that *'ehyeh* means, "I shall be present."[12] Regardless, "I AM" in Ex 3.14 represents a self-identification, i.e., an explanation of the meaning of God's name.[13]

Because God's name has four letters, scholars call it "the Tetragrammaton." This Greek word conjoins the two words *tetra* ("four") and *grammaton* ("letter" or "writing") to mean "four letters." The shortened form of YHWH consists of the two letters YH, which appears fifty times in the MT. Since the ancient Hebrew script did not have vowels, how did the Hebrews, and succeeding Jews, pronounce the Divine Name? The pronunciation of the name of the God of Israel has a long and complex history.

The most significant thing about the history of God's name is that the Jews gradually quit pronouncing and writing it. They had various reasons. First, during the exile the Jews were forced to change their language from Hebrew to Aramaic, the sister language of their captors, the Babylonians. Second, as early as the 3rd century BCE Judaism treated the name YHWH as "ineffable," meaning both "indescribable" and "inexpressible." Third, Jews changed their understanding of the Third Commandment, and this was the most influential factor of all. It reads, "You shall not take the name of the LORD your God in vain" (Ex 20.7; Deut 5.11).[14] To avoid taking the name of God in vain, Jews quit taking

---

[9] *NBD* 479. However, scholars generally regard the appearance of YHWH earlier in Genesis as redaction.
[10] See also, e.g., Ex 6.2-3, 7-8; 15.3; 34.6; Ps 83.18.
[11] Both the RSV and NIV provide the following alternative reading: "I will be what I will be."
[12] Martin Buber, *Moses* (Oxford: East & West Library, 1946), 46-55.
[13] R.E. Brown [*John (i-xii)*, 533] claims Ex 3.14 is "the all important text for the meaning of 'Yahweh.'"
[14] Technically, the Third Commandment can be broken only by taking the name "Yahweh," not the word "God," in whatever language, in vain. But for English-speaking society, esp. in North America and the UK, the capitalized word "God" represents a proper noun that is associated strongly with the God of the Bible, so that for some, vainly uttering the word "God" seems close to breaking the Third Commandment.

it altogether! By the 1st century BCE, even though Jews may have still written the Tetragrammaton and only priests spoken it in the temple, Jews probably no longer spoke the Tetragrammaton in synagogue worship or pronounced it in the public reading of Scripture, no matter what language they used.[15] Instead, other words were substituted as surrogates for YHWH, mostly the Hebrew word *adon(ay)*, the Aramaic *mare*, or the Greek *kurios*,[16] all of which are translated "lord" in English.

Consequently, soon after the destruction of the Second Temple, in 70 CE, all recollection of the correct pronunciation of the Tetragrammaton was lost.[17] The name YHWH thereafter existed only as a written symbol, not as a living word.[18] Yet God had entrusted Israel with His name, and He had decreed that Jerusalem's temple be built as the sole shrine for His name on earth (e.g., 2 Sam 7.13; 1 Chr 22.10). And so much of the OT commands people to proclaim, sing, and praise God's peculiar name, but, of course, to do so with great reverence for God and His name. Hans Bietenhard thus alleges, "There happened to the name of Yahweh precisely what the OT had said should not happen. Yahweh became a God with a secret name, like any other god."[19]

Closely associated with this practice of avoiding the writing and pronouncing of the Tetragrammaton was that, in the 3rd and 2nd centuries BCE, purportedly seventy Jewish scholars in Egypt were selected to translate the entire Hebrew Bible into Greek. It was called the "Septuagint," the Latin word for "seventy." To this day, the literary symbol for the Septuagint is the Roman numerals for the number seventy, which is "LXX."

Whenever translators of the LXX encountered the Tetragrammaton in the Hebrew Bible, we now know they usually transliterated it. Christian copies made centuries later substituted for it the Greek word *kurios* (lord). They substituted *kurios* for YHWH 6,156 times of its total 6,823 occurrences. Down through the centuries, this LXX translation tradition was continued in other language versions of the Hebrew Bible, too. So, English Bibles usually translate the Tetragrammaton as "LORD," which is set in small capitals to distinguish it from "Lord/lord," the English translation of the Hebrew word *adon*.

After the LXX came into existence, for some time the Hebrew Bible was still used in synagogue worship; but it gradually fell into disuse. The Bible used in the temple and synagogue worship during the time of Jesus was the LXX or Aramaic paraphrases of it, called "targums." A millennium after the LXX was produced, Jewish medieval scribes, called "Masoretes," meticulously recovered their Scriptures in their Hebrew language. Their compilation was called "the Masoretic Text," abbreviated MT. Centuries later, when translators came to the Tetragrammaton, to facilitate pronunciation of it they arbitrarily inserted into it the vowel points from the word *adonay*. The result was "*YaHoWaH*," which was first translated into English in the 16th century as "Jehovah" (Y=J; W=V).

---

[15] Some earlier MSS of the LXX do not substitute *kurios* for the Tetragrammaton, but transliterate it. Some scholars allege that the substitution of *kurios* for YHWH in later copies of the LXX represents interpolation by Christian scribes. But this view is generally regarded as no longer tenable. Authority Joseph A. Fitzmyer (*A Wandering Aramean: Collected Aramaic Essays* [Missoula, MT: Scholars, 1979], 115-42) argues that (1) MSS of the LXX that contain the word YHWH are sparse, (2) Greek synagogues substituted *kurios* for YHWH, and (3) whenever NT authors quote YHWH texts in the OT, they always translate *kurios* for YHWH.
[16] G. Vermes, *The Changing Faces of Jesus*, 187.
[17] Karl Georg Kuhn, "*theos*," in *TDNT* 3:93; cf. Werner Foerster, "*kurios*," in *TDNT* 3:1082.
[18] K. Kuhn, *TDNT* 3:93.
[19] Hans Bietenhard, "*onoma*," in *TDNT* 5:269.

But neither "Yahowah" nor "Jehovah" represents a proper rendering of the Tetragrammaton.

So, what vowels should be inserted into the Tetragrammaton in order to know how to pronounce it? The consensus of modern Christian scholars is that YHWH ought to be written "Yahweh." Some Jewish scholars and others prefer "Yahveh" or "Yehvah."

Ascribing a name to God is a personal thing and suggests strictly an "individual divine person."[20] Trinitarianism therefore seems incompatible with the concept of God having a name. Perhaps that is partly why Christians have avoided calling God by His Name. Trinitarians interpret the name YHWH in the OT of both the Father and the triune Godhead, just as they usually do with the word "God" (Heb. *elohim*; Gr. *theos*) in the entire Bible. Each time YHWH appears in the MT (translated "LORD" in English Bibles), careful Trinitarians usually must decide, as with *elohim* (or *theos* in the LXX and Greek NT), whether it refers to their concept of "the Godhead" or "the Father." Having to constantly make such determinations is belaboring and can be quite confusing. Thus, it seems more reasonable for the name YHWH to refer exclusively to the Father.

Christians pray and sing about the "name" of their God, yet most of them don't even know what it is. If asked, they would probably answer, "the Father." A few scholars have.[21] Yet Christians have this strong tradition about Jesus teaching His disciples to pray in this manner, "Our Father, who is in heaven, hallowed be Your name" (Mt 6.9; cf. Lk 11.2). Did Jesus change God's name to "Father" in this model prayer? No way! He would not have abrogated God's Name in the Torah (cf. Mt 5.17). Therein, God told Moses, "The LORD [YHWH],... This is My name forever" (Ex 3.15). And God begins the Decalogue, "I am the LORD" (YHWH: Ex 20.2/Deut 5.6). Two psalmists declare, "You, O LORD [YHWH], abide forever; and Your name to all generations," and "Your name, O LORD [YHWH], is everlasting" (Ps 102.12; 135.13). Such language seems to forbid God's people desisting from pronouncing His Name.

Besides, the word "Father" in Jesus' prayer is not a name but a title that connotes an image, and it is the same with the word "Lord." "Your name" in Jesus' model prayer does not refer to "Father" but *Hashem*, a word Jews used as a circumlocution for YHWH. Jesus gave no indication of doing otherwise. So, "Your name" in the so-called "Lord's Prayer" refers to YHWH. Just as Messiah's name is "Jesus," God's name is "Yahweh."

Then why don't we read in the NT that Jesus called God by His name rather than always calling Him "Father"? Jesus may have had several reasons for doing so. One, it seems, is that He respected Jewish sensibilities on this subject—in which Jews regarded the pronunciation of the Tetragrammaton as an infraction of the Third Commandment—and thus deemed it unimportant. Another possible reason is that He lived and ministered in Israel. Jesus lived in an almost entirely Jewish society among people who believed only in one God. In lands where other gods are worshipped it might be necessary, if not respectful to those worshippers, to identify the God of Israel by His name.

The Messiah

Closely associated with the God of the Bible is "the Messiah." In the history of religion, the Judeo-Christian concept of the Messiah is unprecedented in

---

[20] G. Quell, "*theos*," in *TDNT* 3:80-81.
[21] E.g., H. Bietenhard, *TDNT* 5:272; idem, "*onoma*," in *NIDNTT* 2:653.

its essence and diversity.[22] It thus embellishes religion with the most noble of humanitarian ideals.

Ironically, nothing has divided Jews and Christians ideologically more than their differing views on two matters: (1) one God, now called "monotheism," and (2) the identity of the promised Messiah of Israel. For instance, the concept of an eschatological Messiah, though it originated with Jews, is unessential to Judaism. Some Jewish scholars argue that belief in a future messianic age is unessential to Judaism. But for Christianity, Jesus Christ is everything! Nearly all Christians agree: without Jesus, there would be no Christianity. Specifically, Jews and Christians are most divided over whether (1) God is a single Person, (2) Jesus is Israel's Messiah, and (3) the Messiah is God.

The idea of an eschatological Messiah was first expounded in non-canonical Jewish literature in the 2nd century BCE. Before that, the Messiah was a rather elusive idea in Judaism, and its exact origin still remains rather obscure. This is most remarkable since Jews afterwards so developed this concept that the anticipation of the coming of this Messiah as the catalyst for either a restorative or utopian age, upon which most Jews pinned their hopes, was to become very imbedded in the Jewish consciousness. And the Jews' reaction to Jesus must be understood, in opposition to some scholars, according to their much developed concept of the Messiah. So, what was their concept of the Messiah?

The English word "Messiah" derives from the Hebrew word *mashiah/mashiach*. This word appears thirty-nine times in the MT. In each case, it is rendered *christos* in the LXX; *christos* is transliterated "Christ" in English; *mashiah* is translated *meshiha* in Aramaic.

The Hebrew word *mashiah/mashiach* is an adjective or noun that corresponds to the Hebrew verb *mashah/mashach*, which means "to smear" or "to anoint" with some substance, usually oil. This concept of anointing first emerges in the Bible when Moses enacts the divine command to anoint Aaron's head with oil in order to signify that He belongs to Yahweh and to consecrate him as the priest of Israel (Ex 29.7; 40.9-15). But later, during the period of the monarchy, the term *mashiah* was mostly used descriptively to refer to the kings of Judah or Israel as Yahweh's "anointed (one)."[23] The priest would inaugurate the new king by anointing his head with oil (e.g., 1 Sam 9.16; 10.1; Ps 89.20, 51). It was believed that this physical act symbolized God's invisible, yet real, anointing of the king with God's spirit (1 Sam 10.6), viz., the holy spirit,[24] in order to consecrate the king for service to both God and the nation. The classic example was when Samuel anointed David with oil to make him king, and immediately "the Spirit of the LORD came mightily upon David from that day forward" (1 Sam 16.13). But the term *mashiah* could also be applied to either priest or prophet because they, too, were inducted into their role as servants of God by being anointed with oil.[25] Thus, in ancient Israel, officially anointing someone with oil designated that person as a *mashiah*, an "anointed (one)," whether priest, prophet, or king. This anointing symbolized that God had chosen that individual for some specific service.

In the post-exilic Judaism of the Second Commonwealth, interest arose in the developing concept of an ideal, eschatological king called *Mashiah*. It seems

---

[22] S. Talmon, "The Concepts of *Mashiah* and Messianism in Early Judaism," in *The Messiah*, ed. J.H. Charlesworth, 83.
[23] About thirty of the thirty-nine instances in the OT, e.g., 1 Sam 24.6; Ps 18.50; 132.10, 17; cf. Ps 2.2, 6.
[24] Christians usually capitalize "Holy Spirit," but Jews do not.
[25] E.g., Ex 28.41; Lev 4.3, 5, 16; 6.22; 1 Kg 19.16. Also, the patriarchs are called *mashiah* in 1 Chr 16.22 and Ps 105.15, and so is Persian King Cyrus in Isa 45.1.

to have begun during the 2nd century BCE among one of the two offshoots of the Pharisees, called "The Apocalyptists." They denounced taking up arms against any political oppressor of Israel. They also believed that this *Mashiah* would be a special Jewish male who would appear in "the end of days" (later also called "the Days of the Messiah"), actually on a particular climactic day called in Scripture "the day of the LORD (Yahweh)" and often shortened to "the day." This *Mashiah* would be a proto-type of both Moses and David who would be the final Deliverer and Redeemer of the nation of Israel. Just as the early Christians later did, Jews searched their Scriptures to gather up prophecies under this rubric even though most of these texts did not include the word *mashiah*.[26] This Jewish trend in messianic interpretation of Scripture is reflected in the Apocrypha, although the term "Messiah" never appears there either. But especially, and more profoundly, the concept of an ideal, eschatological Messiah appears frequently in the apocalyptic literature of the Pseudepigrapha and the DSS,[27] and so does the term "Messiah."

Yet there is very scanty evidence for a personal, eschatological Messiah in pre-Christian, non-canonical Jewish literature. Consequently, some recent scholars, especially Reformed Jewish scholars, have further alleged that this concept does not appear in the OT by its namesake, unless maybe in Ps 2.2. They, and many prior Jewish sages, have therefore alleged that later Judaism went astray in its emphasis upon, if not expectation of, an ideal, eschatological Messiah. For instance, the later Talmud makes the astounding exaggeration that "all the prophets prophesied only of the days of the Messiah."[28]

Nevertheless, these scholars have rightly claimed that the Jewish Bible highlights the messianic era. Yet they have further reasoned that God alone will redeem Israel and always be its king. They also cite that, during the Second Commonwealth, Judaism no longer inducted either priests or kings of Judah into office by anointing them with oil.

While these Jewish scholars are correct about some of their assertions, especially their denouncements of some Jewish medieval legends about the Messiah, their primary conclusion depends far too heavily on the absence of the word *mashiah* in the Hebrew Bible, i.e., as it refers to an eschatological Messiah. Rather, such a Messiah is portrayed often in the OT in various images, e.g., the "star" of Jacob (Num 24.17); the "branch" of David (Isa 4.2; 11.1; Jer 23.5; 33.15; Zech 3.8; 6.12); Yahweh's "Shepherd" (Zech 13.7; cf. Eze 37.24); Yahweh's "Son" (Ps 2.7, 12); arguably Daniel's "Son of Man" (Dan 7.13); Yahweh's suffering "Servant" in Deutero-Isaiah and Isaiah's messianic epithets in Isa 7.14 and 9.6. Furthermore, both ideas about God and Messiah being king of Israel are not incompatible; God will reign as king in the messianic kingdom through the Messiah as His co-regent, just as God did through Israel's kings in the ancient monarchy. Finally, in the Eighteen Benedictions (now nineteen)—the chief prayer of Judaism that is supposed to be repeated thrice daily by all Jews— the Fifteenth is about the Messiah. (So is the twelfth article of "the Articles of Faith" drafted by Maimonides.) Granted, Jews have never been certain when the Eighteen Benedictions were drafted. Emil Schurer claims that they "must

---

[26] Esp. Gen 49.9-10; Num 24.17; Ps 2; 110.1; Isa 9.6-7; 11.1-5; Jer 23.5-6; 33.15; Dan 7.13-14; 9.26; Mic 5.1-15; Zech 9.9; 12.10; 13.7. J.M. Roberts ("The Old Testament's Contribution to Messianic Expectations," in *The Messiah*, ed. J.H. Charlesworth, 41) relates how remarkable it is that Jews and Christians have consistently selected the same OT texts as messianic.

[27] In pre-Christian Pseudepigrapha: *1 Enoch*; *Psalms of Solomon*; *Testament of the Twelve Patriarchs*.

[28] *Sanh.* 99a; *Ber.* 34b.

have been given the form of eighteen benedictions in around 70-100 CE; but the underlying foundation of the Prayer is certainly much older."[29]

Still, by the time of Jesus this Jewish picture of an eschatological King-Messiah was not as clear as one might think.[30] Oscar Cullmann rightly says of that time, "Judaism had by no means a single fixed concept of the Messiah."[31] Most Jews believed that there would be only one eschatological Messiah, which they designated "Messiah ben David" and is verified in the NT gospels.[32] But many Jews also believed in other eschatological figures, e.g., that a special Moses-like prophet would appear someday, in accordance with Deut 18.15-19 (cf. Jn 1.21, 25; 6.14; 7.40). Jews had no consensus about the relation between these two figures. And, in accordance with the promise of Mal 4.5, they had another strong tradition about Elijah returning as a forerunner of the Davidic Messiah, which belief is affirmed in the NT as well (Mt 16.14 par.; 27.47, 49 par.; Jn 1.21, 25).

Furthermore, the DSS reveal that as early as the 2nd century BCE, the Qumran Community conceived of another eschatological Messiah who would be only a priest. It labeled him the "Messiah of Aaron" and alleged that he would supersede the Davidic Messiah, calling him the "Messiah of Israel." But this ought not surprise us since the Qumran Community was founded by a priest, called "the Teacher of Righteousness," and this separatist Jewish sect was super-controlled by a priesthood. Moreover, post-exilic Israel was usually a priestly-ruled theocracy with no monarchy.

This idea of two co-existing messiahs arouses the question of their possible rivalry. But Zechariah prophesies about the priest Joshua foreshadowing Messiah under the rubric "Branch." He says, "He will be a priest on His throne," thus uniting the two offices of king and priest (Zech 6.12-13). This seems to rule out the idea of two messiahs.

Following the Bar Kochba Revolt, in 132-135 CE, normative Judaism embraced the concept of two eschatological Messiahs. But its view differed from that of Qumran. Messiah ben David would rule as king over Israel, but a secondary messiah would shortly precede him, being called "Messiah ben Joseph" (or Ephraim). He would be a warrior who would be slain in the battle of Gog and Magog described in Eze 38-39.[33]

Distinguished Jewish scholar Joseph Klausner informs that this belief in Messiah ben Joseph arose quite logically due to the supposition that the lofty, spiritual character of Messiah, as described in Isa 42.1-2 (cf. Isa 61.1), is incompatible with the vengeful character of a warrior-king.[34] (Indeed, some Jews regarded Torah observance and political ambition as conflicting interests.) Most Christians probably would agree, since the pre-Easter Jesus taught personal non-violence as well as love of enemies. Klausner argues convincingly that the idea of Messiah ben Joseph being a warrior was not prompted in order to justify

---

[29] Schurer, 2:459.
[30] James H. Charlesworth, "From Messianology to Christology: Problems and Prospects," in *The Messiah*, ed. J.H. Charlesworth, 28, 31-32; G. Vermes, *The Changing Faces of Jesus*, 28.
[31] O. Cullmann, *Christology*, 111.
[32] Mt 2.2-6; 16.13-16 par.; Lk 2.26; Jn 1.20, 25, 41; 3.28; 7.26-27, 31, 40-43; 9.22; 10.24; 11.27; 12.34.
[33] Ezekiel 38.2 has "Gog of the land of Magog," thus presenting one personage. But another Jewish tradition has "Gog and Magog," which Jews have preferred. This tradition actually coincides with Rev 20.4-9 which depicts a war with "Gog and Magog" that occurs after the 1,000-year reign of Jesus Christ. Jews have debated whether Eze 38-39 will occur near the beginning or end of Messiah ben David's kingly reign. They have speculated on the time-span of Messiah's reign, some allotting 40 years and others, 400.
[34] J. Klausner, *The Messianic Idea in Israel*, 501.

Simon bar Kosiba's failed messianic movement; rather, he alleges that this belief emerged mostly to explain the Messiah being "pierced," recorded in Zech 12.10, and to make sense of the battle of Eze 38-39.[35]

However, these two ideas are not incompatible. Isaiah presents Messiah ben David as the receptor of Yahweh's Spirit, even listing His spiritual qualities (Isa 11.1-5; 42.1-4; 61.1-2), while elsewhere describing Him as a fierce warrior (Isa 9.4-5; 11.4b; 63.1-6). Indeed, King David, from whom this Messiah's title derives, was the consummate warrior-king as well as "the sweet psalmist of Israel" (2 Sam 23.1).[36]

Thus, it seems that neither Scripture nor the title Messiah ben David supports this revised Jewish tradition. Rather, Israel's Messiah will be like David, excelling magnificently both militarily and politically as a conquering warrior-king as well as spiritually as an ethical and righteous leader-priest.

Raphael Patai concurs and further explains,

> This splitting of the Messiah in two persons, which took place in the Talmudic period, achieved another purpose besides resolving the dilemma of the slain Messiah. According to an old tradition, the Messiah was perfectly prefigured in Moses. But Moses died before he could lead the Children of Israel into the Land of Promise. Consequently, for the parallel to be complete, the Messiah, too, had to die before accomplishing his great task of ultimate Redemption. Since, however, the Messiah would not be the True Redeemer of God if he did not fulfill that ultimate task, the only solution was to let one Messiah, like Moses, die, and then assign the completion of the work of Redemption to a second Messiah.[37]

In addition, Second Temple Judaism espoused different traditions about the origin of the idea of the Davidic Messiah. And these traditions were prominent during the time of Jesus (Mt 2.4-6; Jn 7.27). One very established tradition was that this Messiah would descend from King David (e.g., Isa 11.1) and be born in David's birthplace—Bethlehem. (Mic 5.2; 7.42) Another, and seemingly conflicting, tradition about this Davidic Messiah emerges in the Similitudes of 1 Enoch. They mention "the Son of Man" thirteen times and equate him with the Davidic Messiah. This apocalyptic book states that the Messiah would be "concealed in the presence of (the Lord of the Spirits) [God] prior to the creation of the world" (*1 En.* 48.6; cf. 62.6-7; *4 Ezra* 12.32; 13.26, 52). But another Jewish tradition was that the Messiah would appear suddenly on earth as an adult and thus have a secret origin, but from where no one knew. Emil Schurer clarifies this seeming paradox by explaining, "the two views are unified by the hypothesis that he would first live in concealment and then suddenly emerge."[38] More precisely, by joining Isa 49.2 and Mal 3.1, the Messiah would be "concealed" until He would "suddenly come to His temple."[39]

The author of the Similitudes may have drawn this idea of the concealing from Isa 49.2 and interpreted that "Servant" as Messiah personally preexisting. Was the idea of a preexisting Messiah held in Judaism? James D.G. Dunn replies, "*there was no conception of a pre-existent Messiah current in pre-Christian Judaism prior to the Similitudes of Enoch.*"[40] Since Christian traditionalists

---

[35] J. Klausner, *The Messianic Idea in Israel*, 485-501.
[36] The titles attached to the canonical Psalms relate that King David composed 73 of them, nearly half.
[37] Rafael Patai, *The Messiah Texts* (New York: Avon, 1979), 166-67.
[38] Schurer, 2:524.
[39] Also in *Pesah.* 54a.
[40] J.D.G. Dunn, *Christology in the Making*, 72. Emphasis not mine.

have believed that Jesus preexisted, and that preexistence necessarily indicates deity, we need to examine more closely this idea of a concealing, and thus the supposed preexistence, of the Servant in Isa 49. It begins:

1 Listen to Me, O islands, and pay attention, you peoples from afar. The LORD called Me from the womb; from the body of My mother He named Me.
2 And He has made My mouth like a sharp sword; in the shadow of His hand He has concealed Me, and He has also made Me a select arrow; He has hidden Me in His quiver.
3 And He said to Me, "You are My Servant, Israel, in Whom I will show My glory."
4 But I said, "I have toiled in vain, I have spent My strength for nothing and vanity; yet surely the justice due to Me is with the LORD, and My reward with My God."

This figure, the "S/servant" of Yahweh, is mentioned several times in Deutero-Isaiah.[41] Sometimes, it clearly refers to the nation of Israel; other times, it identifies a particular individual who is "chosen" as representative of the nation (e.g., Isa 42.1; 49.7). And in a few of these texts there appears to be some blending of the two figures. Here, in Isa 49, this "Servant" clearly refers exclusively to that chosen individual. For, v. 7 identifies this "Servant" as "the despised One, to the One abhorred by the nation," in which "the nation" is corporate Israel and "My Servant" is the individual Messiah. Indeed, this idea is further elaborated in the renown passage of Isa 52.13—53.12, in which Israel regards this Servant as "despised and forsaken of men" as well as "stricken, smitten of God" (Isa 53.3-4). Zechariah confirms that this Servant is the Messiah by saying of Him on behalf of Yahweh, "I am going to bring in My Servant the Branch" (Zech 3.8). The "Branch" is unquestionably the Messiah (Isa 11.1-2; Jer 23.5; 33.15).

Actually, this idea in Isa 49 of a concealing of the Servant-Messiah coincides quite well with the Christian belief of the synoptic pre-Easter Jesus, His ascension, and His future second coming, without requiring that He preexisted. Christianity has always interpreted this Servant, in especially Isa 49 and 52.13—53.12, as Jesus (e.g., Ac 8.32-35). Jesus' own people, the Jews, despised Him because they could not grasp His true identity. Christians have further alleged that these Jews could not believe because Isaiah had prophesied of them that their hearts would be insensitive, rendering them spiritually blind.[42] It was as if this Servant, Jesus, toiled in vain among His people because His true identity was *concealed and hidden* from their sight. Yet the Jews' rejection of Jesus was by divine design due to the hardness of their hearts. So, Jesus having ascended to heaven, He now sits alongside God in God's throne as an arrow in God's quiver, awaiting His return. On that awesome and glorious day, God will rise up, metaphorically shoot His select arrow—Jesus—and it will fly speedily to the earth. Then God will bend Judah as His bow (Zech 9.13-14), unleashing all His pent-up fury against His and Israel's enemies.

Thus, Deutero-Isaiah skips back and forth between Israel as God's disobedient "servant" and Messiah as God's righteous "Servant." In Isa 42.1-8, the latter is in view. Therein, Yahweh extols the virtues of His Servant-Messiah and reveals how He will make Him a covenant to the people and a light to the nations, which clearly connects this Servant-Messiah to Isa 9.1-2. Then God proclaims, "I am the LORD, that is My name; I will not give My glory to another" (42.8; cf. 48.11).

---

[41] Isa 41.8-9; 42.1, 19; 43.10; 44.1-2, 21; 44.26; 45.4; 48.20; 49.3, 5-7; 50.10; 52.13; 53.11.
[42] Isa 6.9-10; 29.20; Mt 13.14-15: Jn 12.39-40; Ac 28.25-27; Rom 11.7-8.

This does not mean that Yahweh will not give His glory to anyone. Rather, it means that Yahweh *will* give His glory to His Servant-Messiah, but He will *not* give it to anyone else.[43] Nevertheless, the idea of Yahweh sharing His glory with His Servant-Messiah does not make Messiah either God or a god. For, Deutero-Isaiah is well known for its statements by Yahweh, in which He proclaims Himself as the only God (e.g., Isa 43.10-12; 44.6, 8-9; 47.8, 10).

Similar to this idea of the concealing of the Messiah, the rabbis taught that God created seven things prior to the creation of the world, and one of them is the name of the Messiah.[44] Likewise, the Similitudes state that the "Son of Man [Messiah in 1 Enoch] was given a name,... Before-Time, even before the creation" (*1 En.* 48.2-3).

Some Jews therefore have thought that Messiah ben David preexisted because of not only the concealing but also the creation of his name before all time (cf. Eph 1.4; 1 Pt 1.20). But most Jews have thought that these two traditions—the concealing of the Messiah and the preexistence of his name—*only signify the idea of the Messiah in the mind of God* and not the actual preexistence of the Messiah, mostly because the latter is never stated in Tannaitic literature.[45] And some prominent Christian scholars agree.[46]

Yet a few Jews and many Christians have thought that the preexistence of the Messiah is indicated in other Jewish Scriptures. For example, Micah predicts that in "Bethlehem" will be born a "ruler in Israel. His goings forth are from long ago, from the days of eternity" (Mic 5.2). Both Jews and Christians have believed that this ruler refers to the Messiah. But the Targum on Micah renders this last clause, "he whose name was mentioned from of old, from ancient times." This means merely that Messiah's name will preexist, not Messiah Himself. And in place of "days of eternity" the NRSV and ESV have "ancient days," while the NIV and NJPS have "ancient times."

Another one of the seven things Jews think God created prior to the creation of the world is the concept of repentance, but not repentance itself. This suggests that these seven things were merely predetermined by God for the outworking of His purposes,[47] which seems to nullify the idea of the literal preexistence of the Messiah.

Regardless, *Jews have never thought that preexistence necessitated deity*. In fact, many Jews embraced traditions about past heroic saints having preexisted. As for those Jews who thought that the Messiah preexisted, they also thought that when he would appear on earth he would be no more than a man.[48]

Church fathers uniformly interpreted "wisdom" in the Scriptures, especially in Prov 8, as indicating the literal preexistence of Jesus. But Prov 8 is poetic genre, in which the author merely intends to portray the personification of wisdom, not an actual person. This often occurs in non-canonical Jewish Wisdom Literature. The Arians endorsed this patristic blunder and made it worse by citing Prov 8.22 to support their contention that the preexistent Son was created. They appealed to the LXX, here, which does translate that wisdom was "created"

---

[43] Does Yahweh make a distinction by saying that He will "give" His glory to His Servant-Messiah and none other, whereas He will only "show" His glory through His servant Israel (Isa 42.8; 49.3; cf. 60.1-2)?

[44] *Pesah.* 54a; *Ned.* 39b; *Tg. Ps.-J.* on Zech 4.7.

[45] J. Klausner, *The Messianic Idea in Israel*, 460.

[46] See T.W. Manson, "The Son of Man in Daniel, Enoch and the Gospels," *BJRL* 32 (1949-50): 183-85.

[47] J.D.G. Dunn, *Christology in the Making*, 71.

[48] Cf. G. Vermes, *Jesus the Jew*, 139.

(Gr. *ktizo*). The MT, however, is to be preferred, which has the corresponding Hebrew verb *qanah*. The NASB renders Prov 8.22 more accurately as saying, "The LORD possessed me at the beginning of His way."

While normative Judaism never adopted any uniformity regarding the Davidic, eschatological Messiah, it certainly never subscribed to the notion that this Messiah would be God incarnate. In both Judaism and Greek religio-philosophy, the idea of God literally descending to earth and becoming a man was not just an alien concept but a repugnant one.[49] Jewish monotheism could permit angel messianology and spirit messianology, but not a Yahweh messianology. It was thought that such a notion would not only nullify the idea of God's transcendence, but eliminate Jewish monotheism all together. Moreover, Yahweh states outright in Scripture, "I am God and not man" (Hos 11.9; cf. Num 23.19). Jewish scholar Leo Landman informs, "The idea of a Messiah in Judaism centered around a human figure. He may have been assigned exceptional qualities of wisdom and understanding; he was to bring peace and a just life to Israel and to mankind, but he was never more than a being of flesh and blood."[50] Joseph Klausner explains likewise, "The Messiah is only an instrument in the hands of God. He is a human being, flesh and blood, like all mortals. He is but the finest of the human race."[51]

Neither does the OT ever indicate that the eschatological Messiah, under whatever rubric, is to be worshipped. And Jews certainly have never believed that he should be. For them, that would be blasphemous. Jewish monotheism demands that only Yahweh be worshipped. However, 1 Enoch does state concerning the Messiah-Son of Man, "All those who dwell upon the earth shall fall and worship before him" (*1 En.* 48.5). But it adds, "they shall glorify, bless and sing the name of the Lord of the Spirits," viz., the name of Yahweh, without saying the same for the Messiah-Son of Man. This text may allude to Isa 45.23 (cf. Phil 2.9-11>). (See Chapter Five/Worshipping Jesus.)

Jews have only debated whether their expected Messiah would be "natural" or "supernatural." The latter means merely an ordinary man who, like a prophet, would possess supernatural powers with which to perform miracles and prophesy. In the Jews' Tannaitic literature (produced in the 2nd century BCE to c. 220 CE), there is no expectation mentioned about the Messiah performing supernatural acts and other wonders. During the 2nd century BCE, most Pharisees advocated the idea of a natural Messiah who did not do miracles. But "the Apocalyptists" of the 1st century BCE appear to have been the first Jewish sect to insist on a supernatural Messiah and thus one who would perform miracles.

During the time of Jesus, sentiment was probably mixed in which some Jews believed in a supernatural Messiah. For example, one time when Jesus attended the Feast of Booths and taught at the temple at Jerusalem, many of the multitude exclaimed to Him, "When the Christ shall come, He will not perform more signs than those which this man has, will He?" (Jn 7.31). George R. Beasley-Murray explains, "Whereas traditionally miracles were not associated with the Messiah in his coming, the merging of the expected prophet like Moses with the Messiah as the 'second Redeemer' led to anticipation of the miracles of Moses in the exodus finding a repetition in the greater than Moses at the second Exodus."[52] And Jewish scholar Solomon Zeitlin observes that after the

---

[49] Regarding Greek religio-philosophy, see Herman Kleinknecht, "*theos*," in *TDNT* 3:78.

[50] Leo Landman, "Introduction," *Messianism in the Talmudic Era*, ed. Leo Landman (New York: KTAV, 1979), xxiii.

[51] J. Klausner, *The Messianic Idea in Israel*, 523.

[52] George R. Beasley-Murray, *John* in WBC (1987), 112. Cf. Mt 24.24/Mk 13.22.

destruction of the Second Temple, and especially after the Bar Kochba Revolt, "The idea of a supernatural *mashiah* became the cornerstone of Jewish survival" due to this suffering.[53]

Jews certainly have never thought a man having power to perform supernatural acts indicates he is God. The people of Israel have always believed that Moses, Elijah, and other prophets performed miracles. Similarly, ancient pagan Gentiles generally believed that gods could grant supernatural powers to humans without the recipients necessarily being gods. Of course, they also could believe that such human recipients were gods, too; but this was rare. Furthermore, in Jesus' time the Pharisees believed that Beelzebul (Satan) and demons could perform supernatural acts through people as well, and that is what they thought of Jesus (Mt 12.24/Mk 3.22).

A major difference between Judaism and Christianity has been that Judaism has allowed considerable diversity of opinion, and thus not been credal, whereas Christianity has been very credal. Nowhere is this more apparent than in comparing messianology and Christology. As the delightfully humorous saying goes: "Two Jews, three opinions!"

Yahweh and Messiah Distinguished

The meaning of *mashiah* requires a marked distinction between two individuals: the anointer and the anointed. As with Yahweh and Messiah, Yahweh is "the Anointer," by means of His Spirit, and the Messiah is "the Anointed (One)." Thus, the Anointer cannot be the Anointed One and the Anointed One cannot be the Anointer. So, it is fundamental to messianology that Yahweh is not Messiah and Messiah is not Yahweh.

Furthermore, Yahweh and Messiah ben David are occasionally mentioned together in the OT, and such juxtapositioning clearly distinguishes them as two separate individuals. The same occurs in the NT regarding God and Christ, only more frequently. All of these instances show that Messiah cannot be Yahweh and Christ cannot be God. Let us consider two examples that Judaism regards as most prominent in its Scriptures; in fact, they are the most oft-quoted OT passages in the NT. Both are psalms composed by King David. He writes in Ps 2, "The kings of the earth take their stand, and the rulers take counsel together against the LORD and against His Anointed" (v. 2; cf. Ac 4.26-27). Thus, Yahweh and His Messiah are juxtapositioned, clearly distinguishing them as two separate individuals. A few verses later, Yahweh calls this anointed one "My King" and "My Son" (vv. 6-7, cf. v. 12). The other psalm in which David juxtapositions Yahweh and Messiah, and thereby clearly distinguishes them, is Ps 110. David begins this psalm by declaring, "The LORD says to my Lord: 'Sit at My right hand, until I make Thine enemies a footstool for Thy feet'" (v. 1). Herein, "LORD" (YHWH) refers to Yahweh, and "Lord" (*Adon*) refers to Messiah. Jesus once quoted this passage, implying that it refers to Him as *Adon* (Mt 22.42-45 par.). In both passages, Yahweh and Messiah are clearly distinguished.

There are other important OT passages in which both Yahweh and Messiah are mentioned together, only Messiah is designated by some other title and sometimes even identified explicitly as a "man." Let us consider three. Most significant and graphic is Dan 7.13, which we will consider later in this chapter in some depth. Part of it reads, "with the clouds of heaven, one like a Son of Man was coming, and He came up to the Ancient of Days and was presented before

---

[53] Solomon Zeitlin, "The Origin of the Idea of the Messiah," in *Messianism in the Talmudic Era*, ed. Leo Landman, 459.

Him." The Ancient of Days identifies Yahweh, and the Son of Man is arguably the Messiah. In the book of the prophet Zechariah, Zech 12.10 describes the crucifixion marks of Jesus at His second coming. This book later hints at Jesus' crucifixion with these words, "'Awake, O sword, against My Shepherd, and against the man, My Associate,' declares the LORD of hosts. 'Strike the Shepherd'" (Zech 13.7). And in the psalms, Ps 80.14-17 presents a request for God to revive and restore Israel, portrayed as a "vine." Verse 17 reads, "Let Thy hand be upon the man of Thy right hand, upon the son of man whom Thou didst make strong for Thyself." A Jewish Targum on this passage substitutes "King Messiah" for "the son of man." Derek Kidner surely grasps the correct meaning in saying, "Israel's calling becomes focused in a single figure who alone fulfills it: the true Vine and Son of man."[54] So, Messiah is depicted in all three passages as either a man or a son of man in close association with God, yet distinguished from Him sufficiently so that He cannot *be* God.

The Jews are right; the conclusion is inescapable; the OT *presents the Davidic Messiah as no more than a man, but a man in very close association with Yahweh.*

Messiah as Yahweh's Agent

Very close! Closer than Jews affirm. Close enough to be Yahweh's prime agent.

The ancient Israelites practiced certain aspects of agency in their religion. For example, once a year on Yom Kippur the high priest entered the holy of holies. With no small fear and trepidation, he stood before the ark of the covenant and the mercy seat to offer prayers to Yahweh on behalf of the congregation of Israel. It was the most solemn occasion of the Jewish year. According to Scripture, if the priest did not properly sanctify himself while preparing to enter the holy of holies, thereby having become defiled, it was guaranteed that he would not come out of there alive! By performing this important ritual, the high priest was called *saliah hassibbur*, meaning the "agent of the congregation."[55] During those tense moments, the members of the congregation were bound to their agent, either for good or for bad. That is why the high priest did not stay long, kept his prayers short, and got out quickly. (Sounds like a formula some parishioners would like invoked at church on Sunday!) That is how it was for an agent of the congregation ministering to Yahweh. What about the opposite—an agent of Yahweh ministering to the congregation?

God is both transcendent and immanent in relation to His creation. Even though His transcendence makes Him otherworldly, God becomes immanent in creation when He makes Himself known to human beings by means of self-revelation. How does He do it? He does it in various ways. He manifests His power to us earthlings through His Holy Spirit; He communicates His thoughts to some by means of His Logos; He unveils His genius to saints through His Wisdom; He shows His glory through the Shekinah. But God also makes Himself known to human beings more indirectly by appointing intermediaries as His messengers or agents. These agents are usually angels or humans beings.

One reason traditionalist Christians think that Jesus was God is that sometimes the NT presents Jesus in such close association with God that they think the two are merged into one, making Jesus effectively God. The same

---

[54] Derek Kidner, *Psalms 73-150: A Commentary on Books III-V of the Psalms* (Liecester, England: Inter-Varsity, 1973), 292.
[55] Indebted to George Wesley Buchanan, "Apostolic Christology," in *SBLSP* (1986), 176.

phenomenon *seems* to occur in OT prophecies about Yahweh and Messiah. Such prophets mention, and/or quote, Yahweh while also describing activity peculiar to Messiah. The result is a blurring of the two individuals. Does this phenomenon create a tension for monotheism?

Ancient Judaism easily accommodated the two concepts of exclusive monotheism and divine agency.[56] Divine agency means that God selects someone to serve as His representative—in word and perhaps in action—to transact some business or activity. In other words, agency means that the word or act of the agent becomes that of the agent's principal. (See Chapter Six/Agent Christology.) Thus, OT texts that conflate the activities of Yahweh and Messiah merely indicate that Messiah acts on behalf of Yahweh as His agent. This scenario occurs in some of Zechariah's prophecies pertaining to the end times. He proclaims, "For thus says the LORD of hosts, 'After glory He has sent me against the nations ... Then you [Israel] will know that the LORD of hosts has sent Me" (Zech 2.8-9). Yahweh speaks of someone He sends yet identifies that person as "Me"! Zechariah next says to Israel, "'I am coming and I will dwell in your midst,' declares the LORD" (v. 10); yet he adds, "and you will know that the LORD of hosts has sent Me to you" (v. 11). Zechariah means that Yahweh sends Messiah as His agent, indicated by the thrice-repeated "Me." This messianic identification is certain since Yahweh identifies "Me" as "My servant the Branch" (Zech 3.8; cf. 6.12; Isa 4.2; 11.1; Jer 23.5; 33.15).

The same thing occurs two other times in the book of Zechariah. In Zech 12, the prophet, speaking on behalf of Yahweh, uses the pronoun "I" in vv. 1-10 for the first person, thus referring to Himself. In v. 10, he switches to "Me" and then the third person pronoun "Him," with the latter surely referring to the Messiah. Thus, the "I" refers to Yahweh and the words, "they will look on Me whom they have pierced; and they will mourn for Him" (v. 10), refer to the Messiah. The Fourth Evangelist quotes this text in Jn 19.37, and he interprets that it was fulfilled when the Jews looked upon the crucified Jesus. But it will be fulfilled again at Jesus' second coming (Mt 24.30; Rev 1.7). Also, Yahweh's word "Me," here, so identifies Himself with Messiah that for Messiah to be pierced, it is as if Yahweh is pierced as well (cf. Mt 25.34-40). Likewise, Zechariah later states on behalf of Yahweh, "I will gather all the nations against Jerusalem ... Then the LORD will go forth and fight against those nations,... And in that day His feet will stand on the Mount of Olives.... Then the LORD, my God, will come" (Zech 14.2-5). The "I" refers to Yahweh and "His feet" are the literal feet of the one Yahweh had just called "My Shepherd,... the man, My Associate" (Zech 13.7; cf. Isa 52.7), which can be none other than the Messiah. Jesus alluded to this image when He called Himself "the good shepherd" (Jn 10.11, 14).

It must be concluded from such passages that the Messiah is so connected to Yahweh as His agent that whenever the Messiah does anything, it is as if Yahweh does it. This functionality is what Jesus had in mind when He said, "I and the Father are one" (Jn 10.30>). But this blurring of individuals in such prophecies should not be misconstrued as an identification of Messiah as being Yahweh. In Judaism, it is God who accomplishes the Redemption of Israel, and He does it through Messiah as His instrument. Thus, God reigns supreme and Messiah merely executes God's will. That is why Judaism generally has emphasized the messianic age more than the Messiah Himself.[57]

---

[56] L.W. Hurtado, *One God, One Lord*, 18.
[57] J. Klausner, *The Messianic Idea in Israel*, 469.

Yahweh as Messiah's God

Three OT texts state that Yahweh is Messiah's God, not that Messiah is Yahweh.

First, King David wrote Ps 22, and Christians have always believed it is full of prophecies about Jesus' suffering on the cross. The first sentence is, "My God, my God, why hast Thou forsaken me?" (v. 1). Yet David, this sufferer who felt estranged from Almighty God, added, "Thou hast been my God from my mother's womb" (v. 10).

Jesus uttered the first sentence of this psalm while hanging on the cross, thus twice calling the Father "My God" (Mt 27.46/Mk 15.34). Matthew and Mark record His quotation as an obvious echo of Ps 22.1. All four gospel Evangelists make other citations or allusions to this psalm, applying them to Jesus' crucifixion as well.[58]

Second, Isaiah tells about a righteous, suffering Servant of Yahweh, whom the NT often identifies as Jesus. (See Chapter Nine/Servant Christology.) Isaiah relates that the Servant says, "The LORD called Me from the womb" (Isa 49.1). The Servant adds, "my reward [is] with My God," and "My God is My strength" (vv. 4-5). According to the NT, Jesus here twice calls Yahweh "My God."

Third, the prophet Micah proclaims that a future ruler of Israel will be born in Bethlehem (Mic 5.2). Both Jews and Christians have always regarded this ruler as the Messiah. Micah adds concerning this ruler, "He will arise and shepherd His flock in the strength of the LORD, in the majesty of the name of the LORD His God" (v. 4). Notice the words, "the LORD His God." Micah declares that the Messiah will not operate in His own strength but that of Yahweh His God, indicating His subordination to Him. The author of the Psalms of Solomon writes similarly, saying that the nation of Israel "will be under the rod of discipline of the Lord Messiah in the fear of his God" (*Pss. Sol.* 18.7).[59]

In sum, all of these texts mean clearly that *the Messiah is not God but has a God.*

The Son of God

Christians believe that Jesus is "the Son of God," and this is amply confirmed in the NT. We saw in Chapter Two that the traditional church dogma that Jesus is the Son of God by means of an ontological, eternal generation requires personal preexistence and means that Jesus is eternally God. Church fathers labeled this "divine Sonship," and this expression continues today among traditionalists. But we also learned that church fathers derived this understanding by comparing this "son of God" title to physical generation. And they appealed to Greek metaphysics for its meaning rather than subscribing to how Judaism understood its use in its Scriptures. Thus, church fathers did not derive their viewpoint from Jesus' religious culture. This is the main reason the institutional church proclaimed more of a Gentile Christ than the Jewish Messiah it should have proclaimed. The Third Quest is currently reclaiming Jesus as a Jewish Messiah, and the identification of Him as "the Son of God" plays an integral part in this reclamation.

The Third Quest repudiates the church's history of anti-Semitism and considers Jewish convictions. Eminent Jewish Bible scholar Geza Vermes alleges that the Nicene Creed's description of Jesus as "God of God" is "the most un-Jewish doctrine." He says "it is no exaggeration to contend that the identification

---

[58] Mt 27.39/Mk 15.29; Mt 27.43; Lk 23.35; Mt 27.35/Mk 15.24/Lk 23.34/ Jn 19.23-24.
[59] Scholars believe that the Psalms of Solomon were probably written in the 1st century BCE.

of a contemporary historical figure with God would have been inconceivable to the first-century CE Palestinian Jew."[60] He adds that "the meaning of a religious title depends more on culture and traditional usage than on etymology.... The primary aim must therefore be to determine the impact of a title in a first-century CE Galilean milieu. If this can be done, there is a good chance of approaching closer to the thought of Jesus and his first disciples."[61] Indeed, Jews in Jesus' time understood the title "son (of God)" as it is used in their Scriptures.

Use of the words "son" and "sons" in relation to God appears only a few times in the OT. ("Son" translates the Heb. *ben*, Aram. *bar*, and Gr. *huios*.) Each instance depicts a subordinate relationship with God. Sometimes, it is further indicated by the genitive case ("of"). The OT uses this imagery in various ways. Sometimes, it designates angels as "sons of God,"[62] which is a corporate description that usually refers to God's royal court.

The OT sometimes calls men of God His "sons." For instance, Moses identified individual Hebrew males as "sons (of God)." He declared, "You are the sons of the LORD your God" (Deut 14.1).[63] He meant that they were Yahweh's people by divine election in accordance with the covenant. Moses writes next, "For you are a holy people to the LORD your God; and the LORD has chosen you to be a people for His own possession" (v. 2).

Other times, the OT calls Israel corporately the "son" of Yahweh.[64] And the OT conversely deems Yahweh as the "father" of Israel.[65] These appellations are based on the covenant Yahweh made with Abraham and his seed of promise, recorded in Gen 15. Israel is the "son" of Yahweh by adoption because Yahweh is Israel's covenant-keeping God. That is, God chose to enter into this covenant relationship with Abraham and, indirectly, with his promised descendants. Thus, the Israelites are "the Chosen People," which is synonymous with being the "son(s)" of Yahweh. It is not that God loved them more than other people, but that they entered into a covenant with Yahweh to be His witness to the nations. God chose them for a task. Their agreement was that if Israel was obedient to the covenant, God would bless Israel; but if Israel was not obedient to the covenant, God would discipline Israel, all because the nation belonged to God as His son.

Furthermore, in non-canonical Jewish Literature a particularly righteous man is designated as a "son of God."[66] This practice became prevalent in later Hellenism. Also, recall that Jesus taught, "Blessed are the peacemakers, for they shall be called sons of God" (Mt 5.9). And Jesus taught that those who love their enemies and do good to them "will be sons of the Most High" (Lk 6.35). Likewise, in Judaism a man who conforms to the Torah shows by his lifestyle that he is a genuine son of God.

During Israel's monarchy, its king was regarded not only as Yahweh's "anointed" but also His "son." Designating the king as God's son merely extended the larger idea of Israel as God's son. A classic text on this is 2 Sam 7.14. Therein, Nathan the prophet speaks on behalf of God to King David regarding Solomon,

---

[60] G. Vermes, *Jesus the Jew*, 192, 212.

[61] G. Vermes, *Jesus the Jew*, 84.

[62] Job 1.6; 2.1; 38.7; Ps 89.7. Genesis 6.2, 4 and Ps 82.6 refer to sons of men, not angels. Psalm 29.1 probably does too, esp. because of v. 11. Daniel 3.25 depicts an angel (v. 28) rather than testifies to the preexistent Christ, as church fathers believed since the 3rd century and the AV incorrectly affirms.

[63] Cf. "(His) sons and daughters" in Deut 32.19; Isa 63.8; Wis 9.7.

[64] E.g., Ex 4.22-23; Hos 11.1; cf. Deut 32.5-6; Isa 1.2, 4; 30.1; 63.16; Jer 3.19-22; 31.9, 20; Wis 18.13; *4 Ezra* 7.28; 13.32, 37, 52; 14.9; Sib Or 3.702; Jub 1.25.

[65] Deut 32.6; Isa 63.16; 64.8; Jer 3.4, 19; 31.9; Mal 2.10; Jub 1.28.

[66] E.g., *Wis. of Sol.* 2.12-20; 5.1-7; *Pss. Sol.* 17.26-27; Ecclesiasticus 4.10.

his son and heir to the throne, by saying, "I will be a father to him and he will be a son to Me" (cf. 2 Chron 22.20; 28.6).

Sometimes, the OT specifically designates Israel's promised Messiah-King as a "son (of God)." Some Jews also applied 2 Sam 7.14a more particularly to this Messiah. Many Jews apparently believed that the supreme biblical text that identifies the Messiah as the son of God is Ps 2.7 and v. 12 (cf. Ps 89.26-27).[67] In fact, the Qumran Community made lists, contained in their DSS, which connect other messianic Scriptures with Ps 2.[68] This psalm mentions Yahweh and Messiah ("His Anointed," v. 2) together and presents Yahweh as calling Messiah "My king" and "My Son," even "the Son" (vv. 6-7, 12).

Psalm 2 is one of the most scholastically debated christological texts in the OT. Its first two verses concern Yahweh's Messiah ("Anointed One"), and they are quoted and applied to Jesus in the NT in Ac 4.25-27. The same thing occurs three more times in the NT concerning "My Son" in Ps 2.7 (Ac 13.33; Rom 1.4; Heb 1.5). In this verse in Ps 2, the Messiah-King declares, "I will surely tell of the decree of the LORD: He said to Me, 'Thou art My Son, today I have begotten Thee.'" The word "begotten" in this verse has nothing to do with such notions as an ontological generation or Adoption Christology. Rather, it refers principally to Jesus' royal coronation in heaven as the Son of Man,[69] as portrayed in Dan 7.13-14>. Presumably, this event immediately precedes Jesus' return to earth and subsequent installation as Israel's Messiah-King on David's throne on Mount Zion (Ps 2.6). Thus, Ps 2 uses the terms "Messiah" and "Son" interchangeably.[70]

Like any other king of Israel, the Messiah would be God's "son" and thus his vice-regent on earth. But Jews also believed that this Messiah-King would be *the* son of God extraordinaire. Nevertheless, they did not reckon that his unique sonship would be due to some metaphysical generation as the surrounding polytheistic nations were apt to ascribe to their gods and human kings and as church fathers later said of Jesus. Rather, the Messiah-King would be God's son in the sense that he would be specially related to Yahweh as His representative and Israel's, too. Trinitarian N.T. Wright cautions against misunderstanding this messianic "son (of God)" title by explaining that "in the first century the regular Jewish meaning of this title had nothing to do with an incipient Trinitarianism; it referred to the king as *Israel's representative*. Israel was the son of YHWH; the king [Messiah] who would come to take her destiny on himself would share this title."[71] G.W.H. Lampe goes further by alleging, "'Son,' however, suggests a being who is not God himself but who coexists beside God and acts as God's agent."[72]

The Shema and Jewish Monotheism

The bedrock of normative Judaism has always been strict monotheism—the belief that there is only one God. Therefore, Rabbinic Judaism has always embraced what is now called "exclusive monotheism." The Jews' maxim, that there is only one God, has always distinguished Jews from their neighbors. It's what made a Jew a Jew. Nations in antiquity were intensely polytheistic, worshipping many gods and sons of gods that they usually depicted by their man-made idols. For Jews, these gods and idols were anathema.

---

[67] G. Vermes, *Jesus the Jew*, 194-95.
[68] 4QFlorilegium 1.10-14 cites 2 Sam 7.14 and applies "son" therein to the "branch" of David in Isa 11.1.
[69] Cf. Georg Fohrer, "huios," in *TDNT* 8:350-51.
[70] Also in the DSS, e.g., 4QFlor. 10-14.
[71] N.T. Wright, *Jesus and the Victory of God*, 485-86. Emphasis not mine.
[72] G.W.H. Lampe, *God as Spirit*, 140.

Jews have always believed that their monotheistic faith is expressed so resolutely in what they call "the Shema." It is recorded in Deut 6.4-5,[73] the Jews' most sacred portion of Scripture. This text is a literary unit that reads as follows in the NASB:

4 "Hear, O Israel! The LORD is our God, the LORD is one!
5 "And you shall love the LORD your God with all your heart and with all your soul and with all your might."

This passage is called "the Shema" because its first word in the Hebrew text is *shama*, a verb translated *shema* in Aramaic which means "to hear." Throughout ancient Israel's existence, Jews always regarded the Shema as not only a confessional statement but also sort of an ethnic, if not a national, creed. The first sentence in Deut 6.4 can be paraphrased, "Listen up, O Israel, for this is what you are about."

There has always existed some ambiguity concerning the proper translation of the second sentence in Deut 6.4. It has been translated into English in four different ways:
- The LORD *is* our God, the LORD *is* one.
- The LORD our God, the LORD *is* one.
- The LORD our God *is* one LORD.
- The LORD *is* our God, the LORD *alone*.

The Hebrew word translated "one" in Deut 6.4 is *echad*. The primary meaning of *echad* is the numeral "one,"[74] and it is so translated over 600 times in the NASB. The second most prominent translation of *echad* in the NASB is the word "each," which is so translated fifty-five times. Thus, *echad* in the Bible usually means numerically "one."

A scribe once asked Jesus, "What commandment is the foremost of all?" (Mk 12.28; cf. Mt 22.36). Jesus answered by quoting Deut 6.4-5 and saying it was "foremost" (v. 29). The scribe replied, "Right, Teacher, You have truly stated that HE IS ONE; AND THERE IS NO ONE ELSE BESIDES HIM" (v. 32). Jesus obviously accepted this statement as correct by replying, "You are not far from the kingdom of God" (v. 34). Did Jesus therefore mean that God was one person and not two or three? Indeed He did.

Rabbinic Judaism has always required that every Jewish adult male recite the Shema twice daily,[75] at "the morning and evening prayer." Nothing ever contributed to the Jews' ongoing monotheistic faith more than this praxis. Actually, the Shema is not regarded as a prayer but a confession. Indeed, its recitation in synagogue services is traditionally followed with a specific rabbinical prayer called "the *Shemoneh Esreh*," which consists of eighteen benedictions commonly known as "the Prayer."

During the 12th century, the wise and learned Rabbi Maimonides compiled thirteen articles of faith that Jews subsequently adopted into their liturgical prayers, and the devout have recited them regularly ever since. One of these articles of faith represents a brief commentary on the Hebrew word *echad* in the Shema. It reads in English, "I believe with a perfect faith that the Creator, blessed

---

[73] Deuteronomy 6.6-9 and its counterparts, Deut 11.13-21 and Num 15.37-41, are also part of the *Shema*.

[74] The ancients did not have a numerical system like Arabic numerals, which were later borrowed for English. Instead, they used either single letters of their alphabet or a word to represent a specific number. The Hebrews used their word *echad* as the numeral "one."

[75] Josephus, *Antiquities* 4.212.

be His name, is an absolute one." The Hebrew word that Maimonides used for "one" is not *echad* but *yachid*. This Hebrew word corresponds unequivocally to our English numeral "one."

Many other portions of the OT affirm the oneness of God declared in the Shema. Deutero-Isaiah (Isa 40-55) is the most prominent. God, speaking through the prophet Isaiah, repeatedly states such things as "there is no God besides Me" or the like.[76]

But this Jewish, exclusive monotheism should not be understood as devoid of other supernatural beings.[77] The Bible is full of information about the existence of angels. But it always presents them as subordinate to the one God, Yahweh, even including those who rebelled against Him—Satan and his angels. The OT can even identify angels as "gods," which should be understood as compatible with exclusive monotheism. (See later in this chapter the subtitle, "Angels Called 'gods' and 'sons of God.")

Trinitarian Monotheism?

Both Binitarian and Trinitarian Christians claim that they are monotheists, thus professing belief that God is "one." But most of them define "one" as a unity rather than numerically. They also believe that this one God exists as either two or three persons.[78] This belief is, at best, an anomaly, and many people deem it a contradiction in terms.

Muslims, with 1.3 billion adherents to Islam, and Jews deny that Trinitarianism is monotheistic. Most of them allege that it is tritheistic, meaning belief in three gods.[79]

So, what is monotheism? Henry More, a Cambridge Platonist philosopher, coined the word "monotheism" in the 17th century. It represents a transliterated conjoining of two Greek words. The word "mono" derives from the Greek word *monos*, meaning "only," "alone," or "single;" but as a prefix it can also mean numerically "one." The word "theistic" derives from *theos*, the Greek word for "god," and thus means "belief in god." Joining these two words together signifies numerically one god/God in contrast to the word polytheism, meaning "many gods" or "more than one god." Yet Trinitarians define the one God of the Bible as three Persons, each being equally God. It therefore seems questionable that Trinitarian Christianity should be categorized as monotheistic. That is one reason some scholars reject the word "monotheism" as a useful category.[80]

During the 17th century, Trinitarians applied the keywords "unit" and "unity" to Polish Socinians for their belief in one God and thereby labeled them as "Unitarians." Although these Socinians rejected this label, it stuck. But the word "unit" can mean a category having one or more persons, things, or

---

[76] Isa 43.10; 44.6, 8; 45.21-22; 46.9; 47.8; cf. 45.5-6, 18.

[77] I am using "exclusive monotheism" to mean, as the Apostle Paul says, that God is the "only Sovereign,... who alone possesses immortality," who is "above" all as "the Most High (God)" (1 Tim 6.15-16).

[78] Much of what is said here about Trinitarianism also applies to Binitarianism.

[79] Some prominent English dictionaries equate Trinitarianism with tritheism. *Webster's New Universal Unabridged Dictionary* defines tritheism as "the doctrine of the existence of three distinct gods; specifically, in Christian theology, the doctrine that the Father, Son, and Holy Spirit are separate and distinct Gods." Of course, Trinitarians vigorously deny such definitions.

[80] E.g., R.W.L. Moberly, "How Appropriate is 'Monotheism' as a Category for Biblical Interpretation?" *Early Jewish and Christian Monotheism*, ed. Loren T. Stuckenbruck and Wendy E.S. North (London: T&T Clarke, 2004), 216-34. Moberly cites and quotes other distinguished Trinitarian scholars who are of this opinion, e.g., Gerhard von Rad and Walter Brueggemann.

abstract concepts. And this is how many Trinitarians think of their belief. Thus, Trinitarianism is more appropriately designated unitarian than monotheistic, and monotheism more appropriately refers to Unitarianism.

Jews have always vehemently defended their exclusive monotheism against Trinitarianism. And they have denied any hint of Trinitarianism in their Scriptures. For many religious Jews, the church doctrine of the Trinity seems blasphemous, and this is surely how Jews would have viewed it in the time of Jesus. R.E. Brown rightly states concerning that era, "For the Jew 'God' meant God the Father in heaven."[81] And Earl Morse Wilbur well observes that "nothing else has proved such an impassable barrier to the reception of Christianity by the Jews, as has the doctrine of the Trinity, which has seemed to them to undermine the very cornerstone of their religion."[82]

Then how should it be determined who is a monotheist and who is not? Larry Hurtado suggests that, despite anomalies, we should "take people as monotheist if that is how they describe themselves."[83] But most Christians don't allow such a loose definition for confessional conversion. Except for Unitarian churches, most other church denominations have established some criteria for deciding who is a true Christian (though they often disagree on the criteria). Indeed, this usually is reflected in their requirements for formal church membership. Thus, Christians generally do not accept a person as one of their own merely because that person professes to be a Christian. Rather, prospective converts must meet the established criteria of that particular church community. In times past, such standards have often been set forth in the form of a catechism or a creed. The NT reveals that the early Jewish Christians required at least the following confessional criteria: Jesus is Lord, Messiah, Son of God, and Savior, and God raised Him from the dead (e.g., Rom 10.9-10; Jn 20.30-31; 1 Cor 15.3-4). Likewise, it seems there could be some criteria for determining who is a monotheist and who is not which goes beyond mere profession. I suggest as a simple formula the etymology of "monotheism" explained above, which definition is in sharp contrast to "polytheism." Accordingly, it is doubtful that either Binitarianism or Trinitarianism can rightly be categorized as monotheistic.

The New History of Religions School

The subject of the early development of church Christology and its relationship to Jewish monotheism has recently come to the forefront in biblical scholarship with much vigor. The reason is that serious questions have always existed regarding the origin of church Christology. The main question is, How could the early Jesus/Christian movement have changed so rapidly, perhaps only in a couple of decades or less, from expounding an exclusive monotheism to proclaiming both the Father and Jesus as God? For, Jesus is depicted as no more than the (Moses-like) prophet-Messiah-Son of God-Son of Man in the Synoptics and Acts, but He is supposedly proclaimed unambiguously as "God" in the later Gospel of John. Another question arises, How could this important christological development have occurred without the NT providing any information about it?

Wilhelm Bousset was the foremost leader of the old History of Religions School. He and Rudolf Bultmann answered this first question as follows: When early Christianity spread into Gentile lands—where the constraint of monotheism was weak or nonexistent and polytheism was widespread—Christianity soon

---
[81] R.E. Brown, *Jesus God and Man*, 87.
[82] E.M. Wilbur, *Our Unitarian Heritage*, 9.
[83] L.W. Hurtado, "What Do We Mean by 'First-Century Jewish Monotheism'?" 355.

became Hellenized by adopting the Gnostic Redeemer myth that had originated in Persia. It was the belief that a preexisting divine being would descend from heaven to earth to become a man and redeem humans.

Christianity did become somewhat Hellenized theologically, but not with the Gnostic Redeemer myth in the 1ˢᵗ century. Later 20ᵗʰ century scholarship discovered that this myth did not exist until the 2ⁿᵈ century, *after* post-apostolic church fathers had already proclaimed Jesus as the preexistent, incarnate God. This discovery rendered this allegation by Bousset and Bultmann as anachronistic, and it contributed significantly to the sharp decline and eventual demise of this liberal History of Religions School.

Partly in reaction to this demise, a rival scholastic movement arose a half-century later, during the past two decades. It is called "the New History of Religions School." Ironically, it consists mostly of conservative-minded traditionalists rather than liberal critics, and they provide an alternate answer to this intriguing question about Christian origins. With their old scholastic counterpart, they share the premise of a development in the NT from a low to a high Christology. Unlike their predecessors, however, they contend that it was not due to a Hellenization of early Christianity, but the early influence of both a preceding and contemporary Judaism that embraced a somewhat elastic, or a very elastic, monotheism which speculated mostly about intermediate, divine figures.[84] These scholars insist that this Jewish model of "inclusivistic monotheism," which includes divine intermediaries, enabled the early Christians to worship Jesus as "divine" or "God" and thereby accomplish their transition from a low to a high Christology.

Consequently, most scholars in this New History of Religions School propose a radically-revised view of Jewish monotheism during the Second Temple period. They assert that this monotheism became quite fluid, allowing for intermediary, divine figures subservient to God if not equal to God. These scholars attempt to show, especially from inter-testamental Jewish Literature,[85] much of it apocalyptic, that principal angels,[86] heavenly exalted human patriarchs,[87] and even powers or attributes of God deemed as *hypostases* separate from God, e.g., Spirit, Word, and Wisdom, exhibit characteristics peculiar to deity and, being worshipped, are thought to be in some sense divine.

---

[84] Leading representatives of this scholastic christological movement, with their principal works on this subject appended in short titles, include: Martin Hengel, *The Son of God* (1976); idem, *Studies in Early Christology* (1995); Alan F. Segal, *Two Powers in Heaven* (1978); Christopher Rowland, *The Open Heaven* (1982); Richard Bauckham, "The Worship of Jesus in Early Christinianity," *ABD* (1981-82); idem, *God Crucified* (1998); Larry W. Hurtado, *One God, One Lord* (1988); idem, *Lord Jesus Christ* (2003); Jarl E. Fossum, *The Name of God and the Angel of the Lord* (1985); Loren T. Stuckenbruck, *Angel Veneration and Christology* (1995); Peter R. Carrell, *Jesus and the Angels* (1997); Crispin H.T. Fletcher-Louis, *Luke-Acts: Angels, Christology and Soteriology* (1997); Charles A. Gieschen, *Angelomorphic Christology* (1998); D.D. Hannah, *Michael and Christ* (1999). For a recent, brief history of this research, see C.A. Geischen, *Angelomorphic Christology*, 16-25.

[85] See the survey provided by L.W. Hurtado, "What Do We Mean by 'First-Century Jewish Monotheism'?" in *SBLSP* (1993), 348-54.

[86] E.g., Michael, Melchizedek in esp. DSS, Metatron or Yahoel as the angel of Ex 23 in esp. 3 *En.* 48.1 (see also "Yahoel" in *Apocalypse of Abraham* 17.13), and other archangels. See esp. L.W. Hurtado, *One God, One Lord*, 71-92.

[87] E.g., Adam (*Life of Adam and Eve*, 12-16); Enoch of Gen 5.18-24 (1 *En.* 46.3-4; 48.5, 52.4; 62.6-9; 71.5, 14; cf. 3 *En.* 4.2-3, 8-9; esp. 12.5); and Moses (Sirach 45.2; Ezekiel the Tragedian's *Exagoge*, lines 68-91). See L.W. Hurtado, *One God, One Lord*, 51-69. But some of these sources merely describe these patriarchs with a celestial glory that supersedes that of angels, which is implied in many Scriptures (e.g., Dan 12.3; 1 Cor 6.3) because of the saints' inheritance in Christ (Heb 1.4).

Many of these scholars have centered their studies on angels. This discipline is now called "angelomorphic Christology." "Angelomorphic" means "angel" that appears human, and angelomorphic Christology means for some that Jesus preexisted as an angel and for others that "angel" only served as an antecedent of high Christology. These scholars compare Jesus with angelic forms and functions in the OT and other ancient Jewish literature. Many of them suggest that the preexistent Jesus was "the angel of the LORD" in the OT who is associated with God. So, these scholars contend that their angel studies contribute to identifying Jesus as a divine being. Except for "the angel of the LORD," it is mostly the post-exilic material in the OT that provides information about angels. Nevertheless, this New History of Religions School relies heavily on angel speculation in non-canonical, apocalyptic, Jewish literature of the Second Temple period.

A few of these scholars, especially Margaret Barker, also cite substantial patristic evidence to support their angel Christology. But Barker's position is extremely radical. She claims to be a Trinitarian, yet distinguishes between the supreme God as Elohim and His inferior Son being Yahweh! And she further confuses matters by identifying Yahweh as "the angel of the LORD" in the OT as well as the preexistent Jesus Christ![88]

Angel messianology did occupy a place in pre-Christian Judaism, though not a conspicuous one. While the eschatological Messiah and certain exalted angels, especially Michael as the patron angel of Israel, were usually distinguished yet associated, some Jewish interpreters regarded these two figures as synonymous.

Some historical-critical scholars claim that Jewish monotheism was not static but dynamic.[89] They insist that ancient Jewish Literature and even the Jewish Bible divulge that in one era Jewish monotheism was very exclusive whereas during another era it was quite flexible. Indeed, Second Temple apocalyptic Jewish Literature did proliferate angel speculation, and sometimes this material seems to compromise strict monotheism. If true, that would mean there existed various Judaisms throughout Jewish history, a concept most authorities now affirm. Accordingly, Jewish monotheism becomes a difficult concept to define precisely as a background for church Christology.

Nevertheless, Rabbinic Judaism has always argued that any departure from strict monotheism which allows for other divine beings, even if of a lesser divinity than that of Yahweh, never represented normative Judaism.[90] This argument is most compelling. For example, rabbis cite Judaism's strong reaction to the Two Powers Heresy of the early 2nd century CE. Therefore, Rabbinic Judaism has explained that angel speculation in this non-canonical literature (1) was representative of fringe elements of Judaism or separatist sects, and (2) sometimes others misinterpreted it with a crass literalism. So, the assertion that angelology weakens monotheism has been amply refuted and characterized as a misunderstanding of Jewish language taken too literally rather than idiomatically.[91]

---

[88] Margaret Barker, *The Great Angel: A Study of Israel's Second God* (London: SPCK, 1992), 190-207.

[89] E. Stauffer (*TDNT* 3:96) says apocalyptic Jewish Literature caused later Judaism to endorse "a dynamic monotheism."

[90] George Foot Moore, "Intermediaries in Jewish Theology: Memra, Shekinah, Metatron," *HTR* 15 (1992): 41-85; cf. Paul A. Rainbow, "Jewish Monotheism as the Matrix for New Testament Christology: A Review Article," *NovT* 33 (1991): 81-83.

[91] L.W. Hurtado, *One God, One Lord*, 37.

Some scholars think Martin Hengel's little book, *The Son of God* (ET 1976), was the catalyst for forming The New History of Religions School.[92] In it, he cites texts from pre-Christian Jewish Literature which he assesses as "substantial building material" that the early church would have used in proceeding from a low to a high Christology twenty years or less after the Christ event.[93] But Hengel can cite only non-canonical sources,[94] most of which Rabbinic Judaism never viewed as reflecting normative Judaism.

Second only to angel studies, some scholars in the New History of Religions School have focused on the Son of Man figure in Dan 7.13-14>. These so-called "Son of Man scholars" examine apocalyptic Jewish Literature of the Second Temple period, especially *1 Enoch* because it contains so much commentary on Daniel's Son of Man. Regardless of whether these scholars deem Daniel's Son of Man figure as depicting Jesus, and most do not, they seek to show that Daniel presents an actual personage who is divine and therefore on a level comparable to that of God. So, as with "the angel of the LORD" in the OT, these scholars regard Daniel's Son of Man as another "bridge" that further enabled the early Christians to cross over from a low to a high Christology.

Most of these members of The New History of Religions School are like evolutionists searching for the "missing link." Thus, Richard Bauckham proposes another explanation within this school. He affirms the traditional rabbinic view of mainstream Second Temple Judaism, that it was strictly monotheistic, and dismisses the relevance of intermediary figures to early Christology.[95] Though Trinitarian, he avoids Trinitarian language and the formulation "Jesus (Christ) is God." Yet he redefines monotheism, as do J.D.G. Dunn and N.T. Wright,[96] by including Jesus along with the Father in a single divine category he repeatedly calls the "unique divine identity."[97] Larry Hurtado joins Bauckham in this conviction but employs his own terminology. Hurtado describes the supposedly early church transition from a low to a high Christology ("easily within the first decade of the Christian movement") as an innovative and unprecedented "mutation in monotheistic devotion," which results in a "binitarian shape of early Christian worship."[98]

In Chapter Six, we will see that nearly a generation ago traditionalists William Barclay and Max Zerwick explained Jn 1.1c by proposing this same divine category that includes both Jesus and the Father, exclusively. But this interpretation of this Johannine clause never escaped the charge of dual gods,

---

[92] Martin Hengel, *The Son of God: The Origin of Christology and the History of Jewish-Hellenistic Religion* [1975], tr. John Bowden (Philadelphia: Fortress, 1976). See also Jarl E. Fossum, "The New *Religionsgeschichtliche Schule*: The Quest for Jewish Christology," in *SBLSP* 30 (1991), 638-46.
[93] M. Hengel, *The Son of God*, 57.
[94] M. Hengel, *The Son of God*, 41-56.
[95] R. Bauckham, *God Crucified*, 4.
[96] J.D.G. Dunn, "Was Christianity a Monotheistic Faith from the Beginning?" 336; N.T. Wright, *What Saint Paul Really Said: Was Paul of Tarsus the Real Founder of Christianity?* (Grand Rapids: Eerdmans, 1997), 65-72, 176. Wright speaks of "christological monotheism."
[97] R. Bauckham, *God Crucified*. So does Hans W. Frei, *The Identity of Jesus Christ: The Hermeneutical Bases of Dogmatic Theology* (Philadelphia: Fortress, 1975); Gerald O'Collins, *Christology: A Biblical, Historical, and Systematic Study of Jesus* (Oxford: University, 1995), 138, 241-42, 250. See also A. Harnack, *History of Dogma*, 1:186.
[98] L.W. Hurtado, *One God, One Lord*, 99; idem, *At the Origins of Christian Worship*, 63. P.M. Casey ("The Deification of Jesus," in *SBLSP* [1994], 709) endorses Hurtado's terminology "binitarian mutation."

and neither does this proposal by these scholars of the New History of Religions School, as Hurtado's straining defense belies.[99]

In contrast, A.E. Harvey, Don Cupitt, and P.M. Casey rightly allege that this New History of Religions School is a futile, misguided effort. They agree with Bauckham and Hurtado that mainstream Second Temple Judaism was strictly monotheistic; but they disagree with them by contending that Christians of the 1st century held to an exclusive monotheism, so that there was no development from a low to a high Christology then.[100] Harvey rightly asserts that it was not until the 2nd century CE, when Christianity "had spread well beyond the confines of its parent Judaism, that it became possible to break the constraint [of strict Jewish monotheism] and describe Jesus as divine; and it is significant that Jewish Christian churches continued to exist for at least a century which refused to take this step…. released from the constraint of Jewish monotheism, gentile Christians began to think of Jesus as also, in some sense, God."[101]

So, Harvey and others affirm the allegation lodged earlier by Bousset, Harnack, and Bultmann, that Christianity became somewhat hellenized theologically. However, Harvey and others rightly disagree with them by insisting that there is no evidence for such a hellenization in the NT, so that the high Christology developed *after* the NT was written, beginning in the early 2nd century CE. Harvey ends his classic book by stating, "there is no unambiguous evidence that the constraint of monotheism was effectively broken by any New Testament writer."[102] Accordingly, this New History of Religions School, like its predecessor, rests on the false assumption that the NT says Jesus is God.

Due to the assertion by post-apostolic church fathers and this New History of Religions School that Jesus preexisted, we now turn to examine the two foremost OT figures purported to have aided the church's transition from a low to a high Christology in the 1st century CE. These are "the angel of the LORD" and Daniel's "Son of Man."

B. The Angel of the LORD

Introduction	Moses and the Guardian Angel of Israel
The Meaning of *malak*	The Transcendence of God
Adam and Eve	Joshua
Hagar	Other Instances of Angel of the LORD
Abraham	The Angels Gabriel and Michael
Isaac and Jacob	Michael as the Guardian Angel of Israel
Manoah and his Wife	Servetus and Michael the Archangel
Moses	

Introduction

Without a doubt, the most mysterious and enigmatic figure in the OT is "the angel of the LORD (=Yahweh)." This expression occurs repeatedly in the OT. This "angel" seems to be very important because of being involved in many of the most important events in the history of Israel that are recorded in the OT. In many

---

[99] L.W. Hurtado, *One God, One Lord*, 121; idem, *At the Origins of Christian Worship*, 70, 90, 101-06.
[100] E.g., A.E. Harvey, *Jesus and the Constraints of History*, 154-78; D. Cupitt, *Jesus and the Gospel of God*; P.M. Casey, *From Jewish Prophet to Gentile God*.
[101] A.E. Harvey, *Jesus and the Constraints of History*, 158, 173.
[102] A.E. Harvey, *Jesus and the Constraints of History*, 178.

instances, a human or humans literally saw, and usually conversed with, this individual. At first sight, these people often mistook this person as a man, and sometimes they concluded that this person was God. In most of these accounts, the angel of the LORD is at least perceived to be other worldly. Yet the OT never expressly, and thus unambiguously, identifies this individual. Consequently, Bible readers usually are quite curious about the identity of this figure in the OT.

There has never been any consensus in Judaism concerning the identity of "the angel of the LORD" in the OT. Rabbinic Judaism usually discouraged belief in angels as intermediaries between God and His people, so that it tended to treat "the angel of the LORD" in its Scriptures as God. It is because there had been many Jewish traditions that venerated angels, and many rabbis thought that these traditions encroached upon Jewish monotheism. Yet Ibn Ezra, Rashbam, and Ramban (Nahmanides)—the three foremost Jewish Bible commentators of medieval times—interpreted the angel of Ex 23 and 33, whom many rabbinic commentators identified as "the angel of the LORD," as the captain of God's angelic armies.[103] Some rabbis further identified him as Michael the archangel.

During post-apostolic church history until modern times, Christian traditionalists generally regarded "the angel of the LORD" in the OT as the Logos-Son and therefore the preexistent Jesus Christ. It has been one of their key scriptural supports in asserting Jesus' preexistence, and they have deemed it substantial OT evidence that Jesus was and is God.

Throughout church history, no one trumpeted this interpretation of "the angel of the LORD" in the OT more than 2nd century church father Justin Martyr did in his *Dialogue with Trypho,* and it had a strong impact on the church. His primary purpose in this book (we don't know if it is fiction or not) is to convince a Jew named Trypho that Christ was God, and one way he does is to equate "the angel of the LORD" in the OT with the Logos-Son as the preexistent Christ and distinguish him from the supreme God, the Father, whom he often calls "Maker of all things." For instance, Justin says to Trypho about the preexistent Christ, "Permit me, further, to show you from the book of Exodus how this same One, who is both Angel, and God, and Lord, and man, and who appeared in human form to Abraham and Isaac, appeared in a flame of fire from the bush, and conversed with Moses."[104] Justin often repeats this interpretation, calling Jesus an "Angel."[105]

It would be strange to identify the supposed preexistence of a man as an "angel." In fact, the writer of Hebrews goes to great lengths to prove that Jesus Christ is superior to angels and all other men. Thus, he clearly distinguishes Jesus from angels, describing Him as "having become as much better than the angels" (Heb 1.4). He then inquires, "For to which of the angels did He ever say" (v. 5), and he then quotes OT scriptures, thereby further distinguishing Jesus from angels. He finally writes, "But to which of the angels has He ever said, 'SIT AT MY RIGHT HAND, UNTIL I MAKE YOUR ENEMIES A FOOTSTOOL FOR YOUR FEET'" (v. 13). Besides, calling the supposed preexistent Christ an "angel" borders on Docetism (Jesus was a god and not man), which the church fervently opposed.

Yet this christological interpretation became well accepted by church fathers.[106] Many centuries later, most Reformation leaders not only embraced it,

---

[103] William H.C. Propp, *Exodus 19-40: A New Translation with Introduction and Commentary* in AB 2A (2006), 287. See Josh 5.14-15.
[104] J. Martyr, *Dialogue with Trypho* in ANF, 59.1.
[105] E.g., J. Martyr, *Dialogue with Trypho* in ANF, 34.1.6; 56.8.1; 60.3.1; 116.1.2; 127.1.5; 128.1.1, 5.
[106] C.F. Keil (K&D, 1:185n1) says a few church fathers, e.g., Augustine and Jerome, thought it an angel.

but some even rendered it essential to orthodoxy. An example was John Calvin. When he and the other pastors of Geneva condemned Servetus as a heretic and got him executed, they included in their list of allegations against him, all of which they deemed as blasphemies worthy of death, Servetus' denial that "the angel of the LORD" in the OT was the preexistent Christ.[107]

Most contemporary, traditionalist, OT scholars do not embrace this interpretation, that "the angel of the LORD" in the OT is the preexistent Christ, though many Evangelicals still do. While there is no scholastic consensus among traditionalists on the relationship of "the angel of the LORD (Yahweh)" with Yahweh Himself,[108] most of them agree with historical critics in interpreting one individual—Yahweh. James D.G. Dunn propounds this view, claiming that "the angel of Yahweh is simply a way of speaking about Yahweh himself."[109] But leading form critic Hermann Gunkel says of "the angel of the LORD" in Gen 16.7-11, "the OT often speaks of this messenger of Yahweh or God as though it were Yahweh or God himself.... This difficulty is not to be alleviated by the acceptance of the unclear notion that the messenger is simultaneously a form of Yahweh himself."[110]

Those who interpret "the angel of the LORD" in the OT as Yahweh are reminiscent of the Sadducees. Since they denied the existence of angels (e.g., Ac 23.8), alleging that scriptural descriptions of angels and their activities are merely manifestations of God Himself, they denied that the angel of the LORD was an actual angel.

Recall that the New History of Religions School, which consists only of a few traditionalist scholars, asserts that the early church was strongly aided in its development from a low to a high Christology by viewing principal angels in the OT, mostly "the angel of LORD," as divine and that this enabled the early Christians to think of Jesus as divine.

Because of these two interpretations among traditionalists—that "the angel of the LORD" in the OT indicates that Jesus is God—we need to examine this complex figure. As we do, keep in mind that the three primary interpretations are that "the angel of the LORD" in the OT is (1) Yahweh Himself, (2) the supposed preexistent Christ, and (3) an angel. A fourth interpretation, the "interpolation theory," means that later scribe(s) inserted the word *mal'ak* before *yhwh* to solve theological problems.[111] But resorting to interpolation always appears as a last resort to solve a difficulty and must be rejected by those who have a higher view of the divine inspiration of Scripture.

The Meaning of *malak*

The expression, "the angel of the LORD," occurs 56x in the OT.[112] The expression, "the angel of God," occurs 10x in the OT.[113] These two expressions occur together in two narratives, indicating that they are synonymous (Jud 6.11-22; 13.3-21).

---

[107] See J. Calvin, *Institutes*, 1.13.11-16; 1.5.11.
[108] G. Wenham, *Genesis 16-50*, 9.
[109] J.D.G. Dunn, *Christology*, 150.
[110] Hermann Gunkel, *Genesis*, 3rd ed. [1910] (rep. Macon, GA: Mercer University, 1997), 186.
[111] Advocated, e.g., by Samuel A. Meier, "Angel of Yahweh," in *DDD*, 58-59.
[112] Gen 16.7, 9-11; 22.11, 15; Ex 3.2; Num 22.22-27, 31-32, 34-35; Jud 2.1, 4; 5.23; 6.11-12, 21-22; 13.3, 13, 15-18, 20-21; 2 Sam 24.16; 1 Kgs 19.7; 2 Kgs 1.3, 15; 19.35; 1 Chr 21.12, 15-16, 18, 30; Ps 34.7; 35.5-6; Isa 37.36; Zech 1.11-12; 3.1, 5-6; 12.8.
[113] Gen 21.17; 31.11; Ex 14.19; Jud 6.20; 13.6, 9; 1 Sam 29.9; 2 Sam 14.17, 20; 19.27.

An important point is that all of these narratives containing these expressions—"the angel of the LORD/God"—involve Israel or a certain Israelite(s). Most of these narratives describe actual events that occurred during Israel's pre-exilic period. Ironically, angels are not mentioned much in the OT during this period, except "the angel of the LORD/God," but more often in its post-exilic writings and especially in inter-testamental Jewish Literature.

Some of these OT accounts mention "the angel of the LORD" as well as "the LORD."[114] Some seem to distinguish the two figures; in others a blending occurs, making the two figures indistinguishable. And in a few of these accounts, "the angel of the LORD" speaks on God's behalf in the first person.[115] This blending and first person are the major reasons most scholars interpret the angel of the LORD as Yahweh Himself. Yet in some of these narratives "the angel of the LORD" speaks in the third person about "the LORD/God," indicating two individuals. And some accounts state that "the angel of the LORD/God appeared" to a certain Israelites(s),[116] while others relate that "the LORD/God appeared."[117] Also, many scholars regard some narratives as depicting the angel of the LORD/God even though they do not include these expressions.[118] In trying to identify the angel of the LORD/God, all of these texts should be examined.

So, many Israelites literally saw "the angel of the LORD/God." Even Balaam's "donkey saw the angel of the LORD" (Num 22.25, 27). Many of these narratives include conversations between this "angel" and these people. Some of these texts identify this figure as "a man," and at first he is sometimes mistaken as a man.[119] Often, this figure is depicted as performing human-like functions, e.g., eating, sitting, standing, touching, walking, moving a hand, even raising a sword.[120] The author of Hebrews likely referred to the account of Abraham in Gen 18 when he wrote, "Do not neglect to show hospitality to strangers, for by this some have entertained angels without knowing it" (Heb 13.2).

Thus, problems arise in trying to identify the angel of the LORD/God in the OT. Foremost among them is whether this figure depicts an actual angel. The Hebrew word *mal'ak* means "messenger" or "representative."[121] It can refer to either a human or an angel, but it usually refers to an angel. Andrew Bowling rightly claims that "'messenger' is an inadequate term for the wide range of tasks carried out by the OT *mal'ak*."[122]

Another problem is whether *mal'ak* in *mal'ak yhwh* should be treated as a definite noun or not. Nearly all English Bible translators render *mal'ak yhwh* in the Hebrew Bible as "the angel of the LORD" even though no definite article appears in these texts. The reason is that translators usually treat *mal'ak* as a definite noun since it is in the Hebrew construct state, in which case a specific figure is indicated. That seems to be why the LXX usually, though not

---

[114] E.g., Gen 22.11-16; Ex 3.2-7; Num 22.22-35; Jud 5.23; 6.11-23; 2 Sam 24.16-25; 2 Kgs 1.3-4, 15-16; 1 Chr 21.12-18, 27-30; Zech 1.11-17; 3.1-10; cf. Ex 6.2-3.
[115] E.g., Gen 16.10; Ex 3.2, 6; Jud 2.1.
[116] Ex 3.2; Jud 6.12; 13.3, 21.
[117] Gen 26.2, 24; 35.1, 9; Deut 31.15; 1 Sam 3.21; 1 Kgs 3.5; 9.2; 2 Chr 1.7; 7.12; cf. Gen 48.3; Ex 3.16; 4.5; 6.3; 24.10; 1 Kgs 11.9.
[118] E.g., Gen 3.8-19; 17.1-22; 18.1-33; 32.24-30 cf. with Hos 12.3-4; Josh 5.13-15.
[119] E.g., Gen 18.1-2, 16, 22, 33; Jud 6.12-22; 13.3-6, 16, 20-22; cf. Gen 32.24-30; Josh 5.13-15.
[120] E.g., Gen 18.4, 8, 16; Num 22.22-26, 31; Jud 6.11, 21; 2 Sam 24.16; 1 Kgs 19.5, 7; 1 Chron 21.15-16, 30; Zech 3.5.
[121] Andrew Bowling, "*mal'ak*," *TWOT*, 1065.
[122] Andrew Bowling, "*mal'ak*," *TWOT*, 1065.

always, translates *mal'ak* as definite.[123] But the New JPS Translation, by Jews, consistently translates the first occurrence of *mal'ak yhwh* in such narratives as "an angel of the LORD" and any subsequent occurrences in the same pericope as "the angel of the LORD," showing that translators thought no specific angel is intended.

English Bible translators do not treat the Greek NT the same way. They translate *angelos (gar/de) kuriou* as "an angel of the Lord" 10x.[124] However, there are two NT narratives in which the article both occurs and doesn't occur.

When Joseph contemplated his fiancé Mary being pregnant with the Child Jesus, "an angel of the Lord appeared to him in a dream, saying, 'Joseph, son of David, do not be afraid to take Mary as your wife; for that which has been conceived in her is of the Holy Spirit'" (Mt 1.20). Then we read, "Joseph arose from his sleep, and did as the angel of the Lord commanded him" (v. 24). In the Greek text, the first occurrence of *angelos* is anarthrous, i.e., without the article, but the second is *ho angelos*, thus with it. But this has no significance, since the article would naturally be included the second time.

The other example is Stephen's speech that brought about his martyrdom, in which he mentions "angel," without "Lord," 3x. He first quotes Ex 3.1, saying that "an angel" appeared to Moses in the burning bush (Ac 7.30). When he mentions it again (v. 35), although the Greek text does not have the article, since *angelou* is the genitive case translators usually render it "the angel." In the third instance he says "the angel who was speaking to him on Mount Sinai," i.e., when Moses received the Law (v. 38). In this case it is *tou angelou*, thus having the article. So, although Stephen refers to two different incidents in Moses' career, we shall see that the angel involved in each incident was the same, being the angel of the LORD, yet Stephen shows that whether the article is included or not is irrelevant in identifying that figure. His saying it both ways may reflect the LXX.

Even if we accept that *mal'ak* in *mal'ak yhwh* in the Hebrew Bible should always be treated as a definite noun, i.e., "the angel of the LORD," we can't be sure it refers to the same angel every time until we get to the book of Daniel nearer the end of the OT.

The Bible is a literary progression of divine revelation. That is why there is much benefit in reading it from cover to cover. This becomes evident when examining its many accounts of the angel of the LORD/God. So, the proper method to use for discovering the identity of the angel of the LORD/God in the Bible is to examine its texts containing this expression in their chronological order, which we will now do. It will be a little tedious, and we won't consider all of them, but this method will payoff at the end of our study.

Adam and Eve

According to the book of Genesis, God made the first man, Adam, and put him in a garden (Gen 2.7-15). Then we read, "the LORD God commanded the man, saying, 'From any tree in the garden you may eat freely, but from the tree of the knowledge of good and evil you shall not eat, for in the day that you eat from it you shall surely die" (v. 16). This narrative does not indicate whether God also appeared to Adam.

Then God made Eve. Satan deceived her, Adam and Eve ate of the forbidden fruit, and for the first time they recognized their nakedness (Gen 3.1-7). Then we read, "And they heard the sound of the LORD God walking in the garden, in

---

[123] E.g., 2 Sam 24.16-17; 1 Kgs 19.5, 7; 1 Chron 21.12, 15-16, 18, 20, 27, 30; Zech 3.1, 3.

[124] Mt 1.20; 2.13, 19; 28.2; Lk 1.11; 2.9; Ac 5.19; 8.26; 12.7, 23. John 5.4 is not in the best Greek mss.

the cool of the day, and the man and his wife hid themselves from the presence of the LORD God among the trees of the garden" (v. 8). Then a most significant dialogue ensues between them.

There are two things we should keep in mind about this second encounter as we examine subsequent encounters between God and his people recorded in Scripture. First, God not only was walking in the garden, but Adam and Eve heard it, so that this was not a vision. Second, God revealed his presence to Adam and Eve. Did He Himself actually walk in their midst? Did they literally see God? We read later in the book of Genesis that Enoch, Noah, and Abraham "walked with God" (Gen 5.22, 24; 6.9; cf. 17.1; 24.40; 26.5).

Hagar

The angel of the LORD is first mentioned in Genesis in stories about the Hebrew patriarchs and a maid. On various occasions, the angel of the LORD appeared and/or spoke to them. These episodes often happened during times of crisis in their lives.

The first episode involves Hagar, the maid of Sarai, Abram's wife. (God later changed Abram's name to Abraham and Sarai's name to Sarah.) Hagar experienced two encounters with the angel of the LORD, and both of them involved her son Ishmael.

In Hagar's first encounter, we only learn that "the angel of the LORD found her" and spoke to her (Gen 16.7-12). The narrative does not say whether this angel appeared to her. But right after their first meeting ended we read, "Then she called the name of the LORD who spoke to her, 'You are a God who sees;' for she said, 'Have I even remained alive here after seeing Him?" (v. 13).[125] So, this angel of the LORD must have appeared to Hagar, because she literally saw him, even though the text does not expressly state it.

This is a key point. Other such biblical narratives do not always include details which the circumstances necessarily require. This angel of the LORD was a stranger who appeared as a man, yet Hagar realized his otherworldly status as he said her name, told her she was Sarai's pregnant maid, and said God would give her a son and descendants.

We read concerning Hagar's second encounter, "God heard the lad [Ishmael] crying, and the angel of God called to Hagar from heaven" (Gen 21.17). Notice that "God heard," but "the angel of God" spoke, which seems to distinguish God from the angel so that the angel was not God. Furthermore, this surely was "the angel of the LORD" who had appeared to Hagar previously. And this narrative introduces a new detail: the angel spoke "from heaven," suggesting that he may not have appeared to Hagar at this time.

Scholars claim that when the Bible depicts God appearing to a human(s), it is a theophany. Such should be distinguished from visions or dreams that have appearances, which are not literally seen. Genesis records six supposed theophanies that involved the patriarchs as follows: 3x to Abraham (Gen 12.7; 17.1; 18.1); 2x to Isaac (Gen 26.2, 24); 1x to Jacob (Gen 35.9). The first five of these narratives state that "the LORD appeared." The sixth one says "God appeared." In all six of these narratives, no angel is mentioned.

---

[125] The Hebrew phrase here rendered "a God who sees" is difficult and can be translated "a God who may be seen." And capitalizing pronouns modifying "the angel of the LORD" in the NASB, as here, indicates that its translators were Trinitarians who believed either that this figure refers to Yahweh or the preexistent Christ.

Abraham

Abraham is a prime example. Sometimes, the book of Genesis only narrates that "the LORD" spoke to Abram, just as it does concerning its first mention of Abram's many encounters with Yahweh (Gen 12.1). Other times, it relates that "the LORD appeared to Abram and said" something to him (Gen 12.7; 17.1; cf. 18.1). The second time this occurs, they finished talking and "God went up from Abraham" (Gen 17.22; Abram's name has now been changed). The third time, "the LORD appeared to him ... [a]nd when he lifted up his eyes and looked, behold, three men were standing opposite him" (Gen 18.1-2; cf. Heb 13.2). One conversed with Abraham while "the two angels" departed to destroy nearby Sodom and Gomorrah (19.1). We read, "Abraham was still standing before the LORD. And Abraham came near" and spoke to him (Gen 18.22-23). Abraham obviously came near an actual personage, so that all three persons appeared as men. The one who stayed behind must have been the LORD or someone representing the LORD.

Then, did Yahweh literally appear to Abraham at this time? Interestingly, these three encounters between Yahweh and Abraham do not mention "the angel of the LORD."

The third mention of the angel of the LORD in Genesis concerns the time when "God tested Abraham" regarding his only son Isaac (Gen 22.1). God spoke to Abraham, commanding him to go to Mount Moriah and sacrifice Isaac there as a burnt offering. He went, and as Abraham took the knife to slay his son "the angel of the LORD called to him from heaven" (v. 11), telling Abraham not to continue. The narrative states, "Then the angel of the LORD called to Abraham a second time from heaven" (v. 15). The angel speaking from heaven suggests that he may not have appeared to Abraham.

So, this incident is the first recorded in Scripture in which Abraham encountered the angel of the LORD. Yet it begins with "God" speaking to Abraham, not "the angel of the LORD." Plus, we have learned that "the LORD appeared to Abram" on two previous occasions (Gen 12.7; 17.1). In all of these incidents, God likely encountered Abraham by means of the angel of the LORD even though some biblical narratives do not say so.

Next, Abraham sent his servant to his relatives at Nahor to get a wife for his son Isaac. Abraham first assured his servant, "the LORD, the God of heaven,... He will send His angel before you" (Gen 24.7). God clearly acted in these circumstances. When the servant arrived at his destination, he told his story to Abraham's relatives, adding that his master had told him, "The LORD, before whom I have walked, will send His angel with you to make your journey successful" (v. 40). These statements by Abraham clearly distinguish an actual angel from Yahweh. Most likely, Abraham refers to that same "angel of the LORD" who had appeared and/or spoken to him on previous occasions.

Isaac and Jacob

Regarding Abraham's son Isaac, we read that "the LORD appeared to him and said" certain things on two different occasions (Gen 26.2, 24). Yet "the angel of the LORD" is not mentioned in either of these two narratives.

It was the same with Isaac's son Jacob. As he traveled to Mesopotamia he stopped to rest at the city of Luz. We read that "he had a dream, and behold, a ladder was set on the earth with its top reaching to heaven, and behold, the angels of God were ascending and descending on it. And behold, the LORD stood above it and said, 'I am the LORD, the God of your father Abraham" (Gen 28.12-13). Then God promised Jacob, as he had Abraham, to give him a land and many descendants. When Jacob awoke from the dream he said, "Surely the LORD is in this place.... This is none other than the house of God, and this is the gate of heaven" (vv. 16-17). So Jacob renamed that city Bethel, which means "house of God." Yet there is no mention of "the angel of the LORD" in this account.

Later, Jacob had another dream which he related to his two wives. He said, "Then the angel of God said to me in the dream,... 'I am the God of Bethel'" (Gen 31.11, 13). So, it was the angel of the LORD/God who appeared and spoke to Jacob in the first dream even though the account does not say. In both, the angel must represent God as His agent.

Jacob had another interesting experience. One night "a man wrestled with him until daybreak" (Gen 32.24). Jacob sensed his superhuman status and asked him for a blessing. When he blessed Jacob and presumably departed, the patriarch exclaimed as Hagar had, "I have seen God face to face, yet my life has been preserved" (v. 30). Again, this indicates it was an actual angel and not God Himself even though it is not so stated.

At the end of Jacob's life he said to his son Joseph, "God Almighty appeared to me at Luz" (Gen 48.3), yet that was in a dream. Then Jacob spoke of "the angel who has redeemed me from all evil" (v. 16). This must include when "a man wrestled with him," whom Jacob here identifies as an "angel," as well as the other appearances to him (28.13; 31.11; 35.9), indicating that it was always the same angel. And Hosea the prophet says Jacob "contended with God. Yes, he wrestled with the angel and prevailed" (Hos 12.4). Hosea surely would not have said "angel," here, if it had actually been "the LORD."

The wrestling angel had said to Jacob, "Your name shall no longer be Jacob, but Israel; for you have striven with God and with men and have prevailed" (Gen 32.28; cf. 35.10). Israel means "contend with God" or "God contends." Then we read, "Then Jacob asked him and said, 'Please tell me your name.' But he said, 'Why is it that you ask my name?' And he blessed him there. So Jacob named the place Peniel, for he said, 'I have seen God face to face, yet my life has been preserved'" (Gen 32.29-30). The angel didn't answer Jacob's question by telling him his name. Why not? Jacob isn't alone in asking it.

Manoah and his Wife

Sometime later, Manoah and his barren wife wanted to have children. We read, "Then the angel of the LORD appeared to the woman" (Jud 13.3). He told her she would bear a son, and he was to become Samson. She went and told her husband, "A man of God came to me and his appearance was like the appearance of the angel of God, very awesome. And I did not ask him where he came from, nor did he tell me his name" (v. 6).

The same angel later appeared to Manoah and his wife and conversed with them. We read, "Then Manoah said to the angel of the LORD, 'Please let us detain you so that we may prepare a kid for you.' And the angel of the LORD said to Manoah, 'Though you detain me, I will not eat your food but if you prepare a burnt offering, then offer it to the LORD.' For Manoah did not know that he was the angel of the LORD" (Jud 13.15-16). The angel clearly distinguishes himself from Yahweh and implies that sacrifices should be offered only to Yahweh and therefore not to himself.

Then we read, "Manoah said to the angel of the LORD, 'What is your name, so that when your words come to pass, we may honor you?' But the angel of the LORD said to him, 'Why do you ask my name, seeing it is wonderful?'" (Jud 13.17-18). Then the angel "performed wonders while Manoah and his wife looked on.... The angel of the LORD ascended in the flame of the altar. When Manoah and his wife saw this, they fell on their faces to the ground... Then Manoah knew that he was the angel of the LORD. So Manoah said to his wife, 'We shall surely die, for we have seen God'" (vv. 19-22). But his wife gave wise reasons why they would not die. Again, Manoah expressed the tradition that a mortal human being who literally sees God will soon die.

So, Manoah told the angel that if his prediction came true, he and his wife would "honor" him. The veneration of angels has often been a problem within both Judaism and Christianity that threatened to bring reproach against their claim to monotheism. This subject even emerges in the NT. John the Revelator says that he "fell down to worship at the feet of the angel who showed me these things. And he said to me, 'Do not do that, I am a fellow servant ... worship God'" (Rev 22.8-9). Yet John had done this same thing earlier, and the angel had made the same reply (19.10-11). These accounts reveal the strong lure to worship angels when they do wonders or give insight. This seems to be the reason the angel of the LORD did not answer Jacob or Manoah when they asked his name.

Moses

Throughout the book of Genesis, we cannot be sure if the several occurrences of the expression "the angel of the LORD" refer to the same figure, whether Yahweh Himself or a real angel. But when we turn to Exodus, the next book of the Bible, that all changes.

One of the most prominent examples of the appearance of the angel of the LORD in the OT is when God first told Moses He was going to deliver Israel from bondage in Egypt through Moses' leadership. We read in this account that "the angel of the LORD appeared to him [Moses] in a blazing fire from the midst of a bush; and he looked, and behold, the bush was burning with fire, yet the bush was not consumed" (Ex 3.2). Moses was intrigued, turned aside, and came closer to investigate this awesome site. Then "God called to him from the midst of the bush," saying, "I am the God of your father, the God of Abraham" (vv. 4, 6). "Then Moses hid his face, for he was afraid to look at God" (v. 6). A very important and extended dialogue then ensues between Moses and this figure.

Notice that the narrative says "the angel of the LORD appeared" to Moses in the flaming bush, "God called" to Moses from the bush, the speaker said "I am the God" of the patriarchs, and Moses was "afraid to look at God." Three things must be concluded from these elements in the narrative: (1) "the angel of the LORD," "the LORD," and "God" are used interchangeably here and in numerous OT narratives to refer to the same figure,[126] (2) Moses was afraid due to the tradition that mortal humans cannot see God and live, and (3) Moses did not die when he saw the angel of the LORD. Therefore, this individual could not have been God Himself; rather, it *seemed* that Moses saw and heard God. This interchangeability is best explained as "the angel of the LORD" representing God as His agent. Consequently, to see or hear the angel is rightly described as seeing or hearing God. Thus, the only reasonable conclusion from this account and those above is that *the angel of the* LORD *was not God Himself but His personal representative.*[127]

Soon afterwards, Moses prayed to God and God spoke to him again, saying, "I am the LORD; and I appeared to Abraham, Isaac, and Jacob, as God Almighty" (Ex 6.3). Yet we have read in some of these narratives about the patriarchs that "the angel of the LORD" appeared to them. God Almighty could not literally have

---

[126] E.g., Gen 16.7, 13; 21.17; 22.15-16; Ex 14.19, 24, 26, 30; Jud 6.11-12, 14, 16, 20, 23.
[127] C. Rowland, *The Open Heaven*, 94-95.

appeared to them or they would have instantly died. So, this statement must mean that *God appeared to the patriarchs by means of the angel of the* LORD *as His personal representative.*

Trinitarian Bruce Waltke well says of the angel of the LORD in the OT, "Like all angels, he is a heavenly being sent from the heavenly court to earth as God's personal agent.... So also the Lord's messenger is treated as God and yet as distinct from God, as God's angel.... Some [scholars] equate him with the second person of the Trinity, yet the New Testament never makes this identification."[128] James D.G. Dunn shows from the NT that "the possibility of equating Jesus with the angel of the LORD had never entered the Evangelists' heads ... *There is no evidence that any* NT *writer thought of Jesus as actually present in Israel's past,* either as the angel of the Lord, or as 'the Lord' himself."[129] Yet the NT reveals that its authors expended much effort in linking Jesus to the Jewish Bible.

Moses and the Guardian Angel of Israel

Another very important incident in which God *seemed* to have appeared to Moses happened at the time He gave Moses the Law on Mount Sinai. Thereupon, God revealed how He would bring the Israelites into the promised land. He told Moses, "Behold, I am going to send an angel before you [Israel] to guard you along the way, and to bring you into the place which I have prepared. Be on your guard before him and obey his voice; do not be rebellious toward him, for he will not pardon your transgression, since My name is in him.... For My angel will go before you and bring you into the land" (Ex 23.20-21, 23). Can anything be clearer than this, that two beings are being depicted, so that this "angel" is not God Himself? Besides, God can't send Himself as His own agent, which is absurd.

God later reiterated to Moses, "My angel shall go before you;... And I will send an angel before you and drive out the Canaanite,... for I will not go up in your midst, because you are an obstinate people, lest I destroy you on the way" (Ex 32.34; 33.2, 3). This text states further, "For the LORD had said to Moses, 'Say to the sons of Israel, "You are an obstinate people; should I go up in your midst for one moment, I would destroy you"'" (Ex 33.5). Herein, God distinguishes Himself from this angel, so that this angel is not God. It is due to God's holiness that He must send this angel as an intermediary.

This angel will "guard" Israel, making him *the guardian angel of Israel.* He will guard the Israelites against their enemies and protect them from the stifling desert heat by providing a pillar of cloud by day and a pillar of fire by night, enabling them to travel either day or night (Ex 13.21-22; 14.19-21, 24). But if they do not obey what the angel commands them to do, and thus rebel against him, he will discipline them.

So, *God Himself did not appear in the following episodes: the burning bush, the deliverance from Egypt, the journey to the promised land, and taking possession of it.* Moses explained in a letter to the king of Edom that "the Egyptians treated us and our fathers badly. But when we cried out to the LORD, He heard our voice and sent an angel and brought us out from Egypt" (Num 20.16). So, God did all of this through His angel.

Stephen, the first Christian martyr affirms this and more. Filled with the Holy Spirit (Ac 7.55), he preached that "an angel appeared" to Moses at the burning bush (v. 30), Moses was "the one whom God sent to be both a ruler and

---
[128] B.K. Waltke, *Genesis: A Commentary*, 253-54.
[129] J.D.G. Dunn, *Christology*, 154, 158. Emphasis his.

a deliverer with the help of the angel who appeared to him in the thorn bush" (v. 35), and Moses was "the one who was in the congregation in the wilderness together with the angel who was speaking to him on Mount Sinai" (v. 38). Thus, Stephen makes it clear that the angel God sent to lead Israel through the wilderness and help take possession of the promised land was the same angel that previously appeared to Moses in the burning bush and on Mount Sinai. Thus, *the angel of the* LORD *is the guardian angel of Israel.*

Although the Torah says that "the LORD came down on Mount Sinai," and "the LORD descended upon it in fire" (Ex 19.20, 18), God did so through His intermediary angel. And Stephen also informs that other "angels" assisted in giving the Law on Mount Sinai (v. 53; cf. Deut 33.2 LXX; Gal 3.19; Heb 2.2). So, *the* LORD *God did not personally give the Law to Moses on Mount Sinai, but the angel of the* LORD *did it as His agent.* "Moses spoke and God answered him with thunder" (Ex 19.19), caused by that angel.

The Transcendence of God

Cited in Chapter Three, Sir Isaac Newton had both angels and humans in mind in stating the maxim that "God does nothing by himself which he can do by another." Another reason God sends such agents is that, in order for Him to interact with His creation, one of His attributes requires it. God's holiness, which is manifested by His glory, results in His relation to creation that theologians call "the transcendence of God." This is most evident in God's giving of the Law.

When God gave Moses the Law, He said thereafter that He would meet Moses at the tent of meeting and speak to him (not with thunder) from above the mercy seat resting atop the ark of the covenant (Ex 25.22). Whenever Moses would enter this tent the people would arise and stand at the entrance of their tents to watch the pillar of cloud "descend and stand at the entrance of the tent; and the LORD would speak with Moses.... Thus the LORD used to speak to Moses face to face, just as a man speaks to his friend" (34.9, 11).

Moses then asked Yahweh, "See, You say to me, 'Bring up this people!' But You Yourself have not let me know whom You will send with me. Moreover, You have said, 'I have known you by name, and you have also found favor in My sight'" (Ex 33.12). Moses' mention of his own name indicates that in his previous sentence he means that God had not told him the name of the angel He would send. Yet God did not answer him.

Moses then asked God, "show me Your glory!" (Ex 33.18). God replied, "You cannot see My face; for no man can see Me and live!" (v. 20, cf. v. 23). Again, God probably spoke to Moses through the angel of the LORD as His personal representative. And this pericope reveals that Jacob was wrong, or he didn't mean it literally, in his first clause when he exclaimed, "I have seen God face to face, yet my life has been preserved" (Gen 32.29-30). So, when OT saints said they saw God, as if literally, they really saw His representative.

Two points need to be understood from this narrative. First, when "the LORD used to speak to Moses face to face, just as a man speaks to his friend" (Ex 33.11), it could not have been literal since God also said, "no man can see Me and live." Thus, it merely means that the voice representing God originated from above the mercy seat in the tent of meeting on the same level as two humans talk, not that there necessarily was any outward manifestation that was the source of that voice. Second, when "the LORD" then said to Moses, "you shall see My back, but My face shall not be seen" (v. 23), this supposed theophany which ensued as Moses was in the cleft of a rock could not have been Yahweh Himself because He had said, "no man can see Me and live" (v. 20), whether His face or His back. Then when "the LORD descended in the cloud and stood there with him [Moses]," and "the LORD passed by in front of him" (34.5-6), it must have been Yahweh's personal representative. Moreover, after this glorious figure passed by Moses we read, "Then God said,... Be sure to observe what I am commanding you this day: behold, I am going to drive out the Amorite before you, and the Canaanite," etc. (vv. 10-12). But we learned that the figure who is going to do that is "an angel" God will send (23.20, 23; 33.2). So, this one that passed before Moses in great glory was the guardian angel of Israel who also showed himself to Moses as Yahweh's personal representative.

A similar event took place at this time. Moses, his three administrators, and the seventy elders of Israel together "saw the God of Israel; and under His feet there appeared to be a pavement of sapphire, as clear as the sky itself. Yet He did not stretch out His hand against the nobles of the sons of Israel; and they beheld God, and they ate and drank" (Ex 24.10-11). Saying that God did not stretch out His hand against them recalls the tradition that if mortal humans literally see God they will immediately die. Since they ate, it was not a vision. This event also must have involved the angel appearing as God.

Other examples of the LORD and/or the angel of the LORD appearing to Israelites and they contemplated whether they would die are when Gideon and his 300 men were about to slay the Midianites (Jud 6.22-23), and Manoah's wife was going to bear their son Samson (Jud 13.20-23). The biblical narratives of these events affirm that these people did not literally see God but His personal agent, who was also the guardian angel of Israel. Gideon spoke to the angel, implying his fear of death, and the angel replied, "Peace to you, do not fear; you shall not die" (Jud 6.23).

It was no different with Jesus. Humans saw Him just as they saw the angel of the LORD, yet they did not die. If either of them had been God, those people would have died. Jesus, John, and Paul affirm this tradition.[130] (See Chapter Six/The Invisibility of God.) So, *God sent His angel as His intermediary to guard Israel because God is transcendent.* Because of His holiness, God transcends fallen, sinful humans and their activities. He dwells in a glorious light,[131] signifying His holiness, making Him unapproachable by mortals. Thus, God sent this angel as His intermediary between Himself and His creation.

Joshua

The Hebrews, after wandering in the wilderness for forty years, arrived at the backside of the land of Canaan to take possession of it as God had promised. Moses died, Joshua replaced him, and the people forded the Jordan River just across from Jericho. We read, "Now it came about when Joshua was by Jericho, that he lifted up his eyes and looked, and behold, a man was standing opposite him with his sword drawn in his hand, and Joshua went to him and said to him, 'Are you for us or for our adversaries?' And he said, 'No, rather I indeed come now as captain of the host of the LORD.' And Joshua fell on his face to the earth, and bowed down, and said to him, 'What has my lord to say to his servant?' And the captain of the LORD's host said to Joshua, 'Remove your sandals from your feet, for the place where you are standing is holy.' And Joshua did" (Josh 5.13-15). Notice that Joshua "bowed down," similar to John the Revelator before the angel, except that here it does not say that he did it "to worship" the angel (Rev 19.10; 22.8).

---

[130] E.g., Jn 1.18; 5.37; 6.46; 1 Tim 1.17; 6.16; 1 Jn 4.12.
[131] E.g., Ps 104.2; cf. Eze 1.4, 28; Dan 7.10.

This "man" with a drawn sword indicates that he is a warrior who is poised to conduct war. The word "host," mentioned repeatedly in the OT, often refers to God's angelic armies in heaven. And this "man" identifying himself as their "captain" indicates that he is the chief of the angelic armies, thus an angel appearing as a man. He obviously is going to fight for the Hebrews as they enter the promised land and take possession of it from the Canaanites. The Greek Orthodox Church adopts a Jewish tradition of identifying this angel as Michael the archangel, the angel of the LORD, and it calls him the "Supreme Commander of the Heavenly Hosts." So, *the guardian angel of Israel is also the chief of the angelic armies of heaven.*

Other Instances of the Angel of the LORD

Several OT Scriptures state that the angel of the LORD spoke to certain Israelites, yet these passages do not explain whether the angel actually appeared to them. Other instances when the angel of the LORD appeared to someone are as follows:
- He killed many people when David sinned in numbering Israel (2 Sam 24; 1 Chr 21).
- He strengthened Elijah with super food to make a forty-day journey (1 Kgs 18.7-8).
- He struck the Assyrian armies and 185,000 died in the camp (2 Kgs 19.35; Isa 37.36).

The strongest evidence that the angel of the LORD in the OT is to be distinguished from Yahweh Himself is those narratives that present these two talking to each other.

The first narrative in which this occurs is about David's sin in numbering Israel. We read, "And God sent an angel to Jerusalem to destroy it; but as he was about to destroy it, the LORD saw and was sorry over the calamity, and said to the destroying angel, 'It is enough; now relax your hand.' And the angel of the LORD was standing by the threshing floor of Ornan the Jebusite. Then David lifted up his eyes and saw the angel of the LORD standing between earth and heaven, with his drawn sword in his hand stretched out over Jerusalem" (1 Chr 21.15-16; cf. 2 Sam 24.15-16). David immediately bought that threshing floor, built an altar on it, and offered burnt sacrifices to the LORD. It seems the angel remained visible with his drawn sword. For we then read, "And the LORD commanded the angel, and he put his sword back in its sheath" (1 Chr 21.27).

Another time when the angel of the LORD and the LORD spoke to one another was in the Prophet Zechariah's vision he had about four angels who rode horses patrolling the earth (Zech 1.10-11). Chief among them was "a/the man" (vv. 8, 10) who was "the angel of the LORD" (v. 12). We read, "Then the angel of the LORD answered and said, 'O LORD of hosts, how long will You have no compassion for Jerusalem and the cities of Judah,... And the LORD answered the angel" (vv.12-13).

As we progress through the OT with our examination, we discover that the angel of the LORD increasingly becomes a distinct personality that is separate from Yahweh and thus in accordance with the portrayal of Israel's guardian angel in Ex 23 and 33.[132]

---

[132] Darrell D. Hannah, *Michael and Christ: Michael Traditions and Angel Christology in Early Christianity* (Tubingen: Mohr Siebeck, 1999), 24.

The Angels Gabriel and Michael

Israel's guardian angel has a special significance beyond being its patron angel. In speaking of him, God told Moses, "My presence shall go with you, and I will give you rest" (Ex 33.14). That is, God's presence would accompany this angel. Isaiah explains about God delivering Israel from bondage in Egypt, that "the angel of His presence saved them" (Isa 63.9), which means literally "the angel of His face saved them" (cf. Mt 18.10).[133] So, Israel's guardian angel has the honor of being associated with God's presence, which further suggests that this angel is God's personal representative.

Although the Bible often mentions angels, it names only two of them: Gabriel and Michael.[134] Gabriel is the only angel mentioned in the Bible who is expressly associated with the presence of God. When Gabriel appeared to the priest Zacharias, announcing that his barren wife Elizabeth would have a son, who would later become John the Baptist, Zacharias questioned it. The angel replied as if slighted, "I am Gabriel, who stands in the presence of God" (Lk 1.19).

Some inter-testamental Jewish Literature mentions, and sometimes names, seven supreme angels.[135] Two are Gabriel and Michael. The book of Daniel probably refers to these seven special angels when it says that the angel "Michael," whom we know to be an "archangel" (Jude 9), is "one of the chief princes" (Dan 10.13). Accordingly, these seven superior angels are called "archangels" and "chief princes." In the book of Revelation, "the seven Spirits who are before His [God's] throne" (Rev 1.4; cf. 3.1; 4.5; 5.6), and "the seven angels who stand before God" (Rev 8.2), probably are the same seven archangels mentioned in this inter-testamental Jewish Literature. (See Chapter Four/The Seven Spirits of God.) So, Gabriel and Michael are surely two of these seven archangels who stand before God's throne in heaven and therefore in God's immediate presence.[136]

The chief of the angelic armies of heaven is Michael the archangel. Revelation says, "And there was war in heaven, Michael and his angels waging war with the dragon. And the dragon and his angels waged war, and they were not strong enough, and there was no longer a place found for them in heaven. And the great dragon was thrown down, the serpent of old who is called the devil and Satan, who deceives the whole world, he was thrown down to the earth, and his angels were thrown down with him" (Rev 12.7-9). So, this text affirms that Michael is "the captain of the host of the LORD" (Josh 5.14).

Michael as the Guardian Angel of Israel

Many scholars think God's announcement to Moses in Ex 23 and 33—that He would send an angel to guard Israel—is seminal to a correct understanding of "the angel of the LORD" in the OT even though this expression does not occur in these two texts.

Pre-Christian Judaism had a widespread rabbinical belief that "the angel of the LORD" was an actual, special angel. Some rabbis called this figure "the great angel." Many identified him as the angel depicted in Ex 23 and 33, which they also designated as "the angel of God's presence" because God said to Moses in the context of this angel, "My presence shall go with you" (Ex 33.14; cf. Is 63.9). Many of these rabbis further identified this great angel with the name "Metatron." This

---

[133] Textual critics think the above MT reading was original and not the LXX. Translated into English it reads, "neither a messenger nor an angel, but His face saved them," i.e., the LORD Himself.

[134] Gabriel: Dan 8.16; 9.21; Lk 1.19, 26. Michael: Dan 10.13, 21; 12.1; Jude 1.9; Rev 12.7.

[135] E.g., *1 En.* 20.1-7, which names six of them; but some mss. of *1 Enoch* name all seven. See also *1 En.* 40.9-10; 54.6; 68.2-4; 71.3, 8-9; *Tobit* 12.15; *Test. of Levi* 3.5.

[136] Cf. Jub. 1.27, 29; 2.1-2; *Test. of Levi* 3.7.

viewpoint is espoused in much non-canonical Jewish Literature. In *3 Enoch*, alone, thirty-four of that book's forty-eight chapters begin, "Metatron (Prince of the Divine Presence) said to me." This Metatron is also called therein "the lesser Yahweh" (*3 En.* 12.5) and identified as the angel of Ex 23. But rabbinic Judaism rejected this provocative assertion as a threat to its monotheism.

Similarly, the Magharians, a pre-Christian Jewish sect, claimed that all mention in the OT of human contact with either "the angel of the LORD" and/or "the LORD" does not pertain to God Himself but an angel who represented the presence of God to Israel.[137]

Larry Hurtado relates this tradition. He says "ancient Judaism embraced the idea that God had a particular angel more exalted than others, whose authority and status made him second only to God." Hurtado identifies this angel as Michael the archangel, the guardian angel of Israel.[138] Darrell Hannah observes, "The tradition of Michael as Israel's angelic champion and guardian was well established in the [Jewish] apocalypses."[139] In fact, the sectarian Qumran Community, which produced the Dead Sea Scrolls, described Michael the archangel as the Angel of Light who, as the commander of the angelic hosts (armies) of heaven, would lead true Israel to victory during the eschaton. Thus, Gerhard von Rad asserts matter-of-factly, "Michael is the guardian angel of Israel."[140]

So far, we have examined most texts in the Pentateuch and the historical books of the OT that contain the expression "the angel of the LORD," and they do not provide much information about this figure's identity. But the book of Daniel, written many years later, implicitly identifies the angel of Ex 23 and 33—Israel's guardian angel—as Michael.

Daniel relates that he mourned and fasted for three weeks and then had a vision (Dan 10.2-6). An unnamed angel, perhaps Gabriel (Dan 8.16; 9.21), came to Daniel and said that he had been trying to come to Daniel's aid since the first day of his fast (v. 12). But he explained, "the prince of the kingdom of Persia was withstanding me for twenty-one days; then behold, Michael, one of the chief princes, came to help me, for I had been left there with the kings of Persia. Now I have come to give you an understanding of what will happen to your people in the latter days" (vv. 13-14). This angel also said that when he was finished delivering his message to Daniel, "I shall now return to fight against the prince of Persia; so I am going forth, and behold, the prince of Greece is about to come" (v. 20). This obviously describes a conflict between God's angels and Satan's angels, and it reveals that certain angels, not necessarily God's, have authority over certain nations.[141] Indeed, if each believer has a guardian angel, why not nations?[142]

Then this angel gave Daniel the longest message in the Bible (Dan 11.2–12.13). It predicts Israel's future and the kingdoms that will affect it. The angel says of the end of the age, "Now at that time Michael, the great prince who stands guard over the sons of your people, will arise" to deliver Israel from its

---

[137] Jarl E. Fossum, "The Magharians: A Pre-Christian Jewish Sect and Its Significance for the Study of Gnosticism and Christianity," *Henoch* 9 (1987), 329.
[138] L.W. Hurtado, *One God, One Lord*, 81-82, 90.
[139] D.D. Hannah, *Michael and Christ*, 38.
[140] Gerhard von Rad, "angelos," in TDNT, 1:79.
[141] This is supported by the LXX rendering of the end of Deut 32.8, translated "according to the angels of God," rather than the MT rendering, which is translated "according to the number of the sons of Israel."
[142] Mt 18.10; Lk 22.43; Ac 12.15; cf. Rev 1.1; *1 En.* 100.5.

greatest "time of distress" (Dan 12.1), and then will occur the resurrection of the righteous dead (v. 2). Daniel is clear; *the guardian angel of Israel, mentioned in Ex 23 and 33, is Michael the archangel.*[143]

Recall that God said of Israel's guardian angel, "My name is in him" (Ex 23.21). Both of the Hebrew words *yhwh* and *el* can be treated as names for God. Michael means "who is like God," in which the *el* in this name means "God."

Perhaps we should address Daniel's account of Babylonian King Nebuchudnezzar having Daniel's three friends cast into the fiery furnace. The king suddenly exclaimed that he saw "four men loosed and walking about in the midst of the fire without harm, and the appearance of the fourth is like a son of the gods" (Dan 3.25). Many Christians have believed that this fourth figure is the preexistent Christ mostly because the KJV translates *lebar-elahin* in the Aramaic text as "the Son of God." But this is anachronistic, reflecting church Christology rather than the king's frame of reference, and no modern English Bible versions render it this way. Besides, the king further exclaimed, "Blessed be the God" of Daniel's friends, "who has sent His angel" to deliver them (v. 28). And when later King Darius reluctantly had Daniel thrown into the den of lions, Daniel survived and explained, "My God sent His angel and shut the lions' mouths" (Dan 6.22).

In sum, by following the progression of revelation in the Bible, here is what we have learned in our examination of the identity of "the angel of the LORD" in the OT:

- *The angel of the LORD in the OT was associated exclusively with Israel.*
- *The angel of the LORD in the OT was not God Himself but His personal representative.*
- *God appeared to certain Israelites by means of the angel of the LORD as His agent.*
- *God did not appear literally to these Israelites or they would have instantly died.*
- *The transcendent God sent His angel as His intermediary to guard Israel.*
- *The angel of the LORD is the guardian angel of Israel.*
- *The guardian angel of Israel is also the chief of the angelic armies of heaven.*
- *The chief of the angelic armies of heaven is Michael the archangel.*
- *Therefore, the guardian angel of Israel is Michael the archangel.*
- *In conclusion, Michael the archangel is the angel of the LORD in the OT.*

Michael Servetus Linked Himself to Michael the Archangel

One of the theological allegations John Calvin brought against Michael Servetus was about the angel of the LORD in the OT. Calvin interpreted this figure as the preexistent Christ; but Servetus interpreted it as Michael the archangel. Calvin therefore wrote, "the impiety of Servetus was the more detestable, when he maintained that God was never manifested to Abraham and the Patriarchs, but that an angel was worshipped in his stead.... he was not a created angel, but one in whom the fullness of the Godhead dwelt." Calvin later explains more succinctly that "in those passages wherein it is stated that the angel of the Lord appeared to Abraham, Jacob, and Moses, Christ was that angel."[144]

Many have honored the day of Michael Servetus' death more than his birth, but Servetus may not have approved of that. He wrote repeatedly of his firm

---
[143] C. Rowland, *The Open Heaven*, 182.
[144] J. Calvin, *Institutes*, 1.13.10.10, 16; 1.14.5.11.

conviction that he was born on September 29th and named Michael because of divine providence. Why? There is much tradition in Christianity about Michael the archangel being a warrior who fights Satan, protects Israel and the church, and is the patron of soldiers and police.

For example, at Rome during the 6th century, September 29th was designated as "St. Michael's Day."[145] It was a feast day in commemoration of Michael the archangel. Later, it became a widespread holy day in Europe and was called "Michaelmas Day." The RCC even made it an obligatory holy day. But during the 18th and 19th centuries, the RCC discontinued making certain holy days obligatory, and one of them was Michaelmas Day.

Michael Servetus viewed himself as the embodiment of Michael the archangel in fighting against Satan and his forces. Therefore, Servetus believed those who resisted his efforts to reform the church and its Christology were controlled by Satan and his demons.

C. The Son of Man

Introduction	The Son of Man as King
Daniel 7	The Worldwide Kingdom
The Two Powers Heresy	The Son of Man as Suffering Servant
The Jewish Saints Interpretation	The Son of Man as "the Highest One"
Dating Daniel	The Son of Man as a Warrior-King
The Worldwide People of God	The Son of Man as a Divine Being?
Heaven's Royal Court	Conclusion

Introduction

The expression *ben adam* appears in the Hebrew Bible 107 times, and it usually is translated "son of man" in English versions. Ninety-three of these occurrences appear in the book of Ezekiel as a form of address or an identification of the author. In eighty-seven of these instances, God calls Ezekiel "son of man," meaning simply "man" or "that man." In the remaining instances, Ezekiel calls himself "son of man."

Almost every time this expression "son of man" appears in the OT, it is a Semitic idiom that means what it literally says or simply "man," "that man," or "child of man." When a speaker or writer uses it as a subtle method of self-identification, it is regarded as a circumlocution. This literary device avoids the personal pronoun "I" or "me," perhaps due to the author's modesty or to intentionally convey a lowly, humble attitude.

However, there is one particular occurrence of a qualified "son of man" ("Son of Man") expression in the OT that scholars debate as to whether it is a circumlocution. If it is not, it has a most profound relevance for both messianology and Christology. This single occurrence is in the apocalyptic book of Daniel, in Dan 7.13. It reads briefly, "one like a Son of Man ... came up to the Ancient of Days." Most peculiarly, this is the only occurrence of these two expressions in the OT, except the latter also appears in v. 9, and neither of them specifies the identity of those two figures. Almost all scholars rightly identify "the Ancient of Days" in Dan 7 as "the Most High God" (Yahweh), which Daniel says often. But the more enigmatic figure—"one like a Son of Man"—arouses many perplexing

---

[145] In the Bible, the word "saint" is always applied only to God's people and never to angels.

questions. For instance, Does it depict a human being? If so, Who is he? Is he the promised Messiah, called "the messianic interpretation"?

For several centuries, biblical scholars have been intensely interested in the Son of Man figure in Dan 7.13. And they have published a vast amount of commentary on it. This subject is most relevant for Christians because Jesus used this title, by far more than any other, as a means of self-identification. Son of Man study is therefore most critical to Christology in seeking to understand the identity of Jesus.

In this section we will launch out beyond our narrow focus of whether the Son of Man in Dan 7.13 is God or divine. One reason is its importance in comprehending Jesus' identity. Another reason is that there is much misunderstanding about this figure.

Daniel 7

The book of Daniel was not written originally in one language. Rather, Dan 2.4–7.28 was written in Imperial Aramaic. The remainder of the book, like the rest of the OT,[146] was written in Hebrew. Imperial Aramaic was a sister language of Hebrew and an official dialect of the neo-Babylonian empire during Daniel's lifetime. It was an early form of the Galilean Aramaic that Jesus and His Galilean disciples later spoke.

The critical christological phrase in Dan 7.13, "one like a Son of Man," translates the Aramaic expression *kebar enash*. *Ke* means "like;" *bar* means "son;" *nash* is the shortened form of *enash*, which means generically "man," "humankind," or "a human being." Both nouns in this expression are anarthrous (indefinite; *enasha* is definite). So the entire expression means literally "(one) like a male human being." Because of the addition of the prefix *ke*, and the fact that both *ben adam* in Hebrew and *bar (e)nash* in Aramaic are often used as a circumlocution, the first question that arises concerning Daniel's Son of Man is whether this figure refers to a particular human being.

To understand Dan 7.13-14, it is necessary to consider the entire context of Dan 7. Scholars debate whether Dan 7 represents a unity that was created by a single author or that later hands edited it and/or added to it. Herein, we will regard Dan 7 as a unity.

Daniel relates that he "saw a dream and visions in his mind as he lay on his bed" (Dan 7.1). An angel afterwards appeared to him to interpret this dream (v. 16). Daniel later wrote a summary of the matter (v. 1). He relates that this dream consisted of four great beasts that symbolize four earthly empire-kingdoms that would arise consecutively out of their respective regions, each bordering on the Mediterranean Sea. At the pinnacle of the dominion of each of these four kingdoms, they are symbolized by their most prominent king (v. 17). The fourth king is also symbolized by a "little horn" that emerges from the fourth beast. This fourth king wages war against "the saints" (v. 21), and he overpowers them for three-and-a-half years (v. 25: "time, times and half a time"). Near the end of this king's reign, Daniel relates a simultaneous scene that occurs in heaven:

9 "I kept looking until thrones were set up, and the Ancient of Days took His seat; His vesture was like white snow, and the hair of His head like pure wool. His throne *was* ablaze with flames, its wheels were a burning fire.

---

[146] However, one-fourth of the book of Ezra is quotations of official Babylonian records written in Aramaic.

10 "A river of fire was flowing and coming out from before Him; thousands upon thousands were attending Him, and myriads upon myriads were standing before Him; the court sat, and the books were opened.
....
13 "I kept looking in the night vision, and behold, with the clouds of heaven one like a Son of Man was coming, and He came up to the Ancient of Days and was presented before Him.[147]
14 "And to Him was given dominion, glory and a kingdom that all the peoples, nations, and men of every language might serve Him. His dominion is an everlasting dominion which will not pass away; and His kingdom is one which will not be destroyed."

There has never been a sustained scholastic consensus in either Christianity or Judaism concerning the meaning or origin of Daniel's Son of Man figure.[148] Christian orthodoxy generally has regarded it as signifying an individual, either the Messiah or the preexistent Logos-Son. But many scholars no longer regard the figure as depicting an individual, but only a symbol of Jewish saints. Yet there still remains no unanimity among Christian scholars, it being a hotly disputed issue.[149] While there is little or no evidence for a Son of Man tradition in pre-Christian Judaism,[150] 1st century Judaism generally interpreted Daniel's Son of Man as the Messiah.[151] But that would soon change.

The Two Powers Heresy

Foreign domination of ancient Israel often resulted in social foment due to the desire for political freedom. Under such circumstances, messianic aspirations were most apt to flourish. Such a time occurred during the Roman domination of the Jewish nation, especially during the Herodian rule and thereafter, up to the Second Revolt, in 132 CE. During this period, numerous false messiahs suddenly appeared and quickly vanished.[152]

In the first part of the 2nd century CE, an increasing interest emerged in Judaism about the interpretation of the Son of Man figure in Dan 7.13. Sometime between 110 and 132 CE, Judean Jewish scholar Elisha ben Abuyah professedly had a vision in which he saw Metatron (the name many Jews attributed to "the angel of the LORD") enthroned in glory. Abuyah exclaimed excitedly, "Truly, there are two divine powers in heaven," viz., Yahweh and

---

[147] Manuscript evidence of the LXX has two variant readings for Dan 7.13. One supports the MT, upon which all English versions rely, as here; but most authorities think the other one reflects the original. It coalesces the two figures into one as follows: "He came as Son of Man and presented as Ancient of Days." Some scholars, e.g., A. Yarbo Collins ("The Son of Man Tradition and the Book of Revelation," in *The Messiah*, ed. J.H. Charlesworth, 555), think this variant came into existence as a scribal error. But A.F. Segal (*Two Powers in Heaven*, 201-02) thinks it may represent a 2nd century CE scribal interpolation by rabbis as a defense against the Two Powers Heresy.

[148] D. Burkett, *The Son of Man Debate*, 5.

[149] J.D.G. Dunn, *Christology in the Making*, 65; Reginal H. Fuller, "Son of man," in *HBD* 981.

[150] This depends largely on whether the Similitudes of Enoch are pre-Christian.

[151] *Hag.* 14a; *Sanh.* 38b; Carsten Colpe, "*ho huios tou anthropou*," in *TDNT* 8:430; G. Vermes, *Jesus the Jew*, 172; A.F. Segal, *Two Powers in Heaven*, 47-48, 48n22; D. Burkett, *The Son of Debate*, 23, 122-23. See also *1 En.* 48.10; 52.4; *4 Ezra* 12.32; Jn 12.34. The Targum calls "the son of man" in Ps 80.17, "King Messiah," and connects it to Dan 7.13.

[152] J. Klausner, *The Messianic Idea in Israel*, 441. For a brief listing of messianic movements in Israel during the 1st century, see R. Bultmann, *Jesus and the Word*, 21-22. For a listing of movements between the two Jewish revolts, see John J. Collins, *The Scepter and the Star: The Messiahs of the Dead Sea Scrolls and Other Ancient Literature* (New York: Doubleday, 1995), 199-203.

Metatron (cf. 3 En 16.3; *b. Hag.* 14a; *b. Sanh.* 38b).[153] Furthermore, Abuyah's contemporary and the preeminent Torah scholar of that period, R. Akiba (c. 50-135 CE), is most known for adopting and popularizing this teaching. A key element was that he transferred Abuyah's assertion concerning the heavenly-enthroned Metatron to Daniel's Son of Man by interpreting the total number of "thrones" set up, in Dan 7.9, as two: one for "the Ancient of Days," i.e., God the Father, and the other for "one like a Son of Man."[154] R. Akiba further identified the latter as "David," referring to the Davidic Messiah.

Some Jews during this period found support for this interpretation of Daniel's Son of Man figure in the non-canonical Similitudes (*1 Enoch* 37-71) and *4 Ezra*. We have already seen that these apocalyptic writings present the Son of Man as a particular individual, viz., the Messiah of Israel (*1 En.* 48.10; 52.4), and they *seem* to characterize Him as having literally preexisted. This preexistence of the Son of Man-Messiah was thought to indicate that He was divine, perhaps a second god.

In 130 CE, Roman Emperor Hadrian imposed stricter measures against Judaism. They included transforming Jerusalem into a pagan city by renaming it *Aelia Capitolina* and banning male circumcision there. A Jew named Simon Bar Kosiba, a political leader, not a spiritual leader, took this restriction as a reproach against Judaism. He reacted by proclaiming himself as the promised Messiah-Deliverer. Rabbi Akiba publicly endorsed Simon Bar Kosiba as the Davidic Messiah-Son of Man. Thus, we read in *y.Ta'an.* 4, 68d, "Again, when R. Akiba saw Bar Kosiba, he cried out, 'This is King Messiah.'" Simon even endorsed this affirmation (*b.Tann.* 93b). Then R. Akiba joined others in renaming him "Simon Bar Kochba." The word *kochba* was a messianic term meaning "son of a star" and drawn from Num 24.17. Moreover, Simon denounced Jewish Christians. He even threatened them with severe punishment if they did not deny Jesus as the Messiah.[155]

Judaism still regards R. Akiba as the greatest Torah scholar of his generation and one of the greatest of all time. Due to this stature, most rabbis of Palestine in that period agreed with R. Akiba's endorsement; but not all of them. When R. Akiba said of Simon, "This is King Messiah," R. Yohanan ben Torta blurted out to him, "Akiba, grass will come out of your cheeks and still the Son of David will not have come!"[156]

So, in 132-135 CE Simon Bar Kochba led Jews of Palestine in armed rebellion against Rome, with R. Akiba as their spiritual leader. This uprising came to be called "the Bar Kochba Revolt" or "the Second Jewish Revolt." They recaptured Jerusalem and established Jewish rule there and in the surrounding countryside. Simon eventually was killed in battle; the conflict ended in disaster for the Jews; and R. Akiba was executed. In revenge, Emperor Hadrian instituted a period of harsh persecution against Jews in their land. The teaching of the Torah was banned and Jews were forbidden to enter Jerusalem, both offences punishable

---

[153] This tradition is reflected in *3 Enoch*, which identifies the angel ("the Angel of the LORD") of Exodus 23 as Yahweh's enthroned associate. It calls him "(The angel) Metatron, Prince of the Divine Presence" thirty-five times. This recalls Abuyah's statement, "There are indeed two powers in heaven" (*3 En.* 16.4). And *3 Enoch* even identifies Metatron most provocatively as "the lesser YHWH" (*3 En.* 12.5).

[154] The Talmud (*Sanh.* 38b) reveals that other rabbis protested against R. Akiba while agreeing that the total number of "thrones" are two. R. Jose explained, "One for justice and the other for mercy;" R. Eleazer ben Azariah suggested, "One for His [God's] throne and one for His footstool."

[155] Justin Martyr, *Apology*, 1.31.6; Eusebius, *Ecclesiastical History*, 4.8.4.

[156] *Ta'an.* 68d.

by death. The emperor even tried to eradicate all Jewish names from the land. Such actions resulted in the final stage of the Jews' worldwide Diaspora.

Despite R. Akiba's stature, rabbinic Judaism as a whole never subscribed to his novel interpretation of Dan 7 or endorse Simon Bar Kosiba as the Messiah. After that revolt, it regarded this movement, and its interpretation of Dan 7, as a serious threat to Jewish monotheism. Rabbis later labeled this messianic movement "the Two Powers Heresy." They refused to call it "the Two Gods Heresy," as if to credit the error.

The "Jewish Saints" Interpretation

As mentioned above, during Jesus' time Jews generally interpreted the Son of Man in Dan 7.13 as the Messiah. Joachim Jeremias informs that prior to the Bar Kochba Revolt, "Dan. 7.13 was interpreted, without exception, not collectively, but in terms of an individual person. In this way 'the man' becomes a title for the redeemer in apocalyptic ... the 'being in human form' of Dan. 7.13 is also identified with the Messiah in Rabbinic literature."[157] Following the Bar Kochba Revolt, in an apparent attempt to ward off any possible repeat of the Two Powers Heresy, and perhaps in opposition to Christian dogma,[158] Rabbinic Judaism abandoned the interpretation that Daniel's Son of Man depicts an individual who is the Messiah and interpreted this figure solely as a symbol collectively depicting "the saints" ("holy ones") mentioned in Dan 7.18, 21-22, 25, 27.[159] It also restricted the identification of these "saints" to persecuted faithful Jews, most probably those living during the end times. Thus, this interpretation represents a reaction to a heretical movement in Judaism that ended in the dissolution of the nation of Israel.

This "corporate" or "collective" interpretation—Daniel's Son of Man figure only symbolizing the Jewish saints of the end times—not only survives to this day in current Judaism but, amazingly, it has been adopted by most contemporary Christian scholars as well.[160] Such an interpretation renders Jesus' practice of calling Himself "the Son of Man" irrelevant to Dan 7.13, i.e., unless it is believed that Jesus used this text as a background for His "Son of Man" language while reshaping its meaning, a view many now hold. One is J.A. Fitzmyer; he admits, "The problem has always been to explain how that collective sense of the phrase would have developed into a title for an individual in the NT."[161]

Dating Daniel

In the century following the Bar Kochba Revolt, this Jewish saints interpretation of Daniel's Son of Man was reinforced by Porphery's revised dating for the composition of the book of Daniel. Porphery (232-303 CE) was a

---

[157] J. Jeremias, *New Testament Theology* (New York: Scribner's Son, 1971), 274-75. Jeremias cites the following apocalyptic literature, with corresponding estimated dates of publication, for support: *Sibylline Oracles*, 70-100 CE; *4 Ezra*, 94 CE; also Justin Martyr, *Dialogue with Trypho*, 32.1, pre-165 CE.

[158] In Allan F. Segal's scholastically-acclaimed book, *Two Powers in Heaven*, he shows that Rabbinic Judaism also applied this label to the developing church Christology, i.e., that both the Father and Jesus being God is a Two Powers Heresy.

[159] However, J.J. Collins (*The Scepter and the Star*, 187) claims that "the collective interpretation is not clearly attested in Jewish sources until Ibn Ezra."

[160] J.G.D. Dunn (*Christology in the Making*, 69n13) claimed in 1980 that this interpretation was "widely recognized" among Christian scholars, and he provided a list of twelve who had written on the subject.

[161] J.A. Fitzmyer, *The Gospel According Luke (i-ix)*, 209.

famous philosopher and the chief skeptic of Christianity in his time. He wrote a book, now non-extant, in which he argued vehemently that someone other than Daniel wrote the book of Daniel and that the author did so during the mid-2nd century BCE, soon following the wars of the Maccabees.[162] This revised date was four centuries later than the traditional one. Porphery, in his source-critical hypothesis, alleges that much of the book of Daniel belies historical dependence on the Maccabean period, so that the author really wrote history rather than prophecy. Accordingly, Porphery interprets the "little horn" in Dan 7 to be Antiochus Epiphanes (reign: 175-163 BCE). He was that Seleucid tyrant who ruled Judea so ruthlessly and provoked Jewish ire in desecrating the temple at Jerusalem by setting up an altar (likely an image) to Zeus and sacrificing a swine on it.

Since the rise of biblical criticism, a large majority of biblical scholars from a wide theological spectrum have subscribed to this late dating of the book of Daniel. But E. Earle Ellis observes, "A Maccabean origin of the Daniel narratives (Dan 1-6) has increasingly given way [scholastically] to the view that they were formed and in use well before the Maccabean period. For a number of reasons the Maccabean origin of the visions (Dan 7-12) is also open to doubt."[163] Here are Ellis's reasons: (1) since the DSS contain early copies of Daniel, it is improbable that visions could have become widely received as the word of God only a few decades after they allegedly were composed, in about 165 BCE, by an author fictitiously posing as a 6th century prophet; (2) any evidence of strictly 2nd century BCE language in Daniel probably would be the result of a necessary rewriting of it due to the need to recopy Scripture, especially Daniel, after its destruction by Antiochus Epiphanes in about 169 BCE; (3) Josephus (*Antiquities of the Jews*, 11.337) records a fascinating story about the Jewish high priest showing Alexander the Great a copy of the book of Daniel, which would have been in the 4th century BCE. This story, which most scholars deem fiction, may be historically accurate since Josephus often relied on the historian Hecataeus of Abdera (c. 300 BCE), who wrote a book on the relationship of the Jews to Alexander.[164]

This hypothesis—a Maccabean origin of the book of Daniel during the 2nd century BCE—has had an enormous impact on the interpretation of Daniel. For example, "the saints" in Dan 7 generally are interpreted as those faithful Jews who were led by the Maccabees in overthrowing Antiochus Epiphanes and regaining control of Jerusalem and Judea. Even some conservative Dispensationalist scholars, who do not restrict the interpretation of "the little horn" in Dan 7 to Antiochus Epiphanes but also apply it to the future Antichrist, still subscribe to "the saints" in Dan 7 being exclusively Jews.[165]

However, the author of the book of Daniel clearly purports to be "Daniel," whose name appears an astonishing seventy-five times and who lived during

---

[162] Jerome was the author of the Vulgate and foremost patristic authority on the book of Daniel. In his own commentary on it, he disputes extensively with Porphery's commentary on Daniel and adheres to the traditional dating and authorship. Jerome (*Jerome's Commentary on Daniel*, tr. Gleason L. Archer, Jr. [Grand Rapids: Baker, 1958], 15) relates that Porphery alleges "that 'Daniel' did not foretell the future so much as he related the past,... inasmuch as he would not have foreknown the future." Thus, late dating Daniel is based on the assessment of a famous skeptic of Christianity who did not believe in prophecy.

[163] E. Earle Ellis, *The Old Testament in Early Christianity: Canon and Interpretation in Light of Modern Research* (Tubingen: Morh-Siebeck, 1991), 43.

[164] E.E. Ellis, *The Old Testament in Early Christianity*, 41n133, 43-44.

[165] E.g., J. Dwight Pentecost, "Daniel," in *The Bible Knowledge Commentary: Old Testament*, eds. John F. Walvoord and Roy B. Zuck (Wheaton, IL: Victor, 1985), 1352-54.

the Media-Persian regimes of the 6th century BCE. The author also provides several historical and some geographical pointers that locate the book's origin in that time and region of the world.[166] Some of this information about Persia likely would have been unknown to a Palestinian Jew living in the 2nd century BCE. Thus, this late date of composition assails the author's integrity. Some conservative Christian scholars allege that if the book originated in the 2nd century BCE, it should have been deemed a fraud and not included in the canon. And if Jews had believed in this late date, they would not have included the book in the canon.

In contrast, Jesus affirmed Daniel's authorship and the book's divine inspiration by mentioning "the ABOMINATION OF DESOLATION which was spoken of through Daniel the prophet" (Mt 24.15 par.; cf. Dan 8.13; 9.27; 11.31; 12.11). Desmond Ford is no doubt right about Jesus' "attitude to the Old Testament. Neither He, nor His contemporaries, thought of the book of Daniel as a pseudonymous production of the 2nd century BCE."[167]

The Worldwide People of God

This exclusively corporate interpretation of Daniel's Son of Man—that it only symbolizes Jewish saints—is much too narrow, and there are several ways to show this.

First, Dan 7 says nothing about Jews and, more particularly, does not identify "the saints" as Jews. In fact, Jews do not come into view (except as a part of the whole of humanity) anywhere in Dan 1-7, and the "saints" only appear in Dan 7. But Jews *do* come into view, and increasingly become the center of attention, in the remainder of this book. For instance, the expressions "your people," "the/thy/my people," "holy people," and "the many" appear often in Dan 8-12 and there only, and in each instance they refer to Daniel's people, the Jews.[168] This seems to be due to the fact mentioned above, that Dan 2.4—7.28 was written in Aramaic whereas Dan 8-12 was written in Hebrew. Gleason Archer explains, "The Aramaic chapters deal with matters pertaining to the entire citizenry of the Babylonian and the Persian empires, whereas the other six chapters relate to peculiarly Jewish concerns and God's special plans for the future of his covenant people."[169] Furthermore, Joyce Baldwin offers an excellent point, that if the author had intended to portray Jewish saints exclusively he likely would have used the figure "son of Israel/Jacob" rather than the universalistic "Son of Man."[170] Indeed, and this expression is key—that the universalistic Son of Man indicates a universalistic scope of the saints.

Second, this distinction between "the saints" in Dan 7 and the Jews in Dan 8-12 also suggests that "the saints" refer to the full racial spectrum of God's people, which includes faithful Jews. So, *"the saints" of Dan 7 are clearly the worldwide people of God who will live on the earth during the latter days and will suffer intense persecution for their faith.* Theses saints "will receive the kingdom" (v. 18), not because they *are* the Son of Man but because they are

---

[166] E.g., Dan 1.1-2; 2.1; 5.1, 31; 6.1, 9; 7.1; 8.1; 9.1-2; 10.1; 11.1.
[167] Desmond Ford, *The Abomination of Desolation in Biblical Eschatology* (Washington, D.C.: University Press of America, 1979), 74.
[168] "Your people:" Dan 9.24; 10.14; 11.14, 12.1; "the/thy/my people:" Dan 9.15-16, 19-20; 11.32-33; "the holy people:" Dan 8.24; 12.7; "the many:" Dan 9.27; 11.33, 39.
[169] Gleason L. Archer Jr., "Daniel," in EBC, 7:6.
[170] Joyce G. Baldwin, *Daniel: An Introduction and Commentary* (Downers Grove, IL: InterVarsity, 1978), 150-51.

connected to the Son of Man who is "given" the kingdom (v. 14), which includes people from all over the world, even Jews.

Third, "the saints (of the Highest One)," in Dan 7.18, 21-22, 25, 27, refer to "all the peoples, nations, and men of every language" in v. 14, who will "serve Him," viz., "one like a Son of Man" (v. 13). Thus, "the sovereignty, the dominion, and the greatness of all the kingdoms under the whole heaven will be given to the people of the saints of the Highest One" (v. 27). This clearly refers to the worldwide kingdom of God and thus cannot be restricted to Jewish saints. And the words that immediately follow—"His kingdom"—refer back to that worldwide kingdom given to the Son of Man. Furthermore, the book of Revelation alludes to Dan 7.14. It records a song sung in heaven about Jesus, "Worthy art Thou ... for Thou wast slain and didst purchase for God with Thy blood men from every tribe and tongue and people and nation. And Thou hast made them to be a kingdom ... and they will reign upon the earth" (Rev 5.9-10; cf. v. 12; 1.6).

Fourth, the ruler of the fourth empire depicted in Dan 7 "was waging war with the saints and overpowering them" (Dan 7.21, cf. v. 25). Many Christian interpreters have rightly regarded this person as the final Antichrist and that he is depicted in Rev 13.7. It reads, "it was given to him to make war with the saints and to overcome them." These "saints" are the same as those in Dan 7, and they clearly refer to God's people throughout the world. These two passages—Rev 13.7 and Dan 7.21—have very similar language.

Fifth, the Son of Man riding on actual clouds infers an individual, not a symbol.

Sixth, to interpret the Son of Man only as a symbol, while everything else in the vision is interpreted literally, is hermeneutically inconsistent. For example, this vision obviously contrasts the Son of Man with the four kings. Such a contrast would seem to require that the Son of Man is a human being as are these four kings.[171] While these four kings are symbolized as beasts, they are clearly interpreted in v. 17 as four literal kings and therefore are four individual human beings. It is inconsistent to interpret the fourth king as a human being, whether Antiochus Epiphanes or the Antichrist, and the Son of Man strictly as a symbol. If the author had intended this Son of Man language strictly as a symbol, and thus not depicting an individual human being, it seems that he would have so informed his readers. Furthermore, the qualifying word "like" (*ke*) in the expression, "one like a Son of Man," seems superfluous if this expression is intended only as a symbol.

Seventh, the same is true of King Nebuchadnezzar's dream in Dan 2. Although many scholars do not think the author of the book of Daniel purposely designed it as a literary unit, nearly all scholars agree that the dream in Dan 2 and the vision in Dan 7 coincide. That dream depicts an idol shaped like a man, whose four specified body parts consist of different metals and designate four earthly kingdoms. These four kingdoms were to rule the Mediterranean world successively, after which the fourth kingdom would be destroyed at the end time and superseded by an everlasting, fifth kingdom that would descend from heaven to earth. This scenario coincides perfectly with the vision in Dan 7, it being an elaboration of Dan 2. So, the everlasting kingdom consists of the saints, i.e., all of God's people of all ages, both Jews and Gentiles.

---

[171] For reasons why Daniel's Son of Man is probably not only an individual, but the Messiah, see G.R. Beasley-Murray, *Jesus and the Kingdom of God* (Grand Rapids: Eerdmans, 1986), 33-35.

Heaven's Royal Court

Daniel 7 presents a series of visions (v. 15). In each of these narratives, Daniel prefaces the vision by saying, "I was/kept looking" (vv. 2, 7, 9, 11, 13, 21). And Daniel's encounter with the angel, as well as the angel's interpretation, must be deemed a vision also (vv. 16-18, 23-27). Thus, Daniel 7.9-10 is a distinct vision of a court scene in which judgment is passed against the king ("little horn") and his fourth kingdom on earth who are waging war against the saints during the end times (vv. 21-22, 25-26; cf. *1 En.* 65.6).

This royal court session is conducted in heaven.[172] On earth, the little horn overpowers the saints "until the Ancient of Days came" forth and "took His seat" (Dan 7.21-22, 9). This "seat" apparently refers to God's heavenly throne or perhaps a special seat used solely for judgment or council meetings (cf. Ps 9.7). The "thrones" in Dan 7.9 likely belong to the members of God's heavenly council.[173] Thrones symbolize rule and therefore authority to judge (cf. Mt 19.28).

Much of the NT book of Revelation serves as a commentary on the book of Daniel and a supplement to it. Thus, Daniel's heavenly court scene in Dan 7.9-10 is quite likely the same one described in Rev 20.4. Accordingly, "the books" opened in Dan 7.9, which presumably contain official records of human acts done on earth,[174] are the same "books" mentioned in Rev 20.12, and the "thrones" mentioned in Dan 7.9 are those mentioned in Rev 20.4, in which "judgment was given" to those who "sat on them."[175] As Jerome rightly interprets,[176] these thrones belong to the twenty-four, crowned elders in heaven (Rev 4.4, 10; 5.6, 8, 11, 14; 19.4).[177] They are the "twenty-four elders, who sit on their thrones before God" (Rev 11.16), and they are seated "around" God's "throne" (Rev 4.4).

So, the thrones mentioned in Dan 7.9 are not two in number, as R. Akiba claimed, but twenty-four, and those who sit on them are heaven's twenty-four elders. The ensuing judgment that is passed against the little horn and his fourth kingdom and in favor of the Son of Man and His saints is probably not a unilateral decision taken by the Ancient of Days, but a corporate one involving Him and these twenty-four elders.

This celestial court scene may be one of Yahweh's council meetings, with council membership consisting only of the twenty-four elders and God as head. The "thrones" in Dan 7.9 appear to be temporal since they are placed quickly.[178]

---

[172] Contra Robert D. Rowe, "Is Daniel's 'Son of Man' Messianic?" in *Christ the Lord*, ed. H. H. Rowdon, 94.

[173] See C.F. Keil, *Commentary on the Old Testament*, 9:229-30; Louis F. Harman and Alexander A. Di Lella, *The Book of Daniel: A New Translation with Notes and Commentary on Chapters 1-9*, AB (New York: Doubleday, 1977), 217; P. Maurice Casey, *Son of Man: The Interpretation and Influence of Daniel* (London: SPCK, 1979). R.D. Rowe ("Is Daniel's 'Son of Man' Messianic?" 95) subscribes to R. Akiba's interpretation, that these thrones are two in number: one for the Ancient of Days and the other for the Son of Man. Rowe insists that in Scripture, "Nowhere is the heavenly host represented as seated beside God," but always "standing," just as are "the myriads" in Dan 7.10 and "the host" in 1 Kg 22.19. But C.F. Keil points out that this generally is true of heaven's innumerable angels, but not all.

[174] Harman and Di Lella, *The Book of Daniel*, 218.

[175] Richard Bauckham, *The Theology of the Book of Revelation* (Cambridge: University, 1993), 106; idem, "thrones," in *DDD* 864.

[176] *Jerome's Commentary on Daniel*, 78.

[177] Jesus chose twelve apostles to signify an embodiment of twelve tribes of a New Israel. Twelve apostles and twelve sons of Israel, together, are a copy of the pattern of twenty-four elders in heaven (cf. Mt 6.10).

[178] C.F. Keil, *Daniel*, in K&D, 9:229. The Hebrew word rendered "set up" is *remah*, meaning "cast" or "throw."

In the book of Revelation, the elders' thrones and crowns symbolize their ruling authority in heaven, indicating that they are "a ruling council." When they "cast their crowns before the throne" of God in praise and worship of Him (Rev 4.10), they do not do so to signify the divesture of their authority, as some interpret, but their absolute subordination to Him. Richard Bauckham well concludes, "The twenty-four 'elders'—a political, rather than cultic term—are the angelic beings who compose the divine council (cf. Isa. 24:23; Dan. 7:9; 2 Enoch 4:1; T. Levi 3:8). As their own thrones and crowns indicate ([Rev] 4:4), they are themselves rulers. They rule the heavenly world on God's behalf."[179]

The Son of Man as King

Many scholars who adopt the Jewish saints interpretation of Dan 7 do not allow for a king for the saints' kingdom since the passage does not state that the Son of Man is an individual, much less a king. Indeed, this Son of Man is only mentioned expressly in the book of Daniel here in vv. 13-14. Such silence is by no means conclusive.

It is inconceivable that a kingdom can exist without a king.[180] Since Daniel's Son of Man is contrasted with four literal human kings, it follows that He is a human king as well. This seems affirmed because we read, "to Him was given dominion, glory and a kingdom" (v. 14). C.F. Keil says of this verse, "Daniel, like the other prophets, knows nothing of a kingdom without a head, a messianic kingdom without the King Messiah."[181]

Daniel's angelic interpreter explains concerning the four kingdoms, "these great beasts, which are four in number, are four kings" (Dan 7.17). That is, the four kings are the *embodiment* of their respective kingdoms. Since the prophecy implicitly compares the Son of Man with these four kings, it follows that *the Son of Man is a king who embodies His kingdom and thus represents His suffering people who comprise His kingdom.*

Daniel 7.13-14 is actually a separate vision in itself. What it depicts immediately follows chronologically the court judgment. Since the Son of Man does not only come "up to the [presumably enthroned] Ancient of Days," but is also "presented before Him" and given a worldwide kingdom, no doubt *this scene in Dan 7.13-14 portrays a royal coronation ceremony in heaven in which the Son of Man is crowned as king*,[182] though He is not enthroned there. John E. Goldingay explains simply, "The humanlike figure comes in order to be invested as king."[183] Thus, for *all* of God's saints, the Son of Man is their archetypal Man, their King because they are citizens of "His kingdom," their Lord and Master because they "will serve and obey Him" (vv. 14, 27). This royal coronation ceremony in heaven therefore resembles Israel's similar royal paradigm on earth.

This royal coronation ceremony corresponds to Rev 19.11-16. John, the author, relates a vision, "And I saw heaven opened; and behold, a white horse, and He who sat upon it is called Faithful and True; and in righteousness He judges and wages war.... And upon His head are many diadems" (vv. 11-12).

---

[179] R. Bauckham, *The Theology of the Book of Revelation*, 34. Yet Revelation also presents the twenty-four elders (and the four living creatures) as guiding the heavenly worship, similar to king-priests.
[180] Cf. R.D. Rowe, "Is Daniel's 'Son of Man' Messianic?" 95.
[181] C.F. Keil, *Daniel*, in K&D, 9:235.
[182] Many scholars regard at least Pss 2 and 110 as royal coronation psalms that are also messianic. It is believed that these psalms were sung when Israel's kings were enthroned at their coronation ceremony.
[183] John E. Goldingay, *Daniel* in WBC, 168.

Diadems are headbands worn as crowns. They indicate what is written on His robe and thigh: "KING OF KINGS, AND LORD OF LORDS" (v. 16). It seems that Daniel's royal ceremony in heaven is immediately followed by this scene, so that this rider on the white horse is the Son of Man (cf. Rev 1.13; 14.14).

Many scholars deny that Daniel's Son of Man depicts an actual human being by insisting that the prophecy does not state that the Son of Man descends to earth with his kingdom.[184] But neither does Dan 7 mention that the kingdom descends to earth, yet this idea is strongly implied. If the Son of Man is given a kingdom, and the saints comprise that kingdom, and they "took possession of the kingdom" on earth (Dan 7.22, cf. vv. 18, 27), then the Son of Man surely must descend to earth bringing the kingdom with him. Besides, in interpreting Dan 7 according to the framework in Dan 2, the stone falling on the feet of the image symbolizes that "the God of heaven will set up a kingdom which will never be destroyed" (Dan 2.44), indicating the Son of Man of Dan 7 will descend to earth with the "everlasting kingdom" that "will not be destroyed" (Dan 7.27, 14).

Furthermore, in the Sanhedrin's interrogation of Jesus, He answered the High Priest, "you shall see the Son of Man ... coming on the clouds of heaven" (Mt 26.64/Mk 14.62; cf. Mt 24.30 par.). Surely, Jesus envisioned Daniel's Son of Man descending from heaven to earth. Geza Vermes points out, "Although Daniel 7:13 could have provided an excellent scriptural basis for the construction of the Christian belief in the resurrection of Jesus, and even more so for his ascension, there is no evidence of its direct use in any other context but that of an earthward journey at the Parousia," i.e., the Second Coming.[185]

Daniel's Son of Man also should be connected to Yahweh's "anointed One" (Messiah) and "Son" portrayed in Ps 2.[186] All three images surely refer to the same individual because Yahweh says that He will install "My Son" as "My King" on Mount Zion (vv. 6-7). Daniel omits mentioning this role of the Son of Man in establishing His kingdom on earth by overthrowing His enemies, a messianic role described particularly in the prophets but usually only regarding Israel. Again, the role of Daniel's Son of Man is more extensive than that of Israel's promised Messiah. The implied chronological order of movements of Daniel's Son of Man is ascent-descent, though neither one is actually stated. The importance of this order will become evident when we later examine the preexistence of Jesus in the Fourth Gospel.

The Worldwide Kingdom

If the kingdom in Dan 7 is given to saints who are from throughout the entire world, that kingdom must be a worldwide kingdom.[187] Indeed, a kingdom that comprises the redeemed of all ages—people who are from all nations, tribes, and languages from throughout the world—can be none other than *the blessed eschatological kingdom of God that will exist upon the earth during the messianic age.*

We have seen that many scholars have thought that Daniel's Son of Man is the Messiah. If "Messiah" is understood in the narrow sense, as only the King of Israel who will vanquish Israel's enemies and sit on David's throne,[188] then Daniel's Son of Man is much more inclusive than that. Such a Messiah is only for

---

[184] Cf. Schurer, 2:522n30.
[185] G. Vermes, *Jesus the Jew*, 187.
[186] C.F.D. Moule, *The Origin of Christology* (Cambridge: University Press, 1977), 26.
[187] C.F. Keil, K&D, 9:239.
[188] However, Ps 2 says that Yahweh will say to "His Anointed" (Messiah), "'Ask of Me, and I will surely give the nations as Thine inheritance, and the very ends of the earth as Thy possession'" (Ps 2.2, 8).

Israel; but *the Son of Man depicted in the book of Daniel is for the whole world and thus the entire human race.*

So, the eternal kingdom of God portrayed in Dan 7 does not refer specifically to the promised, future kingdom of Israel. Rather, it includes the sovereignty and dominion of all the kingdoms existing on the earth at the time of the end (Dan 7.27), including Israel, making it *a worldwide kingdom*. And this interpretation corresponds to the kingdom portrayed in Dan 2 that came from heaven and "filled the whole earth" (v. 35).

That kingdom described in Dan 2 is characterized by a double metaphor. One metaphor is the "stone cut out without hands" (v. 34), indicating divine origin. The other metaphor is that this stone "became a great mountain and filled the whole earth" (v. 35). Since it "will never be destroyed" and therefore "endure forever" (v. 44), this kingdom must be the same one described in Dan 7 as "an everlasting kingdom" that "will not be destroyed" (vv. 27, 14). *This eternal kingdom of God is therefore described in both Dan 2 and 7 as a worldwide kingdom, so that the kingdom of Israel, and therefore the believing Jews, are no doubt included in it, but they are not mentioned as particularly in view.*

The Son of Man as Suffering Servant

While Daniel's Son of Man depicts a literal human being, and therefore is *not a symbol* indicating the saints, He nevertheless *represents* the saints.[189] As pointed out above, as with the four kings the Son of Man is the embodiment of His kingdom and therefore His people. Although Dan 7 does not describe Him as suffering, *for the Son of Man to completely identify with His suffering people as their ultimate representative, it is necessary that He, too, suffer*. The fact that the saints must endure suffering before being awarded the kingdom logically requires the same of their representative. Otherwise, it does not seem just that God would make Him king rather than one of the suffering saints.

Thus, Daniel's Son of Man is none other than the suffering "Servant/servant" of Yahweh foretold by the prophet Isaiah.[190] Isaiah mentions this servant figure twenty times in Isa 41-53. Sometimes, it refers to disobedient Israel (and perhaps the prophet himself); but in many of these instances it indicates a renowned individual. The prophet's most well known mention of this figure is in Isa 52.13—53.12. It begins with Isaiah quoting Yahweh as saying, "Behold, My Servant will prosper, He will be high and lifted up, and greatly exalted" (52.13). Isaiah next recapitulates by relating that the Servant will first suffer. Then, "as a result of the anguish of His soul, He will see it and be satisfied" (53.11). That is, this Servant will suffer and afterwards be satisfied because of His being exalted and rewarded. Indeed, Yahweh "will allot Him a portion with the great" (v. 12).

Nowhere in Scripture is someone lifted up highly and exalted more than is the Son of Man in Dan 7.13-14. We read that He "came up to the Ancient of Days," referring to God. God is often pictured in the OT as enthroned and elevated above all other citizens of heaven. That is why He is called repeatedly in Daniel

---

[189] F.F. Bruce, "The Background to the Son of Man Sayings," in *Christ the Lord*, ed. H.H. Rowdon, 55. The two views that Jesus, in identifying Himself as the suffering Son of Man, either drew exclusively, or nearly so, from Isa 53 and not also from Dan 7.13 (e.g., R.T. France) or vice versa (e.g., C.K. Barrett, M.D. Hooker) are too one-sided in my judgment.

[190] However, the legitimacy of conjoining these two motifs has been much debated in recent times. It was opposed most fully by M.D. Hooker (*Jesus and the Servant* [1959]). But D. Burkett (*The Son of Man Debate*, 47n10, n11) lists thirty reputable scholars in the 20th century who combined Daniel's Son of Man with Isaiah's suffering Servant in a synthesis that depicts the same individual, which seems more correct.

"the Most High (God)." The Aramaic verb here translated "came up" is *metah*. It usually means "to reach" or "to attain;" but here it means "come unto."[191] The Son of Man therefore attains a most lofty position by being ushered into the very presence of God. That is what Isa 52.13 means, that Yahweh's Servant "shall be exalted and lifted, and shall be very high" (NRSV).

Jesus taught the same thing. He said the Son of Man must suffer, be rejected, and afterwards be exalted, all in that order (e.g., Mk 8.31 par.; Lk 24.26; cf. Ac 17.3; 26.23). He meant that God had so decreed, it having been written as Holy Scripture, especially in Isa 52.13—53.12. Many of Jesus' Son of Man sayings concern this theme of suffering. Luke alludes to the lifting up, mentioned in both Isa 52.13 and Dan 7.13, when he reports that at Jesus' ascension He literally was "lifted up" and "a cloud received Him" as He went "into heaven" to be greatly "exalted" there (Ac 1.9, 11; 2.33; 5.31).

Many of Jesus' Son of Man sayings are predictions of His impending sufferings. And He sometimes explained that His disciples would suffer due to their association with Him. As their Master, He must suffer too, for he said that "a slave [servant] is not greater than his master" (Jn 13.16; cf. Mt 10.24). Likewise, it should be assumed from Dan 7 that the Son of Man will be the suffering Exemplar for His people—the saints.

Moreover, the Apostle Peter claimed likewise, that all the OT prophets predicted the sufferings of the Christ. Peter had preached, "But the things which God announced beforehand by the mouth of all the prophets, that His Christ should suffer, He has thus fulfilled.... all the prophets who have spoken, from Samuel and his successors onward, also announced these days" (Ac 3.18, 24). "All" must include Daniel. There is nowhere else in the book of Daniel where this can be construed other than in Dan 7.

Isaiah also shows that Yahweh's Servant will restore the nation of Israel, a role that belongs solely to the Messiah. Yet Isaiah informs that God goes further by telling His suffering Servant, "It is too small a thing that You should be My Servant to raise up the tribes of Jacob, and to restore the preserved ones of Israel; I will also make You a light of the nations so that My salvation may reach to the end of the earth" (Isa 49.6). Indeed, Dan 7.14 also portrays this same worldwide role for the Son of Man. And Jesus applied this role to Himself in a universalistic, and not just a nationalistic, sense.[192] So, all three of these OT figures—the Messiah, the suffering, righteous Servant, and the Son of Man—though portraying different features and perhaps roles, refer to the same individual.

The "Son of Man" as "the Highest One"

Next, we need to consider briefly a linguistic complexity. The Aramaic word *illay* appears ten times in the Aramaic portion of the book of Daniel. English versions usually translate it "the Most High."[193] *Illay* is an adjective that is always emphatic and means "highest." In its first nine appearances in Daniel, *illay* refers to God.[194] The tenth one, in Dan 7.25, is usually translated "the Most High," and no doubt it refers to God as well.

---

[191] B-D-B, 1100.

[192] J. Jeremias, *New Testament Theology*, 274-75.

[193] Dan 3.26; 4.2, 17, 24, 25, 32, 34; 5.18, 21; 7.25.

[194] Indicated by their context, this is further supported by the word *elaah* being attached to *illay* in Dan 3.26, 4.2, 5.18, and v. 21. *Eloah* is the Heb/Aram. word for "god/God," usually translated "the Most High God."

Daniel 7.25 is also one of the four verses in Dan 7 that contain the expression, "the saints of the Highest One" (NASB), which translates *qaddise elyonin* in the Aramaic text. (The others are vv. 18, 22, and 27.) But most Bible translators and exegetes render it, "the saints of the most/Most High" (e.g., AV, JB, NIV), thus treating *elyon(in)* as God.

Like *illay, elyon* is an adjective used in both Hebrew and Aramaic that means "high." Both appear often in the OT as a proper noun for God, usually translated "the most/Most High." But *elyon* can also be used to describe a human ruler, such as a king, or an angel.[195] Plus, in the many instances in which *elyon(in)* appears in the Hebrew Bible, it rarely is without a modifier that signifies God as the referent; yet all four instances in Dan 7 have no modifier. Thus, it is likely that these instances of *elyonin* in Dan 7—vv. 18, 22, 25, and 27—do not refer to God but to the Son of Man who will be king of the saints.

In addition, *elyon* derives from the primitive root verb *alah*, meaning "to go up" or "to ascend." *Elyon* therefore is akin to the verb *metah*, which we learned is in Dan 7.13 and translated "came up." That is, the Son of Man "came up to the Ancient of Days."

This interpretation is supported by the fact that in Dan 7.22 and v. 25, both God (v. 22: "the Ancient of Days;" v. 25: "the Most High") and "the Highest One" (*elyonin*) are mentioned. It seems redundant if "the Highest One," placed second in both verses, also refers to God. If the author had intended this reference, he more likely would have substituted for *elyonin* the equivalent of "his saints" (as indeed the NIV unjustly renders it in v. 25) or words to that effect. Instead, it appears that *two beings are depicted in both Dan 7.22 and v. 25*, so that "the Highest One" refers to the Son of Man since He ascends to the Ancient of Days to become the highest of all other beings in heaven, except God.

Son of Man scholar Chrys C. Caragounis adopts this interpretation. Although he translates *elyonin* in Dan 7 as "Most High," he explains that it is a double plural in v. 25:

> This shows that the author distinguishes the "Most High" spoken of in connection with the saints from the Most High as referring to God. In the author's conception these two are different entities. That this is so is confirmed strikingly by vs. 22, where again the author distinguishes between the Ancient One and the "Most High" spoken of in relation to the saints. It ought therefore to admit of no doubt that the "SM" [Son of Man] is interpreted as being none other than the "Most High" of the expression "saints of the Most High" (of vv. 18, 22, 25 and 27), and that the Being is distinguished from the Most High in reference to the Ancient One, or God."[196]

Moreover, Dan 7.27 is a recapitulation of v. 14, so that "His kingdom" in v. 27, i.e., the kingdom of "the Highest One" (*elyonin*), refers to "His kingdom" in v. 14, i.e., the kingdom of the Son of Man. Also, certain words that occur in Dan 7.27—"serve," "dominion(s)," and "everlasting"—surely echo the same words that appear in v. 14. And the phrase "serve and obey Him" in v. 27 surely echoes "serve Him" in v. 14. Thus, the kingdom of the saints is the kingdom of the Son of Man, who is also "the Highest One."

Finally, the Son of Man became "the Highest One" (in comparison to all others besides God) when He *came up* to the Ancient of Days, who alone is "the Most High God." For, God apparently says of this Son of Man through Jeremiah the prophet, "And I will bring him near and he shall approach Me; for who would dare to risk his life to approach Me?" (Jer 30.21; cf. 50.44) The Son of Man

---

[195] B-D-B, 751.
[196] Chrys C. Caragounis, *The Son of Man: Vision and Interpretation* (Tubingen: Mohr, 1986), 75.

therefore possesses a loftier, more majestic dignity than all other beings except God. Indeed, God is "awesome above all those who are around Him," including those called "gods" (Ps 89.7; cf. 97.9; 135.5).

All of this suggests that all four occurrences of *elyonin* in Dan 7 do not refer to the Ancient of Days—God—but to the Son of Man, so that the saints are said to belong to Him.[197] This corresponds with Jesus repeatedly stating that the Father gave Him His genuine disciples, so that they belong to Him (e.g., Jn 6.37, 39; 10.29; 17.2, 6, 9, 24).

This interpretation answers the objection of those who adopt the Jewish saints interpretation of Dan 7, in which they allege that the Son of Man is never mentioned again after vv. 13-14, but only the saints are mentioned.[198] And this fourfold mention of the saints belonging to the Son of Man solidifies his identification with their suffering.

The Son of Man as a Warrior-King

Most Christian scholars who affirm that Daniel's Son of Man portrays a human being nevertheless deny that he is a warrior-king who fights earthly battle. Some even repudiate altogether the strong Jewish tradition that the future Davidic Messiah will wage war against Israel's enemies, deliver the suffering nation, and thereby establish it as the head of the nations. These scholars, usually due to their ecclesiology, conceive of only a peaceful establishment of an ethical worldwide kingdom. Many of them think that this is the background of Jesus' entire teaching about the kingdom of God.[199]

On the contrary, although the loving Jesus emphasized ethics, which included peacemaking, the Messianic Destruction is well attested in the prophets.[200] That is why it has always been a fundamental precept of Judaism. There is no evidence that Jesus ever taught contrary to this literal interpretation of these many prophecies. To insist otherwise creates many irresolvable problems. Christians living in the last days most likely will not object to it, since The Antichrist will be slaughtering millions of them.

At this point, some readers might object, "Then why didn't Jesus ever talk about this final war and His role in it as a warrior-king?" Any such talk very well could have risked alarming Roman authorities, resulting in Jesus' premature execution. Plus, He didn't want His disciples to think that that time had arrived (cf. Ac 1.6-7).

Now, it is true that Dan 7 is silent about the Son of Man personally engaging in earthly battle. But that is because this prophecy does not expressly tell us anything about the Son of Man's role in establishing His eschatological kingdom on earth. However, it does so implicitly; for, the heavenly coronation ceremony, in vv. 13-14, should be viewed as *chronologically preceding* the destruction of

---

[197] C.C. Caragounis, *The Son of Man*, 213, 227. However, S.P. Tregelles (*Remarks on the Prophetic Visions in the Book of Daniel* [1863], 7th ed. [repr. London: Sovereign Grace Advent Testimony, 1965], 48) provides the interesting translation, "saints of the most high places," which signifies the lifting up of the saints due to their connection to the Son of Man (cf. Eph 1.20; 2.6).

[198] E.g., Harman and Di Lella, *The Book of Daniel*, 218-19.

[199] E.g., R. Bultmann, *Theology of the New Testament*, 1:4-5; C.C. Caragounis, *The Son of Man*, 215-19, 238-40.

[200] E.g., Isa 9.4-5; 11.1-4; 34.2-8; 35.4; 40.10; 42.13; 61.2; 63.1-66.15-16; Joel 2.11; 3.2, 12-14; Obadiah 15-18; Mic 4.11-13; 5.4-15; Zeph 3.8, 17; Zech 9.13-15; 10.3-6; 12.3-9; 14.2-3, 12-14. These prophecies present the militant victor(s) as either Yahweh, Messiah, God's people (usually Jews), or two or more of them. Thus, all of them will participate in the Messianic Destruction on the eschatological Day.

the fourth kingdom and its king.[201] That is, the Son of Man receives His kingdom and brings it to earth, and this arrival becomes the occasion whereby "the beast was slain, and its body was destroyed and given to the burning fire" (v. 11b), or similarly, "his dominion will be taken away, annihilated and destroyed forever" (v. 26). In other words, the same Son of Man who receives the heavenly kingdom likely will be the conquering hero who leads His kingdom in militarily defeating the fourth king and his kingdom in a Messianic Destruction.

The eschatological Day is the day of God's vengeance (Deut 32.41-43; Isa 34.8; 35.4). Isaiah says of that day, "The LORD will go forth like a warrior, He will arouse His zeal like a man of war. He will utter a shout; yes, He will raise a war cry. He will prevail against His enemies" (Isa 42.13; cf. Zeph 3.17). "Behold, the LORD God will come with might, with His arm ruling for Him" (Isa 40.10). His "arm," here, is a metaphor for God's Messiah-Servant (Isa 49.6-7; 52.10; 53.1; 59.16; 63.5). Therefore, God will exercise His vengeance as a mighty warrior on "that day" and prevail against His enemies. And He will accomplish it by means of Messiah as His vice-regent (Isa 59.16-20; 61.1-2; 63.4).

There are many ways to show from Scripture that the same person who fulfills the role of Daniel's Son of Man will also do earthly battle on the eschatological Day. For example, we have already determined that in Dan 2 the kingdom symbolized by the stone that falls on, and crushes, the feet of the image corresponds to the kingdom presented to the Son of Man in Dan 7.13-14. Daniel 7 only informs that the dominion of the fourth king will be "taken away, annihilated and destroyed" (v. 26); but it does not reveal how this will happen. But Dan 2 tells how: "And in the days of those kings the God of heaven will set up a kingdom which will never be destroyed, and that kingdom will not be left for another people; it will crush and put an end to all these kingdoms, but it will itself endure forever" (Dan 2.44). God's kingdom will not gradually overcome these other kingdoms through a prolonged process of peaceful influence and coexistence, as most Christian expositors have proclaimed throughout church history.[202] Rather, the displacement will happen instantly and violently. God's kingdom will fall from the sky like a giant, meteoric "stone" and "crush" the hostile powers on earth with a massive destruction (v. 34-35). Those defeated kingdoms will then vanish quickly, like the wind carrying chaff from the summer threshing floor (v. 35), or like being "given to the burning fire" (Dan 7.11). And if God's kingdom crushes those kingdoms with such a violent overthrow, it seems that the Son of Man will be that warrior-king who will command and lead the massacre with God's power and ingenuity operating behind the scenes.

Another way to show that Daniel's Son of Man will engage in eschatological battle is that His kingdom will encompass the whole earth (Dan 7.14, 27). This is never stated in the OT of any other person than God's Messiah. For example, in Ps 2 Yahweh says to "His Anointed" (v. 2: the Messiah), whom He also calls "My King" and "My Son" (vv. 6-7), "Ask of Me, and I will surely give the nations as

---

[201] S.P. Tregelles, *Remarks on the Prophetic Visions in the Book of Daniel*, 37. Ancients thought more thematically and modern westerners think more chronologically. Thus, the implicit decision rendered by the court in v. 10—a decision favoring the saints and against the fourth kingdom and its king—is executed in v. 11 whereas vv. 13-14 backtrack to an earlier theme: how and why the saints will receive the kingdom.

[202] That is why Jesus taught, "For just as the lightning comes from the east, and flashes even to the west, so shall the coming of the Son of Man be" (Mt 24.27; cf. Lk 17.24). And this is how *taxus* probably should be understood in the Gr. text of Rev 20.7, 12 and v. 20. That is, Jesus will not return "soon," as some English versions render it; rather, when the appointed time arrives, He will return very "quickly," almost instantly, just as the lightning flashes across the sky. See BAGD, 807.

Thine inheritance, and the very ends of the earth as Thy possession. Thou shalt break them with a rod of iron, Thou shalt shatter them like earthenware" (v. 8). Yahweh calls this same individual "Lord" and says to Him, "Sit at My right hand until I make Thine enemies a footstool for Thy feet" (Ps 110.1). When that time arrives, on the eschatological Day, this "Lord" will "shatter kings" and "judge among the nations" (vv. 5-6). At least Ps 2 clearly reveals that that monarch's war-gained dominion will be worldwide, just as it does in Dan 7.13-14.

In addition, although Daniel is silent about the Son of Man waging earthly battle, the NT certainly is not. The book of Revelation describes "one like a son of man," a warrior-king who unquestionably refers to Jesus Christ (Rev 1.13; 14.14).[203] From "out of His mouth came a sharp two-edged sword" (Rev 1.16; cf. 2.12), and with it He will "smite the nations" (Rev 19.15). This same "sword," or "rod" as it is usually designated in the OT (the shepherd carried a rod with which to fend off predators), depicts military prowess. Isaiah portrays it as protruding from the mouth of not only the Davidic Messiah (Isa 11.4; cf. 2 Thes 2.8), but even Yahweh's "Servant" (Isa 49.2-3), the latter being He who will suffer (Isa 52.13—53.12). This apocalyptic Son of Man in Revelation is also described as "a Lamb" who was "slain" (Rev 5.6). The nations "will wage war against the Lamb, but the Lamb will overcome them" (Rev 17.14; cf. 19.15, 19).

Finally, there is one other apocalyptic account of the Son of Man in The Revelation that very convincingly presents Him as a warrior-king. The revelator writes, "And I looked, and behold, a white cloud, and sitting on the cloud was one like a son of man, having a golden crown on His head, and a sharp sickle in His hand" (Rev 14.14). The cloud and crown were not mentioned in the earlier description of the Son of Man, in Rev 1.13-16, because He had not been made king by the time depicted in that vision. But now, having been crowned at His coronation ceremony in heaven (Dan 7.13-14), perhaps the same cloud that carried Him before the Ancient of Days now transports Him to earth, where He will be installed as king over all the earth (cf. Ps 2.6, 8). As this Cloud-Man enters earth's atmosphere and hovers above the land of Israel, perhaps assessing the enemies' forces as would a military commander, an angel-messenger comes out of the temple in heaven and cries out to Him in a loud voice, "Put in your sickle and reap, because the hour to reap has come, because the harvest of the earth is ripe" (Rev 14.15; cf. Isa Rev 16.14-16; 19.11-21). Those behind the scenes have been causing the nations' armies to gather together in the Kidron Valley just outside East Jerusalem (e.g., Joel 3.2; Zech 12.9; 14.2; Rev 14.19). The prophet Joel says that place will be "the valley of decision" on the "great and awesome day of the LORD" (Joel 3.14; 2.31). From the clouds above, the Son of Man descends upon His enemies—perhaps many are kings and senior military officers—gathered together in the valley and tightly compacted to become a footstool for His feet (Ps 110.1). He then destroys the nations' armies as if trampling grapes in a winepress (Rev 14.20; cf. 16.14-16; 19.15; Isa 63.1-6; Zech 14.2-4).

The Son of Man as a Divine Being?

With this brief analysis of Dan 7 now complete, we arrive at our purpose for examining Daniel's Son of Man. Recall that church fathers thought that Jesus' practice of calling Himself "the Son of Man" indicated His human nature and that His status as "the Son of God" indicated His divine nature, which latter meant that He was God. But it has only been in modern times that some traditionalist scholars have abandoned this old position and actually taken the

---

[203] The NASB is inconsistent by capitalizing "Son of Man" in Dan 7.13, but not in Rev 1.13 and 14.14.

opposite view, citing Dan 7.13 to support their belief that Jesus is God.²⁰⁴ For instance, B.B. Warfield insisted that the three primary OT passages that affirm "the deity of the Messiah" are Ps 45.6, Isa 9.6, and Dan 7.13.²⁰⁵ Oscar Cullmann claimed that Jesus drew upon Daniel's Son of Man figure and "that by means of this very term Jesus spoke of his divine heavenly character."²⁰⁶ I. Howard Marshall alleged that Jesus' use of Daniel's Son of Man figure indicates both His humanity and "divine origin" because "he comes from heaven."²⁰⁷ Strangely, a few non-traditionalist scholars have adopted the radical position that Daniel's Son of Man represents a second deity,²⁰⁸ perhaps a young god approaching the aged god to receive blessing.²⁰⁹

Many modern Christian scholars, both traditionalists and non-traditionalists, have interpreted Daniel's Son of Man as an individual who is "divine," "deity," or "god/God" simply because He comes "with the clouds of heaven" (Dan 7.13).²¹⁰ For support, they cite parallel OT texts that describe God riding on clouds or being pictured in clouds.²¹¹ They insist that riding on, or in, clouds is a prerogative that belongs only to God.

But this assessment about riding on clouds is an arbitrary assumption. Recall that Judaism always repudiated the notion that Messiah is God, whether He comes on clouds or not. Thus, *b. Sanh.* 98a explains that if Jews ever become "deserving," their Messiah will come to them triumphantly "with clouds of heaven;" but if not, He will come "lowly and riding upon an ass."²¹² And Judaism taught that when Moses died he ascended on a cloud to heaven.²¹³ So, in Judaism, the idea of riding on clouds was not restricted to deity.

Christians should not think someone being in/on clouds necessarily indicates that person is divine. The Apostle Paul taught about the resurrection of the saints, that they "shall be caught up ... in the clouds to meet the Lord [Jesus] in the air" (2 Th 4.17).

---

²⁰⁴ E.g., C. Rowland, *The Open Heaven: A Study of Apocalyptic in Judaism and Early Christianity* (New York: Crossroad, 1982), 97-98; Seyoon Kim, *The "Son of Man" as the Son of God* (Tubingen: Mohr, 1983), 36; C.C. Caragounis, *The Son of Man*, 79-81; B. Witherington, *The Christology of Jesus*, 233-62.

²⁰⁵ Benjamin Breckinridge Warfield, *Christology and Criticism* [1929] in *The Works of Benjamin B. Warfield* [1929], 10 vols. (repr. Grand Rapids: Baker, 1991), 3:47.

²⁰⁶ O. Cullmann, *Christology*, 162.

²⁰⁷ I. Howard Marshall, "Son of Man," in *DJG* 780-81.

²⁰⁸ E.g., M. Barker, *The Great Angel*, 92.

²⁰⁹ E.g., John Day, *God's Conflict with the Dragon and the Sea: Echoes of a Canaanite Myth in the Old Testament* (Cambridge: University, 1985), 162.

²¹⁰ Conservative traditionalists include E.W. Hengstenberg, *Christology of the Old Testament* [1835], tr. Ruel Keith (repr. Grand Rapids: Kregel, 1970), 115; B.B. Warfield, *Christology and Criticism*, 3:42; John F. Walvoord, *Daniel: The Key to Prophetic Revelation* (Chicago: Moody, 1971), 167; Darrell L. Bock, *Blasphemy and Exaltation in Judaism and the Final Examination of Jesus: A Philological-Historical Study of the Key Jewish Themes Impacting Mark 14:61-64* (Tubingen: Mohr-Siebeck, 1998), 201-02. Moderate traditionalists include C. Rowland, *The Open Heaven*, 181-82; James D.G. Dunn and John W. Rogerson in their edited volume, *Eerdmans Commentary on the Bible* (Grand Rapids: Eerdmans, 2003), 671-72.

²¹¹ Ex 13.21; (cf. 14.19-20); 19.9, 16; 20.21; 1 Kg 8.10-11; Ps 18.12; (cf. 68.4); 97.2; 104.3; Isa 19.1; Nah 1.3; cf. Deut 33.26 LXX. Some scholars also cite Ps 68.33, treating *araba* as reflecting a Ugaritic word meaning "clouds."

²¹² This is remarkable in light of Christian belief and the tradition that Jesus rode into Jerusalem on a donkey on Palm Sunday (Mt 21.4-7/Jn 12.14-15; cf. Zech 9.9).

²¹³ *Yoma* 4a; *Pesiq. Rab.* 20:4.

Some contemporary scholars assert that Daniel's Son of Man is an angel, and a few of them identify a particular angel.[214] A few scholars interpret Daniel's Son of Man as a transcendent, heavenly being who resembles a divine being. While the Bible sometimes describes the appearance of an angel on earth as "a man," there is no biblical justification for identifying Daniel's Son of Man as an angel.

Many scholars also think that Daniel's Son of Man depicts an individual who is both human and divine because of His heavenly status, which many conclude necessitates preexistence. James D.G. Dunn rightly counters, "It by no means follows that a figure in an apocalyptic vision is pre-existent simply because he appears before God in heaven."[215]

Some scholars cite the Similitudes (*1 Enoch* 37-71), and maybe *4 Ezra*, to support that the Son of Man preexisted His human life and therefore is a divine being (*1 En.* 48.6; 62.7; *4 Ezra* 12.32; 13.3, 26).[216] The Similitudes do mention "the Son of Man" fourteen times, and we have seen that both the Similitudes and *4 Ezra* identify Him as "the Messiah" (*1 En.* 48.10; 52.4; *4 Ezra* 7.28-29; 12.32). They also *seem* to proclaim His preexistence (*1 En.* 48.2, 6; 62.6-7; *4 Ezra* 12.32; 13.26). But these apocalyptic books should be regarded as *dependent* on Daniel and therefore no more than a commentary on Daniel's Son of Man as well as other OT motifs, e.g., the Messiah and Isaiah's suffering Servant.[217] In addition, normative Judaism always allowed for the belief that various human beings preexisted, e.g., the ante-diluvian Enoch, the priest-king Melchizedek, Moses (*Ass. Mos.* 1.14), and the prophet Elijah, and such beliefs were never thought to imperil normative Judaism's strict monotheism.

Most English Bibles state that all the citizens of the Son of Man's kingdom will "serve" Him (Dan 7.14, 27: AV, NASB, NRSV); the NIV has "worship(ped)." The Aramaic word is *pelach*, meaning "to revere" or "serve." This can be said of either a god or a man.

The traditional Christian perspective has always been, and rightly so, that the risen Jesus ascended into heaven where God rewarded and exalted Him by inviting Him to sit down with Him in His throne as His heavenly co-regent, awaiting His heavenly coronation as king and simultaneous reception of the kingdom and then to bring it with Him to earth. This scenario is quite compatible with Dan 7. That is, Daniel's Son of Man could have lived a human existence on earth *prior to* His reception of the kingdom in heaven, in which case He merely would have awaited the long intervening period. The chronological order of events would be: (1) the Son of Man lives an earthly life; (2) then occurs His death, resurrection, ascension into heaven, and exaltation to God's right hand; (3) a long time interval transpires; (4) the heavenly court passes judgment on the fourth kingdom on earth; (5) the royal coronation ceremony immediately follows, in which the Son of Man is given the kingdom and crowned as its king;

---

[214] E.g., J.J. Collins ("The Son of Man in First Century Judaism," NTS 38 [1992]: 451) identifies him as Michael. J.E. Fossum (*The Name of God and the Angel of the Lord*, 279n61) and C. Rowland (*The Open Heaven*, 181-82) think he is Gabriel.

[215] J.D.G. Dunn, *Christology in the Making*, 74.

[216] Some conservative readers may wonder why I often cite such ancient, non-canonical Jewish Literature. Oscar Cullmann (*Christology*, 140) explains concerning *1 Enoch*, "This late Jewish writing is very important in general for understanding the beginnings of Christianity."

[217] The Similtudes generally are regarded as having been written during the 1st century BCE and *4 Ezra* in about CE 100. But the DSS do not contain any MS evidence of *1 Enoch*, yet the Qumran Community was very centered on eschatology. Some authorities therefore think that The Similitudes are post-Christian. As for the DSS, they allot little significance to Daniel's Son of Man figure and do not interpret it as preexistent.

(6) He then descends to earth, bringing His kingdom with Him; (7) He destroys the fourth kingdom on earth and replaces it with His eternal kingdom. This is what Jesus taught in His parable of the nobleman (Lk 19.11-27), referring to Himself. He said, "A certain nobleman went to a distant country to receive a kingdom for himself, and then return" (v. 12). Upon his return the nobleman announced, "these enemies of mine, who did not want me to reign over them, bring them here and slay them in my presence" (v. 27; cf. Mt 25.30).

Summary
In sum, Daniel's prophecy about "one like a Son of Man" riding on clouds and appearing in heaven before the enthroned Almighty God, in Dan 7.13-14, does not depict a symbol of Jewish saints but an actual man who will be king of God's people. And neither His heavenly exaltation nor his association with clouds require that He preexisted His human life or that He is either divine or God. Besides, even if this Son of Man did preexist, that does not necessitate that he is deity. Consequently, Dan 7.13-14 does not support the belief, held by some scholars, that Daniel's Son of Man is God.

D. Problem Passages

1. Is the Trinity in the book of Genesis?

Introduction	Cherubim
Switching from Plural to Singular	Seraphim
Four Primary Interpretations	Angels Called "gods" and "sons of God"
The Form of God and Angels	The Council of the Holy Ones
Man in the Image of God	The Seven Spirits of God
Elohim	Conclusion

Introduction
Throughout most of church history, Trinitarians have regarded three texts in the book of Genesis as the foremost OT passages that support their doctrine of the Trinity. These passages are Gen 1.26, 3.22, and 11.7. Ante-Nicene church fathers often cited these texts in asserting that Jesus preexisted. For example, the Epistle of Barnabas—written in about 100 CE and full of Mosaic inaccuracies, absurd interpretations of Scripture, and ludicrous allegories[218]—twice asserts that God said to His Son during creation, "Let us make man in our image,"[219] which is surely a quotation of Gen 1.26.

These three verses in the book of Genesis read as follows in the NASB:

1.26 "Then God said, 'Let Us make man in Our image, according to Our likeness'"
3.22 "Then the LORD God said, 'Behold, the man has become as one of Us, knowing good and evil'"
11.7 "And the LORD said,... 'Come, let Us go down and there confuse their language'"

Notice that in all three of these passages, God is the speaker. But we are not informed of the identity of those He addresses. They are indicated by the plural

---

[218] According to editors Alexander Roberts and James Donaldson in *ANF*, 1:133-34.
[219] *Barn.* 5.6; 6.26.

pronoun "Us" and the twice-repeated word "Our" in Gen 1.26. Trinitarians assume that God the Father is the speaker and that "Us" and "Our" indicate the other two members of the Trinity, viz., Jesus as the preexistent Logos and the Holy Spirit.

Also notice that the word "Us" is capitalized. Ancient Hebrew script did not have upper and lower case. Yet some English versions, like the NASB, capitalize the word "Us" in all three passages as well as the word "Our" in Gen 1.26. Capitalizing these personal pronouns indicates a Trinitarian interpretation by translators. But most English versions do not capitalize these words (e.g., AV, RSV, JB, NEB, NIV).

The immediate context of these Genesis passages provides no support for the idea that "Us" and "Our" refer to two members of a supposed Trinity. Trinitarians cite a much earlier context for support, it being in the very beginning of the first chapter of Genesis. It reads, "God created the heavens and the earth" (Gen 1.1; cf. v. 27),[220] and "the Spirit of God was moving over the surface of the waters" (v. 2). The Word of God (preexistent Logos) is no doubt indicated by the repeated expression "God said" (vv. 3, 6, 9, 14, 20, 24, 26, 28-29). The NT affirms that God accomplished His creation by means of His Logos (Jn 1.3; Col 1.16). However, Genesis 1 does not clarify that the Spirit and the implicit Logos each constitute a separate *hypostasis*, or personality, to be distinguished from that of "God."

Switching from Plural to Singular

But what about this creation account switching from the plural pronouns "Us" and "Our" to the singular pronoun "His" in Gen 1.26-27? The text changes from "Let *Us* make man in our image" to "God created man in His own image,... male and female He created them." And the contexts of the other two passages do the same.

All three Genesis texts—Gen 1.26, 3.22, and 11.7—reveal that God decided upon, and expressed, a plan that was presumably to be undertaken by Him and someone else or a plurality of beings. Yet God Himself is said to have accomplished the fulfillment of that plan. (See Gen 1.26-27; 3.22-24; 11.7-8.) Does this switch from plural to singular mean that "God" can be understood as a Godhead subsisting in three co-equal persons, as Trinitarians insist?

There are other possible explanations for the switch from the plural word "Us" to "God/ LORD" in these three Genesis passages. This sort of thing occurs in other portions of Scripture. For example, two angels described as "men" went down to Sodom and appeared to Lot, Abraham's nephew. They told Lot, "we are about to destroy this place,... the LORD has sent us to destroy it" (Gen 19.13). Yet the narrative continues, "Then the LORD rained on Sodom and Gomorrah brimstone and fire from the LORD out of heaven, and He overthrew those cities,... God destroyed the cities" (vv. 24-25, 29). Did God destroy the place or did the angels do it? The correct answer is surely that God sent His angels as His agents, commanding them to cause the brimstone and lightning to descend.

So, this narrative about the destruction of Sodom and Gomorrah also switches from plural to singular, as in Gen 1.26-27. But, in this account of Sodom and Gomorrah it is clear that the plural refers to angels and the singular refers to God. Could it be likewise with these "us" passages in Genesis, i.e., that God is speaking to angels? And must we think only of God using His angels for destruction on earth, but not for the creation of it?

---

[220] Trinitarians arbitrarily presume that "God" in Gen 1 refers to the Father rather than their triune Godhead.

Four Primary Interpretations

The four primary interpretations of the words "us" and "our" in Gen 1.26 are as follows: (1) Philo,[221] most rabbis,[222] and others have interpreted these words as God's communication to a special group of angels who gather closely around God's throne in heaven and constitute His royal court or council;[223] (2) post-Nicene church fathers almost unanimously understood the Father to be speaking to the other two members of the Trinity;[224] (3) many commentators just before and during the 20th century interpreted these words as a plural of majesty, which allows for Trinitarian belief but does not necessitate it;[225] or (4) God's address to Himself. How one interprets Gen 1.26 usually determines how one treats Gen 3.22 and 11.7, with all three passages being interpreted the same.

Thus, the Jews generally held that these "us" and "our" passages in Genesis indicate God consulting with the angelic members of His heavenly court.[226] Philo viewed Gen 1.26 as God speaking to "other beings," and he identified them as God's "assistants," implying angels.[227] Church father Justin Martyr acknowledged that in his lifetime, rabbis taught "that God spoke to angels" in Gen 1.26. Justin opposed this interpretation by asserting that God thereupon spoke to His "Son."[228] Tertullian later affirmed the same.[229]

Interestingly, C.F. Keil and F. Delitzsch, in their classic ten-volume commentary on the OT, disagree on this one. Keil embraces the traditional, Trinitarian exposition of Gen 1.26 whereas Delitzsch interprets the council of angels.[230] Delitzsch further remarks about the words "our image" in Gen 1.26, "since man is in the image of God, he is at the same time in the likeness of an angel."[231] Of course, Delitzsch does not mean that angels have physical bodies, but that they have spiritual bodies that appear as those of humans.

Contemporary commentators generally regard only the first and fourth above interpretations as viable, that God (1) spoke to His angels, more particularly His heavenly court of angels,[232] or (2) He spoke to Himself as a single entity.[233] But where in Scripture does God speak to His Holy Spirit?[234] Gordon Wenham observes that it is "universally admitted" by distinguished, contemporary

---

[221] Philo, *On the Creation*, 72-75; idem, *On the Confusion of Tongues*, 168-179.

[222] E.g., Rashi, Ibn Ezra, and Sforno. See esp. *b. Sanh.* 38b-39b.

[223] Non-Jewish, modern commentators who've held this view are H. Gunkel, G. von Rad, and W. Zimmerli.

[224] Justin Martyr (*Dialogue with Trypho*, 62) seems to have been the first patristic writer to interpret these Genesis "us" and "our" passages as the Father speaking to the preexistent Jesus as the Logo-Son.

[225] However, Claus Westermann (*Genesis 1-11* [1974], tr. John J. Scullion [Minneapolis: Augsburg, 1984], 145) states that "this older explanation has been completely abandoned today" for a plural of deliberation because of the discovery that "the plural of majesty does not occur in Hebrew."

[226] *Sanh.*, 38b.

[227] Philo, *On the Creation*, 75. Also, the Nag Hammadi text, *Treatise on the Three Natures*, relates that some Jews "say that God is the creator of that which exists; others say that he created through his angels."

[228] Justin Martyr, *Dialogue with Trypho*, 62.

[229] Tertullian, *Against Praxeas*, 21.

[230] F. Delitzsch, *Psalms*, K&D, 5:154.

[231] F. Delitzsch, K&D, 5:154.

[232] E.g., Gerhad Kittel, "*angelos*," in *TDNT* 1:82.

[233] Gordon Wenham, *Genesis 1-15* in WBC (1987), 28; Bruce K. Waltke with Cathi J. Fredricks, *Genesis: A Commentary* (Grand Rapids: Zondervan, 2001), 64-65.

[234] Buzzard and Hunting, *The Doctrine of the Trinity*, 13.

scholars that the author of Genesis could not have meant this plural of majesty as the Trinity.[235]

The Form of God and Angels

Both rabbinic and Christian scholars have embraced the concept of God creating man in His own image and in the image of angels. But they have asserted this only with regard to the soul of man and not man's physical body. They presume that, because Scripture verifies that both God and angels are spirits (e.g., Jn 4.24), neither God nor angels have form. But this viewpoint raises critical questions because it fails to further address the constitution of both God and angels. For example, how can angels literally make themselves visible to human beings, appearing as men? To be sure, neither God nor angels possess a physical body (e.g., Lk 24.37-43). But according to much Scripture, humans have both seen and conversed with angels while at first mistaking them for humans.[236] In addition, consider that the angels, the four living creatures, and the twenty-four elders in heaven fall on their "faces" to worship God (Rev 7.10-11; cf. 11.16). Also, Jesus taught that "angels in heaven continually behold the face of My Father who is in heaven" (Mt 18.10; cf. Ps 17.15; Rev 22.4). Do angels have faces? And what about God?

God is sometimes described in the Bible as having human-like form. His having form and literally sitting on a throne is what Jewish Merkabah mysticism is about. The foremost OT text for this is the "ancient of Days" sitting on a throne in Dan 7.9-14. Add to this Isaiah's vision of Yahweh in Isa 6.1 and Ezekiel's "visions of God" in Eze 1. And the OT is replete with such descriptions as God having a "face," "eyes," "mouth," "arm," "hand," "finger," and "feet," or that He "sees," "hears," "speaks," "sits," and "walks." Most of these many instances do not include "the angel of the LORD" in their context.

Throughout the history of biblical interpretation, most scholars have maintained that such biblical descriptions of God are anthropomorphisms, i.e., ascribing human-like form to God even though He does not really posses such form. They explain that this is done to accommodate human understanding. But is not such an interpretation disparaging to the human intellect? And such instances can rarely be substantiated from their context. The notion smacks of Greek dualism, in which the human soul and spirit are regarded as pure whereas flesh, and therefore manifested form, is regarded as evil. In reality, it is the result of overcaution against the fear of fashioning idols as replicas of God's form.

Along with interpreting this biblical data as anthropomorphic, the old Christian dogmatics often did the same with many of the emotions ascribed to God in the Bible. Called an "anthropopathism," it refers to attributing human-like emotions to God even though it is asserted that God is impassible, i.e., incapable of passion. Hardly any Christians believe this anymore—that God is not an emotional being. Yet most still think that describing God with human-like form is anthropomorphic. Where is the consistency?

We don't know much about the spirit world. Most of what we can know must be gleaned from Scripture. Even when Scripture reveals information about the spirit world, e.g., about God, angels, and heaven, much of it is apocalyptic. This esoteric literature can seem so strange to us humans compared to what we know of our physical universe.

---

[235] G. Wenham, *Genesis 1-15*, 27.
[236] E.g., Gen 18.3; 19.2; Mt 28.2-7; cf. Mk 16.5; Lk 24.4; Heb 13.1.

Man in the Image of God

Ironically, the first Genesis passage that Trinitarians offer in support of their doctrine is Gen 1.26; yet it contains a brief, fundamental statement about man's creation that weighs heavily against Trinitarianism. Irrespective of the identity of "Us" and "Our" therein, God says, "Let Us make man in Our image, according to Our likeness." The author makes a summary statement in the next verse, saying that "God created man in His own image, in the image of God He created him; male and female He created them" (v. 27). This concept, about God creating human beings in His image, is a fundamental precept about God and His creation that is repeated in other places in the Bible.[237]

To review, Trinitarianism means that there is only one God and that this God is three co-equal Persons subsisting in one essence, often called "the Godhead." Trinitarians thus refer to this God as "the triune God," which makes God a tri-personal being. *If God is a tri-personal being, as Trinitarians claim, and humans are made in the image and likeness of God, then it would seem that humans would have to be tri-personal as well.*

Now, human beings are generally regarded as tripartite: having a body, soul, and spirit. Some Trinitarians cite this concept as evidence that humans bear the image and likeness of the triune God. But this comparison is a false parallelism because the human body, soul, and spirit are not individual persons, as in Trinitarianism.

Throughout the history of Trinitarianism, its proponents have offered several analogies drawn from all manner of God's creation in order to explain their doctrine. But analogies do not prove its veracity, which most Trinitarian scholars now concede.

Since man is made in the image of God, even though this image is marred by the fall, we can grasp a rudimentary knowledge of God simply by having a basic knowledge of ourselves. *Since man is uni-personal, man being made in the image of God requires that God be uni-personal too.* This is not making God in our image, as some allege. On the contrary, it is based on the divine revelation that man represents the image of God and therefore reflects something about the nature of God. Since man is a personal and usually a rationale being, so is God. Since man is an intellectual being who thinks, investigates, learns, works, and plans, so is God. Since man is an emotional being who experiences love, compassion, sorrow, anger, and hatred, so does God. The closest that man comes to a tri-personality is schizophrenia, which is a mental disorder that does not reflect God.

Elohim

The Hebrew word translated "God" in the Bible is *elohim*, the plural of *eloah*. *Elohim* is often shortened to the proper name *El*. *Elohim* occurs about 2,570 times in the OT, either as a common noun or a divine name.[238] Most past Trinitarians insisted that *elohim* indicates that God subsists in a plurality of persons, which would support their view of a trinity of Persons in a single Godhead.[239] Most contemporary Christian scholars, not to mention all Jewish scholars, dismiss this viewpoint as an error. They contend that the plural word

---

[237] E.g., Gen 1.26; 5.1; 9.6; 1 Cor 11.7; Jam 3.9.
[238] Dennis Pardee, "eloah," in *DDD* 287; Karel van der Toorn, "*elohim*," in *DDD* 352.
[239] The Talmud, e.g., *Sanh.* 38b, reveals that post-apostolic Christians questioned rabbis about the plurality of the word *elohim* in the Jewish Bible as a reference to Yahweh, as if they thought that it referred to God the Father as well as Jesus preexisting as the Logos-Son.

elohim merely indicates intensity, expressing the dignity or greatness of God. Jack B. Scott observes that most scholars insist that this "plural ending is usually described as a plural of majesty and not intended as a true plural when used of God. This is seen in the fact that the noun *elohim* is consistently used with singular verb forms and with adjectives and pronouns in the singular."[240] Then he cites no less of an authority on antiquities than William F. Albright, who suggests that this plural of majesty was used commonly in the ancient Near East to express the "totality of manifestations of a deity."[241] Gesenius, the "father of Greek grammar," likewise explained concerning Hebrew, "the language has entirely rejected the idea of a numerical plurality in *elohim* (whenever it denotes one God) and is proved especially by its being almost invariably joined with a single attribute."[242] Many contemporary Trinitarian scholars no longer disagree with this assessment. Trinitarian F.F. Bruce explains that the word *elohim* indicates no more than "a plural denoting God as including within Himself all the powers of deity."[243]

Besides, how could the most frequently used word for God (excluding YHWH) in the Hebrew Bible accommodate a Gentile idea that God is three persons? The idea seems ludicrous! First of all, such a definition contradicts strict Jewish monotheism, and to Jews it smacks of polytheism. Secondly, it seems presumptuous for Gentiles to tell Jews what their Hebrew words mean. Thirdly, the same can be said of the correct understanding of the word *echad* in the Shema, in Deut 6.4>. Fourthly, few church fathers knew Hebrew, and their theology suffered considerably due to it. Jewish scholar Louis Israel Newman alleges, "If all the Greeks had understood Hebrew, the Greek church fathers would not have caused us so much trouble in their interpretation of the various names of God."[244]

Cherubim

The Bible provides much information about angels, though many of our questions about them may remain unanswered. Primarily, its post-exilic OT writings reveal that God accomplishes His purposes by means of angels acting on His behalf as intermediaries or agents. The NT book of Revelation has numerous prophecies about God causing natural calamities involving lightning, fire, heat, earthquakes, darkness, and stars befalling the earth, and all of these things are said to be accomplished through the agency of angels.

One of the best OT examples is the account of God giving His Law to Moses on Mount Sinai (Ex 19—24); yet only the NT informs that He accomplished this monumental task through His angels (Ac 7.35, 38, 53; Gal 3.19). This verifies that, sometimes, angelic agency is presumed in Scripture without being expressly stated. This is probably how we should understand Gen 1.26-27. That is, the "us" and "our" therein refer to a particular class of angels who were involved in creation. Not a few Jews probably embraced this view prior to the Christian era, and some certainly did in its 1st century.[245]

---

[240] Jack B. Scott, "*elohim*," in *TWOT* 1:93.

[241] J.B. Scott, *TWOT* 1:93.

[242] *Gesenius' Hebrew Grammar*, ed. E. Kautzsch (Oxford: Clarendon, 1910), 399.

[243] F.F. Bruce, *Answers to Questions* (Exeter: Paternoster, 1972), 2.

[244] Louis Israel Newman, *Jewish Influence on Christian Reform Movements* (New York: Columbia University, 1925), 534.

[245] *Tripartite Tract*, 112.19—113.1; Justin Martyr, *Dialogue with Trypho*, 62.3. Cf. Josephus' apparent rebuttal of Philo in *Against Apion*, 2.192.

The book of Genesis provides two accounts of creation, being in Gen 1.1—2.3 and Gen 2.4—3.24. The mention of angels in this second account suggests their involvement in creation. We read that after Adam and Eve ate the forbidden fruit,

22 Then the LORD God said, "Behold, the man has become like one of Us, knowing good and evil; and now, lest he stretch out his hand, and take also from the tree of life, and eat, and live forever"—
23 therefore the LORD God sent him out from the garden of Eden, to cultivate the ground from which he was taken.
24 So He drove the man out; and at the east of the garden of Eden He stationed the cherubim, and the flaming sword which turned every direction, to guard the way to the tree of life.

Thus, mention of the cherubim suggests that "us" refers corporately to them and God. However, Isa 44.24 appears to oppose this interpretation (cf. *2 En.* 33.4; *4 Ezra* 3.4), in which Yahweh states, "I, the LORD, am maker of all things, stretching out the heavens by Myself, and spreading out the earth all alone." Philo apparently sought to reconcile this passage with his angel interpretation of the Genesis "us" passages by asserting that God created all of creation, "not being urged on by any prompter ... but guided by his own sole will," except that angels assisted Him only in the creation of man.[246]

Cherubim are mentioned ninety-one times in the OT and once in the NT, in Heb 9.5. Most of these instances concern the mercy seat. God had instructed Moses to make two human-looking winged-cherubim of gold and put them end-to-end on the mercy seat with their faces facing each other (Eze 1.5 cf. with 10.15; Ex 25.18-20). Then, whenever Moses would stand before the tent of meeting and God would speak to him, the voice of God would always come "from above the mercy seat, from between the two cherubim" (v. 22). Thus, cherubim were important in Israel's worship of God.

No one in the OT is ever characterized as being literally closer to God than the cherubim. This is certainly depicted in the construction of the mercy seat. But it does not pertain only to Israel's worship of God by humans on earth. Scripture sometimes informs that things on earth are patterned after things in heaven (e.g., Heb 8.5; 9.23). Indeed, the heavenly reality is that God "is enthroned above the cherubim" (Ps 99.1).[247] This is true of both God's stationary throne as well as His chariot throne (Eze 1, 10). Consequently, when God spoke the words recorded in Gen 3.22, it is possible that He directed them to those closest to Him, who would have been the cherubim.

Seraphim

Or consider Isaiah's vision of God, in which he "saw the LORD sitting on a throne, lofty and exalted" (Isa 6.1). Some rather human-looking, six-winged "seraphim stood above Him" (v. 2). These "seraphim" are mentioned twice in this vision, and they are not mentioned anywhere else in Scripture. They are no doubt a class of angels, or other heavenly creatures, similar to the cherubim mentioned in Genesis and the four living creatures in Revelation.[248] All three groups are associated with God's throne.

---

[246] Philo, *On the Creation*, 23, 75.
[247] Cf. 1 Sam 4.4; 2 Sam 6.2; 1 Chr 13.6; 2 Kgs 19.15; Ps 80.1; Isa 37.16.
[248] E.g., Gen 3.24; Rev 4.6-8.

The word "seraphim" means "burning." In the Bible, fire often symbolizes purification, resulting in holiness. Thus, the very name of these beings suggests that they represent the holiness of God. Indeed, this is the very subject that they proclaim (Isa 6.6).

Isaiah continues the account of his vision. He hears God inquiring, "Whom shall I send, and who will go for Us?" (Isa 6.8). Again, notice that the NASB translators have translated the word "Us" from a Trinitarian perspective. To whom does "Us" refer?

Isaiah relates that God wants to send someone to preach holiness to Israel. Since this subject concerns the very identity of the seraphim, one of them flies to the prophet Isaiah and touches his mouth with a burning coal. This act symbolically signifies the purification of Isaiah to prepare him to be sent on his holy mission. Thus, God includes these seraphim as His associates, identifying them with His purposes. The "us" in Isa 6.8 therefore seems to refer to God and the seraphim rather than a trinity of Persons in a Godhead, a concept unknown not only in the book of Isaiah but the entire OT.

Angels Called "gods" and "sons of God"

The Bible sometimes calls angels, probably a certain class of angels, "sons of God/the mighty."[249] Job relates that when God finished creating the universe, "all the sons of God shouted for joy" (Job 38.7). This expression, "sons of God," probably refers to a certain class of angels. But why did they shout for joy when creation was completed? Did they only watch its proceedings or participate in the process? This scene renders it unlikely that creation, as in Gen 1, spanned millions of years rather than six literal days.

Similarly, the OT even identifies angels, or a certain class of angels, as "gods" (Heb. *elohim*). In some cases, however, it may be difficult to tell whether the writer refers to angels or pagan gods and/or idols. The psalmist probably intends angels in Ps 86.8; 95.3; 96.4; but it is certain he does so in Ps 97.7. It says regarding God, "worship Him, all you gods." The author of the NT book of Hebrews quotes this and probably "sons of God" in Deut 32.43 in the LXX and renders them, "let all the angels of God worship Him" (Heb 1.6). And sometimes the Bible calls the God of Israel "(the) God of gods" (Deut 10.17; Ps 136.2; Dan 11.36; cf. 2.47).

Yet the OT, especially Isaiah, distinguishes the God of Israel as the only God.[250] A frequent OT pattern is to identify God as "the Most High (God)" or "God Most High" in relation to other so-called "gods," thus referring to angels. (We can make a distinction by using capitalization whereas the ancients did not have this literary luxury.) This language of loftiness is intended to portray God in heaven literally seated above His angels (e.g., Isa 6.1), which symbolizes His superiority over them. That these angels can rightly be called "gods" is seen in the following psalms:

- "Thou art the LORD Most High ... exalted far above all gods" (Ps 97.9).
- "For I know that the LORD is great, and that our Lord is above all gods" (Ps 135.5).

---

[249] E.g., Ps 29.1; 89.6. Hebrews 1.6 quotes Deut 32.43b in the LXX (relocated in the MT), but it changes "sons (of God)" to "angels." Psalm 29.1 may refer to "His people" (vv. 10-11) rather than angels. "The sons of God" in Gen 6.2 and v. 4 surely refers to men, not angels (cf. Mt 22.30/Mk 12.25/Lk 20.35-36).

[250] E.g., Isa 43.10; 44.6, 8; 45.5-6, 18, 21-22; 46.8.

The Council of the Holy Ones

Throughout Jewish history, certain religious authorities have rejected the idea of angels in order to protect Jewish monotheism. It was thought that the concept of angels performing the divine will could easily be distorted, thus being viewed as gods who had infringed upon Yahweh's power and majesty. It was concluded that whatever could be described as an act of God, God actually performed it Himself without employing any ontological agency. The most renowned example was the Sadducee sect which ruled Israel's religious life in the time of Jesus. The Sadducees rejected belief in the existence of angels, the supernatural, and the resurrection of the dead. In order to hold these views, they had to regard the Pentateuch as superior to the biblical "writings and prophets."

Regarding God's acts, it is shortsighted to presume that He decides everything unilaterally without inviting suggestions from others. Such an idea ignores the perspicuity of God's intelligent subjects, stifles their creativity, and fails to comprehend that God delights in the fellowship gained and the honor bestowed by consulting with others in a monarchial, democratic process in formulating His plans. Notwithstanding Isa 40.13-14, James D.G. Dunn explains, "the more servants and councilors attributed to Yahweh the greater *his* majesty as the one true God supreme over all."[251]

Indeed, Scripture attests that the Most High God meets, probably regularly, with a court of advisors who are apparently His angels. For instance, the psalmist attests to "the assembly of the holy ones" and that Yahweh is "a God greatly feared in the council of the holy ones, and awesome above all those who are around Him" (Ps 89.5, 7).[252] And Job probably describes one of these periodic council meetings by relating that "the sons of God came to present themselves before the LORD" (Job 1.6; 2.1). Also, the non-canonical, apocalyptic Similitudes affirm "the court of the Lord" (*1 En.* 65.6). All of these narratives suggest that conferences have always been convened regularly in heaven at which times God requires certain attendants to give an account of their activities. Such a heavenly hierarchy involving delegated responsibility is, of course, similar to human government.

The idea of Yahweh being the head of a heavenly council of angels, wherein He passes judgment and issues forth decrees based on angelic counsel, is strikingly similar to Canaanite mythology.[253] E.T. Mullen informs that even "the terminology used to denote the divine council and its members in Canaanite and Hebrew literature is markedly similar."[254] Moreover, the undisputed king of the pantheon of Canaanite gods, who issued uncontested decrees from his council of the gods, was called "El." This is the same (abbreviated) name for "God" (Hcb. *elohim*) in the Hebrew Bible.

So, the Bible reveals that the members of Yahweh's heavenly council are not merely static supporters of His decrees. Sometimes, Yahweh inquires of them how they might treat some issue on earth. One vivid instance occurred during the days of Israel's wicked King Ahab. Yahweh decided that Ahab must die. At that

---

[251] James D.G. Dunn, "Was Christianity a Monotheistic Faith from the Beginning?" *SJT* 35 (1982), 312. Emphasis his.
[252] For a possible contrary view, see *1 En.* 14.23; 65.6. The words in *2 En.* 33.4, that "there is no advisor ... to my creation," may mean no more than Philo (*On the Creation*, 23) does, that God needed no "prompter."
[253] E.g., see Frank Moore Cross, *Canaanite Myth and Hebrew Epic: Essays in the History of the Religion of Israel* (Cambridge, MA: Harvard University, 1973); E. Theodore Mullen, Jr., *The Divine Council in Canaanite and Early Hebrew Literature* (Chico, CA: Scholars, 1980).
[254] E.T. Mullen, *The Divine Council in Canaanite and Early Hebrew Literature*, 119.

time, "the LORD [was] sitting on His throne, and all the host of heaven standing by Him on His right and on His left" (1 Kg 22.19). Then Yahweh asked them who would volunteer to go to the earth and entice King Ahab to make war and fall in battle. A discussion ensued among the members of Yahweh's council about the best way to handle this situation. We read, "One said this while another said that. Then a spirit [angel] came forward and stood before the LORD and said, 'I will entice him.' And the LORD said to him, 'How?' And he said, 'I will go out and be a deceiving spirit in the mouth of all his prophets.' Then He said, 'You are to entice him and also prevail. Go and do so.'" (vv. 20-22).[255] This narrative, however, does not reveal if this was a scheduled council meeting.[256]

Nevertheless, here is an example of God and His angels discussing a problem, one of them offering a creative solution, and God approving and sanctioning it as His plan. This demonstrates that God encourages creative thinking among certain of his angels and sometimes decides to adopt their suggestions as His will.[257]

Either the Creator cannot, or more likely chooses not to, do *directly* all His works Himself. Instead, He *indirectly* accomplishes many things through His angels as His agents. Recall from Chapter Three that Sir Isaac Newton explained, "God does nothing by himself which he can do by another." Furthermore, *Sanhedrin* 38b states, "the Holy One, blessed be he, does nothing without consulting his heavenly court." Thus, the contemporary rabbinical consensus is probably reflected in the highly-acclaimed *JPS Torah Commentary*, which states concerning "us" in Gen 1.26, "The extraordinary use of the first person plural evokes the image of a heavenly court in which God is surrounded by His angelic host. Such a celestial scene is depicted in several biblical passages."[258]

If God did employ angels in accomplishing His work of creation, what, then, were His reasons for doing so? Philo answers rather shrewdly that only God knows.[259]

Some people think such divine acquiescence detracts from the wisdom and power of God. And some even allege, "If God used any of His creatures to help Him in creating the world, He wouldn't be Almighty God." If true, then why did He employ angels in accomplishing His many other plans, to which the Scriptures abundantly attest? For God often commissions "His angels, mighty in strength, who perform His word, obeying the voice of His word!" (Ps 103.20).

If God often employed special angels to carry out His plans on earth, isn't it conceivable that He could have consulted with them, or at least solicited their aid, at the time of its creation?[260] Surely creation was a foremost activity among the great decrees and acts of God. And, if so, shouldn't we expect

---

[255] A similar example is when "an evil spirit from the LORD" was sent to terrorize King Saul (1 Sam 16.14).

[256] In Dan 7.9-10, the members of the council presumably take their seats ("thrones"), but the remainder of heaven's citizens were "attending" to God and "standing before Him" (v. 10), apparently as observers.

[257] One human example is when God acquiesced to Abraham's inquiry in the destruction of Sodom and Gomorrah (Gen 18). Another is when God was so angry with the Israelites that He intended to destroy them, but Moses intervened and persuaded God to change His mind and relent (Exo 32; Num 14).

[258] Nahum M. Sarna, *Genesis*, in JPSTC (1989), 12.

[259] Philo, *On the Creation*, 72, 75.

[260] Non-canonical Jubilees 2.2 says God created the angels on the first day of the week of creation. But the Bible does not even affirm the idea that God created the angels.

His angelic council was involved?[261] Donald Gowan remarks concerning Gen 1.26-27 and 3.22:

> There is no support in the OT for most of the proposed explanations: the royal "we," the deliberative "we," the plural of fullness, or an indication of a plurality of persons in the Godhead.... The only theory that uses the language of the OT itself is that which claims God is here addressing the heavenly court, as in Isa 6:8. That God was believed to consult with spiritual creatures in heaven is revealed by the scenes described in 1 Kgs. 22:19-22 and Job 1:6--2:6. Hence the consultative "we" has support from other texts, and it fits both the Gen. 1:26-27 and 3:22 on the assumption that Israel believed there were creatures in the heavenly realm ("the host of heaven," 1 Kgs. 22:19) whose identity had something in common both with God and with human beings. The familiar objection that angels could not have participated in creation is a theological judgment about what is possible in heaven.[262]

Simon B. Parker says of Yahweh's word "Us" in Isa 6.8, "With the first person plural of v 8, Yahweh speaks for the divine court as a whole; so also in the divine resolutions of Gen 1:26; 3:22; 11:7."[263] Gregory Boyd agrees,[264] and he well explains concerning these angelic council members, which he calls "gods:"

> These gods never rival the Creator's authority. They are never construed as major competing deities. Herein lies the central difference between the Old Testament and pagan conceptions of the heavenly council. But it is important to note that the Old Testament certainly accepts that some such council exists, and that the members of this council have some say in how things are done. In sharp contrast to the later Augustinian monopolizing view of divine sovereignty, the sovereign One in this concept invites and responds to input from both his divine and human subjects. The supplications and decisions of his creatures genuinely affect him, to the point where he may even alter previous plans in response to his creatures' requests and behavior (e.g., Ex 32:14-15; Jon[ah] 3:4-10; Is 38:1-5; Jer 18:6-11).
> The classical-philosophical theistic tradition has judged all of this scriptural talk to be anthropomorphic. It has had to, not because anything in Scripture suggests this but because of a nonbiblical philosophical presupposition. At the heart of this concept of God is the Hellenistic philosophical assumption that divine perfection means changelessness, impassibility, immutability, pure actuality and so on. Such a concept rules out the idea that God could ever be affected by, let alone receive advice from, angelic or human beings.[265]

The Seven Spirits of God

Two books of the Bible that should be compared are the first and the last, viz., Genesis and Revelation. The author of Revelation begins his salutation by mentioning a heavenly trinity of sorts, but not *the* Trinity. He writes, "Grace to you and peace, from Him who is and who was and who is to come; and from the seven Spirits who are before His throne; and from Jesus Christ" (Rev 1.4-5). The author therefore reveals that the grace and peace of God comes from not only God (the Father) and Jesus Christ but from "the seven Spirits" who are before God's throne.

---

[261] J.D.G. Dunn (*Christology in the Making*, 105) tentatively thinks so.
[262] Donald E. Gowan, *From Eden to Babel: A Commentary on the Book of Genesis 1-11* (Grand Rapids: Eerdmans, 1988), 27-28.
[263] Simon B. Parker, "Council," in *DDD*, 206.
[264] Gregory A. Boyd, *God at War: The Bible and Spiritual Conflict* (Downers Grove, IL: InterVarsity, 1997), 131-32. Boyd (p. 129) asserts that theodicy is due to refusal to believe in "spiritual cosmic struggle."
[265] C.A. Boyd, *God at War*, 130. Interpreting Scripture anthropomorphically, not literally, is often forced.

Some Trinitarians interpret "the seven Spirits" in Rev 1.4 as the Holy Spirit and thereby supposedly affirm their doctrine of the Trinity. In support, they cite the supposed sevenfold attributes of "the Spirit of the LORD" enumerated in Isa 11.2. But these interpretations of Rev 1.4 and Isa 11.2 flounder for the following reasons:
1. The LXX translation of Isa 11.2 lists seven attributes. The more reliable MT has six attributes, as in the DSS, rabbinic literature and so rendered in most English Bibles.
2. As with the words "Us" and "Our" in the three Genesis passages mentioned above, the NASB translates *pneumaton* (spirits) in Rev 1.4 by capitalizing it, suggesting that it refers to the supposed sevenfold Spirit of God, viz., the Holy Spirit.[266] But in doing so, translators have followed the tradition of the AV, which represents interpretation. Most modern English versions do not capitalize this word in Rev 1.4.[267]
3. "The Spirit," i.e., the Holy Spirit, appears only a few verses later in Rev 1 and twelve other times in The Revelation. Such evidence suggests that "the seven spirits" are to be distinguished from, not equated with, "the Spirit" which is the Holy Spirit.
4. Nowhere else in the Bible is the Holy Spirit designated as "the seven spirits."
5. These seven spirits are located "before" God's throne and symbolized as "lamps of fire" (Rev 4.5), neither of which can properly be said of the Spirit of God. Scripture never depicts the Spirit of God as being located *before* the throne of God or symbolized as a vessel for that matter. It is just the opposite; the Holy Spirit fills vessels, animates, and energizes them. (Moreover, the Holy Spirit being "before" God's throne seems to designate an inferior status to that of the Father and Christ.)
6. These seven spirits are further symbolized as the Lamb's "seven eyes ... sent out into all the earth" (Rev 5.6). Surely they are what Zechariah calls "the seven ... eyes of the LORD which range to and fro throughout the earth" (Zech 4.10; cf. 2 Chr 16.9).

Trinitarian George Ladd asserts that "it is certain" that these seven spirits are "a reference to God the Holy Spirit, thus including all persons of the Godhead" because the Father and Christ are mentioned along with them.[268] However, if just one passage of Scripture can be found with a triune formula of God, Christ and angels or spirits, Ladd's certainty appears ill-founded. And there is one; Paul wrote, "I solemnly charge you in the presence of God and of Christ Jesus and of His chosen angels" (1 Tim 5.21). David Aune, in his three-volume commentary on Revelation, says of this Holy Spirit interpretation of the seven spirits in Revelation, "All these explanations are artificial and unconvincing. In part this is because of the later conceptualization of God in terms of three interrelated persons, Father, Son, and Holy Spirit."[269]

The seven spirits of God in Revelation therefore appear to be actual angels.[270] That is, they are special angels who wait upon God before His throne to be sent

---

[266] When the Greek NT was written, as with the Hebrew Bible, Greek writing consisted only of uncials, i.e., all capitals. So, there was no lower case and therefore no capitalization. Written Greek was not changed into upper and lower case letters until the 4th and 5th centuries, long after the NT documents were written.
[267] E.g., RSV, TEV, JB, NEB, NIV.
[268] George Eldon Ladd, *A Commentary on the Revelation of John* (Grand Rapids: Eerdmans, 1972), 25.
[269] David E. Aune, *Revelation 1-5*, in WBC (1997), 34.
[270] Are we to distinguish between spirit beings and angels, as a few scholars insist? Or are these spirits of the angels (cf., eg., Ac 23.8-10; Heb 1.13-14; Rev 16.14)?

out by Him, search throughout the earth, and report back to Him as if they are God's eyes.

John probably identifies these seven spirits of God when he writes, "And I saw the seven angels who stand before God, and seven trumpets were given to them" (Rev 8.2). The definite article being attached—*tous hepta angelous* (the seven angels)—is significant for two reasons: (1) it specifies seven particular angels and (2) implies that readers are familiar with them. Indeed, John also says that these seven angels "stand before God" as do the seven spirits mentioned previously. This suggests that the seven angels are familiar to the reader, being the seven spirits mentioned earlier. Note that the Greek words *angelos* ("angel" or "messenger") and *pneuma* ("spirit") are often used interchangeably in Scripture to refer to angels.[271]

Interestingly, the inter-testamental Jewish apocalyptic books of *1 Enoch* and Tobit tell of seven archangels. *1 Enoch* contains very detailed descriptions of these seven archangels and names them (*1 En.* 20).[272] These seven archangels have special tasks assigned to them in overseeing the earth. Some contemporary, conservative interpreters of Revelation equate the seven archangels of *1 En.* 20 with John's seven angels in Rev 8.2.[273] Tobit relates that an angel named Raphael is "one of the seven holy angels who present the prayers of the saints and enter into the presence of the glory of the Holy One" (Tobit 12.15; cf. Rev 8.2-6).[274] These seven angels are called "angels of the presence," literally "face," i.e., the face of Yahweh (cf. Isa 63.9; Jubilees 1.27, 29; 2.1-2, 18; 15.27; 31.14). In other words, these seven angels are distinguished from all others by being in the immediate presence of Yahweh, presumably awaiting his bidding in performing their duties. Furthermore, two of these seven angels named in *1 Enoch* are the only angels named in the Bible: Michael and Gabriel. And the NT quotes Gabriel as saying, "I am Gabriel, who stands in the presence of God" (Lk 1.19).

The Bible also affirms the existence of archangels (1 Thes 4.16), and it identifies Michael as one of them (Jude 1.9). In the book of Daniel we learn that the angel Gabriel told Daniel that the angel "Michael" was "one of the chief princes" as well as "your prince" (Dan 10.13), i.e., the guardian angel of Israel. We should probably understand "chief princes," here, as synonymous with "archangels" and that there are others besides Michael and Gabriel. David Aune surely rightly concludes, "The seven spirits of Rev 1:4 are equivalent to 'the seven spirits of God' of 3:1, 4:5, 5:6 and must be identified with 'the seven angels who stand before God' in 8:2. Thus the view that the seven spirits are the seven archangels (*TWNT* 6:450) seems correct."[275]

Conclusion

The book of Genesis provides no substantial evidence for the doctrine of the Trinity. It appears that those beings to whom God said the words "us" and "our"—in Gen 1.26, 3.22, and 11.2—were a special class of angels. Perhaps they were the

---

[271] Some commentators have therefore identified the seven angels of the seven churches in Rev 2-3 with the seven spirits of God. However, Rev 3.1 distinguishes one of these seven angels—the angel of the church in Sardis—from the seven spirits of God, which reveals that they cannot be the same.
[272] See also *1 En.* 90.21; Tobit 12.15.
[273] E.g, G.R. Beasley-Murray, *The Book of Revelation* in *NCBC* (1974), 156; Wilfrid J. Harrington, *Revelation* in *SPS* (1993), 16:103.
[274] Peter R. Carrell (*Jesus and the Angels: Angelology and the Christology of the Apocalypse of John* [Cambridge: University, 1997], 21) seems to equate the seven angels of Rev 8.2 with those of both *1 Enoch* 20 and Tobit 12.15.
[275] D.E. Aune, *Revelation 1-5*, 35.

members of God's heavenly royal council or "the seven spirits of God" in the book of Revelation, i.e., "the seven angels who stand before God" (Rev 1.4; 8.2). Maybe they are the seven archangels, which seems quite likely. The following reasons support the latter interpretation: (1) they obviously occupy a very lofty position in heaven, standing "before the throne of God," (2) John the Revelator singles them out among all the angels in heaven and classifies them in the select company of God the Father and the Lamb, who is Christ (Rev 1.4-5), and, (3) because John the Revelator, in this book of last things in the Bible, wishes for his readers that grace and peace will proceed from not only God the Father and Jesus Christ but from these seven spirits as well, it seems appropriate that the Almighty God would address these same seven angels when He says "us" and "our" in the book of first things in the Bible, in Gen 1.26, 3.22, and 11.2. Finally, if Genesis alludes to later NT revelation about the supposedly preexistent Christ, it would only be the apparently impersonal Logos as God's spoken word, in Gen 1.

2. Is Messiah called "Mighty God" in Isaiah 9.6?

Introduction	The Context
English Versions	Commentators
The Hebrew and Greek Texts	Messianic Agency
	Conclusion

Introduction

Both Jews and Christians have always correctly interpreted Isa 9.1-7 as messianic. Christians have rightly applied all of the epithets in the second half of v. 6 to Jesus. The particular epithet that most concerns Christology is *el gibbor* in the Hebrew text of Isa 9.6. It is usually translated "Mighty God" in English versions,[276] which indirectly calls Jesus "God." After the "us" passages in Genesis, traditionalists usually cite these words, "Mighty God" in Isa 9.6, as the next strongest OT passage which supports their thesis that Jesus is God. But is "Mighty God" the correct translation of *el gibbor* here?

Hymns have always played a significant role in Christian worship. This rendering "Mighty God" in Isa 9.6 has inspired many church hymns about Jesus. Most memorable to many Westerners is the final, heart-stirring ensemble in Handel's magnificent *Messiah*. It is often performed by church choirs at Christmastime. But hymnology is no substitute for sound theology. When hymns reflect Christian theology, they should do so accurately and therefore scripturally.

In both translating and interpreting the words *el gibbor* in Isa 9.6 in the MT, many scholars regard its context as crucial. All of Isa 9.1-7 reads as follows in the NASB:

1 But there will be no more gloom for her who was in anguish; in earlier times He treated the land of Zebulun and the land of Naphtali with contempt, but later on He shall make it glorious, by the way of the sea, on the other side of Jordan, Galilee of the Gentiles.
2 The people who walk in darkness
Will see a great light;
Those who live in a dark land,
The light will shine on them.

---
[276] Calling Messiah "Eternal Father" in Isa 9.6 can be understood as "father of eternity" (cf. Jn 5.21).

3 Thou shalt multiply the nation,
Thou shalt increase their gladness;
They will be glad in Thy presence
As with the gladness of harvest,
As men rejoice when they divide the spoil.
4 For Thou shalt break the yoke of their burden and the staff on their shoulders;
The rod of their oppressor, as at the battle of Midian.
5 For every boot of the booted warrior in the battle tumult,
And cloak rolled in blood, will be for burning, fuel for the fire.
6 For a child will be born to us, a son will be given to us;
And the government will rest on His shoulders;
And His name will be called Wonderful Counselor,
Mighty God, Eternal Father, Prince of Peace.
7 There will be no end to the increase of His government or of peace,
On the throne of David and over his kingdom,
To establish it and to uphold it with justice and righteousness
From then on and forevermore.
The zeal of the LORD of hosts will accomplish this.

English Versions

All English versions have not translated *el gibbor* in Isa 9.6 alike. The AV has "the mighty God," and many subsequent English versions render it "Mighty God" (RV, RSV, NASB, JB, NIV, ESV). But a few English versions translate *el gibbor* in Isa 9.6 so that it *does not* call Messiah "God," as the following reveal:
- "God-Hero" (NAB)
- "Godlike hero" (Goodspeed)
- "a divine hero" (Moffatt)
- "in battle God-like" (NEB; also CBCNEB, 1973)

In addition, some notable Reformers did not translate *el gibbor* as "mighty God." Martin Luther, in his German translation, rendered *el gibbor* in Isa 9.6 with the German words "*Kraft-held*," which means "Strength-Hero." Luther explains that this epithet "belongs not to the person of Christ, but to his work and office."[277]

Furthermore, a few Christian scholars have translated *el* in Isa 9.6 as "god/God" while treating it qualitatively, so that it does not exactly call Jesus "God." For instance, J. Skinner translates *el gibbor* in Isa 9.6 as "Hero-God." He explains, "The Messiah may be a superhuman Personage—a demi-god; but not Jehovah incarnate."[278]

The Hebrew and Greek Text

Do the Hebrew words *el gibbor* in Isa 9.6 mean "Mighty God"? *El* in the singular is the Hebrew primitive root for "god" or "God." It occurs 230 times in the OT. Twenty-three of these occurrences appear in the book of Isaiah. Sometimes in the OT, *el* identifies men and not God. When this occurs, it is usually translated "the mighty (one)," "chief," "leader," or the like. Sometimes the OT uses the plural form—the more familiar *elohim*—to designate men as "gods," e.g., Ps 58.1 and 82.1 and v. 6. Also, many OT characters bore the word *el* in their names as a designation for "God," e.g., the word "Israel." This was not intended to indicate that they were

---
[277] Cf. *Luther's Works*, ed. Jaroslav Pelikan, 55 vols. (Saint Louis: Concordia: 1958-86), 16:101.
[278] J. Skinner, *The Book of the Prophet Isaiah: Chapters 1-39* in CBSC (1930), 83. Otto Kaiser (*Isaiah 1-12: A Commentary*, 2nd ed., tr. John Bowden [London: SCM, 1983], 204) translates it "divine hero."

God but that they belonged to God. Isaiah calling the Messiah *el gibbor* is similar to calling Him "Immanuel" in Isa 7.14>, in which *el* is not intended to identify the Messiah as "God" but "God with us" (cf. Mt 1.23>).

The Hebrew word *gibbor* occurs over 150 times in the MT in its singular and plural form. In over half of these instances the NASB renders it "mighty" or "mighty man" or "men." In thirty-eight of them it is translated "warrior(s)." This evidence shows that *el gibbor* can be treated as an adjective or a substantive (noun) that designates men. Context and associated words are the determining factors. Consequently, like Martin Luther, R.E. Brown denies that *el gibbor* in Isa 9.6 means "Mighty God." He insists that Isaiah intended to describe Messiah as "god/God," but as in a royal psalm, e.g., Ps 45.6.[279]

The LXX translates *el gibbor* in Isa 9.6 as *Megales boules angelos*. *Angelos* is the Greek word from which we derive our English word "angel." But *angelos* often has the wider meaning of "messenger." So, this entire expression in the LXX is usually translated, "messenger of mighty counsel."[280] Consequently, the LXX translators did not think *el gibbor* in Isa 9.6 identifies God. This is significant because these pre-Christian Jewish translators could not have been biased against the later, Christian interpretation, i.e., that *el gibbor* identifies Jesus of Nazareth as "God."

The Context

While both Jews and Christians generally have regarded Isa 9.2-7 as messianic, Jews, of course, have not agreed with Christians that Jesus fulfilled vv. 1-2 as the Light from Galilee, which Matthew explicitly affirms and John implies (Mt 4.14-16; Jn 7.52—8.12).[281] But both orthodox Jews and conservative Christians generally have agreed that Isa 9.3-5 foretells the Messianic Destruction on the eschatological Day. This scenario is graphically depicted in Isa 11.4, 34.1-8, and 42.13 ("The LORD will go forth like a warrior"). But it is especially prominent in Isa 63.1-6, a passage that inspired the composition of the USA's patriotic national anthem, "The Battle Hymn of the Republic."

That Isa 9.3-5 describes the Messianic Destruction indicates that *el gibbor*, in the next verse, should be translated according to this context. The foremost suggestions for translating it in this context have been "mighty warrior" and "divine warrior."[282] These suggestions, along with those in the above versions,

---

[279] R.E. Brown, "Does the New Testament Call Jesus God?" 563; idem, *Jesus God and Man*, 25n42. Cf. Raymond E. Brown, *The Birth of the Messiah: A Commentary on the Infancy Narratives in the Gospels of Matthew and Luke* [orig. 1977], new updated ed. (New York: Doubleday, 1993), 425; idem, *The Death of the Messiah: From Gethsemane to the Grave: A Commentary on the Passion Narratives in the Four Gospels*, 2 vols. (New York: Doubleday, 1994), 1:473.

[280] This is how the DSS translate it. Cf. Mal 3.1. The *Alexandrine Text* renders it "Mighty One."

[281] The pericope of the woman caught in adultery, recorded in Jn 7.53—8.11, does not appear in either Codex Sinaiticus or Codex Vaticanus, the two oldest and complete MSS of the NT. While most scholars regard it as an authentic story, the NASB typically sets it in brackets to indicate doubt regarding Johannine authenticity. Thus, Jn 7.52, which tells about no prophet arising from Galilee, should be immediately followed with Jesus' pronouncement in 8.12, "I am the light of the world," thus alluding to Isa 9.1-2.

[282] E.g., George Woosung Wade, *The Book of the Prophet Isaiah* in WC (1911), 10:66; A.S. Herbert, *The Book of the Prophet Isaiah: Chapters 1-39* in CBCNEB (1973), 1:75; R.E. Clements, *Isaiah 1-39* in NCBC (1980), 108; John F.A. Sawyer, *The Daily Study Bible (Old Testament)*, 2 vols. (Philadelphia: Westminster, 1984), 2:100; Owen C. Whitehouse, *The New Century Bible*, 2 vols. (Oxford: University, 1905), 1:151.

do not imply that the child will be God but that, as an adult, God will infuse Him with supernatural prowess for leadership in battle.[283] God apparently will do similarly with the surviving Israelite adult males, whom Messiah will lead in battle (Zech 10.3-7; 12.1-10; 14.3-4, 14).

Many Christians have resisted the idea of the loving Jesus returning to earth as a military conqueror. They suppose that the Jews in Jesus' day were misguided in thinking that Messiah will militarily deliver Jews from their enemies and make Israel the greatest nation on earth. On the contrary, these Jews thought right; they just didn't understand God's timing. That is, they did not foresee Messiah Jesus' cross before His crown. For, the OT is full of prophecies about Messiah militarily delivering Jews from their enemies at the end of the age, and Isaiah tells much about it.

Commentators

Most Christian scholars and many Jewish scholars have agreed in interpreting the "child" in Isa 9.6 as Messiah. Of course, Christians have interpreted it of Jesus (cf. Mic 5.2; Mt 2.4-6; Lk 2.4; Jn 7.42). To avoid conflict about Jesus, some rabbis, such as Ibn Ezra, have insisted that the "child" refers only to King Hezekiah or his son.

Jews and Christians have not agreed on the construction, and thus the application, of these epithets in Isa 9.6. While both the Targum on Isaiah and later rabbinical commentators interpret the "child" as Messiah, e.g., the preeminent Rashi and Kimchi,[284] they also interpret *el gibbor* as referring to God and not the Messiah, thereby avoiding calling Messiah "God." These rabbinical scholars have either (1) applied only *el gibbor* to God and the other epithets to Messiah, as in the first column below, or (2) rendered all of the titles to God except the latter, as in the second column.

| "the mighty God has called his name Wonder, Counsellor, eternal Father, Prince of Peace" | "the God, who is called Wonder, Counselor, mighty God, eternal Father, calls him Prince of Peace" |

Christian scholars have contended that both of these constructions are forced, thus charging these rabbis with bias. And since Matthew quotes Isa 9.1-2 and refers it to Jesus (Mt 4.14-16; cf. Lk 1.79), many Christian scholars have insisted that its close proximity to v. 6 suggests that those epithets should be applied to the Messiah as well.

Translators of some Jewish Bibles seem to have trouble with Isa 9.6. For instance, *The Holy Scripture According to the Masoretic Text* (1917) transliterates all of its epithets; yet it appends the marginal translation, "Wonderful in counsel is God the Mighty, the Everlasting Father, the Ruler of peace,"[285] thus applying all of these titles to God. And the NJPS renders the debated clause, "He has been named 'The Mighty God is planning grace; the Eternal Father, a peaceable ruler.'"

---

[283] R.E. Clements, *Isaiah 1-39*, 108.
[284] Ibn Ezra, however, applied all of the epithets in Isa 9.6 to the Messiah.
[285] *The Holy Scriptures According to the Masoretic Text* (Philadelphia: Jewish Publication Society of America, 1917), 489. It is noteworthy that this publication contains very few transliterations.

Messianic Agency

El gibbor occurs only one other time in the MT, in Isa 10.21.[286] This passage predicts that, on the eschatological Day,[287] a portion of Israelites (cf. Isa 6.13; Zech 13.8-9) will survive an attack and return to Yahweh to forevermore rely upon Him. It is presumed that *el gibbor* refers to Yahweh, here (v. 20: "LORD"), so that it is translated "the mighty God" in the NASB. For these reasons, plus its close proximity to Isa 9.6, many Christian scholars regard *el gibbor* in Isa 10.21 as conclusive evidence that *el gibbor* in Isa 9.6 should be rendered likewise, so that it calls Jesus "Mighty God."

However, Isa 10.20-21 will probably be accomplished by means of messianic agency, as in Isa 9.3-7.[288] That is, the surviving Jewish remnant will return to Yahweh on the eschatological Day by literally presenting themselves in servitude before Messiah their King, whom Yahweh will send to be their Deliverer. For, immediately following Isa 9.6 the prophet says concerning the military success and governmental reign of Messiah, that "the zeal of the LORD of hosts will accomplish this" (v. 7), i.e., through the Messiah. Thus, *el gibbor* in both Isa 9.6 and 10.21 may refer to the Messiah.

Conclusion

So, the evidence is inconclusive that *el gibbor* in Isa 9.6 should be translated "Mighty God," as if from the Christian perspective it calls Jesus "God." This is further doubtful because Christian traditionalists cannot muster even one other OT passage that clearly identifies Messiah as "God." Rather, translating *el gibbor* in Isa 9.6 as "mighty warrior" or the like fits the context better. Accordingly, Jesus will return to the earth as a mighty warrior to destroy all those who oppress true Israel without cause.

3. What about *alma* and *Immanuel* in Isaiah 7.14?

Isaiah 7.14 has been a pivotal text in the debate about Jesus' virgin birth. This verse is about the prophet Isaiah prophesying to King Ahaz, "Therefore the Lord Himself will give you a sign: Behold, a virgin will be with child and bear a son, and she will call His name Immanuel." The Hebrew word here translated "virgin" is *alma*. There has been a long-running scholastic debate about whether *alma* means "a virgin" or "a young, married woman." Most contemporary scholars think the latter. Regardless, this issue lies outside the scope of our study, since our concern is with the meaning of "Immanuel" herein. (For the discussion about Immanuel in this verse, see Chapter Five/Mt 1.23>.)

---

[286] A similar construction, *el haggibbor*, refers to God in Deut 10.17, Neh 9.32, and Jer 32.18.

[287] Isaiah 10.20-34 should not be disconnected from vv. 12-19. Yahweh will not complete His work on Mount Zion and Jerusalem (v. 12) until the eschatological Day, depicted by "in that day" in vv. 20, 25.

[288] E.g., cf. Isa 45.23 with Phil 2.10. Other OT examples are Zech 12.10 and 14.3-4. "You," mentioned 3x in Isa 9.3-4 (NRSV), refers to Yahweh (cf. v. 7e), signifying He will destroy by means of Messiah.

4. Is the Davidic Messiah called "Yahweh" in Jeremiah 23.6?

Prior to the 20th century, most traditionalist biblical commentators interpreted Jer 23.6 to mean that the Davidic Messiah is indirectly identified as Yahweh.[289] Jeremiah prophesies in the previous verse about this Messiah, calling Him "a righteous Branch" who will someday deliver Judah and Israel. Jeremiah declares concerning that time, "And this is His name by which He will be called, 'The LORD [Yahweh] our righteousness'" (v. 6). Jeremiah does not mean that Messiah *will be* Yahweh but that Messiah will both bear the name of Yahweh and be the righteousness of Yahweh for Israel in the messianic age.[290] In strikingly similar language, Jeremiah also foretells that the same name and meaning will be conveyed upon Jerusalem at that time. For he states, "In those days Judah shall be saved, and Jerusalem shall dwell in safety; and this is the name by which she shall be called; the LORD is our righteousness" (Jer 33.16). Obviously, this same identification does not mean that the city of Jerusalem is Yahweh, and this parallel strongly suggests that neither is Messiah called "Yahweh" in Jer 23.6.

---

[289] So says C.F. Keil, *Jeremiah*, in K&D, 8:352.
[290] C.F. Keil, K&D, 8:353-54.

Part Three
Christology of the New Testament

Chapter Five
Christology of the Synoptists

A. Introduction

The Synoptic Gospels and their Authors	The Holy Spirit in the Life of Jesus
The Authenticity of the Sayings of Jesus	Acts of the Holy Spirit in Jesus' Life
Priority and Dates of Authorship	The Temptations of Jesus
Oral Tradition	The Humanity of Jesus
The Christ, the Son of God	Angels Ministering to Jesus
Only the Father is God	The Miracles of Jesus
The Baptism of Jesus	The Resurrection of Jesus
The Voice Out of the Heavens	Summary

The Synoptic Gospels and their Authors

The first three gospels of the NT are purportedly historical narratives that portray many significant events in the life of Jesus. Except for the genealogies and birth-infancy narratives in the gospels of Matthew and Luke, all three gospels focus almost entirely on the brief, public ministry of Jesus. These documents tell us how He gathered disciples to Himself in Galilee and that, as a rabbi, He taught them. These gospels also inform us of what Jesus said and did as He traveled about with His disciples, especially in Galilee, as an itinerant preacher and a prophet. Oftentimes, He attracted large crowds as He healed people and performed exorcisms. And a significant portion of each of these documents concerns the last week of Jesus' life plus His death, called "Passion Week," as well as accounts of His empty tomb and subsequent post-resurrection appearances. Scholars refer to these gospel accounts of Jesus' life, death, and resurrection as "narrative Christology."

Scholars call these first three gospels of the NT "Synoptic Gospels" because they often provide summaries of the same events in the life of Jesus. The etymology of the word "synoptic" is that the Greek word *syn* means "with" and *opt* means "see" or "view," hence "view together." Indeed, viewing these three gospels together represents the very heart of NT gospel study and any examination of the life of the historical Jesus.

The so-called "Synoptic Problem" arises in comparing the same sayings and events of Jesus that are recorded in the Synoptic Gospels. It refers to such questions as, What are the sources of these gospels? Why are they so much alike? How are they different? What do these differences imply? In modern times, it has been widely believed that these accounts of same incidents in Jesus' life often indicate literary dependence or interdependence because of the same or similar wording in the reports themselves. This seems even more evident regarding quotations of characters, especially the sayings of Jesus. Trying to determine how these Synoptic Gospels were compiled, composed, and perhaps edited is called "gospel criticism." Thus, the Synoptic Problem is the complex relationship between these first three gospels, especially their sameness and differences.

The Synoptic Gospels do not seem to originally have had titles. Apparently, church fathers later appended the respective titles because they believed that these documents were so authored or at least went back to those named as if they were the primary source.

All three Synoptic Gospels are therefore anonymous. Anonymity was a common literary practice by authors of religious literature in antiquity. The synoptic Evangelists may have employed this custom with the sole intention of remaining unknown. Why? They may have been sensitive to the fact that their documents were largely not their own literary creations but compilations that had their primary source in the preexisting written materials and oral tradition of church communities (Lk 1.1; cf. 2 Thes 2.15).

The modern scholastic consensus is that all three synoptic Evangelists compiled their gospels primarily by copying and editing previously written sources available to them. Luke informs, "Inasmuch as many have undertaken to compile an account of the things accomplished among us, just as those who from the beginning were eyewitnesses and servants of the word have handed them down to us" (Lk 1.1-2). The last half of this statement refers to oral tradition. Certainly Luke, who seems to have been a Gentile, was not privy to these events in the life of Jesus; Mark probably wasn't either; but the Apostle Matthew, if he compiled and authored the gospel bearing his name, indeed was.

According to modern literary standards, the Synoptic Gospels are not exactly biographies of the life of Jesus. Except for the birth narratives, we know almost nothing about Jesus' life prior to the time of His public ministry, which lasted perhaps only two to three years. But these Synoptic Gospels *are* comparable to the type of biographies written in antiquity.[1] While they furnish little information about Jesus' interior life, and therefore His psychology, we have seen that they do provide substantial information about Jesus' self-consciousness regarding especially His relationship with God as well as His identity. So, these three gospels are critical sources for determining who Jesus thought He was.

Besides being purportedly historical narratives, the Synoptic Gospels must be regarded as rhetorical, theological documents. That is, their authors were not impartial reporters; rather, their primary purpose was either to convince or affirm readers of who they believed Jesus was, what He did, and how He fitted into the plan of God and thus ultimately His significance for humankind. Scholars refer to these things as "salvation history." Accordingly, earlier form critics labeled these gospels "proclamation" or "witness" documents.[2] N.T. Wright captures recent scholastic sentiment by identifying their genre as "theologically reflective biographies."[3] So, the synoptic Evangelists were biographical historians who wrote with theological designs.

Finally, most contemporary scholars think that at least the gospels of Mark and Matthew were written primarily for their respective church communities.

---

[1] C.C. Caragounis (*The Son of Man*, 247) cites ancient, secular sources as examples. See also James D.G. Dunn, *Jesus Remembered* (Grand Rapids: Eerdmans, 2003), 184-86.
[2] See William L. Lane, *The Gospel of Mark: The English Text with Introduction, Exposition and Notes*, in NICNT, 1.
[3] N.T. Wright, *Who Was Jesus?* (Grand Rapids: Eerdmans, 1992), 96, cf. 73-74.

The Historical Authenticity of the Sayings of Jesus

Like Judaism, Christianity has always claimed to be a very historical religion. Indeed it is, and this is nowhere more evident than in the NT gospels. In Chapter One of this book, it was stated that the NT gospel sayings of Jesus are historically reliable. The development of historical-critical scholarship over the past two centuries, however, requires that we consider this issue further before launching more deeply into our study.

Since the rise of biblical criticism, the NT gospel sayings of Jesus have undergone a scrutiny from historical-critical scholars that is by far unparalleled in the history of literature. Consequently, for the first time in church history the historical reliability of the NT gospels was seriously challenged from both inside and outside the church. Many NT scholars no longer subscribed to a conservative view of the inspiration of the Bible, as the church previously had done. So, these scholars did not regard some of the NT sayings of Jesus as historically authentic. Instead, they dismissed some as fictional creations of the respective church communities (or schools) that they believed were behind these gospels.

Scrutinizing whether Jesus said things accredited to Him in the NT gospels is a detailed process of historical inquiry much like detective work or, better yet, thousands of lawyers cross-examining witnesses in a court of law. Yet in so many instances, there is insufficient evidence upon which to base a truly scientific investigation. Consequently, critical evaluations that dismiss gospel sayings of Jesus as historically inauthentic are often quite subjective, and methodologies employed are sometimes suspect.[4] Specialists establish a criterion of principles that they apply, each of which has been shown to have weaknesses. Most of their assessments therefore represent no more than varying degrees of probability. In this process, gospel criticism has frequently gone to the extreme of abandoning accepted standards of impartial analysis in historical investigation by being unduly skeptical of the historical authenticity of these documents.

On the contrary, the NT gospel Evangelists ought to be considered innocent until proven guilty of producing any fraudulent history. The tendency of historical critics of the Bible is to do the opposite. Besides, the theological message of these gospels is patently dependent on honest, accurate reporting of history. No one would have been more aware of this than the authors themselves. Also, these gospel writers appear to have depended on previous written sources and a strong, stable oral tradition. And its origin must have been not much removed in time from the reported events themselves. Moreover, these gospels were soon circulated among the churches. Some of these churches would have included eyewitnesses to some of these recorded accounts about Jesus. And the testimony of these eyewitnesses would have prevented the circulation of a fraudulent history about Jesus.

C.H. Dodd asserts that the gospel sayings of Jesus have "an unmistakable stamp. It is impossible to suppose that they are merely the product of skillful condensation by early Christian teachers. They have the ring of originality. They betray a mind whose processes were swift and direct, hitting the nail on the head without waste of words."[5] Indeed, brevity is the mark of oral tradition.

This author believes that, as this long, drawn-out process of critical analysis matures, the NT gospel sayings of Jesus will stand the test of time and be found to be quite trustworthy. This conviction is supported by predictions made by Moses and Jesus.

---

[4] See, e.g., Humphrey Palmer, *The Logic of Gospel Criticism* (London: Macmillan, 1968).
[5] C.H. Dodd, *The Founder of Christianity*, 37.

We already have seen that Moses predicted that a most significant prophet, one like himself, would someday arise in Israel. Moses quoted Yahweh as saying of this prophet, "I will put My words in his mouth, and he shall speak to them [the Israelites] all that I command him. And it shall come about that whoever will not listen to My words which he shall speak in My name, I Myself will require it of him" (Duet 18.18-19).[6] Assuming that the Christian interpretation of this prophecy is correct—that Jesus is that prophet—Moses presupposes that the sayings of Jesus would become widely known.

Similarly, Jesus predicted that His words would be recorded for all posterity through the missionary activity of His apostles (Jn 17.8, 20). He explained to them that after His ascension into heaven, the Holy Spirit would come and "teach you all things, and bring to your remembrance all that I said to you" (Jn 14.26). Jesus proclaimed that the result would be that "heaven and earth will pass away, but My words will not pass away" (Mk 13.31 par.). Not only that, He asserted what Moses implied above, that Jesus' words would become the standard rule on judgment day. For, Jesus said most solemnly, "he who rejects Me, and does not receive My sayings, has one who judges him; the word I spoke is what will judge him at the last day" (Jn 12.48; cf. Mk 8.38/Lk 9.26). For those who accept these pronouncements as reliable, they presuppose that Jesus' words would be preserved and become well known. What else could Jesus have meant than the words attributed to Him in the four gospels of the NT?

Jesus often spoke of "the Scripture(s)" (Gr. *tas graphas*), referring to the OT. Sometimes, He quoted them with the introductory words, "it is written" (Gr. *gegraptai*). Since Jesus quoted the Torah, the prophets, and the writings, He obviously differed with the Sadducees, and agreed with the Pharisees, by including all three divisions as Scripture that was equally inspired by God. Moreover, Jesus Himself seems to have had a very conservative view of Scripture. He once said, "the Scripture cannot be broken" (Jn 10.35). And He apparently taught more than once, "until heaven and earth pass away, not the smallest letter or stroke shall pass away from the Law, until all is accomplished" (Mt 5.18; cf. Lk 16.17). Jesus surely would have endorsed what the Apostle Paul later wrote, "All Scripture is inspired by God" (2 Tim 3.16). The critical question is this: What are the Scriptures? Would Jesus have disagreed with critics and included all of His purported sayings in the NT gospels as Scripture that cannot be broken?

One of the main criterions that critics use in assessing the authenticity of Jesus' gospel sayings is called "dissimilarity." According to this criterion, Jesus' frequent self-designation, "Son of Man," verifies the authenticity of those sayings that contain it. For, neither the gospel Evangelists nor the later church applied this title to Jesus (except Ac 7.56; cf. Rev 1.13; 14.14). If many of Jesus' gospel sayings are embellishments of church communities, these communities surely would not have quoted Jesus as calling Himself by such an ambiguous expression as "the Son of Man" if they themselves did not apply it to Him. Such dissimilarity suggests that all of Jesus' Son of Man sayings are authentic.

Also, many contemporary scholars think that central to Jesus' kerygma was the eschatological kingdom and that He believed it would appear soon, no later than 70 CE. Since this "imminent kingdom" did not appear, this situation presented a serious problem for Christology. If this scholarly assessment is correct (I don't think it is), and the dating of the gospels is post-70 CE, as commonly believed nowadays, the synoptic Evangelists certainly would not have

---

[6] The accountability mentioned here is not to be restricted to those Jews who actually heard Jesus but also to succeeding generations familiar with His sayings (e.g., Jn 5.45-47).

included any such embarrassing sayings of Jesus. Since they did, this evidence favors the view that such sayings are historically reliable.

It is most reasonable to accept that the gospel sayings attributed to Jesus are His.

Priority and Dates of Authorship

The church's acceptance of the four gospels into the NT canon depended on several factors, mostly their authorship and content. Modern scholars have regarded their dates of composition and chronological order of origin as quite important.

Church fathers generally believed that the Gospel of Matthew was written first and that all three Synoptic Gospels were written independently of each other. Clement of Alexandria (c. 150-215 CE) wrote that the chronological order of composition of the Synoptics was Matthew-Luke-Mark. Augustine differed by proposing Matthew-Mark-Luke. In 1783 and 1789, J.J. Griesbach claimed that Matthew and then Luke were written earliest, with Mark representing a condensation of both. This "Griesbach Hypothesis," now called "Matthean priority," thereafter held sway among scholars until modern times.

In the 20th century, a large majority of NT scholars overthrew Matthean priority. They insisted that the Gospel of Mark was written first and that both Matthew and Luke used it in compiling their gospels. About 90% of Mark is included in both Matthew and Luke. This Markan priority hypothesis reigns supreme today, though it is not without its challengers. Consequently, most scholars now regard Mark as the most important NT gospel for discovering the historical Jesus, since they believe that it was written first.

The gospels of Matthew and Luke also contain some reports about same events in the life of Jesus that are not included in Mark, and these accounts have the same or very similar wording. Scholars refer to this material as "Q," which represents an abbreviation of the German word *quell*, meaning "source." Scholars use "Q" to refer to a hypothetical, non-extant document consisting mostly of sayings of Jesus that they think preexisted the Synoptic Gospels. So, most contemporary scholars believe that the authors of the gospels of Matthew and Luke used the Gospel of Mark plus Q in compiling their gospels. This view is called "the Two-Source Hypothesis."[7] The smaller amount of material peculiar to Matthew-Mark and Mark-Luke has given rise to "the Four-Source Hypothesis."

The dates in which the Synoptic Gospels were written and published are uncertain. A few scholars think they could have been written in the 60s.[8] But most believe Mark was written in the early 70s and Matthew and Luke were written in the late 70s or 80s.

Oral Tradition

During the interim period between the Christ event and the time in which it was committed to writing, the early Christians verbally preserved a history of Jesus in what is called "oral tradition." It consisted of how Jesus' followers remembered him. Jesus had been their master-teacher who had taught in ways that enhanced memory. Early church communities must have carefully developed units of oral tradition about Jesus in a way that further aided

---

[7] It was first established among German scholars by H.J. Holtzmann in 1863 and later among English-speaking scholars by B.H. Streeter in *The Four Gospels: A Study of Origins* (London: Macmillan, 1924).

[8] See John A.T. Robinson, *Redating the New Testament* (London: SCM, 1976), esp. p. 116.

memory and accommodated preaching. This oral tradition played a vital role in preserving the whole Jesus tradition. It seems the synoptists must have been more dependent upon this oral tradition than literary sources than has been previously thought.[9]

Eventually, this oral tradition came to be written down. How much later we can't be sure, perhaps twenty years or more. Even after the gospels were written, church fathers claimed that oral tradition continued to be prominent in many church communities. As inferred above, such a short time-period between the formation of the Jesus oral tradition and its commitment to writing is hardly conducive to the formation of falsified reports.

Analyzing these units of written, oral tradition in the NT gospels is called "form criticism." Some radical form critics have regarded the pre-gospel, oral tradition as loose, imprecise, and heavily influenced by later, more-developed christological beliefs. Thus, they generally have regarded the NT gospels as historically suspect.

Recent research suggests to the contrary, and it may prove formidable in future biblical studies. Peter J. Tomson explains, "While on the road or when resting, Jesus taught continuously. Just as with the rabbis, the disciples must have learned the more important lessons and rules by heart. For western readers this may seem unlikely, but there still are cultures where whole collections of stories or law are transmitted orally. The Quran, too, is recited by heart. The church fathers report that the transmission of Jesus' words continued to be done orally for a long time. This is understandable in a culture in which Jesus lived."[10] Indeed, not many people were literate.

Some scholars now believe that the earliest church communities employed careful systems of memorization through repetition and perhaps repeatedly re-enacting dramatic performances of events in the life of Jesus in order to help preserve not only the memory of his actions but the accuracy of his sayings.[11] D.A. Carson insists, "Oral traditions, especially religious oral traditions, are not conducive to tampering and falsification but are remarkably stable."[12] James D.G. Dunn alleges regarding the undue dependence of form-critical analysis on several supposed layers of literary tradition that underwent an extensive editorial process, that this "perspective which has dominated the study of the history of Synoptic tradition is simply wrong-headed."[13] Richard Bauckham is calling for a disengagement from the distinction between the historical Jesus and the Christ of faith. He asserts that the gospels depend mostly on eyewitnesses rather than literary sources.[14]

---

[9] E.g., Birger Gerhardsson, *Memory and Manuscript, Oral Tradition and Written Transmission in Rabbinic Judaism and Early Christianity*, tr. Eris J. Sharpe (Lund: Gleerup, 1961); idem, *The Reliability of the Gospel Tradition* (Peabody: Hendrickson, 2001); J.D.G. Dunn, *Jesus Remembered*, 192-210.

[10] Peter J. Tomson, *Presumed Guilty: How the Jews Were Blamed for the Death of Jesus* (Minneapolis: Fortress, 2005), 44.

[11] Kenneth E. Bailey, "Informal Controlled Oral Tradition and the Synoptic Gospels," *AJT* 5 (1991): 34-54; idem, "Middle Eastern Oral Tradition and the Synoptic Gospels," *ExpT* 106 (1995): 363-67; C.L. Blomberg, "Form Criticism," in *DJG* 247; James D.G. Dunn, "Messianic Ideas and Their Influence on the Jesus of History," in *The Messiah*, ed. J.H. Charlesworth, 371-72; idem, *Jesus Remembered*, 238-54.

[12] D.A. Carson, "Matthew," 9.

[13] J.D.G. Dunn, *Jesus Remembered*, 248.

[14] Richard Bauckham, *Jesus and the Eyewitnesses: The Gospels as Eyewitness Testimony* (Grand Rapids: Eerdmans, 2006).

Thus, the units of oral tradition about Jesus that were committed to writing and came to be included in the NT gospels have a high probability of historical accuracy. The various believing communities that produced these oral traditions no doubt would have included several eyewitnesses of the events. These members of church communities would have discussed these matters among themselves in order to achieve the most accurate account remembered of what Jesus both did and said. Their final kerygma might have been subjected to the scrutiny of those outside the believing communities who were eyewitnesses themselves. Since there existed a network of early church communities in and near Israel, there might have been some comparison of each other's units of oral tradition to further help achieve accuracy. Of this we can be sure: the Synoptic Gospels were closely linked to a preceding oral tradition that would have been quite historically reliable in itself. Besides, central to the Christian message is the concept of truth, which involves honesty and integrity. The NT gospel pericopes are so imbedded with purported history that to discredit their history would also discredit their theological import.

Finally, not to be overlooked, but outside the scope of historical criticism, is the concept of the guidance of the Holy Spirit in preserving the true history of Jesus. For, if we can believe that Jesus and His apostles did miracles by means of the Holy Spirit, and that Jesus arose from the dead, is it any more difficult to believe that the same Spirit of God could have brought to the remembrance of the disciples, who were eyewitnesses (Jn 14.26), either Jesus' exact words or a reasonable facsimile thereof, such as a paraphrase?

Believers therefore can rest assured that the NT gospel sayings of Jesus, which depended upon a stable oral tradition, are reasonably representative of Jesus' voice.[15]

The Christ, the Son of God

What do these Synoptic Gospels say about the identity of Jesus? They say that, prior to Jesus' resurrection, His closest disciples regarded Him as a *hasid* ("holy man"), an eschatological prophet and an itinerant preacher, a rabbi and a wisdom teacher, a healer and a charismatic miracle-worker, an exorcist and therefore a deliverer from demonic evil, the King of Israel, their Master and Lord, and even the Savior of the world. But most of all, *all three Synoptic Gospels proclaim that Jesus is the promised Messiah of the Jewish Scriptures as well as the Son of God.*[16] This was most clearly stated by the Apostle Peter while Jesus and His entourage were traveling in Caesarea Philippi. Jesus questioned His disciples about who people thought He was. Then "He said to them, 'But who do you say that I am?' And Simon Peter answered and said, 'Thou art the Christ, the Son of the living God'" (Mt 16.15-16 par.).

In the Synoptics, Jesus is identified as, or questioned as being, "the Son (of God)" 16x in Matthew, 8x in Mark, and 12x in Luke. All three Synoptists relate that at two of the most significant events in Jesus' life—His baptism and transfiguration—a voice from above proclaimed Him as "My beloved Son" (Mt 3.17 par.; 17.5 par.). When Jesus was soon tempted in the wilderness, the devil prefaced his temptation by saying, "If You are the Son of God" (Mt 4.3, 6/Lk 4.3, 9). And two Synoptists record the Q logion about "the Son" and "My/the Father" in Mt 11.27 and Lk 10.22. Then there is the soldier at the cross who exclaimed, "Truly this man was a son of God" (Mt 27.54/Mk 15.39 NEB).

---

[15] See C.L. Blomberg, "Gospels (Historical Reliability)," 291-97.
[16] E.g., Mt 1.1, 16, 18; Mk 1.1; Lk 1.1-4; Jn 20.30-31.

The foremost critical question for our study is this: Do these Synoptic Gospels say that Jesus is God? The overwhelming consensus among contemporary NT scholars is that *there is nothing in the Synoptic Gospels to indicate that Jesus, His disciples, or the synoptic Evangelists believed or proclaimed that Jesus is God by being the Son of God.*[17]

Then, what do these Synoptic Gospels mean by saying Jesus is the Son of God? Perhaps the best way to discover the answer to this question is to consider the voice from heaven at Jesus' baptism and transfiguration. The following is a conflation of all three synoptic quotations of both sayings, "This is My beloved Son, in/with whom I am well-pleased."[18] The voice at the transfiguration adds, "listen to Him." In this transfiguration saying, Luke omits the word "beloved" and adds after "Son," "My Chosen One."

The current scholarly consensus is that these pronouncements at Jesus' baptism and transfiguration represent a conflation of Isa 42.1 and Ps 2.7, with Isa 42.1 being dominant.[19] In Isa 42.1 Yahweh states, "Behold, My Servant, whom I uphold, My chosen one in whom My soul delights." Of course, "with whom I am well-pleased" corresponds with "in whom My soul delights." If scholars are correct about the voice alluding to Isa 42.1, as it seems, this substitution of "Son" for "chosen one," and Luke's inclusion of both, surely indicates that Jesus being the Son of God means that He is the Chosen One. Yet Jesus' status of being divinely chosen does not mean that He is God.

In sum, the Synoptics never equate the title "Son of God" with the word "God."

Only the Father Is God

The synoptists sometimes use the words "God" and "Father" interchangeably in their sayings of Jesus. For instance, Matthew writes that Jesus said, "For whoever does the will of My Father who is in heaven, he is My brother and sister and mother" (Mt 12.50). Mark, on the other hand, quotes the same saying verbatim, but includes the phrase "the will of God" instead of "the will of My Father who is in heaven" (Mk 3.35).

Occasionally, the synoptists use the words "God" and "Father" interchangeably in the same context, even in Jesus' sayings. It occurs in Matthew's account of Jesus' famous Sermon on the Mount, in which Jesus speaks of both "your heavenly Father" and "God" (Mt 6.26, 30, 32). The same thing happens in Mark's account of Jesus cursing the fig tree. Mark quotes Jesus as saying, "Have faith in God" (Mk 11.22), after which Mark adds that Jesus said, "your Father also who is in heaven" (v. 25).

Such evidence shows that for Jesus and the synoptic Evangelists, "God" and "(the) Father" were interchangeable terms that referred to the same divine being.

The Baptism of Jesus

Jesus' baptism served to launch His brief public career. Oscar Cullmann writes that it "provides the introduction to an understanding of the whole life of Jesus—and of all Christology."[20] Indeed, Jesus' baptism seems to have even

---

[17] Contra Rudolf Karl Bultmann (*History of the Synoptic Tradition* [1921], tr. John Marsh, rev. ed. [ET 1963; repr. Peabody, MA: Hendrickson, n.d.], 358, 367), who asserts that both Matthew and Luke make Jesus "divine" with the birth narratives and calling Jesus "Lord."

[18] Baptism: Mt 3.17/Mk 1.11/Lk 3.22; Transfiguration: Mt 17.5/Mk 9.7/Lk 9.35.

[19] W.D. Davies and Dale C. Allison, *The Gospel According to Saint Matthew*, 3 vols. (London: T&T Clark, 1988), 1:338.

[20] O. Cullmann, *Christology*, 284.

played a pivotal role in the development of His God-consciousness even though that was a continuous process.[21]

All three synoptists narrate the baptism of Jesus. His cousin, John, performed the blessed ritual. Matthew records that "after being baptized, Jesus went up immediately from the water; and behold, the heavens were opened, and he saw the Spirit of God descending as a dove, and coming upon Him, and behold, a voice out of the heavens, saying, 'This is My beloved Son, in whom I am well-pleased'" (Mt 3.16-17 par.). This voice identified Jesus as God's "Son" due to His piety rather than ontologically. We have seen that one of the identifications of "son of God" in Judaism was a *hasid*—a pious one.

Thus, two significant manifestations of divine revelation occurred when Jesus was baptized: (1) the Holy Spirit of God descended upon Him in the form of a dove, and (2) a voice sounded forth simultaneously from the sky above. That these two manifestations were literally seen and heard by eyewitnesses seems evident, though uncertain.[22]

Some have thought this heavenly utterance at Jesus' baptism affirms Adoption Christology, i.e., that at that moment Jesus became God's Son by means of adoption. Other Adoptionists have cited Jesus' resurrection as the defining moment of adoption, supporting it with Rom 1.4. On the contrary, the issue in the NT that gives rise to Adoption Christology is not *when* Jesus became the Son of God but when this status was revealed from heaven, which occurred multiple times. For example, Jesus was divinely declared "the Son of God" just prior to His conception (Lk 1.32, 35).

More importantly, Christianity has always struggled with the idea that Jesus was baptized. Why? John was "preaching a baptism of repentance for the forgiveness of sins" (Mk 1.4 par.), baptizing people as they were "confessing their sins" (v. 5). When Jesus came to be baptized, John expressed dismay (Mt 3.14); for he had previously admitted his own unworthiness compared to Jesus (v. 11 par.). Indeed, the NT repeatedly proclaims Jesus' sinlessness, so that He did not need divine forgiveness. Nevertheless, Jesus replied to John, "it is fitting for us to fulfill all righteousness" (v. 15). This enigmatic answer apparently means that Jesus, even though He was without sin, came to be baptized as an act of identification with all of humankind regarding the frailty of our humanity, i.e., the weakness of the flesh, and perhaps as a symbol of the New Israel or the New Humanity. Any implicit admission of weakness, if correct, does not seem to coincide with Jesus being God. Yet Jesus' baptism may merely signal His divine consecration for service.

We saw in Chapter Four that "Messiah" means the "anointed (One)" and that pre-Christian Judaism expected the Messiah to be anointed by the Spirit of God, just as King Saul and King David were. Thus, the Spirit-anointing of Jesus at His baptism emerges as one of the first acts that subtly indicates His divine chosenness, if not His messiahship.

Jesus' baptism and simultaneous reception of the Holy Spirit indicate His subordination to, and dependence upon, God, which are contrary to His being God. For, John would have baptized Jesus in The Name, viz., Yahweh, and thereupon the Spirit of Yahweh descended upon Jesus. Adolf Harnack explains,

---

[21] Friedrich Schleiermacher, *The Life of Jesus* [1864], ed. Jack C. Verheyden, tr. S. Maclean Gilmour (Mifflintown, PA: Sigler, 1997), 267.
[22] See Jn 1.31-34. The narratives imply that the people present, especially John and Jesus, heard the voice. Cf. Mt 17.5-6 par.; Jn 12.28-30.

"The formula, *eis to onoma* [in the name], expresses that the person baptised is put into a relation of dependence on him into whose name he is baptised."[23]

The Voice Out of the Heavens

Rabbinical Judaism has always taught that the earthly activity of "the holy spirit" ceased when the age of the prophets ended, in about 400 BCE. Rabbis have further believed that, after that, divine revelation was conveyed to humans on rare occasions by means of what they called the heavenly "daughter of a voice" (Heb. *bat qol*). That is, in rare instances God spoke in heaven and an echo of His voice was heard by divinely-selected people on earth. Interestingly, Jewish scholar Geza Vermes compares this rabbinic tradition about *bat qol* with the heavenly voice heard at Jesus' baptism.[24]

The voice that sounded out of the heavens at Jesus' baptism was undoubtedly intended to represent that of the transcendent Almighty God, whom Jesus often called "the/My Father." That it was actually the Father's voice is doubtful. It may not have been *bat qol* because Jesus told "the Jews" concerning God the Father, "You have neither heard His voice at any time, nor seen His form" (Jn 5.37).

The NT gospels record a total of three incidents in Jesus' life when a voice sounded from above. They were (1) Jesus' baptism, (2) His transfiguration, and (3) when He prayed on Palm Sunday during Passion Week.[25] Curiously, all scriptural accounts of these three events do not identify the source of the voice.

The third incident is particularly intriguing, and only the Fourth Evangelist reports it. A few days prior to Jesus' unforgettable prayer and subsequent arrest in the Garden of Gethsemane, He said His soul was "troubled" as He anticipated His imminent, violent death. So He prayed, indicating His willingness to undergo this final baptism of death. Instantly, "there came therefore a voice out of heaven," proclaiming that God's Name was about to be glorified in Jesus (Jn 12.28). "The multitude therefore who stood by and heard it were saying that it had thundered; others were saying, 'An angel has spoken to Him'" (v. 29). That Jesus referred to it merely as "this voice" (v. 30), without designating it precisely as the voice of the Father, suggests that it was not the Father's actual voice. Were some hearers correct, that the source of the voice was either thunder or an angel?

It may have been both. Maybe the answer can be discovered in the most important event in Israel's history prior to the Christ event. That would be when Moses received the Law on Mount Sinai. At that time, "the LORD spoke to Moses" (Ex 19.21); but it was not literally with His own voice. Rather, "Moses spoke and God answered him with thunder" (vv. 19; cf. Rev 10.3-4). Indeed, God had told Moses, "Behold, I shall come to you in a thick cloud, in order that the people may hear when I speak with you" (Ex 19.9). The thick cloud was necessary to produce the thunder, so that all of the Hebrew people who were standing at the foot of the mountain could hear that God was speaking to Moses.

Later, the first Christian martyr—Spirit-filled Stephen—preached about Moses receiving the Law. He explained that Moses received it by means of "the angel who was speaking to him on Mount Sinai" (Ac 7.38). Stephen also identified God's spokesperson at Mount Sinai as "the angel who appeared to him [Abraham] in the thorn bush" (v. 35), viz., "the angel of the LORD" (Ex 3.2). And Stephen further related that Israel "received the law as ordained by angels" (Ac 7.53).

---

[23] A. Harnack, *History of Dogma*, 1:79n2.
[24] G. Vermes, *The Changing Faces of Jesus*, 189-90.
[25] Mt 3.17; 17.5; Mk 1.11; 9.7; Lk 3.22; 9.35; Jn 12.28.

Thus, a likely candidate for God's spokesperson on the three occasions that the heavenly voice is recorded in the NT is an angel, perhaps "the angel of LORD" in the OT. If so, that angel may have affected that speech on behalf of God by using thunder to form the audible words. Regardless, such evidence indicates both God's transcendence as well as His involvement with His earthly creation by means of angelic agency.

The Holy Spirit in the Life of Jesus[26]

Jesus' earthly life, from beginning to end, was completely immersed in the Holy Spirit. First, His supernatural conception was accomplished by the power of the Holy Spirit (Mt 1.18, 20; Lk 1.35). Second, at His baptism He was anointed with the Holy Spirit (Lk 4.18; Ac 10.38). Prior to that blessed event, the Holy Spirit no doubt influenced Jesus' life; but it is doubtful that Jesus ever performed any miraculous deeds prior to His baptism.[27] The NT makes it clear that the Spirit-anointing of Jesus at His baptism was something quite new and pivotal in His life and that it was necessary in order to assist Him in His imminent mission.[28] Third, Jesus indicated His reliance upon the Holy Spirit early in His public ministry when He quoted from Isaiah, "THE SPIRIT OF THE LORD IS UPON ME, BECAUSE HE ANOINTED ME TO PREACH THE GOSPEL TO THE POOR," etc. (Lk 4.18). He then explained, "Today this Scripture has been fulfilled in your hearing" (v. 21). Fourth, soon after Jesus died He was resurrected through the power of the Holy Spirit. Eduard Schweizer concludes, "the Spirit of God presides over the whole life of Jesus."[29]

That is what people thought about Jesus, at least those who knew Him best. Take the Apostle Peter; soon after Jesus' ascension into heaven Peter preached to thousands on the day of Pentecost, saying, "Men of Israel,... Jesus the Nazarene [was] attested to you by God with miracles and wonders and signs which God performed through Him in your midst" (Ac 2.22). Later, Peter explained about "Jesus of Nazareth, how God anointed Him with the Holy Spirit and with power, and how He went about doing good and healing all who were oppressed by the devil; for God was with Him" (Ac 10.38).

Some scholars therefore conclude that the fulness of the Holy Spirit in Jesus' life is primarily what made Him so unique. Eduard Schweizer also thinks that the NT church "community had ascribed to the Spirit that which distinguished Jesus from all other men, even the greatest of the prophets."[30] James D.G. Dunn observes regarding the NT gospels, *"Jesus is presented consistently as a man of the Spirit during his life and ministry."*[31] Scholars label this phenomena "Spirit Christology."[32]

---

[26] Included here are a few other NT passages that depict the operation of the Holy Spirit in Jesus' life.

[27] It is doubtful that Jesus ever performed miracles prior to the Spirit-anointing at His baptism. Some non-canonical, spurious writings assert otherwise. Satan's temptation that Jesus turn stones into bread suggests that Jesus might have been able to do so due to past experiences. But only the Fourth Evangelist records Jesus' miracle of turning water into wine, adding, "This beginning of His signs Jesus did in Cana of Galilee" (Jn 2.11). This seems to mean that it was the first miraculous act of any sort that Jesus ever did.

[28] James D.G. Dunn, *Jesus and the Spirit: A Study of the Religious and Charismatic Experience of Jesus and the First Christians as Reflected in the New Testament* (London: SCM, 1975), 65.

[29] Eduard Schweizer, *The Holy Spirit*, tr. Reginald H. and Ilse Fuller (Ger. orig. 1978; Philadelphia: Fortress, 1980), 56.

[30] E. Schweizer, *The Holy Spirit*, 57.

[31] J.D.G. Dunn, *Christology in the Making*, 141. Emphasis his.

[32] See esp. G.W.H. Lampe, *God as Spirit*.

Despite Peter's bold and important proclamations about the Holy Spirit in Jesus' life, a century ago Abraham Kuyper made the insightful and profound observation that "the church has never sufficiently confessed the influence of the Holy Spirit exerted upon the work of Christ."[33] Indeed it has not! It is because *the concept of the Holy Spirit empowering Jesus to do His mighty works does not accord well with the traditional belief that Jesus was God.* That is surely why Eduard Schweizer observes, "There is a dearth of scholarly works on the Holy Spirit"?[34] How much more regarding the Holy Spirit in the life of Jesus? Athanasius even unwittingly acknowledged the following Arian argument, which is very sound: If Jesus was "Very God," as the Nicene Creed states, He would not have needed the Holy Spirit.[35] In fact, Justin Martyr had earlier framed this argument and put it in the mouth of Trypho the Jew, suggesting that it was a prominent argument at that time.[36] To defend the developing traditional Christology during Justin's time, he asserted flatly that Jesus did not "need" the Holy Spirit.[37]

On the contrary, *the power of the Holy Spirit is what enabled Jesus to accomplish His miracles.* Traditionalist Gerald Hawthorne explains, "the Spirit so fully motivated Jesus' speech and actions that the miracles he performed and the words he spoke he spoke and performed, not by virtue of his own power, the power of his own divine personality, but by virtue of the power of the Holy Spirit at work within him and through him."[38] Hawthorne asserts that although Jesus was "divine," he needed the Holy Spirit.

So, *Jesus' reliance upon the Holy Spirit indicated His need of the Holy Spirit.* But classical theism, which traditionalists have generally adopted, maintains that God, being totally self-sufficient, does *not* need anything; otherwise, He would not be God. Indeed, we have seen that the very meaning of God's Name, YHWH, is the self-sufficient One. If Jesus was God, it would have been impossible for the Holy Spirit to have even assisted Him. Yet, without the Holy Spirit's aid, Jesus surely could not have accomplished His divinely appointed mission, which included performing many miracles. The Johannine Jesus implied this when He said, "the Son can do nothing of Himself" (Jn 5.19; cf. v. 30).

Athanasius contended otherwise. He asserted that Jesus' miracle-working power came from the source of His deity as the Logos-Son.[39] But this assertion is not confirmed anywhere in the NT. James D.G. Dunn remarks, "If we spell out Jesus' own religious experience, his experience of God, solely in terms of sonship, we misunderstand Jesus almost totally. Jesus' experience was also of God as Spirit."[40]

Whatever impact the incarnation had on Jesus—that is, the Logos taking flesh to become the man, Jesus—it must not have satisfied Jesus' need of empowerment of the Holy Spirit in order for Him to accomplish His mission. Thus, there must be a profound difference between "the word of God" and

---

[33] Abraham Kuyper, *The Work of the Holy Spirit*, tr. Heiligen Geest (New York: Funk & Wagnalls, 1900), 97. Cited by Gerald Hawthorne, *The Presence and the Power: The Significance of the Holy Spirit in the Life of Jesus* (Dallas: Word, 1991), 2-3.

[34] E. Schweizer, *The Holy Spirit*, 135.

[35] Athanasius, *Orations Against the Arians*, 3.26.

[36] Justin Martyr, *Dialogue with Trypho*, 47.2-3.

[37] E.g., Justin Martyr, *Dialogue with Trypho*, 88.1, 4.

[38] G. Hawthorne, *The Power and the Presence*, 145-46, cf. 148, 154-55, 160, 162. See also J.D.G. Dunn, *Jesus and the Spirit*, 87.

[39] E.g., Athanasius, *Orations Against the Arians*, 3.31.

[40] J.D.G. Dunn, *Jesus and the Spirit*, 89.

"the Spirit of God" even though they are closely associated. Perhaps the main difference is that the Logos has to do with God's spoken word whereas the Spirit has to do with God's power manifested through His works (cf. Isa 11.1). We often read in the OT that "the Spirit of the LORD/God came" upon someone, especially a prophet, and that prophet either did or said something that came from God. More often we read that "the word of the LORD came" upon some prophet and that prophet spoke the word of the LORD. Yet the Holy Spirit sometimes speaks to people as well. Perhaps the Spirit's empowerment provides the animation, and what is actually spoken represents the word of God. If so, the Logos embodying Jesus does not preclude Jesus' need of empowerment from the Holy Spirit. Surely God's Word and Spirit are to be distinguished, yet they worked together in the life of Jesus.

Jesus' miracle-working power therefore was not intrinsic to Himself. This is most evident from Jesus' response to His opponents' accusations that He was doing miracles in the power of Satan. He replied, "whoever shall speak a word against the Son of Man, it shall be forgiven him; but whoever shall speak against the Holy Spirit, it shall not be forgiven him" (Mt 12.32). Herein, Jesus clearly attributes His mighty works to the Holy Spirit working in and through Him. And He distinguishes this power from Himself as the Son of Man. Thus, if Jesus' miracle-working power was an essential part of His nature, then, to speak against this power would be to speak against Him rather than against some entity other than Him, viz., the Holy Spirit.

Surprisingly, the Gospel Evangelists do not furnish much information about the Holy Spirit empowering Jesus. And they rarely report that Jesus acknowledged the Holy Spirit as the source of His miraculous power. They seem to have presumed it by what they earlier related about his baptism. E. Schweizer explains, "there can be no doubt that the three evangelists are trying to tell us that the Holy Spirit which descended upon Jesus [at His baptism] will be manifested in all his life to come."[41] Besides, Isaiah predicted that the Messiah would come in the power of the Holy Spirit (Isa 11.2; cf. 42.1; 61.1).

Was Jesus reluctant to talk about the Holy Spirit's presence and empowerment in His life? If so, one reason could have been that the prophet Joel had predicted that the Holy Spirit would be poured out on all of God's people as the principal sign of the in-breaking of the glorious messianic age (Joel 2.28-29). Jesus may have wanted to avoid unnecessarily encouraging His disciples into thinking that that blessed time was imminent (cf. Ac 1.6-7).[42] E. Schweizer gives a pragmatic reason, that "the best way to teach about the Holy Spirit is simply to ... let the Spirit permeate one's life."[43] Jesus sure did that.

Apparently, the idea of the Holy Spirit indwelling and empowering Jesus is synonymous with God being in Him. Jesus explained, "the Father abiding in Me does His works" (Jn 14.10).[44] In other words, God the Father indwells the earthly Jesus by means of His Spirit. Schleiermacher, who we have seen was a strong proponent of a solely God-in-Christ Christology, puts it this way, "the existence of God in the Redeemer is posited as the innermost fundamental

---

[41] E. Schweizer, *The Holy Spirit*, 52.
[42] Contra A. Schweitzer (*The Quest of the Historical Jesus*) and many modern scholars who postulate that Jesus preached an imminent eschatological kingdom, but subsequent history proved Him wrong.
[43] E. Schweizer, *The Holy Spirit*, 50.
[44] This saying suggests that the Father indwells Jesus by means of His Spirit, so that the Spirit is not a separate *hypostasis* from the Father and therefore not a separate Person.

power in Him."⁴⁵ That power was the Spirit of God. In conclusion, NT *accounts of the Holy Spirit in the life of Jesus emerge as significant evidence that Jesus was not God but that God was in Him by means of His Holy Spirit.*

Acts of the Holy Spirit in the Life of Jesus

Nevertheless, a few synoptic reports do indicate that Jesus constantly depended on being led by the Holy Spirit. For example, immediately following Jesus' baptism the Holy Spirit "led" Him forth so that He thereafter accomplished all of His healings, other miracles, and exorcisms in "the power of the Holy Spirit" (Lk 4.14; cf. Mt 4.1; 12.28; Ac 2.22). This was soon confirmed most explicitly by Jesus Himself when He attended the synagogue in His hometown of Nazareth and read to the congregation from Isa 61.1: "THE SPIRIT OF THE LORD IS UPON ME, BECAUSE HE ANOINTED ME TO PREACH THE GOSPEL TO THE POOR. HE HAS SENT ME TO PROCLAIM RELEASE TO THE CAPTIVES, AND RECOVERY OF SIGHT TO THE BLIND, TO SET FREE THOSE WHO ARE DOWNTRODDEN" (Lk 4.18; cf. Isa 35.5-6; 42.1; Mt 11.5/Lk 7.22; Mt 12.18). Then Jesus explained, "Today this Scripture has been fulfilled in your hearing" (Lk 4.21). Obviously, He applied this text to Himself to mean that He accomplished His mighty deeds because the Spirit of God was upon Him.

Occasionally, Jesus indicated the same thing implicitly. For instance, when the imprisoned John the Baptist questioned whether Jesus was the Promised One of the OT Scriptures, Jesus sent a message of assurance back to John, His cousin. He told him that He was indeed the Promised One, drawing his attention to His miracles and quoting some of Isa 61.1 as being fulfilled in Himself as the Promised One (Mt 11.2-5/Lk 7.18-22).

Another time was when Jesus healed a deaf and dumb man by casting a demon out of him. Witnesses alleged, "He casts out demons by Beelzebul, the ruler of the demons" (Lk 11.15). According to Luke, Jesus retorted, "I cast out demons by the finger of God" (v. 20). Matthew reports the same incident but substitutes Luke's metaphor, "the finger of God," with "the Spirit of God" (Mt 12.28). James Dunn suggests that, not just for exorcisms, "This was evidently Jesus' own explanation for his success as a healer."⁴⁶

Of course, Jesus was not the only one who ever did miracles in the power of the Holy Spirit. According to the OT and other Judaic traditions, as indicated by those who accused Jesus, prior prophets did too. But Christians believe that the extent to which the Holy Spirit impacted the life of Jesus was far greater than it was with them. In OT times the Spirit *came upon* individuals, such as kings and prophets, only temporarily and, assumedly, partially. And it is questionable whether the Holy Spirit ever actually indwelt anyone prior to the Spirit-anointing of Jesus.

In contrast, during the Christian era the Holy Spirit indwells believers (e.g., Jn 7.38-39; Rom 8.9). But the current universal indwelling of the Holy Spirit in God's people is only partial and therefore not the same as it was with Jesus (despite Eph 3.19). In contrast, God gave His Holy Spirit to Jesus "without measure," so that "the fulness" of God dwelt most uniquely in Jesus (Jn 1.16; 3.34; Col 1.19>; 2.9>).

To sum, the Synoptic Gospels imply that Jesus could only have accomplished His mission by means of the Holy Spirit. Jesus' *need* of supernatural power—a power He acquired through God's Spirit in order to perform His divinely-

---

⁴⁵ F. Schleiermacher, *The Christian Faith*, 397.

⁴⁶ J.D.G. Dunn, *Christology in the Making*, 137.

ordained mission—shows that such power *did not* reside intrinsically in Jesus as a part of His nature. Accordingly, Jesus could not have been God. Jesus' uniqueness as a miracle-worker can be explained only by His filial relationship with God and thus His empowerment by God's Holy Spirit. Therefore, classical incarnation Christology is incompatible with this Spirit Christology.

The Temptations of Jesus

All three synoptists attest that, immediately after Jesus' baptism, the Holy Spirit led Him into the wilderness to be tempted by the devil (Mt 4.1-11 par.). Only Matthew and Luke delineate three specific temptations. In each one, Jesus quoted Scripture, all from the Torah. His response to these temptations illustrates His complete reliance upon the word of God and the Spirit of God. Consequently, the devil "departed from Him until an opportune time" (Lk 4.13). While this confrontation with Satan was apparently a momentous occasion in Jesus' life, it would not be his last (e.g., Mk 8.33 par.)

An obvious question arises from these temptations: How can Jesus be God if He was tempted? For we read, "God cannot be tempted by evil" (Jam 1.13). This question leads to another: If Jesus was God, were His temptations real? That is, could Jesus have possibly succumbed to temptation and therefore have sinned? Orthodox Christianity has struggled with these two christological questions that relate to our lives as much as any.

Classical Christian theism answers these two questions with a resounding, "No!" Its main argument is that Jesus, being God, could not have sinned because deity is both impassible (no emotion) and immutable (no change). Here is one of the main reasons orthodox Christianity has always tended toward Docetism.

On the contrary, human beings have moral choice. If Jesus was fully human, He must have had moral choice; if not, He wasn't fully human. Surely the Apostle Paul would not have compared Jesus to Adam if Paul had thought Jesus did not possess the freedom of moral choice, as Adam had. (See Chapter Seven/Adam Christology.) But if Jesus' supposed divine nature so programmed Him that He could not have sinned, He did not have moral choice and therefore was not as human as Adam and Eve were prior to the fall. J.A.T. Robinson well explains, "Jesus' obedience was certainly not automatic or necessary.... He must have had the freedom to sin or not to sin ... He was fallible—yet when the crunch time came, he did not fail."[47] Praise Jesus!

Jesus' complete freedom of moral choice was most evident at the time of His arrest and just prior to it. In the Garden of Gethsemane He prayed to the Father, "remove this cup from Me; yet not what I will, but what Thou wilt" (Mk 14.36; cf. Mt 26.39; Lk 22.42). He endured an inner struggle with the temptation to abort the divine mission. Moments later, when He was arrested, Peter drew his sword, swung it, and cut off the ear of the high priest's slave. Jesus exclaimed to Peter, "do you think that I cannot appeal to My Father, and He will at once put at My disposal more than twelve legions of angels?[48] How then shall the Scriptures be fulfilled, that it must happen this way?" (Mt 26.53-54). Yes, there existed a tension here between Jesus' freedom of choice and the divine will; yet Jesus clearly revealed that He had choice in the matter. Otherwise, the Johannine Jesus could not have said, "I lay down My life ... I lay it down on My

---

[47] J.A.T. Robinson, *The Human Face of God*, 93-94.
[48] As Jn 5.19, 30, here is an antidote to the claim that Jesus possessed the divine attribute of omnipotence.

own initiative. I have authority to lay it down, and I have authority to take it up again" (Jn 10.17-18).

In sum, it is only plausible to think of Jesus' prayerful temptations as real, and that is surely how they are presented in the NT. Consider His intense struggle in the Garden of Gethsemane immediately prior to His arrest (Mk 14.32-38 par.). Moreover, the fact that Jesus was greatly rewarded upon His entrance into heaven suggests that He was not programmed, that He could have succumbed to temptation and aborted His mission. But Jesus once said something that is most pertinent to the seeming dilemma between divine sovereignty and human free will: "with God all things are possible" (Mt 19.26 par.; cf. Mk 9.23; 11.22-24 par.; 14.36). God was *with* Jesus, and that is how He accomplished His mission, not because He *was* God.

The Humanity of Jesus

Thus, the Synoptic Gospels present compelling evidence that Jesus was a human being in every sense. Physically, He got hungry (Mt 21.18/Mk 11.12), and He got tired Mk 6.31). Emotionally, Jesus loved (Mk 10.21), rejoiced (Lk 10.21), got angry (Mt 21.12 par.; Mk 3.5; 10.14), grieved (Mk 3.5; Mt 26.37-38/Mk 14.33-34), became distressed (Mt 26.37/Mk 14.33), wept profusely (Lk 19.41; 22.44), and obviously felt compassion for those He healed (Mt 14.14/Mk 6.34).

Gerald Hawthorne surmises that church fathers and many other traditionalists have emphasized Jesus' deity so much that they have thereby diminished His humanity. For a traditionalist, Hawthorne offers this surprising protest:

> to preserve at all costs the deity of Jesus Christ, many contemporary teachers of the church have followed the lead of the ancient fathers and have become *de facto* Docetists,... often neglecting the clear New Testament teaching of the full humanity of Jesus, many of these have not adequately stressed that Jesus was made like us "in every respect" (Heb. 2:17), except in the matter of sin (Heb. 4:15), have refused to accept the fact that there were things that Jesus did not know (Matt. 24:36), have rejected out of hand the idea that there were things he could not do (Mark 6:5), and have overlooked that he performed his miracles by the Spirit of God (cf. Matt. 12:28). They have preferred rather to side with the fathers who taught that Jesus as man may have been limited, but that the very same person at the same instant was unlimited as God—that he was weak as a man, but that he knew all things as God. Such teaching, however, while claiming in theory to hold fast to the humanity of Jesus, in reality lets it slip away.[49]

According to all three synoptists, Jesus foretold His disciples of His death, burial, and resurrection (Mk 8.31 par.; 9.31 par.; 10.33-34 par.). Many historical-critical scholars dismiss these accounts as literary embellishments that are thus historically inauthentic. Moderate traditionalist John Macquarrie rejects them "on the grounds that it diminishes the humanity of Jesus by attributing to him a supernatural knowledge."[50] What? Jesus could have understood from Scripture about His impending death.[51] Besides, prophets were given supernatural knowledge and performed supernatural acts that were miracles, and no one thinks these powers diminished their humanity.

---

[49] G. Hawthorne, *The Presence and the Power*, 205.
[50] J. Macquarrie, *Jesus Christ in Modern Thought*, 358.
[51] E.g., Ps 16.10 (cf. Ac 2.31; 13.35); 22.1, 14-16; Hos 6.2; Jonah 1.17; Isa 52.13–53.12; Zech 12.10.

Angels Ministering to Jesus

Jesus, the par excellent Minister, sometimes needed others to minister to Him. All three synoptists provide varying degrees of evidence showing that on rare occasions Jesus needed and received ministering from angels. One such incident occurred following His temptations, when "the devil left Him; and behold, angels came and began to minister to Him" (Mt 4.11 par.). Another time was during Passion Week, when He took His three inner core of disciples with Him to pray in the Garden of Gethsemane about His imminent suffering and death. He "began to be very distressed and troubled. And He said to them, 'My soul is deeply grieved to the point of death'" (Mk 14.33-34). Only Luke adds, "an angel from heaven appeared to Him, strengthening Him" (Lk 22.43).[52]

If Jesus was God, how could He get depressed and need ministering from others? Moreover, how could an angel impart strength to God? Couldn't Jesus' supposed divine nature have sustained Him? Recall that God's self-ascription— "I AM WHO I AM" (Deut 3.14)—means, "I am the Self-Existent One." Thus, God is always totally self-sufficient. In contrast, certain events in the life of Jesus, such as angels ministering to Him in His time of need, demonstrate that He was not self-sufficient and therefore was not God.

The Miracles of Jesus

The Synoptics are distinguished for their many accounts of Jesus' healings and other miracles. Do such things attest that Jesus was God? That is what many church fathers and many other Christians have thought.[53] Neil MacDonald observes, "with the advent of Enlightenment, a necessary condition of affirmation of the rational status of the divinity of Christ was belief in the miracles attested in the Gospels, and in particular, in what is taken to be the greatest miracle of all—the resurrection of Jesus Christ."[54]

This assessment is merely a biblically-unjustified overreaction to Enlightenment. Those who think that such evidence attests to Jesus being God seem to have carelessly overlooked that the OT prophets and Jesus' apostles did miracles as well. If Jesus was God simply because He performed miracles, then the prophets and apostles must have been God as well, which is absurd. While some godly people have performed miraculous acts comparable to those of Jesus,[55] He surely accomplished far more than any others did either before or after Him (Jn 9.32; 15.24). Yet that does not make Him God.

Jesus researcher E.P. Sanders addresses the significance of Jesus' miracles. He explains, "A lot of Christians, and possibly even more non-Christians, think that central to Christianity is the view that Jesus could perform miracles because he was more than a mere human being.... Like other ancient people, Jews believed in miracles but did not think that the ability to perform them proved exalted status.... Historically, it is an error to think that Christians must

---

[52] However, Lk 22.43-44 has weak MS attestation as indicated in some modern English versions.
[53] E.g., Origen, *De Principiis*, 2.6.1; Athanasius, *On the Incarnation*, 18.4; 38.3-4; 49.1, 4; idem, *Orations Against the Arians*, 32. Modern traditionalists include M. Harris, *Jesus as God*, 289, 315; Paul E. Little, *Know Why You Believe: New Edition, Revised and Updated* (Downers Grove, IL: InterVarsity, 2000), 40, 44; R.M. Bowman and J.E. Komoszewski, *Putting Jesus in His Place*, 201-04. Athanasius (e.g., *Orations Against the Arians*, 3.31, 40) often asserts that Jesus' miracles attest to His being the Logos, which Athanasius regards as synonymous with Jesus' deity.
[54] Neil MacDonald, "Enlightenment," in *DHT*, 180.
[55] Elijah and Elisha performed some miracles that can be compared to those of Jesus (e.g., 1 Kgs 17.17-24; 2 Kgs 4.18-37). And the Apostle Paul accomplished a resuscitation from the dead (Ac 20.9-12).

believe that Jesus was superhuman, and also an error to think that in Jesus' own day his miracles were taken as proving partial or full divinity."[56] Yes, Jews believed God could do, and did, miracles through His prophets (e.g., Jn 3.2). The Jewish religious authorities never questioned whether Jesus performed miracles; rather, they accused Him of doing them in the power of Satan (Mt 12.22-24/Mk 3.22).

Many fairly conservative traditionalist scholars affirm what Sanders here says. For instance, D.A. Carson acknowledges, "the value of miracles as proof of Jesus' deity is not so conclusive as some conservative expositors have thought."[57] N.T. Wright puts it more decisively by claiming that Jesus' miracles were "certainly not in themselves indications or hints that Jesus was 'divine' (whatever that might be deemed to mean)."[58]

Apparently, Jesus could not heal and do other miracles indiscriminately, and this phenomenon further indicates that He was not God. For instance, on one Sabbath day Jesus began to teach in His hometown synagogue of Nazareth. Matthew relates that the parishioners discussed among themselves, "'Where did this man get this wisdom, and these miraculous powers?'.... And they took offense at Him" (Mt 13.58 par.). Jesus must have done miracles in their midst or else they knew of His reputation for it. Mark says of this episode, "He could do no miracle there except that He laid His hands upon a few sick people and healed them. And He wondered at their unbelief" (Mk 6.5-6 par.). Indeed, it was "because of their unbelief" that Jesus could not perform miracles there (Mt 13.58).

So, Jesus' power to heal depended to some degree on the faith of the beneficiary. That is how it was with the paralytic. To get into the overcrowded house where Jesus was, the man's four friends carried him on his bed and let him down through the roof. Only Luke explains, "the power of the Lord was present for Him to perform healing" on the man (Lk 5.17; cf. 6.19). Again, this suggests that Jesus did not always have power to heal, indicating He was not God. But He had the power that day because of "seeing their faith" (Lk 5.20), i.e., the faith of the paralytic man and his friends. Sometimes, Jesus healed people and told them, "your faith has made you well" (Mt 9.22/Mk 5.34/Lk 8.48; Mk 10.52/Lk 18.42). J.D.G. Dunn well states concerning Jesus, "Faith was the necessary complement to the exercise of God's power through him, hence his inability to perform any mighty work in Nazareth ... Faith in the recipient as it were completed the circuit so that the power could flow,"[59] i.e., the power of the Holy Spirit through Jesus to others.

One time the flow of power to heal was not even turned on by Jesus. A woman with a hemorrhage of blood for twelve years seems to have activated it. She was in a big crowd where people were pressing upon Jesus. When she purposely touched His clothes, hoping to be healed, Jesus was not aware of her touch. He only felt a surge of healing power go through His body (Mk 5.24-34 par.). Perhaps it was like an electrical charge of low voltage. In this case, Jesus was not sovereign in the exercise of His miracle-working power. Instead, God the Father was in control by means of His Spirit. Such things do not coincide well with the notion that Jesus was God, since God is supposed to be sovereign.

---

[56] E.P. Sanders, *The Historical Figure of Jesus*, 133, 135.

[57] D.A. Carson, "Matthew," 36. See also D. Cupitt, *Jesus and the Gospel of God*, 14.

[58] N.T. Wright, *Jesus and the Victory of God*, 196, cf. 186; similarly, idem, *The Resurrection of the Son of God* (Minneapolis: Fortress, 2003), 577. See also M. Borg, *Jesus: A New Vision*, 70.

[59] J.D.G. Dunn, *Jesus and the Spirit*, 74-75.

These and other examples show that Jesus' power to perform miracles was never intrinsic to His own being. Instead, it was derived from God through God's Holy Spirit. Even though Jesus acknowledged that He healed people (e.g., Jn 7.23), His miracles cannot be ascribed to either His supposed deity (divine nature) or, as traditionalist and systematic theologian Charles Hodge strangely puts it, "the works of his human nature."[60]

In sum, Jesus' miracles did not attest that He was God but that He was sent by God, acted on behalf of God, and was empowered by God, so that God was with Him.[61]

The Resurrection of Jesus

All four NT gospels culminate with an account of Jesus' empty tomb and bodily resurrection. These reports relate several post-resurrection appearances of Jesus that occurred during the next forty days, when His disciples literally saw, touched, and talked with Him. Despite the difficulty in harmonizing these accounts in order to provide a historically-accurate composite, Jesus' resurrection was most critical to the development of Christianity. C.H. Dodd asserts, "It is the central belief about which the church itself grew, without which there would have been no church and no gospels."[62] William Lane Craig, an authority on Jesus' resurrection, states, "The origin of Christianity therefore hinges on the belief of the early disciples that God had raised Jesus from the dead."[63]

Only in the past two centuries have professing Christian scholars, challenged by the emergence of rationalism and biblical criticism, begun to doubt the literal, bodily resurrection of Jesus. Yet in the mid-20th century, the pendulum began to swing back to the traditional, literal view of Jesus' resurrection, even among some historical-critical scholars. Thus, in the 1960s and 1970s a rash of books appeared, some even written by neo-Bultmanian scholars, which defended the historical reality of Jesus' resurrection.

Some traditionalists have contended that Jesus' resurrection is prime evidence of His incarnation and thus that He is God.[64] Paul E. Little, in his best-selling book, *Know Why You Believe*, asserts, "Jesus' supreme credential to authenticate his claim to deity was his resurrection from the dead."[65] And preeminent Evangelical theologian Alister McGrath states, "The central and decisive Christian doctrine of the divinity of Jesus Christ is grounded in his

---

[60] Charles Hodge, *Systematic Theology* [1871-1873], 3 vols. (repr. Grand Rapids: Eerdmans, 1986), 2:630.
[61] E.g., Mt 12.28; Lk 11.20; Jn 3.2; 5.36; 9.31-33; 10.24-25, 38; 14.10-11; Ac 2.22; 10.38.
[62] C.H. Dodd, *The Founder of Christianity*, 28.
[63] William Lane Craig, *Knowing the Truth about the Resurrection* (Ann Arbor, MI: Servant, 1988), 117.
[64] New Testament scholars include Wolfhart Pannenberg, *Jesus God and Man* [1964], 2nd ed., tr. Lewis L. Wilkins and Duane A. Priebe (Philadelphia: Westminster, 1977), 108, 150, 152-53, 209, 325; Carl E. Braaten, "The Significance of New Testament Christology for Systematic Theology," in *Who Do You Say that I Am?: Essays on Christology*, eds. Powell and Bauer, 221; Brian Hebblethwaite, "The Myth and Truth Debate," in *Crisis in Christology*, ed. W.R. Farmer, 3; tentatively, M.M.B. Turner, "The Spirit of Christ and Christology," in *Christ the Lord*, ed. H.H. Rowdon, 173; Norman L. Geisler, *The Battle for the Resurrection* (Nashville: Thomas Nelson, 1989), 36; Darrell L. Bock, *Breaking the Da Vinci Code* (Nashville: Thomas Nelson, 2004), 108.
[65] P.E. Little, *Know Why You Believe*, 45.

resurrection from the dead."[66] Those who make this assertion invariably do so arbitrarily by failing to provide any rationale or biblical support.[67]

Most contemporary, traditionalist scholars would surely disagree with such an extreme position.[68] World-renown Jesus researcher and traditionalist N.T. Wright rightly alleges that it is "a frequent misunderstanding" that "the resurrection somehow proves Jesus' divinity."[69] Wright explains that in much of Judaism in Jesus' time, "resurrection was what was supposed to happen to all the dead, or at least all the righteous dead, and there was no suggestion that this would simultaneously constitute divinization."[70]

Indeed, if Jesus' resurrection attests that He was God, the future resurrection of the saints will verify that they are gods too! Wright adds, "When the New Testament predicts the resurrection of all who belong to Jesus, there is no suggestion that they will thereby become, or be shown to be, divine. Clearly, therefore, resurrection by itself could not be taken to 'prove' the 'divinity' of Jesus; if it did, it would prove far too much. The over-simple apologetic strategy one sometimes encounters ('he was raised from the dead, therefore he is the second person of the Trinity') makes no sense."[71]

Early Jewish Christians preached that Jesus' empty tomb and post-resurrection appearances indicated God vindicated Him, and they further claimed this as evidence that He was the Christ, the Son of God, but not that He was God (e.g., Ac 2.31, 36; Rom 1.4). These positive maxims were the heart of their kerygma. Wright calls this connection "the key move in early Christology."[72] James D.G. Dunn compares these principal axioms and concludes, "The belief that God raised Jesus from the dead is, if anything, of even more fundamental importance to Christian faith than the belief in Jesus as the Son of God."[73]

Indeed, the book of Acts reveals that the early Christians made Jesus' resurrection the chief cornerstone of their kerygma.[74] They never preached that Jesus was God but that God raised Jesus from the dead and that they were witnesses of it by afterwards having seen the risen Jesus (e.g., Ac 3.15). Subsequent church fathers reversed this early church kerygma, asserting that the foundation of Christian faith was that Jesus Christ was God. In so doing, they made Jesus' resurrection a secondary element in their kerygma.[75]

Jesus' resurrection further substantiates His dependence upon God, which also affirms that He is not God. For, the NT unequivocally and repeatedly proclaims that *God raised Jesus from the dead*. Jesus was not sovereign in

---

[66] Alister E. McGrath, *"I Believe:" Exploring the Apostles' Creed* (Downers Grove, IL: Inter-Varsity, 1991), 64, cf. 43, 45. Similarly, idem, *Christian Theology: An Introduction*, 3rd ed. (Oxford: Blackwell, 2001), 375, 381, 404; I. Howard Marshall, "Incarnational Christology in the New Testament," in *Christ the Lord*, ed. H.H. Rowdon, 16.

[67] W. Pannenberg (*Jesus-God and Man*, 153) states concerning Jesus' resurrection, "the inner logic of the matter indicates that Jesus was always one with God," in which Pannenberg clearly means Jesus was God.

[68] E.g., Robert L. Reymond, *Jesus, Divine Messiah* (Ross-shire, Scotland: Christian Focus, 2003), 19-20.

[69] N.T. Wright, "The Divinity of Jesus," in M. Borg and N.T. Wright, *The Meaning of Jesus: Two Visions*, 163; idem, *The Challenge of Jesus*, 108, 130. See also D. Cupitt, *Jesus and the Gospel of God*, 14.

[70] N.T. Wright, *The Challenge of Jesus*, 108; similarly, idem, *The Resurrection of the Son of God*, 573.

[71] N.T. Wright, *The Resurrection of the Son of God*, 573.

[72] N.T. Wright, *The Resurrection of the Son of God*, 576.

[73] J.G.D. Dunn, *The Evidence for Jesus*, 53, 43.

[74] E.g., Ac 2.32; 3.15; 4.33; 5.32; 10.39, 41; 13.31.

[75] Peter Carnley, *The Structure of Resurrection Belief* (Clarendon, England: Oxford, 1987), 7-10.

accomplishing His resurrection.[76] Instead, He completely depended upon God for His vindication through resurrection.

In the minds of many Christians, their belief in classical incarnation—that God became man—overshadows Jesus' resurrection and thus renders it of lesser importance. Some Christians have reasoned that Jesus' resurrection was the necessary outcome of His being God. Thus, it is Jesus being God that is most important, not His resurrection, which merely testifies to His being God. But this reasoning does not correspond to especially Luke's book of Acts. Therein, he shows that the early Christians repeatedly proclaimed Jesus' resurrection, but he never relates that they proclaimed that He was God.

Summary

In sum, all three synoptic Evangelists clearly reveal that they believed that the most important things that can be said about the identity of Jesus are that He is "the Christ" and "the Son of God." And they never identify Him as God or present Him as claiming to be God. Neither do they ever indicate that Jesus' sinless life, miracles, or resurrection testify that He was God, as many conservative traditionalists still claim.[77]

So far, we have considered those christologies that the synoptists held in common. Now we will examine those christologies that are peculiar to each of the synoptists.

B. Christology of Matthew

The Author and his Readers	Worshipping Jesus
Form, Structure, and Style	Jesus' Authority to Perform Miracles
The Christ, the Son of God	The God of Jesus Christ
The Virgin Birth	Summary

The Author and his Readers

According to church tradition, Matthew was a former tax collector who became one of Jesus' twelve apostles.[78] (He is also named Levi, a Jewish name.) This church tradition also holds that this same Matthew wrote the NT gospel that bears his name. Most historical critics propose that this gospel is the product of a particular Jewish church community that the Apostle Matthew probably led. Since Matthew remains the best candidate for the authorship of this gospel, we will refer to him tentatively as its author.

The Gospel of Matthew is an apologetic work that emphasizes the teaching of Jesus; but it also includes extensive information about His deeds, death, and resurrection. The book's main purpose is to proclaim Jesus as the Messiah promised in the OT. The author attempts to do so mostly by quoting OT prophecies, many of them messianic, and interpreting them as having been fulfilled by Jesus.[79] Furthermore, Matthew distinctively identifies Jesus as "the Son of David," which is one of several Jewish idioms in his book.

---

[76] Despite Jn 2.19-21; 10.11, 15, 17-18. See herein Chapter Six/Introduction/The Resurrection.

[77] E.g., R.M. Bowman and J.E. Komoszewski (*Putting Jesus in His Place*) claim that Jesus is "God" due to His miracles (pp. 201-04) and since He is "the Word" (p. 216), "the Son of God" (p. 78), "Lord" (pp. 157-70, 272, 279), "Savior" (p. 210), "Immanuel" (pp. 137, 272), and "Son of Man" (pp. 68-69, 86, 246-47).

[78] Mt 9.9/Mk 2.14/Lk 5.27; 10.3; Mk 3.18/Lk 6.15

[79] Matthew has about 125 quotations from, and allusions to, the OT; Mark has over 60; Luke has 90-100.

In fact, the Gospel of Matthew is packed with Judaica, giving it a peculiarly Jewish orientation. This indicates that the author was a Jew and that his primary intended readers were Jews who possessed a keen knowledge of Judaism and the Jewish Bible. The author also portrays the conflict between Jesus and the religious officials (and perhaps implicitly that conflict between the later synagogue and church) more precisely than the other synoptists do. In sum, Matthew was not anti-Semitic, as he has so often been characterized of late; rather, he was a Jew who designed his gospel for Jewish Christians partly as a polemical defense against their opposition from Judaism.

Form, Structure, and Style

A church tradition seems to relate that the Gospel of Matthew existed originally in some other form than the one in which it has come down to us. In about 130-140 CE, church father Papias (80-155 CE) penned these words: "Matthew composed/collected the oracles/sayings [Gr. *ta logia*] in the Hebrew [Aramaic?] dialect and each one interpreted them as he was able,"[80] i.e., presumably translating them especially into Greek. Some modern scholars have proposed that Papias refers to what they identify as "Q" (see Glossary) and that Matthew's gospel therefore represents an expanded version of Q. However, recent scholarship has shifted more to the view that this gospel was originally composed in Greek with a Jewish style.[81]

This First Gospel is so Jewish that some recent authorities view the Matthean Jesus as "the New Moses."[82] Indeed, this gospel is full of Moses typology. Events in Jesus' life are constructed as parallels to Moses' life, e.g., infancy narrative, trip to Egypt, fasting forty days and nights, on a mountain concerned with the Law and being transfigured. Yet this typology is never stated and the two persons are never explicitly compared. Some scholars also point out that Matthew's gospel is structured in five divisions (Mt 5-7, 10, 13, 18, 24-25), although all do not agree in identifying them. These divisions are believed to correspond to the OT, particularly the Pentateuch. Comparing Jesus with the man Moses seems to militate against Jesus being God. If Jesus is God, how can He legitimately be compared to another man?

A comparison of the Synoptic Gospels appears to indicate that Matthew edited his written sources more than the other synoptists did. Such redaction sometimes results in some peculiar Matthean expressions. For example, while Mark and Luke characterize Jesus as constantly teaching about "the kingdom of God," Matthew often substitutes "the kingdom of heaven" (32x) as well as "My/your Father who is in heaven" (12x) or simply "My/your Father." His use of "heaven" is a Jewish idiom for "God." Matthew may have substituted "kingdom of heaven" for "kingdom of God" to avoid using the word "God" due to sensitivity to the Jews' reluctance in pronouncing, and even writing, "the Name" (Heb. *Hashem*, which refers to God's name: YHWH).[83] However, Jesus may have shared this Matthean concern so that Matthew's expressions actually represent Jesus' *ipsissima verba*. If so, it is Mark who makes this substitution, likely to

---

[80] So states church historian Eusebius (*Ecclesiastical History*, 3.39.16).
[81] See, e.g., Scot McKnight, "Gospel of Matthew," in *DJG* 527-28.
[82] See esp. Dale C. Allison, Jr., *The New Moses: A Matthean Typology* (Minneapolis: Fortress, 1993).
[83] S. McKnight, *A New Vision for Israel*, 28-30, 28n47. However, Matthew is inconsistent in this, writing "kingdom of God" four times. And he records that Caiaphas questions Jesus if He is "the Son of God" (Mt 26.63), whereas Mark quotes Caiaphas asking Jesus if He is "the Son of the Blessed One" (Mk 14.61).

more clearly communicate to his Gentile readers and perhaps so translate for Peter's hearers, as we will soon learn.

Matthew also has Jesus calling God "My/the Father" much more often than do the other synoptists (Mt 43x; Mk 5x; Lk 16x; Jn 103x). On the other hand, Matthew only has Jesus using the expression "kingdom of God" four times whereas Mark has Him saying it thirteen times. Matthew's style of substituting "Father" for Mark's "God" in Jesus' sayings shows that Matthew regarded "God" exclusively as the "Father" and not a triune Godhead (e.g., Mt 12.50 par. Mk 3.35; Mt 26.29 par. Mk 14.25).

Matthew's gospel has certain stylistic features that make it unique compared to the other Synoptic Gospels. For instance, it is more thematic, organized, liturgical, rhetorical, less chronologically-arranged,[84] and contains more pericopes. So, Matthew's gospel is larger than the other two Synoptic Gospels, being almost twice the size of Mark. For these and other reasons, Matthew's gospel has always been more popular.

The Gospel of Matthew is always arranged first in NT versions because it has always come down to us in this order in Greek MSS when accompanied with the other gospels. One reason for this is that scribes and church fathers believed that, among the Synoptic Gospels, the Gospel of Matthew was written first. But we have seen that this view is no longer held by most contemporary scholars. Another reason offered is that, because Matthew is the most Jewish gospel, it was placed first in the NT canon to provide the best link to the OT. Indeed, Matthew makes it most evident that the life of Jesus can be best understood in accordance with the background setting of the OT.

Since a Jew undoubtedly wrote the Gospel of Matthew particularly for Jews, and Jews were strict monotheists, it is inconceivable that this author could have believed in a triune God (despite Mt 28.19>). Rather, for Matthew, God was the covenant-keeping "God of Israel" (Mt 15.31), "THE GOD OF ABRAHAM, AND THE GOD OF ISAAC, AND THE GOD OF JACOB" (Mt 22.32), whom devout Jews always understood as a single individual.

The Christ, the Son of God

Matthew establishes early in his gospel that his primary theme is the identification of Jesus as the Christ, the Son of God. He begins his gospel with a "genealogy of Jesus Christ," which ends with the words, "Jesus, who is called Christ" (Mt 1.17). Three times Matthew joins Jesus' name and the Christ title to form the proper name "Jesus Christ" (Mt 1.1, 18; 16.21).[85] Then, following his account of the birth of Jesus, Matthew becomes the only synoptist to record the visitation of the magi to Jerusalem. He relates that they ask where "the King of the Jews" was born, who is identified as "the Christ" (Mt 2.2, 4).

We have already seen that Matthew identifies Jesus as the Son of God more often than do the other synoptists. He is so-called during the devil's temptations, His baptism, and the later transfiguration. Additional pericopes that do so are as follows:
- The escape of Joseph and Mary to Egypt with the Child Jesus, and their return, fulfilled Hos 11.1: "OUT OF EGYPT DID I CALL MY SON" (Mt 2.15).
- When Jesus walked on the water and then got into a boat, His disciples exclaimed, "You are certainly God's Son" (Mt 14.33; *huios* is anarthrous here and Mt 27.43).

---

[84] However, it is very uncertain how much Lk 10.1--18.14 is arranged chronologically.
[85] In the other Synoptics, the proper name "Jesus Christ" only appears once, in Mk 1.1.

- The ridiculing remark that the passing protagonists hurled at the crucified Jesus, "If You are the Son of God, come down from the cross" (Mt 27.40).
- The religious authorities mocked Jesus by recounting, "HE TRUSTS IN GOD; LET HIM DELIVER *Him* now,... for He said, 'I am the Son of God" (Mt 27.43).
- Jesus' saying about the baptismal formula includes, "and the Son" (Mt 28.19>).

The Virgin Birth

Only Mathew and Luke record pronouncement-birth narratives about Jesus (Mt 1.18-25; Lk 1.26-38; 2.1-21). Their accounts also include infancy narratives (Mt 2.1-23; Lk 2.22-39). They relate that the virgin Mary miraculously conceived in her womb by the power of the Holy Spirit (and remained a virgin until Jesus was born).

This tradition is called "the virgin birth" (better, the Virginal Conception). Later, it was to become an integral, if not an essential, element of church doctrine. Throughout church history, Catholics have tenaciously defended the doctrine of the virgin birth and connected to it the veneration of Mary as "the Mother of God." The early Protestants also embraced the doctrine of the virgin birth but never accepted the designation of Mary as "the mother of God." In modern times, the virgin birth doctrine has come under attack and therefore been abandoned in certain Protestant circles.

The virgin birth eventually came to be regarded as the incarnation of the divine, and therefore preexistent, Son of God.[86] The miraculous nature of the virgin birth was thought to verify that Jesus was God. And this view is still maintained today by some conservative traditionalist scholars.[87] For example, leading Evangelical theologian, Alister McGrath, boldly asserts, "The way Jesus was conceived confirms ... that Jesus is indeed both God and man."[88] And Roman Catholic systematic theologian Gerald O'Collins explicates, "Traditionally the major value of his virginal conception has been to express Jesus' divine origin. The fact that he was born of a woman pointed to his humanity. The fact that he was born of a virgin pointed to his divinity."[89]

However, if the miraculous virgin birth indicates that Jesus is either God or divine, it is surprising that neither Matthew nor Luke expressly say so in their birth narratives. And if Jesus was God, He had to have preexisted. Yet no less of an authority on this subject than R.E. Brown concludes concerning especially the birth narratives, "Matthew and Luke show no knowledge of preexistence" of Jesus.[90] Such silence strongly suggests that they did not believe that Jesus preexisted or that He was God.

The angel announced at Jesus' birth that He "shall be the Son of God" (Lk 1.35, cf. v. 32),[91] not because of an ontological preexistence but His supernatural conception. This miracle merely signaled that He would have a special relationship with God. Indeed, Jesus' conception being accomplished by God's Spirit is the basis for identifying Him as the Son of God.[92] Moderate traditionalist Reginald H. Fuller explains that Jesus is called "the Son of the Most High (God)"

---

[86] So says G. Vermes, *Jesus the Jew*, 214; R.E. Brown, *The Birth of the Messiah*, new updated ed., 141-42.

[87] So observes R. Funk, *Honest to Jesus*, 283.

[88] A. McGrath, *"I Believe:" Exploring the Apostles' Creed*, 45, 64

[89] G. O'Collins, *Christology*, 276.

[90] R.E. Brown, *The Birth of the Messiah*, 31n17.

[91] *Huios* (Son) is anarthrous in Lk 1.32 and v. 35, so that there is no article modifying "Son."

[92] Eduard Schweizer, "huios," in *TDNT* 8:382.

in this birth-pronouncement "because of the salvation he is to accomplish in history, not because of his inherent nature."[93]

Logically, the virgin birth *does not* indicate that Jesus is God simply because of its miraculous nature. Miracles only point to a supernatural source. God did a miracle by causing a virginal conception; but that doesn't indicate that the miracle itself is God.

Consider the first man, Adam. Accepting the two biblical accounts of his creation as literal (Gen 2-3), like Jesus, Adam became a human being due to the direct creation of God. Yet no one thinks Adam's supernatural origin makes him god/God.

Many traditionalists have further insisted that the virgin birth is an essential element of Christian belief. In other words, they have insisted that a person must believe in the virgin birth in order to be a genuine Christian. However, no such teaching exists in the NT. This silence is significant in the two recorded birth narratives, but especially in the evangelistic sermons recorded in Acts and the writings of the Apostle Paul. Moreover, the subject of Jesus' miraculous conception is not even mentioned anywhere else in the NT, unless implicitly and sarcastically by Jesus' opponents in Jn 8.41. Many scholars think that, since the Apostle Paul died before Matthew and Luke published their gospels, Paul didn't even know about the virgin birth. Regardless, N.T. Wright well observes, "The virginal conception of Jesus is not, in itself, a central, major doctrine of the New Testament."[94] And Hans Kung states, "belief in Christ in no way stands or falls with the confession of the virgin birth."[95]

If the virgin birth *does not* indicate that Jesus had a divine nature, making Him God, does it have any impact on Christology? Most scholars who deny the virgin birth think not. They would agree with Ellen Flesseman-van Leer's assertion that the virgin birth has no "theological relevance" and "is utterly unimportant for salvation."[96]

However, the virgin birth seems to complement Adam Christology, especially if Augustine's view of original sin is correct. That is, Jesus' virgin birth enabled Him to come into this world without inheriting a sin nature, similar to Adam being created sinless. (See Chapter Seven/Adam Christology.) Likewise, Daniel's distinctive language, "One like a Son of Man" (Dan 7.13), seems to imply the virgin birth.

Worshipping Jesus

The Gospel of Matthew is *the* liturgical gospel in the NT. By comparing it with the other two Synoptics, scholars think Matthew often edited his written sources in order to make some of his material conducive for liturgical use and teaching.

The most prominent liturgical theme in religion is "worship." The Gospel of Matthew is unique among the NT gospels in that it often portrays people who "worship" Jesus in public.[97] But do such acts indicate that these people believed

---

[93] Reginald H. Fuller, *Christ and Christianity: Studies in the Formation of Christology*, comp. and ed. Robert Kahl (Valley Forge, PA: Trinity, 1994), 106.
[94] N.T. Wright, *Who Was Jesus?* 84.
[95] H. Kung, *Credo*, 44.
[96] E. Flesseman-van Leer, *A Faith for Today*, 71.
[97] *Proskuneo* appears in the Greek text of the Gospel of Matthew in Mt 2.2, 8, 11; 8.2; 9.18; 14.33; 15.25; 20.20; 28.9, 17. Cf. Mt 17.14; 27.29. There are only two instances in the other gospels, in Mk 5.6 and Jn 9.38, in which a person is described as performing *proskuneo* before Jesus.

Jesus was God? Many traditionalists have believed that they do, or that at least Matthew and his church community thought so.[98] A few traditionalists have even posited that Jesus' acceptance of such behavior suggests that He thought of Himself as God. But Trinitarian David Brown concedes concerning Jesus in the NT gospels, "there is good evidence to suggest that he never saw himself a suitable object of worship."[99]

Scholars of the NT often neglect in their writings to define their use of the word "worship," particularly as applied to Jesus. This omission causes misunderstanding about the significance of instances recorded in the NT in which people "worshipped" Jesus.

The word in the Greek NT that is usually translated "worship" is *proskuneo*. It and its cognates occur sixty-one times in the NT. Most of these occurrences are in the Gospel of Matthew and the book of Revelation. The etymology of *proskuneo* is that *pros* means "motion," either "from" or "towards" some object, and *kuneo* means "to kiss." Lexical authority Walter Bauer informs that *proskuneo* was "used to designate the custom of prostrating oneself before a person and kissing his feet, the hem of his garment, the ground, etc."[100] He adds that *proskuneo* can be translated "*(fall down and) worship, do obeisance to, prostrate oneself before, do reverence to, welcome respectfully.*"[101]

Therefore, during antiquity the Greek word *proskuneo* merely signified a physical act. It indicated the oriental custom of either genuflection, i.e., bowing down by bending the knee(s), or prostration. Practitioners, however, adopted either of these two postures toward a superior in order to convey their humble attitude of respect, honor, and perhaps submission in the sense of readiness to defer to the will of that superior. They frequently performed *proskuneo* towards those possessing imperial authority, especially kings. Such physical acts usually were associated with no more than a humble attitude of submission.

Now, it is true that when citizens in some ancient pagan cultures performed either genuflection or prostration before their monarch they in some sense regarded that person as deity. But such a belief could not be ascertained from the physical act alone. On the other hand, genuflection or prostration before an idol in ancient temples did indeed signify that the devotee was paying tribute to the supposed god represented by that idol.

In contrast, our English word "worship," whether used as a noun or a verb, does not designate a physical act. So, it does not serve as a suitable translation of *proskuneo*. Furthermore, the definition of our word "worship" has a wide range of meanings. To be sure, the primary use of the word "worship" is for religious purposes, i.e., the recognition of, and reverence for, a deity. But any good English dictionary shows that "to worship" can also mean merely to admire, adore, respect, or honor any human being by exhibiting an intense love and devotion toward that person. Thus, mutual lovers can "worship" each other, meaning to adore each other. The Anglican Church's *Book of Common Prayer* still contains the traditional words cited during the "Marriage Service," in which both bride and groom repeat to each other, "With my body I thee worship." And British sometimes officially call a mayor of a city, "His/Her Worship." So, to translate *proskuneo* in the NT with the English word "worship" can be quite ambiguous if not misleading.

---

[98] E.g., Larry W. Hurtado, "Pre-70 CE Jewish Opposition to Christ-Devotion," *JTS* 50 (1999): 35-58.
[99] David Brown, *The Divine Trinity* (London: Duckworth, 1985), 108.
[100] BAGD, 716.
[101] BAGD, 716. Emphasis not mine.

Proskuneo appears over 150 times in the LXX, which usually translates the word *shachah* in the Hebrew text. Most of these acts of obeisance are directed toward God or false gods, indicating that the word is used in a cultic sense. Yet many of these acts are directed toward some human being, e.g., a king, with no suggestion of deification.[102] So, there are distinct differences in the meaning of the act of *shachah* as presented in the OT.

It is the same with the NT and thus the Gospel of Matthew. For example, Satan tempted Jesus to "worship" (Gr. *proskuneses*) him (Mt 4.9 par.). Jesus responded by quoting Deut 6.13: "YOU SHALL WORSHIP THE LORD YOUR GOD, AND SERVE HIM ONLY." Jesus was using the term in a cultic, and thus an exclusive, sense reserved only for God. This use indicates that God is the only Creator and Sovereign Ruler of the universe.

In contrast, several acts of *proskuneo* directed toward Jesus in Matthew's gospel do not necessarily indicate that those practitioners thought of Him as deity.

Jesus' parable of an unforgiving servant-slave seems decisive. Matthew records He said, "The slave therefore falling down, prostrated [Gr. *proskuneo*] himself before" his master, begging him for leniency regarding the slave's indebtedness to his master (Mt 18.26). Jesus certainly did not mean that the slave was worshipping his master as a deity. Notice that translators render *proskuneo*, here, as "prostrated" rather than "worshipped."

When the gospel Evangelists report that someone performed *proskuneo* toward Jesus, translators invariably show their bias as traditionalists by translating it "worship," suggesting that that person thought of Jesus as either "divine" or "God." But when the Evangelists relate that a person performed *proskuneo* toward someone other than Jesus, translators render it "bowed down," "bend the knee," or "prostrate." So, they render it "worship" when done to Jesus, but a physical act when done to someone else.

Sometimes, *proskuneo* is accompanied in the NT with the word *pipto*, meaning "to fall down" physically. For instance, Matthew relates that the magi from the east "fell down and worshiped" (Gr. *pesontes prosekunesan*) the Christ Child (Mt 2.11). That is, they bent down and prostrated themselves before the baby Jesus to honor Him, showing their respect for Him. This act surely does not indicate they worshiped Jesus as God.

Matthew provides three other significant episodes when Jesus was "worshipped." One was when He walked on water, and the other two were His post resurrection scenes (Mt 14.33; 28.9, 17). When Jesus walked on water, Matthew relates that He afterwards got into a boat with His disciples and they "worshipped" Him (Mt 14.33). Both Matthew and Mark reveal that the disciples' response was also affected by a strong wind that had stopped immediately when Jesus got into the boat. Matthew's word *proskuneo* in the Greek text probably is intended to reflect no more than Mark's "greatly astonished" (Gr. *existemi*; Mk 6.51). The disciples did not think of Jesus as "God" even though Matthew says that they then acknowledged Him as "a son of God" (Gr. *theou huios* is anarthrous).

In Chapter Three, we learned of theologian James Denney's objection to the dogma that Jesus is God. Here is more of what he said, "If a man does not worship Christ, I do not care what he thinks of Him—he does not see what is there; and I have missed the mark completely in what I have written if I have not made it clear that all men should honour the Son even as they honour

---

[102] L.W. Hurtado, "The Binitarian Shape of Early Christian Worship," 188-89.

the Father.... For me, to worship Jesus as God is worshipped, to trust Him as God is trusted, to owe to Him what we can owe to God alone, is the essence of Christianity."[103] Denney thus equates the worship of Jesus with honoring Him, alluding to Jn 5.23. In that text Jesus said, "that all may honor the Son, even as they honor the Father." While Denney firmly insisted that Jesus ought to be worshipped, i.e., honored as the Father is honored, Denney did not believe that Jesus was God.

An increasing number of conservative, traditionalist scholars are acknowledging that acts of *proskuneo* that were directed toward Jesus and recorded in the NT gospels do not necessarily indicate that those practitioners believed that He was God.[104] For instance, D.A. Carson cautions regarding the Gospel of Matthew, "it is very doubtful if *proskyneo* by itself or in connection with *pipto* suggests anything more than obeisance, homage."[105] And J. Lionel North asserts that there is "nothing" in the NT "that requires us to conclude that Jesus is regarded as divine because he is worshipped."[106] Wendy North and Loren T. Stuckenbruck conclude that what should be "gained from the New Testament" is "that 'worship' is too imprecise a word to point necessarily to the conclusion that Jesus is divine."[107] Non-traditionalist D. Cupitt alleges that such exploitation of the NT word *proskuneo* by many past traditionalists is evidence of the weakness of their case.[108]

In conclusion, *the Gospel of Matthew, as well as the other NT gospels, does not provide any evidence that people who genuflected or prostrated themselves in front of the Jesus of the ministry conceived of Him at that time as being God.*[109] For Jews, such a notion would not only have been preposterous but blasphemous! (For more on "worship" see Chapter Ten.)

Jesus' Authority to Perform Miracles

Also, more than the other two synoptists, Matthew focuses on Jesus' authority to perform healings and other miracles. Matthew makes it clear that this authority is not intrinsic to Jesus, but derived from God (the Father). For example, when Jesus healed the paralytic let down through the roof, only Matthew adds, "when the multitudes saw this, they were filled with awe, and glorified God, who had given such authority to men" (Mt 9.8). Thus, Matthew relates that these people did not think that Jesus was God on account of this healing, but that God had given Jesus the authority and ability to heal the man. They glorified God because they rightly perceived that He ultimately made it happen.

The God of Jesus Christ

The NT clearly establishes that Jesus had a God, He worshipped His God, and His God was the God of Israel, the God of the Scriptures, whom He called

---

[103] V. Taylor, "Does the New Testament Call Jesus God?" 116.

[104] E.g., M.M.B. Turner, "The Spirit of Christ and Christology," 169-70.

[105] D.A. Carson, "Christological Ambiguities in the Gospel of Matthew," in *Christ the Lord*, ed. H.H. Rowdon, 109.

[106] J. Lionel North, "Jesus and Worship, God and Sacrifice," in *Early Jewish and Christian Monotheism*, eds. Stuckenbruck and North, 189.

[107] Wendy North and Loren T. Stuckenbruck, "Introduction," in *Early Jewish and Christian Monotheism*, ed. Stuckenbruck and W. North, 12.

[108] D. Cupitt, *Jesus and the Gospel of God*, 19.

[109] E.g., R.T. France, "The Worship of Jesus: A Neglected Factor in Christological Debate," 26; D.A. Carson, "Christological Ambiguities in the Gospel of Matthew," 109.

"my/the Father." For instance, we saw in Chapter Four that both Matthew and Mark narrate that Jesus uttered His famous cry of dereliction while hanging on the cross, crying out, "MY GOD, MY GOD, WHY HAST THOU FORSAKEN ME?" (Mt 27.46/Mk 15.34). (Small caps in the NASB indicate an OT quotation, in this case from Ps 22.1.) These words that proceeded from the parched lips of the crucified Jesus evoke the thought-provoking question, If Jesus is God, how could He have said, "My God, my God," let alone pray to God? Put more succinctly, How can Jesus be God and have a God? Colin Brown observes concerning this saying, "From earliest times the cry has been felt to raise problems for christology."[110]

Many Christians have also questioned how God, as the loving Father, could have abandoned Jesus in so sublime a moment as His crucifixion and thereby cut off their very intimate fellowship? The standard answer has been that, since Jesus then bore our sins on the cross, it was soteriologically necessary that the Holy Father separate Himself from His Son at that moment because He could not have fellowship with sin. If correct, how could Jesus' divine nature remain a part of Him as He suffered for our sins? What is the difference? Orthodoxy says Jesus' divine nature is as much God as the Father is God.

On the contrary, God did not abandon Jesus. Scripture clearly attests that God never abandons the righteous. He declares of those who abide in Him, "I will be with him in trouble" (Ps 91.1, 15). Moses told Joshua, "the LORD your God is the one who goes with you. He will not fail you or forsake you" (Deut 31.6, cf. v. 8). David told his son Solomon, "the LORD God, my God, is with you. He will not fail you or forsake you until all the work for the service of the house of the LORD is finished" (1 Chron 28.20).

Another psalmist reveals that God stays with the faithful in distress. He says, "In my distress I called upon the LORD,... He heard my voice," meaning God was with him. We read next, "the earth shook and quaked" and there was "thick darkness" (Ps 18.6-9). Both of these natural phenomena occurred when Jesus hung on the cross (Mt 27.45-51).

More particularly, Isaiah declares that God never forsakes His obedient Servant. The prophet presents God the Father as saying of Jesus, "Behold, My Servant, whom I uphold ... I will also hold you by the hand and watch over you" (Isa 42.1, 6).

So, God did not abandon Jesus at any time while He was suffering on the cross. The Johannine Jesus had said, "He who sent Me is with Me; He has not left Me alone" (Jn 8.29; cf. 16.32). Since God only forsakes those who forsake Him (2 Chron 15.2), how much more will He not forsake His only Son while He is doing the work of salvation?

Then, what is the meaning of Jesus' words, "MY GOD, MY GOD, WHY HAST THOU FORSAKEN ME"? *In Jesus' dereliction cry—about God forsaking Him while He hung upon the cross—Jesus was not expressing a fact, but how He felt. God the Father was with Him, perhaps even feeling His pain, without Jesus perceiving it.* Colin Brown explains that David and Jesus suffered "without the conscious awareness of God's presence."[111]

David wrote this psalm from which Jesus quoted, so it was David's experience too. Jesus applied it to Himself, as did NT writers (Jn 19.24; Heb 2.12; Mt 27.43). Later in this psalm David says of God, "He has not despised nor abhorred the

---

[110] Colin Brown, *NIDNTT* 2:82. This is reflected in MS variants for "My God" in Mt 27.46 and the interpolated quotation of it in the *Gospel of Peter*: "My power, O power, thou hast forsaken me" (5:19).
[111] C. Brown, *NIDNTT* 2:82.

affliction of the afflicted; neither has He hidden His face from him; but when he cried to Him for help, He heard" (Ps 22.24). The writer of Hebrews tells the same thing about Jesus, saying that "He offered up both prayers and supplications with loud crying and tears to the One able to save Him from death, and He was heard because of His piety" (Heb 5.7).

Thus, during the righteous suffering of David and that which Jesus endured while hanging on the cross, God did not turn His face from either of these righteous servants and abandon them; rather, He heard their cry for help, signifying that He was with them.

This interpretation of Jesus' dereliction cry has profound application for God's people. When we suffer for righteousness sake, God does not abandon us but somehow feels our pain. Isaiah says of Israel and God, "In all their affliction He was afflicted" (Isa 63.9; cf. 46.4). David writes in another psalm, "Blessed be the Lord, who daily bears our burden" (Ps 68.19; cf. 55.22). One time, when Israel repented of its sins, God reached His breaking point; for we read, "He could bear the misery of Israel no longer" (Jud 10.16).

How does God experience our pain? Is it not by His Holy Spirit? Beyond this, can we know any more? Surely, this is another profound mystery of our compassionate God.

In conclusion, Jesus addressing the Father as "My God" indicates that Jesus is not God but that only the Father is the one and only, true and living, God of Jesus Christ.

Summary

In sum, Matthew's primary purpose for writing his gospel was to prove that Jesus was the Christ, the Son of God. He did so by emphasizing Jesus' connection to the OT, especially His fulfilling of many of its prophecies. Neither Matthew's account of the virgin birth, nor Jesus performing healings and other miracles, nor Matthew's several recorded episodes of people bowing down before Jesus necessarily indicate that Jesus was God or that those worshippers thought that He was God. Moreover, Matthew does not portray Jesus being worshipped as God but Jesus worshipping God.

C. Christology of Mark

The Author and his Readers	The Messianic Secret
Structure and Style	Summary
The Author's Purpose	

The Author and his Readers

There is very strong patristic evidence that the anonymous author of the Gospel of Mark was the person whom Luke refers to as "John who was also called Mark" (Ac 12.12, 25). Apparently, his given name was John and his Christian name was Mark. This same John-Mark sometimes accompanied his cousin Barnabas and the Apostle Paul on their evangelistic missionary journeys (Col 4.10; Ac 12.25; 13.5; 15.37, 39; 2 Tim 4.11). According to legend, John-Mark's affluent mother was a close friend of the Apostle Peter, she owned the Upper Room, and that is where Jesus and His apostles ate the Last Supper (Mk 14.15; Ac 1.13; 12.12).

This early patristic testimony also asserts that John-Mark wrote the Gospel of Mark while accompanying the apostle Peter on his evangelistic missionary journeys in Italy as Peter's interpreter (cf. 1 Pt 5.13), and he later published it in Rome.[112] If so, this gospel no doubt represents Peter's reminiscences of stories and sayings of Jesus. In addition, this gospel is detailed and contains the *ipsissma verba* of Jesus' sayings more often than do the other Synoptics,[113] both of which further suggest an eyewitness. This avowed connection between Peter and this gospel ensured its inclusion in the NT canon.

The Gospel of Mark seems originally to have been intended for Gentile readers. Internal evidence supports this view. For example, Mark provides the fewest quotations and allusions to the OT than do the other Synoptics. It also contains very few Jewish idioms or geographical references to Judea, and it includes some Latin words not found in the other Synoptics.[114] It therefore seems that the author of the Gospel of Mark expected his readers to have little or no knowledge of Judea, Judaism, and its Scriptures.

Structure and Style

The Gospel of Mark is the smallest of the Synoptic Gospels. Compared to the other Synoptics, its pericopes are usually more brief, compact, direct, fast-paced, and exciting. It therefore conveys a sense of urgency not found in the other Synoptics. For instance, the word "immediately" (Gr. *euthys*) appears forty-one times in Mark. However, scholars explain that this word was intended only as a connector so that, as with the other synoptists, Mark's purpose was not to piece together a strictly chronological arrangement of events in the life of Jesus but a topical arrangement. Nevertheless, Mark's order of events is probably more chronological than that of the other synoptists.

In contrast especially to Matthew, Mark peculiarly records what Jesus *did* more than what He *said*. For example, Mark does not include Jesus' renowned Sermon on the Mount/Plain (Mt 5-7; Lk 6.17-49). But Mark does provide quite a dramatic, action-packed account of Jesus' ministry. Scholars therefore regard the Gospel of Mark as the premier gospel of action, and some characterize it as "Enacted Christology."[115]

Since the consensus of contemporary scholarship is that the Gospel of Mark was written first of the Synoptic Gospels, scholars therefore deem it as seminal to a correct understanding of the historical Jesus.

The Author's Purpose

Throughout this Second Gospel (so-called because of its traditional arrangement in the Bible), readers often wonder: How did Jesus accomplish His mighty acts? This question inevitably leads to another, more important, question: Who is Jesus? Christopher Tuckett observes, "even more than in the Gospels of Matthew and Luke, the question of who Jesus is provides the central focus of Mark's narrative."[116]

---

[112] E.g., Eusebius (*Ecclesiastical History*, 3.39.15) records that in about 130-140 CE, Papias, bishop of Hierapolis, cites from a work now lost a quotation by "the Elder"—supposedly "John the Elder," believed to have been a disciple of the apostle John—in which he states that Mark was Peter's interpreter in Italy.

[113] G. Vermes, *The Changing Faces of Jesus*, 221.

[114] W.L. Lane, *The Gospel of Mark*, 24.

[115] E.g., Elizabeth Struthers Malbon, "The Christology of Mark's Gospel: Narrative Christology and the Markan Jesus," in *Who Do You Say that I Am?* eds. Powell and Bauer, 34-37.

[116] Christopher Tuckett, *Christology and the New Testament: Jesus and His Earliest Followers* (Louisville, KT: Westminster John Knox, 2001), 109.

Mark answers this question about who Jesus is at the very beginning of his gospel. He writes, "The beginning of the gospel of Jesus Christ, the Son of God" (Mk 1.1). Since these words do not represent a complete sentence, many scholars think Mark intended them as the title of his book. Regardless, they indicate Mark's purpose for writing his gospel; it was to proclaim who Jesus is, that He is the Christ, the Son of God. In mentioning the proper name—"Jesus Christ"—Mark means that Jesus is the Christ.[117] L.W. Hurtado further observes, "Mark's christological affirmation which permeates the whole of his gospel [is that] Jesus,... is the Son of God."[118]

Indeed, Mark repeatedly applies both of these titles to Jesus in his gospel. For example, just as the other two synoptists do, Mark portrays Peter declaring Jesus as "the Christ" (Mk 8.29). All three synoptists also record that, at Jesus' baptism as well as His transfiguration, a voice from above identified Jesus as the "Son (of God)" (Mk 1.11 par.; 9.7 par.). In Mark, Jesus is further declared to be "(the) Son (of God)" by demons (3.11; 5.7; cf. 1.24), Jesus Himself, implicitly in parabolic form (Mk 12.6) and explicitly in His Olivet Discourse (13.32), Caiaphas (Mk 14.61-62), and the centurion (Mk 15.39).

But what did Mark mean by calling Jesus "the Son of God"? He surely would not have intended a Hellenistic, mythological understanding of gods procreating sons of gods. Such pagan, polytheistic concepts clashed with Jewish monotheism. Nor could he have understood it in the sense that later church fathers did, that Jesus had an ontological preexistence due to an eternal generation. Rather, the "life setting" (Ger. *sitz im leben*) must determine what Mark, Jesus, and the early Christians meant when they applied the expression, "son of God," to Jesus. That is, it must be understood in its Jewish context because Jesus and the earliest Christians were Jews. And we saw in Chapter Four that Jews typically applied this expression to their king or perhaps to a particularly holy man to mean no more than one specially favored by God.

The Messianic Secret

The synoptists never reveal that Jesus admitted that He was Israel's Messiah until His examination before the Sanhedrin. Sometimes, He instructed people not to publicly broadcast that He was the Messiah or that He did miracles, though He sometimes told His apostles they could do so after His death. This censorship is particularly prominent in the Gospel of Mark.[119] William Wrede (1859-1906) wrote about it in his renowned book, *The Messianic Secret of the Gospels* (1901, ET 1971). Many historical-critical scholars have followed Wrede in calling this phenomenon "the Messianic Secret" and concluding that Jesus never claimed or thought that He was the Messiah.[120]

Let us have a little peek at the biblical evidence. Once Jesus inquired of His apostles as to whom they thought He was. Peter answered that He was the Messiah (Mk 8.29 par.). Mark adds that Jesus "warned them to tell no one about Him" (v. 30). Mark implies that Jesus accepted Peter's identification of Him and commanded the disciples not to tell it to anyone. Had Peter been wrong in identifying Jesus as the Messiah, his Lord surely would have corrected him.

---

[117] R.A. Guelich, "Gospel of Mark," in *DJG* 518.
[118] L.W. Hurtado, "God," in *DJG* 272.
[119] Mk 1.25, 34, 44; 3.11-12; 5.43; 7.36; 8.26, 29-30; 9.9, 30-31.
[120] Wrede *tentatively* argued in this book that the Messianic Secret was a fiction designed by the Markan church community. But he later conceded that it truly reflected Jesus' messianic consciousness.

Matthew goes further, adding that Jesus explained that the Father had revealed this to Peter (Mt 16.17).

Mark was especially interested in Jesus' exorcisms. When Jesus encountered demon-possessed people, Mark reports that the demons might say things to Jesus like, "I know who You are—the Holy One of God" (Mk 1.24), or "You are the Son of God" (Mk 3.11). Mark informs that on such occasions Jesus commanded the demon(s) not to make this known (Mk 1.25; 3.12). Mark explains that Jesus "was not permitting the demons to speak, because they knew who He was" (Mk 1.34). If the demons knew who Jesus was, wouldn't they have more readily acknowledged that He was God, if indeed He was, than the seemingly lesser status as the Holy One or Son of God?

Sometimes, the same thing happened when Jesus healed people. Mark records three episodes in which Jesus healed someone and then told the healed person, as well as the witnesses, not to tell anybody about it (Mk 1.43-44; 5.43; 7.36; cf. 8.26).

Jesus did likewise on the Mount of Transfiguration. Soon after His inner core of three apostles witnessed that glorious event He said to them, "Tell the vision to no one until after the Son of Man has risen from the dead" (Mt 17.9; cf. Mk 9.9). When Caiaphas the High Priest later questioned Jesus before the Sanhedrin, Jesus finally admitted publicly for the first time that He was the Messiah, the Son of God (Mk 14.61-62 par.).

Many scholars think the Messianic Secret indicates that Jesus disagreed with contemporary Jewish views about the Messiah being a warrior-king who would deliver and redeem Israel by conquering its enemies. On the contrary, Jesus never disavowed this popular viewpoint. Such expectations were, in fact, based upon a literal understanding of many OT prophecies, and Jesus' silence indicates that He most likely accepted them. He merely envisioned the cross before the crown (e.g., Lk 24.21, 25-26).

Jesus no doubt had reasons for not publicly disclosing His messianic identity at that time. For one thing, He wanted to prevent a premature arrest and execution, which would have preempted God's timing. That may have happened once, if He had not prevented a great multitude from fulfilling their desire "to take Him by force, to make Him king" (Jn 6.15). That is why Jesus quickly departed.

So, Jesus only revealed that He wanted His messianic identity kept secret until after His death. Matthew makes it evident that Jesus was seeking to avoid a premature death when he writes, "the Pharisees went out, and counseled, as to how they might destroy Him. But Jesus, aware of this, withdrew from there. And many followed Him, and He healed them all, and warned them not to make Him known" (Mt 12.14-16).

Actually, the Messianic Secret occurs in all four NT gospels, just more often in Mark. For example, when Peter confessed Jesus as "the Christ," all three synoptists add that Jesus warned His apostles not to tell anyone (Mt 16.20/Mk 8.30/Lk 9.21). And the same theme appears in the Fourth Gospel, only in another form (e.g., Jn 10.24-25).[121] In addition, the Messianic Secret coincides with Jesus' veiled identity in His parables.

Since only the Fourth Gospel records Jesus' early ministry, it seems to provide the main reason He adopted the Messianic Secret. During a feast at Jerusalem, He healed a man on the Sabbath (Jn 5.5). John informs, "The man

---

[121] See C.K. Barrett, *The Gospel According to St. John: An Introduction with Commentary and Notes on the Greek Text*, 2nd ed. (Philadelphia: Westminster, 1978), 71.

went away, and told the Jews that it was Jesus who had made him well" (v. 15). Apparently, Jesus had not instructed the man otherwise. John adds, "for this reason the Jews were persecuting Jesus" and "seeking all the more to kill Him" (vv. 16, 18). After that, "Jesus was walking in Galilee; for He was unwilling to walk in Judea, because the Jews were seeking to kill Him" (Jn 7.1). As another feast approached, Jesus' unbelieving sibling brothers began chiding Him, saying, "no one does anything in secret, when he himself seeks to be known publicly. If You do these things, show Yourself to the world" (v. 4). At that time, they were obviously "of the world" and not "born of the Spirit" (Jn 3.6; 7.5; 15.19; 17.14, 16). In contrast to their advice, Jesus went to the feast, "not publicly, but as it were, in secret" (v. 10). So, Jesus' Messianic Secret ought to be compared to His reluctance to walk in Judea and His suppression of publicity concerning His attendance at feasts in Jerusalem. All of this was to forestall His capture and arrest until the proper "time" or "hour" would come (Jn 2.4; 7.6, 8, 30,; 8.20; 12.23, 27; 13.1; 17.1), which had long ago been decided by God.

With the Messianic Secret, Jesus imitated God. The OT often portrays Yahweh as the covenant-keeping God who nonetheless turns His face away and "hides" Himself from disobedient Israel.[122] Thus, Jesus' Messianic Secret is like this "Yahweh Secret."

Yet a man claiming to be Israel's Messiah was not against the Mosaic Law. And Jesus' reluctance to identify Himself as the Messiah, and prohibiting others from doing so, appears superfluous if He identified Himself as God.

Only the Father Is the One God

Mark records two incidents in the life of Jesus in which he relates that only the Father is God. One is recorded in Mk 10.17-27, particularly v. 18, and we will consider it in the Problem Passages section of this chapter. We will consider the other incident now.

The Jews categorized the Law of Moses into 613 laws. They often discussed which one was the most important. One time a Pharisee asked Jesus this question. He replied by quoting the Shema, saying, "HEAR, O ISRAEL! THE LORD OUR GOD IS ONE LORD" (Mk 12.29). Only Mark records that the scribe responded, "Right, Teacher, You have truly stated that HE IS ONE; AND THERE IS NO ONE ELSE BESIDES HIM" (v. 32), thereby quoting the last half of Deut 4.35.[123] Of course, they were talking about the God of Israel, whom Jesus often called "the/My Father."

The Pharisee's answer, as recorded in the Greek text of Mk 12.32, does not allow for a plurality of persons in a godhead/Godhead, as Trinitarianism asserts. The text reads, *ouk estin allos plen autou*, literally meaning, "there is not another besides him." The word *allos* (another) specifies a single entity, and the word *autou* (him) is a personal pronoun which represents only one individual. This response means that God is an individual and there is no other God, so that Jesus cannot be God.

Finally, Jesus showed His approval of the man's remark, and thus Deut 4.35, by replying, "You are not far from the kingdom of God" (v. 34).

Summary

In sum, Mark's purpose for writing his gospel was the same as that of the other synoptists. It was that Jesus is "the Christ, the Son of God." But Jesus

---

[122] Deut 31.17-18; 32.20; Isa 1.15; 8.17; 30.20; 45.15; 54.8; 57.17; 59.2; 64.7; Eze 39.23-24, 29; Hos 5.6, 15; 9.12.
[123] See also Deut 8.10; Isa 45.5-6, 18, 21-22; 46.9; 43.10-11.

sometimes told people not to broadcast who he was until after His death, a phenomenon that is most prominent in the Gospel of Mark. In so warning His disciples, Jesus did not intend to deny His messiahship but to avoid a premature death. This Messianic Secret makes it even more evident that no one during Jesus' ministry ever thought that He was God, much less that He thought He was God. If they had, we can be sure that Jesus would have needed to engineer far more than just a Messianic Secret to forestall a premature death.

D. Christology of Luke

The Author and his Readers	Glorifying and Praising God
Structure and Style	Jesus in Prayer
"Christ, the Son of God"	Preaching Jesus as "the Christ"
"the Most High (God)"	Preaching "the word"
Jesus' Physical and Moral Development	Resurrection, Ascension, Exaltation
Jesus' Dependence upon the Holy Spirit	Summary
Jesus as Prophet	

The Author and his Readers

Tradition is surely correct that a man named "Luke" wrote both the Gospel of Luke and The Acts of the Apostles. He apparently was a Gentile because "Luke" is a Gentile name. If so, he was the only Gentile author of the NT. The Apostle Paul calls this same Luke "the beloved physician" because he was a medical doctor and one of Paul's associates on some of his missionary journeys (Col 4.14; 2 Tim 4.11; Philemon 24). In fact, Luke and Paul emerge as the two most prolific authors of the NT, with their combined writings representing over half of that canon. Thus, the multi-talented Luke was a physician, a medical missionary, a theologian, a historian, and an author.

Like the other Synoptic Gospels, the Gospel of Luke is purportedly a historical account of significant events in the life and death of Jesus that also includes some of His post-resurrection appearances. We saw earlier that Luke divulges that he did not witness these events; instead, he tells about two categories of traditions: oral and written. He says of the oral traditions, "eyewitnesses and servants of the word have handed them down to us;" and he adds concerning the written traditions, "many have undertaken to compile an account" (Lk 1.1-2). Luke thus informs that he made use of these traditions in compiling his gospel, "having investigated everything carefully from the beginning" (v. 3).

Luke's book of Acts is also a historical account. But it relates the development of the post-Easter Jesus Movement and therefore the growth and geographical spread of early Christianity. The last half of this book concerns exclusively Paul's missionary activity. Therein, Luke provides his own eyewitness account of many of these events.[124]

Unlike the other NT gospels, Luke wrote both his gospel and Acts to a specific person. Luke calls him "most excellent Theophilus" (Lk 1.3; cf. Ac 1.1). But we know nothing else about him. His Greek name and this description suggest that he was a distinguished Gentile, perhaps a Roman government official or an influential or affluent citizen, who provided financial support for Luke's ministerial activities. Regardless, he must have been either a Christian believer or someone sympathetic to Luke's spiritual endeavors. For, Luke explains that

---

[124] Luke repeatedly uses the plural pronoun "we," e.g., Ac 16.10-17; 20.5-15; 21.1-18; 27.1--28.16.

he is writing his gospel to Theophilus "so that you might know the exact truth about the things you have been taught" (v. 4). Like the Gospel of Mark, the Gospel of Luke seems specially suited to Gentile readers.

Since Luke and Acts represent a two-volume work, in this section Luke's Christology will be gleaned from both volumes.

Structure and Style

Structurally, the Gospel of Luke is a book wide in scope. Most notably, it reflects the author's keen sense of God's salvation-history and therefore emphasizes divine providence. In other words, God will accomplish His redemptive plan for humankind by means of Jesus' sacrificial death (Ac 2.22-24). Luke therefore presents Jesus as being sharply focused on going to Jerusalem,[125] resolutely determined to complete His mission there by being nailed to an old rugged cross.

Since Luke was a medical doctor, he emphasizes Jesus' compassion for people. Luke records several episodes about Jesus' care for the ailing, the underprivileged, and the oppressed, regardless of their ethnicity. Luke especially tells of Jesus' concern for the sick, the poor, women and children, and other social outcasts.

Luke's style in his gospel reveals some distinctive theological features. One is that he uses the word "God" (Gr. *theos*) 122 times and "Father" (Gr. *pater*) only 19 times. The other synoptists use these two words with equal frequency. This usage indicates that Luke felt no compunction to identify "God" as "the Father," which is surely implied. Another one of Luke's distinctive features is that he often applies the word "Lord" exclusively to Jesus, perhaps as a result of his close association with the Apostle Paul, who did the same.

Scholars generally believe that the title, "The Acts of the Apostles," was appended to Luke's second volume, probably no earlier than the late 2nd century. It has often been said that this book would be more accurately entitled, "The Acts of the Holy Spirit," or the like. Indeed, in Acts 1 Luke quotes Jesus' last words to His disciples before ascending into heaven, saying, "you shall receive power when the Holy Spirit has come upon you; and you shall be My witnesses both in Jerusalem, and in all Judea and Samaria, and even to the remotest part of the earth" (Ac 1.8). Luke uses this prophetic statement as a sort of rudimentary outline for this book. He next records how the Holy Spirit filled the disciples on the day of Pentecost in order for them to speak the word of God in foreign languages. In the remainder of the book, Luke tells how the Holy Spirit enabled the disciples to do some miracles and mostly inspired them to preach "the word" about the resurrected Jesus. Luke recounts how "the word" spread just as Jesus had predicted, starting in Jerusalem and going all the way to Rome. Luke ends his book with Paul at Rome, "preaching the kingdom of God, and teaching concerning the Lord Jesus Christ" (Ac 28.31, cf. v. 23).

Thus, Luke recounts in his book of Acts how the Jesus Movement developed from a small Jewish sect into predominantly Gentile Christianity. He relates a major turning point in Ac 16.46, in which the Apostle Paul brings to the attention of the Jews of Galatia their rejection of the gospel. He then announces to them, "we are turning to the Gentiles" (cf. Ac 28.28). Luke therefore emphasizes in both of his volumes the universality of the good news about Jesus Christ and His kingdom, which is also the kingdom of God.

---

[125] Lk 9.51; 13.22, 32-33; 17.11; 18.31; 19.11, 28.

Luke also records in his book of Acts various lengthy sermons preached by especially Peter, Stephen, and Paul. And we saw in Chapter One that these sermons are very important to identity Christology in that they clearly *do not* identify Jesus as God, just as the Synoptics clearly do not either.

Christ, the Son of (the Most High) God

Luke, like the other synoptists, begins his gospel by soon introducing Jesus as the Christ, the Son of God. He does so by providing an extended narrative about Jesus' birth. He reveals that the angel Gabriel appeared to Mary to announce that she would soon become pregnant with the baby Jesus by means of a supernatural act of the Holy Spirit. Gabriel (and perhaps another angel) prophesied about the Child as follows:

- "He will be great, and will be called the Son of the Most High; and the Lord God will give Him the throne of His father David" (Lk 1.32).
- "The holy offspring shall be called the Son of God" (Lk 1.35).
- "There has been born for you a Savior, who is Christ the Lord" (Lk 2.11).

At least two important points regarding identity Christology should be understood from Luke's birth narrative about Jesus. First, the angels announced that Jesus "shall be called the Son of God," not "God." Second, Luke makes Jesus' conception the basis for His *being* "the Son of God,"[126] not just being *called* the Son of God.[127] Perhaps a third point should be mentioned; in both of these Lucan instances in which the angel called Jesus "Son of God," this title is anarthrous (without the article).[128]

Thus, Luke seems to know nothing of the later Church dogma about Jesus having preexisted as the Son of God. R.E. Brown observes, "there is no evidence that Luke had a theology of incarnation or preexistence; rather for Luke (1:35) divine sonship seems to have been brought about through the virginal conception."[129] Joseph A. Fitzmyer concurs and adds, "In Lucan theology there is no question of Jesus' preexistence or incarnation.... neither of these aspects of his existence emerge in the Lucan portrait of him."[130] These two christological omissions are significant since Luke wrote much of the Christian story.

"the Most High (God)"

Also, notice that Gabriel called Jesus "the Son of the Most High," and he further distinguished the Child Jesus from "the Lord God." "The Most High" is an expression that appears forty-one times in the OT and nine times in the NT,[131] with seven of the nine occurring in Luke's writings. Luke's filial use of this expression affirms clearly that "the Most High" always refers exclusively to God (the Father) in the OT. It means that, at least until the heavenly exaltation of Jesus, God the Father was the single highest-ranking personage in heaven and therefore superior over all. This is further signified by Isaiah's description of God's throne as being "lofty and exalted" above all others (Isa 6.1).[132]

---

[126] Otto Procksch, *"hagios,"* in *TDNT* 1:101; Walter Grundmann, *"dunamai/dunamis,"* in *TDNT* 2:300, 300n56; E. Schweizer, *"huios,"* in *TDNT* 8:382.

[127] R.E. Brown, *The Birth of the Messiah*, 289, 291.

[128] Also in Mt 27.54; Mk 15.39; Jn 10.36; 19.7. The article only appears with *theos* in Mt 4.3, 6; Lk 4.3, 9.

[129] R.E. Brown, *The Birth of the Messiah*, 432, cf. 31n17, 291.

[130] Joseph A. Fitzmyer, *The Gospel According to Luke (i-ix): Introduction, Translation, and Notes*, in AB (New York: Doubleday, 1970), 197.

[131] The NT occurrences are Mk 5.7; Lk 1.32, 35, 76; 6.35; 8.28; Ac 7.48; 16.17; Heb 7.1.

[132] Heaven's twenty-four elders have their own thrones (Rev 4.4; 11.16; cf. 20.4; Dan 7.9).

In comparison, calling Jesus such things as "great," "the Son of the Most High," and "the Son of God" all together suggests that these are the grandest ascriptions, and therefore the highest christological appellations, that can be rightly applied to Him.

Jesus' Physical and Moral Development

We have seen that one of the detriments of traditional Christology is that it tends toward Docetism and thereby diminishes Jesus' humanity. That perspective makes it difficult to picture Jesus growing up as a Jewish boy who, in most respects, lived like other lads by undergoing physical and psychological development as He matured into adulthood. Oscar Cullmann insists that "the life of Jesus would not be fully human if its course did not manifest a *development*."[133] Karl Rahner states more specifically, "We may speak without any embarrassment of a spiritual, indeed religious development of Jesus."[134] R.E. Brown acknowledges the common resistance among Christians to recognize Jesus' psychological development and that He had various human needs. Observes Brown, "there are believers who transfer the picture of the glorified Jesus back into his public ministry, imagining him to have walked through Galilee with an aura about him, almost wearing a halo. They cannot visualize him as being like other men."[135] Indeed, but they may be able to if they immerse themselves in the Gospel of Luke.

Dr. Luke also provides the most comprehensive narrative concerning Jesus' birth and His growth as a youth. Luke attests to the following characteristics of Jesus' human development, first with respect to His childhood and adolescence and then His adulthood:

- "And the Child continued to grow and become strong, increasing in wisdom; and the grace of God was upon Him" (Lk 2.40).
- "And Jesus kept increasing in wisdom and stature, and in favor with God and men" (Lk 2.52).

The same Greek word, *charis*, is translated "grace" in both of these verses in the AV, NIV, and NASB; but it is translated "favor" in these verses in the RSV, NRSV, JB, and NEB. The meaning is the same in both renderings: God favored Jesus. The concept of the patriarchs finding "favor with God" appears often in Genesis-Exodus.

Notice that Luke says Jesus *increasingly* found favor with God. Vincent Taylor calls Lk 2.40 and v. 52 "one of the greatest of Christological truths" in the NT.[136] On account of these two statements alone, it cannot be denied that God's favor toward Jesus increased as a result of His moral development. And, as with all other human beings, Jesus' moral development was largely a result of His upbringing and His many choices.

How could Jesus increasingly gain favor with God if He *was* God? For, credal Christianity asserts that Jesus was always consubstantial with the Father so that the Father must have *always* favored Jesus completely. Athanasius acknowledges that the Arians' posed this question as one of their primary arguments against the orthodox party.[137]

---

[133] O. Cullmann, *Christology*, 97. Emphasis his.

[134] Karl Rahner, "Dogmatic Considerations on Knowledge and Consciousness in Christ," in *Dogmatic vs. Biblical Theology*, ed. H. Vorgrimber (Baltimore: Helicon, 1964), 261.

[135] R.E. Brown, *An Introduction to New Testament Christology*, 27.

[136] Vincent Taylor, *The Person of Christ in New Testament Teaching* (London: MacMillan, 1958), 303.

[137] Athanasius, *Orations Against the Arians*, 3.26.

This concept of God increasingly favoring Jesus due to His moral development emerges in Luke's sole account of Jesus' consciousness of His special filial relation with, and mission for, God at the tender age of twelve (Lk 2.41-49). Thus, Jesus' moral development probably should be viewed as a progression from innocence to the attainment of righteous perfection. Jesus' life therefore contrasts with that of Adam, who digressed from original innocence to sin. (See Chapter Seven/Adam Christology.)

The fact that Jesus grew in wisdom also shows that He did not always possess complete wisdom and certainly not "the beatific vision" as propounded by Thomas Aquinas. Athanasius acknowledged that the Arians argued that if Jesus was fully God, He could not have advanced in wisdom.[138] Athanasius responded by applying the two-nature grid, i.e., interpreting that Jesus increased in wisdom in His human nature only.[139]

Jesus' Dependence upon the Holy Spirit

In the introduction to this chapter, we considered the subject of the Holy Spirit in the life of Jesus. The Holy Spirit is mentioned more in the Gospel of Luke than in any of the other three gospels. As for Luke's book of Acts, he mentions the Holy Spirit a total of fifty-four times, far more than in any other NT book or letter. Most of these references are not relevant to Christology since they concern the Holy Spirit's activity in the lives, and thus the ministries, of the disciples. It should be recognized, however, that two Spirit-induced phenomena stand out as contributing to the disciples' realization of Jesus' true identity and His significance for humankind: (1) the evidence for the resurrection of Jesus, consisting of the empty tomb and His post-resurrection appearances, and (2) the Pentecostal anointing of the Holy Spirit upon the disciples to empower them as bold witnesses.

Far more than the other gospel writers, Luke emphasizes in his gospel Jesus' dependence on the Holy Spirit for the anointing, guiding, and empowerment of His life. Luke relates that (1) "Jesus, full of the Holy Spirit ... was led about by the Spirit" (Lk 4.1), (2) after which He returned to Galilee "in the power of the Spirit" (Lk 4.14), and (3) at Jesus' hometown synagogue of Nazareth He read and applied to Himself the following words from Isaiah, "The Spirit of the Lord is upon Me, because He anointed Me to preach the gospel to the poor" (Lk 4.18; cf. Isa 61.1). And, in the Q logion of Mt 11.25-27/Lk 10.21-22, only Luke includes the introductory words, "At that time He rejoiced greatly in the Holy Spirit" (v. 21). Luke also infers the Holy Spirit when he tells about Jesus healing the bedridden paralytic let down through the roof, saying "the power of the Lord was present for Him to perform healing" (Lk 5.17).

Luke does the same in his book of Acts. He begins his history of the apostolic church by recounting that, just prior to Jesus' ascent to heaven, "He had by the Holy Spirit given orders to the apostles" to remain in Jerusalem (Ac 1.2). Luke adds that Jesus said, "you shall be baptized with the Holy Spirit not many days from now" (Ac 1.2, 5). When the Spirit came upon them on the day of Pentecost, Peter preached that Jesus was "a man attested to you by God with miracles and wonders and signs which God performed through Him" (Ac 2.22). And Peter later proclaimed, "God anointed Jesus of Nazareth with the Holy Spirit and with power;... for God was with Him" (Ac 10.38 NRSV).

---

[138] Athanasius, *Orations Against the Arians*, 3.26.
[139] Athanasius, *Orations Against the Arians*, 3.51-53.

In conclusion, *Jesus' power to accomplish supernatural acts was not intrinsic to His own being but derived from the Holy Spirit of God. Such dependence on the Holy Spirit is further evidence that Jesus was not God.*

Jesus as Prophet

Among the synoptists, Luke paints the largest portrait of Jesus as a leader-prophet and, of course, one who is clearly distinguished from God. Twice Luke relates that Jesus designated Himself as a miracle-working prophet (Lk 4.24; 13.33). And Luke presents the multitudes as indeed perceiving Jesus as a prophet (Lk 9.18-19). For instance, only Luke records about Jesus raising the dead man at Nain, when the people responded, "A great prophet has arisen among us!" (Lk 7.16). Again, only Luke records the pericope about the two disciples walking on the road to Emmaus, when they said among themselves that Jesus was "a prophet mighty in deed and word in the sight of God and all the people" (Lk 24.19). So, Jesus being a prophet *in the sight of God* shows Him to be distinct from God.

The picture is very similar in Acts. Luke informs that in Peter's first two sermons he identifies Jesus as a "prophet" (Ac 2.30; 3.23). In Peter's second sermon, Luke has Peter quoting Moses' prediction in Deut 18.15 about a great prophet and identifying Him as Jesus (Ac 3.22). Luke later adds that Stephen did the same (Ac 7.37). Geza Vermes observes, "the Acts of the Apostles contain nothing that could possibly be interpreted as pointing to a divine Jesus.... Far from considering Jesus as God ... Peter qualifies him in the first public christological statement of the Acts as a Jewish prophet."[140]

Thus, Luke, in both his gospel and Acts, presents a very primitive Christology. It is that Jesus was a Moses-like prophet sent by God. And neither Luke nor any of the characters he portrays give any indication that they believed that this prophet was God.

Glorifying and Praising God

Another unique feature of Luke's Gospel is his "theology of glory." He often portrays Jesus as healing someone, after which they and/or the attending crowds respond by "glorifying" and/or "praising" "God."[141] Perhaps the best example is Jesus' so-called "triumphal entry" into Jerusalem on Palm Sunday, which is recorded by all three synoptists. The crowds following Jesus were shouting liturgical phrases of worship that were inscribed in the OT. Yet only Luke appends the theological explication, "the whole multitude of the disciples began to praise God joyfully with a loud voice for all the miracles which they had seen" (Lk 19.37). In such instances, Luke does not mean that the people glorified and/or praised Jesus as being God, but that they rightly recognized God the Father as the Source of Jesus' miraculous power (cf. Ac 2.22).

A similar situation arises concerning Luke's portrayal of the exorcised demoniac of Gerasenes (Gadarenes?). After casting the demons out of this man Jesus commanded him, "Return to your house and describe what great things God has done for you" (Lk 8.39). Yet Luke interjects that the man "went away, proclaiming throughout the whole city what great things Jesus had done for him" (v. 39). Does this account mean that Jesus indirectly referred to Himself as "God"? Hardly! Euthymius Zigabenus rightly explains, "Christ indeed modestly

---

[140] G. Vermes, *The Changing Faces of Jesus*, 145.
[141] Lk 5.25-26; 7.16; 13.13; 17.15; 18.43; 19.37-38; cf. 2.14, 20; 24.53. Such instances in the other Synoptics occur only in Mt 9.8; 15.31; Mk 2.12.

attributed the work to the Father; but the healed man continued gratefully to attribute it to Christ."[142]

Luke provides other instances in which God was praised, blessed, and/or glorified for what Jesus did.[143] One story that is told only by Luke highlights what some scholars call Luke's "theology of glory." It is about Jesus healing the ten lepers. Only one of them, a Samaritan, "turned back, glorifying God with a loud voice" (Lk 17.15). Jesus inquired of those witnesses, "Was no one found who turned back to give glory to God, except this foreigner?" (v. 18). Both Luke and Jesus here indicate that God healed through Jesus. Moreover, this incident points to Israel's failure to recognize God's visitation through Jesus (cf. Lk 19.24) and that on this account God will soon turn His attention from the Jews to the Gentiles (Ac 1.8; 13.45-48; 18.4-6).

Jesus in Prayer

We have seen that there is perhaps no better demonstration of Jesus' dependence upon God than His frequent praying to God. And, more than the other synoptists, Luke portrays Jesus as a man of prayer. In fact, the synoptists record a total of twelve times that Jesus either prayed or they mention his praying, and only Luke relates eight of them.[144] For example, all three synoptists report Jesus' baptism and transfiguration, but only Luke adds that Jesus was praying when both of these glorious events began to transpire (Lk 3.21; 9.28-29). And only Luke tells that Jesus "would often slip away to the wilderness and pray" (Lk 5.16). Again, only Luke informs that right before Jesus chose His twelve apostles, "He went off to the mountain to pray, and He spent the whole night in prayer to God" (Lk 6.12). As stated earlier, this practice of Jesus making petitionary prayers to God demonstrates His need of God's help and therefore His dependence upon God.

In all of Jesus' prayers recorded in the NT gospels, He addresses God as "Father" every time except one, which is His dereliction cry while hanging on the cross. But that is because He was quoting Ps 22.1 and claiming it as His experience. Jesus calling God His own Father represents an innate recognition of One who possesses a greater authority, and therefore rank, than His own, which is what the Johannine Jesus revealed when He said, "the Father is greater than I" (Jn 14.28>).

Preaching Jesus as "the Christ"

Since Luke was a synoptist, we will consider briefly his second volume: the Acts of the Apostles. We discover that his recorded acts refer mostly to their preaching and otherwise spreading the message about Jesus. In their message they focus on Jesus' identity, His work, and His significance. They usually identify "Jesus" as "(the) Christ." Occasionally, they identify Him as "the Son of God," "Prince," "Savior," or "Lord." The following includes all of the titles in the book of Acts that the early Jewish Christians used to identify Jesus in their preaching and teaching:

- Peter proclaimed, "God has made Him both Lord and Christ—this Jesus" (2.36)
- Peter and other apostles said, "God exalted ... as a Prince and a Savior" (5.31)
- The apostles "kept right on teaching and preaching Jesus as the Christ" (5.42)
- Paul "began to proclaim Jesus ..., saying, 'He is the Son of God'" (9.20)

---

[142] Quoted by H.A.W. Meyer, MCNT, 2:65. See also I.H. Marshall, *Luke*, 341.
[143] Lk 1.46, 68; 2.13-14, 20, 28; 10.21; 23.47; 24.53.
[144] Lk 3.21; 5.16; 6.12; 9.18, 28-29; 11.1; 23.34, 46. The only others: Mk 1.35; Mt 11.25-27/Lk 10.21-22; Mt 14.33/Mk 6.46; Mt 26.39-44/Mk 14.35-39/Lk 22.41-45.

- Paul preached, "proving that this Jesus is the Christ" (9.22)
- Paul said, "God has brought to Israel a Savior, Jesus" (13.23)
- Paul said, "This Jesus whom I am proclaiming to you is the Christ" (17.3)
- Paul was "testifying to the Jews that Jesus was the Christ" (18.5)
- Apollos "powerfully refuted the Jews ... that Jesus was the Christ" (18.28)

Mostly, the early Christians simply referred to Jesus as "(the) Christ" (Ac 3.18, 20; 8.5; 26.23). Eventually, they dropped the article in the expression, "Jesus the Christ," and called him by the name "Jesus Christ" (Ac 4.10; 8.12; 10.36, 48; 11.17; 20.21). They also cited certain OT Scriptures that mention the "Christ" or God's "Son," and they applied these to Jesus too (Ac 4.26 cf. with Ps 2.2; Ac 13.33 cf. with Ps 2.7).

In conclusion, according to Luke the early Christians identified Jesus mostly as "the Christ," and they stressed the necessity of believing this about Jesus in order to receive forgiveness of sins and therefore eternal salvation. *In light of traditional Christology, it is very illuminating to realize that Luke's book of Acts, which records the early Christians preaching evangelistically about the identity of Jesus, never relates that they proclaimed that Jesus is God.* I believe that this evangelistic silence is the second most important phenomenon about silence in the NT. It indicates that Jesus is not God, and it is second in importance only to the four gospels never relating that Jesus identified Himself as God.

Preaching "the word"

Thus, as mentioned earlier, Luke's book of Acts represents a historical record about the early Christians (not only the apostles) spreading "the word" about Jesus. In the NT the expression "the word (of God)" appears mostly in Acts, and it occurs there no less than forty times. It usually translates *ho logos* (occasionally *rhema*) in the Greek text and means simply "the good news" (gospel) about Jesus. This good news includes Jesus' identity as the Christ, the Son of God, Lord, and Savior as well as both the fact and significance of His sufferings, death, resurrection, and ascension.

Every one of these occurrences of the expression "the word" in the book of Acts clearly refers to *the spoken word*. For instance, Jesus' disciples spoke "the word of God" with much "confidence" and "boldness" (Ac 4.29, 31). The method they used to deliver "the word" was usually through preaching or teaching (Ac 8.4; 18.11). Recipients would "hear the word" (Ac 13.7, 44), and many of them "received the word" by faith (Ac 2.41; 8.14; 11.1; 17.11). As a result, "the word of God kept on spreading" (Ac 6.7). In the book of Acts, therefore, "the word" does not exactly refer to the Scriptures but to the spoken word about Jesus that these early Christians delivered in the power of the Holy Spirit.

We shall see later that the Johannine writings occasionally call Jesus "the Word." This concept, while similar, ought to be distinguished from "the word" that appears so frequently in Luke's book of Acts.

Jesus' Resurrection, Ascension, and Exaltation

The main focus of Luke's book of Acts is not the identity of Jesus, however important that is, but His resurrection.[145] For, Jesus' resurrection became the catapult of Christianity and thus the basis of its growth and continuing existence.

Surprisingly, Luke is the only Evangelist who mentions what happened to Jesus after His resurrection appearances.[146] He relates that Jesus led His

---
[145] Ac 1.22; 2.24-32; 3.15; 4.1-2, 10, 33; 5.30; 10.40-41; 13.30-37; 17.3, 18, 31-32; cf. 23.6-8; 24.15; 26.23.
[146] All contemporary NT scholars believe that Mk 16.9-20, which includes mention of Jesus' ascension in v. 19, is an addendum that was probably added by another author.

disciples up the Mount of Olives and "departed from them" (Lk 24.51). Luke further informs in Acts that Jesus "was lifted up while they were looking on, and a cloud received Him out of their sight" (Ac 1.9). Luke adds that two angels immediately appeared, standing with the disciples and explaining to them that Jesus had been "taken up from you into heaven" (v. 11).

Later in Acts, Luke adds that when Jesus arrived in heaven God invited Him to sit down at His right hand on His throne, which He did (Ac 2.33-34; 5.31; cf. 7.55-56). This act fulfills the OT Scripture in which God says to His Messiah, "Sit at My right hand, until I make Thine enemies a footstool for Thy feet" (Ps 110.1). This passage is quoted in the NT more than any other OT passage. It is one of the most important messianic fulfillments of the OT because it represents God's ultimate vindication of His suffering Servant. Theologians refer to the ascended Jesus' initial sitting at God's right hand in His throne as "the session." Jesus' ascension and session, taken together, are His exaltation.

Although God and Jesus sitting together on God's throne may appear to signify their equality, the NT never says this or suggests that they are two Gods. Rather, "to sit at the right hand" is a Jewish idiom signifying the custom of a dignitary honoring someone. In the case of a king, it would be the place of highest honor for any of his subordinates. Therefore, Jesus' session merely signifies His exaltation to the place of highest honor in heaven, but not that He is God.

Perhaps no act distinguishes Jesus and God the Father more clearly, and shows that only the Father is God, than Jesus sitting beside God on God's throne. God inviting Jesus to do so strongly illustrates God's superiority over Jesus and Jesus' dependence upon God. So does the idea of God making Jesus' enemies a footstool for His feet.

Moreover, Luke presents Jesus' session as something new and different for Jesus (cf. Phil 2.9). Such honor had never been bestowed on Him or anyone else, even among God's angels (Heb 1.4, 13). Jesus' session therefore suggests philosophically that He cannot be God because, according to classical theism, God cannot be exalted to a higher status than He previously possessed. That would represent an improvement in deity, and, according to classical theism, God cannot improve.

Finally, neither Luke nor any of the other NT authors ever indicate that Jesus' resurrection, ascension, or heavenly session resulted in some kind of divinization or deification of Him or a reclaiming or reactivation of deity or attributes of deity, as if to confirm the later Church dogma determined at Nicae—of Jesus being "Very God."[147] We have no biblical evidence suggesting that the essence of the heavenly Jesus has been any different from that of the pre-Easter Jesus. The pre-Easter Jesus was no more than a man, and the same is true of the post-Easter, heavenly Jesus. The only difference is that, before, Jesus had a physical body that was subject to death; now, He has a resurrection, spiritual body that is glorified, immortal, and eternal. But He is still no more than a man.

Summary

Thus, Luke highlights Jesus' humanity by documenting His physical and moral development as a human being. And Luke repeatedly shows that when Jesus performed healings and other miracles, He accomplished them through the power of the Holy Spirit, thus demonstrating His dependence upon God. People didn't praise Jesus for it, but God. They believed that these signs that Jesus did signified what Peter later preached, that He was "a man attested ... by

---

[147] Contra M. Borg, *Jesus: A New Vision*, 6-7.

God" (Ac 2.22). So, Luke emphasizes that Jesus was a man who, through prayer and the power of the Holy Spirit, always depended upon God to accomplish His divinely-appointed mission to bring salvation to not only the Jews but the whole world. And when His disciples later went out preaching this good news, they never proclaimed that Jesus was God.

E. The Limited Knowledge of Jesus

Introduction	Jesus' Ignorance of Mundane Matters
Textual Variance	Jesus' Supernatural Knowledge
History of Interpretation	Did Jesus "know all things"?
Jesus' Ignorance of Other Matters	Conclusion

Introduction

In 1980, solely due to my personal study of the Bible, I became perplexed about the subject of what Jesus knew. Now we will examine that startling saying of Jesus that first caused my consternation about Jesus' knowledge which led to my lengthy quest for the identity of Jesus and the writing of this book.

A few days before Jesus was crucified, He led His apostles eastward from the temple at Jerusalem and up the nearby Mount of Olives. As they sat down overlooking Jerusalem, Jesus taught them an overview of the future, which included details about His second coming. He divulged that He did not know the time when He would return, but only the Father knew (Mt 24.36 and Mk 13.32). All three synoptists relate this discourse, but only Matthew and Mark include this admission by Jesus.

Jesus' disclosure about His apparent ignorance of the time of His return is a major christological saying that presents serious difficulty for the traditional view that He is God.[148] It raises the question: How could Jesus not know something if He is God, since God the Father knows? This saying of Jesus has stirred much scholarly debate. But before considering it, we need to look at MS discrepancy regarding the relevant texts.

Textual Variance

There is no textual variance in Mk 13.32.[149] It reads as follows:

32 "But of that day or hour no one knows, not even the angels in heaven, nor the Son, but the Father *alone*."[150]

Matthew provides almost the same quotation, in Mt 24.36. But the majority of Greek MSS of the Gospel of Matthew omit the words *oude ho huios* ("nor the

---

[148] So admits traditionalist Robert Stein (*Difficult Passage in the Gospels*, 97-100). R.E. Brown (*Jesus God and Man*, 39-42) indicates as much. T.E. Pollard (*Johannine Christology and the Early Church*, 240n3) informs that the Arians cited it as well as Lk 2.52, Jn 11.34, and Mk 6.38 to support their thesis that Jesus was God, yet not absolutely, and therefore that Jesus was not omniscient.

[149] Nonetheless, Gustaf Dalman (*The Words of Jesus Considered in the Light of Post-biblical Jewish Writings and the Aramaic Language*, tr. D.M. Kay [Edinburgh; T.&T. Clark, 1902], 194) and J. Jeremias (*The Prayers of Jesus* [Naperville, IL: A.R. Allenson, 1967], 37) regard the words in Mark's account—"nor the Son, but the Father"—as an assimilation to those MSS which include these words in Mt 24.36.

[150] The italicized word "*alone*," in Mk 13.32, indicates that it does not appear in the Greek text. Thus, its insertion by NASB translators can only be regarded as an unwarranted assimilation of Mk 13.32 to Mt 24.36.

Son").[151] In addition, all Greek MSS of Matthew include the word *monos* ("only" or "alone") at the end of this sentence, whereas those of Mark do not.

This variation in the MS evidence of Mt 24.36 compared with Mk 13.32 is often reflected in English versions. For instance, the AV appears more judicious than does the NASB by omitting the phrase "nor the Son" in Mt 24.36 while including it in Mk 13.32. Regardless, many versions, e.g., NRSV and NIV, include the questionable phrase in both passages and append a footnote at Mt 24.36, informing that some Matthean MSS omit it.

What are we to make of this MS variance in Mt 24.36? Textual critics generally reason that it would have been very unlikely for early church scribes to create a phrase that they surely would have understood as theologically difficult. Most contemporary scholars agree that the phrase, "nor the Son," is genuine in Mt 24.36 but that later scribes omitted it in their copies due to the "doctrinal difficulties it caused the church."[152] Indeed, Bruce Metzger, a member of the UBS Committee, explains, "The omission of the words because of the doctrinal difficulty they present is more probable than their addition by assimilation to Mk 13.32."[153] This assessment is substantiated by the fact that the omission appears late chronologically in the MS evidence, thus after the Arian controversy and the drafting of the Nicene Creed. Of course, if the original text had omitted *oude ho huios*, yet included *monos*, the meaning would be the same: only the Father knows.

Some patristic writers attest to the authenticity of the questionable Matthean phrase. During the 2nd century, Iranaeus included it in his quotation of this saying, apparently taken from Mt 24.36, as if he was unaware of any uncertainty about it.[154]

History of Interpretation

Now we will consider the history of interpretation of this saying of Jesus, a saying that was not controversial at the time Jesus said it but became so generations later.

Orthodox Christianity recognizes Iranaeus as the most capable biblical commentator and theologian of the 2nd century. On the basis of this single saying, in Mt 24.36/Mk 13.32, Irenaeus argued extensively that Jesus *really did not know* the time of His return. He asserted, "the Son was not ashamed to ascribe the knowledge of that day to the Father only."[155]

We have already seen that, like the other apologists, Iranaeus believed that Jesus was God, but with certain qualifications. Thus, he could call Christ "God" while also saying that "the Father Himself is alone called God" and that "God holds the supremacy over all things," including over Christ.[156] Iranaeus then quoted Jn 14.28 ("The Father is greater than I") to support that the Father does indeed "excel" Christ in knowledge.[157]

---

[151] This omission caused the Committee of the United Bible Societies" (UBS) *Greek New Testament* to give this phrase in Mt 24.36 a C rating (="a considerable degree of doubt" of its authenticity). But there are no variants regarding Mk 13.32 and thus no such doubt about its authenticity.
[152] B. Witherington, *The Christology of Jesus*, 229.
[153] B.M. Metzger, *A Textual Commentary*, 62. See also D.A. Carson, "Matthew," 508.
[154] Iranaeus, *Against Heresies*, 28, 6. Iranaeus apparently quoted Matthew's account because he included the word "alone."
[155] Iranaeus, *Against Heresies*, 28, 6.
[156] Iranaeus, *Against Heresies*, 28, 4, 6.
[157] Iranaeus, *Against Heresies*, 28, 8.

However, most succeeding church fathers did not agree with these declarations. They maintained that Jesus Christ possessed unlimited knowledge, called the maximalist view. They did so because they adopted Greek religio-philosophical thinking, in which it was supposed that deity was perfect and that absolute omniscience (all-knowing, including complete knowledge of the future) was the supreme perfection (cf. 1 Cor 1.22). (Recall that Irenaeus had spurned Greek philosophy.) Nearly all church fathers therefore insisted that Jesus, being God and therefore perfect, must be omniscient.

Athanasius acknowledged that the Arians disagreed with this maxim by arguing that if Jesus was "Very God" He could not have been ignorant of the day of His return.[158] Athanasius replied by applying the two-nature method of exegesis, that Jesus did not know in His human nature but He did know in His "Godhead,"[159] i.e., His divine nature. Athanasius further reasoned that if Jesus had predicted certain events to precede His return, He must have also known the day of His return.[160] But this reason fails to account for the OT prophets not knowing the day of Messiah's coming in glory although they made predictions that would occur just prior to it.

We have already seen that, during the Middle Ages, Thomas Aquinas and the Scholastics adopted a romantic perspective about Jesus' knowledge, called "the beatific vision." That is, Jesus was viewed as supernaturally possessing perfect knowledge of everything, so that He would have been able to expound extemporaneously, and most brilliantly, on any topic and thereby show Himself to surpass all human knowledge during all ages, both past and future.

On the contrary, Scripture does not confirm the notion of Jesus possessing beatific knowledge. For, according to the NT Jesus' perfection regarded His righteousness, which had nothing to do with knowledge of future events (e,g., 2 Cor 1.21; Heb 2.10; 4.15; 5.9; 7.26). Moreover, it may well be argued that this Greek concept of divine omniscience is neither commensurate with being human nor a perfection for humanity.[161]

Through the centuries the RCC steadfastly adhered to the maximalist view and thus opposed the teaching that Jesus possessed only limited knowledge. For instance, under Pope Vigilius in 553 the Church condemned the teaching of Nestorius—that Jesus was ignorant of both the time of His return and the day of judgment. And in about 600, Pope Gregory offered a rather confusing interpretation of Mk 13.32, that Jesus knew in His human nature the time of His return, but the source of His knowledge of it was His divine nature! However, these papal opinions never were binding on Roman Catholics.[162]

The primary interpretations of this saying of Jesus recorded in Mt 24.36 and Mk 13.32 that have emerged throughout church history can be summarized as follows, with some corresponding objections appended:

1. Jesus pretended ignorance (most church fathers as well as Thomas Aquinas).
    Rebuttal: This view unwittingly undermines the integrity of Jesus, implying that He was dishonest in making such an admission.
2. Similar to the above, Jesus knew in His divine nature the time of His return, but He did not know in His human nature (Athanasius). (See Chapter Seven/Phil 2.5-11.) That is, at the moment of incarnation the Logos voluntarily laid aside some of His divine attributes, or during His incarnation He chose not

---

[158] Athanaius, *Orations Against the Arians*, 3.26.
[159] Athanasius, *Orations Against the Arians*, 3.34, 37-38.
[160] Athanasius, *Orations Against the Arians*, 3.42.
[161] R.E. Brown, *An Introduction to New Testament Christology*, 28.
[162] R.E. Brown, *Jesus God and Man*, 78n59.

to exercise such attributes. (In the late 19th century, these views came to be called "kenotic theories.") When the Arians asserted the inferiority of the Son by citing Jesus' ignorance in Mt 24.36/Mk 13.32, Athanasius replied by applying to it the two-nature method of exegesis, that Jesus knew as "the Word" but that He was "ignorant" of it in His "human nature."[163]

Rebuttal: First, a two-nature Christology is not supported by Scripture, and it is both anthropologically and psychologically unsound. Second, this interpretation is contradictory because Jesus' use of the word "Son" (Son of God), according to orthodoxy, signifies His divine nature. Third, all kenotic theories diminish deity and fail to escape the charge of rendering Jesus as a deceiver, if not a liar.

3. It was not the Father's will at that time for Jesus to either know or reveal the date of His return; yet Jesus might become so informed at a later time (Augustine).

Rebuttal: This view is mere speculation. Some who adopt it suppose that Jesus, upon entering heaven, was at that time informed of the time of His second coming and that He later revealed it to John when he wrote the book of Revelation (Rev 1.1).[164] But this defense does not escape impugning Christ's deity, since the pre-Easter Jesus did not possess this knowledge. The Apocalypse only informs that certain future events will transpire, e.g., the second coming. It does not provide any definitive knowledge of their chronological order or timing, much less from some fixed date.[165]

4. Jesus really did not know the time of His return. His acknowledgment of ignorance concerning the timing of this event was not original with Him but echoes Zech 14.7: "On that day there will be no light, no cold or frost. It will be a unique day, without daytime or nighttime—a day known to the LORD" (NIV).[166] The last phrase means "that day" is known *only* to Yahweh. But it was not only the timing of the inbreaking of the Day of the LORD (Yahweh) that Jesus did not know. The Johannine Jesus said that He had divulged to His disciples all that He knew, i.e., all that the Father had told Him (Jn 8.26; 15.15). There must have been many other facets of knowledge, at least concerning the future, which Jesus did not know because the Father had not told Him.

When biblical criticism arose in the early 19th century, mostly among Protestants, the traditionalists' maximalist view of both Jesus' knowledge and foreknowledge was questioned. Kenotic theories flourished in the latter part of that century, first in Germany and then Britain. These theories were an attempt to resolve the dilemma of how Jesus could be God and yet not know the time of His return. (See Chapter Seven/Phil 2.5-11.)

However, by the mid-20th century most non-Catholic Bible scholars had rejected these kenotic theories. They reasserted that Jesus had not in any way feigned ignorance of the time of His return. For instance, in 1961 distinguished, moderate, form critic Vincent Taylor insisted, "The Gospels clearly show that the knowledge of Jesus was limited, that He asked questions for the sake of information."[167] By 1973, J.A.T. Robinson stated concerning distinguished

---

[163] Athanasius, *Orations Against the Arians*, 3.42-45.
[164] E.g., John Albert Bengel, *Bengel's New Testament Commentary* [1742], 2 vols. (repr. Grand Rapids: Kregel, 1981, 1:278, 364; W.G.T. Shedd, *Shedd's Dogmatic Theology*, 2:277.
[165] Even the predictions in Daniel and Revelation about the 3 1/2 years, 42 months, and 1260 days do not provide a beginning or ending of these time periods to enable calculation of the exact day of Christ's return.
[166] See also *Pss. Sol.* 17.23. This assertion is based on the view that Yahweh refers only to the Father.
[167] V. Taylor, "Does the New Testament Call Jesus God?" 118.

biblical scholars, "There would be few today who would question that Jesus' knowledge was limited."[168]

The RCC always unofficially adhered to the traditional, maximalist view of Jesus' foreknowledge because its dogmatic theologians, rather than its exegetes, controlled the discussions on this subject.[169] Then, in the mid-20th century the RCC began to question its prolonged opposition to biblical criticism as well as its unofficial maximalist view of Jesus' foreknowledge. First, Vatican II (1964) finally provided official assent for Catholic scholars to employ literary criticism to the Bible as well as their church creeds. Then, in 1984 The Pontifical Biblical Commission issued its extensive critique on christological methods, entitled *Bible et christologie*.[170] This important and excellent document acknowledges approvingly that "some questions ... have been recently examined anew, e.g., the 'knowledge' of Christ and the development of his personality" (1.1.1.2c).

Since 1967, esteemed RCC scholar R.E. Brown wrote extensively on the subject of Jesus' knowledge. He insists that the earthly Jesus had limited knowledge not only of the future but regarding other things as well.[171] Brown acknowledges that those who conclude as he does, that Jesus Christ *was not* omniscient, open themselves up to the charge of "denying the divinity of Jesus," a charge which Brown vehemently rejects.[172] He observes concerning his church, "We know of no Church statement that forbids the interpretation of the literal sense of Mk 13.32,"[173] i.e., that the entire Person—Jesus Christ—actually did not know the time of His second coming. Brown later adds, "It is important to emphasize that there is no dogma of the church on the extent of Jesus' knowledge.... the church ... has not entered authoritatively in historical questions such as the one we are asking: How much did Jesus know in his lifetime?"[174] Finally, in 1994 he notes that "the theological climate has changed, and very prominent Roman Catholic theologians now allow for limitations in Jesus' knowledge."[175]

Another RCC scholar who has adopted a minimalist view of Jesus' knowledge has been the brilliant theologian Karl Rahner. He dismisses the two-nature exegesis of the gospels and even rejects the Greek religio-philosophical idea, adopted by so many traditionalists, that omniscience is a necessary perfection of deity. Rahner concludes that Jesus' knowledge, even His knowledge of God, developed throughout His earthly life.[176]

Thus, in modern times there have been many reputable scholars who have believed that Jesus was God, yet they did not believe that He was omniscient.[177]

---

[168] J.A.T. Robinson, *The Human Face of God*, 71.
[169] R.E. Brown, *Jesus God and Man*, 39.
[170] See an English translation of this document by J.A. Fitzmyer, *Scripture and Christology*, 3-53.
[171] R.E. Brown, *Jesus God and Man*, 39-102; idem, *An Introduction to New Testament Christology*, 31-59. Other NT examples of Jesus having limited knowledge may be in Mk 5.30-31; 9.21; Lk 8.45-46; Jn 11.34. But I do not subscribe to some of Brown's interpretations of other passages as indicating Jesus' ignorance.
[172] R.E. Brown, *Jesus God and Man*, 41.
[173] R.E. Brown, *Jesus God and Man*, 78n59.
[174] R.E. Brown, *An Introduction to New Testament Christology*, 29n31.
[175] R.E. Brown, *An Introduction to New Testament Christology*, 29. Brown (*Jesus God and Man*, 44) wrote in 1967 that "almost all Catholic scholars today admit a limited experiential knowledge on Jesus' part." His colleague, J.A. Fitzmyer (*A Christological Catechism*, 101), agreed.
[176] Karl Rahner, "Dogmatical Reflections on the Knowledge and Self-Consciousness of Christ," 203-12.
[177] Besides Roman Catholic scholars—e.g., K. Rahner, R.E. Brown, and J.A Fitzmyer—Protestant scholars include the following: W. Barclay, *Jesus As They Saw Him*, 37; V. Taylor, *The Person of Christ*, 291-92; G. Hawthorne, *The Presence and the Power*, 209; B. Witherington, *Christology of Jesus*, 227-28, 233.

Jesus' Ignorance of Other Eschatological Matters[178]

Some may counter that Jesus only *seemed* to portray ignorance (and its associated essential subordination) during His earthly life, but that afterwards He no longer did so. For according to kenotic theory, either at the time of His resurrection or His ascension, Jesus reclaimed all those divine attributes that He had either laid aside or did not exercise. On the contrary, there are other Scriptures that indicate otherwise.

Jesus sometimes spoke of God the Father's unique authority as being greater than His own. One time the apostles James and John accompanied their mother as she asked Jesus to grant that her two sons sit beside Him in the future, glorious kingdom. Jesus replied, "to sit on My right and on My left, this is not Mine to give; but it is for those for whom it has been prepared by My Father" (Mt 20.23; cf. Mk 10.40). Does this omission infer that Jesus *did not know* who would be awarded these positions of honor?

Just prior to Jesus' ascension into heaven, He again revealed to His disciples His limited knowledge about eschatological matters. His disciples asked Him if, at that time, He was going to restore the promised kingdom to Israel. Jesus replied that all "times and epochs ... the Father has fixed by His own authority," especially the eschatological Day (Ac 1.7; cf. 17.31; Zech 14.7).[179] In other words, the Father alone determines the ages and their timing. Jesus' reply suggests at least two things concerning Christology: (1) the earthly Jesus did not inherently foreknow the timing of certain ages, and (2) this unshared authority of the Father renders Him superior to all, including Jesus (cf. Jn 14.28).

Not only did Jesus' status as the Son not enable Him to foreknow all of the future, neither did it cause Him to inherently know all of God's activities and plans.[180] For Jesus said, "the Father loves the Son, and shows Him all things that He Himself is doing" (Jn 5.20). This implies that Jesus only knows what the Father does as the Father shows Him.

The book of Revelation is prime evidence of this. It begins, "The Revelation of Jesus Christ, which God gave Him to show to His bond-servants, the things which must shortly take place" (Rev 1.1).[181] So, God told the exalted Jesus things about the future that He previously did not know. This truth exposes the error of kenosis theories, which project Jesus as taking back His divine attributes, e.g., omniscience, at His heavenly exaltation. Ben Witherington rightly explains that Jesus' limited knowledge "implies the inferiority of the son [Jesus] to the Father in knowledge of eschatological matters."[182]

The Apostle Paul portrays God's unique and superior authority in eschatological matters by characterizing Him as the director and producer of

---

[178] By applying the words "ignorant" and "ignorance" to Jesus, I do not intend them in a pejorative sense.

[179] Also see the eschatological "appointed time" of the end, in Ps 102.13 and Dan 8.19 (cf. Dan 11.27, 29, 35, 40; 12.4, 9, 13), which time is presumably decided by God.

[180] The Q logion of Mt 11.27/Lk 10.22 does not imply that Jesus knew everything about the Father's plans.

[181] The Greek words *en tachei* are here translated "shortly" in the NASB. But the literal translation—"with speed" or "speedily" ("quickly")—is preferred. "Shortly" suggests "soon" whereas "speedily" or "quickly" does not. History affirms that many of these predictions have not happened. Besides, a similar word in this book—*tachys*—is consistently translated "quickly" in the NASB (Rev 2.5, 16; 3.11; 11.14; 22.7, 12, 20).

[182] B. Witherington, *The Christology of Jesus*, 233.

Jesus' second coming. Paul wrote that God the Father, according to His timing, "will bring about at the proper time" Christ's return because God is the "only Sovereign," thus being over Christ (1 Tim 6.15).

Jesus' Ignorance of Mundane Matters

Further evidence that Jesus did not possess omniscience is that He often lacked knowledge of mundane matters. The following incidents either attest or suggest His lack of knowledge. The fundamental question that often needs to be asked is whether Jesus expressed an apparent ignorance only for the purpose of informing those present:

1. Jesus once entered the country of Gadarenes (Gerasenes?) and encountered a wild, naked man who was possessed by many demons. As Jesus commanded the demon(s) to come out of the man, He engaged the chief demon in conversation. Jesus asked him, "'What is your name?' And he said to Him, 'My name is Legion; for we are many'" (Mk 5.9 par.). Luke explains that "many demons had entered him" (Lk 8.30). Jesus apparently did not know the chief demon's name. This ignorance seems further confirmed by the fact that the chief demon did not object to Jesus' inquiry by saying Jesus knew his name.
2. Shortly thereafter, as Jesus was walking along, a woman touched His garment and instantly was healed of a twelve-year hemorrage. "And Jesus said, 'Who is the one who touched Me?' And while they were all denying it, Peter said, 'Master, the multitudes are crowding and pressing upon You.' But Jesus said, 'Someone did touch Me, for I was aware that power had gone out of Me'" (Lk 8.45-46; cf. Mk 5.30-31). This account seems pretty clear and straight forward; Jesus did not know who touched Him.
3. All four Evangelists record Jesus' miraculous feeding of the 5,000 men (Mt 14.21; perhaps a total of 10,000 people with the inclusion of women and children). Only Mark relates that Jesus asked His disciples, "How many loaves do you have?" (Mk 6.38). Jesus may not have known a boy had five loaves and two fish (Jn 6.9).
4. When Jesus saw the unclean spirit throw a boy into convulsions, He "asked his father, 'How long has this been happening to him?' And he said, 'From childhood'" (Mk 9.21). Jesus appears to have not known the answer to His question.
5. One time Jesus "became hungry. And seeing at a distance a fig tree in leaf, He went to see if perhaps He would find anything on it; and when He came to it, He found nothing but leaves," so He promptly cursed the tree and it withered (Mk 11.12-13; cf. Mt 21.18-19). Apparently, Jesus didn't know if the tree had fruit when He first saw it.
6. As Jesus approached Bethany to raise Lazarus from the dead, He supernaturally knew for days that His beloved friend was dead (Jn 11.14). But He apparently did not know exactly for how long. For John writes, "So when Jesus came, He found that he had already been in the tomb four days" (v. 17). Neither did Jesus know the location of the tomb. For when He saw the people weeping because of Lazarus' death, He asked them, "Where have you laid him?" (v. 34). Neither of these points can be attributed to a feigned lack of knowledge in order to inform those present because they knew.
7. When Pilate asked Jesus if He was a king, Jesus answered, "Are you saying this on your own initiative, or did others tell you about Me?" (Jn 18.34).

8. Jesus' dereliction outcry while hanging on the cross—"My God, My God, why hast Thou forsaken Me?" (Mt 27.46 par.)—seems to indicate that, at that moment, He felt separated from the Father due to a disruption in their fellowship, which He did not comprehend. Vincent Taylor cites this saying as evidence that, for Jesus, "there must have been times when knowledge was less clear, and even clouded."[183]

Jesus' Supernatural Knowledge

Sometimes Jesus supernaturally knew the future and the thoughts or previous actions of others (cf. Jn 4.19; 1 Cor 14.24-25). This does not indicate that Jesus was omniscient, but merely that He possessed some piece of supernatural knowledge, which was typical of Spirit-inspired prophets. Consider the following examples:

1. When Jesus met Nathanael, He said to him, "'Behold, an Israelite indeed, in whom is no guile!' Nathanael said to Him, 'How do You know me?' Jesus answered and said to him, 'Before Philip called you, when you were under the fig tree, I saw you'" (Jn 1.47-48). In other words, Jesus previously had a vision of Nathanael under a fig tree.
2. Jesus, having never known the Samaritan woman at the well, told her, "You have had five husbands, and the one whom you now have is not your husband" (Jn 4.18).
3. When Jesus forgave the sins of the paralytic, He revealed to certain scribes who were sitting there that He knew what they were thinking (Mk 2.5-9). Mark relates that Jesus was "aware in His spirit that they were reasoning that way within themselves" (v. 8).
4. We read, "Jesus knew from the beginning who they were who did not believe and who it was that would betray Him" (Jn 6.64).
5. Just before His arrest, Jesus foreknew that Judas would be accompanied by officials and that they were about to arrive to arrest Him (Mt 26.46 par.). He also foreknew "all the things that were coming upon Him" (Jn 18.4).

The following points indicate that Jesus' possession of some item of supernatural knowledge *cannot* rightly be regarded as evidence of His being omniscient:

1. Each instance in which Jesus supernaturally foreknew something only verifies that He possessed that piece of knowledge, not that He was omniscient of all other things.
2. Jesus' capacity to supernaturally know something does not necessitate that the source of His knowledge was an attribute intrinsic to His own nature. Rather, Jesus acquired His supernatural knowledge from the Father, no doubt by means of the Holy Spirit.
3. The Bible furnishes many examples of other biblical characters who demonstrated supernatural knowledge about something, e.g., prophets, and no one would argue that such evidence proves that they were omniscient as well.

A.N.S. Lane argues forcefully that Jesus was *not* omniscient. He makes the alarming allegation that *the traditional dogma that Jesus possessed omniscience actually undermines the humanity of Jesus*. Lane explains:

> It is true that the Christ of the Gospels taught with a supreme authority and manifested supernatural knowledge. But neither of these can be equated with omniscience. The affirmation

---
[183] V. Taylor, *The Person of Christ*, 303.

of the omniscience of the historical Jesus has no biblical basis and indeed runs counter to the teaching of the Gospels.... it undermines his true humanity as taught in Scripture. It is hard to see how an omniscient man could be genuinely tempted to do something that he *knew* that he would not do.... But the New Testament nowhere bases the authority and reliability of Jesus' teaching on his omniscience. Indeed the contrary is affirmed in that Jesus' teaching is not his own but his Father's. It is strange how often those who have sought to defend the authority of Jesus' teaching have done so by invoking a doctrine which he himself explicitly denied.[184]

So, Lane says Jesus often said that His teaching, which included knowledge, was not His own but the Father's. If Jesus was co-equal in essence with the Father, then His teaching would be just as much His own as the Father's. On the contrary, the Father gave Jesus His words, teaching, and miraculous works, making the Father their source.

Did Jesus "Know All Things"?

Twice the apostles said to Jesus, "You know all things" (Jn 16.30; 21.17). A few exegetes assert that these affirmations show that Jesus possessed omniscience.[185]

The first incident occurred in the Garden of Gethsemane just prior to Jesus' arrest. The Master told His disciples of some things and they responded, "Now we know that You know all things, and have no need for anyone to question You; by this we believe that You came from God" (Jn 16.30; cf. Mt 6.8). Taking this statement out of context, it appears to say that Jesus is omniscient. Rather, it refers to what Jesus had just said, in which He obscurely foretold His death and resurrection appearances. But the disciples did not understand. "Jesus knew that they wished to question Him" about what He had just said (v. 19). So He told them what they were questioning in their minds and answered those very questions. R.E. Brown says of "the Jewish idea that the ability to anticipate questions and not to need to be asked is a mark of the divine.... When the disciples recognize that he knows questions before they are asked, they recognize automatically that he came forth from God."[186] Maybe call it mind reading; but it isn't omniscience.

The other incident occurred when the resurrected Jesus subtly and tenderly confronted Peter about his previous three denials that He knew Jesus (Mt 26.31-35 par.). Jesus' purpose was surely to restore His beloved apostle to full fellowship with Himself, partly in anticipation of Peter's future mission for His Lord. Penitent Peter responded rather shyly, "Lord, You know all things" (Jn 21.17). Peter did not mean that Jesus was omniscient, but that *Jesus knew everything about Peter's heart*, including that Peter truly did love Jesus. The author of the Fourth Gospel probably also intended for this narrative to echo what he had written earlier, that Jesus "knew what was in man" (Jn 2.25).

So, Jesus certainly did not know everything. For instance, at the end of His earthly ministry the Johannine Jesus informed the Eleven, "all things that I have heard from My Father I have made known to you" (Jn 15.15). The Father never told Jesus anything Jesus did not make known to His apostles. "All things" does not include knowledge of science, mathematics, etc., but all spiritual truth the Father had told Him. Ben Witherington well explains, "this relationship between Father and son does not entail that the son knows all the things the Father knows.... Jesus' special and unique 'communion' with God did not include a knowledge of every truth or secret God might have unveiled to him."[187]

---

[184] A.N.S. Lane, "Christology Beyond Chalcedon," in *Christ the Lord*, ed. H.H. Rowdon, 271.
[185] E.g., M. Harris, *3 Crucial Questions about Jesus*, 67.
[186] R.E. Brown, *John (xiii-xxi)*, 725-26.
[187] B. Witherington, *The Christology of Jesus*, 233, 228.

Conclusion

Jesus clearly did not know the time of His second coming; only the Father knew. Kenosis theories offered to explain otherwise are not biblically based nor theologically or anthropologically sound. They suggest Jesus was dishonest, perhaps schizophrenic, and thus impugn His integrity. We must conclude that (1) when Jesus possessed supernatural knowledge it was because the Father revealed it to Him, and (2) when Jesus did not know something it was because the Father had not revealed it to Him.

In sum, (1) Jesus' knowledge was limited, (2) the Father has a greater knowledge than Jesus does, and (3) the Father is superior to Jesus so that (4) Jesus is not God.

F. The Trial of Jesus

Introduction	The Trial before Pilate
The Sanhedrin's Examination of Jesus	The Crucified Jesus
The Charge of Blasphemy	Conclusion
No Charge of Jesus Claiming to Be God	

Introduction

Throughout the history of Christianity, so many devout Christians have thought that Jesus was condemned and executed for claiming to be God. To examine if this is correct, we now turn to some of the most important evidence for determining who Jesus claimed to be. It is the NT gospel accounts of (1) the examination of Jesus by the Jewish Council (Sanhedrin), (2) the official Roman trial of Jesus, and (3) the crucifixion scene. But before we do, we will consider the authorities' pretexts for arresting Jesus.

We have already seen that according to the NT gospels the religious authorities at Jerusalem had become jealous of Jesus' popularity with the Jewish people (Mt 27.18; Mk 15.10). This envy became the root cause of their growing enmity toward Him. We even read that "they were afraid of Him" (Mk 11.18). This is most evident from their reaction to Jesus' parable that He delivered immediately after His so-called "cleansing" of the temple during Passion Week. Those Pharisees listening to Jesus knew that this parable of the wicked tenant farmers referred to them (Mt 21.45/Mk 12.12/Lk 20.19; cf. Mt 22.7).

In recent NT scholarship, it is common to deem Jesus' cleansing of the temple during Passion Week as the Jewish religious leaders' primary, if not only, pretext for arresting Jesus.[188] On the contrary, the Fourth Evangelist reports that very early in Jesus' public ministry "the Jews were seeking all the more to kill Him, because [they thought] He not only was breaking the Sabbath, but also was calling God His own Father, making Himself equal with God" (Jn 5.18). Also early in Jesus' career, when some Pharisees saw Him heal a man of a withered arm they counseled together, discussing "how they might destroy Him" (Mt 12.14/Mk 3.6). Later, when Jesus raised His friend Lazarus from the dead, "the chief priests and Pharisees convened a council" against Jesus, and "from that day on they planned together to kill Him" (Jn 11.47, 53). Therefore, Jesus' cleansing of the temple during Passion Week merely represents a legitimate act of a reformer prophet (cf. Zech 14.20 NRSV). The fact that "the chief priests and the scribes" thereafter "kept looking for a way to kill him" (Mk 11.18 NRSV) suggests that this

---

[188] Esp. E.P. Sanders, *Jesus and Judaism*, 301-05; idem, *The Historical Figure of Jesus*, 253-65.

temple cleansing only exacerbated their already growing hostility toward Jesus and thus fueled their continuing determination to kill Him.

Matthew reveals the Jews' motive for arresting Jesus. He alleges that Governor Pilate "knew that because of envy they had delivered Him up" (Mt 27.18). Indeed, the chief priests and Pharisees had convened that council meeting to discuss Jesus' raising of Lazarus. For they said of Jesus, "What are we doing? For this man is performing many signs. If we let Him go on like this, all men will believe in Him, and the Romans will come and take away our place and our nation" (Jn 11.47-48). Thus, the motive of these rulers for arresting Jesus was clearly their jealousy of Him, their fear of losing their prestigious position as Council members, and perhaps the peril of a messianic uprising.

During the latter part of Jesus' public ministry, the scribes and Pharisees were constantly questioning Him about His teachings, mostly those regarding Torah. Being Torah experts themselves, they sought to find Jesus guilty of teaching something contrary to the Torah or in some way violating it. For example, whenever they encountered Jesus healing on the Sabbath, they would accuse Him of breaking the Sabbath and perhaps dismiss that miracle as inspired by Beelzebul/Satan (Mt 12.22-32/Mk 3.22-30; Lk 11.14-26). Other times, they took counsel to destroy or even kill Him.[189] Jesus' enemies were united in seeking a pretext against Him (Jn 7.1, 19, 25; 8.37, 40; 10.31-33), it being mostly "that they might catch Him in some statement, so as to deliver Him up to the rule and the authority of the governor" (Lk 20.20).

In the providence of God, the Apostle Judas carried out that most wicked deed by going to the chief priests at Jerusalem to betray Jesus to them. At that time, Jerusalem was teeming with a mass of visitors who were preparing to celebrate the Passover Festival (Mk 14.10 par.). To avoid a mob riot, the chief priests secretly conspired with Judas to betray Jesus apart from the multitudes (Mt 21.46 par.; 26.3-16 par.; Jn 11.53). So, at night Judas led an armed multitude to Jesus. The mob included the chief priests, the temple guards, and a cohort of Roman soldiers. A Roman cohort usually consisted of 600 men; but it could be as few as 200. They found Jesus with His other apostles, praying in His favorite place—the Garden of Gethsemane (Mt 26.47-57 par.). Then the cohort arrested Jesus and brought Him to Caiaphas the High Priest for questioning.[190]

The Examination of Jesus by the Sanhedrin

The high council of the religious authorities at Jerusalem was called "the (Great) Sanhedrin" (Gr. *synedrion*; Heb. *bet din*, i.e., "court"). As the highest tribunal in Israel, it was comparable to the U.S. Supreme Court. The Sanhedrin, however, was comprised of not nine but seventy members. They consisted of the chief priests (Sadducees), scribes (usually Pharisees), and elders (male heads of tribal families), over which a High Priest presided as the president and thus the seventy-first member (e.g., Mk 15.1). Presumably, this body was numerically constituted after the pattern of Num 11.16 (cf. Ex 18.25-26; Deut 17.8; 19.17-18). Ideally, the Sanhedrin was to be composed of the best scholars in the land and that they possessed equal authority. In reality, it was an aristocratic body in which the chief priests, especially the High Priest, possessed decisive authority.[191]

---

[189] Mt 12.14/Mk 3.6/Lk 6.11; Jn 5.18; Mk 11.18/Lk 19.47; Mt 26.4/Mk 14.1/Lk 22.2.

[190] Jesus probably was first taken to Annas' house temporarily (Jn 18.12). Sanhedrin members were then summoned to Caiaphas' house, where he conducted the main interrogations. In the early morning, the necessary quorum of Sanhedrin members probably met at the temple and officially condemned Jesus.

[191] Schurer, 2:200-26.

At this time, Israel still considered itself a theocracy, though under partial Roman subjugation. Its government operated by means of a complex and fully integrated system of religion, law, and politics. This system, called *halakhah*, was administered by a religious court that, at that time, remained under the jurisdiction of Roman rule.

All four NT gospels provide an abundance of details about the Sanhedrin's interrogation of Jesus. Concerning this important episode in the life of Jesus, these gospel accounts relate that the Sanhedrin vigorously questioned Jesus throughout much of the night in an attempt to bring formal charges against Him (Mt 26.59). They preferred to find Him guilty of a capital crime in accordance with Roman law; if not, then it would be religious blasphemy based on the Torah. Apparently, they felt pressed for time.[192] If Jesus was crucified on Friday morning, as Christian tradition claims, the Sanhedrin had only a few hours until the weekly Sabbath was to begin, at sundown Friday evening. According to *halakhah*, criminals could not be executed during the weekly Sabbath.

Especially during the latter half of the 20th century, several scholars conducted extensive studies comparing the NT gospel accounts of the Sanhedrin's examination of Jesus with Jewish jurisprudence known to have existed at that time and thereafter.[193] The prevailing view among these scholars, as well as most other distinguished scholars, has been that the NT gospels are anti-Semitic. The NT does place the major portion of blame for the condemnation and crucifixion of Jesus on the Jewish religious establishment and only secondarily on the Roman governmental authorities.[194] But Western guilt incurred from so many centuries of Catholic anti-Semitism, as well as the Western World's failure to provide a safe haven for Jews seeking to escape the Holocaust of WWII, resulting in an overreaction in which many western Christian theologians and biblical exegetes no longer regarded the Jewish religious establishment of Jesus' time as predominantly culpable for His condemnation and execution.

Many of these scholars further alleged that, largely due to this anti-Semitism, the NT gospels do not transmit an authentic history of the Sanhedrin's examination of Jesus.[195] Their primary argument has been that the gospel record does not coincide with known Jewish jurisprudence of that time. For example, Jesus endured a Jewish trial at night and was executed the next day; but the Mishnah includes rules for criminal jurisprudence regarding capital cases which expressly (1) prohibits nighttime trials and (2) requires a minimum of two days so that (3) such trials bringing a conviction could not be held on the day before either the weekly Sabbath or a festival day.[196] Also, many of these 20th century scholars were opposed to Jn 18.31, which states that Jews had no right to adjudicate capital crimes, by insisting that the Sanhedrin did indeed have this right.

In contrast, many scholars have accepted the historical reliability of the NT gospel records concerning the Sanhedrin's interrogation of Jesus and accused the Sanhedrin of illegalities, irregularities, or both, regarding proper Jewish jurisprudence in this case. In fact, some Jewish scholars have adopted

---

[192] D.A. Carson, "Matthew," 550-52.
[193] For a survey of this scholarship, see D. Bock, *Blasphemy and Exaltation*, 5-29.
[194] E.g., Lk 24.20; Jn 19.11; Ac 2.23, 36; 3.13-15; 4.10; 7.52; cf. Deut 30.1-6; Zech 12.10-14; Mt 27.24-25.
[195] Hans Lietzmann ("Der Prozess Jesu," in *Sitzungsberichte der (koniglichen) Preussischen Akademie der Wissenchaft* [1931], 313-22) first championed this viewpoint rather powerfully and succinctly.
[196] *Sanh.* 4.1.

this perspective as a defense lodged against the allegation that succeeding generations of Jews are culpable for the condemnation and death of Jesus. Some of these alleged illegalities are that (1) the Sanhedrin's examination of Jesus was conducted at night, (2) its judgment was rendered on a feast day, (3) this judgment was based on a confession elicited from the accused, and (4) it was pronounced prior to securing the full council's judgment. Also, Jewish criminal law did not allow questioning of the accused, but only permitted the testimony of witnesses.

While some Sanhedrin irregularities may have occurred, perhaps for the sake of expediency, the gospels never describe the Sanhedrin's interrogation of Jesus as an actual trial. It was more likely a judicial inquiry,[197] better yet, a hearing,[198] so that these rules did not apply. In fact, this all-night vigil was held in the High Priest's house (Lk 22.54; cf. Mt 26.58 par.), hardly a suitable site for a trial. The Sanhedrin's official condemnation apparently occurred later, at dawn, in the Sanhedrin's "council chambers" (Lk 22.66), perhaps in accordance with *halakhah*. Regardless of all of this, authority David Catchpole concludes, "the debate about illegalities should be regarded as a dead end, and at most able to make only a minor contribution" toward understanding the condemnation of Jesus by the Sanhedrin.[199] In other words, nothing in the synoptic narratives regarding the Sanhedrin's examination of Jesus clearly negates their historical authenticity because it cannot be determined with certainty whether some matters were legal or not.

One thing is certain: the Sanhedrin would have left no stone unturned in its intense effort to find Jesus guilty of teaching against, or in some way violating, the Torah. But its interrogation of Him only produced conflicting witnesses, resulting in their false and inconsistent testimony. These witnesses could only muster the false charge that Jesus had threatened to destroy the temple at Jerusalem (Mt 26.59-61/Mk 14.55-59).

This allegation reflects a widespread, Near Eastern custom in antiquity in which political governments respected religious traditions by designating any impairment of temples and shrines as a capital offense against the state, punishable by death. This charge was elicited because, early in Jesus' ministry, He declared publicly in the temple, "Destroy this temple, and in three days I will raise it up" (Jn 2.19). The Fourth Evangelist, however, explains, "But He was speaking of the temple of His body" (v. 21).

There is a strong connection in the OT between the Messiah and Jerusalem's temple. For example, the prophet Malachi predicts that the Messiah "will suddenly come to His temple" (Mal 3.1). And Zechariah says of the one named Branch, "He will build the temple of the LORD" (Zech 6.12; cf. vv. 13-15; 3.8). Jews debated if this Branch was only Joshua the High Priest (v. 11) or also the Messiah, as predicted by Isaiah and Jeremiah (Isa 4.2; 11.1; Jer 23.5; 33.15). Consequently, Jesus' earlier statement about destroying and raising the temple

---

[197] G.B. Caird (*New Testament Theology*, 358-59) insists, "Clearly it was not a trial but an inquiry." R.E. Brown (*The Death of the Messiah*, 557) tentatively states similarly, "This was probably not a courtroom trial in the technical sense." Likewise, C.H. Dodd, *The Founder of Christianity*, 155.

[198] D. Bock, *Blasphemy and Exaltation*, 189-92, 235. For support, Bock cites esp. Otto Betz ("Jesus and the Temple Scroll," in *Jesus and the Dead Sea Scrolls*, ed. J.H. Charlesworth, 87-88), who cites authority A.N. Sherwin-White, author of *Roman Society and Roman Law in the New Testament* (Oxford: Clarendon, 1963).

[199] David R. Catchpole, *The Trial of Jesus: A Study in the Gospels and Jewish Historiography From 1770 to the Present Day* (Leiden: Brill, 1971), 268-67. See also E.P. Sanders, *Jesus and Judaism*, 299.

would have led the Sanhedrin to question if He claimed to be the Messiah. Regardless, this question was "in the air" (Jn 7.26, 40-43; 9.22; 10.24).

Caiaphas the High Priest demanded an unequivocal answer from Jesus concerning His identity. According to Matthew, Caiaphas exclaimed, "I adjure You by the living God, that You tell us whether You are the Christ, the Son of God" (Mt 26.63 par.). How did the High Priest know that Jesus claimed to be the Messiah? Albert Schweitzer is probably right, here, that it was Judas. No one knew this Messianic Secret except Jesus and the Twelve. Caiaphas must have learned it from Judas when he betrayed Jesus to the chief priests.[200] Thus, Schweitzer states, "the decisive thing was the betrayal of the messianic secret.... But the difficulty was that Judas was the sole witness. Therefore the betrayal was useless so far as the actual trial was concerned unless Jesus admitted the charge. So they first tried to secure His condemnation on other grounds, and only when these attempts broke down did the High Priest put, in the form of a question, the charge."[201] Similarly, Judas must have told them about Jesus' prediction that He would rise from the dead on the third day (Mt 27.62-66), which He had only told the Twelve.

Jesus answered Caiaphas' question somewhat obscurely, yet affirmatively, "You have said it yourself" (Mt 26.64). There is no longer a need for the Messianic Secret because His hour has come. Jesus voluntarily added, "nevertheless I tell you, hereafter you shall see THE SON OF MAN SITTING AT THE RIGHT HAND OF POWER, and COMING ON THE CLOUDS OF HEAVEN" (v. 64). This statement is a clear self-designation as the Son of Man of Dan 7.13-14. The word "POWER" is surely a Jewish euphemism for "God;" more precisely, and literally, it refers to God's power. And regarding the expression, "sitting at the right hand," Jews well understood it as a reference to Ps 110.1, if not also Ps 80.17.[202] For the first time, Jesus unequivocally claimed publicly to be the Messiah-the Son of God-the Son of Man. It is certainly the most thoroughgoing self-identification Jesus ever made. He fully revealed who He was, and He did not say that he was God. Rather, this remark by Jesus represents a clear claim that God would vindicate Him to the utmost.

That did it; the High Priest exploded with rage! First, he invoked a long-held tradition, based on 2 Kgs 18.37, of tearing (Heb. *keriah*) his robe as a symbolic gesture indicating mourning. It was due either to grief or anger, in this case, mourning on account of this last remark uttered by Jesus.[203] Then, according to Matthew, Caiaphas formally charged Jesus as a blasphemer. All present Sanhedrin members consented to the High Priest's allegation (Mt 26.66/Mk 14.64). R.E. Brown explains, "Jesus' claim of relationship to God was the decisive factor in the hostility of the authorities toward him."[204] Notice that Brown says "claim of relationship" rather than claim to be deity.

The Charge of Blasphemy

One of the most perplexing questions about the whole saga of the life and death of Jesus of Nazareth is this: *What did Jesus claim about His identity that so infuriated the Sanhedrin, causing it to condemn Him to death?*

---

[200] Mt 26.14-16/Mk 14.10-11/Lk 22.3-6.
[201] Albert Schweitzer, *The Quest of the Historical Jesus: First Compete Edition*, ed. John Bowden, 353.
[202] C.H. Dodd, *According to the Scriptures: The Sub-structure of New Testament Theology* (London: Nisbet, 1952), 101-02; C.F.D. Moule, *The Origin of Christology*, 24-26.
[203] *Sanh.* 7.5 requires that any judges who hear the accused utter blasphemy are to tear their clothes.
[204] R.E. Brown, *John (xiii-xxi)*, 877.

To answer, we must first ask, How did the Jews define blasphemy in the time of Jesus? Blasphemy was based on the Torah. Leviticus 24.15-16 has the narrow definition: "If anyone curses his God,... blasphemes the name of the LORD [s/he] shall surely be put to death." But Num 15.30-31 is more inclusive by stating, "the person who does anything defiantly,... that one is blaspheming the LORD; and that person shall be cut off ... because he has despised the word of the LORD." To be "cut off" meant either exile or execution.

The Sanhedrin's charge of blasphemy against Jesus has been much debated by both Jewish and Christian scholars. The NT passion narratives do not seem to show that Jesus violated the law of blasphemy as it appears in the Torah, especially in Lev 24. However, ancient Jewish literature reveals that the Jews' definition of blasphemy during this time was quite elastic on account of Num 15. Bruce Corley informs that Judaism interpreted these two Torah laws of blasphemy with a "wider significance in the NT period ... Blasphemy referred to acts or words which violate God's power and majesty, a claiming of prerogatives which belong to God alone."[205]

Apparently, it was not until the 2nd or 3rd century CE that Rabbinic Judaism restricted the definition of blasphemy to a single crime, as verified in *m. Sanh.* 7.5.[206] Strange to us moderns, that crime was merely uttering the sacred name of the God of Israel, YHWH, assumedly pronounced "Yahweh." Most scholars now agree that to expect that the Judaism of Jesus' day shared this narrow definition is anachronistic.[207]

Did Jewish authorities think Jesus' admission of being the Messiah violated either God's power or majesty, provoking their charge of blasphemy? Not at all. The Fourth Gospel alone contains several strands of evidence which implicitly indicate that the Jews believed that simply being the Messiah would not in and of itself usurp God's majesty.[208] Moreover, Jews never perceived messianic imposters, of which there were many, as blasphemers. Judaism only accused such pretenders of heresy, not blasphemy. Maurice Casey explains, "messiahship is a part of Jewish identity, not a threat to it."[209] Indeed, most recent Jewish authorities agree that Jesus did claim before the Sanhedrin to be the Messiah but that it did not constitute blasphemy,[210] and many contemporary Christian exegetes concur.[211] N.T. Wright explicates more precisely, "confessing to being Messiah was not blasphemous" because it was "not in itself an affront to YHWH."[212]

Then what about Jesus' admission to being the Son of God? Did the Sanhedrin deem it a claim to be God, as most devout Christians and their scholars have supposed? No. Caiaphas' question, and Jesus' reply, must be understood according to how Jews understood their appellation, "the Son of God," and not according to Hellenism.

We learned in Chapter Four that the ancient Israelites applied this title to their king as God's anointed one through whom God acts on behalf of the

---

[205] Bruce Corley, "Trial of Jesus," in *DJG* 852. Cf. Philo, *On the Life of Moses,* 2.38; Josephus, *Antiquities of the Jews,* 4.8.6.
[206] *Sanh.* 7.5.
[207] R.E. Brown (*The Death of the Messiah,* 531) examines the Greek stem *blasphem* in the LXX and the writings of Josephus and Philo, whereby he shows that it never refers to uttering the Divine Name.
[208] E.g., Jn 1.19-20, 25; 3.28; 4.29 (Samaritans); 7.26-27, 31, 41-42; 10.24; 11.27.
[209] P.M. Casey, *From Jewish Prophet to Gentile God,* 176.
[210] So says D. Catchpole, *The Trial of Jesus,* 75.
[211] E.g., R.E. Brown, *The Death of the Messiah,* 534-35.
[212] N.T. Wright, *The Challenge of Jesus,* 119.

nation of Israel. In fact, the Qumran Community used the concepts of the Davidic Messiah and a/the son of God interchangeably. Jews could designate an extraordinarily holy man as being "a son of God," indicating no more than his very intimate relationship with God.

So, Caiaphas and these other Sanhedrin members either understood the expression "the Son of God" synonymously with the term "Messiah" or as an explanation of it. Similarly, some Sanhedrin members may have regarded the two titles synonymously only when joined together.[213] That may be why Caiaphas, according to Matthew (similarly Mark), phrased his question by saying, "I adjure You by the living God that You tell us whether You are the Christ, the Son of God" (Mt 26.63 par.). Traditionalist William Lane elucidates that "the second clause stands in apposition to the first and has essentially the same meaning. In Jewish sources contemporary with the NT, 'son of God' is understood solely in a messianic sense.... The question of the high priest cannot have referred to Jesus' deity, but was limited to a single issue: do you claim to be the Messiah?"[214]

However, Joseph A. Fitzmyer remarks, "To give 'Son' (or even 'Son of God') in the Lucan Gospel exclusively the meaning of messiah is simply not convincing. On the other hand, it is not necessary to load it with the explicit affirmation of divine sonship that it acquires in the patristic writings or in the definition of the Council of Nicaea."[215]

Accordingly, like the Messiah title, a claim to be the Son of God would not conjure up the charge of blasphemy.[216] Yet the curious fact that the High Priest posed this dual question may suggest that he thought that if Jesus answered in the affirmative, such a confession would be an indictment of some sort against Himself.

A.E. Harvey convincingly establishes that identifying Jesus as "(the) Son of God" meant no more than his being God's representative, His agent par excellence, on earth.[217] He explains, "to call oneself 'Son of God' was not in itself blasphemous or punishable by law (though it might be unjustified and reprehensible).... it would be understood as a claim to be speaking or acting with the authorisation of God."[218] So, the Sanhedrin may have felt that this self-designation by Jesus infringed upon its own divine authorization.

Since claiming to be the Messiah or the Son of God does not appear to violate the Torah,[219] most recent scholars have suggested that the Sanhedrin's charge of blasphemy was provoked more by Jesus' implicit identification of Himself as the heavenly-exalted, eschatological Son of Man of Dan 7.13-14.[220] Indeed, this identification seems to be the reason the Sanhedrin stoned the first Christian martyr, Stephen, to death (Ac 7.55-60).

Many Sanhedrin members no doubt had previously heard Jesus identify Himself as "the Son of Man." Yet we have no evidence they ever objected to it. What is different now? With no qualification, there was a certain ambiguity about it (e.g., Jn 12.34). But with Jesus mentioning the clouds of heaven, for the first time He clearly specifies that He is that Son of Man of Dan 7.13-14 to whom God will grant worldwide dominion and thus authority. Also, by quoting the

---

[213] Luke, however, separates the two titles in Lk 22.67 and v. 70 to form two separate questions.
[214] W.L. Lane, *The Gospel of Mark*, 535.
[215] J.A. Fitzmyer, *The Gospel According to Luke (i-ix)*, 793-94.
[216] So says G. Vermes, *Jesus the Jew*, 36.
[217] A.E. Harvey, *Jesus and the Constraints of History*, 154-73.
[218] A.E. Harvey, *Jesus and the Constraints of History*, 171.
[219] Contra J.C. O'Neill, *Who Did Jesus Think He Was?* 48-49.
[220] So says R.E. Brown, *The Death of the Messiah*, 537.

words, "SITTING AT THE RIGHT HAND OF POWER," Jesus identifies Himself as that heavenly-exalted figure called *Adonai* ("Lord") in Ps 110.1. With Jesus invoking these two strong, heavenly images, He claims to share in the divine authority, power, and glory. These religious rulers probably thought that no human being, much less a Galilean prophet from Nazareth (Jn 1.46), had a right to make such claims.

Also, Jews generally connected Ps 110 with Ps 2. In so doing, they identified *adonai* (lord) in Ps 110.1 as *mashiah* (messiah) in Ps 2.2. In both texts, *adonai* and *mashiah* are described in close association with Yahweh. Yahweh calls *mashiah* "My King" in Ps 2.6, moreover, "My/the Son" in vv. 7, 12. Yahweh says He will install His Messiah-King-Son on Mount Zion, apparently on the eschatological Day. He adds, "Now therefore, O kings, show discernment; take warning, O judges of the earth.... Do homage to the Son, lest He become angry, and you perish in the way" (vv. 11-12). If Jesus was this Messiah-King-Son, here is a warning directed specifically to those members of the Sanhedrin who are judging Him. So, Ps 2 seems to use the titles Messiah, king, and Son synonymously. And Jews did identify these three figures with *adonai* in Ps 110.1.

Knowing this connection between Ps 110 and Ps 2, especially the warning for kings and judges respecting their treatment of Yahweh's Son, may have raised the ire of Sanhedrin members. Regardless, many Jews interpreted Mic 5 as messianic (cf. Mt 2.2-6), and it states that a "ruler" born in Bethlehem will be the "judge of Israel" (Mic 5.1-2).

Yet Jesus had previously claimed unambiguously that, as the Son of Man, He would be the eschatological Judge. But He seems to have taught it only privately to His disciples (Mt 16.27 [echoes Ps 62.12b]; 19.28; 25.31-46). At least once He taught it publicly in Jerusalem, with some of His opponents being present. He claimed that God "gave Him authority to execute judgment, because He is the Son of Man" (Jn 5.27; cf. Mk 2.1-12 par.). Worldwide, everlasting "dominion" is indeed ascribed to the Son of Man in Dan 7.14, which also implies that He will be earth's supreme Judge.

There has never been any certainty in Judaism about whether God or the Messiah will conduct the judgment.[221] However, the Son of Man is most clearly identified as the eschatological Judge in the non-canonical Similitudes of *1 Enoch*. Assuming they predate Christianity,[222] Jewish scribes would have surely known them well. The Similitudes depict the Son of Man-Chosen/Elect One-Messiah (*1 En.* 48.2, 6, 10; 49.4; 62.1-9), and they assert that "He shall judge the secret things" when He "sits on the throne of his glory" on "the day of judgment" (*1 En.* 49.3; 62.3).[223] Assuming that the non-canonical Psalms of Solomon are also pre-Christian, they state concerning Messiah that "he will judge the tribes of the people" of Israel, and "he will judge peoples and nations" (*Pss. Sol.* 17.26, 29). So, with Jesus identifying Himself as the Messiah, Son of God, and Son of Man, and thus alluding to Ps 110.1 and Dan 7.13, in effect He declares Himself to be the eschatological Judge.[224] Ironically, these Sanhedrin members are now Jesus' judges; but Jesus declares, as He had previously taught (Mt 16.27; 25.31-46; Jn 5.22), that in the future He will be their Judge. Peter Stuhlmacher sums

---

[221] A. Harnack, *History of Dogma*, 1:146n2.
[222] Matthew Black ("The Messianism of the Parables of Enoch: Their Date and Contribution to Christological Origins," in *The Messiah*, ed J.H. Charlesworth, 162) observes that even though The Similitudes are absent from the DSS, most authorities now regard *1 Enoch* 37-69 as pre-Christian.
[223] Cf. *1 En.* 61.8; *4 Ezra* 12.32-34; *2 Bar.* 40.1-2.
[224] E.g., D. Bock, *Blasphemy and Exaltation*, 28, 201-02, 208, 236. On p. 26 he informs of a growing consensus among contemporary scholars that this is the key to the blasphemy charge.

it up well by explaining, "Jesus openly confessed his messianic mission before his Jewish judges and expressed his expectation that he would be exalted to the right hand of God according to Ps 110:1 and installed in the end-time office of the Son of Man to execute the final judgment 'coming with the clouds of heaven' (Dan 7.13)."[225] Indeed, Jesus will be the Judge because, as the Son of Man, He is the archetypal, ideal man (Jn 5.27; Mk 2.10 par.). Darrell Bock well concludes of Jesus, "The claim of such authority is what caused him to be crucified."[226]

Jesus' claim to such authority and divine exaltation simply proved too much for the Sanhedrin, especially its High Priest. In Caiaphas' mind, this Jesus, this upstart pseudo-prophet who hailed from the obscure village of Nazareth, this untrained quasi-rabbi from the disreputable Galilee, from which no prophet had ever risen (Jn 7.52), this (step) son of a common laborer, He had finally claimed too much! Caiaphas and the other Sanhedrin members may have regarded Jesus' entire confession involving the three titles, but certainly the last one, as a self-designation that infringed upon the divine majesty and perhaps endangered Israel's citizens with Rome due to threat of possible riot. R.E. Brown probably represents the consensus of modern scholarship by concluding, "*the only likely historical charge would have been that Jesus arrogantly claimed for himself status or privileges that belonged properly to the God of Israel alone and in that sense implicitly demeaned God.*"[227] Furthermore, for Jesus to insinuate that He would be their Judge on judgment day, human nature being what it usually is, that settled it; He had to go![228]

This scenario is reminiscent of Joseph and his eleven brothers. Joseph is a type of the exalted Christ. And Joseph's brothers, being jealous of him and therefore hating him, typify these religious authorities doing likewise toward Jesus (Gen 37.8).

So, in accordance with the Jews' understanding of the Torah in the time of Jesus, we must conclude that Jesus did not blaspheme. Rather, these religious leaders, especially the chief priests, had increasingly personalized their conflict with Him so that their jealousy was the primary underlying cause of their charging Him with blasphemy. It came down to this question: Who possessed authority bestowed from heaven—the Sanhedrin or Jesus? Most Sanhedrin members believed that, as legal successors of Moses the Lawgiver, only they had divine authority to judge. So, they must have concluded that Jesus was acting defiantly as a blasphemer toward themselves—the divinely-approved earthly council—and thereby indirectly toward God in accordance with Num 15.30.

No Charge of Jesus Claiming to be God

Perhaps the second strongest biblical evidence, though indirect, which indicates that Jesus never claimed to be God is that the Sanhedrin never leveled this charge against Him during its interrogation of Him. Had the Sanhedrin suspected Jesus of claiming to be God, it surely would have regarded this as a more substantial blasphemy, and thus a greater offense against God, than Jesus' claim to be the Christ-Son of God-Son of Man. And it certainly would not have failed to pursue such an infraction of Torah.

---

[225] Peter Stuhlmacher, "The Messianic Son of Man: Jesus' Claim to Deity," in *Biblical Theology of the New Testament*, tr. D.P. Bailey (Grand Rapdis: Eerdmans, 2005), 343-44.
[226] Darrell L. Bock, "The Reign of the Lord Christ," in *Dispensationalism, Israel and the Church: The Search for Definition*, ed. Craig A. Blaising and Darrell L. Bock (Grand Rapids: Zondervan, 1992), 53.
[227] R.E. Brown, *The Death of the Messiah*, 531. Emphasis his.
[228] In no way whatsoever did Jesus' answer violate the Torah (e.g., Ex 22.28).

Granted, this is an argument from silence; but such silence is surely impossible if any members of the Sanhedrin had suspected that Jesus had ever claimed to be God. Few scholars have recognized the strength of this argument. J.A.T. Robinson surely did.[229] He insisted that *if Jesus had ever claimed to be God, "it is inconceivable,... that it should not come out in the charges against him at the trial, where again the worst that can be said about him is that he claimed to be 'God's son'"* (emphasis mine).[230]

So, throughout Jesus' public career the sum of the religious rulers' allegations, or lack thereof, against Him is that they went from (1) accusing Him earlier of claiming to be equal with God (Jn 5.18>), (2) then charging Him with making Himself out to be God (Jn 10.33>), and, finally, (3) the highest religious tribunal in the land indicting Him for only claiming to be the Christ, the Son of God, the Son of Man. Apparently, those who made these early allegations either were persuaded otherwise by Jesus' immediate replies or upon subsequent reflection. *If the Sanhedrin never accused Jesus of claiming to be God, how can later Christians justify their assertion that Jesus made such a claim?*

The Trial before Pilate[231]

Under Roman rule, the Great Sanhedrin was permitted to pronounce the death penalty upon the criminally accused. Whether this Sanhedrin possessed civil authority to carry out executions at this particular time in history, or the Roman Empire reserved final consent regarding any Sanhedrin death sentences, uncertainty still prevails among the best authorities.[232] The situation appears to have been somewhat fluid throughout much of the 1st century,[233] which seems to have been the case at this time.

Apparently, Sanhedrin officials had hoped to convince the Roman governor to rubber-stamp their indictment and carry out their death sentence. To consummate their diabolical scheme, they brought Jesus to Pontius Pilate, Roman procurator (governor) of Judea (26-37 CE), and presented Him as a criminal deserving of death. They no doubt knew that they had no capital case against Jesus with respect to Roman law and that their charge of religious blasphemy was irrelevant to it. So Pilate had to ask them, "'What accusation do you bring against this Man?' They answered and said to him, 'If this Man were not an evildoer, we would not have delivered Him up to you'" (Jn 18.29-30).

Ha! What a lame, arrogant reply. And it has no specifics for due process of law. Since that didn't fly with the governor, they next accused Jesus of claiming to be a king. That seems to have gotten Pilate's attention; for he promptly took the accused into his judgment chambers for private questioning.

There was a sect of Judaism, called "the Zealots," that advocated the overthrow of Roman domination of Israel. It seems that one of Jesus' twelve

---

[229] So does M.M.B. Turner, "The Spirit of Christ and Christology," 170.

[230] J.A.T. Robinson, *The Priority of John*, 387.

[231] For purposes of consolidation, Johannine information respecting this episode is included in this section.

[232] Schurer, 2:219-23, 219n80; Eduard Lohse, "*sunhedrion*," in *TDNT* 7:865-66. However, Jn 18.31 seems to indicate that the Jews had no civil authority to execute criminals.

[233] After the Romans installed a governor in Judea, in 6 CE, it appears that thereafter the Sanhedrin no longer possessed authority to execute criminals. Sometime after Jesus' death, however, it did sentence and execute Stephen and James, Jesus' brother (Ac 7.59-60; Josephus, *Antiquities of the Jews*, xx, ix, 1). Yet both *Sanh*. 18a and 24b state, "The right to try capital cases was taken from Israel forty years before the destruction of the Temple." Historians generally think the number "forty" may be inaccurate.

apostles, "Simon the Zealot," was a former member of this group (Mk 3.18 par.). But as a follower of Jesus, he must have abandoned the Zealots and their ideology. For, His Master certainly was no political revolutionary. This is evident when Jesus gave the reply to the question of paying taxes, "Render to Caesar the things that are Caesar's" (Mk 12.17 par.). More than any other Jews, Zealots detested paying taxes to Rome.

So, Jesus admitted to the governor that His destiny was indeed to be the king of Israel but that His kingdom was not of this world (Lk 23.2; Jn 18.33-37). Pilate clearly did not regard such an answer as seditious; for he returned to the Jewish religious officials and announced, "I find no guilt in this man" (Lk 23.4; cf. Jn 18.38).

But that didn't matter to them; they already had their minds mind up, and nothing the governor said was going to change them. Thus, they persisted in demanding Jesus' death. The governor tolerated them by returning to question Jesus again and then going back out a second time to announce the same thing. Pilate wanted to free Jesus (Ac 3.13).

Pontius Pilate had an unsavory reputation for cruelty and anti-Semitism.[234] He therefore cared little, or nothing, about accommodating Jews. But at this particular time he appears to have been concerned about the possibility of a mob riot breaking out. Such possible disturbances had always loomed large at the Jews' festivals while their country remained under Roman domination. Indeed, their history of the Maccabean Wars, as well as their civil war in 90-85 BCE, would cause most any subsequent Roman administrator of governance and justice to be concerned about any possible rebellious outbreak. That is why an extra large company of Roman soldiers was kept stationed at Antonia Fortress, attached to the north wall of the temple grounds, during such Jewish festivals.

None of the allegations that Sanhedrin rulers brought against Jesus impressed the governor until they exclaimed to him, "We have a law, and by that law He ought to die because He made Himself out to be the Son of God" (Jn 19.7; "a son of God").[235] And when Jesus later hung on the cross, Sanhedrin officials stood gawking at Jesus and mocked, "He said, 'I am the Son of God'" (Mt 27.43; "a son of God"). It appears from this allegation that they *may not* have equated the titles "Messiah" and "Son of God" but that, in their minds, the latter represented Jesus' highest claim for Himself and one that usurped the divine authority believed to have been invested in the Sanhedrin. Regardless, this evidence further affirms that *Sanhedrin authorities did not interpret Jesus' claim to be (the) Son of God as a self-identification as God.*

Recall in Chapter Four that one common messianic view of that time was that the Davidic Messiah-King would be concealed prior to his earthly appearance, suggesting preexistence, and so have a mysterious origin (*1 En.* 62.7).[236] That is why some Jews said to Jesus, "whenever the Christ may come, no one knows where He is from" (Jn 7.27).

This belief in a Messiah "from who knows where" was reminiscent of Graeco-Roman mythology. Most of those pagans believed in myths about gods

---

[234] Philo, *On the Virtues*, 301-02.

[235] *Huios* ("Son") is anarthrous (without the article "the") in Jn 10.36 and 19.7, as well as Mt 14.33, 27.43 and v. 54, in both UB⁴ and NA²⁷, the two most recent Greek NT texts. The NEB rendering of Jn 19.7 is thus more accurate: "he has claimed to be Son of God." And "(a) son/Son" is more natural in all of these texts.

[236] Cf. *1 En.* 48.6; *4 Ezra* 12.32. However, scholars debate if *1 En.* 48.2-6 means that the Son of Man preexisted creation or merely that His "name," and therefore implicitly God's plan for Him, preexisted. Either way, these two passages in *1 Enoch* seem to represent a commentary on Isa 49.2.

procreating other gods, to be called a "son of god," and some of their offspring coming down to earth in human form. For example, in Greek mythology Zeus was the son of the gods Kronos and Rhea. Zeus was believed literally to have cohabited with mortal women on earth and thereby to have fathered both gods and men. In fact, Stoics believed that Zeus was the father of all men. In addition, many Greeks thought the god Apollos sired the famous philosopher—Plato. Or take the NT; one time the Apostle Paul healed a man born lame and the Gentile multitude shouted, "The gods have become like men and have come down to us" (Ac 14.11). Another time a poisonous viper bit Paul; but when he didn't swell up and die, as expected, the people "began to say that he was a god" (Ac 28.6).

Pilate would have been familiar with such pagan lore and probably the Jews' law of blasphemy. Yet he cared little for these Sanhedrin officials or their religion (cf. Jn 18.35). Besides, Jewish religious law, called *halakah*, was subservient to Roman jurisprudence. On account of *Pax Romana* (Roman Peace), Roman administrators of the government were only required to formally respect local religions and their traditions, i.e., those religions Rome had officially sanctioned.

But did Pilate believe at all in mythology? He *did* become "more afraid" when these Jewish religious rulers reported to him that Jesus had "made Himself out to be the Son of God" (Jn 19.7). Alarmed, Pilate quickly returned to his chambers to ask Jesus, "Where are You from?" (v. 9), and he didn't mean Galilee. The governor had already asked Him about that (Lk 23.6-7).

Could Pilate have surmised if Jesus was a god in human form, maybe possessing magical powers due to His reputation for healings and exorcisms?[237] The later Jewish Babylonian Talmud alleges, "Yeshua of Nazareth" was executed "because he practiced sorcery and enticed Israel to apostasy."[238] This assessment must have gone back to the time of Jesus. Plus, while Pilate was interrogating Jesus, he received a startling message from his wife that read, "Have nothing to do with this righteous Man; for last night I suffered greatly in a dream because of Him" (Mt 27.19). This letter must have rattled Pilate's composure because he tried more earnestly to defend Jesus and release Him.[239]

Now, there was a tradition during the Passover Festival in which the governor was accustomed to set free a single prisoner selected by the multitude. When Pilate offered to release Jesus, the multitude shouted back, "Not this Man, but Barabbas" (Jn 18.40). Barabbas apparently was the leader of a group of imprisoned insurrectionists who had committed robbery and murder (Mk 15.7). At first, Pilate ignored this request. Instead, he tried to appease their unrelenting wrath by scourging the accused and announcing for the third time that he found no guilt in Him (Lk 23.22; Jn 18.38; 19.4, 6). But Pilate's efforts proved to no avail, since the chief priests had stirred up the multitude (Mk 15.11). So, the people yelled repeatedly, "Crucify, crucify Him!" (Lk 23.21 par.).

Jesus' crafty opponents had one last ploy in their diabolical scheme to overcome the governor's resistance. They solemnly declared, "If you release this Man, you are no friend of Caesar; everyone who makes himself out to be a king opposes Caesar" (Jn 19.12). This charge recalls the frequent manipulation

---

[237] Suggested by R.E. Brown (*John [xiii-xxi]*, 877-78), who also cites C.H. Dodd (*Historical Tradition in the Fourth Gospel* [Cambridge: University, 1963], 113-14) and R. Bultmann (*John*, 512) for support. Bultmann (*John*, 661) claims that the question really means, "Are you a man or a divine being?"

[238] *Sanh.* 43a.

[239] The NT assessment of the Roman trial of Jesus was that the Jewish religious authorities were determined to get Jesus executed whereas Governor Pilate wanted to release Him (Ac 3.13-15; cf. Lk 24.20).

of the Roman treason law for political gain,[240] and it *really* got the governor's attention. Disloyalty to Caesar was the worst charge that could be leveled against a Roman official. Loyalty to Caesar was the highest law in the land. Members of the Roman Senate were called "Friend of Caesar."

This Jewish charge against the governor was ingenious because of what happened earlier. Pilate had set up in his Jerusalem headquarters several golden shields dedicated to Emperor Tiberius. The Judeans protested these imageless shields, likening them to idols. When Pilate refused to remove them, these Judeans took their complaint to the emperor. Pilate suffered disgrace when the emperor sent him a letter ordering that the shields be removed and warning him to uphold Jewish religious traditions.

Paul L. Maier, an authority on Pontius Pilate, claims that "the episode of the golden shields *is critically important in understanding Pilate's conduct at the trial*" of Jesus.[241] Maier adds a paraphrase to the Jews' allegation, "you recall Tiberius' threatening letter to you five months ago: if he upheld us then in the case of the golden shields, he'll uphold us now in a far more serious manner. You, Pilate, will have to leave your exclusive club of the Friends of Caesar.... You will make your exit via the usual means for disgraced members: exile, or compulsory suicide."[242]

Pilate evidently was quite shaken at this challenge to the sincerity of his imperial allegiance. But he was also worried that "a riot was starting" to break out (Mt 27.24). So the governor finally succumbed to the Jews' political pressure, charged Jesus with implicit treason for having kingly aspirations, and condemned Him to death. It appears from secular sources that, at least at this time, only the highest Roman official in equestrian provinces, in this case, Pontius Pilate, had authority to execute criminals.[243]

Ironically, these Jewish religious rulers, in condemning Jesus to death, sealed their own condemnation before God. Apparently due to the heightened passion of the moment, the chief priests had also exclaimed to Pilate, "We have no king but Caesar" (Jn 18.15). By blurting out this most irrational statement for a religious Jew, they not only rejected Jesus as their Messiah-King but unwittingly rejected the messianic concept itself and,[244] above all, the OT injunction to make God their king!

Here is the sum of this judicial process that brought about Jesus' condemnation and execution: (1) some Sanhedrin members held a preliminary hearing in which they charged Jesus guilty of blasphemy for claiming to be the Christ, the Son of God, the Son of Man, (2) shortly thereafter the Sanhedrin officially condemned Jesus to death, and (3) the Sanhedrin then brought Jesus to the Roman governor, who conducted an official trial of his own in which he condemned Jesus to death on a trumped-up charge of insurrection and thereupon had Him crucified. *Throughout the two entire legal proceedings, no one accused Jesus of ever having claimed to be God.*

---

[240] A.N. Sherwin-White, *Roman Society and Roman Law in the New Testament*, 47.

[241] Paul L. Maier, *First Easter: The True and Unfamiliar Story in Words and Pictures* (New York: Harper & Row, 1973), 59. Emphasis his.

[242] P.L. Maier, *First Easter*, 72-73.

[243] So says E.P. Sanders (*The Historical Figure of Jesus*, 310-11n28) by consulting contemporary Roman historians and citing authority Sherwin-White in *Roman Society and Roman Law in the New Testament*.

[244] Rudolf Karl Bultmann, *The Gospel of John: A Commentary*, tr. G.R. Beasley-Murray (Philadelphia: Westminster, 1971), 665; G.R. Beasley-Murray, *John*, 343.

The Crucified Jesus

There is light at the cross. Whenever Roman officials crucified capital criminals, they usually chose locations that were very accessible to the local population in order to warn potential evildoers. Golgotha was located just outside Jerusalem and apparently adjacent to a prominent thoroughfare. That is why, regarding the crucified Jesus, pedestrians "passing by were hurling abuse at Him, wagging their heads, and saying,... 'If You are the Son of God, come down from the cross'" (Mt 27.39-40). Such taunts suggest that Jesus' answer to the High Priest's question had quickly circulated throughout the city and that it served as the basis, or part of the basis, for the charge of blasphemy. In addition, the religious rulers likewise chimed in sarcastically by quoting Ps 22.8: "HE TRUSTS IN GOD; LET HIM DELIVER HIM NOW, IF HE TAKES PLEASURE IN HIM; for He said, 'I am the Son of God'" (Mt 27.43). By quoting from this psalm, which the NT repeatedly interprets as messianic and therefore applies it to Jesus, these rulers indicted themselves as those who "sneer" and "wag the head" at Messiah (Ps 22.7). Also, by quoting this psalm they acknowledged, although sarcastically, that Jesus claimed to *trust* in God, and they acknowledged un-sarcastically that Jesus distinguished Himself from God. These disparaging remarks therefore emerge as further evidence that those Jewish religious authorities never perceived that Jesus had ever claimed to be God.

Conclusion

Thus, *the NT accounts of the two legal proceedings conducted against Jesus, as well as the crucifixion scene, provide overwhelming evidence that Jesus' accusers no longer perceived Him as ever having claimed to be God.* Earlier, they had indeed made this allegation on two separate occasions, recorded in Jn 5.18> and 10.33>. But when we come to Chapter Six, we will see that in each case Jesus denied their charge. So, the fact that the Sanhedrin never accused Jesus of ever claiming to be God suggests that those Jews who made this earlier allegation had by now accepted Jesus' denial of it.

Even though a large majority of contemporary scholars insist that the Synoptic Gospels do not contain any evidence that either Jesus or His disciples believed that Jesus was God, there are still some traditionalist scholars who think otherwise. Therefore, we must cast our fishing line farther and deeper into the crystal-clear, christological waters of the Synoptic Gospels to try to fish for, catch, and examine a few small problem passages that are swimming around out there.

G. Problem Passages

1. Does calling Jesus "Immanuel" in Matt. 1.23 mean He is "God"?

Matthew says Jesus' birth fulfilled Isa 7.14. He quotes it and explains as follows:

Mt 1.23 "'BEHOLD, THE VIRGIN SHALL BE WITH CHILD, AND SHALL BEAR A SON, AND THEY SHALL CALL HIS NAME IMMANUEL,' which translated means, 'GOD WITH US.'"

Because of the doctrine of Jesus' virgin birth, Isa 7.14 and Mt 1.23 have received considerable attention throughout church history. The reason is that

Isaiah's Hebrew word *almah* has aroused much scholarly debate as to whether it means "a virgin." If it does not, Isa 7.14 does not seem to be a prophecy of Jesus' mother, the Virgin Mary.

However, our subject concerns another issue in Mt 1.23. Put in question form, How did Matthew understand Isaiah's ascription of the word "Immanuel" to a child? Regardless of whether Isaiah intended his prophecy in Isa 7.14 to be messianic, which also has been much debated among critical scholars, Matthew obviously understood it that way. And he treats "Immanuel" as a title, not a proper name, for Jesus. For he had just related in v. 21 that the angel had instructed Joseph, "you shall call His name Jesus."

This word "Immanuel" represents the joining of two Hebrew words: *immanu* and *el*. Since *el* is the shortened Hebrew form for "God" (Heb. *elohim*), some traditionalists assert that ascribing the title "Immanuel" to Jesus effectively identifies Him as God.[245]

On the contrary, joining these two words means exactly what Matthew says it does: "God with us."[246] That is, calling Jesus "Immanuel" merely indicates that God is present with His people through Jesus as His agent. It means what someone exclaimed when Jesus raised the widow's dead son to life: "God has visited His people" (Lk 7.16). The Apostle Peter once preached likewise, saying that Jesus "went about doing good and healing" people because "God was with Him" through the anointing of "the Holy Spirit" (Ac 10.38). Jewish scholar Geza Vermes rightly explains, "Jews would have known that the name Emmanuel ('God is with us') signified not the incarnation of God in human form, but a promise of divine help to the Jewish people."[247]

Some traditionalists, to support their view that "Immanuel" in Mt 1.23 indicates that Jesus is God, also connect Isa 7.14 with the distinctly messianic Isa 9.6>, which applies the Hebrew title *el gibbor* to Messiah. But we saw in Chapter Four that *el gibbor* in Isa 9.6> should be translated "mighty warrior," or the like, rather than "Mighty God."

Calling Jesus "Immanuel" is similar to the names of some OT saints. For example, Israel, Elijah, Elisha, Daniel, Michael, Ezekiel, and Joel contain *el*, meaning "God;" but those parents who so named their child did not intend it as a declaration that their child was God. The same is true of those names that contain the shortened form of Yahweh.

Most traditionalist authorities now concede that Mt 1.23 does not identify Jesus as "God." For instance, Murray Harris dismisses the argument that it does so by explaining, "Matthew is not saying, 'Someone who is "God" is now physically with us,' but 'God is acting on our behalf in the person of Jesus.'"[248] And A.W. Wainwright points out that Matthew's explanation can be understood in two ways: either as (1) "God with us," implying that Jesus is God, or as (2) "God *is* with us," which means no more than that God mystically indwells Jesus. Wainwright concludes, "because of its ambiguity this passage cannot be used as evidence that Jesus was called God."[249]

---

[245] E.g., John C. Fenton, "Matthew and the Divinity of Jesus," in *Studia Biblica 1978/Sixth International Congress on Biblical Studies, Oxford 3-7 April 1978*, ed. Elizabeth A. Livingstone (Sheffield: University, 1979-80).

[246] The Greek text in Mt 1.23, *meth amon ho theos*, is translated "God with us" in AV, RV, RSV, NASB, NIV; but it is translated "God is with us" in NEB, TCNT, TEV, JB, NRSV. Both translations mean the same.

[247] G. Vermes, *The Changing Faces of Jesus*, 212.

[248] M. Harris, *Jesus as God*, 258.

[249] A.W. Wainwright, *The Trinity in the New Testament*, 72.

This idea of God being *with* Jesus is similar to the ending of Matthew's gospel, in which the risen Jesus said to His disciples, "lo, I am with you always" (Mt 28.20).

2. Is the Doctrine of The Trinity in Matthew 28.19?

The most well-known Trinitarian passage in the NT is Mt 28.19. It tells about the resurrected Jesus appearing to His disciples and entrusting to them His program for world evangelism, now often called "the Great Commission." There has been some controversy regarding these words of Jesus. The entire saying reads as follows:

18 And Jesus came up and spoke to them, saying, "All authority has been given to Me in heaven and on earth.
19 Go therefore and make disciples of all the nations, baptizing them in the name of the Father and the Son and the Holy Spirit,
20 teaching them to observe all that I commanded you; and lo, I am with you always, even to the end of the age" (Mt 28.18-20).

We should not be surprised that critics have dismissed this purported *logion* of Jesus as unauthentic. They have regarded it as the creation of the Matthean church community in a late stage of doctrinal development of the NT documents. Church fathers, on the other hand, embraced a conservative view of the inspiration of Scripture and therefore assessed *most* of this saying as the authentic expression of Jesus, and that is how it shall be treated herein. There is, however, a textual problem in the latter half of Mt 28.19. A few patristic writings and versions quote v. 19, but omit its second clause that begins with the word "baptizing." And the parallel passage in Mk 16.15 suggests the same omission. That is partly why critical scholars reject this entire saying of Jesus in Mt 20.18-20 as being more historically unreliable than any other synoptic saying of Jesus. Nevertheless, this second clause in v. 19 has strong MS attestation.

Another problem with Mt 28.19b is that it has been the source of much debate concerning the question of what is the proper formula to be uttered during the Christian rite of water baptism. Throughout church history, priests, ministers, and pastors usually have uttered the Matthean formula while baptizing converts. This practice continues in most churches today, but certainly not all. The United Pentecostal Church does not use it. It contends that converts should be baptized "in Jesus name only" in accordance with the baptismal wording recorded in the book of Acts. (This Pentecostal praxis relates to their Sabellian Christology, that God is one person existing in three distinct modes: Father, Son, and Spirit.) Indeed, Acts shows that the early Christians did baptize solely "in the name of (the Lord) Jesus (Christ),"[250] and it provides no information that they baptized according to this seemingly later Matthean formula. So, the overall NT evidence seems to support this Pentecostal contention, especially if one puts credence in the concept of a developmental Christology in the NT period. However, it does not appear from the NT that the early church adopted rigid liturgies, specifically that it sanctioned only one baptismal formula over others. So, the instruction in Mt 28.19 does not preclude another formula.

Since United Pentecostals are anti-Trinitarian, they also insist that this Matthean formula does not substantiate the doctrine of the Trinity because the

---
[250] Ac 2.38; 8.16; 10.48; 19.5; cf. Rom 6.3; 1 Cor 6.11.

word "name," in the phrase "in the name" (Gr. *eis to onoma*), appears in the singular. They argue that if the early Christians had intended for this formula to indicate separate persons, it would be plural—"in the names." Indeed, *eis to onoma* is a unique and difficult expression. Some scholars dismiss this argument and treat the phrase as a rendering of the Hebrew word *hashem*, translating it "with respect/regard to"[251] or "with fundamental reference to."[252]

Contrary to popular opinion, NT formulas like that in Mt 28.19 do not substantiate either that Jesus is God or that the doctrine of the Trinity is correct. Juxtapositioning the Father, Jesus Christ, and the Holy Spirit only bears witness to their association and unity of purpose. Thus, the Father giving Jesus authority suggests that Jesus was not co-equal in essence with the Father. (See Appendix A: The Doctrine of the Trinity.)

3. Does Jesus' authority to forgive sins in Mark 2.5-7 mean He is God?

During antiquity, both rabbinical theologians and Greek theistic philosophers taught that God possesses certain prerogatives that belong only to Him. Rabbis insisted that one of those prerogatives is the forgiveness of sins, and Christian traditionalists later accepted this axiom. They therefore asserted that since Jesus claimed the authority to forgive sins, and only God can forgive sins, this indicates that Jesus was God.

The synoptists report two instances in which Jesus verbally forgave someone's sins that were *not* committed personally against Jesus. Only Luke relates one instance, in which a woman of ill repute anointed Jesus' feet with perfume while she simultaneously wept profusely (Lk 7.36-50). Then Jesus said to her, "Your sins have been forgiven" (v. 48). Those present wondered to themselves, "Who is this man who even forgives sins?" (v. 49). A similar episode happened that is reported by all three synoptists, and their accounts are more developed. Jesus healed a paralytic man who was let down through the roof in a house while he was lying helplessly on his bed-pallet (Mt 9.1-8; Mk 2.1-12; Lk 5.17-26). In Mark's account, the portion that pertains to Christology is as follows:

5 And Jesus seeing their faith said to the paralytic, "My son, your sins are forgiven."
6 But there were some of the scribes sitting there and reasoning in their hearts,
7 "Why does this man speak that way? He is blaspheming; who can forgive sins but God alone?"
8 And immediately Jesus, aware in His spirit that they were reasoning that way within themselves, said to them, "Why are you reasoning about these things in your hearts?
9 "Which is easier, to say to the paralytic, 'Your sins are forgiven;' or to say, 'Arise, and take up your pallet and walk?'
10 "But in order that you may know that the Son of Man has authority on earth to forgive sins"—He said to the paralytic—

---
[251] E.g., H. Bietenhard, *TDNT* 5:274.
[252] E.g., Nils Alstrup Dahl, *Jesus the Christ: The Historical Origins of Christological Doctrine*, ed. Donald H. Juel (Minneapolis: Fortress, 1991), 177; R. Gundry, *Matthew: A Commentary on His Handbook*, 596. Regardless, most contemporary scholars, including some conservatives like D.A. Carson ("Matthew," 598), do not regard this post-resurrection saying of Jesus as His *ipsissima verba* (actual words).

11 "I say to you, rise, take up your pallet and go home."
12 And he rose and immediately took up the pallet and went out in the sight of all; so that they were all amazed and were glorifying God, saying, "We have never seen anything like this."

Scribes were the biblical scholars of that time, the recognized authorities in interpreting the Law of Moses. Luke more specifically identifies "Pharisees and teachers of the law sitting there" (Lk 5.17). Jesus no doubt posed His question for the benefit of the crowd, which would have been aware of the traditional precept behind the scribes' thinking. The common answer to Jesus' question would be that it would be impossible for anyone to heal a paralytic; if Jesus healed him, it would seem to demonstrate that He had the authority to forgive the man's sins as well. In Judaism, lameness and sins were thought to be inter-related (e.g., Jn 5.14; 9.2), and so were healing and divine salvation, which includes divine forgiveness (e.g., Isa 35.4-5).

These scribes inwardly accused Jesus of blasphemy because of their tradition that the authority to forgive sins in a final sense is a prerogative that belongs only to God. Judaism had determined that even the promised Messiah could not forgive sins. So, these scribes took Jesus' assertion as an affront to God's majesty, if not an implied claim to be God. In the Torah, insulting God's dignity was the primary basis of blasphemy.

Christian traditionalists have usually agreed with these Jewish scribes, and their tradition, that only God can forgive sins. And they have further alleged that Jesus' claim to forgive sins was an indirect claim to be God. But were these scribes right, that only God can forgive sins and that if anyone else professes to do so it is blasphemy? E.P. Sanders claims that "such a pronouncement would not be regarded as blasphemy by any known Jewish law or by any known interpretation."[253] If Sanders is correct, that must be why this accusation was never made later, at Jesus' examination before the Sanhedrin.

Jesus' announcement of forgiveness, in Mk 2.5, is in the passive voice and thus is somewhat ambiguous.[254] Indeed, the scribes seem to have been rather perplexed as to what Jesus meant. Did He mean that God had forgiven the paralytic and that Jesus was merely exercising His prophetic office by announcing that fact? That is what the prophet Nathan did when he said to penitent King David, "The LORD also has taken away your sin" (2 Sam 12.13). However, in v. 10 Jesus made it perfectly clear that He possessed authority to forgive sins. Surely, any such decision on His part would not be contrary to the divine will but commensurate with it. Indeed, the Johannine Jesus explained, "if I do judge, My judgment is true; for I am not alone in it, but I and He who sent Me" (Jn 8.16).

In addition, when Jesus healed the paralytic the attending crowd responded by "glorifying God" (Mk 2.12; Lk 5.25-26). This does not mean that they glorified Jesus *as* God. Matthew explains, "But when the multitudes saw this, they were filled with awe, and glorified God, who had given such authority to men" (Mt 9.8). In other words, the people glorified God because they rightly recognized that God had given Jesus authority to heal as well as to forgive sins. And it is evident from the last clause that this was Matthew's understanding as well. Traditionalist M.M.B. Turner further explains, "the significance which Jesus attaches to his pronouncement of forgiveness and the corroborating miracle, is

---
[253] E.P. Sanders, *The Historical Figure of Jesus*, 213.
[254] Dieter Zeller, "Jesus," in *DDD* 468.

not that he shares the divine essence but rather that he already has the authority of the Son of man to execute God's judgment (Mk 2:10)."[255]

This probably was the first time during Jesus' public ministry that He claimed authority to forgive sins. But it was not His last. At least two more times Jesus expressly claimed authority to judge on judgment day (e.g., Mt 16.27; 25.31-46). Surely such authority includes the right to do so prior to that time, e.g., at that moment when the paralytic was brought to Him. Besides, the Johannine Jesus seems to have not restricted His authority to forgive only on judgment day because He announced, "For not even the Father [alone] judges anyone, but He has given all judgment to the Son" (Jn 5.22).

Furthermore, the authority to forgive sins in a final sense is a prerogative that God has delegated to others besides Jesus. And when He has done so, the recipients of such authority have not been perceived as being God.[256] As we saw in Chapter Four, the best OT example is "the angel of the LORD." God had instructed the wandering Israelites regarding this patron angel, "Be on your guard before him and obey his voice; do not be rebellious toward him, for he will not pardon your transgression" (Ex 23.21). The implication is that the Angel of the LORD has authority to forgive Israel's sins.

Also, Jesus' instructions to His disciples about binding and loosing allude to a networking of forgiveness between God and men. The first time this occurred was when Jesus gave Peter the keys of the kingdom of God and told him that he would be the first of the apostles to open and close the door(s) to the kingdom. In other words, whatever Peter chose to bind or loose on earth would be bound or loosed in heaven, with heaven being a euphemism meaning that God would approve of it (Mt 16.19; cf. 18.18). The second time this occurred, Jesus was more specific. It seems to have involved, among other things, both forgiving sin and refusing to forgive sin by calling down judgment from heaven. For, Matthew records that this promise of Jesus was given in the context of forgiveness (Mt 18.15-17, 21-35).

Jesus made this even clearer during one of His post-resurrection appearances, when He mysteriously breathed the Holy Spirit onto His disciples. Then He said to them, "If you forgive the sins of any, their sins have been forgiven them; if you retain the sins of any, they have been retained" (Jn 20.23). R.E. Brown illuminates the meaning of the first clause by paraphrasing it, "When you forgive men's sins, at that moment God forgives those sins and they remain forgiven."[257] This bestowal of the Holy Spirit as well as Jesus' associated proclamation about the authority to forgive sins represents the transference of power and authority from Jesus unto His disciples. The result, of course, is a continuation of Jesus' ministry on earth following His ascension into heaven.

It must therefore be concluded that if God grants authority to forgive sins to angels or men, and it does not indicate that they are God, Jesus' authority to forgive sins does not necessarily imply that He is God either. Neither does Jesus' authority to judge on the day of judgment necessarily make Him God. And this prerogative does not belong to Jesus inherently but has been granted to Him by the Father (Jn 5.22, 27; 8.16).

Finally, when church fathers interpreted that Jesus forgiving sins, in Mk 2.5-7, means that He was God, they contradicted another aspect of their theology. They insisted that the prerogative to forgive sins belongs only to deity

---

[255] M.M.B. Turner, "The Spirit of Christ and Christology," 171.
[256] See D. Cupitt, *Jesus and the Gospel of God*, 16-17.
[257] R.E. Brown, *John (xiii-xxi)*, 1024.

and thus Jesus' divine nature. Yet Jesus had said that the reason He possessed this authority to forgive sins was that He was "the Son of Man." Church fathers, and many subsequent traditionalists, believed that Jesus' status as the Son of Man referred exclusively to His human nature.

4. Did Jesus imply He was God to the rich young man in Mark 10.18?

All three synoptists record the conversation between Jesus and the rich young ruler. This account has left an indelible mark on Christian tradition for several reasons, mostly Jesus' picturesque but hyperbolic remark, "It is easier for a camel to go through the eye of a needle than for a rich man to enter the kingdom of God" (Mk 10.25 par.).

This pericope has been much disputed in the past because some traditionalists thought it contains christological implications. But, before addressing this issue, we need to consider the harmonizing difficulty that exists between the synoptic accounts.

Mark and Luke relate that a rich young ruler ran up to Jesus, knelt down, and asked Him, "'Good Teacher, what shall I do to inherit eternal life?' And Jesus said to him, 'Why do you call Me good? No one is good except God alone'" (Mk 10.17-18/Lk 18.18-19). On the other hand, Matthew recounts the conversation quite differently: "And behold, one came to Him and said, 'Teacher, what good thing shall I do that I may obtain eternal life?' And He said to him, 'Why are you asking Me about what is good? There is only One who is good'" (Mt 19.16-17).[258] Jesus' question has christological implications. His critical words in these two different accounts can be arranged as follows:

Mk 10.18/Lk 18.19 "Why do you call Me good? No one is good except God alone."
Mt 19.17 "Why are you asking Me about what is good? There is only One who is good."

The apparent discrepancy in accounts is probably attributed to Mark and Luke providing the *ipsissma verba* (exact words) whereas Matthew has typically editorialized Jesus' words to clarify a potential misunderstanding about Jesus' sinlessness.[259]

But we are most concerned with the christological implications of Jesus' words. Indeed, church fathers seized on this Mark-Luke account as proof that Jesus herein indirectly claimed to be God. Later, John Bengal argued likewise in his dispute with the Socinians.[260] Today, however, most traditionalist scholars correctly differ with these doctrinal forebears, dismissing the passage as having no christological significance.

This pericope is pregnant with meaning regarding Judaism and its view of Torah. As for the man calling Jesus "Good Teacher," he may have meant no more than a respectful address suitable for rabbis, though this usage is not found in Jewish sources.[261]

---

[258] The AV has, "*there* is none good but one, *that is*, God," which represents a scribal assimilation to the Synoptics. See B.M. Metzger, *The Text of the New Testament*, 193.
[259] Walter Grundmann, "*agathos*," in *TDNT* 1:15-16.
[260] J. Bengal, *Bengal's New Testament Commentary*, 1:352.
[261] W.L. Lane, *The Gospel of Mark*, 365.

It is important to ask what Jesus' purpose was in answering the man's question. It could not have been to identify Himself as God; that response would have been irrelevant to the man's question. Neb Stonehouse states, "Jesus is not occupied here with questions of Christology."[262] Even John Calvin, who never passed an opportunity to defend Christ's supposed deity, admits that Jesus "is not therefore affirming the essence of His deity."[263]

During the early and mid-20th century, B.B. Warfield was one of America's leading conservative and staunchly Trinitarian theologians. He provides what many conservative scholars have regarded as a classic treatment of Mk 10.18/Lk 18.19. He asserts, "The question of the relation of Jesus to this God does not emerge: there is equally no denial that He is God, and no affirmation that He is God."[264] Warfield quotes five other biblical scholars of his time who held the same view. One of them was Presbyterian J.A. Alexander, whose father founded Princeton Theological Seminary. Alexander remarks on this passage, "The goodness of our Lord Himself and His divinity are then not at all in question, and are consequently neither affirmed nor denied."[265]

Then what did Jesus mean when He said, "no one is good but God alone"? In the OT,[266] Judaism, and especially Hellenistic theism,[267] only God was recognized as "good" in an *absolute* sense. And this must be Jesus' intended meaning. Human beings were called "good" only in a *derived* sense,[268] with God recognized as the Source of their goodness. Characterizing God as perfectly good was thought to bring honor to Him. So, Jesus' remark reflects the common belief at that time about God. It has nothing to do with the use of the word "good" in distinguishing moral differences between human beings.

Similarly, the NT often describes Jesus as "holy."[269] Yet in the Apocalypse, those who will overcome the Antichrist will eventually sing a song, saying of God the Father, "O Lord God, the Almighty;... Thou alone art holy" (Rev 15.3-4). Apparently, they mean this in an absolute sense, since Jesus' holiness is derived from God the Father.

Actually, Jesus was contrasting the rich man's lack of goodness with that absolute perfect goodness of God. This man thought that he was good; yet he also recognized that Jesus was good. Jesus exposed the man's lack of goodness, to which the man was blind, when He said to him, "If you want to be perfect, go, sell your possessions and give to the poor,... Then come, follow me" (Mt 19.21 NIV; cf. AV, RSV, JB). If the man would have done what Jesus advised, he would have fulfilled the commandment given in Lev 19.18, to love your neighbor as yourself. In fact, Matthew adds that Jesus explained goodness by quoting some of the Ten Commandments, ending with this catchall precept (v. 19).

---

[262] Ned B. Stonehouse, *Origins of the Synoptic Gospels: Some Basic Questions* (Grand Rapids: Eerdmans, 1963), 105.
[263] John Calvin, *A Harmony of the Gospels Matthew, Mark and Luke* in *Calvin's Commentaries* [1572], 3 vols., (repr. Grand Rapids: Eerdmans, 1972), 2:254.
[264] B.B. Warfield, *Christology and Criticism*, 3:107.
[265] Quoted by B.B. Warfield, *Christology and Criticism*, 3:107, n24.
[266] E.g., Ps 16.2; 106.1; 136.1; 118.1, 29; cf. 1 Chr 16.34; 2 Chr 5.13.
[267] W. Grundmann, *TDNT* 1:12-13; Erich Beyreuther, "*agathos*," in *NIDNTT* 2:99.
[268] E.g., Prov 12.2; 13.22; 14.14; Eccl 9.2; Mt 12.35; 25.31; Lk 6.45; 8.15.
[269] Lk 1.35; 4.34; Jn 6.69; Ac 3.14; 4.30; 1 Pt 1.15-16; 1 Jn 2.20; Rev 3.7; cf. Ac 2.27; 13.35.

In saying that God "alone" is good, Jesus was *not* denying His own sinlessness or righteousness.[270] But He *was* implying that His righteousness was in some respect less than that of God His Father. Warfield quotes H.R. Mackintosh approvingly, who well explains, "What Jesus disclaims, rather, is *God's* perfect goodness. None but God is good with a goodness unchanging and eternal;... Jesus, on the contrary, learnt obedience by the things which He suffered, being tempted in all points like as we are (Heb 5.8; 4.15).... the holiness of Jesus, as displayed in the record of His life, is no automatic effect of a metaphysical substance, but in its perfected form the fruit of continuous moral volition pervaded and sustained by the Spirit."[271] Indeed, Jesus underwent a maturing process in attaining goodness (Lk 2.40, 52). It is assumed that God has always been perfectly good.

It must be concluded that Jesus did not in any way identify Himself as God in Mk 10.18/Lk 18.19. Rather, this passage attests that only the Father is God and that He alone possesses an unrivaled and absolutely perfect goodness. R.E. Brown explains, "A frequent patristic interpretation is that Jesus is trying to lead the man to a perception of his [Jesus'] divinity,... One cannot but feel that such an exegesis is motivated by an apologetic concern for protecting the doctrine of the divinity of Jesus. Other interpreters stress that Jesus is trying to direct attention away from himself to his Father. This is undoubtedly true, but it should not disguise the fact that this text strongly distinguishes between Jesus and God, and that a description that Jesus rejects is applicable to God. From this text one would never suspect that the evangelist thought of Jesus as God."[272]

---

[270] See Ac 3.14; 2 Cor 5.21; Heb 4.15; 7.26; 1 Pt 2.22.
[271] Quoted by B.B. Warfield, *Christology and Criticism*, 3:130. See also Vincent Taylor, *The Gospel According to St. Mark* (London: Mac Millan, 1963), 427.
[272] R.E. Brown, *Jesus God and Man*, 6-7.

Chapter Six
Christology of John

A. Introduction

Preamble	The Meaning of *theos* in John
The Author and his Readers	The Invisibility of God
"The Jews"	Distinguishing God and Christ
The Traditional Interpretation of John	The Subordination of the Son to God
Comparing John with the Synoptics	The Dependence of the Son upon God
Alleged Disparity/Consequent Dismissal	Truth and Life in the Son
Reinterpreting John	The Resurrection of the Son
Christocentric or Theocentric?	The Holy Spirit
The Prologue	The Superiority of God the Father
The Word	Only the Father Is God
Wisdom Christology	The Son of God
The Humanity of Jesus	The Revealer of God
The Incarnation	The Purpose of the Fourth Gospel
Agent Christology	Summary

Preamble

The traditional understanding that Jesus is God rests mostly on the Gospel of John. It arguably says more about the identity of Jesus than the rest of the NT. This gospel also has had the most profound impact on the development of Christology. Christians have cited this gospel more than the entire rest of the Bible in asserting that Jesus is God.

Geza Vermes is a Jewish Christian scholar, a distinguished Jesus researcher, and the world's preeminent authority on the Jewishness of Jesus. He does not believe that Jesus is God. Vermes' busy academic schedule includes much public speaking. He claims that Christian Evangelicals and Fundamentalists are most aghast at his denial that Jesus is God. He relates that when they address their inquiries to him, "Nine times out of ten, the traditionalists' bewildered question derives from some passage in the Fourth Gospel."[1]

So, those who care about Jesus' identity need to focus their attention very acutely on this Fourth Gospel. We will first do so by examining its overall presentation of Jesus. Then we will analyze in detail its most formidable texts

---

[1] G. Vermes, *The Changing Faces of Jesus*, 6.

that supposedly support the view that Jesus is God. *This lengthy chapter is therefore the most important part of this book.*

The Author and his Readers

The Fourth Gospel is entitled "The Gospel According to John." Scholars think it originally had no title and that church fathers later appended this title to it.

Like the synoptists, the Fourth Evangelist never expressly identifies himself. He seems to have been a Jew because he conveys an extensive knowledge of Jewish customs and life in general in especially Judea. And he appears to have been an eyewitness of most of the events recorded in this gospel. Thus, there is some evidence, both internally and externally (patristic writings), which indicates that the Apostle John—the son of Zebedee and younger brother of James—was the primary source for this gospel.[2] Church fathers generally believed that the beloved Apostle John wrote it during his old age.

However, historical-critical scholars contend for another, and later, initial author (Jn 21.24). Many propose "John the Elder," a presbyter mentioned in patristic writings who was professedly a disciple of the Apostle John. These critics surmise that this John was the first author among other subsequent redactor(s) who were all members of some particular Johannine church community or school,[3] perhaps located at Ephesus,[4] but some think Antioch, and that these several hands were all involved in the book's multi-stage development. In antiquity, a purported author of a book was not necessarily its writer, but the authority upon which the book was based. R.E. Brown explains that "frequently the men whose names were attached to biblical books never set pen to papyrus."[5]

A plausible mediating scenario for the authorship of the Gospel of John goes like this: the Apostle John, who probably was "the disciple whom Jesus loved,"[6] while leading a church community or school related most of the contents of this gospel to his associates, and one of them, perhaps John the Elder acting as an amanuensis,[7] first wrote its contents. But several other possible scenarios have been suggested. Most Johannine scholars believe that this gospel's last chapter is a later appendage, by whom is unknown.

---

[2] J.A.T. Robinson (*The Priority of John*, xiii) has been one of the few modern Johannine scholars who believed concerning the Gospel of John that the apostle "John wrote it."

[3] E. Kasemann (*The Testament of Jesus*, 27-33) admits his perplexity that this gospel furnishes little evidence of a developed ecclesiology, which would seem to accompany its supposedly higher Christology.

[4] So says church father Irenaeus, *Against Heresies*, 3.1.1; cf. Eusebius, *Ecclesiastical History*, 3.23, 31. But Ignatius wrote to the church at Ephesus sometime between 110 and 117 CE without mentioning John.

[5] R.E. Brown, *John (i-xii)*, lxxxvii.

[6] Jn 13.23; 19.26-27, 35; 20.2-10; 21.7, 20, 24. Ancients often wrote anonymously when producing a historical compilation that included other sources. "The disciple whom Jesus loved" was probably the apostle John. He had to be one of the Eleven because he was present at the Last Supper, having leaned back on Jesus' breast to question His Master (Jn 13.25; 21.20). Comparing Jn 21.2 with v. 7 narrows his identity to four disciples. However, it appears that the actual writer of this gospel was someone else (Jn 21.24).

[7] R.E. Brown, *John (i-xii)*, xcviii. See also J.H. Bernard, *A Critical and Exegetical Commentary on the Gospel According to St. John*, 2 vols (Edinburgh: T. & T. Clark, 1928), 1:lvii-lxx. Johannine scholar J.A.T. Robinson (*Twelve More New Testament Studies*, 65-66) persuasively contends that the entire Gospel of John is a literary unit without dislocations and composed by a single author, whom he (*The Priority of John*, xiii, 122) identifies as the apostle John.

Due to this scholarly uncertainty about the authorship of this gospel, I will simply refer to him as "John" without specification. Since the Johannine epistles reflect a similar or same theology and use the same terminology as that of the Fourth Gospel, I will include discussion of them in this chapter and regard their author also as simply "John."

Some Johannine scholars think that, like the Epistle to the Hebrews, the Gospel of John was written primarily to Jews.[8] Many debate whether it was intended originally for Christians or non-Christians. Regardless, throughout the succeeding centuries both Jews and Gentiles, believers and non-believers, have read the Gospel of John with much profit. In fact, Christians generally have esteemed it their favorite book in the Bible. *This author is of the opinion that the Gospel of John is the most masterful,[9] well-crafted book in the Bible. I further contend that the identification of Jesus in the Gospel of John has been widely misunderstood throughout post-apostolic church history, even to the present time.*

"The Jews"

One of the many distinguishing (and many today think troubling) features of the Gospel of John is that it depicts a heightened tension between Jesus and the religious establishment at Jerusalem. John often refers to these opponents of Jesus as "(the) Jews" (Gr. *Ioudaioi*). Aside from the fact that all four NT gospels call Jesus "the King of the Jews" by quoting Pilate and citing the inscription on Jesus' cross, the term "(the) Jews" occurs only three other times in the Synoptics, whereas it appears about seventy times in the Fourth Gospel. Historical critics contend that such an inordinate use of this term reflects not so much Jesus' conflict with the Jews, but the later conflict between church and synagogue. But such a view impugns this book's historical authenticity. Furthermore, many of these critics, as well as most rabbinical scholars, criticize this gospel's frequent use of this term as being polemically based and therefore anti-Semitic.[10]

It is both unfair and unproven to accuse the Fourth Evangelist of employing the term "(the) Jews" in a pejorative sense and thereby of being anti-Semitic.[11] For one thing, as stated above, he seems to have been a Jew writing predominantly to Jews. Besides, he clearly uses this word in different ways, not always polemically.[12] Sometimes, he applies it without malice to the Jewish multitude (e.g., Jn 6.41, 52; 10.19; 11.19; 12.9), of whom he says that some believe in Jesus and some do not (Jn 7.31; 8.31; 10.19-21; 12.11). Moreover, he uses

---

[8] E.g., Jacob Jervell, *Jesus in the Gospel of John* [1978], tr. Harry T. Cleven (Minneapolis: Augsburg, 1984), 79-83. I am using the term "(the) Jews" interchangeably with "(the) Jewish people."

[9] R.E. Brown (*John [xiii-xxi]*, 791, xlix) writes of "John's genius" as "the theologian par excellence;" J.D.G. Dunn (*Christology in the Making*, 249) calls his gospel "inspired genius;" and J.A.T. Robinson (*The Priority of John*, 93) describes it as "the most mature piece of writing in the New Testament."

[10] E.g., Maurice Casey, *Is John's Gospel "True"?* (London: Routledge, 1996), 3; idem, "The Deification of Jesus," 706-10. But see Felix Just's review (*Is John's Gospel "True"?* JBL [Fall 1999]: 558-60), in which he implies that it is not John but subsequent commentators on his gospel, e.g., John Chrysostom and Martin Luther, as Casey also points out, who have unjustly made it a springboard for their anti-Semitic invectives.

[11] James D.G. Dunn, "The Question of Anti-semitism in the New Testament," in *Jews and Christians: The Parting of the Ways: AD 70 to 135*, ed. James D.G. Dunn (Grand Rapids: Eerdmans, 1999), 203; N.T. Wright, *Jesus and the Victory of God*, 542.

[12] Concerning the various Johannine uses of the term "the Jews," see J.D.G. Dunn, "The Question of Anti-semitism in the New Testament," 195-203. As a historian, Luke uses the term "(the) Jews" non-polemically in Acts sixty-seven times, sometimes quoting the Apostle Paul.

the word twice to refer specifically to those who *did* believe in Jesus (Jn 8.31; 11.45). Nevertheless, this Fourth Evangelist *does* predominantly use this term polemically to refer specifically to the religious rulers at Jerusalem, viz., the chief priests (Sadducees), scribes (Pharisees), and elders of the people. They are the ones who decided matters of faith and controlled the religious life of all Israeli Jews. Because they were generally hostile toward Jesus, in some sense John is being anti-Judaic, not anti-Semitic. And all four gospel Evangelists provide ample reasons to justify this position: (1) these rulers were envious of Jesus' popularity (Mt 27.18/Mk 15.10), (2) they felt a loss of prestige with the people because of Jesus, and (3) they perceived Jesus as an indirect threat to their office because the Romans would violently squash any political, messianic movement (Jn 11.47-48; 12.19). John writes that ordinary folk feared these religious rulers (Jn 7.1, 13; 9.22; 19.38; 20. 19), who were "persecuting Jesus" and "seeking ... to kill Him" (Jn 5.16, 18). Thus, the only just criticism of John's use of the term "(the) Jews" is that he exhibits an anti-Judaism bent but, more specifically, a discriminatory attitude toward Judaism's leadership in Judea during the time of Jesus.

Besides, if the Johannine sayings of Jesus are accepted as historically reliable, such criticism must be directed mostly at Jesus. Many scholars cite one particular denunciation of the Jews by Jesus when He said, "You are of your father the devil" (Jn 8.44). This is the most caustic language directed towards the Jews in the Fourth Gospel. But Jesus merely said this in the tradition of the Hebrew prophets, who did not overlook self-righteous hypocrisy, nor mince words about it, but declared the truth by exposing it.

The Traditional Interpretation of John

Of course, our narrow interest in investigating the Fourth Gospel concerns the question of whether it identifies Jesus as "God" (Gr. *theos*). From as early as the 2nd century and continuing to the present, the almost unanimous testimony of the church has been that it does. Also, most scholars have assessed the Fourth Gospel as the foremost NT document that unequivocally proclaims Jesus as God. Most contemporary scholars would concur with the conclusion of traditionalist Murray Harris, that the "paramount importance" and "cruciality of the Johannine testimony" is that Jesus is God.[13]

More particularly, *the Fourth Gospel contains the two most formidable passages in the Bible that have been traditionally interpreted as declaring unequivocally that Jesus is God.* These are Jn 1.1c—traditionally translated, "and the Word was God"—and Jn 20.28, in which the Apostle Thomas exclaimed to Jesus, "My Lord and my God." It is especially because of these two, brief passages that this chapter is so important.

More precisely, does John present Jesus as claiming to be God? Or is it only John who says that Jesus is God? While John presents many claims of Jesus concerning His own identity, most contemporary scholars would agree with traditionalist R.E. Brown, who maintains that this gospel affirms that Jesus is God but admits that "even the Fourth Gospel never portrays Jesus as saying specifically that he is God."[14]

It can hardly be overstated how much traditional Christology was founded on the understanding that the Gospel of John identifies Jesus as God. T.E. Pollard relates, "it was St John's Gospel, with its Logos-concept in the Prologue

---

[13] M. Harris, *Jesus as God*, 284.
[14] R.E. Brown, *Jesus God and Man*, 30. John 10.30> will be examined later.

and its emphasis on the Father-Son relationship, that raised in a most acute way the problems which led the church to formulate her doctrines of the trinity and of the person of Christ."[15] Pollard shows that during the Arian controversy of the 4th century, both Arius and Athanasius drew heavily on this gospel to support their differing theses. In fact, they made the Gospel of John the primary battlefield for their controversy so that, according to Pollard, without this sacred text neither of these enemies would have needed to be confuted.[16] Geza Vermes explains:

> The great doctrinal controversies of Christianity during the first millennium of its history and throughout the heated debates of its ecumenical councils from Nicaea (325) to Chalcedon (451) and Constantinople (553) mostly revolved around ideas first mooted in the pages of the Fourth Gospel. The orthodox doctrines relating to Christology—the one person and two natures of Jesus Christ—and to the Holy Triad or triune Deity, through which the various great heresies of the ancient church from Arianism to the *Filioque* controversies were rebutted, all spring from the theology of the spiritual Gospel of John.[17]

Most historical critics have also interpreted the Gospel of John as identifying Jesus as "God." In doing so, they have followed F.C. Baur by dismissing its historicity altogether, alleging that it presents a fictional Jesus. Wilhelm Bousset, a subsequent pioneer of the History of Religions School, ridicules the Johannine Jesus as "God, sojourning upon the earth."[18] A half-century later, Bultmanian scholar Ernst Kasemann, who ironically is credited with re-opening the quest for the historical Jesus, sarcastically characterizes the Johannine Jesus as "God, descending into the human realm" and "going about on the earth," and, "John changes the Galilean teacher into the God who goes about on the earth." Kasemann doesn't let up with his assault on John's gospel, twice describing the Johannine "Jesus as God walking on the face of the earth." And Kasemann concludes his diatribe by accusing John of a "naïve docetism."[19] Plus, we saw in Chapter Three that the current Jesus Seminar has also rendered the Johannine Jesus as fictional.

Yet, in the latter half of the 20th century an increasing number of critical scholars accepted the witness of the Gospel of John as reliable. Most interpreted it to mean that in some sense Jesus is "divine." At the same time, they refrained from either verbalizing or writing the formula, "Jesus is God," simply like that. One reason is the complete absence of this expression in not only the Fourth Gospel but the entire NT. Consequently, some of these scholars preferred the parlance "divinity" or "deity of Christ" in describing Jesus' uniqueness. (See Glossary.) Yet this language is also absent from Scripture. Besides, many scholars use it synonymously with the maxim, "Jesus is God."

Comparing John with the Synoptics

To adequately understand NT Christology, the christologies of the Gospel of John and those of the synoptists must be compared. To do so, the approximate

---

[15] T.E. Pollard, *Johannine Christology and the Early Church*, xi.
[16] T.E. Pollard, *Johannine Christology and the Early Church*, 3, 13, 146-64, 185-87.
[17] G. Vermes, *The Changing Faces of Jesus*, 53-54.
[18] Wilhelm Bousset, *Kyrios Christos: A History of the Belief in Christ from the Beginnings of the Christianity to Iranaeus* [1913], tr. John Steely, 5th ed. (Nashville, TN: Abingdon, 1970), 217, cf. 220. However, Bousset asserted that such portraits did not represent the historical Jesus.
[19] E. Kasemann, *The Testament of Jesus*, 13, 8-9, 26-27, 73, 75, 77, cf. 66. Kasemann (pp. 9, 27) cites the writings of the following German scholars who hold this view: F.C. Baur, G.P. Wetter, E. Hirsch, J. Grill, W. Heitmuller. Late in Kasemann's career he disavowed himself of these assertions.

dates of composition of these gospels need to be established. We learned in Chapter Five that a large majority of contemporary scholars believe that the Gospel of Mark was written first, all three Synoptics were written in the 70s and 80s, and the Gospel of John was written last, with the consensus being that it was produced in the 90s.[20]

In addition, church fathers believed that the Apostle John wrote his gospel with full knowledge of the Synoptic Gospels, so that he supplemented them. But modern historical critics have soundly refuted this view. Instead, the Gospel of John is now regarded as reflecting traditions that are generally independent of those that undergird the Synoptics.[21] And an increasing number of Johannine scholars think that this gospel goes back to even earlier traditions than the Synoptics do.[22] One reason regards the early development of omitting the article from the formula, "Jesus (is) the Christ," to form the proper name "Jesus Christ;" yet the article is retained with the word "Christ" in the Fourth Gospel much more often than in the Synoptics, which suggests an earlier tradition.

How does the Gospel of John compare *structurally* with the Synoptic Gospels? One reason for the viewpoint that John most likely drew upon traditions independent of those that undergird the Synoptic Gospels is that almost 90% of John's material does not appear in the Synoptics. While the Synoptics relate many wondrous deeds of Jesus, most of them accomplished in Galilee, they also focus on His parabolic teaching and other short, pithy, didactic statements, much of which involves information about entering the kingdom of God. In contrast, the idea of entering the kingdom of God is only mentioned once in the Fourth Gospel (Jn 3.3-5). This gospel's emphasis is on receiving eternal life by believing that God sent Jesus, that Jesus spoke God's words, and that Jesus is the Christ, the Son of God. The Fourth Gospel therefore distinguishes itself as an *extremely* theological narrative centered mostly on the identity of Jesus. It does so by narrating eight sign-miracles interwoven with Jesus' discourses and extended, argumentative dialogue with the religious authorities at Jerusalem. The Synoptics are journalistic in their rapid reporting of many events in Jesus' life, whereas the Fourth Gospel is quite selective and reflective in its reports. *The Gospel of John provides the ultimate reality, i.e., the spiritual meaning lying behind Jesus' words and actions.* And, like the Synoptics, John relates an account of Passion Week and various subsequent resurrection appearances of Jesus.

How does the Gospel of John compare *theologically* with the Synoptic Gospels? Some traditionalists have insisted that not only does John clearly reveal the deity of Christ but that this idea is *seminal*, and thus somewhat *hidden*, in the Synoptics. C.F.D Moule was well known for putting forth this "developmental" approach. He insisted that "all the various estimates of Jesus reflected in the New Testament" are "only attempts to describe what was already there from the beginning" concerning the real Jesus.[23]

But many recent traditionalist authorities disagree with this hypothesis. They argue for an "evolutionary" approach, in which the Synoptics *do not* seminally portray Jesus as having preexisted or that He was God but that the Fourth Gospel

---

[20] For the compelling argument that all of the NT materials were written prior to the destruction of Jerusalem, in 70 CE, see J.A.T. Robinson, *Redating the New Testament*, esp. pp. 311, 352.
[21] See esp. P. Gardner-Smith, *St John and the Synoptic Gospels* (Cambridge: University, 1938; C.H. Dodd, *Historical Tradition in the Fourth Gospel*; J.A.T. Robinson, *The Priority of John*, 10-35.
[22] C.H. Dodd, *Historical Tradition in the Fourth Gospel*; J.A.T. Robinson, *The Priority of John*, esp. 34.
[23] C.F.D. Moule, *The Origin of Christology*, 2-3. Likewise, M. Hengel, *The Son of God*, 2; idem, *Studies in Early Christology*, 383, 389.

does both.²⁴ Yet Moule alleges, and rather provocatively for a traditionalist, that the Fourth "Gospel comes within an ace of presenting only a 'docetic' [Christ] ... and suggesting a divine Being who is merely disguised as a man and has not really become a man."²⁵ C.K. Barrett claims the Synoptics make us "think of a human Christ, a venerated teacher and leader who was perhaps the best of men but not God," whereas "(t)he Fourth Gospel has often been taken as the bastion of orthodox Christology."²⁶ Indeed, the history of Christology is closely linked with the history of the interpretation of John's gospel. Many scholars conclude as does J. Jocz, "The Christology of the Church is essentially Johannine."²⁷

Many contemporary scholars debate as to when this supposed transition from a "low" to a "high" Christology occurred, and the same goes for Binitarian (or Trinitarian) monotheism. We saw in Chapter Four that L.W. Hurtado is representative of traditionalist scholars who insist on a very early transition. He claims that "the cultic veneration of Jesus as a divine figure apparently began among Jewish Christians,... within the first two decades of Christianity."²⁸ Other scholars, e.g., P.M. Casey,²⁹ insist on a later transition, toward the end of the 1st century, and that it is only reflected in the Gospel of John. (See Appendix C: Modern Christologies.)

Alleged Disparity and Consequent Dismissal

Most historical-critical scholars have contended that the synoptic Jesus and the Johannine Jesus are in sharp conflict. The first to powerfully allege this disparity were D.F. Strauss and F.C. Baur. We encountered them in Chapter Three regarding Baur's Tubingen School in Germany. They are well known for spurning supernaturalism and dismissing the Fourth Gospel as fiction and thus not a reliable source for determining the faith of the earliest Christians.³⁰ Albert Schweitzer observes, "The necessity of choosing between John and the Synoptists was first fully established by the Tubingen school."³¹

Strauss seemed determined to destroy the Christian faith, whereas Baur proposed diplomatically and convincingly that a proper understanding of who Jesus really was must be based on the critical study of Christian origins. Members of the Tubingen School thus recognized the value of investigating the historical Jesus as He is presented in the first three gospels while rejecting the historicity of the Fourth Gospel. Baur sought to either revive the old critical assessment of

---

[24] F.F. Bruce (*The New Testament Documents: Are They Reliable?* [1943], 5th ed. [repr. Grand Rapids: Eerdmans, 1994], 58) is one of the few modern traditionalists who insists, "There is, in fact, no material difference in Christology between John and the three Synoptists."
[25] C.F.D. Moule, *The Holy Spirit*, 54. Cf. E. Kasemann, *The Testament of Jesus*.
[26] C.K. Barrett, "'The Father is greater than I' (Jo 14, 28): Subordinationist Christology in the New Testament," in Barrett's *Essays on John* (Philadelphia: Westminster, 1982), 20.
[27] Jakob Jocz, "The Invisibility of God and the Incarnation," *Judaica* 17 (1961): 196.
[28] L.W. Hurtado, *One God, One Lord*, 11. But on p. 5 he seems to say this same phenomena transpired "easily within the first decade of the Christian movement." Cf. his *At the Origins of Christian Worship*, 5.
[29] P.M. Casey, *From Jewish Prophet to Gentile God*, 36; idem, "The Deification of Jesus," 697-714.
[30] See esp. F.C. Baur's essay, *Ueber die Composition und den Charakter den joh. Evangeliums* (1844); David Friedrich Strauss, *Leben Jesu* [1835], ET *The Life of Jesus Critically Examined*, ed. Peter C. Hodgson, tr. and ed. from the 4th Ger. by George Eliot (Philadephia: Fortress, 1972). However, in a letter (H. Harris, *The Tubingen School*, 33) Baur responds to such allegations by denying that he had ever "thrown overboard the historical authority of the Gospel of John." Baur did deny that the apostle John wrote the Fourth Gospel, and he decided wrongly that it was written in the late 2nd century.
[31] A. Schweitzer, *The Quest of the Historical Jesus*, 11, cf. 82.

the Gospel of John (The Alogi had alleged that John was written by the Gnostic Cerinthus) or allege that it merely had a Gnostic basis.

Many subsequent German exegetes of Scripture, especially those of the later History of Religions School, adopted this anti-Johannine bias. For instance, Wilhelm Bousset asserted that the author of the Fourth Gospel "thought of the work, so far as we can see, not as a supplement but as a substitute for the Synoptic Gospels."[32] Bultmann later followed Bousset in putting forth the Gnostic Redeemer myth as the primary basis of Johannine Christology, comparing it to the supposed descent-ascent scenario in Jn 6. He alleged that the myth "provides the terminology for the christology of John."[33]

This myth, which originated in Persia (Iran), and was prevalent in the Hellenistic world, was a story about a god who appeared (so it seemed) as a man in order to rescue human civilization by imparting some secret knowledge of salvation and returning to heaven, thus the descent-ascent scenario. But the 1945 discovery of the Nag Hammadi Library in Upper Egypt, which contains Gnostic literature produced in the late 4th century CE, seemed to prove that this Gnostic Redeemer myth originated in the 2nd century CE. So, scholars deemed it anachronistic, dismissing it as the basis for crafting the Fourth Gospel. But did this myth influence later traditionalists in their understanding of this gospel?

E. Kasemann sounded like he wanted to excise the entire Fourth Gospel from the NT. He contended that "the reception of the Fourth Gospel into the canon is but the most lucid and most significant example of the integration of originally opposing ideas and traditions into the ecclesiastical tradition." Then he added a scathing attack, contending that it causes "many theological contradictions" in the NT and that "its acceptance into the Church's canon took place through man's error and God's providence" because the Church was "misled by the picture of Jesus as God walking on the face of the earth."[34]

Geza Vermes argues likewise. He says "it is obvious to any religiously unbiased reader that if the Fourth Evangelist is right, his forerunners [synoptists] must be mistaken or vice versa."[35] He concludes, "The difference between the ideas of John's Jesus and the Jesus of the first three Gospels is particularly striking: they are indeed irreconcilable."[36]

Some recent, even moderately traditionalist, scholars are not much different about it than these critics. Take C.K. Barrett; he acknowledges concerning Jesus' identity, "It is impossible to harmonize the Johannine and synoptic narratives."[37] James D.G. Dunn agrees and therefore cautions against attempting a synthesis of such NT christologies.[38]

Popular author Tom Cahill likewise asserts, "neither Mark nor Matthew, neither Paul nor Luke, none of the apostles and none of the disciples who gathered around Jesus and then formed the early church considered Jesus to be God. This would have seemed blasphemy to them. Their belief in Christ was,

---

[32] W. Bousset, *Kyrios Christos*, 220. Bousset concludes that the author of the Fourth Gospel failed in his supposed attempt to supplant the synoptic portrait of Jesus with his own because the Synoptic Gospels "had already sunk roots too deeply into the primitive Christian community life."

[33] R. Bultmann, *Theology of the New Testament*, 175.

[34] E. Kasemann, *The Testament of Jesus*, 75-76.

[35] G. Vermes, *The Changing Faces of Jesus*, 8, cf. 38.

[36] G. Vermes, *The Changing Faces of Jesus*, 22.

[37] C.K. Barrett, *John*, 179.

[38] J.D.G. Dunn, *Unity and Diversity in the New Testament: An Inquiry into the Character of Earliest Christianity*, 2nd ed. (Harrisburg, PA: Trinity, 1990), 226-27; idem, *Christology in the Making*, 266-67.

after all, a form of Judaism; and Judaism was the world's only monotheism.... By the end of the first century, however, [in] the Fourth Gospel,... we find, for the first time, Jesus acclaimed as God."[39]

If these authors are correct—that the Johannine Jesus differs substantially from the synoptic Jesus, so as to pose a blatant contradiction about Him—then this situation presents a serious problem of discontinuity in the NT. Independent, diverse traditions about Jesus that can possibly dovetail are one thing; but independent traditions about Jesus that are unequivocally incompatible are quite another thing. Such a scenario must be deemed a discontinuity regarding a most fundamental aspect of the Christian message about Jesus during the 1st century CE. One might characterize this state of affairs as two opposing Christianities: a Synoptic Christianity and a Johannine Christianity.

However, it is important to recognize that this alleged disparity between the Synoptic Gospels and the Gospel of John, and the consequent rejection of the Gospel of John by most historical-critical scholars as historically inauthentic, is based on the traditional interpretation of this gospel. Rather than questioning this exegesis, these scholars accepted it as viable. They concluded that it was imperative to make a choice between these two contrasting portraits as to which one represented the historical Jesus. They chose the synoptic portrait and rejected the Johannine one. At least these scholars are to be commended for recognizing the incongruity between these two interpretations.

More and more recent scholars have come to the same conclusion.[40] We have already referred to the rejection of the historical authenticity of the Fourth Gospel by the radically liberal Jesus Seminar. Perhaps the most notable and moderately conservative scholar who adopts this approach is the moderately traditionalist James D.G. Dunn. In his highly acclaimed *Christology in the Making* (1980), Dunn alleges that the Fourth Gospel is not "a historical documentary." He explains,

> despite the renewal of interest in the Fourth Gospel as a historical source for the ministry of Jesus, *it would be verging on the irresponsible to use the Johannine testimony on Jesus' divine sonship in our attempt to uncover the self-consciousness of Jesus himself*.... The Johannine Christology of conscious pre-existent sonship, of self-conscious divinity, belongs most clearly to the *developed* tradition and not to the original.... Consequently, in looking for the origin of a Christology of sonship in the sayings and life of Jesus we are forced back upon the Synoptic material.[41]

And Maurice Casey, Dunn's former colleague, alleges likewise by claiming that

> the deity of Jesus was deliberately expounded in the Johannine community ... [this] development of New Testament Christology cannot be an example of the Holy Spirit guiding the church into all truth. The Holy Spirit could hardly lead the church into an evaluation of the Jesus of history which Jesus in his revelatory ministry could not hold,... John's misleading picture of Jesus is at the centre of this. It makes him divine ... If Christianity is to remain a viable option for honest and well-informed people, it should surely undo that process of development, and emerge as something nearer to the religion of Jesus of Nazareth.[42]

---

[39] Thomas Cahill, *Desire of the Everlasting Hills: The World before and after Jesus* (New York: Nan A. Talese/Doubleday, 1999), 257.
[40] E.g., M. Wiles, *Theology* 85 (1982), 94-95, 325-26; G. Vermes, *The Changing Faces of Jesus*, 25.
[41] J.D.G. Dunn, *Christology in the Making*, 31-32. Emphasis his.
[42] P.M. Casey, *From Jewish Prophet to Gentile God*, 176, 178.

Such scholars have posited various reasons for this supposed change in NT Christology. Many surmise that the infant church altered its primitive, monotheistic Christology, from Jesus being merely a healing prophet and perhaps the Jewish Messiah to His being God. And many of them have concluded that this change took place during the last quarter of the 1st century. (Radical critics and some traditionalists decide on an earlier date.) Many have insisted that this change occurred because the infant Jewish church soon spread into Gentile lands where it was transformed to consist predominantly of Gentiles and thereby become Hellenized enough to dogmatize Jesus as God.[43] And they have explained that this is confirmed by the dates of composition of the gospels. That is, there must have been a sufficient *time gap* between the dates of composition of the earliest written sources used in compiling the Synoptic Gospels and the date of the Gospel of John and its sources in order to account for this christological change witnessed in the Gospel of John.[44] This supposed Johannine development is referred to as a "Late, Hellenized Christology." (See Appendix C: Modern Christologies.)

We should not think that historical-critical scholars generally dismiss the Gospel of John as inauthentic only because of its supposed deity of Christ. They have many other reasons. Suffice it to say that their proposed obstacles against Johannine authenticity are not insurmountable. Let us consider only one. Critics often allege that the structural and stylistic differences between the Synoptics and the Fourth Gospel indicate the latter's historical unreliability. That is, in the Synoptics Jesus teaches ethical parables; but in the Fourth Gospel He engages with opponents in argumentative, theological dialogue. This supposed disparity is thought to indicate that the Johannine Jesus is a fictional caricature.

On the contrary, the two different settings sufficiently account for these structural and stylistic differences. Until Passion Week, the setting of the Synoptics is usually about Jesus teaching multitudes in Galilee, where Pharisees and scribes likely did not reside and were seldom in His audiences.[45] But the setting of the Fourth Gospel is primarily at the temple in Jerusalem during the festivals, and Jesus' audiences there would have often included Pharisees and perhaps other religious authorities. Plus, it is plausible that Jesus could have tailored his words and style to accommodate the two different life settings.

This dismissal of the Gospel of John as a reliable source for discovering the historical Jesus resides mostly with scholarship. Christian laity does not accept it. J.D.G. Dunn acknowledges this incongruity between scholarship and laity and explains about it, "Probably no issue marks off the bulk of New Testament scholarship so sharply from the piety of the pews than the issue of how the fourth Gospel should be understood."[46]

In contrast, Johannine scholar John A.T. Robinson differed with so many of his colleagues by insisting that the Gospel of John is very historically reliable

---

[43] E.g., A.E. Harvey, *Jesus and the Constraints of History*, 173; esp. P.M. Casey, *From Jewish Prophet to Gentile God*.
[44] However, for the view that John used written sources predating Q, see C.H. Dodd (*Historical Tradition in the Fourth Gospel*) and J.A.T. Robinson (*Priority of John*).
[45] Josephus was the commander-in-chief of the revolutionary Jewish forces in Galilee when the First Jewish Revolt began, in 66 CE. G. Vermes (*The Changing Faces of Jesus*, 229) cites that Josephus' only mention (*Life*, 189-98) of Pharisees in Galilee were delegations dispatched from Jerusalem. Vermes concludes, "it is highly unlikely that Jesus came across Galilean Pharisees of note during his activity in the province."
[46] J.D.G. Dunn, "Let John Be John: A Gospel for Its Time," 298.

and therefore does not conflict with the Synoptics.⁴⁷ This is the view espoused in this book.

Reinterpreting John

But have these accomplished critical scholars been right in concluding that the traditional interpretation of the Gospel of John is correct, i.e., that the Johannine Jesus is God? In 1984, John A.T. Robinson pointed out that "a considerable reaction has more recently set in in New Testament circles against writing off the historical value of the Johannine tradition—a reaction with which I have long been in sympathy." Citing A.M Hunter and C.H. Dodd as examples, Robinson concludes that "when it comes to the central issue of all, the picture which John gives us of Jesus and the use that we can make of it for doctrine, the criteria have not, I think, been adequately reassessed."⁴⁸

Indeed, *church fathers and all subsequent traditionalists have misunderstood Jesus' identity mostly because they have misinterpreted key passages about Him in the Gospel of John, and most critical scholars have endorsed these misinterpretations. Consequently, the primary purpose of this chapter is to heed John A.T. Robinson's call for a reexamination of the Johannine Jesus and thereby show that this gospel does not present Jesus as God and therefore does not conflict with the synoptic portrait of Jesus*. Robinson rightly contends that the Johannine Jesus is *not* "God dressed up as a human being. He is not a divine being who came to earth,"⁴⁹ as critics E. Kasemann, P.M. Casey, and other distinguished historical-critical scholars have sarcastically alleged.

Christocentric or Theocentric?

This supposed christological difference between the Synoptics and the Fourth Gospel has also caused the common impression, held by conservatives and critics alike,⁵⁰ that the Synoptics are *theocentric* whereas the Fourth Gospel is *christocentric*. That is, the Synoptics characterize Jesus as constantly preaching about God and His kingdom, but not in the Gospel of John. For instance, John Stott, for a leading conservative Evangelical, asserts surprisingly that the Johannine "Jesus ... was constantly talking about himself." Stott even insists on a "self-centeredness of the teaching of Jesus."⁵¹ R. Bultmann wrote similarly, that the Johannine Jesus "speaks only of his own person."⁵²

These observations are skewed. To be sure, the Johannine Jesus talked often about Himself; but this talk often centered on a combination of His mission and His relationship with God as His Father. A typical Johannine picture is of Jesus talking about His identity and/or mission so that people might believe in Him and thereby be reconciled to God. His classic statement on this theme is Jn 14.6: "I am the way, and the truth, and the life; no one comes to the Father, but through Me." *The Johannine Jesus thus spoke often about Himself, but often in the sense that He was the lifeline to God*. Besides, whatever the Johannine Jesus said about Himself, according to His repeated testimony He did so *not* on account of His own initiative but because God had so instructed Him to speak.

---

⁴⁷ J.A.T. Robinson, *The Priority of John*, 32.
⁴⁸ J.A.T. Robinson, *Twelve More New Testament Studies*, 141. For the historical reliability and truth of John's portrait of Jesus, see esp. ch. 9.
⁴⁹ J.A.T. Robinson, *The Priority of John*, 393-94.
⁵⁰ As observed by J.A.T. Robinson, *The Priority of John*, 349. During the 20ᵗʰ century, Christian process theologians were the leading advocates of the view that Jesus was theocentric in His theology.
⁵¹ J.R.W. Stott, *Basic Christianity*, 23.
⁵² R. Bultmann, *Theology of the New Testament*, 2:4.

In fact, rather than being self-centered, the Johannine Jesus could go so far as to say, "He who believes in Me does not believe in Me, but in Him who sent Me" (Jn 12.44).

Self-centeredness is self-absorption, the antithesis of self-denial. Jesus not only emphasized self-denial, He perfectly modeled it. *The Johannine Jesus was not self-centered but God-centered and very theocentric in His theology.*[53] J.A.T. Robinson well observes, "an essential point about the theology of the Fourth Gospel is that the centre of the picture is not Jesus but the Father."[54] J.D.G. Dunn says too, "for the fourth evangelist, theology (in the narrower sense) is more important than *Christology*."[55] Marinus de Jonge concludes, "Johannine Christology, with all its statements about Jesus' unity with God, remains theocentric.... Jesus' Christology was 'theocentric' from beginning to end."[56]

If Jesus talked incessantly about Himself, being self-centered He brought glory to Himself. But the Johannine Jesus said, "I do not seek My glory" (Jn 8.50, cf. v. 54). Hans Kung rightly explains, "even conservative Christian theologians today concede that Jesus did not proclaim himself, but the kingdom of God:... He did not put his own role, person, dignity at the centre of his preaching."[57] Indeed, Jesus said, "He who speaks of himself seeks his own glory; but He who is seeking the glory of the one who sent Him, He is true, and there is no unrighteousness in Him" (Jn 7.18). That is what the Johannine Jesus did: He constantly alerted peoples' attention to the One who sent Him.

Thus, familiarity with the Gospel of John breeds this result: *it is difficult to think of the Johannine Jesus without also thinking of God, whom He often called "the Father."* This is even truer of the Fourth Gospel than the Synoptics. Another example of this truth is when the Johannine Jesus denounced His Pharisaic adversaries, declaring, "You know neither Me, nor My Father; if you knew Me, you would know My Father also" (Jn 8.19).

Related to this issue is the cherished Protestant-Evangelical tradition of preserving a "Christ-centered" faith. Neo-orthodox scholar Karl Barth is well known from his *Church Dogmatics* for emphasizing this viewpoint in opposition to Liberal Theology. On a popular level in the U.S., C.I. Scofield exemplified this viewpoint in the Preface of his Study Bible with this statement, "the central theme of the Bible is Christ."[58] Not at all; the central theme of the Bible is God. *The Christian faith is properly viewed as a God-centered faith made possible by saving faith in Jesus, in which God forgives people for breaking His Law and reconciles them to Himself when they believe in Jesus.*

In conclusion, the Johannine Jesus was no more christocentric in His teaching than He was theocentric, and He certainly was not self-centered. Neither was the Johannine Jesus more theocentric than the synoptic Jesus. The

---

[53] See, e.g., C.K. Barrett, *John*, 97; idem, *Essays on John*, 158; N.A. Dahl, *Jesus the Christ*, ed. D.H. Juel, 153-63. A. Harnack (*What Is Christianity?*, 144, emphasis his) goes too far with his renowned assertion that "*the gospel*, as Jesus proclaimed it, has to do with the Father only and not the Son." Harnack (*History of Dogma*, 1:72) also stated, "the Person of Christ is the central point of the [Christian] religion."

[54] J.A.T. Robinson, *The Priority of John*, 350. D. Cupitt (*Jesus and the Gospel of God*, 70) insists likewise, claiming that Jesus' "message and outlook was wholly God-centered."

[55] J.D.G. Dunn, "Let John Be John," 318. Emphasis his.

[56] M. de Jonge, *God's Final Envoy*, 140, 144, cf. 109.

[57] H. Kung, *Credo*, 78.

[58] *Scofield Reference Bible*, vi. Strictly speaking, a person is not a theme. Jesus being the Christ is a theme.

Johannine Jesus and the synoptic Jesus are quite compatible regarding both theo- and christo- centricity.

The Prologue

Now let us consider briefly the christological content of the Fourth Gospel.

The Gospel of John is unique in that it begins with a profound prologue consisting of poetry, prose, and history that is interwoven and tightly compacted into eighteen verses. Many critics regard this prologue, or portions of it, as a preexisting church hymn. Some critics think one of the Johannine redactors attached it later to this gospel. Both proposals seem implausible because the prologue is so integrated with the gospel text.[59]

The word "prologue" means, "to say beforehand."[60] John's prologue therefore represents a preliminary introduction appended to the beginning of his gospel that serves as a sort of outline of principal theological themes that he develops throughout his gospel text.[61] R.H. Strachan concludes that this prologue "cannot be fully understood except after studying the Gospel itself; for what is expressed in the prologue in the abstract, is expressed more in concrete and in detail in the body of the Gospel."[62] Accordingly, John intends that certain portions of his gospel text, usually sayings of Jesus, be connected to their corresponding themes in the prologue. This connection is called "linkage."[63]

In sum, John's prologue is mostly a poem that was created like an artist sketching the outer form of an object. John's gospel text is therefore comparable to the artist filling in the forms with colors. The finished canvass presents a clear, christological portrait of Jesus,[64] one that is more like the synoptic portrait than has generally been recognized.

The Word

John's prologue begins with the phrase, "In the beginning was the Word." This expression, "the Word," is also a unique feature of John's gospel. But what does it mean? And what is its significance in this gospel?

The message of John's prologue may be summarized thus: (1) God created all things by means of His Word; (2) this Word took flesh to become the man, Jesus Christ; (3) this man reveals God and thereby exhorts people to believe in Himself so that they may become enlightened with the truth of God and be born spiritually as children of God.

"The Word" in John's prologue translates *ho logos* in its Greek text. There is no English word that adequately conveys the wide breadth of meaning of this Greek term. Most philologists translate it "word," referring to the spoken word that reflects God's self-expression. But a few prefer the more precise definition of "reason" or "mind," indicating God's rational thought that prompts His spoken word. Still others suggest "deed," signifying both God's self-revelatory and redemptive activity.

The Logos was a well-known concept in the OT, Judaism, Hellenism, and many cultures in antiquity. By the time of Jesus, a plethora of theological and

---

[59] J.G.D. Dunn, "Let John Be John," 313n7/8.
[60] *The Webster Reference Dictionary of the English Language: Encyclopedic Edition.*
[61] Cf., J.A.T. Robinson, *Twelve More New Testament Studies*, 68, cf. 71.
[62] R.H. Strachan, *The Fourth Gospel*, 67.
[63] Robin Scroggs (*Christology in Paul and John: The Reality and Revelation of God* [Philadelphia: Fortress, 1988], 64) calls this connection "a spiral technique."
[64] Contra C.K. Barrett (*John*, 98), who alleges, "There is no straightforward, clearcut Christology in John."

philosophical ideas about the Logos had circulated throughout the Hellenistic world. Since then, countless volumes have been written on what these ancients meant by "the Logos."

No one popularized the Logos concept more than Philo (c. 20 BCE—50 CE). He was a Jewish philosopher and theologian from Alexandria, Egypt, and a slightly older contemporary of Jesus. Philo was not an original ideologue, but more of a spokesperson of theological and philosophical ideas then current, some of which we have considered. He combined Judaic and Greek thought into a complex system that portrays the Logos as a conduit for God's power, revelation, or speech to humans. Hence, Philo depicted the Logos as an intermediary between the transcendent God and humankind, in which God, who is unknowable, can be known only through His Logos. Philo further claimed that this Logos is described in Gen 1 and other Jewish Scriptures as God's agent in creation.

We saw in Chapter Two that the apologists of the 2nd and 3rd centuries made the Logos concept the centerpiece of their Christology, which some scholars now call "Logos Christology." Since these apologists were influenced by neo-Platonic ideas, they adopted various cosmological, metaphysical theories about the Logos. Many of these apologists, like Philo, equated the preexistent Logos and Son of God. Many modern scholars have thought that this direction was misguided and that these apologists should have focused christologically on Jesus' Sonship, to which church fathers did return in the 4th century.

But how do the Logos teachings of John and Philo compare? Both define the Logos as God's self-revelation in so far as He may be known by us humans. The major difference between them is that John's Logos takes flesh to become a man whereas Philo's Logos does not, which reflects his neo-Platonic dualism. The apologists insisted that Philo's Logos is only a personification of God's power whereas John's Logos depicts a distinct *hypostasis* (somewhat like our word "person"), separate from God the Father, which became flesh as the man Jesus. Later church fathers agreed with these earlier apologists, that the Logos was a complete rational being distinct from the Father. But they differed from the apologists by putting forth their new concept of eternal generation, insisting that the Logos *always* existed in eternity past. So, they rejected more acutely any similarity between the Logos teachings of John and Philo than the apologists had done.

Some distinguished, modern Johannine scholars have renewed the apologists' view of a strong affinity between Philo and John about the Logos. C.H. Dodd proposes that John's prologue "would inevitably find suggested here a conception of the creative and revealing *logos* in many respects similar to Philo; and it is difficult not to think that the author intended this."[65] And J.A.T. Robinson quotes T.W. Manson, who was probably right about John, "I very much doubt that he thought of the Logos as a personality."[66]

So much patristic discussion about John's Logos was speculative, now called "Logos speculation." Church fathers delved into many questions that the Scriptures shed little or no light upon. For example, prior to the incarnation did the Logos subsist as an entity distinguishable from God or merely represent an attribute or power of God, later emanating from Him to become a separate and distinct personality through whom God then created the universe? During the incarnation, did the Logos merely subsume human nature, called

---

[65] C.H. Dodd, *The Interpretation of the Fourth Gospel* (Cambridge: University, 1953), 277.
[66] J.A.T. Robinson, *The Priority of John*, 391. Quoted from T.W. Manson, *On Paul and John: Some Selected Theological Themes*, ed. Matthew Black (Naperville, IL: A.R. Allenson, 1963), 156.

Monophysitism? Or, at the incarnation did the Logos retain an identity or nature distinct from Jesus' human nature? If so, doesn't that require that Jesus had two minds and two wills, as indeed was determined at the Sixth Ecumenical Church Council? Was the preexistent Logos also the Son of God, as many prominent church fathers said, so that it was the Logos-Son who undertook the incarnation? Did the Logos impact the earthly Jesus as He lived His righteous life and, if so, to what extent? And how does this correlate with the Holy Spirit's influence in Jesus' life? Moreover, can we detect from the gospels any awareness of these matters by Jesus? For example, was Jesus conscious of having preexisted? If so, did He have cosmic memory? Speculation notwithstanding, church fathers often established answers to some of these questions as orthodoxy and required all Catholic Christians to subscribe to such dogma or risk excommunication.

Although John's Logos is a very unique feature of his gospel, after the prologue he surprisingly never mentions it again. Thus, John never designates the Logos as "the Son (of God);" yet he calls Jesus "the Son (of God)" numerous times. Consequently, many modern scholars would concur with T.E. Pollard's dismissal of the relevance of the Logos by asserting, "the subject of John's gospel is Jesus Christ, not the Logos."[67]

Then, why does John mention the Logos at all? Is it not because his readers live in a Hellenistic world full of religio-philosophical ideology that incorporates a multitude of Logos theories,[68] some with which they are familiar? Vincent Taylor therefore concludes that John "believes Jesus to be 'the Christ, the Son of God' (xx. 31), which reminds him of the Logos."[69] Accordingly, John's primary, if not only, purpose for mentioning the Logos is for it to serve as a point of contact for his readers and the world they live in.[70]

But this does not fully suffice, either. We have seen that the purpose of John's prologue is to introduce themes he further elaborates upon in his gospel text. While Jesus is never precisely identified in the gospel text as the Logos (only Jn 1.14 of the prologue), this gospel's most prominent theme is that God sent Jesus to speak God's words and teach His truth.[71] Robert Gundry posits the compelling argument that Jesus' identification as the Logos in the prologue, though never mentioned again in the gospel text, is very thoroughly developed in the gospel text to mean that Jesus speaks the words of God.[72]

Yet why doesn't John expressly state, either in his prologue or in his gospel text, that "Jesus is the Word" or the like? Perhaps it is incorrect to conclude that there is an exact equivalence between the man Jesus and the preexistent Logos, even though Jesus is identified as "the Word of God" in Rev 19.13. Maybe the most that can be safely adduced about the Logos in John's gospel is that *Jesus was the man that the Logos became.*[73]

In conclusion, John's focus throughout his gospel is not Logos speculation but the identity of Jesus as the Christ, the Son of God, who speaks and acts on behalf of God because of Jesus' very intimate, filial relationship with God as His Father.

---

[67] T.E. Pollard, *Johannine Christology and the Early Church*, 13.
[68] E.g., J.H. Bernard, *A Critical and Exegetical Commentary on the Gospel According to St. John*, 1:cxlii.
[69] V. Taylor, *The Person of Christ*, 108.
[70] Similarly, R.N. Longenecker, *The Christology of Early Jewish Christianity*, 147.
[71] E.g., Jn 6.44-46; 7.14-17; 8.26-28; 14.24; 17.8.14. John mentions Jesus' "word(s)" about forty times.
[72] Robert H. Gundry, *Jesus the Word According to John the Sectarian* (Grand Rapids: Eerdmans, 2002), 1-50.
[73] Cf. J.D.G. Dunn, *Christology in the Making*, 244; idem, *Unity and Diversity*, 221.

Wisdom Christology

Logos and Wisdom were two related concepts prevalent in Hellenism, Judaism, early Christianity, and proto-Gnosticism. All four NT gospels, and especially the non-canonical Gospel of Thomas, depict Jesus as possessing wisdom par excellence. The Fourth Gospel goes further than the Synoptics, characterizing Jesus as that personified Wisdom described in the OT and other Jewish Wisdom Literature.[74] Perhaps the Fourth Evangelist intended to present Jesus' preexistence in the same manner, i.e., an impersonal yet personified Logos. G.B. Caird explains, "Neither the Fourth Gospel nor Hebrews speaks of the eternal Word or Wisdom of God in terms which compel us to regard it as a person."[75] Caird adds that all Jewish Wisdom Literature is mere personification.[76] Many Johannine scholars identify what they call a "Wisdom Christology" or a "Wisdom-Logos Christology" in the Fourth Gospel, and some deem it no more than personification.

Jewish Wisdom Literature of the OT, and that produced in the intertestamental period, is rich in imagery. The best OT example is Prov 8.[77] It depicts personified wisdom as a woman (Gr. *sophia*, "wisdom," is feminine in gender) who shouts in the streets and city-square and utters sayings at the entrance to the city. This wisdom says, "The LORD possessed me at the beginning of His way, before His works of old. From everlasting I was established, from the beginning, from the earliest times of the earth. When there were no depths, I was brought forth,... When He established the heavens, I was there,... then I was beside Him, as a master workman; and I was daily His delight, rejoicing always before Him" (Prov 8.22-24, 27, 30).

Church fathers applied Prov 8 to Jesus. In doing so, they misunderstood its poetic language by taking it literally as personal preexistence. In contrast, R.E. Brown compares Prov 8 to John's prologue and states, "in the OT presentation of Wisdom, there are good parallels for almost every detail of the Prologue's description of the Word."[78] That is why Brown interprets "the personification of 'the Word' in the Prologue to John."[79]

James D.G. Dunn may be the preeminent, contemporary authority on Christology. He contends that John's Logos is not described anywhere in his prologue as a personal being, except that in Jn 1.14 "we have an explicit statement of *incarnation*, the first, and indeed only such statement in the NT."[80] Dunn quotes several personified Wisdom texts in Jewish inter-testamental literature to show that they strongly parallel John's Logos poem, but also other NT texts.[81] Both Dunn and Brown insist that this Wisdom-Logos motif is prevalent not only in John's prologue but in his gospel text in its language and imagery.[82] Indeed, Christopher Tuckett likewise observes, "It has long been recognized that much of the language of the prologue in John 1:1-18 can be paralleled in language about Wisdom, and the same also applies to virtually all of John."[83]

---

[74] R.E. Brown, *John (i-xii)*, cxxii.
[75] G.B. Caird, "The Development of the Doctrine of Christ in the New Testament," in *Christ for Us Today*, ed. Norman Pittenger (London: SCM, 1968), 79-80.
[76] Ibid, 76.
[77] See esp. Prov 1.20-21, 22-33; 7.4; 8.1-36; 9.1-6.
[78] R.E. Brown, *John (i-xii)*, 523.
[79] R.E. Brown, *John (i-xii)*, 519.
[80] J.D.G. Dunn, *Christology in the Making*, 241-44. Emphasis his.
[81] J.D.G. Dunn, *Christology in the Making*, 164-67.
[82] R.E. Brown, *John i-xii*, cxxii-cxxv; J.D.G. Dunn, "Let John Be John," 314.
[83] C. Tuckett, *Christology of the New Testament*, 165.

These strong parallels of personified Wisdom in the OT and other Jewish literature with John's Logos make it likely that John does not intend for the Logos to be understood as a personal being distinct from God. Dunn insists, "we are dealing with personifications rather than persons, personified actions of God rather than an individual divine being as such. The point is obscured by the fact that we have to translate the masculine Logos as 'he' throughout the poem. But if we translated *logos* as 'God's utterance' instead, it would become clearer that the poem did not necessarily intend the Logos in vv. 1-13 to be thought of as a personal divine being."[84] Dunn further explains in a later publication, "The key is to recognize that what John draws on is the Wisdom tradition *within* Judaism— where Wisdom/Logos is not understood as a divine being distinct from God,... but rather where Wisdom is understood precisely as the expression of God's *immanence*."[85] Dunn adds, "Wisdom/Logos is not a heavenly being over against God, but ... God in his self-manifestation, God insofar as he may be known by the human mind."[86]

In conclusion, John's Logos likely should be understood just as Wisdom is often portrayed in the OT and other Jewish literature: merely personified and thus not a person.

The Humanity of Jesus

The widespread belief that Jesus preexisted as God by possessing a divine nature has always led the church to de-emphasize Jesus' humanity and thereby succumb to the tendency toward Docetism. And most Christians, including many traditionalist scholars, have continued to promote this imbalance. R.E. Brown acknowledges, "Many Christian believers do not sufficiently appreciate the humanity of Jesus."[87] Nowhere has this been more evident than the manner in which the Gospel of John has usually been expounded. In the extreme, 2nd century philosopher Cerinthus heralded so-called "Christian Gnosticism" by strongly embracing the Gospel of John and interpreting it as portraying Jesus as God while not being entirely human.

While it has been believed that the Gospel of John presents the supreme scriptural evidence that Jesus is God, it also provides even more evidence for Jesus' humanity than do the Synoptics.[88] It is well known among scholars that this gospel, and especially the comparable epistle of 1 John, opposes incipient Gnosticism, which touted that the Logos could not have been human. In contrast, examples of the Johannine Jesus' physical needs are that He got tired (Jn 4.6), thirsty (Jn 4.7; 19.28), and hungry (Jn 4.31). Also, the Johannine Jesus experienced such human emotions as love of friends,[89] sorrow (11.33, 38), crying (v. 35), and anxiety (Jn 12.27; 13.21). J.E. Davey states, "the Christ of John is actually more 'human' than in almost any of the other New Testament writings."[90]

---

[84] J.D.G. Dunn, *Christology in the Making*, 243.

[85] J.D.G. Dunn, "Let John Be John," 320. Emphasis his.

[86] J.D.G. Dunn, "Let John Be John," 314. Cf. J.D.G. Dunn, "Was Christianity a Monotheistic Faith from the Beginning," 320.

[87] R.E. Brown, *Jesus God and Man*, ix.

[88] J.A.T. Robinson, *The Human Face of God*, 169-79. See also Marrianne Meye Thompson, *The Humanity of Jesus in the Fourth Gospel* (Philadelphia: Fortress, 1988); Martin Hengel, *The Johannine Question* (London: SCM, 1989), 69-72.

[89] E.g., Jn 11.3, 5, 11, 36; 13.1, 23, 34; 15.9, 12; 19.26; 20.2, 7, 20; 21.7, 20.

[90] J.E. Davey, *The Jesus of St. John: Historical and Christological Studies in the Fourth Gospels* (London: Lutterworth, 1958), 89.

In fact, more than all three Synoptics combined,[91] the Gospel of John repeatedly and expressly calls Jesus "a man" (Jn 1.30; 4.29; 9.11-12, 16; 19.5). R. Bultmann asserts that the Johannine Jesus was "nothing but a man" and that this is how people who knew Him took Him to be.[92] Indeed, the Johannine Jesus once called Himself "a man" (Jn 8.40). In light of traditional Christology, it is remarkable how He did so; for He replied to His interlocutors, "you are seeking to kill Me, a man who has told you the truth, *which I heard from God*" (Jn 8.40; emphasis mine). Notice the distinction of Himself and God.

It is difficult to reconcile the concepts of full humanity and personal preexistence. This assessment is supported by the two relatively new disciplines of anthropology and psychology. And due to Jesus Research, a slew of scholarly studies have issued forth in recent decades affirming and emphasizing Jesus' humanity by focusing on His being a Jewish man who lived in a Jewish culture in the Galilee. It thus becomes questionable if Jesus can be considered fully human like ourselves (yet without sin) if He had preexisted.

Some moderately traditionalist scholars now adamantly propound this conclusion. John Knox stoutly contends, "We can have the humanity without the pre-existence and we can have the pre-existence without the humanity. There is absolutely no way of having both."[93] John Macquarrie agrees and boldly alleges that the "claim that Jesus Christ had prior to his birth a conscious, personal pre-existence in 'heaven,' this is not only mythological but is, I believe, destructive of his true humanity."[94]

Even more irreconcilable, conceptually, is the conjoining of humanity and deity in one person. Traditionalist theologians call it "the hypostatic union." It may be judicious to also question whether someone who is both God and man is a genuine human being. A God-man, in the sense of a demi-god, perhaps; a man, likely not. Dutch theologian Ellen Flesseman-van Leer is a proponent of a strictly God-in-Christ Christology and thus not a traditionalist. She well concludes that by "replacing the expression 'God and man' with 'God in this man'... justice can better be done to the true humanness of Jesus Christ."[95]

The Incarnation

The ideas of the personal preexistence of the Logos and the humanity of Jesus remind us of the church doctrine of the incarnation. Throughout most of church history, *Christians have been taught that the incarnation is one of the most essential doctrines, if not the most essential doctrine, of the Christian faith.* But what is it?

The incarnation has not been well defined by either the church or its doctors of theology.[96] In fact, throughout church history there have been many different

---

[91] John A.T. Robinson, "Dunn on John," *T* 85 (1982): 334.

[92] R. Bultmann (*Gospel of John*, 62-63, 63n1) cites evidence in Jn 4.29; (5.12); 7.46, 51; 9.16; 11.47, 50; 18.14, 17, 29.

[93] J. Knox, *The Humanity and Divinity of Christ*, 106. See his presentation of the irreconcilability of these two concepts on pp. 53-72, 93-112.

[94] J. Macquarrie, *Jesus Christ in Modern Thought*, 57. Similarly, J.A.T. Robinson, "Dunn on John," 332.

[95] E. Flesseman-van Leer, *A Faith for Today*, 66.

[96] J. Hick ("Is There a Doctrine of the Incarnation," in *Incarnation and Myth: The Debate Continued*, ed. M.D. Goulder, 48) states, "there is nothing that can be called *the* Christian doctrine of the incarnation." Emphasis his. See also M.F. Wiles, "A Survey of Issues in the Myth Debate," in *Incarnation and Myth: The Debate Continued*, ed. M.D. Goulder, 3-5; J.D.G. Dunn, *Christology in the Making*, 115, 125.

definitions of the incarnation.⁹⁷ The Nicene Creed states, "Jesus Christ, the Son of God,... came down [presumably from heaven to earth] and became incarnate, becoming man." But the name "Jesus Christ" refers to a man. So, this statement seems to claim that Jesus was a man *prior to* His incarnation, which is incorrect. Yet many church fathers believed this.

In order to define the incarnation, several questions first need to be answered, including some of those mentioned above concerning the Logos. For example, does the incarnation mean that the preexistent Logos became the man, Jesus of Nazareth? Does the incarnation mean the Logos was fully God, so that God became the man Jesus? And does the incarnation indicate that the man Jesus preexisted as God, or only the Logos did?

The theological term "incarnation" derives from the Latin word *incarnatus*, which means "in flesh," or better, "enfleshment." Latin fathers applied this word to the Logos in Jn 1.14. Consequently, Johannine Christology has been characterized as an "incarnational Christology." This is due to John's Logos teaching in his prologue as well as his several gospel texts concerning Jesus' apparent preexistence. Yet surprisingly, Jn 1.14 contains the only NT statement that confirms the idea of the enfleshment of the Logos.⁹⁸ It reads:

14 And the Word became flesh, and dwelt among us, and we beheld His glory, glory as of the only begotten from the Father, full of grace and truth.

In this brief statement, its author identifies Jesus' preexistence as "the Word" (Gr. *logos*). Accordingly, it seems the church doctrine of the incarnation means that the Logos somehow assumed a physical body to become the man Jesus. As far back as the patristic era, many theologians have used the term, "the Incarnate Word," to refer to this concept.

However, the classical definition of the incarnation goes much further; it asserts that *God actually became the man Jesus*. This definition does not mean merely that God indwelt the man Jesus,⁹⁹ the exact meaning of God-in-Christ Christology; rather, the Nicene Creed's description of Jesus as "very God" means unequivocally that God became the man Jesus so that Jesus is properly identified as "God." More precisely, and in accordance with the doctrine of the Trinity, the classical doctrine of the incarnation means that the Second Person of the Trinity—the Logos-Son—became the man Jesus. Most recently, Martin Hengel has asserted, "no greater thought has been conceived than that of the one God who, for the salvation of all, became a human being in Jesus of Nazareth."¹⁰⁰ Hengel even joins Jurgen Moltmann and Richard Bauckham in following Martin Luther, who called the crucified Jesus "the crucified God."¹⁰¹

---

⁹⁷ J. Hick, "Is there a Doctrine of the Incarnation?" 47; K. Runia, *The Present-Day Christological Debate*, 105.
⁹⁸ J.D.G. Dunn, *Chistology in the Making*, 241.
⁹⁹ N.T. Wright ("Jesus and God," 147) explains, "*Incarnation* means 'embodiment:' in Jesus, God became embodied, the Word became flesh." Emphasis his. But is "embodiment" a synonym for "became flesh"?
¹⁰⁰ M. Hengel, *Studies in Early Christology*, xviii.
¹⁰¹ M. Hengel, *Studies in Early Christology*, 383; Jurgen Moltmann, *The Crucified God: The Cross of Christ as the Foundation and Criticism of Christian Theology*, tr. R.A. Wilson and John Bowden (London: SCM, 1974), 200-290; Richard Bauckham, *God Crucified: Monotheism and Christology in the New Testament* (Grand Rapids: Eerdmans, 1998), 68-69, 72.

Many traditionalist expositors interpret the Gospel of John as indicating that God became man by comparing Jn 1.14 with the traditional translation of Jn 1.1c. Their reasoning goes like this: (1) the Word was God; (2) the Word became flesh, i.e., the man Jesus Christ; therefore, (3) Jesus Christ is God. (But notice that this reasoning depends on the traditional translation of Jn 1.1c>, which we will soon see is quite suspect.) This was Ignatius' reasoning. We have already seen that he was the first patristic writer to state expressly and repeatedly that God became a man. In more recent times, E. Stauffer has boldly asserted, "God himself had become man." But by 1974, traditionalist George Ladd said of this maxim, "most scholars think that Stauffer defends an extreme position."[102]

Indeed, the classical doctrine of the incarnation has been seriously challenged in modern times.[103] James Dunn informs, "since the Enlightenment the traditional doctrine of the incarnation has come under increasing pressure to explain and justify itself."[104] In the 19th century, this challenge was precipitated by the Tubingen School and accelerated by the History of Religions School. That opposition picked up steam in 1977 with the controversial British publication, *The Myth of God Incarnate*.[105] In 1982, A.E. Harvey surmised, "In the last few years it has come to be questioned whether the resultant construction of Jesus as 'God Incarnate' is either credible or intelligible ... the earliest Christians were constrained to stop considerably short of this" incarnation Christology.[106]

Some scholars warn of the dangers involved in adopting incarnation Christology. Don Cupitt claims, "those who continue today to affirm a strong [=classical] doctrine of the incarnation risk destroying belief in God," in which "attempts to prolong the life of incarnational theology are now too costly. It would be much better to go back to Jesus and the New Testament and try to produce a better account."[107]

During the 20th century, an increasing number of scholars attempted to redefine the incarnation more biblically. For example, even staunch Trinitarian and systematic theologian L. Berkhof conceded, "it is better to say that the Word became flesh than that God became man."[108] Indeed, many biblical scholars now call Jesus "the Incarnate Word" and refrain from calling Him "the Incarnate God."

Some scholars caution against speculating precisely how the Logos "became flesh." J.H. Bernard maintains concerning Jn 1.14, "To explain the exact significance of *egeneto* [became] in this sentence is beyond the powers of any interpreter."[109] And Hans Kung thinks that neither Jn 1.14 nor the entire Gospel of John identifies Jesus as God. He boldly alleges, "Certainly the category 'becoming man' is alien to Jewish and originally Jewish-Christian thought and derives from the Hellenistic world.... The Greek conceptual model of 'incarnation' must to some degree be buried.... The man Jesus did not act as God's double

---

[102] George Eldon Ladd, *A Theology of the New Testament* (Grand Rapids: Eerdmans, 1974), 251.
[103] Brian Hebblethwaite, *The Incarnation: Collected Essays in Christology* (Cambridge: University, 1987), 2.
[104] J.D.G. Dunn, *Christology in the Making*, 2. Also see W. Pannenberg, *Jesus-God and Man*, 11.
[105] J. Hick, ed., *The Myth of God Incarnate*.
[106] A.E. Harvey, *Jesus and the Constraints of History*, 173.
[107] D. Cupitt, "Mr. Hebblethwaite on the Incarnation," in *Incarnation and Myth: The Debate Continued*, ed. Michael D. Goulder, 45.
[108] L. Berkhof, *Systematic Theology*, 4th rev. ed. (Grand Rapids: Eerdmans, 1939), 333.
[109] J.H. Bernard, *John*, 1:20.

('second God'). Rather, he proclaimed, manifested and revealed the word and will of the one God."[110] And Kung quotes Jn 17.3 for support.

In sum, neither the Gospel of John nor any of the Bible, for that matter, supports the classical definition of the incarnation. In the latter half of the 20th century, scholars steadily abandoned classical incarnation. Indeed, instead of God becoming a man, it is best to simply understand Jn 1.14a to mean that *Jesus is the man the Logos became*.

Agent Christology

Actually, the foremost christological motif in the Fourth Gospel is not incarnation Christology but "agent Christology." John informs us no less than forty times that the Father "sent" Jesus or did "send" Him as His agent. Some have labeled this concept a "Sending Christology." Jesus claimed similarly, that He "came" or did "come" from the Father. J.A.T. Robinson explains concerning this abundant data, "The picture which John presents is of Jesus as the Father's agent."[111] Indeed, church father and former lawyer, Tertullian, explains regarding the Johannine Jesus, "He had shown Himself to be the Father's Commissioner, through whose agency even the Father could be seen in His works, and heard in His words."[112] G.B. Caird states similarly, "Jesus is God's agent because he acts on behalf of God and because God is present in him."[113]

The writer of Hebrews calls Jesus an "apostle" (Heb 3.1). An apostle was an envoy, a sent agent. The word "apostle" (Gr. *apostolos*) combines the Greek word *apo* ("from) and *stello* ("to send") to mean "one sent." The Greek word *apostellein*, meaning "messenger," was used frequently in the Hellenistic world. It occurs 700x in the LXX and 135x in the Greek NT. An apostle in the NT was thus the agent of the sender.[114] The term "apostle" emphasizes the agency or commission rather than the agent himself.[115]

While Agent Christology is most prominent in the Fourth Gospel, it does not appear only there. E.P. Sanders summarizes Jesus' message in all four gospels, "He said, in effect, 'Give up everything you have and follow me, because I am God's agent.'"[116]

Only recently has this important concept of christological agency received much scholarly attention. Peder Borgen and, soon afterwards, A.E. Harvey, both produced compelling articles on Agent Christology as the primary key for understanding the "sent/came" terminology of the Fourth Gospel as it is applied to Jesus.[117] Borgen informs, "John's Christology and soteriology are molded on Jewish rules for agency."[118]

---

[110] H. Kung, *Credo*, 60-61.
[111] J.A.T. Robinson, *The Priority of John*, 350. Robinson notes several scholars who affirm likewise.
[112] Tertullian, *Against Praxeas*, 24.17.
[113] G.B. Caird, *New Testament Theology*, 414.
[114] Karl Heinrich Rengstorf, *Apostolate and Ministry* (St. Louis: Concordia, 1969), 27.
[115] Karl Heinrich Rengstorf, "*apostello*," in *TDNT* 1:404.
[116] E.P. Sanders, *The Historical Figure of Jesus*, 238.
[117] Peder Borgen, "God's Agent in the Fourth Gospel," in *The Interpretation of John*, ed. John Ashton (repr. Philadelphia/London: Fortress, SPCK, 1986), 67-78; first published in *Religions in Antiquity: Essays in Memory of Erwin Ramsdell Goodenough*, ed. Jacob Neusner (Leiden: Brill, 1968)]; A.E. Harvey, *Jesus and the Constraints of History*, esp. ch. 7; idem, "Christ as Agent," in *The Glory of Christ in the New Testament: Studies in Christology in Memory of George Bradford Caird*, eds. L.D. Hurst and N.T. Wright (Oxford: Clarendon, 1987), 239-50.
[118] P. Borgen, "God's Agent in the Fourth Gospel," 67.

Borgen and Harvey explain that, during antiquity, agency was practiced widely in business and law in the Near East, including in Israel.[119] Here's how it worked: a man as principal would select a man as a reliable agent, delegate his authority to him, and send him out as his representative to speak and/or act on his behalf. The one sent thus became the embodiment of the authority of the sender. A man's agent was like himself. So, to be in the presence of a man's agent was like being in the presence of that man himself.

In 1977, J.A. Buhner became the first Christian scholar to produce a book on Agent Christology.[120] Harvey claims, "This book is the first major study to have been devoted to the Jewish law of agency in relation to the New Testament, and in my opinion it makes a conclusive case for understanding much of the language used of Jesus in the Fourth Gospel as drawn from juridical practice."[121]

Both Jesus and the Judaism of His day applied the principle of agency to religion. For instance, Judaism endorsed the two axioms, "an agent is like the one who sent him,"[122] and "the sender is greater than the sent" (*Gen. R.* 78.1).

The primary issue in the ancient practice of agency was its proof. In order for an agent to conduct business on behalf of his principal, the agent had to verify that he indeed possessed the authority of his principal. That is why Jesus' opponents sometimes inquired of Him about His authority to teach and perform miracles, usually healings (Mt 21.23-27 par.). And that is an important reason why the Fourth Gospel, which has often been called "the book of signs," is structured around eight miraculous "signs" Jesus did. These signs testify to Jesus' authority as God's agent par excellence. Ernst Kasemann explains, "To be sent by God means, to begin with, nothing else than 'to be authorized'" by Him.[123]

To rightly understand the Johannine Jesus, Agent Christology can hardly be over-emphasized. It is the corrective to the misinterpretation of some Johannine texts in which Jesus is wrongly depicted as God or as God becoming a man.

Moreover, John portrays Jesus as teaching that Agent Christology, i.e., Sending Christology, should be the primary focus of saving faith for the believer. For example, the Johannine Jesus said that His works bear witness "that the Father has sent Me" (Jn 5.36). He added, "This is the work of God, that you believe in Him whom He has sent" (Jn 6.29; cf. 5.24, 38). Later, when Jesus anticipated His imminent resuscitation of Lazarus from the dead, He thanked God "that they [who would soon witness it] may believe that Thou didst send Me" (Jn 11.42). At the close of the teaching ministry of the Johannine Jesus His disciples said to Him, "Now we know ... [and] believe that You came from God" (Jn 16.30). Soon afterwards, He prayed to the Father that His disciples had "truly understood that I came forth from Thee, and they believed that Thou didst send Me" (Jn 17.8).

But how are we to understand Agent Christology regarding the Johannine Jesus' supposed preexistence? Does God sending Jesus require personal preexistence? Hardly! In the prophetic tradition, God has always sent His messengers. He asked Isaiah, "Whom shall I send"? The prophet replied, "Send

---

[119] P. Borgen, "God's Agent in the Fourth Gospel," 67-72. A.E. Harvey (*Jesus and the Constraints of History*, 161n50; "Christ as Agent," 242n12) cites authorities who provide bibliographic support. In modern times, the type of agency that we are perhaps most familiar with is real estate agency.
[120] J.A. Buhner, *Der Gesandte und sein Weg im 4. Evangelium* (Tubingen, 1977).
[121] A.E. Harvey, "Christ as Agent," 241.
[122] *Mek.* on Ex 12.3, 6; cf. *m. Ber.* 5.5; *b. Hag.* 10b; *b. Menah.* 93b.
[123] E. Kasemann, *The Testament of Jesus*, 11.

me" (Isa 6.8). That is like the Fourth Evangelist describing John the Baptist as "sent from God" (Jn 1.6). No one (except maybe Origen!) would assert that God sending prophets implies their preexistence. Moderate traditionalist Christopher Tuckett explains, "The idea of Jesus as the one who is 'sent' certainly need not imply any very 'high' Christology.... The language of 'sending' on its own is thus probably rooted in prophetic traditions showing Jesus as a true prophet figure."[124]

Moreover, if God sending Jesus implies that Jesus preexisted in heaven and came to earth to accomplish the incarnation, then the Johannine Jesus says the same of His apostles, which, of course, is absurd. For, during Jesus' High Priestly Prayer He said to the Father, "As Thou didst send Me into the world, I also have sent them into the world" (Jn 17.18). The word "as" (Gr. *kathos*) indicates comparison and therefore means "just as."[125] So, Jesus says that just as the Father sent Him, so He has sent His apostles.

Jacob Jervel insists that the idea of God sending Jesus must be understood from a Jewish rather than a Hellenistic (and therefore a metaphysical, ontological) perspective. Recall that the author of the Fourth Gospel is a Jew writing to Jews. Jervel contends that for Jews, God sending the Messiah merely meant that He delegated full, divine authority to Him. Jervell rightly asserts, "It is a misunderstanding to believe that the gospel of John makes Jesus into God, or identical with God. The gospel permits the Jews to bring the accusation of blasphemy against Jesus, that is, that he equates himself with God (5.18). This criticism is pushed aside in the gospel. Jesus is not God but God's representative, and, as such, so completely and totally acts on God's behalf that he stands in God's stead before the world."[126] AMEN!

In sum, *as God's supreme agent, Jesus functions as God without being God.* That is what many scholars mean when they speak of an exclusively functional Christology.

The Meaning of *theos* in John

In English, the word "God" is generally understood as a proper name. In Christian theology, such usage would seem to restrict its application exclusively to the Father.

Theos is the Greek word for "God." It appears in the Greek text of the Gospel of John either 82 or 83 times.[127] Traditionalists concede that, in all but three of these cases, *theos* refers only to the Father. They insist that Jn 1.1c, 1.18, and 20.28 are the three exceptions in which *theos* should be treated as a title rather than a proper name.[128]

However, the following paramount reasons are against any such exceptions:
1. Such frequent Johannine application of *theos* to the Father suggests otherwise.
2. All four Evangelists often quote Jesus as using "God" (*theos*) and "the/Father" (Gr. *pater*) interchangeably,[129] showing that Jesus treated these words synonymously.

---

[124] C. Tuckett, *Christology in the New Testament*, 161.
[125] BAGD, 391.
[126] J. Jervell, *Jesus in the Gospel of John*, 21. Yet Jervell (pp. 16-17) recognizes Jesus as "divine."
[127] The second occurrence of *theos* in John 1.18> is textually questionable.
[128] E.g., M. Harris, *Jesus as God*, 124.
[129] Jesus would have spoken the Aramaic word for "Father," *abba*, and the Aramaic word for "God," *elah*.

3. How the Evangelists' employ *theos* likely would not differ from their record of how Jesus used it in His sayings, which was always as a reference to the Father.
4. The Evangelists would likely not differ between themselves in their use of *theos*.

Moreover, this traditionalist argument about exceptions may be ill framed. For, some contemporary commentators think *theos* in the Fourth Gospel indicates a category rather than represents either a title or a proper name. (See comments on Jn 1.1c>.)

The Invisibility of God

Like Paul (1 Tim 1.17; 6.16), the Fourth Evangelist affirms the OT teaching that God is invisible to human sight (e.g., Ex 33.20; Deut 4.12). He first introduces this idea at the end of his prologue by saying, "No man has seen God at any time" (Jn 1.18; cf. 5.37). He takes up the subject again by quoting Jesus as affirming the same thing when He said, "Not that any man has seen the Father, except the One who is from God, He has seen the Father" (Jn 6.46), referring to Himself. And the first Johannine epistle affirms, "No one has beheld God at any time" (1 Jn 4.12). People will see God in the resurrection (Job 19.26; Ps 17.15; Mt 5.8). The logical conclusion is inescapable: *If humans have not literally seen God, yet people saw Jesus, then Jesus cannot be God.*

Distinguishing God and Christ

Like much of the NT, the Fourth Evangelist frequently distinguishes God from Christ. This is most clear in the following examples:
- Jesus - "Me, a man who has told you the truth, which I heard from God" (Jn 8.40).
- Martha to Jesus - "whatever you ask of God, God will give You" (Jn 11.22).
- John on Jesus – "He had come forth from God, and was going back to God" (Jn 13.3).
- Jesus to His apostles - "believe in God, believe also in Me" (Jn 14.1).
- The apostles to Jesus - "we believe that You came from God" (Jn 16.30).

In all of these texts, "God" is axiomatically understood as "the Father."

Besides Jn 17.3, which we will examine soon, nowhere else does the Fourth Gospel distinguish Jesus and God more clearly as separate beings than in Jn 7.16-17: "Jesus therefore answered them, and said, 'My teaching is not Mine, but His who sent Me. If any man is willing to do His will, he shall know of the teaching, whether it is of God, or whether I speak from Myself.'"

The Fourth Gospel sometimes further distinguishes God and Christ by stating the genitive case for "God" in the Greek text (Gr. *theou*), that Jesus is "from God" (Jn 3.2; 6.46; 9.33; 16.30), which the Johannine Jesus can readily admit Himself (Jn 8.42).

The Subordination of the Son to God

Another very distinctive feature of Johannine Christology is the subordination of the Son to the Father.[130] This is most evident in the Fourth Gospel, not only in sending the Son but in His investiture as well. That is, the Father has given "all things" to the Son (Jn 3.35; 13.3; 17.7, 10), alluding to Dan 7.14. For example, the Johannine Jesus claims that the Father has already given Him future authority

---

[130] Contra Mark L. Appold, *The Oneness Motif in the Fourth Gospel: Motif Analysis and Exegetical Probe into the Theology of John* (Tubingen: Mohr-Siebeck, 1976), 22.

to raise the dead (Jn 6.39-40), give eternal life (Jn 5.21, 26; 6.27), and judge and execute judgment (Jn 5.22, 27). Since Jesus discloses that His authority to do these things is derived from the Father, this implies His subordination to Him. The paramount question is whether the Fourth Evangelist portrays Jesus as *essentially* subordinate to the Father or merely *functionally* subordinate to Him. According to classical incarnation, Jesus could only have been the latter.

In classical incarnation, two factors—Christ's deity and His subordination to God the Father—present a striking paradox, especially as viewed in the Fourth Gospel. A few traditionalist scholars admit that this paradox is a problem for their position.[131] For instance, traditionalist R.E. Brown acknowledges that "even in the New Testament works that speak of Jesus as God, there are also passages that seem to militate against such a usage."[132] In contrast, traditionalist L.W. Hurtado maintains, "There is no indication whatsoever that the Fourth Evangelist noticed any tension between the subordinationist theme and his exalted view of Christ as one with the Father."[133]

But there is no paradox, and thus no tension, in John's gospel if the most exalted status it assigns to Jesus is that God mystically indwells Him, resulting in a completely functional unity between God and Jesus. Philip Harner explains that John "frequently weaves together the themes of unity and subordination in the same passage, indicating in this way that they must be seen in close interrelationship with one another."[134]

Closely associated with the subordination of the Son is His obedience to God the Father. Yet Jesus *being* God and *obeying* God are incompatible concepts. C.K. Barrett asserts concerning Jn 8.28>, "It is simply intolerable that Jesus should be made to say, 'I am God, the supreme God of the Old Testament, and being God I do as I am told.'"[135]

The Dependence of the Son upon God

In order for Jesus to accomplish all that He did, *He had to depend totally on the Father*. Nowhere is this more evident than in the Gospel of John, and it is usually Jesus who says so. As with subordination, we encounter an irresolvable paradox between the Johannine Jesus' supposed deity and His dependence on the Father. The two foremost Johannine sayings of Jesus that indicate His inadequacy, and therefore require His total dependence on the Father, are the following: (1) "I can of mine own self do nothing," and (2) "I can do nothing on My own initiative" (Jn 5.19, 30). Yet Jesus could also say, "all things are possible with God" (Mk 10.27). So, Jesus depended completely upon God's adequacy and not His own. Martinus de Jonge remarks concerning the Johannine Jesus, "Although he himself may be called 'god,' he remains dependent on the Father."[136] De Jonge does not capitalize "god," here, because he does not believe Jesus is fully God. He asserts correctly concerning the Johannine Jesus, "Jesus, a human being, has not usurped the prerogatives of the one and only God;... his close relationship as Son to the Father in no way led to his deification or to an infringement on monotheism."[137]

---

[131] E.g., A.W. Wainwright, "The Confession 'Jesus Is God' in the New Testament," 289n2; R.E. Brown, *An Introduction to New Testament Christology*, 176; G.R. Beasley-Murray, *John*, 11.
[132] R.E. Brown, *Jesus God and Man*, 33.
[133] L.W. Hurtado, "God," *DJG*, 274.
[134] P. Harner, *The 'I Am' in the Fourth Gospel*, 53-54. These passages are Jn 5.17-24; 10.29-32; 17.19-26.
[135] C.K. Barrett, *Essays on John*, 12.
[136] M. de Jonge, *God's Final Envoy*, 125.
[137] M. de Jonge, *God's Final Envoy*, 140-41.

The Johannine Jesus clearly derived His miraculous powers from the Father in order to perform signs (Jn 5.19-30; 8.28-29; 17.2, 4). And He often attributed these works to the Father.[138] Moreover, the Johannine Jesus disclosed explicitly that He was given these gifts because He always depended upon the Father (Jn 11.22; 17.7-8). Thus, *not only were Jesus' astounding powers not intrinsic to His own nature, but their bestowal on Him was conditioned by His subordination to, and dependence upon, God.*

The Johannine Jesus also depended on the Father as the source of His wisdom. He frequently divulges that the Father gave Him both His words and His teaching.[139] Jesus proclaimed that Moses wrote about Him (Jn 5.46-47; cf. 12.48-49), referring to Deut 18.18-19. Therein, Yahweh said, "I will put My words in his mouth, and he shall speak to them all that I command him" (v. 18). Jesus explains, "I did not speak on My own initiative, but the Father Himself who sent Me has given Me commandment, what to say, and what to speak" (Jn 12.49). Thus, a major role the Johannine Jesus fulfills is Moses' prediction of "that prophet" like himself. He would be God's mouthpiece,[140] whom some scholars now call "the New Moses." Ernest Davey alleges that Jesus' dependence upon God is "the chief constituent in Christ's experience of God the Father; one might indeed call this dependence the ruling element in John's portrait of Christ. The so-called 'Johannine Christ'...is a myth; a Christ, I mean, who is omniscient, omnipotent, self-determining and independent."[141]

Truth and Life in the Son

Two other prominent themes in the Fourth Gospel are that both truth and life reside in the Son. These, too, are a strong witness to Jesus' dependence upon the Father.

The words "true" and "truth" (Gr. *alethes, aletheia*) appear in the Gospel of John 21x and 27x, respectively. Yet they hardly occur in the Synoptics. The first occurrence is in John's prologue, in which the Law coming through Moses is contrasted with grace and truth coming through Jesus Christ (Jn 1.14, 17).

But how did the Johannine Jesus attain truth? We learned earlier that He once told His opponents, "you are seeking to kill Me, a man who has told you the truth, which I heard from God" (Jn 8.40). Jesus did not claim to intrinsically possess the truth, as would be expected of one who was God. Rather, *Jesus claimed to receive the truth from God.*

The Fourth Gospel also says Jesus told the "truth."[142] In a very sublime moment reported only in this gospel, Jesus informs Governor Pilate, "Everyone who is of the truth hears My voice" (Jn 18.37). Pilate responds, "What is truth?" and then walks out (v. 38). Thereafter, Jesus has nothing more to say to the governor, even when he asked Jesus. (This ought to be a warning to all non-believers who hear the gospel.) But the supreme "truth" passage in John's gospel is when Jesus said to His disciples, "I am the way, the truth, and the life; no one comes to the Father but through Me" (Jn 14.6). Jesus doesn't just *tell* the truth; He *is* the truth. But that doesn't make Him God, just *the way* to God.

The same is true of the Johannine Jesus about the concept of life. The word "life" (Gr. *zoe* or *psuche*) appears 47x in the Fourth Gospel, more than all three Synoptics combined. In over one-third of these occurrences, it is qualified as

---

[138] Jn 5.19, 36; 9.3-4; 10.25, 32, 37-38; 14.10; 17.4.

[139] Jn 7.16; 8.28; 12.49; 14.24; 17.8, 14.

[140] Cf. Deut 18.18-19 with esp. Jn 12.48-50.

[141] J. Ernest Davey, *The Jesus of St. John* (London: Lutterworth, 1958), 77.

[142] Jn 5.33; 8.40, 45-46; 16.7; 18.37.

"eternal life." This theme about life is first set forth in the prologue with the assertion about Jesus, that "in Him was life" (Jn 1.4). This life is probably the abundant life Jesus describes in Jn 10.10, which He lays down for His disciples. His resurrection manifests eternal life, which is given to all who believe in Him (Jn 3.15-16, 36; 5.24; 6.40, 47). Yet, like truth, eternal life was not intrinsic to Jesus. For He said, "just as the Father has life in Himself, even so He gave to the Son also to have life in Himself" (Jn 5.26; cf. Rev 1.18). So, it is derived.

Perhaps nothing attests more clearly to Jesus' utter dependence on God than God giving Him the truth and eternal life.

The Resurrection of the Son

We saw in Chapter Six that some traditionalists have insisted that the resurrection of Jesus indicates that He was God. This issue centers on the question: Did Jesus raise Himself from the dead or did God? If Jesus did, it is thought to support that He is God.

Luke repeatedly proclaims in his book of Acts that *God raised Jesus from the dead*. Yet John seems to present Jesus teaching otherwise. For instance, John records that early in Jesus' public ministry He said to the crowd at one of the Passover feasts at the temple at Jerusalem, "Destroy this temple, and in three days I will raise it up" (Jn 2.19). John adds, "He was speaking of the temple of His body" (v. 21). Gerald Hawthorne explains, "But then John immediately goes on to say about Jesus that 'when he *had been raised* from the dead, his disciples recalled what he had said' (John 2:22). His use of the passive voice here, 'had been raised,' indicates that in the final analysis a power other than Jesus' own power brought about his resurrection."[143]

John continues this theme. He quotes Jesus as saying, "I am the good shepherd. The good shepherd lays down His life for the sheep" (Jn 10.11, cf. v. 14-15). Jesus further reveals, "For this reason the Father loves Me, because I lay down My life that I may take it again" (v. 17). Does Jesus mean He will accomplish His own resurrection? Yes and No. He adds, "No one has taken it away from Me, but I lay it down on My own initiative. I have authority to lay it down, and I have authority to take it up again. This command I received from My Father" (v. 18). He means that His authority, and assumedly His power, to resurrect Himself comes from the Father. These words anticipate what He said later, "all things that the Father has are Mine" (Jn 16.15; cf. 17.10). A primary theme of the Fourth Gospel is that the Father gives Jesus His works (e.g., Jn 5.36). So, everything that Jesus does is God doing it through Him, including His own resurrection from the dead.

Accordingly, there is no contradiction between God raising Jesus from the dead and Jesus raising Himself. R.E. Brown explains, "Since in Johannine thought the Father and the Son possess the same power (x 28-30), it really makes little difference whether the resurrection is attributed to the action of the Father or of the Son."[144] Thus, if Jesus somehow participated in raising Himself from the dead, it does not indicate that He possessed deity because He would have done so by the power given to Him by God.

As with so many other attributes of Jesus, if He was God He would have innately possessed the authority and power to raise Himself from the dead. But this would conflict with what He said earlier, that "the Son can do nothing of

---

[143] G. Hawthorne, *The Presence and the Power*, 185. Emphasis not mine.
[144] R.E. Brown, *John i-xii*, 399. In debt to G. Hawthorne (*The Presence and the Power*, 196n17) for quote.

Himself" (Jn 5.19, cf. v. 30). The truth is the Father gave Jesus eternal life, which culminates in resurrection (Jn 5.26).

The Holy Spirit

In Chapter Six we learned that everything Jesus said and did was accomplished by the Spirit of God. The Holy Spirit is more prominent in the Fourth Gospel than in the Synoptics. But this Johannine material regards mostly Jesus' predictions about baptizing His disciples in the Holy Spirit and this Paraclete thereafter guiding and empowering them (Jn 1.33; 7.39; 14-16; 20.22). Indeed, the most prominent events that fired up the early Christians, eventually causing later Christians to "turn the world upside down," were (1) Jesus' empty tomb, (2) His post-resurrection appearances, and (3) the Holy Spirit coming upon the disciples on the day of Pentecost in great power to manifest the charismata and give them wisdom and boldness to proclaim the message of their risen Lord Jesus. Yet this Paraclete teaching in John is irrelevant to identity Christology.[145]

However, John does relate that God "gives the Spirit without measure" to Jesus (Jn 3.34; cf. Col 1.19>; 2.9>). Consequently, the following question only arises in the Gospel of John: If Jesus was God due to the Incarnate Logos, of what use was the Holy Spirit to Jesus? (To answer with some kenotic theory proves unsatisfactory, as we shall see in Chapter Seven/Phil 2.5-11>.) Irrespective of the relation of the Logos to Jesus, God's infusion of wisdom and miraculous power in Jesus must have come from the Holy Spirit (e.g., Isa 11.2). How the Logos and the Holy Spirit are to be precisely differentiated in Jesus—beyond the Logos being viewed as the *expression* of God and the Holy Spirit as the *power* of God—will probably remain a mystery to be revealed in the Age to Come.

The Superiority of God the Father

Jesus is most known in the Gospel of John for calling God His "Father." He does it about 120x and calls Himself God's "Son" 27x. The main purpose of these appellations is to signify the extraordinarily intimate relationship between Jesus and God.

Similar to the subordination and dependence themes, and, again, more than the synoptists do, the Fourth Evangelist occasionally puts forth the motif that the Father is superior to the Son. And again, on each occasion this teaching is by Jesus Himself (Jn 5.19; 7.16; 10.29; 14.28). Foremost among these types of sayings of Jesus are His words recorded in Jn 14.28, which He uttered after the Last Supper. The Master informs His disciples that He would soon leave them and go to His Father in heaven. Then He adds:

28 "You have heard that I said to you, 'I go away, and I will come to you.' If you loved Me, you would have rejoiced, because I go to the Father; for the Father is greater than I."

The critical words for Christology are the last clause: "the Father is greater than I."

This comparative disclosure by Jesus became the subject of much christological dispute during the Arian-Nicene Controversy of the 4th century.[146]

---

[145] But this was not true of orthodoxy. The foremost disagreement between the RCC and the Eastern Orthodox Church (EOC) has been an issue regarding both pneumatology and Christology: whether the Holy Spirit proceeds from the Father through Christ (RCC) or only from the Father (EOC).

[146] In contrast, T.E. Pollard (*Johannine Christology and the Early Church*, 154) disputes this but acknowledges that few Arian writings are extant.

The Arians used this statement to support their position that the Father is superior to the Son regarding their essence or nature. And they cited both Tertullian and Origen for support.[147]

Church fathers' response to this Arian assertion is weak because three different interpretations of Jn 14.28 prevailed among them. These are as follows, with rebuttals:

1. This saying only concerns generation, and not essence, by expressing a distinction between the Father as Unbegotten and the Son as Only-begotten (e.g., Origen, Tertullian, Alexander of Alexandria, Athanasius, Basil, and Gregory of Nazianzus).

    Rebuttal: R.E. Brown rejects this viewpoint, saying it is "anachronistic to imagine that John had Jesus speaking to his disciples of inner trinitarian relationships."[148]

2. Jesus speaks from His humanity and not His deity, meaning that He is less than the Father only because of His incarnation, i.e., His being a man (Augustine). This view is a further refinement of view #1.

    Rebuttal: C.K. Barrett argues that Jn 14.28 cannot "be simply explained away as having reference only to the humanity or incarnate life of our Lord."[149] And we have already discussed that this two-nature exegesis is neither biblical nor sustainable on either anthropological or psychological grounds.

3. Jesus intended only a comparison of office, or function, and not personal essence.

    Rebuttal: Many traditionalist scholars are inconsistent in their interpretation of Jn 10.30 and 14.28. For we have just seen that many of them insist arbitrarily that Jn 10.30 speaks of the essence of the Father and Christ but deny the same in Jn 14.28, and they often do so without recognizing this inconsistency, much less defending it.

The Greek word translated "greater" in Jn 14.28 is *meizon*, which means greater in "rank and dignity."[150] Obviously, a difference in rank or dignity between the Father and Christ does not accord well with the traditional view of their supposed co-equality.

The context that immediately precedes Jn 14.28 implies an essential subordination of Jesus to the Father. In fact, this was the view of both the Arians and Eusebius. The conjunctive word "for" (Gr. *hoti*="because"), at the beginning of this clause, points to the words that immediately precede it. These words—"I go to the Father"—further hint at the Father being greater than Christ in essence. How so? Christ going to the Father recalls His initial commission, i.e., that God elected, consecrated, and sent Christ as His agent. Also, Jesus had just said at the Last Supper, "a slave is not greater than his master; neither is one who is sent greater than the one who sent him" (Jn 13.16; cf. Mt 10.24; Lk 6.40).

Why should Jesus' disciples rejoice that He would soon leave them? The answer is that He will soon ascend into heaven to be exalted and glorified. They should rejoice not only for their Lord but *for their own selves*. Only then will

---

[147] M.F. Wiles, *The Spiritual Gospel*, 122. P. Schaff (*History of the Christian Church*, 3:619) observes, "The roots of the Arian controversy are to be found partly in the contradictory elements of the Christology of the great Origen," viz., his doctrines of eternal generation and the essential subordination of the Son.

[148] R.E. Brown, *John (xiii-xxi)*, 654.

[149] C.K. Barrett, *John*, 91. However, see Barrett's comment on p. 468, which seems to contradict.

[150] BAGD, 498a.

the Father send His Spirit on the day of Pentecost to recall many things to their minds about Jesus and to further enlighten, guide, and empower them in their mission.

The context that follows Jn 14.28 concerns the Son's obedience and thus portrays His essential subordination to the Father. So does Jesus' conclusion of this discourse, in which He says, "as the Father gave Me commandment, even so I do" (Jn 14.31).

The Father rewarding His Son demonstrates the Father's superiority over His Son. For, the OT portrait is of the one God enthroned above His worshipping angels in heaven and enveloped in a magnificent, shining glory (e.g., Eze 1). Contrast this with the lowly position of Jesus as the Son of Man on earth, enduring humiliation in a world system engulfed in sin and death and ruled by evil cosmic powers. The Son's reward for His perfect obedience while living in this sinful world was to be enthroned and honored equally alongside God, His heavenly Father. Such reward indicates that the God-Father was always greater in rank and dignity than His Son.

The Father sending His Son presupposes the Father's superiority over His Son as well. And this concept is not new here; it has appeared subtly in Jn 5.19, 30 and 10.29.

The converse of the Father's superiority over His unique Son must be true as well. Though it is never stated in Scripture, this one-of-a-kind Son is necessarily inferior to the Father. Vincent Taylor tries to soothe the feelings of those traditionalists who bristle at this converse idea by remarking, "subordination is robbed of all the sting of inferiority in the manifold relationship of love which exists between the Father and the Son."[151]

This interpretation of Jn 14.28—the Father is essentially greater than the Son—is supported in several ways. One is the Jewish Midrash, "The sender is greater than the one sent."[152] Another regards typology, in which Joseph was a type of Christ and Pharaoh a type of God. Pharaoh made Joseph second highest rank in Egypt and said, "all my people shall do homage" to you; "only in the throne I will be greater than you" (Gen 41.40).

In conclusion, *Jesus' statement that God the Father is greater than Himself emerges as very substantial evidence that Jesus cannot be God.*

Only the Father Is God

The fact that the Son worships the Father, yet the Father does not worship the Son, further demonstrates the inferiority of the Son to the Father. Recall that this concept surfaces here in the Fourth Gospel, in which the Samaritan woman at Jacob's well questions Jesus about worship. The Samaritans had always contended with the Jews that the proper place to worship God was on their Mount Gerizim rather than at the Temple Mount in Jerusalem. Due to this background, Jesus replied to the Samaritan woman, "You worship that which you do not know; we worship that which we know, for salvation is from the Jews" (Jn 4.22). Notice that Jesus said "we," thereby including Himself among Jews who worship God. Note also in this dialogue that Jesus interchanges "God" and "the Father" (vv. 21, 23-24). The question therefore arises, How can Jesus be God if He worships God? And, if so, how does this affect Jewish monotheism?

---

[151] V. Taylor, *The Person of Christ*, 97.
[152] *Gen. Rab.* 78.1.

John the Evangelist was a strict monotheist, and that is how he presents Jesus.[153] John quotes Jesus as calling the Father, "the one and only God" (Jn 5.44). This phrase alludes to the Shema (cf. Mk 12.29 par.). John A.T. Robinson claims "that John is as undeviating a witness as any in the New Testament to the fundamental tenet of Judaism, of unitary monotheism. There is the one true and only God (John 5:44; 17:3)."[154]

The strongest monotheistic statement in the NT *is probably Jn 17.3. It is surely the premier* NT *text which shows that only the Father is God and that Jesus Christ is not God.* Most significantly, Jesus said it. As He lifted up His eyes to heaven, Jesus began to pray His longest prayer recorded in the NT. He begins as follows:

1 "Father, the hour has come, glorify Thy Son, that the Son may glorify Thee,
2 even as Thou gavest Him authority over all mankind, that to all whom Thou hast given Him, He may give eternal life.
3 And this is eternal life, that they may know Thee, the only true God, and Jesus Christ, whom Thou hast sent" (Jn 17.1-3).[155]

Furthermore, *nowhere else in the* NT *gospels does Jesus more clearly distinguish Himself from God than in Jn 17.3.* Also, He therein succinctly stresses the necessity for people to believe in both God and Himself in order for them to obtain eternal life (cf. Jn 14.1). However, elsewhere in this gospel Jesus makes it clear that if a person genuinely believes in Him, that person automatically believes in God who sent Him (e.g., Jn 12.44).

We have seen that Arius, Eusebius, and Socinus all employed Jn 17.3 as their primary scriptural support for their respective christologies. All three men interpreted these words in the same manner, i.e., that the Father, being "the only true God," is essentially superior to the Son so that the Son is God only in a derivative sense. The Arians apparently cited statements in Isaiah for additional support, in which Yahweh pronounces Himself as the only God (Isa 43.10-11; 44.6; 45.5-6, 18, 21-22; 46.9).

Some church fathers made rather feeble attempts to reconcile Jn 17.3 with their Christology. For example, Athanasius sought to refute the Arians with a most ludicrous interpretation of Jn 17.3, in which Jesus did not exclude Himself from the concept of "the only true God" but only contrasted it to all gods falsely so-called.[156] And Augustine, who did not know Greek, arbitrarily rearranged the verse to read, "That they may know Thee and Jesus Christ, whom Thou hast sent, as the only true God."[157] On the other hand, Roman Catholic traditionalist R.E. Brown acknowledges, "the 'one true God' and 'Jesus Christ' are not identified" as

---

[153] D. Cupitt (*Jesus and the Gospel of God*, 18) rightly assesses that the entire NT is strictly monotheistic.
[154] J.A.T. Robinson, *Twelve More New Testament Studies*, 175. The Greek word in these texts is *monos*.
[155] Not only form-critical scholars dismiss this third person designation—"Jesus Christ"—as redactional and therefore inauthentic. C.K. Barrett (*John*, 503) avoids this conclusion by suggesting that John intended v. 3 as his own parenthetic insertion, like a footnote, to define eternal life. Regardless, the Christology of v. 3 remains intact and true whether the words are those of Jesus, John, or later editors.
[156] Athanasius, *Orations Against the Arians*, 3.7-9. Athanasius (3.8) also argues that God said His "I am" pronouncements, in Isaiah (Isa 41.4; 43.10, 13; 48.12), by His Logos, so that His Logos was not excluded either. And Athanasius (3.9) asserts that Jesus is called "the true God" in 1 Jn 5.20>.
[157] Augustine, *Homilies on the Gospel of John* in NPNF¹, 7:105, 3.

the same individual in Jn 17.3. He therefore tepidly admits that "this verse runs somewhat contrary to other verses in John that call Jesus 'God.'"[158]

According to Jn 17.3, Jesus clearly believed that there is only one true God and that the Father is that one God. The logical deduction is that Jesus *did not* believe that He Himself was the one God. Actually, this verse conceivably might be interpreted in such a manner as to worry traditionalists. Jesus could have meant that for a person to receive eternal life, that individual must believe that the Father is the only true God and that this God sent Jesus, so that only the Father is God and Jesus is not God. But God looks more on our hearts rather than whether our minds grasp the perfect theology.

The Son of God

The identification of Jesus as "the Son of God" must be understood in accordance with His religious culture and thus the OT and Judaism. We saw in Chapter Four that this epithet could be applied to angels, the king of Israel, or an extraordinarily righteous man. The Fourth Evangelist provides nothing to indicate otherwise. Therefore, he does not give any reason for his readers to think that his application of this title to Jesus indicates an ontological, preexistent generation of the Son, as church fathers later insisted.

Jesus is called "the Son" (Gr. *ho huios*) in the Gospel of John much more often than anywhere else in the NT. John applies this title to Jesus 27x,[159] with Jesus sometimes being the speaker. John usually, but not always,[160] adds the definite article "the." It designates Jesus as the special Son of God and thus one more prominent than any other son.

In the NT, the Apostle Paul most often designates believers as "sons (of God)."[161] This further demonstrates that calling Jesus "a/the Son of God" does not indicate deity. (Capitalizing "Son" as a designation for Jesus, compared to identifying believers as "sons," is not based on the Greek text and therefore does not indicate deity.) Yet John in his gospel seems to distinguish a difference between Jesus' Sonship and that of Jesus' disciples by calling the latter "children (of God)" rather than "sons (of God)."

Examining instances in which the Fourth Evangelist designates Jesus as "(the) Son (of God)" should help us in understanding the meaning of this epithet as applied to Jesus.

John the Baptist is the first person recorded in the Gospel of John to call Jesus "the Son of God" (Jn 1.34). He made this designation because, when he baptized Jesus, he heard the voice from above proclaim, "This is My beloved Son, in whom I am well-pleased" (Mt 3.17 par.). The idea of Jesus being well-pleasing to God seems to establish the primary meaning of His being "the Son (of God)." That is, Jesus is the Son of God because He lives His life before God as an obedient son lives before his righteous father, the son imitating what he sees his beloved father doing (e.g., Jn 5.19-20). So, *designating the Johannine Jesus as the Son of God signifies, first and foremost, that God highly favors Him and He has an extraordinary relationship with God, which seems to be because of His piety.*

The second occurrence of Jesus being designated "the Son of God" in the Gospel of John is when Jesus told a bit of supernatural knowledge to Nathanael

---

[158] R.E. Brown, *John (xiii-xxi)*, 741.
[159] It is 28x, if Jn 1.18 has "Son." And 1 Jn includes this expression 22x.
[160] Jn 10.36; 19.7. See also Mt 27.54; Mk 15.39; Lk 1.32, 35.
[161] Rom 8.14-15, 19, 23; 9.4; 9.26/Hos 1.10; 2 Cor 6.18; Gal 3.26; 4.5-6; Eph 1.5.

about himself. In response, "Nathanael answered Him, 'Rabbi, You are the Son of God; You are the King of Israel'" (Jn 1.49). Because Nathanael was influenced by Judaism and the OT, he seems to have used these titles synonymously.[162] For, the title "son of God" was applied to the king of Israel in the OT (2 Sam 7.14; Ps 2.6-7, 12; 89.26-27) and the DSS. Nathanael must have been identifying Jesus as the Messiah as in Ps 2, where Messiah, Son of God, and King of Israel are all brought together as epithets for the same Person. So, *calling the Johannine Jesus "the Son of God" signifies His future role as the Messiah-King of Israel.*

Furthermore, John's account of how Jesus so often identified God affirms Jesus' filial relationship to God. For, the Johannine Jesus calls God "My/the Father" just over 100x. This in itself, of course, implies that Jesus is the Son of God, God being His Father.

But the most prevalent occurrences of the Johannine Jesus being identified as "(the) Son (of God)" are in a context of the Father *sending* Jesus to speak the Father's words and do His works. This act of sending *does not* indicate or require an ontological, preexistent generation;[163] rather, *God sending His Son indicates Agent Christology.*

Indeed, the Sonship of Jesus is the epitome of Agent Christology. A man's best agent was usually his adult son. Who could he trust more? And who knew the man better than his own son? As God's agent, Jesus said, "whatever the Father does, these things the Son also does in like manner" (Jn 5.19). A son naturally imitates what he sees his father doing. Jesus also said, "no one knows the Father except the Son" (Mt 11.27 NRSV; cf. Lk 10.22). *Jesus being the unique Son of God marks Him as God's agent par excellence.*[164]

Recall that church fathers, being influenced by Greek metaphysics, obliterated the Jewish distinction between "God" and "the Son of God." This practice has continued among so many traditionalist scholars to this day,[165] even among a few distinguished historical-critical scholars.[166] Some of them indicate as much by applying the expression "divine Sonship" to Jesus, which terminology traces to the patristic era. These scholars believe that identifying Jesus as "the Son (of God)" indicates His deity and therefore His preexistence. Moderate traditionalist James D.G. Dunn states, "Only in the Fourth Gospel does the understanding of a personal pre-existence fully emerge, of Jesus as the divine Son before the world began."[167] But moderate traditionalist G.B. Caird points out, as did Michael Servetus, that "John never uses 'Son' of the pre-existent logos, only of the incarnate logos, the human Jesus." Thus, "Son" in the Fourth Gospel, as well as especially in Lk 1.32, 35, refers exclusively to "the historical Jesus,"[168] if not also the risen Jesus.

The Revealer of God

So, *in calling Jesus "the Son of God," John does not depict Jesus as God but the Revealer of God*. This is perhaps the best way to explain the meaning of Jesus' Sonship, that He perfectly reveals God because the Father can be

---

[162] G. R. Beasley-Murray, *John*, 27.

[163] K.H. Rengstorf, *TDNT* 1:405.

[164] Cf. C.H. Dodd, *The Interpretation of the Fourth Gospel*, 254-62; P. Borgen, "God's Agent in the Fourth Gospel," 68-69; A.E. Harvey, "Christ as Agent," 241.

[165] An example is M. Harris, *Jesus as God*, 208, 293, 317.

[166] E.g., P.M. Casey, *From Jewish Prophet to Gentile God*, 23-25, 33, 37, 156-57.

[167] J.D.G. Dunn, *Christology in the Making*, 61.

[168] G.B. Caird, *New Testament Theology*, 296-97, 322. Caird (p. 320) further insists that for both the Apostle Paul and the author of Hebrews, "'the Son' is a title for the human Jesus."

spiritually seen in the Son (cf. Jn 1.18; 12.45; 14.9, 11). Bultmann well explains that John identifying Jesus as the Son of God means that "Jesus is the Revealer, in whom God encounters man."[169]

Greek philosophers always maintained that the Logos was the Revealer of God. But they shared no consensus on how this could be. And their dualism would not permit them to conceive that the Logos, which they regarded as pure spirit, could become flesh since they believed intercourse with the material world would taint the Logos with evil.

In contrast, John's deepest conviction is that the Logos became a man, having a physical body of flesh and bones, and that this man—Jesus Christ—was the Revealer of God.[170] B.F. Westcott insightfully explains concerning the Johannine Jesus, "He never speaks of Himself as God (cf. vv. 17-18), but the aim of His revelation was to lead men to see God in Him."[171] And E. Kasemann, despite his frequent assertions that the Johannine Jesus was God walking on the earth (which Kasemann later refuted), nevertheless states that John "is concerned exclusively throughout with the presence of God in Christ."[172]

The Johannine Jesus was most evident as the Revealer of God when He said, "He who has seen Me has seen the Father" (Jn 14.9). This identification is like the Apostle Paul and the author of Hebrews describing Jesus metaphorically as the image of God, or Paul stating, "God was in Christ reconciling the world to Himself" (2 Cor 5.19). R.E. Brown says of the latter, "this is scarcely the same as saying that Christ was God."[173]

Jesus as the Revealer of God portrays perfectly a God-in-Christ Christology. And it dovetails with a Sending/Agent Christology. Putting it all together, *Jesus Christ was sent by God as God's agent to perfectly reveal God by God being in Christ.*

The Purpose of the Fourth Gospel

Finally, John cannot be saying that Jesus is God because that would conflict with his purpose for writing his gospel, which he states at close of his book, in Jn 20.30-31, as follows:[174]

30 Many other signs therefore Jesus also performed in the presence of the disciples, which are not written in this book;
31 but these have been written that you may believe that Jesus is the Christ, the Son of God; and that believing you may life in His name.

Thus, John says that he wrote his book to persuade his readers to believe, or continue to believe, or both, that Jesus is the Christ, the Son of God. And he likely meant that not only these "signs," but the dialogues as well, are intended for this purpose.[175]

---

[169] R. Bultmann, *John*, 93n1.
[170] J.H. Bernard, *John*, 1:cxlii.
[171] Brooke Foss Westcott, *The Gospel According to St. John: The Greek Text With Introduction And Notes* [1902], 2 vols. (repr.; Grand Rapids: Eerdmans, 1954), 2:356.
[172] Ernst Kasemann, *New Testament Questions of Today* (Philadelphia: Fortress, 1969), 174.
[173] R.E. Brown, *Jesus God and Man*, xii.
[174] Most contemporary scholars regard Jn 20.31 as the end of this gospel as originally planned and that Jn 21 is an addendum added later by the same author or someone else.
[175] R. Bultmann (*John*, 698) insists John here meant "signs," referring to the whole gospel, because they are expounded in Jesus' corresponding discourses. Thus, the supreme sign in Jn 13-20 is Jesus' resurrection.

Therefore, it cannot be overemphasized that *the entire Gospel of John must be understood in light of the author's stated purpose recorded in Jn 20.30-31.* Moreover, this statement makes it clear that the author believed that it is sufficient to believe that Jesus is the Messiah, the Son of God, in order to obtain eternal life (cf. 1 Jn 4.15).[176]

Summary

The Gospel of John is the premiere NT book of misunderstanding. In its interior, its characters constantly misunderstand Jesus because they think literally when He speaks figuratively.

Readers of this gospel often make the same mistake. The foremost example is the traditional interpretation that, more than anywhere else in Scripture, the Gospel of John unambiguously declares that Jesus is God. Surprisingly, most historical critics accept this interpretation. Using their terminology, they allege that the Jesus of history (mostly in the Synoptic Gospels) and the Christ of faith (mostly in the Gospel of John, which they believe identifies Jesus as God) are in sharp conflict. Many of these critics therefore demand that a choice be made concerning this alleged discontinuity. They choose to dismiss much or all of the Gospel of John, rendering it historically inauthentic, and favor the Synoptic Gospels as providing the more accurate portrait of the real, historical Jesus.

On the contrary, John's gospel presents truth, and the traditional understanding of it does not. This interpretation that the Johannine Jesus is "God" rests so much on a mistreatment of Greek grammar in Jn 1.1c, misunderstandings about several of Jesus' claims about Himself, and, most of all, a misunderstanding of Thomas' Confession in Jn 20.28. Thus, identity Christology in the Fourth Gospel does not conflict with that of the Synoptics but presents a portrait that coincides with them—that *Jesus was a man and not God.* The Fourth Evangelist's stated purpose for writing his gospel is not that Jesus is God; rather, it is the same as that of the synoptists: *Jesus is the Christ, the Son of God.*

To verify this identification of Jesus as a man and not God, we need to analyze in some detail several important christological texts in the Gospel of John that have been thought to either expressly or implicitly identify Jesus as God.

B: Problem Passages

1. Is the Logos identified as "God" in John 1.1c?

Introduction	The Anarthrous *theos* in John 1.1c
The Mini-Prologue	The Colwell Rule?
English Versions and the Greek Text	Harner vs. Colwell
Dissecting the Three Clauses	"what God was, the Word was"
Grammatical Problems	"the Word had the same nature as God"
"the Word was divine"	Linkage
"the Word was a god"	Comparing John & the Hebrews Author
The Jehovah's Witnesses	Summary
"the Word was God"	

---

[176] Contra M. Harris (*Jesus as God*, 103), who surprisingly, and arbitrarily, asserts that John "indicates that the acknowledgment of the messiahship of Jesus (20.31) necessarily involves belief in his deity."

Introduction

Throughout church history, almost all biblical scholars have insisted that the two primary NT passages that identify Jesus as "God" are Jn 1.1c ("and the Word was God") and Thomas' confession in Jn 20.28> ("My Lord and my God"). One would expect that such texts would be rather copious. Not so; both consist of only one small phrase having a total of only five words in most English Bible versions.[177] Regardless of the brevity of these two portions of Scripture, due to their importance for Christology more attention will be devoted to them in this book than to any other passages in the NT, although the treatment of Phil 2.5-11 is extensive as well.

While Jn 1.1c does not expressly identify Jesus as God, comparing it with Jn 1.14 ("And the Word became flesh") seems to imply that it does. James D.G. Dunn says of this verse, "Here we have an explicit statement of *incarnation*, the first, and indeed only such statement in the NT."[178] So, Jn 1.1c is so critical for Christology, partly due to v. 14.

We will now examine Jn 1.1c: "and the Word was God." This brief phrase has caused Christians to believe that Jesus is God more than any other portion in the Bible.

The Mini-Prologue

Recall that the first verse of the Gospel of John is a single sentence consisting of three short clauses. This introductory sentence serves as a mini-prologue for the entire gospel. C.K. Barrett explains, "John intends that the whole of his gospel shall be read in the light of this verse."[179] Garrett C. Kenney says likewise, "If John 1:1 provides the thesis statement of the gospel, which is likely,... then the body of the gospel should cohere."[180] Accordingly, the purpose of John's mini-prologue is the same as for his entire prologue: to link its themes to corresponding texts in the body of this gospel. Therefore, these texts throughout the gospel explain or elaborate the introductory prologue themes.

There seems to be no difficulty in linking Johannine gospel texts with the two themes in the first two clauses of John's mini-prologue. But identifying portions of John's text that correlate with the traditional translation of the third clause in Jn 1.1 has not proved an easy task. This subject of linkage will be resumed at the end of this section.

English Versions and the Greek Text

The Greek text of John 1.1 usually has been translated as in the AV and NASB:

1 In the beginning was the Word, and the Word was with God, and the Word was God.

Post-apostolic, Greek-speaking church fathers understood Jn 1.1c to mean the same as this traditional English translation.[181] And this is how subsequent church leaders and scholars have usually understood it, and thus translated it,

---

[177] The Greek NT has five words in Jn 1.1c and seven words for Thomas' Confession in Jn 20.28.
[178] J.D.G. Dunn, *Christology in the Making*, 241. Emphasis his.
[179] C.K. Barrett, *John*, 156.
[180] Garrett C. Kenney, *John 1:1 as Prooftext: Trinitarian or Unitarian?* (Lanham, MD: University Press of America, 1999), 20.
[181] E.g., Irenaeus, *Against Heresies*, 1.8.5.

ever since. By comparing Jn 1.1c with v. 14, this rendering of Jn 1.1c effectively calls Jesus Christ "God."

However, Jn 1.1c has not always been so translated. This can be observed in the following list of English versions that serve as a brief history of the translation of Jn 1.1c.

- "and god was the worde" (Wycliffe 1380)
- "and the worde was god" (Tyndale 1525)
- "and God was the worde" (Coverdale 1535)
- "and that Worde was God" (Geneva Bible 1560)
- "and God was that Word" (Bishop's Bible 1568)
- "and God was the Word" (Rheims 1582, similarly Luther in his German translation)
- "and the Word was God" (AV, RV, NAB, ASV, RSV, NASB, NIV, JB, Berkeley, ESV)
- "and the Logos was divine" (Moffatt 1935, Berkeley 1959)
- "and the Word was divine" (Goodspeed 1923)
- "and he was the same as God" (TEV, GNB)
- "and what God was, the Word was" (NEB, REB)
- "the Word was the very same as God" (Cassirer 1989)

This variety of translations shows that during the past 500 years or more, the traditional translation of Jn 1.1c has not always been fully accepted. While this translation continues to dominate to the present, some reputable modern English versions translate this clause so that it *does not* call the Word "God." Several contemporary commentators agree. It will probably come as a surprise to most faithful Bible believers that *scholastic support for the traditional translation of Jn 1.1c has declined considerably in recent years*. John 1.1 reads as follows in the Greek NT, with an attached interlinear translation:

Jn 1.1a - *En arche en ho logos,*
  In [the] beginning was the word,
Jn 1.1b - *kai ho logos en pros ton theon,*
  and the word was with the God,
Jn 1.1c - *kai theos en ho logos.*
  and God was the word.

Dissecting the Three Clauses

Let us first examine briefly the entire sentence of Jn 1.1 in order to determine what the problems are in its third clause.

Most scholars agree that the independent clause that begins the Fourth Gospel—"In the beginning was the Word"—alludes to the independent clause that begins the book of Genesis—"In the beginning God created the heavens and the earth." Accordingly, John's introductory prepositional phrase, "In the beginning," refers to the time that God created the universe. This observation is further substantiated by the remainder of John's first clause—"was the Word." That is, "the Word" existed at the time of creation because Gen 1 repeatedly records concerning that time, "Then God said,... and it was so." (Yet the context of Genesis does not resolve the question of whether at the time of creation God's spoken word existed as a personal entity to be distinguished from God's own being.)

The second clause in Jn 1.1—"and the Word was with God"—means that the Word existed in some mode of association with God at the time of creation. Indeed, Gen 1 implies that in some mysterious way God's spoken word consisted of more than mere sound in accomplishing His creation. The NT expressly states that God *created* the world through, or by means of, His Word, viz., Jesus Christ (Jn 1.3, 10; Col 1.16; Heb 1.2).

But who is "God" in this second clause of Jn 1.1? Most contemporary scholars would agree with Trinitarian Murray Harris, who rightly states that "there can be little doubt that *ho theos* in 1.1b designates the Father." Therefore, Harris denies that it refers to "the trinitarian God."[182] Indeed, "the Word" and "God" (as the Father) are clearly distinguished in this second clause. Moreover, the two occurrences of "the Father" in the prologue seem to further identify all of the several occurrences of "God" in the prologue.

Grammatical Problems

In proceeding to the third clause in Jn 1.1, we notice that there are two major differences between the second and third clauses in the Greek text. One is that *logos* precedes *theos* in the second clause, whereas their order is reversed in the third clause. This change in word order is the first problem encountered in Jn 1.1c. That is why John Wycliffe, Martin Luther and others translated *theos* as the subject and *ho logos* as the predicate, resulting in, "and God was the Word." The other major difference is that *theos* is anarthrous (without the article; Gr. *ho* and Eng. "the") in the third clause whereas it is articular (*ton theon*, with the article) in the second clause. A noun with an article usually makes it definite—e.g., "the god/God." An anarthrous noun makes it indefinite—"a god." In fact, this anarthrous *theos* emerges as the formidable problem in Jn 1.1c.

Several questions arise due to these two major differences in Jn 1.1. First of all, is *theos* the subject or the predicate of this third clause? If it is the predicate, as in the traditional translation, doesn't this negate the distinction established in the second clause between the Logos and God? If not, then what does this anarthrous *theos* refer to: (a) God personally, (b) God's essence (nature), or (c) only the nature of the Logos? If it refers to God's essence, is it hermeneutically justifiable to interpret *ton theon* in the second clause as the Person of God the Father while interpreting the anarthrous *theos* in the third clause quite differently, i.e., of God's essence? Moreover, is the anarthrous *theos* to be treated as a substantive (noun) or as adjectival? If adjectival, is it qualitative in meaning or not?

Obviously, these questions demonstrate that the translation and interpretation of Jn 1.1c are *extremely* complicated.[183] Most of these questions concern Greek grammar. Due to the importance that traditionalists attach to Jn 1.1c in support of their doctrine, the following analysis will be the most complex in this book and thus test the patience of most readers. Yet I will attempt to address these difficult issues with the non-Greek reader in mind while also endeavoring not to oversimplify this matter. In the process, we will examine not only the traditional translation of Jn 1.1c, but other translations of it too.

"the Word was divine"

Notice, above, that a few English versions translate Jn 1.1c, "and the Word was divine." So do some distinguished, 20th century commentators.[184] Among them is Max Zerwick,[185] an eminent Roman Catholic NT grammarian.

---

[182] M. Harris, *Jesus as God*, 55.

[183] R.E. Brown, *Introduction to NT Christology*, 187; M. Harris, *Jesus as God*, 67.

[184] E.g., William Temple, *Readings in St. John's Gospel: Its Significance and Environment*, 2 vols. (London: MacMillan, 1939), 1:4; R.H. Strachan, *The Fourth Gospel*, 3rd ed., 99; V. Taylor, *The Person of Christ*, 109; Ernst Haenchen, *John 1: A Commentary on the Gospel of John: Chapters 1-6* in Hermeneia, 109.

[185] Max Zerwick and Mary Grosvenor, *A Grammatical Analysis of the New Testament*, 3rd ed. (Rome: Pontifical Biblical Institute, 1988), 285.

Translating the anarthrous *theos* in Jn 1.1c as "divine" renders it as an adjective and therefore makes it qualitative. In this case, it does not exactly call Jesus "God." Nevertheless, translating *theos* as "divine" in Jn 1.1c is dubious for the following reasons:
1. If John had wanted to say "divine" he surely would have used the Greek word *theios* ("divine") that was available to him.
2. This word *theios* only appears twice in the Greek NT. In neither instance is it applied to Christ.[186] This makes it further unlikely that *theos*, here, means *theios*.
3. The English word "divine" is an unsuitable translation for *theos* because "divine" has a much wider range of meaning in English than does the English translation of the Greek word *theos*, which is "God." Moreover, even traditionalists admit that *ho theos* is almost always used in a narrow sense in the Greek NT, i.e., to identify the one and only God, who is the Father.[187]

"the Word was a god"

During the Nicene era the Arians insisted that Jn 1.1c meant either that "the Word was god/God" or "a god," but not "God" absolutely.[188] Over a millennium later Socinians and Unitarians concurred. We have already seen that Arius drew support from Origin's writings. Indeed, Origen once wrote that Jesus Christ, as Logos, was "the second god."[189]

There is one example of the anarthrous *theos* being translated "a god" in the NT. It appears in Luke's account of the Apostle Paul being bitten by a poisonous viper on the Mediterranean island of Malta. When Paul did not physically swell up and die, as was to be expected, the natives "began to say that he was a god" (Ac 28.6). Of course, Luke's use of the anarthrous *theos*, here, is justifiably translated "a god" because of the common pagan belief in a pantheon of gods. So, the translation of *theos* in this instance depends on its context, a subject to which we will soon return.

The Jehovah's Witnesses

The growing sect called "the Jehovah's Witnesses" (JWs) is the most formidable group in modern times that has adopted this Arian-Unitarian interpretation of Jn 1.1c. In their *New World Translation* (*NWT*), they translate Jn 1.1 as follows: "Originally the Word was, and the Word was with God, and the Word was a god."[190] Many traditionalist expositors denigrate this translation.

---

[186] Paul used *theios* in Ac 17.29 to refer to God the Father as "the Divine Nature." And Peter used *theios* in 2 Pt 1.3 to refer to God's "divine power." Paul also used *theiotos* in Rom 1.20 to describe God as "divinity" or "divine nature" and *theotetos* in Col 2.9 to describe God's nature as "deity" indwelling Jesus.

[187] E.g., M. Harris (*Jesus as God*, 47) explains, "When *ho theos* is used, we are to assume that the NT writers have *ho pater* [the Father] in mind unless the context makes this sense of *ho theos* impossible."

[188] The original NT books and letters were written in uncials (all capitals instead of upper and lower case) so that there was no means of distinguishing between "God" and "god" in the Greek language of that time.

[189] Origen, *Fragment of Hebrews contra Celsum*, 5.39

[190] The JWs' first translation of the NT was the *New World Translation of the Christian Greek Scriptures*. It was published by their Watchtower Bible and Tract Society, located in Brooklyn, New York, in 1950 and revised in 1951. In 1961, they published their translation of the entire Bible, entitled the *New World Translation of the Holy Scriptures*. This later edition left the former essentially intact, according to Robert H. Countess ("The Translation of *Theos* in the New World Translation,"

However, it is bias to reject a translation primarily because it is proposed by what many Christians identify pejoratively as "a cult."

Actually, this *NWT* of Jn 1.1c is worthy of some consideration because it furnishes a rather respectable, critical apparatus of nearly four pages in length.[191] In this apparatus the JWs may be correct in their assertion "that John's saying the Word or Logos 'was divine' is not saying that he was God with whom he was. It merely tells of a certain quality about the Word or Logos, but it does not identify him as one and the same as God."[192] Many ante-Nicene church fathers would have agreed with this statement.

Surprisingly, some very distinguished, 20th century NT scholars have provided more support for this Arian-Unitarian-JW translation of Jn 1.1c than they have for the traditional translation. For instance, R. Bultmann asserts flatly that in the NT, "Christ is looked upon and worshipped as a divine figure ... as a god, but not simply as God."[193] And J.G. Griffiths argued that *theos* in Jn 1.1c can be rendered with equal force either as "(the) God" or "(a) God."[194] Also, James D.G. Dunn regards the pre-Incarnate Logos in Jn 1 as an "impersonal personification" and thus translates Jn 1.1c similar to Origen, "and the Word was god."[195] Finally, C.H. Dodd, the general editor of the NEB, explains quite well concerning Jn 1.1c, "If translation were a matter of substituting words, a possible translation of *theos en ho logos* would be, 'The Word was a god.' As a word-for-word translation it cannot be faulted.... The reason why it is unacceptable is that it runs counter to the current of Johannine thought, and indeed of Christian thought as a whole."[196]

So, it is indeed grammatically possible to translate *theos* in Jn 1.1c as "god" or "a god," as in Ac 28.6.[197] However, such a translation is unjustifiable contextually. And there is no evidence that John, or any other NT writer for that matter, ever intended to identify Jesus as "a god." (However, see Jn 10.30>.)

"the Word was God"

The traditional translation of Jn 1.1c—"and the Word was God"—has been advocated by an overwhelming majority of church fathers and NT scholars ever since. But even though this translation has stood the test of time, it has always incurred significant theological and literary difficulties which include the following:

1. It is very unlikely that an author—presumably a strict monotheistic Palestinian Jew—would usurp the majesty of the one God of Israel by calling a man *theos* who had no ruling authority in Israel (cf. Ps 82.6; Jn 10.34),

---

JETS 10 [1967]: 153). Herein, I refer to their 1950 edition since it contains appendices pertaining to Jn 1.1 not included in the 1961 edition.

[191] *NWT*, 773-77. R. Countess ("The Translation of *Theos* in the NWT," 160) commends the JWs for this.

[192] *NWT*, 773.

[193] R. Bultmann, *Essays*, 279, cf. 278. Yet Bultmann (*Gospel of John*, 33) accepts the traditional translation of Jn 1.1c, insisting that it "cannot be taken as meaning: he was a god, a divine being." However, Bultmann does not contradict himself. He believed that the NT teaches that the Logos, as both the preexistent and the resurrected Jesus, was "God" but that the earthly Jesus of the ministry was not.

[194] J.Gwyn Griffiths, "A Note on the Anarthrous Predicate in Hellenistic Greek," *ExpT* 62 (1950-51): 315.

[195] J.D.G. Dunn, *The Making of Christology*, 58.

[196] C.H. Dodd, "New Testament Translation Problems II," *BT* 28 (1977): 101-102.

[197] M. Harris (*Jesus as God*, 60), e.g., affirms this.

especially without some explanation in this prologue or support in the gospel text.
2. It is very unlikely that the author would contradict himself by distinguishing *ho logos* and *ton theon* in Jn 1.1b, thus treating them as two separate entities,[198] and dissolve this distinction in the next clause, in Jn 1.1c, as the traditional translation does.
3. Traditionalist M. Harris admits that this traditional, English translation is troublesome since "in normal English usage 'God' is a proper noun, referring to the person of the Father or corporately to the three persons of the Godhead"[199] and thus not to Christ.
4. Many exegetes justify the traditional translation of Jn 1.1c by linking it to Thomas' Confession in Jn 20.28. But this is circular reasoning.

Following Jn 1.1, in the next three verses the most distinguished modern versions have four masculine pronouns that refer to the masculine *logos* in v. 1 (e.g., RSV, NASB, NRSV, NIV, ESV). Greek nouns and pronouns have gender, but this does not establish the gender of their object. In the Greek text, the first pronoun is *houtos* and the other three are *autos*. John 1.2 thus reads, "He was in the beginning with God," in which "He" refers to "the Word" in v. 1. Both *houtos* and *autos* can be treated as either personal or impersonal pronouns, as "he," "she," "it," or "this (one)." The context is the determining factor. So, whether these pronouns are rendered personal or impersonal depends on one's view of "the Word" in v. 1, to which they refer. If "the Word" is viewed as a personal entity, then these pronouns will be treated as personal pronouns and translated "he" or "him." But if "the Word" in v. 1 is viewed as an impersonal entity, then these pronouns in vv. 2-4 will be treated as impersonal pronouns and translated "it" or "this (one)." So, how one treats these four pronouns in the Greek text of Jn 1.2-4 is a matter of interpretation. People read these personal pronouns in Jn 1.2-4 in English versions and think "the Word" is a Person.

Due to these several difficulties, many prominent 20th century NT scholars did not feel comfortable with the traditional translation of Jn 1.1c or most other translations of it. For example, William Barclay cautioned, "To say that the Word was God is too much; to say that the Word was Divine is too little."[200] So, Murray Harris assesses concerning his colleagues, "Therefore few will doubt that this time-honored translation needs careful exegesis,... The rendering cannot stand without explanation."[201] What needs explaining the most of all about Jn 1.1c is its grammar.

The Anarthrous *Theos* in John 1.1c

Shortly before NT writings came into existence, Philo distinguished a difference in meaning in the Greek language between *ho theos* and *theos*. He consistently took *ho theos* to mean the one and only true God and the anarthrous *theos* to refer to the Logos. Philo therefore subscribed to a supposed, two-part, Greek rule of grammar at that time: (1) when *theos* has the article it always refers to the one and only, true God, and (2) when *theos* does not have the article, it does not refer to the one and only true God.

Similarly, Origen later emerged as the first church father to insist that *ho theos* in the NT refers exclusively to God the Father and the anarthrous

---

[198] Not to mention the same with *houtos* ("He" refers to *ho logos* in v. 1) and *ton theon* in v. 2.
[199] M. Harris, *Jesus as God*, 69.
[200] William Barclay, "Great Themes of the New Testament: II John 1.1-14," *ExpT* 70 (1958-59): 114.
[201] M. Harris, *Jesus as God*, 69.

theos refers only to the Logos-Son, who became the man Jesus Christ. In his commentary on the Gospel of John, Origen even regards *theos* without the article as an indication that the Son derives His "divinity/deity" from the Father, so that the Son is essentially subordinate and therefore inferior to the Father.[202] In his discussion of both occurrences of *theos* in Jn 1.1, Origen asserts that John "uses the article, when the name of God refers to the uncreated cause of all things, and omits it when the Logos is named God."[203] Origen's words, "uncreated cause," suggest the practice of the ante-Nicene fathers in distinguishing God the Father as "Uncreated," "Unoriginate," and "First Cause" from Jesus as "God the Logos-Son," "Originate," and "Second Cause," words borrowed from Greek metaphysics.

But modern scholarship has for some time rejected these supposed distinctions between the articular and non-articular *theos*. And it has been shown that there are no such distinctions in Hellenistic Greek writings, either.[204] Murray Harris cites numerous NT examples to show that *theos* and *ho theos* are nearly always interchangeable in the NT, both of them referring only to God the Father.[205]

Furthermore, most scholars now regard *theos* in the NT as a proper noun. And it is well known among NT scholars that, in both classical and biblical (*koine*) Greek, proper nouns have no precision with regard to the accompanying of the article or not.[206]

The Colwell Rule?

Nevertheless, 20th century biblical scholarship witnessed sharp debate about the use of anarthrous nouns in Greek, more particularly, how this affects the translation of Jn 1.1c. For example, in 1933 the prestigious *Journal of Biblical of Literature* published an article by the distinguished Professor Ernest C. Colwell of the University of Chicago that concerned the relation of word order to the use of the article with predicate nouns in the Greek language during antiquity.[207] In this study, Colwell sought to establish whether anarthrous nouns preceding the verb were regarded as definite or indefinite. His primary conclusion, called "the Colwell rule," was that "a definite predicate nominative has the article when it follows the verb; it does not have the article when it precedes the verb."[208]

One of Colwell's purposes in this study was to affirm the traditional translation of Jn 1.1c. We have seen that in the Greek text of Jn 1.1c the anarthrous *theos* precedes the verb. For Colwell, this anarthrous *theos* is definite and should be translated "God."

Since then, many American traditionalist scholars have cited Colwell's rule approvingly, that anarthrous predicate nouns preceding the verb are definite. They have hailed its application to Jn 1.1c as substantial proof of the traditional translation of it.

---

[202] Origen, *Commentary on John*, 2.3.
[203] Origen, *Commentary on John*, 2.2.
[204] E.g., see J. Gwyn Griffiths, "A Note on the Anarthrous Predicate," 314-16; H.G. Meecham, "The Anarthrous *Theos* in John 1.1 and 1 Corinthians 3.16," *ExpT* 63 (1951-52): 126.
[205] M. Harris, *Jesus as God*, 37.
[206] E.g., J.N.D. Kelly, *A Commentary on the Pastoral Epistles Timothy I & II, and Titus* in HNTC (1960), 246; M. Harris, *Jesus as God*, 38.
[207] Ernest C. Colwell, "A Definite Rule for the Use of the Article in the Greek New Testament," *JBL* 52 (1933): 12-21.
[208] E.C. Colwell, "A Definite Rule," 13.

On the other hand, traditionalist Murray Harris surprisingly refutes Colwell's supposed rule, especially its application to Jn 1.1c. Harris alleges that some scholars, e.g., Bruce Metzger,[209] who defends the traditional translation of Jn 1.1c by citing Colwell's rule, have exceeded even Colwell's certainty of the application of his rule to that phrase.[210] Indeed, Colwell had admitted that there were exceptions to his rule. And he applied it to Jn 1.1c with the following remark:

> a predicate nominative which precedes the verb cannot be translated as an indefinite or a "qualitative" noun solely because of the absence of the article; if the context suggests that the predicate is definite, it should be translated as a definite noun in spite of the absence of the article.
>
> ....
>
> The opening verse of John's Gospel contains one of the many passages where this rule suggests the translation of a predicate as a definite noun. *Kai theos en ho logos* looks much more like 'And the Word was God' than 'And the Word was divine' when viewed with reference to this rule. The absence of the article does not make the predicate indefinite or qualitative when it precedes the verb; it is indefinite in this position only when the context demands it. The context makes no such demand in the Gospel of John, for this statement cannot be regarded as strange in the prologue of the gospel which reaches its climax in the confession of Thomas.[211]

So, Colwell admitted that the primary exception to his supposed rule was if the context demands otherwise. As Harris observes about Jn 1.1c, "It is clearly the context of the verse in the Fourth Gospel that encourages Colwell to see an application of the grammatical rule here."[212] Colwell even argued that the larger context of the Fourth Gospel, especially including Thomas' Confession in Jn 20.28, affirms the application of his rule to Jn 1.1c and thus its traditional translation. But this is circular reasoning.

Harner vs. Colwell

Philip B. Harner has had a profound impact on this grammatical debate about Jn 1.1c.[213] His critical analysis of Colwell's study appeared forty years later, in 1973, in the same journal that published Colwell's study.[214] In this article Harner explains, "Colwell was almost entirely concerned with the question whether anarthrous predicate nouns were definite or indefinite, and he did not discuss at any length the problem of their qualitative significance."[215] Harner shows that when an anarthrous predicate noun precedes the verb, as in Jn 1.1c, it has a distinct qualitative force that is more prominent than its definiteness or indefiniteness, whichever the case may be.[216] Both opposite and the same as Colwell, he maintains that it is qualitative unless the context

---

[209] Bruce M. Metzger, "The Jehovah's Witnesses and Jesus Christ," *ThTo* 10 (April 1953): 75-76; idem, "On the Translation of John 1.1," *ExpT* 63 (1951-52): 125-26. See also Nigel Turner, *Grammatical Insights into the New Testament* (Edinburgh: T. & T. Clark, 1965), 17; M-H-T, 3:183.
[210] M. Harris, *Jesus as God*, 62.
[211] E.C. Colwell, "A Definite Rule," 20-21.
[212] M. Harris, *Jesus as God*, 62.
[213] See this assessment by R.E. Brown (*An Introduction to New Testament Christology*, 187).
[214] Philip B. Harner, "Qualitative Anarthrous Predicate Nouns: Mark 15:39 and John 1.1," *JBL* 92 (1973): 75-87.
[215] P.B. Harner, "Qualitative Anarthrous Predicate Nouns," 76. Harner (p. 85) observes that heretofore no Johannine scholar had considered this either.
[216] P.B. Harner, "Qualitative Anarthrous Predicate Nouns," 77-84.

demands otherwise. And Harner further argues that neither the "meaning or context" of Jn 1.1c requires that *theos* is definite.[217] He also demonstrates that the availability of other possible word orders for Jn 1.1c further strengthens his case. Harner concludes, "In John 1.1 I think that the qualitative force of the predicate is so prominent that the noun cannot be regarded as definite."[218]

Furthermore, in *koine* Greek a word placed at the beginning of a sentence or clause usually makes it more emphatic. That is why Harner says concerning Jn 1.1c, "the word *theos* is placed at the beginning for emphasis."[219] Indeed, Colwell had admitted that another exception to his rule was an author's emphasis.[220] Thus, the anarthrous *theos* in Jn 1.1c is emphatic, which further enhances its being qualitative.

So, according to Harner's analysis the traditional translation of Jn 1.1c ("and the Word was God") is incorrect. To date, his determinations in this article, and thus his conclusions in it about the proper rendering of Jn 1.1c, have not been thwarted. Rather, it seems that an increasing number of scholars now endorse his compelling viewpoint.[221] Harner ends his argument by endorsing the NEB translation of Jn 1.1c.

"what God was, the Word was"

Why is the word order reversed in Jn 1.1c from the previous clause? C.F.D. Moule suggests that it was done deliberately to make a theological point, that "God" describes the nature of the Logos without signifying any equivalence.[222] This is what both the NEB and REB do by translating it, "and what God was, the Word was." This translation treats the anarthrous *theos* as adjectival, thus qualitative, without translating it "divine." This rendering, which some scholars deem a paraphrase, is obviously endorsed by the general editor of the NEB, C.H. Dodd, as well as one of its translators, J.A.T. Robinson. Both of them were very distinguished British scholars.[223] C.H. Dodd is recognized as the greatest British NT scholar of the 20th century. Robinson insists concerning *theos* in Jn 1.1c, "it is impossible to represent it in a single English word." He says the NEB rendering "steers carefully between the two" translations that call Jesus either "divine" or "God."[224]

Dodd also suggested that Jn 1.1c paralleled personified wisdom in Prov 8 and other ancient Jewish Literature, including in Philo.[225] A.E. Harvey observed that Dodd's "analysis precludes the meaning 'The Word was (a second) God' or 'The Word was (identical with) God' ... the phrase can only mean that the word was (an expression or reflection of) God."[226]

The TEV translates Jn 1.1c, "he was the same as God," which is very similar to the NEB. Similar to Harner's rendering, these translations in the NEB, REB, and TEV avoid all of the difficulties listed above that the traditional translation fails to overcome.

---

[217] P.B. Harner, "Qualitative Anarthrous Predicate Nouns," 86.
[218] P.B. Harner, "Qualitative Anarthrous Predicate Nouns," 87.
[219] P.B. Harner, "Qualitative Anarthrous Predicate Nouns," 85.
[220] E.C. Colwell, "A Definite Rule," 18.
[221] E.g., M. Harris, *Jesus as God*, 70, 312-13.
[222] C.F.D. Moule, *An Idiom Book of New Testament Greek* (Cambridge: University, 1960), 116.
[223] The NEB renders Heb 1.8 and v. 9 so as to call Jesus "God," showing that they were not biased.
[224] J.A.T. Robinson, *Honest to God*, 71.
[225] C.H. Dodd, *The Interpretation of the Fourth Gospel*, 280.
[226] A.E. Harvey, *Jesus and the Constraints of History*, 176-77.

"the Word had the same nature as God"

Some contemporary NT scholars have suggested translations of Jn 1.1c that are very similar in the NEB, REB, and TEV, but based on a slightly different reasoning. That reasoning is that the anarthrous *theos* does not refer to an individual person or thing but to a class or sphere to which that subject belongs. Their translation usually goes like this: "the Word has the same nature as God does." William Barclay translates it, "the nature of the Word was the same as the nature of God."[227] He explains:

> When in Greek two nouns are joined by the verb 'to be,' and when both have the definite article, then the one is fully identified with the other; but when one of them is without the article, it becomes more an adjective than a noun, and describes rather the class or the sphere to which the other belongs.
>
> ....
>
> .... The *Logos*, therefore, is not identified as God or with God; the word *theos* has become adjectival and describes the sphere to which the *Logos* belongs. We would, therefore, have to say that this means that the *Logos* belongs to the same sphere as God; without being identified with God the *Logos* has the same kind of life and being as God. Here the NEB finds the perfect translation: "What God was, the Word was."
>
> This passage then does not identify the *Logos* and God; it does not say that Jesus was God, nor does it call him God; but it does say that in his nature and being he belongs to the same class as God, and is in the same sphere of life as God.[228]

Max Zerwick earnestly agrees. He refutes Colwell's rule and explains:

> In fact, predicates commonly lack the article, but this is not in virtue of any rule about predicates in particular,... for in the nature of things, the predicate commonly refers not to an individual or individuals as such, but to the class to which the subject belongs, to the nature or quality predicated of the subject; e.g., Jn 1.1c [*kai theos en ho logos*], which attributes to the Word the divine *nature*.[229]

The weakness of this treatment of Jn 1.1c that is advocated by Barclay, Zerwick, and others is that it comes precipitously close to asserting dual gods. John Macquarrie thus rightly objects to it by alleging, "to turn *theos* into an adjective is not only to usurp the usage of an already existing adjective, it is also to suggest that there is a class of divine beings to which the Word belongs, and such an idea would have been intolerable from the point of view of Jewish monotheism."[230]

Some modern commentators who translate the anarthrous *theos* in Jn 1.1c as qualitative and thus similar to the NEB are as follows, with their translations appended:

- P.B. Harner - "and the Word had the same nature as God."[231]
- Cassirer - "and the Word was the very same as God"
- M. Harris - "and the Word was identical with God the Father in nature"[232]

---

[227] W. Barclay, *The New Testament* (1968).
[228] W. Barclay, *Jesus As They Saw Him*, 21-22.
[229] Max Zerwick, *Biblical Greek: Illustrated by Examples*, English ed. adapted from the 4th Latin ed. by Joseph Smith (Rome: Scripta Pontificii Instituti Biblici, 1963), 55.
[230] J. Macquarrie, *Jesus Christ in Modern Thought*, 110.
[231] P.B. Harner, "Qualitative Anarthrous Predicate Nouns," 87. M. Harris (*Jesus as God*, 70) admits that Harner's translation "most accurately represents the evangelist's intended meaning." Yet Harris curiously clings to the traditional translation while also proposing his own, which resembles Harner's.
[232] M. Harris, *Jesus as God*, 70.

Linkage

Now we will consider that linkage mentioned earlier, i.e., the concept that each of the three clauses of Jn 1.1 correspond to various passages in the body of John's Gospel. (The same can be done with much of the remainder of the prologue.) There seems to be no difficulty in linking Jn 1.1a ("In the beginning was the Word") with Johannine texts portraying the supposed preexistence of Jesus (e.g., Jn 1.2, 15, 30; 8.58; 17.5, 24). And Jn 1.1b ("and the Word was with God") can justifiably be linked with Johannine passages that concern the union of Jesus with God (e.g., Jn 1.2, 18; 3.2; 8.29; 16.32; 17.5). But, as stated earlier, identifying portions of John's gospel which correlate with the traditional translation of Jn 1.1c has proved difficult. Indeed, *with the exception of the traditional interpretation of Jn 20.28>, the traditional translation of Jn 1.1c cannot reasonably be linked to any Johannine text, and this lack of linkage weighs heavily against it.*

In contrast, the NEB translation of Jn 1.1c—"and what God was, the Word was"—links quite well with the following sayings of Jesus in the Gospel of John:
- "the Father is in Me, and I in the Father" (Jn 10.38, cf. 30).
- "And he who beholds Me beholds the One who sent Me" (Jn 12.45).
- "He who has seen Me has seen the Father" (Jn 14.9)
- "I am in the Father, and the Father is in Me" (Jn 14.11, cf. v. 20).

We will examine these verses later. For now, suffice it to say that Jn 12.45 and 14.9 provide the same meaning that John intended in Jn 1.1c. Furthermore, Jn 1.18d, 10.38, 14.10-11, and v. 20 explain how this is so. That is, when Jesus said, "He who has seen Me has seen the Father," He meant that, with respect to moral character, He was just like God. Therefore, everything that God is in His relative attributes of love, righteousness, justice, etc., Jesus is also. And this is so, not because Jesus and the Father possess the same essence or nature, but because the Father fully indwells Jesus, which is the same thing as saying that "God was in Christ" (2 Cor 5.19). Accordingly, *Jesus' words in Jn 14.9—"He who has seen Me has seen the Father"—explain the Greek text of Jn 1.1c.*

Comparing John and the Author of Hebrews

Finally, there is an expression elsewhere in the NT that says the very same thing as do the NEB and TEV renderings of Jn 1.1c. It is that which the author of The Epistle to the Hebrews wrote in his introduction. He states that the Son "is the radiance of His [God's] glory and the exact representation of His nature" (Heb 1.3). In other words, Jesus Christ reflects perfectly the character of God. That the writer of Hebrews refers to the character of God rather than His entire essence is most apparent. For he writes that Jesus was superior to all men and even angels (Heb 1.4; 3.1-6), not by possessing some divine nature but because of His piety (Heb 2.18; 4.15-16; 5.7-9; 7.26).

Summary

In sum, we have seen that Jn 1.1c has been traditionally translated, "and the Word was God." Comparing v. 14 with this translation makes the author indirectly call Jesus Christ "God" here. However, the proper translation of Jn 1.1c, and therefore its meaning, is not a settled issue among NT scholars today. The main reason is that the grammar of this phrase is problematic in the Greek text, being exceedingly complex. Throughout much of the 20th century, traditionalist scholars thought that the supposed "Colwell rule" for anarthrous nouns undergirded their traditional translation. However, P.B. Harner's analysis of anarthrous nouns in the NT has shown decisively that Colwell misapplied his supposed rule to the anarthrous *theos* in Jn 1.1c. Consequently, an increasing number of contemporary scholars no longer subscribe to the traditional translation of Jn 1.1c. Rendering the clause, "and the Word was divine," or the like, fails to suffice. Instead, an increasing number of scholars now agree with Harner in treating the anarthrous *theos* therein as qualitative and therefore advocate the NEB translation (or its equivalent): "what God was, the Word was." That is why Marinus de Jonge remarks, "The author of this Prologue clearly wants to identify 'the Word' and God as closely as possible without infringing the belief in the One God."[233] Finally, as is so often the case, William Barclay explains the situation beautifully, "When John said *the word was God* he was not saying that Jesus was identical with God; he was saying that Jesus was so perfectly the same as God in mind, in heart, in being that in him we perfectly see what God is like."[234]

2. Did Jesus Preexist in Heaven?

Introduction	"He...Comes from Heaven" in Jn 3.31
The Spiritual Gospel	The Bread from Heaven in John 6.25-65
"He Existed before Me" in Jn 1.15, 30	Wisdom Christology
Angels Ascending/Descending, Jn 1.51	"I Am from Above" in John 8.23
Jesus Ascending/Descending in Jn 3.13	"The Glory...I had...Before" in Jn 17.5

Introduction

Most contemporary biblical scholars agree that the Synoptic Gospels do not present Jesus as having preexisted as a person or *hypostasis* prior to His existence as a human being.[235] We have seen that even the birth narratives about Jesus in the gospels of Matthew and Luke provide no hint of Jesus having preexisted. In fact, Luke presents the angel Gabriel declaring the Child Jesus as "the Son of God" merely on the basis of Jesus' supernatural conception (Lk 1.35, cf. v. 32).

The Gospel of John, on the other hand, provides much teaching about what has been widely recognized as the preexistence of Jesus.[236] Actually, the Logos teaching in John's prologue seems to presuppose it. Moreover, this gospel's repeated mention of the apparent preexistence of Jesus stands out as one of its distinctive features. Using mostly the Prologue as a guide, John's overall message about this preexistence of Jesus can be summarized literally as follows: (1) before the creation of the world the Logos existed in glory (Jn 1.1a; 17.5; cf. 12.37), was with God (Jn 1.1b, 18), and was loved by God (Jn 3.16; 17.24); (2) after that the Logos came down from heaven into the world to take flesh and in some mysterious fashion become the man, Jesus Christ (Jn 1.14; 6.33-63).

Following his Prologue, John supports this seemingly ontological view of Jesus with a flurry of preexistence passages. In a few of these texts, he *explicitly* presents Jesus' supposed preexistence (Jn 1.15, 30; 3.13; 8.58; 17.5, 24). More often, John *implicitly* describes it, usually by quoting Jesus Himself.[237] For

---

[233] Marinus de Jonge, *Christology in Context: The Earliest Christian Response to Jesus* (Philadelphia: Westminster, 1988), 198.
[234] William Barclay, *The Gospel of John*, rev. ed., 2 vols. (Philadelphia: Westminster, 1975), 1:39.
[235] Contra Simon J. Gathercole, *The Pre-existent Son: Recovering the Christologies of Matthew, Mark, and Luke* (Grand Rapids: Eerdmans, 2006).
[236] Jn 1.1-3, 9-10, 14-15, 30; 3.13; 6.33-63; 8.23, 58; 17.5, 24.
[237] Jn 5.43; 6.14; 7.28; 9.39; 10.10; 11.27; 12.46; 15.22; 18.37.

example, the Johannine Jesus claims that (1) God "sent" Him into the world,[238] (2) He had "come" or "came" from God/into the world or merely was "from" God/the Father,[239] and, more precisely, (3) He had "come" or "came (down) from/out of heaven."[240]

Justin Martyr (d. 165 CE) emerges in patristic literature as the first church father to assert that Jesus "pre-existed."[241] Traditionalists ever since have regarded the Johannine picture of the supposed preexistence of Jesus as incontrovertible evidence that He is God. But is this conclusion logical? The notion of preexisting personages had widespread currency in late, mainstream Second Temple Judaism; yet Jews did not think such speculation compromised their strict monotheism.

Friedrich Schleiermacher, the so-called "father of Liberal Theology," was the first Christian theologian to launch a serious attack against the church doctrine of the two natures and therefore the preexistence of Jesus Christ.[242] Ironically, he based his theology for the most part on the Gospel of John. He stated concerning all the gospel sayings of Jesus, "Nowhere does Christ speak of a real consciousness that he had of a preexistent state." Schleiermacher concludes that preexistence is incompatible with being human.[243]

In modern times, the idea that Jesus preexisted has aroused many anthropological questions and thus undergone close scrutiny even by several notable traditionalists. For example, some staunch traditionalists avow that the preexistence of Jesus requires that His human mind, ego, and moral character preexisted. In that case, Jesus did not undergo development of human character. This viewpoint seems not only non-human but a blatant contradiction that Jesus grew up and was "increasing in wisdom" (Lk 2.40, 52). Moderate traditionalist Norman Pittenger, the leading process theologian of the 20th century, deems this assertion "absurd and impossible. Hence, we must reject outright any idea of a pre-existence of *Jesus* and along with this rejection an incredible amount of pious error and confusion. Something *did* pre-exist; it was the Eternal Word of God who is incarnate in Jesus."[244] Accordingly, and as stated earlier, Jesus may be characterized as the Incarnate Word but not the Incarnate God. J.A.T. Robinson adds, "the ego of the human Jesus,... is no more pre-existent than that of any other human being."[245] William Barclay thus states that "one of the most difficult of all ideas [is] the idea of the preexistence of Jesus."[246]

The Spiritual Gospel

Should the Johannine passages about the preexistence of Jesus be taken literally? In the 3rd century, church father Clement of Alexandria called the Fourth Gospel "the spiritual gospel,"[247] and scholars ever since have endorsed this description. It is because the Johannine Jesus used so much figurative language in His discourses and dialogues. For example, at the end of His ministry the

---

[238] Jn 3.17, 34; 4.34; 5.23-24, 30, 36-37; 6.29, 38-39, 44, 57; 7.16, 18, 28-29; 8.16, 18, 26, 29, 42; 9.4; 10.36; 11.42, 12.44-45, 49; 13.20; 14.24; 15.21; 16.5; 17.3, 8, 18, 21, 23, 25; 20.21.
[239] Jn 3.2; 6.46; 7.29; 8.42; 9.33, 39; 12.46; 13.3; 16.27-28, 30; 17.8; 18.37.
[240] Jn 6.38, 41-42, 50-51, 58; cf. 3.13, 31; 8.23.
[241] E.g., Justin Martyr, *Dialogue with Trypho*, 48.3-6.
[242] F. Schleiermacher, *The Life of Jesus*, 81-87.
[243] F. Schleiermacher, *The Life of Jesus*, 268.
[244] W.N. Pittenger, *The Word Incarnate*, 218-19. Emphasis his.
[245] J.A.T. Robinson, *Twelve More New Testament Studies*, 167.
[246] W. Barclay, "Great Themes of the New Testament: II John 1.1-14," 114.
[247] Cited by Eusebius, *Ecclesiastical History*, 6.14.10.

Johannine Jesus said to The Eleven, "I have spoken to you in figurative language; an hour is coming when I will speak no more to you in figurative language but will tell you plainly" (Jn 16.25; cf. 10.6). He then explained His mission briefly and forthrightly. The disciples replied, "Lo, now You are speaking plainly, and are not using a figure of speech" (Jn 16.29).

Consequently, the Johannine Jesus is frequently misunderstood because His speech contains so many metaphors. This phenomenon occurs in the Synoptic Gospels as well, just not nearly as often. The following are perhaps the three most well-known examples of the Johannine Jesus using metaphorical language that is misunderstood as literal: (1) Jesus said at the temple in Jerusalem, "Destroy this temple and in three days I will raise it up;" but John explains that He meant it of His body, whereas the Jews thought that He intended it literally (Jn 2.19-21; cf. Mk 14.58 par.); (2) Jesus told Nicodemus that he needed to be "born again;" but Nicodemus thought He meant a second physical birth (Jn 3.3); (3) when Lazarus died, Jesus told His disciples that His friend had "fallen asleep ... but they thought that He was speaking of literal sleep" (Jn 11.11, 13). Some other examples are drinking water (Jn 4.10-15), being free (Jn 8.31-36), and being blind (Jn 9.39-41). No wonder the Johannine Jesus was so misunderstood; and no wonder church fathers called this gospel "the spiritual gospel." *The Gospel of John distinctively and repeatedly portrays the spiritual reality of things, which is the ultimate reality.*

Most of the Johannine preexistence passages describe Jesus as having "come down" either "from heaven" or "from above." Traditionalists have interpreted these texts literally, in which Jesus personally preexisted in heaven. But the spiritual nature of the Gospel of John should caution us in quickly adopting this interpretation. God sending Jesus may mean no more than it does in the prophetic tradition, e.g., John the Baptist was a prophet "sent from God" (Jn 1.6).[248] Similarly, Nicodemus did not infer preexistence when he said to Jesus, "You have come from God" (Jn 3.2; cf. 9.16, 33). Also, several Johannine passages that describe God's sending of Jesus use the Greek verb *apostello*, from which we derive our English word "apostle." None of these passages connote a locus of departure, e.g., heaven, in the divine commissioning.[249]

Nonetheless, whether the Fourth Evangelist believed that Jesus preexisted as a complete personal being does not seem to be a fundamental element of his message and therefore the message of the Johannine Jesus.[250] If it were, the Evangelist likely would not have left us in doubt. Rather, the main elements of John's Christology are these: (1) Jesus was sent by God and thus came from God (e.g., Jn 16.27-30; 17.3, 8), (2) God was with Jesus (e.g., Jn 1.1; 16.32), (3) as the Revealer of God Jesus perfectly reflects God (the Father) because God was in Jesus (e.g., Jn 14.9,11), and (4) Jesus was the Christ, the Son of God (e.g., Jn 20.30-31). None of these require literal preexistence.

"He Existed Before Me" in John 1.15, 30

Besides Jn 1.14, the first occurrence in the Gospel of John of the supposed preexistence of Jesus is in two brief, identical statements made by John the Baptist. Therein, he declares concerning Jesus, "He who comes after me has a

---

[248] Scholars who reject the interpretation that God sending Jesus indicates Jesus preexisted include the following: E. Schillebeeckx, *Christ: The Christian Experience in the Modern Word* (London: SCM, 1980), 317; J.A.T. Robinson, *John*, 383.
[249] Cf. J.D.G. Dunn, *Christology in the Making*, 39.
[250] Neither is it an element included in the evangelistic messages of Acts.

higher rank than I, for He existed before me" (Jn 1.15, 30). In the first clause, the Baptist refers to his earlier statement about Jesus,[251] which is recorded only by the synoptists. It reads, "After me One is coming who is mightier than I" (Mk 1.7 par.). The meaning is obvious: Jesus has a higher rank of authority in the kingdom of God than John the Baptist does. Critical to Christology is the second clause, in which, according to the NASB, the Baptist states that Jesus existed before he himself did. Since John the Baptist was born six months earlier than Jesus was (Lk 1.24-31), this independent clause would require that Jesus preexisted His own birth. However, the AV, RSV, and NIV translate this second clause differently: "he was before me." This translation is not about preexistence but represents a reiteration of the first clause, i.e., that Jesus outranks John the Baptist. Accordingly, C.H. Dodd well paraphrases the second clause, "he is and always has been essentially my superior."[252]

The Fourth Evangelist records again that John the Baptist declared that Jesus was greater than himself. The Baptist said, "He must increase, but I must decrease. He who comes from above is above all,... He who comes from heaven is above all" (Jn 3.30-31). The twice-repeated phrase, "above all," translates *epano panton*. It is figurative and means "over all" in the sense of rank.[253] The clauses, "He who comes from above" and "He who comes from heaven," are commonly thought to be synonymous, referring to Jesus preexisting in heaven.[254] We will consider this issue later, in Jn 6 and 8.23.

Angels "Ascending and Descending" in John 1.51

Jesus apparently did not know much, or anything, about Nathanael until they met. As Nathanael approached, Jesus spoke as a prophet to him, "Behold, an Israelite indeed, in whom is no guile!" (Jn 1.47). Thus, Jesus implicitly contrasted Nathanael with the patriarch Jacob (Israel), who, at his mother's insistence, became a beguiler (Gen 27). Then Jesus again exercised His role as a prophet by telling Nathanael that He had just seen him (in a vision?) under a fig tree. Nathanael replied to Jesus' supra-terrestrial knowledge by exclaiming, "Rabbi, You are the Son of God; You are the King of Israel" (v. 49). Nathanael thus draws these two titles together to signify the same individual—Jesus—and this identification of Jesus serves as the author's purpose for writing his gospel (cf. Jn 20.30-31; Christ=King). Jesus then responded to Nathanael, "You shall see greater things than these.... Truly, truly, I say to you, you shall see heaven opened, and the angels of God ascending and descending upon the Son of man" (vv. 50-51 RSV). Here occurs for the first time the Johannine theme of ascending/descending. Wayne Meeks remarks, "It is used exclusively to identify Jesus ... as the Stranger *par excellence*."[255]

Jesus talking about angels ascending and descending alludes to Jacob's most well-known dream. He "had a dream, and behold, a ladder was set on the earth with its top reaching to heaven; and behold, the angels of God were ascending and descending on it" (Gen 28.12). This dream is a prophecy of the future unification of earth and heaven, more precisely, and apparently, the heavenly New Jerusalem (Rev 21.2). Simultaneously, God will consummate His New Covenant by regenerating a New Israel—True Israel—on earth. Jesus, who

---

[251] R. Bultmann, *John*, 75.
[252] C.H. Dodd, *Historical Tradition in the Fourth Gospel*, 274.
[253] BAGD, 283.
[254] The words "from above" in Jn 3.31 translate *anothen* in the Greek text. Jesus uses this word (actually, its Aram. equivalent) in Jn 3.3 and v. 7 when he tells Nicodemus he must be born "again."
[255] Wayne A. Meeks, "The Man from Heaven in Johannine Sectarianism," *JBL* 91 (1972): 50.

embodies perfectly this New and True Israel, points to Nathanael as a prototype of a true Israelite. Upon hearing this supernatural revelation about himself, Nathanael instantly manifests a startling and exemplary faith in Jesus.

Jesus interprets Himself as the ladder in Jacob's dream. He means that He *literally* joins heaven and earth together. This unification will be consummated at a particular moment in time, i.e., on the eschatological Day. That is when God's angels accompany Jesus from heaven to earth at His second coming (Mt 16.27; 2 Thes 1.7; Jude 14; Rev 19.14). Jesus will then fulfill His mission as the eschatological bringer of salvation, viz., "the Savior of the world" (Jn 4.42; cf. 1.29). Actually, He doesn't merely *show* the way of salvation; Jesus *is* "the way." It extends from earth upwards to the "Father's house," viz., heavenly New Jerusalem, and therefore to "the Father" Himself (Jn 14.1-6).

But Jesus also intends that His words in Jn 1.51 be understood *spiritually*. That is, during His earthly ministry Jesus was already mystically and ideally joining heaven and earth together. He did so by exercising His spiritual access to heaven while here on earth, which was His uninterrupted communion with God. The idea of Jesus as Jacob's ladder relates to that item in Jesus' so-called Lord's Prayer, "Thy kingdom come. Thy will be done, on earth as it is in heaven" (Mt 6.10). This divine goal is being spiritually, and thus partially, accomplished during this age. But it will be fully consummated on "that day."

Jesus does not join heaven and earth together by means of His own personal resources but by the Spirit of God. John the Baptist testified concerning Jesus, "I saw the Spirit descend as a dove from heaven, and it remained on him" (Jn 1.32 RSV). The Baptist elaborates on the idea of the Spirit remaining on Jesus by adding, "to him God gives the Spirit without limit" (Jn 3.34 NIV; cf. Col 1.19>; 2.9>). John the Baptist thereby draws an implicit contrast; in the past, God always gave His Holy Spirit to His prophets. But it was with measure, so that the Spirit came upon them temporarily, partially, and then departed, only to return again at a later time.[256] But Jesus is more than a prophet, being *the* Son of Man and *the* Son of God, so that the Spirit of God always remains on Him (cf. Isa 11.2). And this unrestricted and unrestrained activity of the Spirit of God in the life of Jesus provides Him with constant and unlimited access, as it were, to a window into heaven, so that He always "sees" what the Father is doing (Jn 5.19). This enables Jesus not only to bring down from heaven the wisdom and knowledge of God, but to actually *reveal* God.

Jesus Ascending and Descending in John 3.13

This ascending/descending motif in Jn 1.51 surfaces again in John's gospel in Jesus' conversation with Nicodemus, recorded in Jn 3.13. But this time Jesus expressly applies the ascending/descending motif to Himself. This verse reads as follows in the AV: "And no man hath ascended up to heaven, but he that came down from heaven, even the Son of man which is in heaven." Traditionalists cite this verse in support of two of their christological precepts, the preexistence and omnipresence of Jesus, and they insist that both of these precepts indicate that Jesus is God. We will first consider preexistence.

Rudolf Bultmann acknowledged the difficulty in interpreting the identity of Jesus in the Fourth Gospel, and he called this problem the "Johannine puzzle." He insisted that, in order for this puzzle to be solved, the attempt must begin with

---

[256] R.E. Brown [*John (I-xii)*, 158] cites the Midrash Rabbah on Lev 15.2, in which R. Aha says, "The Holy Spirit rested on the prophets by measure." Brown says this idea was not uncommon in rabbinic literature.

the ascending and descending of Jesus as the Son of Man.[257] Indeed, this theme is an important key to discovering the identity of the Johannine Jesus.[258] But Bultmann, like most scholars, reversed the ascending/descending order of Jn 3.13 and thereby affirmed the traditional incarnation/ascension scenario.[259] He also interpreted that the Evangelist was influenced by Gnosticism, having used the Gnostic Redeemer myth as his source. But this myth was later discovered to be anachronistic and abandoned by scholars as an interpretation here.

Nevertheless, most scholars, including traditionalists and non-traditionalists, have thought that Jesus' words in Jn 3.13 require that the descent precedes the ascent and that emphasis is on the descent. So, they have interpreted that the first clause refers implicitly to Jesus' upcoming ascension into heaven and the second clause refers to His already past descent from heaven to earth at His incarnation. But there are several problems with this interpretation: (1) it does not fit the prior context, (2) it reverses the chronological order of the ascending and descending in Jn 1.51 and 3.13, (3) the use of the Greek verb *anabebeken* ("has ascended") is inexplicable if its perfect tense is taken as a completed action in the past, since Jesus' ascension had not yet occurred,[260] (4) it is without parallel in the NT,[261] and (5) it does not correlate with the overall biblical pattern, in which the righteous Servant-Son of Man must first suffer before He is not only exalted and glorified but even experiences any such thing. Traditionalist R.N. Longenecker cites a textual "ambivalence that defies precise designation of the nature of the descent involved."[262]

Much more compelling is the interpretation that accepts the ascending/descending order as it stands in the text because it fits the context. The context of Jn 3.13 is that Jesus is in the midst of giving a discourse to Nicodemus, a member of the Sanhedrin and a distinguished Torah teacher in Israel (Jn 3.1, 10). Jesus informs Nicodemus that he must be born "from above" (Gr. *anothen*), i.e., anew in spirit, in order to enter the kingdom of God (vv. 3, 7). Perplexed, Nicodemus responds crassly, as most people usually did to the Johannine Jesus: he interprets Jesus literally and thus misunderstands Him (vv. 3-9).

Jesus now speaks to Nicodemus about seeing spiritual things. He says, "we speak that which we know and bear witness of that which we have seen, and you [plural] do not receive our witness" (Jn 3.11). "We" may refer to Jesus and John the Baptist, but perhaps His genuine apostles also. The Fourth Evangelist later relates that John the Baptist spoke similarly of Jesus, "What He has seen and heard, of that He bears witness; and no man receives His witness" (v. 32; cf. 1.11-12). The Evangelist later amplifies this theme by quoting Jesus as saying, "the Son can do nothing of Himself, unless it is something He sees the Father doing;... For the Father loves the Son, and shows Him all things that He Himself

---

[257] Rudolf Bultmann, "Die Bedeutung der neuerschlossenen mandaischen und manichaischen Quellen fur das Verstandnis des Johannesevangeliums," *ZNW* 24 (1925), 102 (repr. *Exegetica* [Tubingen: Mohr, 1967], 57). Taken from W.A. Meeks, "The Man from Heaven in Johannnine Sectarianism," 47n12.

[258] W.A. Meeks, "The Man from Heaven in Johannine Sectarianism," 60-61.

[259] R. Bultmann, *John*, 147-51.

[260] H.A.W. Meyer, MCNT, 3:128. R.E. Brown [*John (i-xii)*, 132] admits concerning this incarnation and ascension interpretation, "The use of the perfect tense is a difficulty, for it seems to imply that the Son of Man has already ascended into heaven."

[261] Ephesians 4.10 is not a parallel because v. 9 shows that Paul refers to Jesus' descent into Sheol at death.

[262] R.N. Lonenecker, *The Christology of Early Jewish Christianity*, 62.

is doing" (Jn 5.19-20). Jesus adds, "No man has seen God at any time," i.e., "except the One who is from God, He has seen the Father" (Jn 1.18; 6.46).

Therefore, Jesus sees, hears, and bears witness to heavenly things, even to God's activities. What Jesus sees is not literal but spiritual. He further explained to Nicodemus, "If I told you earthly things and you do not believe, how shall you believe if I tell you heavenly things?" (v. 12). In this first clause, Jesus refers to what He has just told Nicodemus about the new birth. Although the nature of the new birth is spiritual, being accomplished "from above" by "the Spirit" (vv. 3, 5), Jesus nevertheless categorizes it as an earthly phenomenon. Nicodemus, like all other men except the Son of Man, is both physically and spiritually confined to the earth with all of his life experiences.[263] John the Baptist testified the same concerning himself by saying, "he who is of the earth is from the earth" (v. 31). He added that only Jesus is "from above," meaning that only Jesus has spiritual access into heaven and thereby spiritually sees, hears, and knows things there.

When Jesus says in the first clause of Jn 3.13, "no man has ascended up to heaven,"[264] He alludes to certain pre-Christian legends prevalent in Jewish apocalyptic literature. These legends characterized past heroic saints as having "ascended into heaven,"[265] some having received divine revelation (heavenly things) there and having brought it back to earth to expound it to others. Jesus also may have had in mind Jewish Merkabah mysticism, which advocated meditating on the chariot-throne vision of Eze 1 in order to conjure up a similar visionary ascent into heaven. But Jesus implicitly rejects all of these legends as well as their import. Instead, He makes the astounding claim that only He *spiritually* ascends into heaven to obtain heavenly secrets, and it happens on account of His being the Son of Man. Such a rich experience of acquiring this esoteric knowledge, consisting of secret things in heaven, was probably like literally being there.

All such legends—about holy men going to heaven to obtain some portion of wisdom and/or knowledge there and bringing it back to earth—are exactly what the sage surmises in Prov 30.3-4. He states therein, "Neither have I learned wisdom, nor do I have the knowledge of the Holy One. Who has ascended into heaven and descended? Who has gathered the wind in His fists?" etc. (Notice the ascent/descent order.) The writer means that no man so far had attained anywhere near the fulness of the wisdom and knowledge of God, let alone gone up to heaven to get any of it and brought it back to earth. This proverb, written in about 1,000 BCE, unwittingly anticipates these later, Jewish legends as well as Daniel's account of the ascending/descending Son of Man and thus Jesus. The Johannine Jesus *is* the personified Wisdom/Logos of God of pre-Christian Judaism.[266] R.E. Brown states regarding Jewish Wisdom Literature, "Wisdom is described as having descended from heaven to dwell with men ... The function

---

[263] Cf. R.E. Brown, *John (i-xii)*, 132.
[264] Second Kings 2.11 states, "Elijah went up by a whirlwind to heaven" (cf. v. 1). If this means Elijah went to the heaven where God dwells, as commonly understood, it conflicts with Jesus' remark here in Jn 3.13. But it might mean that Elijah was only taken up into the earth's atmosphere, not heaven where God dwells.
[265] J.D.G. Dunn ("Let John Be John," 306) lists some of these legends contained in ancient Jewish sources that postulate a heavenly ascension for the following figures: Adam (*Life of Adam and Eve* 25-29), Enoch (*1 En.* 14.8ff.; 39.3ff.; 70-71; *2 En.* 3ff.), Abraham (Test. Abr. 10ff.; *Apoc. Abr.* 15ff.; cf. *4 Ezra* 3.14; *2 Bar.* 4.4), Levi (Test. Levi 2.5ff.), Baruch (*2 Bar.* 76; *3 Bar.*), Isaiah (*Ascen. Isa.* 7ff.; cf. *Sir.* 48.24-25). Add to this list Moses on Mt. Sinai (Philo, *Vita Mosis*, I.158). Although some of this literature is not pre-Christian, it contains legends that no doubt were pre-Christian in origin.
[266] J.D.G. Dunn, "Let John Be John," 314.

of Wisdom among men is to teach them of the things that are above (Job 11.6-7; Wis 9.16-18), to utter truth (Prov 8.7; Wis 6.22),... This is precisely the function of Jesus as revealer, as portrayed in numerous passages in John."[267] The Apostle Paul writes likewise of Jesus, "in whom are hidden the treasures of wisdom and knowledge" (Col 2.3; cf. 1 Cor 1.24, 30).

Jesus identifies Himself as "the Son of Man" twelve times in the Fourth Gospel. The first two are recorded in Jn 1.51 and 3.13. In Jn 3.13, He clearly presents Himself as the ascending/descending Son of Man. Recall from Chapter Four that Daniel's Son of Man first ascends on heavenly clouds to God in heaven to receive a kingdom; then He implicitly descends to earth to establish that kingdom with the saints. So, Daniel presents the Son of Man as first ascending and later descending, the same order as Jesus states in Jn 3.13 regarding Himself. This chronological order, of course, is the opposite of the incarnation/ascension scenario. And it seems that when the Johannine Jesus designates Himself as the Son of Man, He usually intends to be understood according to Dan 7.[268]

Just as Jesus' saying in Jn 1.51 has both a literal and a spiritual connotation, so it seems to be the case with His saying in Jn 3.13. A one-time literal ascending of the Son of Man in Jn 3.13 is implied in the next verse, in which Jesus says, "And as Moses lifted up the serpent in the wilderness, even so must the Son of Man be lifted up" (v. 14). Here, Jesus speaks of His future crucifixion by being lifted up on the cross. This lifting up of the Son of Man is another Johannine theme (Jn 8.28; 12.32, 34; cf. Isa 52.13). For the Fourth Evangelist, Jesus' crucifixion signifies His glory by becoming a prelude to His glorious resurrection and ascension into heaven. Later, Jesus will even describe both this scandalous lifting up on the cross and subsequent heavenly ascension as "the Son of Man ascending [Gr. *anabainonta*] where He was before" (Jn 6.62).[269]

Now let us examine this ascending and descending of the Son of Man from a grammatical perspective. The English words in Jn 3.13, "came down" from heaven, are past tense and therefore also give the impression that the descent must precede the ascent, thus favoring the traditional view. But these words translate the aorist participle *katabas* in the Greek text, which derives from the verb *katabaino* ("I go/come down"). The Greek aorist tense only indicates kind of action, not time of action. However, grammarians used to think that one of the rules of Greek grammar was that the action of an aorist participle precedes in time the action of the main verb. Accordingly, Jn 3.13 would have to be understood as descent/ascent, favoring the incarnation/ascension scenario. But it has recently been discovered that this is incorrect and that the tense of a Greek aorist participle is determined just as with an English participle: according to its context.

So, what is the context of Jn 3.13? Jesus' identification of Himself as the Son of Man in this verse indicates that He intends to be understood in accordance with Daniel's prophecy of the Son of Man in Dan 7. Daniel's Son of Man presumably is literally going to come down from heaven on the eschatological Day with His kingdom. Daniel 7 thus requires that *katabas* in Jn 3.13 be translated "coming down" or "(the one who) comes down" or the like, which is compatible with a future tense, but not "came down" or "descended," which is past tense. Thus,

---

[267] R.E. Brown, *John (i-xii)*, cxxiii.
[268] W.A. Meeks ("The Man from Heaven in Johannine Sectarianism," 52) states, "There is a curiously close connection throughout the gospel [of John] between this title and the descent/ascent language." Indeed, although Meeks writes constantly of a descent/ascent order instead of the ascent/descent order in the text.
[269] E.g., R. Bultmann, *John*, 445; G.R. Beasley-Murray, *John*, 96.

Jesus means in Jn 3.13 that the One who will descend from heaven on the eschatological Day is the One who now ascends spiritually into heaven and descends spiritually as well, so that this ascent precedes the descent, just as Dan 7 suggests.[270] Furthermore, R.E. Brown insists concerning the tense of these verb forms for ascent and descent, "In the Johannine references to Jesus there is a strange timelessness or indifference to normal time sequence that must be reckoned with."[271]

In conclusion, Jn 3.13 ought to be understood according to the background of the Son of Man in Dan 7 and that that figure's descent is therein implied, so that His literal ascent precedes His literal descent. It also needs to be recognized that whenever this ascent-descent motif is expressly stated in Scripture,[272] it is always in this order and never in the reverse. Accordingly, Jesus' ascent/descent in Jn 3.13 refers to His spiritual access to heavenly secrets and bringing them down to earth as well as His later, literal ascension into heaven and subsequent literal descent from heaven to earth at His second coming.

Now we will consider the supposed omnipresence of Jesus in the last clause of Jn 3.13 in the AV. Many traditionalists have endorsed these words as authentic, interpreting them to mean that at the moment Jesus uttered them He also existed in His human nature simultaneously in heaven and presumably throughout the entire universe.[273] But this idea is unprecedented in the NT, let alone the sayings of Jesus. Most contemporary scholars therefore dismiss this AV clause as nonsensical and inauthentic.

Indeed, MS attestation for retaining the last phrase in Jn 3.13—"which is in heaven"—is weak.[274] English versions are about evenly divided on including it or not. The committee for the United Bible Societies' Greek NT, though divided, dismissed it as spurious.[275] A majority of the members were impressed with its omission in the external evidence. Thus, they deemed it "an interpretative gloss, reflecting later Christological development."[276] Accordingly, some textual critics have suggested that it is a later scribal assimilation to the questionable reading of *theos* in Jn 1.18>. However, the clause could be authentic if it means no more than that Jesus had constant spiritual access to heaven.

Note that this idea of the omnipresence of Jesus in Jn 3.13 is not the same as the post-resurrected Jesus being spiritually present with all of His disciples everywhere (Mt 18.20; 28.20; Jn 14.23). (See Appendix B: The Nature of the Holy Spirit.)

"He Who Comes from Heaven" in John 3.31

The speaker throughout Jn 3.27-36 is John the Baptist. The first mention in the Gospel of John of Jesus being from "above" is in this speech, in v. 31. We have already briefly considered it. The Baptist says of Jesus, "He who comes from above is above all,... He who comes from heaven is above all." Obviously, the Baptist uses these prepositional phrases—"from above" and "from heaven"—interchangeably and thus synonymously. Church fathers interpreted such

---

[270] J.D.G. Dunn ("Let John Be John," 313n76) cites J.A. Buhner (*Der Gesandte und sein Weg im 4. Evangelium*, 1977, 353-62), who insists the language in Jn 3.13 implies that ascent precedes descent.
[271] R.E. Brown, *John (i-xii)*, 132.
[272] E.g., Gen 28.12; Prov 30.4; cf. Deut 30.12; Ps 68.18; Eph 4.8.
[273] E.g., C.K. Barrett, *John*, 73; M. Harris, *3 Crucial Questions*, 67.
[274] It is only included in a few late Greek MSS and Syriac versions.
[275] See B.M. Metzger, *Textual Commentary*, 203-04. Both UBS[1] and UBS[2] render it "virtually certain" as being spurious; but UBS[3] admits to "a considerable degree of doubt" in rejecting it.
[276] B.M. Metzger, *Textual Commentary*, 204.

passages literally, and they included this concept in the Nicene Creed. It states concerning Jesus, "For us men and our salvation he came down from heaven," signifying preexistence and incarnation.

But does the Baptist intend that his language be understood literally, i.e., that Jesus actually came from heaven? Couldn't John have meant it figuratively? Indeed, the word "heaven" in both Jn 3.31 and Jn 6 is a periphrasis for the word "God."[277]

Now let us consider these two independent clauses in the Greek text of Jn 3.31. We saw earlier that the words "above all" translate *epano panton* and mean "rank," as in Jn 1.15, 30. Since they do not connote preexistence in heaven, confusion is avoided by translating them "over all." John the Baptist later explained that this phrase indicates sovereignty, not heavenly origin, when he said, "The Father loves the Son, and has given all things into His hand" (v. 35; cf. Mt 11.27/Lk 10.22), which echoes Dan 7.14, 27.

In addition, the Greek verb twice translated "comes" in Jn 3.31 is *erchomenos*. It corresponds to the descending motif in v. 13. Therefore, we see that these preexistence passages in the Gospel of John are very intertwined. In fact, the idea that Jesus comes from heaven appears most often in His Bread of Life discourse.

The Bread from Heaven in John 6.25-65

Many Christians think the foremost preexistence passage in the Gospel of John is Jesus' lengthy Bread of Life discourse in Jn 6.25-65, which contains a lot of descent language. Yet this graphic picture that Jesus draws is full of metaphors. For instance, Jesus describes Himself as "the (living) bread that came down out of heaven" (Jn 6.41, 51, 58). Even though He obviously did not mean that He was literal bread, nearly all readers of this gospel and most scholars have thought Jesus meant that He literally came down from heaven to earth, thus inferring a personal preexistence and incarnation. Yet Jesus also said in this discourse that people need to eat His flesh and drink His blood, and if they do they will never hunger or thirst again but live forever (vv. 50-58). Many of Jesus' hearers grumbled that these were difficult words (vv. 41, 60-61), and many of His disciples no longer followed Him because of it (v. 66). Yet Jesus had just explained outright that He was speaking figuratively by saying, "the words that I have spoken to you are spirit and are life" (v. 63). If the bread, flesh, blood, hunger, and thirst are strictly metaphors, thus intended to be understood spiritually and not literally, can we justify treating the idea of Jesus coming down from heaven any differently? Yet, as with His sayings in Jn 1.51 and 3.13, Jesus here seems to have intended both a spiritual and a literal descent from heaven, the latter in accordance with the implied descent in Dan 7.

Jesus begins His lengthy Bread of Life discourse in Jn 6 following His miraculous feeding of the multitude, recorded in vv. 1-15. He exhorts this audience, "Do not work for the food which perishes, but for the food which endures to eternal life, which the Son of Man shall give to you" (v. 27). So, at the very beginning of this discourse Jesus identifies Himself as the Son of Man of Dan 7 (also Jn 6.53, 62). Jesus' ensuing message reminds the multitude of Israel's wilderness experience, when God, through Moses as His agent, gave the Israelites manna from heaven to eat (Ex 16). Of course, we should understand that the manna in the wilderness did not literally come down from the heaven

---

[277] J.A.T. Robinson, *The Priority of John*, 371.

where God dwells but that this language is figurative, so that the manna came into existence because of a decision made in heaven by God, with heaven serving as a circumlocution for "God."

Jesus replies that it is not Moses but "My Father who gives you the true bread out of heaven. For the bread of God is that which comes down out of heaven, and gives life to the world.... I am the bread of life;... everyone who beholds the Son and believes in Him, may have eternal life; and I Myself will raise him up on the last day" (vv. 32-33, 35, 40). Jesus does not mean that He literally came down from heaven, just as the parallel manna did not literally come down from heaven.

Yet Jesus also means that on the eschatological Day He will descend from heaven as the Son (of Man), i.e., the true bread of God from heaven. When He does He will raise the dead saints (cf. 5.21, 25-26), thereby consummating for them their gift of eternal life. But to do so, Jesus must first literally ascend into heaven. So, this literal understanding of Jesus' words in Jn 6.33-63, based on Dan 7, results in a necessary ascent-descent order, not the descent-ascent order of incarnation/ascension.

Also, John quotes Jesus using the word *katabas* three times in His Bread of Life discourse. Jesus first says, "I am the bread of life that came down [*katabas*] from heaven" (Jn 6.41). And the other two passages containing *katabas* are similar (vv. 51, 58). Recall from Jn 3.13 that *katabas* is an aorist participle in which the tense is determined only by the context. Therefore, these three occurrences of *katabas* in Jn 6 do not necessarily indicate the past tense, as often rendered in English versions. Interpreting it according to the ascent-descent scenario in Dan 7, these three occurrences of *katabas* can be translated "coming down," or even "the one who comes down," thus possibly indicating a future tense. R.E. Brown says concerning *katabas* in Jn 6.51, "The aorist here may be compared with the present 'comes down' in vs. 50."[278]

Some scholars wrongly interpret Jesus' Bread of Life discourse in Jn 6 as echoing the Eucharist that He later instituted at the Last Supper.[279] This interpretation depends heavily on the Gospel of John being a church document that relates the later conflict between church and synagogue and thus does not represent Jn 6 as an actual, historical discourse delivered by Jesus. Besides, alluding to the later institution of the Eucharist would be anachronistic and unintelligible to the hearers participating in this scene.[280]

Wisdom Christology

Another way to understand Jesus' Bread of Life discourse in Jn 6 is through Wisdom Christology. In the OT and Jewish Wisdom Literature,[281] Wisdom is personified as a woman because the Hebrew word for "wisdom," *hokma*, is feminine in gender. This Wisdom is even identified as Torah in Sirach 24.23 and Baruch 4.1. Thus, R. Bultmann asserts, "There can be no doubt, in fact, that a connection exists between the Judaic Wisdom myth and the Johannine Prologue."[282] R.E. Brown reveals several affinities between

---

[278] R.E. Brown, *John (i-xii)*, 282.
[279] R.E. Brown [*John (i-xii)*, 272] provides an overview of three different interpretations, listing those scholars who adopt them, of the Bread of Life discourse in Jn 6 that incorporates a Eucharistic theme.
[280] D.F. Strauss, *The Life of Jesus*, 374.
[281] E.g., Job 28; Prov 1-9; Bar 3.9—4.4; Sir 1; 4.11-19; 6.18-37; 14.20—15.10; 19.20-30; 24; Wis 6-10.
[282] R. Bultmann, *John*, 22.

this personified Wisdom and the Johannine Jesus.[283] More specifically, he and Peder Borgen show that some of the same metaphors that Jesus used in His Bread of Life discourse in Jn 6, e.g., eating and drinking, are also applied to Wisdom in the OT and Jewish Wisdom Literature.[284] Such vivid connections between this personified Wisdom and the preexistence of the Johannine Jesus, especially as the Bread of Life come down from heaven, suggest that Jesus' preexistence in the Fourth Gospel is personified as well. For example, both personified Wisdom and the Johannine Jesus (1) existed with God before creation,[285] (2) are everlasting light from God,[286] and (3) descend from heaven to dwell on the earth.[287] Brown states, "in John, Jesus is personified Wisdom."[288]

Summing up Jesus' Bread of Life discourse in Jn 6, He identifies Himself as the Son of Man of Dan 7 who, yet in the future, will literally come to earth from heaven. In addition, Jesus probably implicitly identifies Himself in Jn 6 as personified Wisdom in the Torah which mythically comes down from heaven to impart life to the world. J.D.G. Dunn sums up this widespread Wisdom motif as applied to the Johannine Jesus, "The key is to recognize that what John draws on is the Wisdom tradition *within* Judaism—where Wisdom/Logos is not understood as a divine being distinct from God,... but rather where Wisdom is understood precisely as the expression of God's *immanence*.[289]

"I Am from Above" in John 8.23

Take Jesus' comparable language in Jn 8.23. He says to His unbelieving Jewish interlocutors, "You are from below, I am from above; you are of this world, I am not of this world." Does He mean that at His incarnation He literally came down "from above," so that He actually preexisted in heaven? If so, then, to treat this antithesis consistently, these unbelieving Jews being "from below" must mean that they literally preexisted in heaven's counterpart, viz., hell (located "below," inside the earth), which is absurd!

In Jn 8.23, most English versions translate *ek ton kato* as "from below" and *ek ton ano* as "from above." But in doing so, they avoid translating the article. This seems unnecessary, especially since it stands alone as a plural in the genitive case. The literal translation is, "You are of the things below, I am of the things above," in which the article *ton* is translated both times. R.E. Brown translates similarly, "You belong to what is below; I belong to what is above."[290] Obviously, neither of these two renderings requires that Jesus literally preexisted in heaven. Furthermore, the second half of this saying, in v. 23, explains the first half. That is, "you are from below" means "you are of this world," and "I am from above" means "I am not of this world." Thus, Jesus is saying that His opponents are from below *in a spiritual sense*, i.e., their values that they live by reflect that they are of the world and therefore without God in their life. In contrast, Jesus

---

[283] R.E. Brown, *John (i-xii)*, cxxiii.
[284] R.E. Brown, *John (i-xii)*, cxxiii; Peder Borgen, *Bread from Heaven: An Exegetical Study of the Concept of Manna in the Gospel of John and the Writings of Philo* (Leiden: Brill, 1981), 154-58, cf. 148-54.
Wisdom: Prov 9.2-5; Isa 55.1-3, 10-11; Sir 24.19-21; 19.21. Jesus: Jn 6.35, 51-58.
[285] Wisdom: Prov 8.22-23; Sir 24.9; Wis 6.22; Jesus: Jn 1.1; 17.5.
[286] Wisdom: Wis 7.26; cf. Sir 1.29; Wis 7.10, 29. Jesus: Jn 1.4-5; 8.12; 9.5; cf. Rev 21.23.
[287] Wisdom: Prov 8.30-31; Sir 24.3, 8; Bar 3.37-38; Wis 9.10. Jesus: Jn 1.14; 3.31; 6.38; 16.28.
[288] R.E. Brown, *John (i-xii)*, cxxv.
[289] J.D.G. Dunn, "Let John Be John," 320. Emphasis his.
[290] R.E. Brown, *John (i-xii)*, 346.

is spiritually "from above" in the sense that His values that He lives by originate with God and therefore come from heaven. Conversely, Jesus means that He is "not of this world" in the sense that He does not belong to this world because He does not live according to its standards. Thus, Jesus does not infer, here, that He literally came from heaven at the moment of an incarnation but that, *ethically, He is of the things of heaven*. Again, we see why the Fourth Gospel has so rightly been called "the spiritual gospel."

It is much the same with the eleven apostles. Jesus prayed to the Father about them, saying, "As Thou didst send Me into the world, I also have sent them into the world" (Jn 17.18; cf. 1.6). If God sending Jesus into the world infers that Jesus literally preexisted, thus affirming the (classical) incarnation, then, to be consistent, Jesus sending His disciples into the world must imply their preexistence and incarnation as well, which is ludicrous! Similarly, if Jesus being "not of this world" (Jn 8.23) parallels His being "from above," and the latter means that He preexisted in heaven, then, to be inconsistent, The Eleven must have preexisted in heaven as well because Jesus prayed to the Father concerning them, "They are not of the world, even as I am not of the world" (Jn 17.16).

Another unique feature of this gospel is that it often contrasts two antithetical metaphors. For example, John (usually quoting Jesus) contrasts light with darkness (Jn 1.5-9; 3.19-21; 8.12; 9.4-5; 12.35-36, 46), life with death (Jn 1.4; 5.21-26, 54; 8.51-52; 11.25), freedom with slavery (Jn 8.32-38), and seeing with blindness (Jn 9.39-41). The same is likely true of Jesus' expressions "from below" and "from above" in Jn 8.23. They are not intended literally of one's origin but to indicate *a spiritual reality*.

This metaphorical interpretation of Jn 8.23 serves as a further explanation of Jn 3.31 and Jn 6.25-65. That is, all three passages mean that the Jesus of the ministry is spiritually, not literally, "from above," i.e., heaven.[291] G.W.H. Lampe well concludes concerning the Johannine ascent/descent language, "to interpret God's saving work in Jesus we do not need the model of a descent of a preexistent divine person into the world.... The model of a descent and an ascent of the Second Person of the Trinity, God the Son, is more likely to confuse ... than the concept of the indwelling presence of God as Spirit, in Jesus himself."[292] This can be called God-in-Christ-by-the-Spirit Christology.

"The Glory Which I Had ... Before the World Was" in John 17.5, 24

Twice during Jesus' so-called "high priestly prayer," uttered shortly before His capture and arrest, He mentioned His preexistent glory. He prayed, "And now, glorify Thou Me together with Thyself, Father, with the glory which I had with Thee before the world was.... My glory which Thou hast given Me; for Thou didst love Me before the foundation of the world" (Jn 17.5, 24). On the surface, these excerpts seem to suggest that Jesus preexisted in heaven prior to the creation of the world and that during that time He possessed a glory He apparently shared with God, which God gave Him out of love.

The glory that Jesus refers to in Jn 17.5 and v. 24 cannot be the same exact glory He had thus far experienced as a man. (See especially Jn 1.14). But Jesus could be referring to the Shekinah glory that accompanied the Israelites during the exodus. They had beheld this glory especially at Mount Sinai, but also repeatedly before the tent of meeting in the wilderness, and subsequently in the

---

[291] J.A.T. Robinson, *The Priority of John*, 369-71.
[292] G.W.H. Lampe, *God as Spirit*, 33.

temple at Jerusalem. It seems most likely that Jesus referred to the Shekinah glory in Jn 17.5 if the Fourth Evangelist has thus far not intended to present Jesus as personally having preexisted. While the glory of the Johannine Jesus has several nuances,[293] it seems doubtful any of them depend on Jesus having personally preexisted. As for Jesus' similar words in Jn 17.5, v. 22, and v. 24, He could have meant that, in the mind of God and before He created the world, God loved His Son whom He foreknew (cf. Eph 1.4; 1 Pt 1.20) and for whom He had predestined the Shekinah glory (cf. Jn 8.12; 9.5 with Isa 9.1-7; 59.20–60.3). Indeed, Judaism taught that the Shekinah glory was predestined for the Messiah.

This is likely what John the Evangelist meant as he quoted about Isaiah's vision of Yahweh. The prophet says, "I saw the Lord sitting on a throne, lofty and exalted" (Isa 6.1, cf. "LORD" in vv. 3, 5). Isaiah then alleges a somewhat divinely-induced obtuseness of the Jews (vv. 9-10). Then John explains, "These things Isaiah said, because he saw His [Jesus'] glory, and he spoke of Him" (Jn 12.41). Does John imply that Isaiah saw the glory of the preexistent Jesus enthroned in heaven? Hardly.

First, the Bible never presents Jesus as occupying a throne in heaven prior to His post-Easter session. Rather, the biblical data suggests it was an unprecedented event.

Second, Isaiah relates that Yahweh says of His suffering Servant that He will appoint Him as "a covenant to the people, as a light to the nations, to open blind eyes" (Isa 42.6-7). This surely refers only to Jesus. Yahweh adds, "I will not give My glory to another" (Isa 42.8). This means Yahweh will give His glory to His Servant, signifying His subordination, and it indicates that the Servant never possessed this glory before.

Third, Isaiah, here, only mentions Yahweh enthroned, thus saying nothing of His glory. This omission has led many commentators to decide that John refers to the Jewish Targum (Aramaic paraphrase) on this passage. It mentions "the glory of the Lord" in Isa. 6.1 and "the glory of the shekinah of the Lord" in v. 5.[294] Thus, John could have had in mind that Isaiah saw in a vision the Shekinah glory and that it would belong to Jesus in the future. Accordingly, John does not intend in Jn 12.41 that Jesus preexisted.

As mentioned earlier, R.E. Brown states that a sort of timelessness pervades the Gospel of John.[295] Indeed, it occurs often in the Johannine sayings of Jesus, especially in those about His glory, e.g., Jn 12.41; 17.5, 22, 24. Isaiah mentions this same glory, but he presents it more chronologically. He portrays Yahweh speaking to His Spirit-anointed Servant, first introduced in Isa 42.1, "I will appoint you as a covenant to the people [Israel], as a light to the nations,... I am the LORD, that is My name; I will not give My glory to another" (v. 6). That is, in light of especially the Gospel of John, Yahweh will share His glory with no one other than His Servant, Messiah Jesus. What Isaiah describes as not yet accomplished in his own day, the Johannine Jesus mentions as if consummated before creation, in which he probably had in mind that God had then merely planned and willed it. For, whatever God decides, it is so absolutely certain that it will come to pass that, from the divine viewpoint, which is timeless, it is as if it is already a done deal!

---

[293] E.g., Jn 1.14; 2.11; 7.39; 12.16, 23; 17.22.
[294] See R.E. Brown, *John (i-xii)*, 486-87.
[295] Cf. John A.T. Robinson, *Jesus and His Coming* (Philadelphia: Westminster, 1957), 170.

3. Is Jesus described as "the only begotten God" in John 1.18?

Introduction The Greek NT and English Versions The Meaning of *Monogenes* Reasons for *Monogenes Theos*	Reasons against *Monogenes Theos* Reasons for *Ho Monogenes Huios* Reasons against *Ho Monogenes Huios* Survey of Scholars Conclusion

Introduction

The last verse in the prologue of the Fourth Gospel is Jn 1.18.[296] This verse emerges as one of the major, debated *theos* texts in the NT. It reads in the NASB:

18 No man has seen God at any time; the only begotten God, who is in the bosom of the Father, He has explained Him.

The problem with Jn 1.18 is mostly textual. It concerns the phrase, "the only begotten God," which identifies Jesus as "God." The MS evidence for this reading is substantial. But variant readings exist, so that some modern English versions here read "the only begotten (Son)" or the like. The question thus arises, Does the correct Greek text of Jn 1.18 contain the word *theos*, thus calling Jesus "God," or does it not?

The Greek New Testament and English Versions

The MS variants in Jn 1.18 can be classified into three categories as witnessed by the major Greek NT texts and the English versions and their marginal readings.[297] One of these categories identifies Jesus as God and the other two do not, as the following shows:
1. *ho monogenes huios* ("only begotten son" or the like: TR, Nestle's[25])
2. *ho monogenes theos* ("only begotten God" or the like: WH, Nestle's[26], UBS[1,2,3])
3. *ho monogenes* ("only begotten" or "only one")

As witnessed above, the majority of modern editions of the Greek NT contain *monogenes theos* in Jn 1.18. This rendering is reflected in the following versions:
- "God the only Son" (TCNT, NRSV)
- "God the only [Son]" (NIV)
- "God the only begotten" (NIVmg[1])
- "the only God" (RSVmg, ESV)
- "the only begotten God" (NASB)
- "the only one, himself God" (NEBmg[2])
- "the only One, who is the same as God" (TEV, cf. ESV)

---

[296] Scholars who identify stanzas of the hymn in the prologue are divided on whether Jn 1.18 belongs to it.
[297] Textual critics compile a Greek NT by consulting three types of witnesses: (1) over 5,000 Greek MSS of the NT and portions thereof, (2) ancient Bible translations (versions), and (3) scriptural quotations in patristic writings. The results of their meticulous scholarship can often be viewed in an apparatus that is sometimes appended to their Greek NT. Such an apparatus shows that three major variants exist in Jn 1.18.

Nevertheless, a slight majority of English versions differ from these listed above by translating Jn 1.18 so that it does not call Jesus "God," as the following show:
- "the only begotten Son" (AV, RV, ASV, NASBmg)
- "the only Son" (RSV, JB, NJB)
- "the only Son" or "the only begotten Son" (NIVmg[2])
- "God's only Son" (NEB)
- "the only one" (NEBmg[1])

The Meaning of *Monogenes*

The word *monogenes* appears nine times in the Greek NT, including here in Jn 1.18 and four other Johannine texts.[298] This somewhat enigmatic word has a long history of being translated "only begotten" in these Johannine passages. But Jn 1.18 is the only instance in the NT in which *monogenes* is attached to *theos* in an identification of Jesus.

The Fourth Evangelist also identifies Jesus in his Greek text by attaching the word *monogenes* to *huios*, meaning "son," in the two much beloved passages Jn 3.16 and v. 18. The traditional translation of *ton huion ton monogene* therein is "the only begotten Son." C.S. Lewis, in his popular book *Mere Christianity*, reasons metaphysically concerning these texts, as church fathers did, by saying, "What God begets is God; just as what man begets is man."[299] But *monogenes* does not mean "only begotten;" it means literally "one-of-a-kind." And there was a Greek word for "only begotten," which was *monogenetos*.[300]

Church father Jerome (347-420) popularized this wrong translation of *monogenes* when Pope Damasus asked him to undertake a revision of the Old Latin Bible, which he did. In each Greek text having *monogenes*, Old Latin Bible MSS translate *unicus*, meaning "only" or "unique." Jerome changed six of these in his Latin Vulgate to *unigenitus*, which means "only begotten."[301] But one of them, Heb 11.17, exposes Jerome's mistranslation. It describes Isaac as an "only begotten" son, which conflicts with Abraham fathering Ishmael prior to Isaac. Yet Isaac was a one-of-a-kind son, being the son of promise.

Many patristic authorities now accuse Jerome of theological bias. They allege that he made these alterations in opposition to Arianism to support the orthodox doctrine of eternal generation.[302] Yet all three parties in the Arian Controversy— viz., Arians, semi-Arians, and orthodox—believed in God's metaphysical begetting of the Son prior to His incarnation. So, the Arians approved of the concept of Jesus being "only begotten;"[303] they only disapproved of the concept that the Son was generated throughout all eternity.

Traditionalist M. Harris represents most recent scholars in his admission that the Johannine "*monogenes* is concerned with familial relations, not manner

---

[298] Lk 7.12; 8.42; 9.38; Jn 1.14, 18; 3.16, 18; Heb 11.17; 1 Jn 4.9.
[299] C.S. Lewis, *Mere Christianity*, 138, cf. 140.
[300] Dale Moody, "God's Only Son: The Translation of John 3:16 in the Revised Standard Version," *JBL* 72 (1953): 213.
[301] Jn 1.14, 18; 3.16, 18; Heb 11.17; 1 Jn 4.9.
[302] E.g., F.J.A. Hort, *Two Dissertations* (London: MacMillan, 1876), 48-53; J. Schneider, *DNTT* 2:75-76; J.A.T. Robinson, *Twelve More New Testament Studies*, 173; Harris, *Jesus as God*, 86; R.E. Brown, *An Introduction to New Testament Christology*, 178n252.
[303] J.H. Bernard (*John*, 1:31) relates that "*monogenes theos* was an expression adopted by Arius and his associate Eunomius as freely as by the orthodox Catholics."

of birth. Neither the virgin birth of Jesus nor the 'eternal generation' of the Son is in John's mind."[304]

Although the Greek word *genos* is remotely related to our English word "beget," there is little justification for translating *monogenes* "only begotten."[305] Etymologically, *mono* literally means "only" or "single," and *genos*, from which we derive our English word "gene," means "kind." So, a good word-for-word translation is "one-of-a-kind." Another possible translation is "only one." Contemporary Johannine scholars often translate the Johannine *monogenes* as "only" or "unique," which emphasizes John's motif of Jesus having a unique relationship with God, it being one-of-a-kind. In three of the other Johannine occurrences of *monogenes*—Jn 3.16, 18; 1 Jn 4.9—this word is linked with *huios* (son), so that Jesus is properly described as "the one-of-a-kind Son (of God)."

Yet some exegetes object to translating *monogenes* either as "only" or "unique." "Only" suggests that God has no other "sons," which is erroneous. In Jn 3.16 and v. 18, *monogenes* actually refers to Jesus' chosenness, as in Isa 42.1. "Chosen" is a better word than "unique" because it does not conjure up the notion of an ontological genesis.

The shorter reading in Jn 1.18—*ho monogenes* ("the only one")—is certainly the most attractive internally. It avoids the problems that arise with the other two renderings. But nearly all textual critics reject it due to its poor external attestation, i.e., by the witnesses,[306] so that it must be rejected. This leaves only two readings as viable: (*ho*) *monogenes theos* ("[the] only God") or *ho monogenes huios* ("the only Son").[307] Now we will consider the most prominent reasons for and against each of these two readings.

Reasons for *Monogenes Theos* ("[the] only Begotten God")

The following reasons support *monogenes theos* as the authentic text of Jn 1.18:

1. The word *theos* has superior attestation in all three classes of the witnesses: Greek MSS,[308] versions, and patristic writings. Regarding MS evidence, many textual critics and other scholars regard the appearance of *monogenes theos* in p^{66} and p^{75} of the Bodmer Papyri, which has a very early MS dating, to the 2nd century, as conclusive that this is the correct reading. Indeed, this variant occurs mostly in the Alexandrian family of MSS, which is the oldest of the MS families and thus the most trustworthy.

2. The exhaustive study by textual critic F.J.A. Hort,[309] which concludes that *monogenes theos* is original, has been widely accepted by modern scholars.

3. *Theos* is the more difficult reading. A principle of textual criticism is that the more difficult, complex, or harsh variant is likely the original. Thus, it is deemed more probable that scribes purposely supplanted *theos* (God) with *huios* (Son) to achieve greater simplicity and smoothness, in this case, to conform to *monogenes huios* in Jn 3.16 and v. 18, than vice versa.

4. *Theos* is the more suitable climax to the prologue by corresponding to *theos* in Jn 1.1c. Hort states that his "careful study" of this contextual reason is

---

[304] M. Harris, *Jesus as God*, 87. Likewise D. Moody, "God's Only Son: The Translation of John 3:16," 214.
[305] E.g., J. Schneider, *DNTT* 2:75.
[306] See B.M. Metzger, *Textual Commentary*, 198. This reading is not in any Greek MSS of Jn 1.18.
[307] We will not consider the complex issue of the variants that include the article and its significance.
[308] It needs to be admitted that most of the oldest and therefore best MSS of Jn 1.18, which support *theos* rather than *huios*, were not discovered until centuries after Erasmus compiled TR and the AV was published.
[309] F.J.A. Hort, *Two Dissertations*.

what primarily caused him to decide unreservedly for *monogenes theos*, and it is generally regarded as his strongest argument.[310] But this depends on Jn 1.1c calling the Logos *theos*.

Reasons against *Monogenes Theos* ("[the] only God")

The following reasons deny *monogenes theos* as the correct text in Jn 1.18:

1. Manuscript attestation for *monogenes theos*, though superior in quality, is largely restricted to only one of the five MS families—the Alexandrian type—whereas MS attestation for *ho monogenes huios* is widespread among all the MS family types.
2. In the ante-Nicene era, Alexandria, Egypt, was already the center in the Roman Empire of belief that Jesus was fully God. This situation, as well as *monogenes theos* appearing mostly in Alexandrian MSS, suggests that early, non-professional scribes living in Alexandria purposely changed *huios* to *theos* because of their theology.[311]
3. God being invisible and the visible Jesus being God are two incompatible concepts.[312] John here affirms the fundamental OT principle that "No man has seen God at any time." And he repeats it later, in Jn 5.37 and 6.46.
4. Neither the words *monogenes theos* nor their concept appear anywhere else in this gospel or the entire NT. Recall that the purpose of the attached prologue is that its themes can be linked with their corresponding elaborations in the gospel text.
5. The concept that only "God" has seen and revealed (explained) "God" (the Father) is bizarre, redundant, and does not appear elsewhere in this gospel or the NT.
6. The concept that "the only (begotten) God" is "in the bosom of the Father" is also strange and does not appear elsewhere in this gospel or the NT.
7. *Monogenes theos* is too developed as a theological concept to occur this early.[313]
8. The concept of *monogenes theos* is incompatible with John's stated purpose for writing his gospel, recorded in Jn 20.31.

Reasons for *Ho Monogenes Huios* ("the only [begotten] Son")

Reasons for the correct text being *ho monogenes huios* in Jn 1.18 are as follows:

1. *Monogenes huios* conforms to Johannine usage (Jn 3.16, 18; 1 Jn 4.9).
2. *Theos* is likely a scribal error due to the similarity in abbreviations of it and *huios*.[314]

---

[310] E.g., M. Harris, *Jesus as God*, 79n30, 82. Harris (p. 103) is representative of many traditionalists who cite three highlights in the Fourth Gospel that designate Jesus' three states of existence as *theos* and argue that these instances are co-supportive interpretatively of each other: the preexistent Logos (Jn 1.1c), the incarnate Son (1.18), and the risen Christ (20.28).
[311] The recognized Christian scribal profession did not come into existence until the 3rd and 4th centuries.
[312] The NT affirms OT teaching that God is literally invisible to mortal humans (Rom 1.20; Col 1.15-16; 1 Tim 1.17; 6.16; Heb 11.27; 1 Jn 4.12, 20). In contrast, Jesus was literally seen and touched (cf. 1 Jn 1.1-3).
[313] This view is based on the following presuppositions: (1) Jn 1.18 is part of the hymn, (2) the hymn was not composed by the author of the Fourth Gospel, which is generally accepted to have been written during the 90s, but preexisted it perhaps decades earlier, (3) this view is further supported if J.A.T. Robinson's conclusion is correct, that the Fourth Gospel was written no later than 70 CE, and (4) Thomas' Confession in Jn 20.28 is not historical. This last presupposition must be rejected.
[314] Allen Wikgren, committee member of the UBS's Greek NT, adopted this view, as cited by B.M. Metzger (*Textual Commentary*, 198).

3. A scribe could have mistakenly substituted *theos* for *huios* due to the immediately preceding proximity of *theou*.[315]
4. Being "in the bosom of the Father" is a Semitic idiom describing the child-father relationship and thus suggests the antecedent *huios*. That is, it conjures up the image of the Son being in the Father, which is supported by the prominent and related Johannine motifs of Father-Son and their Mutual Indwelling (Jn 10.38; 14.10-11, 20).
5. A corollary Johannine theme is that the Son declares, explains, or makes known God the Father by speaking and acting on His behalf (Jn 3.11-13; 5.19; 14.9-11; 15.15).

Notice that most reasons that support *ho monogenes huios* as authentic are contextual.

Reasons against *Ho Monogenes Huios* ("the only [begotten] Son")

Here is one reason that *ho monogenes huios* in Jn 1.18 is a spurious variant:
1. Scribes purposely changed *theos* to *huios* to conform to Johannine usage.

Survey of Scholars

The majority of prominent NT scholars over the past century have favored the Alexandrian MS evidence and therefore opted for Jn 1.18 calling Jesus "God." M. Harris has garnered a list of these scholars during this time-period who have decided between the two primary variants in Jn 1.18.[316] His list can be condensed as follows:

ho monogenes huios	*monogenes theos*
2 textual critics	5 textual critics
5 commentators	11 commentators
3 general studies	16 general studies

Conclusion

The three external witnesses and modern scholarship clearly favor *monogenes theos* ("[the] only God") as the original text in Jn 1.18, in which Jesus is called "God." On the other hand, modern English versions as well as the internal evidence of the Fourth Gospel decidedly support *ho monogenes huios* ("the only Son") as the authentic text in Jn 1.18, in which Jesus is not called "God." R. Bultmann and, tentatively, C.K. Barrett preferred this reading due to the internal evidence within the verse.[317]

Overall, the arguments seem about evenly divided for either variant. But the following point is decisive: if Jn 1.1c, 5.18, 10.30-38, and 20.28 are interpreted as not calling Jesus *theos* ("God"), as in this book, then Jn 1.18 cannot be linked to any corresponding text in the body of this gospel. And we have seen that the concept of linkage is the very purpose of the prologue. On the other hand, the reading *ho monogenes huios* is clearly linked to Jn 3.16 and v. 18. On account of this conformity, the authentic text of Jn 1.18 is most likely not *monogenes theos* but *ho monogenes huios*, so that this verse likely does not call Jesus "God."

---

[315] Ezra Abbot, *The Authorship of the Fourth Gospel and Other Critical Essays*, 2 vols. (Boston: Ellis, 1888), 1:270, 283.

[316] M. Harris, *Jesus as God*, 83.

[317] R. Bultmann, *John*, 81, 82n2; C.K. Barrett, *John*, 169.

4. Who said in John 5.18 Jesus was "making Himself equal with God"?

Introduction	Equality with God?
Healing on the Sabbath	Jesus' Disclaimer of Deity
Keeping the Sabbath Holy	Summary

Introduction

Early in Jesus' ministry, His adversaries misunderstood some of His claims about His identity. Only John records these incidents because he is the only gospel writer who told about Jesus' early ministry. It includes several of Jesus' appearances at the temple in Jerusalem during the festivals and therefore provides more exposure to His opponents.

On one occasion, Jesus' antagonists accused Him of making Himself "equal" with God. On a later occasion, His enemies accused Him of claiming actually to *be* God. Such allegations allude to the cause of Adam's Fall (Gen 3.5). For now, we will examine the charge that Jesus was "making Himself equal with God," recorded in Jn 5.18. Later, we will consider the similar allegation, recorded in Jn 10.33, that Jesus claimed to be God. To understand these texts we need to ask, Do these allegations indicate that Jesus made these claims? Or are these texts intended to mean that this is how Jesus' interlocutors understood Him at that time, and they erred in doing so?

Healing on the Sabbath

The first occasion that prompted such an allegation took place when Jesus and His disciples were attending one of the feasts at Jerusalem. One Sabbath day during this feast, Jesus healed a man who had been paralyzed for thirty-eight years (Jn 5.2-9). Jesus had commanded him, "Arise, take up your pallet and walk" (v. 9). So the fellow did just that; he picked up his mattress and took off!

Now, the Law of Moses clearly forbade physical labor on the Sabbath. Accusing a Jew of doing work on the Sabbath was a serious charge. It could invoke the death penalty. For, the Torah reads unequivocally, "whoever does any work on the sabbath day shall surely be put to death" (Ex 31.15; cf. v. 14).

But what constitutes work? There are no easy answers. E.P. Sanders explains, "The written law is very incomplete; in theory it covers all of life, but it often lacks details. Consequently, it had to be extended and applied in all kinds of ways."[318] That is why Judaism later interpreted and condensed the Torah into 613 laws, 39 of which were about Sabbath-breaking, in which some activities are specifically identified as "work."

Sometimes Jesus exposed religious error, either in doctrine or practice. When He did, He often pointed out that some of these 613 laws of Judaism did not accurately reflect the Torah but were actually misinterpretations of it.

One of these thirty-nine Judaic laws regarding Sabbath-keeping forbade the carrying of anything on the Sabbath. The load carried was regarded as a "burden," so that the activity was deemed to be "work." Consequently, "the Jews" told the healed man that he was not permitted to carry his pallet on the

---

[318] E.P. Sanders, *The Historical Figure of Jesus*, 209.

Sabbath because it was a burden (Jn 5.10). The man replied by informing them that Jesus had told him to do it. Thus John writes,

16 And for this reason the Jews were persecuting Jesus, because He was doing these things on the Sabbath.
17 But He answered them, "My Father is working until now, and I Myself am working."
18 For this cause therefore the Jews were seeking all the more to kill Him, because He not only was breaking the Sabbath, but also was calling God His own Father, making Himself equal with God.

Many traditionalists have understood the sentence in Jn 5.18 to be the assessment of not only "the Jews" but the author as well, and they have believed that it is correct.[319] In other words, John and "the Jews" believed Jesus was breaking the Sabbath and making Himself equal with God. Even a few critics have thought this.[320] In fact, the Athanasian Creed reads that the Son "is equal to the Father according to divinity." So, the traditional viewpoint is that Jesus is co-equal with the Father in all of the Father's divine attributes.

It is difficult to determine from the Evangelist's statement in Jn 5.18 whether he is reporting (1) both his own and the Jews' assessment of Jesus, or (2) the Jews' assessment. Even some traditionalists admit that substantial lines of evidence indicate that *in Jn 5.18 the author expresses the Jews' assessment of Jesus, which is not his own.*[321]

Keeping the Sabbath Holy

When Jesus healed this paralytic and told him to carry his bed, Jesus' opponents could rightly accuse Him of breaking two of these thirty-nine laws of Judaism regarding Sabbath-keeping. One was that it was unlawful to heal on the Sabbath. The other was the prohibition against carrying something on the Sabbath. John says that is why "the Jews were persecuting Jesus because He was doing these things on the Sabbath" (v.16).

It should be clear to NT gospel readers that *Jesus never broke the Sabbath.* He *did* break some of Judaism's thirty-nine laws, or rules, concerning the Sabbath (*Sabb.* 7.2). But breaking *man's laws* is not the same as breaking *God's laws.*[322] In fact, Jesus often corrected Pharisaical misinterpretations of the Torah, especially about Sabbath-keeping.

Pre-Christian Judaism debated what constituted "work" and a "burden." A few years before Jesus conducted His public ministry, Philo had argued that God never ceases His creative activity, even on the Sabbath.[323] Rabbis uniformly agreed that God performs His moral work as Revealer and Judge everyday.[324] And some rabbis even insisted that God could do anything He wanted to on the Sabbath without ever breaking it.[325] Moreover, rabbis of the 1st century further distinguished between God's *original* work of creation and His *subsequent* work

---

[319] Many distinguished, contemporary biblical commentators hold this view, e.g., R.E. Brown [*John (i-xii)*], 408), C.K. Barrett (*John*, 256-57), J.N. Sanders, and B.A. Mastin (*John*, 164).
[320] E.g., P.M. Casey, *From Jewish Prophet to Gentile God*, 28.
[321] E.g., L.W. Hurtado, *How on Earth Did Jesus Become a God?* 52.
[322] The Bible often calls the Torah "the Law of God" and "the Law of Moses." God gave it through Moses.
[323] Philo, *On the Cherubim*, 87.
[324] R. Bultmann, *John*, 245-46.
[325] C.K. Barrett, *John*, 256.

of *sustaining* that creation, even on the Sabbath.³²⁶ Healing would be regarded as sustaining creation.

Consequently, it logically follows that if God creates (works) on the Sabbath, then surely there is nothing wrong with a human being doing likewise, e.g., restoring people to good health (considered a form of creation) on the Sabbath. Indeed, the Judaism of that time clearly permitted medical doctors to work on the Sabbath if an illness or injury was imminently life threatening.³²⁷

But what if the physical problem *was not* life threatening? Did doing cures in such situations constitute work? There was no consensus among Jews on this question. Pietist sects, e.g., Pharisees and Essenes, forbade treating minor ailments on the Sabbath.³²⁸ Yet most Jews were not so strict. This is evident from the crowds' response to Jesus' healing on other Sabbath days. For, aside from the Fourth Gospel, the synoptists report that Jesus healed three different people on three separate Sabbath days: (1) a man with a withered hand (Mk 3.1-6 par.), (2) a woman bent double for eighteen years (Lk 13.10-17), and (3) a man who suffered from dropsy (Lk 14.1-5). In all three incidents the question was broached, either by Jesus or His opponents—scribes, Pharisees, or a synagogue official—about whether it was lawful to heal on the Sabbath. Authority Geza Vermes concludes, "the form of healing by word of mouth or touch which Jesus had adopted did not really count as 'work' prohibited on the sabbath."³²⁹

Nevertheless, Jesus' opponents insisted that His healings were "work" and thus not lawful on the Sabbath. But each time Jesus replied by questioning the men present as to who among them would not rescue their own sheep that had fallen into a pit or their own son or ox that had fallen into a well on a Sabbath day. He also called their attention to the fact that all men satisfy their donkey's thirst on the Sabbath by untying the animal and leading it from the stall to the water, which act should be regarded as Sabbath-breaking according to their rules. Finally, Jesus usually concluded His remarks by asking them how much more value a human being is than an animal.

So, in light of these things that Jesus said on other occasions about Sabbath-keeping, His reply in Jn 5.17 must represent a refutation of the Jews' objection to His healing on the Sabbath and an allusion that the two rabbinical laws regarding Sabbath-keeping, mentioned above, are defective. Also, Jesus implies that His heavenly Father never ceases working on the Sabbath (cf. Jn 9.3-4), and He associates His deeds with those of His Father. In fact, John has already quoted Jesus when He identified His work as that of the Father (Jn 4.34). Therefore, if the idea of Jesus healing on the Sabbath was actually the Father working through Him, as indeed it was, then it follows that Jesus did not break the Sabbath because God the Father does not break the Sabbath.

Jesus appears to have further substantiated this argument when He claimed on another occasion to be "Lord of the Sabbath" (Mt 12.8 par.). By claiming such authority, like God, He does not break the Sabbath.

In light of these points, John is surely contrasting the true and therefore divine viewpoint of Jesus healing on the Sabbath with the faulty viewpoint of His accusers. That is, John correctly reports that Jesus "was doing these things on the Sabbath" (v. 16); in contrast, John means that the Jews falsely alleged that Jesus "was breaking the Sabbath."

---

³²⁶ R.H. Strachan, *The Fourth Gospel: Its Significance and Environment*, 2nd ed. (Edinburgh: SCM, 1917), 114.

³²⁷ G.B. Caird, *New Testament Theology*, 387.

³²⁸ E.P. Sanders, *The Historical Figure of Jesus*, 208.

³²⁹ G. Vermes, *The Changing Faces of Jesus*, 196.

Moreover, John reports another instance of Jesus healing on the Sabbath (Jn 9.6-7, 16), and, as mentioned above, the synoptists tell of three other occasions when He did so. On all of these occasions Jesus' opponents accused Him of breaking the Sabbath (Mt 12.9-13 par.; Lk 13.10-17; 14.1-6). Yet, in none of these reports do any of the gospel writers indicate that they agreed with the Jews' accusation.

Early in Jesus' ministry, He declared His intention to keep all of the Torah. It included keeping the Sabbath day holy. He announced, "Do not think that I came to abolish the Law or the Prophets; I did not come to abolish, but to fulfill" (Mt 5.17). E.P. Sanders thinks Jesus "did not act in such a way as to cause people ... to believe that he had denied the validity of the sabbath law, which would mean denying its divine origin. Jesus lived, on the whole, as a good Jew," which included Sabbath-keeping.[330]

Jesus' accusers must have realized afterwards that their allegation was incorrect. For when the Sanhedrin later interrogated Jesus, no one charged Him with Sabbath-breaking or, more importantly, with teaching against keeping the Sabbath day holy.

Equality with God?

If we accept that, in Jn 5.18, John is *not* relating his own assessment of Jesus healing on the Sabbath, but that of "the Jews," to be consistent we must treat the other allegation the same. That is, *John the Evangelist is not reporting that he himself says that Jesus was "making Himself equal with God," but that it is Jesus' opponents who say this.*

Some traditionalists seem to erroneously disconnect Jesus "calling God His own Father" and "making Himself equal with God," in Jn 5.18b, as if the one has nothing to do with the other. On the contrary, the first clause is the cause of the second clause. Some translators of English versions appear to have anticipated this error and so have translated (or paraphrased) it more clearly as follows: (1) "he had said that God was his own Father, and in this way had made himself equal with God" (TEV); (2) "by calling God his own Father, he claimed equality with God" (NEB); (3) "he spoke of God as his own Father, and so made himself God's equal" (JB).

Jesus may have been the first Jewish rabbi to personally call God his "Father" and thereby go beyond the OT declaration of God as "father" of Israel, which is strictly in a corporate sense.[331] These Jews, who apparently heard it for the first time, were outraged because they thought it tantamount to claiming equality with God. But Christians should be under no such illusion. Jesus calling God "My Father" is not at all evidence that He was posturing Himself equal with God, nor could this have been the author's perception. For, Jesus had earlier taught His disciples to address God in prayer as "Father" (Mt 6.9 par.). Thus, Christians certainly have never thought that their constant practice of calling God their "Father" is tantamount to claiming that they themselves are equal with God!

Apparently, these Jews were also upset with Jesus associating His works with those of the Father, as in Jn 5.17. They thought He was evaluating His

---

[330] E.P. Sanders, *The Historical Figure of Jesus*, 223.
[331] See J. Jeremias (*The Prayers of Jesus*), although some of his main points have since been nullified; e.g., see James Barr, "Abba Isn't "Daddy,'" *JTS*, N.S., 39 (April 1988): 28-47. G. Vermes (*Jesus the Jew*, 210-11) is only able to show that certain Hasidim had previously acknowledged God as their "Father." Thus, F. Hahn (*The Titles of Jesus in Christology*, 307) may still be correct in asserting that calling God *abba* was "unthinkable in the prayer language of contemporary Judaism."

works on the same level with those of God.[332] In their minds, such an assessment was an affront to the divine Majesty and a claim to equality with God. And they probably thought that any man who equates himself with God simultaneously acts independently of Him.[333]

It has often been said—and there is a sense in which it is true—that "Jesus never made Himself out to be anything." He let God do that while He simply remained obedient (e.g., Mt 3.17 par.; 17.5). For, the Johannine Jesus repeatedly claimed no more than to have been sent by God and that God gave Him His works and His words. Accordingly, the supreme Johannine testimony, coming from Jesus Himself, is that His miraculous works are "signs" which testify that God sent Him (e.g., Jn 5.36; 10.37).

It was the same with Moses; he did not make himself out to be anything, either. In fact, he did the opposite (Ex 3.11), and *that* angered God (Ex 4.10-17). God sent Moses to deliver Israel and, by means of miracles, made him as "god to Pharaoh" (Ex 7.1).

In sum, John the Evangelist must mean in Jn 5.18 that the Jews thought Jesus was making Himself equal with God, not that John himself thought this.[334] Thus, these Jews were mistaken in thinking that Jesus was claiming equality with God.[335] William Temple concludes that this assessment of Jesus in v. 18 was "introduced by His enemies."[336] George Beasley-Murray calls it "a misleading interpretation of the declaration of Jesus" in v. 17.[337] And J.C. Fenton explains most succinctly concerning v. 18, "this is what the Jews wrongly supposed, not what John believes, as the speech which follows shows."[338]

Jesus' Disclaimer of Deity

Indeed it does. Jesus' lengthy discourse in Jn 5.19-47 represents a clear disclaimer to the Jews' allegation in v. 18 that He makes Himself equal with God.[339] John implies this by explaining, "Jesus therefore answered and was saying to them" (v. 19). He means that, due to the Jews' allegation in v. 18 (verbalized or not), Jesus begins in v. 19 to answer His critics by explaining His statement in v. 17 about the association of His works and the Father's works. He promptly admits His own inadequacy and thus affirms His utter dependence upon, and essential subordination to, the Father. He says that "the Son can do nothing of Himself," and "I can do nothing on My own initiative" (vv. 19, 30). Jesus makes Himself nothing—though by human standards He is really something!—so that God His Father may be everything.[340] Here is a summary of Jesus' disclaimer:

- Jesus cannot do miracles in His own initiative (vv. 19, 30).
- The Father shows Jesus what He is doing so that Jesus can do it, too (vv. 19-20).

---

[332] B.F. Westcott, *The Gospel According to St. John: The Greek Text with Introduction and Notes*, 1:187.

[333] So claims W.F. Howard, *Christianity According to St. John* (London: Duckworth, 1943), 71.

[334] A.E. Harvey, *Jesus and the Constraints of History*, 168; J. Jervell, *Jesus in the Gospel of John*, 21; L.W. Hurtado, "God," 275.

[335] Craig S. Keener, *The Gospel of John: A Commentary*, 2 vols. (Peabody, MA: Hendrickson, 2003), 1:647.

[336] W. Temple, *Readings in St. John's Gospel*, 1:110.

[337] G.R. Beasley-Murray, *John*, 75, cf. 390.

[338] J.C. Fenton, *John*, 71. See also G.B. Caird, *New Testament Theology*, 402.

[339] G.R. Beasley-Murray, *John*, 175; C.S. Keener, *The Gospel of John*, 1:647-48. Contra C.K. Barrett, *John*, 72; P.M. Casey, *From Jewish Prophet to Gentile God*, 24, 38.

[340] Similarly, J.A.T. Robinson, *The Priority of John*, 393.

- The Father gives Jesus His miraculous works (v. 36).
- The Father gives Jesus authority to raise dead saints to eternal life (vv. 21, 26).
- The Father gives Jesus authority to judge and execute judgment (vv. 22, 27, 30).

The Jews of that time were convinced that it was blasphemous for a man to claim prerogatives or powers that they deemed to be the sole possession of God. But they wrongly presumed that such non-transferable powers included the giving of life to the dead and exercising justice on judgment day.[341] Jesus, in making these claims contained in vv. 19-47, also made it perfectly clear that these powers were not intrinsic to His own nature but delegated to Him by the Father. Therefore, the question arises, *How can Jesus be God if He cannot do any of His miraculous works in His own power?*

Jesus further revealed that it is also the Father's purpose, in bestowing such grand authority and power upon Him, that "all may honor the Son, even as they honor the Father" (v. 23). Traditionalists usually insist that such homage indicates worship and thus requires that Jesus is God. But how can this be if Jesus' answer represents a clear denial to claiming equality with God? Rather, the Son attains all such privileges because He is "worthy," having obediently fulfilled His destiny as the archetypal Son of Man (v. 27; cf. Rev 5.12-13). James M. Robinson hits the mark squarely by saying, "Jesus did not need to be deified to receive the high honor he deserves" on the basis of His worthiness.[342]

Moreover, Jesus concluded His response herein by providing incontrovertible evidence that He never made Himself equal with God or claimed to be God. He called the Father, "the one and only God" (5.44; Gr. *tou monou theou*). This alludes to Israel's cherished Shema (Deut 6.4). So, Jesus, in calling Yahweh "My Father" and "the one and only God," implicitly denies that He claims either equality *with* God or identity *as* God.

Finally, we have already considered that John, later in this gospel, unambiguously presents the Father as essentially superior to the Son, which nullifies the notion of their equality, by quoting Jesus as saying, "The Father is greater than I" (Jn 14.28; cf. 10.29).

Summary

In sum, John the Evangelist does not say in Jn 5.18 that Jesus was either breaking the Sabbath or making Himself equal with God. Rather, he represents this assessment as that of the Jews, with which he surely disagrees. Moreover, Jesus' lengthy response to His accusers, recorded in vv. 19-46, represents a clear disclaimer to their allegation. In contrast, He reveals His utter dependence upon, and subordination to, God His Father. Finally, the fact that no witness at Jesus' interrogation by the Sanhedrin ever alleged that He claimed to be God suggests that Jesus had convinced these Jews of His disclaimer.

---

[341] Str-B, 1:523, 895; 4:1199-1212.
[342] James M. Robinson, "Very Goddess and Very Man: Jesus' Better Self," *Encountering Jesus: A Debate on Christology*, ed. Stephen T. Davis (Atlanta: John Knox, 1988), 111.

5. Did Jesus claim implicitly, in John 8.24, 28, 58, "I am Yahweh"?

Introduction	Jesus' "I am" Sayings with a Predicate
"I am" in Exodus 3.14 and Isaiah	The "Son of Man" in John 8.28
Messianic Interpretation of John 8.24	Preexistence of Jesus in John 5.58?
Jesus as "the Light of the World"	A Different "I am" Saying
Context of Jesus' "I am" in John 8.24	Jesus' "I am" Saying in John 18.5
Jesus' Message from the Beginning	Summary

Introduction

The Gospel of John is unique in that it relates several utterances by Jesus that scholars refer to as "the 'I am' sayings of Jesus." Although this expression, "I am," is recorded in the Greek NT as *ego eimi*, Jesus no doubt spoke it in Aramaic. So, His actual Aramaic words likely were *ani hu*, similar to the Aramaic *ana hu*. John the Evangelist included these important *ego eimi* sayings to fill in his portrait of the identity of Jesus.

Most of Jesus' "I am" sayings in the Fourth Gospel have a predicate nominative attached to them, some of which are metaphors. Two renowned examples are "I am the bread of life" and "I am the light of the world" (Jn 6.35; 8.12; 9.5). In such instances, Jesus made a clear self-identification. Some of these types of Jesus' "I am" sayings allude to messianic OT passages (e.g., Isa 9.2; cf. Mt 4.14-16).

However, a few of Jesus' *ego eimi* sayings do not have an attached predicate nominative.[343] While some of these merely mean, "It is me,"[344] a few do not, resulting in some ambiguity. The latter type are when Jesus spoke of believing that "I am *He*," with the personal pronoun added. Three of these obscure types appear in Jn 8 as follows:

21 He said therefore again to them, "I go away, and you shall seek Me, and shall die in your sin; where I am going, you cannot come."
22 Therefore the Jews were saying, "Surely He will not kill Himself, will He, since He says, 'Where I am going, you cannot come'?"
23 And He was saying to them, "You are from below, I am from above; you are of this world, I am not of this world.
24 "I said therefore to you, that you shall die in your sins; for unless you believe that I am *He*, you shall die in your sins."
25 And so they were saying to Him, "Who are You?" Jesus said to them, "What have I been saying to you from the beginning?
....
28 Jesus therefore said, "When you lift up the Son of Man, then you will know that I am *He*, and I do nothing on My own initiative, but I speak these things as the Father taught Me.
....
56 "Your father Abraham rejoiced to see My day, and he saw it and was glad."
57 The Jews therefore said to Him, "You are not yet fifty years old, and have You seen Abraham?"

---

[343] Mk 14.62; Jn 8.24, 28; 8.58; 13.19; 18.5-6. In some of these the NASB adds the word "He" in italics.
[344] Mt 14.27; Lk 24.39; Jn 18.5-6. R.E. Brown [*John (i-xii)*, 533] renders *ego eimi*, "It is I" or "I am the one." C.K. Barrett (*John*, 342) says, "As it stands alone, *ego eimi* is in Greek a meaningless expression."

58 Jesus said to them, "Truly, truly, I say to you, before Abraham was born, I am."
59 Therefore they picked up stones to throw at Him; but Jesus hid Himself, and went out of the temple.

Note that the "I am" sayings in vv. 24 and 28 are followed by the italicized word "*He*." It indicates that this word does not appear in the Greek text, and translators have added it for clarification. (Notice, however, that the NASB translators omit *He* in v. 58.)[345]

The "I AM" Sayings in Exodus 3.14 and Deutero-Isaiah

Many traditionalist scholars contend that these *ego eimi* sayings of Jesus without the predicate, in Jn 8.24, v. 28, and v. 58, allude to Yahweh's self-designation, "I AM," in Ex 3.14, which the LXX translates *ego eimi*. For Jesus to make this connection, these traditionalists assert that He indirectly identified Himself as Yahweh.[346] R.E. Brown makes the astounding assertion concerning these three occurrences, "No clearer implication of divinity is found in the gospel tradition."[347]

Exodus 3 relates the very important episode in the early development of the Hebrews' religion, in which "the angel of the LORD [Yahweh]" appeared to Moses in a burning bush and spoke to him on behalf of Yahweh. The pertinent text reads as follows:

13 Then Moses said to God, "Behold, I am going to the sons of Israel, and I shall say to them, 'The God of your fathers has sent me to you.' Now they may say to me, 'What is His name?' What shall I say to them?"
14 And God said to Moses, "I AM WHO I AM"; and He said, "Thus you shall say to the sons of Israel, 'I AM has sent me to you.'"
15 And God, furthermore, said to Moses, "Thus you shall say to the sons of Israel, 'The LORD, the God of your fathers, the God of Abraham, the God of Isaac, and the God of Jacob, has sent me to you.' This is My name forever, and this is My memorial-name to all generations."

Those traditionalist scholars who connect Jesus' "I am" sayings in Jn 8 with the "I AM" of Ex 3.14 do so largely because none of these Johannine occurrences contain a predicate, which these scholars generally assume is the case with Ex 3.14. However, a predicate is implied in Ex 3.14 because in the next sentence God commands Moses to tell Israel, "'The LORD,... has sent me to you.'" In other words, when God said at that time, "I AM," He clearly meant, "I am Yahweh."

More particularly, the words in Ex 3.14, "I AM WHO I AM," translate the Hebrew words *'ehyeh ser 'ehyeh*. Thus, "I AM" translates *'ehyeh*. This word, *'ehyeh*, derives from the Hebrew verb *hayah* (also *hawa*), which is usually translated "(be)came," "become," or "be," and herein means "the Self-Existent One," "the Self-Subsistent One," or the like. Thus, the "I AM" in Ex 3.14-15 represents a self-identification and, more precisely, an explanation of the meaning of Yahweh's name.[348]

---

[345] In this book, this is the only place in the NASB where its italicized words are left intact.
[346] E.g., J.H. Bernhard, E. Stauffer, R. Snackenburg, R.E. Brown, Leon Morris.
[347] R.E. Brown, *John (i-xii)*, 367.
[348] R.E. Brown (*John [i-xii]*, 533) claims Ex 3.14 is "the all important text for the meaning of 'Yahweh.'"

Jesus, on the other hand, identified Himself in entirely the opposite manner. Rather than claiming self-existence, He disclosed His inadequacies by acknowledging that He was completely dependent upon the Father, not only for His words, authority, works, and power, but even His possession of eternal life (e.g., Jn 5.19, 26, 30; 8.28). Obviously, self-subsistence is independence and therefore the opposite of dependence.

Many recent traditionalist scholars have exchanged this Ex 3.14 interpretation of Jesus' "I am He" sayings in Jn 8 for four "I am He" (Heb. *ani hu*) sayings of Yahweh in Isa 41.4; 43.10, 13; 48.12.[349] Therein, Yahweh extolls Himself as the only God by saying, "I am He." The LXX here translates the Hebrew *ani hu* with *ego eimi*, the same words that appear in the Greek text of Jn 8.24, v. 28, and v. 58. Nevertheless, these scholars who change their references from Ex 3.14 to these Deutero-Isaiah passages end up with the same result: the Johannine Jesus is represented as claiming to be Yahweh.

Interpreting Jesus' words "I am He," in Jn 8.24, 28, or v. 58, as referring to those in either Ex 3.14 or Isaiah, and thereby indirectly identifying Jesus as Yahweh, appears most arbitrary. Many distinguished NT scholars object to it. For example, John Calvin states concerning Jn 8.24, "Some of the ancient writers have deduced from this passage the Divine essence of Christ; but this is a mistake."[350] R. Bultmann asserts concerning Jn 8, "We should, however, reject the view that *ego eimi* means: 'I (Jesus) am God,' i.e., that the sentence identifies Jesus with God."[351] C.K. Barrett deems any OT interpretation of these "I am" sayings in Jn 8 as contextually "impossible."[352] He alleges concerning v. 24, "It is not however correct to infer either from the present passage or from the others in which *ego eimi* occurs that John wishes to equate Jesus with the supreme God of the Old Testament.... *Ego eimi* does not identify Jesus with God." Barrett adds cogently, "He pronounces *ego eimi*, not to identify himself with God in any exclusive and final sense, but to draw attention to himself as the one in whom God is encountered and known."[353]

Besides, if the Jews had understood Jesus' "I am" sayings in Jn 8 as an intended allusion to Yahweh's "I am" saying in either Exodus or Isaiah, they no doubt would have promptly charged Jesus with blasphemy and reached for the rocks! (Cf. Jn 8.59; 10.31.) For, Judaism later held that simply pronouncing the divine name was blasphemy and thus deserving of death.[354] How much more if a man claimed to be Yahweh?

The large majority of scholars treat all three of Jesus' "I am" sayings in Jn 8 alike. That is, (1) they assert that they *allude* to Ex 3.14 or the Isaiah passages, so that Jesus *indirectly claims* to be God, or (2) they conclude that these sayings *do not allude* to these OT references so that Jesus *does not* herein claim to be God. A few commentators interpret them as echoing OT references, but only in the sense of Jesus associating Himself with Yahweh by bearing His name,[355] which is not a claim to being Yahweh.

Perhaps the worst thing about this Ex 3.14/Isaiah interpretation of Jn 8.24 is that it presents Jesus as saying that people must believe that He is Yahweh in order for them to be saved. Accordingly, Jesus' words in v. 24 can be paraphrased,

---

[349] E.g., D.A. Carson, *The Gospel According to John* (Grand Rapids: Eerdmans, 1991), 343.
[350] John Calvin, *Calvin's Commentaries*, 22 vols. (repr. Grand Rapids: Baker, 1984), 17:333.
[351] R. Bultmann, *John*, 327.
[352] C.K. Barrett, *John*, 342.
[353] C.K. Barrett, *John*, 342, 98; similarly, idem, *Essays on John*, 71.
[354] *Sanh.* 7:5.
[355] E.g., E. Stauffer, "ego," in *TDNT* 2:352.

"unless you believe that I am Yahweh, you shall die without having your sins forgiven." This interpretation is preposterous! Can we accept that Jesus would make such an inflammatory remark as a Jewish religious reformer without making it more clear? Not only do the gospels reveal that He never claimed to be Yahweh (God), we saw in Chapter One that His chosen apostles never preached this precept, let alone made it an essential article of faith.

The Messianic Interpretation of John 8.24

Now we will consider the alternative proposals offered by scholars for Jesus' "I am" sayings in Jn 8.24, v. 28, and v. 58, in which Jesus is regarded as not alluding to either Ex 3.14 or the Deutero-Isaiah texts and thus not identifying Himself as Yahweh.

Several commentators have thought that Jesus meant in Jn 8.24 that He was the Christ. H.A.W. Meyer posits that Jesus meant, "namely, *the* Messiah, the great name which every one understood without explanation,... which was the *most present thought* both to Jesus and the Jews, especially in all their discussions.... The Jews understand the *hoti ego eimi* well enough, but refuse to recognize it."[356] Indeed, sometimes when the multitudes saw Jesus heal or heard Him speak, there was much inquisitiveness and debate among them as to whether He was the Messiah, and John is not remiss in recording it.[357]

Jesus' Olivet Discourse *may* support this messianic interpretation of Jn 8.24. Mark quotes Jesus as saying, "Many will come in My name, saying, 'I am He!' and will mislead many" (Mk 13.5; cf. Lk 21.8). While Mark and Luke assume the predicate, "He" (not in Gr.), Matthew includes it with the words, "I am the Christ" (Mt 24.5). Why this difference in quotation? Mark and Luke must relate the *ipsissma verba* (exact words) whereas Matthew typically editorializes in order to provide Jesus' exact meaning of what might otherwise be construed as an ambiguous declaration.

Sometimes Jesus' use of the "I am" without a predicate does not allow "God" as the implied predicate. One example is the important dialogue He had with His apostles at Caesarea Philippi. Mark and Luke report that Jesus asks them, "Who do people/the multitudes say that I am?" (Mk 8.27/Lk 9.18).[358] All three synoptists record that He adds, "Who do you say that I am?" Peter answers that Jesus is "the Christ." This answer infers that Jesus' use of "I am," here, means that he is the Christ. Another example is when the Johannine Jesus washed the apostles feet immediately prior to the Last Supper. Jesus said, "You call Me Teacher and Lord; and you are right, for so I am" (Jn 13.13).

Jesus as "the Light of the World"

To understand Jesus' "I am" saying in Jn 8.24, we ought to first consider His preceding "I am" saying with the predicate. For John records only twelve verses earlier, "Again therefore Jesus spoke to them, saying, 'I am the light of the world'" (Jn 8.12; cf. 1.4, 9; 3.19, 21; 9.5). Who was Jesus' audience, whom John calls "them?"

All English versions of the Gospel of John include the pericope about a woman caught in adultery and brought to Jesus, recorded in Jn 7.53—8.11. But many modern versions enclose it in brackets, as does the NASB, and/or they explain in a footnote that this story does not appear in most Greek MSS

---

[356] H.A.W. Meyer, MCNT, 3:270. Emphasis his.
[357] See Jn 4.29; 7.26-27, 31, 41.
[358] Matthew substitutes "the Son of Man" for "I" (Mt 16.13), thus blending it with "the Christ" (v. 16).

(and ancient versions). A few MSS include it, but in another location in this gospel, or they have it solely in the Gospel of Luke. Textual critics regard this story as probably authentic, partly because it conforms to the character of Jesus' ministry. But they do not think that it originally was penned by the Fourth Evangelist.[359] Indeed, literary analysis shows that this pericope differs linguistically from the remainder of the Fourth Gospel,[360] and it arguably does not fit this location well. Consequently, this gospel should probably be read as if Jn 8.12 immediately follows Jn 7.52. Accordingly, v. 53, which reads, "And everyone went to his home," originally was not a part of this gospel either. In other words, the people in the previous scene(s) did not go home. This viewpoint is further supported by the word "Again" and the conjunctive "therefore" in Jn 8.12. Accordingly, the word "them" in Jn 8.12 refers to the same people Jesus had been speaking to in Jn 7.

In Jn 7, the Evangelist relates that Jesus attended the last day of the feast of Tabernacles (*Sukkoth*) at the temple in Jerusalem (Jn 7.2, 37). On that day, called *Hashana Rabba*, water was poured out in front of the altar as a ritual. Probably, as this was being done, "Jesus stood and cried out, saying, 'If any man is thirsty, let him come to Me and drink. He who believes in Me, as the Scripture said, 'From his innermost being shall flow rivers of living water'" (v. 37). It is uncertain what OT Scripture(s) Jesus had in mind. It was probably those passages which relate the time when the wandering Israelites complained of thirst in the desert at Meribah.[361] That is when God commanded Moses to strike a rock, which he did, and out flowed drinking water (Ex 17.6; Num 20.11).

This connection to Moses caused the multitude to question whether Jesus was "the prophet," predicted by Moses, or the Christ (Jn 7.40-41). Some people insisted that the Christ would not come from Galilee, where Jesus lived, but from Bethlehem (vv. 41-42), as prophesied in Mic 5.2. (Apparently, these people did not know where Jesus was born.) Thus, there arose a division among them (v. 43).

At this point in the narrative, the author interjects a sidebar. He had mentioned that the chief priests and Pharisees had sent officers to seize Jesus (v. 32). He resumes this subject by relating that these officers had returned and must give an answer to the chief priests for their failure to arrest Jesus (v. 45). Nicodemus—a Pharisee, a Torah teacher, and by now a secret disciple of Jesus (cf. Jn 3.1-21)—spoke up and argued for justice on behalf of Jesus. The scribes and other Pharisees answered sarcastically, "You are not also from Galilee, are you? Search, and see that no prophet arises out of Galilee" (v. 52). Why did they say that? Judeans regarded Galileans as spiritually ignorant and deemed Galilee a land of spiritual darkness. It seems no prophet had come from Galilee.

Now let us review. So far, John the Evangelist has related two separate scenes on this last day of the feast. In both of them, people denied that Jesus could be "that prophet" predicted by Moses or the Messiah because they concluded that no prophet could come from Galilee, though Jonah had (2 Kgs 14.25). With this, John has finished the sidebar concerning the failure to arrest Jesus, and we must skip over the story of the adulterous woman, in Jn 7.53—8.11. Thus, in Jn 8.12 the Evangelist resumes the interaction between Jesus and the multitude.

---

[359] See B.M. Metzger, *Textual Commentary*, 219-22.
[360] E.g., R.E. Brown, *John (i-xii)*, 336.
[361] Some scholars, e.g., R.E. Brown [*John (i-xii)*, 322-23], add Eze 47.12; Zech 14.8; Rev 22.1, 17.

Jesus is about to respond to the erroneous assumption of the groups mentioned in the two previous scenes that no prophet or the Messiah can possibly originate in Galilee. He does so rather obscurely by proclaiming, "I am the light of the world" (Jn 8.12). This statement of identity clearly alludes to Isaiah's identification of the Messiah as "the great light" who comes "by the way of the sea" in "Galilee of the Gentiles" (Isa 9.1-2). These Jews have obviously overlooked it. But Matthew, having the advantage of hindsight, has not; he quotes this passage and interprets that it was fulfilled when Jesus relocated from Nazareth to Capernaum, located on the Sea of Galilee (Mt 4.15-16). So, by proclaiming Himself as the light of the world, Jesus clearly makes an indirect messianic claim.

The Context of Jesus' Predicateless "I Am" Saying in John 8.24

Next, Jesus and His opponents argue about the ethics of His personal testimony. Then Jesus asserts, "I am from above;... I am not of this world" (v. 23). Note that these statements are "I am" sayings *with* predicates. Jesus continues, "for unless you believe that I am He, you shall die in your sins." As above, this time Jesus uses the "I am" without a predicate. If He does not allude to Ex 3.14 or the Deutero-Isaiah passages, thereby indirectly calling Himself God, what does He mean?

Philip Harner explains that Jesus' predicateless "I am" sayings in Jn 8.24 and v. 28 are "merely a convenient expression of everyday speech" (cf. 2 Sam 2.20 LXX).[362] Accordingly, in and of themselves they are meaningless, as in the LXX. Also, Georg Braumann claims that "*ego eimi* in the LXX is not an exclusively religious title."[363]

Nonetheless, a predicate can rightly be assumed from the immediately preceding context, showing that Jesus is the One who is from above, viz., heaven, and not of this world. Verses 23-24 can thus be paraphrased, "I said therefore to you, that you shall die in your sins; for unless you believe that I am from above, viz., heaven, and therefore not of this world, you shall die in your sins."[364]

John Calvin says concerning the "I am" in Jn 8.24, "we must supply all that the Scripture ascribes to the Messiah" as the predicate.[365] Bultmann interprets both v. 24 and v. 28 more precisely, saying "he is everything which he has claimed to be.... [which] is gathered up in the title 'Son of Man.'"[366] The NIV translators even insert in v. 24 a bracketed statement to the effect, "I am [the one I claim to be]."[367] The NEB goes further in both v. 24 and v. 28 by saying, "I am what I am." J.A.T. Robinson, an NEB editor, explains that these two renderings "do not carry with them the implication that he is Yahweh."[368]

These claims by Jesus echo His earlier Bread of Life pronouncements in John 6. We have learned of them that Jesus did not mean He literally came

---

[362] Philip B. Harner, *The "I Am" of the Fourth Gospel: A Study in Johannine Usage and Thought* (Philadelphia: Fortress, 1970), 15.

[363] Georg Braumann, "*ego eimi*," in *DNTT* 2:278.

[364] D.A. Carson (*John*, 343) cites G.C. Nicholson (*Death as Departure: The Johannine Descent-Ascent Schema* [London: Scholars, 1983], 113) as putting forth this view.

[365] J. Calvin, *Calvin's Commentaries*, 17:333.

[366] R. Bultmann, *John*, 349. Bultmann apparently means "Son of Man" in v. 28.

[367] The imprisoned John the Baptist spoke similarly when he sent word to inquire of Jesus, "Are You the Expected One" (Mt 11.3/Lk 7.19), viz., the One promised in the OT. Much of Jesus' self-revelation consisted of both sayings and acts that alluded to what had already been written about Him in the OT.

[368] J.A.T. Robinson, *Twelve More New Testament Studies*, 168.

down from heaven, but that He lives by the moral principles and spiritual insight that originate there.

Jesus' Message "From the Beginning"

Nevertheless, these Jews are perplexed and flustered by what seems to them such provocative claims by Jesus. So they ask Him bluntly, "Who are You?" (Jn 8.25).

The translation of Jesus' brief answer is rather uncertain. Since older Greek MSS lacked punctuation and space between words, the Greek text of Jn 8.25 can be translated in two primary ways.[369] Most English versions render Jesus' response in the form of a question: "What have I been saying to you from the beginning?" or the like (NASB, AV, RSV, JB, NEB, NIV).[370] But a few versions provide the sarcastic reply, "Why should I speak to you at all?" (NEB, cf. RSVmg, JBmg). This latter reading does not fit the next sentence and therefore seems meaningless. Thus, the former translation is to be prefered.[371]

Accordingly, what do Jesus' words in Jn 8.25—"the beginning"—refer to? This expression cannot echo the same words in Jn 1.1a, which refer to the time of creation. Neither does Jesus mean the beginning of "wisdom" as in Prov 8.22, which many church fathers interpreted as referring to the pre-existent Christ. And it cannot refer to Jesus' identification of Himself as the Messiah to the woman at the well (Jn 4.25-26). For she was a Samaritan whereas Jesus' question, "what have I been saying to you," refers to the Jews. "The beginning" could refer to the beginning of Jesus' public ministry (Lk 1.2; Ac 10.37), or perhaps His slightly earlier baptism by John (cf. Jn 15.27; Ac 1.22). Most likely, and in accordance with the immediate and overall context of this gospel, it refers more specifically to the beginning of Jesus' public ministry among "the Jews" at Jerusalem.[372] Since only John provides information about Jesus' earlier ministry, recorded in Jn 2-5, he means "the beginning" of Jesus' public ministry in Jerusalem as being when Jesus attended His first Passover following the beginning of His public ministry (Jn 2.13). That is when Nicodemus came secretly at night to Jesus to discuss spiritual matters (Jn 3.1-2). Most significantly, Jesus then twice identified Himself to Nicodemus as "the Son of Man" (vv. 13-14). Recall that Nicodemus was a member of the Sanhedrin and "*the* teacher of Israel" (v. 10, emphasis mine). Nicodemus' word "we," in v. 2, suggests that he was associated with others in his inquiry of Jesus. Perhaps he later shared with them what Jesus had said, including His term of self-designation.

So, what has Jesus been saying to "the Jews" at Jerusalem since the beginning of His public ministry to them? He has been saying that He is "the Son of Man." Thus, Jesus' answer in Jn 8.25 makes it quite clear that His "I am" statement in v. 24 means, "I am the Son of Man," just as He earlier disclosed to Nicodemus. In fact, this is the one title of self-designation that constantly falls from the lips of Jesus no matter where He is.

So, there is no evidence in the NT gospels that during Jesus' public ministry He ever declared expressly or implicitly that He was Yahweh. Neither does Jesus' "I am" saying in Jn 8.24 allude to either Ex 3.14 or the Deutero-Isaiah passages.

---

[369] See B.M. Metzger (*Textual Commentary*, 223-24), who lists three possible renderings.
[370] The NIV does not put it in question form but has, "Just what I have been claiming all along."
[371] C.K. Barrett, *John*, 343.
[372] Cf. R.E. Brown, *John (i-xii)*, 350.

Jesus' "I Am" Sayings with a Predicate

As mentioned earlier, there are several other "I am" sayings of Jesus in the Fourth Gospel that have a predicate nominative, and some of these allude to OT, messianic prophecies. If any of these predicates that Jesus applies to Himself are also applied to God in the Bible,[373] this does not necessarily indicate that Jesus is God but merely that God manifests Himself as such through Jesus as His agent.[374] For example, Jesus is "light" because "God is light" (Jn 1.4, 7-9; 1 Jn 1.5). The "I am" sayings of Jesus that have a predicate are as follows, with some corresponding OT passages appended:

- "I am the bread of life" (Jn 6.35): alludes to combining Deut 8.3 and 18.15-19.
- "I am the light of the world" (Jn 8.12; 9.5): alludes to Isa 9.1-2; 42.6; 49.6; 60.1-3.
- "I am the door of the sheep" (Jn 10.7, 9)
- "I am the good shepherd" (Jn 10.11, 14): alludes to Ps 23.1-2; 78.52; 80.1; Isa 40.10-11; Jer 31.10; Eze 34.12-16; Zech 13.7.
- "I am the resurrection and the life" (Jn 11.25)
- "I am the true vine" (Jn 15.1, 5): alludes to Isa 4.2; 5.1-7; 11.1; 27.2-3; 53.2; Jer 12.10; 23.5; 33.15; Zech 3.8; 6.12; Ps 80.8-17.
- "I am the way, and the truth, and the life" (Jn 14.6)

Since Jesus' *ego eimi* sayings with predicates do not represent a claim to be Yahweh, shouldn't we expect the same of His *ego eimi* sayings without a predicate?

"The Son of Man" Interpretation of John 8.28

This question about the meaning of Jesus' predicateless "I am" saying in Jn 8.24 reemerges four verses later. In v. 28, Jesus says to these Jews, "When you lift up the Son of Man, then you will know that I am He." This expression, "lift up," refers to Jesus' imminent crucifixion (Jn 12.32-34); "you" lifting Jesus up refers to the Jewish religious leaders' participation in that future wicked deed. The "I am," here, clearly refers to Jesus being "the Son of Man." This sentence may therefore be paraphrased simply, "When you lift up the Son of Man, then you will know that I am the Son of Man." Whereas Jesus hinted in v. 25 that He meant in v. 24, "I am the Son of Man," here in v. 28 He expressly declares it. Bultmann explains concerning the "I am" in both v. 24 and v. 28, "Thus everything that he is can be referred to by the mysterious title 'Son of Man.'"[375]

This remark by Bultmann arouses a question debated by modern scholars: Did Jesus ever mix or blend OT images referring to Himself, e.g., Daniel's Son of Man, Isaiah's Suffering Servant, or the Messiah? The NT sometimes does so, and it even presents Jesus as doing so (e.g., Lk 24.26, 46). Here, in Jn 8.28, Jesus' words, "lift up," seem to echo Isaiah's words about the Suffering Servant being "lifted up and greatly exalted" (Isa 52.13). The Hebrew word translated "lifted up," which is *nasah*, has three meanings: (1) literally lifted up, (2) bear guilt, and (3) take away guilt.[376] All three reflect Jesus' atoning death on the cross. Then, too, "lifted up" and "greatly exalted" perhaps describe Jesus' ascension and subsequent exaltation as the Son of Man in Dan 7.13-14.[377]

---

[373] R.E. Brown (*John [i-xii]*, 397-98) refutes R. Bultmann (*John*, 279) by affirming that Jesus draws from the OT background in some of His "I am" sayings with a predicate.

[374] Cf. Mark Allan Powell, *Fortress Introduction to the Gospels* (Minneapolis: Fortress, 1998), 132.

[375] R. Bultmann, *John*, 349. Contra R.E. Brown, [*John (i-xii)*, 348], who denies Bultmann's affirmation.

[376] B-D-B, 669d.

[377] Cf. R.E. Brown, *John (i-xii)*, 146.

Post-Nicene church fathers could not have seen, and therefore endorsed, this Son of Man interpretation of Jn 8.24 and v. 28. Their faulty understanding of Jesus as the Son of Man prevented them from doing so. We have already seen that they regarded this title as referring exclusively to Jesus' humanity. Thus, they would have reasoned that Jesus could not have meant that people could have their sins forgiven, and thus receive eternal life, merely by believing in Jesus' humanity.

John provides additional evidence that this Son of Man interpretation in Jn 8.28 is correct. As in the case of the restored blind man in Jn 9.35-38, John here adds concerning Jesus, "as He spoke these things, many came to believe in Him" (v. 30). Believe what? They believed Jesus was the Son of Man sent by God, who was "with" Him (vv. 28-29).

The evidence is overwhelming that Jesus' "I am" sayings without the predicate, in Jn 8.24 and v. 28, *do not* equate Himself with Yahweh's "I am" in either Ex 3.14 or Isaiah but simply mean, "I am the Son of Man who brings light to the world."

The Preexistence of Jesus in John 8.58?

Jesus continued to dialogue with these Jews (Jn 8). Three times they mention their forefather Abraham. Then they inquire of Jesus, "Surely You are not greater than our father Abraham,... whom do You make Yourself out to be?" (Jn 8.53, cf. v. 25).

This is the second time in this dialogue that Jesus' interlocutors have asked Him who He is. Jesus responds, "Abraham rejoiced to see My day" (v. 56). Did He mean that the deceased patriarch, looking from far off in Paradise, actually saw Jesus on earth? No. Since Jesus said "My day," not "Me," He could have referred to a legend then current and contained in pre-Christian Jewish Literature. It claimed that during Abraham's lifetime he saw in a vision "the end of days," which rabbis call "the days of Messiah." Or Jesus could have inferred Abraham's near offering of Isaac as a type of Jesus' impending crucifixion.

Regardless, as usual Jesus' antagonists thought literally and thus misunderstood Him again. They replied, "You are not yet fifty years old, and have You seen Abraham?" (v. 57). Their response represents a reversal of thought, going from the idea of Abraham seeing Jesus to Jesus seeing Abraham. Why this switch? Apparently, they did it to avoid the appearance of acknowledging Jesus' superiority over Abraham.

Jesus answered their question by asserting, "before Abraham was born, I am" (v. 58). Scholars generally think this is the strongest statement in the NT gospels in which Jesus claimed to have preexisted. And we have seen that traditionalists generally have thought that if Jesus preexisted, He must have been God. But, both logically and according to Judaism, preexistence does not necessarily indicate deity. M.M.B. Turner observes, "other beings than God were thought by the Judaism of the day to pre-exist Abraham."[378]

Scholars debate if Jesus meant in Jn 8.58 that He had a *personal* preexistence. Some have insisted that He intended less, e.g., that He preexisted only in the sense that He outranked Abraham in the kingdom of God. Others have proposed that what Jesus had in mind was that the

---

[378] M.M.B. Turner, "The Spirit of Christ and Christology," 171. Origen would have surely denied that preexistence indicates deity. He embraced the Platonic teaching of the preexistence of all souls, which the Catholic Church later condemned, and rightly so.

messianic concept merely preexisted in the mind, and therefore the plan, of God. Some apocalyptic Jewish Literature seems to depict the Messiah preexisting creation (e.g., *1 En.* 48.2-4; 62.7; 4 *Ezra* 12.32). But Judaism has debated whether it means this or merely that the name of the Messiah had already been predetermined before creation. For Jews, the preexistence of Messiah's name indicates His superiority over all other human beings, including Abraham.

This latter interpretation accords well with the entire narrative in Jn 8.31-59. Recall that the Jews asked Jesus if He was greater than Abraham. But they reversed the order of Abraham seeing Jesus' day to avoid the appearance that they assented to Jesus being superior to Abraham. Accordingly, Jesus' response in v. 58 might be paraphrased, "Before Abraham existed, in the mind of God I was greater than Abraham." Infuriated at Jesus' claim to be superior to Abraham, they reached for the rocks to stone Him to death.

Did Jesus' hearers regard His assertion in Jn 8.58 as blasphemy? Traditionalists think so because they interpret the Jews' attempt to stone Him as evidence that they rightly understood His words as an indirect claim to be God.[379] C.K. Barrett counters, "Stoning was the punishment for blasphemy ... but this does not mean that Jesus had claimed to be God."[380] Moreover, if they had understood this saying as a claim to be God, it surely would have surfaced at Jesus' subsequent hearing before the Sanhedrin.

A Different "I Am" Saying

So, Jn 8.58 presents the third and final time in this dialogue in which Jesus pronounced the predicateless "I am He." Does it differ from the previous two?

Philip Harner produced a highly acclaimed scholarly treatment of Jesus' "I am" sayings in the Fourth Gospel.[381] We have seen that he interprets Jesus' first two "I am He" sayings, in Jn 8.24 and v. 28, as an insignificant, common expression in which only the context can supply an implied predicate. He therefore dismisses these two *ego eimi* sayings of Jesus as having no correlation with Yahweh's "I am" sayings in the OT.

However, Harner interprets Jesus' "I am He" saying in Jn 8.58 differently. He maintains that this one is "a distinct, self-contained expression that is complete and meaningful in itself. It is an 'absolute' phrase, in the sense that it does not need to be completed by any predicate derived from the context."[382] For support, Harner cites C.H. Dodd and C.K. Barrett as adopting this "absolute" usage interpretation of v. 58, in contrast to that of vv. 24 and 28, and connecting it to Yahweh's "I am" sayings in Deutero-Isaiah.[383] In so doing, they seem to acknowledge that, in Jn 8.58, Jesus indirectly claimed to be Yahweh. Harner, on the other hand, only concedes that the connection indicates the unity of the Father (Yahweh) and the Son while the Father, as God, still remains numerically one.[384] Harner is careful to maintain that "this unity does not violate the integrity of monotheistic belief,"[385] insinuating that the traditionalist view does.

---

[379] E.g., J.H. Bernard, *John*, 322; D.A. Carson, *John*, 358.
[380] C.K. Barrett, *John*, 352.
[381] P.B. Harner, *The "I AM" of the Fourth Gospel*.
[382] Ibid., 3.
[383] Ibid., 4.
[384] Ibid., 49-57.
[385] Ibid., 56.

George Beasley-Murray says substantially the same thing. He states, "This use of *ego eimi* in v. 58 is slightly different from those in vv. 24 and 28, where 'I am he' is clearly in mind, whereas no predicate is intended here. Nevertheless the OT revelation formula [in especially Deutero-Isaiah] is in the background.... Is then the statement an assertion that Jesus is God? Not in terms of identification. It is an affirmation of Jesus as the revelation of God,... As such it entails *unity* with God, as John 1.1."[386]

Jesus' "I am" Saying in John 18.5

Recall that Judas had led the Jewish religious officials and Roman soldiers during the darkness of night to the Garden of Gethsemane to locate and arrest Jesus. Only John the Evangelist informs that, as they approached, Jesus "went forth, and said to them, 'Whom do you seek?' They answered Him, 'Jesus the Nazarene.' He said to them, 'I am He.' And Judas also who was betraying Him, was standing with them. When therefore He said to them, 'I am He,' they drew back and fell to the ground" (Jn 18.4-6).

The traditional Christian interpretation of this multitude falling to the ground has been that, upon hearing Jesus' words—"I am He" (Gr. *ego eimi*)—a supernatural force exuded from Jesus, knocking them to the ground. Some commentators have linked these words of Jesus with Ex 3.14, just as they have with those thrice-repeated in Jn 8. For example, R.E. Brown asserts regarding this text, "the Johannine tradition 'I am' serves virtually as a divine name with the power to cast men to the ground (18.5)."[387]

Such an interpretation is both unnecessary and unwarranted, especially if our interpretation of the thrice-repeated "I am" in Jn 8 is correct. Rather, the multitude was surprised when Jesus courageously "went forth" to meet His enemies. J.H. Bernard puts it well, "the men who came to make the arrest (some of whom at least did not previously know Jesus even by sight) were so overcome by His moral ascendancy that they recoiled in fear."[388] Indeed, this episode alludes to David's words in Ps 27.2, "When evildoers came upon me to devour my flesh, my adversaries and my enemies, they stumbled and fell." Accordingly, those in the foreground, startled by Jesus' bold response, quickly drew back. As they did, they may have bumped into others behind them, causing many to stumble and fall. Perhaps it was like the Three Stooges! Whether God resorts to the use of supernatural power, He still causes His enemies to appear as stooges.

Summary

In sum, Jesus did not intend that His "I am" sayings without the predicate, in Jn 8.24 and v. 28, allude to either Ex 3.14 or the Deutero-Isaiah passages and thereby indirectly identify Himself as Yahweh. Rather, the predicate is implied from the context of Jesus' speech. On these occasions He indirectly claimed to be the promised One of the OT, the One sent by Yahweh, perhaps the Messiah or the Suffering Servant, but certainly the Son of Man of Dan 7.13. Jesus may have purposely uttered His "I am" saying in v. 58 as an allusion to Yahweh's "I am" sayings in Deutero-Isaiah. If He did, it was only to highlight the unity between Himself and Yahweh His God.

---

[386] G.R. Beasley-Murray, *John*, 139.
[387] R.E. Brown, *The Death of the Messiah*, 488.
[388] J.H. Bernard, *St. John*, 2:586-87.

6. What did Jesus mean in John 10.30, "I and the Father are One"?

> Introduction
> Verse-by-verse Exposition
> Summary

Introduction

Did Jesus ever claim to be God? "Yes," answer most Christians, confidently. And many of them will add that Christ's deity is the most important of all Christian doctrines. Ask Bible students for scriptural support for this answer, and many of them will offer as their chief text Jesus' brief saying in Jn 10.30: "I and the Father are one."[389] Some notable traditionalist scholars agree.[390] That is what Jesus' antagonistic listeners thought, too, when He uttered these words. So they accused Him of claiming to be God, charging Him with blasphemy. But in the dialogue that transpired, Jesus denied their allegation by explaining what He meant by being "one" with the Father. The following account informs us of when, where, and how this heated exchange took place:

22 At that time the Feast of Dedication took place at Jerusalem;
23 it was winter, and Jesus was walking in the temple in the portico of Solomon.
24 The Jews therefore gathered around Him, and were saying to Him, "How long will You keep us in suspense? If You are the Christ, tell us plainly."
25 Jesus answered them, "I told you, and you do not believe; the works that I do in My Father's name, these bear witness of Me.
26 "But you do not believe, because you are not of My sheep.
27 "My sheep hear My voice, and I know them, and they follow Me;
28 and I give eternal life to them, and they shall never perish; and no one shall snatch them out of My hand.
29 "My Father, who has given them to Me, is greater than all; and no one is able to snatch them out of the Father's hand.
30 "I and the Father are one."
31 The Jews took up stones again to stone Him.
32 Jesus answered them, "I showed you many good works from the Father; for which of them are you stoning Me?"
33 The Jews answered Him, "For a good work we do not stone You, but for blasphemy; and because You, being a man, make Yourself out to be God."
34 Jesus answered them, "Has it not been written in your Law, 'I SAID, YOU ARE GODS'?
35 "If he called them gods, to whom the word of God came (and the Scripture cannot be broken),
36 do you say of Him, whom the Father sanctified and sent into the world, 'You are blaspheming,' because I said, 'I am the Son of God'?
37 "If I do not do the works of My Father, do not believe Me;
38 but if I do them, though you do not believe Me, believe the works, that you may know and understand that the Father is in Me, and I in the Father."
39 Therefore they were seeking again to seize Him, and He eluded their grasp.

---

[389] G. Vermes (*The Changing Faces of Jesus*, 6) says this is most true of Evangelicals and Fundamentalists.
[390] E.g., M. Hengel, *Studies in Early Christology*, 367.

Verse-by-Verse Exposition

Due to the peculiar and extensive nature of this dialogue, I will depart from the usual method used in this book and provide a verse-by-verse exposition of this entire account in order to best ascertain what Jesus meant by being "one" with the Father.

v. 24 *If You are the Christ.* Jesus has never told "the Jews" at Jerusalem explicitly who He is. Even when they asked Him shortly before this episode, "Who are You?" (Jn 8.25), we have seen that He answered rather ambiguously. This answer caused them to inquire again, "whom do you make Yourself out to be?" (Jn 8.53). Indeed, Jesus has regularly identified Himself to them in enigmatic, often figurative, language. Consequently, there has arisen much questioning in Jerusalem about whether Jesus is the Messiah and/or that Moses-like prophet predicted by Moses (Jn 6.14; 7.26-27, 40-43; cf. Deut 18.15-19).

Jesus seems to have provoked this inquiry by these Jews by describing Himself to them as "the good Shepherd" (Jn 10.11-16).[391] By invoking this metaphor, He alludes to the OT portrayal of both Yahweh and Messiah as a shepherd (Eze 34.11-16; 37.24-25; 40.11; Zech 13.7). More particularly, the prophet Zechariah draws a contrast between the future, good "Shepherd" of God, who will be struck down (Zech 13.7; cf. Mt 26.31/Mk 14.27), and a future "foolish" and "worthless shepherd" (Zech 11.15-17).

tell us plainly. If He does, they will not believe in Him (Lk 22.67). Therefore, He will not say so unequivocally (even later, arguably, before the Sanhedrin).

v. 25 *I told you.* He does not mean that He has already told them explicitly, "I am the Christ." Nor does He have in mind His dialogue with the Samaritan woman (Jn 4.25-26).[392] Rather, He means that He has already answered this question implicitly, e.g., in Jn 5.36, by telling them what He says here, "the works that I do in My Father's name, these bear witness of Me." His works are the best witness because they are the witness that "the Father who sent Me bears witness of Me" (Jn 8.18). Indeed, to verify that Jesus was a true prophet, the Jews often required of Him a sign from heaven to prove that He speaks the truth.[393] So, He means that His works are a witness that He is the Promised One of the OT,[394] viz., the Anointed One, Son of God, Son of Man, and Suffering Servant.

Earlier, Jesus had answered John the Baptist the same way. When the imprisoned Baptist began to waiver in his faith that Jesus was "the Expected One" prophesied in the (OT) Scriptures, Jesus sent word back to John telling about His miraculous works of healing and quoting Isaiah's prophecies about His works (Mt 11.2-6; Is 35.5-6; 61.1). Thus, Jesus did not answer John explicitly either, but implicitly, citing His works as the witness that He was the Expected/Promised One.

We might ask why Jesus did not answer plainly, as the Jews had asked. One reason is that a picture speaks louder than a thousand words. Rather than stating it outright, Jesus demonstrated to His Jewish interlocutors that He was the Promised One by performing miraculous works before their very eyes in fulfillment of the Scriptures (e.g., Jn 5.1-9; 9.1-34). In addition, His works confirm that He is that prophet predicted by Moses, who himself performed miraculous works. In sum, Jesus' works are a testimony to His being sent by God; but these "Jews" refuse to believe it.

---

[391] R.E. Brown, *John (i-xii)*, 406.

[392] His private, implicit, messianic self-disclosure to the Samaritan woman in Samaria is not the same as telling "the Jews" of Judea, explicitly and publicly, that He is the Christ.

[393] E.g., Mt 12.38-40; Mt 16.1-4/Mk 8.11-12; Lk 11.16; Jn 2.18; 6.30.

[394] E.g., Isa 35.5-6; 61.1; Mt 11.5/Lk 7.22; Lk 4.18.

the works. Jesus has already divulged that the Father has given Him His works and that they bear witness that the Father has sent Him (Jn 4.34; 5.17-20, 36). So He tells them again. His works therefore also testify that He enjoys a very intimate union with God, a concept He has heretofore hinted at by calling God His "Father." He now begins to divulge further to them about His filial relationship with God.[395]

v. 26 *My sheep*. They are genuine ("true") disciples of Jesus their Shepherd, i.e., their Master (cf. Jn 8.31).

v. 27 *hear ... and they follow Me*. They hear Jesus' teaching (Jn 8.47), believe in Him (v. 26), follow Him (Jn 3.36; 10.4-5), and abide in Him (Jn 8.31; 15.4-8).

v. 28 *never perish* (cf. Jn 3.16; 17.12). The true disciples, i.e., all those the Father will give Jesus, will be with Jesus throughout eternity and will behold His glory (Jn 17.24).

no one shall snatch them. The true disciples are safeguarded (Jn 17.11-12; cf. Rom 8.28-39). Therefore, "those who believe" in Jesus, God will "keep from the evil one" (Jn 17.15, 20).

v. 29 *given them to Me* (cf. Jn 6.37). To become a true disciple, one must come to the Father by faith in the Son (Jn 14.6). But it will not happen unless the Father first draws them (Jn 6.44, 65; cf. Mt 16.16 par.; Mt 11.27/Lk 10.22). In so doing, the Father does not make arbitrary, capricious selections. Rather, He draws those who desire to know the truth and therefore have seeking hearts (Jn 5.40, 44; 7.17; cf. Mt 23.37).

greater than all.[396] The Father is "greater" in rank and dignity, thus superior and sovereign over all (1 Tim 6.15). "All" must include Jesus Himself (cf. Jn 14.28). His reason is that the Father, being the Benefactor, "has given them to Me."

the Father's hand. Jesus again associates Himself with the Father by explaining that the true disciples are safely in both His hand and the Father's hand. So, He will lose none of them (Jn 6.39; 17.24). Put colloquially, the Father and the Son "work hand in glove." This analogy about their mutual work is preparatory for what Jesus says next.

v. 30 *one*. Does Jesus mean "one" ontologically or only functionally?[397] This important christological word (Gr. *hen* is neuter for *heis*), reportedly spoken by Jesus (He would have actually used the Aram. *chad*), stirred much controversy during the patristic era.

> Since the 4th century, traditionalists have generally understood "one" in Jn 10.30 ontologically. That is, they have insisted that Jesus thereupon claimed that both He and the Father were "one in essence," sharing equally the divine nature and therefore all of the divine attributes. If true, since the Father is God, Jesus also implicitly identifies Himself as God. This ontological interpretation of Jn 10.30 became the main weapon that the orthodox party used against the Monarchians of the 3rd century and the Arians of the 4th century.[398]
>
> In contrast, the earlier modalistic Monarchians, e.g., Noetus, Paul of Samasota, and Sabellius, took *hen* in Jn 10.30 numerically as one Person, interpreting that Jesus claimed to be the Father. For support they cited His saying in Jn 14.9, "He who has seen Me has seen the Father."

---

[395] R.E. Brown, *John (xiii-xxi)*, 633; G.R. Beasley-Murray, *John*, 175.

[396] Codex Vaticanus contains this variant in v. 29 (ET): "what the Father has given me is greater than all," or the like. Many authorities conclude that this variant, which appears in only a few MSS, is an interpolation that crept into the textual tradition quite early.

[397] Those who say only a functional unity do not believe this indicates Jesus is God.

[398] T.E. Pollard, "The Exegesis of John X.30 in the Early Trinitarian Controversies," *New Testament Studies* 3 (1956-57), 335, 339. The Sabellians tried to preserve the unity of God, but denied the distinction in the personalities of the Father and Jesus. The Arians attempted to preserve the distinction of Persons, but inadvertently denied the unity of God by designating the Father and the Son as two "Gods" or "gods."

Although Origen opposed modalistic Monarchianism, he paraphrased Jn 10.30 likewise, "I and the Father are one God."[399] Did Origen contradict himself, since he called Jesus "a second god"?[400] No, he insisted that Jesus said that He and the Father were "one" from the perspective of His divine nature. Previous church fathers had distinguished a divine and human nature in Jesus, some accrediting the divine nature to "the Christ" title and the human nature to His name "Jesus." But Origen appears to have been the first church father to extend this concept further by employing the two-nature method in interpreting all of Jesus' words and deeds.[401]

Hippolytus, and later Tertullian, had opposed all of these interpretations by treating *hen* in Jn 10.30 as "one by power and harmony of attitude" and thus a functional unity, i.e., a unity of fellowship.[402] They further insisted that since this is the only possible meaning for the word *hen* in Jn 17.11, 21-23, it must be the same here. So, both of these church fathers argued contrary to what the Nicene fathers later decided.

The Nicene fathers contended against the Arians by asserting both a functional and an ontological meaning of *hen* in Jn 10.30. Athanasius argued that an external and functional unity between the Father and Son depended upon an internal unity of essence between them.[403] Some contemporary commentators still agree.[404] However, Athanasius rambles in a lengthy defense of this exegesis, contradicts himself, and flounders miserably.[405] In contrast, the Arians interpreted *hen* in Jn 10.30 as Hippolytus and Tertullian had, also citing Jn 17.11, 21-22 for support.

Hippolytus, Tertullian, and the Arians were right: the same word that Jesus used in Jn 10.30, translated "one," He used five times in His prayer recorded in Jn 17 (vv. 11, 21-23). However Jesus meant "one" in Jn 10.30, He must have meant the same thing in all five uses of the same word in Jn 17 (cf. 1 Cor 3.8). In that prayer, He asked the Father concerning the Eleven, "that they may be one, even/just as We are" (vv. 11, 22). Thus, if Jesus meant "one in essence" in Jn 10.30, as many church fathers and succeeding traditionalists have claimed, He must have asked the Father to make the Eleven "one in essence," which is ludicrous! Moreover, the addition of the words, "even/just as We are (one)," clearly means that Jesus was praying that the Eleven would be "one" in the same manner that He and the Father were "one," which can only mean to be unified relationally. Thus, *Jesus' fivefold-use of the word "one" in Jn 17 clearly indicates that His use of the same word in Jn 10.30 means that He and the Father have a relational unity which results in a functional unity, not a unity of essence.*[406]

Furthermore, this interpretation of Jn 10.30 fits the immediately preceding context. In vv. 28-29, Jesus reveals that He and the Father are unified in their purpose of protecting the disciples. Interestingly, that is Jesus' subject in Jn 17 when He introduces the word "one" (v. 11). In contrast, the traditional interpretation of Jn 10.30 does not fit this context. Jesus could not have meant "one in essence" because He said, (1) "My Father,... is greater than all," which must include Himself (v. 29; cf. Jn 14.28), and (2) the Father consecrates (sets apart for a task) and sends the Son (v. 36), and He who sends is greater in dignity than He who is sent.

---

[399] Indebted to T.E. Pollard, *Johannine Christology and the Early Church*, 101.
[400] Origen, *Fragment on Hebrews contra Celsum*, 5.39.
[401] M. Wiles, *The Spiritual Gospel*, 112-13.
[402] Hippolytus, *Against Noetus*, 7; Tertullian, *Against Praxeas*, 22.
[403] Cited by T.E. Pollard, "The Exegesis of John X.30," 341-42.
[404] E.g., M. Harris, *Jesus as God*, 125, n94; D.A. Carson, *John*, 395.
[405] Athanasius, *Orations Against the Arians*, 3:10-24. See also T.E. Pollard, *Johannine Christology and the Early Church*, 227-32; idem, "The Exegesis of John X.30," 341-44.
[406] M.M.B. Turner, "The Spirit of Christ and Christology," 171-72; Rudolf Schnackenburg, *The Gospel According to St. John*, 3 vols. (New York: Crossroads, 1968-82), 2:313; R.V.G. Tasker, *John*, 136; G.R. Beasley-Murray, *John*, 174. For the first extensive study of this functional unity motif in this gospel, see M.L. Appold, *The Oneness Motif in the Fourth Gospel*.

John Calvin says of Jn 10.30, "the ancients made a wrong use of this passage to prove that Christ is of the same essence with the Father (*homoousis*). Christ does not argue about the unity of substance, but about the agreement that he has with the Father."[407] William Barclay well explains, "When Jesus said: 'I and the Father are one,' he was not moving in the world of philosophy and metaphysics and abstractions; he was moving in the world of *personal relationships*. No one can really understand what a phrase like 'a unity of essence' means; but any one can understand what a unity of heart means.... He was one with God because he loved and obeyed him perfectly."[408]

v. 31 *took up stones again* (cf. Jn 8.59). They perceive that Jesus has blasphemed (v. 33). But the Evangelist does not give any evidence that he subscribes to their perception.

v. 32 *I showed you many good works.* They have seen some of His miracles, yet they still do not believe (cf. Jn 5.40, 44; 6.44, 65; 12.39-40; Mt 11.27/Lk 10.22; cf. Lk 16.31). Due to our scientific age, moderns are often perplexed at such unbelief because they think "seeing is believing." But that is not always true, partly due to a difference in cultures, and these Jews are proof of it. They believe that Satan can also perform miracles.

from the Father. Jesus' works are the works of the Father (Jn 5.36; 17.4). This is further evidence of His dependence upon the Father. If He was co-equal with the Father, Jesus surely would do His miracles in His own power and thus not depend upon anyone else, much less admit that His works belonged to someone else. But He has already testified that He can do nothing, i.e., of eternal value, in His own power (Jn 5.19, 30).

v. 33 *and.* This conjunctive indicates that Jesus' accusers have two reasons to stone Him: (1) for blasphemy due to His having identified His works as those of the Father, in v. 25 and v. 29 (cf. Jn 5.17-18), and (2) for His claiming to be "one" with the Father.

blasphemy. (See Chapter Five/The Trial of Jesus.)

make Yourself out to be God. The NIV has, "you ... claim to be God."[409] Again, this recalls Jn 5.18>, when the Jews similarly accused Jesus of "making Himself equal with God." Many traditionalist scholars have understood that the Jews' perception was correct, that Jesus had indirectly claimed in v. 30 to be God.[410] But some traditionalists now insist that Jesus *did not* herein claim to be God, so that the Jews' allegation in v. 33 is wrong.[411] Accordingly, Jesus' response in

---

[407] J. Calvin, Calvin's *Commentaries*, 17:417.

[408] W. Barclay, *John*, 2:75-76.

[409] Since *theon* is anarthrous the NEB translates it, "You ... claim to be a god." Some translators and other scholars (e.g., lexicographer J.H. Thayer in his *Greek-English Lexicon of the New Testament* [1886] [repr. Grand Rapids: Zondervan, 1962], 287) have thought that these Jews accused Jesus of claiming to be "a god" or "divine," as if comparing Himself with past judges of Israel as "gods," which He did by quoting Ps 82.6. However, since *theos* is anarthrous in several NT instances that are clear references to "God" (BAGD, 357), it is more likely that *theon* in v. 33 should be treated as a definite noun and thus translated "God."

[410] Contemporary scholars include the following: O. Cullmann, *Christology*, 302; R.E. Brown, *John (i-xii)*, 408, 411; C.K. Barrett, *John*, 378, 384, 542; M. Harris, *Jesus as God*, 125; M. Hengel, *Studies in Early Christology*, 367; D.A. Carson, *John*, 395, 399; P.M Casey, *From Jewish Prophet to Gentile God*, 23, 30.

[411] E.g., R.V.G. Tasker, *The Gospel of John* in TNTC (1960), 136; M.M.B. Turner, "The Spirit of Christ and Christology," 170-71; J.A. Fitzmyer, *Scripture and Christology*, 59-60; idem. *A Christological Catechism*, 97; G.R. Beasley-Murray, *John*, 174.

vv. 34-36 represents a clear disclaimer.[412] Critic Ernst Haenchen well explains, "The Jews are therefore completely mistaken when they accuse him [Jesus] of blasphemy: he makes himself equal to God. He actually stands in the place of God as the one sent by him."[413]

A surprising rejection of this traditional interpretation of Jn 10.30 comes from the RCC's prestigious Pontifical Biblical Commission. In its very important and excellent document on Christology, *Bible et christologie* (1983), this elite group of twenty scholars suggests that those who espouse classical (Nicene-Chalcedonian) Christology tend to be obstinate, "*not being open*" to critical investigation, resulting in their appeal to Scripture only defensively.[414] The Commission chose American Catholic Joseph A. Fitzmyer to produce a commentary on this document. He explains that "the Commission is pointing its critical finger at Catholic fundamentalism, often associated with this approach to Christology. An example of this sort of use of the NT would be the appeal to Jn 10:30, 'I and the Father are one,' to establish the divinity of Christ."[415] Fitzmyer means that neither he nor the commission members believe that Jesus here claimed that He was God.

v. 34 *Jesus answered them.* Here recurs the particularly Johannine theme of Jesus being a misunderstood man.[416] As in Jn 5.19-47, He proceeds in vv. 34-36 to deny the allegation and correct their misunderstanding of what He has just said in v. 30. He does so by giving a typical midrashic argument, in which He asks a question about the (OT) Scriptures to show that their accusation lacks a scriptural basis, thereby denying their allegation.[417]

YOU ARE GODS. Jesus here quotes the God-inspired psalmist, who said of the "rulers" who were judges of ancient Israel, "You are gods, and all of you are sons of the Most High" (Ps 82.6).[418] The word in the Hebrew text, here quoted in the NT Greek text as *theoi* ("gods"), is *elohim*. It is the most common word in the Hebrew Bible, other than YHWH, to designate the God of Israel. But *elohim* is not used in the Bible exclusively for God.[419] Indeed, the psalmist here calls these human rulers "gods," which he intends as the equivalent of what follows: "sons of the Most High." Both expressions mean that God granted these judges authority to rule Israel on His behalf (cf. 2 Chron 19.6). Yet, note that the psalmist also chastised these rulers for judging wickedly (Ps 82.6; cf. 58.1). Obviously, in

---

[412] Contra scholars such as P.M. Casey (*From Jewish Prophet to Gentile God*, 24), who asserts flatly that "Jesus does not deny the charge."

[413] Ernst Haenchen, *John 2: A Commentary on the Gospel of John, Chapters 7-21*, in *Hermeneia* (1984), 30.

[414] *Bible et christologie*, 1.2.1.2. Emphasis not mine.

[415] J.A. Fitzmyer, *Scripture & Christology*, 59-60; idem, *A Christological Catechism*, 97. Yet even some distinguished scholars have clung to this interpretation, e.g., M. Hengel ("Christological Titles in Early Christianity," in *The Messiah*, ed. J.H. Charlesworth, 431); H.P. Liddon (*The Divinity of Our Lord and Saviour Jesus Christ*, 2nd ed. [London: Rivingtons, 1868], Lecture iv).

[416] Other examples include cf. Jn 2.19-21 with Mt 26.61; Jn 3.4; 5.18; 6.52, 60, 63; 7.35-36; 8.22, 27, 33, 43, 48, 52-53; 9.16, 29, 39-41; 10.6, 20.

[417] F. Scheiermacher, *The Christian Faith*, 423-24; A.E. Harvey, *Jesus and the Constraints of History*, 157n26; J.A.T. Robinson, *Twelve More New Testament Studies*, 175; idem, *The Priority of John*, 351, 387-89; apparently G.R. Beasley-Murray, *John*, 175. Contra the following scholars who think otherwise: T.E. Pollard, *Johannine Christology and the Early Church*, 16; R.E. Brown, *John (i-xii)*, 411.

[418] Cf. Ex 4.16; 7.1; Ps 58.1; cf. 97.7 with Heb 1.6. Since Jesus said this in the temple (cf. Ps 82.1), does He imply ironically that Sanhedrin officials, being rulers of Israel, can rightly be called "gods" also?

[419] Sometimes the word *elohim* is used in the MT to designate angels, perhaps in Ps 95.3; 96.4; 135.5; 136.2; 138.1. Certainly this is the case in Ps 97.7, which can be cf. with Heb 1.6 and Dan 11.36.

antiquity the Hebrew word *elohim* sometimes was used in a wider sense than we are accustomed in using our word "God" with a capital "G."

vv. 35-36 Jesus' argument can be paraphrased as follows: "If the rulers of Israel were rightly called 'gods' and 'sons of God,' how can you charge Me with blasphemy since I have been given a higher, divine commission than they were, thereby having been consecrated and sent into the world to perform unprecedented miracles and even become the Savior of the world; yet I have merely identified Myself with what would *seem to be* a nominally lesser title— 'a son of God.' If you therefore do not charge the psalmist with blasphemy for calling them 'gods,' how can you so charge Me?"[420]

I said, 'I am the Son of God.' This response does not signify a tacit acceptance of their allegation, as some contemporary traditionalists insist.[421] Such reasoning is usually based on the patristic practice of equating the terms "God" and "the Son of God." Rather, with these words Jesus made the following important points: He (1) denied the Jews' allegation that He claimed to be God, (2) distinguished Himself from God, and (3) clearly affirmed His true identity as a/the son/Son of God.[422]

In a departure from most English versions, the NEB quotes Jesus here as saying, "I am God's son." This is because the Greek word *huios* (son) is anarthrous (without the article). So, the literal translation of this clause is, "I am a son of God."[423] Since Jesus was comparing the Jews' allegation against Him with the psalmist identifying Israel's rulers as "gods," He thereby implied that He could rightly be called "a god" with the meaning that the psalmist intended for Israel's rulers.[424] Since this scene occurred in the temple, Jesus' interlocutors may have included Sanhedrin rulers, in which case Jesus may have cleverly hinted that the psalmist's words also applied to them! Additionally, Jesus may have had in mind the scriptural (OT) practice of calling Israel's king a son of God. Better yet, the oneness context suggests that Jesus used the term to refer to His intimate association with God, and therefore to identify Himself as a *hasid*, i.e., an extraordinarily holy man whom Jews labeled "a son of God." Regardless, *Jn 10.36 is the only passage in the NT that provides scriptural authorization for calling Jesus "(a) god," and it comes from Jesus Himself. But, in doing so, Jesus clearly did not mean either that He was the one and only God or a divine being* (cf. Jn 5.44; 17.3). For, the psalmist clearly distinguishes these "gods" from "the Most High," viz., the God of Israel, which is surely what Jesus meant. A.E. Harvey well explains, "Jesus' reply makes the semantic point that there is precedent in his own culture for using the word *theos* for beings who are other than the one God."[425]

Due to Jesus' well-known reticence to apply titles other than "the Son of Man" to Himself (e.g., Lk 4.34-35, 41), even some moderate critics have denied that He said here, "I am a/the son/Son of God."[426] But Jesus' constant practice of calling God His Father, which all critics affirm, represents an implicit claim to be a/the son/Son of God. Also, this claim by Jesus in Jn 10.36 appears authentic

---

[420] Those who adopt a similar paraphrase include A.M. Hunter, *The Gospel According to John* in CBCNEB (1965), 108; R.V.G. Tasker, *John*, 134; G.R. Beasely-Murray, *John*, 175.

[421] E.g., Leon Morris, *The Gospel According to John* (Grand Rapids: Eerdmans, 1971), 525; Barnabas Lindars, *The Gospel of John* (Greenwood, SC: Attic, 1972), 373.

[422] J.A.T. Robinson, *The Priority of John*, 387.

[423] The anarthrous *huios* is also applied to Jesus in Mt 14.33; 27.43, 54/Mk 15.39; Lk 1.35; Jn 19.7. Yet almost all English versions add the article and capitalize "Son" in these texts.

[424] So G.R. Beasely-Murray, *John*, 175. Note that Mic 5.1-2 calls Messiah "judge" and "ruler" of "Israel."

[425] A.E. Harvey, *Jesus and the Constraints of History*, 157n26.

[426] E.g., C.K. Barrett, *John*, 385.

since it corresponds to the remainder of the verse from which He quoted, which reads, "And all of you are sons of the Most High."

A few earlier expositors were correct in interpreting Jesus' response in Jn 10.34-36 as a disclaimer. Socinian Johann Crellius (1590-1633) remarks, "when it was objected against him, that he made himself God, he purposely declined the name of *God*, and professed himself the *Son of Go*d, so far was he from professing or endeavoring to demonstrate that he was the most high God."[427] Unitarian Joseph Priestly highlights what is missing in Jesus' response by arguing cogently, "Now if Christ had been conscious to himself that he was the *true and very God*, and that it was of the utmost consequence to mankind that they should regard him in that light, this was certainly a proper time for him to have declared himself, and not to have put his hearers off with such an apology as this."[428] C. Luthardt approvingly cites W. Beyschlag, who, like the above Unitarians thinks "this statement stands in irreconcilable contradiction with the church doctrine of the Trinity."[429]

There are two reasons these Jews must have accepted Jesus' response, in vv. 34-38, that He denied their allegation. First, they never brought this charge against Him at His hearing before the Sanhedrin. Second, "the Jews" afterwards exclaimed to Pilate concerning Jesus, "He ought to die because He made Himself out to be the Son of God" (Jn 19.7).[430] So, they changed their charge that Jesus claimed to be God to Him claiming to be a/the Son of God. Notice that they distinguished "God" and "a/the Son of God."

v. 37 *do not believe Me*. In contrast to some religious figures in human history, Jesus taught that an acclaimed prophet or *hasid* should be judged by his works (Mt 7.15-19).

v. 38 *believe the works*. (cf. Jn 14.11). A tension exists between two strains of Jesus' gospel sayings about His miraculous works. He has heretofore chastised this "evil and adulterous generation [that] seeks after a sign" (Mt 16.4; cf. 12.39). But now He exhorts those who do not believe in Him to believe His works as a possible bridge to believing both Him and His teaching. Indeed, the Gospel of John is constructed as a book of signs intended to convince its readers of the truth, i.e., the truth about Jesus.[431]

the Father is in Me, and I in the Father (cf. Jn 14.10-11; 17.21). Jesus explains what He means in v. 30,[432] that He and the Father are "one" in the sense of a reciprocal immanence. Many scholars label this theme "the Mutual

---

[427] Johann Crellius, *Two Books Touching One God the Father* (1665), 79. Emphasis not mine. I have altered this quotation from Old English into modern English.
[428] Joseph Priestly, *Three Tracts*, 3 vols. (London: Unitarian Society, 1791), 1:18. Emphasis not mine.
[429] Christoph Ernst Luthardt, *St. John's Gospel Described and Explained According to Its Peculiar Character*, tr. Caspar Rene Gregory, 2 vols. (Edinburgh: T.&T. Clark, 1877), 2:389. See also Willibald Beyschlag, *Die Christologie des Neuen Testaments* (Berlin, 1866), 68-69.
[430] Again, *huios* in the Greek text of Jn 19.7 is anarthrous and therefore should be translated "a son," which is exactly what Jesus had claimed in Jn 10.36. Nevertheless, all three synoptists include the article with *huios* in the question directed to Jesus at His hearing before the Sanhedrin (Mt 26.63/Mk 14.61/Lk 22.70).
[431] E.g., Jn 1.14, 17; 3.21; 4.23-24; 8.32, 40, 45-46; 14.6; 18.37-38.
[432] H.A.W. Meyer, MCNT, 3:333; R. Bultmann, *John*, 391; R. Schnackenburg, *John*, 2:313; D.A. Carson, *John*, 400; J.N. Sanders and B.A. Mastin, *A Commentary on the Gospel According to St. John* (New York: Harper, 1968), 260; M. de Jonge, *Christology in Context*, 147. Contra these scholars who indecisively or contradictorily interpret a oneness of essence in v. 30 while insisting that v. 38 explains v. 30: J.A. Bengel, *Bengel's New Testament Commentary*, 1:651, 653; C.K. Barrett, *John*, 382, 386; D.A. Carson, *John*, 395, 400.

Indwelling."[433] God-in-Christ Christology obviously expresses one side of the Mutual Indwelling. So, this explanation in v. 38 negates the interpretation of v. 30 that Jesus and the Father are "one in essence."

So, Jesus is not God but the One in whom God dwells in full measure (cf. Jn 3.34; Col 1.19; 2.9). Earlier, the Johannine Jesus taught the mutual indwelling as a mutual abiding (Jn 6.56). He will teach both aspects again, recorded in Jn 14.9-11 and 17.23.

seeking again to seize Him. Their attempt to seize Him is probably not because they reject His disclaimer and still think that He postures Himself as God.[434] Rather, it is because He (1) still associates His and the Father's works together and (2) claims such an intimate relationship with the transcendent God. These Jews apparently still think that such assertions infringe upon the divine majesty and are therefore blasphemous.

Summary

In sum, when Jesus said in Jn 10.30, "I and the Father are one," He did not mean that He and the Father were one in essence but one relationally, which results merely in a functional unity. This is the only interpretation that fits the preceding context. Plus, it is exactly how Jesus used the same word in Jn 17. Since these Jews misunderstood this saying of Jesus as a claim to be God, in vv. 34-36 He denies their allegation and clarifies that He claimed to be "a son of God," which is not the same thing as claiming to be "God." At the end of this encounter, Jesus clearly explains that His being "one" with the Father means that He and the Father mutually indwell each other.

So, when Jesus said, "I and the Father are one," He clearly did not claim to be God. If this verse is the best in the Bible that traditionalists can muster to support their belief that Jesus claimed to be God, we can be pretty sure He never made such a claim.

7. Did Thomas call Jesus "My God" in John 20.28?

Introduction	"The Only True God"
The Thomas Incident	Jesus as the Father's Agent
Authenticity of Thomas' Confession	*Seeing* the Father in Jesus
History of Interpreting the Confession	The "God in Christ" Interpretation
An Address to Jesus	Source of Enlightenment & Glorification
Nominatives as Vocatives?	Jesus' Response
Ascribing Divinity to Jesus	More History of Interpretation
"The Lord"	The Purpose of John's Gospel
"My God and Your God"	Conclusion

Introduction

Throughout church history, an overwhelming majority of biblical scholars have regarded the two brief statements in Jn 1.1c and Jn 20.28 as foremost in the Bible that unequivocally identify Jesus as "God." Yet we have seen that an increasing number of 20th century scholars no longer translated Jn 1.1c in the traditional way—"the Word was God"—and many of them did not believe this

---

[433] E.g., B. Lindars, *The Gospel of John*, 371, 376; G.R. Beasley-Murray, *John*, 177. Some scholars label it a "Oneness Christology," which can be misconstrued as Sabellianism.
[434] Contra B.M. Metzger, "The Jehovah's Witnesses and Jesus Christ," 73.

clause calls Jesus "God." But what about Thomas' words in Jn 20.28, in which he exclaimed to the resurrected Jesus, "my Lord and my God"? Don't most scholars believe Thomas therein called Jesus "God"?

Indeed they do. In 1975, B.A. Mastin provided a brief but substantial survey of contemporary, exegetical authorities who interpreted the major *theos* texts in the NT which generally have been believed to call Jesus "God." He concluded that only Jn 20.28 "is universally accepted" by NT scholars as calling Jesus "God."[435] Popular commentator, William Barclay, is a prime example. We have already seen that he treats the anarthorous *theos* in Jn 1.1c as qualitative and therefore rejects the traditional translation of that clause. Hence, Barclay did not believe Jn 1.1c identifies Jesus as "God." But regarding Thomas' confession Barclay states, "There is only one passage in the New Testament, Jo. 20:28, where there is no doubt that Jesus is called God."[436]

Form critics are no different. R. Bultmann asserts that "the only [NT] passage in which Jesus is undoubtedly designated or, more exactly, addressed as 'God,' is John 20.28."[437] And we learned that V. Taylor raises serious objections as to whether the NT calls Jesus "God." Yet, like Bultmann, he concedes that in Jn 20.28 Thomas said his words to Jesus, so that "there is no doubt that the name 'God' is assigned to Him."[438] Taylor adds that in the NT it is "the one clear ascription of Diety to Christ."[439]

On the other hand, we have seen that an array of recent Bible scholars do not believe that Jesus was God. Many of them, e.g., most Fellows of the Jesus Seminar, believe that the Bible identifies Jesus as "God" but that it is wrong in doing so. However, such historical-critical scholars usually do not believe in the supernatural and therefore that Jesus performed miracles and literally arose from the dead. Then there are the notable British theologians who were contributing writers to the controversial book, *The Myth of God Incarnate* (1977). These include its editor John Hick as well as contributors Francis Young, Michael Goulder, and Don Cupitt, all of whom do not believe that Jesus was God. But there are a significant number of renown theologians and biblical exegetes who have a more conservative view of the NT gospels—believing that Jesus did miracles and arose from the dead—who also do not believe Jesus was God. These include Roman Catholic theologians Piet Schoonenberg, Edward Schillebeeckx, and Hans Kung, plus Protestant theologians Ellen Flesseman van-Leer and Hendrikus Berkhof, all Europeans. Not to be forgotten are those few scholars, e.g., Maurice Casey, who affirm Jesus' miracles and resurrection, deny that Jesus was God, yet, like the Fellows of the Jesus Seminar, insist that the Gospel of John teaches that Jesus was God but allege that it is erroneous. Then there are Johannine scholars who affirm Jesus' miracles and resurrection and treat the Fourth Gospel as historically reliable, yet reject that it teaches that Jesus was God (the view of this author), such as John A.T. Robinson and Jacob Jervell. However, a perusal of the writings of all of these scholars shows

---

[435] B.A. Mastin, "A Neglected Feature of the Christology of the Fourth Gospel," *NTS* 22 (1975-76): 33. Also, A.W. Wainwright ("The Confession 'Jesus is God' in the New Testament," 294) observes that Jn 20.28 "is more or less universally accepted" by modern scholars as calling Jesus "God." Surprisingly, patristic writings rarely cite Thomas' Confession to support their constant assertion that Jesus is God.
[436] W. Barclay, *Jesus As They Saw Him*, 33.
[437] R. Bultmann, "The Christological Confession of the World Council of Churches," in Bultmann's *Essays*, 276.
[438] V. Taylor, "Does the New Testament Call Jesus God?" 117.
[439] V. Taylor, "Does the New Testament Call Jesus God?" 118.

that, in their denial that Jesus is God, they either ignore Jn 20.28b in their writings, presumably because they do not see any recourse to the traditional interpretation of it, or they provide an alternative exegesis of Jn 20.28b that is not convincing.[440]

So, *Thomas' words in Jn 20.28 emerge as the most formidable in the Bible that purportedly support the traditional view that Jesus is God.* Yet we have seen that up to this place in John's Gospel, near its end, it has *not* called Jesus "God." *Is it possible that there is only one verse in the* NT—*Jn 20.28— that clearly identifies Jesus as God?* Most scholars probably would agree with Millard Erickson's assertion concerning Thomas' Confession, "Nowhere in the New Testament is Jesus more clearly identified as God."[441] Therefore, this Thomas incident certainly demands our utmost attention.

The Thomas Incident

The first evening after Jesus arose from the dead His disciples gathered together in the Upper Room (Jn 20.19). But Thomas was not among them. The risen Jesus then appeared to them. Afterwards, they told Thomas, "'We have seen the Lord!' But he said to them, 'Unless I shall see in His hands the imprint of the nails, and put my finger into the place of the nails, and put my hand into His side, I will not believe'" (Jn 20.25). That is how this apostle got his legacy as "doubting Thomas." Even though he had seen Jesus do miracles, like so many people he still wanted proof. Thomas had to see the risen Jesus.

Eight days later Thomas got his wish. Jesus appeared again in the Upper Room to His gathered disciples, with Thomas present. Jesus, aware of Thomas' disbelief uttered the prior week, said to him, "Reach here your finger, and see My hands; and reach here your hand, and put it into My side; and be not unbelieving, but believing" (Jn 20.27).

The text does not say that Thomas did so. Most scholars think he didn't. But this question is irrelevant to our study. The main point of this narrative is that Thomas literally saw and heard the resurrected Jesus, and he at least visually witnessed Jesus' marks of crucifixion. What John records next is most important for Christology:

28 "Thomas answered and said to Him, 'My Lord and my God!'"
29 Jesus said to him, "Because you have seen Me, have you believed? Blessed are they who did not see, and yet believed."

Scholars call Thomas' five words in v. 28 (seven in the Gr. NT), "Thomas' Confession."

Doubting Thomas has been a symbol of hope to countless believers ever since. Though this skeptical apostle wavered in faith, upon literally seeing the risen Jesus his faith was strengthened immeasurably. And he apparently remained steadfast in this faith the rest of his life. According to tradition, Thomas preached the gospel as far away as India with remarkable results. His mission even reputedly included fascinating miracles.

---

[440] E.g., H. Berkhof, *Christian Faith*, 294; J.A.T. Robinson, *The Priority of John*, 393. Recall from Chapter Three that Hans Kung's writings avoid discussing Jn 1.1c and 20.28, and J.A. Fitzmyer faults him for this.
[441] Millard J. Erickson, *The Word Became Flesh: A Contemporary Incarnational Christology* (Grand Rapids: Baker, 1991), 461.

Most scholars agree that Thomas' Confession represents a fitting climax to the Fourth Gospel,[442] and they have correctly connected it to Jn 1.1c. However, like Jn 1.1c, *Thomas' words to Jesus, "My Lord and my God," have been exceedingly misunderstood.*

Authenticity of Thomas' Confession

Before we examine this misunderstanding of Thomas' Confession in Jn 20.28, we need to consider whether he really spoke these words. Until modern times, there had never been any doubt about it. As E.W. Hengstenberg remarked over a century ago, "We have here the first passage in which Jesus is expressly by His disciples called God—a confession which was soon to be the common one of the whole Christian Church."[443]

How times have changed. D.A. Carson relates that the historicity of Thomas' Confession "has come under grave suspicion" by many scholars,[444] not only by radical form critics. Surprisingly, some are distinguished traditionalists who accept the Thomas incident as historical yet reject that Thomas uttered the purported words in Jn 20.28.[445] Instead, they insist that this brief confession is a liturgy created by the Johannine church community and that the Fourth Evangelist has fictitiously placed it on Thomas' lips.

Scholars who adopt this non-historical approach to Thomas' Confession posit substantial reasons for their skepticism which should not be ignored. First, they correctly recognize that the NT gospels never present Jesus as expressly calling Himself "God." Second, they rightly insist that, besides Thomas' Confession, the gospels never portray Jesus' disciples as calling Him "God." [446] Third, some of these scholars well observe that none of the evangelistic messages recorded in Acts identify Jesus as "God."[447] In light of these substantial omissions, rendering Thomas' Confession as non-historical ought to be regarded as a serious and important attempt to explain these significant omissions.

As mentioned above, some of these exegetes who doubt the historicity of Thomas' Confession are traditionalists who think some of the debatable, NT *theos* passages *do* call Jesus "God." But they claim that the NT writings that call Jesus "God" were written between the late 50s and 90s, some thirty to sixty years after the Christ event. Such scholars therefore postulate that calling Jesus "God" must have been a later christological development, beginning decades after the Christ event. (See Appendix C: Modern Christologies.) Roman Catholic R.E. Brown adopts this view. He explains that in the NT, "the title 'God' is not directly given to the Jesus of the ministry."[448] He adds that in the time of the writing of the NT

---

[442] Most contemporary Johannine scholars regard Jn 21 as a later appendage, it being much debated whether written by the original author of this gospel or someone else.
[443] E.W. Hengstenberg, *Commentary On The Gospel Of St. John* [1865], 2 vols. (repr. Minneapolis: Klock & Klock, 1980), 2:462. It also is the only passage in the NT gospels in which someone supposedly calls Jesus "God." Such silence suggests that Thomas did not call Jesus "God."
[444] So says D.A. Carson, *John*, 657. For a review of this debate, see M. Harris, *Jesus as God*, 111-19.
[445] E.g., A.W. Wainwright, *Trinity*, 63; R.E. Brown, *Jesus God and Man*, 30n52, 34-36; idem, *John xiii-xxi*, 1019, 1047; idem, *An Introduction to New Testament Christology*, 190n280; Reginald H. Fuller, *The Formation of the Resurrection Narratives* [1971] (repr. Philadelphia: Fortress, 1980), 143; tentatively C.K. Barrett, *John*, 573. Many historical-critical scholars, e.g., W. Bousset (*Kyrios Christos*, 317, 322n309, 330-31), have regarded the entire Thomas pericope as non-historical.
[446] Traditionalist R.E. Brown (*An Introduction to New Testament Christology*, 190n280) admits that Thomas calling Jesus "God," with no similar NT evidence, is a serious problem for traditionalists.
[447] E.g., R.E. Brown, *Jesus God and Man*, 30; idem, *An Introduction to New Testament Christology*, 190.
[448] R.E. Brown, *Jesus God and Man*, 36.

documents, "the NT use of 'God' for Jesus is not yet truly a dogmatic formulation, but appears in a liturgical or cultic context."[449] Reginald H. Fuller states likewise, "The earlier strata of the New Testament never designates Jesus unequivocally as God. The practice begins in the later writings of the New Testament."[450] Due to this supposedly late and scanty scriptural evidence, these scholars conclude that Thomas could not possibly have called Jesus "God."

The RCC's Pontifical Biblical Commission disagreed with this dismissal of the historicity of Thomas' words. Its important document, *Bible et christologie*, states: "*But all these* [NT gospel] *testimonies must be accepted in their totality* ... No one of them can be rejected on the grounds that, being the product of a secondary development, it would not express the *true* image of Christ,... The interpretation of the texts, which remains quite necessary, should by no means end up by throwing out any of their content."[451]

Some scholars who are skeptical of the historicity of Thomas' Confession suggest that the Johannine community borrowed this phrase from Ps 35.23 in fictitiously creating Thomas' words.[452] The relevant words in this psalm are "my God and my LORD" (AV, RSV, NASB). But the circumstances and nature of the psalmist's formula and Thomas' formula differ in three significant ways: (1) the two formulas are arranged in opposite order, (2) although both Ps 35.23 in the LXX and Thomas' Confession in the Greek NT have *kurios* (lord), the psalmist clearly addresses Yahweh (MT) while Thomas addresses Jesus, and (3) the pronoun "my" occurs twice in Thomas' Confession, which favors the Two Person view, viz., Jesus and God the Father, while the psalmist employed this pronoun only once, which favors the One Person view, viz., the Father. Some scholars cite examples in the LXX of the familiar conjunction "Lord (my/our) God" (*kurie/kurios ho theos [mou/hemon]*) as evidence that the Johannine community used these liturgical formulas in its worship of Jesus and thus applied it anachronistically to Thomas.[453]

Some historical-critical scholars further speculate that the Johannine community's fictitious creation of Thomas' Confession is a reaction to developments in the imperial cult under Emperor Domitian (reign: 81-96 CE).[454] Their reasoning is as follows: (1) the Fourth Gospel was written at Ephesus during Domitian's reign, (2) Domitian declared himself *dominus et deus noster* (I.. "our Lord and God"), which incidentally many Roman citizens mocked and mimicked, and (3) due to this common usage it would have been natural for Roman Christians to apply this epithet, or its likeness, to Jesus.

What are we to make of this scholarly doubt concerning the historical authenticity of Thomas' Confession? While these scholars are to be commended for recognizing serious problems regarding the traditional interpretation of Thomas' Confession, their methodology unnecessarily impugns the historical integrity of the Gospel of John.[455] To accept the theological import of Thomas' words, but not their historicity, is begging the question. Most Bible believers will toss this viewpoint into the wastebasket, along with any demythologizing

---

[449] R.E. Brown, *John xiii-xxi*, 1047.
[450] R.H. Fuller, *The Formation of the Resurrection Narratives*, 143.
[451] *Bible et christologie*, 2.2.2.2. Empasis not mine.
[452] E.g., R.E. Brown, *John (xiii-xxi)*, 1047.
[453] See M. Harris (*Jesus as God*, 120-21n68, n69, n70, n72, n73) for about forty examples in the LXX.
[454] E.g., B.A. Mastin, "A Neglected Feature of the Christology of the Fourth Gospel," 46; tentatively R.N. Longenecker, *The Christology of Early Jewish Christianity*, 140.
[455] For a defense of the historical reliability of Thomas' Confession, see M. Harris, *Jesus as God*, 111-19.

of the Gospel of John, and rightly so. Though many scholars will deem this as naivete, how can a reader trust any of the account of the Evangelist when he fraudulently and knowingly misrepresents history? Rather, it is better to accept Thomas' Confession as historically authentic and search for a better interpretation of it.

History of the Interpretation of Thomas' Confession

Let us begin this search by considering the history of the interpretation of Jn 20.28. From the 2nd to the 6th century CE, patristic writings reveal that church fathers unanimously interpreted it to mean that Thomas identified Jesus as "God." But in the 6th century a renowned scholar decided otherwise, and it landed him in a heap of trouble.

Theodore of Mopsuestia (350-428 CE) has generally been regarded by modern scholars as the most capable biblical exegete from the apostolic era to his own time. Accordingly, he superceded the interpretive skills of stalwarts Origen, Augustine, and Jerome. Theodore interpreted that Thomas' entire confession referred only to the Father. And much later, so did Faustus Socinus.

This new interpretation started quite a furor. It even caused the Roman Emperor Justinian I—an ardent advocate of the decrees of the Council of Chalcedon—to condemn Theodore's writings in 543-544 CE in the emperor's "Three Chapters" edict. In 551 CE, the emperor issued another edict in preparation for the Second Council of Constantinople (Sixth Ecumenical Council). It again attacked Theodore of Mopsuestia, quoting him as saying, "The words which Thomas, after feeling Him, spoke: 'My Lord and my God' (S. John xx.28), had reference not to Christ, but to God who raised Christ up." So, Theodore applied all of Thomas' Confession to God the Father and none of it to Jesus. He insisted that Thomas' Confession was "an exclamation of gratitude to God for the wonder of the miracle of the resurrection, rather than an affirmation of faith in the divinity of Jesus."[456]

The Second Council of Constantinople was convened two years later, in 553 CE. It condemned Theodore of Mopsuestia as a heretic, only for his interpretation of Thomas' Confession, and excommunicated him from the Catholic Church. The council declared, "this confession of Thomas referred to Christ and was not simply an expression of glory to God the Father" (NAB, 167). It made no difference to the council that Theodore still affirmed the Nicene Creed and Chalcedonian two-nature Christology.[457]

This denunciation of Theodore of Mopsuestia therefore continued the practice that began at Nicea of anathematizing heretics. (Anathema means "to curse.") But this council went a step further by proclaiming in its Article 11: "Whoever defends Theodore thus blaspheming, and does not anathematize him and his adherents, let him be anathema."[458]

For the next thousand years, the traditional interpretation of Thomas' Confession held firm in Christendom, thus without any opposition. Then some Unitarians temporarily revived Theodore's interpretation. But in modern times, Theodore's interpretation finds few advocates.[459]

---

[456] Cited in B.A. Mastin, "A Neglected Feature of the Christology of the Fourth Gospel," 42.

[457] B.A. McDonald, "Theodore of Mopsuestia," *Historical Handbook of Major Biblical Interpreters*, ed. Donald K. McKim (Downers Grove, IL: InterVarsity, 1998), 68-69.

[458] This severe condemnation was engineered by the Alexandrians in revenge for the condemnation of Origen ten years prior. See J.A.T. Robinson, *The Human Face of God*, 205.

[459] So says R.E. Brown, *Jesus God and Man*, 28.

An Address to Jesus

All traditionalist scholars, and many historical-critical scholars, have steadfastly contended on grammatical grounds that Thomas addressed the entire contents of his confession to Jesus and that this fact necessitates that Thomas called Jesus "God." John did write, "Thomas ... said to him," viz., Jesus. The words in the Greek text, *eipen auto*, mean "said to/unto him." So, Thomas clearly addressed his entire confession to Jesus. These scholars have reasoned that if Thomas merely intended to praise the Father for raising Jesus from the dead, as Theodore of Mopsuestia had insisted, John would not have used the words *eipen auto*. They further assert that if Thomas had not intended to direct any of his confession to Jesus, John likely would have made this clear as well. Consequently, traditionalists generally have centered their interpretation of Jn 20.28 on the idea that Thomas spoke his entire confession to Jesus.

However, without opposing this reasoning, Unitarian George E. Ellis raised an interesting inquiry by stating concerning Thomas' words in Jn 20.28, "the Trinitarian insists that he applied both terms to the Saviour. But must Thomas be precluded from the possibility of having both Christ and God in his mind in that moment of surprise and earnest outbursting of emotion?"[460] That is exactly what John Milton, the 17th century famed English poet and dedicated Christian, had contended. He wrote a lengthy book on Christology in which he secretly proposed the interpretation that Thomas called Jesus "my Lord" and the Father "my God."[461] But Milton did not provide any rationale for it.

In modern times, the Jehovah's Witnesses have sought to revive this viewpoint adopted by Milton and others. Bruce Metzger, early in his career, opposed the Jehovah's Witnesses on this by alleging, "It is not permissable to divide Thomas' exclamation.... Such a high-handed expedient overlooks the plain introductory words, 'Thomas said to him.'"[462] R.H. Strachan, however, had earlier cautioned concerning Thomas' Confession, "In interpreting the words 'my God' as addressed to Jesus, we must bear in mind that the risen Jesus never usurps the place of God in New Testament thought."[463]

Nominatives Treated as Vocatives?

Interpreters who adopt the traditional interpretation of Thomas calling Jesus "God" often argue on grammatical grounds. They assert that the two nominatives with the articles—*ho kurios mou kai ho theos mou* ("the Lord of me and the God of me")—are vocatives, so that Thomas spoke of Jesus' Person, i.e., that He was God.

But G.B. Winer, the preeminent NT grammarian of the 19th century, disagreed.[464] He conceded that the nominative with the article is frequently used as an address, "particularly in calling or commanding;... instead of the Vocative, which was intended for this purpose ... On the other hand, Jno.(sic) xx. 28, though directed to Jesus, is rather exclamation than address; and, in the

---

[460] George E. Ellis, *A Half-Century of the Unitarian Controversy* (Boston: Crosby, 1857), 136.
[461] John Milton, *Complete Poems and Major Prose*, 946.
[462] B.M. Metzger, "The Jehovah's Witness and Jesus Christ," 71n13.
[463] R.H. Strachan, *The Fourth Gospel*, 3rd ed., 332. Strachan (p. 99) is one of the few conservative exegetes who translates Jn 1.1c, "the logos was divine."
[464] New Testament Greek grammar was almost totally disregarded by NT philologists until the outstanding work of G.B. Winer in the 19th century.

Greek authors, such a nominative has early and strong prominence."[465] In other words, Winer insisted that Thomas' words "Lord" and "God" are to be taken strictly as nominatives and not as vocatives so that these words, despite being addressed to Jesus, do not necessarily say something about His nature. (This is apparently why the NEB and JB do not translate *auto* and thus omit the words "unto Him.") Accordingly, Thomas' words "Lord" and "God" are ascriptions uttered in exclamation, so that he did not intend to say something about Jesus' identity.[466]

Ascribing Divinity to Jesus?

In more recent times, some prominent NT scholars have adopted what amounts to a mediating position between the traditional interpretation of Jn 20.28 and the Theodore-Unitarian interpretation of it. These scholars interpret Thomas' words "my God" to mean the ascription of some form of divinity to Jesus, but not that He is fully God. (This is similar to the views of the apologists and Arians, who identified Jesus as "God," but only derivatively and therefore essentially less than "the one true God"—the Father.) For example, C.E. Luthardt offers the rather weak grammatical argument that Thomas' word "God" (*theos*) should be treated as a predicate ascribing divinity to Jesus, which we have seen is how some commentators treat *theos* in Jn 1.1c>. Then Luthardt takes an Origenist perspective by insisting, "He is not *ho theos* ["the God"] in the subject, the one whom we call God, but God in the predicate; *theotes* ('divinity') is true of him."[467]

C.H. Dodd forged quite a different route but arrived at the same destination. He suggested that "my Lord" refers to Jesus and "'my God' is a theological evaluation of his Person."[468] Dodd also favorably recalled, "I remember hearing F.C. Burkitt paraphrase Thomas' confession thus: 'Yes: it is Jesus!—and He is Divine!'"[469]

Moderate traditionalist Reginald H. Fuller steered on a slightly different track. He explains, "Thomas is not making a metaphysical statement, but a confession of faith that in Jesus he has encountered the eschatological presence of God at work."[470] Obviously, this view does not make Thomas attribute divinity to Jesus or recognize Him as God.

Traditionalists argue convincingly against interpreting *theos* in either Jn 1.1c or 20.28 to mean that Jesus is "divine." They insist that if John had intended to so describe Jesus, he surely would have used the Greek word *theotes* (divine) which was available to him.[471] So, Thomas clearly did not intend to call Jesus "divine."

---

[465] G.B. Winer, *A Grammar of the Idiom of the New Testament Prepared as a Solid Basis for the Interpretation of the New Testament*, 7th ed., rev. Gottlieb Lunemann, tr. J. Henry Thayer (London: Draper, 1869), 183. Winer cites addional NT evidence of a nominative used as exclamation, e.g., Lk 12.20; 1 Cor 15.36; Phil 3.18-19. A.T. Robertson (*A Grammar of the Greek New Testament in the Light of Historical Research*, 466) unjustly undermines Winer's credibility by alleging, "Winer calls this exclamation rather than address, apparently to avoid the conclusion that Thomas was satisfied as to the deity of Jesus by his appearance to him after the resurrection."
[466] R. Bultmann (*John*, 695n1) claims that "it makes no difference whether the words are understood as an address (nominative form used as vocative).... or as an exclamation of the confessor."
[467] Christoph Ernst Luthardt, *Clark's Foreign Theological Library: Luthardt on the Gospel of St. John*, 3 vols. (Edinburgh: T. & T. Clark, 1878), 3:342.
[468] C.H. Dodd, *The Interpretation of the Fourth Gospel*, 430n2.
[469] C.H. Dodd, *The Interpretation of the Fourth Gospel*, 430n2.
[470] R.H. Fuller, *The Formation of the Resurrection Narratives*, 144.
[471] As mentioned above, the word *theotes* only appears once in the Greek NT, in Col 2.9.

Moreover, it is most unlikely that Thomas called Jesus either "God" or "divine" because the NT gospels contain no other narratives in which either Jesus or His disciples ever made such a claim about Him. Although this argument from silence is not decisive, it ought to alert us to search carefully for another interpretation of Thomas' words.

One of the most important principles in interpreting a document is to consider its context. Indeed, *context is the key to a proper understanding of Thomas' Confession.*

"The Lord"

We have seen that the title "Lord" (Gr. *kurios*) is by far the most common epithet applied to Jesus in the NT. John records twenty-eight instances in which one or more of the disciples called Jesus "Lord," and several of these appear in his gospel near Thomas' Confession. In fact, in Jn 20-21 John reports that Jesus' disciples called Him "Lord" ten times. One of these instances is particularly significant for discovering the true meaning of Thomas' Confession. It is when Mary Magdalene called Jesus "my Lord" (Jn 20.13), the same two words Thomas uttered only a few days later. This evidence and it proximity suggests that John means that Thomas also called Jesus "my Lord," to which nearly all interpreters agree. But did John also mean that Thomas called Jesus "my God"? One of the literary clues to the correct answer is found in Jesus' message that he gave Mary.

"My God and Your God"

What the risen Jesus' said to Mary Magdalene in Jn 20.17 strongly suggests that the Fourth Evangelist did not mean that Thomas called Jesus "God." John records only a few verses before the Thomas incident that the resurrected Jesus told Mary Magdalene to tell His disciples, "Go to My brethren, and say to them, 'I ascend to My Father and your Father, and My God and your God'" (Jn 20.17). For obvious literary reasons, John would not present Jesus as calling the Father "My God" and soon follow it with Thomas calling Jesus "my God." That would be utter confusion, besides a denial of Jewish monotheism. If the Father is the God of Jesus, and there is only one God, then Jesus can't also be God.

In addition, in Jesus' message that he gave Mary Magdalene to give to His (other) disciples, Jesus' identification of the Father as "your God" indicates exclusivity. That is, only the Father, and not also Jesus, is "God" to the disciples.

Furthermore, the words "my God" occur at least ten other times in the NT,[472] and most of them are represented to be sayings of Jesus. It is certain from their contexts that all of them refer to God the Father. Such evidence makes it even more likely that Thomas' words, "my God," refer to the Father as well.

Thus, the near context of John 20.28 necessitates that the author of the Fourth Gospel purposefully chose and arranged his material with the intent that Thomas' words "my Lord" identify Jesus and Thomas' words "my God" echo those of Jesus in v. 17, thus referring to the Father. Recall that this was the interpretation proposed by both John Milton and George Ellis. And we will learn in Chapter Seven that this interpretation follows St. Paul's practice of exclusively calling Jesus "Lord" and the Father "God."

"The Only True God"

Moreover, recall that John reports three chapters prior that only a few days earlier Jesus had prayed, calling the Father "the only true God" (Jn 17.3; cf. v. 1).

---

[472] E.g., Mt 27.46; Mk 15.34; Jn 20.17, 28; Rom 1.8; 1 Cor 1.4; 2 Cor 12.21; Phil 1.3; 4.19; Rev 3.12.

Surely John would not have recorded this clear identification of the Father if he had believed that Thomas' words identified Jesus as "God." Again, that would be utter confusion!

In sum, while Thomas did address his entire confession to Jesus, *it is contextually unacceptable to interpret the second half of Thomas' Confession as calling Jesus "God."* But can we be more certain that Thomas' words "my God" refer to the Father? Searching further into the context of the Fourth Gospel, we discover that we can indeed.

Jesus as the Father's Agent

John repeatedly portrays Jesus as teaching that to *believe in* Him, or words to that effect, is to do likewise regarding the Father.[473] Similarly, Jesus explains that if anyone knows and has the Son, they also know and have the Father, for the Son is the Father's envoy, representative, or agent par excellence. A.E. Harvey, in his commentary on the NT, remarks insightfully on Jn 20.28, "We have seen how this gospel portrays Jesus as God's agent on earth; and we have noted the principle that 'a man's agent is as himself.' At this moment, perhaps, Thomas recognized, not that Jesus was God himself (let alone some other god), but that Jesus was representing God in the fullest sense it was possible to imagine: addressing him, he was (as it were) addressing God himself."[474]

John relates most wonderfully how Jesus is the Father's agent in some brief and rather poetic quotations of Jesus that can be summarized as follows:
- To know Jesus is to know the Father-God (Jn 8.19; 14.7).
- To believe in Jesus is to believe in the Father-God (Jn 12.44).
- To behold Jesus is to behold the Father-God (Jn 12.45).[475]
- To receive Jesus is to receive the Father-God (Jn 13.20; cf. Mk 9.37).
- To honor Jesus is to honor the Father-God (Jn 5.23; cf. Phil 2.11)

But there is one more Johannine saying of Jesus that needs to be added to this list. It is the only NT account of a dialogue between Jesus and Thomas.[476] By including it, *John intends that his readers should understand Thomas' words "my God" in light of the earlier dialogue between Jesus and Thomas, recorded in Jn 14.5-11.* Unfortunately, this interpretation has received very little attention throughout the history of Christianity.

Seeing the Father in Jesus

John records in Jn 14.1-3 that ten days prior to the Thomas episode, during the Last Supper, Jesus divulged to the Eleven rather obscurely that He was about to depart from this world and ascend to His Father in heaven. (Interestingly, He begins this discourse by interchanging "God" with "My Father" in vv. 1-2; cf. Jn 13.3.) We now break into this very important teaching session of Jesus with His apostles, which includes His interaction with both Thomas and Philip.

4 "And you know the way where I am going."
5 Thomas said to Him, Lord, we do not know where You are going, how do we know the way?"

---

[473] The reverse is true as well. That is, whoever believes in God the Father will also believe in Jesus (e.g., Jn 8.41-42, 54-55). Similarly, whoever rejects Jesus also rejects the Father (Lk 10.16; cf. Jn 5.23).

[474] A.E. Harvey, *A Companion to the New Testament*, 2nd ed. (Cambridge: University, 2005), 382.

[475] The NASB translates the double use of *theoreo* in Jn 12.45 as "behold;" the RSV and NIV render it "sees."

[476] Only John provides one other quotation by Thomas, recorded in Jn 11.16.

6 Jesus said to him, "I am the way, the truth, and the life; no one comes to the Father but through Me.
7 "If you had known Me, you would have known My Father also; from now on you know Him, and have seen Him."
8 Philip said to Him, "Lord, show us the Father, and it is enough for us."
9 Jesus said to him, "Have I been so long with you, and yet you have not come to know Me, Philip? He who has seen Me has seen the Father; how do you say, 'Show us the Father'?
10 "Do you not believe that I am in the Father, and the Father in Me? The words that I say to you I do not speak on My own initiative, but the Father abiding in Me does His works.
11 "Believe Me that I am in the Father, and the Father in Me; otherwise believe on account of the works themselves.
....
18 "I will not leave you as orphans; I will come to you.
19 "After a little while the world will behold Me no more; but you will behold Me,...
20 "In that day you shall know that I am in My Father;..."
....
29 "And now I have told you before it comes to pass, that when it comes to pass, you may believe."

In this dialogue-discourse in Jn 14, the critical words for Christology are in vv. 7-11. *The key to unlocking the true understanding of Thomas' words "my God" in Jn 20.28 is found in what Jesus said earlier to Thomas, in Jn 14.7, "If you had known Me, you would have known My Father also; from now on you know Him, and have seen Him." And Jesus restates more precisely in v. 9, "He who has seen Me has seen the Father."*[477]

In discussing Jn 14.9, it is surprising how many Christians sound like they have been talking to the heretic Sabellius! Why? They think Jesus identifies Himself as the Father in this verse. That is exactly what Sabellius had taught; for Jn 14.9 was one of his main prooftexts for his modalistic monarchianism, which the Catholic Church rightly condemned as heresy. Let us recount the steps in their deductive reasoning process: (1) the Father is God; (2) Jesus said that He is the Father; (3) therefore, Jesus is God. Their colossal error is reason #2, that Jesus meant that He was *literally* the Father. Jesus is *not* the Father! Everywhere in the NT, Jesus and the Father are distinguished as two separate individuals. This deduction is, again, a failure to understand the "spiritual gospel."

What Jesus first broaches in Jn 14.7, about seeing the Father, He states more explicitly in v. 9. But He explains it clearly in vv. 10-11: "the Father is in Me," and again, "I am in the Father, and the Father is in Me." He means the Mutual Indwelling that we encountered in Jn 10.37. So, Jesus does not mean in Jn 14.7 and v. 9 that literally seeing Him is *literally seeing* the Father. Yet that apparently is what Philip thought Jesus meant. For he then asked Him, "show us the Father" (v. 8).

John's readers should not make this mistake. For John's prologue states, "No man has seen God at any time" (Jn 1.18). And the Johannine Jesus has already

---

[477] Johannine scholar Jacob Jervell (*Jesus in the Gospel of John*, 21, 22) says he does not "believe that the gospel of John makes Jesus into God, or identical with God." Then he adds, "A crucial statement for our understanding of who Jesus is in the Fourth Gospel occurs in 14:9." Unfortunately, he does not elaborate.

said, "Not that any man has seen the Father" (Jn 6.46). These declarations affirm the fundamental OT teaching that God is invisible to mortal humans. If they were to literally see God, they would instantly die. So, Jesus must have intended that His words in v. 7 and v. 9, about seeing the Father, be understood *mystically*. That is, to see and know Jesus relationally was to *spiritually* see and know the Father, who is God, because *God was in Christ*.

What Jesus next said to Thomas and Philip is quite sobering. He said, "Believe Me that I am in the Father, and the Father in Me; otherwise believe on account of the works themselves" (v. 11). What Jesus here means can be paraphrased, "Believe my miraculous works because they testify that what I am saying to you is true, that I am in the Father and the Father is in Me."

The "God-in Christ" Interpretation

This teaching of Jesus in Jn 14.7-11—about seeing the Father in Jesus—must have made a strong impression on Thomas. He surely recalled it ten days later when he first saw the resurrected Jesus. *Thomas' Confession thus indicates more than a mere recognition that God raised Jesus from the dead. Rather, Thomas' words "my God" also indicate that this previously doubting apostle now understands what Jesus had taught ten days earlier, that God the Father fully indwells, and therefore completely permeates, the life of Jesus. Thus, the Father is spiritually seen, that is, comprehended, in Jesus Christ. So, Thomas' words "my God," while addressed to Jesus, represent a faith response to the God who revealed Himself to Thomas in the risen Jesus.*

Finally, Jesus concluded His remarks on this subject by predicting that when the Eleven would literally see Him in His resurrection body they would believe (v. 29). Believe what? He didn't mean believing that He was the Christ, the Son of God (Jn 20.30-31). They had already done that. And that is why their sins were forgiven and they belonged to God and Christ (e.g., Mt 16.16; Jn 13.10-11). Instead, Jesus meant that, when the Eleven would literally see Him in His resurrection body, they would believe that He was indeed in the Father and the Father in Him. Although Jesus had already explained this Mutual Indwelling to them, recorded in Jn 10.37, they had not comprehended it and therefore had not believed it.

The merit of this "God-in-Christ" interpretation of the latter half of Thomas' Confession is that it is based on another important and simple hermeneutical principle: let Scripture interpret Scripture. More precisely, this interpretation has to do with Jesus' earlier teaching to Thomas, recorded only in Jn 14.7-11 in the NT. As Bultmann so aptly puts it, "Thomas has now seen Jesus in the way that Jesus wills to be seen and ought to be seen."[478] We might add that it is the way Jesus had earlier instructed Thomas to see Him. Vincent Taylor's observation applies especially well here, that John's "deepest conviction is that God is made known, and can be seen, in Christ."[479] *God being fully in Christ, not Christ being God, is what gives significance to Jesus Christ.*

A.E. Harvey concludes the same via Agent Christology. He explains, "when the son is known to be acting as the father's agent, it is as if the father is actually

---

[478] R. Bultmann, *John*, 695. Bultmann says of Thomas' Confession, "it sees in Jesus God himself." He then quotes Jn 14.9 and cites 12.45 without elaboration. Yet in the same paragraph he endorses the traditional interpretation of Jn 20.28 and 1.1c, asserting that Jesus "is now recognized [by Thomas] as the *theos* that he was from the beginning (1.1)." Bultmann believed this gospel does not view the pre-Easter Jesus as God.

[479] Vincent Taylor, *Forgiveness and Reconciliation* (London: MacMillan, 1941), 126.

present in the son."[480] Moreover, Harvey applies this explanation to the Thomas incident and insists that the doubting apostle now recognizes "the presence of God himself" in Jesus, and he understands that speaking to Jesus "was as if to speak to God himself."[481]

So, this God-in-Christ interpretation of the latter half of Thomas' Confession accords perfectly with the overall tenor of the Fourth Gospel as the "spiritual gospel." That is, Thomas' words "my God" mean that he now spiritually sees and acknowledges God the Father as indwelling Jesus, which is a spiritual interpretation. In contrast, the traditional view of Thomas' words "my God" is a literal interpretation that repeats the common error of failing to comprehend "the spiritual gospel" and the Johannine Jesus.

The Source of Enlightenment and Glorification

Another reason which supports this God-in-Christ interpretation of Thomas' words "my God" in Jn 20.28 is that the Fourth Evangelist has already verified that all human insight into Jesus' identity ultimately derives from the Father. People are born again, not by the will of the flesh or the will of man "but of God" the Father (Jn 1.13). The Johannine Jesus explains that the Father does so by drawing people to His Son and enlightening them about Him (Jn 6.44, 65). Then Jesus quotes from Isa 54.13, "they shall be taught of God" (Jn 6.45). God enlightens some and not others due to the condition of their hearts (vv. 33, 38, 41; cf. Mt 11.20, 25; 18.3-4).[482] A well known synoptic example is when Jesus asked His disciples who He was. Peter answered that He was "the Christ (the Son) of God." Jesus commended Peter and explained that his insight came from the Father (Mt 16.16-17). We might therefore expect an enlightened Thomas to praise God for his renewed faith, since it is the Father who reveals the truth about Jesus. R.H. Strachan explains about Thomas' insight, that this "faith is not his own creation."[483]

Jesus' Response

Some NT commentators have conceded that Thomas called Jesus "God," but have alleged that he was wrong in doing so. A few American Unitarian expositors have further reasoned that Thomas' opinion was not credible because of his previous disbelief.[484] And some expositors have supposed that Thomas recognized Jesus as "God" only with his heart and not with his mind. That is, Thomas uttered his words in a moment of ecstasy without sufficiently pondering their theological import.

Traditionalists are right that such interpretations are without merit in light of Jesus' response to Thomas' Confession. He readily accepted Thomas' words

---

[480] A.E. Harvey, *Jesus and the Constraints of History*, 166.
[481] A.E. Harvey, *Jesus and the Constraints of History*, 172. Marianne Meye Thompson ("The Living Father," in *God the Father in the Gospel of John*, ed. Adele Reinhartz [Atlanta: Society of Biblical Literature, 1999], 27) remarks similarly, "This category of agency is often deemed helpful in interpreting certain passages in John, such as, 'Whoever has seen me has seen the Father.'"
[482] God is neither capricious nor dictatorial, but just. He shows mercy, gives grace, and enlightens those who diligently seek Him, doing none of this arbitrarily. Cf. Ex 33.19 with 34.6-7 and Rom 9.15; 11.20-23.
[483] R.H. Strachan, *The Fourth Gospel*, 3rd ed., 332. I would say, "faith is not *entirely* his own creation."
[484] E.g., Andrews Norton, *A Statement of Reasons for Not Believing the Doctrines of Trinitarians Concerning the Nature of God and the Person of Christ*, 15th ed. (Boston: American Unitarian Association, 1876), 303-04; Willaim G. Eliot, *Discourses on the Doctrines of Christianity* (Boston: American Unitarian Association, 1890), 78-79.

as true (but not that its latter half meant that Thomas called Jesus "God"). Jesus explained that Thomas' words reflected that he believed because he saw the evidence of the nailprints in Jesus' hands and the sword-pierced hole in His side. Believed what? Not that Jesus was God but what his companions had told him earlier, that Jesus had risen from the dead.

Furthermore, if Thomas' words had been ill-conceived, in that He had called Jesus "God," we may well presume that His Lord would have corrected him. For we have already seen in John's gospel that Jesus' opponents accused Him of claiming to be God, and He denied the charge (Jn 10.33-36). Moreover, we have considered how the Synoptic Jesus objected to a much lesser description of Himself when the young rich man called Him "good" (Mk 10.17-18/Lk 18.18-19). How much more would He have objected if He thought one of His apostles had called Him "God"?

Other scholars propose that it was permissible for Thomas, and anyone else, to declare Jesus as "God" in ecstatic acts of worship, e.g., liturgies and hymns, but not in doctrinal or credal statements.[485] Thus, James D.G. Dunn calls Thomas' Confession "the extravagance of worship rather than the careful formulation of a [creedal] confession."[486]

It is also significant that John does not explain the meaning of Thomas' utterance. *If John thought Thomas called Jesus "God," in Jn 20.28, this account of such an alarming departure from Jewish monotheism must be judged a serious literary blunder because he failed to make this meaning clear.*

More History of the God-in-Christ Interpretation

Early in the 3rd century, Artemon and his friend Theodotus the Tanner affirmed Jesus' virgin birth, sinlessness, and miracles, but alleged He was only a man and the doctrine of the deity of Christ was an innovation, a relapse into heathen polytheism.[487]

Centuries later, the most widely acclaimed Socinian scholar of all time, Samuel Crellius (1657-1747), grandson of Johann Crellius, wrote an erudite book on Johannine Christology under the pseudonym "Artemonius" and adopts Artemon's argument.[488] Crellius exegetes most of the major biblical proof texts for traditional, deity Christology and concludes that none of them identify Jesus as "God" in an absolute sense.[489] More specifically, Crellius attempts to refute the two-nature exegesis of Thomas' Confession, which some traditionalists had embraced, in which "my Lord" refers to Jesus' human nature and "my God" refers to His divine nature. Crellius insists that Thomas' words "my Lord" refer to "the man Christ Jesus, moreover with these words *my God*, God the Father Himself existing inseparably in Christ."[490] Recall that George Ellis and John Milton, both of whom lived after Crellius' time and apparently were unfamiliar with his work, also suggested this interpretation. Although they failed to provide

---

[485] E.g., W. Barclay, *Jesus As They Saw Him*, 24, 33, 37.
[486] J.G.D. Dunn, *Unity and Diversity*, 54.
[487] P. Schaff, *History of the Christian Church*, 2:574. See also Eusebius, *Ecclesiastical History*, 5.28.
[488] Samuel Crellius, *Initium evangelii S. Joannis apostoli ex antiquitate ecclesiastica resitutium*, (n.p., 1726), 656 ff.
[489] E.g., Crellius exegetes Isa 9.6; Jn 1.1; 5.17-18; 10.29-38; Ac 20.28; Rom 9.5; Phil 2.6-11; 1 Tim 3.16; Tit 2.13. See a critique of this book in John Albert Bengel, *Gnomon of New Testament* [1743], 2nd ed., 2 vols. (repr. Edinburgh: T.&T. Clark, 1863], 2:235-36).
[490] S. Crellius, *Initium evangelii S. Joannis*.

a rationale for it, Crellius does by convincingly citing Jn 14.9-11 as the key for this interpretation. He explains:

> Thomas, believing now again, recalls these very words in his own mind, that truly the Father, the God of Thomas, is in Christ, and where the one is there also the other one is, and he who sees the one, also sees the other; therefore he shouts with joy, *ho kurios mou kai ho theos mou* [my Lord and my God. This means,] *Behold that one is my Lord, and behold that one is my God*, whom I saw before and recognized! Behold I see my Lord (Jesus Christ), and behold I see my God, God the Father, who is in Christ my Lord.[491]

Crellius also suggests concerning this memory and insight on Thomas' part that it "does not seem to have happened without a special intervention of the H. Spirit."

Later, John A. Bengel (1687-1752), in his commentary on the whole NT, argues extensively against Crellius' contention that the NT does not identify Jesus as the one true God. He quotes Crellius' interpretation of Thomas' words "my God," that it means "the Father who exists in Him inseparably," and argues, "If this had been the intention of Thomas, John would not have added the words *unto Him*. Thomas had not before expressly rejected faith in God the Father, but he had, in the case of Christ: therefore now it is not in the Father that he declares expressly his believing again, but in Christ."[492]

Bengel is so unconvincing here. First of all, the Eleven had long ago individually exercised saving faith in Jesus,[493] and their Master had verified this at the Last Supper when He pronounced them "clean" (Jn 13.10). Second, a person cannot reject (disbelieve) Jesus without also rejecting God the Father (Lk 10.16; cf. Jn 8.42). Third, we already have seen that this argument, about the phrase "unto Him," is weak.

The Purpose of John's Gospel

Finally, *the most significant literary reason which supports that Thomas could not have called Jesus "God," in Jn 20.28, is that this interpretation does not accord with the immediately following context, which is John's stated purpose for writing his gospel*. We have already considered it in the introduction to this chapter; but now let us review it.

30 Many other signs therefore Jesus also performed in the presence of the disciples, which are not written in this book;
31 but these have been written that you may believe that Jesus is the Christ, the Son of God; and that believing you may have life in His name.

---

[491] S. Crellius, *Initium evangelii S. Joannis*. Emphasis his. Crellius reveals that he became convinced of this interpretation of Thomas' Confession, and its relevance to Jn 14.7-11, through the writings of Theophylactus. I decided on this solely God-in-Christ interpretation of Thomas' words "my God" when I first read Bultmann's commentary on John, wherein he connects these words to Jn 14.9-11, but without any explanation. I regard this discovery as the pinnacle of my research for this book. Fifteen years later I discovered Crellius' rare book while doing research at Harvard University. I am unaware of any modern writer who advocates a solely God-in-Christ interpretation of Thomas words "my God" on the basis of Jn 14.7-11. *The New Interpreter's Bible* (9:850) connects Jn 14.7 and v. 9 with Thomas' words "my God;" but its commentary on this is confusing, sounds Sabellian, and still retains the traditional view.
[492] J.A. Bengel, *Bengel's New Testament Commentary*, 1:494-95. This is an abridged edition.
[493] They believed that Jesus was the Christ, the Son of God (e.g., Mt 16.16 par.; cf. Jn 1.49). Their faith in Jesus' imminent atonement and resurrection would come later, after these particular events had transpired.

For John to write that one of Jesus' apostles called Him "God," and immediately add this stated purpose, would be anticlimactic and reductionist, if not contradictory, if the terms "God" and "Son of God" are distinguished, as indeed they should be.[494] And the immediate proximity of these two statements makes them clash even more.

In contrast, this God-in-Christ interpretation of the latter half of the Thomas Confession fits nicely with John's stated purpose. For, the idea of God indwelling Jesus coincides with Jesus being the Christ and the Son of God. Indeed, Jesus' Sonship actually serves as an *explanation* of Thomas' words "my God." That is, God fully indwells Jesus because Jesus is God's unprecedented agent, being His one-of-a-kind Son.

Finally, most traditionalists assert that Thomas' words "my God" serve as a fitting climax to the Fourth Gospel because they perfectly parallel the traditional translation of Jn 1.1c—"the Word was God"—and that they therefore confirm each other. Thomas' words "my God" *do indeed* perfectly parallel Jn 1.1c, but *not* as traditionalists think. Thomas means that God was *in* Jesus, and this concept perfectly fits the NEB rendering of Jn 1.1c: "what God was, the Word was." That is, the Word-become-flesh is exactly like God the Father in His moral character because the Father, in all of His fulness, indwells Jesus Christ (cf. Jn 3.34; Col 1.19>; 2.9>).

Conclusion

In conclusion, the traditional interpretation of Thomas' Confession in Jn 20.28b is incompatible with the following contextual elements, (1) Jesus' description of the Father as "the only true God" (Jn 17.3), (2) Jesus saying to Mary Magdalene that the Father is "My God and your God" (Jn 20.17), and (3) John's stated purpose for writing his gospel (Jn 20.30-31). Rather, when Thomas uttered his words "my God," he acknowledged what Jesus had taught him earlier, in Jn 14.10-11, that the Father is *in* Him. Indeed, at that enlightening moment, Thomas' reaction affirms what was stated in the introduction of this chapter, that "it is difficult to think of ... Jesus without also thinking of His Father."

This God-in-Christ interpretation of the second half of Thomas' Confession is superior to the traditional interpretation because it accomplishes six important things:
1. It links up with the correct understanding of Jn 1.1c in the prologue, that the Word-become-flesh perfectly reflects God's character.
2. It better affirms the primary overall Johannine theme of Jesus as the Revealer of God.
3. It coincides well with two other important Johannine themes, i.e., the subordination and dependence of Christ to God, whereas the traditional interpretation does not and creates a problematic paradox with these themes.
4. It is a spiritual interpretation, which conforms to this gospel as the "spiritual gospel."

---

[494] Some traditionalists assert the opposite, e.g., Robert L. Reymond, *Jesus, Divine Messiah: The New Testament Witness* (Phillipsburg, NJ: Presbyterian and Reformed, 1990), 214); Martin Hengel, *Studies in Early Christology* (Edinburgh: T. & T. Clark, 1995), 367. They argue that the immediate proximity of Thomas' words "my God" with John's stated purpose, in Jn 20.30-31, indicates that Jesus is God. But they do so by wrongly equating the expression "the Son of God," as applied to Jesus, with the word "God."

5. Perhaps most important of all, it does not go beyond any synoptic claims regarding the identity of Jesus, especially the Synoptic Jesus' own claims about Himself.
6. It accords with all that is said herein about pertinent christological texts in this gospel.

Finally, this God-in-Christ interpretation of Thomas' Confession wonderfully affirms John's masterful, Spirit-led craftmanship in authoring his gospel. Yet the ultimate Master is God, acting through Christ, crafting these events that John has told the world.

8. Is denial that Jesus is the Christ, in 1 John 2.22, a denial of incarnation?

It is surprising that more than a few traditionalists insist that three separate verses in the epistles of John indicate classical incarnation. The first one reads, "Who is the liar but the one who denies that Jesus is the Christ? This is the antichrist, the one who denies the Father and the Son" (1 Jn 2.22). Leading Evangelical expositor John Stott says of this text, "they [the liars] denied that the man Jesus and the Eternal Son were and are the same Person, possessing two perfect natures, human and divine. In a word they denied the incarnation."[495] Stott surely would not deny that to properly understand this and the other two similar texts in these epistles, we need to know something about their background.

There is much similarity between the Gospel of John and the epistles of John. Consequently, scholars generally believe that this Johannine literature originated in what they call a "Johannine community." (The word "we" occurs 17x in the first ten vv. of 1 Jn.) This literature reveals opposition to proto-Gnosticism, and the epistles of John seem to more particularly oppose proto-Docetism. The latter asserted that Jesus only "seemed" (Gr. *doceo* means "to seem") to have possessed a physical body, but He was really a phantom. Later so-called "Christian Gnostics" conceptually separated Jesus and the Christ by designating the Christ as preexistent and divine. These views were predicated on dualism, that spirit is pure but the material, including flesh, is the source of evil if not evil itself, so that the Christ could not have been human.

It seems that due to this opposition the author of 1 Jn begins his epistle by saying that he and others in the Johannine community saw and touched "the Word of Life," viz., "Jesus Christ" (1 Jn 1.1-3). That is, they testify as eye-witnesses that Jesus possessed a physical body. For, the author later states, "every spirit that confesses that Jesus Christ has come in the flesh is from God; and every spirit that does not confess Jesus," i.e., that Jesus has come in the flesh, "is not from God" (1 Jn 4.2). The next epistle states similarly, "For many deceivers have gone out into the world, those who do not acknowledge Jesus Christ as coming in the flesh. This is a deceiver and the antichrist" (2 Jn 7).

Indeed, the author of 1 Jn reveals that some of these liars and deceivers had been members of their Johannine community. But he informs, "They went out from us, but they were not really of us; for if they had been of us, they would have remained with us" (1 Jn 2.19). So, the author makes a distinction between "us" and these secessionists in an attempt to protect the true believers of his community, further warning them that "many false prophets have gone out into the world" (1 Jn 4.1).

---
[495] John R.W. Stott, *The Epistles of John: An Introduction and Commentary* (1964) in TNTC, 111.

Therefore, all three of these epistolary, Johannine texts should be understood from the perspective of that community's opposition to incipient Gnosticism. Accordingly, to deny that "Jesus is the Christ" means essentially the same as to deny that "Jesus Christ has come in the flesh." Taking these passages together, the author is saying that Jesus is the Christ and that he possessed a physical body.

Traditionalists argue that the author of 1 Jn embraces classical incarnation when he writes, "This is the antichrist, the one who denies the Father and the Son" (1 Jn 2.22b). Traditionalists assert that denying that Jesus is the Son means to deny the incarnation. But this interpretation is due to their presupposition that Jesus being "the Son (of God, the Father)" means that he preexisted as God and became the God-man.

On the contrary, there is no evidence in the Johannine epistles that their author(s) believed in classical incarnation, i.e., that God became the man Jesus Christ, let alone that they knew about such teaching. Rather, the author of 1 Jn is using the words "Christ" and "Son" interchangeably in 1 Jn 2.22.[496] That is, he says that to deny that Jesus is the Christ is also to deny that he is the Son because "the Christ" and "the Son" refer to the same individual—the man Jesus. The author indicates as much at the beginning of this epistle by stating, "our fellowship is with the Father, and with His Son Jesus Christ" (1 Jn 1.3; cf. 5.20). The difference between the terms Christ and Son, as applied to Jesus, is that Christ/Messiah, meaning "anointed one," indicates His divine *mission* whereas Son (of God) indicates no more than His *relationship* to God as His Father. God anointed Jesus because He was His Son, as revealed at His baptism. Relationship comes before mission.

9. Is "the Trinity" in 1 John 5.7?

| Introduction | Evidence Against 1 Jn 5.7 Authenticity |
| Erasmus and Textus Receptus | Conclusion |

Introduction

Nothing in the NT substantiates the church doctrine of the Trinity more than does 1 Jn 5.7-8 in the AV. Yet all modern English versions exclude this Trinitarian fragment and therefore apportion the verses differently, as the following comparison reveals:

AV	NIV	NRSV
7 For there are three that bear record in heaven, the Father, the Word, and the Holy Ghost: and these three are one. 8 And there are three that bear witness in earth, the spirit, and the water, and the blood: and these three agree in one.	7 For there are three that testify: 8 the Spirit, the water, and the blood; and the three are in agreement.	7 There are three that testify: 8 the Spirit and the water and the blood, and these three agree.

---

[496] Cf. Mk 1.1; Mt 16.16; Mt 26.63/Mk 14.61; Jn 11.27; esp. 20.31.

Notice that the two modern versions exclude the entire sentence in v. 7 of the AV and divide v. 8 in the AV into two verses—vs. 7-8. The reason is that the portion in v. 7 of the AV does not appear in any Greek editions of the NT published after TR. (And they omit the words, "in earth," in the sentence that follows.) Why? This Trinitarian sentence is without question a spurious addition due to its almost complete lack of MS evidence. There is an interesting story about how it crept into the NT tradition.

Erasmus and Textus Receptus

Erasmus (c. 1469-1536) was the distinguished, Christian humanist scholar who compiled TR. Published in 1516, it was the first Greek NT produced since Jerome's translation (Vulgate) of the Old Latin Bible, over 1,000 years earlier. Erasmus' TR essentially became the Greek text used by translators of the AV, nearly a century later.

Erasmus' compilation was affected by the recent invention of the printing press. He hastily prepared his TR in order to beat the RCC's Polyglot Bible to the press because it contained a Greek text of the NT as well. Erasmus succeeded, so that his TR edition became the first Greek NT published by the printing press.[497] Then he spent part of the remainder of his life making necessary emendations to it in several subsequent editions.

Shortly after TR was published, one of the Catholic editors of the Polyglot Bible accused Erasmus of wrongly omitting the above Trinitarian sentence in his edition. Textual critic and Trinitarian Bruce Metzger relates this intriguing story:

> Erasmus replied that he had not found any Greek manuscript containing these words, though he ... examined several.... In an unguarded moment Erasmus promised that he would insert [it] ... in future editions if a single Greek manuscript could be found that contained the passage. At length such a copy was found—or was made to order! As it now appears, the Greek manuscript had probably been written in Oxford about 1520 by a Franciscan friar named Froy (or Roy), who took the disputed words from the Latin Vulgate. Erasmus stood by his promise and inserted the passage in his third edition (1522), but he indicates in a lengthy footnote his suspicions that the manuscript had been prepared expressly in order to confute him.[498]

If correct, how did the passage find its way into Jerome's Latin Vulgate, compiled in the 5th century CE? Metzger reveals that Jerome evidently did not originally include the questionable sentence in his translation. For, it does not appear in any extant copies of Jerome's Latin Vulgate produced before 800 CE, although it does appear in some copies afterwards. Metzger answers that later scribes presumably inserted it in their copies of the Vulgate because one or more of their copies of the Old Latin Bible, which preceded Jerome's Vulgate, included it. Indeed, Metzger traces the citation back beyond biblical MSS to a 4th century Latin treatise. Due to the custom of scribes attaching marginal notes, just as many devout Bible students do today in their Bibles, Metzger concludes that our passage "may have been written as a marginal gloss in a Latin manuscript of 1 John, whence it was taken into the text of the Old Latin Bible during the fifth century."[499]

---

[497] The RCC decided against publishing its Polyglot Bible; but it never explained why.
[498] B.M. Metzger, *The Text of the New Testament*, 101.
[499] B.M. Metzger, *The Text of the New Testament*, 102.

In 1897, the RCC made an authoritative pronouncement that the questionable sentence in 1 Jn 5.7 was authentic and warned against rejecting it. But in 1968 Metzger observed that "modern Roman Catholic scholars, however, recognize that the words do not belong in the Greek Testament."[500]

Evidence Against the Authenticity of 1 John 5.7
The following external evidence shows that 1 Jn 5.7 in the AV is spurious:
1. No patristic writings of the Sabellian or Arian eras cite this sentence to support their Christology, demonstrating that it must not have been in their copies of NT literature.
2. Except for the Old Latin text cited above, this sentence does not exist in any other extant ancient versions, e.g., Syriac, Coptic, Armenian, Ethiopic, Arabic, or Slavonic.
3. The sentence only begins to appear in some writings of Latin church fathers of the 5th century and in some MSS of the Old Latin Bible from the 6th century onwards.

The following internal evidence shows that 1 Jn 5.7 in the AV is spurious:
1. The Trinity appears as a spurious intrusion unrelated to the immediate context.
2. The two classes of witnesses are disconnected.
3. The NT never conjoins "the Father" and "the Word" together.
4. The Trinity as a witness in heaven seems unnecessary since there is no need for it.

Conclusion
Modern scholarship overwhelmingly dismisses as spurious the AV sentence in 1 Jn 5.7: "For there are three that bear record in heaven, the Father, the Word, and the Holy Spirit: and these three are one." No modern, Greek NT contains this sentence. Metzger says, "these words are spurious and have no right to stand in the New Testament."[501]

(Here is prime evidence that modern versions of the NT are generally superior to the AV because they are based on modern, and therefore improved, editions of the Greek NT. All modern editions of the Greek NT are superior to the TR because they are based on thousands of Greek MSS of the NT, or portions thereof, whereas the TR was based on only a bare few MSS that were not as old. When it comes to biblical MSS, older is better.)

10. Who is "the true God" in 1 John 5.20?

Introduction	*Houtos* Refers to God the Father
English Versions	Commentators
Houtos Refers to Jesus Christ	Conclusion

Introduction
Later church fathers unanimously cited 1 Jn 5.20 as a primary text which supports their belief that Christ is God. It is one of the major *theos* texts debated

---
[500] B.M. Metzger, *The Text of the New Testament*, 102.
[501] B.M. Metzger, *Textual Commentary*, 715.

by scholars as to whether it calls Christ God. It, and its preceding context, read as follows in the NASB:

19 We know that we are of God, and the whole world lies in the power of the evil one.
20 And we know that the Son of God has come, and has given us understanding, in order that we might know Him who is true, and we are in Him who is true, in His Son Jesus Christ. This is the true God and eternal life.

The christological debate regarding 1 Jn 5.20 is all about grammar. That is, what does the pronoun, "This" (Gr. *houtos*), refer to? If *houtos* refers to the nearest antecedent, as it usually does in English, which is "Jesus Christ," the passage indirectly calls Him "God." But if *houtos* refers to the subject of the previous clause, which is "Him who is true," which refers to "God" the Father, it does not call Jesus Christ "God."

English Versions
English versions do not render 1 Jn 5.20 alike, as may be gleaned below:

- "in him that is true, even in his Son Jesus Christ. This is the true God" (AV)
- "in him who is true, in his Son Jesus Christ. This is the true God" (RSV, ESV)
- "in him who is real, since we are in his Son Jesus Christ. This is the true God" (NEB)
- "in him who is true—even in his Son Jesus Christ. He is the true God" (NIV)
- "in the true God—in his Son Jesus Christ. This is the true God" (TEV)
- "in the true God, as we are in his Son, Jesus Christ. This is the true God" (JB)

Notice that the TEV and JB translate this portion of 1 Jn 5.20 so that "This" (*houtos*) seems to refer to God, who is the Father. Also, the NAB translates "Him who is true" and further provides Jn 17.3 and Eph 1.17 as marginal references for this phrase. This indicates its translators believed that *houtos* refers to God the Father. Furthermore, the NAB, REB, NRSV, and NJB render *houtos* as "He" rather than "This," which seems to refer back to "Him who is true," viz., God the Father.

Reasons for *Houtos* Referring to Jesus Christ
The view that *houtos* in 1 Jn 5.20 refers to "Jesus Christ," thus identifying Him as "the true God," dominated biblical scholarship from the 4th century until the last two centuries. Reasons that support this view, with corresponding rebuttals, are as follows:
1. Proper grammar requires that *houtos* refers to the immediately preceding antecedent, which is "Jesus Christ."
    Rebuttal: Such usage, while correct in modern English, has not been sufficiently proved to have been an established principle of Greek grammar when NT documents were written.[502] Furthermore, many Greek grammarian authorities, who surely would tend to favor a grammarian interpretation, identify the referent of *houtos* as the Father. For instance, J.H. Huther alleges, "the dispute cannot be settled on grammatical lines."[503] And B.F. Westcott explains, "As far as the grammatical

---
[502] Similarly, M. Harris, *Jesus as God*, 246.
[503] J.H. Huther, MCNT, 10:623.

construction of the sentence is concerned the pronoun *houtos* may refer either to 'Him that is true' or to 'Jesus Christ.' The most natural reference however is to the subject not locally nearest but dominant in the mind of the apostle ... This is obviously 'He that is true,' further described by the addition of 'His Son.' Thus the pronoun gathers up the revelation indicated in the words which precede ... [so] to know God as Father is eternal life."[504]

2. No author would be so repetitive, calling the Father "true" three times in a brief space.
   Rebuttals:
   a) Repetition is this author's style.
   b) The author is not repeating himself a third time but further identifying his previously vague expression—"the true One"—as "the true God."
   c) It is unlikely that in one verse an author would refer twice to the Father as "true" and then switch to calling Jesus Christ "true" without explication.
   d) This last sentence in 1 Jn 5.20 represents a summary of what precedes.

3. The expression "eternal life" must refer to Jesus Christ—making Him "the true God"—because Jesus Christ is called "life" in 1 Jn 1.1-2; Jn 11.25; 14.6.
   Rebuttal: But the prologue of 1 Jn shows clearly that eternal life originates solely "with the Father, and was manifested unto us" through "his Son Jesus Christ" (1 Jn 1.2-3; cf. 5.11). The Father is also called in Scripture, "the living God/Father" (e.g., Mt 26.63; Jn 6.57; 1 Thes 1.9). This is because He is the ultimate source of eternal life for all, including Christ (Jn 5.26; 6.57). Therefore, the words, "This is ... eternal life," in 1 Jn 5.20, more aptly apply to the Father.

4. Church fathers interpreted 1 Jn 5.20 as calling Christ "God."
   Rebuttal: The ante-Nicene fathers did not regard 1 Jn 5.20 as calling Jesus Christ "the true God" because they insisted that only the Father is so identified in Scripture. Recall from Chapter Two that the apologists believed that Christ was God, but not absolutely, i.e., without qualification. On the other hand, the Nicene and post-Nicene fathers, in their controversy with the Arians, did indeed adopt this interpretation of 1 Jn 5.20; but it was arguably on dogmatic rather than exegetical grounds.[505]

Reasons for *Houtos* Referring to God the Father

But in the last two centuries, many NT scholars have treated *houtos* in 1 Jn 5.20 as referring to God the Father. The following points sustain this view:

1. While the NT calls both the Father and Jesus Christ "true," it only calls the Father "the true God," in accordance with the OT and Judaism.[506] Paul calls

---

[504] B.F. Westcott, *The Epistles of St. John: The Greek Text with Notes* [1892], 3rd ed. (repr. Grand Rapids: Eerdmans, 1966), 196; J.A.T. Robinson, *Twelve More New Testament Studies*, 175.

[505] Henry Alford, *The Greek New Testament*, 4 vols. (London: Gilbert and Rivington, 1849-61), 2:514.

[506] Rudolf Bultmann, *The Johannine Epistles*, tr. Philip O'Hara (ET Philadelphia: Fortress, 1973), 89.

the Father, "a living and true God," while also distinguishing Him from "His Son" (1 Thes 1.9-10). Moreover, Jesus calling the Father "the only true God" in prayer, recorded in Jn 17.3, ought to finally settle this question in 1 Jn 5.20, that *houtos* refers to God the Father.[507]

2. *Houtos* must refer to the subject of the previous clause, and thus not the immediately preceding antecedent, because of the author's established practice of two similar constructions in these epistles. These are as follows:

   a) "For many deceivers have gone out into the world, those who do not acknowledge Jesus Christ as coming in the flesh. This is the deceiver and the antichrist" (2 Jn 7). Here, the author obviously did not intend for *houtos* ("This") to refer to the immediately preceding antecedents, "flesh" and "Jesus Christ."

   b) "Who is the liar but the one who denies that Jesus is the Christ? This is the antichrist" (1 Jn 2.22). Here, also, *houtos* ("This") obviously was not intended to modify the immediately preceding substantive, which is "Christ," but the subject of the immediately preceding clause—"the one" who denies Christ.

3. The central thought in v. 18 and thereafter is "God." C.H. Dodd is often quoted for explaining concerning 1 Jn 5.20, "The writer is gathering together in his mind all that he has been saying about God ... and *this*, he adds *is the real God,... is eternal life*."[508]

4. The warning in 1 Jn 5.21 to avoid (literal?) "idols," since idolatry permeated Roman culture, further suggests that "the true God" refers to the Father because God and idols are frequently contrasted in Jewish thought. In other words, this is an antithetical construction in which idols (and the gods they represent) are implicitly characterized as false whereas the one God, i.e., the Father, is "true."

5. Since the author has just written that "no man has ever seen God" (1 Jn 4.12 RSV; cf. Jn 6.46), he would seem to be contradicting himself if he intended to call the visible man—Jesus Christ—"God" in 1 Jn 5.20.

6. The author uses the word "God" elsewhere in this epistle in three different ways, and in all three he demonstrates that he does not intend to call Christ "God" in 1 Jn 5.20: (1) he uses the words "God" and "the Father" interchangeably, showing that they are synonymous; (2) he juxtapositions "God" and "the/his Son" (1 Jn 4.9-10, 14-15; 5.9-11), thereby distinguishing them; and (3) he calls Christ "his Son," indicating God's possession (1 Jn 1.3, 7; 4.10; 5.9-11), as he does in the expression in the genitive case, "the Son of God" (1 Jn 3.8; 4.15; 5.12-13).

7. The brief, second sentence in v. 20 is a summary of the longer, preceding sentence.

---

[507] J.A.T. Robinson (*Twelve More New Testament Studies*, 175) contends that the last sentence in 1 Jn 5.20 "deliberately echoes" the similar language in Jn 17.3.
[508] C.H. Dodd, *The Johannine Epistles*, in MNTC (1946), 140. Emphasis his.

Commentators

Scholarly opinion is about evenly divided on whether *houtos* in 1 Jn 5.20 refers to the preceding "Jesus Christ" or "God."[509] A few notable commentators think the question is irresolvable. Walter Bauer says of both 1 Jn 5.20 and 2 Pt 1.1> that "the interpretation is open to question."[510] William Barclay decides likewise, saying, "It is hardly possible to be certain ... the doubt is such that we could not base any firm argument on the passage."[511]

Conclusion

All arguments considered, it seems doubtful that the author of 1 John intended to call Jesus Christ "God" in 1 Jn 5.20, especially without providing any explanation for it. Regardless, this verse provides no more than tenuous support for traditional Christology.

---

[509] M. Harris, *Jesus as God*, 240. For a listing of scholars, see Ezra Abbot, "On the Construction of Titus ii.13," *JBL* 1 (1881): 19; R.E. Brown, *The Epistles of John*, 625; M Harris, *Jesus as God*, 249, 253. Modern traditionalist authorities who do not interpret that 1 Jn 5.20 calls Jesus "God" include V. Taylor, A.W. Wainwright, and M. Harris; those who do think it calls Jesus "God" include E. Stauffer, O. Cullmann, R.E. Brown (probable), and R.N. Longenecker. R. Bultmann (*Gospel of John: A Commentary*, 695n4) is representative of most historical critics who think it "is doubtful" that *houtos* here refers to Jesus.

[510] BAGD, 357.

[511] W. Barclay, *Jesus As They Saw Him*, 26.

Chapter Seven
Christology of Paul

A. Introduction

Saul the Pharisee	Adam Christology
Paul the Monotheistic Theologian	God-in-Christ Christology
Paul the Evangelist	Lordship Christology
Paul's Gospel	Yahweh Texts Applied to Jesus
Keeping the Gospel Pure	Subordination Christology
Only the Father is God	The Invisibility and Immortality of God
The God and Father of Jesus Christ	"Maranatha"
Distinguishing God and Christ	The Spirit & Kingdom of God & Christ
Distinguishing God and His Son	The Preexistence of Jesus?
Christ as the Perfect Image of God	The Cosmic Christ
	Summary

To embark on a quest for the historical Jesus, or to discover Christian orgins, it is incumbent upon the researcher to reach as far back in history as possible. In doing so, we encounter a man named "Paul."

This Paul had an enormous impact on the dissemination of the Christian gospel. He also had a major influence on the doctrinal development of early Christianity. Yet Paul never met the earthly Jesus. Paul was converted two to four years after the Christ event, at about the age of twenty-four. He became an apostle, meaning "one sent out," when the church at Antioch sent him out to preach (Ac 13.4). Since Paul was not one of the twelve apostles he had to constantly defend his apostleship (e.g., 1 Cor 9.2).

The Apostle Paul wrote several letters to his associates in ministry and various churches in cities. His extant letters comprise more than one-fourth of the NT.[1] This corpus is superseded quantitatively only by the writings of Paul's missionary accomplice, Dr. Luke. Also, Paul probably wrote his letters earlier than all of the other NT documents except James. Therefore, the christological statements contained in Paul's letters express a viewpoint formed soon after the Christ event. Most significantly, Paul's letters provide several partial credal statements and hymnal fragments which he borrowed from other Christians

---

[1] Historical critics usually assess the pastoral epistles as non-Pauline. Herein, Paul is regarded as the author.

that reflect a prior Christology.² Regarding identity Christology in the NT, Paul's life and letters are perhaps only surpassed in importance by the NT gospels.

Saul the Pharisee

Paul was a Jew born in a Gentile land, in the city of Tarsus, Cilicia (present Turkey). Apparently, his Jewish name was "Saul" and his Roman name was "Paul."

Saul came from a family of Pharisees (Ac 22.3; 23.6). The Pharisees were the strictest of the three major sects of Judaism (Ac 26.5). The other two were the Sadducees and the Essenes. The Pharisees distinguished themselves by their devotion to the study of all the Scriptures they held sacred. Their tripartite Scriptures consisted of the Torah, the Prophets, and the Writings, i.e., the entire Hebrew Bible, called the "Tanakh" in Hebrew. Josephus relates that during the 1st century, Pharisees were well respected by the Jewish populace and recognized as the preeminent experts in interpreting the Tanakh.³

As a Pharisee, Saul's education would have begun at home, with his father as his instructor. At about age five, Saul's formal education would have begun at the synagogue school in his hometown of Tarsus. Boys were required to study the Torah and the Hebrew language from perhaps about age five to age thirteen. After that, Paul relates that he was "brought up in this city [Jerusalem], educated under Gamaliel, strictly according to the law of our fathers, being zealous for God" (Ac 22.3; cf. 26.4). Gamaliel was a prominent Jewish rabbi and leader of the Pharisees. Paul further testifies that, concerning "my former manner of life in Judaism,... I was advancing in Judaism beyond many of my contemporaries among my countrymen, being more extremely zealous for my ancestral traditions" (Gal 1.13-14).

This Saul was a religious zealot who violently opposed the new Jesus Movement.⁴ He later testified, "I thought to myself that I had to do many things hostile to the name of Jesus of Nazareth. And this is just what I did in Jerusalem; not only did I lock up many of the saints in prisons, having received authority from the chief priests, but also when they were being put to death I cast my vote against them. And as I punished them often in all the synagogues, I tried to force them to blaspheme; and being furiously enraged at them, I kept pursuing them even to the foreign cities" (Ac 26.9-11).

While Saul was journeying from Jerusalem to Damascus to undertake one of his hostile missions against Jewish Christians, he had a vision of Jesus speaking to him that instantly and dramatically converted him to faith in Jesus (Ac 9.1-19; 22.3-21; 26.4-18). For the remainder of his life he went by his Roman name Paul, traveling in much of the Roman world conducting an evangelistic, church-planting missionary movement. As a result, this indefatigable worker had a profound impact on the history of Christianity.

Partly because of Paul's background as a Pharisee, Hans Kung observes, "Paul can only be understood from his origin in Judaism."⁵

---

² Both V. Taylor (*Person of Christ*, 35-37) and R. Bultmann (*Theology of the New Testament*, 1:27, 46-47, 50-52, 81, 98, 125, 129, 131-32) observe that Paul demonstrates some originality, but that he largely adopts primitive church Christology, witnessed by his frequent inclusion of credal and hymnal fragments.
³ Josephus, *The Life of Flavius Josephus*, 38; idem, *Wars of the Jews*, 2.8.14.
⁴ Ac 8.1-3; 9.1-2; 22.4-5, 19-20; Gal 1.13, 23; 1 Cor 15.9.
⁵ H. Kung, *Christianity: Essence, History, and Future*, 91.

Paul, the Monotheistic Theologian

As a former Pharisee, Paul used his knowledge of (OT) Scripture to become an astute Christian theologian.[6] The OT was a very important source of teaching for Paul, just as it was for most of the other early Jewish Christians.[7] His doctrines of God and the Messiah were firmly rooted in the OT. That is partly why Paul is never accused in the book of Acts of abandoning his monotheistic, ancestral tradition.[8] V. Taylor observes, "First, we note the dominating place of monotheism in St. Paul's Christology.... Always in his Christological statements the emphasis is upon God."[9] Indeed, even as a Christian theologian the Apostle Paul remained very monotheistic.

So, Paul clearly affirmed the Shema in his epistles, that God is numerically "one." He wrote to the saints at Rome that "God ... is one" (Rom 3.30). And he completed this epistle with the doxology, "to the only wise God, through Jesus Christ, be the glory forever" (Rom 16.27). Paul also wrote to the Galatians that "God is only one" (Gal 3.20). And in his first epistle to Timothy, Paul describes the Father as "the only God," and more explicitly, "for there is one God" (1 Tim 1.17; 2.5). *But the two most prominent Pauline statements that reflect the Shema and clearly establish that (1) there is one God, the God of the OT, (2) this one God is the Father only, and (3) this one God and Jesus Christ are to be distinguished as two separate beings, so that Jesus Christ is not God, are 1 Cor 8.4, 6 and Eph 4.4-6.* These two passages allude to the Shema and read as follows:

- "We know that ... there is no God but one.... there is but one God, the Father, from whom are all things, and we exist for Him; and one Lord, Jesus Christ, by whom are all things, and we exist through Him" (1 Cor 8.4, 6).[10]
- "There is ... one Lord, one faith, one baptism, one God and Father of all" (Eph 4.4-6)

Some scholars think these two texts may be pre-Pauline confessional statements. Frances Young rightly concludes from these verses concerning Paul and his converts, "their God was the God of the Old Testament and their Lord, Jesus, was 'God's Vicegerent [sic].'"[11] It is surprising how not a few traditionalist scholars cite 1 Cor 8.6 to support that Jesus is God since it says all things are by Him, but they ignore it says that only the Father is God.

All of the above allusions to the Shema are clear evidence that the Apostle Paul never recoiled from his upbringing in strict Jewish monotheism.[12] As V. Taylor rather cleverly puts it of this dedicated apostle of Christ, "He will not compromise his belief that God is One God, not even for Christ's sake."[13] Thus,

---

[6] Eminent NT textual critic Kurt Aland (*The Text of the New Testament*, 52) calls Paul a "rabbinic scholar."
[7] Maurice F. Wiles, *The Making of Christian Doctrine* (Cambridge: University, 1967), 42.
[8] P.M. Casey, "The Deification of Jesus," 704.
[9] V. Taylor, *The Person of Christ*, 60; idem, "Does the New Testament Call Jesus God?" 116.
[10] Some church fathers and recent traditionalist scholars have cited 1 Cor 8.6 as evidence that Jesus is God, either because it affirms His Lordship or implies He preexisted. N.T. Wright ("'Constraints' and the Jesus of History," *SJT* 39 [1986]: 208-09) asserts concerning Jesus' Lordship in 1 Cor 8.6 that it automatically includes Him within Jewish monotheism and thus affirms the incarnation. So does L.W. Hurtado (*At the Origins of Christian Worship*, 97). D. Cupitt (*Jesus and the Gospel of God*, 18-19) refutes this view, and K. Kuschel (*Born Before All Time?* 285-91) cites several distinguished contemporary scholars who do too. J.D.G. Dunn (*Christology in the Making*, 182) says of 1 Cor 8.6, "It asserts simply that Christ is the action of God, Christ embodies the creative power of God. In other words, Christ is being identified here not with a pre-existent being but with the creative power of God."
[11] F. Young, "A Cloud of Witnesses," 20.
[12] Contra M. Harris, *Jesus as God*, 167.
[13] V. Taylor, *The Person of Christ*, 60; idem, "Does the New Testament Call Jesus God?" 116.

Paul's clear teaching on this unity (oneness) of God does not allow for either of the later church doctrines of Binitarianism or Trinitarianism.[14] Preeminent Jewish scholar Joseph Klausner is therefore correct, "Paul the Jew did not go so far as to call Jesus "God.""[15] Albert Schweitzer stated likewise, "The Pauline Christ, even though He is called the Son of God, is not God."[16]

Paul the Evangelist

The earliest NT accounts of the early Christians preaching evangelistically are in the book of Acts and Paul's letters. A cursory reading of these texts reveals that the core of Paul's evangelistic message was no different than that of Peter or the other apostles; they all preached that two cardinal elements of Jesus' identity were that He was *the Christ* and *the Son of God*. After Paul was converted to faith in Jesus, "immediately he began to proclaim Jesus in the synagogues, saying, 'He is the Son of God'" (Ac 9.20). And Paul was "confounding the Jews who lived at Damascus by proving that this Jesus is the Christ" (v. 22). Paul attempted to prove that Jesus was Israel's Messiah by citing OT messianic prophecies and interpreting them as having been fulfilled in Jesus' life, death, and resurrection. Paul thereafter undertook his missionary journeys throughout many Mediterranean countries, "testifying to the Jews that Jesus was the Christ" (Ac 18.5). Again, we read that "he powerfully refuted the Jews in public, demonstrating by the Scriptures that Jesus was the Christ" (v. 28; cf. 17.3). As with Paul's strict monotheism, there is no evidence that he ever altered this basic message by proclaiming Jesus as God.

Paul's Gospel

So, we learn from the NT that Paul traveled about the Mediterranean world preaching "the gospel." What is the gospel?

"Gospel" means "good news." Jesus preached "the gospel of the kingdom (of God/heaven)" (e.g., Mt 4.23; 9.35; 24.14; Lk 16.16; cf. Mk 1.15). It means that God reigns supreme as sovereign king in this kingdom or realm. Jesus taught how to enter it (e.g., Jn 3.3-8). And He once mentioned how Isaiah prophesied the "good news" about this kingdom.[17]

But we saw in Chapter Six that Mark the Evangelist begins his book, "The gospel of Jesus Christ." Is there a difference between the gospel of the kingdom of God and the gospel of Jesus Christ? Slightly. The principal good news that the twelve apostles first preached was that Jesus was risen from the dead (Ac 2.22-32; 3.15; 4.10, 33). But that wasn't all there was to the core of their gospel about Jesus.

When Paul wrote his letters, addressed to believers, he usually cared most about imparting knowledge of the soteriological benefits of the gospel. Sometimes he defined his evangelistic message in "the/my gospel" (Rom 2.16; 16.25; 2 Tim 2.8). For instance, he wrote to the church at Corinth, explaining that "the gospel" is "that Christ died for our sins according to the Scriptures, and that He was buried, and that He was raised on the third day according to the Scriptures," and that He afterwards appeared to many of the disciples

---

[14] Contemporary Pauline scholars who do not think Paul believed that Jesus was God include the following: R. Scroggs, *Christology in Paul and John*, 52; J.D.G. Dunn, *Unity and Diversity*, 53; idem, *The Theology of Paul the Apostle* (Edinburgh: T&T Clark, 1998), 255-57.

[15] J. Klausner, *The Messianic Idea in Israel*, 528.

[16] Albert Schweitzer, *Paul and His Interpreters: A Critical History* [1912], tr. W. Montgomery (New York: MacMillan, 1951), 223.

[17] Mt 11.5/Lk 7.22 cf. with Isa 35.5-6; 40.9; 52.7; 61.1.

(1 Cor 15.1-8). Paul further explains, in what may be an adopted credal formula,[18] "that if you confess with your mouth Jesus as Lord, and believe in your heart that God raised Him from the dead, you shall be saved" (Rom 10.9).

So, Paul preached and wrote that for people to be saved—to enter the kingdom of God and thus possess eternal life—they must do two things: (1) genuinely *believe* that Jesus is the Christ, the Son of God, that He died for their sins, was entombed, was raised from the dead, and (2) publicly *confess* Jesus as "Lord," which involves some degree of obedience to Jesus' teachings. In all of the definitions of his gospel (e.g., Rom 1.1-4; 1 Cor 15.1-8), as well as his evangelistic sermons and testimonials recorded in the book of Acts,[19] *Paul never wrote or proclaimed that Jesus was God.*

Paul was a careful, theological logician. He surely would not have failed to clarify that Jesus is God if that was indeed what he believed, and he certainly would not have refrained from boldly preaching it. Which is greater, that Jesus is the Christ, the Son of God, or that He is God? The answer is obviously the latter.

The fact that Paul, a Jew, often wrote his letters in response to known problems in churches, many of which were doctrinal, makes it evident that he did not preach or teach that Jesus was God. If he had, he surely would have mentioned it in his letters. Paul's letters contain much evidence of controversy in these churches,[20] and these were of far less importance than this issue would have been, especially to Jews.

Second century church father Justin Martyr, a Gentile, is a case in point. He wrote a lengthy tome, entitled *Dialogue with Trypho*, which is a conversation between himself and a Jew named "Trypho." In chapters 48-64, Justin attempts to convince Trypho that Jesus was and is God. He concludes, "Now I have proved at length that Christ is called God."[21] By this time, there was nothing Jews and Christians disagreed about more than whether the Messiah would be God. If Paul had preached, as Justin, that Jesus was God, we surely would learn in his letters of the controversy it would have stirred among Jews.

Keeping the Gospel Pure

In fact, Paul became quite concerned about the veracity of his gospel message. He wanted to ensure that it did not differ from that of Jesus' apostles who had preceded him, as if he was preaching in vain. Consequently, seventeen years after Paul's conversion this successful yet humble and determined servant of God traveled to Jerusalem to procure the apostles' scrutiny of his gospel message. Paul writes, "I submitted to them the gospel which I preach among the Gentiles" (Gal 2.2). Paul relates that their judgment was that his gospel was substantially the same as their own (Gal 2.7-10; cf. Ac 15).

We have seen that many traditionalists now concede to the critics' allegation that traditional Christology represents a substantial change from the primitive Christology. But they usually insist that the church was divinely authorized to do so. If true, then why did the Apostle Paul feel compelled to submit His gospel to His predecessors for their approval? Was it not because Paul wanted to be sure that He had not changed the original gospel about Jesus Christ, the gospel that was handed down by Jesus' twelve apostles?

---

[18] R. Bultmann, *Theology of the New Testament*, 1:81.
[19] E.g., Ac 13.16-41; 17.22-31; 22.3-21; 23.1-6; 24.10-21; 26.2-29.
[20] P.M. Casey, "The Deification of Jesus," 702-03.
[21] Justin Martyr, *Dialogue with Trypho*, 124.11.

According to the NT, Paul had much experience defending his gospel. He went out preaching it everywhere—synagogues, marketplaces, wherever. But whenever he did so, and he was confronted and forced to defend his gospel, like the apostles before him he never went christologically beyond identifying Jesus as the Christ, the Son of God.

Thus, Paul took great care in protecting what he called the "simplicity and purity" of his gospel (2 Cor 11.3), and he challenged others to do likewise. For example, he cautioned the church at Corinth to discriminate "if one comes and preaches another Jesus whom we have not preached,... or a different gospel" (v. 4). Paul likewise warned the brethren of Galatia not "to distort the gospel of Christ" with unnecessary additions and thereby create "a different gospel" (Gal 1.6-7). He declared most solemnly, "But even though we, or an angel from heaven, should preach to you a gospel contrary to that which we have preached to you, let him be accursed.... if any man is preaching to you a gospel contrary to that which you received, let him be accursed" (Gal 1.8-9; cf. 2 Tim 2.2). According to these solemn statements, some might question whether preaching that Jesus is "God" is "another Jesus" and "a different gospel" from the one Paul preached.

Regardless, *Paul absolutely forbade altering the gospel he preached and passed on to others.* Neither did he tolerate theological speculation of his gospel and Jesus' identity. Paul wrote about his missionary teams, "We are destroying speculations and every lofty thing raised up against the knowledge of God" (2 Cor 10.5).

These excerpts from Paul's letters suggest that he would have disagreed with later church fathers in their development of Christology by changing the primitive gospel of Jesus as no more than a man to His being God. *The original gospel of Jesus Christ did not need to be developed; it already was. Paul merely expected his successors to receive and preach it as he had, not to change it.* Paul surely would have objected to Carl Braaten saying, "A Christology that settles for anything less than the true divinity of Jesus Christ, along with his full humanity, has ripped the heart out of the gospel."[22]

Only the Father Is God

In Paul's letters, he constantly follows Jesus' practice of identifying "God" as "the Father." And Paul implies that *the Father is exclusively God* by conjoining the two terms fourteen times to form the expression "God the Father" or "God our Father" (Gr. *theou patros [amon]*).[23] These expressions are always anarthrous (without the article), being translated literally "(our) God Father." Interestingly, this expression, "God the/our Father," never appears in the NT gospels, and its development seems to have preceded Paul.

The expression, "God the Father," is not a NT category to be distinguished from the term "God" (or "godhead/Godhead"), as Trinitarians imply and some expressly assert. If it was, in accordance with Trinitarianism we also ought to expect to read the expression "God the Son" in Paul's writings, if not elsewhere in the NT. But we don't.

Perhaps nowhere in Paul's corpus is it more evident that he believed that the Father is exclusively God than in his use of the expression "the/our God and Father" (Gr. *[ho] theos kai pater [amon]*), which occurs twelve times.[24] In each

---

[22] Carl E. Braaten, "The Significance of New Testament Christology for Systematic Theology," in *Who Do You Say that I Am?: Essays on Christology*, ed. Mark Allan Powell and David R. Bauer, 225.

[23] 1 Cor 1.3; 2 Cor 1.2; Gal 1.1; Phil 2.11; Col 1.2, 3; 3.17; 1 Thes 1.1; 2 Thes 1.1, 2; 1 Tim 1.2; 2 Tim 1.2; Tit 1.4; cf. 2 Thes 2.16.

[24] Rom 15.6; 1 Cor 15.24; 2 Cor 1.3; 11.31; Gal 1.4; Eph 1.3; 4.6; 5.20; Phil 4.20; 1 Th 1.3; 3.11, 13.

instance, the two Greek nouns are joined together with the conjunction "and." English versions sometimes translate it "God, even the Father," as in Eph 5.20.[25] This gives the same sense as "one God and Father," as in Eph 4.6. The addition of the conjunction "and" strongly suggests that God is exclusively the Father.

Paul, more than any other NT author, constantly interchanges the words "God" and "the Father." This praxis even further indicates that Paul believed that *only the Father is God*. Roman Catholic Trinitarian theologian Karl Rahner asserts that whenever *ho theos* appears in not only the Pauline corpus but the entire Greek NT, it never refers to the triune God but always to "the Father," with the possible exception of 1 Jn 5.20>.[26]

The Apostle Paul taught that prayer generally should be directed to the one God, the Father.[27] Paul often does this in his letters right after his salutations, in which he gives thanks to God the Father for those to whom he writes.[28] Paul repeatedly states elsewhere in his letters that praying to the Father is both his practice and that of other Christians.[29] When he so informs he often mentions Christ, thus distinguishing God and Christ; yet he does not acknowledge directing such prayers to Christ. Paul often explains that he prays to God *through* Christ,[30] praying in Jesus' name, as Jesus taught. Geza Vermes observes, "Paul's prayers and liturgical blessings are regularly addressed to God or the Father, and not to, though often through, Jesus Christ."[31] Paul can, however, pray to either the Father or Jesus when he asks for strength (e.g., 2 Cor 12.8-10; Eph 3.14-16; cf. Phil 4.13).

The God and Father of Jesus Christ

Just as the OT calls Yahweh "the God of Abraham, the God of Isaac, and the God of Jacob" (Ex 3.6; cf. Mk 12.26 par.), so the Apostle Paul occasionally writes likewise about *the God of Jesus Christ*. He says God is the Father of Jesus Christ and, conversely, that the Father is the God of Jesus Christ. These Pauline portions are as follows:

- "the God and Father of our Lord Jesus Christ" (Rom 15.6; 2 Cor 1.3; Eph 1.3)
- "The God and Father of the Lord Jesus" (2 Cor 11.31)
- "the God of our Lord Jesus Christ, the Father of glory" (Eph 1.17)
- "God, the Father of our Lord Jesus Christ" (Col 1.3)

Notice that all of these passages can be read, "(the) God ... of ... Jesus (Christ)."

Conversely, the NT never says that Jesus Christ is "the God" of the Father. The implication is obvious: *if Paul says that Jesus Christ has a God, who is the Father, and Paul also says that there is only one God, then, for Paul, Jesus Christ cannot be God.*

Paul can also call the Father "our God" or "my God" (e.g., 1 Cor 1.3-4; Phil 1.2-3; 4.19-20). Conversely, he never calls Jesus Christ "our God" or "my God," as Ignatius often does. In fact, in Rom 1.8 Paul even distinguishes between "my God" and "Jesus Christ." The God of the Apostle Paul, this former Pharisee, is the God of his fathers (Ac 24.14; cf. 22.14; 2 Tim 1.3), the God of the OT, who is none other than Yahweh.

---

[25] This is how W. Bauer (BAGD, 391) renders it in 1 Cor 15.24; 2 Cor 1.3; 11.31; Eph 1.3; Jam 1.27.
[26] K. Rahner, *Theological Investigations*, 1:135, 143, 146.
[27] P.M. Casey, "Monotheism, Worship and Christological Development in the Pauline Churches," in *The Jewish Roots of Christological Monotheism*, ed. C.C. Newman et al., 219-20.
[28] Rom 1.8; 1 Cor 1.4; Phil 1.3-4; Col 1.3; 1 Thes 1.2; 2 Thes 1.3; 2 Tim 1.3; Philemon 1.4.
[29] E.g., Rom 6.17; 10.1; 15.30; 1 Cor 1.14; 11.13; 14.18; 2 Cor 2.14; 8.16; 9.12, 15; 13.7; Eph 1.16-17; Phil 4.6; Col 1.12; 3.16; 4.3; 1 Th 2.13; 3.9; 2 Th 2.13; cf. Rom 1.10; 1 Tim 2.1-3; 5.5.
[30] E.g., Rom 1.8; 7.25; Col 3.17; cf. 1 Cor 15.57; Eph 5.20.
[31] G. Vermes, *The Changing Faces of Jesus*, 79, cf. 80, 97.

Distinguishing God and Christ

Paul also repeatedly distinguishes "God" and "(Jesus) Christ" in his letters, as the above juxtapositioning reveals. In fact, he does so more than any other NT writer. Paul often does it without using the fuller expression, "God the Father." He does so in many ways, most notably regarding God's involvement in the foremost events of Jesus' life: (1) God sending His Son (e.g., Rom 8.3; Gal 4.4), (2) God raising Jesus Christ from the dead (e.g., Rom 8.34; 10.9; 1 Cor 6.14; Gal 1.1), and (3) God inviting Jesus Christ to sit with Him in His heavenly throne at His right hand (e.g., Rom 8.34; Col 3.1; cf. Ps 110.1).

Since juxtapositioning indicates distinction,[32] this practice also reveals that Paul regards God exclusively as the Father. Nowhere in Paul's letters is this literary style more prominent than in his salutations. They consistently mention "God the/your Father" and "(Jesus) Christ" with the same or a very similar wording. For example, the following sentence appears verbatim in the salutation of seven of Paul's ten NT letters: "Grace to you and peace from God our Father and the Lord Jesus Christ."[33] And Paul's three other salutations have a similar wording with regard to God and Christ.[34] Moreover, in all of these epistolary salutations Paul first mentions God the Father and immediately thereafter mentions the Lord Jesus Christ. This consistent order further suggests that Paul regards God the Father as superior, and therefore essentially preeminent, to Jesus Christ.

Many NT commentators acknowledge that Paul characteristically distinguishes God and Christ. H.A.W. Meyer even asserts that Paul "*always* accurately distinguishes God and Christ."[35] And Ezra Abbot admits, "I do not see how anyone can read the Epistles of Paul without perceiving that,... he constantly uses *theos* as a *proper name*, as the designation of the Father in distinction from Christ."[36]

Furthermore, Paul mentions both God and Christ in these salutations without ever mentioning the Holy Spirit. In light of Trinitarianism, this silence is most conspicuous. Such an omission strongly suggests that the Apostle Paul did not regard the Holy Spirit as co-equal with God the Father and/or Jesus Christ.

Regarding the doctrine of the Trinity, Paul has several triadic formulas in his corpus. In most of them he specifies "God" without further identifying Him as "the Father" (Rom 15.30; 1 Cor 12.4-6; 2 Cor 13.14; Gal 4.6; 2 Thes 2.13).[37] This evidence suggests that Paul assumes that his readers know quite well that "God" is "the Father." In contrast, Trinitarians constantly feel compelled to identify "God" as "the Father" in their triadic statements in order to distinguish this so-called "First Member" of the Trinity from the triune Godhead.

What must be concluded from all of this Pauline evidence is this: *for the Apostle Paul, "God" is exclusively "the Father," so that there can be no one else who is God*. Accordingly, Binitarianism and Trinitarianism would have been

---

[32] M. Harris, *Jesus as God*, 42.
[33] Rom 1.7; 1 Cor 1.3; 2 Cor 1.2 (cf. v. 3); Gal 1.3; Eph 1.2 (cf. vv. 3, 17); Phil 1.2; Philemon 3.
[34] Col 1.3; 1 Thes 1.1; 2 Thes 1.1-2; 1 Tim 1.2; 2 Tim 1.2; Tit 1.4.
[35] H.A.W. Meyer, MCNT, 5:119. Emphasis not mine.
[36] Ezra Abbot, "On the Construction of Romans ix5," *JBL* (1881): 121. Emphasis not mine.
[37] To identify any scriptural quotations as "Trinitarian" is an anachronistic use of that term, suggesting that those texts affirm Trinitarianism. On this see Gerd Ludemann, *Heretics: The Other Side of Early Christianity* [1995], tr. John Bowden (Louisville, KT: Westminster John Knox, 1996), 187n635.

foreign concepts to the Apostle Paul's mind since they would have clashed with his strict monotheistic theology.

Distinguishing God and His Son

Neither did Paul obliterate the distinction between the terms "God" and "the Son (of God)," as post-apostolic church fathers did. Some modern expositors still continue in this error. For instance, Herman Ridderbos writes most succinctly that for Paul, "Christ's being the Son of God is none other than being God himself."[38] On the contrary, Paul often distinguishes the epithets "God" and "the Son of God" or the like,[39] just as he does with "God" and "Christ." Yet Paul only uses the expression "the Son of God" four times and "the/His Son" thirteen times in his corpus. Vincent Taylor rightly explains of Paul's writings, "In the passages which speak of 'the Son' and 'His Son' a new point emerges; the terminology is used because Jesus Christ is mentioned over against God."[40]

So, for Paul "the Son of God" is a relational expression which he applies to Christ to *distinguish* Him from "God." Jewish scholar Geza Vermes says, "Paul's subconscious Jewish mind instinctively distinguished between God the Father and the Son of God. His prayers are automatically addressed to the Father either directly or through the mediation of the Christ Jesus, the Son, who is above ordinary mortals, but indubitably below the transcendent deity." Vermes concludes, "Paul stops short of declaring Jesus divine."[41]

Interestingly, approximately twenty-five times in Paul's corpus he gives thanks "to God" without adding the qualifying word "Father." This evidence shows that (1) Paul regarded the Father as the preeminent recipient of thanksgiving, and (2) he did not deem it necessary to append the words "the Father" because he expected his readers to know that only the Father is God. Twice Paul thanks God "through Jesus Christ" (Rom 1.8; 7.25; cf. Col 3.17). Only once does he qualify his thanksgiving "to God, the Father" (Col 1.3). And only once does he write that he gives thanks "to the Father" without appending the word "God" (Col 1.12). And, again, only once does Paul thank Christ when he says, "I thank Jesus Christ our Lord," adding, "who has strengthened me" (1 Tim 1.12).

Paul may hint that the church will not achieve unity and a correct understanding about Jesus being the Son of God until the end of the age. For he writes to the saints at Ephesus about Christ giving gifted men to the church for its edification, "until we all attain to the unity of the faith and of the knowledge of the Son of God, to a mature man, to the measure of the stature which belongs to the fulness of Christ" (Eph 4.13).

Christ as the Perfect Image of God

Paul is the only NT writer who describes Jesus Christ as God's "image" (Gr. *eikon*=Eng. "icon"). He writes of "Christ, who is the image of God" (2 Cor 4.4), and "He is the image of the invisible God, the first-born of all creation" (Col 1.15).[42]

---

[38] Herman Ridderbos, *Paul: An Outline of His Theology* [1966], tr. John Richard De Witt (Grand Rapids: Eerdmans, 1975), 77.
[39] E.g., Rom 1.1-4, 9; 5.10; 8.3, 28-29; 1 Cor 1.9; 15.28; Gal 4.4; 1 Thes 1.9-10.
[40] V. Taylor, *The Person of Christ*, 46.
[41] G. Vermes, *The Changing Faces of Jesus*, 80, 108, cf. 79.
[42] Arius employed this passage and Rev 3.14 to support his view that the preexistent Logos-Son had a beginning. On the contrary, "first-born" is not to be taken literally and ontologically, but as a metaphor referring to Christ's preeminence over creation due to His resurrection (vv. 17-18; Rom 8.29; cf. Gen 49.3).

Some Christians have thought that Jesus' status as "the image of God" indicates that He is God. On the contrary, "God created man in His own image, in the image of God He created him; male and female He created them" (Gen 1.27). Although Adam and Eve were made in the image of God, this status did not make them Gods.

Even Jesus being the perfect image of God by means of His sinlessness does not make Him God. Geza Vermes rightly states, "Paul described Christ as the 'likeness,' or icon, of God ... it cannot be taken as being anywhere close to inferring divinity."[43]

The word "image" can be defined as "an imitation or a representation of a person or thing."[44] A good example is a reflection in a mirror. So, an image is a representation of an original, not the original itself. That is what the writer of the book of Hebrews means in describing Jesus as "the exact representation" of God's nature (Heb 1.3), which echoes the correct interpretation of Jn 1.1c. Traditionalist C.K. Barrett states concerning Jesus, "what Christians behold is not God, viewed directly; such direct vision is not for this world." Barrett further explains that Jesus Christ is "the means by which the invisible God becomes visible."[45] Aloys Grillmeier puts it similarly by remarking, "*God* himself becomes visible in Christ, his image."[46] That is exactly what Jesus meant when He said, "He who has seen Me has seen the Father" (Jn 14.9). Logically, it must be concluded that Jesus cannot be both the image of God and God Himself, who is invisible to mortals.

Adam Christology

Designating Jesus Christ as the perfect image of God alludes to the first man, Adam. In fact, "adam" is the Hebrew word for "man." As stated above, "God created man in His own image," that is, "in the likeness of God" (Gen 1.27; 5.3; cf. 9.6).

The Apostle Paul is unique as a NT author by teaching in his letters a contrast between Adam and Jesus (Rom 5.14-19; 1 Cor 15.45-47; cf. Phil 2.6). Scholars call this contrast "Adam Christology." Paul compares Adam and Jesus by relating that Jesus was the ideal, archetypal man whereas Adam, who apparently was created for this purpose, did not attain that lofty goal. Instead, Adam failed the test that God put before him in the Garden of Eden and thereby brought ruination upon the earth and all of humankind.

Paul expounds an Adam Christology by calling Jesus Christ "the second man" (1 Cor 15.47). And he writes that Adam was "a type of Him who was to come," viz., Jesus Christ (Rom 5.14). Paul further explains, "So also it is written, 'The first man, Adam, became a living soul.' The last Adam [Jesus] became a life-giving spirit" (1 Cor 15.45; cf. Gen 2.7). Since this last verse appears credal, many scholars have thought that Adam Christology was quite primitive, widespread, and did not originate with Paul.[47]

Adam Christology signifies that Jesus became what God originally had intended man to be.[48] What Adam lost through the fall, Jesus more than gained

---

[43] G. Vermes, *The Changing Faces of Jesus*, 109.
[44] *Webster's New Universal Unabridged Dictionary*, deluxe 2nd ed. (New York: Simon and Schuster, 1983).
[45] C.K. Barrett, *A Commentary on the Second Epistle to the Corinthians*, in HNTC (1973), 125.
[46] A. Grillmeier, *Christ in Christian Tradition*, 25. Emphasis his.
[47] E.g., J.D.G. Dunn, *Christology in the Making*, 114-15, 125. Other distinguished, scholarly proponents of Adam Christology include O. Cullmann, J. Murphy-O'Connor, M.D. Hooker, and there are many more.
[48] J.D.G. Dunn, "Was Christianity a Monotheistic Faith from the Beginning," 327.

by means of His righteous life, suffering, and atoning death for others. The first man—Adam—disobeyed God and thereby marred his created status as the image of God; the last Adam—Jesus—perfectly obeyed God, attained the divine goal as the Righteous One, and in the future will consummate a complete restoration of what Adam lost.

In Chapter Two, we learned that many traditionalists have insisted that Jesus had to be God because only God could live a sinless life and thus qualify as the Redeemer. But this notion is arbitrary, without scriptural support, and contrary to Adam Christology. E. Flesseman-van Leer explains that Jesus' "complete obedience was not superhuman,... Jesus acted in harmony with being man,... and we act in conflict with it."[49]

Furthermore, according to Adam Christology, Jesus was the exact counterpart of Adam. That is, *Jesus was just as human as Adam was. In order for this to be so, Jesus had to have been just as capable of disobeying God and becoming a sinner as Adam was*. But if Jesus was God, He could not have been capable of sinning because "God cannot be tempted by evil" and therefore sin (Jam 1.13).

To ask if Jesus could have sinned or not have sinned is, of course, a hypothetical question. Yet it is an important one that needs to be addressed when considering Jesus' identity. For, *if Jesus could not have sinned, He was not fully a man*. Adam was fully man; he could have sinned; he did sin. Believers should forever praise Jesus that He did not succumb to temptation and sin, but that He provided for us so great salvation!

In the Apostle Paul's lengthy explanation of resurrection, he seems to deny that Jesus preexisted as a supernatural being. Therein, Paul twice calls the resurrection body a "spiritual body" (1 Cor 15.44). Then he explains that "the spiritual [body] is not first, but the natural; then the spiritual" (v. 46). If Paul meant to apply this to the resurrection body of Jesus as well as those of the saints, as it seems, he meant that Jesus first existed only as a human being, just as all other human beings do, and "then the spiritual," referring to Jesus' resurrection body. James D.G. Dunn says confidently of this verse, "Paul explicitly denies that Christ precedes Adam" with a preexistence.[50]

Some scholars who emphasize Adam Christology rightly deny that Paul believed Jesus preexisted.[51] They insist that if He did, Jesus could not have been a complete type of Adam since Adam never preexisted. When Paul further explained, "the second man is from heaven" (1 Cor 15.47), the context that follows, in 1 Cor 15.48-49, shows that he does not mean Jesus preexisted in heaven but that His resurrection body had its origin in heaven. So, God created Jesus' resurrection body in heaven, as with others (2 Cor 5.1).

Paul also implies that the hope of the resurrection of the saints depends on Jesus being a man just like pre-fallen Adam was, not a preexistent God-man. Paul states, "since by a man came death, by a man also came the resurrection of the dead" (1 Cor 15.21).

This comparison of Adam and Jesus only makes sense if Jesus is a sufficient parallel to Adam. Jesus preexisting and/or being God disqualifies Him as a suitable equivalent of Adam capable of recovering what he lost. This comparison begins with the virgin birth.

---

[49] E. Flesseman-van Leer, *A Faith for Today*, 67.

[50] J.D.G. Dunn, *Christology in the Making*, 308n41.

[51] E.g., J.D.G. Dunn, *Christology in the Making*, 113-28.

Most critical scholars dismiss the virgin birth of Jesus as having no theological or christological relevance for modern Christianity, even alleging that it detracts from it.[52] On the contrary, the virgin birth has a profound relevance to Adam Christology. In order for Jesus to regain what Adam lost in Paradise, Jesus had to be like pre-fallen Adam in every way, especially regarding temptation. Although both men came into existence by different means, the result was the same in that both were man and no more, and both were equally sinless prior to their comparable tests involving Satan as their tempter.

Interestingly, Paul writes frequently about the righteousness of Christ; yet neither he nor any NT writers ever accredit it to Jesus' virgin birth (virginal conception).

One reason Paul adopted Adam Christology may be that he wanted to distinguish Jesus and Adam in a category separate from all other human beings. If so, he probably had in mind that they were both comparable and unique, both having been without sin.

Even the Koran expounds Adam Christology. We saw in Chapter Three that it affirms Jesus' virgin birth. Also, the Koran correctly makes Jesus' virgin birth the basis for Adam Christology by declaring, "Jesus is as Adam" before the fall (Susa 3:59).

In sum, Adam Christology is nullified if Jesus is essentially different from Adam. Again, *Jesus cannot rationally be compared to Adam if Jesus is a God-man; they must be exact parallels. This is why many traditionalists refrain from adopting Adam Christology.*

God-in-Christ Christology

Paul also affirms a God-in-Christ Christology. He explicitly writes about "God in Christ (Jesus)" (Eph 4.32; 1 Thes 2.14). Paul's most well-known passage containing this concept is 2 Cor 5.19: "God was in Christ, reconciling the world to Himself."[53]

An exclusive God-in-Christ Christology, as opposed to traditional God-is-Christ Christology, is fundamentally a theocentric Christology. So it is with Paul; he writes right before 2 Cor 5.19: "Now all things are from God, who reconciled us to Himself through Christ" (v. 18). Hans Kung well explains that Paul's "christocentricity remains grounded in and culminates in a theocentricity: 'from God through Jesus Christ.'"[54]

It should be obvious that God being in Christ does not make Christ God anymore than both God and Christ indwelling believers makes them gods or christs. Paul's favorite expression for the concept of the spiritual position of believers is that they are "in Christ."

Paul's God-in-Christ Christology presents one side of the Mutual Indwelling that was taught by the Johannine Jesus (Jn 10.38; 14.11). But Paul teaches the other side as well in his words "Christ in God" (Col 3.3). Consequently, God is in believers because they are in Jesus Christ; and since Jesus Christ is in God, believers are also "in God."

---

[52] E.g., E. Flesseman-van Leer, *A Faith for Today*, 71.
[53] Some scholars, e.g., V. Taylor (*The Person of Christ*, 60), suggest that this is an incorrect translation of 2 Cor 5.19, so that it should be like the NEBmg: "God was reconciling the world to himself by Christ." But NEB editor J.A.T. Robinson (*The Human Face of God*, 181) claims either translation "makes no difference to the centrality of the agency of God," but that each portrays Christ as God's agent in reconciliation.
[54] H. Kung, *Christianity: Essence, History, and Future*, 113, cf. 96.

Therefore, for Paul, Jesus is the perfect image of God primarily because God, in all of His fulness, dwells in Jesus Christ (e.g., Col 1.19; 2.9), which does not make Him God.

Lordship Christology

The earliest credal statement of the Jesus Movement was that "Jesus is Lord." No NT writer reflects this brief, christological confession more than does the Apostle Paul. He applies the word "Lord" to Jesus nearly 230 times in his epistles, whereas he attaches the term "Son (of God)" to Jesus only 17 times. The Lordship of Jesus Christ is without a doubt the dominant theme in Pauline Christology.

Paul, unlike other NT writers, applies the title "Lord" (Gr. *kurios*) exclusively to Jesus in his corpus and thus never to the Father. This pattern can be quickly gleaned from all ten Pauline verses mentioned above in the section entitled, "The God of Jesus Christ." For Paul, God is "the Father" and Jesus Christ is "the Lord," exclusively. We already have considered 1 Cor 8.4-6 as the most prominent Pauline passage that conveys this distinction. Another is where Paul writes to the Corinthians about the resurrection of the saints, saying, "Now God has not only raised the Lord, but will also raise us up" (1 Cor 6.14). Again, notice that Paul distinguishes "God" from "Lord," the latter being Jesus.

But what does it mean to call Jesus "Lord"? It means simply that Jesus ought to be obeyed regarding His instruction in righteousness. This is very interesting, since Paul is the great proponent of the grace of God, even being accused falsely of antinomianism.

Many traditionalists contend otherwise, alleging that the NT designation of Jesus as "Lord" indicates He is God due to the LXX practice of translating *kurios* for YHWH. But Paul provides no evidence that his application of *kurios* to Jesus should be taken as a substitute for the tetragrammaton, as if implying that Jesus is YHWH.[55] J.D.G. Dunn says of the word "lord" in Paul's writings, "*kyrios* is not so much a way of identifying Jesus with God, but if anything more a way of *distinguishing* Jesus from God.[56]

Besides, now there is a consensus among authorities that 1st century CE copies of the LXX did not substitute words for the tetragrammaton. In 1978, George Howard stated,

> Recent discoveries in Egypt and the Judaen desert show that in the pre-Christian Greek Bible the tetragrammaton was never represented by the surrogate *kurios* and in addition was usually left untranslated. It was reproduced in archaic-Hebrew or square Aramaic letters or in the transliterated form of IAΩ.... The practice of surrogating the divine name in writing with *kurios*, as we find it in the Christian copies of the Septuagint, is a Christian innovation that in no way reflects the appearance of the Bible which the NT writers used.... the early church was accustomed to seeing the Hebrew word יהוה written in their Greek OT, not the surrogate *kurios*.[57]

In fact, Jewish copies of the LXX consistently replace *kurios* with the Tetragrammaton![58]

---

[55] Contra many traditionalist scholars, e.g., M. Hengel, *The Son of God*, 77.
[56] J.D.G. Dunn, *The Theology of Paul the Apostle*, 254. Emphasis his.
[57] George Howard, "Phil. 2:6-11 and the Human Christ," *CBQ* 40 (1978): 383-84. See esp. George Howard, "The Tetragram and the New Testament," *JBL* 96 (1977): 63-83.
[58] Robert Hanhart, "Introduction," in Martin Hengel, *The Septuagint as Christian Scripture: Its Prehistory and the Problem of Its Canon* (Grand Rapids: Baker, 2002), 7-8.

For many traditionalists, an important passage in this regard is Paul's renowned statement about salvation in Rom 10.9. It reads, "if you confess with your mouth Jesus as Lord, and believe in your heart that God raised Him from the dead, you shall be saved." These traditionalists think confessing Jesus as "Lord" implicitly affirms that He is God. On the contrary, Paul here juxtapositions "Jesus" and "God," which actually distinguishes them. Calling someone "lord" merely indicates either a respectful address or submission to a monarch or master. The latter is meant whenever Jesus' disciples called Him "Lord."

Even Oscar Cullmann takes this traditionalist track. He asserts, "The question of the deity of Christ in the New Testament should be asked in terms of the *Kyrios* title and its implications for the absolute lordship of Christ over the whole world…. The New Testament unquestionably presupposes the deity of Christ, but it does so in connection with faith in the lordship he exercises…. Thus in connection with the *Kyrios* title we could already speak of the occasional use in early Christianity of the name 'God' (*theos*) for Jesus, for this name by no means indicates, as we are inclined to think, a higher dignity than the unsurpassable *Kyrios* designation."[59]

Gustaf Dalman disagrees. He relates that (1) Jesus and the early Jewish Christians of Palestine did not call God "Lord" in their languages, and (2) the Jews' substitution of the word "Lord" (Heb. *adonai*) for God's Name—YHWH—had begun among Hellenistic Jews only.[60] Dalman says of the NT gospels, "We do not find expressed the idea of God's becoming man, or of a twofold nature united in a single person."[61]

James D.G. Dunn postulates that soon after Jesus' resurrection the early Jewish Christians applied the title "Lord" to Jesus to indicate a divinity that was not fully God.[62] Dunn further explains, "Paul calls Jesus *kyrios*, but he seems to have marked reservations about actually calling Jesus 'God'…. *Paul can hail Jesus as Lord not in order to identify him with God, but rather, if anything, to distinguish him from the one God.*"[63]

Paul calling Jesus "Lord" arouses the question of whether he worshipped Jesus. As explained elsewhere in this book, this question depends on how the word "worship" is defined. Dunn says Paul's writings "should certainly make us hesitate before asserting that Paul 'worshiped' Christ, since the evidence clearly indicates otherwise." Dunn further explains that if we make the historic distinction between certain words, e.g., "worship," "veneration," and "adoration," "we could say that Jesus was worshiped, meaning by that something short of the adoration reserved for God alone."[64]

In sum, the NT accounts of the early Christians calling Jesus "Lord" indicate no more than their recognition of His God-given authority to rule and their corresponding voluntary submission to be ruled by Him. And Paul, the premiere proponent of Lordship Christology in the NT, gives no reason to venture further, by equating "Lord" with "God."

---

[59] O. Cullmann, *Christology*, 235, 237. Cullmann (p. 236n2) quotes Ethelbert Stauffer (*New Testament Theology*, tr. John Marsh [New York: Macmillan, 1955], 114) as saying, "But of all the christological titles [in the NT] the richest is that of 'Lord'…. [which is] the divine honouring of Jesus Christ."

[60] G. Dalman, *The Words of Jesus*, 179-80.

[61] Ibid., 287.

[62] J.D.G. Dunn, *Unity and Diversity*, 52-53.

[63] J.D.G. Dunn, *Unity and Diversity*, 53. Emphasis his. Similarly, J.D.G. Dunn, "Was Christianity a Monotheistic Faith from the Beginning?" 328.

[64] J.D.G. Dunn, *The Theology of Paul the Apostle*, 259-60.

Yahweh Texts Applied to Jesus

Some traditionalists also contend that Paul's occasional practice of applying OT passages about Yahweh to Jesus indicates that he believed that Jesus was Yahweh.[65] The most prominent examples are Paul's quotation of Joel 2.32 in Rom 10.13 and Isa 45.23b in both Rom 14.11 and Phil 2.10-11 (cf. Ps 145.21). In Rom 10.13, he quotes the prophet Joel, "WHOEVER WILL CALL UPON THE NAME OF THE LORD WILL BE SAVED" (Joel 2.32). "THE LORD," here, translates YHWH, and Paul *seems* to apply it to Jesus. But in doing so, Paul does not mean that Jesus is Yahweh but that calling upon Jesus is the same thing as calling upon Yahweh (God the Father), since access to Yahweh is attained through Jesus, His agent. And by Paul applying Isa 45.23b twice to Jesus, bowing the knee to Him and confessing His name represents adoration directed toward both Jesus and God. For Jesus had taught specifically that whoever receives, honors, beholds, and believes the Son does likewise regarding the Father (Mt 10.40; Jn 5.23; 12.44-45; 13.20). Finally, Paul quotes Yahweh from Isa 40.13 by writing, "For WHO HAS KNOWN THE MIND OF THE LORD, THAT HE SHOULD INSTRUCT HIM? But we have the mind of Christ" (1 Cor 2.16; cf. Rom 11.34). The meaning is surely no more than that the risen Christ and Yahweh think alike.

The author of Hebrews quotes two OT texts about Yahweh and applies them to Jesus. The first is Ps 97.7 (cf. Deut 32.43 LXX), which says of God in the MT, "Worship Him, all you gods." But the author of Hebrews quotes this clause from the LXX and applies it to Jesus, "And let all the angels of God worship Him" (Heb 1.6). Thus, the LXX interprets "gods" as "angels." And in Heb 1.10-12 the author quotes Ps 102.25-27, which concerns both creation and its eschatological transformation, and he applies it to Jesus.

A bare few scholars have alleged that Jesus occasionally applied OT Yahweh texts to Himself, or He approved of such, thus regarding Himself as Yahweh. For instance, Jesus quoted from the Hillel psalm in Ps 118.22, "the stone which the builders rejected, this became the chief cornerstone" (Mt 21.42/Mk 12.10/Lk 20.17). Then Jesus added, "he/everyone who falls on this/that stone will be broken to pieces; but on whomever it falls, it will scatter him like dust" (Mt 21.44/Lk 20.18). This statement seems to allude to Yahweh's similar words in Isa 8.14, as if Jesus indirectly identifies Himself as Yahweh.[66]

Some traditionalists argue that Jesus is Yahweh because Paul identifies the eschatological "day of the LORD (Yahweh)" in the OT as "the day of the/our Lord Jesus (Christ)."[67] But we have already seen that "that day," as it is sometimes abbreviated in both the OT and Paul's writings,[68] is the day when Yahweh will fully consummate His purposes through Christ, His agent. So, "that day" belongs to both God and Christ.

It should be concluded that in most instances in which the NT quotes or alludes to an OT text that refers to Yahweh and applies it to Jesus, it indicates agency. So, in such cases Jesus is not being identified as Yahweh but as Yahweh's agent. It is the same with Eph 4.8, in which Paul quotes about Yahweh in Ps 68.18 and applies it to Jesus.

---

[65] See esp. David B. Capes, *Old Testament Yahweh Texts in Paul's Christology* (Tubingen: Mohr, 1992); idem, "YHWH Texts and Montheism? A Contribution to the Discussion of Christian Monotheism," in *Early Jewish and Christian Monotheism*, ed. Stuckenbruck and North, 120-137.

[66] Richard T. France, *Jesus and the Old Testament: His Application of Old Testament Passages to Himself and His Mission* (London: Tyndale, 1971), 152-53.

[67] The expression, "the day of the Lord," appears in 1 Thes 5.2; 2 Thes 2.2. "The day of the/our Lord Jesus/Christ" is in 1 Cor 1.8; 5.5; 2 Cor 1.14. "The day of Christ (Jesus)" is in Phil 1.6, 10; 2.16.

[68] Isaiah: Isa 2.11, 20; 3.7, 18; 4.1-2; 11.10-11; 12.1, 4; 24.21; 27.13; 29.18. Paul: 1 Cor 3.13; 2 Thes 1.10.

Yet Paul's application of the title "Lord" to Jesus, and his indication that blessing proceeds from both God and Jesus, shows that Paul viewed his Lord Jesus Christ with a very lofty status, making Him worthy of the utmost adoration. An oft-repeated example is that in eight of Paul's ten salutations in his ten letters, he writes these introductory words, "Grace to you and peace from God our/the Father and the Lord Jesus Christ."[69]

Subordination Christology

Like the Fourth Evangelist, Paul is well known for teaching on the subordination of Christ to God. His letters set forth such things as God's possession of, and headship over, Christ. Perhaps nowhere is this demonstrated more vividly than in the following: "Christ belongs to God" and "God is the head of Christ" (1 Cor 3.23; 11.3).

But what exactly does Paul mean by this subordination of Christ to God? Does he mean a mere *economic* or *functional* subordination, i.e., only in rank? Or does Paul teach an *essential* subordination, which renders the Father superior to the Son regarding their nature or essence? Paul's NT corpus indicates the latter.

Paul further relates God's authority over Christ by revealing that it is God the Father "who is the blessed and only Sovereign" (1 Tim 6.15). This will be demonstrated when the Father "will bring about at the proper time" the second coming of Christ. If the Father is the "only Sovereign" (Gr. *monos dunastes*), and Paul states this in relation to Christ and His return, then Christ cannot also be equal in sovereignty to God the Father.

The signal signpost of Jesus' essential subordination to God is Paul's prophecy about Jesus' final, revelatory act regarding the kingdom. For, Paul writes of Jesus, "when He delivers up the kingdom to the God and Father,... then the Son Himself also will be subjected to the One who subjected all things to Him, that God may be all in all" (1 Cor 15.24, 28; cf. 1 Chron 29.11). Here is the ultimate subordination act, and it seems to be a voluntary one. Oscar Cullmann calls it "the key to all New Testament Christology."[70]

What is so surprising about this future act—Jesus giving the kingdom back to the Father—is that, having experienced the ultimate in political power and human adulation, who would voluntarily give that up? Ask those who govern and they will probably admit that authoritarian power is addictive. Yet, after Jesus' successful thousand-year reign on earth (Rev 20), He will give up that authority. He will willingly forfeit it all and even succumb to some kind of mysterious absorption of His own identity into that of God His Father, and all saints will do likewise.[71] Robin Scroggs well explains that thereafter, and throughout all eternity, "God remains the only and single power who is God."[72]

Christ's subordination to God is also seen in Paul's prayers. After the salutations in his letters, Paul often adds that he gives thanks to God in prayer concerning those to whom he writes.[73] And even though he occasionally appends Jesus' name to his petitions and heart-felt thanks made in prayer, Paul relates his view about the Father's essential preeminence over Jesus by always addressing these prayers solely to "God (the Father)."

---

[69] 1 Cor 1.3; 2 Cor 1.2; Gal 1.3; Eph 1.2; Phil 1.2; 2 Thes 1.2; 2 Thes 1.2; Philemon 1.3. Emphasis mine.
[70] O. Cullmann, *Christology*, 293.
[71] O. Cullmann (*Christology*, 248) calls it "a complete eschatological absorption of the Son in the Father."
[72] R. Scroggs, *Christology in Paul and John*, 45.
[73] Rom 1.8; 1 Cor 1.4; Phil 1.3-4; Col 1.3; 1 Th 1.2; 2 Tim 1.3; Philemon 4.

The Invisibility and Immortality of God

Like the Fourth Evangelist (Jn 5.37; 6.46; cf. 1.18), Paul teaches the "invisibility" of God the Father. We have already seen that he calls Christ "the image of the invisible God" (Col 1.15). He also pens a doxology to God the Father as being "the King eternal, immortal, invisible, the only God" (1 Tim 1.17).

In both of these texts, Paul uses the Greek word *aoratos*. Translated "invisible," it literally means "unseen." Thus, God is not invisible; rather, He is unseen by mortals.

Paul later explains why it is so in another doxology to "God," the Father, since Paul distinguishes "God" and "Christ Jesus" in each context (1 Tim 1.1; 2.5; 6.13). He says, "who alone possesses immortality and dwells in unapproachable light; whom no man has seen or can see" (6.16; cf. Rom 1.23). In this last clause Paul affirms the OT portrayal of God dwelling in a glorious light and/or fire, making Him unapproachable by mortal humans and thereby unseen by them (Ps 104.2; Eze 1.4, 28; Dan 7.9; Ex 33.20). As stated in the previous chapter, *if it is impossible for mortal human beings to literally see God, how could Jesus be God since He was certainly seen by humans?*

Notice that these two Pauline statements to Timothy also state that only God the Father possesses immortality. Thus, Jesus did not possess either immortality or eternal life intrinsically during His earthly sojourn (cf. Jn 5.26). Rather, the Father raised Jesus from the dead and thereby *conferred upon Him immortality*. Traditionalist J.N.D. Kelly correctly explains that these two Timothy passages are "not intended to deny immortality to other beings, but to bring out that it belongs inherently and by right only to God, as the very source of life."[74] Accordingly, if immortality was not an intrinsic attribute of Jesus Christ's nature (see Jn 5.26), then He cannot be co-equal with God the Father in all of His relative attributes, which all Christians insist includes immortality.

The dogma that Jesus is God and that He died has always been a problem for classical, incarnational Christology. One of the correct and well-accepted presuppositions of classical theism is that God is immortal and therefore cannot die. Since Jesus died, the question arises, How can Jesus be God if God cannot die? Traditionalists reply that it is only Jesus' human nature and physical body that underwent death, not His divine nature. The notion of a "crucified God" who died on a cross, which is still expounded by some traditionalist scholars,[75] is impossible. Yet God does feel the pain of His people.[76]

Since the late 19th century, some traditionalists have addressed these issues of God's invisibility and immortality by employing one of the kenosis theories, e.g., that Jesus in some way relinquished His immortality and other relative divine attributes during His incarnation. But we have already seen in Chapter Three that the idea of God relinquishing any of His divine attributes necessarily makes Him less than God.

Notice also that Paul says God "dwells in unapproachable light." He means that if mortal humans literally approached God, they would be destroyed before they got close enough to literally see Him. Jesus cannot be God because people saw and touched Him. When Jesus was transfigured on a mountain with three apostles present (Mt 17.2 par.), His magnificent, Moses-like illumination (Ex 34.30) was only a glimpse of the Shekinah glory which God's resurrected and

---

[74] J.N.D. Kelly, *Pastoral Epistles Timothy I & II, and Titus*, 146.
[75] Esp. J. Moltmann, *The Crucified God*; R. Bauckham, *God Crucified*. See also M. Hengel, *Studies in Early Christology*, 383.
[76] E.g., Jud 10.16; Ps 68.19; Isa 63.9.

glorified people will see emanating from their Lord Jesus Christ at His second coming (Rev 21.23; 22.5). Only then will people be able to approach and literally see God because they will possess immortality (Mt 5.8; 1 Cor.51-54; 1 Jn 3.2). Thus, it seems that Jesus could *not* have literally approached God and sat down with Him on His throne until Jesus had received immortality at His resurrection.

"Maranatha"

Paul uses the Aramaic word *maranatha* only in 1 Cor 16.22.[77] This use indicates that Greek-speaking Christians borrowed this transliterated word from the early Aramaic-speaking Jewish Christians of Judea and Galilee and made it a part of their own liturgy. Its meaning is complex.[78] If parsed *marana tha*, it is a request and means "our Lord, come;" but if parsed *maran atha*, it is a confession and means "our Lord has come."

Some scholars have thought that this early Christian use of *maranatha* in mostly a liturgical setting indicates that its meaning is to be found in its application to the Eucharist. In that case, it could mean either of the above. However, it is more likely that Paul mostly employed it eschatologically, i.e., "our Lord, come," to indicate the Christians' hopeful, expectant attitude concerning Jesus' promised return to earth in glory. Accordingly, some NT scholars, not just traditionalists, think that *maranatha* in 1 Cor 16.22 is a prayer which verifies Paul's sanction of praying to Jesus,[79] thus asking Him to return soon. But this concept conflicts with subordinationist elements in NT eschatology and Christology: (1) Paul's teaching that only the Father will "bring about" Christ's return (1 Tim 6.14-15) and Jesus' two revelations that (2) He did not know the time of His return (Mt 24.36/Mk 13.32>) and (3) only the Father decides the timing of such events (Ac 1.7). Also, Daniel calls "the end" of the age "the appointed time,"[80] meaning that God long ago "decreed" it (Dan 9.27), so that it is fixed and cannot be changed. So, this Christian use of *maranatha* likely expresses merely the heart's desire for Jesus to return rather than it being an actual prayer request for Him to return soon. Such a view accords with "Come, Lord Jesus," in Rev 22.20, which may represent the translation of *maranatha*. Many scholars compare it to the Kaddish prayer about Messiah, "May he reveal himself speedily in our days."

Geza Vermes and others trace this early Christian use of *maranatha* back to Jesus' words in His so-called Lord's Prayer, "Thy kingdom come" (Mt 6.10/Lk 11.2).[81] This is a prayer directed to "Our Father," not Jesus. Even if *maranatha* represents a prayer asking Jesus to return, it would be the same as praying to the Father, "Thy kingdom come," since Jesus is the embodiment of the kingdom of God. And this connection may suggest that the early church employed *maranatha* liturgically, perhaps at the Eucharist, but only in the sense of asking Jesus to be in their midst, which would have been synonymous with requesting the presence of the Holy Spirit.

The Spirit, Kingdom, Gospel, Day, and the Judgment of God and Christ

Some traditionalist expositors assert that Christ is God because Paul interchanges these two nouns in his corpus when associating them with various themes.

---

[77] *Maranatha* also appears in *Didache* 10.6.
[78] Gordon D. Fee, *The First Epistle to the Corinthians*, in *NICNT* (1987), 838.
[79] O. Cullmann, *Christology*, 209-16; L.W. Hurtado, *One God, One Lord*, 106.
[80] Dan 9.26; 11.27, 29, 35, 40; 12.9, 13.
[81] G. Vermes, *The Changing Faces of Jesus*, 201.

First, Paul employs the terminology, "the Spirit of God" and "the Spirit of Christ."[82] Does he thereby imply that Christ is "God?" Hardly! For instance, in Rom 8.9 Paul evidently interchanges the two expressions, making them synonymous. By such usage, he simply refers to the Holy Spirit. For, Paul properly designates the Holy Spirit as both "of God" and "of Christ" because the Spirit is sent by God through Jesus in Jesus' name (cf. Jn 14.16, 26; 15.26). This subject is called "the procession of the Holy Spirit," and disagreement on it caused the official split in the Catholic Church, in the year 1054.

Second, Paul does the same regarding the kingdom. Like Jesus, he sometimes styles it "the kingdom of God."[83] Yet Paul depicts the kingdom as belonging to both God and Christ (Col 1.13; 2 Tim 4.1, 18). With this usage, does Paul intend to indirectly call Christ "God?" Indeed not; he only means that the kingdom belongs to both God and Christ, just as he says outright in Eph 5.5: "the kingdom of Christ and God."[84] Moreover, Jesus had taught that the Father, to whom the kingdom belongs (e.g., Mt 26.29), had given the Son "all things" (Mt 11.27/ Lk 10.22), so that the kingdom afterwards belongs to both God and His Son (Dan 7.13-14; Mt 16.28; Lk 19.15; 22.29-30).

Third, Paul does the same thing regarding the gospel. Ten times in his corpus he mentions "the gospel of Christ;" and seven times he writes of "the gospel of God." Such usage does not imply that Christ is God but that "the gospel" belongs to both of them.

Fourth, Paul does the same with "the/that day,"[85] which is the abbreviated form for "the day of the LORD" in the OT. Paul writes of "the day of the Lord" (1 Th 5.2; 2 Th 2.2); but he also pens "the day of the/our Lord Jesus (Christ)" (1 Cor 1.8; 5.5; 2 Cor 1.14) and "the day of Christ (Jesus)" (Phil 1.6, 10; 2.16). Whose day is it? It belongs to both.

Fifth, Paul does likewise regarding the judgment day. He states:
- "For we shall all stand before the judgment seat of God" (Rom 14.10).
- "For we must all appear before the judgment seat of Christ" (2 Cor 5.10).

Notice the difference of "God" and "Christ." Paul does not intend to call Christ "God" in Rom 14.10. Neither does he indicate in these two verses that God and Christ will preside separately over two different tribunals, or that there will be one tribunal in which Christ, as Judge, will reveal that He is God.[86] For, God the Father "has given all judgment to the Son" (Jn 5.22). Yet Bultmann observes that the Son is "not alone in it;" i.e., the Father will also participate (Jn 8.16). Bultmann explains, "our responsibility to Christ is identical with our responsibility to God. God as judge becomes concrete for us in Christ."[87]

The Preexistence of Jesus?

It is generally thought that the Apostle Paul believed that Jesus had preexisted. Although Paul does not state this explicitly in his letters, it is thought

---

[82] "Spirit of God:" Rom 8.9, 11, 14; 1 Cor 2.11, 14; 3.16; 6.11; 7.40; 12.3; 2 Cor 3.3, 17-18; Eph 3.16; 4.30; Phil 3.3. "Spirit of (Jesus) Christ:" Rom 8.9; Phil 1.19; cf. Gal 4.6. However, note how Paul distinguishes these two expressions in Rom 8.16-17; 1 Cor 6.11; 12.3; 2 Cor 13.14; Eph 2.18.

[83] The Matthean Jesus almost always says "kingdom of heaven," which means "kingdom of God." "Kingdom of heaven" is a Jewish idiom or circumlocution for God in order to avoid offending the Jews' sensitivity, thus refraining from pronouncing the divine name. It probably represents the *ipsissima verba*.

[84] Contra M. Harris (*Jesus as God*, 316), who asserts that joint possession alots "divine status" to Jesus.

[85] Rom 13.12-13; 1 Cor 3.13; 1 Th 5.4; 2 Th 1.10; 2 Tim 1.12, 18; 4.8.

[86] Contra M. Harris, *3 Crucial Questions*, 86-87.

[87] R. Bultmann, *Essays*, 283.

that he implies it in the following ways: (1) Christ's involvement in creation (1 Cor 8.6; Col 1.16), (2) God sending His Son to be born of a woman (Rom 8.3; Gal 4.4), and (3) disputably in 2 Cor 8.9> and Phil 2.6-7> (cf. 1 Cor 10.4, 9; 15.47). Gerhard Kittel concludes, "Christological pre-existence sayings are a constituent part of the whole of Paulinism."[88]

But how did Paul conceive of Jesus preexisting? Did he think it was a personal subsistence or merely a personification? We have seen that church fathers believed that the Fourth Gospel, Paul's letters, and the book of Hebrews reflect that Jesus preexisted eternally as the Logos-Son, i.e., as a complete *hypostasis* or Person. But we saw in the previous chapter that the spiritual character of the Fourth Gospel suggests otherwise. So do Paul's writings. Karl-Josef Kuschel cites distinguished scholars for support and says, "there is no sign of any unambiguous and explicit statement about pre-existence in the Christology outlined by Paul."[89] Hans Kung, his colleague, explains that in Paul, "the sending of the Son is to be understood metaphorically, in the tradition of the Old Testament prophets."[90] Kuschel adds, "Paul's confessions ... about preexistence are not about a temporally isolated 'existence' before the creation of the world."[91]

Many traditionalists cite the sending of the Son motif in Gal 4.4 as indicating that Paul taught the actual preexistence and incarnation of the Son rather than merely the Logos. It reads, "But when the fulness of time came, God sent forth His Son, born of a woman, born under the Law."[92] But there is nothing explicit here about preexistence. Moreover, the context is soteriology, not Christology. God's sending of His Son should be understood according to the Jewish prophetic tradition of divine commissioning.

A few traditionalists insist that Paul teaches that Jesus possessed His humanity in heaven prior to His incarnation. Some cite Paul's brief treatise on resurrection, in which he contrasts Adam and Jesus as follows: "The first man was of the dust of the earth, the second man from heaven," twice calling Jesus "the man from heaven" (1 Cor 15.47-49 NIV). Paul does not here refer to either a preexistence or incarnation of Jesus.[93] Rather, in accordance with his context, Paul means that Jesus' resurrection body had its origin in heaven, making it adaptable to both the physical and spirit realms. Moderate traditionalist John Macquarrie well insists that Paul did not go beyond primitive Christology, so that he did not think that Jesus was either "a 'man from heaven' or a preexistent divine being."[94]

Some traditionalists also cite 1 Cor 10.4, which is about Israel's exodus from Egypt, to support that Paul believed in the actual preexistence of Jesus. This verse recalls the thirsty Israelites encamped at Meribah and complaining bitterly to Moses of a lack of water. Upon God's direction, Moses struck a rock and out came water for them to drink (Ex 17.6). Paul explains, "all drank the

---

[88] Gerhard Kittel, "*lego*," in *TDNT* 4:130.
[89] Karl-Josef Kuschel, *Born Before All Time? The Dispute Over Christ's Origin* [1990], tr. John Bowden (New York: Crossroad, 1992), 303.
[90] K. Kuschel, *Born Before All Time?* 305; H. Kung, *Credo*, 59.
[91] K. Kuschel, *Born Before All Time?* 306.
[92] The main non-Johannine NT passages that depict the sending of the Son are Rom 8.3; Gal 4.4; 1 Jn 4.9.
[93] Lincoln D. Hurst ("Re-enter the Pre-existent Christ in Philippians 2.5-11?" *NTS* 32 [1986]: 455n21) follows J.D.G. Dunn (*Christology*, 308n41) by rightly explaining, "The pre-existence of Christ as man cannot be argued from 1 Cor 15.47-49, where he is referred to as 'the man from heaven' (in contrast to Adam, 'the man of dust'), since Paul makes it clear that the heavenly man *follows* Adam rather than precedes him." Emphasis his.
[94] J. Macquarrie, *Jesus Christ in Modern Thought*, 64.

same spiritual drink, for they were drinking from a spiritual rock which followed them; and the rock was Christ" (1 Cor 10.4). Does Paul mean Christ preexisted and secretly accompanied Israel during the exodus? A rabbinical legend says a literal rock followed the Israelites in the wilderness. Some traditionalists interpret that Paul means that the physical rock Moses struck symbolized the Messiah and that the spiritual rock refers to the Messiah following them. But Paul more likely means the literal rock typified the future Messiah as the One who would spiritually provide individuals with (or *be* to them?) living water, i.e., signifying a spiritually abundant and fruitful life so they would not spiritually thirst again (e.g., Jn 4.13-14; 7.37-38; 10.10).

Like John Macquarrie, many contemporary NT scholars reject the idea that Jesus literally preexisted. Instead, they embrace the apologists' teaching that He only preexisted as the impersonal Logos prior to His incarnation or He merely preexisted ideally in the mind of God.[95] James D.G. Dunn likewise contends, "There is no good evidence that Jesus thought of himself as a pre-existent being" or that Paul thought that Jesus either preexisted or possessed deity.[96] Dunn concludes that much of Paul's language about preexistence is personified Wisdom language (e.g., 1 Cor 10.4; Col 1.15-20), as in "Christ the power of God and the wisdom of God" (1 Cor 1.24), and that Paul never intended for it to be understood as literal preexistence.[97] Dunn asserts that by the time Paul wrote Romans, in the mid-50s, "there is no evidence that Christian thought had so far evolved the idea of incarnation, or that the language of preexistence when referred to Christ (1 Cor 8:6) would as yet be taken to imply his personal preexistence, or that talk of his being 'sent' (Rom 8:3) was as yet understood to imply a descent from heaven."[98]

Some scholars think that belief in the preexistence of Jesus has a negative effect on more than just Jesus' humanity. Moderate traditionalist John Knox raises the alarming concern that "the more fully the logic of pre-existence is allowed to work itself out in the story [about Jesus], the less important the [His] resurrection is bound to become."[99]

More importantly, Paul never indicates in any of his epistles that people need to believe that Jesus literally preexisted in order for them to obtain eternal salvation.[100] In fact, the preexistence of Jesus is not an essential element in Pauline Christology. Robin Scroggs insightfully observes that Paul only refers to this theme by "citing or alluding to formulas created by others in the church. Nowhere does he develop the motif in his own theological reflections. Preexistence clearly does not have an essential function in his christological structure."[101] Dunn states succinctly and importantly concerning Jesus, "Paul was not seeking to win men to belief in a pre-existent being."[102]

---

[95] E.g., J. Knox, *The Humanity and Divinity of Christ*; J.A.T. Robinson, *The Human Face of God*; Maurice F. Wiles, *The Remaking of Christian Doctrine* (London: SCM, 1974); Michael Goulder, "Jesus, the Man of Universal Destiny," in *The Myth of God Incarnate*, ed. J. Hick, 79, 85; D. Cupitt, *The Debate About Christ*.
[96] J.D.G. Dunn, *Unity and Diversity*, 225-26, 221.
[97] J.D.G. Dunn, *Christology in the Making*, 176-96, 255-56; idem, *The Theology of Paul the Apostle*, 266-93. In addition, Philo (*Allegorical Interpretation*, 2.86) identifies the rock in apparently Ex 17.6, which Paul calls "a spiritual rock" in 1 Cor 10.4, as "the wisdom of God."
[98] J.D.G. Dunn, *Romans 9-16*, 615.
[99] J. Knox, *The Humanity and Divinity of Christ*, 37.
[100] The same is true of Jesus' Virgin Birth, which Paul never mentions in his corpus.
[101] R. Scroggs, *Christology in Paul and John*, 44.
[102] J.G.D. Dunn, *Christology in the Making*, 195.

Regardless, traditionalists generally have concluded that if Jesus preexisted temporally as a complete personal being, He must be God. But this reasoning is both illogical and biblically unsupported. We saw in Chapter Four that mainstream Judaism allowed for the preexistence of beings, which included some exalted humans, yet Jews never perceived that this idea infringed on their monotheism. Besides, traditionalist D.A. Carson is right in stating categorically, "pre-existence does not entail deity."[103]

The Cosmic Christ

Paul further teaches that the exalted Jesus presently reigns over the universe as cosmic Lord (1 Cor 8.6; Col 1.16-17; cf. Heb 1.6-13; 1 Pt 3.22). *But Jesus acting on God's behalf as His vice-regent, thus functioning as God, is not the same as being God.* Paul makes this distinction clear in his use of the following prepositions (emphasis mine):

God, the Father	**the Lord Jesus Christ**
"*from* Him and *through* Him and *to* Him are all things" (Rom 11.36)	
"*from* whom are all things, and we exist *for* Him" (1 Cor 8.6)	"*by* whom are all things, and we exist *through* Him" (1 Cor 8.6)
	"*by* Him all things were created ... all things have been created *by* Him and *for* Him" (Col 1.16)

The information in this table may be summarized as follows: (1) all things are *from/of* (Gr. *exi*) and *to* God the Father, exclusively, but (2) all things were made *by, through*, and *for* (Gr. *di, eis*) both God and Christ. The apologists sometimes cited such evidence for their designation of God the Father as "First Cause" and "Originate" and, conversely, for their designation of Christ as "Second Cause" and "Unoriginate."

Summary

The Apostle Paul was the great proponent of three prime axioms of the Christian faith: *God is one, He is the Father, and Jesus is Lord*. In all of his teaching and preaching recorded in the NT, Paul never discusses whether Jesus is God. (There are only a few brief Pauline phrases in which traditionalists insist Paul calls Jesus "God.") Thus, it must not have been an issue in Paul's time. Yet in his letters Paul repeatedly affirms the Shema, constantly distinguishes between God and Jesus Christ, and identifies God exclusively as the Father. Indeed, as a former Pharisee, this apostle never abandoned his monotheistic roots. It is inconceivable that this accomplished theologian of the early church could have believed that Jesus was God and not explicitly stated and clearly explained it in either his evangelistic sermons in Acts or in his several extant letters, especially when his audience was Jewish. For Paul, as for the rest of the Christian community at that time, God was a single being—the Father—and the Lord Jesus Christ was another.

---

[103] D.A. Carson, *Divine Sovereignty and Human Responsibility: Biblical Perspectives in Tension* (Atlanta: John Knox, 1981), 147.

In light of this substantial evidence, the burden of proof rests upon those biblical commentators who think that Paul *does* identify Jesus Christ as God in his NT epistles. To those debated Pauline passages we now turn.

B. Problem Passages

Introduction to Problem Passages

A most important principle of hermeneutics (interpretation) is that an author's ambiguous words or phrases should never be made the centerpiece of his or her supposed belief system. That is why, in the formulation of Christian doctrine, scholars caution that a biblical author's ambiguous passages should be interpreted by his clear passages on the same subject that appear elsewhere in his writings. This is especially true when there is grammatical ambiguity. Regardless of theories of inspiration of Scripture, objectivity concludes that the NT authors occasionally wrote something ambiguous. Sometimes, it was because they did not conceive of later developments. Plus, Greek lacked punctuation and space between words, which certainly contributed to grammatical ambiguity.

This hermeneutical principle about grammatical ambiguity should be considered in examining those Pauline texts that are debated as to whether they call Jesus "God." We have just seen that in many other places in Paul's corpus, he writes very clearly that (1) there is only one God, (2) this one God is distinguished from the man, Christ Jesus, and (3) only the Father is "God" and Christ is "Lord." Since Paul uses the word "God" over 500 times in his corpus, and his praxis is to use it interchangeably with "the Father," we may safely conclude that in these few ambiguous passages we are about to consider, this careful and consistent theologian does not intend to divert from this established practice.

Another matter to consider is the type of material in which these grammatical difficulties occur. Murray Harris well states, "It is highly improbable that Paul would introduce a profound, unqualified doctrinal affirmation (Christ is *theos*) in an incidental manner, in a context where the assertion is not crucial to the flow of argument."[104]

It is clear in Paul's writings that he never outright calls Jesus Christ "God," i.e., *ho theos*, or writes, "Jesus is God" or the like. Roman Emperor Julian, despite his later apostasy from the Christian faith, was correct when he asserted, "Paul never calls Christ 'God.'" Many contemporary scholars agree.[105]

Some scholars suggest that Paul and other NT writers purposefully avoided describing Christ's supposed divinity in precise language in order to prevent the idea of Him being a second god.[106] But there is no evidence in Paul's corpus that he designedly avoided critical christological issues in order to sidestep a possible misunderstanding. Rather, such silence indicates that the question of whether Jesus was God simply was not an issue for Paul or the Christian communities in which he ministered.

In determining whether Paul calls Christ "God," his christological discussions in his writings may be more significant than his few brief phrases that arguably apply *theos* to Jesus. For example, Paul strains to the utmost in describing Jesus' likeness to God in Phil 2.5-11 and Col 1.15-19 (cf. 2.9), yet in such cases he never explicitly calls Jesus "God." Here, Paul's subject matter is Jesus identity, whereas

---

[104] M. Harris, *Jesus as God*, 262. Yet he thinks the deity of Christ is integral to Paul's argument in Rom 9.5.
[105] E.g., F. Young, "A Cloud of Witnesses," 21; J.D.G. Dunn, *Unity and Diversity*, 221. See also J.G.D. Dunn, *The Theology of Paul the Apostle*, 255-57.
[106] E.g., V. Taylor, *The Person of Christ*, 133; M. Harris, *Jesus as God*, 283.

in Rom 9.5 and Tit 2.13 it is not. And it is in these christological discussions that we should expect Paul to identify Jesus as God, if that is what he believed, but he never does. Robert M. Grant puts it well, "Even in Paul's highest christological moments he hesitates to speak of Christ as God."[107]

And we might add that the same is true of the many times Paul ascribes functions and dignities to Jesus which many scholars think were reserved only for God.[108] In none of these instances does Paul even indirectly call Christ "God." Moderate form-critic and traditionalist Vincent Taylor concludes from Paul's NT epistles, "He speaks of Christ as divine, applies to Him names and titles which give Him no less a status, assigns to Him soteriological functions such as no man or demi-god can exercise, gives Him a place in the creation of the universe, and all but identifies Him with the Spirit of God. Above all, he represents Him as the object of worship,... And yet, he does not call Him God, but distinguishes Him from God, and presents Him in a relation of subordination to God!"[109]

Keeping this introduction in mind, we will now examine those Pauline passages that traditionalists have put forward as indicating that Paul identifies Jesus Christ as God.

1. Does "the church of God" in Acts 20.28 indicate that Jesus is God?

| Introduction | Two *Theou* Translations |
| The Greek Text and Versions | Conclusions of Commentators |

Introduction

Some traditionalists list Ac 20.28 to support that Jesus Christ is God. In this verse, Luke records that the Apostle Paul, while journeying to Jerusalem, met with the elders of the church at Ephesus and spoke to them, saying,

28 "Be on guard for yourselves and for all the flock, among which the Holy Spirit has made you overseers, to shepherd the church of God which He purchased with His own blood."

Three problems about the identity of Jesus emerge from Ac 20.28. Two of them are textual and the other one is grammatical.

The Greek Text and English Versions

The first problem to consider in Ac 20.28 is whether the Greek text should have *theou* (Gr. for "God") or *kuriou* (Gr. for "Lord").[110] English versions slightly favor *theou*:
- "the church of God" (AV, RVmg, RSV, NASB, TEV, JB, NEBmg, NIV, ESV)
- "the church of the Lord" (RV, RSVmg, NASBmg, NEB, NIVmg).

---

[107] Robert M. Grant, *Jesus After the Gospels: The Christ of the Second Century* (Louisville, KT: Westminster/John Knox, 1990), 37.

[108] E.g., David F. Wells, *The Person of Christ: A Biblical and Historical Analysis of the Incarnation* [1984] (repr. Alliance, OH: Bible Scholar Books, 1992), 64-65.

[109] V. Taylor, *The Person of Christ*, 59.

[110] Several other variant readings in Ac 20.28 are poorly attested in the MS evidence. They are (in English): "the church of God and Lord," "the church of the Lord and God," "the church of the Lord God" (or "Lord Jesus [Christ]"). Authorities regard these variants as scribal conflations of the two well-attested readings.

But the MS evidence, as well as other external witnesses, is about evenly divided:[111]
- *ten ekklesian tou theou* (Codex Vaticanus, Codex Sinaiticus, Latin Vulgate)
- *ten ekklesian tou kuriou* (Codex Alexandrinus, Codex Bezae, some minor versions).

On the whole, textual critics seem about evenly divided between which of these two, well-attested readings in the MS evidence is to be preferred as authentic. The Committee for the United Bible Societies' Greek New Testament (and many scholars) tentatively concluded that *theou* is the authentic reading in Ac 20.28. However, they gave it a C-rating, meaning that they had "a considerable degree of doubt" about it.[112]

Much of the discussion among textual critics as to whether *theou* or *kuriou* is the authentic word in Ac 20.28 regards reasons why copyists might have changed *theou* to *kuriou* or vice versa. These reasons are actually principles of textual criticism. It is quite likely that a scribe changed the original text of *theou* by substituting *kuriou* because he considered *theou* to be confusing, since "God" does not personally possess a physical body consisting of flesh and "blood" while the "Lord" Jesus did. On the other hand, it is plausible, but less likely, that a scribe did the opposite—substituting *theou* for *kuriou*—in opposition to Patripassianism.[113]

One piece of internal evidence supports that Ac 20.28 should read "God." It is that the phrase, "the church of God," appears eleven times in Paul's writings whereas "the church of the Lord" does not appear in the NT.

The other textual problem with Ac 20.28 regards whether the word *idiou* ("own") is to be taken as an adjective or a noun. That is, is the correct text *tou idiou haimatos* ("his own blood") or *tou haimatos tou idiou* ("the blood of his own;" some would also translate it "his own blood")? The former reading lends itself to calling Jesus "God." Indeed, this reading is usually found in MSS that have *theou*.

The UBS' Committee also rendered *tou haimatos tou idiou* ("blood of his own") as the correct reading and gave it a B-rating, meaning that they had "some degree of doubt" about it.[114] This UBS text of Ac 20.28 therefore translates, "the church of God which he purchased with the blood of his own (One/Son)."

Two *Theou* Translations

So, if *theou* is authentic in Ac 20.28 there are two primary translations of it and three ways to understand it. They are as follows, with commentary appended:

1. "To shepherd the church of God which he purchased with his own blood." This translation suggests that "God" refers to Jesus since the Father does not have blood. Traditionalist A.W. Wainwright admits, "it is difficult to imagine that the divinity of Christ should have been stated in such a blunt and misleading fashion."[115] However, this translation can also be understood to mean that God the Father purchased the church with Jesus' blood, which belongs to both the Father and Jesus (cf. Jn 17.10).

---

[111] B.M. Metzger, *Textual Commentary*, 480.
[112] B.M. Metzger, *Textual Commentary*, 480-81.
[113] Patripassianism, classified as modalistic Monarchianism, was condemned by the majority of church fathers in the 3rd century. It means Jesus was divine yet had no personality distinct from that of the Father.
[114] B.M. Metzger, *Textual Commentary*, 482.
[115] A.W. Wainwright, *The Trinity in the New Testament*, 74.

2. "To shepherd the church of God which he purchased with the blood of his own (One/Son)." This rendering of the UBS Greek text clearly makes "God" refer to the Father, "the blood" belongs to Jesus, and "his own" means the Father's own Son, viz., Jesus Christ.[116] This translation, which is preferred by a majority of scholars, does not call Jesus "God." Its meaning is encapsulated in a new song sung to Jesus in heaven, "Thou wast slain, and didst purchase for God with Thy blood men" (Rev 5.9).

Conclusion of Commentators

A very large majority of biblical exegetes render Ac 20.28 as a text that does not identify Jesus as God. Even most contemporary traditionalist commentators, especially those who have written extensively that the NT calls Jesus "God," conclude that Ac 20.28 does not do so. Here are some examples among them: R.E. Brown says, "we are by no means certain that this verse calls Jesus God;"[117] M. Harris deems it "unlikely, although not impossible;"[118] A.W. Wainwright admits, "this passage cannot be adduced as convincing evidence that Jesus was called God in New Testament times."[119]

2. Does Paul call Christ "God" in Romans 9.5?

Introduction	Reasons for the One Person View
Modern Greek New Testaments	Reasons for the Two Persons View
Versions that Call Christ "God"	Survey of Commentators
Versions that Do Not Call Christ "God"	Conclusion

Introduction

Traditionalist authorities regard Rom 9.5 as a foremost debatable christological text in the NT that calls Jesus "God." Scholars have probably analyzed the translation of Rom 9.5, and thus its meaning, more than that of any other NT text.[120] Bruce Metzger says F.C. Burkitt did not exaggerate in saying of Rom 9.5 that its "punctuation has probably been more discussed than that of any other sentence in literature."[121] James D.G. Dunn concludes, "So far as Paul's own theology is concerned, the issue hangs on Rom. 9.5."[122]

The problem with Rom 9.5 (actually 9.5b) is the Greek language. Paul wrote his letter in koine Greek. Up to that time, Greek had no punctuation and no spaces between letters, with all letters being capitalized, called "uncials." Punctuation, spacing between letters, and upper and lower case were not incorporated into the Greek language until the 3rd and 4th centuries CE. So, NT grammarians admit that the correct rendering of Rom 9.5b cannot be decided on the basis of Greek grammar that did not exist then. The question is how to punctuate the Greek text

---

[116] B.M. Metzger (*Textual Commentary*, 481) observes that "this absolute use of *ho idios* [his/her/one's own] is found in Greek papri as a term of endearment referring to near relatives."
[117] R.E. Brown, *Jesus God and Man*, 12.
[118] M. Harris, *Jesus as God*, 141.
[119] A.W. Wainwright, "The Confession 'Jesus is God' in the New Testament," 294.
[120] W. Sanday and A.C. Headlam, *A Critical and Exegetical Commentary on the Epistle to the Romans*, in ICC (1896), 233; M. Harris, *Jesus as God*, 144.
[121] Bruce M. Metzger, "The Punctuation of Rom. 9:5," in *Christ and Spirit in the New Testament: Festschrift in Honour of C.F.D. Moule*, ed. Barnabas Lindars and Stephen S. Smalley (Cambridge: University, 1973), 95. See also F.C. Burkitt, "On Romans ix 5 and Mark xiv 61," *JTS* 5 (1904): 451-55.
[122] J.D.G. Dunn, *The Theology of Paul the Apostle*, 257.

and translate it into English. Thus, whether Rom 9.5b calls Jesus "God" is all about grammar, which in this case involves mostly interpretation.

The primary question about how to punctuate the Greek text of Rom 9.5b can be stated as follows: in accordance with later, punctuated Greek, should a colon (a raised period) or a full stop (a period) be inserted after the word *sarka* ("flesh") in the Greek text that is not punctuated? If either should be, then an independent clause begins after it as a doxology to God the Father, and the passage does not call Christ "God." Since Rom 9.5b mentions both God and Christ, God presumably being the Father, this rendering is called the Two Persons view. But if another form of punctuation is placed after *sarka*, such as a comma, or the sentence is punctuated in some other place, the verse continues with Christ in view. In this case it becomes a doxology to Christ, thus calling Him "God." Since only Christ is in view in this grammatical construction, it is called the One Person view. Ezra Abbot, in his thorough article on this question, shows seven possible ways to punctuate Rom 9.5b.[123] But these two constructions predominate among contemporary NT scholars.

A comment is needed about the later, punctuated Greek NT MSS. From the time scribes began inserting punctuation in their copies of Greek NT documents, extant copies thereafter are mixed. Some have a full stop after the word *sarka* and some do not. Abbot claims that a thorough examination of miniscules (cursive lower case) shows a notable majority have a full stop.[124] Greek expert M. Harris states, "At most one may say that many ancient scribes regarded a pause after *sarka* as natural or necessary,"[125] showing they considered the verse a doxology to God the Father. But B.M. Metzger observes, "The presence of marks of punctuation in early manuscripts of the New Testament is so sporadic and haphazard that one cannot infer with confidence the construction given by the punctuator."[126] W. Sanday and A.C. Headlam therefore conclude, "the punctuation of the MSS is interesting in the history of interpretation, but has no other value."[127]

A subordinate question concerning Rom 9.5b concerns whether the ascription, "who is over all," should be applied to "Christ" or "God."

Modern Greek New Testaments

Modern NT Greek texts render Rom 9.5b as if it had a colon (raised period) after *sarka*, so that it does not call Christ "God," or as if it had a comma after *sarka*, so that it calls Christ "God." The punctuation in Rom 9.5b in modern Greek NT texts is as follows:

Two Persons View: Christ not God	**One Person View**: Christ is God
Nestle-Aland[25], United Bible Societies[1, 2, 3]	Nestle-Aland[26, 27]

Versions that Call Christ "God"

The following English versions render the One Person view of Rom 9.5b:

- "Christ came, who is over all, God blessed for ever." (AV)
- "Christ ... who is over all, God blessed forever." (RV)

---

[123] E. Abbot, "On ... Romans ix.5," 89-90.
[124] Indebted to M. Harris, *Jesus as God*, 149.
[125] M. Harris, *Jesus as God*, 149.
[126] B.M. Metzger, *A Textual Commentary*, 521n2.
[127] W. Sanday and A.C. Headlam, *Romans*, 233.

- "Christ, who is God over all, blessed for ever." (RSVmg, cf. ESV)
- "Christ ... who is over all, God blessed forever." (NASB)
- "Christ who is above all, God for ever blessed!" (JB)
- "sprang the Messiah, supreme above all, God blessed forever." (NEBmg¹)
- "Messiah, who is God, supreme above all and blessed for ever." (REBmg¹)
- "Christ, who is God over all, forever praised!" (NIV)
- "Christ who is above all, God, blessed for ever." (NJB)
- "The Messiah, who is over all, God blessed forever." (NRSV)
- "Messiah, who is God over all, blessed forever." (NRSVmg¹)

Versions that Do Not Call Christ "God"

The following English versions render the Two Person view of Rom 9.5b:

- "Messiah ... Blessed forever be God who is over all!" (NAB)
- "Christ. God who is over all be blessed for ever." (RSV)
- "Christ. (Blessed for evermore be the God who is over all! Amen.)" (Moffatt)
- "Christ came—God who is over all be blessed forever!" (Goodspeed)
- "Christ,... May God, who rules over all, be praised forever!" (TEV)
- "Messiah. May God, supreme above all, be blessed for ever." (NEB)
- "the Messiah, who is supreme above all. Blessed be God for ever!" (NEBmg²)
- "Christ, who is over all. God forever be praised!" (NIVmg¹)
- "Christ. God who is over all be forever praised!" (NIVmg²)
- "Messiah. May he who is God over all be blessed forever." (NRSVmg²)

Reasons for the One Person View

The One Person view is based mostly on narrow grammatical and exegetical grounds. The following reasons are proposed by commentators who insist that Rom 9.5b calls Christ "God," with rebuttals appended:

1. Almost all church fathers regarded Rom 9.5b as calling Christ "God."[128]

Rebuttal: H.A.W. Meyer claims, "In the Arian controversies our passage was not made use of. But at a later period it was triumphantly made available against the Arians."[129] This shows that scribes prior to and during the Arian controversy did not think Rom 9.5b calls Christ "God" in the unpunctuated Greek text. Bruce Metzger, who thinks the text calls Christ "God," admits of later fathers that "their dogmatic interests may have swayed (and in many instances undoubtedly did sway) their interpretation" of Rom 9.5b.[130] Members of the editorial committee for the United Bible Societies' Greek NT (3rd ed.) "agreed that evidence from the church fathers, who were almost unanimous in understanding the passage as referring to *ho Christos* ["the Christ"], is of relatively minor significance."[131]

2. A doxology of praise to God in Rom 9.5b would be out of place with Paul's expressed sorrow and regret recorded previously, in vv. 1-3.

Rebuttal: But Paul's enumerated privileges for Israel, a major theme in the book of Romans (Rom 3.1-2), constitutes a change of subject in the interim of vv. 4-5a which fits well with a concluding doxology to God.

---

[128] M. Harris (*Jesus as God*, 144) cites H.M. Faccio (*De divinitate Christi juxta S. Paulum, Rom. 9,5*, 64-101, 135), who shows in a detailed monograph that church fathers almost unanimously accepted without any debate that Rom 9.5b calls Christ "God."
[129] H.A.W. Meyer, in MCNT, 5:360-61.
[130] B.M. Metzger, "The Punctuation of Rom. 9:5," 103.
[131] B.M. Metzger, *Textual Commentary*, 520-21.

3. The normal word order in OT doxologies is not used, in which the word "blessed" precedes "LORD/God" (e.g., Gen 9.26; 24.27; Ex 18.10; 1 Sam 25.32; Ps 41.13).

Rebuttal: But the doxology in Rom 1.25 is very similar to Rom 9.5b: "God ... the Creator, who is blessed forever. Amen." This pronoun "who" refers to "God," effectively making "God" precede "blessed" as in Rom 9.5b (cf. pronoun for God preceding "glory" in Gal 1.5; 2 Tim 4.18). Also, Paul does not seem concerned about this particular syntax since he writes it both ways in another letter: "Blessed be the God and Father of our Lord Jesus Christ" and "the God and Father ... He who is blessed forever" (2 Cor 1.3; 11.31).

4. In other Pauline doxologies (e.g., Rom 1.25; 11.36; 2 Cor 11.31; Gal 1.3-5; Eph 3.20-21; Phil 4.20), the word "God" is not mentioned first, as in Rom 9.5b.[132]

Rebuttal: The same argument above holds true here, in which the pronoun for "God" appears first in Rom 1.25 and 2 Cor 11.31.

5. Pauline doxologies are never asyndetic (without a conjunction), as here, which would be unnatural and render the articular participle *ho on* ("who is") as superfluous.[133] That is, Paul's doxologies *usually* exist in the same sentence and thus link with what precedes, whereas a stop after *sarka* unnaturally begins a new sentence and/or a new subject.

Rebuttal: If Pauline doxologies do not *always* take this form, in which Rom 11.36 and 2 Cor 11.31 are exceptions, then this reason lacks weight. M. Harris cites twelve NT texts that contain the same or similar articular participle which is asyndetic. This shows that such a construction is not unnatural, though Harris thinks it "unconscionable" to divorce it in this case from the preceding subject of "Christ."[134]

Reasons for the Two Persons View

Notice that, in contrast to the above, most of the following reasons given for the Two Persons view—that Rom 9.5b *does not* call Christ "God" but is a doxology to God the Father—do not concern the text and therefore its proper grammatical construction. This is because most scholars who adopt the Two Person view insist that the question cannot be settled according to grammar or punctuation (and some would even add exegesis) but must be explored in the style, usage, and theology of Paul's writings.

1. Paul, the former zealous Pharisee, could not have called Christ "God" because monotheism still remained a dominant feature of his theology.[135]

Rebuttal: M. Harris asserts, "Paul shows that his Christian experience and reflection have forced him to redefine his hereditary monotheism so as to include Christ within the category of Deity."[136]

On the contrary, we do not have any sufficient evidence to indicate that Paul ever changed his early and basic evangelistic message about Jesus' identity as recorded in the book of Acts. That message is that Jesus is the Christ, the Son of God (Ac 9.20-22), not that Jesus is Deity. Thus, Paul never compromised his former, strict monotheism. In this epistle Paul says "God ... is one" (Gr. *hen*), and he means it numerically because he also writes of "the One, Jesus Christ" (Rom 3.30; 5.17).

---

[132] Paul also has doxologies to God the Father in Rom 16.27; 1 Tim 1.17; 6.15-16.

[133] N. Turner, *Grammatical Insights*, 15.

[134] M. Harris, *Jesus as God*, 157, 159n45. See M. Harris (*Jesus as God*, 152-165) for other grammatical reasons. See E. Abbot's ("On ... Romans ix.5," 95-101) rebuttal that this participle is superfluous.

[135] E.g., Rom 3.29-30; 1 Cor 8.6; Eph 4.4-6; 1 Tim 1.17.

[136] M. Harris, *Jesus as God*, 167.

2. Paul could not have called Jesus Christ "God" because he constantly distinguished God and Jesus Christ throughout this letter as well as all of his NT letters.[137]

3. Paul never directly calls Christ "God" in his NT letters. Scholars who think otherwise can muster only Tit 2.13 and perhaps 2 Th 1.12 for support. However, since Paul uses the word *theos* for the Father over 500 times in his NT corpus, such uniform usage suggests that he did not depart from it in a bare few ambiguous texts, such as Rom 9.5b.[138]

Rebuttal: Murray Harris argues that Paul's infrequent application of *theos* to Christ can be accounted for by the following reasons: (1) the distinction between the Father and the Son is maintained, (2) the Son's subordination to the Father is intact, (3) Jesus' humanity would have been jeopardized otherwise, and (4) applying *theos* as a proper noun to Jesus would have resulted in the charge that Jesus is "another God."[139]

But how does the lack of frequency affect any of these points? If the Bible only once identifies Jesus as "God," then He is God and these points are without merit.

4. Paul, being an astute theologian and gifted communicator, would not call Christ "God" without explanation. Much less would he do so in a brief clause that begins a lengthy treatise on an altogether different subject, especially it being about Israel, as he does in Rom 9-11. Even if he did, he would anticipate a strong reaction and therefore attach an apologetic response. Although A.W. Wainwright tentatively thinks Paul calls Christ "God" in Rom 9.5b, he admits that authorities who share his persuasion "have not shown how it fits in with the rest of the apostle's thought. If he wished to introduce this clear proclamation of the divinity of Christ into his epistles, why did he not do so more often? Why did he not expand and explain the idea, instead of thrusting it forward abruptly and passing immediately to another theme?"[140]

5. The frequency of six out of the total of seven other doxologies in Paul's corpus being clearly addressed to God the Father[141] suggest the same in Rom 9.5b.[142]

6. Paul never applies the Greek expression *epi panton* ("over all"), or its corollary, *pantokrator* ("Almighty"), to Christ, and neither does any other NT author. To do so would contradict Paul's teaching that Christ is subordinate to God. For he says elsewhere that "Christ belongs to God" (1 Cor 3.23), "God is the head of Christ" (1 Cor 11.3), and that there is "one God and Father of all who is over all" (Eph 4.6; cf. 1 Cor 15.27-28). This evidence strongly suggests that Paul intends this same meaning in Rom 9.5b. Also, in Eph 4.6 the "Lord" (Jesus Christ) is juxtapositioned with "God the Father," thereby distinguishing the two while also signifying that the Father is both the God of Christ and over Christ. Moreover, the nearby doxology to God the Father, in Rom 11.36 ("to Him are all things"), effectively means the same as "over all."[143] In other words, God the Father is over

---

[137] E.g., Rom 1.7-8; 2.16; 3.22; 5.1, 10-11; 6.11, 23; 8.3, 34; 10.9; 15.6; 16.27.

[138] E. Abbot, "On ... Romans ix.5," 113.

[139] M. Harris, *Jesus as God*, 170. Ironically, Harris appears impervious to the fact that all four of his points are actually arguments proposed by those who do not believe that the NT calls Jesus Christ "God."

[140] A.W. Wainwright, *The Trinity in the New Testament*, 57-58.

[141] Rom 1.25; 11.36; 2 Cor 11.31; Gal 1.3-5; Eph 3.20-21; Phil 4.20. His sole Jesus doxology is 2 Tim 4.18.

[142] See OT doxologies in Ps 41.13; 66.20; 72.18; 89.52; 106.48; praising God and Christ in Rev 5.13; 7.10.

[143] E. Abbot, "On ... Romans ix.5," 106.

all, including over Christ. H.A.W. Meyer thus rightly insists that calling Christ "over all" and "the Almighty" "is absolutely incompatible with the entire view of the NT as to the dependence of the Son on the Father."[144]

Rebuttal: Paul elsewhere calls Christ "head over all things" (Eph 1.22), thereby insinuating that He is God.

On the contrary, both Christ's authority over, and possession of, all things is said to be given to Him by the Father.[145] Only the Father remains over all, including Christ.

7. Taking the words as "God over all" alludes to OT parallels which suggest a doxology to God here. For example, Ps 104.19-20 reads, "The LORD has established His throne in the heavens; and His sovereignty rules over all. Bless the LORD." And the end of 1 Chron 29.11 reads, "Thine is the dominion, O LORD, and Thou dost exalt Thyself as head over all." The first part of this last verse influenced Christian scribes to add it to the end of the so-called "Lord's Prayer," in Mt 6.13. This demonstrates that they thought Yahweh referred exclusively to the Father in 1 Chron 29.11. And 1 Cor 11.3 apparently alludes to 1 Chron 29.11 as well. So, in Rom 9.5b and 1 Cor 11.3, Paul likely alludes to 1 Chron 29.11, thereby implying that Yahweh, not Christ, is "God" and "head over all."

8. The Greek adjective *eulogetos* ("blessed") is never applied to Christ, either in Paul's corpus or anywhere else in the NT. Rather, in all seven instances in which *eulogetos* appears in the NT, it is applied to God the Father. In addition, expressions like "Blessed be the LORD/God" frequent the OT about thirty times. In accordance with this Jewish usage (e.g., Mk 14.61; Lk 1.68), former Pharisee Paul applies *eulogetos* to God (the Father) in Rom 1.25 and elsewhere (2 Cor 1.3; 11.31; Eph 1.3; cf. 1 Pt 1.3), which suggests that he does the same in Rom 9.5b.[146]

Rebuttal: Paul's infrequent use of *eulogetos*, occurring only four other times in his writings, is too small of a sample upon which to establish a fixed usage.

9. Paul elsewhere writes that God is the "only Sovereign" (1 Tim 6.15), which seems incompatible with Christ being "over all." In other words, God alone is the ultimate Source and Bestower of all gifts and blessings (Jam 1.17; cf. Jn 3.27), including these enumerated privileges granted to Israel.[147]

10. Including Christ in a list of eight advantages given Israel seems incompatible with Paul describing one of those presumably God-given privileges as "God over all."[148]

Survey of Commentators

As mentioned above, later church fathers regarded Rom 9.5b as calling Christ "God." Erasmus, who was essentially the compiler of TR, from which the AV was translated, was the first notable scholar to critically examine Rom 9.5b and thereby question that it called Christ "God." What about more recent scholarship?

M. Harris has produced a survey of fifty-six commentators regarding how they treat Rom 9.5b. In it he shows that thirty-nine favor the One Person view, thirteen prefer the Two Persons view, and seven are non-commital.[149] But it

---

[144] H.A.W. Meyer, in MCNT, 5:362.

[145] E.g., Mt 28.19; Mt 11.27/Lk 10.22; Jn 3.35; 13.3; 16.15; 17.10.

[146] Contra N. Turner (*Grammatical Insights*, 15), who applies the doxology in 2 Cor 11.31 to Christ. Paul indicates otherwise in 2 Cor 1.3. See F.C. Burkitt, "On Romans ix 5 and Mark xiv 61," 452.

[147] See Ernst Kasemann, *Commentary on Romans* [1973], tr. and ed. by Geoffrey W. Bromiley (Grand Rapids: Eerdmans, 1980), 260. Cf. Jn 14.16, 26; 16.26.

[148] J.D.G. Dunn, *Romans 9-16*, 529.

[149] M. Harris, *Jesus as God*, 172.

should be noted that Harris' survey encompasses the past few centuries rather than scholars of more recent vintage.

Some scholars claim that a significant shift has been occurring in contemporary scholarship toward the Two Persons rendering of Rom 9.5b. As early as 1961, Vincent Taylor claimed, "it is well known that the greatest of commentators range themselves on each side" of the issue. Yet he claims that the balance of recent scholarship up to his time had adopted the Two Persons view.[150] *The Interpreter's Bible* affirms likewise.[151] But in 1994, M. Harris objected by alleging that A.E. "Harvey (*Jesus*) was unjustified in claiming (in 1982) that 'the great majority of recent commentators and translators take Rom. 9:5b as an independent doxology to God.'"[152] Indeed, the prior year J.A. Fitzmyer had provided the most up-to-date and thorough assessment. Surveying seventy modern scholars who had written commentaries on Romans, he lists thirty-five who interpret Rom 9.5b as calling Christ "God" and thirty-five who interpret that it does not call Christ "God."[153] However, no doubt a large majority of those scholars believed that Christ is God.

Then there are scholars who offer a tentative opinion on Rom 9.5b or insist that its proper rendering is too uncertain. W. Barclay states, "Here again is a case in which few will wish to be dogmatic. Both punctuations are equally possible, although, to express no more than an opinion, we would say that the Greek reads more naturally as an ascription of praise to God."[154] F.F. Bruce favors a doxology to Christ but admits, "the legitimacy of the alternative punctuation must be conceded" as "equally permissable."[155] Other notable commentators who regard the rendering of Rom 9.5b as uncertain are T.W. Manson,[156] James D.G. Dunn,[157] and William Sanday.[158]

The majority of the members of the editorial committee for the *United Bible Societies' Greek New Testament* (3rd and 4th eds.) preferred either a colon or a full stop after *sarka* in Rom 9.5b, making what follows it a doxology to God the Father. They regarded none of the reasons for the One Person view as "decisive" and considered it "tantamount to impossible" that Paul would have called Christ "God blessed forever."[159]

Conclusion

It must be concluded that Rom 9.5b is ambiguous since the earliest and therefore most reliable Greek MSS of the NT, or portions thereof, were written in uncials without punctuation. So, the proper translation of Rom 9.5b cannot be determined with certainty on the basis of either grammar or exegesis. In such cases, Paul's clear statements made elsewhere on the same subject should

---

[150] V. Taylor, "Does the New Testament Call Jesus God?" 117.

[151] IB, 9:540.

[152] M. Harris, *Jesus as God*, 154n22.

[153] J.A. Fitzmyer, *Romans: A New Translation with Introduction and Commentary*, in AB 33 (1993), 548. He shows that O. Michel has held either view at different times.

[154] W. Barclay, *Jesus As They Saw Him*, 29.

[155] F.F. Bruce, *The Letter of Paul to the Romans: An Introduction and Commentary*, 2nd ed., in TNTC (1985), 186.

[156] T.W. Manson, in PCB, 824.

[157] J.D.G. Dunn, *Christology in the Making*, 45. Dunn later changed and adopted the Two Persons view in *Romans 9-16*, 528-29, 535-36; idem, *The Theology of Paul the Apostle*, 255-57.

[158] William Sanday, *The Epistle to the Romans* (London: Cassel, Peter, Galpin, nd), 103.

[159] B.M. Metzger, *Textual Commentary*, 522. The members of the editorial committee were Kurt Aland, Matthew Black, Carlo M. Martini, Bruce M. Metzger, and Allen Wikgren.

serve as the primary determining factor in assessing his intent in Rom 9.5b. Paul's unambiguous passages, such as 1 Cor 8.6 and Eph 4.5-6, his frequent affirmation of strict monotheistic belief throughout his letters, his constant practice of distinguishing between God and Christ, his clear subordination of Christ to God, and other features in his corpus indicate that Paul could not have intended to call Christ "God" in Rom 9.5b. Regardless, this grammatically ambiguous passage should not be used as a proof text to support the traditional belief that Jesus Christ is God.

3. Does 2 Corinthians 8.9 indicate Jesus preexisted?

Most Christians have thought that 2 Cor 8.9 echoes Phil 2.6-8> by presenting a concise summary of Jesus' preexistence and incarnation. It reads:

9 For you know the grace of our Lord Jesus Christ, that though He was rich, yet for our sakes He became poor, that you through His poverty might become rich.

The common view has been that the word "rich" indicates the personal preexistence of Jesus in heaven as the Father's equal, and the words "poor" and "poverty" signify Jesus abandoning this lofty status at His incarnation. Karl-Josef Kuschel observes, "Traditional exegesis has always interpreted this passage in terms of pre-existence Christology and incarnation, as have present-day exegetes right across all confessional camps."[160]

However, both James D.G. Dunn and Maurice Casey insist otherwise, that this passage only concerns Adam Christology.[161] Dunn explains rather cogently about both Phil 2.6-8 and 2 Cor 8.9, "Though he could have enjoyed the riches of an uninterrupted communion with God, Jesus freely chose to embrace the poverty of Adam's distance from God, in his ministry as a whole, but particularly in his death, in order that we might enter into the full inheritance intended for Adam in the first place."[162] Traditionalist and systematic theologian John Macquarrie thinks "Dunn's interpretation allows us to see Paul's general Christology as much more coherent than it would otherwise appear."[163] Dunn later explained that "2 Cor 8.9 is as a vivid allusion to the tremendous personal cost of Jesus' ministry ... this self-impoverishment ... That Paul intended an allusion to the preexistent Christ's self-abasement in incarnation must be judged unlikely."[164]

Indeed, this interpretation of 2 Cor 8.9 conforms better with its context. The entire chapter of 2 Cor 8 is about the collecting of monies for the saints at Jerusalem. They had fallen into financial poverty by enduring persecution for their faith in Jesus. Paul reveals that many churches he ministered to were serving these brethren by giving of their own financial resources and thereby following their Lord Jesus Christ in being a servant to others. For, Jesus had said, "the Son of Man did not come to be served, but to serve, and to give His life a ransom for many" (Mt 20.28/Mk 10.45). Both this saying and 2 Cor 8.9 allude to Isaiah's portrait of the righteous, suffering "Servant" in Isa 52.13—53.

Perhaps Paul had something more specific in mind. Dunn thinks 2 Cor 8.9 depicts "evidently a one-stage act of abasement."[165] Until Jesus was thirty years

---
[160] K. Kuschel, *Born Before All Time?* 295.
[161] J.D.G. Dunn, *Christology in the Making*, 114-21; P.M. Casey, "The Deification of Jesus," 702-03.
[162] J.D.G. Dunn, *Christology in the Making*, 123.
[163] J. Macquarrie, *Jesus Christ in Modern Thought*, 59.
[164] J.D.G. Dunn, *The Theology of the Apostle Paul*, 292.
[165] J.D.G. Dunn, *The Theology of the Apostle Paul*, 291.

old, He probably enjoyed an emotionally rich and fulfilling life as the eldest of four brothers and several sisters (Mk 6.3). And He must have had a good reputation as the carpenter of Nazareth and its vicinity. But in a most profound and untold *single act of self-denial*, He laid aside this comfortable lifestyle by leaving home, going to the Jordan River to be baptized by John, and undertaking His public ministry. Choosing this divine mission would lead to financial poverty and even forfeiture of life. It was like when His disciples left all to follow Him (Lk 5.11, 28 par.; 18.28). Jesus admitted to such financial poverty after being run out of Nazareth, when He said to His disciples, "The foxes have holes, and the birds of the air have nests; but the Son of Man has nowhere to lay His head" (Mt 8.20/Lk 9.58).

Jesus also epitomized a poverty of spirit. He taught it in His Sermon on the Mount (cf. Mt 5.3). Isaiah prophesied that Jesus would be "despised and forsaken of men, a man of sorrows, and acquainted with grief," "oppressed and ... afflicted" (Isa 53.3, 6).

Jesus also became "poor" by choosing to undergo death (Jn 10.17-18. It seems that He never would have died by natural causes. Due to His virgin birth, He did not inherit a sin nature. Thus, the death principle did not pass naturally unto Him (Rom 5.12).

When Jesus was crucified, most people thought He was "smitten of God" (Isa 53.4). He cried out, "MY GOD, MY GOD, WHY HAST THOU FORSAKEN ME" (Mt 27.46/Mk 15.34). In this way, He "bore the sin of many" to "justify the many" (Isa 53.11).

All of this is what Paul meant by Jesus becoming poor to make "the many" rich.

4. Does Galatians 2.20 say "Son of God" or "God and Christ"?

Only biblical scholars know about Gal 2.20 as a possible text that calls Christ "God." It is due to a textual variant which appears in a bare few, though important, Greek MSS.[166] The well-attested Greek text, its variant and translations are as follows:

Well-attested Text	Variant Text
en pistei zo te tou huiou tou theou	*en pistei zo te tou theou kai Christou*
"I live by faith in the Son of God"	"I live by faith in God and in Christ" or
	"I live by faith in (the) God and Christ"

Editors of the primary Greek NT and translators of all modern English versions reject the above variant because of its scarcity of MS evidence. And commentators almost unanimously reject it as well. R.E. Brown remarks that these words are "never found elsewhere in the Pauline writings, and so is suspect. Thus, this text should not be counted among those passages which call Jesus God."[167]

How did this variant creep into the MS tradition? Bruce Metzger explains that the standard text "is widely attested by a broad spectrum of Greek, versional, and patristic witnesses. It is probable that in copying, the eye of the scribe passed immediately from the first to the second *tou*, so that only *tou theou* was written

---

[166] These are P45, *Codex Vaticanus*, and *Codex Bezae*.
[167] R.E. Brown, *Jesus God and Man*, 11.

(as in ms. 330); since what followed was now incongruous, copyists either added *tou huiou* or *kai Christou*."[168]

5. What about "the kingdom of Christ and God" in Ephesians 5.5?

A minor text that some allege calls Christ "God" is Eph 5.5. The critical phrase in the NASB is, "the kingdom of Christ and God." A few 19th century scholars thought this phrase in the Greek text could give the sense, "the kingdom of Christ who is God."[169] Grammarians N. Turner and M. Zerwick think it plausible;[170] but a large majority of scholars now do not.[171] No English versions have this rendering; some even indicate otherwise by including another genitive, "the kingdom of Christ and of God" (AV, RSV, NAB, NEB, NIV, NRSV, REB, ESV). A few have only "the kingdom of God" (JB, NJB).

The kingdom belongs to both God and Christ. Jesus often talked of "the kingdom of God." Yet that same kingdom also belongs to Jesus (Dan 7.14; Lk 19.12; 1 Cor 15.24; Rev 11.15). All the Father has belongs to Jesus (Mt 11.27; 28.18; Jn 16.15; 17.7, 10).

The same is true of Judgement Day. Paul uses the expressions "the judgment seat of God" and "the judgment seat of Christ" (Rom 14.10; 2 Cor 5.10; cf. Jn 5.27). He says of that time, "God will judge the secrets of men through Christ Jesus" (Rom 2.16). While God "has given all judgment to the Son" (Jn 5.22), both will participate that Day (v. 30).

Also, Paul clearly distinguishes God and Christ six times in this epistle.[172] Such internal evidence makes it likely that he intended the same in Eph 5.5. One instance is Paul's foremost passage that identifies the Father exclusively as God and Jesus as Lord: "There is ... one Lord, one faith, one baptism; one God and Father of all" (Eph 4.4-6).

6. Does Philippians 2.6 say Jesus preexisted equal with God?

Introduction	"The Form of a Bond-Servant"
Two Interpretations	Being Born and Becoming a Man
Adam Christology as Background	"He Humbled Himself"
Gnostic Redeemer Myth as Background	"God Highly Exalted Him"
Servant and Son of Man as Background	"The Name ... Above Every Name"
"The Form of God"	"The Name of Jesus"
"Equality With God"	"Every Knee Bow and Tongue Confess"
"A Thing to Be Grasped"	Jesus Christ is Lord to God's Glory
"Emptied Himself"	Paul's Applies the Hymn Personally
	Conclusion

---

[168] B.M. Metzger, *Textual Commentary*, 593.
[169] M. Harris (*Jesus as God*, 261n18) cites T.F. Middleton, F. Godet, and H.P. Liddon.
[170] N. Turner (*Grammatical Insights*, 16) asserts without explanation that this phrase should be translated, "the kingdom of Christ who is God." Cf. Max Zerwick, *Biblical Greek: Illustrated by Examples*, 185.
[171] E.g., E. Abbot ("On ... Titus ii. 13," 3) claims that "a large majority of the best commentators" in his time, i.e., the late 19th century, adopted the Two Persons view of Eph 5.5.
[172] Eph 1.16; 2.4, 6; 4.4-6, 32; 5.2.

Introduction

Philippians 2.5-11, particularly vv. 6-7, is one of the most important christological texts in the Bible. One reason is that NT scholars regard it as the earliest christological portion in the NT, thus rendering it such a critical source for discovering Christian origins. Traditionalists usually cite Phil 2.5-11, even though it is not a *theos* text, as one of their chief biblical texts in support of their view that Jesus both preexisted and was and is God.

Even though scholars agree that there is no concept of the preexistence of Jesus in His synoptic sayings, H.E. Todt informs, "Christological doctrine has been developed in Protestantism mainly with regard to the concepts expressed in Phil. 2. The synoptic texts were interpreted to conform to this passage."[173] It should have been vice versa.

Philippians 2.5-11 has also been one of the most hotly debated passages in the history of NT interpretation.[174] N.T. Wright attests that it "is one of the most notoriously complex passages in Paul," i.e., in his NT letters.[175] Ralph P. Martin informs, "Philippians 2:5-11 taxes the skill of the translator, as many of the key words, especially to do with the presentation of Christ's role in the text, baffle the lexicographer's mind and offer a wide, often puzzling, variety of choice and interpretation.... Many of the terms under examination are rare in biblical Greek and even rarer in the Pauline vocabulary; hence the translator's difficulty is compounded."[176] Gerald Hawthorne echoes previous scholars by humorously stating about Phil 2.5-11, "the number of genuine exegetical problems and the sheer mass of books and articles it has called forth leaves one ... well-nigh stricken with mental paralysis."[177] Therefore, this critical christological text, which is full of compact and rare phraseology, requires that we examine what scholars say about it as we try to unpack its author's intended meaning and the Apostle Paul's purpose for using it.

Ernst Lohmeyer's 1928 monograph on Phil 2.6-11 proved pivotal in this scholarly discussion.[178] The consensus ever since has been that Phil 2.6-11 is a hymn (perhaps a hymnal fragment) or a psalm that is probably pre-Pauline.[179] Most scholars think Paul has incorporated it into this letter as a model of humility and its divine reward. So, this hymn or psalm is liturgical, instructional, and doctrinal. It reads as follows in the NASB:

5 Have this attitude in yourselves which was also in Christ Jesus,
6 who, although He existed in the form of God, did not regard equality with God a thing to be grasped,
7 but emptied Himself, taking the form of a bond-servant, and being made in the likeness of men.

---

[173] H.E. Todt, *The Son of Man in the Synoptic Tradition* [1963], tr. Dorothea M. Barton, 2nd ed. (London: SCM, 1965), 295, cf. 13-14, 19-20.

[174] Lincoln D. Hurst, "Christ, Adam, and Preexistence Revisited," in *Where Christology Began*, ed. R. Martin and B. Dodd, 84.

[175] N.T. Wright, "A Biblical Portrait of God," in *The Changing Faces of God: Lincoln Lectures in Theology* (n.p.: Lincoln Cathedral Publications, 1996), 23.

[176] Ralph P. Martin, "*Carmen Christi* Revisited," in *Where Christology Began*, eds. Ralph P. Martin and Brian J. Dodd (Louisville, KT: WJK, 1998), 2.

[177] G.F. Hawthorne, *Philippians* in WBC 43, 76.

[178] Ernst Lohmeyer, *Der Brief an die Philipper* [1928], 9th ed., rev. W. Schmauch, 1953 (Gottingen: Vandenhoeck and Ruprecht, 1930).

[179] See Eph 5.19-20. Most scholars think Paul inserts hymnic material in Col 3.16-17 and 1 Tim 3.16. A few scholars, e.g., G. Fee and R. Gundry, recently have denied that Phil 2.6-11 was originally a hymn.

8 And being found in appearance as a man, He humbled Himself by becoming obedient to the point of death, even death on a cross.
9 Therefore also God highly exalted Him, and bestowed on Him the name which is above every name,
10 that at the name of Jesus every knee should bow, of those who are in heaven, and on earth, and under the earth,
11 and that every tongue should confess that Jesus Christ is Lord, to the glory of God the Father.

Since this hymn in Phil 2.6-11 has had a profound impact on church Christology, we will briefly examine each of its phrases and consider their possible OT background as important elements in their interpretation.

Two Interpretations

Two contrasting interpretations of Phil 2.6-11 have prevailed among NT scholars. These are the traditional "incarnational" or "preexistent interpretation,"[180] which has dominated to the present time, and the exclusively "anthropological" or "human interpretation,"[181] which recently has been increasing in favor with scholars.[182] The preexistent interpretation means that vv. 6-7 of the hymn present Jesus as personally existing in heaven prior to His earthly life—being equal with God the Father presumably as the Logos of Jn 1.1-18—and He humbled Himself by means of an incarnation in becoming a man. In contrast, the human interpretation means that vv. 6-8 refer only to Jesus' earthly life, thus having nothing to do with preexistence or incarnation.[183] Nearly all conservative scholars think vv. 9-11 necessitate Jesus' resurrection, ascension, and heavenly exaltation. And many scholars have disputed whether the hymn is ethical, soteriological, and eschatological.

This Phil 2 hymn consists of six verses comprising two halves of equal length in vv. 6-8 and vv. 9-11. Scholars have focused intently on how to arrange them into stanzas. Most have endorsed Ernst Lohmeyer's structural analysis of six

---

[180] Principal authorities who advocate the preexistent interpretation include J.B. Lightfoot, *St. Paul's Epistle to the Philippians* [1885] (London: Macmillan, 1927), 109-15; Ernst Lohmeyer, *Kyrios Jesus: Eine Untersuchung zu Phil. 2,5-11* (Sitzungsberichte der Heidelberger Akademie der Wissenschaft, Philosophisch-historische Klasse, Jahrgang 1927/1928, 4 Abhandlung; Heidelberg: Carl Winter, Universitatsverlag, Zweite Auflage, 1928, ²1961); Ernst Kasemann, "A Critical Analysis of Philippians 2:5-11," in *God and Christ: Existence and Province*, ed. Hebert Braun, tr. Alice F. Carse, (Tubingen: Mohr-Siebeck, 1968), 45-88; Ralph P. Martin, *Carmen Christi: Philippians ii.5-11 in Recent Interpretation and in the Setting of Early Christian Worship* [1967], rev. ed. (Grand Rapids: Eerdmans, 1983).
[181] Leading advocates of the human interpretation are H. Wheeler Robinson, *The Cross in the Old Testament* (London: SCM, 1955), 57, 103-05; Charles H. Talbert, "The Problem of Pre-existence in Phil. 2:6-11," *JBL* 86 (1967): 141-53; F.H. Borsch, *The Son of Man in Myth and History* (Philadelphia: Fortress, 1967), 250-56; J.A.T. Robinson, *The Human Face of God*, 162-69; idem, *The Priority of John*, 383; H.-W. Bartsch, *Die konkrete Wahrheit und die Luge der Spekulation* (Frankfurt-Main: Peter Lang, 1974); Jerome Murphy-O'Connor, "Christological Anthropology in Phil. 2:6-11," *RB* 83 (1976): 25-50; G. Howard, "Phil 2:6-11 and the Human Christ," 368-87; J.D.G. Dunn, *Christology in the Making*, 114-21. In this treatment of the hymn, all scholars cited who advocate its human interpretation are traditionalists except Robinson.
[182] Peter T. O'Brien, *The Epistle to the Philippians: A Commentary on the Greek Text*, in NIGTC (Grand Rapids: Eerdmans, 1991), 266.
[183] R. Martin (*A Hymn of Christ*, 63-66) relates how 19th century Lutheran scholars first set forth this view.

strophes having three lines each.[184] Accordingly, the first three strophes, in vv. 6-8, present what Jesus did; the last three strophes, in vv. 9-11, tell what God does for Jesus because of what Jesus did.

Each of these two interpretations of Phil 2.6-11 must necessarily address several christological questions that it arouses. For example, what is "the form of God" as well as "equality with God"? What was it Jesus "emptied Himself" of? What does it mean to call Jesus "Lord"? Was the hymn crafted against the background of any particular Scriptures? We will examine these questions in light of these two interpretations of Phil 2.6-11, yet bypass the complex structural analysis of the hymn that some scholars have undertaken.

It is surprising how scholars who promote the preexistence interpretation of this hymn rarely mention the human interpretation of it, let alone interact with it. Yet there is no clear evidence in Paul's corpus indicating that he believed Jesus preexisted. Therefore, proponents of the human interpretation of Phil 2.6-11 frequently accuse those who adopt the preexistent interpretation of it of being non-objective by viewing the hymn through their theological grid. For example, in 1976 now renowned Roman Catholic scholar Jerome Murphy-O'Connor accused the majority of NT scholars of "an uncritical acceptance of the current consensus, an acceptance that is facilitated by the dogmatic understanding of Christ as the Second Person of the Trinity and by certain statements of Paul which *seem* to imply the pre-existence of Christ."[185]

Larry Hurtado is an example of those who assume Christ's preexistence. He well states concerning this hymn, "the way it is used in Philippians practically requires us to think that Paul expected his readers to recognize and affirm either the passage (i.e., as an early ode/hymn known to them) or at least what the passage expresses *as reflective of what they already knew and affirmed about Jesus.*"[186] Yet Hurtado presumes that what they knew was a preexistent, incarnate Jesus. Since Paul's biblical corpus does not include any evidence that this is what he believed, this hymn more likely reflects only a human Jesus or else Paul surely would have explained otherwise.

Adam Christology as Background

From early times, church fathers and NT scholars, regardless of whether they have adopted the preexistent or human interpretation of Phil 2.6-11, have claimed that it belies an Adam Christology or typology that is based on the creation and fall of Adam and Eve recorded in Gen 1-3.[187] (See this chapter/Introduction/Adam Christology.) This means that the first man, Adam, and Jesus are contrasted as parallels even though Adam is never mentioned in the hymn. The turning point between these two primary interpretations of this hymn is where this Adam-Christ contrast begins. Scholars who advocate the human interpretation claim that it starts at the beginning of the hymn, in v. 6, so that Jesus therein is not said to have preexisted but merely to have existed as a man.

But an Adam Christology at the beginning of this Phil 2 hymn seems to favor the human interpretation in its entirety. Consequently, the trend in NT scholarship in recent decades has been to adopt an Adam Christology of the hymn and abandon, either partially or altogether, the preexistent interpretation

---

[184] E. Lohmeyer, *Der Brief an die Philipper*, 90. There still is no consensus on the hymn's correct structure.
[185] J. Murphy-O'Connor, "Christological Anthropology in Phil. 2:6-11," 31. Emphasis mine.
[186] L.W. Hurtado, *How on Earth Did Jesus Become a God?* 87. His emphasis.
[187] Markus Bockmuehl ("'The Form of God' [Phil. 2.6] Variations on a Theme of Jewish Mysticism," *JTS*, n.s., 48 [1997]: 9) says it started in patristic writings with those of Irenaeus and Augustine.

and adopt the human interpretation of it.[188] Yet many scholars who have done so have been traditionalists and remained so, insisting that the Bible elsewhere teaches that Jesus is God. For instance, Oscar Cullmann asserts that apart from Adam Christology, Phil 2.6 "can scarcely be understood."[189]

Some scholars who have adopted a strictly human interpretation of this hymn have restricted its background to Adam Christology and/or Wisdom Christology and linked it to texts scattered about in the NT or ancient, non-canonical Jewish Literature. Of course, NT parallels cannot serve as the hymn's background, since they were written later.

Gnostic Redeemer Myth as Background

Rudolf Bultmann and other earlier form-critics interpreted that in Phil 2.6-11 Paul used the Iranian-Gnostic Redeemer myth and Christianized it.[190] This myth was about a divine being who came down from heaven to earth, imparted to humans some secret knowledge to save them, and returned to heaven. In the first half of the 20th century, it was thought that this myth was pre-Christian, thus known in Israel in the 1st century CE. But it was discovered later that this myth originated during the 2nd century CE. Thus, this mythical interpretation proved anachronistic and was largely abandoned by scholars.

For nearly three decades, traditionalist James D.G. Dunn has been the leading advocate of the human interpretation of Phil 2.6-11. He raises the question of the possible influence of this Gnostic myth on the interpretation of Phil 2.6-11 by Christians in the 2nd century CE and afterwards. He alleges of Paul's readers in the 1st century CE, "the idea of a heavenly being becoming man in order to die would be strange to them." He adds, "It may even be that the pre-existence-incarnation interpretation of Phil. 2.6-11 etc. owes to the later Gnostic redeemer myth."[191] If so, this may apply to other NT texts traditionalists like Dunn cite for support.

Servant and Son of Man as Background

The NT amply attests that the early Jewish Christians, in order to comprehend the Christ event more fully, searched for prophecies and types in their Scriptures (OT) which they believed Jesus fulfilled. In doing so, they gathered a litany of OT texts to support their traditions of Jesus they were forming based on their personal experiences with Him. Thus, the NT has many quotations of, and allusions to, OT texts that are applied to Jesus.

In contrast, traditionalist scholars must rely solely on the NT to support their doctrine of incarnation. Likewise, those who advocate the preexistent interpretation of Phil 2.6-11 also must search for parallels in the NT, not the OT, to support this view.

Since Phil 2.6-11 seems to begin with a subtle Adam-Christ contrast, and the hymn ends with a clear quotation from Isa 45.23, this situation raises the question of whether there are other OT portions the author intended as background for his hymn. If any can be found, these should provide further insight into the author's intended meaning.

---

[188] Larry J. Kreitzer, "When He at Last Is First," in *Where Christology Began*, eds. Martin and Dodd, 118.
[189] O. Cullmann, *Christology*, 177.
[190] R. Bultmann, *Theology of the New Testament*, 1:175.
[191] J.D.G. Dunn, *Christology in the Making*, 128.

Since Paul uses this hymn to teach humility and servitude, could its author have purposely drawn upon certain OT portions which predict a servant figure that has nothing to do with preexistence or incarnation and applies to Jesus? If such a background can be reasonably established as the intention of the hymn's author, the preexistent interpretation is significantly weakened. Dunn explains that understanding the hymn depends mostly on "the background against which the hymn has to be set, the context of thought to which the author was indebted, which the first readers would presuppose, and on which consequently a faithful exegesis of the hymn must depend to a decisive degree."[192]

Interestingly, from the beginning of the Jesus Movement the first Christians, all of them Jews, stressed the idea of Jesus being God's "servant" (Heb. *ebed*; Gr. *pais, doulos*). (See Chapter 9/Servant Christology.) In doing so, they relied heavily on the only portion of the OT that presents the figure of a suffering, righteous Servant of the LORD whom He greatly exalts. It is four cryptic poems or songs in Isa 42—53.[193] The most important NT passages that link to this material tell of the voice from heaven uttered at Jesus' baptism and transfiguration. These pronouncements are based on Isa 42.1.[194] But the NT is very rich in teaching about Jesus fulfilling this Servant role as depicted in Isa 52.13—53.12.[195]

We need look no further than 1 Pt 2.21-25.[196] Verse 21 says Christ suffered as an example for us, which is Paul's purpose for including the Phil 2 hymn. Verse 22 quotes Isa 53.9 about the Servant not committing sin. Verse 23 echoes Isa 53.7 about the Servant not opening His mouth to defend against His revilers. Verses 24-25 are soteriological, thus going beyond this Philippian hymn by echoing Isa 53.5-12 about the Servant bearing the sins of others unto death because they were "sheep having gone astray."

Likewise, Phil 2.7-11 has clear links to Isa 42—53. Sometimes, Isaiah's servant figure depicts sinful Israel.[197] Other times, it refers to a righteous person.[198] Occasionally, the two concepts are blended together, e.g., Isa 49.3, in which the righteous Servant is the embodiment of Israel. The idea that Isa 42—53 serves as the principle background for this Phil 2 hymn is also suggested by both of these texts being of the same genre—poetry.

Two portions of Phil 2.7-11 have clear links to Isa 42—53. One is about Jesus being "a bond-servant" (Phil 2.7), which connects especially to Isa 42.1 and 52.13. The other is the quotation of Isa 45.23 in Phil 2.10-11 about bowing and confessing. These two clear links of this Philippian hymn to the OT suggest that there may be others.

---

[192] J.D.G. Dunn, *Christology in the Making*, 114.
[193] The servant motif actually begins in Isa 41.8-9, where it depicts the collective people of Israel. The four poems or songs are identified as follows: (1) Isa 42.1-4; (2) 49.1-6; (3) 50.4-9; (4) 52.12—53.12.
[194] Baptism: Mt 3.17/Mk 1.11/Lk 3.22. Transfiguration: Mt 17.5/Mk 9.7/Lk 9.35. Express quotations from Isa 42—53 include Mt 12.18-21; 8.17; Mk 15.28; Lk 22.37; Jn 12.38; Ac 8.32-33.
[195] For a listing of all the NT texts and their connection to Isa 52.13—52.12, see C.H. Dodd, *According to the Scriptures: The Sub-structure of New Testament Theology* (New York: Scribner's Sons, 1953), 92-94. For a treatment of this linkage of all of these NT passages, see Joachim Jeremias, "*pais thou*," in *TDNT* 5:700-17. In his letters Paul quotes or alludes to portions of Isa 52.13—53.12 in Rom 4.25; 10.16; 15.21; 1 Cor 15.3.
[196] J. Jeremias (*TDNT* 5:712) says the hymn in 1 Pt 2.22-25 "almost seems to be a short summary of Is. 53."
[197] Isa 41.8-9; 42.19; 44.1-2, 21, 26; 45.4.
[198] Isa 42.1-8; 49.1-8; 50.4-10; 52.13—53.12.

Indeed. The hymn begins with Adam Christology and then presents a full-blown Servant Christology that is based on a blending of a righteous Servant figure in Isa 42—53 and a Son of Man figure in Dan 7.13,[199] with the Servant figure more prominent.[200] Oscar Cullmann rightly concludes about Phil 2.6-11, "This text, which is extremely rich Christologically, unites three concepts: 'Son of Man,' 'Servant of God,' and *Kyrios*."[201] The difference is that the Servant links to Israel and the Son of Man to all of humanity.

Scholars who deny that Isa 52.13—53.12 provides any background for this Phil 2 hymn often advance two objections. First, they assert that if that was the case, the author of the hymn would have included some soteriological remark since the Servant dying for the sins of others is the major theme in Isa 52.13—53.12. But none of the identifications of Jesus as God's servant in the book of Acts include any soteriological remark. Robert Gundry therefore replies, "we cannot expect NT use of the OT to incorporate all elements of the OT text," and he shows that both texts omit subjects the other includes.[202] Second, those scholars who posit an Isa 52.13—53.12 background usually advocate an ethical interpretation of the hymn; but some scholars, e.g., E. Kasemann, object to this by rightly asserting that the hymn contains no such ethical directive. The author may have decided to omit this since Jesus' soteriological sacrifice cannot serve as a model to be imitated. Jesus humbled Himself, and that we can imitate; but *the way* in which He did so was peculiar to Himself as the sinless Lamb of God, and that we cannot imitate. Most scholars nevertheless agree that the purpose of the hymn is to teach that God rewards humility.

"The Form of God"

Most traditionalists who adopt the preexistent interpretation of this Phil 2 hymn view it in three stages: preexistence in v. 6, incarnation in vv. 7-8, and exaltation in heaven in vv. 9-11. So, they interpret "form of God" in v. 6 as Jesus having preexisted eternally as a distinct *hypostasis* or Person, being the Logos of Jn 1.1-18, by possessing the same divine nature as that of God the Father, which makes Him equal with the Father.

How one interprets the expression, "in the form of God" (Gr. *en morphe theou*), largely determines the interpretation of the remainder of the hymn. This critical phrase is difficult partly because, except for cognates, *morphe* ("form") occurs only twice in the Greek NT, both being here in vv. 6-7.[203] In most Greek literature, *morphe* means "outward appearance," i.e., what can be perceived only by the senses.[204] So, "form of God" seems to refer to Jesus' bodily existence instead of a pre-temporal, ontological one. Such a view avoids a problem for those traditionalists who assert that because God is spirit (Jn 4.24) He cannot have outward form. However, some avoid this by defining *morphe* as essence.

---

[199] E. Lohmeyer (*Kyrios Jesus*) links the hymn to all three of these OT sources.
[200] However, we saw in Chapter Four that the Son of Man figure in Dan 7.13 indicates only an individual (denying the collective interpretation) who necessarily suffers as a model for the members of his kingdom.
[201] O. Cullmann, *Christology*, 174.
[202] Robert H. Gundry, "Style and Substance in 'The Myth of God Incarnate According to Philippians 2:6-11," in *Crossing the Boundaries: Essays in Biblical Interpretation in Honour of Michael D. Goulder*, eds. Stanley E. Porter, Paul Joyce, and David E. Orton (Leiden: Brill, 1994), 293.
[203] The word *morphe* also appears in Mk 16.12, but scholars regard Mk 16.9-20 as a later addendum.
[204] BAGD, 528; J. Behm, "*morphe*," in *TDNT* 4:745-46; G. Hawthorne, *Philippians*, 82.

Proponents of the human interpretation of Phil 2.6-11 link this concept of Jesus existing "in the form of God" with Adam being made in the "image (of God)," as in Gen 1.27; 5.3. In support, Paul elsewhere describes Jesus as God's "image" (Gr. *eikon*; 2 Cor 4.4; Col 1.15). Plus, the LXX renders *eikon* for the Hebrew *tselem* (likeness) in Gen 1.26 and 5.1 in the MT. Some think *morphe* and *eikon*, if not *tselem*, are nearly synonyms.[205] They say the hymn does not imply Jesus preexisted but that He and Adam are parallels. J. Murphy-O'Connor proposes that "one should begin with the working hypothesis that the author views Christ [only] as man, and only if this hypothesis fails to explain the rest of the evidence should one envisage the hypothesis that he is a being of a higher order."[206]

Some proponents of the preexistent interpretation disagree. They counter that *eikon* cannot serve as a synonym for *morphe* in Phil 2.6 since it would have to do the same for "form of a slave" (Gr. *morphen doulou*) in v. 7, yet "image of a slave" makes no sense.[207] But hymns are poetry set to music, and poets often must take such liberties. So, the author of the hymn probably used *morphe* to create a parallel in an artful composition.

Gerald Hawthorne follows Ernst Kasemann in focusing on the word "in" in this phrase, "in the form of God." Hawthorne asserts, "not 'Christ *was* the form of God,' but Christ was '*in* the form of God,' as if the form of God were a sphere in which Christ existed."[208] If so, it does not seem that the Logos can be counted as one God if the Logos existed in the same sphere that included "God," since that would suggest two Gods.

Peter O'Brien and other scholars insist that "form of God" refers non-personally to God's glory that is often presented in the OT.[209] This rendering arguably coincides with what Jesus said in Jn 17.5 about His previous "glory." And the author of Hebrews affirms this idea by describing the earthly Jesus as "the radiance" of God's glory (Heb 1.3).

Therefore, an increasing number of scholars, while still representing a minority, now deny that "the form of God" in Phil 2.6 implies that Jesus preexisted and claim that it only indicates that Jesus was like all humans—made in the image of God. So, the hymn begins by saying Jesus was in the image of God, implying like Adam was.

"Equality with God"

What does Paul mean by saying that Jesus "did not regard equality with God a thing to be grasped"? Most traditionalists explain that it, too, is about the preexistence of Jesus as the Logos. That is, prior to the incarnation the Logos possessed "equality with God" (Gr. *isa theo*), but relinquished it at the moment of incarnation. A serious problem with this explanation is that if the preexistent Jesus, as the Logos, could have grasped at equality with God, He did not possess it and thus could not have been equal with God.[210]

In Chapter Seven, we learned that the Jews wrongly accused Jesus of "making Himself equal with God" (Jn 5.18>; cf. 10.33>). In the Greek NT, the same word

---

[205] E.g., J.D.G. Dunn, "Christ, Adam, and Preexistence," 76-77; cf. O. Cullmann, *Christology*, 175.
[206] J. Murphy-O'Connor, "Christological Anthroplogy in Phil. 2.6-11," 39.
[207] L.W. Hurtado (*How on Earth Did Jesus Become God?* 98-100) argues against the equivalence of these two expressions and supports it by a survey of their use in the Bible.
[208] G. Hawthorne, *Philippians*, 81. Emphasis his. See also P.T. O'Brien, *The Epistle to the Philippians*, 206.
[209] P.T. O'Brien, *The Epistle to the Philippians*, 210-11.
[210] G. Hawthorne, *Pilippians*, 84.

(Gr. *ison*, but with a different ending, of course) is used in Jn 5.18 as here in Phil 2.6. But we also learned that Jesus denied their charge by explaining, "whatever the Father does, these things the Son does in *like* manner" (Jn 5.19, emphasis mine). Jesus meant that He acts *like God* in how He lives (cf. Jn 14.7, 9), thus denying that He is *equal* with God.

As a background for this Phil 2 hymn, "equality with God" links to "like God" (Heb. *kelohim*) in Gen 3.5, which indicates Adam Christology. Recall that Adam sinned because Satan deceived Adam's wife, Eve, telling her that if she ate the forbidden fruit, "you will be like God, knowing good and evil" (Gen 3.5). This lie meant that Adam and Eve could attain "equality with God" in the realm of knowledge and wisdom (Gen 3.6).

George Howard insists that, due to the syntax of Phil 2.6, the verb *einai* should not be disconnected from the clause *einai isa theo*, as most scholars do. He thus translates it, "being like God." He supports this by relating that linguist Pierre "Grelot convincingly argues that *isa* in LXX Greek is equivalent to the Hebrew, k-, "like/as."[211]

"A Thing to Be Grasped"

This idea of "equality with God," or "being like God," turns on the meaning of the adjacent expression—"a thing to be grasped" (Gr. *harpagmon hegesato*). This is the only occurrence of *harpagmos* in the Greek NT, and it is very rare in classical Greek. It has been variously translated as follows: (1) "did not consider equality with God something to be grasped" (NIV, cf. NRSV, ESV), and 2) several recent authorities render it "did not regard equality with God something to be exploited" or "used to one's own advantage."

Grasping at being like God recalls Adam's sin that resulted in the fall (Gen 3.1-7). So, an increasing number of recent scholars have adopted an Adam Christology in Phil 2.6-7, and some have insisted that it indicates no more than that.[212] They claim that Jesus' disavowal of self-aggrandizement contrasts with the sin of Adam and Eve, in which they sought to usurp the majesty of God by selfishly grasping at His knowledge and wisdom.

Traditionalist O. Cullmann adopted the preexistent interpretation of Phil 2.6-11, yet he also endorsed an Adam Christology in it. He even claims, "All the statements of Phil. 2.6 ff. are to be understood from the standpoint of the Old Testament history of Adam."[213] Cullmann warns that by ignoring this comparison, as church fathers did, "we become lost in tangential theological speculations foreign to early Christianity." [214]

John A.T. Robinson insists that the more plausible background is that Paul, as a former Pharisaic theologian, is reflecting Judaism in its earthy idealization of Adam.[215]

---

[211] G. Howard, "Phil 2:6-11 and the Human Christ," 377. Pierre Grelot, "Deux expressions difficiles de Philippiens 2, 6-7," *Bib* 53 (1972): 498-501; idem, "Deux notes critiques sur Philippiens 2, 6-11," *Bib* 54 (1973): 185. So also J. Murphy-O'Connor, "Christological Anthropology in Phil. 2.6-11," 39.

[212] E.g., C.H. Talbert, "The Problem of Pre-existence in Philippians 2:6-11," 141-53; J.A.T. Robinson, *The Human Face of God*, 162-66; idem, *The Priority of John*, 383; J.D.G. Dunn, *Christology in the Making*, 114-121; C. Tuckett, *Christology in the New Testament*, 52-56.

[213] O. Cullmann, *Christology*, 181, cf. 175. So also J.D.G. Dunn, *Christology in the Making*, 114, 119; P.M. Casey, *From Jewish Prophet to Gentile God*, 112; tentatively F. Young, "A Cloud of Witnesses," 44n22.

[214] O. Cullmann, *Christology*, 177.

[215] J.A.T. Robinson, *The Human Face of God*, 163. Others have taken this view, including E. Lohmeyer.

By allowing Adam Christology to be the guide for understanding at least Phil 2.6, the meaning of *harpagmon hegesato* and *isa theo* would be as follows: Jesus did not grasp at equality with God as did Adam and Eve, who acted on Satan's deception that eating the forbidden fruit would give them knowledge and wisdom like that of God.

In sum, if this Adam Christology interpretation of Phil 2.6 is correct, then it is more likely that the whole hymn does not teach that Jesus preexisted or that He is God.

"Emptied Himself"

In Chapter Three, we learned of various "kenosis theories" that past traditionalists put forth to support their doctrine of the incarnation. Now we will examine what is about the only NT source for their Kenotic Christology, which is the word "emptied" in Phil 2.7.

The idea that Jesus "emptied Himself" (Gr. *heauton ekenosen*) of something occurs in the NT only in Phil 2.7. These two words have stirred more debate among NT scholars in the past 150 years than any other two words conjoined in the Bible. But what did Jesus empty Himself of? The hymn does not expressly say, and neither does Paul.

Most traditionalist scholars connect the two expressions in Phil 2.6-7—"form of God" and "emptied Himself"—and treat them as referring to the supposed preexistent Jesus. That is, Jesus preexisted in the form of God as the personal Logos and emptied Himself of some divine attributes at the moment of incarnation. Many of these scholars cite 2 Cor 8.9> ("He was rich,... He became poor") as implying the same sense.

But this preexistent interpretation of Phil 2.6-7 does not accord with the Apostle Paul's purpose for including this hymn in this letter. It is to teach humility and its divine reward by citing Jesus as the archetypal model to imitate. For, Paul immediately prefaces this hymn with the exhortation, "Do nothing from selfish or empty conceit, but with humility of mind let each of you regard one another as more important than himself.... Have this attitude ... which was also in Christ Jesus" (Phil 2.3, 5).

As mentioned above, we can relate to the earthly Jesus' humble self-denial (Phil 2.5), but not to His doing so by incarnation.[216] Some traditionalists have felt the force of this argument and so have divorced the hymn from its context in order to deny any ethical interpretation of it.[217] But to reject the hymn's context in order to avoid this problem for the incarnation weakens the preexistent interpretation, and scholars have not supported it. Also, the ethical interpretation of the hymn better supports the human interpretation of it.

Neither can we relate to an incarnation by kenosis. Recall from Chapter Three that exponents of Kenotic Christology interpreted the idea of Jesus having "emptied Himself" mostly in one of two ways: (1) He divested Himself of His relative divine attributes, or (2) He merely chose not to exercise some of His divine attributes during His incarnation. But we also learned that an insurmountable difficulty arose in which scholars concluded that (1) a divesture of some relative divine attributes—e.g., omniscience, omnipresence, and omnipotence—was necessary because these are incompatible with being human, yet (2) a divesture of any divine attributes necessarily results in something less

---

[216] E. Kasemann, "A Critical Analysis of Philippians 2:5-11;" R. Martin, *A Hymn of Christ*, 84-91, 287-91.

[217] Esp. E. Kasemann, "A Critical Analysis of Philippians 2:5-11," 45-88.

than full deity. Consequently, by the early second half of the 20th century, all kenosis theories had fallen out of favor with most distinguished NT scholars.[218]

Even some conservative Evangelicals now regard that this Christ-hymn in Phil 2 has nothing to do with the idea of a preexistent Christ emptying Himself of certain divine attributes. D.A. Carson soundly reasons that "a being cannot readily be separated from his attributes."[219] And G. Hawthorne well explains that "there is no basis for any of these speculative answers in the text of the hymn, simply because it gives no clue whatsoever as to what it was that Christ emptied himself of.... It is not necessary, therefore, to insist that ... Christ emptied himself *of something*.... Rather, it is a poetic, hymn-like way of saying that Christ poured out himself, putting himself totally at the disposal of people."[220]

Indeed, Paul means in Phil 2.6-7 that Jesus emptied Himself of *self* by submitting to God's plan for His life which culminated in death on a cross.[221] It is the cross of Christ, not incarnation, which is the epitome of Jesus' self-denial depicted in the NT. It is only in this sense, rather than incarnation, that Paul can legitimately set forth an example for his readers to follow. *So, Jesus did not deny Himself by suppressing or laying aside certain divine attributes at His birth, but by doing acts of moral character throughout His life.*[222]

The author of the hymn seems to have intended that "emptied Himself" (Gr. *heauton ekenosen*) echoes "poured out Himself to death" (Heb. *nephesho lamoot herah*) in Isa 53.12.[223] J. Jeremias has been the most distinguished scholar who has championed this background for "emptied Himself." He explains, "The decisive proof of the thesis that the Christology of Phil. 2:6-9 is rooted in Is. 53 HT lies in the fact that the expression *heauton ekenosen* (Phil. 2:7),... is an exact translation of *naphesho ... herah* (Is. 53:12)." Of this expression in Phil 2.7 he alleges, "The use of Is. 53:12 shows that the expression *heauton ekenosen* implies the surrender of life, not the *kenosis* of the incarnation."[224]

Yet Jesus' surrender of life should not be restricted to His death. His colossal self-denial began with His decision to obey God by leaving home and undertaking His public ministry that led to His death. Isaiah 53.12 means literally, "poured out *his life* to death."

"Taking the Form of a Bond-Servant"

In Phil 2.7, the NASB translates "bond-servant" for the Greek word *doulos*, which means "slave" or "servant." While *doulos* is the most common word for "slave" in Greek, most NT versions translate it "servant." These two expressions— "form of God" and "form of a servant"—are set in contrast. Traditionalists usually interpret "form of God" as indicating Jesus' preexistence and "form of a servant/ slave" as His incarnation. But the Bible does not portray being human as slavery, i.e., apart from the effects of the fall. And if the author of this Philippian hymn derived "form of God" from "image of God" in Gen 1.26-27, in the very next verse

---

[218] So says V. Taylor, *The Person of Christ*, 78.
[219] D.A. Carson, *The Farewell Discourse and Final Prayer of Jesus: An Exposition of John 14-17* (Grand Rapids: Baker, 1980), 36.
[220] G. Hawthorn, *Philippians*, 85-86.
[221] J.A.T. Robinson (*Honest to God*, 74) says it means Jesus "emptied himself utterly of himself."
[222] G. Hawthorn, *Philippians*, 86.
[223] C.H. Dodd, *According to the Scriptures*, 93; H. Wheeler Robinson, *The Cross in the Old Testament* (London: SCM, 1955), 103-05; L.J. Kreitzer, "When He at Last is First," 126n39.
[224] J. Jeremias, "*pais theou*," in *TDNT* 5:711, n445. HT refers to the MT. See also J. Jeremias, "Zu Phil. 2:7: HEAUTON EKENOSEN," *NovT* 6 (1963): 182-88.

God said to pre-fallen Adam and Eve, "fill the earth, and subdue it; and rule" over the animal kingdom (v. 28), which is the opposite of slavery.

Ernst Kasemann sought to skirt the ethical interpretation of this Phil 2 hymn by asserting that Jesus taking the form of a slave refers to His incarnation subjecting Him, as with other humans, to the bondage of Satan and demons.[225] Nothing could be farther from the truth! The Synoptic Gospels repeatedly reveal that Jesus thwarted Satan's temptations and often demonstrated His God-given authority over demons by performing exorcisms.

So, Jesus taking the form of a servant/slave must not refer to an incarnation but to the undertaking of His mission that God set before Him, which was to serve others. And that is how Jesus explained Himself and His mission. He said of Himself, "even the Son of Man did not come to be served, but to serve, and to give His life a ransom for many" (Mk 10.45; cf. Mt 20.28). These words, "a ransom for many," clearly link to the righteous Servant who "bore the sin of many," in Isa 53.12. And Jesus washing His disciples' feet just prior to the Last Supper demonstrated His being a Servant, just as He explained (Jn 13.3-17). Moreover, the Eucharist that He then instituted reflects much of Isa 53.[226]

The Hebrew word for "servant" is *ebed*. It occurs twenty times in Isa 41—53 in the MT. In this portion, the LXX translates *ebed* with the Greek words *pais* or *doulos*.[227] Both words mean "servant," though *pais* also can mean "child" or "son."[228]

The background of "taking the form of a bond-servant" seems to be God saying, "Behold, My Servant, whom I uphold, My chosen one in whom My soul delights" (Isa 42.1). God adds, "I have called you in righteousness" (v. 6). This means that God calls His Servant to undertake the mission He sets forth, which includes righteous living.

Being Born and Becoming a Man

Jesus "being made in the likeness of men," in Phil 2.7b, is better translated in the NRSV as "being born in human likeness."[229] Either way, "likeness" (Gr. *homoioma*) seems to allude to the word "like" (*ke*) in "One like a Son of Man" (Aram. *ke bar enash*) in Dan 7.13>. Both "likeness" and "like" in these two texts seem to imply Jesus' virgin birth. If not, what is their purpose? Why not just say that Jesus was born a human being? So, these two words seem to hint that Jesus is fully human yet sinless partially due to His virgin birth, although Paul never mentions it in his corpus. "Likeness," here, recalls Adam and Eve being made in God's "likeness" (Heb. *demuth*; Gen 1.26; 5.1), i.e., the image of God before the fall. Paul uses *homoioma* similarly in Rom 8.3, where he declares that Jesus came "in the likeness of sinful flesh." Therefore, Jesus appeared in the likeness of God as well as the likeness of human beings, making Him perfectly-suited as their Mediator.

---

[225] E. Kasemann, "A Critical Analysis of Philippians 2:5-11," 81.

[226] Also, cf. "covenant" in Mt 26.28/Mk 14.24/Lk 22.20 with the Servant as "covenant" in Isa 42.6; 49.8.

[227] The LXX translates *doulos* for *ebed* in Isa 42.19; 48.20; 49.3, 5. But the 2nd century CE Greek version by Aquila translates *doulos* more often in Isa 41—53, even rendering *morphe doulou* in Isa 52.14 and 53.2.

[228] "Form of a servant" in Phil 2.7 may relate to "form" (Heb. *toar*) of the Servant in Isa 52.14 and 53.2.

[229] P.T. O'Brien (*The Epistle to the Philippians*, 225) says *homoioma* keeps a "distinction from the original."

Jesus "being found in appearance as a man," in Phil 2.8a, seems to repeat the prior statement, again implying His sinlessness due to His virgin birth. However, the prior statement refers to Jesus' physical birth, whereas this one refers to His adulthood. The word "appearance" translates the Greek word *schema*, meaning the outward appearance of a person or an object.[230] It echoes the Hebrew word *mareh* in the MT and the Greek word *eidos* in the LXX, both of which mean outward appearance, in Isa 52.14 and 53.2.

E. Lohmeyer was probably right in breaking new ground by connecting the phrase "as a man" (Gr. *hos anthropos*), here in Phil 2.8a, with "as a son of man" (Gr. *hos huios anthropou*) in the LXX and "One like a Son of Man" (Aram. *ke bar enash*) in the MT of Dan 7.13 and treating them as equivalents even though this Philippian phrase does not include the word "son" (Gr. *huios*).[231] But Lohmeyer also insisted that the background of this clause was *1 En.* 46 and the Iranian-Gnostic heavenly redeemer myth, which latter we've seen proved anachronistic so that scholars abandoned it.

"He Humbled Himself"

Again, Paul's purpose for quoting this hymn is to relate that Jesus demonstrated much humility and self-denial (Phil 2.1-4, 12), and Paul exhorts his readers to imitate His example (v. 5). Jesus chose not to make His life His own but gave Himself unreservedly to God and others in accord with God's plan for His life. Such an attitude was reflected in one of Jesus' most quoted sayings in the synoptics. He said, "For whoever wishes to save his life shall lose it; but whoever loses his life for My sake and the gospel's shall save it" (Mk 8.35 par.; cf. Mt 10.39; Lk 17.33). On the last day of His earthly life, Jesus suffered at the hands of mortal men by enduring their taunts, spitting, hair-pulling, and blood-letting by beating, flogging, thorns, and crucifixion. So, Jesus underwent the supreme act of self-denial, forfeiting His life to a most painful death on behalf of others. What a model of self-denial the apostle calls his readers to follow!

The intended OT background of "He humbled Himself by becoming obedient to the point of death" is that "He poured out Himself to death" (Isa 53.12).[232] This humility demonstrates the Servant not opening his mouth against his oppressors in self-defense (Isa 53.7), which corresponds to Jesus not answering Caiaphas, Pilate, or Herod.[233]

This mention of humility is the only place in the hymn where a divine mission is implied. It infers Jesus' monumental decision to undertake His divine calling to leave home, go to the Jordan River, be baptized by John, and begin His public ministry leading to death. This humble obedience is subtly contrasted with Adam's act of disobedience.

Since Jesus was sinless, He was *not* subject to death by natural causes. The reason "death spread to all [other] men" was "because all sinned" (Rom 5.12).

---

[230] BAGD, 797.

[231] E. Lohmeyer, *Kyrios Jesus*, 39-40, 69. R. Martin (*A Hymn of Christ*, 209n4) lists the following scholars who do likewise: A.E.J. Rawlinson, *The New Testament Doctrine of the Christ: The Bampton Lectures for 1926* (London: Green, 1926), 125; C.K. Barrett, "New Testament Eschatology, ii," *SJT* 6 (1953): 235; E.M. Sidebottom, *The Christ of the Fourth Gospel: In Light of First-century Thought* (London: SPCK, 1961), 91-92; C.H. Dodd, *The Interpretation of the Fourth Gospel*, 243.

[232] C.H. Talbert ("The Problem of Pre-existence in Philippians 2.6-11," 153) says of Phil 2.7-8 that "'he emptied himself' and 'he humbled himself,' are, therefore, to be read against the background of Isa 53."

[233] Caiaphas: Mt 26.62-63/Mk 14.60-61; Pilate: Mt 27.12-14/Mk 15.4-5; Herod: Jn 19.9.

Jerome Murphy-O'Connor well contends that since Jesus was sinless He was incorruptible and would have lived forever. He adds, "death had no claim on Christ,... he could have chosen not to die ... he permitted himself to be put to death."[234] C.A. Wanamaker explains likewise, "Christ, who was without sin (2 Cor 5.21) stood outside the legitimate rule of death. Death only had power over Christ because he humbled himself."[235] The Johannine Christ did predict that He would willingly lay down His life (Jn 10.17-18). Even when the time came, He explained that He could summon legions of angels to protect Him (Mt 26.53).

So, in accordance with the human interpretation of this Phil 2 hymn, its first half can be rendered as follows: "the One who existed in the form (image) of God did not consider grasping at being equal with God, but emptied Himself of self by taking the form of a servant. And being born in human likeness, and being found as a human being, he humbled himself, becoming obedient unto death, even death of a cross."[236] This rendering only relates acts that the historical Jesus did, not cryptic statements about His supposed preexistence, and these earthly acts feature His moral trait of humility.

"God Highly Exalted Him"

So far, this Phil 2 hymn is christocentric, focusing on Jesus' attitude and its effect on His life. Verse 9 begins with the conjunction "Therefore" (Gr. *dio*), which signals the start of the hymn's second half, which tells of God honoring Jesus due to His humility.

The hymn now turns eschatological by focusing on what God does. While it does not mention Jesus' resurrection, ascension, and session, these eschatological events are assumed in the clause, "God highly exalted Him." That these events are omitted in Isa 42—53 and Dan 7 further suggests that these texts are the hymn's intended background.

Because Jesus did not do as Adam did—grasp at obtaining God's knowledge and wisdom in order to become like, or equal with, God—in a certain sense that is what God rewarded Jesus with. Paul writes that the "true knowledge of God's mystery" is "Christ Himself, in whom are hidden all the treasures of wisdom and knowledge" (Col 2.3).

Because Jesus so humbled Himself, God highly exalted Him, even to a position of honor and authority equal to His own (cf. Jn 5.23; Rev 5.13). The NT often affirms that when Jesus ascended into heaven He sat down at the right of hand of God the Father on the Father's throne, fulfilling Ps 110.1. This heavenly session symbolizes the Father sharing His sovereign authority with Jesus, resulting in their joint rule of both heaven and earth (Mt 28.18).[237] According to the book of Revelation, angels have so honored Jesus along with the Father ever since. O. Cullmann well surmises of Jesus in this Phil 2 hymn by stating that "because of his obedience, complete equality with God in the exercise of divine sovereignty is added.... the equality with God he did not grasp as a 'robbery.'"[238]

Here in Phil 2.9, the ethical interpretation becomes most evident. Two contrasting scriptural principles are: "pride goes before ... a fall" (Prov 16.18

---

[234] J. Murphy-O'Connor, "Christological Anthropology in Phil. 2:6-11," 42, 45, 40.
[235] C.A. Wanamaker, "Philippians 2.6-11: Son of God or Adamic Christology?" *NTS* 33 (1987): 189.
[236] Similar to the translation by James D.G. Dunn, "Christ, Adam, and Preexistence," in *Where Christology Began*, eds. Martin and Dodd, 76.
[237] W. Foerster, *TDNT* 3:1089.
[238] O. Cullmann, *Christology*, 181. Cullmann seems to here assert a lesser deity for Jesus' preexistence.

NRSV), and "humility goes before honor" (Prov 18.12). Jesus often taught, "whoever exalts himself shall be humbled; and whoever humbles himself shall be exalted" (Mt 23.12; cf. Lk 14.11; 18.14). This hymn's Adam-Christ contrast reflects these principles. Adam suffered humiliation by means of the fall; Jesus was exalted to a position of great honor due to His humility.

Many Reformers and scholars, in order to protect the doctrine of incarnation, have denied that this Phil 2 hymn indicates that God rewarded Jesus. But they have recoiled at this idea due to their overreaction to Catholicism's works-merit system.[239] Thus, they have contended that faith and reward are mutually exclusive. On the contrary, the author of Hebrews says, "without faith it is impossible to please God,... he rewards those who seek him" (Heb 11.6 NRSV). And he adds, "Jesus,... who for the joy set before Him endured the cross" (Heb 12.2). Jesus' joy obviously comes from God rewarding His obedience. Moreover, Isaiah quotes the suffering Servant as saying, "surely the justice due to Me is with the LORD, and My reward [is] with My God" (Isa 49.4).

Jesus being "highly exalted" (Gr. *huperuphosen*) suggests that He was given a higher rank than He ever previously possessed.[240] If so, this clashes with the traditional view, which can only accept that Jesus reclaimed a prior position. The reason is that classical theism says God is always sovereign and thus cannot be rewarded or exalted. Plus, *God exalting Jesus requires that God is essentially superior to Jesus*.

The intended background of the words "God highly exalted Him" is the statement, "Behold, My servant will prosper, He will be high and lifted up, and greatly exalted" (Isa 52.13). Both of these passages allude to two OT texts: (1) "The LORD [God the Father] says to my Lord [Jesus]: 'Sit at My right hand'" (Ps 110.1); and (2) Jesus, as "One like a Son of Man ... came up to the Ancient of Days," who is God the Father (Dan 7.13). The prefix *huper* (highly), as in *huperuphosen* here in Phil 2.9a, means to "raise someone to the loftiest height."[241] There is no higher place than the throne of "the Most High God" in heaven. The NIV translates Phil 2.9a, "Therefore God exalted him to the highest place."

"The Name Which Is Above Every Name"

Nearly all scholars claim that "the name which is above every name," in Phil 2.9, refers to the word "Lord" two verses later, in v. 11. For instance, R.E. Brown says of this clause, "the name bestowed on Jesus is not 'God' but 'Lord.'"[242] Brown surely is right about "God;" but is he right about the hymn saying the name given to Jesus is "Lord?"

This question is irrelevant to identity Christology except for one thing: some traditionalists contend that Jesus being given "the name" of "Lord" (Gr. *kurios*), here, supports their assertion that Jesus is Yahweh because the LXX translates YHWH as *kurios* (lord). For example, John Macquarrie states concerning Phil 2.9-11, "he receives the name above every name, the name that belongs to God,"[243] viz., "Lord." And Reginald H. Fuller makes the same assertion and connects this clause in Phil 2.9 to Ex 3.14.[244]

---

[239] R.P. Martin, *A Hymn of Christ*, 231-33.
[240] E.g., E. Lohmeyer, *Der Brief an die Philipper*, 97.
[241] BAGD, 842.
[242] R.E. Brown, *Jesus God and Man*, 9n16.
[243] J. Macquarrie, *Jesus Christ in Modern Thought*, 372.
[244] R.H. Fuller, *Christ and Christianity*, 51.

On the contrary, "Lord" is not a name but a title,[245] and God's name is not "Lord" but "YHWH." Plus, the Hebrew word *hashem* ("the name") in the MT refers only to YHWH. And we have seen that the substitution of *kurios* for YHWH in the LXX occurred centuries later, in Christian copies of it. (See Introduction/Lordship Christology in this chapter.)

Furthermore, Phil 2.9 says God gave Jesus "the name" as if He never possessed it previously. Traditionalists who insist that the name is "Lord" are in a similar predicament as they are with Jesus being rewarded and exalted.[246] That is, the incarnation requires that Jesus always was "Lord" of creation in His preexistence, so that He could not have been given this name anew; rather, He could only have abandoned it and later reclaimed it.

"The Name of Jesus"

Moreover, identifying "the name" in Phil 2.9 as "Lord" does not fit what follows in the next clause, in v. 10, which is "the name of Jesus." Laying aside all christological presuppositions, the hymn naturally proclaims that it is "the name of Jesus," not "Lord," that is "above every name." Otherwise, to avoid confusion the hymn's author should have written in v. 10, "the name of Lord." C.F.D. Moule says of this Phil 2 hymn, "verses 9-11 concern the name 'Jesus,' not the title 'Lord.'" Moule well explains that "when the name of 'Jesus' is uttered" publicly for all to hear, all people will then call Him "Lord."[247]

Paul often highlights "the name" of "Jesus" in his corpus. Nine times in his letters he pens the words, "the name of (the/our) Lord Jesus (Christ)."[248] So, for Paul, "Jesus" is a name, and "Jesus Christ" became a name, but nowhere in Paul's letters does he indicate that "Lord," by itself, is a name. Paul wrote to the saints at Ephesus about God exalting Jesus to His right hand, saying Jesus is "far above ... every name that is named" (Eph 1.21; cf. Heb 1.4). And Paul surely accepted the solid Christian traditions of praying, baptizing, and exorcising demons in the name of Jesus.

The NT provides additional evidence of a very early and strong Christian tradition concerning Jesus' name. The Apostle Peter proclaimed regarding Jesus' name, "there is no other name under heaven that has been given among men, by which we must be saved" (Ac 4.12). And the author of Hebrews wrote that Jesus had even "inherited a more excellent name than" any of the angels had (Heb 1.4).[249]

---

[245] Cf. G. Quell, "*kurios*," in *TDNT* 3:1062.

[246] Traditionalist Stephen E. Fowl (*Philippians* [Grand Rapids: Eerdmans, 2005], 104-05) acknowledges this problem. He attempts to resolve it by appealing to two solutions advocated by Thomas Aquinas. These are (1) Ambrose's solution that it indicates the deification of Jesus' human nature and (2) Augustine's solution that it recognizes what was eternally true. The first view introduces a presupposition foreign to Paul and the hymn, and both views find virtually no support today from scholars except Fowl.

[247] C.F.D. Moule, "Further Reflexions on Philippians 2:5-11," in *Apostolic History and the Gospel: Biblical and Historical Essays Presented to F.F. Bruce on his 60th Birthday*, eds. W. Ward Gasque and Ralph P. Martin (Grand Rapids: Eerdmans, 1970), 270. See also Moises Silva, *Philippians*, 2nd ed. (Grand Rapids: Baker, 1992), 110-11.

[248] 1 Cor 1.2, 10; 5.4; 6.11; Eph 5.20; Col 3.17; 2 Th 1.12; 3.6.

[249] Contra Hugh Montefiore (*A Commentary on the Epistle to the Hebrews* [New York: Harper & Row, 1964], 39) and William L. Lane (*Hebrews 1-8*, in WBC [1991], 17, 25), who interpret "name" as "Son." What do they intend as Jesus' name where the author of Hebrews pens, "Jesus the Son of God" (Heb 4.14).

So, "Jesus" is a name, but "Lord" is a title. The NT exhorts its readers to believe in the name of "Jesus," not "Lord," which is not a name. We are told to pray and heal in the name of Jesus, confess, praise and proclaim the name of Jesus, and suffer for the name of Jesus.

The Fourth Gospel says of Jesus that only "those who believe in His name" can "become the children of God" (Jn 1.12). What does it mean to believe in Jesus' name (cf. Jn 2.23; 3.18; 1 Jn 3.23; 5.13)? Recall that the name "Jesus" is the translation of the Aramaic name "Yeshua/Yeshu." It means "Yahweh saves," since Ye in Yeshua is the abbreviation of the name YHWH and *shua* means "salvation." To believe in Jesus' name is to believe that Yahweh saves through Yeshua, viz., Jesus. The Johannine Jesus said, "I have come in My Father's name" (Jn 5.43), inferring that the Father's name "YHWH" is incorporated into Jesus' name "Yeshua." The Johannine Jesus also prayed for The Eleven, saying, "Holy Father, keep them in Thy name, the name which Thou hast given Me" (Jn 17.11, cf. v. 12). Again, Jesus means that the name "YHWH," i.e., its shortened form, is contained in His name "Yeshua." Thus, Jesus does not bear God's name by being named "Lord" or "YHWH" but by being named "Jesus," which has the name "YHWH" in it.

However, does the context of Phil 2.9 indicate God gave Jesus "the name" at the time of His heavenly exaltation? If so, that would require that "the name" is "Lord," not "Jesus." But could the hymn refer to God giving Jesus His name at His birth?

We have seen that pre-Christian, apocalyptic Judaism had a strong tradition about God having determined Messiah's name prior to creation. The Similitudes state that the "Son of Man was given a name, in the presence of the Lord of the Spirits [God] ... before the creation" (*1 En.* 48.2). It adds, "he was concealed in the presence of (the Lord of the Spirits) prior to the creation of the world" (v. 6; cf. *1 En.* 62.7; *4 Ezra* 12.32; 13.26). Rabbinical authorities dispute whether this last verse means that Messiah preexisted and was concealed or, as most think, that merely his name preexisted and was concealed.

This tradition about Messiah's name is based on a single OT text. It is about the Servant saying of God, "while I was in my mother's womb he named me" (Isa 49.1 NRSV). The next verse adds, "He has concealed Me,... He has hidden Me." This text seems to be the background of Phil 2.9—that God "bestowed on Him [Jesus] the name which is above every name." Both texts were fulfilled when an angel told Joseph and pregnant Mary on two occasions to name the Child "Jesus" (Mt 1.21; Lk 1.31).

"Every Knee Bow" and "Every Tongue Confess"

The hymn finally identifies Jesus, in v. 10, as the person characterized throughout. The image of every knee bending before Jesus and every tongue confessing Him as Lord raises christological, eschatological, and soteriological questions. Is it worship? Do they call Jesus "Yahweh?" When will this happen? And does it mean all will be saved?

This Phil 2 hymn seems to quote Isa 45.23 from a targum. Yahweh declares in this passage, "to Me every knee will bow, every tongue will swear allegiance" (cf. Ps 145.21). While the hymn describes universal (includes heaven) homage to Jesus, Isaiah's text renders it to Yahweh. As for the hymn, it does not say that Jesus is Yahweh; rather, such acknowledgment honors Jesus as Yahweh's agent, which brings glory to Yahweh. This fulfills the Johannine Jesus' sayings, "He who beholds Me beholds the One who sent Me" (Jn 12.45; cf. v. 44), and "all may honor the Son, even as they honor the Father. He who does not honor the Son does not honor the Father who sent Him" (Jn 5.23).

Paul also alludes to, or quotes, Isa 45.23 in Rom 14.11. He prefaces it by saying, "we shall all stand before the judgment seat of God" (v. 10). So, bowing and confessing to Jesus will occur at the judgment. And Isa 45.24 says of Yahweh, "all who were angry at Him shall be put to shame," which may refer to the judgment as well (cf. *1 En.* 62.3).

While Paul may have intended that this bowing and confessing in Phil 2.10-11 be applied to the present church, the overall context of Isa 45.23-24 seems to be the future messianic kingdom on every Sabbath and new moon. For Isaiah later relates that Yahweh says of those times, "all mankind will come to bow down before Me" (Isa 66.23). These texts seem to correspond with Rev 5.13, which describes "every created thing which is in heaven and on the earth and under the earth" as honoring God and Christ the Lamb.

This bowing and confessing should not be construed as worship of Jesus as God. For, this universal homage will include the faithful as well as those who feign allegiance. Yet this does not infer the universal salvation of all humans and even demons. Rather, it may be the same idea King David wrote about in a psalm, saying that "foreigners pretend obedience to me; as soon as they hear, they obey me" (2 Sam 22.45).

1 Enoch vividly relates feigned allegiance to the Son of Man on judgment day:

> On the day of judgment, all the kings, the governors, the high officials, and the landlords shall see and recognize him—how he sits on the throne of his glory,… they shall be terrified and dejected; and pain shall seize them when they see that Son of Man sitting on the throne of his glory. (These) kings, governors, and all the landlords shall (try to) bless, glorify, extol him who rules over everything,… and those who rule[d] the world shall fall down before him on their faces, and worship and raise their hopes in that Son of Man; they shall beg and plead for mercy at his feet. But the Lord of the Spirits [God] himself will cause them to be frantic, so that they shall rush and depart from his presence. Their faces shall be filled with shame, and their countenances shall be crowned with darkness. So he will deliver them to the angels for punishments in order that vengeance shall be executed on them" (*1 En.* 62.3, 5-6, 9-11; cf. 48.5, 8-10; 63).

Will demons pretend allegiance to Jesus and God the Father? Hardly. Jesus taught that at the Judgment He will say to the wicked, "Depart from Me, accursed ones, into the eternal fire which has been prepared for the devil and his angels" (Mt 25.41). Scripture does not inform of the location of that eternal lake of fire (cf. Rev 20.10-11, 14-15). Apparently, the demons will be cast into it either at the Judgment or just prior to it.

"Jesus Christ is Lord, to the Glory of God the Father"

It seems that this last clause contains several allusions to the OT that serve as the author's intended background. First, bowing to Jesus and confessing that "Jesus Christ is Lord" seems to allude to what God twice proclaims of His righteous Servant, "I have (kept you and) given you as a covenant to the people," i.e., the Israelites (Isa 42.6; 49.8). Ancient law codes had authority over their people, and lordship is all about authority. So, Jesus is the covenant to His people by being their Lord. God making Jesus the Lord of all creation parallels His making Adam the lord of the earth (Gen 1.28). Dunn well states that the two contrast when Jesus "attains a far higher glory than the first Adam lost."[250]

Second, this universal bowing and confessing to Jesus alludes to Yahweh saying of His righteous Servant, "I will allot Him a portion with the great" (Isa 53.12). This seems to be reflected in what Jesus said, "All authority has been given to Me in heaven and on earth" (Mt 28.18; cf. Jn 16.15; 17.10). This universal authority of Jesus was made possible by God promising His Servant, "It is too small a thing that You should be My Servant to raise up the tribes of Jacob, and to restore the preserved ones of Israel; I will also make You a light of the nations so that My salvation may reach to the end of the earth.... Kings shall see and arise, princes shall also bow down" (Isa 49.6-7). All of these texts link to the Son of Man being given "a kingdom, that all the peoples, nations, and men of every language might serve Him" (Dan 7.14).

Third, the intended background of this universal homage to Jesus, which brings glory to God, is in two passages in Deutero-Isaiah.[251] In the first passage, Yahweh says of His righteous Servant, "I will not give My glory to another" (Isa 42.8; cf. Isa 49.3; Jn 17.5). This implies that God will give His glory to His righteous Servant and Him *only*. Yet through this Servant God will share His glory with one nation, and that one *only*—Israel (Isa 46.13; 48.11; 60.1-2). In the second passage, the righteous Servant says of Yahweh, "And he said to me, 'You are my servant, Israel, in whom I will be glorified'" (Isa 49.3 NIV).[252] Calling this righteous Servant "Israel" means that He is the embodiment of true Israel due to His being its Redeemer. There is no evidence in these texts that this righteous Servant possessed this glory previously, as if during a preexistence.

Concerning this final clause in the hymn, it reflects Paul's constant practice of distinguishing between Christ and God by restricting the title "Lord" to Christ and "God" to the Father, which always shows that Christ is not God. H.A.W. Meyer well observes, "Paul, particularly, even where he accumulates and strains to the utmost expressions concerning the Godlike nature of the exalted Christ (as Phil. ii.6ff; Col. i.15ff., ii.9), does not call Him *theos*, but sharply and clearly distinguishes Him as *kurios* from *theos*."[253]

Indeed, all three occurrences of the word "God" in the hymn refer to God the Father, which seems to preclude that the hymn in any way portrays Jesus Christ as God.

Moreover, Isaiah's righteous Servant calls Yahweh "My God." He says, "My reward [is] with My God," and "My God is My strength" (Isa 49.4-5). Also, Yahweh repeatedly declares such things in Isa 42—53 as "I am God, and there is no other" (Isa 45.21; 46.9). Such declarations establish that this righteous Servant cannot be God. Since Isa 42—53 clearly is background for the Phil 2 hymn, such declarations strongly suggest that it was not the intent of the hymn's author to present Jesus as God.

Ending the hymn with a doxology, and it being that honoring Jesus will abound "to the glory of God the Father," suggests Jesus is essentially subordinate to the Father.[254]

---

[250] J.D.G. Dunn, *Christology in the Making*, 118.
[251] Also, the Greek word *doxa* (glory) appears three times in the LXX in Isa 52.13-14; 53.2.
[252] Some modern Bible versions, e.g., the NIV, do not capitalize the word "servant" in Isa 42-53.
[253] H.A.W. Meyer, in MCNT, 5:362.
[254] G.B. Caird, *New Testament Theology*, 339-40.

Paul's Personal Applications of the Hymn

In this Philippian epistle Paul reiterates several concepts in its hymn and applies them to himself, his co-workers, and his readers. Sometimes, this is apparent only if the hymn is interpreted of Jesus' earthly life and heavenly exaltation. For instance, Paul exhorts his readers, "Do nothing from selfishness ... but with humility of mind" (2.3), which links to both the hymn describing Jesus as having "humbled Himself" and Paul's life (cf. 1.17; 2.21). Paul mentions several things he attained as a good Jew but forfeited to serve God and Jesus (3.4-8), and this links to Jesus having "emptied Himself." Paul describes himself and Timothy as "bond-servants of Christ Jesus" (1.1), and he tells of Timothy and Epaphroditus being servants (2.22, 25), all of which resembles Jesus "taking the form of a bond-servant." Paul also relates, "it has been granted for Christ's sake, not only to believe in Him, but also to suffer for His sake" (1.29; cf. v. 7), which parallels Jesus as the Servant in especially Isa 52.13—53.12. Paul repeatedly mentions his risk of death in ministering the gospel (1.20-21; 3.27-30), and this parallels Jesus "becoming obedient to the point of death." Twice Paul exhorts his readers to follow his own example (3.17; 4.9), which links to his exhortation to follow Jesus' example (2.5). And the apostle envisions his reward by revealing, "I press on toward the goal of the prize of the upward call" (3.14), which corresponds to Jesus being "highly exalted" as a reward for His obedience. Some of these items are parallels only in accord with the human interpretation of the hymn, which further suggests it is the correct interpretation.

Finally, Paul ends the letter with this doxology—"Now to our God and Father be the glory forever and ever" (4.20; cf. 1.11). It echoes the one at the end of the hymn, which suggests that Jesus is essentially subordinate to the Father, as in 1 Cor 15.24, 28.

Conclusion

Deciding on the proper interpretation of Phil 2.5-11 is difficult. Although most scholars desire to be objective in their approach to the Bible, determining how to interpret this hymn seems to depend so much on the exegete's christological presuppositions.[255] Traditionalists invariably decide on the preexistent interpretation of the hymn, and non-traditionalists usually opt for the human interpretation of it. But if this hymn is interpreted within its ethical context as an example, the human interpretation is more plausible.

Yet it is factors external to this epistle that are most determinative in favoring the human interpretation of its hymn. These factors are stated in this chapter's introduction and thus can be summarized: Paul did not believe Jesus was, or is, God because in his corpus (1) he reveals that he was a strict monotheist both before and after his conversion to Jesus, (2) he never provides any sort of treatise, argument, or discussion as to whether Jesus Christ preexisted or that He is God, (3) he often distinguishes God and Christ, and (4) he provides much evidence showing he believes that only the Father is God.

One appeal of the preexistent interpretation of this Phil 2 hymn is that it views all of its events chronologically whereas the human interpretation does not.[256] It recapitulates in vv. 7-8, from Jesus taking the form of a servant to being born, becoming a man, and then reiterating the servant theme with "humbled

---

[255] L.J. Kreitzer, "When He at Last Is First," 118. Two exceptions are E. Kasemann and J.D.G Dunn.
[256] See N.T. Wright, "*Harpagmos* and the Meaning of Philippians 2: 5-11," *JTS*, n.s., 37 (1986): 336.

Himself." Plus, interpreting "the name" in v. 9 as "Jesus" breaks the chronology of events, too. Such recapitulations, however, are not without precedence in Paul's recorded hymns, e.g., 1 Tim 3.16; Col 1.15-20.

Another attractive feature of the human interpretation of this Phil 2 hymn is that it is quite simple and straightforward. Most of its scholarly proponents therefore differ only on the details of the author's intended background. In contrast, J. Murphy-O'Connor points out that "the great variety of interpretations prevalent among those who accept" the preexistent interpretation suggest that this interpretation is incorrect.[257]

Even if this Philippian hymn does teach the personal preexistence of Jesus, it is stated repeatedly in this book that preexistence does not necessarily indicate deity.

But the most determining factor that favors the human interpretation of this Phil 2 hymn is its linkage to three OT figures and their sole texts which the hymn's author surely drew upon as the hymn's background: Adam in Gen 1.3, Yahweh's Servant in Isa 42—53, and the Son of Man in Dan 7.13-14. The reason is that there is nothing in the passages about these last two personages that indicate their preexistence or incarnation.

Thus, C.H. Talbert asserts that "the modern confidence in an interpretation of Phil 2.6-11 which sees there the pre-existence of Jesus followed by his incarnation and subsequent exaltation does not stand up ... it means to speak only of the human existence of Jesus."[258] Therefore, this Philippian hymn does not infer Jesus is God.

7. Does "fulness" in Colossians 1.19 and 2.9 mean Jesus is God?

Traditionalists generally cite the Apostle Paul's concept of "the fulness" that dwells in Jesus Christ, in Col 1.19 and 2.9, as evidence that Paul implicitly identifies Jesus as God. Many historical-critical scholars maintain that in Col 1.15-20 Paul quotes from a preexisting church hymn. Most scholars agree that in this passage Paul depicts Jesus Christ as the Logos-Wisdom of God by whom, for whom, and in whom God the Father created the universe. In this letter, Paul writes concerning Jesus Christ:

- "For it was the Father's good pleasure for all the fulness to dwell in Him" (Col 1.19).
- "For in Him all the fulness of Deity dwells in bodily form" (Col 2.9).

But what does Paul mean by his twice-repeated expression, "the fulness (of Deity)"?

The Greek word translated "fulness" in both Col 1.19 and 2.9 is *pleroma*, which means "full measure," "fulness," or "completeness." Many theologians and biblical exegetes interpret "the fulness" in these two verses as referring to all of God's divine attributes.[259] They conclude that if all divine attributes reside in Christ, He must be God.

---

[257] J. Murphy O'Connor, "Christological Anthropology in Phil. 2.6-11," 31.
[258] C.H. Talbert, "The Problem of Pre-existence in Philippians 2.6-11," 153.
[259] E.g., M. Harris, *Jesus as God*, 168, 287-88, 316; idem, *3 Crucial Questions*, 66.

On the contrary, the "fulness" mentioned in Col 1.19 and 2.9 indicates God's total self-revelation to humankind.[260] That is, God has fully revealed Himself in Jesus Christ. This interpretation coincides with Paul's context, "that they may have the full riches of complete understanding, in order that they may know the mystery of God, namely, Christ, in whom are hidden all the treasures of wisdom and knowledge" (Col 2.2-3 NIV).

The author of the Fourth Gospel thought similarly of the *pleroma*. He explains in his prologue that Jesus was "full of grace and truth" and that "of His fulness we have all received" (Jn 1.14, 16).[261] He means that the fulness is God's grace and truth as revealed in Jesus Christ. Paul concurs in another one of his letters, saying that those who belong to Christ "may be filled up to all the fulness of God" (Eph 3.19).

Both Paul and the Fourth Evangelist are eager to tell of this "fulness" because they were combating proto-Gnosticism. Regarding Paul's interests, a syncretistic religion prominent in Colossae was infiltrating the church there. It represented a fusing of Judaic rituals, ascetic practices due to Platonic dualism, the worship of astral powers, and some other incipient Gnostic beliefs. The latter had especially to do with the identity of Jesus.

Gnostics believed that the transcendent God revealed Himself in His totality to humankind by means of an order of aeons (spirits?), collectively known as the *pleroma*. They regarded the Logos as merely one of the aeons in the *pleroma*, thus representing only a portion of it. So-called Christian Gnostics viewed Jesus as the Logos in this *pleroma*. Valentinian Gnostics deemed the Logos-Jesus as its supreme aeon.

Paul's purpose in this epistle therefore was partly polemical, i.e., to counter this Colossian error.[262] He uses the word *pleroma* in the same sense that the proto-Gnostics did by referring to God's revelation. Paul thereby opposed this Gnostic belief by arguing that the entire fulness of God dwells in Jesus Christ.

Notice that Paul explains that the fulness dwells *in* Christ and not that Christ *is* that fulness. There is a big difference. Francis Young explains, "the fulness *was pleased* to dwell in him (*eudokesen*); it was choice, will, purpose, election, rather than essential derivative nature."[263]

In sum, what Paul meant by the fulness of Deity dwelling in Christ is the same thing as saying that *God was in Christ*, not that Christ is God.

8. Is Jesus Christ "our God" in 2 Thessalonians 1.12?

| English Versions | Reasons for the One Person View |
| Reasons for the Two Persons View | Conclusion |

Some traditionalist NT commentators cite 2 Thes 1.12, Tit 2.13, and 2 Pt 1.1 to support their belief that Jesus is God. All three of these passages have a similar syntax (word order) that makes them somewhat ambiguous. Thus, the dispute between non-traditionalists and traditionalists over these three passages

---

[260] R. Schippers, "*pleroo*," in *DNTT* 1:740. This view seems more correct than Gerhad Delling's ("*pleroma*," in *TDNT* 6:303-04) narrower interpretation, which makes *pleroma* refer only to God's power.

[261] Cf. J.A.T. Robinson, "Dunn on John," 333.

[262] R.N. Longenecker, *The Christology of Early Jewish Christianity*, 57.

[263] F. Young, "A Cloud of Witnesses, 45n23.

concerns only a phrase and its grammar. Yet, many traditionalist scholars who cite Tit 2.13 to support their view that Jesus is God also deny that 2 Thes 1.12 and 2 Pt 1.1 do likewise.[264]

English Versions
Most English versions translate the problematic phrase in 2 Thes 1.12 so that two Persons are in view, so that it does not call Christ "God," as the following table shows:

Two Persons View	One Person View
"the grace of our God and the Lord Jesus Christ" (AV, RV, RSV, NASB, NIV, JB, TEV, NEB, NJB, NEB, NRSV, ESV)	"the grace of our God and Lord(,) Jesus Christ" (NAB, NIVmg)

Reasons for the Two Persons View
The following reasons support the Two Persons view of 2 Thes 1.12, so that its critical phrase *does not* call Jesus Christ "God:"
1. In the Greek text, Paul's use of the word *theos* elsewhere in this epistle shows that he intends for it to refer here also to the Father. For instance, twice in his salutation in this epistle Paul pens the words, "God our Father and the Lord Jesus Christ" (vv. 1-2). And he writes in 2 Thes 2.16, "our Lord Jesus Christ Himself and God our Father." (Cf. 2 Thes 1.8.) In addition, in 1 and 2 Thessalonians each of the epithets—"our God" and "God our Father"—occur four times as a title for the Father.[265] So "our God" and "Lord Jesus Christ" in 2 Thes 1.12 should be distinguished as two Persons. Traditionalist R.E. Brown remarks concerning 2 Thes 1.12, "Most commentators accept this distinction, and the latest and most comprehensive Catholic commentary says that it must be accepted. So, this text cannot be used as an example of the use of the title 'God' for Jesus."[266]
2. The word "our" separates the two titles.
3. Since the words "our God" in 2 Thes 1.11 obviously refer to God the Father, the same is likely true of the words "our God" in v. 12, both of which occur in the same sentence.
4. Since Paul writes in his salutation, "Grace to you and peace from God the Father and the Lord Jesus Christ" (v. 2), he intends the same about "grace" in v. 12. That is, this grace is from both "God (the Father) and the Lord Jesus Christ."

Reasons for the One Person View
The following reason (with rebuttal) is given for the One Person view in 2 Thes 1.12, in which case its critical phrase *does* call Jesus Christ "God:"
1. The absence of the definite article preceding *kurios* ("Lord") unites the two genitives, so that "our God" refers to "Lord Jesus Christ."

Rebuttal: "Lord Jesus Christ" had by then become a fixed formula, i.e., a separate, common entity that makes the article unnecessary for distinguishing God and Christ.

---
[264] E.g., William Hendricksen, *Exposition of the Pastoral Epistles*, in NTC (1957), 375.
[265] 1 Thes 1.3; 2.2; 3.9, 11, 13; 2 Thes 1.1, 11; 2.16.
[266] R.E. Brown, *Jesus God and Man*, 15-16.

Conclusion

The above table shows that the versions overwhelmingly favor the Two Person view of 2 Thes 1.12—eleven-to-one—so that it does not call Jesus "God." This coincides with Paul's other epistles, which indicate he did not believe Jesus was God.

9. Is Christ Jesus "the God-man" in 1 Timothy 2.5?

Introduction	Christ as Mediator
God is "One"	Conclusion
The God-man?	

Introduction

Certain church fathers called Jesus "the God-man," and traditionalists have been doing it ever since. For example, Emil Brunner, in his classic defense of traditional Christology, repeatedly calls Jesus Christ the "God Man."[267] Those who employ this ascription mean that God literally became the man, Jesus Christ, which is classical incarnation. And they often cite 1 Tim 2.5 as their sole biblical support. It reads:

- For there is one God, and one mediator also between God and men, the man Christ Jesus.

God is "One"

Many scholars think that in 1 Tim 2.5, Paul cites a liturgy commonly used in churches of that time (cf. 1 Cor 8.6). If so, this would explain why he did not feel it necessary to explain the meaning of what would have been familiar to Timothy.

Note that the first word in 1 Tim 2.5 is "For," a conjunction that refers to what precedes it, which is "God our Saviour." Does this phrase refer to God the Father or to Christ Jesus? The answer is found in the words which follow: "For there is one God." This "one God" therefore refers back to "God our Savior," who must be the Father.

This interpretation of 1 Tim 2.5 is confirmed in Paul's salutation of this letter. He begins it by claiming that his apostleship derives from "God our Savior, and of Christ Jesus" (1 Tim 1.1). He ends this opening sentence by writing, "God the Father and Christ Jesus our Lord" (v. 2). So, in this salutation "God our Savior" is clearly "God the Father."

This "one God" in 1 Tim 2.5 also refers back to the "invisible,... only God" in 1 Tim 1.17 (cf. 6.15-16), who can be none other than the Father as well.

Thus, this liturgical saying in 1 Tim 2.5 establishes the first precept of the truth about God, that He is numerically one, therefore alluding to the Shema (Deut 6.4).

Trinitarians argue that the Shema, and biblical allusions to it, do not define God as numerically one but as a unity, thereby allowing for their doctrine of God as a unity of three Persons. But Paul's juxtaposition of the "one God, and one mediator" in 1 Tim 2.5 clearly distinguishes two Persons. In other words, if "the one mediator" identifies one Person, viz., Christ Jesus, then the parallel

---

[267] Emil Brunner, *The Mediator: A Study of the Central Doctrine of the Christian Faith* [1927], tr. Olive Wyon (Philadelphia: Westminster, 1947). See also W.N. Pittenger, *The Word Incarnate*, 132-45.

expression, "the one God," would seem to identify numerically one Person as well, viz., God the Father. Thus, rather than 1 Tim 2.5 indicating that Jesus is the "one God," it distinguishes Him from the one God.

The God-Man?
Some past scholars objected to applying the ascription "God-man" to Jesus. Schleiermacher and others had earlier pointed out that this term appears neither in 1 Tim 2.5 nor anywhere else in the Bible, so that this term requires scrutinizing.[268] Indeed, this non-biblical term and its concept parallels the pagan notion of mythological demigods who are both god and man. Interestingly, proto-Gnostics sometimes even described these mythological redeemer figures as the "God man."[269]

It seems strange that Christians would call Jesus "the God-man" based on 1 Tim 2.5. This verse indicates the opposite because it clearly (1) distinguishes God from Christ, (2) affirms that God is a single Person, (3) calls Jesus only a "man," and (4) thus does not call Him either "God" or "the God-man." Non-traditionalist theologian Hendrikus Berkhof cites 1 Tim 2.5 as evidence that Jesus "is not a dual being,"[270] meaning that He does not have a human nature and a divine nature to be a God-man.

Also, if Paul believed that Jesus was God, it seems unlikely that he would here overlook providing some explanation that the mediator is indeed both man and God.

Finally, identifying Jesus Christ as "the God-man" seems to diminish His humanity. For, how can anyone be a God-man and still be fully human?

Christ as Mediator
In this prescribed formula of 1 Tim 2.5, Paul probably intends to describe Jesus polemically as the one mediator in contrast to the proto-Gnostic belief in a *pleroma* of many aeons as a chain of mediators linking God and humankind.

Jesus is described as "mediator" three other times in the NT, all in the book of Hebrews (Heb 8.6; 9.15; 12.24). These texts and their contexts contribute to the view that Jesus was uniquely qualified to mediate between God and humankind. As God's Son and a perfectly righteous man, Jesus was intimately associated with holy God.

What is a mediator? In the Greek NT, the word translated "mediator" is *mesites*, meaning "one who stands in the middle," literally a "middleman." B.F. Westcott defines *mesites* as "one who, standing between the contracting parties, shall bring them into fellowship."[271] So, a mediator is a third party who attempts to reconcile two parties at variance. The two parties in this case are God and humankind. The mediator—Jesus Christ—attempts to reconcile them. Rather than 1 Tim 2.5 offering support for Jesus being God, it does the opposite by necessitating that the mediator, as the middleman, is neither God nor another sinful human being alienated from God.

The Bible teaches that God the Father is the One with whom human beings are alienated and therefore the One with whom they need to be reconciled. Paul tells the Corinthians, "be reconciled to God" (2 Cor 5.21; cf. Rom 5.10). Interestingly,

---
[268] F. Schleiermacher, *The Christian Faith*, 424.
[269] A. Grillmeier, *Christ in Christian Tradition*, 81.
[270] H. Berkhof, *Christian Faith*, 291.
[271] Cited by W. Barclay, *Jesus As They Saw Him*, 334.

the Bible never tells us to be reconciled to Jesus Christ. Why? God is the One to whom human beings are accountable because we have broken His laws.

Yet God is the ultimate source of our reconciliation. He plans and accomplishes it through Christ, whom He sent as the Redeemer. So, Paul further informs the believing Corinthians that "God ... has reconciled us to Himself through Christ" (2 Cor 5.18).

Some traditionalists think that Jesus' mediatorship requires that He is God. For example, William Barclay asserts, "Jesus is therefore the only possible mediator between God and man, because he is perfectly God and man."[272] On the contrary, 1 Tim 2.5 does not identify Jesus as being either of the two disputant parties, as Barclay claims. Instead, Paul employs the word "men" to refer to the category of all human beings, other than Jesus, who are estranged from God. Jesus is not included in this category because He was sinless. In other words, as mediator between these two disputants, Christ Jesus is neither the "one God" nor among the category of sinful "men." Yet Christ Jesus is uniquely and intimately associated with both, which further serves to qualify Him as mediator.

Conclusion

It must be concluded that it is incorrect to call Jesus Christ either "God" or "the God-man" based on 1 Tim 2.5. Logically, Jesus Christ as a third party cannot reconcile us to God and at the same time be God. Finally, the TEV well paraphrases Paul's intended meaning in 1 Tim 2.5 as follows: "For there is one God, and there is one who brings God and mankind together, the man Christ Jesus."

10. Is Christ Jesus "God manifest in the flesh" in 1 Timothy 3.16?

Scholars regard the six strophes in 1 Tim 3.16 as an excerpt from a pre-Pauline church hymn. They think each of these strophes refers to major events in the life of Jesus that are arranged in chronological order. The hymn reads as follows in the AV:

16 And without controversy great is the mystery of godliness:
God was manifest in the flesh,
Justified in the Spirit,
Seen of angels,
Preached unto the Gentiles,
Believed on in the world,
Received up into glory.

Many past traditionalists insisted that the first strophe in 1 Tim 3.16 identifies Jesus as God. But in the Greek MSS of the NT there is weak evidence for *theos*, translated "God." The earliest, and therefore the best, evidence for it appears only in the 8th and 9th century Byzantine family of MSS, which is very late. And it is quite rare in the other MS families. The AV was translated from TR, which depended solely on Byzantine MSS and thus has *theos*.

The entire MS evidence provides much stronger support for *hos* ("who") or *ho* ("he" or "the one") in the first strophe of 1 Tim 3.16. Consequently, the four

---
[272] W. Barclay, *Jesus As They Saw Him*, 337.

foremost modern Greek NT texts have *hos* rather than *theos*.²⁷³ Accordingly, nearly all major, modern English versions of the NT have "He" (RSV, NEB, JB, NASB, NIV, NJB, NRSV, REB), or "Who" (NAB, RSVmg, NIVmg, NRSVmg), rather than "God," as in the AV.

Textual critic and traditionalist Bruce Metzger assesses the patristic writings. He concludes concerning the variant *theos* in 1 Tim 3.16, "all ancient versions presuppose *hos* or *ho*; and no patristic writer prior to the last third of the fourth century testifies to the reading *theos*."²⁷⁴ So, *ho* must be a justifiable correction of *theos* by later scribes.²⁷⁵

Most modern exegetes therefore agree that *hos*, not *theos*, appeared in the original autograph of 1 Tim 3.16. R.E. Brown concludes regarding this *theos* variant, "The attestation for such a reading is not strong enough to warrant serious consideration."²⁷⁶

How did this corrupt reading get into the MS evidence? In Greek MSS that are in uncials (all capitals), the difference in appearance between an omicron (Gr. letter for Eng. "O") and a theta (Gr. letter for Eng. "TH") is very minute. A scribe could have innocently miscopied it. Metzger suggests that it could have occurred either as an interpretation of the six strophes of the hymn or as dogmatic support for the Trinitarian doctrine.²⁷⁷

Why does this hymn have the ambiguous *hos* rather than a noun to clearly identify Christ? Murray Harris answers by citing Westcott and Hort's critical apparatus in their Greek NT. In it, they speculate that Paul did not quote the entire hymn, so that *hos* refers to an antecedent in the preceding unquoted portion.²⁷⁸ J.N.D. Kelly agrees, explaining that since this preceding hymnal portion no doubt expressly identifies Christ,

> This evidently caused difficulty to early exegetes and scribes, some of whom tried to amend the text so as to produce a smooth-flowing sentence. Thus the majority of Western witnesses substitute the neuter *ho* ("which") for *hos*, so linking the clause with "the mystery of [godliness]." A number of later MSS read *theos* ("God") for *hos*, which gives the translation "God was manifested ..." (so AV). Both these variants are clearly secondary, being attempts to eliminate the superficial disjointedness of the true text. Unquestionably *hos* has the best MSS support and represents the true text, and there can in any case be no doubt that Christ, not God, must be the subject of the following verbs.²⁷⁹

Regardless of these variants and how they got into the MS evidence, we can rest assured that Paul would not have contradicted himself by saying that "God was manifest in the flesh," meaning to appear and literally be seen by human eyes.²⁸⁰ He wrote in the same epistle that God is "invisible," "whom no man has seen or can see" (1 Tim 1.17; 6.16). Here, Paul means the same thing about Jesus as John did in his first epistle: "we have seen with our eyes, what we beheld and our hands handled, concerning the Word of Life—and the life was manifested" (1 Jn 1.1-2). Thus, human beings literally saw Jesus whereas none (other than the resurrected, exalted Jesus) have ever literally seen God.

---

²⁷³ E.g., Nestle²⁶, UBS¹,²,³
²⁷⁴ B.M. Metzger, *Textual Commentary*, 641.
²⁷⁵ M. Harris, *Jesus as God*, 267.
²⁷⁶ R.E. Brown, *An Introduction to New Testament Christology*, 177.
²⁷⁷ B.M. Metzger, *Textual Commentary*, 641.
²⁷⁸ M. Harris, *Jesus as God*, 268.
²⁷⁹ J.N.D. Kelly, *Pastoral Epistles Timothy I & II, and Titus*, 89.
²⁸⁰ BAGD, 853.

A related issue concerns the implication of the verb "manifest" in the first strophe, which means "appeared" (cf. 2 Tim 1.10). Some exegetes think this word signifies the preexistence of Jesus. But James D.G. Dunn refutes this idea, citing J. Jeremias, R.H. Gundry, and E. Schillebeeckx as support. Dunn explains concerning the hymn, "the contrast is between pre-Easter earthly existence and the Easter exaltation to heaven."[281]

11. Is Christ Jesus "our great God and Saviour" in Titus 2.13?

Introduction	Two Persons View
The Greek Text and English Versions	Survey of Scholars
One Person View	

Introduction

Traditionalists offer Tit 2.13 as their second-best Pauline text that they think calls Christ "God," with Rom 9.5b being foremost. The entirety of Tit 2.13 reads as follows in the AV: "Looking for that blessed hope, and glorious appearing of the great God and our Savior Jesus Christ." But this verse reads differently in the NASB: "looking for the blessed hope and the appearing of the glory of our great God and Savior, Christ Jesus." As for "the blessed hope," it refers to the yet future resurrection of the saints (cf. 1 Thes 4.13-18). This event will accompany Jesus' return, which is the "appearing" (Gr. *epiphaneia*). The critical words for Christology are the last clause in Tit 2.13. As in the AV, some English versions translate so that it *does not* call Jesus Christ "God." But, as in the NASB, other versions translate it so that it *does* call Jesus Christ "God," as the following shows:

AV: The Two Persons View	NASB: The One Person View
"great God and our Savior Jesus Christ"	"our great God and Savior, Christ Jesus"

At least three christological questions arise in Tit 2.13. First, does Paul call Christ "God"? Second, if not, does the "appearing" also refer to "the great God," so that God the Father appears with Christ at Christ's return? Third, how should the anarthrous *soteros* ("Savior" without the article) in the Greek text be treated?

The Greek Text and English Versions

The Greek text of Tit 2.13 reads as follows, with an interlinear translation added:

prosdechomenoi ten makarian elpida kai epiphaneian tes doxes tou megalou
  looking for the blessed hope and appearing of the glory (of) the great

theou kai soteros hemon Christou Iesou
  God and savior of us Christ Jesus

---

[281] J.D.G. Dunn, *Christology in the Making*, 237, 345n88.

A survey of Tit 2.13 in major English versions shows that they are about evenly divided between calling Christ "God" or not. Of the first seven printed English Bible versions—from Tyndale through the AV—none of them call Christ "God" in Tit 2.13. Rather, they unanimously render the Two Persons view as follows: "the mighty/great God(,) and our Savior Jesus Christ" (or "Christ Jesus"). But major English versions since the AV was published, in the year 1611, have not been in agreement; the majority have favored the One Person translation, which calls Christ "God," as the following shows:

Two Persons View	One Person View
"of the great God and our Savior Jesus Christ" (or "Christ Jesus") AV, RVmg, ASV, RSVmg, NEBmg, NRSVmg "of the great God and of our Savior Jesus Christ" NAB, cf. NWT	"of our great God and Savior(,) Jesus Christ" (or "Christ Jesus") RV, RSV, NASB, JB, NEB, TEV, NIV, NJB, NRSV, NJB, REB, NRSV, ESV

Notice that some versions have an alternate reading, signified by "mg" meaning "marginal reading." For example, if a version translates Tit 2.13 as calling Christ "God," its alternate reading does not call Jesus Christ "God," or vice versa. Also, some versions translate "the appearing of the glory," whereas others have "the glorious appearing."

One Person View

As with Rom 9.5, those commentators who espouse the One Person interpretation of Tit 2.13 do so primarily on grammatical grounds. Their detailed and often complex discussions are largely beyond the understanding of non-Greek readers and therefore the scope of this book. So, we will only briefly consider these grammatical issues.

Reasons for the view that Paul *does call* Christ "God" in Tit 2.13 are as follows:

1. The absence of the definite article (anarthrous) immediately preceding the noun *soteros* (Savior) in Tit 2.13 requires that it be conjoined with the noun *theou* (God), thus making both refer to *Iesou Christou* (Jesus Christ). Many past scholars, e.g., Baptist A.T. Robertson,[282] based this argument on Granville Sharp's so-called "rule" of koine (biblical) Greek grammar, established in 1798.[283] Sharp's rule states that when only one article precedes the first of two nouns joined together by a copulative (e.g., conjunction "and"), thus making the second noun anarthrous, these two nouns are conjoined and have the same referent, which is "Jesus Christ" in Tit 2.13. Based on this rule, Sharp translated the One Person view in the following passages: Eph 5.5; 2 Thes 1.12; Tit 2.13; 2 Pt 1.1.

Rebuttal: Many grammarians have since insisted that Sharp's supposed rule is uncertain.[284] Some add that a second article is unnecessary in Tit 2.13

---

[282] A.T. Robertson, *A Grammar of the Greek New Testament in Light of Historical Research*, 4th ed. (Nashville, TN: Broadman, 1934), 786.
[283] Granville Sharp, *Remarks on the Uses of the Definite Article in the Greek Text of the New Testament; Containing Many New Proofs of the Divinity of Christ, from Passages Which are Wrongly Translated in the Common English Version* [1798], 3rd ed. (London: Vernor & Hood, 1803), 4-5.
[284] E.g., M-H-T, 3:181. Also, E. Abbot ("On ... Titus ii.13," 16) quotes grammarian Alexander Buttmann, who opposes applying this "rule" to Tit 2.13; 2 Pt 1.1; Jude 4.

because *soteros* (Savior) is sufficiently qualified by the pronoun *hemon* (our).[285] In 1881, Ezra Abbot observed that Sharp's construction of Tit 2.13 and the above passages was supported by only a "few scholars."[286] Grammarian Nigel Turner admits, "Unfortunately, at this period of Greek we cannot be sure that such a rule is really decisive."[287] J.N.D. Kelly adds, "the absence of the article cannot count as decisive, for 'Savior' tended to be anarthrous (cf. 1 Tim 1.1), and in any case the correct use of the article was breaking down in the late Greek."[288] Grammarian G.B. Winer admitted that either view is grammatically possible; but he added, "only doctrinal conviction, deduced from Paul's teaching, that this apostle could not have called Christ *the great God*, induced me to show that there is also no grammatical obstacle to taking *kai ... sotaros ... Christou* by itself as a second subject."[289]

Other grammarians have insisted that there is an exception to Sharp's rule, in which the second article can be omitted when the author knows that his/her readers will assume a distinction in subjects. Ezra Abbot explains that the same is sometimes true in English. He gives the example that "the Secretary and Treasurer" means one person, but "the Secretary and the Treasurer" means two persons. However, if you said, "I saw the President and Treasurer" of some well-known corporation, listeners would understand that you meant two persons, thus rendering the second article unnecessary.[290] So, with one article readers decide if the two titles more sensibly indicate one or two persons.

2. Since the phrase *tou megalou theou* (the great God) does not appear anywhere else in the NT, it seems more appropriate to apply it to Jesus Christ rather than to the Father.

Rebuttals:

a. On the contrary, J. Jeremias, a past authority on 1st century Palestinian Judaism, alleges, "The application of the formula 'great God' to Jesus which was a title for God firmly rooted in late Judaism would be completely unique in the New Testament."[291] In the NT, similar epithets are applied to the Father much more than to Christ (e.g., 1 Tim 1.11, 17; 4.10; 6.15-16), witnessed by its many doxologies to God the Father.

b. The only NT instances in which the adjective "great" is applied to Jesus is when He is implicitly compared to other human beings (e.g., Lk 1.32; 7.16; Heb 4.14; 10.21). And since Jesus said, "The Father is greater than I" (Jn 14.28), it seems best to take this phrase—"the great God"—as a reference to God the Father.

c. The substantival form of *megalou—megaleiotes* (greatness)—is applied to the Father in the NT four times (Lk 9.43; Heb 1.3; 8.1; Jude 25), but only once to Christ (2 Pt 1.16).

d. It seems more appropriate to call God the Father "great," rather than to call Jesus Christ "great," in this context. For, it is the Father who will ultimately

---

[285] E.g., G.B. Winer, *A Treatise on the Grammar of New Testament Greek*, tr. W.F. Moulton (Edinburgh: T. & T. Clark, 1877), 162.

[286] E. Abbot, "On ... Titus ii.13," 3.

[287] N. Turner, *Grammatical Insights*, 16. M. Harris (*Jesus as God*, 307-08) appears to misrepresent Turner by appealing only to his earlier publication.

[288] J.N.D. Kelly, *Pastoral Epistles Timothy I & II, and Titus*, 246. For a thorough and complex discussion of the anarthrous *sotaros* in Tit 2.13, see M. Harris, *Jesus as God*, 179-82, 307-10.

[289] G.B. Winer, *A Grammar of the Idiom of the New Testament*, 130.

[290] E. Abbot, "On ... Titus ii.13," 14.

[291] Quoted by J. Schneider, *DNTT* 2:82.

bring about the glorious second coming of Christ (1 Tim 6.14b-15a; cf. Ac 1.7; 3.20; 1 Thes 4.14).

3. Regarding the translation, "the glorious appearing of the great God," the Greek NT never applies the word *epiphaneia* (appearing) to God the Father. O. Cullmann reflects this view by remarking concerning Christ's return, "A simultaneous 'appearing' of God and Christ does not correspond to the usual expectation."[292]

Rebuttal: Indeed, the Father, who is invisible to us mortal humans (Jn 1.18; 6.46; 1 Tim 1.17; 6.16), does not appear with Christ at His return. The word *epiphaneia* occurs five times in the Greek NT, all in Paul's letters and applied exclusively to Christ. Four of these five instances pertain to Jesus' return (2 Thes 2.8; 1 Tim 6.14; 2 Tim 4.1, 8). This usage, as well as other reasons, requires that the words *epiphaneian tes doxes* should be translated, "the appearing of the glory" (RV, RSV, NASB, ESV), rather than "the glorious appearing" (AV, NIV) in apposition to that in v. 11, "the grace of God has appeared." This rendering provides that "the appearing" is "the glory" and not "the great God;" i.e., it is God's glory and Jesus Christ that will appear at Jesus' return and not the Father who will appear.[293] Jesus verifies this, telling of "the glory of His Father" which will accompany Him at His return (Mt 16.27; Mk 8.38). (This appearing of glory is therefore manifested as the work of the Father since Jesus comes "sitting on the right hand of Power" [Mt 26.64 and par.]). However, Luke records this same saying of Jesus differently, with Jesus referring to three glories to be revealed at His return: "when He [the Son of Man=Jesus] comes in His glory, and the glory of the Father and of the holy angels" (Lk 9.26).

4. The majority of post-Nicene fathers adopted this view.

Rebuttal: But it should be acknowledged that these fathers were biased due to their theological motives arising from the Arian controversy. And Murray Harris admits that the ancient versions, of which nearly all translate the Two Persons view, are worthy of much more weight than the testimony of the Nicene and post-Nicene church fathers due to their bias.[294] Furthermore, many of these versions were translated and published earlier than the writings of these church fathers, giving those versions more weight.

5. In the NT era, the phrase "God and Savior" was applied to some Roman emperors. So it would be natural, and a counteracting polemic, for Paul to say the same of Jesus.[295]

Rebuttal: For Paul to call Jesus "God" is a serious theological proposition and a major departure from his strong monotheistic background that would require a thorough explanation. Moreover, we would not expect Paul to develop his theology in reaction to how the world viewed its rulers and what titles they attributed to them.

Two Persons View

As with Rom 9.5b, those interpreters who espouse the Two Persons view of Tit 2.13 do so primarily because of Paul's teaching and usage throughout his other epistles. J.E. Huther typically remarks, "It cannot be decided on purely grammatical grounds.... The question can only be answered by an appeal to NT usage."[296]

---

[292] O. Cullman, *The Christology of the New Testament*, 314.
[293] E. Abbot, "On ... Titus ii.13," 5.
[294] M. Harris, *Jesus as God*, 185; J.N.D. Kelly, *Pastoral Epistles Timothy I & II, and Titus*, 246.
[295] E.g., N. Turner, *Grammatical Insights*, 16.
[296] J.E. Huther, MCNT, 9:302.

Reasons for the view that Tit 2.13 *does not call* Jesus Christ "God" are as follows:

1. The word "our" likely modifies "Savior" and not "God" since the NT does not contain the following expressions: "our God Jesus Christ," "God Jesus Christ," or "Jesus Christ our God." Also, Paul and other NT writers frequently attach the word "our" to "Lord" and "Savior." If NT authors had believed that Jesus Christ was God, one would expect these simple phrases to appear in their writings, just as they do in Ignatius' letters.

2. Excluding Rom 9.5 and Tit 2.13, everywhere else in his writings Paul always uses the word *theos* (God) exclusively for "the Father." Ezra Abbot explains most convincingly, "In the case of a grammatical ambiguity of this kind in any classical author, the first inquiry would be, 'What is the usage of the writer respecting the application of the title in question?' Now this consideration, which certainly is a most reasonable one, seems to me here absolutely decisive. While the word *theos* (God) occurs more than five hundred times in the Epistles of Paul,... there is not a single instance in which it is clearly applied to Christ."[297] Abbot continues, "In the case of a question between two constructions, either of which is grammatically possible, should we not adopt that which accords with a usage of which we have 500 examples, without one clear exception, rather than that which is in opposition to it?... The habitual, and I believe uniform, usage of Paul corresponds with his language [in] 1 Cor. viii.6."[298]

Rebuttal: M. Harris argues that "every NT author must be permitted the luxury of some stylistic, verbal or theological" departures from that writer's "habitual usage."[299]

3. Paul consistently and repeatedly distinguishes "God" and "(Jesus) Christ" throughout his corpus as two separate and distinct Persons or Beings. He therefore would not have obliterated this distinction in perhaps only two instances, i.e., Rom 9.5 and Tit 2.13. Johannes Schneider and Colin Brown generally reflect the viewpoint of those scholars who adopt the Two Persons view of Tit 2.13 by admitting that the One Person view "is linguistically possible but contradicts the otherwise rigorously maintained distinction in the Pastorals between God and Christ."[300] In this letter to Titus alone, Paul makes this distinction clear in his salutation by saying, "Paul, a bond-servant of God and an apostle of Jesus Christ,... God the Father and Christ Jesus our Savior" (Tit 1.1, 4).

4. Applying the adjective "great" to "God" suggests that "God" is an independent subject to be distinguished from "Jesus Christ."[301]

Survey of Scholars

In 1881, Ezra Abbot provided an impressive list of forty-five commentators and theologians, going back to the Reformation, who sided with all major English versions up to that time, from Tyndale to the AV, in translating the Two Persons view in Tit 2.13, so it does not call Christ "God."[302] For instance, in the Reformation both Erasmus and Martin Luther adopted the Two Persons view of Tit 2.13 while John Calvin was non-commital.

---

[297] E. Abbot, "On ... Titus ii.13," 10.
[298] E. Abbot, "On ... Titus ii.13," 10.
[299] M. Harris, *Jesus as God*, 176-77.
[300] Johannes Schneider and Colin Brown, "*soter*," in *DNTT* 3:220. See also J.E. Huther, MCNT, 9:303.
[301] J.E. Huther, MCNT, 9:303.
[302] E. Abbot, "On ... Titus ii.13," 12.

In 1961, Vincent Taylor surveyed the scholarly landscape concerning this issue in Tit 2.13. He concluded that "the grammarians range themselves on both sides.... The theologians are also divided."[303]

In 1994, Murray Harris provided the following survey dating back a century:[304]

One Person View	**Two Persons View**
8 grammarians	1 grammarian
5 lexicographers	0 lexicographers
31 commentators & theologians	12 commentators & theologians

Harris admits that some of these scholars he lists for the one Person view do so "with varying degrees of assurance."[305] Actually, some of them are quite noncommittal.[306]

Conclusion

Thus, we have seen that since the Reformation most English Bible versions have favored the One Person view of Tit 2.13, yet there has been no decisive consensus among NT scholars as to whether it identifies Jesus Christ as "God." Concerning all of Paul's NT writings, most of these scholars have regarded only the two phrases in Rom 9.5b and Tit 2.13 as serious contenders for whether Paul calls Jesus "God."[307] Yet considering Paul's strong monotheism, the likelihood is he did not intend for these somewhat grammatically ambiguous passages to call Jesus "God."

---

[303] V. Taylor, "Does the New Testament Call Jesus God?" 117.
[304] M. Harris, *Jesus as God*, 185n50, 51, 52, 53, 54.
[305] M. Harris, *Jesus as God*, 185.
[306] E.g., M. Harris includes Catholic scholars R.E. Brown and M. Zerwick. However, Brown (*Jesus God and Man*, 17-18) remarks concerning Tit 2.13, "It is very difficult to come to a definite decision.... no certainty can be reached, here." And M. Zerwick (*Biblical Greek: Illustrated by Examples*, 60) remarks, "Sometimes the use of but one article with more than one noun seems even to suppose and express the divinity of Christ, e.g., Eph 5,5 ... Tit 2,13 ... One must however say that such examples *seem to suggest* the divinity of Christ, and not that they are proofs of it."
[307] M. Harris, *Jesus as God*, 169.

Chapter Eight
Christology of the Author of Hebrews

A: Introduction

The Author and his Style	The Preexistence of Jesus?
Structure and Purpose	Jesus as the Son of God
The Prologue	Distinguishing God and Christ
The Superiority of Jesus	The Subordination of the Son
The Sinless Humanity of Jesus	Jesus' Prayers and Exaltation

The Author and His Style

The Epistle to the Hebrews was written anonymously. Throughout church history, there has been much speculation about this author's identity. All NT scholars agree that the content of the epistle reveals that he must have been a Jew. Many church fathers thought the Apostle Paul was the author; but hardly any scholars think that anymore. The main reasons are that certain stylistic features of the work significantly surpass those of the Apostle Paul's letters, e.g., its articulate method, extensive vocabulary, rich imagery, and the quality of Greek, which experts say is the finest in the NT. However, the author personally knew Timothy and thus presumably Paul (Heb 13.23). Some scholars suggest Barnabas as the author, but there are no compelling reasons for this suggestion.

The most likely candidate for the authorship of the Epistle to the Hebrews is none other than Apollos.[1] Luke says he was "an eloquent man," "mighty in the Scriptures," "fervent in spirit," "teaching accurately the things concerning Jesus," and "he powerfully refuted the Jews in public, demonstrating by the Scriptures that Jesus was the Christ" (Ac 18.24-28). Whew! Apollos was perhaps the premiere apostolic apologist. All of these enumerated abilities of his were characteristic of the author of Hebrews. In addition, no other NT author demonstrates such a thorough knowledge of the OT as does the author of Hebrews. He quotes it no less than thirty-five times and appends as many OT allusions in proving that Jesus is the Promised One of the Scriptures.[2] Apollos was such an eloquent speaker and expositor of Scripture that Paul could compare him to himself and Peter as seemingly the three most effective preachers in Asia (1 Cor 1.12; 3.22). Paul, on the other hand, admitted that he himself was "unskilled in speech" (2 Cor 11.6).

---
[1] E.g., H. Montefiore, *Hebrews*, 9-28.
[2] H. Montefiore, *Hebrews*, 4.

Structure and Purpose

The Epistle to the Hebrews is an apologetic work written to Hellenistic Jewish Christians. They may have lived in or near Rome,[3] and this author may have previously ministered to them (Heb 13.19). The letter reveals that its recipients had manifested some evidence of God's salvific work in their lives; yet some of them were in serious danger of lapsing back into a form of legalistic Judaism (Heb 2.1; 3.12; 6.1-12; 10.26-29). The author's purpose was to exhort his readers to continue in their professed faith in Jesus, thereby persevering in the trials of their faith, in order to actualize the precious goal of obtaining eternal salvation (Heb 3.6, 14; 10.35-39; 13.22). The author does so primarily by laboring at length to prove that Jesus is worthy of their faith as their Savior.

This epistle is also a very important biblical resource for determining the identity of Jesus. The Arians seem to have used it as their primary biblical support for their subordinationist Christology as well as their emphasis on Jesus' humanity. Indeed, the Epistle to the Hebrews contains several descriptions of both of these features, and these do not accord easily with the traditional view that Jesus is co-equal with God the Father.

It is highly unlikely that the author of this epistle would identify Jesus as "God." This is substantiated by the simple fact that this letter is the only NT document written specifically to Jews, thus the book's title. If there is a most suitable place in the NT where there should be a thorough discussion of Jesus being God, if indeed He was, it is here in this epistle. For the author's Jewish readers likely would have had a strong monotheistic religious background, so that such a discourse would have been most relevant to them. But, alas, we find no such discussion. Also, internal evidence suggests that this letter was written quite early, probably in the early fifties.[4] That would be prior to the time when most NT scholars think the church began to develop its supposedly high Christology.

Nonetheless, traditionalists cite Heb 1.8 as evidence supporting their Christology that Jesus is God. In fact, authorities are unanimous that Heb 1.8 is one of the nine major, debated *theos* texts in the NT concerning whether Jesus is God. In this passage, the author quotes Ps 45.6-7 and thereby *seems* to call Jesus "God." Before examining these two texts, we will consider the overall Christology of the Epistle to the Hebrews.

The Prologue

The Epistle to the Hebrews begins with a short prologue consisting of four verses. This introductory statement contains significant christological assertions about Jesus that set the stage for the remainder of this epistle. First, it clearly distinguishes "God" and "His/his Son" (Gr. *huios*) in most English versions of Heb 1.1-2 (AV, NASB, JB, NEB, NIV). But since *huios* is anarthrous, some versions have "a Son" (RSV, NRSV). Second, this prologue mentions the Son's apparent preexistence (vv. 2-3). Third, it arguably has the most important christological statement in the epistle, which says of God that "the Son ... is the radiance of His glory and the exact representation of His nature" (v. 3).[5] In other words, Jesus perfectly reflects both God's glory and His nature. So, the question arises regarding traditional Christology, How can Jesus perfectly represent God if He is God?

---

[3] W.L. Lane, *Hebrews 1-8*, lviii-lx.
[4] H. Montefiore, *Hebrews*, 12, 28.
[5] The words, "the Son," do not represent a correct translation in Heb 1.3. The Greek text has *hos*, meaning "who," as in the AV, so that it does not allow for a new sentence, as most English versions have it.

This prologue in Heb 1.1-4 is comparable to John's prologue in Jn 1.1-18. Both depict Jesus as the One through whom God has spoken His Word (Jn 1.1; Heb 1.1-2). And both establish Jesus' apparent preexistence by God creating the world through Him as the Logos (Jn 1.3; Heb 1.2, 10; cf. 11.3). Most importantly, Jesus being "the exact representation" of God's nature, in Heb 1.3, means virtually the same thing that John does in Jn 1.1c>, which the NEB translates, "what God was the Word was." And this idea coordinates with Paul's description of Jesus as the "image" of God (2 Cor 4.4; Col 1.15).

The word "representation" in Heb 1.3 translates the Greek word *charakter*, from which we derive our English word "character." A *charakter* was an engraving tool. The question arises, Does the word *charakter* in Heb 1.3 refer to God's entire essence, to include His ontological nature, or merely His moral character. While the immediate context does not furnish an answer, the overall tenor of this epistle is that the Son is exactly like God in moral character. Logically, Jesus could not be *like* God and *be* God.

This prologue next states that Jesus "sat down at the right hand of the Majesty on high, having become as much better than the angels" (Heb 1.3-4). So, by means of Jesus' heavenly exaltation He attained a higher stature than that of the angels. Prior to that, He was "LOWER THAN THE ANGELS" (Heb 2.7; cf. Ps 8.5). How could Jesus have been lower than the angels during His earthly life and then, by means of resurrection and heavenly exaltation have become superior to angels if, all along, He was God?

Therefore, in this prologue the author introduces the following themes that he will develop at length: Jesus attaining superiority over all human beings and angels by living a perfectly righteous life and then forfeiting it as an atoning sacrifice for the sins of others.

The Superiority of Jesus

Thus, the primary theme of the book of Hebrews is the superiority of Jesus Christ. The author goes to great lengths to prove that Jesus is superior to the angels (Heb 1.4-14), the OT prophets, most particularly Moses (Heb 3.1-6), and Jewish priests (Heb 4.14—5.5; 7.26—9.28; 10.21), even Melchizedek (Heb 5.6-10; 7.1-17). For six chapters the author argues for the superiority of Christ's priesthood (Heb 5-10). And he cites Scripture to prove three things about Jesus: (1) "ALL THE ANGELS OF GOD WORSHIP HIM" (Heb 1.6), (2) He is properly called "Lord" (Heb 2.3; 7.14; 13.20) and God's eschatological "Son" of Ps 2.7 (Heb 1.5; 5.5), and (3) God has given Him authority over all of creation (Heb 2.7-8).

The strongest argument for the view that the author of Hebrews did not believe Jesus was God is that, if he did, he labored superfluously to prove Jesus' superiority. All he had to do was claim that Jesus is God and that would have sufficed. For, all observant Jews believe that God is superior to all. Moreover, the author's entire argument for Jesus' superiority is inherently based on the presupposition that He is no more than a man.

The Sinless Humanity of Jesus

The humanity of Jesus shines forth more brightly in the book of Hebrews than anywhere else in the NT, and the same is true of His sinlessness. The author of Hebrews emphasizes Jesus' perseverance through sufferings and temptations. He says that Jesus "was tempted in that which He has suffered" (Heb 2.18; cf. 13.12). He therefore depicts Jesus as someone who can "sympathize with our weaknesses,... who has been tempted in all things as we are, yet without sin"

(Heb 4.15). The author of Hebrews further describes Jesus as "holy, innocent, undefiled, separated from sinners" (Heb 7.26). And he adds this classic, two-fold statement, "Although He was a Son, He learned obedience from the things which He suffered. And having been made perfect, He became to all those who obey Him the source of eternal salvation" (Heb 5.8-9). Thus, according to the author of Hebrews, Jesus struggled against temptation and human frailty much as the rest of us human beings do, yet He completely overcame all such obstacles and did not sin. But Jesus could not have been God because "God cannot be tempted with evil" (Jam 1.13).

The converse of Jesus' sinlessness is His perfection. As stated above, the author of Hebrews says that Jesus was "made perfect" (Heb 5.9; 7.28). How so? He explains that God made Jesus "perfect through suffering" (Heb 2.10 NIV; cf. 1 Pt 4.1). So, by means of suffering Jesus emerged sinless and attained righteous perfection. But if Jesus was God, how could He have achieved perfection since God has always been perfect?

The question of whether Jesus could have succumbed to temptation, and therefore have sinned, is a hypothetical one that Scripture does not address. Yet traditionalists have generally contended that it was impossible for Jesus to have sinned, since He was God and God cannot be tempted to sin (Jam 1.13). If correct, it seems that Jesus' temptations could not have been *real* in the same sense that they are for the rest of us human beings. But we have seen that the author of Hebrews relates that Jesus was "tempted in all things as we are" (Heb 4.15). And he explains that Jesus "had to be made like His brethren in all things,... For since He Himself was tempted in that which He has suffered, He is able to come to the aid of those who are tempted" (Heb 2.17-18).

So, Jesus was just as human as pre-fallen Adam was, and He had to be in order for His temptations to have been real. If He was not really tempted like we are, He would not have qualified to aid us who are tempted. It must be concluded from the letter of Hebrews that Jesus was in complete solidarity with all men and women regarding our humanity. If he actually preexisted, let alone if He was a God-man, He certainly was not like us.

The Preexistence of Jesus?

The author of Hebrews clearly emphasizes Jesus' humanity more than any other NT writer, and some would argue the same about Jesus' preexistence. Concerning the latter, the author affirms that God "made the world" through Jesus and that, afterwards, "He comes into the world" by God giving Him "a body" (Heb 1.2, 10; 10.5). And God not only created the world through Jesus, He sustains the entire universe through Him (Heb 1.3). In fact, Jesus is the heir of all things, God having "put the world to come ... in subjection to" Him (Heb 1.2; 2.5). Yet J.D.G. Dunn states boldly that "the author of Hebrews has no place in his thinking for pre-existence as an ontological concept."[6]

One thing seems to rule out the actual preexistence of Jesus in this Hebrews letter. For Jesus to be both Savior and High Priest, He had to be like us in every way except sin. The author of Hebrews explains concerning Jesus, "He had to be made like His brethren in all things, that He might become a merciful and faithful high priest" (Heb 2.17). Again, this requires that Jesus did not literally preexist since the rest of us humans did not. It thus seems that God created the world "through" Jesus simply by having Him in mind.

---

[6] J.D.G. Dunn, *Christology in the Making*, 52.

Distinguishing God and Christ

In Hebrews, we also encounter the typical NT pattern of distinguishing God and Christ. This praxis always negates that Jesus Christ is God, as the following verses show:
- Jesus says of God, "I WILL PUT MY TRUST IN HIM" (Heb 2.13; cf. Isa 8.17 LXX)
- Jesus "is able to save forever those who draw near to God through Him" (Heb 7.25)
- "Christ ... enter[ed] ... into heaven ... in the presence of God" (Heb 9.24)
- "Christ, who ... offered Himself without blemish to God" (Heb 9.14)
- Jesus "SAT DOWN AT THE RIGHT HAND OF GOD" (Heb 10.12; cf. 1.3, 13; 12.2)
- Jesus is "a great priest over the house of God" (Heb 10.21)
- "God ... brought up from the dead ... Jesus our Lord" (Heb 13.20)
- "But you have come to ... God,... and to Jesus, the mediator" (Heb 12.22-24)

The Subordination of the Son

While the author of Hebrews affirms the heavenly exaltation of Jesus, as a Jew he still remains faithful to his monotheistic roots. This is quite apparent in his presentation of Jesus' essential subordination to God, so that Jesus cannot be God. He states that the Son was subordinate to God, and thus dependent upon Him, for (1) His appointment as heir (Heb 1.2; 3.2), (2) the securing of His priestly office (3.2; 5.5, 10), (3) the possession of His physical body (10.5), (4) the power to perform His miracles (2.4), (5) the experience of His resurrection (13.20), and (6) His ascension and exaltation (1.13). The author of Hebrews does not attribute the source of Jesus' miraculous power to Jesus but God, saying, "God also bearing witness [by Jesus] both with signs and wonders, with various miracles, and gifts of the Holy Spirit" (2.4; cf. Ac 2.22). The author further writes that Jesus "has been counted worthy of more glory than Moses" (Heb 3.3), being "crowned with glory and honor" (2.9). This indicates that Jesus' heavenly exaltation was a divine reward for His righteous life and undeserved suffering. And the fact that He trusted in God also indicates His essential subordination to God (2.13).

Like the author of the Fourth Gospel, the author of Hebrews does not see any need to reconcile the two themes of Jesus' exaltation and His subordination to God.[7]

Jesus' Prayers and Exaltation

We have seen that assessing Jesus as God arouses serious questions about His life, such as the temptations that He endured. We have considered the irreconciliabilty of Jesus making petionary prayer to God if He was God. The author of Hebrews states that Jesus "offered up both prayers and supplications with loud crying and tears," and "He was heard because of His piety" (Heb 5.7). So, Jesus prayed and God answered, not because Jesus possessed a divine nature or some lesser degree of divinity or ontological status, but because of His righteous life on earth (cf. Mk 1.11 par. with Jam 5.16-18).

Although Jesus had never possessed an ontological status, the NT often states that He obtained such when He ascended into heaven and sat down at the right hand of God on God's throne. No authors of Scripture emphasize this heavenly exaltation of Jesus more that does the author of Hebrews (Heb 1.3, 13; 8.1; 10.12; 12.2). And, like other Scripture writers, he explains that Jesus' heavenly exaltation fulfills Ps 110.1.

---

[7] V. Taylor, *The Person of Christ*, 96.

This brings us back to the prologue in this epistle, which states that Jesus became superior to the angels through His heavenly exaltation. Why did God exalt Jesus? Again, it was because of His righteous life and the fulfillment of His divinely-appointed mission. Neither the author of Hebrews nor any NT writer ever indicates that when Jesus sat down at God's right hand, He reclaimed a position He previously had held. Jesus' exaltation signified that it was something new He acquired which He had not previously possessed.

In conclusion, *God rewarding Jesus for His obedient life by inviting Him to sit with Him on His throne is one of the strongest evidences that Jesus cannot be God.*

B: Problem Passages

1. What does it mean in Hebrews 1.6 to worship Jesus?

One of the seven OT quotations listed in Heb 1 is about worshipping Jesus. Some traditionalists cite this verse as evidence that Jesus is God. Mentioned above, it reads, along with its introduction, "And when He again brings the first-born into the world, He says, 'AND LET ALL THE ANGELS OF GOD WORSHIP HIM'" (Heb 1.6).[8] The word "worship" translates *proskuneo* in the Greek text. The words in small caps indicate in the NASB that they represent an OT quotation. This quotation is from the Song of Moses recorded in Deut 32.43 (cf. Ps 97.7). However, this portion from Deut 32.43 is found only in the LXX and the DSS, not in the MT upon which English translations usually depend most heavily.

We learned in Matthew's Christology, in Chapter Five, that people who displayed *proskuneo* before Jesus indicated genuflection (bowing the knee), which does not mean they necessarily believed He was God. Since the author's purpose in selecting this text was to prove Jesus' superiority over angels, it does not seem he meant that worshipping Jesus indicated that He was God. (See "Worshipping Jesus" in Chapters Five and Ten.)

The author of Hebrews likely meant that the angels of heaven worship Jesus in the same way Paul describes in Phil 2.10>. He therein says of the exalted Jesus, "at the name of Jesus EVERY KNEE SHOULD BOW, of those who are in heaven [viz., the angels], and on earth, and under the earth." So, in the eschaton everyone will perform genuflection at the public announcement of Jesus' name, which act does not necessarily indicate He is God.

2. Is "the Son" called "God" in Hebrews 1.8-9?

Introduction	English Versions of Hebrews 1.8-9
English Versions of Psalm 45.6-7	Grammar of Hebrews 1.8-9
Grammar of Psalm 45.6-7	Context of Hebrews 1.8-9
Setting of Psalm 45	Literary Reasons
Jewish Monotheism	Scholastic Uncertainty
	Summary

---

[8] "First-born" in Heb 1.6 merely means that, in the divine scheme, Jesus outranks all other human beings.

Introduction

Traditionalists have always cited Heb 1.8 (some include v. 9) as a major NT *theos* text that calls Jesus "God." This has been no less true of their 20th century authorities.

Of all the major debatable *theos* texts, Heb 1.8-9 is the only one that presents a quotation from the OT, viz., Ps 45.6-7 (English Bible).[9] The author of Hebrews quotes it from the LXX almost verbatim.[10] So, both the Greek text of Heb 1.8-9 and its equivalent in the LXX have *ho theos* (lit. "the God"), and both these and the MT, which has *elohim* ("god"), must be considered in order to ascertain the correct meaning of Heb 1.8-9.

In all three texts there is a grammatical problem. Should the first two occurrences of *ho theos* in Heb 1.8-9 and *elohim/ho theos* in Ps 45.6-7 be treated as a vocative or as a nominative (noun)? This choice affects their translation. As in Jn 1.1c, this grammatical issue is exceedingly complex. Consequently, we will only attempt to summarize the technical issues involved. Our purposes will be to seek to (1) understand what each author—viz., the psalmist and the author of Hebrews—intended to mean in these two passages, (2) assess each author's possible theology, and (3) compare the two. To do so, we will first examine Ps 45.6-7 and then consider its quotation in Heb 1.8-9.

English Versions of Psalm 45.6-7

Psalm 45.6-7 reads as follows in the NASB:

6 Thy throne, O God, is forever and ever;
A scepter of uprightness is the scepter of Thy kingdom
7 Thou hast loved righteousness, and hated wickedness;
Therefore God, Thy God, has anointed Thee
With the oil of joy above Thy fellows.

The pertinent christological portion of this Scripture is the first clause (line) in v. 6. English versions vary considerably in how to translate it. The following versions treat both *elohim* ("O God") in the MT and *ho theos* ("[the] God") in the LXX as a vocative and therefore translate it so that the king is called "God:"

- "Your throne, O God" (AV, RV, ASV, Berkeley, NASB, JB, NAB, NIV, NRSV, ESV)
- "Your kingdom, O God, will last forever" (TEV)

In contrast, the following English versions treat *elohim/ho theos* in Ps 45.6a as an adjective, genitive, subject, or predicate, so that the king is not called "God:"

- "your divine throne" (RSV)
- "your throne is a throne of God" or "your throne, O God" (RSVmg)
- "your throne is a throne of God" (NRSVmg)
- "the throne that God has given you" (GNB)
- "God is your kingdom" (TEVmg)
- "Your throne is like God's throne" (NEB)
- "your throne is from God" (NJB)

---

[9] The numbering system for this text varies between English versions, the MT, and the LXX, so that Heb 1.8-9=Ps 45.6-7 in English Bibles (used herein)=Ps 44.7-8 in the LXX=Ps 45.7-8 in the MT.
[10] See M. Harris' (*Jesus as God*, 209-12) discourse of minor variants in Ps 45.6-7 in the LXX and Heb 1.8-9.

Grammar of Psalm 45.6-7

Scholars of the OT have regarded Ps 45.6a as one of the most difficult, brief portions in the OT to both translate and interpret.[11] One reason is that *elohim* is anarthrous (without the article) in the MT whereas its equivalent in the LXX (*ho theos*) has the article. We have already seen how problematic the anarthrous *theos* is in the Greek text of Jn 1.1c, and this situation is similar to it. For, in Hebrew the word *elohim* usually has the article when treated as a vocative, just as *theos* usually does in Greek. That is why the RSV renders this anarthrous *elohim* in Ps 45.6a as adjectival ("your divine throne"), just as some scholars likewise render the anarthrous *theos* in Jn 1.1c ("the Word was divine").[12]

Setting of Psalm 45

Psalm 45 is a wedding song entitled "a song of love." It was composed for the royal marriage of some particular king of Israel, perhaps King Solomon. So, it is a poetic hymn. In Chapter One, we learned that scholars do not regard poetic genre as a very dependable source upon which to construct theology.[13] In fact, the psalmist poet begins by admitting his own exuberance (v. 1: "My heart overflows"), which some historical critics, perhaps unnecessarily, regard as indicating exaggeration on his part.

Psalm 45 seems to refer to an idealic, godlike king. A Targum and many rabbis, including the esteemed Ibn Ezra and Kimchi, interpret it messianically.[14] So does the author of Hebrews and most subsequent Christian exegetes. Therefore, from the Christian perspective, what the psalmist says of a presumably contemporary king applies to Jesus.

This context of Ps 45 favors that *elohim/ho theos* in v. 6a does not call the king/Messiah "God." "God" is clearly distinguished from the king/Messiah in v. 2 ("God has blessed Thee") and in v. 7 ("God, Thy God, has anointed Thee"). This is further amplified in both passages, in which God is actually portrayed as acting upon the king/Messiah. To also call the king/Messiah "God" in such a context would introduce the most inexplicable ambiguity—God acting upon God. Don Cupitt well explains, "No exegete would suggest that the Hebrew writers thought of either their present king or their ideal future king as literally and co-equally divine.... the meaning is rather that the king rules by divine right and is endued with the fullness of God's power."[15]

Jewish Monotheism

There is an obvious theological reason why the psalmist would not have identified King-Messiah as the God of Israel, and neither would his readers have so understood it. As Hebrews, they were strict monotheists,[16] and nothing has changed since. For example, the modern Jewish diglot publication—*The Holy Scriptures According to the Masoretic Text*—provides the following interlinear English rendering, which is similar to the above versions that do not call Jesus

---

[11] M. Harris, *Jesus as God*, 190.

[12] Recall that biblical MSS in early Hebrew and Greek did not have upper and lower case. Whether *elohim* or *theos* should be rendered "God" or "god" is always an unavoidable interpretive decision for translators.

[13] E.g., M. Harris (*Jesus as God*, 202n71) cites J.L. McKenzie, "The Appellative Use of El and Elohim," *CBQ* 10 (1948): 177.

[14] Gunter Reim, "Jesus as God in the Fourth Gospel: The Old Testament Background," NTS 30 (1984): 159.

[15] D. Cupitt, *Jesus and the Gospel of God*, 19.

[16] D. Cupitt, *Jesus and the Gospel of God*, 19.

God, "Thy throne given of God is forever." And the New JPS Translation renders it likewise, "Your divine throne is everlasting." These Jewish translations seem to be supported by 1 Chron 29.23, which reads, "Then Solomon sat on the throne of the LORD as king." In other words, the king's throne was also God's throne.

Indeed, we have seen that the kings of Israel occupied the God-ordained "throne of David" and were thereby recognized by both God and the people as God's vice-regent on earth. Similarly, Israel recognized its king as God's "son." Yet there is some scriptural precedent for ascribing an even greater title to the rulers of Israel than "son (of God)."

We have already seen that the ancient Israelites used *elohim*—their Hebrew word for "god/God"—rather fluidly. For instance, Israel's psalmists occasionally identify the rulers or judges of Israel as *elohim* ("gods:" Ps 82.6; cf. 58.1).[17] So, we should not be surprised if the author of Ps 45 may have done likewise by indirectly calling a particular king of Israel "*elohim*." Jesus acknowledged that a psalmist, also under the inspiration of God's Spirit, rightly called Israel's rulers "*elohim*" (Jn 10.34-35). But such identifications are never intended to encroach upon Yahweh as the only God, as in deutero-Isaiah.

Translating Hebrews 1.8-9

So, what about the quotation of Ps 45.6-7 in Heb 1.8-9? It reads in the NASB:

8 But of the Son He says, "Thy throne, O God, is forever and ever, and the righteous scepter is the scepter of His kingdom.
9 "Thou hast loved righteousness and hated lawlessness; therefore God, Thy God, hath anointed Thee with the oil of gladness above Thy companions."

As mentioned above, the Greek text of Heb 1.8 quotes almost verbatim the LXX translation of Ps 45.6-7. Nearly every modern, major English version of the Bible translates Heb 1.8 so that it *does* call the Son "God," as the following attest:
- "But unto the Son he saith, 'Thy throne, O God'" (AV)
- "but of the Son, 'Your throne, O God'" (NAB)
- "But of the Son (he says), 'Thy throne, O God'" (RSV, NASB, NEB, REB, RV similarly)
- "to his Son he says: 'God, your throne shall'" (JB)
- "But about/of the Son he says, 'Your throne, O God'" (NIV, ESV)
- "About the Son, however, God said, 'Your throne, O God'" (TEV)

Yet the following versions and scholars translate this critical clause in Heb 1.8 so that it *does not* call the Son "God:"[18]
- "God thy seat shall be" (Tyndale)
- "thy throne is divine" (Ewald)
- "thy throne represents God" (Wickham)
- "God is thy/your throne" or "thy/your throne is God" (Grotius, Moffatt, Goodspeed, Cassirer, TCNT, RSVmg, NEBmg, NRSVmg)
- "thy throne is founded on God, the immovable Rock" (Westcott & Hort)

Grammar of Hebrews 1.8-9

While a few leading English versions translate Ps 45.6 so that it *does not* address the king as "God," nearly *every* English version translates Heb 1.8 so that it *does* address Jesus as "God." Why? The problem in Heb 1.8 is the same

---

[17] All three instances are in Psalms, which is poetic, not didactic, literature. *Elohim* is singular or plural.
[18] Other scholars include Bleek, de Wette, Kurtz, Grimm, and Alford.

as in Ps 45.6—grammatical. That is, should *ho theos* in Heb 1.8 be rendered as a vocative, as proper names and noun-objects usually are in Greek when being addressed; or should it simply be treated as a nominative (noun), either as the subject, a predicate, or effectively as an adjective? (We have already encountered this same question regarding *theos* in Thomas' Confession in Jn 20.28>.) If *ho theos* is taken herein as a vocative, it is translated, "Thy throne, O God," which calls Jesus "God;" but if it is treated as a nominative, it can be either the subject or predicate of the clause. As the subject, it would be translated, "God is your throne." As a predicate nominative, it would be translated, "your throne is God." (Ewald treats *theos* as adjectival, translating it "divine.") Either way, Jesus is not called "God." Traditionalist and grammarian A.T. Robertson admits that either rendering "makes good sense."[19]

Moderate form-critic Vincent Taylor insists that *ho theos* in Heb 1.8 should be treated as a nominative. Yet he argues that "nothing can be built upon this reference, for the author shares the reluctance of New Testament writers to speak explicitly of Christ as 'God.'"[20] Taylor contends that Heb 1.8 "supplies no ground at all for the supposition that the author thought and spoke of Christ as God.... Like Paul and John the writer frequently uses the name 'the Son,' and he does so in introducing this very quotation. He has no intention of suggesting that Jesus is God."[21]

A lesser grammatical problem in Heb 1.8-9 concerns another appearance of *ho theos*, in v. 9. In fact, it actually occurs twice. This raises the question, again, of whether to treat this first *ho theos* in v. 9 as a vocative or a nominative. While most scholars treat *ho theos* in v. 8 as a vocative due to grammar, they render the first *ho theos* in v. 9 as a nominative on account of its context. Their reasoning is that the second occurrence of *ho theos* in v. 9 clearly identifies the first occurrence therein as being the "God" of Christ.

Why not do the same with Heb 1.8 and Ps 45.6, thus rendering *ho theos* according to the context? That would make both nominatives. Indeed, the author's purpose in Heb 1.8 is not to establish that the Son is God but that the Son will have a throne and that it, and the dominion which it symbolizes, will last forever (cf. Dan 7.13 with 1 Cor 14.28). William L. Lane states likewise, "The writer's primary interest in the quotation is not the predication of deity but of the eternal nature of the dominion exercised by the Son."[22]

The different ways in which English versions have translated Heb 1.8-9 can be divided into the following three categories:

1. The expression *ho theos* in Heb 1.8 is rendered as a vocative, in which case Christ is called "God," e.g., "Thy throne, O God, is for ever and ever." However, v. 9 is translated so that it does not call Christ "God."
2. While the expression *ho theos* in Heb 1.8 is rendered as a vocative, it is treated rather irregularly as a nominative with *estin* (is) being supplied, in which case it does not call Christ "God," e.g., "God is thy throne for ever and ever."
3. The first two instances of *ho theos* in Heb 1.8-9 are translated so as to call Christ "God," e.g., "Thy throne, O God, is for ever and ever.... Therefore, O God, thy God has set thee ..." (NEB, REB).

---

[19] A.T. Robertson, *A Grammar of the Greek New Testament*, 465; idem, *Word Pictures in the New Testament*, 5 vols. (New York: Harper and Brothers, 1932), 5:339.
[20] V. Taylor, *The Person of Christ*, 96.
[21] V. Taylor, "Does the New Testament Call Jesus God?" 117.
[22] W.L. Lane, *Hebrews 1-8*, 29.

Context of Hebrews 1.8-9

Similar to Ps 45.6-7, the context preceding Heb 1.8-9 seems to forbid the author from calling Jesus "God." We have already seen that this epistle begins with a prologue that is comparable to John's prologue, except there is no question about it identifying Jesus as God. In vv. 1-4, this author (1) clearly distinguishes God and His Son (vv. 1-2),[23] (2) says the Son is the "exact representation" (imprint) of God's nature (v. 3a), rather than intrinsically possesses God's nature, and (3) declares that the Son is superior to angels due to His saviorhood as well as His session at God's right hand (vv. 3b-4; cf. Mt 1.21).

Following this prologue, the author lists seven OT quotations in Heb 1.5-14 as a barrage of support for his assertion that Jesus is superior to angels. Some modern scholars have proposed that the author of Hebrews chose these quotes from a previously written source—a collection of OT passages no longer extant that church fathers cited and called "the *testimonia*"—that was circulated among the early churches to prove that Jesus was the promised One of the OT.[24] If so, the author of Hebrews apparently made use of them because some Jews had believed that Jesus was an angel.[25] If such an early *testimonia* did exist, surely it was not compiled for the purpose of proving that Jesus was God.

Furthermore, these seven OT quotations are no doubt designed to support what is stated christologically in the prologue.[26] In other words, since the prologue does not assert that Jesus is God, surely the author does not intend that his appended list of scriptural quotations and commentary do either. G.W. Buchanan concludes, "For the author, the Son was the first-born, the apostle of God, the reflection of God's glory, and the stamp of his nature (1:3, 6), but he was not God *himself*."[27]

The overall context of Hebrews indicates the same. For instance, traditionalist A.W. Wainwright believes that the Son is called "God" in Heb 1.8; yet he admits, "The belief that Christ is God is not the keystone of the Christology of the Epistle of Hebrews ... the writer does not include the deity of Christ within the scheme of thought which he presents in the epistle."[28]

Literary Reasons

Besides the context, there are at least three other literary reasons why the author of Hebrews did not intend to address Jesus Christ as "God" in Heb 1.8.

First, it is highly unlikely that the author, being a Jew, would intend to call Jesus "God" by quoting Scripture, much less without providing any explanation. He simply quotes the psalmist without altering his language or explaining it. Though his text is the LXX (*ho theos*), he must have known that this passage in the Hebrew Bible applied the word *elohim* to the king. Yet he only supplies this and the other quotations to support his thesis that Jesus is superior to angels, not that He is God. The other six quotations do not even remotely call Jesus "God." The author's argument can be summarized as follows: the angels only serve God as spirits who minister to humans who will inherit salvation, whereas Jesus is

---

[23] Mention of the "Son," here, does not indicate deity, as M. Harris (*Jesus as God*, 207) seems to suppose.

[24] E.g., C.H. Dodd, *According to the Scriptures*, 108. During the 3rd century, church father Cyprian produced his own *Testimonia*.

[25] H. Montefiore, *Hebrews*, 41.

[26] William Manson, *The Epistle to the Hebrews* (London: Hodder & Sloughton, 1951), 91-92.

[27] George Wesley Buchanan, *The Epistle to the Hebrews: Translation, Comment, and Conclusions*, in *AB* 36 (1972), 21.

[28] A.W. Wainwright, *The Trinity in the New Testament*, 67.

superior to angels because, when God created the heavens and the earth He had Jesus in mind, and because of it Jesus now enjoys a filial relationship with God as His Anointed, sitting at God's right hand on God's throne, awaiting His own enthronement on earth (vv. 5-14), which privileges angels do not experience. Nothing here suggests that Jesus is God.

Second, the author of Hebrews spares no effort in attempting to prove Christ's superiority. He devotes over half of this letter to proving that Jesus Christ is superior to all angels and prophets, including Moses, and Israel's priests, even Melchizedek. So, as stated earlier, it appears superfluous for the author to strenuously posit such things when his strongest argument for Christ's superiority would have been to unequivocally declare Him as God if that was indeed what he believed, and consequently meant, in Heb 1.8.

Third, if the author had intended to call Christ "God," the same argument can be adduced even more aptly here than for the Apostle Paul. For, this Jewish writer would no doubt have perceived that his calling Jesus "God" would have stirred up a hornets' nest among his monotheistic Jewish readers. Not providing any reasons at all for such a bold assertion would have represented a serious literary lapse.

Scholastic Uncertainty

There exists some uncertainty among conservative NT scholars as to whether Heb 1.8 calls Jesus "God." For example, F.F. Bruce tentatively believed that Heb 1.8 calls Christ "God" while admitting that the RSV marginal reading—"Thy throne is God"—is "quite convincing."[29] William Barclay, though not exactly a conservative, again well summarizes the situation, "This is a passage in which no one would wish to be dogmatic. In both cases both translations are perfectly possible ... But, whatever translation we accept, we once again see that the matter stands in such doubt that it would be very unsafe to base any firm argument upon it."[30]

Summary

While a large majority of English versions and NT scholars render *ho theos* in Heb 1.8 as a vocative, thus calling Jesus "God," the context of both it and the source of this quotation—Ps 45.6—as well as the psalmist's likely fluid use of *elohim*, suggests that neither the psalmist nor the author of Hebrews intended to call the king/Messiah "God."

---

[29] F.F. Bruce, *The Epistle to the Hebrews*, rev ed., in NICNT (1990), 19.
[30] W. Barclay, *Jesus As They Saw Him*, 25-26.

Chapter Nine
Christology of Peter

A. Introduction

Peter: The Leader of the Apostles	Jesus Is the Christ
Servant Christology	The Holy One of God Belongs to God
God Empowered Jesus to Do Miracles	The God of Jesus Christ
Distinguishing God and Christ	Summary

Peter: The Leader of the Apostles

So far, we have examined the christologies of Matthew, Mark, Luke, John, Paul, and the author of Hebrews, in this order. What is the Christology of the Apostle Peter? Whatever he said or didn't say about Jesus is *extremely* important to Christology.

Simon Peter is the most interesting character among Jesus' twelve apostles. Much more is recorded about him in the NT than the other apostles. He was an impetuous man, a fellow who lived largely by his emotions. Peter seems to have been physically strong. He certainly was a gregarious leader. None of Jesus' twelve apostles He chose had as many emotional and spiritual ups-and-downs as did Simon Peter. Yet, even though he denied his Master three times, Jesus truly changed Peter from a fisherman into a fisher of men. Peter was so committed to Jesus for the rest of his life, he even died a martyr's death for Him. Among the twelve apostles, Peter has first place in the hearts of most Bible readers.

Peter was sort of a spokesperson as well as the most important member of Jesus' twelve apostles. That is why Peter is always mentioned first in lists of the twelve chosen apostles recorded in the Synoptic Gospels (Mt 10.2-4/Mk 3.16-19/Lk 6.13-16). Peter also was one of the three members of Jesus' inner core of apostles—Peter, James, and John. During certain momentous occasions in Jesus' life, He took only these three with Him. He did it at His transfiguration on the mountain and when He prayed in Gethsemane just before His arrest (cf. Lk 8.51). And whenever the synoptists mention this inner core and list their names, Peter is always mentioned first.[1] Moreover, the synoptists mention Peter talking with Jesus an inordinate number of times compared to any of the other apostles. And it was to Peter that Jesus gave "the keys of the kingdom of heaven" (Mt 16.19; cf. Ac 1.8). Peter used them to open doors when he became the first

---

[1] Mk 5.37; Mt 17.1/Mk 9.2/Lk 9.28; Mt 26.37/Mk 14.33/cf. Mk 13.3.

to preach the gospel to the Jews at Jerusalem (Ac 2.14-40), the Samaritans (Ac 8.14-25), and Gentiles (Ac 10).

Because of Peter's prominence in knowing Jesus personally, and him afterwards leading the early Jesus Movement, what this apostle believed about Jesus' identity would arguably be more important than what any other NT characters thought about it. Thus far, we have seen glimpses of Peter's Christology, most of them indirectly in the Gospel of Luke and directly in Luke's book of Acts. Now we will briefly review mostly Luke's accounts about Peter in the book of Acts and examine the two epistles attributed to Peter. We will focus on features of Peter's Christology which indicate that Jesus *is not* God.

Servant Christology

During antiquity in the east, it was common practice in hospitality for a person to identify himself or herself to someone of upper class as "your servant." This custom appears often in the OT. Yahweh is sometimes quoted as calling one of His prophets or Israel's righteous kings, "My servant" (Heb. *ebed*; Gr. *pais*). Conversely, OT saints would present themselves to Yahweh their God as "your servant." William Barclay informs, "In the OT the greatest title of honour that any man can have is the servant of God."[2]

This servant of Yahweh motif emerges most significantly in the OT eighteen times in four songs in Isa 42—53. Two different servant figures are presented. One servant is Yahweh's chosen, yet disobedient, nation of Israel.[3] As for the other Servant (sometimes capitalized in versions to refer to Jesus and distinguish the two), Yahweh will empower Him with His Spirit and share with Him His glory (Isa 42.1, 8).[4] Why the contrast? This other Servant will be obedient to Yahweh, endure considerable suffering, bear the sins of many, and unjustly be killed (Isa 50.5, 10; 52.13—53.12). Yet He will prosper not only by healing and redeeming sin-laden Israel, but by also being a light to the nations (53.5; 49.5-6). So, the destinies of these two servants of Yahweh are mysteriously and intricately interwoven. The fulfillment of the divine mission of the righteous, suffering Servant will make possible the realization of Yahweh's promise to His other servant, Israel, to become the head of the nations and a blessing to all the families of the earth. Isaiah never clearly identifies God's suffering, obedient Servant. But the pre-Christian Targum on Isaiah does; it interprets the Servant in Isa 52.13—53.12 as the Messiah.[5]

The NT identifies this righteous Servant of Deutero-Isaiah as Jesus. Matthew does twice (Mt 8.16-17; 12.18-21; cf. Isa 53.4; 42.1, 4), and John once (Jn 12.38; cf. 53.1). Luke says Jesus identified Himself as this suffering Servant who would be "NUMBERED WITH TRANSGRESSORS," thus crucified between two thieves (Lk 22.37; cf. Isa 53.12).

The book of Acts is most prominent in the NT in identifying Jesus as the Servant of God. It tells of the Ethiopian eunuch reading Isa 53.7-9 and Philip explaining to him that that suffering Servant is Jesus (Ac 8.32-35). And in Peter's second public sermon, he twice calls Jesus God's "servant/Servant" (Ac 3.13, 26). Another time, when Jesus' disciples were gathered together, they prayed to

---

[2] W. Barclay, *Jesus As They Saw Him*, 160.
[3] Isa 41.8-9; 42.19; 43.10; 44.1-2, 21, 26; 45.4; 48.20.
[4] Isa 42.1; 49.3, 5-7; 50.10; 52.13; 53.11. Sometimes, there may be overlap between Isaiah's two servant motifs, as perhaps in Isa 49.3; other times, there is a clear distinction between them, as in Isa 49.5.
[5] See J. Jeremias, *"pais theou," TDNT* 5:683-87.

God about "Thy holy servant Jesus" (Ac 4.27, 30). Then, in Peter's first epistle he explains Jesus' role as the suffering Servant by quoting from Isa 53.9 (1 Pt 2.22). Peter thus emerges as the foremost NT character who identifies Jesus as God's "servant." Although Jesus is not often expressly identified in the NT as God's suffering Servant of Deutero-Isaiah, there are many other allusions to it.[6]

Thus, we can speak of a Servant Christology in the Bible, and we can be sure that this idea was primitive in the Jesus Movement. William Barclay concludes, "It might well be said that the title Servant is the title in the light of which all the other titles of Jesus must be seen."[7] Indeed, that is true of Jesus' use of His favorite title—the Son of Man.[8]

Early church fathers occasionally identified Jesus as God's "servant" (Gr. *pais*),[9] but those later discontinued applying this most precious title to Him. This is remarkable since Isa 52.13—53.12 had become one of the most contested passages in the OT between Christians and Jews, especially because the pre-Christian Targum on Isaiah inserts "the Messiah" into Isa 52.13. Joachim Jeremias observes that "the designation of Jesus as *pais theou* [servant of God] is found in Gentile Christian writings up to 170 CE only at 11 places and in three works.... It does not make its way into dogmatic usage, but remains confined to the liturgy and lofty speech. From the 5th century *pais* disappears completely as a term for Christ.... Jesus as God's servant was alive in Palestinian Christianity.... To the Gentile Church it was offensive from the very first because it did not seem to bring out the full significance of the majesty of the glorified Lord."[10]

Jesus as Servant clashed with the institutional Church's view that He is God. Yet the Koran says of Him, "The Messiah does not disdain to be a servant of God" (4:172).

God Empowered Jesus to Do Miracles

When Peter preached his first evangelistic message, he affirmed that Jesus had accomplished His mighty deeds, not by His own power, but by the power of God. Peter preached about "Jesus the Nazarene, a man attested to you by God with miracles and wonders and signs which God performed through Him" (Ac 2.22). And at Cornelius' house Peter attested, "You know of Jesus of Nazareth, how God anointed Him with the Holy Spirit and with power,... for God was with Him" (Ac 10.38). Here are some of the strongest statements in holy writ that Jesus was not God, but empowered by God. Again, notice in these two statements how Peter clearly distinguishes Jesus and God.

Distinguishing God and Christ

Peter often distinguished God the Father and Jesus Christ, which verifies that Christ is not God. In Peter's second evangelistic sermon, he proclaimed to men of Israel that "the God of Abraham, Isaac, and Jacob, the God of our

---

[6] See J. Jeremias, "*pais theou*," TDNT 5:700-17.
[7] W. Barclay, *Jesus As They Saw Him*, 160.
[8] Christopher Rowland, *Christian Origins: An Account of the Setting and Character of the Most Important Sect of Judaism* (London: SPCK, 1985), 176; G.B. Caird, *New Testament Theology*, 311-16. For a contrary view, in which these figures are not blended together in the NT, see Morna D. Hooker, *Jesus and the Servant: The Influence of the Servant Concept of Deutero-Isaiah in the New Testament* (London: SPCK, 1959). The Similitudes blend these two figures and the Messiah. Jesus seems to do the same.
[9] E.g., *Didache* 9.2-3; 10.2-3.
[10] J. Jeremias, "*pias theou*," TDNT 5:702-03.

fathers, has glorified his servant Jesus" (Ac 3.13). Peter also distinguished God and Christ by preaching or writing of the following categories, both past and future, about the life of his Lord Jesus Christ:
- Deeds: (mentioned above)
- Sufferings: "the things which God announced ... His Christ should suffer" (Ac 3.18)
- Salvation: "Christ also died for sins ... that He might bring us to God" (1 Pt 3.18)
- Resurrection: "God" raised "Jesus" from the dead (Ac 2.24, 32; 3.15; 4.10; 1 Pt 1.21)
- Exaltation: "God has made Him both Lord and Christ" (Ac 2.36)
- Session: "Jesus Christ, who is at the right hand of God" (1 Pt 3.21-22; cf. Ac 2.33-34)
- Judgment: He was "appointed by God as Judge of the living and the dead" (Ac 10.42)

Jesus Is the Christ

The foremost identification of Jesus by His disciples recorded in the NT is Peter's confession at Caesarea Philippi. That's when Jesus asked His disciples who He was. Peter answered, according to Matthew, "Thou art the Christ, the Son of the living God" (Mt 16.16 par.). If at that time Peter had believed that Jesus was God, we can well expect that he would have declared Him as such, rather than this seemingly lesser identification.

From that time forward, Jesus began to tell His disciples that He must suffer many things at the hands of the religious authorities at Jerusalem and be killed there. Matthew then records that "Peter took Him aside and began to rebuke Him, saying, 'God forbid it, Lord! This shall never happen to You'" (Mt 16.22). If Peter believed that Jesus was God, he most certainly would not have rebuked Him. Also, notice how Peter distinguishes between "God" and Jesus as "Lord" like the Apostle Paul regularly does in his epistles.

The Holy One of God Belongs to God

Jesus belonged to God. We see this in the NT in many ways. One is applying appellatives to Jesus in the genitive case, indicated by the word "of." For example, the angel Gabriel announced Jesus' virgin birth by saying, "the holy offspring shall be called the Son of God" (Lk 1.35). Jesus being the Son *of* God means that He belongs to God and therefore cannot be God. Another example is demons and the Apostle Peter rightly calling Jesus "the Holy One of God" (Mk 1.24/Lk 4.34; Jn 6.69). Jesus being *of* God indicates His essential subordination to God, so that He cannot be God.

In accord with the OT, Peter also calls God the Father "the Holy One" (1 Pt 1.15-16). The OT repeatedly identifies Yahweh as "the Holy One."[11] But one OT passage calls the Messiah, "Thy Holy One," i.e., the Holy One *of* God. It is Ps 16.10, the one passage that both Peter and Paul apply to the blessed act of God raising Jesus from the dead (Ac 2.31-32; 13.35-37).

So, Peter applied appellatives to Jesus that are in the genitive case, e.g., "Servant of God," "the Son of God," and "the Holy One of God." These distinguish Jesus from God and show that He belongs to God, both of which negate that He was or is God.

---

[11] E.g., 2 Kgs 19.22; Job 6.10; Ps 71.22; 78.41; 89.18; cf. Lev 11.44-45; 19.2.

The God of Jesus Christ

Like the Apostle Paul, the Apostle Peter believed that Jesus had a God. He wrote, "Blessed be the God and Father of our Lord Jesus Christ" (1 Pt 1.3). Peter also wrote to his readers about Jesus by saying, "Through him you have come to trust in God, who raised him from the dead and gave him glory, so that your faith and hope are set on God" (1 Pt 1.21 NRSV). It is unlikely that Peter could have written such statements and also believed Jesus is God.

But there is more. Peter surely knew that Jesus called the Father "the only true God" (Jn 17.3). Plus, Peter would have known that Jesus prayed on the cross, "MY GOD, MY GOD, WHY HAVE YOU FORSAKEN ME" (Mt 27.46/Mk 15.34). And the risen Jesus told Mary Magdalene, "go to My brethren and say to them, 'I ascend to My Father and your Father, and My God and your God'" (Jn 20.17).

Summary

The Apostle Peter's first two evangelistic sermons recorded in the book of Acts provide some of the most substantial scriptural evidence that Jesus cannot be God. Like most NT characters and writers, Peter constantly distinguishes God and Jesus Christ. Plus, in his first epistle he declares that Jesus had a God, who was the Father. It thus seems impossible that Peter could have thought that Jesus was God. Yet this is what many traditionalists assert that he says in 2 Pt 1.1, if he wrote it. To this text we now turn.

B. Problem Passages

1. Is Jesus called "our God and Savior" in 2 Peter 1.1?

Introduction	Reasons for the Two Persons View
The Greek Text and English Versions	Commentators
Reasons for the One Person View	

Introduction

The NT has two epistles whose authorship is accredited to the Apostle Peter. As stated earlier, titles of books and letters of the Bible were often penned after they were written and probably by a different hand. The early church unanimously accepted "First Peter" as written by the Apostle Peter. But for centuries the church disputed whether he wrote "Second Peter." Most modern, historical-critical, NT scholars have rejected that Peter wrote it. Since its salutation attests to his authorship, I am inclined to accept it.

The only problem passage in First and Second Peter that has to do with whether Jesus is God is 2 Pt 1.1. It contains grammatical problems that are very similar to the ones in Tit 2.13 and 2 Thes 1.12, which mostly concern word order. The question is, Does the last phrase in 2 Pt 1.1 mention Two Persons, viz., the Father and Christ, or One Person, viz., Christ? The One Person view calls Christ "God;" the Two Persons view does not.

The Greek Text and English Versions

The problematic phrase in 2 Pt 1.1 reads in the Greek text as follows, with an interlinear translation supplied below it:
- *tou theou hemon kai soteros Iesou Christou*[12]
- the God of us and Savior Jesus Christ

Only a few English versions translate this phrase in 2 Pt 1.1 with two Persons in view, in which case it *does not* call Jesus Christ "God." In contrast, almost all English versions translate it with one Person in view, viz., Jesus Christ, so that it *does* call Jesus "God." The versions render this problematic clause as follows:

Two Persons View:
- "of God and our Savior Jesus Christ" (AV)
- "of our God and the Savior Jesus Christ" (ASV, RSVmg, NRSVmg, NWT)

One Person View:
- "of our God and Savior(,) Jesus Christ" (RV, NAB, TCNT, RSV, NEB, JB, NASB, NIV, NJB, REB, NRSV, ESV)

Reasons for the One Person View

The following reasons support that 2 Pt 1.1 *does* call Jesus Christ "God:"

1. In the Greek text, the absence of an article preceding *soteros* (Savior) indicates that the pronoun *hemon* (our) applies only to *theou* (God).

   Rebuttal: What J.N.D. Kelly says of Tit 2.13 applies here as well. He states that in Greek the word "'Savior' tended to be anarthrous [without the article] (cf. 1 Tim 1.1), and in any case the correct use of the article was breaking down in late Greek."[13]

2. The doxology to Christ in 2 Pt 3.18 suggests that the author could call Christ "God."

   Rebuttal: Doxologies addressed to Christ are irrelevant as to whether He is called "God" because Jesus said of the Father, "it is his will that all should pay the same honour to the Son as to the Father" (Jn 5.23 NEB).

3. Since the writer employs pagan religious language—and it was common practice in Hellenistic lands to call religious and political figures "our God"—it would have been natural for him to call Christ "our God and Savior."

   Rebuttal: Divine inspiration prohibits pagan influence.

4. The nearby compound construction with its anarthrous *soteros* (Savior), in 2 Pt 1.11 ("our Lord and Savior Jesus Christ"), parallels "God" and "Savior" in v. 1, suggesting that it is a compound title as well.[14]

   Rebuttal: The compound title, "Lord and Savior," appears nowhere else in the NT except in 2 Pt, and it occurs a surprising four times (2 Pt 1.11; 2.20; 3.2, 18). This evidence, along with the generally accepted late date of authorship for 2 Pt, suggests that the words, "Lord and Savior," had by then become a fixed formula, making an article preceding "Savior" assumed. Thus, the repeated compound title, "Lord and Savior," in 2 Pt is not a suitable parallel for the words "God" and "Savior" in 2 Pt 1.1.

---

[12] Codex Sinaiticus has *tou kuriou hemon kai soteros Iesou Christou*. Scholars deem it a conforming gloss.
[13] J.N.D. Kelly, *Pastoral Epistles Timothy I & II, and Titus*, 246.
[14] R.E. Brown, *Jesus God and Man*, 22.

Reasons for the Two Persons View

The following reasons support that 2 Pt 1.1 *does not* call Jesus Christ "God:"
1. The author would not call Jesus Christ "God" in v.1 and then inject confusion by distinguishing clearly the Two Persons in the second half of the same sentence, in v. 2, with the words, "the knowledge of God, and of Jesus our Lord" (e.g., AV, RSV, JB, NASB, NIV). So, this ambiguity in v. 1 should be interpreted by the clarity of v. 2.[15]

    Rebuttal: If the author had wanted to distinguish the Father and Christ in v. 1 he would have clearly done so, as in v. 2.

2. The expression, "our/the Lord and Savior (Jesus Christ)," which appears four times in this epistle, as mentioned above, had become a fixed formula so that the use of "God" here in v. 1 must be intended to distinguish the Two Persons.[16]

    Rebuttal: Writers should be reckoned as free to vary a stereotyped expression.[17]

3. The position of the pronoun *hemon* (our) occurring between the two substantives (nouns)—*theou* (God) and *soteros* (Savior)—separates and thus distinguishes them.[18]

    Rebuttal: When two substantives have a single article, as here in v. 1, a single personal pronoun applies to both.[19]

4. If Peter authored both epistles (which is not accepted by most scholars), he would not write, "the God and Father of our Lord Jesus Christ" in his first epistle (1 Pt 1.3) and then call Christ "God" in his second epistle. Plus, in Peter's evangelistic speeches recorded in Acts, he applies various titles to Jesus without calling Him "God."

Commentators

Murray Harris has thoroughly surveyed the scholarly landscape concerning this dispute in 2 Pt 1.1. He informs us that the One Person view of it is "endorsed by the great majority of twentieth-century commentators with varying degrees of assurance."[20] It should be noted, however, that only a few prominent NT exegetes wrote commentaries on 2 Pt in the 20th century, partly because most of them concluded that the Apostle Peter did not write it, and some of them classified it as non-canonical. Preeminent lexicographer Walter Bauer is typical of those scholars who are non-commital by insisting concerning both 2 Pt 1.1 and 1 Jn 5.20, "the interpretation is open to question."[21]

---

[15] Jerome H. Neyrey, *2 Peter, Jude: A New Translation with Introduction and Commentary*, in AB 37C (1993), 148; Pheme Perkins, *First and Second Peter, James and Jude* (Louisville, KY: WJK, 1995), 167; idem, "Christ in Jude and 2 Peter," in *Who Do You Say that I Am?* eds. Powell and Bauer, 159.

[16] E. Kasemann, *Essays on New Testament Themes*, 183n2.

[17] R. Bauckham, *Jude, 2 Peter* in WBC 50 (1983), 168.

[18] G.B. Winer, *A Grammar of the Idiom of the New Testament*, 130; E. Stauffer, *TDNT* 3:106n268.

[19] M. Harris, *Jesus as God*, 231.

[20] M. Harris, *Jesus as God*, 238.

[21] BAGD, 357.

Chapter Ten
Christology of The Apocalypse

A: Introduction

Introduction and the Author	The Throne of God
Structure and Style	Why No Holy Spirit?
Jesus' Limited Knowledge	"The Throne of David"
God and Christ Distinguished	The Meaning of "Hallelujah"
The God of Heaven and of Jesus Christ	Agent Christology
"The Lamb" and "the Word"	

Introduction and the Author

The last book in the Bible is entitled "(The) Revelation to John."[1] "Revelation" is taken from the book's first word in its Greek text—*apocalupsis*. That is why the book also is called "The Apocalypse." *Apocalupsis* means "uncovering" or "unveiling." This book presents the glorious unveiling of Jesus Christ regarding especially His second coming; but it mostly foretells events that lead up to it. Until Jesus returns, He remains in heaven like God: hidden from the world but unveiled spiritually to His people on earth.

The author of The Revelation identifies himself merely as "John" (Rev 1.4, 9). Many Christians have thought he is the Apostle John. Several strands of evidence, however, indicate otherwise. Some patristic testimony claims it was "John the Elder." What is important is that the author claims to have written this book while under the inspiration of the Holy Spirit of God. He says he did so while on the isle of Patmos in the Aegean Sea, probably as a prisoner (Rev 1.9-10; cf. 6.9; 12.17). Due to this uncertainty regarding the authorship of The Revelation, we will refer to him simply as "John."

Structure and Style

The Revelation is the most fascinating book in all of apocalyptic literature. It is packed full of visions, religious images, and symbols. Its several visionary scenes often switch venue between heaven and earth. This pattern shows that there exists a mysterious link between what happens on earth and in heaven. Many of these scenes depict divine judgments that descend from heaven to fall upon the wicked on earth. As for the saints (believers) on earth, they undergo the most severe persecution for their faith in God and His Christ. Their sufferings are to be distinguished from the several divine judgments. Contrast this saintly

---

[1] This title, occasionally accompanied with "of/to (St.) John," was prefixed after its publication.

suffering on earth with glorious, heavenly scenes of innumerable angels, twenty-four elders, and seven spirits surrounding God's throne along with four strange-looking creatures on each side of it, all of them worshipping God. Then there are various frightening, rather indescribable, otherworldly creatures on earth that either kill or sting humans, not to mention the most unholy triumvirate: the dragon (the devil), the beast (the Antichrist), and the false prophet. Undoubtedly, The Apocalypse is the most mysterious book in the Bible, if not in all of apocalyptic literature. It certainly is the most difficult portion of Scripture to interpret. To adequately do so requires a comprehensive understanding of the OT and maybe a firm grasp on a bottle of Pepto-Bismol!

Throughout the history of Christianity, many persecuted Christians have rightly found comfort and hope by applying prophecies of the book of Revelation to their own time and circumstances. One of the main purposes of The Revelation is to encourage the saints of all ages to persevere and thereby overcome trials and tribulations perpetrated upon them on account of their faith in God and Christ. God promises that in the future He will reign supreme on the earth, just as He always has in heaven (Mt 6.10). And when He does, He will reward the over-comers by causing them to reign with Christ on earth.[2]

While some historical events over the past 1900 years have foreshadowed events prophesied in The Revelation, the complete fulfillment of most of its prophecies, at least those following Rev 6.8, seems to still lie in the future. These prophecies lead up to and include the following major eschatological events of the Bible: (1) Jesus' return, (2) the resurrection of the saints, (3) the judgment, (4) the establishment of the kingdom of God on earth, and (5) the unveiling of the holy city New Jerusalem. The purpose of The Revelation is to teach that Almighty God now reigns supreme in heaven and that He will do likewise someday on earth, thus fulfilling all that He has promised in Holy Scripture.

Even though The Revelation features the second coming of Christ, the book is very theocentric.[3] For example, the original source of this revelation is God, not Christ (Rev 1.1), and the many judgments it depicts are said to come from God and not Christ. Nevertheless, God and Christ are often mentioned as enthroned together in heaven. More often, only God is pictured on His throne. While Christ will wage war on earth at His second coming (Rev 17.14; 19.11, 19), this battle is properly called "the war of the great day of God, the Almighty" because it is God who orchestrates it (Rev 16.14). Moreover, the bright hope of the OT will be realized after this war, when God the Father will literally dwell with His people in the holy New Jerusalem, and they literally will see His face.[4]

Despite such rich imagery and intimate association of God and Christ, *the book of Revelation has received little attention as to whether Christ is God*. It is mostly because it provides substantial evidence that Christ is not God and that it has no problem passages.

Jesus' Limited Knowledge

John begins his book with the following introduction that serves as an elaborate title: "The Revelation of Jesus Christ, which God gave Him to show His bond-servants, the things which must shortly take place; and He sent and communicated it by His angel to His bond-servant John" (Rev 1.1). Accordingly, this book presents an unveiling of future events that are to transpire both in

---

[2] Rev 3.21; 5.10; 14.12-13; 20.6; 22.5; cf. 2 Tim 2.12.
[3] R. Bauckham, *The Theology of the Book of Revelation*, 23.
[4] Rev 21.3; 22.4; cf. Mt 5.8; 18.10. The "face" of God 71x in OT; cf. Ex 33.20; Ps 17.15; Zech 2.10-11.

heaven and on earth. These events culminate in the glorious return of Jesus Christ to the earth at His second coming and the appearing of the holy New Jerusalem. That "God gave" this revelation to the exalted Jesus strongly implies that Jesus did not know these things previously. This revelation even includes information about Jesus' second coming, which suggests that He did not previously know it. Similarly, we already learned in Chapter Five that the earthly Jesus divulged that He did not know the day of His return (Mt 24.36/Mk 13.32>). And The Revelation suggests that at the time these visions were imparted to John, the exalted Jesus Christ still did not know when His return would occur. Such lack of knowledge testifies to three things: God's superiority over Christ; God and Christ are unequal; thus, Christ is not God.

God and Christ Distinguished

God and Christ may be distinguished more clearly in Revelation than anywhere else in the NT. Geza Vermes calls it "a clear-cut distinction."[5] We have seen throughout the NT that distinguishing God and Christ always indicates that Christ is not God. The following passages in The Revelation clearly distinguish God, who is often described as "Him who sits on the throne," from Christ, who is often identified as "the Lamb:"

- "The Revelation of Jesus Christ, which God gave Him" (Rev 1.1)
- "from Him who is ... and from Jesus Christ" (Rev 1.4-5)
- "Thou wast slain, and didst purchase for God with Thy blood men" (Rev 5.9)
- "Thou hast made them to be a kingdom and priests to our God" (Rev 5.10)
- "to Him who sits on the throne, and to the Lamb" (Rev 5.13)
- "Him who sits on the throne, and from the wrath of the Lamb" (Rev 6.16)
- "Salvation to our God who sits on the throne, and to the Lamb" (Rev 7.10)
- "the Lamb in the center of the throne ... God shall wipe away every tear" (Rev 7.17)
- "the kingdom of our Lord, and of His Christ" (Rev 11.15)
- "the kingdom of our God and the authority of His Christ" (Rev 12.10)
- "the commandments of God and ... the testimony of Jesus" (Rev 12.17)
- "to God and to the Lamb" (Rev 14.4)
- "they will be priests of God and of Christ" (Rev 20.6)
- "the Lord God, the Almighty, and the Lamb" (Rev 21.22)
- "the throne of God and of the Lamb" (Rev 22.1, 3)[6]

P.M. Casey rightly concludes from all of this evidence that "the lamb is carefully distinguished from God, and he is not said to be divine."[7]

The God of Heaven and of Jesus Christ

It is recorded ten times in The Revelation that heaven's citizens call the One who sits on the throne "our God," who is the Father.[8] And twice the Father is called "the God of heaven" (Rev 11.13; 16.11). Yet this book never portrays heaven's citizens as calling Jesus Christ "our God" or "the God of heaven." Most striking is when God the Father and Jesus Christ are juxtaposed in The Revelation, with the Father being called "our God." In one such instance, a great multitude of people who came "out of the great tribulation" are "standing before the throne and before the Lamb," and they cry loudly, "Salvation to our God who

---

[5] G. Vermes, *The Changing Faces of Jesus*, 56.
[6] Cf. Rev 1.2; 12.17; 14.12; 15.3.
[7] P.M. Casey, *From Jewish Prophet to Gentile God*, 142.
[8] Rev 4.11; 5.10; 7.3, 10, 12; 12.10 (2x); 19.1, 5-6 (2x).

sits on the throne, and to the Lamb" (Rev 7.9-10, 14). This strongly suggests that only the Father, and not Christ the Lamb, is the God of heaven.

Also, as we have seen in other portions of the NT, Jesus is presented in The Revelation as having a God. John writes about "Jesus Christ" in his salutation, saying, "He has made us to be a kingdom, priests to His God and Father" (Rev 1.6). This sentence not only distinguishes Jesus Christ from God, and identifies this God as the "Father" of Jesus Christ, but the Father is more precisely designated "His God," i.e., the God of Jesus Christ. Thus, The Revelation shows that *Jesus Christ cannot be God because He has a God*. John later extends this theme further by relating that Jesus calls the Father "My God" no less than five times (Rev 3.2, 12 [4x]; cf. Mt 27.46/Mk 15.34).

"The Lamb" and "the Word"

Perhaps a brief explanation is needed about the terminology "the Lamb" and "the word/Word (of God)." "The Lamb" is by far the most prominent title or metaphor applied to Jesus in The Revelation, occurring twenty-eight times. This "Lamb," which is depicted as having been slain, is a symbol of Jesus' crucifixion as the passive, Passover Lamb (Rev 5.6, 9, 12; 13.8; cf. 7.14; 12.11). But The Revelation also presents another picture, and a very different one, of "the Lamb" as One who vents His wrath upon His enemies by engaging them in actual battle and emerging victoriously (Rev 6.16-17; 17.14; 19.11-21). Most scholars reject a literal interpretation of this data. But it can only be this apocalyptic image of a conquering Lamb that John the Baptist had in mind when he identified Jesus as "the Lamb of God who takes away the sin of the world" (Jn 1.29, 36).[9] The Revelation presents both of these perspectives of the same metaphor: a passive, sacrificial Lamb and a militant Lamb. These figures are conjoined in Rev 5.5-6, in which the angel announces to John the seer, "behold, the Lion that is from the tribe of Judah." Thereafter, John sees "a Lamb standing, as if slain, having seven horns" that signify power.

The Revelation continues this image of a militant Lamb. It depicts Him as "The Word of God" who leads His angelic forces into earthly battle (Rev 19.13-16). Whether this appellation refers to Jesus as the preexistent Logos, as in Jn 1.1-14, is difficult to tell; but it certainly portrays Him as a mighty warrior,[10] thus the conquering Lamb of God. The word *logos* (word) appears eight times in the Greek text of The Revelation, and only in Rev 19.13 does it refer to Jesus; the other instances indicate the spoken word of God.[11]

The Throne of God

The OT presents a rich tradition of Yahweh seated on a throne in heaven,[12] with His innumerable angels gathered around Him and some attending Him.[13] Thus arose among the Jews the study of Merkabah mysticism, with much speculation about God's enthronement.

---

[9] C.H. Dodd, *The Interpretation of the Fourth Gospel*, 230-38. John the Baptist was bewildered during his imprisonment. Like Jesus' disciples, he did not understand that the One he identified as "the Lamb of God" must suffer and die. There was no tradition in normative Judaism for the Davidic Messiah to suffer and die.

[10] Cf. Isa 9.6; 63.1-6; cf. 40.10; 42.13; Wisdom 18.15-16.

[11] Rev 1.2, 9; 3.8, 10; 6.9; 12.11; 20.4. "The word (of God)," being that which is spoken, and "Jesus (Christ)/the Lamb" are juxtapositioned in most of these passages, thereby distinguishing them.

[12] E.g., 1 Kgs 22.19/2 Chr 18.18; Ps 9.4, 7; 11.4; 47.8; 89.14; 93.2; 97.2; 103.19; Isa 6.1-5; Lam 5.19; Eze 1.26; 10.1; 43.2-7; Dan 7.9-10, 14.

[13] Dan 7.10; cf. Deut 33.2; 1 Kgs 22.19/2 Chr 18.18.

The NT has an even greater tradition about God's heavenly enthronement. In fact, God's throne is the most prominent image in The Revelation. It is mentioned an amazing thirty-eight times and only six times in the remainder of the NT. This book often describes God the Father as "Him who sits on the throne," sometimes with an innumerable number of "angels around the throne" (Rev 5.11; cf. Dan 7.10). The Apostle Paul writes that God is the "only Sovereign" (1 Tim 6.15). God's sovereignty over His creation is the most prominent theme in The Revelation, and it is symbolized by His heavenly throne.

Nevertheless, The Revelation also presents Jesus Christ as "the Lamb" who sits on God's throne alongside of God. So, God, in fulfillment of Ps 110.1, shares His throne with Jesus Christ (Rev 3.21; 7.17; 12.5; 22.1, 3). This shared throne symbolizes the Lamb's divine authority in heaven and earth (Mt 28.18; Jn 16.15; 17.10). "Him who sits on the throne" always refers to the Father, and this clause infers His preeminence over all.

While The Revelation portrays God's throne as a symbol of His sovereignty, His throne should still be interpreted literally. The two concepts are not necessarily mutually exclusive. Those who argue otherwise usually cite that God is spirit (Jn 4.24), thereby presuming that He cannot sit, or that He is omnipresent and therefore cannot be confined locally, so that it must be concluded that such symbols are anthropomorphisms.

Such assertions reflect a misunderstanding of the spirit world. If God is indeed omnipresent, so that He cannot be confined spatially by literally sitting in a certain locale, e.g., on a throne, then how can the risen and exalted Jesus literally sit on God's throne beside Him, specifically, at His right hand? Does the resurrected man Jesus literally sit on God's heavenly throne at His right hand while God Himself does not sit there? Hardly!

God being spirit does not negate the possibility of Him also possessing form (Jn 4.24; 5.37). Spirit-forms can manifest themselves, even to human sight. The Bible records many instances in which human beings literally saw and conversed with spirits or angels. Jesus' resurrection body may be similar to that of the angels, and thus it will be so with the resurrected bodies of the saints at the resurrection (Mt 22.30 par.; 1 Jn 3.2). The Apostle Paul, in his treatise on resurrection, explains, "There are also heavenly bodies and earthly bodies, but the glory of the heavenly is one, and the glory of the earthly is another.... So also is the resurrection of the dead.... it is sown a natural body, it is raised a spiritual body. If there is a natural body, there is also a spiritual body.... And just as we have borne the image of the earthly, we shall also bear the image of the heavenly" (1 Cor 15.40, 42, 44, 49). So, Paul calls the resurrection body "a spiritual" and "heavenly" body.

Since man is made in God's image, perhaps God's image is a spiritual body too, like that of the angels. This would enable Him to sit on His throne, with Jesus at His side. Isaiah writes, "I saw the Lord sitting on a throne" (Isa 6.1). And Ezekiel relates that he saw in visions "something resembling a throne" having "a figure with the appearance of a man," it being "the appearance of the likeness of the glory of the LORD" (Eze 1.26, 28).

The idea of God inviting Jesus to sit with Him on His throne does not necessarily suggest that Jesus is essentially equal with God and thus possesses deity.[14] Rather, this exaltation magnifies Jesus' *dependence* upon God and

---

[14] Contra Richard J. Bauckham, "The Throne of God and the Worship of Jesus," in *The Jewish Roots of Christological Monotheism*, eds. C.C. Newman et al., 53, 59-60, 66; C. Geischen, *Angelomorphic Christology*, 93-94.

manifests His *subordination* to God. Otherwise, *if Jesus is God, and therefore co-equal with the Father in essence, we would expect Jesus to have His own separate throne in heaven*, perhaps alongside of the Father's and certainly at the same height. The Father's throne in heaven is the highest of all other thrones there. This situation renders Him "the Most High (God)" (e.g., Dan 7.9, 25). God's throne belonging to Him, and its being high and lifted up (Isa 6.1; cf. 52.13), symbolizes His exalted rank and thus His superior dignity over all, including Christ.

The existence of one throne in heaven for God, with Christ at His side, affirms a strict monotheism and thus nullifies both Binitarianism and Trinitarianism. Traditionalist R.H. Bauckham acknowledges, "In Second Temple Judaism, then, the throne of God in the highest heaven became a key symbol of monotheism."[15] And Marinus de Jong insists, "God on his heavenly throne remains the center of all worship (Rev 7:11-17), and adoration of the Lamb in no way endangers or diminishes the worship due him."[16]

In sum, *the most formidable image that refutes the notion that Jesus is God is the one God, the Father, literally sitting on His throne in heaven with Jesus sitting alongside of Him. The reason is that, if Jesus is equally God, no manner of mental gymnastics can escape the allegation that such an image presents two co-equal Gods sitting together. This may be the main reason many traditionalists deny that God literally sits on a throne.*

Why No Holy Spirit?

Following the first three chapters in The Revelation, the Holy Spirit is hardly ever mentioned again in this book. In fact, in the many instances in which God and Christ are mentioned together in it, the Holy Spirit is never included. Due to the church doctrine of the Trinity, this absence becomes most conspicuous. This is especially so in the book's heavenly scenes of praise and adoration directed to both God and Christ. If the doctrine of the Trinity is correct, shouldn't we expect three equal thrones in heaven: one for the Father, one for the Son, and one for the Holy Spirit? If not, at the very least we would expect that the Holy Spirit would be mentioned as sharing the Father's throne with Him and Christ. On the contrary, in the book of Revelation the Holy Spirit is never mentioned in association with God's throne.[17] Such silence strongly suggests that the Holy Spirit is not co-equal with God the Father and Jesus Christ nor even a full-fledged Person.

In Chapter Four, we learned that Trinitarians generally interpret "the seven Spirits (of God)," mentioned four times in Revelation (Rev 1.4; 3.1; 4.5; 5.6), as the Holy Spirit in a seven-fold character or mode.[18] But these seven spirits are described as being "before His throne" (Rev 1.4), i.e., the Father's throne, rather than *on* His throne, as with Jesus the Lamb. And being before God's throne indicates essential subordination to God. Trinitarian G.H. Dix recognized this problem with his belief. He thus concludes, "the invisible Spirit cannot be represented as upon the throne."[19] Dix infers that the Holy Spirit, being spirit, is invisible whereas the Father is not. But the Apostle Paul wrote that to mortal humans the Father is "invisible, the only God" (1 Tim 1.17; cf.

---

[15] R. Bauckham, "The Throne of God and the Worship of Jesus," 53.
[16] M. de Jong, *God's Final Envoy*, 138.
[17] Erik Sjoberg, "*pneuma*," in *TDNT* 6:387, cf. 388.
[18] See Chapter Four/The Big "Us" for comments on "the seven spirits" of Rev 1.4; 3.1; 4.5; 5.6.
[19] G.H. Dix, "The Seven Angels and the Seven Spirits," *JTS* 28 (1927): 250.

Col 1.15). Moreover, Jesus said to the Samaritan woman, "God is spirit" (Jn 4.24), referring to "the Father" (vv. 21, 23). The confusion vanishes by understanding that God is invisible to fleshly, sinful, mortal humans but visible to angels and probably risen saints in the future.

There are other notable silences about the Holy Spirit in the book of Revelation that reflect negatively on the doctrine of the Trinity. For example, the Holy Spirit is never given a name in the Bible, which suggests a lack of full personhood. And the 144,000 have the name of God and the name of the Lamb "written on their foreheads," signifying to whom they belong (Rev 7.3; 14.1; cf. Eze 9.4); yet nothing is said about them having the name of, or belonging to, the Holy Spirit. Furthermore, those who participate in the first resurrection and the subsequent millennial reign of Christ on earth "will be priests of God and of Christ" (Rev 20.6); yet, again, the Holy Spirit is never mentioned there. Also, the exalted Jesus says of those who overcome, "I will confess his name before My Father, and before His angels" (Rev 3.5), but not the Holy Spirit. Such glaring omissions weaken the Trinitarian position, so that the Holy Spirit does not appear to be a co-equal member of a supposed Trinity or even a full-fledged Person as we understand personhood.

"The Throne of David"

Although Jesus now shares the Father's throne with Him in heaven, someday Jesus will have His own throne (Mt 25.31; Rev 3.21). It will be located on earth at Jerusalem in the messianic age. It will be called "the throne of David" because Jesus is "the Son of David," being a descendant of King David (Lk 1.32; 3.31). Then Jesus will be not only the Messiah-King of Israel but also "KING OF KINGS, AND LORD OF LORDS" over all the earth (Rev 19.16). His earthly throne will symbolize His kingly authority, and therefore His sovereignty, over not only Israel but the entire earth (Rev 12.5; 19.16).

When God the Father gives Jesus His own kingdom and the throne of David (Dan 7.13-14; Lk 19.12), both to exist on earth, it will further demonstrate Jesus' dependence upon God. For, heaven's citizens exclaim loudly and unitedly, "Worthy is the Lamb that was slain to receive power and riches and wisdom and might and honor and glory and blessing" (Rev 5.12). Jesus is not worthy because He possesses deity but because of His obedience to God's will, the epitome of which is that He became the slain Lamb.

Jesus' title in Rev 19.16, "KING OF KINGS, AND LORD OF LORDS," distinguishes him from God's title as "God of gods and the Lord of lords" (Deut 10.17; cf. Ps 136.2-3). However, Paul also calls God "King of kings, and Lord of lords" (1 Tim 6.15).

The Meaning of "Hallelujah"

The word "Hallelujah" has always been such a cultic fixture in Christian praise, song, and worship. Yet most people, even Christians, have no idea about its meaning. "Hallelujah" is a Hebrew word which appears in the MT fifteen times, all in the Psalms. It is parsed as follows: *halal* means "boast" or "praise", *lu* means "be to", and *jah* is the abbreviated form of Jahveh (Yahweh). Thus, "Hallelujah" is a liturgical word that means "praise be to Yah(weh)." The Hebrew people seem to have used it in their festivals.

The word "Hallelujah" only appears in the NT in the book of Revelation. Of course, it is a transliteration. Four times in Rev 19, heaven's citizens worship and praise God by exclaiming "Hallelujah" (Rev 19.1, 3, 4, 6). The occasion is God's destruction of the great harlot, called "Mystery, Babylon the Great" (Rev 17.5; 19.2). In each instance, "Hallelujah" is clearly directed only to "our God," more precisely, "the Lord our God, the Almighty" (vv. 1, 5-6), and thus not to Christ. To do so would depict Christ as Yahweh.

Heaven's use of this cultic word, "Hallelujah," demonstrates that even its citizens can call God by His personal name given to Israel, which is YHWH. Because heaven's citizens apply this word exclusively to God further substantiates what we learned in Chapter Four, that "Yahweh" is the exclusive name of God the Father, so that Messiah Jesus is never identified as "Yahweh" in the Bible.

Agent Christology

Jesus' second coming is more prominent in The Revelation than anywhere in the Bible. When that blessed event occurs, Agent Christology will manifest itself brilliantly.

We learned in Chapter Four that the expression, "the day of the LORD," as it relates to the *eschatos*, signifies when Yahweh will display His awesome power as never before. The OT reveals that He will do it by "coming" to the earth "with vengeance" to fight "like a warrior," prevail against His enemies, and thereby "judge the earth."[20]

Yet the Bible teaches that God is transcendent and invisible to mortal humans. If the presence of God ever literally came down to the earth, all mortal humans would instantly be annihilated because God dwells in a glorious light that they cannot approach (Ex 33.5; Ps 104.2; 1 Tim 6.16). Consequently, God will come to the earth on "that day" in the Person of Messiah Jesus as God's agent par excellence (Rev 6.17; 11.15-18; 19.11-16). That event will affirm Agent Christology. At that time Jesus, as God's representative, will fulfill God's promises by coming to the earth to exercise judgment and restore creation to Edenic conditions that existed prior to the fall of Adam and Eve and more.

The Revelation ends by portraying a future, glorious, "holy city, new Jerusalem" (Rev 21.2). This city does not need the sun or moon, "for the glory of God has illumined it, and its lamp is the Lamb" (Rev 21.23; cf. 22.5). God will be the Source of the light that will illuminate this holy New Jerusalem, and Christ the Lamb will be God's agent as the conduit of that light. Thus, the Father, as the one and only God, is the ultimate Source of all things, and Jesus is the Way by which the glorious light of God will be reflected.

B. Problem Passages

1. Is Jesus called "the Lord God ... the Almighty" in Revelation 1.8?

Despite such strong evidence in the book of Revelation that Jesus Christ is *not* God, a few traditionalist expositors assert otherwise concerning Rev 1.8.[21] This passage reads as follows in the NASB: "'I am the Alpha and the Omega,' says the Lord God, 'who is and who was and who is to come, the Almighty.'" These traditionalists assume that Jesus Christ is the speaker in v. 8 because He is the subject of the three previous verses.

---

[20] E.g., Ps 96.13; 98.9; Isa 35.4; 40.10; 66.15; Zech 14.3-4.
[21] E.g., Athanasius, *Orations Against the Arians*, 3.4; John F. Walvoord, *The Revelation of Jesus Christ* (Chicago: Moody, 1966), 40; Josh McDowell, *More Than a Carpenter* (Wheaton, IL: Tyndale, 1977), 11.

In modern times, nearly all scholarly authorities on the book of Revelation have interpreted the speaker in Rev 1.8 as God the Father, not Jesus Christ.[22] And they usually don't even deem it necessary to substantiate this interpretation. G.R. Beasley-Murray says of Jesus therein, "Older expositors sometimes thought that He is the speaker here also, but clearly the view is mistaken; it is spoken by the 'Lord God' (RV) ... the Almighty," which he regards as God the Father.[23] And Hans Georg Link states, "In Rev 1:8 God is the subject of the sentence,... while in Rev 1:17f. the Son of man speaks."[24]

The following reasons affirm that God the Father is the speaker in Rev 1.8:

1. There is no logical reason why the author, John the Revelator, could not have changed speakers immediately following v. 7.
2. The same words that describe the speaker in v. 8—"who is and who was and who is to come"—also describe God the Father in both v. 4 and Rev 4.8.
3. The expression, "Lord God, the Almighty" (Gr. *kurios ho theos ho pantokrator*), occurs six times in The Revelation,[25] and "God, the Almighty" (Gr. *tou theou tou pantokratoros*), occurs twice therein.[26] The Greek word *pantokrator* means "ruler over all," and it only occurs one other time in the Greek NT, in 2 Cor 6.18 (cf. Amos 3.13). Aside from Rev 1.8, scholars concur that in all seven other instances in The Revelation, *pantokrator* refers only to God the Father. The best example is Rev 21.22 because it juxtapositions God and Christ and makes God ruler over all, including over Christ. It reads as follows: "the Lord God, the Almighty, and the Lamb."
4. Due to slight MS variance in Rev 1.8, the TR has only *kurios* and therefore reads only "Lord" in the AV. But MS authority heavily favors *kurios ho theos*, as rendered in all modern Greek NTs, so that all modern English versions have "the Lord God."
5. God's self-annunciation in v. 8 designedly follows the description of the second coming of Christ, in v. 7, because it is God the Father who will orchestrate that event.

In The Revelation, four similar phrases of identity are applied to God the Father, Jesus Christ, or both. The speaker in Rev 1.8 applies two of these epithets to Himself, and it behooves us to have a brief look at all four of them. These passages are as follows:

"I am the Alpha and the Omega"	"who is and who was and who is to come"	"the first and the last"	"the beginning and the end"
Rev 1.8=Father	Rev 1.4=Father	Rev 1.17=Christ	Rev 21.6=Father
Rev 21.6=Father	Rev 1.8=Father	Rev 2.8=Christ	Rev 22.13=Christ
Rev 22.13=Christ	Rev 4.8=Father	Rev 22.13=Christ	

---

[22] E.g., R.H. Charles, *The Revelation of St. John, With Introduction, Notes and Indices*, 2 vols. (Edinburgh: T. & T. Clark, 1920), 1:20; George Eldon Ladd, *A Commentary on the Revelation of John* (Grand Rapids: Eerdmans, 1972), 29; Robert H. Mounce, *The Book of Revelation* (Grand Rapids: Eerdmans, 1977), 73; G.R. Beasley-Murray, "The Revelation," in NBC (1970), 2nd ed., 1170; idem, *The Book of Revelation*, 59-60; Wilfrid J. Harrington, *Revelation*, in SPS (1993), 16:47; G.B. Caird, *New Testament Theology*, 193; P.R. Carrell, *Jesus and the Angels*, 116; R. Bauckham, *The Theology of the Book of Revelation*, 25, 50; C. Tuckett, *Christology and the New Testament*, 183; D.E. Aune, *Revelation 1-5*, 58.

[23] G.R. Beasley-Murray, "The Revelation," 1170.

[24] Hans Georg Link, "ego eimi," in *DNTT* 2:282.

[25] Rev 4.8; 11.17; 15.3; 16.7; 19.6; 21.22.

[26] Rev 16.14; 19.15.

The words "Alpha" and "Omega" identify the first and last letters in the Greek alphabet. Claiming to be "the Alpha and the Omega" is synonymous with claiming to be "the first and the last." The above table shows that, in The Revelation, both God the Father and Jesus Christ are identified as "the Alpha and the Omega," whereas only Jesus Christ is called "the first and the last." However, "the first and the last" echoes Yahweh's self-designation in Isaiah: "I am the first and I am the last" (Isa 44.6; cf. 41.4; 48.12). So, the Bible calls God and Christ "the Alpha and the Omega" and "the first and the last."

Isaiah's application of the expression, "the first and the last," to Yahweh likely means that Yahweh is the eternal One, or at least that He preexisted all living things on earth. Calling Jesus Christ "the first and the last" probably means the same as in Rev 3.14, in which He calls Himself "the Beginning of the creation of God." This phrase was an important text for the Arians in their attempt to refute the orthodox party's doctrine of eternal generation. The Arians interpreted it to mean that Jesus preexisted the creation of the world as the Logos-Son. On the contrary, these words have nothing to do with either metaphysics or creation. Rather, they designate Jesus as the "head" or "chief" (Gr. *arche*) of the new creation of God because He was the first One resurrected from the dead. And this is likely what Paul means when he calls Jesus "the first-born of all creation" (Col 1.15). For, three verses later Paul explains, "He is the beginning, the first-born from the dead; so that He Himself might come to have first place in everything" (v. 18).

Those who maintain that the speaker in Rev 1.8 is Jesus Christ often cite Rev 22.13 for support. Therein, Christ calls Himself "the Alpha and the Omega, the first and the last, the beginning and the end" (cf. Rev 1.17). However, in Rev 21.6 a speaker says, "I am the Alpha and the Omega, the beginning and the end." That speaker is "He who sits on the throne" (v. 5), which we have seen always refers to God the Father, who expressly identifies Himself in v. 7 as "God." Both God and Christ calling themselves "the Alpha and the Omega" and "the beginning and the end" do not make Christ God, just as calling both God and Christ "Lord" does not make Christ God (e.g., 4.8, 11; 11.15, 17; 22.6, 21).

The speaker in Rev 1.8 identifies Himself as one "who is and who was and who is to come." While the other three identical expressions of identity in The Revelation are applied to Jesus Christ, this one is not. The reason may be that this language alludes to Yahweh's self-identification in Ex 3.14 as the "I am," which probably means the Self-Existent One. Self-existence is incompatible with the self-revelation of the Johannine Jesus, which is most obvious in Jn 5.19-30. Indeed, only four verses earlier in The Revelation, in Rev 1.4, John writes to his readers, "Grace to you and peace, from Him who is and who was and who is to come," who certainly is God the Father.

In addition, John the Revelator relates that the four living creatures are located in and around God's throne (4.6). They unceasingly proclaim of the "One sitting on the throne" (4.2), who is God the Father, "Holy, holy, holy, is the Lord God Almighty, who was and who is and who is to come" (4.8). The thrice-repeated word "holy" alludes to the same in Isa 6.3, which identifies Yahweh. The remainder of Rev 4.8, along with the same words in Rev 1.4, is further evidence that the speaker in Rev 1.8 is God the Father.

Finally, only God the Father can rightly be described as "the Almighty" for the following reasons: (1) He is greater than all, including Christ (Jn 10.29; 14.28), (2) Christ actually belongs to Him, and (3) God the Father is the ultimate source of all things.[27]

---

[27] E.g., Mt 11.27; 28.18; Jn 3.35; 14.8; 1 Cor 3.23; 8.6; 11.3; 15.28.

2. Does Revelation 13.8 say the Lamb was slain at the time of creation?

Some English versions strangely translate Rev 13.8 as if Jesus preexisted as a human being and that He was crucified during this preexistence! On the contrary, the context of this verse is a prophecy about Christian believers enduring The Antichrist's reign of terror in the end times. This passage reads as follows in the AV, which is similar to the NIV: "And all that dwell upon the earth shall worship him [The Antichrist], whose names are not written in the book of life of the Lamb slain from the foundation of the world." The word order of the last clause in this translation is exactly the same in the Greek text. However, the word order is rearranged in most English versions. Thus, the NASB reads, "And all who dwell on the earth will worship him [The Antichrist], everyone whose name has not been written from the foundation of the world in the book of life of the Lamb who has been slain." (Similarly, RSV, NEB, JB, NIV.) Of course, this reading does not have Christ being crucified prior to His incarnation. And it is to be preferred due to the similar wording in Rev 17.8 in the Greek text, which the AV has, "whose names were not written in the book of life from the foundation of the world."

3. Does worshipping Jesus in Heaven indicate that He is God?

Christian worship has been an important subject regarding the question of whether Jesus is God. Most Christians believe that only God should be worshipped. Since the NT relates some accounts of people worshipping Jesus, it is generally believed that these accounts indicate that He is God. The book of Revelation presents very vivid and striking accounts of the angels doing homage to Jesus in heaven. Many modern scholars think that the early church made a transition from a low to a high Christology, in which Jesus is fully God, and that it happened mostly because of Christians on earth, and angels in heaven as depicted in The Revelation, worshipping the heavenly-exalted Jesus Christ.[28]

We saw in Chapter Five/Matthew that the word in the Greek NT that is usually translated "worship" is *proskuneo*. And we learned that *proskuneo* indicates the oriental custom of either genuflection (bending the knee[s] to the ground) or "prostrating oneself before a person and kissing his feet, the hem of his garment, the ground, etc."[29] Such physical acts directed toward some individual usually indicate an attitude of obeisance or reverence toward that person, but not necessarily veneration of that person as a deity. It was concluded in Chapter Five that when it is recorded in the Synoptic Gospels that someone performed *proskuneo* at the feet of the pre-Easter Jesus, it indicates no more than that that devotee demonstrated his or her sincere respect and honor for Jesus.

---

[28] E.g., Richard J. Bauckham, "The Worship of Jesus in Apocalyptic Christianity," NTS 27 (1981): 322; R.T. France, "The Worship of Jesus: A Neglected Factor in Christological Debate," 33-36; M.M.B. Turner, "The Spirit of Christ and Christology," 168-69; L. Hurtado, *One God, One Lord*, esp. 11; idem, *At the Origins of Christian Worship*.
[29] BAGD, 716.

A change in the meaning of *proskuneo* occurs twice in the NT gospels. Only in Satan's temptation of Jesus and Jesus' encounter with the Samaritan woman at the well does *proskuneo* connote a religious experience (Mt 4.10/Lk 4.8; Jn 4.20-24). Yet both of those discussions are about worshipping the God of heaven, who is the Father, not Jesus.

Worship is far more prominent in The Revelation than in any other NT book. This Apocalypse is full of rich insight into the communal worship in heaven, which consists mostly of singing hymns and uttering liturgies. For instance, the word *proskuneo* appears fifty-nine times in the Greek NT, with twenty-four occuring in the book of Revelation, and nearly all of these have religious significance. The Revelation contains six heavenly scenes of corporate worship. In each case, heaven's citizens perform *pipto* ("fall down") followed by *proskuneo*.[30] In most of these scenes, devotees seem to direct their worship toward both God and Christ. If so, does their act of *proskuneo* indicate that they believe that Christ is also God? P.M. Casey rightly observes that in The Apocalypse, Jesus Christ "is not actually hailed as divine even in the pictures of him being praised in heaven."[31]

Indeed, The Revelation nowhere declares precisely that Jesus Christ is "God." Even though *proskuneo* frequently exhibits some sort of religious significance in this book, sometimes it clearly does not, in which case *proskuneo* is directed toward others besides God and Christ. For example, Jesus says to the faithful believers at Philadelphia, "I will cause those of the synagogue of Satan,... to come and bow down at your feet" (Rev 3.9). "Bow down," here, translates *proskuneo*. Or take the two instances when John the Revelator fell at the angel's feet to "worship" (*proskuneo*) him. John surely did not intend to convey by these acts that he believed that that angel was God. Nevertheless, both times the angel forbade John's action and commanded him, "worship God," i.e., the Father (Rev 19.10; 22.9; cf. 14.7). Obviously, the angel regarded John's act of *proskuneo* as indicating more than mere respectful honor; otherwise, he would not have forbade it.

But did the angel mean that John should worship only the Father and not Christ? Interestingly, the angel told John, "worship God," without telling him to worship Christ.

Eight times in the Greek text of The Revelation it is clear that *proskuneo* applies exclusively to God the Father.[32] And, of the twenty-four occurrences of *proskuneo* in this book, there is only one instance, in Rev 5.14, in which it conceivably might be applied to Christ. This text relates that "the elders fell down and worshiped," without specifying the object of their worship. On two occasions, John the Revelator relates that the twenty-four elders in heaven "fell down/on their faces and worshiped God" (Rev 11.15-16; 19.4). In both cases, John says nothing about them worshipping Christ. Similarly, in two instances both God and Christ are praised and immediately the twenty-four elders "worshipped God" without anything being said respecting Christ (Rev 7.10-11; 11.16). Why does John often portray heaven's citizens worshipping God, yet he never says they worship Christ?

Because of such evidence, recall from Chapter Three that the early Unitarians of Transylvania deemed it appropriate to worship only God the Father and thus not Christ. Also recall that Sir Isaac Newton and Samuel Clarke

---

[30] Rev 4.8-11; 5.8-14; 7.9-12; 11.15-18; 15.2-4; 19.1-7.
[31] P.M. Casey, *From Jewish Prophet to Gentile God*, 143.
[32] Rev 4.10; 7.11; 11.16; 14.7; 15.4; 19.4, 10; 22.9.

took a mediating position on this. It was that Jesus should be worshipped, but to a lesser extent than the Father is worshipped. Newton even alleged that to worship the Father and Christ equally, as in the doctrine of the Trinity, was to break the First Commandment—"You shall have no other gods before Me" (Ex 20.3/Deut 5.7)—and thus to be found guilty of committing idolatry! Origen had earlier insisted more convincingly that *true worship is directed toward God through the Son, but not to the Son.*[33] This view coincided with his belief that the Son is essentially subordinate to the Father. Indeed, God comes to us through Christ, and we come to God through Christ. Perhaps it is no stretch to say that everything pertaining to a Christian's relationship of God is accomplished through Christ, even their worship of God.

In sum, the idea of heaven's citizens performing *proskuneo* toward Jesus Christ and showering praises on Him does not necessarily indicate that they believe He is God. Yet it is unclear in The Revelation if *proskuneo* is ever directed toward Jesus. Even if it is, it probably means no more than what the earthly Jesus taught—that it is the Father's will that "all may honor the Son, even as they honor the Father" (Jn 5.23; cf. Rev 5.12-13). Such honoring of the Son does not necessitate believing that He is God. Although The Revelation presents the slain Lamb—Jesus Christ—as God's exalted associate, God the Father still remains supremely central to all worship and praise in heaven.

---

[33] Origen, *De Oratione*, 15. Indebted to M. Wiles (*Archetypal Heresy*, 22) for this source.

Appendix A: The Doctrine of the Trinity

Introduction	Contradictory, Confusing, Incomprehensible
Historical Development	Restitution of True Doctrine of God &Christ
No Biblical Basis	

Introduction

While this book is about Christology, many readers may wonder, "What about the doctrine of the Trinity?" Trinitarian Philip Schaff states, "The Trinity and Christology, the two hardest problems and most comprehensive dogmas of theology, are intimately connected."[1] Yes they are. In fact, the doctrine of the Trinity was later formed because the Church finally settled on its dogma that Jesus is fully God. Even though we touched on the doctrine of the Trinity in Chapter Two,[2] we will now briefly consider it further.

We have seen that the Catholic Church decided on its final formulation of the doctrine of the Trinity in the late 4th century. It was that God, also called "the Godhead," is one *ousia* (substance or essence) consisting of three co-equal and co-eternal *hypostases* (subsistences, similar to beings): God the Father, God the Son, and God the Holy Spirit. The Church officially made belief in this doctrine essential for acquiring salvation. That is, if you did not believe in the doctrine of the Trinity—or, more specifically, after having known about it you refused to believe it, or after having believed it you disbelieved it—the Church deemed that you were not a genuine Christian.

This dogma sustained throughout the Protestant Reformation and remains the official teaching in all mainline church denominations to the present. That is why eminent Presbyterian, systematic theologian A.A. Hodge could assert, "it is essential to salvation to believe in the three persons in one Godhead."[3] Yet Hodge wrote in the same volume, "A church has no right to make anything a condition of membership which Christ has not made a condition of salvation."[4] Did Jesus Christ make belief in three co-equal and co-eternal Persons in one Godhead a requirement for salvation? Chapter and verse, please!

The deity of Christ is the foundation of the doctrine of the Trinity. Without it, the doctrine of the Trinity collapses. G.W.H. Lampe rightly explains, "The

---

[1] P. Schaff, *History of the Christian Church*, 3:705.
[2] See also Chapter Four/Is the Trinity in Genesis?/Man in the Image of God.
[3] Archibald Alexander Hodge, *Outlines of Theology* (London: Thomas Nelson & Sons, 1886), 198.
[4] A.A. Hodge, *Outlines of Theology*, 114.

Trinitarian distinctions,... had originally been developed in order to affirm that Jesus is God."[5]

Nathaniel Micklem even questions if it is legitimate to speak of "the doctrine of the Trinity," as if there is and always has been only one. He informs, "There are many doctrines of the Trinity." Then he cites a few, including those of Augustine, Abelard, L. Hodgson, Karl Barth, and Paul Tillich, showing that they all "differ greatly."[6] Of course, church denominations have identified *the* doctrine of the Trinity as the one the Catholic Church deemed official in the 4th century and thus have endorsed it as the correct one.

Historical Development

No matter who you listen to, the doctrine of the Trinity has proven to be the most technical and complex teaching in the history of church dogma. To assess it, we need to review briefly its historical development, which occurred in the following stages:

- *1st century*: Advocating a strict Jewish monotheism, that God is "one" (Person or Being), so that only the Father is God. Thus, Jesus Christ is not identified as God.
- *2nd century*: God is two un-equal Persons—the Father and His inferior Logos-Son. Jesus Christ temporally preexisted as the Logos-Son prior to His incarnation as man.
- *3rd century*: God is two un-equal Persons—the Father and His inferior Logos-Son. But the Father generates the Logos-Son to become an eternally preexisting Person.
- *early 4th century*: God is two co-equal and co-eternal Persons: the Father and the Son. So far, nothing has been decided about the constitution of the Holy Spirit.
- *late 4th century*: God is three co-equal and co-eternal Persons—the Father, the Son, and the Holy Spirit—and all three members of this Trinity share the same substance.

So, the final formula of the doctrine of the Trinity did not obtain until the late 4th century. (For a semantic discussion of words Church authorities used to identify the one God and distinguish the three members of the Trinity from this Godhead, see subheads The Nicene Creed and The Council of Constantinople in Chapter Two.)

This prolonged, historical development of the doctrine of the Trinity raises serious questions. Why would it take so long for such a supposedly important doctrine to be discovered from the revered books and letters that became the NT? Doesn't such a lengthy period of development undermine its credibility? And how can Trinitarians claim that all professing Christians must believe this doctrine in order to be saved, since all generations of Christians prior to its final formulation in the late 4th century had never heard of it?

No Biblical Basis for the Word "Trinity"

The word "Trinity" is not in the Bible. Church father Tertullian coined it in 192 CE. Many people ask, "Why all the fuss about a word that isn't even

---
[5] G.W.H. Lampe, *God as Spirit*, 225.
[6] Nathaniel Micklem, *Ultimate Questions* (Nashville: Abington, 1955), 135.

in the Bible?" We learned in Chapter Two what a fuss there was about the word *homoousios* in the Nicene Creed, which is not in the Greek NT either. Distinguished NT grammarian Nigel Turner, although a staunch Trinitarian, admits, "Most of the distortions and dissensions which have vexed the Church,... have arisen through the insistence of sects and sections of the Christian community upon using words which are not found in the New Testament."[7] Amazingly, neither is the word "Trinity" in any of the early ecumenical creeds.

Many distinguished Christian scholars now acknowledge that the doctrine of the Trinity is not biblical and does not represent primitive Christianity. Roman Catholic Hans Kung, one of the most celebrated theologians in the world for the past several decades, asks concerning the NT, "Why is there never talk of the 'triune God'?... throughout the New Testament, while there is **belief in God the Father, in Jesus the Son and in God's Holy Spirit**, there is **no doctrine of one God in three persons** ... no doctrine of a 'triune God,' a 'Trinity.'[8] He further observes, "If we wanted to judge Christians of the pre-Nicene period after the event, in the light of the Council of Nicaea, then not only the Jewish Christians would be heretics but also almost all the Greek church fathers."[9]

The Encyclopedia Americana rightly recounts the historical development of the Trinitarian doctrine. It says, "Unitarianism as a theological movement began much earlier in history; indeed it antedated Trinitarianism by many decades. Christianity derived from Judaism, and Judaism was strictly Unitarian.... Fourth-century Trinitarianism did not reflect accurately early Christian teaching regarding the nature of God; it was on the contrary a deviation from this teaching."[10] William Penn—a Quaker and the first governor of the State of Pennsylvania—wrote, "the origin of the Trinitarian doctrine ... is not from the Scriptures, nor reason,... it was born about three hundred years after the ancient gospel was declared; it was conceived in ignorance, brought forth and maintained by cruelty."[11] Kung thus concludes, "The theology which became manifest at the [first six ecumenical] councils led to a considerable **alienation from the New Testament**."[12]

The mere fact that the word "Trinity" does not appear in the Bible suggests that the doctrine of the Trinity is not there either. God had forewarned the Israelites through Moses concerning the Law, "You shall not add to the word which I am commanding you, nor take away from it" (Deut 4.2). And Proverbs states rather somberly, "Do not add to His words lest He reprove you, and you be proved a liar" (Prov 30.6; cf. Rev 22.18-19). It appears that Trinitarians have added their doctrine of the Trinity to God's truth.

---

[7] Nigel Turner, *Christian Words* (Edinburgh: T&T Clark, 1980), viii.
[8] H. Kung, *Christianity: Essence, History, and Future*, 94-95. Emphasis his.
[9] H. Kung, *Christianity: Essence, History, and Future*, 103.
[10] *EA* 27 (1956), 2941. Cited by Buzzard and Hunting, *The Doctrine of the Trinity*, 19. Of course, the word "unitarianism" is being used here synonymously with "monotheism."
[11] Quoted by J.H. Broughton and P.J. Southgate, *The Trinity: True or False?* 376.
[12] H. Kung, *Christianity: Essence, History, and Future*, 193. Emphasis his.

APPENDIX A: THE DOCTRINE OF THE TRINITY

Trinitarians generally offer the following NT texts to substantiate their doctrine.[13]

Matthew 28.19	2 Corinthians 13.14	Ephesians 2.18	1 Peter 1.2
"Go therefore and make disciples of all the nations, baptizing them in the name of the Father and the Son and the Holy Spirit"	"The grace of the Lord Jesus Christ, and the love of God, and the fellowship of the Holy Spirit, be with you all."	"for through Him [Jesus Christ] we both have our access in one Spirit to the Father."	"according to the foreknowledge of God the Father, by the sanctifying work of the Spirit, that you may obey Jesus Christ"
Romans 15.30	1Corinthians 12.4-6	Ephesians 4.4, 6	Jude 20-21
"Now I urge you, brethren, by our Lord Jesus Christ and by the love of the Spirit, to strive together with me in your prayers to God for me"	"Now there are varieties of gifts, but the same Spirit. And there are varieties of ministries, and the same Lord. And there are varieties of effects, but the same God"	"*There* is one body and one Spirit,... one Lord, one faith, one baptism, one God and Father"	"praying in the Holy Spirit; keep yourselves in the love of God, waiting anxiously for the mercy of our Lord Jesus Christ"

The most well-known biblical formulation that brings together the so-called "three members of the Trinity" is in Mt 28.19>, quoted above. It has been the church's most popular baptismal formula. Yet most contemporary Trinitarian scholars now admit that all of these above passages *only mention* the Father, the Son, and the (Holy) Spirit without substantiating their Trinity doctrine. Thus, many of them would agree with V. Taylor's assessment that "the Trinity is not an express New Testament doctrine."[14]

Many Trinitarian scholars concede that their doctrine represents no more than a *deduction* from Scripture. J.N.D. Kelly says of the NT, "Explicit Trinitarian confessions are few and far between; where they do occur, little can be built upon them."[15] Johannes Schneider admits, "The NT does not contain the developed doctrine of the Trinity."[16] And staunch Trinitarian D.A. Carson concedes, "Individually these texts do not prove there is any Trinitarian consciousness in the NT, since other threefold-phrases occur."[17]

The NT has other triune formulas which mention angels instead of the Holy Spirit. For example, Paul writes, "I solemnly charge you in the presence of God and of Christ Jesus and of His chosen angels" (1 Tim 5.21). And Jesus spoke of the time when "the Son of Man ... comes in His glory, and the glory of the Father

---

[13] See also 2 Cor 1.21-22; Heb 9.14.
[14] V. Taylor, *The Person of Christ*, 248.
[15] J.N.D. Kelly, *Early Christian Creeds*, 22.
[16] Johannes Schneider, "*theos*," in *NIDNTT* 2:84.
[17] D.A. Carson, "Matthew," 598.

and of the holy angels" (Lk 9.26; cf. Mt 16.27/Mk 8.38). He also said, "But of that day and/or hour no one knows, not even the angels of/in heaven, nor the Son, but the Father alone" (Mt 24.36/Mk 13.32).

Interestingly, Trinitarians have always felt compelled to prove that Jesus is God and that the Holy Spirit is a Person, whereas they have never felt any compulsion at all to prove that the Father is God. However, the latter is axiomatic because the NT *constantly* interchanges the word "God" with "the Father" and never "God" with the "Son." For instance, a comparison of the first two passages listed in the above table—Mt 28.19 and 2 Cor 13.14—seems to show that the Father should be reckoned exclusively as God.

In the past, Trinitarians identified the three members of the Trinity as God the Father, God the Son, and God the Holy Spirit, and they further denominated them as "the first member of the Trinity," "the second member of the Trinity," and "the third member of the Trinity," respectively. But most contemporary Trinitarian scholars have abandoned these numerical designations since they imply rank and thus varying levels of dignity, concepts which seem to contradict their co-equality. Yet these Trinitarians continue the traditional arrangement and rarely if ever alter it, a practice that also implies rank. Notice that none of the eight passages cited above follow this fixed order. Instead, the supposed three members of the Trinity are arranged in five different orders in which God, who is the Father, is mentioned in the first position in only two of these eight passages.

Contradictory, Confusing, and Incomprehensible

So, the primary *scriptural* argument against the doctrine of the Trinity is that neither the word "T/trinity" nor its meaning are found anywhere in Scripture, but only that the Father, Son, and (Holy) Spirit are occasionally mentioned together.

The primary *philosophical* argument against Trinitarianism is that it postulates an abstract, tri-personal Godhead, a concept that is contrary to Nature. This Trinitarian God is not even reckoned as a Person or (arguably) a Being. That is why Trinitarian C.S. Lewis explains, and assents, that "in Christianity God is ... not even a person."[18]

The primary *logical* arguments against the doctrine of the Trinity are that it is contradictory, confusing, and incomprehensible. It is contradictory in that Trinitarianism professes to be monotheistic (one God) while insisting that the Father, Son, and Holy Spirit all have separate identities as full-fledged Persons, each being God, yet they are not three Gods. In fact, post-Nicene patristic writings often contain a statement explaining that the three Persons of the Trinity are one Godhead, not three Gods.

Trinitarians readily admit that their doctrine is a paradox and a mystery. Jews, Muslims, and other non-Trinitarian believers in the one God vehemently deny that such a view is monotheistic. They usually allege it is tritheistic—the worship of three Gods.

Trinitarians defend their doctrine by arguing that it merely *seems* contradictory. When pressed to explain its seeming illogicalness and its contradictions, they frequently resort to their very irrational argument about its incomprehensibility. That is, just about all Trinitarians admit that their doctrine is humanly incomprehensible, explaining that it is because God is inscrutable. Traditionalist L.S. Chafer says of this subject, "If all of this seems

---

[18] C.S. Lewis, *Mere Christianity*, 152.

incomprehensible, it is only because the finite mind is unable to grasp infinite truth."[19] John F. Walvoord, in his revised edition of one of Chafer's books, remarks, "this doctrine [of the Trinity] should be accepted by faith on the basis of scriptural revelation even if it is beyond human comprehension and definition."[20]

Talk about confusion, not to mention circular reasoning! Those who advance such arguments do not seem to grasp that, if their doctrine is incomprehensible, how can *they* comprehend it, let alone explain it?[21] And why should anyone believe the originators of this doctrine, since according to their assertions *they could not have understood it either*?

Trinitarians are well known for offering a multitude of analogies to explain their doctrine. But analogies are not rationale and thus prove nothing regarding the truth.

Christians can get so mixed up about their doctrine of the Trinity. Most of them intellectually affirm that God is tri-personal and thus an abstract Godhead. Yet in their worship they often betray belief in a uni-personal God by acknowledging Him as their "Father." In prayer, many Trinitarian Christians, even some who are well taught, inter-change "the Father" and "Jesus" as if they are one and the same individual.

How strange it is that some Trinitarians are actually fond of asserting the veracity of their doctrine while simultaneously admitting its incomprehensibility! One time Daniel Webster was asked, "How can an intelligent man like you believe that three is one?" He replied, "I do not pretend to understand the arithmetic of heaven." Mr. Webster was like most Trinitarians, who accept their doctrine by blind faith as an unfathomable mystery that originated in heaven even though they assent to its utter incomprehensibility.

Abraham Lincoln (1809-1865) was perhaps the greatest president in U.S. history and one of the greatest men of God in his generation. As a U.S. Senator campaigning to become the sixteenth U.S. president, the media asked him why he had never joined a church. Being a lawyer, Mr. Lincoln replied, "It's because I can't understand their creeds." One wonders if he had in mind mostly Trinitarianism. Lincoln came from the region where the anti-Trinitarian Christian Church denomination was centered.

Many Trinitarians, both clergy and laity, insist that their doctrine is so complex that it is best to *believe it and leave it*. They mean, "leave it only for scholars to discuss." Trinitarians have a famous ditty that can strike fear into the heart of most any Trinitarian who might be considering arguments for the implausibility of their doctrine. It is this:

> Try to explain the doctrine of the Trinity and you'll lose your mind.
> But try to deny it and you'll lose your soul.[22]

---

[19] Lewis Sperry Chafer, *Major Bible Themes* (Grands Rapids: Dunham, 1926), 21.
[20] Lewis Sperry Chafer, rev. John F. Walvoord, *Major Bible Themes: 52 Vital Doctrines of the Scripture Simplified and Explained* (Grand Rapids: Zondervan, 1974), 41.
[21] Cf. D. Cupitt (*Jesus and the Gospel of God*, 14), who effectively makes the same arguments against the classical Incarnation dogma.
[22] Cited by Millard J. Erickson, *Introducing Christian Doctrine*, ed. L. Arnold Hustad (Grand Rapids: Baker, 1992), 105. According to Lewis Sperry Chafer (*Systematic Theology*, 8 vols. [Dallas: Dallas Theological Seminary, 1947], 1:288), Robert South (*Works*, 2:184) penned the original as follows: "As he that denies it may lose his soul; so he that too much strives to understand it may lose his wits."

Restitution of the True Doctrine of God and Christ

Hans Kung critiques the doctrine of the Trinity as it relates to inter-religious dialogue between adherents of Judaism, Christianity, and Islam. He then states:

> I shall try to sum up in three sentences what seems to me to be the biblical nucleus of the traditional doctrine of the Trinity, in light of the New Testament, considered for today:
> — To believe in God the Father means to believe in the one God, creator, preserver and perfecter of the world and humankind: Judaism, Christianity and Islam have this belief in one God in common.
> — To believe in the Holy Spirit means to believe in God's effective might and power in human beings and the world: Jews, Christian and Muslims also have this belief in God's Spirit in common.
> — To believe in the Son of God means to believe in the revelation of the one God in the man Jesus of Nazareth who is thus God's Word, Image and Son.[23]

Here is a restitution of the Bible's teaching on God the Father, Jesus Christ, and the Holy Spirit. I couldn't have said it better myself. Without admitting it, Kung redefines the doctrine of the Trinity as follows: (1) the one God is exclusively the Father, (2) the Holy Spirit is the power of God, and (3) Jesus' uniqueness is that God the Father has revealed Himself fully in Him. Kung adds, "For the New Testament, as for the Hebrew Bible, the principle of unity is clearly the one God (*ho theos*: the God = the Father)."[24]

---

[23] Hans Kung, *Credo: The Apostles' Creed Explained for Today* (ET 1992; repr. Eugene, OR: Wipf and Stock, 2003), 154.
[24] Ibid.

Appendix B: The Nature of the Holy Spirit

The Church Doctrine of the Holy Spirit	Apply Personal Pronouns to Holy Spirit
The Spirit of God and the Spirit of Man	Personifying the Holy Spirit
The Holy Spirit in the Old Testament	Impersonal Functions of the Holy Spirit
The Holy Spirit in the New Testament	Holy Spirit as the Spirit of the Father
Capitalizing Holy Spirit	Does Scripture Say Holy Spirit is God?

The Church Doctrine of the Holy Spirit

Although the subject of this book is whether or not Jesus is God, as with the doctrine of the Trinity many readers would be disappointed if this book did not address the nature of the Holy Spirit. This is especially so since, according to the church doctrine of the Trinity, the Holy Spirit is a full-fledged Person, co-equal and co-eternal with both God the Father and Jesus Christ.[1]

In Chapter Two, we learned that during the 2nd and 3rd centuries there was no consensus among Christian apologists regarding the constitution of the Holy Spirit. Most did not consider it an important matter. In fact, there was a widespread fluidity of ideas among Christians about it. Some thought the Holy Spirit was an impersonal power. Others ascribed full personality to the Holy Spirit. As quoted earlier, Philip Schaff observes, "the doctrine of the Holy Spirit was far less developed, and until the middle of the fourth century was never a subject of special controversy."[2]

Consequently, both the Apostles' Creed and the Nicene Creed only state, "I/We believe ... in the Holy Spirit." Due to this brevity, it is absurd for later Trinitarians to assert that a person must believe that the Holy Spirit is a full-fledged Person, even God, to be a Christian. This view renders all previous, professing Christians as non-Christian.

In the Arian-Nicene Controversy of the 4th century, all three parties to the conflict agreed that the Holy Spirit is a separate hypostasis (subsistence) from that of the Father and Son. Arius regarded the essence of the Holy Spirit as unlike that of the Father or Son. Eusebius, church historian and leader of the middle party, said the Holy Spirit is inferior in essence to that of the Father and Son and "a third power" in "third rank" to them.[3]

---

[1] Identifying the Holy Spirit as a "Person," as modern English-speaking Trinitarians generally have done, is historically problematic. Greek-speaking Eastern church fathers identified the Holy Spirit mostly with their word *hypostasis*. We have no corresponding, common English word for it except that "being" comes close.

[2] P. Schaff, *History of the Christian Church*, 2:560.

[3] Eusebius, *The Ecclesiastical Theology*, 3, 6, 3. Indebted to J.N.D. Kelly, *Early Christian Doctrines*, 255.

Nothing changed for decades after the Nicene Creed. Thus, R.P.C. Hanson also relates, "When we examine the creeds and confessions of faith which were so plentifully produced between the years 325 and 360, we gain the overwhelming impression that no school of thought during that period was particularly interested in the Holy Spirit."[4] A few fathers only argued that the Holy Spirit is a distinct hypostasis essentially subordinate to both the Father and the Son, thus rendering the Holy Spirit unequal with both.

Gregory of Nazianzus, one of the three Cappadocians who composed the final formulation of the doctrine of the Trinity with their treatises, wrote in 380 about belief in the Holy Spirit, "But of the wise men amongst ourselves, some have conceived of him as an Activity, some as a Creature, some as God; and some have been uncertain which to call Him, out of reverence for Scripture, they say, as though it did not make the matter clear either way. And therefore they neither worship Him nor treat Him with dishonour, but take up a neutral position," which latter Gregory deems "very miserable."[5]

The Constantinopolitan Creed (381) changed all of this. It declares, "We believe ... in the Holy Spirit ... who proceeds from the Father." The western branch of the Catholic Church later added to their Latin translation the word *filioque*, meaning "and the Son," which the eastern branch rejected. This "*Filioque* Controversy," which later divided the Church, is irrelevant to whether the Holy Spirit is a full-fledged Person.

Then this creed adds concerning the Holy Spirit, "Who with the Father and the Son is together worshipped and together glorified." This was the Church's first official declaration of a three co-equal hypostases, thereby claiming the Holy Spirit is personal and God. It says the Holy Spirit is to be worshipped. Yet the NT never states or describes worship of the Holy Spirit.[6]

Since the Church made this statement of the doctrine of the Trinity official, it has prevailed in all mainline churches to the present. These church leaders have insisted that to be a real Christian a person must believe that the Holy Spirit is a full-fledged Person as well as fully God, and they usually have required this confession for church membership.

Yet in church history, some professedly Christian sects have denied that the Bible teaches that the Holy Spirit is a full-fledged Person. Sabellians and other monarchians of the 3rd century, as well as the Socinians of the Reformation, contended that the "spirit of God" is merely the power of God. Recall that this was also the view of Michael Servetus.

While the orthodox had argued that the Holy Spirit is a hypostasis in the Godhead, R.P.C. Hanson claims "Athanasius ... never directly calls the Holy Spirit 'God.'"[7] And Hanson says of Basil of Caesarea, one of the three Cappadocians, "Basil carefully refrains from ever directly calling him God (*Theos*) ... Basil is,... troubled by his realization that it is impossible to find in the Bible full and wholly adequate support for the doctrine that the Holy Spirit is a separate *hypostasis* within the Godhead" since "the Bible ... evidence was not sufficient to support ... the full divinity of the Spirit as a third *hypostasis*."[8] Yet Basil often supports his

---

[4] R.P.C. Hanson, *The Search for the Doctrine of God: The Arian Controversy, 318-381* [1988] (repr. Grand Rapids: Baker, 2005), 741.
[5] Gregory of Nazianzen, *The Fifth Theological Oration: On the Holy Spirit*, NPNF: Second Series, 5.5-6.
[6] L.W. Hurtado, *At the Origins of Christian Worship*, 63-64.
[7] R.P.C. Hanson, *The Search for the Christian Doctrine of God*, 752.
[8] R.P.C. Hanson, *The Search for the Christian Doctrine of God*, 776-78.

view by citing the triune baptismal formula in Mt 28.19>. All three Cappadocians had no answer for what constituted the nature of the Holy Spirit.[9]

Since Christians profess to base their beliefs on the Bible, the question arises: Is there sufficient information in the Bible to determine the nature of the Holy Spirit? I think it contains enough information to decide some things that the Holy Spirit *is not*. For one thing, *the Bible indicates that the Holy Spirit is not a full-fledged Person as we moderns understand personhood*. Or, to return to the era when Greek church fathers formulated their doctrine of the Trinity, *the Holy Spirit is not a hypostasis independent of the Father*.

We will now consider very briefly what the Bible says about the nature and the activities of the Holy Spirit. But before we do, it should be understood that "the Holy Spirit," "the Spirit of God," "the Spirit of the LORD (YHWH)," and "the Spirit" are synonymous expressions in the Bible that refer to the same entity. English Bible versions usually translate "spirit" for both the Hebrew word *ruach* in the MT of the OT and *pneuma* in the LXX and Greek NT because that is the primary meaning of these words.

As for the translation "the Holy Ghost" in the KJV, no modern Bible versions use it. It merely reflects a different time, when the word spirit meant ghost. The expression, "give up the ghost," used to refer to the departing of the human spirit at death.

The Spirit of God and the Spirit of Man

The best place in the Bible to first learn about the nature of the Holy Spirit is at its beginning. The book of Genesis tells how "the Spirit of God" participated in creation (Gen 1.2). We read, "God created man in His own image" (Gen 1.27),[10] and "the LORD God formed man of dust from the ground, and breathed into his nostrils the breath of life; and man became a living being" (Gen 2.7; cf. 7.22). The word "breathed" is *neeshmat* in the Hebrew text. Sometimes, it is used synonymously in the OT with *ruach*, meaning "breath" or "spirit."[11] Thus, God made man a living being by giving man a spirit.

Man is a tripartite being consisting of body, soul, and spirit. (This is no analogy for the Trinity since these elements are not persons.) *Because man was made in God's image, man's spirit corresponds to God's Spirit*. Binitarian C.F.D. Moule says "there is a certain kinship between God and man—between Spirit and spirit."[12] Indeed, and *it should be concluded from man's creation that the Spirit of God is to God what the spirit of man is to man*. Graeser, Lynn, and Schoenheit state this, but inversely, by saying, "The spirit bears the same relation to man as the spirit of God bears to God (1 Cor 2:11)."[13] So, creation reveals that the Spirit of God is a part of God just as the spirit of a living human being is a part of that human being. In other words, since the spirit of a human being is not a separate person, or hypostasis, from that human being, neither is the Spirit of God a separate Person, or hypostasis, from God, who is exclusively the Father.

It is surprising that church fathers and few subsequent Bible scholars recognized this. Some church fathers used the analogy of the relationship between the human spirit and the human self to explain the relationship of the

---

[9] R.P.C. Hanson, *The Search for the Christian Doctrine of God*, 786.
[10] God speaks of both His own "soul" (Heb. *nephesh*) and "Spirit" (Heb. *ruach*) in Isa 42.1.
[11] E.g., Job 27.3; Isa 42.5.
[12] C.F.D. Moule, *The Holy Spirit* (Grand Rapids: Eerdmans, 1978), 7.
[13] Graeser-Lynn-Schoenheit, *One God & One Lord*, 597.

Holy Spirit to God; but they did not emphasize this analogy due to its stronger support of monarchianism than trinitarianism.[14]

The creation account in Gen 2.7—about God breathing into the first man—was an act in which God imparted spirit to Adam, described as "the breath of life," thus making him "a living being." Accordingly, *man's spirit is what imparts life to man's body.* Moses implies this twice in the Pentateuch by referring to Yahweh as the "God of the spirits of all flesh" (Num 16.22; 27.16). Eduard Schweizer explains concerning the LXX, "the Greek translators often render 'breath of life' or 'life' as 'spirit.'"[15]

Consequently, the spirit departs from the body when a human being or an animal dies. James makes this quite clear of humans by stating, "the body without the spirit is dead" (James 2.26). As Moses infers, even animals have spirit as their source of life. Therefore, the psalmist says to God concerning animals, "You take away their spirit, they expire and return to their dust. You send forth Your Spirit, they are created" (Ps 104.29).

Two graphic examples in the NT testify to this truth. Only Luke informs that Jesus quoted Ps 31.5 while praying on the cross, "Father, INTO THY HANDS I COMMIT MY SPIRIT" (Lk 23.46). The Fourth Evangelist adds, "Jesus ... said, 'It is finished!' And He bowed His head and gave up His spirit" (Jn 19.30). So, when Jesus died His human spirit went back to the Father who gave it. Later, when Stephen, the first Christian martyr, was being stoned to death he cried out, "Lord Jesus, receive my spirit!" (Ac 7.59), and then he died.

Jannes Reiling contrasts the Bible's teaching with the traditional teaching about the Holy Spirit by rightly alleging, "Within the Bible neither *ruah* nor *pneuma* are used as a divine name. They are not worshipped as divine beings.... The OT does not represent the spirit as a divine being connected with, yet distinct from, God. It is always functioning as an intermediary between God and mankind.... In the NT the spirit is not envisaged as a divine being (hypostasis), but as an instrument of divine action or revelation."[16]

The Holy Spirit in the Old Testament

Lexicons and dictionaries of the OT show that the Hebrew word *ruach/ruah* not only means "spirit" but also "wind" or "breath." In the OT, the NASB translates *ruach* as "Spirit/spirit" 203x, "wind" 95x, and "breath" 31x.

Surprisingly, the expression, "the Holy Spirit," never occurs in the OT. But "Holy Spirit," without the article, appears 3x in the OT. Twice in the NASB it occurs as "His Holy Spirit," in Isa 63.10-11, and once as "Your Holy Spirit," in Ps 51.11. The addition of these personal pronouns signifies that this Spirit belongs to God. Also in the OT, "the/His Spirit" appears 36x; "the Spirit of the LORD" appears 22x; "the Spirit of God" appears 11x; "Your good Spirit" appears 2x; and "the Spirit of the LORD God" appears 1x.

In the OT, the Spirit of God is sometimes mentioned interchangeably with God. For instance, we read that "the Spirit of the LORD departed from [King] Saul" (1 Sam 16.14); yet "Saul was afraid of David, for the LORD was with him but

---

[14] Jaroslav Pelikan, *The Christian Tradition: A History of the Development of Doctrine: The Emergence of the Catholic Tradition* (Chicago: University, 1971), 214-15. Concerning those church fathers who did so, he cites Athanasius, Gregory of Nazianzus, and Basil of Caesarea along with their writings.

[15] Eduard Schweizer, *The Holy Spirit* [1978], tr. Reginald H. and Ilse Fuller (Philadelphia: Fortress, 1980), 37. He cites the following Scriptures as evidence: 1 Kings 17:17; Job 34:14; Dan. 5:23; 10:17; Isa. 38:12.

[16] Jannes Reiling, "Holy Spirit," in *DDD*, 418, 420, 423.

had departed from Saul" (18.12). Also, the OT often relates interchangeably the words, "God/the LORD said" and "the Spirit said."[17] But this identification of the Spirit with God does not require that the Spirit *is* God in all of His fulness; it only means God spoke by means of His Spirit.

In the OT, the Spirit of God often signifies God's manifestation of His power or His activity, if not His presence. James D.G. Dunn explains that in the OT, "'Spirit of God' is simply a way of speaking of God accomplishing his purpose in his world and through men."[18] Dunn further observes, "'Spirit of God' in Judaism denoted the power of God."[19] Dunn thus concludes concerning both the OT and pre-Christian Judaism, "The idea of God's Spirit as a power and presence (i.e., God's) which can be experienced in this world—that thought is well established.... But *of the Spirit as an entity in any sense independent of God, of Spirit as a divine hypostasis, there is nothing.*"[20]

When traditionalist theologians try to support their belief that God is omnipresent, they often cite Ps 139.7 as their foremost biblical text. It says, "Where can I go from Your Spirit? Or where can I flee from Your presence?"[21] King David wrote this, and he clearly implies therein that God's Spirit is everywhere. But David indicates that God Himself is not everywhere, for he writes a few verses earlier, "You know when I sit down and when I rise up; you discern my thoughts from far away" (v.2 NRSV), i.e., in heaven.

To assert that such texts mean God is everywhere borders on pantheism. Rather, the Bible portrays God as spatial, residing in heaven and seated on a throne;[22] yet it also depicts His Spirit as being everywhere.[23] Jesus spoke of God's locality, saying, "My/your Father who is in heaven" (13x in Mt), as if the Father is *only* in heaven. Solomon made the matter plain by saying, "God is in heaven and you [man] are on the earth" (Eccle 5.2).

God explains in the OT *how* His Spirit is everywhere. To the Prophet Zechariah, God gave a vision about seven lamps on a lampstand (Zech 4.1-3), and He said, "Not by might nor by power, but by My Spirit" (v. 6). Then He explained concerning the lamps, "these are the eyes of the LORD which range to and fro throughout the earth" (v. 10). That is, God's Spirit is like seven lamps that see like eyes throughout the whole earth. Earlier, Hanani the seer had explained to King Baasha of Israel, "For the eyes of the LORD move to and fro throughout the earth" (2 Chr 16.9). God later said to the Prophet Jeremiah, "My eyes are on all their ways" (Jer 16.17). So, God sees all things everywhere by His Spirit.

When King Solomon built the temple at Jerusalem and dedicated it, he indicated God's all-seeing ways by praying to Him, "heaven and the highest heaven cannot contain You; how much less this house" (2 Chr 6.18). Later, God said through the Prophet Isaiah, "Heaven is My throne, and the earth is My footstool" (Isa 66.1). And God made all of this clearer when He said through the Prophet Jeremiah, "'Can a man hide himself in hiding places, so I do not see

---

[17] E.g., cf. Isa 6.9 with Ac 28.25; cf. Jer 31.31, 33-34 with Heb 10.15.
[18] J.D.G. Dunn, *Christology in the Making*, 133. So also G.W.H. Lampe, *God as Spirit*, 50.
[19] J.D.G. Dunn, *Jesus and the Spirit*, 47.
[20] J.D.G. Dunn, *Christology in the Making*, 136. Emphasis his.
[21] Some scholars cite the non-canonical text, "The Spirit of the Lord fills the whole earth" (*Wisdom* 1.7).
[22] E.g., 1 Kgs 22.19; 2 Chron 18.18; Ps 9.4, 7; 11.4; 45.6; 47.8; 89.14; 93.2; 97.2; 99.1; 103.19; Isa 6.1; Eze 1.26-28; 43.7; Dan 7.9; Mt 5.34; 23.22; Heb 12.2; and God sitting on His heavenly throne in Rev 13x.
[23] See also 1 Kgs 8.27; 2 Chr 2.6; 6.18; Isa 66.1; Ac 7.49. I am not endorsing pantheism or other like -isms.

him?' declares the LORD. 'Do I not fill the heavens and the earth?' declares the LORD" (Jer 23.24). Yes, and it happens by means of His all-seeing Spirit.

The NT book of Revelation depicts Jesus as "a Lamb standing, as if slain, having seven horns and seven eyes, which are the seven Spirits of God, sent out into all the earth" (Rev 5.6). Though Jesus resides in heaven, He sees all by means of these spirits.

The Holy Spirit in the New Testament

The expression, "the Holy Spirit," i.e., with the article, is a NT phenomenon which appears therein 92x. "Holy Spirit" appears in two other forms in the NT: "His Holy Spirit" in 1 Th 4.8 and "a Holy Spirit" in Ac 19.2. About half of all instances of "(Holy) Spirit" in the NT are anarthrous, i.e., without the article.[24] Some scholars have thought that this suggests that the Spirit is not a Person. But it likely is no more than stylistic.[25] Yet readers are more likely to accept no capitalized "holy spirit" when there is no article, and they are more likely to conceive of holy spirit without the article as not being a person.

We have seen that the NT says God manifests Himself to the world by means of His Spirit through Jesus Christ. In Chapter Five/Acts of the Holy Spirit in the Life of Jesus, we saw that Matthew reports Jesus said, "But if I cast out demons by the Spirit of God, then the kingdom of God has come upon you" (Mt 12.28). Luke records this same saying, but he replaces "Spirit of God" with "finger of God" (Lk 11.20). This difference shows that the early Christians thought of God's Spirit as synonymous with God's power.

We also have seen that the NT often states that Jesus sits alongside God the Father on the Father's throne in heaven; yet the NT never states that the Holy Spirit sits there alongside them. This absence of the Holy Spirit indicates that there is no Trinity and that the Holy Spirit is not a Person, or hypostasis, separate from either God the Father or Jesus Christ. E. Flesseman-van Leer explains that the Holy Spirit is "not an independent entity alongside God, but the evidence of God's active presence in the world."[26]

In Chapter Seven, we learned that one would not think the Apostle Paul believed in the Trinity or that the Holy Spirit is a Person because he mentions God the Father and Jesus in the salutations of all ten of his NT letters without mentioning the Holy Spirit.[27] Similarly, the book of Revelation presents heavenly scenes in which the angels praise and honor both God (the Father) and Jesus Christ, yet the Holy Spirit is not mentioned. Some Trinitarian laypeople have deemed such silence a failure to provide equal recognition of the Holy Spirit and thus a slight; but they think that only because of their Trinitarianism.

Moreover, Paul provides significant insight into the relationship of God's Spirit to God by comparing it to the relationship of man's spirit to man. He does so by saying about future blessings that God will give His people, "these things God has revealed to us through the Spirit; for the Spirit searches everything, even the depths of God. For what human being knows what is truly human except the human spirit that is within? So also no one comprehends what is truly God's except the Spirit of God" (1 Cor 2.10-11 NRSV).

---

[24] Then why do translators always insert the article? Is it because they think it supports Trinitarianism?
[25] Gordon D. Fee, *God's Empowering Presence: The Holy Spirit in the Letters of Paul* (Peabody, MA: Hendrickson, 1994), 15-24.
[26] E. Flesseman-van Leer, *A Faith for Today*, 83-84.
[27] It is the same with salutations in other NT epistles, e.g., Jam 1.1; 2 Pt 1.1-2; 1 Jn 1.3; 2 Jn 1.3; Jude 1.1.

So, the Spirit of God resides in God, being intrinsic to God's nature, just as man's spirit resides in man as part of man's nature. And only God's Spirit knows God's mind, just as only man's spirit knows man's mind. Notice Paul distinguishes between God's mind and Spirit, although they are related, just as he sometimes does with man's mind and man's spirit. This Pauline language in 1 Cor 2.10-11 seems to negate the view that the Spirit of God is a full-fledged Person independent of God.

There may be a slight parallel between God's Spirit and man's spirit regarding the ability to extend beyond their being. For instance, Paul believed that he could be present in spirit but bodily separate from an assembly of believers. For he writes to the saints at Colossae, "For even though I am absent in body, nevertheless I am with you in spirit" (Col 2.5; cf. 1 Th 2.17). And he writes the same to the saints at Corinth (1 Cor 5.3-4).

Regarding the risen Jesus in the NT, "the Spirit of Jesus/Christ" is sometimes used interchangeably with "the Spirit of God." For instance, Paul writes to the saints at Rome, "the Spirit of God dwells in you. But if anyone does not have the Spirit of Christ, he does not belong to Him" (Rom 8.9; cf. Ac 16.6-7; Gal 4.6; Phil 1.19). Paul implicitly explains this when he writes of "one Spirit" (1 Cor 12.13; Eph 2.18; 4.4-6), thus equating Jesus' Spirit with God's Spirit. Yet James D.G. Dunn says of the NT, "However much the Spirit can be understood as the Spirit of Christ, the Spirit is still primarily the Spirit of God."[28]

Capitalizing Holy Spirit

One reason Christians think the Holy Spirit is a full-fledged Person is that English Bible versions usually capitalize "Holy Spirit" and "Spirit" when associated with God.[29] Yet, there is no upper and lower case in Hebrew. And ancient Greek had only capitals until upper and lower case were developed in the early Middle Ages. So, all of the early, extant, Greek MSS of the OT and the NT do not have upper and lower case for deciding "holy spirit" or "Holy Spirit."

Consequently, some capitalization in Bible versions represents interpretation by translators, and this is no less true of the "Holy Spirit" or "Spirit (of God)." Capitalizing these words likely indicates that those translators were Trinitarians. (The Holy Spirit is capitalized in this book to conform to its capitalization in the NASB, but not to indicate a divine Person.)

In contrast, Jews do not capitalize "Holy Spirit" or "Spirit (of God/LORD)" since they do not think these words indicate a separate Person from God. Instead, Jews generally believe the Spirit of God/LORD represents the power of God and perhaps in some sense God's presence. That is why Jewish translations of the Jewish Bible (OT) in English, e.g., the *New JPS Translation*, have "holy spirit" and "spirit of God/LORD."

Applying Personal Pronouns to the Holy Spirit

Most Christians also think the Holy Spirit is a full-fledged Person because nearly all Bible versions ascribe personal pronouns to the Holy Spirit.[30] Systematic theologian Charles Hodge therefore asserts, "The first argument

---

[28] J.D.G. Dunn, *Christology in the Making*, 148.
[29] For the inconsistency, and therefore ambiguity, of English Bible versions in capitalizing "Holy Spirit" or not, see Garrett C. Kenney, *Translating H/holy S/pirit: 4 Models: Unitarian, Binitarian, Trinitarian, and Non-Sectarian* (Lanham, MD: University Press of America, 2007).
[30] An example of those that don't is Edgar J. Goodspeed's *The New Testament: An American Translation*.

for the personality of the Holy Spirit is derived from the use of the personal pronouns in relation to Him."[31] The best example of this is what Jesus said about the Paraclete, recorded in the Gospel of John.

John relates that at the Last Supper, Jesus told the Eleven that He would leave them. He added, "I will ask the Father, and He will give you another Helper, that He may be with you forever" (Jn 14.16). "Helper" translates the masculine word *paracleton* in the Greek text, meaning "one called alongside" or "counselor." Jesus identified the counselor as "the Holy Spirit" (v. 26), which He called "the Spirit of truth" (Jn 14.17; 15.26; 16.13).

The Greek language has masculine, feminine, and neuter nouns and pronouns. In Greek grammar, an article attached to a noun, and a pronoun that refers to a noun, is usually in the same gender as its noun. Yet gender is usually irrelevant in Greek. Thus, little or nothing should be made of a pronoun that has the same gender as its referent. For instance, *pneuma*, the word for "spirit" in the Greek NT, is neuter in gender. If its gender is significant, any pronoun attached to it should be translated "it" rather than "he" or "she." Instead, the only way to decide which of these three translations is correct is to first determine the true gender of *pneuma*. So, whether to translate pronouns in the NT which refer to the Holy Spirit as "he" or "it" is decided by whether the Holy Spirit is a Person.

The same is true of other pronouns in Jesus' Johannine discourse on the Paraclete. For instance, the pronoun *ekeinos* appears therein five times in reference to *paracletos*, viz., the Holy Spirit (Jn 14.26; 15.26; 16.8, 13-14). This pronoun is in the masculine gender only because *paracletos* is masculine, thus rendering its gender insignificant. So, in these passages translators treat *ekeinos* either as "he" or "it" strictly on the basis of whether they believe the Holy Spirit is a Person, which, of course, is interpretation.

The same is true of some verbs in Jesus' discourse on the Paraclete, in Jn 14-16. For instance, three verbs in the Greek text of Jn 16.13 describe the Paraclete's activities, and these three verbs are in the future, active, indicative, third person singular. Whether they are translated "He will guide" and "He will (not) speak," or the English masculine pronoun "He" is replaced with the neuter "it," depends on whether one believes that "the Spirit of truth," which is the Holy Spirit, is a Person.

But there are many other NT examples of personal pronouns being applied to the Holy Spirit. Luke's book of Acts is all about the Holy Spirit ministering through the early Christians. Luke says of the Apostle Peter, "the Spirit said to him, 'Behold, three men are looking for you.... I have sent them'" (Ac 10.20). Luke later relates concerning the church at Antioch, "the Holy Spirit said, 'Set apart for Me Barnabas and Saul for the work to which I have called them'" (Ac 13.2). As they went about preaching the gospel, Luke says they were "forbidden by the Holy Spirit to speak the word in Asia" (Ac 16.6).

Therefore, Bible versions can differ on how they treat pronouns referring to God's "S/spirit." For instance, the Apostle Paul wrote to the saints at Rome, "The Spirit Himself bears witness with our spirit that we are children of God" (Rom 8.16; cf. v. 26). Most NT versions translate the pronoun *auto* in the Greek text, which refers to the first occurrence of *pneuma* (spirit), as "Himself" or "himself" (RSV, NRSV, NASB, NIV, JB, NEB, TEV, ESV). This rendering suggests that those translators were Trinitiarians who believed it refers to a Person. Yet the AV renders *auto* in both Rom 8.16 and v. 26 as "itself."

---

[31] C. Hodge, *Systematic Theology*, 1:524.

Binitarian C.F.D. Moule explains regarding the Bible applying personal pronouns to the Holy Spirit, "the appeal to Scripture,... proves nothing as to the eternal 'being' of the Spirit. It only shows that 'Spirit' is a word for a personal God's personal activity." Moule concludes, "the fact that Spirit is the mode by which a personal God is present does not seem, in itself, to necessitate the recognition of Spirit as essentially personal;... it seems gratuitous to insist on using a personal pronoun" for the Holy Spirit.[32]

The manifestation of God's Spirit to humans seems to signify God's presence even though His Being is localized on a heavenly throne. Yet we learned in Chapter Four that God told Moses His presence would go with Israel as a guardian angel.[33]

Personifying the Holy Spirit

Another reason most Christians think the Holy Spirit is a Person is that the Bible personifies the Holy Spirit just as it does God's Word and Wisdom. This makes it *seem* that Spirit, Word, and Wisdom are real persons when in reality they are not. Thus, when the Bible relates that the Holy Spirit said something, this should not be understood as attributing personality to the Holy Spirit. Jesus once said, "wisdom is vindicated by her deeds/children" (Mt 11.19/Lk 7.35). Another time He said, "the wisdom of God said, 'I will send to them prophets and apostles'" (Lk 11.49). Neither time did He intend to depict wisdom as a person. The best OT example of the personification of wisdom is in Prov 8—9.6. (See Chapter Six/Wisdom Christology.) The Bible frequently personifies inanimate objects and human attributes; yet their authors do not mean that these are actual persons.

The same misunderstanding has occurred in Judaism. Erik Sjoberg informs:

> The autonomy of the Spirit in Judaism is surprising. In Rabbinic writings the Spirit is often spoken of in personal categories. There are many instances of the Spirit speaking, crying, admonishing, sorrowing, weeping, rejoicing, comforting etc.... For this reason it has often been thought that the Spirit is regarded in Judaism as a hypostasis, as a personal angelic being. But this is to introduce ideas which are not in keeping with the Jewish view. The Spirit is no angelic or heavenly being.[34]

The Bible personifies the Holy Spirit by ascribing personal activities to the Spirit. For instance, the Spirit participated in creation, spoke the Word of God through prophets, and imparts life. With regard to believers, the NT says the Holy Spirit indwells, guides, empowers, teaches, and seals them for the day of redemption. It is God the Father who does these things, and He accomplishes them through Jesus by means of God's Spirit.

A most important activity of the Holy Spirit is the spreading of the Word of God. The Apostle Peter explains about OT prophecy, that "men moved by the Holy Spirit spoke from God" (2 Pt 1.21). So, God speaks His Word by the instrumentation of His Spirit.

Another activity of the Holy Spirit is the giving of spiritual gifts to believers. Paul informs that "there are varieties of gifts, but the same the Spirit" who gives them (1 Cor 12.4). The author of Hebrews explains that "the Holy Spirit" gives these gifts "according to His own will" (Heb 2.4). (The words "His own" translate the pronoun *auto*, which, again, can be translated "he," "she," or "it.") The Spirit

---

[32] C.F.D. Moule, *The Holy Spirit*, 45-46, 50-51.
[33] E.g., Ex 23.20, 23; 32.34; 33.2, 14-15; cf. Isa 63.9; Lk 1.19.
[34] Erik Sjoberg, "pneuma," in *TDNT*, 3:387.

having a "will" indicates that the mind of God is connected to His own Spirit (cf. 1 Cor 2.11). Although these gifts are given by the Holy Spirit, Paul says they are "from God" and Christ (1 Cor 7.7; cf. Rom 11.29; 2 Tim 1.6; Eph 4.7-11). Even the Holy Spirit is a gift from God (Ac 2.38; 10.45).

It seems the primary activity of the Holy Spirit is teaching and sanctifying God's people. Jesus told His disciples that He would send the Paraclete to "teach you all things, and bring to your remembrance all that I said to you" and "convict the world concerning sin, and righteousness, and judgment" (Jn 14.26; 16.8). Paul says "the Spirit helps our weaknesses; for we do not know how to pray as we should, but the Spirit Himself intercedes for us with groanings" (Rom 8.26). (Again, the word "Himself" translates the pronoun *auto*.) Paul writes of being "sanctified by the Holy Spirit" (Rom 15.16). Peter writes of "the sanctifying work of the Spirit" (1 Pt 1.2). All of this corresponds to Jesus asking the Father concerning His disciples, "Sanctify them in the truth" (Jn 17.17).

When the early Christians disputed among themselves about the Law of Moses, they convened a council at Jerusalem and came to an agreement about the matter. Then they issued a letter that included the words, "it seemed good to the Holy Spirit and to us" (Ac 15.28). This ascribes a thinking process to the Holy Spirit, thus a link to God's mind.

Does ascribing these personal activities to the Holy Spirit indicate that the Spirit is a Person? Not at all. *Any activity of the Holy Spirit represents the mind of God revealing His will or unleashing His power (1 Cor 2.4-5). Thus, God's mind or power is the best way to think of the Holy Spirit.* James D.G. Dunn explains, "*Spirit of God is in no sense distinct from God*, but is simply the power of God, *God himself acting powerfully in nature and upon men.*"[35]

A Christian should never conclude from her or his experiences of the Holy Spirit that these are evidence that the Spirit is a Person. That is mere subjectivism. The only proper course in comprehending our experiences is to rely upon what Scripture says.

The Bible also personifies the Holy Spirit by attributing emotions to it. Isaiah says of God that Israel "rebelled and grieved His Holy Spirit" (Isa 63.10). Paul warns, "do not grieve the Holy Spirit of God" (Eph 4.30), and "(d)o not quench the Spirit" (1 Th 5.19).

The Bible often ascribes body parts to God without saying they are physical. Most interpreters claim that these are anthropomorphisms, i.e., assigning a function to God that should not be understood as literally true of Him. For example, the Bible ascribes to God the following external body parts, e.g., head, hair, eyes, face, mouth, nostrils, back, arm, hand, and feet. The Bible also attributes to God internal things, e.g., heart, soul, mind, and will. And the Bible describes God as seeing, hearing, smelling, walking, and sitting.

But the Bible never ascribes body parts to the Holy Spirit,[36] and it never describes the Holy Spirit as walking or sitting. We saw in Chapter Ten that the book of Revelation often describes God (the Father) and Jesus Christ the Lamb as sitting together on God's throne in heaven; yet it never says the same of the Holy Spirit. Such evidence suggests that God really does walk and sit, but His Spirit does not do either as a separate entity.

---

[35] J.D.G. Dunn, *Christology in the Making*, 133. Emphasis his.
[36] When Jesus said He casts out demons by "the finger of God" (Lk 11.20), Luke does not correlate it with the Holy Spirit. This should not be understood as ascribing a body part to the Holy Spirit. A comparison of other sayings of Jesus indicates that it is a figure of speech referring to the *power* of the Holy Spirit.

The OT commands us to worship God and Him only (esp. Isa 45-47). The NT tells us to believe in God the Father and in His Son, Jesus Christ. The Johannine Jesus says of Himself that, in the future, "all may honor the Son, even as they honor the Father" (Jn 5.23). Yet the Bible never commands us to believe in, worship, praise, or honor the Holy Spirit.

Finally, Jesus often prayed to God the Father, and so taught his disciples, but there is no evidence in the NT gospels that Jesus ever prayed to the Holy Spirit.

To sum, all personification of the Holy Spirit in the Bible does not indicate that the Spirit is a Person or a hypostasis to be distinguished from God the Father.

Ascribing Impersonal Functions to the Holy Spirit

Sometimes, the Bible ascribes impersonal functions to the Holy Spirit, i.e., actions that do not seem characteristic of personhood. For example, the Prophet Joel proclaims on behalf of Yahweh regarding the last days, "I will pour out My Spirit on all mankind;... Before the great and awesome day of the LORD comes" (Joel 3.28-31). The Apostle Peter quoted this prophecy on the church's first Day of Pentecost, claiming it happened then, surely as a partial fulfillment (Ac 2.16-21). The act of pouring out the Spirit does not seem to fit personhood. Jannes Reiling explains, "in the NT the spirit is not envisaged as a divine being (*hupostasis*), but as an instrument of divine action or revelation."[37]

Neither does the baptism of the Holy Spirit seem conducive to personhood. John the Baptist announced that Jesus would "baptize you with the Holy Spirit" (Mt 3.11/Mk 1.8/Lk 3.16; cf. Jn 1.33). The resurrected Jesus appeared to His disciples and performed a preliminary event to baptism when He "breathed on them, and said to them, 'Receive the Holy Spirit'" (Jn 20.22). And ten days before Jesus ascended into heaven, He told His disciples, "you shall be baptized with the Holy Spirit not many days from now" (Ac 1.5).

The Apostle Peter later evangelized Cornelius and his household. Cornelius was a Roman centurion and a devout believer in God. Then "the Holy Spirit fell upon all those who were listening to the message.... they were ... speaking in tongues and exalting God" (Ac 10.44, 46). Peter later told this event to his skeptical brethren at Jerusalem, saying, "the Holy Spirit fell upon them, just as He did upon us at the beginning" (Ac 11.15). (Here, the NASB inserts "He did" even though it is not in the Greek text.) So, the baptism of the Holy Spirit is equated with the Spirit falling on these new believers and anointing them (2 Cor 1.21; 1 Jn 2.20, 27; cf. Ac 4.27; 10.38).

The result of the Spirit's initial baptizing and outpouring is that the Spirit *fills* believers. On that Day of Pentecost, the Spirit baptized and "filled" Jesus' disciples who were gathered together at Jerusalem (Ac 2.1-4). Afterwards, the NT relates that on eight different occasions one of Jesus' disciples (or a group of them) was "filled with the Holy Spirit."[38] Paul says believers are "sealed ... with the Holy Spirit" (Eph 1.13), and he commands them to "be filled with the Spirit" (Eph 5.18). He explains, "we were all made to drink of one Spirit" (1 Cor 12.13). These acts—baptizing, filling, pouring, sealing, and drinking—are incompatible with personhood. G.W.H. Lampe states, "'the Spirit of God' is to be understood,

---

[37] J. Reiling, "Holy Spirit," 423.
[38] Lk 1.15, 41, 67; Ac 2.4; 4.8, 31; 9.17; 13.9; Eph 5.18.

not as referring to a divine hypostasis distinct from God the Father ... but as indicating God himself as active towards and in his human creation."[39]

According to the NT, Jesus spoke often of His relationship with God. The best evidence is His constant practice of calling God "the/My Father." But the NT never tells of a personal relationship of God or Jesus with the Holy Spirit. For example, it never says God or Jesus loves the Holy Spirit, or vice versa. Similarly, the Bible often mentions the love of God, which indicates personhood. The reason for these omissions seems to be that the Holy Spirit is not a Person. Yet Paul informs about the fruits of the Holy Spirit, the first being love (Gal 5.22). And he mentions "the love of the Holy Spirit" (Rom 15.30). Perhaps God loves by means of His Spirit.

A curious anomaly for Trinitarianism is that the Holy Spirit does not have a name. It is a personal thing to have a name. All humans have names. Even angels have names. God has a name—YHWH. "Holy Spirit" is not a name,[40] despite what a few scholars say. So, *another reason the Holy Spirit is not a Person is that the Spirit does not have a name.*

The Holy Spirit as the Spirit of the Father

The NT has much evidence demonstrating that *the Holy Spirit is a part of God's nature and therefore cannot be a separate, independent entity from Him.* Since the NT identifies God exclusively as the Father, it sometimes designates the Holy Spirit, either explicitly or implicitly, as the Spirit of the Father. For instance, Matthew records that when Jesus sent out seventy disciples to minister and preach, He instructed them about opposition, saying, "do not become anxious about how or what you will speak;... For it is not you who speak, but it is the Spirit of your Father who speaks in you" (Mt 10.20). He meant the Holy Spirit since Mark records that Jesus said the same thing in His Olivet Discourse and explained, "it is not you who speak, but it is the Holy Spirit" (Mk 13.11). And Luke has Jesus saying, "the Holy Spirit will teach you in that very hour what you ought to say" (Lk 12.12). To conclude otherwise—that the Holy Spirit and the Spirit of the Father are not the same—is to attribute two Spirits to God the Father.

According to Luke, Jesus is the Son of God because of His Virgin Birth. For, the angel Gabriel told Mary, "The Holy Spirit will come upon you, and the power of the Most High [God the Father] will overshadow you; and for that reason the holy offspring shall be called the Son of God" (Lk 1.35). If the Holy Spirit is a hypostasis, i.e., a separate subsistence from God the Father, shouldn't Jesus be called "the son of the Holy Spirit"?[41] But Luke indicates that the Spirit is not a hypostasis or Person, but "the power" of God.

Paul clearly identifies the Spirit of God as the Spirit of the Father. He writes to the saints at Rome of "the Spirit of God" and "the Spirit of Him who raised Jesus from the dead," who was the Father (Rom 8.9, 11). Paul writes similarly to the saints at Ephesus, "I bow my knees before the Father," adding that he prays for them to be "strengthened with power through His Spirit" (Eph 3.14, 16).

Does Scripture Identify the Holy Spirit as God?

Trinitarian Karl Rahner admits that there is little scriptural support that the Holy Spirit is a Person. And he says, "*ho theos* [God] is never used in the New

---

[39] G.W.H. Lampe, *God as Spirit*, 11.
[40] See Chapter Five/Is the Doctrine of the Trinity in Matthew 28.19?
[41] Cf. Greaser-Lynn-Schoenheit, *One God & One Lord*, 599; James H. Broughton and Peter J. Southgate, *The Trinity: True or False?* (Nottingham, England: "The Dawn" Book Supply, 1995), 102.

Testament to speak of the *pneuma agion* [Holy Spirit]," and "*theos* is still never used of the Spirit."[42] Murray Harris echoes this in saying, "the NT never uses *ho theos* of the Holy Spirit.[43]

Yet many Trinitarians cite Peter's words in Ac 5.4 as their primary NT support that the Holy Spirit is God.[44] The background of this text is that the early Christians gathered at Jerusalem and agreed to share all of their properties among themselves. They treated them "in common;... sharing them with all as anyone might need" (Ac 2.44-45). Later, "a certain man named Ananias, with his wife Saphira, sold a piece of property, and kept back some of the price for himself, with his wife's full knowledge, and bringing a portion of it, he laid it at the apostles' feet. But Peter said, 'Ananias, why has Satan filled your heart to lie to the Holy Spirit, and to keep back some of the price of the land?... You have not lied to men, but to God'" (Ac 5.1-4). Trinitarians insist that their lying "to the Holy Spirit" and "to God" implies the Spirit is God. On the contrary, the most that can be deduced from this is that by lying to the Spirit they lied to God, since God sent His Spirit.

John Calvin cited this statement by Peter, as well as Paul's teaching on the Spirit indwelling the saints, as evidence that the Spirit is God. Paul wrote inquiring of the saints at Corinth, "Do you not know that you are a temple of God, and that the Spirit of God dwells in you?" (1 Cor 3.16; cf. 6.19). Calvin here wrongly equates "God" and "the Spirit of God;"[45] instead, it means simply that God indwells believers by means of His Spirit.

So, some scholars equate God with His Spirit.[46] This doesn't quite seem correct since the Spirit is a part of God's Being, just as a human spirit is a part of a human being.

Jesus said "God is spirit" (Jn 4.24). Most versions do not capitalize "spirit," here, indicating that those translators, most of whom were surely Trinitarians, did not think that Jesus referred to the Holy Spirit. Indeed, He did not mean this as a definition of God but that God belongs to the realm of spirit.[47]

Paul writes similarly, apparently of Jesus, by saying "the Lord is the Spirit" (2 Cor 3.17). This has been variously interpreted. It likely means that the Spirit represents Jesus, not that Jesus is identified as the Spirit.

To sum, *the Spirit of God is to God what the spirit of man is to man because man was made in the image of God.* So, the Holy Spirit is not a Person or a hypostasis separate from God the Father but His very life and power. This impersonal Spirit is inherent in not only the Father but now in His Son, Jesus Christ, and it emanates throughout the universe.

---

[42] Karl Rahner, *Theological Investigations*, tr. Cornelius Ernst, 14 vols. (Baltimore: Helicon, 1961), 1:143, 138.
[43] M. Harris, *Jesus as God*, 43.
[44] E.g., Stanley D. Toussaint, "Acts," in *The Bible Knowledge Commentary: An Exposition of the Scriptures by Dallas Seminary Faculty: New Testament*, eds. John F. Walvoord and Roy B. Zuck (Wheaton, IL: Victor, 1983), 365.
[45] J. Calvin, *Institutes*, 1.13.15.
[46] E.g., G.W. H. Lampe, *God as Spirit*.
[47] Similarly, J.G.D. Dunn, *Jesus and the Spirit*, 353.

Appendix C: Modern Christologies

High and Low Christologies	Judaical/Anthropological Christologies
A Hellenized Christology	Functional/vs. Ontological Christology
A Late, Liturgical Christology	Process Theology
Development/Evolutionary Christology	

An introduction to Christology would be incomplete without at least a brief consideration of the prominent christologies that have been formulated in modern times. Partly as a result of biblical criticism and the History of Religions School, the 20th century witnessed an explosion in scholarly investigation of the identity of Jesus.[1] Some of these christological approaches emerged in reaction to the traditional, Nicaea-Chalcedonian Christology of church fathers. Even the RCC's venerable Pontifical Biblical Commission acknowledged in its important christological document, *Bible et christologie*, that the recent, christological gains achieved from biblical criticism and historical investigation should not be ignored. The commission even cautioned against the ultra-conservative, fundamentalist mentality, which it admitted was still quite prevalent in its own church, that only cared about defending traditional Christology (classical Trinitarianism).[2] R.E. Brown advocates a judicious attitude by insisting, "Despite the differences among scholars ... Christology is so important ... that one should not express judgments without seriously looking at the evidence."[3]

High and Low Christology

Years ago, traditionalists introduced the terms "high" and "low" Christology. The Nicene-Chalcedonian faith was labeled a "high Christology." The liberal view, in which Jesus was regarded as no more than a man and as a model example, was deemed a "low Christology." In deciding on this terminology, traditionalists argued that it was more prudent theologically to adhere to a high Christology than a low Christology. They meant that it would be better to ascribe *too much* to Jesus than *too little*, i.e., to believe that Jesus *is* God rather than that He *is less* than God. Maurice Wiles explains, "In the case of Nicene Christology, it is tempting to suggest that it was the true development because it gave the 'highest' account of the person of Christ, because it took most seriously the worshipping tradition of the church. But such criterion is clearly unreliable."[4]

---

[1] L.W. Hurtado, *One God, One Lord*, 12.
[2] *Bible et christologie*, 1.1.1.2; 1.1.3.3; 1.2.1.2; 1.2.3. See also J.A. Fitzmyer's (*Scripture and Christology*, 54-96) critique of this important document.
[3] R.E. Brown, *Introduction to New Testament Christology*, 11.
[4] M. Wiles, *The Making of Christian Doctrine*, 168.

Indeed, you can err by ascribing too much to Jesus just as you can by ascribing too little. For example, consider the Catholic Church's veneration of Mary.[5] Protestants allege that the RCC adopts a far higher view of Mary than does the Bible.[6] Such exaltation of Mary results in Catholic parishioners failing to give Jesus His due, i.e., that Jesus is Lord. *Similar to the Catholic Church's veneration of Mary, Christians who advocate high Christology—that Jesus is God—allot too much to Jesus and thereby fail to give God the Father His due, i.e., that God is the sovereign Lord over all, including Christ.* J.A.T. Robinson explains, "There has been a problem of 'over-belief,' of *having* to ascribe everything to Jesus for fear of under-belief."[7]

More recently, scholars have sort of redefined this high and low terminology, thus rendering the former meanings somewhat obsolete. A high Christology is now called a Christology "from above" or "descent Christology." It means that one approaches the identity of Jesus either from the perspective of the Incarnation of the Logos and Jesus' filial relation to God or, more traditionally, from the credal perspective of Jesus as the ontological God-man (Nicaea) with a two-nature (Chalcedon) Christology. A low Christology, on the other hand, is now reckoned as a Christology "from below" or "ascent Christology." It means that one begins an examination of the identity of Jesus from the perspective of the historical Jesus, i.e., that Jesus was a Jewish man who was born and lived in the Galilee and had a Jewish culture and religion.[8] Most contemporary scholars intend by these definitions that neither of these two categories, which merely represent starting points for one's quest for Jesus' identity, is superior theologically to the other.[9]

A Hellenized Christology

One result of the History of Religions School was that Wilhelm Bousset theorized in his book, *Kyrios Christos* (1913), that the primitive Palestinian Christian community was strictly monotheistic but that the veneration of Jesus as God was developed later by the Gentile Christian communities after Christianity had spread into Gentile lands. Bousset speculated that these Gentiles, influenced by Greco-Roman polytheistic culture, attached themselves to the Jesus Movement and compromised its former monotheism.

Many critical scholars used to embrace this viewpoint. They alleged that this late NT Christology began no earlier than the 50s, witnessed by Paul's letters, and that it did not become prevalent until near the end of the 1st century or later, as first evidenced in the Gospel of John. Yet, if this is true we should expect that the parent church communities in Judea and Galilee would have scrutinized such a significant departure from Jewish monotheism and that this

---

[5] Examples of the RCC's veneration of Mary are its doctrines of the Immaculate Conception, the Assumption of Mary, and that Mary is "the Mother of God." The Immaculate Conception means that Mary, like Jesus, did not possess a sin nature and thus never sinned. The Assumption of Mary means that at her death she was bodily transported to heaven. Moreover, there is currently a strong movement within the RCC to officially recognize Mary as the Co-Redemptrix, which means that she shares equally with Jesus in the saving work of redemption.
[6] Catholics have gone too far in praising Mary; Protestants have overreacted, not giving Mary her due.
[7] J.A.T. Robinson, *The Human Face of God*, 74. Emphasis his.
[8] E.g., see The Pontifical Biblical Commission's statement on Christology, entitled *Bible et christologie* (1981), in *Scripture & Christology: A Statement of the Biblical Commission with a Commentary*, tr. Joseph A. Fitzmyer, S.J. (New York: Paulist, 1986), 1.1.11 (= 17), 90.
[9] J.A. Fitzmyer, *Scripture & Christology*, 90.

would be evident in the literature. But it isn't. Besides, this Hellenized view of Christianity is now rendered virtually untenable,[10] i.e., except for one thing. Bousset was right about the subsequent deifying of Jesus; but it occurred at a later stage in the development of church Christology, i.e., perhaps beginning no earlier than in the early 2nd century, and therefore it does not emerge in any of the NT documents.

A Late, Liturgical Christology

A similar but more conservative approach now being advocated by several distinguished scholars is that traditional Christology was a late, liturgical Christology that developed in the latter half of the 1st century but was not Hellenized.[11] These traditionalist scholars postulate that the early Christians of the first decades of Christianity did not call Jesus "God" but that this practice developed later, beginning *only* with their worship and therefore *not* their didactical literature. For example, R.E. Brown regards that Jn 1.1c, 18, 20.28, Rom 9.5, Heb 1.8, and 2 Pt 1.1 are hymns or doxologies that call Jesus "God."[12] He claims that when these documents were written, "the NT use of 'God' for Jesus is not yet truly a dogmatic formulation, but appears in a liturgical or cultic context."[13] He says, "the title 'God' was applied to Jesus more quickly in liturgical formulae than in narrative or epistolary literature."[14] He further observes that these particular texts that call Jesus "God" only describe Jesus either during His preexistence or after His resurrection and therefore not during His earthly life. Brown therefore asserts that in NT usage, "the title 'God' is not directly given to the Jesus of the ministry" or "to define Jesus essentially."[15] He concludes that "there is no reason to think that Jesus was called God in the earliest layers of New Testament tradition."[16] Therefore, calling the earthly Jesus "God" was "a post-New Testament development" apparently attributable to Ignatius of Antioch.[17]

While R.E. Brown and others are no doubt correct about many of these points, their late, liturgical Christology impugns the integrity of the Fourth Gospel. For it requires that Thomas' confession, in Jn 20.28>, is not historical but a fictional creation of the Johannine church community inserted into that truly historical pericope.[18] But this interpretation seems to beg the question. Brown defends it

---

[10] L.W. Hurtado, *One God, One Lord*, 3-15.

[11] R.E. Brown, *Jesus God and Man*, 29-38=*An Introduction to New Testament Christology*, 190-95; A.W. Wainwright, "The Confession Jesus Is 'God' in the New Testament," *SJT* 10 (1957): 295; Joseph A. Fitzmyer, "The Semitic Background of the New Testament *Kyrios*-Title," *A Wandering Aramaean: Collected Aramaic Essays: SBL Monograph 25* (Missoula: 1979), 131; idem, *A Christological Catechism: New Testament Answers*, rev. ed. (New York: Paulist, 1991), 97-98; R.T. France, "The Worship of Jesus: A Neglected Factor in Christological Debate," *Christ the Lord*, 17-36; Ralph P Martin, "Some Reflections on the New Testament Hymns," *Christ the Lord*, 49; J.D.G. Dunn, *Unity and Diversity in the New Testament*, 2nd ed., 226. R.N. Longenecker (*The Christology of Early Jewish Christianity*, 139-41) tentatively subscribes to a mixture of this view with others. M. Harris (*Jesus As God*, 276) cites J.L. D'Aragon (*Jesus: De l'histoire a la foi* [Montreal: Fides, 1974], 201) as currently the foremost spokesperson of this view.

[12] R.E. Brown, *John (i-xii)*, 24. See table 1 above.

[13] R.E. Brown, *John (xiii-xxi)*, 1047.

[14] R.E. Brown, *John (i-xii)*, 24.

[15] R.E. Brown, *Jesus God and Man*, 36-37.

[16] R.E. Brown, *Jesus God and Man*, 30; idem, *An Introduction to New Testament Christology*, 190.

[17] R.E. Brown, *Jesus God and Man*, 37.

[18] E.g., R.E. Brown, *John (xiii-xxi)*, 1047-48.

by insisting, "Were the title 'God' used for Jesus so soon after the resurrection, one could not explain the absence of this title in Christian confessions before the 60's."[19] This is a most significant point which traditionalists need to seriously consider. Yet, this point is irrelevant to the christological viewpoint of this book, which treats Thomas' confession as historical though not an affirmation that Jesus is God.

Traditionalist Robert L. Reymond rightly rejects this late, liturgical theory as the "offspring" of radical form criticism. He argues cogently that the notion

> "that the early church could confess in worship what it neither could conceptualize nor dare to express in nonliturgical prose or narrative is to impute an uncommonly low level of reflective capability to the first-century Christians and their leaders and to suggest that it was not their primary concern that their worship be in accordance with truth and fact. Worship must be grounded in sound doctrine. Any confession of faith must be sound likewise. Are we to suppose that the early church did not understand this? The biblical evidence would indicate that [it did] ... The apostles and the early church were deeply concerned with sound doctrine, and aberrations were not tolerated."[20]

Indeed, it seems just the opposite; church leaders would have only allowed the introduction of hymns into their corporate worship that corresponded with their already established sound doctrine and not that hymnal lyrics and ecstatic utterances of worship would dictate doctrine. Yet Reymond ignores the problem which Brown highlights for traditionalists: "How do you explain the absence of Jesus being called 'God' in the early layers of NT tradition?" R.N. Longenecker, who tentatively subscribes to this late, liturgical Christology, nevertheless acknowledges that "a convincing rationale for this phenomena seems yet to be forthcoming,"[21] and he doubts that it ever will.[22]

That is exactly what the New History of Religions School is attempting to do. (See Chapter Four.) These traditionalist scholars argue that a much shorter period of time elapsed between the Christ event and the early Christians first claiming that Jesus was God, a time period of perhaps only a few years to a maximum of twenty years.

Developmental vs. Evolutionary Christology

C.F.D. Moule championed a hypothesis he called "developmental Christology" as opposed to the "evolutionary Christology" of "Late, Hellenized Christology" and "Late, Liturgical Christology." That is, Moule accepted the view that the explicit identification of Jesus as God in the NT was a late development therein; yet he insisted that it derived from primitive Christology. In other words, Moule contended that the NT does not introduce any substantially new christological features, e.g., the deity of Christ, beyond what is found in the synoptics and Acts, and he even traces the identification of Jesus as God back to Jesus Himself. Moule thus sees "all the various estimates of Jesus reflected in the New Testament as, in essence, only attempts to describe what was already there from the beginning."[23]

---

[19] R.E. Brown, *Jesus God and Man*, 30n52.
[20] R.L. Reymond, *Jesus, Divine Messiah*, 319.
[21] R.N. Longenecker, *The Christology of Early Jewish Christianity*, 139.
[22] R.N. Longenecker, *The Christology of Early Jewish Christianity*, 140.
[23] C.F.D. Moule, *The Origin of Christology*, 2-3.

Judaical and Anthropological Christologies

In the ongoing Third Quest for the historical Jesus, both rabbinical and Christian scholars are rightly emphasizing the Jewishness of Jesus, that He was an eschatological prophet who lived among Jews and participated in the Jewish religio-culture in His Jewish homeland. In contrast, when classical Christology was developed, the Church failed to adequately recognize Jesus as a Jew largely because it was composed of mostly Gentiles and had become somewhat anti-Semitic. These scholars are therefore attempting to correct the traditional perception of a somewhat Gentile Jesus.

Many anthropological christologies were also formed during the 19th and 20th centuries which focused on Jesus only philosophically as the archetypal man, i.e., the perfect model for a supposedly evolving society, who provides profound meaning to human existence. Others, e.g., the recent Jesus Seminar, are based on a bare-bones, primitive portrait of Jesus derived only from the supposedly earliest strata of the NT gospel testimony.

Most of these Judaic and anthropological christologies have one thing in common: they are humanistic because they regard Jesus as no more than a famous, itinerant preacher-prophet, if not a sage. Nevertheless, a few scholars who propose an anthropological Christology adhere to the fundamentals of the Christian gospel, i.e., that Jesus became the resurrected, exalted Redeemer.

Functional vs. Ontological Christology

Returning to a more traditional approach, in the second half of the 20th century many notable Christian scholars proposed various christologies as an explication for the dearth of biblical evidence supporting an ontological Christology, i.e., that Jesus is God by nature. One of these is "functional Christology." We saw in Chapter One that many scholars who avoid the formulation, "Jesus is God," nevertheless conclude that a bare, few biblical texts do indeed call Him "God." Primarily on the basis of this scanty evidence, they propose that the NT only calls Jesus "God" functionally.[24] Some of them outright deny that Jesus was God ontologically;[25] but others do not.[26] (It is well known that Luther preferred to describe the relationship between God and Christ in functional terms rather than the customary metaphysical language of trinitarian formulations.) But in doing so, aren't these scholars following a similar path as that forged by the apologists, who designated Christ as "God" with qualifications? As suggested earlier, such a God is logically less than full deity.

Scholars who adopt this functional Christology, and therefore find the NT very restrained in calling Christ "God," hold a position very close to that set forth in this book. Sometimes, the only difference is that they regard only a few biblical texts, in some cases only Jn 20.28,[27] as calling Jesus "God."

Process Theology

Process theology emerged during the last quarter of the 20th century. This growing movement rightly challenges some aspects of classical theism that relate to Christology, e.g., that God is absolutely transcendent, unconditionally

---

[24] E.g., O. Cullmann, *Christology*, 3-4; G.H. Boobyer, "Jesus As 'Theos' in the New Testament," 250, 260.
[25] E.g., G.H. Boobyer, "Jesus As *'Theos'* in the New Testament," 250, 260; E. Flesseman-van Leer, *A Faith for Today*, 69.
[26] E.g., O. Cullmann, *Christology*, 306-14.
[27] E.g., R. Bultmann, *Essays*, 276.

sovereign, totally omniscient, inertly immutable, and stoically impassible. More particularly, process theology generally denies the two-nature Christology and the doctrine of the Trinity. But while affirming the complete humanity of Jesus as well as God's immanence in Him, like the old liberals, most process theologians stray from the NT mooring by denying Jesus' resurrection and any supernaturalism to His works. Despite the critical gains of process theology over classical theism, its Christology represents a resurgence of Ebionism, with some process thinkers even positing that Jesus sinned.[28]

For other christologies not explained in this appendix, see Kenotic Christology in Chapter Three, Agent (=Sending) Christology in Chapters Six and Ten, and both Adam Christology and God-in-Christ Christology in Chapter Seven.

---

[28] Bruce Demarest, "Process Reduction of Jesus and the Trinity," *Process Theology*, ed. Ronald Nash (Grand Rapids: Baker, 1987), 69.

Glossary

ANTI-SEMITISM. Prejudice against Jews. (However, in fairness to other Semitic peoples, e.g., Arabs, it should be recognized that this term is used more narrowly than it otherwise connotes.)

APOCALYPTIC. The "revealing" (Gr. *apocalypse*) about the end times, i.e., how God mysteriously and secretively intervenes in human affairs to establish justice and righteousness on earth through His kingdom.

APOSTOLIC FATHERS. Church fathers who lived during the age immediately following the NT period.

ATONEMENT. Jesus' suffering and death on the cross were expiatory in that He mystically bore the sins of others. To be distinguished from the atonement of OT sacrifices, which only temporarily covered sins.

BIBLICAL CRITIC. One who employs biblical criticism.

BIBLICAL CRITICISM. The literary discipline of a detailed analysis of the Bible. It includes the origin of its books and letters according to authorship, dates of composition, and possible written sources used (source criticism), the forms of oral tradition preceding composition (form criticism), and subsequent editorializing of MSS (redaction criticism). "Biblical criticism" does not necessarily imply a critical or negative view of the Bible.

BINITARIANISM. Belief in the Father and Jesus as two Persons who are either equally or unequally God, with either no opinion or a variety of opinions on the identity of the Holy Spirit, but not that He/it is God.

CHRIST EVENT, THE. Jesus' earthly life, death, resurrection, and ascension to heaven.

CHRISTOCENTRIC. Jesus Christ is emphasized more than God the Father is.

CHRISTOLOGY. Narrowly, the study of Jesus as the Christ. Broadly, the study of everything about Jesus. In orthodoxy, it usually refers only to how Jesus is God and man. Herein, it refers only to Jesus' identity.

DEITY CHRISTOLOGY. The belief that Jesus Christ is both God and man.

DEITY OF CHRIST, THE. A theological expression not found in the NT but fashioned by traditionalists to indicate that Jesus Christ is fully "God" by means of a divine nature. "Deity" derives from *Deus*, the Latin word for God. Past traditionalists restricted "deity" to "Christ," as if "Christ" is to be associated exclusively with His supposed divine nature and "Jesus" only with His human nature. "The deity of Christ" is biblically correct if defined as God indwelling Christ, i.e., God-in-Christ. But traditionalists have not so defined it.

DEUTERO-ISAIAH. Used herein to refer to Isa 40-55.

DIASPORA, THE. The dispersion of the Jews from their ancestral land, which first occurred in the Exile of the 6th century BCE by the Babylonians and again in the 2nd century CE while under Roman subjugation.

DIVINE, DIVINITY. Besides quotations, these terms are not used herein to describe Jesus Christ. (See Preface.) Traditionalists have used the terms "divine," "divinity," "deity," "God," and "Godhead/godhead" interchangeably to identify Jesus Christ. Some recent scholars have distinguished "deity" and "divinity," with "deity" meaning "God" or "Godhead/godhead" and "divinity" referring to something less. What about words in the Gr. NT that can be translated "divine" or "divinity"? *Theios* appears only twice in the NT: in 2 Pt 1.3 as an adjective with *dunamis*, usually translated "divine power," and in Ac 17.29 as a noun that is translated "Godhead" (AV), "the Deity/deity" (RSV, NEB, JB), or "divine being" (NIV). *Theiotes* derives from *theios* and appears only in Rom 1.20, being translated "Godhead" (AV), "diety" (RSV, NEB, JB), or "divine nature" (NIV, TEV). These words should be distinguished from *theotes*, which appears only in Col 2.9 and is there translated "Godhead" (AV, NEB), "fulness of (the) deity/Deity" (RSV, NIV), "fulness of divinity" (JB), or "divine nature" (TEV). None of these Gr. words are ever used in the Gr. NT to identify Jesus.

DOCETISM. The belief that Christ only seemed (Gr. *dokeo* ="to seem") to have a human body and suffer. Docetism usually meant that Jesus Christ was God and not man, mostly on the basis of Gr. dualism.

DUALISM (GREEK). Man's flesh is corrupt and evil whereas man's soul is pure, good, and immortal.

ESCHATOLOGY. The study of last things (Gr. *eschatos*="last things"), i.e., the end times and beyond.

ELEVEN, THE. Jesus' apostles excluding Judas after his betrayal and prior to his replacement by Matthias.

ETERNAL GENERATION. God generated Jesus in His preexistent state as the Logos-Son throughout all past eternity, so that there never was a time when the Logos-Son did not exist as a full *hypostasis*/Person.

ETERNAL SONSHIP. Jesus has always preexisted metaphysically throughout past eternity as a complete Person and called "the Son of God." Eternal Sonship relates to the doctrine of Eternal Generation.

EVANGELISTS, THE. The original, supposed, four authors of the four gospels of the NT.

FORM CRITICISM. The study of forms in a document that are presumably based on oral tradition.

GNOSTICISM. A widespread movement that flourished in the 2nd century BCE and continued as late as the 4th century CE. It claimed an esoteric, superior wisdom or knowledge (Gr. *gnosis*="knowledge") of mysteries and thus spiritual truth. Not easily defined, it was a synthesis of Gr. and Oriental philosophies mixed with elements from Judaism and Christianity. Its fundamental precepts included belief in a supreme God and a lesser god that was called "the Demiurge" and perceived as the god of the OT and thus the creator of the universe. Fully-developed Gnosticism viewed the Demiurge as evil. Most Gnostics embraced Gr. dualism. So-called "Christian Gnostics" usually believed in Docetism as well.

GODHEAD, THE. A word that Trinitarians created during medieval times to describe God existing in His totality as three separate and distinct Persons. They created it to accommodate their doctrine of the Trinity, perhaps mostly to solve the problem of applying singular, personal pronouns to the triune God. "Godhead" appears in the AV three times, in Ac 17.29 (Gr. *theios*), Rom 1.20 (Gr. *theiotes*), and Col 2.9 (Gr. *theotes*). They are translated "deity/Deity" in the RSV. For Trinitarians, "Godhead" is synonymous with "triune God."

GOSPEL. Derives from the Anglo-Saxon expression "god spell," meaning "good news." It well translates *euangelion* in the Gr. NT, meaning "good news," and therein has some nuances of meaning. Jesus probably used it in allusion to Isa 40.9 and 61.1, referring to kingdom blessings. The early Christians usually used it to refer to the good news about eternal salvation, i.e., the forgiveness of sins and eternal life. Used in this manner, "the gospel" refers to the essence of Christian faith, and this is how the term is used in this book.

GOSPELS, THE FOUR NT. Not exactly biographies of Jesus by modern standards, they are collections of narratives about Him and sayings by Him that are designed to evoke a faith response from readers.

HELLENISM. A term applied to Gr. culture during the period from Alexander the Great to the early stages of the Roman Empire and thus the beginning of the Christian era, after which its influence continued.

HISTORICAL JESUS, THE. Herein, the real pre-Easter Jesus, not only as He can be recovered by methods of modern historical research, but as He actually was and presumably is portrayed in the NT gospels.

HOLY SPIRIT, THE. The following expressions are used synonymously in the Bible: "the Holy Spirit (of God)," "the Spirit (of God)," and "God's Spirit." (See Appendix B: The Nature of the Holy Spirit.)

IDENTITY CHRISTOLOGY. The study of the identity of Jesus, which includes His being the Christ.

JEWISH BIBLE, THE. The Hebrew Bible and the Septuagint. Jews call the Hebrew Bible "the Tanakh." Christians call both "the Old Testament."

MESSIANIC SECRET, THE. Not used herein to deny that Jesus is the Messiah/Christ, but to refer to Jesus' efforts to keep His messianic identity a secret from the public until the time of His death.

MONOTHEISM. "Strict (rigid, exclusive) monotheism" means to restrict divine status only to the one God as a single Being (Person). "Flexible (inclusive) monotheism" attributes divine status to both God and some intermediate figure(s) between God and man. "Monotheism" is used herein to refer to "strict monotheism."

MUTUAL INDWELLING, THE. A theological expression indicating that God the Father completely indwells His Son, Jesus Christ, and the Son indwells the Father. Also called "the reciprocal indwelling."

ONE PERSON VIEW, THE. The viewpoint of a passage of Scripture in which it is interpreted as mentioning only God the Father and thus not Jesus Christ as well.

ORAL TRADITION. As applied to Christianity, the memorized and performed oral transmissions about Jesus that soon arose among early Christian communities, some of it written and included in the NT gospels.

ORTHODOX(Y), (CHRISTIAN). Not used herein in its primary meaning of *right opinion*, but in its secondary meaning of *conformity* to Christianity as represented by the ancient church councils and creeds. "Orthodox" is used herein interchangeably with "traditionalist" unless otherwise stated.

GLOSSARY

PASSION WEEK. The last days of Jesus' earthly life between His arrival in Jerusalem on Palm Sunday and His resurrection on the following Sunday.

PENTATEUCH. A technical term for the first five books of the Bible.

PERICOPE. Pronounced pe rik' o pe-e. A Gr. word that literally means "something cut out." It is a self-contained unit of tradition, e.g., a narrated story or a teaching discourse.

PERSON. In English a self-conscious, rational being distinct from other beings that are not so. Herein distinguished from the Gr. word *hypostasis*, meaning "subsistence," i.e., that which underlies an object.

Q. A supposed, non-extant document containing sayings of Jesus. About 90 percent of the Gospel of Mark is contained in the other two synoptics, in which all three gospels often have the same or similar wording. Most modern NT scholars therefore presume that Matthew and Luke used Mark in compiling their gospels. In addition, Matthew and Luke contain a smaller amount of the same material, with the same or similar wording, which is not in Mark. Scholars thus conclude that they borrowed this material from a now non-extant document, which apparently consisted only of sayings of Jesus (cf. Lk 1.1-2). Scholars refer to these phenomena as "the two-source hypothesis." German scholars used the capitalized letter "Q" as an abbreviation for their word "Quell," meaning "source," to designate this non-extant, sayings document.

PREEXISTENCE OF CHRIST, THE. Jesus existed pre-temporally as a complete *hypostasis* or Person.

RABBINIC JUDAISM. Following CE 70, it replaced former Judaism, which had been centered at Jerusalem and its Temple, with a renewed focus on learning and its center of worship being in synagogues.

REDACTION CRITICISM. The study of a presumed editorializing of a document following its original composition, usually done by other hands and perhaps many years later.

SECOND TEMPLE PERIOD, THE. Relating to Judaism during the time of Jerusalem's Second Temple, which existed soon after the return from Exile to its destruction, from 570 BCE to CE 70.

SANHEDRIN. The supreme court of ancient Israel. It tried cases regarding both religious and civil law.

SAYINGS OF JESUS (=JESUS' SAYINGS). Restricted herein to the words of Jesus in the NT gospels.

SEPTUAGINT (LXX). The Gr. translation of the Hebrew Bible by Jewish scholars at Alexandria, Egypt, in the 3rd century BCE. Legend attributes seventy or seventy-two translators, hence its name "Septuagint," meaning "seventy," which is also signified as an abbreviation by the Roman numeral LXX.

SOURCE CRITICISM. The identification and study of written sources used in composing a document.

SYNOPTIC GOSPEL(S). The first three gospels of the NT, viz., Matthew, Mark, and Luke. The Gr. word *syn* means "with" or "together," and *opt* means "see" or "view." Hence, "synoptic," which derives from "synopsis," means "a viewing together." Thus, the first three NT gospels are called "synoptics" because all three record many of the same events in the life of Jesus, so that they can with profit be viewed together.

SYNOPTIC PROBLEM. The complex relationship between the first three gospels of the NT. It arouses questions as to how and why these three gospels came to be either the same or different.

SYNOPTISTS. The three supposed, original authors of the first three gospels of the NT.

TEXTUAL CRITICISM (of the Bible). A literary discipline which seeks to recover the authentic text of the Bible by analyzing sources. Concerning the NT, three types of extant literature are analyzed: (1) Gr. MSS or fragments believed to go back to the original NT documents, (2) patristic writings containing NT quotations, and (3) versions. Primary emphasis is on the Gr. MSS that, prior to the invention of the printing press, were copied by professional scribes. Due to human frailties, mistakes were unavoidable. Different wording within MSS are called "variants." Editors (textual critics) who compile a biblical text must choose between variants.

THEOCENTRIC. God the Father is emphasized more than Jesus Christ is.

TORAH. A Hebrew word meaning "teaching" or "instruction." Generally, the Pentateuch; specifically, "the Law (of Moses/of God)."

TRADITIONAL CHRISTOLOGY. Minimally, the church dogma that Jesus Christ is both man and God. Maximally, the doctrine of The Trinity. Herein, it equates with "orthodoxy" and "classical Christology."

TRADITIONALIST, A. Herein, it refers to one who embraces either binitarian or trinitarian Christology.

TRINITY, THE (DOCTRINE OF THE). The one, true, and living God consists of one essence subsisting in three co-equal and co-eternal Persons: the Father, the Son (Jesus Christ), and the Holy Spirit.

TRINITARIAN, A. One who believes in the doctrine of the Trinity.

TRINITARIANISM. Belief in the doctrine of the Trinity.

TWELVE, THE. The twelve apostles Jesus chose as His disciples at the beginning of His public ministry.

TWO-NATURE CHRISTOLOGY. Jesus Christ possesses both a human nature and a fully divine nature.

TWO PERSON VIEW, THE. The interpretation of a Bible text in which it is viewed as mentioning both God the Father and Jesus.

UNITARIANISM. Belief in one God as a uni-personal Being.

Selected Bibliography

In the following works, these distinguished authorities thoroughly address exegetically the question of whether the New Testament identifies Jesus as "God."

Books

Barclay, William. "God." Pages 20-37 in his *Jesus As They Saw Him: New Testament Interpretations of Jesus*. Grand Rapids: Eerdmans, 1962.

Brown, Raymond E. "Does the New Testament Call Jesus God?" Pages 1-38 in his *Jesus God and Man: Modern Biblical Reflections*. New York: MacMillan, 1967. (This portion is a slightly modified version of his 1965 journal article cited below.)

--------. "Did New Testament Christians Call Jesus God?" Pages 171-95 in his *An Introduction to New Testament Christology*. New York: Paulist, 1994.

Bultmann, Rudolf Karl. "The Christological Confession of the World Council of Churches." Pages 273-90 in his *Essays Philosophical and Theological* [1951-52]. Translated by James C.G. Greig. New York: MacMillan, 1955.

Cullmann, Oscar. "The Designation of Jesus as 'God.'" Pages 306-14 in his *The Christology of the New Testament* [1957]. Translated by Shirley C. Guthrie and Charles A.M. Hall. Rev. ed. Philadelphia: Westminster, 1963.

D'Aragon, J.L. "Jesus de Nazareth etait-il Dieu?" Pages 193-217 in *Jesus: De l'histoire a la foi*. Edited by J.L. D'Aragon et al. Montreal: Fides, 1974.

Fitzmyer, Joseph A. *Scripture and Christology: A Statement of the Biblical Commission with a Commentary*. New York: Paulist, 1986.

Harvey. A.E. "Appendix III: The Divinity of Jesus in the New Testament." Pages 175-78 in his *Jesus and the Constraints of History*. London: Duckworth, 1982.

-------. "Son of God: the Constraint of Monotheism." Pages 154-73 in his *Jesus and the Constraints of History*.

Harris, Murray J. *Jesus As God: The New Testament Use of Theos in Reference to Jesus*. Grand Rapids: Baker, 1992.

--------. "Is Jesus God?" Pages 65-103 in his *3 Crucial Questions about Jesus*. Grand Rapids: Baker, 1994.

Longenecker, Richard N. "God." Pages 136-41 in his *The Christology of Early Jewish Christianity* [1970]. Repr. Grand Rapids: Baker, 1980.

O'Collins, Gerald. "Saviour and God." Pages 143-46 in his *Christology: A Biblical, Historical, and Systematic Study of Jesus*. Oxford: University, 1995.

Rahner, Karl. "Theos in the New Testament." Pages 1:135-38 in his *Theological Investigations*. 14 vols. Translated by Cornelius Ernst. Baltimore: Helicon, 1961.

Reymond, Robert L. Pages 212-14, 243-79, 288-91, 296-321 in his *Jesus, Divine Messiah: The New Testament Witness*. Phillipsburg, NJ: Presbyterian and Reformed, 1990.

Robinson, John A.T. Pages 70-75 in his *Honest to God*. Philadelphia: Westminster, 1963.

Schneider, Johannes. "Christ as God." In *TDNT* 2:80-82.

Stauffer, Ethelbert. "Christ as *Theos* in Early Christianity." In *TDNT* 3:104-106.

Taylor, Vincent. "St. Paul's View of Christ's Relationship to God." Pages 55-61 in his *The Person of Christ in New Testament Teaching*. London: Macmillan, 1958.

Turner, Nigel. "Jesus Is God." Pages 13-17 in his *Grammatical Insights into the New Testament*. Edinburgh: T. & T. Clark, 1965.

Warfield, Benjamin B. *The Lord of Glory: A Study of the Designations of our Lord in the New Testament with Especial Reference to His Deity* [1907]. Repr. Grand Rapids: Zondervan, n.d.

Journal Articles

Boobyer, G.H. "Jesus As 'Theos' in the New Testament." *BJRL* 50 (1967-68): 247-61.

Brown, Raymond E. "Does the New Testament Call Jesus God?" *JTS* 26 (1965): 545-73.

Mastin, B.A. "A Neglected Feature of the Christology of the Fourth Gospel." *NTS* 22 (1975-76): 32-51.
Wainwright, Arthur W. "The Confession 'Jesus Is God' in the New Testament." *SJT* 10, no. 1 (March 1957): 274-99.
Taylor, Vincent. "Does the New Testament Call Jesus 'God'?" *ExpT* 73 (1961-62): 116-18. Reprinted on pages 83-89 in his *New Testament Essays*. London: Epworth, 1970.

****

The following works advocate the same God-in-Christ Christology presented in this book, except that the doctrine of the Trinity and Chalcedonian Christology are affirmed but redefined functionally.
Books
Berkhof, Hendrikus. *The Christian Faith: An Introduction to the Study of Faith* [1979]. Translated by Sierd Woudstra. Rev. ed. Grand Rapids: Eerdmans, 1986.
Kung, Hans. *On Being a Christian*. New York: Doubleday, 1976.
-------. Pages 87-110 in his *Christianity: Essence, History and Future* [1994]. New York: Continuum, 1995.
Schillebeeckx, Edward. *Jesus: An Experiment in Christology* [1974]. Translated by Hubert Hoskins. New York: Seabury, 1979.
Schoonenberg, Piet. *The Christ: A Study of the God-man Relationship in the Whole of Creation and in Jesus Christ* [1969]. Translated by Della Couling. New York: Herder and Herder, 1971.

****

The following works adhere very closely to the exclusive God-in-Christ Christology in this book:
Books
Bible et christologie. Pages 1-53 in Joseph A. Fitzmyer's *Scripture and Christology: A Statement of the Biblical Commission with a Commentary*. New York: Paulist, 1986. Drafted in 1983 by the Pontifical Biblical Commission of the Roman Catholic Church (RCC).
De Jonge, Marinus. "The One God and Jesus." Pages 130-42 in his *God's Final Envoy: Early Christology and Jesus' Own View of His Mission*. Grand Rapids: Eerdmans, 1998.
Jervell, Jacob. *Jesus in the Gospel of John* **[1978]**. Translated by Harry T. Cleven. Minneapolis: Augsberg, 1984.

****

The following works advocate the same exclusive God-in-Christ Christology as in this book—that God the Father indwells Jesus Christ as God's ultimate self-revelation to humankind, yet Jesus Christ is no more than a man. Some of these authors affirm Jesus' Virgin Birth, literal resurrection from the dead, and ascension into heaven, as in this book, while some of them do not affirm all of these teachings.
Books
Cupitt, Don. Pages 7-23 in his *Jesus and the Gospel of God*. Guildford, England: Lutterworth, 1979.
Broughton, James H., and Peter J. Southgate, *The Trinity: True or False?* (Nottingham, England: "The Dawn Book Supply, 1995 [except pp. 280-84].
Flesseman-van Leer, E. Pages 65-72, 83-9 in her *A Faith for Today* [1972]. Translated by John E. Steely. Macon, GA: Mercer University, 1980.
Graeser, Mark H., John A. Lynn, and John W. Schoenheit. *One God & One Lord: Reconsidering the Cornerstone of the Christian Faith*. 3rd ed. Indianapolis, IN: Christian Educational Services, 2003.
Harvey, A.E. Pages 154-73, 176-78 in his *Jesus and the Constraints of History*. London: Duckworth, 1982.
Hick, John, ed. *The Myth of God Incarnate*. Philadelphia: Westminster, 1977.

****

Finally, I regard the approximately fifty-page document entitled *Bible et christologie*, produced by the RCC's Pontifical Biblical Commission and published in 1983, as the most informative, and perhaps the most important, piece of literature on Identity Christology that has appeared in modern times.

General Bibliography

A: Primary Works Cited

Letters of Gaius Plinius Caecilius Secundus. In *The Harvard Classics.* Translated by William Melmoth. Revised by F.C.T. Bosanquet. 51 vols. New York: P.F. Collier, 1909.
Pliny Letters and Panegyricus in Two Volumes with ET by Betty Radice. In *The Loeb Classical Library.* Edited by E.H. Warmington. Cambridge, MA: Harvard, 1969

General Bibliography (continued)

B: Secondary Works Cited

A

Abbott, Ezra. *The Authorship of the Fourth Gospel and Other Critical Essays*. 2 vols. Boston: Ellis, 1888.

-------. "On the Construction of Romans ix.5." *JBL* 1 (1881): 87-154.

-------. "On the Construction of Titus ii.13." *JBL* 1 (1881): 3-19. Repr. in Abbott, *Authorship*, 439-57.

-------. "On the Reading 'Church of God,' Acts XX.28." *BSac* 33 (April 1876): 313-53. Repr. in Abbot, *Authorship*, 294-31.

-------. "Recent Discussions on Romans ix.5." *JBL* 3 (1883): 90-112.

Akers, John N., and John H. Armstrong, John D. Woodbridge, gen. eds. "The Gospel of Jesus Christ: An Evangelical Celebration." Pages 239-48 in *This We Believe: The Good News of Jesus Christ for the World*. Grand Rapids: Zondervan, 2000.

Aland, Kurt, and Barbara Aland. *The Text of the New Testament: An Introduction to the Critical Editions and to the Theory and Practice of Modern Textual Criticism* [1981]. Translated by Erroll F. Rhodes: Leiden: Brill, 1987.

Alford, Henry. *The Greek New Testament*. 4 vols. London: Gilbert and Rivington, 1849-61.

Allison, Jr., Dale C. *The New Moses: A Matthean Typology*. Minneapolis: Fortress, 1993.

-------. *Resurrecting Jesus: The Earliest Christian Tradition and Its Interpreters*. New York: T. & T. Clark, 2005.

Althaus, Paul. *The Theology of Martin Luther*. Translated by Robert C. Schultz. Philadelphia: Fortress, 1966.

Anselm, *Cur Deus Homo*

Appold, Mark L. *The Oneness Motif in the Fourth Gospel: Motif Analysis and Exegetical Probe into the Theology of John*. Tubingen: Mohr-Siebeck, 1976.

Aquinas, Thomas. *Summa Theologica*.

Archer Jr., Gleason L. "Daniel." In *EBC* (1985).

Ashton, John, ed. *The Interpretation of John*. Repr. Philadelphia: Fortress, 1986.

Audet, Jean Paul. *Didache: Instructions des apotres*. Paris: J. Gabalda, 1958.

Aune, David E. *Revelation 1-5*. In WBC (1997).

B

Bailey, Kenneth E. "Informal Controlled Oral Tradition and the Synoptic Gospels." *AJT* 5 (1991): 34-54.

-------. "Middle Eastern Oral Tradition and the Synoptic Gospels." *ExpT* 106 (1995): 363-67.

Baillie, Donald Macpherson. *God Was in Christ: An Essay on Incarnation and Atonement*. New York: Scribner's Sons, 1948.

Baldwin, Joyce G. *Daniel: An Introduction and Commentary*. Downers Grove, IL: InterVarsity, 1978.

Barclay, William. *The Gospel of John*. Rev. ed. 2 vols. Philadelphia: Westminster, 1975.

-------. "Great Themes of the New Testament: II John 1.1-14." *ExpT* 70 (1958-59): 78-82, 114-17.

-------. *Jesus As They Saw Him: New Testament Interpretations of Jesus*. London: SCM, 1962.

-------. *The New Testament: A New Translation*. 2 vols. London: Collins, 1968-69.

Barker, Margaret. *The Great Angel: A Study of Israel's Second God*. London: SPCK, 1992.

Barnes, Timothy D. *Constantine and Eusebius*. Cambridge, MA: Harvard, 1981.

Baron, Richard. *Cordial for Low Spirits*. 3 vols. London, 1763.

Barr, James. "Abba Isn't 'Daddy.'" *JTS*, N.S. 39 (April 1988): 28-47.

Barrett, C.K. "Christocentric or Theocentric? Observations on the Theological Method of the Fourth Gospel." Pages 1-18 in Barrett's *Essays on John*.

———. *A Commentary on the Second Epistle to the Corinthians*. In HNTC (1973). Repr., Peabody, MA: Hendrickson, 1987.
———. *Essays on John*. Philadelphia: Westminster, 1982.
———. "'The Father is Greater than I' (Jo 14, 28): Subordinationist Christology in the New Testament." Pages 19-36 in Barrett's *Essays on John*.
———. *The Gospel According to St. John: An Introduction with Commentary and Notes on the Greek Text*. 2nd ed. Philadelphia: Westminister, 1978.
———. "New Testament Eschatology, ii." *SJT* 6 (1953): 225-43.
Barth, Karl. *Church Dogmatics*. Edited by G.W. Bromiley and T.F. Torrance. Translated by G.W. Bromiley. 14 vols. Edinburgh: T. & T. Clark, 1975.
———. *Dogmatics in Outline*. London: SCM, 1949.
Bauckham. Richard J. *God Crucified: Monotheism and Christology in the New Testament*. Grand Rapids: Eerdmans, 1998.
———. *Jesus and the Eyewitnesses: The Gospels as Eyewitness Testimony*. Grand Rapids: Eerdmans, 2006.
———. *Jude, 2 Peter*. In WBC 50 (1983).
———. *The Theology of the Book of Revelation*. Cambridge: University, 1993.
———. "The Worship of Jesus in Apocalyptic Christianity." *NTS* 27 (1981): 322-41.
Beasley-Murray, George Raymond. *The Book of Revelation*. In NCBC (1974).
———. *Jesus and the Kingdom of God*. Grand Rapids: Eerdmans, 1986.
———. *John*. In WBC (1987).
———. "The Revelation." In NBC (1970). 2nd ed.
Behm, Johannes. "morphe." In *TDNT* 4:742-52.
Bengel, John Albert. *Bengel's New Testament Commentary* [1742]. 2 vols. Repr. Grand Rapids: Kregel, 1981.
Berkhof, Hendrikus. *Christian Faith: An Introduction to the Study of Faith* [1979]. Translated by Sierd Woudstra. Rev. ed. Grand Rapids: Eerdmans, 1986.
Berkhof, Louis. *Systematic Theology*. 4th rev. ed. Grand Rapids: Eerdmans, 1939.
Bernard, J.H. *A Critical and Exegetical Commentary on the Gospel According to St. John*. 2 vols. Edinburgh: T. & T. Clark, 1928.
Betz, Otto. "Jesus and the Temple Scroll." Pages 75-103 in *Jesus and the Dead Sea Scrolls*. Edited by James H. Charlesworth.
Beyreuther, Erich. "agathos." In *NIDNTT* 2:98-102.
Beyschlag, Willibald. *Die Christologie des Neuen Testaments*. Berlin, 1866.
Biddle, John. *Twelve Questions or Arguments drawn out of Scripture, wherein the commonly received Opinion touching the Deity of the Holy Spirit is clearly and fully refuted*. 1647.
Bietenhard, Hans. "onoma." In *NIDNTT* 2:648-55.
———. "onoma." In *TDNT* 5:242-83.
Black, Matthew. "The Messianism of the Parables of Enoch: Their Date and Contribution to Christological Origins." In *The Messiah*. Edited by J.H. Charlesworth.
Blomberg, Craig L. "Form Criticism." Pages 243-50 in *DJG*.
———. "Gospels (Historical Reliability)." Pages 291-97 in *DJG*.
Bock, Darrell L. *Blasphemy and Exaltation in Judaism and the Final Examination of Jesus: A Philological-Historical Study of the Key Jewish Themes Impacting Mark 14.61-64*. Tubingen: Mohr Siebeck, 1998.
———. *Breaking the Da Vinci Code*. Nashville: Thomas Nelson, 2004.
———. "The Reign of the Lord Christ." Pages 37-67 in *Dispensationalism, Israel and the Church: The Search for Definition*. Edited by Craig A. Blaising and Darrell L. Bock. Grand Rapids: Zondervan, 1992.
Bockmuehl, Markus. "'The Form of God' (Phil. 2.6) Variations on a Theme of Jewish Mysticism," *JTS*, n.s., 48 (1997): 1-23.
Boobyer, G.H. "Jesus As '*Theos*' in the New Testament." *BJRL* 50 (1967-68): 246-61.
Borg, Marcus J. *Jesus: A New Vision: Spirit, Culture, and the Life of Discipleship*. San Francisco: HarperSanFrancisco, 1987.
Borg, Marcus J., and N.T. Wright. *The Meaning of Jesus: Two Visions*. New York: HarperCollins, 1999.
Borgen, Peder. *Bread from Heaven: An Exegetical Study of the Concept of Manna in the Gospel of John and the Writings of Philo*. Leiden: Brill, 1981.
———. "God's Agent in the Fourth Gospel." Pages 67-78 in *The Interpretation of John*. Edited by John Ashton. Repr., Philadelphia: Fortress, 1986. Repr. from *Religions in Antiquity*, 1968.
Borsch, F.H. *The Son of Man in Myth and History*. Philadelphia: Fortress, 1967.
Bousset, Wilhelm. *Kyrios Christos: A History of the Belief in Christ from the Beginnings of the Christianity to Iranaeus* [1913]. Translated by John Steely. 5th ed. Nashville, TN: Abingdon, 1970.
Bowman Jr., Robert M., and J. Ed Komoszewski. *Putting Jesus in His Place: The Case for the Deity of Christ*. Grand Rapids: Kregel, 2007.

Boyd, Gregory A. *God at War: The Bible and Spiritual Conflict.* Downers Grove, IL: InterVarsity, 1997.
Braaten, Carl E. "The Significance of New Testament Christology for Systematic Theology." Pages 216-27 in *Who Do You Say that I Am?: Essays on Christology*, eds. Mark Allan Powell and David R. Bauer.
Braumann, Georg. "*ego eimi.*" In *NIDNTT* 2:278-81.
Broughton, James H., and Peter J. Southgate. *The Trinity: True or False?* Nottingham, England: "The Dawn" Book Supply, 1995.
Brown, Colin. "*kenos.*" In *NIDNTT* 1:546-49.
-------. "*theos.*" In *NIDNTT* 2:82-83.
Brown, Colin, and Johannes Schneider. "*soter.*" In *NIDNTT* 3:216-21.
Brown, David. *The Divine Trinity.* London: Duckworth, 1985.
Brown, Raymond E. *The Birth of the Messiah: A Commentary on the Infancy Narratives in the Gospels of Matthew and Luke* [1977]. New updated ed. New York: Doubleday, 1993.
-------. *The Death of the Messiah: From Gethsemane to the Grave: A Commentary on the Passion Narratives in the Four Gospels.* 2 vols. New York: Doubleday, 1994.
-------. "Does the New Testament Call Jesus God?" *JTS* 26 (1965): 545-73. Repr. in Brown, *Jesus God and Man*, 1-38.
-------. *The Epistles of John: Translated with Introduction, Notes, and Commentary.* In AB 30 (1982).
-------. *The Gospel According to John (i-xii): Introduction, Translation and Notes.* In AB 29 (1966).
-------. *The Gospel According to John (xiii-xxi): Introduction, Translation and Notes.* In AB 29A (1970).
-------. *An Introduction to New Testament Christology.* New York: Paulist, 1994.
-------. *Jesus God and Man: Modern Biblical Reflections.* New York: MacMillan, 1967.
Bruce, F.F. *Answers to Questions.* Exeter: Paternoster, 1972.
-------. "The Background to the Son of Man Sayings." Pages 50-70 in *Christ the Lord.* Edited by H.H. Rowdon.
-------. *The Epistle to the Hebrews.* Rev. ed. In NICNT (1990).
-------. *The Letter of Paul to the Romans: An Introduction and Commentary.* 2nd ed. In TNTC (1985).
-------. *The New Testament Documents: Are They Reliable?* [1943]. 5th ed. Repr., Grand Rapids: Eerdmans, 1994.
Brunner, Emil. *The Mediator: A Study of the Central Doctrine of the Christian Faith* [1927]. Translated by Olive Wyon. Philadelphia: Westminister, 1947.
Buber, Martin. *Moses.* Oxford: East & West Library, 1946.
-------. *Two Types of Faith.* 1951.
Buchanan, George Wesley. *The Epistle to the Hebrews: Translation, Comment, and Conclusions.* In AB 36 (1972).
-------. "Apostolic Christology." Pages 172-82 in *SBLSP* (1986).
Buhner, J.A. *Der Gesandte und sein Weg im 4. Evangelium.* Tubingen, 1977.
Bultmann, Rudolf Karl. "The Christological Confession of the World Council of Churches." Pages 273-90 in R. Bultmann, *Essays, Philosophical and Theological* [paper delivered in 1951].
-------. "Die Bedeutung der neuerschlossenen mandaischen und manichaischen Quellen fur das Verstandnis des Johannesevangeliums." *ZNW* 24 (1925).
-------. *Essays, Philosophical and Theological.* Translated by J.C.G. Greig. London; SCM, 1955.
-------. *The Gospel of John: A Commentary.* Translated by G.R. Beasley-Murray. Philadelphia: Westminster, 1971.
-------. *History of the Synoptic Tradition* [1921]. Translated by John Marsh. Rev. ed. ET 1963. Repr., Peabody, MA: Hendrickson, n.d.
-------. *Jesus and the Word* [1926]. Translated by Louise Pettibone Smith and Erminie Huntress Lantero. New York: Scribner's Sons, 1934.
-------. *The Johannine Epistles: A Commentary on the Johannine Epistles.* Philadelphia: Fortress, 1973. Translated by R. Philip O'Hara. Philadelphia: Fortress, 1973.
-------. *Theology of the New Testament* [1948-53]. Translated by Kendrick Grobel. 2 vols. London: SCM, 1951-55.
Burkitt, F.C. "On Romans ix 5 and Mark xiv 61." *JTS* 5 (1904): 451-55.
Bury, Arthur. *The Naked Gospel.* 1690.
Bushnell, Horace. *God in Christ.* Hartford: Brown and Parsons, 1848.
Buzzard, Anthony F., and Charles F. Hunting. *The Doctrine of the Trinity: Christianity's Self-Inflicted Wound.* Morrow, GA: Atlanta Bible College and Restoration Fellowship, 1994.

C

Cahill, Thomas. *Desire of the Everlasting Hills: The World before and after Jesus.* New York: Doubleday, 1999.
Caird, G.B. "The Development of the Doctrine of the Christ in the New Testament." Pages 66-80 in *Christ for Us Today.* Edited by Norman Pittenger. London: SCM, 1968.
-------. *New Testament Theology.* Edited by L.D. Hurst. Oxford: Clarendon, 1994.

Calvin, John. *Calvin's Commentaries*. 22 vols. Repr., Grand Rapids: Baker, 1984.
-------. *Commentary on the Gospel According to John*. Translated by William Pringle. Grand Rapids: Eerdmans: 1949.
-------. *A Harmony of the Gospels Matthew, Mark and Luke* in *Calvin's Commentaries* [1572]. 3 vols. Repr. Grand Rapids: Eerdmans, 1972.
Capes, David B. *Old Testament Yahweh Texts in Paul's Christology*. Tubingen: Mohr, 1992.
-------. "YHWH Texts and Montheism? A Contribution to the Discussion of Christian Monotheism." Pages 120-137 in *Early Jewish and Christian Monotheism*. Edited by Stuckenbruck and North.
Caragounis, Chrys C. *The Son of Man: Vision and Interpretation*. Tubingen: Mohr, 1986.
Carnley, Peter. *The Structure of Resurrection Belief*. Clarendon, England: Oxford University, 1987.
Carrell, Peter R. *Jesus and the Angels: Angelology and the Christology of the Apocalypse of John*. Cambridge: University, 1997.
Carson, D.A. "Christological Ambiguities in the Gospel of Matthew." Pages 97-114 in *Christ the Lord*. Edited by H.H. Rowdon.
-------. *Divine Sovereignty and Human Responsibility: Biblical Perspectives in Tension*. Atlanta: John Knox, 1981.
-------. *The Farewell Discourse and Final Prayer of Jesus: An Exposition of John 14-17*. Grand Rapids: Baker, 1980.
-------. *The Gospel According to John*. Grand Rapids: Eerdmans, 1991.
-------. *The King James Version Debate: A Plea for Realism*. Grand Rapids: Baker, 1979.
-------. "Matthew." In EBC 8 (1984).
Casey, P .Maurice. "The Deification of Jesus." Pages 697-714 in *SBLSP* (1994).
-------. *From Jewish Prophet to Gentile God: The Origins and Development of New Testament Christology*. Cambridge: James Clarke, 1991.
-------. *Is John's Gospel "True?* London: Routledge, 1996.
-------. "Monotheism, Worship and Christological Development in the Pauline Churches." Pages 214-33 in *The Jewish Roots of Christological Monotheism*. Edited by Carey C. Newman et al.
-------. *Son of Man: The Interpretation and Influence of Daniel*. London: SPCK, 1979.
Cassirer, Heinz W. *God's New Covenant: A New Testament Translation*. Grand Rapids: Eerdmans, 1989.
Catchpole, David R. *The Trial of Jesus: A Study in the Gospels and Jewish Historiography from 1770 to the Present Day*. Leiden: Brill, 1971.
Chafer, Lewis Sperry. *Major Bible Themes*. Grands Rapids: Dunham, 1926.
-------. *Major Bible Themes: 52 Vital Doctrines of the Scripture Simplified and Explained*. Revised by John F. Walvoord. Grand Rapids: Zondervan, 1974.
-------. *Systematic Theology*. 8 vols. Dallas: Dallas Theological Seminary, 1947.
Charles, R.H. *The Revelation of St. John, with Introduction, Notes and Indices*. 2 vols. Edinburgh: T. & T. Clark, 1920.
Charlesworth, James H. "From Messianology to Christology: Problems and Prospects." Pages 3-35 in *The Messiah*. Edited by J.H. Charlesworth.
Charlesworth, James H., ed. *The Messiah: Developments in Earliest Judaism and Christianity*. Minneapolis: Fortress, 1992.
-------. *Jesus and the Dead Sea Scrolls*. New York: Doubleday, 1992.
Clements, R.E. *Isaiah 1-39*. In NCBC (1980).
Collins, A. Yarbo. "The Son of Man Tradition and the Book of Revelation." Pages 536-68 in *The Messiah*. Edited by J.H. Charlesworth.
Collins, John J. *The Scepter and the Star: The Messiahs of the Dead Sea Scrolls and Other Ancient Literature*. New York: Doubleday, 1995.
-------. "The Son of Man in First Century Judaism." *NTS* 38 (1992).
Colpe, Carsten. "ho huios tou anthropou." In *TDNT* 8:400-77.
Colwell, Ernest C. "A Definite Rule for the Use of the Article in the Greek New Testament." *JBL* 52 (1933): 12-21.
Corley, Bruce. "Trial of Jesus." Pages 841-54 in *DJG*.
Cotterell, F.P. "The Christology of Islam." Pages 282-98 in *Christ the Lord*. Edited by H.H. Rowdon.
Countess, Robert H. "The Translation of *Theos* in the New World Translation." *JETS* 10 (1967).
Craig, William Lane. *Knowing the Truth about the Resurrection*. Ann Arbor, MI: Servant, 1988.
Crellius, Johann. *The Two Books Touching One God the Father* (London: 1665).
Crellius, Samuel. *Initium evangelii S. Joannis Apoftoli ex Antiquitate Ecclefiaftica reftitutum*. 1726.
Cross, Frank Moore. *Canaanite Myth and Hebrew Epic: Essays in the History of the Religion of Israel*. Cambridge, MA: Harvard University, 1973.
Cullmann, Oscar. *The Christology of the New Testament*. Rev. ed. Translated by Shirley C. Guthrie and Charles A.M. Hall. Philadelphia: Westminster, 1963.
Cupitt, Don. "The Christ of Christendom." Pages 133-47 in *The Myth of God Incarnate*. Edited by J. Hick.
-------. *The Debate About Christ*. London: SCM, 1979.

-------. *Jesus and the Gospel of God*. London: Lutterworth, 1979.
-------. "Jesus and the Meaning of God." Pages 31-40 in *Incarnation and Myth: The Debate Continued*. Edited by M.D. Goulder.
-------. "Mr. Hebblethwaite on the Incarnation." Pages 43-46 in *Incarnation and Myth: The Debate Continued*. Edited by M.D. Goulder.
-------. "Religion and Critical Thinking." *Theology* 86 (1983): 243-49.

D

Dahl, Nils Alstrup. *Jesus the Christ: The Historical Origins of Christological Doctrine*. Edited by Donald H. Juel. Minneapolis: Fortress, 1991. 153-63.
Dalman, Gustaf. *The Words of Jesus Considered in the Light of Post-biblical Jewish Writings and the Aramaic Language*. Translated by D.M. Kay. Edinburgh: T. & T. Clark, 1902.
Davey, J. Ernest. *The Jesus of St. John*. London: Lutterworth, 1958.
Davies, W.D., and Dale C. Allison. *The Gospel According to Saint Matthew*. 3 vols. London: T&T Clark, 1988.
Davis, Stephen T., ed. *Encountering Jesus: A Debate on Christology*. Atlanta: John Knox, 1988.
Day, John. *God's Conflict with the Dragon and the Sea: Echoes of a Canaanite Myth in the Old Testament*. Cambridge: University, 1985.
De Beer, E.S. *The Correspondence of John Locke*. 8 vols. Oxford: Clarendon, 1979.
de Jonge, Marinus. *Christology in Context: The Earliest Christian Response to Jesus*. Philadelphia: Westminster, 1988.
-------. *God's Final Envoy: Early Christology and Jesus' Own View of His Mission*. Grand Rapids: Eerdmans, 1998.
Delling, Gerhard. "*pleroma*." In *TDNT* 6:298-305.
Denney, James. *Letters of Principal James Denney to W. Robertson Nicoll (1883-1917)*. London: Hodder and Stoughton, 1920.
-------. *The Methodist Recorder*. 1939.
Dibbs, M.T. *Servetus, Swendenborg and the Nature of God*. Lanham, MD: University Press of America, 2005.
Dix, G.H. "The Seven Angels and the Seven Spirits." *JTS* 28 (1927).
Dodd, C.H. *According to the Scriptures: The Sub-structure of New Testament Theology*. London: Nisbet, 1952.
-------. *The Founder of Christianity*. New York: Macmillan, 1970.
-------. *Historical Tradition in the Fourth Gospel*. Cambridge: University, 1963.
-------. *The Interpretation of the Fourth Gospel*. Cambridge: University, 1953.
-------. *The Johannine Epistle*. In MNTC (1946).
-------. "New Testament Translation Problems II." *BT* 28 (1977).
Draper, Edythe, ed. *The Almanac of the Christian World* [1991-92 ed.]. Wheaton, IL: Tyndale, 1990.
Dunn, James D.G. "Christ, Adam, and Preexistence." Pages 74-83 in *Where Christology Began*. Edited by R.P. Martin and B.J. Dodd.
-------. *Christology in the Making: A New Testament Inquiry into the Origins of the Doctrine of the Incarnation*. Philadelphia: Westminster, 1980.
-------. *The Evidence for Jesus*. Philadelphia: Westminster, 1985.
-------. *Jesus Remembered*. Grand Rapids: Eerdmans, 2003.
-------. *Jesus and the Spirit: A Study of the Religious and Charismatic Experience of Jesus and the First Christians as Reflected in the New Testament*. London: SCM, 1975.
-------. "Messianic Ideas and Their Influence on the Jesus of History." Pages 365-81 in *The Messiah*. Edited by J.H. Charlesworth.
-------. *A New Perspective on Jesus: What the Quest for the Historical Jesus Missed*. Grand Rapids: Baker, 2005.
-------. "The Question of Anti-semitism in the New Testament." Pages 177-211 in *Jews and Christians: The Parting of the Ways*. Edited by J.D.G. Dunn.
-------. *Romans 9-16*. In WBC (1988).
-------. *The Theology of Paul the Apostle*. Edinburgh: T&T Clark, 1998.
-------. *Unity and Diversity in the New Testament: An Inquiry into the Character of Earliest Christianity*. 2nd ed. Harrisburg, PA: Trinity, 1990.
-------. "Was Christianity a Monotheistic Faith from the Beginning?" *SJT* 35 (1982): 303-36.
Dunn, James D.G., ed. *Jews and Christians: The Parting of the Ways: A.D. 70 to 135* [1992]. Repr. Grand Rapids: Eerdmans, 1999.
Dunn, James D.G., and John W. Rogerson, eds. *Eerdmans Commentary on the Bible*. Grand Rapids: Eerdmans, 2003.

E

Eadie, John. *The Epistle to the Philippians*.
Eliot, William G. *Discourses on the Doctrines of Christianity*. Boston: American Unitarian Association, 1890.

Ellis, E. Earle. *The Old Testament in Early Christianity: Canon and Interpretation in Light of Modern Research*. Tubingen: Morh-Siebeck, 1991.
Ellis, George E. *A Half-Century of the Unitarian Controversy*. Boston: Crosby, 1857.
Enelow, H.G. *A Jewish View of Jesus*. New York, 1920.
Erickson, Millard J. *Introducing Christian Doctrine*. Edited by L. Arnold Hustad. Grand Rapids: Baker, 1992.
-------. *The Word Became Flesh: A Contemporary Incarnational Christology*. Grand Rapids: Baker, 1991.

F

Faccio, H.M. *De divinitate Christi juxta S. Paulum, Rom. 9,5*.
Farmer, William R., ed. *Crisis in Christology: Essays in Quest of Resolution*. N.p.: Truth, 1995.
Fee, Gordon D. *The First Epistle to the Corinthians*. In NICNT (1987).
Fennema, D.A. "John 1.18: 'God the Only Son.'" *NTS* 31 (1985): 124-35.
Fenton, John C. "Matthew and the Divinity of Jesus." Pages 79-82 in *Studia Biblica 1978/Sixth International Congress on Biblical Studies, Oxford 3-7 April 1978*. Edited by Elizabeth A. Livingstone. Sheffield: University, 1979-80.
Ferre, N.F.S. "Is the Basis of the World Council Heretical?" *ExpT* 74 (1962-63): 66-68.
Fitzmyer, Joseph A. *A Christological Catechism: New Testament Answers*. Rev. ed. New York: Paulist, 1991.
-------. Bible et christologie [1984]. In Scripture & Christology.
-------. *The Gospel According to Luke (i-ix): Introduction, Translation, and Notes*. In AB 28 (1970).
-------. *The Gospel According to Luke (x-xxiv): Introduction, Translation, and Notes*. In AB 28A (1985).
-------. *Romans: A New Translation with Introduction and Commentary*. In AB 33 (1993).
-------. *Scripture and Christology: A Statement of the Biblical Commission with a Commentary*. New York: Paulist, 1986.
-------. *A Wandering Aramean: Collected Aramaic Essays*. Missoula, MT: Scholars, 1979.
Flesseman-van Leer, Ellen. *A Faith for Today* [1972]. Translated by John E. Steely. Macon, GA: Association of Baptist Professors of Religion, 1980.
Fletcher-Louis, Crispin H.T. *Luke-Acts: Angels, Christology and Soteriology*. Tubingen: Mohr Siebeck, 1997.
Foerster, Werner. "*kurios*." In *TDNT* 3:1081-95.
Fohrer, Georg. "*huios*." In *TDNT* 8:340-54.
Ford, Desmond. *The Abomination of Desolation in Biblical Eschatology*. Washington, D.C.: University Press of America, 1979.
Ford, Paul Leicester. *The Name of God and the Angel of the Lord: Samaritan and Jewish Concepts of Intermediation and the Origin of Gnosticism*. Tubingen: Mohr, 1985.
-------. "The New *Religionsgeschichtliche Schule*: The Quest for Jewish Christology." *SBLSP* 30 (1991).
Ford, Paul Leicester, ed. *The Works of Thomas Jefferson*. 14 vols. 1904-05.
France, Richard T. "Christology." Pages 182-84 in *NTCERK*.
-------. *Jesus and the Old Testament: His Application of Old Testament Passages to Himself and His Mission*. London: Tyndale, 1971.
-------. "The Worship of Jesus: A Neglected Factor in Christological Debate?" Pages 17-36 in *Christ the Lord*. Edited by H.H. Rowdon.
Frei, Hans W. *The Identity of Jesus Christ: The Hermeneutical Bases of Dogmatic Theology*. Philadelphia: Fortress, 1975.
Frend, W.H.C. *The Rise of Christianity*. Philadelphia: Fortress, 1984.
Fuller, Reginal H. *Christ and Christianity: Studies in the Formation of Christology*. Compiled and edited by Robert Kahl. Valley Forge, PA: Trinity, 1994.
-------. *The Formation of the Resurrection Narratives* [1971]. Repr. Philadelphia: Fortress, 1980.
-------. *The Foundations of New Testament Christology*. New York: Scribner's Sons, 1965.
-------. "Son of man." Page 981 in *HBD*.
Funk, Robert W., and Roy W. Hoover. *The Five Gospels: The Search for the Authentic Words of Jesus*. New York: Polebridge, 1993.
-------. *Honest to Jesus: Jesus for a New Millennium*. New York: HarperSanFrancisco, 1996.

G

Gardner-Smith, P. *St John and the Synoptic Gospels*. Cambridge: University, 1938.
Gathercole, Simon J. *The Pre-existent Son: Recovering the Christologies of Matthew, Mark, and Luke*. Grand Rapids: Eerdmans, 2006.
Gerhardsson, Birger. *Memory and Manuscript, Oral Tradition and Written Transmission in Rabbinic Judaism and Early Christianity*. Translated by Eris J. Sharpe. Lund: Gleerup, 1961.
-------. *The Reliability of the Gospel Tradition*. Peabody: Hendrickson, 2001.

Gibbon, Edward. *The History of the Decline and Fall of the Roman Empire*. 7 vols. London: Methuen, 1909.
-------. *The History of the Decline and Fall of the Roman Empire*. 3 vols. New York: Modern Library, 1932.
Gieschen, Charles A. *Angelmorphic Christology: Antecedents and Early Evidence*. Leiden: Brill, 1998.
Goldingay, John E. *Daniel*. In WBC (1987).
Gore, Charles. *Dissertations*. 1895.
-------. *Lux Mundi*. 1889
Goulder, Michael D. "Jesus, the Man of Universal Destiny." Pages 48-63 in *The Myth of God Incarnate*. Edited by J. Hick.
-------. "The Two Roots of the Christian Myth." Pages 64-86 in *The Myth of God Incarnate*. Edited by J. Hick.
Goulder, Michael D., ed. *Incarnation and Myth: The Debate Continued*. Grand Rapids: Eerdmans, 1979.
Gowan, Donald E. *From Eden to Babel: A Commentary on the Book of Genesis 1-11*. Grand Rapids: Eerdmans, 1988.
Graeser, Mark H., John A. Lynn, and John W. Schoenheit. *One God & One Lord: Reconsidering the Cornerstone of the Christian Faith*. 3rd ed. Indianapolis: Christian Educational Services, 2003.
Grant, Robert M. *Greek Apologists of the Second Century*. Philadelphia: Westminster, 1988.
-------. *Jesus After the Gospels: The Christ of the Second Century*. Louisville: Westminster John Knox, 1990.
Green, Michael, ed. *The Truth of God Incarnate*. Grand Rapids: Eerdmans, 1977.
Gregg, Robert C., and Dennis E. Groh. *Early Arianism: A View of Salvation*. Philadelphia: Fortress, 1981.
Grelot, Pierre. "Deux expressions difficiles de Philippiens 2, 6-7," *Bib* 53 (1972): 498-501.
-------. "Deux notes critiques sur Philippiens 2, 6-11," *Bib* 54 (1973): 169-86.
Griffiths, J.Gwyn. "A Note on the Anarthrous Predicate in Hellenistic Greek." *ExpT* 62 (1950-51): 314-16.
Grillmeier, Aloys. *Christ in Christian Tradition* [1965]. Translated by Alois Grillmeier. Philadelphia: Westminster, 1975.
-------. *Christ in Christian Tradition: Volume Two, From the Council of Chalcedon (451) to Gregory the Great (590-604)* [1986]. Translated by Pauline Allen and John Cawte. Atlanta: Knox, 1987.
Gross, Jules. *The Divinization of the Christian According to the Greek Fathers* [1938]. Anaheim, CA: A&C, 2002.
Grundmann, Walter. "*agathos*." In *TDNT* 1:10-17.
-------. "*dunamai/dunamis*." In *TDNT* 2:284-317.
Guelich, R.A. "Gospel of Mark." Pages 512-25 in *DJG*.
Gundry, Robert H. *Jesus the Word According to John the Sectarian*. Grand Rapids: Eerdmans, 2002.
-------. *Matthew: A Commentary on His Handbook for a Mixed Church Under Persecution*. 2nd ed. Grand Rapids: Eerdmans, 1994.
-------. "Style and Substance in 'The Myth of God Incarnate According to Philippians 2:6-11." Pages 271-93 in *Crossing the Boundaries: Essays in Biblical Interpretation in Honour of Michael D. Goulder*. Edited by Stanley E. Porter, Paul Joyce, and David E. Orton. Leiden: Brill, 1994.
Gunkel, Hermann. *Genesis*. 3rd ed., 1910. Translated by Mark E. Biddle. Repr. Macon, GA: Mercer University, 1997.

H

Haenchen, Ernst. *John 1: A Commentary on the Gospel of John: Chapters 1-6*. In *Hermeneia*
-------. *John 2: A Commentary on the Gospel of John: Chapters 7-21*. In *Hermeneia*
Hafemann, Scott J. "F.C. Bauer." Pages 285-89 in *Historical Handbook of Major Biblical Interpreters*. Edited by D.K. McKim.
Hahn, Ferdinand. *The Titles of Jesus in Christology: Their History in Early Christianity*, 1963. Translated by Harold Knight and George Ogg. London: Lutterworth, 1969.
Hanhart, Robert. "Introduction." Pages 1-17 in Martin Hengel, *The Septuagint as Christian Scripture: Its Prehistory and the Problem of Its Canon*. Grand Rapids: Baker, 2002.
Hannah, Darrell D. *Michael and Christ: Michael Traditions and Angel Christology in Early Christianity*. Tubingen: Mohr Siebeck, 1999.
Hanson, R.P.C. *The Search for the Christian Doctrine of God: The Arian Controversy, 318-381* [1988]. Repr. Grand Rapids: Baker, 2005.
Harman, Louis F., and Alexander A. Di Lella. *The Book of Daniel: A New Translation with Notes and Commentary on Chapters 1-9*. In AB 23 (1977).
Harnack, Adolf von. *History of Dogma* [1886-89]. 7 vols. Translated by N. Buchanan et al. London: Williams and Norgate, 1896-1899.

-------. *What Is Christianity?* [1899-1900]. 2nd ed. Translated by Thomas Bailey Saunders. New York: Putnam's, 1902.
Harner, Philip B. *The "I Am" of the Fourth Gospel: A Study in Johannine Usage and Thought.* Philadelphia: Fortress, 1970.
-------. "Qualitative Anarthrous Predicate Nouns: Mark 15:39 and John 1:1." *JBL* 92 (1973).
Harrington, Wilfrid J. *Revelation.* In SPS (1993).
Harris, Horton. *The Tubingen School: A Historical and Theological Investigation of the School of F.C. Baur* [1975]. Repr., Grand Rapids: Baker, 1990.
Harris, Murray J. *Jesus as God: The New Testament Use of Theos in Reference to Jesus.* Grand Rapids: Baker, 1992.
-------. "References to Jesus in Early Classical Authors." Pages 343-68 in *The Jesus Tradition outside the Gospels.* Edited by David Wenham. Sheffield, England: JSOT, 1985.
-------. *3 Crucial Questions About Jesus.* Grand Rapids: Baker, 1994.
-------. "Titus 2:13 and the Deity of Christ." Pages 262-77 in *Pauline Studies: Essays Presented to Professor F.F. Bruce on His 70th.* Edited by Donald A. Hagner and Murray J. Harris. Grand Rapids: Eerdmans, 1980.
Harvey, Anthony E. "Christ as Agent." Pages 239-50 in *The Glory of Christ in the New Testament: Studies in Christology in Memory of George Bradford Caird.* Edited by L.D. Hurst and N.T. Wright. Oxford: Clarendon, 1987. 239-50.
-------. "Christology and the Evidence of the New Testament." Pages 42-55 in *God Incarnate: Story and Belief.* Edited by A.E. Harvey. London: SPCK, 1981.
-------. *A Companion to the New Testament.* 2nd ed. Cambridge: University, 2005.
-------. *Jesus and the Constraints of History.* London: Duckworth, 1982.
Hawthorne, Gerald F. *Philippians.* In WBC 43 (1983).
-------. *The Presence and the Power: The Significance of the Holy Spirit in the Life of Jesus.* Dallas: Word, 1991.
Hebblethwaite, Brian. *The Incarnation: Collected Essays in Christology.* Cambridge: University, 1987.
-------. *"The Myth* and Christian Faith." Pages 15-16 in *Incarnation and Myth: The Debate Continued.* Edited by M.D. Goulder.
-------. "The Myth and Truth Debate." Pages 1-11 in *Crisis in Christology.* Edited by W.R. Farmer.
Hendrickson, William. *Exposition of the Pastoral Epistles.* In NTC (1957).
Hengel, Martin. "Christological Titles in Early Christianity." Pages 425-48 in *The Messiah.* Edited by J.H. Charlesworth.
-------. *Crucifixion in the Ancient World and the Folly of the Message of the Cross.* Philadelphia: Fortress, 1977.
-------. *The Johannine Question.* London: SCM, 1989.
-------. *The Pre-Christian Paul* [1991]. Translated by John Bowden. London: SCM, 1991.
-------. *The Son of God: The Origin of Christology and the History of Jewish-Hellenistic Religion* [1975]. Translated by John Bowden. Philadelphia: Fortress, 1976.
-------. *Studies in Early Christology.* Edinburgh: T&T Clark, 1995.
Hengstenberg, E.W. *Christology of the Old Testament* [1835]. Translated by Ruel Keith. Repr., Grand Rapids: Kregel, 1970.
-------. *Commentary on the Gospel of St. John* [1865]. 2 vols. Repr. Minneapolis: Klock & Klock, 1980.
Hick, John. "Critique by John Hick." Pages 66-69 in *Encountering Jesus: A Debate on Christology.* Edited by Stephen T. Davis et al. Atlanta: John Knox, 1988.
-------. "Is there a Doctrine of the Incarnation?" Pages 47-50 in *Incarnation and Myth: The Debate Continued.* Edited by M.D. Goulder.
-------. *The Metaphor of God Incarnate: Christology in a Pluralistic Age.* 2nd ed. Louisville: WJK, 2005.
-------. "Preface." Pages ix-xi in *The Myth of God Incarnate.* Edited by J. Hick.
Hick, John, ed. *The Myth of God Incarnate.* Philadelphia: Westminster, 1977.
Higgins-Biddle, John C., ed. *John Locke's The Reasonableness of Christianity, As Delivered in the Scriptures: Edited with an Introduction and Notes.* Oxford: Clarendon, 1999.
Hillar, Marian, with Claire S. Allen. *Michael Servetus: Intellectual Giant, Humanist, and Martyr.* Lanham, MD: University Press of America, 2002.
Hodge, Archibald Alexander. *Outlines of Theology.* London: Thomas Nelson & Sons, 1886.
Hodge, Charles. *Systematic Theology* [1871-73]. 3 vols. Repr., Grand Rapids: Eerdmans, 1986.
Hooker, Morna D. *Jesus and the Servant: The Influence of the Servant Concept of Deutero-Isaiah in the New Testament.* London: SPCK, 1959.
Hort, F.J.A. *Two Dissertations.* London: MacMillan, 1876.
Howard, George. "The Tetragram and the New Testament." *JBL* 96 (1977): 63-83.
-------. "Phil 2:6-11and the Human Christ." *CBQ* 40 (1978): 368-87.
Howard, W.F. *Christianity According to St. John.* London: Duckworth, 1943.

Hudson, Bob, and Shelley Townsend. *A Christian Writer's Manual of Style*. Grand Rapids: Zondervan, 1998.
Humphrey, J. Edward, *Emil Brunner*. In *Makers of the Modern Theological Mind*. Edited by Bob E. Patterson. Waco, TX: Word, 1976.
Hunter, A.M., *The Gospel According to John*. In CBCNEB (1965).
Hurst, Lincoln D. "Christ, Adam, and Preexistence Revisited." Pages 84-95 in *Where Christology Began: Essays on Philipppians 2*. Edited by R.P. Martin and B.J. Dodd.
-------. "Re-enter the Pre-existent Christ in Philippians 2.5-11?" *NTS* 32 (1986): 449-57.
Hurtado, Larry W. *At the Origins of Christian Worship: The Context and Character of Earliest Christian Devotion*. Grand Rapids: Eerdmans, 1999.
-------. "The Binitarian Shape of Early Christian Worship." Pages 187-213 in *The Jewish Roots of Christological Monotheism*. Edited by C.C. Newman et al.
-------. "God." Pages 270-76 in *DJG*.
-------. *How on Earth Did Jesus Become a God? Historical Questions about Earliest Devotion to Jesus*. Grand Rapids: Eerdmans, 2005.
-------. *Lord Jesus Christ: Devotion to Jesus in Earlist Christianity*. Grand Rapids: Eerdmans, 2003.
-------. *One God, One Lord: Early Christian Devotion and Ancient Jewish Monotheism*. London: SCM, 1988.
-------. "Pre-70 CE Jewish Opposition to Christ-Devotion." *JTS* 50 (1999): 35-58.
-------. "What Do We Mean by 'First-Century Jewish Monotheism'?" *SBLSP* (1993), 348-68.
Huther, J.H. *Critical and Exegetical Handbook to the Epistles to Timothy and Titus*. In MCNT 9.
-------. *The General Epistles of James, Peter, John, and Jude*. In MCNT 10.

J

Jeremias, Joachim. *New Testament Theology*. New York: Scribner's Sons, 1971.
-------. "*pais theou*." In *TDNT* 5:677-717.
-------. *The Prayers of Jesus*. Naperville, IL: A.R. Allenson, 1967.
-------. "Zu Phil. 2:7: HEAUTON EKENOSEN." *NovT* 6 (1963): 182-88.
Jerome. *Jerome's Commentary on Daniel*. Translated by Gleason L. Archer, Jr. Grand Rapids: Baker, 1958.
Jervell, Jacob. *Jesus in the Gospel of John* [1978]. Translated by Harry T. Cleven. Minneapolis: Augsberg, 1984.
Jocz, Jakob. "The Invisibility of God and the Incarnation." In *Judaica* 17 (1961).
-------. *The Jewish People and Jesus Christ: A Study in the Relationship Between the Jewish People and Jesus Christ*. London: SPCK, 1949. 3rd ed. Grand Rapids: Baker, 1979.
Jung, Carl G. *Aion*. In *The Collected Works of C.G. Jung*. New York: Routledge, 1959.
Just, Felix. *Is John's Gospel "True"? JBL* (Fall 1999).

K

Kahler, Martin. *The So-Called Historical Jesus and the Historic, Biblical Christ* [1896]. Translated and edited by Carl E Braaten. Philadelphia: Fortress, 1964.
Kaiser, Otto. *Isaiah 1-12: A Commentary*. 2nd ed. Translated by John Bowden. London: SCM, 1983.
Kasemann, Ernst. *Commentary on Romans* [1973]. Translated and edited by Geoffrey W. Bromiley. Grand Rapids: Eerdmans, 1980.
-------. "A Critical Analysis of Philippians 2:5-11." Pages 45-88 in *God and Christ: Existence and Province*. Edited by Herbert Braun et al. Translated by Alice F. Carse. Tubingen: Mohr-Siebeck, 1968.
-------. *Essays on New Testament Themes*. London: SCM, 1964.
-------. *New Testament Questions of Today*. Philadelphia: Fortress, 1969.
-------. *The Testament of Jesus: A Study of the Gospel of John in the Light of Chapter 17* [1966]. Translated by Gerhard Krodel. Philadelphia: Fortress, 1968.
Kautzsch, E., ed. *Gesenius' Hebrew Grammar*. Oxford: Clarendon, 1910.
Keck, Leander E. "Christology of the New Testament: What, Then, Is New Testament Christology." Pages 185-200 in *Who Do You Say that I Am?: Essays in Christology*. Edited by Powell and Bauer.
Keener, Craig S. *The Gospel of John: A Commentary*, 2 vols. Peabody, MA: Hendrickson, 2003.
Keil, C.F. *Daniel*. In K&D 9.
Kelly, J.N.D. *The Athanasian Creed: The Paddock Lectures for 1962-1963*. London: Adam & Charles Black, 1964.
-------. *A Commentary on the Pastoral Epistles Timothy I & II, and Titus*. In HNTC (1960).
-------. *Early Christian Creeds*. 3rd ed. Essex, England: Longman, 1972.
Kenney, Garrett C. *John 1:1 as Prooftext: Trinitarian or Unitarian?* Lanham, MD: University Press of America, 1999.
Kidner, Derek. *Psalms 73-150: A Commentary on Books III-V of the Psalms*. Liecester, England: Inter-Varsity, 1973.
Kiljn, A.F.J. *The Jewish Christian Gospel Tradition*. Leiden: Brill, 1992.

Kim, Seyoon. *The "Son of Man" as the Son of God*. Tubingen: Mohr, 1983.
Kinzig, Wolfram. "The Nazoraeans." Pages 463-487 in *Jewish Believers in Jesus*. Edited by O. Skarsaune and R. Hvalvik.
Kittel, Gerhard. *"angelos."* In *TDNT* 1:80-87.
-------. *"lego."* In *TDNT* 4:91-136.
Klausner, Joseph. *Jesus of Nazareth, His Life, Times and Teaching*. Translated by Herbert Danby. New York: Macmillan, 1925.
-------. *The Messianic Idea in Israel: From Its Beginning to the Completion of the Mishnah*. Translated by W.F. Stinespring. New York: MacMillan, 1955.
Kleinknecht, Herman. *"theos."* In *TDNT* 3:65-79.
Klinghoffer, David. *Why the Jews Rejected Jesus: The Turning Point in Western History*. New York: Doubleday, 2005.
Knox, John. *The Humanity and Divinity of Christ: A Study of Pattern in Christology*. Cambridge: University, 1967.
Kreitzer, Larry J. "When He at Last Is First." Pages 111-27 in *Where Christology Began*. Edited by R.P. Martin and B.J. Dodd.
Kuhn, Karl Georg. *"theos."* In *TDNT* 3:92-94.
Kung, Hans. *On Being a Christian* [1974]. Translated by Edward Quinn. Garden City: Doubleday, 1976.
-------. *Christianity: Essence, History, and Future* [1994]. Translated by John Bowden. New York: Continuum, 1995.
-------. *Credo: The Apostles' Creed Explained for Today* [1992]. Repr., Eugene, OR: Wipf and Stock, 2003.
-------. *Does God Exist?: An Answer for Today*. Translated by Edward Quinn. Garden City, NY: Doubleday, 1980.
Kuschel, Karl-Josef. *Born Before All Time? The Dispute Over Christ's Origin* [1990]. Translated by John Bowden. New York: Crossroad, 1992.
Kuyper, Abraham. *The Work of the Holy Spirit*. Translated by Heiligen Geest. New York: Funk & Wagnalls, 1900.

L

Ladd, George Eldon. *A Commentary on the Revelation of John*. Grand Rapids: Eerdmans, 1972.
-------. *A Theology of the New Testament*. Grand Rapids: Eerdmans, 1974.
Lampe, G.W.H. *God as Spirit: The Bampton Lectures, 1976*. Oxford: Clarendon, 1977.
Landman, Leo. "Introduction." Pages xi-xxxv in *Messianism in the Talmudic Era*. Edited by Leo Landman. New York: KTAV, 1979.
Lane, A.N.S. "Christology Beyond Chalcedon." Pages 257-281 in *Christ the Lord*. Edited by H.H. Rowdon.
Lane, William L. *The Gospel of Mark: The English Text with Introduction, Exposition and Notes*. In NICNT (1974).
Latourette, Kenneth Scott. *A History of Christianity: Volume I:Beginnings to A.D. 1500*. Rev. ed. New York: Harper & Row, 1975.
Lawton, John Stewart. *Conflict in Christology*. New York: MacMillan, 1947.
Leer, E. Flesseman-van. *A Faith for Today*. Translated by John E. Steely. Macon, GA: Association of Baptist Professors of Religion, 1980.
Lewis, C.S. *The Case for Christianity*. New York: MacMillan, 1943.
-------. *Mere Christianity*. New York: MacMillan, 1943.
-------. *The Screwtape Letters*. New York: 1st Touchstone, 1942.
Liddon, H.P. *The Divinity of Our Lord and Saviour Jesus Christ*. 2nd ed. London: Rivingtons, 1868.
Lietzmann, Hans. "Der Prozess Jesu." In *Sitzungsberichte der (koniglichen) Preussischen Akademie der Wissenchaft* [1931].
Lightfoot, J.B. *The Apostolic Fathers Clement, Ignatius, and Polycarp: Revised Texts with Introduction, Notes, Dissertations, and Translations* [1889-1890]. 5 vols. Repr., Grand Rapids: Baker, 1981.
-------. *Saint Paul's Epistle to the Philippians* [1878]. 6th ed. London: Macmillan, 1881.
Lindars, Barnabas. *The Gospel of John*. Greenwood, SC: Attic, 1972.
Link, Hans Georg. *"ego eimi."* In *NIDNTT* 2:281-83.
Little, Paul E. *Know Why You Believe: New Edition, Revised and Updated* [1967]. Downers Grove, IL: InterVarsity, 2000.
Locke, John. *The Reasonableness of Christianity, As Delivered in the Scriptures*. London, 1695.
Lohmeyer, Ernst. *Der Brief an die Philipper*. 9th ed. Revised by W. Schmauch, 1953. Gottinger: Vandenhoeck and Ruprecht, 1930.
-------. *Kyrios Jesus: Eine Untersuchung zu Phil. 2,5-11* (1928).
Lohse, Eduard. *"sunhedrion,"* In *TDNT* 7:860-71.

Loisy, Alfred. *The Gospel and the Church* [1903]. Translated by Christopher Home. Repr., Philadelphia: Fortress, 1976.
Longenecker, Richard N. *The Christology of Early Jewish Christianity*. London: SCM, 1970; repr. Grand Rapids: Baker, 1981.
Ludemann, Gerd. *Heretics: The Other Side of Early Christianity* [1995]. Translated by John Bowden. Louisville, KT: Westminster John Knox, 1996.
Luomanen, Petri. "Ebionites and Nazarenes." Pages 81-118 in *Jewish Christianity Reconsidered: Rethinking Ancient Groups and Texts*. Edited by Matt Jackson-McCabe. Minneapolis: Fortress, 2007.
Luthardt, Christoph Ernst. *Clark's Foreign Theological Library: Luthardt on the Gospel of St. John*. 3 vols. Edinburgh: T. & T. Clark, 1878.
-------. *St. John's Gospel Described and Explained According to Its Peculiar Character*. Translated by Caspar Rene Gregory. 2 vols. Edinburgh: T.&T. Clark, 1877.

M

MacDonald, Neil. "Enlightenment." Pages 175-83 in DHT.
Mackey, James. *The Christian Experience of Trinity*. London: SCM, 1983.
Macquarrie, John. "Christianity without Incarnation? Some Critical Comments." Pages 140-44 in *The Truth of God Incarnate*. Edited by Michael Green.
-------. *Jesus Christ in Modern Thought*. London: SCM, 1990.
Maier, Paul L. *First Easter: The True and Unfamiliar Story in Words and Pictures*. New York: Harper & Row, 1973.
Malbon, Elizabeth Struthers. "The Christology of Mark's Gospel: Narrative Christology and the Markan Jesus." Pages 33-48 in *Who Do You Say that I Am?* Edited by M.A. Powell and D.R. Bauer.
Manson,Thomas Walter. *The Epistle to the Hebrews*. ET London: Hodder & Sloughton, 1951.
-------. *On Paul and John: Some Selected Theological Themes*. Edited by Matthew Black. Naperville, IL: A.R. Allenson, 1963.
-------. "The Son of Man in Daniel, Enoch and the Gospels." *BJRL* 32 (1949-50): 1-17.
-------. *The Teaching of Jesus* [1931]. Cambridge: University, 1935.
Manson, William. *The Epistle to the Hebrews*. London: Hodder & Sloughton, 1951.
Marshall, I. Howard. *The Gospel of Luke: A Commentary on the Greek Text*. In NIGTC (1978).
-------. "Incarnational Christology in the New Testament." Pages 1-16 in *Christ the Lord*. Edited by H.H. Rowdon.
-------. *The Origins of New Testament Christology*. Leicester, England: Inter-Varsity, 1977.
-------. "Son of Man." Pages 775-81 in *DJG*.
Marshall, John. *John Locke, Toleration and Early Enlightenment Culture*. Cambridge: University, 2006.
Martin, Ralph P. *Carmen Christi: Philippians ii.5-11 in Recent Interpretation and in the Setting of Early Christian Worship*. London: Cambridge University, 1967. Rev. ed. Grand Rapids: Eerdmans, 1983.
-------. "*Carmen Christi* Revisited." Pages 1-5 in *Where Christology Began*. Edited by R.P. Martin and B.J. Dodd.
-------. "Some Reflections on New Testament Hymns." Pages 37-49 in *Christ the Lord*. Edited by H.H. Rowdon.
Martin, Ralph P., and Brian J. Dodd, eds. *Where Christology Began: Essays on Philippians 2*. Louisville, KT: WJK, 1998.
Mastin, B.A. "A Neglected Feature of the Christology of the Fourth Gospel." *NTS* 22 (1975-76): 32-51.
McCloughry, Roy. "Basic Stott: Candid Comments on Justice, Gender, and Judgment." In *Christianity Today*, January 8, 1996.
McDonald, B.A. "Theodore of Mopsuestia." Pages 65-69 in *Historical Handbook of Major Biblical Interpreters*. Edited by D.K. McKim.
McDowell, Josh. *More Than a Carpenter*. Wheaton, IL: Tyndale, 1977.
McGiffert, A.C. *A History of Christian Thought*. New York: Scribner's Sons, 1954.
McGrath, Alister E. *Christian Theology: An Introduction*. 3rd ed. Oxford: Blackwell, 2001.
-------. "*I Believe:*" *Exploring the Apostles' Creed*. Downers Grove, IL: Inter-Varsity, 1991.
-------. "The Two Nations: Disillusionment with Academic Theology." Pages 120-55 in McGrath's *The Future of Christianity*. Oxford: Blackwell, 2002.
McKenzie, J.L. "The Appellative Use of El and Elohim." *CBQ* 10 (1948): 170-81.
McKim, Donald K., ed. *Historical Handbook of Major Biblical Interpreters*. Downers Grove, IL: InterVarsity Press, 1998.
McKnight, Scot. "Gospel of Matthew." Pages 526-41 in *DJG*.
-------. *A New Vision for Israel: The Teachings of Jesus in National Context*. Grand Rapids: Eerdmans, 1999.
Meecham, H.G. "The Anarthrous *Theos* in John 1.1 and 1 Corinthians 3.16." *ExpT* 63 (1951-52).

Meeks, Wayne A. "The Man from Heaven in Johannine Sectarianism." *JBL* 91 (1972).
Meier, Samuel A. "ANGEL OF YAHWEH." Pages 53-59 in *DDD*.
Metzger, Bruce M. "The Jehovah's Witnesses and Jesus Christ." *ThTo* (April, 1953): 75-76.
-------. "On the Translation of John 1.1." *ExpT* 63 (1951-1952): 125-26.
-------. "The Punctuation of Rom. 9:5." Pages 95-112 in *Christ and Spirit in the New Testament: Festschrift in Honour of C.F.D. Moule*. Edited by Barnabas Lindars and Stephen S. Smalley. Cambridge: University, 1973.
-------. *The Text of the New Testament, Its Transmission, Corruption, and Restoration*. 2nd ed. New York: Oxford University Press, 1968.
-------. *A Textual Commentary on the Greek New Testament*. Stuttgart, Germany: United Bible Societies, 1971.
Micklem, Nathaniel. *Ultimate Questions*. Nashville: Abington, 1955.
Milton, John. "The Christian Doctrine," Book I, Chapter 5. In *John Milton's Complete Poems and Major Prose* [n.d.]. Edited by Merritt Y. Hughes. Repr., New York: Odyssey, 1957.
Moberly, R.W.L. "How Appropriate is 'Monotheism' as a Category for Biblical Interpretation?" *Early Jewish and Christian Monotheism*. Edited by Loren T. Stuckenbruck and Wendy E.S. North. London: T&T Clarke, 2004.
Moltmann, Jurgen. *The Crucified God: The Cross of Christ as the Foundation and Criticism of Christian Theology*. Translated by R.A. Wilson and John Bowden. London: SCM, 1974.
Montefiore, C.G. *Some Elements of the Religious Teaching of Jesus*. London, 1910.
-------. *The Synoptic Gospels*. 2 vols. London, 1909).
Montefiore, Hugh. *A Commentary on the Epistle to the Hebrews*. New York: Harper & Row, 1964.
Moody, Dale. "God's Only Son: The Translation of John 3:16 in the Revised Standard Version." *JBL* 72 (1953): 213-19.
Moore, George Foot. "Intermediaries in Jewish Theology: Memra, Shekinah, Metatron." *HTR* 15 (1992).
Morris, Leon. *The Gospel According to John*. Grand Rapids: Eerdmans, 1971.
Moule, C.F.D. "Further Reflexions on Philippians 2:5-11." Pages 264-76 in *Apostolic History and the Gospel: Biblical and Historical Essays Presented to F.F. Bruce on his 60th Birthday*. Edited by W. Ward Gasque and Ralph P. Martin. Grand Rapids: Eerdmans, 1970.
-------. *The Holy Spirit* [1978]. Repr., Grand Rapids: Eerdmans, 1979.
-------. *An Idiom Book of New Testament Greek*. Cambridge: University, 1960.
-------. *The Origin of Christology*. Cambridge: University, 1977.
Mounce, Robert H. *The Book of Revelation*. Grand Rapids: Eerdmans, 1977.
Mullen, Jr., E. Theodore. *The Divine Council in Canaanite and Early Hebrew Literature*. Chico, CA: Scholars, 1980.
Murphy-O'Connor, Jerome. "Christological Anthropology in Phil. 2:6-11." *RB* 83 (1976): 25-50.

N

Neusner, Jacob, and Bruce Chilton. *Jewish-Christian Debates: God, Kingdom, Messiah*. Minneapolis: Fortress, 1998.
Neusner, Jacob, ed. *Religions in Antiquity: Essays in Memory of Erwin Ramsdell Goodenough*. Leiden: Brill, 1968.
Newman, Carey C., James R. Davila, and Gladys S. Lewis, eds. *The Jewish Roots of Christological Monotheism: Papers from the St. Andrews Conference on the Historical Origins of the Worship of Jesus*. Leiden: Brill, 1999.
Newman, Louis Israel. *Jewish Influences on Christian Reform Movements*. New York: Columbia University, 1925.
Newton, Isaac. *Paradoxical Questions concerning the morals of Athanasius and his followers*. Early 1690s. Keynes Ms. 10
Neyrey, Jerome. H. *2 Peter, Jude: A New Translation with Introduction and Commentary*. In AB 37C (1993).
Nicholson, G.C. *Death as Departure: The Johannine Descent-Ascent Schema*. London: Scholars, 1983.
Nock, Arthur Darby. *Essays on Religion and the Ancient World*. Edited by Zeph Stewart. 2 vols. Oxford: University, 1972.
Noll, Mark A. *The Scandal of the Evangelical Mind*. Grand Rapids: Eerdmans, 1994.
North, J. Lionel. "Jesus and Worship, God and Sacrifice." Pages 186-202 in *Early Jewish and Christian Monotheism*. Edited by Stuckenbruck and W. North.
North, Wendy E.S., and Loren T. Stuckenbruck. "Introduction." Pages 1-13 in *Early Jewish and Christian Monotheism*. Edited by Stuckenbruck and W. North.
Norton, Andrews. *A Statement of Reasons for Not Believing the Doctrines of Trinitarians Concerning the Nature of God and the Person of Christ*. 15th ed. Boston: American Unitarian Association, 1876.
Norwood, Michael. *Is Jesus God? Finding Our Faith*. New York: Crossroad, 2001.

O

O'Brien, Peter T. *The Epistle to the Philippians: A Commentary on the Greek Text.* In NIGTC (1991).

O'Collins, Gerald. *Christology: A Biblical, Historical, and Systematic Study of Jesus.* Oxford: University, 1995.

O'Neill, J.C. *Who Did Jesus Think He Was?* Leiden: Brill, 1995.

P

Palmer, Humphrey. *The Logic of Gospel Criticism.* London: Macmillan, 1968.

Pannenberg, Wolfhart. *Jesus-God and Man* [1964]. 2nd ed. Translated by Lewis L. Wilkins and Duane A. Priebe. Philadelphia: Westminster, 1977.

Pardee, Dennis. "ELOAH." Pages 285-88 in *DDD*.

Parker, Simon B. "COUNCIL." Pages 204-08 in *DDD*.

Patai, Rafael. *The Messiah Texts.* New York: Avon, 1979.

Pelikan, Jaroslav. *The Christian Tradition: A History of the Development of Doctrine: The Emergence of the Catholic Tradition.* Chicago: University, 1971.

Pelikan, Jaroslav. *The Christian Tradition: A History of the Development of Doctrine: The Spirit of Eastern Christendom (600-1700).* Chicago: University, 1974.

Pentecost, J. Dwight. "Daniel." Pages 1323-75 in *The Bible Knowledge Commentary: An Exposition of the Scriptures by Dallas Seminary Faculty: Old Testament.* Edited by John F. Walvoord and Roy B. Zuck. Wheaton, IL: Victor, 1985.

Perkins, Pheme. "Christ in Jude and 2 Peter." Page 155-65 in *Who Do You Say that I Am?* Edited by M.A. Powell and D.R. Bauer.

------. *First and Second Peter, James and Jude.* Louisville, KY: WJK, 1995.

Pittenger, W. Norman. *The Word Incarnate: A Study of the Doctrine and Person of Christ.* New York: Harper, 1959.

Pollard, T.E. "The Exegesis of John X.30 in the Early Trinitarian Controversies." *NTS* 3 (1956-57): 334-49.

------. *Johannine Christology and the Early Church.* Cambridge: University, 1970.

Powell, Mark Allan, and David R. Bauer., eds. *Fortress Introduction to the Gospels.* Minneapolis: Fortress, 1998.

------. *Who Do You Say that I Am?: Essays on Christology.* Louisville, KT: WJK, 1999.

Priestly, Joseph. *Three Tracts.* 3 vols. London: Unitarian Society, 1791.

Pritz, Ray A. *Nazarene Jewish Christianity: From the End of the New Testament Period until Its Disappearance in the Fourth Century.* Leiden: Brill, 1988.

Procksch, Otto. "hagios." In *TDNT* 1:100-10.

Propp, William H.C. *Exodus 19-40: A New Translation with Introduction and Commentary.* In AB 2A (2006).

Q

Quell, G. "kurios." In *TDNT* 3:1058-81.

------. "theos." In *TDNT* 3:79-89.

R

Rahner, Karl. "Dogmatic Considerations on Knowledge and Consciousness in Christ." In *Dogmatic vs. Biblical Theology.* Edited by H. Vorgrimber. Baltimore: Helicon, 1964.

------. "Dogmatical Reflections on the Knowledge and Self-Consciousness of Christ," *TI* 5 (1966).

------. *Theological Investigations.* Translated by Cornelius Ernst. 14 vols. Baltimore: Helicon, 1961.

------. "Theos in the New Testament." Pages 1:79-148 in Rahner's *Theological Investigations.* 20 vols. Baltimore: Helicon, 1961.

Rainbow, Paul A. "Jewish Monotheism as the Matrix for New Testament Christology: A Review Article." *NovT* 33 (1991).

Rawlinson, A.E.J. *The New Testament Doctrine of the Christ: The Bampton Lectures for 1926.* London: Green, 1926.

Reiling, Jannes. "Holy Spirit." Pages 418-24 in *DDD*.

Reim, Gunter. "Jesus as God in the Fourth Gospel: The Old Testament Background." *NTS* 30 (1984).

Rengstorf, Karl Heinrich. "apostello." In *TDNT* 1:398-406.

------. *Apostolate and Ministry.* St. Louis: Concordia, 1969.

Reymond, Robert L. *Jesus, Divine Messiah.* Ross-shire, Scotland: Christian Focus, 2003.

------. *Jesus, Divine Messiah: The New Testament Witness* [1989]. Phillipsburg, NJ: Presbyterian and Reformed, 1990.

Richard, Earl. *Jesus: One and Many: The Christological Concept of New Testament Authors.* Wilmington, Delaware: Michael Glazier, 1988.

Richardson, Alan, and John Bowden, eds. *The Westminster Dictionary of Christian Theology.* Philadelphia: Westminster, 1983.

Ridderbos, Herman. *Paul: An Outline of His Theology* [1966]. Translated by John Richard De Witt. Grand Rapids: Eerdmans, 1975.

Roberts, J.M. "The Old Testament's Contribution to Messianic Expectations." Pages 39-51 in *The Messiah*. Edited by J.H. Charlesworth.
Robertson, A.T. *A Grammar of the Greek New Testament in the Light of Historical Research*. 4th ed. Nashville, TN: Broadman, 1934.
-------. *Word Pictures in the New Testament*. 5 vols. New York: Harper and Brothers, 1932.
Robinson, H. Wheeler. *The Cross in the Old Testament*. London: SCM, 1955.
Robinson, James M. "Very Goddess and Very Man: Jesus' Better Self," *Encountering Jesus*. Edited by Stephen T. Davis.
Robinson, John A.T. "Dunn on John." *Theology* 85 (1982).
-------. *Honest to God*. Philadelphia: Westminster, 1963.
-------. *The Human Face of God*. Philadelphia: Westminster, 1973.
-------. *Jesus and His Coming*. Philadelphia: Westminster, 1957.
-------. "Need Jesus Have Been Perfect?" In *Christ, Faith and History: Cambridge Studies in Christology*. Edited by S.W. Sykes and J.P. Clayton. Cambridge: University, 1972.
-------. *The Priority of John* [1985]. Amer. ed. Edited by J.F. Coakley. Oak Park, IL: Meyer-Stone, 1987.
-------. *Redating the New Testament*. London: SCM, 1976.
-------. *Twelve More New Testament Studies*. London: SCM, 1984.
Rowdon, Harold H., ed. *Christ the Lord: Studies in Christology presented to Donald Guthrie*. Downers Grove, IL: Inter-Varsity, 1982.
Rowe, Robert D. "Is Daniel's 'Son of Man' Messianic?" Pages 71-96 in *Christ the Lord*. Edited by H.H. Rowdon.
Rowland, Christopher. *Christian Origins: An Account of the Setting and Character of the Most Important Sect of Judaism*. London: SPCK, 1985.
-------. *The Open Heaven: A Study of Apocalyptic in Judaism and Early Christianity*. New York: Crossroad, 1982.
Rubenstein, Richard E. *When Jesus Became God: The Epic Fight over Christ's Divinity in the Last Days of Rome*. New York: Harcourt Brace, 1999.
Runia, Klaas. "'Continental' Christologies." Pages 13-24 in *Crisis in Christology*. Edited by W.R. Farmer.
-------. *The Present-Day Christological Debate*. Downers Grove, IL: Inter-Varsity, 1984.

S

Sanday, William, and Arthur C. Headlam. *A Critical and Exegetical Commentary on the Epistle to the Romans*. In ICC (1896).
-------. *The Epistle to the Romans*. London: Cassel, Peter, Galpin, nd.
Sanders, E.P. *The Historical Figure of Jesus*. New York: Penguin, 1993.
Sanders, J.N., and B.A. Mastin. *A Commentary on the Gospel According to St. John*. New York: Harper, 1968.
Sarna, Nahum M. *Genesis*. In JPSTC (1989).
Sawyer, John F.A. *The Daily Study Bible (Old Testament)*. 2 vols. Philadelphia: Westminster, 1984.
Schaff, Philip. *History of the Christian Church* [1910]. 8 vols. Repr., Grand Rapids: Eerdmans, 1985.
Schillebeeckx, Edward. *Christ: The Christian Experience in the Modern World*. London: SCM, 1980.
-------. *Jesus: An Experiment in Christology* [1974]. Translated by Hubert Hoskins. New York: Seabury, 1979.
Schippers, R. "*pleroo*." In *NIDNTT* 1:733-41.
Schleiermacher, Friedrich. *The Christian Faith* [1830]. Translated by H.R. Mackintosh and J.S. Steward. 2nd ed. Philadelphia: Fortress, 1928.
-------. *The Life of Jesus* [1864]. Edited by Jack C. Verheyden. Translated by S. Maclean Gilmour. Mifflintown, PA: Sigler, 1997.
Schnackenburg, Rudolf. *The Gospel According to St. John*. 3 vols. New York: Crossroads, 1968-82.
Schneider Johannes. "*theos*." In *NIDNTT* 2:66-67, 70-82.
Schneider, Johannes, and Colin Brown. "*soter*." In *NIDNTT* 3:216-21.
Schoonenberg, Piet. *The Christ: A Study of the God-man Relationship in the Whole of Creation and in Jesus Christ* [1969]. Translated by Della Couling. New York: Herder and Herder, 1971.
Schweitzer, Albert. *Out of My Life and Thought: An Autobiography* [ET 1933]. Translated by C.T. Campion. Postcript by Everett Skillings. Repr., New York: Henry Holt, 1949.
-------. *Paul and His Interpreters: A Critical History* [1912]. Translated by W. Montgomery. New York: MacMillan, 1951.
-------. *The Quest of the Historical Jesus: A Critical Study of Its Progress from Reimarus to Wrede* [1906; ET 1910]. Translated by W. Montgomery. 3rd ed. London: A. & C. Black, 1954.
--------. *The Quest of the Historical Jesus: First Complete Edition*. Translated and edited from 2nd Ger. ed. by John Bowden. Minneapolis: Fortress, 2001.
Schweizer, Eduard. *The Holy Spirit* [1978]. Translated by Reginald H. and Ilse Fuller. Philadelphia: Fortress, 1980.
-------. "*huios*." In *TDNT* 8:363-92.

Scofield, C.I. *Scofield Reference Bible*.
Scott, Bernard B. "Introduction." Pages xi-xiii in A. Loisy's *The Gospel and the Church*.
Scott, Jack B. "elohim." *TWOT*.
Scroggs, Robin. *Christology in Paul and John: The Reality and Revelation of God*. Philadelphia: Fortress, 1988.
Segal, Alan F. *Two Powers in Heaven: Early Rabbinic Reports about Christianity and Gnosticsm*. Leiden: Brill, 1977.
Servetus, Michael. *Dialogues on the Trinity*. 1532.
———. *On the Errors of the Trinity. In seven books, by Michael Servetus, Spaniard from Aragonia, also known as Reves*. 1531.
———. *On the Justice of Christ's Reign*. 1532.
———. *The Restitution of Christianity*. 1553.
Sharafuddin, Abdus-Samad. *About "The Myth of God Incarnate:" An Impartial Survey of its Main Topics*. Jeddah, Saudi Arabia, 1978.
Sharp, Granville. *Remarks on the Uses of the Definite Article in the Greek Text of the New Testament; Containing Many New Proofs of the Divinity of Christ, from Passages Which are Wrongly Translated in the Common English Version* [1798]. 3rd ed. London: Vernor & Hood, 1803.
Shedd, William G.T. *Shedd's Dogmatic Theology*. 2nd ed. 3 vols. N.p., n.d.; repr. Nashville: Nelson, 1980.
Sherwin-White, A.N. *The Letters of Pliny: A Historical and Social Commentary*. Oxford: Clarendon, 1966.
———. *Roman Society and Roman Law in the New Testament*. Oxford: Clarendon, 1963.
Sidebottom, E.M. *The Christ of the Fourth Gospel: In Light of First-century Thought* (London: SPCK, 1961.
Silva, Moises. *Philippians*. 2nd ed. Grand Rapids: Baker, 1992.
Sjoberg, Erik. "*pneuma*." In *TDNT* 6:368-89.
Skarsaune, Oskar, and Reidar Hvalvik, eds, *Jewish Believers in Jesus: The Early Centuries*. Peabody, MA: Hendrickson, 2007.
Skinner, J. *The Book of the Prophet Isaiah: Chapters 1-39* in CBSC (1930).
Smalley, Stephen. *1, 2, 3 John*. In WBC 51 (1984).
Snobelen, Stephen. "Isaac Newton, heretic: the strategies of a Nicodemite." In www.isaac-newton.org
Sproul, R.C. *Getting the Gospel Right: The Tie that Binds Evangelicals Together*. Grand Rapids: Baker, 1999.
Stauffer, Ethelbert. "ego." In *TDNT* 2:343-62.
———. *New Testament Theology*. Translated by John Marsh. New York: Macmillan, 1955.
———. "theos." In *TDNT* 3:90-92, 94-119.
Stein, Robert. *Difficult Passage in the Gospels*. Grand Rapids: Baker, 1984.
Stonehouse, Ned B. *Origins of the Synoptic Gospels: Some Basic Questions*. Grand Rapids: Eerdmans, 1963).
Stott, John R.W. *Basic Christianity*. 2nd ed. Downers Grove, IL: Inter-Varsity, 1971.
Strachan, R.H. *The Fourth Gospel: Its Significance and Environment*. 2nd ed. Edinburgh: SCM, 1917.
———. *The Fourth Gospel: Its Significance and Environment*. 3rd ed. London: SCM, 1941.
Strauss, D.F. *The Christ of Faith and the Jesus History* [1865]. Translated and edited by L.E. Keck. Philadelphia: Fortress, 1977.
———. *The Life of Jesus Critically Examined* [1835]. Translated by George Eliot. Repr., London: SCM, 1973.
Strecker, Georg. "Appendix 1: On the Problem of Jewish Christianity." Pages 241-85 in *Orthodoxy and Heresy in Earliest Christianity* [1934]. Walter Bauer. Translated by John E. Steely et al. Edited by Robert Kraft and Gerhard Krodel. 2nd ed. Philadelphia: Fortress, 1971.
Streeter, Burnett Hillman. *The Four Gospels: A Study of Origins*. London: Macmillan, 1924.
Stuckenbruck, Loren T. *Angel Veneration and Christology: A Study in Early Judaism and the Christology of the Apocalypse of John*. Tubingen: Mohr-Siebeck, 1995.
Stuckenbruck, Loren T., and Wendy E.S. North. "Introduction." Pages 1-13 in *Early Jewish and Christian Monotheism*. Edited by Stuckenbruck and W. North.
Stuhlmacher, Peter. "The Messianic Son of Man: Jesus' Claim to Deity." Pages 126-45 in *Biblical Theology of the New Testament*. Translated by D.P. Bailey. Grand Rapids: Eerdmans, 2005.

T

Talbert, Charles H. "The Problem of Pre-existence in Phil. 2:6-11." *JBL* 86 (1967): 141-53.
Talmon, S. "The Concepts of *Mashiah* and Messianism in Early Judaism." Pages 79-115 in *The Messiah*. Edited by J.H. Charlesworth.
Tasker, R.V.G. *The Gospel of John*. In TNTC (1960).
Taylor, Vincent. "Does the New Testament Call Jesus God?" *ExpT* 73 (1961-62): 116-18.

-------. *Forgiveness and Reconciliation*. London: MacMillan, 1941.
-------. *The Gospel According to St. Mark*. London: MacMillan, 1963.
-------. *The Names of Jesus*. London: MacMillan, 1954.
-------. *The Person of Christ in New Testament Teaching*. London: MacMillan, 1958.
Temple, William. *Christus Veritas: An Essay*. London: MacMillan, 1924.
-------. *Readings in St. John's Gospel: Its Significance and Environment*. 2 vols. London: MacMillan, 1925.
Thayer, J.H. *Greek-English Lexicon of the New Testament* [1886]. Repr., Grand Rapids: Zondervan, 1962.
Thomasius, Gottfried. *Christi Person und Werke*. 1853.
Thompson, Marrianne Meye. *The Humanity of Jesus in the Fourth Gospel*. Philadelphia: Fortress, 1988.
Todt, H.E. *The Son of Man in the Synoptic Tradition* [1963]. Translated by Dorothea M. Barton. 2nd ed. London: SCM, 1965.
Tomson, Peter J. *Presumed Guilty: How the Jews Were Blamed for the Death of Jesus*. Minneapolis: Fortress, 2005.
Toussaint, Stanley D. "Acts." Pages 349-434 in *The Bible Knowledge Commentary: An Exposition of the Scriptures by Dallas Seminary Faculty: New Testament*. Edited by John F. Walvoord and Roy B. Zuck. Wheaton, IL: Victor, 1983.
Tregelles, S.P. *Remarks on the Prophetic Visions in the Book of Daniel*. 7th ed. London: Sovereign Grace Advent Testimony, 1863.
Tuckett, Christopher. *Christology and the New Testament: Jesus and the His Earliest Followers*. Louisville, KT: Westminster John Knox, 2001.
Turner, M.M.B. "The Spirit of Christ and Christology." Pages 168-90 in *Christ the Lord*. Edited by H.H. Rowdon. 168-90.
Turner, Nigel. *Christian Words*. Edinburgh: T&T Clark, 1980.
-------. *Grammatical Insights into the New Testament*. Edinburgh: T. & T. Clark, 1965.
Tyrrell, George. *Christianity at the Cross-Roads*. London: Longmans, 1909.
V
van der Horst, Pieter W. "THEOS." Pages 365-69 in *DDD*.
van der Toorn, Karel. "ELOHIM." Pages 352-65 in *DDD*.
Vermes, Geza. *The Changing Faces of Jesus*. London: Penguin, 2000.
-------. *Jesus in His Jewish Context*. Minneapolis: Fortress, 2003.
-------. *Jesus the Jew: A Historian's Reading of the Gospels*. Philadelphia: Fortress, 1973.
W
Wade, George Woosung. *The Book of the Prophet Isaiah*. In WC (1911).
Wainwright, A.W. "The Confession 'Jesus is God' in the New Testament," *SJT* 10 (March 1957): 274-99.
-------. *The Trinity in the New Testament*. London: SPCK, 1962.
Waltke, Bruce K., with Cathi J. Fredricks. *Genesis: A Commentary*. Grand Rapids: Zondervan, 2001.
Walvoord, John F. *Daniel: The Key to Prophetic Revelation*. Chicago: Moody, 1971.
-------. *The Revelation of Jesus Christ*. Chicago: Moody, 1966.
Wanamaker, C.A. "Philippians 2:5-11: Son of God or Adamic Christology?" *NTS* 33 (1987): 179-93.
Warfield, Benjamin Breckinridge. *Christology and Criticism* [1929]. In *The Works of Benjamin B. Warfield*. 10 vols. Repr., Grand Rapids: Baker, 1991.
Weiss, Johannes. *Jesus' Proclamation of the Kingdom of God* [1892]. Translated and edited by Richard Hyde Hiers and David Larrimore Holland. Philadelphia: Fortress, 1971.
Wells, David F. *The Person of Christ: A Biblical and Historical Analysis of the Incarnation* [1984]. Repr., Alliance, OH: Bible Scholar Books, 1992.
Wenham, Gordon. *Genesis 1-15*. In WBC (1987).
Westcott, Brooke Foss. *The Epistles of St. John: The Greek Text with Notes*. 3rd ed. 1892; repr. Grand Rapids: Eerdmans, 1966.
-------. *The Gospel According to St. John: The Greek Text with Introduction and Notes* [1902]. 2 vols. Repr., Grand Rapids: Eerdmans, 1954.
Westermann, Claus. *Genesis 1-11* [19740. Translated by John J. Scullion. Minneapolis: Augsburg, 1984.
Whiston, William. *Historical Memoirs of the Life and Writings of Dr. Samuel Clarke*. London, 1730.
-------. *Primitive Christianity Revived*. 5 vols. London, 1711 12.
-------. "Suspicions Concerning Athanasius." Pages 1-47 in *An Historical Preface to Primitive Christianity Revived*. London, 1711.
Whitehead, Alfred North. *Process and Reality*. Cambridge: University, 1929.
Whitehouse, Owen C. *The New Century Bible*. 2 vols. Oxford: University, 1905.
Wilbur, Earl Morse. *A History of Unitarianism*. 2 vols. Cambridge, MA: Harvard, 1952.
-------. *Our Unitarian Heritage: An Introduction to the History of the Unitarian Movement*. Boston: Beacon, 1925.

-------. *The Two Treatises of Servetus on the Trinity*. In *The Harvard Theological Studies*. Translated by Earl Morse Wilbur. 1932. Repr., New York: Kraus, 1969.
Wiles, Maurice F. *Archetypal Heresy: Arianism Through the Centuries*. Oxford: Clarendon, 1996.
-------. "Can We Still Do Christology?" Pages 229-38 in *The Future of Christology: Essays in Honor of Leander E. Keck*. Edited by Abraham J. Malherbe and Wayne A. Meeks. Minneapolis, MN: Fortress, 1993.
-------. "Christianity without Incarnation? Pages 1-10 in *The Myth of God Incarnate*. Edited by J. Hick.
-------. *Explorations in Theology 4*. London: SCM, 1979.
-------. *The Making of Christian Doctrine*. Cambridge: University, 1967.
-------. "Person or Personification? A Patristic Debate about Logos." Pages 281-89 in *The Glory of Christ in the New Testament: Studies in Christology in Memory of George Bradford Caird*. Edited by L.D. Hurst and N.T. Wright. Oxford: Clarendon, 1987. 281-89.
-------. *The Remaking of Christian Doctrine*. London: SCM, 1974.
-------. "Some Reflections on the Origins of the Doctrine of the Trinity." *JTS* n.s. 8 (1957): 92-106.
-------. *The Spiritual Gospel: The Interpretation of the Fourth Gospel*. Cambridge: University, 1960.
-------. "A Survey of Issues in the Myth Debate." Pages 1-12 in *Incarnation and Myth: The Debate Continued*. Edited by M. Goulder.
Williams, G.H. *The Radical Reformation*. Philadelphia: Westminster, 1962.
Williams, Rowan. *Arius: Heresy and Tradition*. London: Darton, Longman and Todd, 1987.
Winer, G.B. *A Grammar of the Idiom of the New Testament, Prepared as a Solid Basis for the Interpretation of the New Testament*. 7th ed. Revised by Gottlieb Lunemann. Translated by J. Henry Thayer. London: Draper, 1869.
-------. *A Treatise on the Grammar of New Testament Greek*. Translated by W.F. Moulton. Edinburgh: T. & T. Clark, 1877.
Witherington, III, Ben. *The Christology of Jesus*. Minneapolis: Fortress, 1990.
Wright, N.T. "The Divinity of Jesus." Pages 157-68 in Borg and Wright, *The Meaning of Jesus: Two Visions*.
-------. "*Harpagmos* and the Meaning of Philippians 2: 5-11." *JTS*, n.s., 37 (1986): 321-52.
-------. *Jesus and the Victory of God*. Minneapolis: Fortress, 1996.
-------. *The New Testament and the People of God*. Minneapolis: Fortress, 1992.
-------. *The Original Jesus: The Life and Vision of a Revolutionary*. Grand Rapids: Eerdmans, 1991.
-------. *The Resurrection of the Son of God*. Minneapolis: Fortress, 2003.
-------. *What Saint Paul Really Said: Was Paul of Tarsus the Real Founder of Christianity?* Grand Rapids: Eerdmans, 1997.
-------. *Who Was Jesus?* Grand Rapids: Eerdmans, 1992.
Wright, N.T., Keith Ward, and Brian Hebblethwaite. *The Changing Face of God: Lincoln Lectures in Theology 1996*. N.p.: Lincoln Cathedral Publications, 1996.

Y

Young, Francis. "A Cloud of Witnesses." Pages 13-47 in *The Myth of God Incarnate*. Edited by J. Hick.
-------. "Two Roots of a Tangled Mass?" Pages 87-121 in *The Myth of God Incarnate*. Edited by J. Hick.

Z

Zeitlin, Solomon. "The Origin of the Idea of the Messiah." Pages 99-111 in *Messianism in the Talmudic Era*. Edited by Leo Landman. New York: KTAV, 1979.
Zeller, Dieter. "*Iesous*." Pages 467-73 in *DDD*.
Zerwick, Max. *Biblical Greek: Illustrated by Examples*. Eng. ed. adapted from the 4th Lat. ed. by Joseph Smith. Rome: Scripta Pontificii Instituti Biblici, 1963.
Zerwick, Max, and Mary Grosvenor. *A Grammatical Analysis of the New Testament*. 3rd ed. Rome: Pontifical Biblical Institute, 1988.

Other Sources

Webster Reference Dictionary of the English Language, The: Encyclopedic Edition.
Webster's New Universal Unabridged Dictionary. Deluxe 2nd ed. New York: Simon and Schuster, 1983.

The Real Jesus

Jesus of Nazareth is the most famous man who has ever lived. But who was he? To learn about his identity, we must turn to the Bible. The New Testament presents Jesus as a seer-prophet, a teaching rabbi, an itinerant preacher, a wisdom sage, a charismatic healer, a miracle worker, and an exorcist. It applies to him the titles Messiah/Christ, Son of Man, Son of God, Savior, and Lord. It says he was born of a virgin, lived a sinless life in obedience to God, and died on a cross due to sinful men. Yet Jesus' suffering and death was according to God's plan as atonement for the sins of others. For those who believe these things about Jesus, God will forgive them of their sins and give them eternal life.

The New Testament also proclaims that God vindicated Jesus by literally raising him from the dead. It reveals that for the next forty days Jesus literally appeared to many of his disciples on multiple occasions, after which he ascended from their midst into heaven. Then God exalted Jesus by inviting him to sit with him on his throne. The New Testament also reveals that Jesus will dramatically return to the earth sometime in the future, bringing with him his promised and glorious kingdom. Then God will bring about the resurrection of the dead as well as judgment day.

During the early centuries of Christianity, the Catholic Church adhered faithfully to these scriptural teachings about Jesus. But in the fourth and fifth centuries, it officially proclaimed that Jesus was not only a man but also God by possessing two natures: a fully human nature and a fully divine nature, the latter called "the deity of Christ." And through the Church's councils and creeds it pronounced that if anyone did not believe that Jesus was fully God—co-equal and co-eternal with God the Father and the Holy Spirit—that person did not really believe in Jesus and thus was not a genuine Christian. Roman Catholic, Greek Orthodox, and Protestant church denominations still officially embrace these additional proclamations, claiming that they reflect the New Testament. And these churches identify the Father, Son, and Spirit as a "Trinity" even though this word is not in the Bible.

When the Catholic Church identified Jesus as "God," it departed from the fundamental, biblical, Judeo-Christian teaching that God is "one," later called "monotheism." It happened because, when the Church expanded into Gentile lands, it gradually (1) became rather anti-Semitic, (2) abandoned the established principle of using only biblical terms and categories with which to identify Jesus, (3) went beyond Scripture by introducing Greek metaphysics into theology in an effort to identify Jesus more precisely, and therefore (4) interpreted Jesus' status as "the Son of God" ontologically, thereby making this title synonymous with the word "God." Instead, Jesus should be understood as the Son of God in a Jewish context, so that this title means One specially favored by God to be Israel's Messiah.

Jesus was not God because of the following biblical evidence or lack thereof:
There is *no* New Testament evidence that Jesus ever *thought* that he was God.
There is *no* New Testament evidence that Jesus ever *claimed* that he was God.
There *is* New Testament evidence that Jesus *denied* that he claimed to be God.
At Jesus' examination before the Sanhedrin, he was *never* accused of ever claiming to be God.
The New Testament regularly *distinguishes* between God and Jesus as two separate individuals.
The New Testament constantly *interchanges* the words "God" and "the Father."
The New Testament repeatedly *identifies* "God" *exclusively* as "the Father."
The New Testament contains *no* unambiguous statement such as "Jesus (Christ) is God."
In the synoptic gospels and evangelistic sermons in Acts, Jesus is *never* identified as "God."

Jesus was not God because Jesus said of himself:
"Why do you call me good? No one is good but God alone" (Mark 10:18).[1]
"The Son can do nothing on his own but only what he sees the Father doing" (John 5:19, cf. v. 30).
"You" are "making yourself God." Jesus replied, "I said, 'I am God's Son'" (John 10:33, 36).
"The Father is greater than I" (John 14:28).
Jesus prayed, "Father,... the only true God, and Jesus Christ whom you have sent" (John 17:1, 3).
"Jesus said to her,... 'I am ascending to my Father ... to my God and your God'" (John 20:17).

Jesus was not God because of the following additional Scriptures:
Jesus was visible, but God is "invisible" to humans (1 John 1:1-3; 1:18; 1 Timothy 1:17).

---

[1] All Bible references are from the New Revised Standard Version, Updated Edition (NRSVue).

Jesus was approachable, but God "dwells in unapproachable light" (1 Timothy 6:16; cf. Psalm 104:2).
Jesus was tempted, but "God cannot be tempted by evil" (Mark 1:13; James 1:13).
Jesus was mortal, dying on a cross, so that "only God" is "immortal" (1 Timothy 1:17; 6:16).
Jesus said the Father is "the one who alone is God" and "the only true God" (John 5:44; 17:3).
Jesus called the Father "my God" several times (Matthew 27:46; John 20:17; Revelation 3:2, 12).
Paul wrote that "God is one" and "the only wise God" (Romans 3:30; 16:27).
Paul wrote that the Father is "the only God" and "only Sovereign" (1Timothy 1:17; 6:15).

Peter did not believe Jesus was God since he distinguished them as follows:
"Jesus of Nazareth, a man attested to you by God with deeds of power, wonders, and signs that God did through him among you" (Acts 2:22).
"Rulers of the people and elders,... Jesus Christ of Nazareth, whom you crucified, whom God raised from the dead" (Acts 4:8, 10).
"God has made him both Lord and Messiah, this Jesus whom you crucified" (Acts 2:36).
"God anointed Jesus of Nazareth with the Holy Spirit and with power;... he went about doing good and healing all who were oppressed by the devil, for God was with him" (Acts 10:38).

Paul the monotheist did not believe Jesus was God because he wrote the following:
"For there is one God; there is also one mediator between God and humankind, Christ Jesus, himself human" (1 Timothy 2:5).
"There is no God but one.... there is one God, the Father, from whom are all things and for whom we exist, and one Lord, Jesus Christ, through whom are all things and through whom we exist" (1 Corinthians 8:4, 6).
"There is ... one Lord, one faith, one baptism, one God and Father" (Ephesians 4:4-6).
"God and Father of our/the Lord Jesus" (Romans 15.6; 2 Corinthians 1:3; 11:31; Ephesians 1:3, 17).
"Christ is God's" because "God is the head of Christ" (1 Corinthians 3:23; 11:3).
"In Christ God was reconciling the world to himself" (2 Corinthians 5:19).
"Grace to you and peace from God our Father and the Lord Jesus Christ" (salutations 6x).

Jesus was not God because of the following logical reasons:
If Jesus did miracles by means of a divine nature, the Father *did not* do the works of Jesus.
If Jesus' ability to do miracles was intrinsic, he did *not need* the power of the Holy Spirit.
God is totally self-sufficient, but Jesus *needed* the miracle-working power of God's Spirit.
There is *no* biblical evidence that Jesus had two natures and two wills, which is non-human.
God transcends his creation, so that being God is *incompatible* with being human.
God foreknew the yet future date of Jesus' return to earth, but Jesus *did not* know it (Mark 13:32).

Thus, the New Testament *does not* teach Jesus was God, but that God *sent* him,[2] God was *with* him,[3] God was *in* him,[4] and God *raised* Jesus from the dead. The traditional view that Jesus is God is based on only a few Bible texts.[5] Most of them have grammatical difficulties partly due to the primitive structure of ancient language; thus, Bible versions often differ as to whether they call Jesus "God." Some are rightly interpreted to mean that *God was in Christ*, not Christ was God. In sum, Jesus was not God but a virgin-born man who endured temptation, suffering, shame, trial, and a violent death to provide salvation for us, and God vindicated and exalted him for it. Praise Jesus and his God!

Kermit Zarley wrote this tract as a condensation of his book, *The Restitution: Biblical Proof Jesus Is Not God*. Visit his website, kermitzarley.com, to print this tract free and learn about him and his several books on biblical studies that are available on amazon.com. Mr. Zarley is known mostly for his lifetime career as a pro golfer on the PGA Tour and its Champions Tour. He was a pioneer in bringing Christianity to American professional sports by co-founding and leading the PGA Tour Bible Study, which still thrives today. Kermit also has been a member of the Society of Biblical Literature since 1999.

---

[2] It is stated over forty times in the Gospel of John that God "sent," or did "send," Jesus.
[3] John 3:2; 8:29; 16:32; Acts 10:38; cf. John 1:1-2.
[4] John 10:38; 14:10-11; 17:21; 2 Corinthians 5:19.
[5] The most prominent are the following: Isaiah 9:6; John 1:1, 18; 10:30; 20:28; Romans 9:5; Philippians 2:6-7; 2 Thessalonians 1:12; Titus 2:13; Hebrews 1:8; 2 Peter 1:1; 1 John 5:20.

Still Here Books
on Bible Prophecy by Kermit Zarley

ISBN: 978-1-933538-43-3

ISBN: 978-0-9815462-2-3

ISBN: 978-1-7352591-0-9

ISBN: 978-1-7352591-2-3

★★★★★
Leave Kermit a review at Amazon.com!

Go to https://amazon.com and search for "Kermit Zarley Books"
Select a book you have read, scroll down and
click on "Write a Customer Review"
Write your review... and THANK YOU!

Other Books
by Kermit Zarley

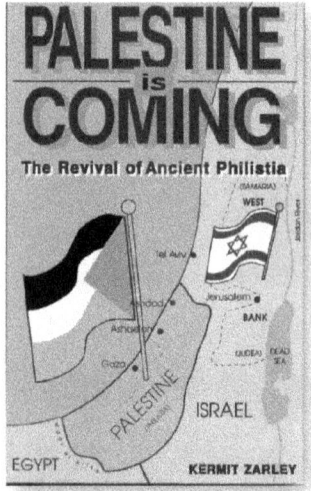

ISBN: 978-1-55635-181-5

ISBN: 978-1-57910-775-8

ISBN: 978-1-7352591-6-1

ISBN: 978-1-4982-2528-1

★★★★★
Leave Kermit a review at Amazon.com!

Go to https://amazon.com and search for "Kermit Zarley Books"
Select a book you have read, scroll down and
click on "Write a Customer Review"
Write your review... and THANK YOU!

www.ingramcontent.com/pod-product-compliance
Lightning Source LLC
Chambersburg PA
CBHW071857160426
43209CB00005B/1090